The Stage in Action

An Introduction to Theatre and Drama

Helen Manfull
Lowell L. Manfull

Department of Theatre Arts
Pennsylvania State University

KENDALL/HUNT PUBLISHING COMPANY
2460 Kerper Boulevard P.O. Box 539 Dubuque, Iowa 52004-0539

Copyright © 1989 by Kendall/Hunt Publishing Company

Library of Congress Catalog Card Number: 88-82426

ISBN 0-8403-6009-6

Printed in the United States of America
10 9 8 7 6 5 4 3

Contents

Preface

In one regard, and a telling one, this is an old-fashioned text for it eschews fancy window dressing in favor of a straightforward, chronological and historical presentation of theatre and drama. It is designed for undergraduate students as an introduction to the fascinating story of The Theatre—where it has been, where it is, and where it is going; what it was, what it is, and what it can be.

Theatre does not and never has existed in a vacuum. So, an attempt has been made to place the theatrical art in its time with a brief socio-political history and a glance at important aspects and developments of the theatre and plays of the period. It is not the intention here to say all that can be said. That task we may safely leave to theatre historians. This is an introduction to the highlights of an art and as such it must, of necessity, neglect the contributions of many great and important artists. However, we hope that, by choosing plays with subject matter which still speaks to young people and by centering our attention on some of the most productive and active moments of theatrical history, we have managed to convey a measure of the importance, excitement and joyous vigor of the art.

The title of this text—*The Stage in Action*—suggests the fundamental view that informs our approach. The theatre is a living, breathing entity, an *active* forum for idea, impressions and emotion. Its plays, too, are active; they are not dead literature but vital, living blueprints for production. The drama imitates action in performance and exists to its fullest only as it is embodied and brought to life on stage before an audience by the artists and craftsmen of the theatre.

We wish to express our sincere appreciation to Jim Hoskins for the drawings, Inge Miller of the Art History Department of Pennsylvania State University, to Charles Mann and Sandra Stelts of the Rare Book Room of Penn State's Pattee Library, Arlette Manfull for her careful reading of the text, and to Tim Lorah and Suzanne Murphy for their valuable assistance with various aspects of this text. A very special and heartfelt thank-you is extended to our colleagues and students in the Department of Theatre at Pennsylvania State University for their unfailing support, understanding and encouragement. If this text were to bear a dedication, it would be addressed to a small and very special company of student actors and directors whose daily presentation of scenes from world drama provide the heart and soul of our introduction to theatre classes.

Helen and Lowell Manfull
Pennsylvania State University

THE GLOBE THEATRE,

On the Bankside.

As it appeared in the reign of King James I.

Enlarged from an engraved view of London.   *made about the year 1612.*

From Londina Illustrata. London: Robert Wilkinson, publisher 1819–1825. (Photo courtesy of The Rare Books' Room, Pattee Library, Penn State University.)

CHAPTER I

Curtain Going Up

The Nature of Theatre

Almost every theatrical season, especially the mercurial Broadway season in New York, is deemed "the worst in years;" heads shake in despair for the frail and ailing theatre. But this "fabulous invalid," as Alexander Woollcott called it, has managed to survive through sickness and health, poverty and prosperity, war and peace for approximately three thousand years. It has changed and will continue to change—declining and advancing—in its traditions, conventions, circumstances, influence, and environment. For just as drama is the story of Mankind, the theatre is the mode or means of presenting that story.

If we go to a dictionary, we can find theatre defined in a number of ways. First of all, theatre means a place. To the Greeks it was a Seeing Place. Interestingly, when we speak of a theatre of operations or theatre of war, we mean that place where the action occurs. Theatre, then, is a place where we see an enactment of deeds. As a place, we can define it as a building for dramatic performances, but a theatre need not be a specific building; it can just as well be a classroom, a street corner, a loft, or a barn. From the point of view of those of us involved in this craft, act or labor of producing plays, we can say that we present or create theatre. From the audience point of view, we can speak of the experience of attending plays as going to the theatre. From the point of view of the uninitiated, we often speak of something theatrical as being overblown, flamboyant, excessive. Putting all of these ideas together, we might say that the theatre is a heightened enactment, prepared by a group of craftspeople for an audience in an appropriate space.

Let us consider for a moment what this theatre has been to various peoples at various times: to primitive man it was a means of placating evil spirits, of securing good fortune and food; to the Greeks it was a religious celebration, commanding the devotion of the best minds in the community; to the Romans in the last days of the empire it became little more than a degraded circus, a project by slaves for the titillation of their masters; to the early Christian Church it was a pagan evil to be crushed along with thievery and prostitution; to the same Church a few centuries later it became a means of teaching the Holy Scriptures; to the Puritans under Cromwell it was perceived as a den of vice; to the realists of the nineteenth century it became a platform of social reform; to the youth culture of the late 1960s it provided a means of protest against the Viet Nam War; to its practitioners from the beginning of history it has been a means of earning a living, no matter how meager; to its spectators it has always been a source of entertainment; and to the great playwrights throughout history, the theatre has been a means of probing honestly and fearlessly the meaning of life and the mystery of existence.

Ultimately, no matter what purpose it serves or how it is perceived, theatre is an art, an interpretation of life expressed in a way that can be universally recognized and understood, and of all the arts it is the closest to life. As Ingmar Bergman so eloquently says in his film, *Fanny and Alexander,* the little world of the theatre helps us understand the big world of life. The little world of the theatre organizes and distills the life experience, freeing it from all the chaos, anarchy, and disarray of life itself.

Leo Tolstoy said, "Art is as human activity which is passed on to others causing them to feel and experience what the artist has felt and experienced. . . . It is a means of communicating between people, uniting them in the same feelings. . . . As soon as the spectator and the hearers are affected by the same feelings which the artist felt—that is art." While Tolstoy was speaking generally of art, his words have enormous relevance to the theatre. For drama, an imitation of an action and a reflection of human experience, enacted in a particular space for a particular audience, is pure communication.

While at the very heart of this experience are three ingredients—story, actor, and audience—theatre is by nature a communal rather than an individual art. It requires the group effort of a large number of artists or craftspeople and hence is very different from the solitary work of the poet in a study or the painter at an easel. To help the reader better understand the nature of theatre and performance as it exists today, we can briefly characterize the roles of the major practitioners in the theatre.

The Playwright

Notice the spelling of the word; we do not speak of the playwrite but rather the playwright. The dictionary meaning of *wright* is workman. Hence the playwright is the play worker or the play maker. He or she conceives of the idea and shapes the play into dialogue, place or scene, characters, time, and action. When the playscript is completed, the playwright hopes to find a performing group to breathe life into the written word. Usually with a new play, writer, director and actors create the living theatre experience together.

The Director

Often the director chooses the play, selects the actors, works with the designers, rehearses the actors and coordinates the technical elements—scenic design, lighting, costumes, make-up and sound—into the concept of the production. Ultimately, the director is responsible for all elements of that production. Moreover, the director is responsible for projecting the meaning of the playwright's work, for making the play relevant to a particular audience, for synthesizing all production elements into a meaningful and cohesive whole, and for perceiving the experience with the eyes and sensibility of the audience. The director is the advocate of the audience.

The Actors

Acting is an ancient art which imitates life. The actor's primary task is to breathe life truthfully into the playwright's character. In the twentieth century, Constantin Stanislavsky, working at the Moscow Art Theatre in Russia, was the first person to systematize a method of acting which is based on such elements as concentration, relaxation, observation, truthfulness, believing in what you are doing, finding the character's wants and needs, and working from moment to moment.

Stanislavsky taught the actor to work in small units, to be very specific, and to study every aspect of the character's internal make-up (needs, goals, attitudes) and his external behavior (looks, movement, voice, age, and station in life.) To become a fine actor is a life-time occupation; even the greatest performers like Laurence Olivier and Meryl Streep constantly study roles and devote themselves to development of the actor's instrument: body, voice, emotional equipment, and intelligence.

Scenic Designer

The scenic designer creates the environment in which the characters live. That environment usually tells us a great deal about the characters: when they lived, where they live, their social and economic class, their taste, their attitudes, even their internal states. The designer also helps convey the mood of the play, and creates a workable, usable space in which the characters function and the story is told.

Lighting Designer

The first obligation of the lighting designer is to make the action of the play and the characters visible to the audience and to control and focus the audience's attention. In order to do this he or she manipulates lighting intensity, direction, and color. As with the scenic designer, the lighting designer creates mood, helps the audience see what the director wants them to see, helps create an environment, and shapes an illusion of the event.

Costume Designer

The costume designer works most intimately with the actors, for he or she must provide the very garments that both cover and enhance the actor's body movements. The costume designer works with line, texture, and color to create the lives of the characters, their taste, position in life, time in which they lived, their habits, mannerisms, and behavior. It is usually when the actors put on their finished costumes and their make-up that they feel most completely one with the characters they are portraying.

Make-Up Designer

The make-up artist's first responsibility is to enhance and project the actor's features. Beyond that, he or she devises special make-ups to emphasize particular aspects of character. Prosthesis, putty, crepe hair, and paint are the make-up artists major tools to convey age, station in life, status, and physical traits. Fantasy and animal make-ups are the particular delights of the make-up specialist.

Sound Designer

The sound designer, working closely with the director, selects the necessary sound for a play: doorbells, telephone, rain, and gun shots. He or she selects the music and effects which help convey the mood, intensity, and emotional quality of the play. Sound may be performed live or be recorded, composed for the production, or selected from existing recordings. The sound designer is also responsible for the quality of the sound: placement of speakers, volume, use of microphones, mixing, acoustical adjustments in the house or auditorium. With our ever increasing emphasis on music and sound, the function of the sound designer has become very active in the theatre.

Technical Director

The technical director is responsible for the ordering, building, and execution of the scenic elements of the production. He or she supervises the crew work, sees that the scene shop runs efficiently, and that the set is built safely and on time.

Stage Manager

The stage manager is not only the director's right hand person but also the link between the director-actor team and the technical staff. The stage manager organizes and calls the rehearsals according to the director's wishes, posts information for actors and technical staff, records blocking, keeps all communication open, and runs every detail of performances, determining when the curtain rises and falls, and precisely when each sound and lighting cue will be executed. It is a demanding and exacting job requiring the organizational skills of a business executive and the personnel skills of a trained psychologist.

In summary, we may look at all of the personnel involved in creating a theatrical production and at the major steps and procedures required to bring the theatrical event about: the script is written, and playwright and director confer; a producing agency and financial backing are arranged; auditions are held and a cast is selected. Meanwhile the production staff of designers and directors meet to discuss concept and style of the production; the scenic designer, working with the director, creates a ground plan; the basic movements of each actor are planned (the blocking). While working rehearsals are conducted, the designers and technicians prepare the setting, lighting, costumes, make-up and sound. Then polishing rehearsals are held, after which technical rehearsals integrate the design elements with the actors' work; finally the costumes are added just a few days before the play is performed before a live audience. After the last performance the production is "struck"; that is the scenery is taken apart, the costumes are taken to the shop where they will be cleaned and stored, all lighting instruments are taken down, all props returned to storage. During this entire process still another team under the leadership of a business manager is selling tickets, promoting the production, working out the contractual arrangements, and planning for the comfort of the audience during the performance. This whole complex process may have taken anywhere from a month to a full year to accomplish.

Besides the communal nature of the theatre with these artists participating in the creation of the event, there are a number of features of the theatrical experience which are distinctive and unique. Just as all artists have a medium—the sculptor marble, the writer pen and ink, the potter clay—so the dramatist uses the tools of the theatre. The primary tool is the actor who in turn uses his or her tools, the self. And as we have said before, the actor is dependent upon the audience for a response. These ingredients—story of the dramatist, actors, and audience—remain at the heart of the theatrical experience. When we add the work of the various craftspersons listed above we find that the materials of the theatre are expanded to include all of the arts: music, painting, sculpture, art, dance. Carrying this idea still one more step, we find that when we add all of the spotlights, shotgun microphones, elevator stages, computerized lighting boards, cinematic projections, or vacuform trim we are expanding our media or materials to include all of the sophistication that modern science and technology can produce. Theatre, then, can be pure, eclectic, or complex.

Throughout history we have grown suspicious of the theatre that relies too heavily upon spectacle, scenic effect or illusion. These accoutrements of the theatre may suggest that the emperor has no clothes, that the story being told is thin and pale, that the drama itself is wanting.

Historical periods of elaborate spectacle and great scenic effect have rarely been periods of great plays; similarly great eras of playwriting have rarely been times of emphasis on scenic display. Nevertheless, the scenic embellishments create the magic, the richness, the excitement, and the illusion of the story. Perhaps theatre works best when these elements fundamentally support the story and work least well when they become a substitution for it.

Continuing our consideration of those qualities that make the theatre unique, we may observe that no two performances are ever alike. Let us suppose that one audience sees the play on Tuesday night, and the second audience on Wednesday night. The production is the same—same actors, same dialogue, same space, same setting. Each night the final curtain falls at 10:47. But on Tuesday night the audience leaves the theatre detached, indifferent, unmoved—even bored. Wednesday night's audience, on the other hand, is uplifted, moved, transformed. While such extreme variance in response is rare, it is nevertheless true that each night the performance is created anew. Some nights the actors go through the play with professional competence; other nights for some unknown and inexplicable reason, the magic occurs; the chemistry between the performers themselves and between the cast and the audience is electric.

Just as no two performances are alike, so a theatre event does not live beyond its own time and place. A poem, a composition, a painting may be immortal; a production is not. When the curtain falls, it is accomplished. Precisely because, as we noted above, no two performances are alike, an evening in the theatre can never be completely recaptured. One may tell us about Laurette Taylor, Eleanore Duse, or Helen Hayes, but their work is lost to us unless we experienced it. The play-script remains but not the theatrical event. For example, you cannot perceive the brilliance of Julie Andrews's talent simply by reading the script of *My Fair Lady.* Similarly, we can flip back the pages of a novel to catch a description or a phrase or return to a museum to see a Picasso or a Vermeer, but we cannot turn back a night in the theatre. With the current popularity of video cassette systems, one can even recapture a moment of a film. A live performance lacks this capability.

Sometimes plays are recorded on film. Theatre buffs may see John Barrymore's *Hamlet,* for example, or the work of Sarah Bernhardt. Often plays are performed on film: Dustin Hoffman's *Death of a Salesman* or Sir Tyrone Guthrie's *Oedipus Rex;* but what we really have is a record of a production, not the production itself. Certainly seeing a play on film is better than not seeing a notable production at all. The major difference lies in the fact that on film the performance cannot change. It exists irrespective of the audience. Yet in the live theatre, how the audience responds—or does not respond—affects and shapes that particular performance. Perhaps more than any other characteristic, it is its aliveness that makes the theatre unique. Actors and audience sharing the same space, working together to create the performance—that is the incomparable magic of the theatre.

Just because both actor and audience are alive in one space, both are fallible. On stage collar buttons fly off, matches refuse to light, crepe hair mustaches come loose. Actors must deal with these problems and still commit to the truthful depiction of the characters' lives. After all, things go wrong in real life, too. These are actors' nightmares but they are incredible challenges as well. Audiences are no less vulnerable. It rains; you have a head cold; you did not feel like going to the theatre tonight with that math test tomorrow. The actors ask, "Is there anybody out there? Are they alive?" Actors and audience can miscue on their interaction or on their commitment to one another. Just as productions do, audiences have their own character. Some are boisterous, some restless, some quiet, some loud, some blood thirsty, some reticent. When actors push results or think themselves cunning, audiences withdraw; when actors are in difficulty with a costume or a prop, audiences become supportive and sympathetic. Audiences most often come to the theatre with what has been called "the willing suspension of disbelief." They come ready to accept what they know is not real, to play the game with the actors, to believe, to empathize, to respond. And every night the actor begins anew and establishes a new place, tells a new story, and lives a new life.

Because we are attempting in this book to bring together the written texts of great plays and notes about the theatre in which they were performed, it must always be remembered that the play is not theatre. The play is the vehicle for theatrical performance. The great English director, Tyrone Guthrie, said that reading a drama is like following the notes of a printed symphony score. Just as very few people can read a score and hear the symphony in all of its beauty and complexity, so very few people can read a play and extract its full meaning and emotional impact. Only when that symphony is performed with the full resonance of a great orchestra in a fine concert hall is it fully realized. Plays may be read with pleasure and insight, but they are not complete experiences until they are performed with a live audience. The play is half the event; it is the performance that makes the theatrical experience.

We have been dealing with the uniqueness of the theatre event. It would be dishonest to suggest that work in the theatre is without difficulty. Few of us would agree to the transient existence, the meager pay, the long hours, and the quixotic nature of the work if we did not love it. If theatre people can do anything else with their lives, they should do so; most of us, however, have no choice. We are willing to gamble and sacrifice in order to pursue a career in the theatre. It fulfills some basic need in our natures: a need to play, to make-believe, to live out other lives, to learn about other worlds than our own, to be transported. We experience a freedom and a joy that are beyond rational understanding. So often, the casual theatre goer will ask why one chooses a career in the theatre. Why does one choose a career in business or plumbing or nursing? We do what we must do. We become the myth makers, the story tellers, the creators of dreams and illusions, the purveyors of truth. For ultimately theatre is about timeless truths and the quality of the lives we lead. That great American director, Alan Schneider, once told a story that distills the meaning and purpose of theatre in our lives. Schneider's own father, a physician, questioned his son's career choice. Were there not, the old doctor asked, more important occupations one could choose? In exasperation, Schneider asked his father what he did for a living. "I save lives," the elder Schneider answered proudly. "Fine," the young director responded, "And I help people live them after you've saved them."

No matter how comfortable theatre practitioners may be with their craft, they often find themselves obliged to answer a series of charges about the profession. One of the major and persistent charges is that the theatre is immoral. Students frequently respond to strong language, progressive ideas, and shocking situations as immoral. It is true that just as the theatre reflects society, many dramatists are champions of new and controversial thought; yet it is rare when a play of any real value advocates negative attitudes. When Ibsen first wrote *A Doll House,* he was branded as a vile monster for suggesting that a woman might be justified in leaving her husband. Today we accept Ibsen's premise as a commonplace. In a recent university production of Caryl Churchill's *Cloud Nine,* some students were offended by the contemporary speech and alternate life styles of the characters but had no disagreement with the play's theme of self-knowledge and self-acceptance. It is always a mystery when audiences are offended by profanity but readily accept an act of murder on stage; almost no one finds *Hamlet* shocking in spite of the many murders that occur. While David Mamet's *Glengarry Glen Ross* contains highly volatile contemporary speech, the play's attack on corrupt business practices is a highly moral one. Just as life is sometimes raw, unkind, ugly, unjust, and brutal, so the theatre must convey the truth of our behavior if it is to help us perceive and create our best selves.

Too often the theatre is accused of being antiquated. Why should anyone who is a product of contemporary society with all of its technology and knowledge go to the theatre? Cannot film and television do the job better? It is true that film and TV offer us a literal and often realistic view of the event and provide us with varied and rapidly changing images. The theatre, then, has a much greater obligation to challenge the imagination of the audience, to tell its story in a non-realistic but truthful way, to employ all of the elements of bold theatricality that will reach its audience. Ultimately, that we must dress, go to a designated space, sit arm against arm with our fellow beings, focus our attention in one direction, involve ourselves in a set of conventions, respond to actors who in turn respond to us—all of these elements simply cannot be experienced in forms of mass media.

Film and television are also relatively inexpensive when compared to the theatre. That theatre is too expensive today, that it has become a plaything for the wealthy when it should be reaching the young is unfortunately too true. Somehow it is going to become necessary to break the patterns of high cost of production and high cost of tickets if the theatre is to prosper. All too frequently the commercial theatre must limit itself to a single set, one person show; or it must offer the extravagant and sure-fire hit musical that can run for ten years and make a profit. An expensive theatre becomes a safe theatre rather than one of risk, daring, and innovation. Fortunately, regional theatres still offer tickets at reasonable rates, and student ticket reductions are often available. Perhaps the only justification of ticket prices exists in the fact that a production, unlike a film, can reach only a small number of people at one time. Similarly, a stage actor can perform only in one place at one time. A film featuring Jack Lemmon may play in hundreds of movie houses across the nation; in New York only a few hundred people can actually see him live in the revival of Eugene O'Neill's *Long Day's Journey into Night*.

With the relative expense of the theatre compared to mass media, with what some critics say is a dearth of vital new plays available to audiences, it is sometimes argued that the theatre is once again in a state of decline. We can only end as we began stating that the theatre will change, grow, prosper, weaken, and grow strong again. The mimetic impulse is too great in us, the story telling desire too strong, the need for personal interaction too vivid for us to ever see the theatre destroyed. It is both relevant and universal. It speaks to us in our own time about our own problems, needs and aspirations, but it also finds the universal patterns of life, the common beliefs and desires of all people in all times. The pain of parent-child relationships as expressed in *King Lear,* the inequities of war in *The Trojan Women,* or the realization that we cannot always control our destinies in *Oedipus Rex*—these are the truths that we continue to reaffirm in the great works of the theatre. As the poet and playwright, Goethe, believed, the theatre offers us three things: on the most basic level it entertains us; next it educates or edifies us; and finally it elevates us, taking us out of ourselves and making us aware of our human potential for right and good.

The Nature of Drama

One hundred years or so after the great playwrights—Aeschylus, Sophocles, and Euripides—had created the golden age of Greek tragedy, an eminent philosopher and scholar gathered his students together in the market place of Athens to examine the nature of drama. Over a period of months, if not years, the great teacher, Aristotle, ruminated on the structure, intention and content of the magnificent tragedies he had seen performed in the theaters of Greece. He questioned their place in the hierarchy of the arts and their function within a society. In spite of what subsequent scholars of the Renaissance have implied, Aristotle did not prescribe a series of laws dictating the nature of drama; he merely described and analyzed for his students what he regarded to be one of the major arts of Greek culture.

For Aristotle, the drama was a *fine* art as opposed to a *practical* art. Therefore, it was not the purpose of drama to imitate in a servile or literal way the surface reality of life, but, rather, to imitate the inner process of reality. Drama was a demonstration of the marshalling of man's psychic forces imitating the striving of the human soul toward some desired goal beyond the surface of everyday life. It dealt not with reality so much as with an impression of reality. As Aristotle saw it, painting and sculpture could render only the outward or physical features of the real world while occasionally suggesting symbolically something of the inner reality. Poetry, music and dance, on the other hand, because they incorporate rhythm and time and movement through space, could convey a more vivid impression of the movement of the psyche or soul. However, even these arts had to content themselves with a symbolic representation of the movement of the human soul.

Drama was obviously superior to the other art forms in Aristotle's eyes because it could achieve by itself everything the other arts accomplished collectively. Furthermore, the drama employed the human being, the live actor, to convey its meaning as part of the form itself. The audience, then, immediately perceived the art as a depiction of human experience and the deeds of men. Dance might show man in action; but in dance man's deeds are still symbolically represented rather than concretely depicted. Only in the art of the drama do we find the representation of the deeds of man directly presented to us as they occur in life in an immediate and comprehensible form.

Aristotle lectured on both tragedy and comedy but, unfortunately, what he had to say about the nature of comedy is now lost to us. His observations on tragedy—his lecture notes, as it were—remain for us, at least in part, in what is called *The Poetics* where he defines tragedy as an *imitation of an action*. By *action* he meant a major deed of profundity and importance, a thing done or performed. He insisted that the enactment took the form of action not narration. That is to say, the spectator *sees* the deed performed rather than being told about it. Novels, short stories and narrative poems tell us of deeds done, but the drama shows us the deed. It becomes obvious, then, why actors are essential to this art form we call drama, for they are the doers, the enacters of deeds. Without the actor's performance the art form does not truly exist. A drama or play only exists in its performance. The play script is merely the blueprint of the enactment, the design or plan for the production.

One of the significant aspects of Aristotle's definition of tragedy is his use of the word *imitation*. Obviously, he means imitation in the sense of a representation or enactment as well as in that sense of something one step removed from reality. The drama is not the real thing but rather a representation—or, if you will, an imitation—of the real thing. But Aristotle, according to what appears in *The Poetics,* also devoted attention in his lectures to another specific aspect of imitation. He reminded his students that it is through the process of imitation that the human being learns much of what he knows. The individual, for example, learns to speak and walk by imitating the behavior of his elders. And, if we can believe Aristotle, we take a particular pleasure in learning through imitating the behavior and accomplishments of others. Implicitly, then, when the great scholar speaks of tragedy as being an imitation he is also thinking of it as a means of learning. We are intended to learn something about the nature of Man and human behavior—and through implication, ourselves—by attending the tragedy. He never goes so far as to say that the drama is a preachment of a moral lesson, for he saw the teaching that transpires in drama as happening obliquely and unobtrusively as the audience witnesses the striving of the human soul toward the accomplishment of a goal.

The spectator emerges from the theatre having learned something of interest about life itself. But, according to Aristotle, the spectator has also benefitted in other ways. By having his emotions as well as his intellect engaged during the enactment of the drama, he leaves the theater feeling uplifted and cleansed of negative feelings. In his lectures on the drama the Greek scholar suggested that the social efficacy of tragedy lay in its ability to purge the audience of pity and fear through the arousal of those emotions during the enactment of the drama. The purgation, or catharsis, came about as the spectator participated in the dramatic experience through empathetically identifying himself with the protagonist and his or her plight. In fact, catharsis—the major aim and intention of a dramatic performance—could only come about if the theater-goer surrendered himself to the enactment to the extent of empathetically feeling what the hero felt and vicariously experiencing what the hero experienced.

Interestingly, the aim and end of tragedy was the purging of negative emotion, and that could only come about through the spectator's empathic surrender to the play itself and not through his intellectual understanding of the meaning of the play. Clearly, the intellectual understanding of what the drama—in this case, tragedy—meant transpired *after* the emotional experiencing of the drama. First, the spectator had to experience vicariously the meaning, *feel* the meaning, before he could intellectually comprehend the meaning of the play. In a sense, Aristotle perceived of tragedy as primarily an *emotional* experience, not an intellectual one. The lessons of tragedy, the intellectual content it possessed, were presented unobtrusively and indirectly to the spectator. Tragedy made its appeal to the emotions and guts of the theater-goer. Comedy, on the other hand, was the form of drama that made its appeal to the intellect or mind. To put it another way, tragedy is the feeling man's drama while comedy is the thinking man's drama.

Today, of course, we no longer believe that the purpose of drama is confined to the catharsis of pity and fear. We tend to believe that the dramatic experience can lead to the purging of many other emotions as well. Nor do we think much about the teaching that transpires in the imitative process of drama. Still, even today we tend to subscribe to the notion that a serious play, or tragedy, should contain ideas of some significance, ideas that potentially make us think, while arousing our emotions to such a degree that we leave the theater feeling awed or uplifted or at least jarred out of our complacency.

Aristotle, then, conceived of tragedy as being the imitation of a major deed or action depicting through its enactment the striving of the human soul toward some goal with the intention of purging negative emotion while teaching oblique lessons of life. In examining the art form with his students, the Greek teacher concluded that tragedy contained six elements or components—plot, character, thought, diction, music and spectacle. Of the elements, three—plot, character and thought—were essentially the subjects of plays; that is to say, plays are about stories and people and ideas. Two of the elements—diction and music—represent the tools or materials playwrights use to fashion their dramas. Dramatists employ words, sound and symbols as well as verse and rhythm and music to create the play script. And the final element, spectacle, relates to the manner in which the art is presented to the consumer—in this case a staged production in a theatre.

Of all the elements, according to Aristotle, plot was the most important; he referred to it as "the first principle," "the soul of tragedy," "the first and most important part of Tragedy," and "the first level of imitation." He was convinced, it would seem, that a play needed a strong story-line in order to accomplish its purpose. He probably reasoned that if you wished to write a play imitating a major action such as "to re-establish God's order in the realm," then the most expeditious and practical way to accomplish your aim was to find a story that could be used to demonstrate such a quest—just as Shakespeare did in *Hamlet*. "Plot," he said, "is the imitation of the action." By "action" in this instance he meant the one major profound deed that the play will depict; and plot now becomes the primary means of depicting or imitating that deed or action.

Later, in the Renaissance, scholars, misinterpreting what Aristotle said, waged numerous, endless, witless and futile battles over a principle they termed "the unity of action" which dictated that a play could have only one plot. There was an obvious tendency to confuse "plot" with "action" and to assume that the terms were synonymous. They were not synonymous, however—certainly not in Aristotle's thinking. When the Greek scholar spoke of the need for a single action in a play, he was referring to the need in each tragedy to focus attention on the accomplishment of only *one* major deed; but accomplishment of that deed could conceivably be imitated by more than one plot so long as all plots in the single play were demonstrating or imitating the one action. It stands to reason that a play which attempted to imitate more than one action would become incredibly confusing to the spectator. However, a play like *King Lear* may have two plots—the main plot involving Lear and the sub-plot having to do with Glouster—without once becoming confusing since both plots develop a single action concerning a father's problem in distinguishing between real and feigned filial love. When Aristotle said, "Tragedy, then, is an imitation of an action," he used the verb "is" in the sense of "equals." "Tragedy" and "imitation of an action" are synonymous terms in this sense. So, *Antigone* may be called a tragedy or *an* imitation of *an* action.

As playwrights constructed their plots, they tended to employ three basic ingredients in varying combinations. Most plots, or so it seemed to Aristotle, incorporated reversals of fortunes, discoveries, and suffering. That is to say, as the hero performed certain acts to accomplish the one major task set for him, he would proceed with great good fortune toward winning his goal only to encounter obstacles from time to time that momentarily defeated him or prevented him from obtaining his goal. At one moment he would seem to be winning, at the next he might appear near defeat. After all, if the hero pursued his goal without encountering obstacles, the story of his accomplishments would lack suspense and interest. The reversals of fortune he experiences in the quest of his goal give the play its tensions and excitement.

Likewise, from time to time in the play the dramatic hero makes important discoveries or recognitions. He may discover the truth of a situation, the real identity of an unknown person, or fundamental truths about himself that he did not recognize before. The recognitions and discoveries are of tremendous help to the hero in solving his problems; they can also be great hindrances to his progress as well. Aristotle was aware of the significant relationship between reversals of fortune and recognitions. One depended upon the other. The reversal of fortune often was the occurrence that made the hero recognize an important truth. On the other hand, the recognition of a particular fact could be the very thing to cause the reversal in the hero's fortunes. Regardless of how the changes of fortune came about the dramatist had to exercise care that those changes did not show an eminently good man brought from prosperity to ill-fortune for such a spectacle would be an outrage to our sense of justice.

In a tragedy, because it deals with serious matters and unfortunate circumstances, reversals of fortune and recognitions ultimately and inevitably lead to situations which cause great pain to the protagonist. By the end of the tragedy the hero suffers mightily because of what he has experienced and what he has learned. Indeed, tragedy is primarily concerned with the suffering of the hero. Aristotle even went so far as to imply that without suffering there could be no tragedy. Perhaps this explains why true tragic heroes are invariably men of great spirit and substance. After all, a small-minded or small-spirited man will possess a limited capacity to suffer. And, if the hero cannot suffer, how can there be tragedy? Still, the mighty heroes bear their agonizing trials with dignity. They suffer in awareness, but they do not feel sorry for themselves. They may bewail their fates crying out "Woe is me!"; but in the final analysis they recognize they have willed their own suffering, that they are not mere victims of fatal forces, that they have brought destruction upon themselves. In their tragic enlightenment they achieve a kind of grandeur and nobility of spirit exceeding that of lesser, ordinary men.

Tragic heroes, then, achieve a kind of magnitude or stature through their suffering; they are revealed to be men of truly noble spirit. But true tragic heroes are men of stature from the outset; the protagonist begins the play as a man a cut above other men. Aristotle described him as "one who is highly renowned and prosperous." During the Renaissance it was argued that the hero of a worthwhile play therefore had to be a king or prince. But that was not Aristotle's meaning. The Greek scholar really meant that the hero had to be a man whose actions and deeds mattered, whose conduct affected the welfare of others. And since the cathartic end of tragedy could not happen without the spectator identifying himself with the hero, this meant that the protagonist consequently had to be "a man like ourselves." Aristotle was an aristocrat who lived in a democracy that believed in slavery and the inferiority of women. So, it is not surprising to hear the Greek scholar declare that you could not write a tragedy about a woman (because few people could become concerned about the plight of an inferior being) or a slave (because no one cared what happened to a worthless being). It becomes inevitable, then, for Aristotle to conclude that the protagonist of a tragedy had to be Greek, male and aristocratic because that, after all, was the kind of being with whom Aristotle himself could readily identify. Even if Aristotle's views on the stature of the tragic hero strike us today as being somewhat snobbish, we must recognize the fundamental validity underlying the principle he is enunciating. The hero of a serious play must be someone whom we can care about, someone whose welfare matters to us. In the American democracy of today we subscribe to the belief that the common man has intrinsic worth and dignity and that what happens to him should concern us all. Consequently, we can see serious plays dealing with rather ordinary human beings—male or female—and become very much involved in their plights through empathic identification.

Aristotle was aware of other implications in the expression "a man like ourselves." Essentially, the words imply that the tragic hero also had to be very human. He could not be a paragon of virtue, the epitome of manliness and dignity, the perfect human being because, if he were, the spectator might be able to admire him immensely but he would never be able to identify with such a protagonist. Besides, as was said before, he would be outraged by the fall of such a perfect man. The hero had to be very good and just but something slightly short of an angel; he had to possess some frailty in his nature or error in his judgment that could cause his fall. (In later centuries we began to refer to that frailty or error as "the tragic flaw.") In a sense, Aristotle was saying that the protagonist had to bring about his own downfall, that he had to deserve his fate. Then we would pity him for what befell him, and we would fear that a similar fate might overtake us because we, like the tragic hero, could be flawed and imperfect in spite of our best intentions. Again, the Greek scholar seemed to be very concerned regarding the spectator's ability to identify with the protagonist of the play because without that identification the cathartic end of the tragedy could not and would not transpire.

Who the character *is* by nature, what he *says* and what he *does* tell us much about ourselves, human nature in general, the life we live and the society that surrounds us. This is all part of the thought content of a play. Every great play contains interesting and significant ideas. In many instances the play has an obvious thesis to present or an argument to propound. The drama may contain themes and messages and morals. That is not to say that each play is a preachment of some sort, a disguised sermon. In fact, the play that does become a sermon or a political tract is in essence defeating itself. It is the function of drama to *show* us the movement of the human soul not tell us about moral or political truths. Aristotle was of the persuasion that the lessons of the drama in the shape of themes or theses or morals should be presented implicitly in the action and activities of the play; the behavior of the characters and the happenings in the plot should demonstrate those profound ideas. The play becomes something less than drama anytime the characters stand on stage and lecture the spectator or tell him stories or preach to him. Still, a play without ideas is a dull thing indeed. If *Hamlet* contained nothing but its plot of revenge, no one would bother to stage it. In fact, it would have vanished long ago and no one would know of the play today. But the splendid array of ideas in *Hamlet*—ideas about the divine right of kings, filial duties, the power of love, the substance of profound character, the acceptance of responsibility, growing up, the nature of justice, the need for truth, superstition, evil, ambition, and on and on— in addition to an exciting story keep the play forever alive.

Aristotle's observations on diction are less profoundly persuasive to us today and yet much that he had to say is of significance. He seemed to be very concerned that the language of a play be clear and understandable above all else. But he was concerned that the language reflect the dignity and elevation of the art form itself through the avoidance of commonplace jargon and lowly speech. The language of the play should have a magnitude that reflects the magnitude of character and idea in the drama. The language should superficially sound like everyday speech but should really be a kind of heightened expression in which poetic elements are in evidence—elements such as meter, rhythm, alliteration, and metaphor and interesting, unexpected turns of phrase which would engage the ear of the spectator delighting his sense but also riveting his attention.

The poetic aspect of the language was inevitable in Aristotle's time because much of the drama was set to music. Large portions of the dialogue—if not all of it—were sung to the accompaniment of a flute and lyre and percussion instruments. The choral passages were certainly composed for musical accompaniment as were the longer speeches of the characters; the hero's long speeches were delivered much like operatic arias. (In fact, opera as an art form was created in the late sixteenth century as an attempt to produce an authentic Greek tragedy.) One portion of the play, the paean, was actually the protagonist's major song of suffering—the aria he sang in the final scene of the play when his suffering was at its peak. While the music served to underscore the dialogue of the Greek tragedy, it also functioned as an accompaniment for the dance movements of the Chorus. As far as we know, the music was improvised afresh for each new play. Aristotle did not have much to say about the music of Greek drama or about the manner in which it was actually incorporated in the play. Or, if he did lecture at length on the subject, his notes have been lost and, therefore, we do not know his thoughts on the subject.

Nor do we know much of what Aristotle had to say about spectacle as an element of drama. He does inform us that by spectacle he meant the scenic embellishment and production aspects of the actual staging of the tragedy. He even suggested that it was of less importance than other elements of the drama because its effect depended more upon the talents of the scenic artist than the talents of the dramatist. However, in interpreting his attitude, we must bear in mind that the plays of Aristotle's day were staged in enormous amphitheaters where detail and subtlety of production would have been lost on most spectators. Scenery, costumes, and stage movement could not have been expected to have much impact in terms of conveying moods or ideas. Notice how different it is for us today in the twentieth century when plays are staged in small, intimate environments (or on a movie screen where we can see detail in close-up). Now, when the audience can see and examine the details of production, even a book on the hero's library shelf can tell us something about the character of the protagonist as can the particular and specific clothing he wears. If, for example, the hero is always dressed in business suits because the public scenes in which he appears demand such attire but his shoes are invariably unpolished, scuffed and dirty, we begin to suspect something about his social attitudes or at least his habits of personal neatness. His shoes might tell us that he is lazy, or indifferent, or poor, or absent-minded or rebellious. The hero's shoes cannot be ignored today. In Aristotle's day such detail would not have been seen too readily. So, if it were to figure importantly in the play in any way, the fact would have to be pointed out in the dialogue for the benefit of the spectators.

To this point our focus has been primarily upon what the great Greek scholar Aristotle told us of the nature of drama in what remains to us of his lecture notes on tragedy because those observations, when they were rediscovered in the Renaissance, influenced and shaped the entire concept of western drama as it exists today. Aristotle doubtlessly lectured on the comedy as well and probably instructed his students that the comedic form was, like tragedy, the imitation of an action. However, he probably went on to say that comedy was the imitation of an action demonstrating the movement of the human psyche that was nonserious in nature or, at least, amusing in its seriousness. He possibly saw the end of comedy being similar to the end of tragedy in that it, too, effected a catharsis. However, in the case of comedy, the spectator was probably purged of absurdity or ridiculousness through an intellectual awareness of his own foibles. In tragedy, mighty forces upset the balance of the world producing a state of chaos on a grand scale; in comedy, on the other hand, the state of imbalance or disruption is not so critical or devastating because the problems confronting the characters are less severe—since the form is, after all, less serious. Consequently, in comedy the spectator tends to be less concerned for the plight of the character because less is at stake. The spectator, then, is more inclined to be interested in *how* the hero goes about solving his problem rather than being concerned about the inevitable outcome of the action in terms of the success or failure of the hero.

While Aristotle provided us a view of drama which determined the course of all future drama in the western civilization, his perception is not the only one nor the only valid one. There are, after all, other ways to look at the drama; there are other perspectives that may serve as tools for helping us to understand what a play is and how it is what it is. For example, it is often informative and helpful to examine a play in terms of its linear structure to see how the dramatist has put the various pieces of the drama together. Then we perceive how he has employed a relatively logical cause-effect pattern to produce a story that moves forward in a believable and suspenseful way to an inevitable and meaningful conclusion.

Examining the linear structure of plays we are made immediately aware of a fundamental difference between the works of Sophocles and Shakespeare and Ibsen, for example. The Greek dramatists based their plays on legends well known to their audiences. They were free, then, to concentrate their attention primarily on the most exciting part of the story knowing that the spectator would be familiar with the important events that lead up to the climactic incident. The practice of starting a play very near its climactic moment is called *late point of attack*. Shakespeare, on the other hand, often dealt with fictitious material and more or less original storylines not completely known to the theater-goer. It became necessary for him, therefore, to stage more of the actual events of the story preceding the climactic moment to avoid confusing and mystifying the spectator. Because he attacked—or began—his story at an earlier point in its development in order to include those significant events, his plays were necessarily longer than those of Sophocles. Later, in the modern drama of the nineteenth century, Ibsen followed the example of Sophocles in the late point of attack so that his plays could be concise, focussed, and unrelenting in their tension. However, Ibsen then had to find a means of relating to the spectator all important information (or *exposition*) regarding characters and happenings which had an impact on the story line preceding the first scene of the play.

In a sense, exposition is information which points backwards or into the past where the story's linear development is concerned. In all plays there is certain background information, or exposition, which the audience must have in order to understand what is happening in the play. In order to understand why the hero is unhappy and depressed at the opening of *Hamlet,* it is necessary to know that Hamlet's father has recently died and his mother has married his uncle. That information is quickly given to us by the dramatist in the opening lines of Shakespeare's play. Notice how often the television drama you are watching begins with a group of characters in front of the camera talking about someone else or about something of importance that has just happened. The television screenwriter is simply laying the groundwork so that you can comprehend what is about to be presented in the development of the plot. If you miss an episode of a serial drama such as "Dynasty" or "Dallas," you may experience difficulty in following the plot-line of the subsequent episode because you have missed certain events of a previous telecast that serve as exposition for the present evening's story. But, then, notice, too, how the screenwriter will often find an excuse for the characters to recall or rehash past events in order to freshen your memory where exposition is concerned so that you might follow more readily what is about to happen in the unfolding saga.

So, the opening scene of most plays contains information that points backwards in time to previous events; but the scene often will contain information that points forward to coming events. In a sense, this information is exposition in reverse. It is called *foreshadowing*. Just as exposition helps the spectator or reader to understand what has already happened in the past, foreshadowing helps the spectator or reader to accept and understand something that will happen in the future.

For example, if, in the final scene of a murder mystery, the heroine is to take a revolver from a desk drawer and shoot the villain who is threatening her life at the moment, the audience is not likely to believe or accept what happens unless it is already informed that such a revolver is, indeed, in the desk drawer and that it is, indeed, loaded. Therefore, the wise playwright will have included a scene in the opening of his play—or certainly well before that final scene—in which someone opens the desk drawer and takes out the revolver for the audience to see while informing them that it is loaded. Not infrequently, and most unfortunately, that task is assigned to a maid or housekeeper who is cleaning the room at the time and who has no other function in the play whatsoever than to perform the task of foreshadowing.

A play, then, frequently begins with a late point of attack when events are ripe for development; and usually in the first few scenes the spectator is given the exposition and foreshadowing he needs to understand and accept the unfolding of the plot. Very soon an event occurs that triggers the action of the play. In *Hamlet,* the action of the drama (the act of imitation that demonstrates the striving of the human psyche) concerns the hero's attempt to re-establish God's order in the realm—to re-establish the "divine right of kings," as it were. The event that triggers Hamlet's activity, that causes Hamlet to act, is the discovery of the truth regarding his father's death. Learning that his father did not die a natural death but was murdered by Claudius sets the hero on the path of revenge in an effort to re-establish the proper order of royal succession. Hamlet first learns the truth when his father's ghost appears to him in the end of Act One of the play. The tale of woe the Ghost tells Hamlet sets the events of the play in motion. Such a dramatic event is referred to as the *inciting incident.*

Following the inciting incident, the playwright generally develops a series of events related through cause and effect which lead up to a *crisis* or turning point in the plot. The crisis is that crucial moment in the play when a decision is either made by the hero or forced upon him which commits him to a course of action from which there is no return. (In most classical drama the hero actively makes the decision himself and, by doing so, becomes a man of commitment. In some contemporary drama, the hero frequently has a course of action forced upon him—or he pursues a direction willy-nilly or indifferently—and, therefore, seems to lack a sense of true commitment.) At the moment of crisis in *A Doll House* Nora discovers that the wonderful thing she has been hoping for—that her husband will understand, forgive, and defend her—is not going to happen, that she has been living with a false perception of her husband, that her marriage has, in effect, been based on a lie. With that discovery Nora knows there is no turning back; things can never be as they were in spite of how much her husband may profess to the contrary. She, therefore, must take the only realistic course of action available to her. And she acts very decisively.

Nora's final exit in *A Doll House* is an extraordinary moment in the play, a high point in the action. But there have been other high points in the development of the story—such as the moment when Nora, feeling trapped and desperate, dances a wild Tarantella. High points such as these are called *climaxes.* A climax is essentially a moment of maximum tension in the story, a point where emotions reach their peak, or a time when events seem very critical, a time when the conflict seems most strained and stressful, or a time when the clash of wills is most vividly apparent. Each scene of a play will tend to have its own individual climax as will each act. The climax of Act Two will exceed that of Act One in importance. The play as a whole will have one outstanding climax. The crisis of the play will inevitably be a scene of major climax; and the final climax of the play will usually correspond to the final outcome of the crisis. The developmental movement of the plot of a play is in a way a series of mounting climaxes with one superseded by the next. This imparts to the play a somewhat undulating pattern of action in which tension builds to a climax and then recedes for a moment only to build again to another, greater climax. The pattern is repeated again and again until the last major climax which caps the crisis of the story. At that moment, we know the outcome of the events. All that is needed now is to tie up the loose threads of the story-line.

When we learn in the final scene of the murder mystery that the butler did it, we are still not totally satisfied. There are, after all, certain other things we want to know. For example, we would feel cheated if we were not told *how* the detective deduced that the butler was the culprit. We also want to be satisfied concerning the motives that prompted the butler to commit murder. And what about the old gardener who was last seen being pursued over the moors by a gigantic hound? Is he dead? Is he safe? Was he involved in the crime in any way? What is more, we really have a right to know also what will happen to the charming and beautiful, but innocent, suspect—the niece of the murder victim—with whom the detective seemed to be smitten. Will our detective confess his love for the young niece? Will they marry and live happily ever after? None of these threads is really essential to apprehending the guilty butler. Yet, each of these side issues engages our attention during the play, and we must know the outcome in each instance to feel fully satisfied by the murder mystery. After all, the *denouement* of the play—the tying up of each loose thread of the plot—is a very important element of the story and a very important part of the play's construction. Without a satisfying, and relatively complete, denouement the play will fail to please the spectator. Without a proper denouement a play will seem unfinished.

With the conclusion of the denouement the play feels complete partly because the world depicted in the play seems to have resumed a sense of safety and sanity; the chaos that has disturbed the balance of the universe, as it is depicted in the play, has been eliminated and the world has returned to its proper state of order. While the play as a whole is the imitation of an action depicting the movement of the human soul or psyche toward the accomplishment of a major deed, it may also be perceived as the depiction of the efforts of human beings to produce a state of order out of a condition of chaos. The major deed, or action, of which Aristotle speaks is, for all intents and purposes and in the general sense, the action taken by the protagonist of a play to re-establish order in his world. That world may be of universal dimension as it is in the Greek tragedies or in Shakespeare's major tragedies; or the world may be a smaller domain such as the individual social environment of a group of characters as it is in *A Doll House;* or the world may be defined as a single household as it is in many comedies such as *Life With Father* or *Ah, Wilderness!* or most of the entertainments you might see nightly on television.

In any event, the drama is an enactment of the deeds, hopes and dreams of Mankind. It may be presented to us realistically or through the fractured prism of Expressionism; it may be romanticized or poetically heightened. It may prompt us to laugh or to weep; it may enlighten us regarding our human condition; it may purge our emotions. Regardless of what it does or how it does it, the drama deals inevitably and ultimately with human experience. If it cannot be perceived as an imitation of human experience, it has no meaning; and lacking meaning, it has little worth. And in the end, drama is the story of Mankind.

The Greek Theatre of Epidaurus. In a theatre such as this
Antigone was probably first staged. (Photo courtesy of the Art
History Department, Penn State University.)

The classical Greek theatre. Drawing by Jim Hoskins.

CHAPTER II

The Golden Age of Greece

The Theatre of the Greeks

Athens, Greece today is a vast, sprawling, congested city with a pollution problem that literally corrodes the art and architecture that, 2,500 years ago, made this city an inspiration for all mankind. One can scarcely imagine what it might have been like living in 442 B.C. when Sophocles is believed to have written *Antigone,* when Pericles and his system of democracy made Athens a model for all ages to come, when Socratic philosophy and thought were innovative and controversial, and when the statues of Phidias (the sculptor of the gods) and the magnificent pediments of the Parthenon, which told the history of a people in richly painted sculpture, were new and dazzling. The fifth century B.C., the full flowering of classical antiquity, was a time of tremendous pride, vitality, and achievement.

Many factors contributed to the "glory that was Greece," not the least of which was the extraordinary natural beauty of the countryside: the sharply cut stones of the hills accentuating the sparse fertility of the land, out-croppings of grass where sheep grazed the hillsides amid glorious spring wildflowers, the sapphire sea shimmering in sunlight, and the islands purple in the luminous air.

Long before the age of Pericles, the Greeks were aware of an ancient and noble heritage: the fabled Trojan War over eight hundred years before and the epic tales of Homer (whose name means hostage) some six hundred years before. At the beginning of the fifth century, the Greeks had gained domination of the world through their victories over the Persian invaders. They had defeated Darius in the battle of Marathon in 490 B.C.; at Thermopylae seven thousand Greeks had stood against Xerxes and two million Persians. Athens had been burned and destroyed only to rise again, glorious and proud, under the long and stable leadership of Pericles. Near the end of the fifth century B.C., Athens again found herself engaged in conflict—the Peloponnesian Wars—which dragged on for twenty-seven years, which provided the inspiration for Aristophanes's great anti-war comedy, *Lysistrata,* and which ultimately became the turning point in Greek history when the great city-state of Athens fell to Sparta in 404 B.C.

Wars such as these were not unfamiliar to the Greeks. They accentuated a fundamental truth of the Greek national temperament: their love of peace after war, their exultation after tragedy, their pleasure in play after hard work. Depressed, gray-minded people did not rejoice just as they did not agonize; but the Greeks were a people of strong, bold contrasts, of passion and of reason. Their entire culture—the first great Western civilization—was based on reason and thought; indeed they possessed a passion for reason and thought. Socrates said, "All things are to be examined and called into question. There are no limits set to thought." Even the Greek word "leisure" means the pursuit of knowledge. The building that dominated the Acropolis, The Parthenon, was dedicated to Athena, the goddess of wisdom and knowledge.

But just as the Greeks were a people who loved reason and intellect, they loved play. Balance, symmetry in life, the perfect mind in tune with the perfect body—these were ideals. Games of all kinds—chariot racing, wrestling, dancing, footraces, drama contests—offered healthy competition, participation, action, and discipline. Artistry, too, was a part of basic Greek life. Whether one were musician, painter, or poet himself or a patron of the arts, life and artistry, reality and creativity fused. Art was not a superficial decoration of life; it was a fact of life that touched the soul of every Athenian.

Besides their sensitivity to their environment and cultural heritage, their love of learning and of play, their passionate and artistic natures, the Greeks of the classical period were also reflective and questioning. Although they believed in an ordered universe, many Greeks of the fifth century rejected the gods of the Homeric myths, embracing instead the more contemporary view that "Man is the measure of all things." The Periclean Greek was too sophisticated to believe any longer that the storms, thunder, lightening and swelling seas were the rages, agonies and suffering of the gods. Over the centuries, the poetic Greek fancy had embellished the adventures of the gods; their lively dramatic and plastic sense had humanized them, giving them failings, jealousies, pettiness, vulnerability, and physical form; their sense of order and unity had reduced their number and combined them into a family with mighty Zeus as the supreme head. Yet the ancient myths remained vital, filled from time to time with deep religious, philosophical, and moral meaning. They were still in essence what they had always been—an explanation; but in the hands of grave and powerful poets, like Aeschylus, Sophocles, and Euripides, they became an explanation of human fallibility and a revelation of triumph over suffering. These myths served the Athenian as Holinshed served Shakespeare, as Job served Archibald MacLeish in his play *J.B.*, as *Antigone* served Anouilh in his modern retelling of the myth—for parables, morals, truths, insights, and interpretations.

One final aspect of the culture that contributed to our monumental perception of golden age Greece was the Periclean concept of the democratic state. True, it was a flawed democracy: women were little more than servants, slaves were kept, over-population was controlled by infanticide and the administering of hemlock to certain citizens over sixty; but they were creating a society such as the world had never known before, one in which, as Pericles said, "Power rests with the majority instead of the few." Moreover the state did not take responsibility for the individual Athenian; instead, the individual Athenian had to take responsibility for the state. To the citizen, the duty of making his own decisions, carrying them out, and accepting the consequences was a necessary part of the life of a free man. "The creed of democracy, spiritual and political liberty for all, and each man a willing servant of the state," was the Greek ideal; in fact, the concept of free individuals unified by spontaneous service to the common life became a model for all the world. We must agree with Pericles who said, "Future ages will wonder at us, as the present age does now."

At the very heart of this extraordinary culture was The City Dionysia, a festival which took place each spring at the end of March or the beginning of April. Uniting church and state, the celebration was planned by a government official and presided over by the priest of Dionysus. It was a competition that engaged the talents of the finest actors and playwrights in all of Greece, a week long celebration of spring, rebirth, poetry, passion, revelry, reverence, mystery—and of life.

The origins of this great communal event probably existed in primitive fertility rites and celebrations dating back hundreds of years. We can only imagine what these revels might have been like, beginning with early dawn processions through the countryside in which neighbor would join neighbor in a journey toward town. A young girl might be chosen as festival queen and reign from a decorated cart. A man, perhaps her father or a distinguished citizen, sang a phallic song, a ballad celebrating fertility. He might have been followed by a clown dressed as a satyr (half man and half goat) who made obscene gestures and jokes. Then everyone probably joined in the parade—called the comus—with the girl, the patron, and the satyr leading. They might snake through town routing people from their beds and getting doused with water for their efforts. Finally the procession would approach the ceremonial grounds on the far side of town—a large cleared field with a flat circular dancing area—which had been leveled. The priest of Dionysus from the local temple might erect an altar for the god's statue in the center of this dancing area or orchestra. The statue of Dionysus would be brought from the temple and placed on its pedestal.

Probably wine kegs were opened and great revelry began. A hymn, or dithyramb, celebrating the exploits of the god Dionysus was sung. A particular hymn, sung as a goat was slaughtered on the altar, was called a goat song or tragos ode; hence our modern word tragedy. When the dithyramb was finished in these ancient rites, everyone tasted the flesh of the slaughtered goat, washing it down with more wine and submitting to more spirited revelry. If the celebration got out of hand and a young maiden became pregnant during the festivities, she was instantly forgiven. The resultant child was taken by the state and raised as a special honor child to Dionysus. The revelry broke up only as a new dawn began. As time passed, these Dionysian revels became so unwieldy that the best voices in the community were chosen to sing the dithyramb, and the first Greek chorus was created. As even more time elapsed the dithyrambs were no longer just in praise of Dionysus but in praise of other Greek heroes; and drama was born. It occurred to a chorus member, a man named Thespis, about 534 B.C., that he might become a solo performer conversing with the chorus; and so the first actor was born.

It should be noted here that this story of the comus is pure conjecture as is so much of our information about the Greek theatre. Historians and scholars never cease to explore, hypothesize, piece together fragments of information, argue and speculate. We do not know, for example, how it was that Dionysus, playful god of wine and fertility, became the patron god of theatre. Interesting in relation to the theatre's focus on youth and life experiences is the belief that Dionysus was the youngest of the gods and the only one to have a mortal parent. Drama, like the crop and the vine, is a rebirth, a recreation, an intimation of immortality. Moreover wine was considered a two-sided gift to man, on the one hand the source of freedom and joyousness, on the other of weakness, brutality, and crudity. Dionysus himself could be merry and gentle or ruthless and powerful. When the gift of wine worked positively, it could uplift man, provide an exultant sense of mastery, take him out of himself—all things the theatre could also do.

The City Dionysia offered a public holiday in which all work stopped, legal proceedings were postponed, and many model prisoners were released from detention for the occasion. The preplanning for the festival began almost a year before when hopeful playwrights submitted their plays—some scholars believe by reading portions of them aloud—to the archon (principle civic magistrate) who selected both the plays to be presented and the choregi, those wealthy Athenian citizens who bore, as a state tax, or as the aforementioned individual service to the state, the various costs of the festival. One choregus was assigned to each dramatic writer, the choregi being chosen by lot in July of the year before so that they had ample time to prepare for the following spring festival. Each choregus paid the salaries, bore the burden of training and costuming the chorus, the flute players, and the extras. While it was considered a high honor to be selected as a choregus, disgrace could be brought to one who cut corners or scrimped on production costs. These choregi, then, served as the first theatrical producers, but it was the playwright himself who directed and shaped the production. How lucky the playwright who was awarded a generous, sympathetic, and imaginative choregus.

Until the time of Sophocles, it is generally believed that the playwrights acted in their own plays, after which they were responsible for selecting the first actor (protagonist), who in turn selected his own second actor (deuteragonist), and third actor (tritagonist). All of the choregi, playwrights, and actors were male; women were rarely seen in attendance at the theatre, at least not respectable women who were at home, often locked in at home, tending to their spinning, weaving, and demanding domestic chores. Pericles once characterized the role of women in Athenian society by saying, "The best reputation a woman can have is not to be spoken of among men either for good or evil." This denigration of women is perhaps surprising when we think of the strength of many of the women in the Greek plays: Clytemnestra, Cassandra, Electra, Antigone, Hecuba, and Andromache, to name just a few. But these women were of royal blood; they were queens, the mothers and daughters of kings. They were, of course, played by male actors. Women acting would be unthinkable.

Each tragic playwright at the City Dionysia did not write just one play but an entire trilogy, a cycle of three plays, and a satyr play or short dramatic afterpiece. Often the satyr play was in the form of the tragedies it followed but comic in tone, burlesquing one of the familiar myths. The choruses in these plays dressed like satyrs, the woodland attendants of Dionysus, who were endowed with special fertility powers and known for lascivious and riotous behavior. They were bestial in countenance, with small horns on the forehead and a tail like a horse or goat.

On the first day of the festival, everyone gathered at a building, the Odeon or listening place, which had been commissioned by Pericles and built close to the Theatre of Dionysus. There was no playbill for the festival so this occasion—called the proagon—was the meeting of the poets competing for the prizes, the actors without their masks and costumes, the choregi, and flute players. There must have been tremendous excitement in the air, like the pep rally before the big game, as a herald announced each participant, the dramatic subjects or myths being treated, and the order of the anticipated events. The proagon was a living theatrical program.

That same night, just at dusk, a huge procession of shouting, dancing and singing revellers snaked through the streets with a cart carrying the statue of Dionysus from the temple to a sacred grove called the Academy. There sacrifices were offered, rites performed—the old Dionysian revels—and finally a subdued torch light procession escorted the statue to the Theatre of Dionysus itself where it was placed on an altar, the thymele, in the center of the orchestra—the god ready to preside over his festival.

On the second day of the celebration, spectators went to the preliminary events: the dithyramb contests, probably the clearest tie with the ancient rites of Dionysus. We believe that until the Peloponnesian Wars, all of these activities were free of charge, the expenses being absorbed by taxes and contribution of the choregi. Certainly this concept went beyond state supported theatre, for the theatre was a function of the state itself. For two days these dithyramb choruses performed. The first day's contest involved ten choruses of boys and the second, ten choruses of men, one from each of the ten tribes of Attica. There were fifty members in each chorus—one thousand dancers and singers, twenty flute players, one for each chorus. The competition was sharp, the spirit and excitement intense.

It may well have been that the fourth day of the Dionysia was devoted to comedy; however, we believe that old comedy, as it was called, found its true home in other festivals, particularly the Lenaia. Yet Greek comedy, as evidenced in Aristophanes's masterpieces—*The Frogs, The Birds,* and *Lysistrata*—was bawdy, farcical, satirical, witty, yet relevant to the audiences, in tune with their everyday lives and the society in which they lived. The comedies were original in plot, rather than based in myth as the tragedies were, and anything was fair game: contemporary politics, art, questions of war and peace, persons and practices disliked by the comic writer. Several characteristics were unique to comedies; their choruses were large, usually consisting of twenty-four members; their costumes consisted of very short chitons, or tunics, worn over flesh colored tights, creating a ludicrous effect of partial nakedness; their use of the phallus—sometimes made of red leather, sometimes a large raw carrot, which dangled from the costumes of most male characters—was a source of much bawdy humor.

The fifth, sixth, and seventh days of the City Dionysia—each day devoted to the work of one tragic playwright—marked the high point of the week's activities. Audience members would begin to fill the Theatre of Dionysus, which with standees was capable of holding approximately twenty thousand people. All of the spectators sat on the south slope of the Acropolis, looking toward the harbor and market place on the right and the open country on the left. Some members of the audience brought cushions for the stone benches carved out of the existing limestone slope. Some wandered home in the course of the day for a meal but most stayed in the theatre from dawn until dusk, enjoying wine, fruit, and cheeses. Convention allowed the audience to express its disapproval by pelting actors with foodstuffs and the pits from olives or dates. The audience in fifth century, B.C. Athens was intelligent, took its drama seriously, applauded vigorously what it liked and vociferously rejected what it disliked. Moreover this audience had an intense interest in the outcome of the various contests. The hundreds competing for prizes, sharpened appetites for victory and success made the event not unlike the Olympic games of today.

The physical environment in which the plays were performed was called the Theatron or seeing place. The audience looked toward a building called the skene, the Greek word for tent, which had once been pulled down and re-erected for each festival. A permanent wooden building and, at a later date, a stone one replaced the improvised skene and acted not only as a background and sounding board to help carry the actors' voices forward into the Theatron but also as a dressing and storage room; three doors in the skene provided entrances and exits of the principle actors. Whether or not the skene was raised slightly or built on level ground is a point of some conjecture; however, it is believed that in the classical theatre actors and chorus mingled freely. The front-of-the-skene acting area was called the proskenion, the roof of the skene called the logeion, and two side wings, the paraskene, each with its own door, offered increased backstage space and further helped to frame the actors.

Besides the three doors in the skene and an additional door in each of the paraskenion, entrances were also made through the parados or passageway on either side of the skene. It was through the parados that both the audience and the chorus made their entrances. In the tragedies, the first entrance of the chorus is called the parados. Characters arriving from another city or great distance away also entered through the parodos. Just in front of the skene was the orchestra, a full circle, approximately sixty-five feet in diameter. It was here that the altar and statue of Dionysus stood, and here that the chorus enriched the tragedy with song and dance. Ringing the orchestra were a series of some sixty seats of honor for priests, archon, high officials, choregi, and in the very center of the circle of seats a kind of throne for the priest of Dionysus.

In the classical period, staging was believed to be extremely simple, properties consisting of dummies of bodies, biers, couches, chariots, and torches. Sophocles is believed to have invented scene painting so the wooden skene was sometimes painted to suggest a specific locale. There were three primary machines associated with the classical Greek plays. First, since Greek tradition preferred acts of violence off stage, the eccyclema, a low cart on casters, was provided for the display of dead bodies. The body of Euridyce in *Antigone* probably was revealed on an eccyclema. Secondly, the mechane was a crane from which a god or other character could be lowerd to the proskenion from the logeion. From this device we derive our modern term, *deux ex machina,* which literally translates as god in a machine but which has come to mean any unexpected, unmotivated, or improbable device used to tie up loose ends of the plot or create a neat conclusion. Finally, the periaktoi were up-ended prisms painted with a different scene on each of the three sides. When the periaktoi were turned a new scene was created. Whether these periaktoi were placed within the doorways of the skene, between the doors, or on the front facade of the paraskene is a moot point.

There is a dearth of solid information concerning the actors of the City Dionysus. We know that all of them were male, that there probably was little training beyond experience, that they were highly respected in society—at least in the classical period—and that they were exempt from military service because of their great cultural service to the state. While the poetry of the plays would suggest simplicity, vigor, and dignity in acting, we know that it must have been a difficult and complex art. Not only did these artists handle strong action, poetic dialogue, prose speeches, recitative, dancing, singing, and flute accompaniment but they had to project vocally and physically in the large out-of-door theatres. Moreover, the three actors were expected to double and triple in roles. Usually a protagonist, like Creon, wore only one mask, but the deuteragonist and tritagonist would have been required to wear two or three throughout the course of a play to portray different characters. Often actors moved from male to female roles within one play; the actor playing Antigone, for example, might well have played the role of Teiresias who appears only after Antigone has been taken away to the cave. There were those actors, we believe, who specialized in female roles. Each protagonist was responsible for the hiring of his second and third actors. Naturally, a superior actor wants to surround himself with the highest possible talent; but there must have been occasions when jealousies and pettiness precluded the finest acting ensemble; by 449 B.C. it was decided that a prize should be given not only to the best playwright but to the best tragic actor as well.

All of the actors wore masks. Practically, they compensated for the size of the theatres, acted as a form of natural megaphone, and facilitated doubling and tripling in roles. The masks were light in weight, having been carved by highly skilled craftsmen out of wood or cork covered with linen. A great actor seemed to become one with his mask, endowing it with vitality and expressiveness that far surpassed the ability of the human face in so vast a setting.

We know that the costumes worn by these actors were bright, colorful, and ornate. The basic garment was the chiton, an oblong piece of cloth wrapped or draped around the body. Patterned sleeves, decorated girdles, crossbands, scepters, and soft buckskin boots with laces completed the attire. While the chiton probably covered more of the body than those worn in everyday life, they added grace to the human form and allowed for fast costume changes. The himation, another oblong piece of cloth, was draped over the upper part of the chiton for outdoor wear. Travelers wore a garment called the chlamys, a short mantle attached at the shoulder. Old men carried staffs; humble characters' chitons were of wool or crude linen; warriors appeared in armor; emblems and insignia were used. The Greeks loved bold, strong color and used it richly in their theatre. While in later periods there may have been some attempts to enlarge the human form with padding and boots, we believe no such convention was employed in the age of Sophocles.

One of the most unique elements of the classical Greek drama involved the chorus. It is from the choruses of fifty singing the dithyrambic hymns that we believe the drama itself evolved. By Sophocles's time the chorus was usually made up of fifteen members. The odd number permitted the solo work of the chorus leader, and two groups of seven each who might respond to one another much as in the responsive readings of many modern church services. Choruses also sang in unison or as individual voices. Some scholars think of the physical movement of the chorus as approaching military drill; others think of it as symbolic and stylized. While usually not trained as solo actors, the choruses were rigorously trained in singing, dancing, hand gestures, and recitation, working with flute accompaniment, to fill that sixty five foot circle with varied, rich, full sound and movement.

The work of the chorus primarily occurred in the choral odes between the episodes and in their dramatic entrance and exit, the parodos and the exodos. The choruses served the drama in a number of vital ways: first, they portrayed minor characters offering opinions, advice, solace to the principle actors; second, in the odes the chorus established the ethical framework of the play; third, they often acted as ideal spectators, reacting to a dramatic situation as the playwright might want the audience to react; fourth, in a drama that was not as highly visual as our theatre today, the chorus set the mood of the play and the dramatic tone; finally, they added color, movement, and spectacle to the whole. In the plays of Sophocles some of the most powerful, evocative, dramatic, and lyrical passages are given to the chorus. No other playwright has ever used it more skillfully.

When the three days of trilogies and satyr plays were over, the judges cast their ballots and the vine garlands and great honors were bestowed. Everything—including the competition—was enjoyed to the utmost. Here was living theatre in its fullest sense; state supported, a respected part of the culture, a sport, a contest, a basic part of existence—a thing loved, participated in, shared.

Only twice in history have there been periods of great tragedy: in the Athens of Pericles and in Elizabethan England. What these two periods had in common, two thousand years and more apart in time, may give us some hint of the nature of tragedy. Far from being periods of darkness and despair, each was a time when life was full, when the individual was hopeful, when the future seemed to offer infinite possibilities. Both were times of national pride—the Greeks at Marathon and Salamis, the Elizabethans defeating the mighty Spanish armada—and of positive energy and prosperity. But this is not the stuff of tragedy, you might say. Isn't the tragic view one of sadness, despair, hopelessness? As Edith Hamilton has so eloquently said, "The temper of mind that sees tragedy in life has not for its opposite the temper that sees joy. The opposite pole to the tragic view of life is the sordid view. When humanity is seen as devoid of dignity and significance, trivial, mean and sunk in dreary hopelessness, then the spirit of tragedy departs." This may go a long way toward explaining why we do not see great contemporary tragedies in our theatre today. Some might say we have become too absorbed with the petty problems of little people and are too mean-spirited and negative in our view of life to approach a tragic vision.

Sophocles

Sophocles, the second of the three great tragic writers of the fifth century B.C.—Aeschylus, Sophocles, and Euripides—was born in 497 B.C. in the district of Colonus near Athens. His well-to-do family provided him with a superior education; he was also an accomplished actor, musician, and gymnast who was selected, in youth, to lead the victory procession after the battle of Salamis. Sophocles wrote, we believe, one hundred twenty-three plays of which only seven are extant. His first award at The City Dionysia—ultimately he was to enjoy eighteen—occurred in 468 when he defeated the famous Aeschylus. He died in 402 B.C., two years after Athens had fallen to Sparta in the Peloponnesian Wars.

One story reports that in his extreme old age Sophocles was brought into court by his son who charged the old man with incompetence in the management of his own affairs. The tragedian's sole defense was to recite passages from his plays. The judge ruled that a man who could write such poetry could never be deemed incompetent, the case was dismissed, and Sophocles left the court honored and triumphant.

Many critics—Aristotle included—name Sophocles the finest tragic writer in the ancient world. He was a gentle spirit, an upholder of established order, well adjusted psychologically, and popular socially. His primary concern in drama was with character, and one of his major contributions was the addition of the third actor, thus allowing for more complex plotting and interaction than had heretofore been achieved. As he developed and probed character, he reduced the role and prominence of the chorus without, however, sacrificing language, power, or the structural importance of choral passages. Manipulation of plot, handling of exposition, use of dramatic irony, revelation of characters by their reactions to changing situations, skilled handling of entrances and exits—all contributed to Sophocles' perfection of style and craftsmanship. One of his most distinguished contributions, however, was his introduction of double motivation, whereby he provided believable human motivation for the character's actions even though that character's deed seem to be dictated by the will of the gods.

But greatest of all was Sophocles' tragic vision. He was able to see beauty and wisdom rising out of wrong-doing, folly, and error. To him tragedy was pain transmuted into exultation. His characters created and directed their own destinies, but Sophocles believed in a natural rhythm and order in the universe that was beyond mortal men. But because he allowed his tragic characters such insight into their own fallibility, Sophocles leaves us with a great sense of the dignity of being human.

Sophocles' Antigone

Antigone, like other Greek tragedies, was an individual play of a trilogy in which all three dramas developed a single idea or theme and were based on the characters and events of one legend. Sophocles employed the same legend for two other important plays—*Oedipus the King* and *Oedipus at Colonus.* These three plays together could make an interesting trilogy even though, as far as we know, they were written years apart; in fact, *Antigone* was probably written fourteen years before *Oedipus the King.* Although we have lost the other plays which formed the separate trilogies, we are fairly certain that each of the extant plays belong to different trilogies because they individually present three distinctive themes.

Of the three plays, *Oedipus the King* is perhaps the best; indeed Aristotle regarded it as the greatest of all the Greek tragedies. But *Antigone* is perhaps the most accessible because its story-line is relatively simple and direct and its conflict is defined with remarkable clarity. Furthermore, its characters are sharply delineated, understandably motivated, and recognizably human. Still, if you are reading the play for the first time—or reading Greek tragedy for the first time—it can seem somewhat confusing at the outset because of its distinctive form. So, before examining the content of the play, it may be wise for us to look for a moment at the manner in which it is physically set down.

The structure of the play is typically that of Greek tragedy and, therefore, is the structure that influences the form of all drama of the western civilization. In its form we find the seeds of the structure used by Shakespeare, Molière, Ibsen and Neil Simon; we simply call the various parts by different names from time to time. The play begins, like many later plays, with a *prologue* in which the playwright informs the audience of the story he is about to relate and sets up the situation by giving us the necessary exposition. The next major division of the play is called the *parodos* which is the first choral passage of the play. It is simply the choral song performed by the chorus of the drama as it enters onto the orchestra of the theatre through the main gate (also called the parodos). The text of the opening choral passage may touch upon one of the major themes of the play while also providing some exposition.

Following the parodos, the typical Greek tragedy moves into a series of five *episodes* interspersed with four choral interludes. Episodes are the portions of the play in which the plot is enacted, the conflict is unfolded and the story is moved forward to its conclusion. Episodes correspond to individual acts of contemporary plays. (Notice that they are five in number just as most Renaissance plays, including the works of Shakespeare, contain five acts.) An episode frequently contains a *monody,* or song for a solo voice, which is very similar to an aria in an opera. In the final episode the monody is the majestic song of suffering, or *paean,* sung by the tragic hero.

Between the episodes are the *stasimon,* or choral passages, in which the chorus of the play—if it is functioning as the Greek chorus should—focuses the play for the spectator. The stasimon not only allowed the three actors performing the tragedy an opportunity to catch their breath, but it also allowed the dramatist a moment to underscore the meaning of the preceding scene or to stress a theme or idea which would prepare the audience for what was to come. To make the stasimon more interesting and variable, and to make them more dramatic as well, the dramatist frequently divided the choral odes into parts—*strophes* and *antistrophes*—that might be sung by halves of the chorus in alternating sequence. The stasimon might end then with an *epode,* or summation speech, that the entire chorus would sing in unison.

Following the fifth and final episode of the tragedy, after the plot has been concluded and the major characters have left the stage, the playwright had to provide material for the chorus to sing as it made its exit from the orchestra. The exit song is called, logically enough, the *exodos,* and it usually contains a summary of the major theme of the play.

For the most part, the structural format outlined above is the form Sophocles employed in composing *Antigone* and his other plays. However, not all translations of *Antigone* will look exactly like what has been stated above. Some translations of the Greek tragedies clearly specify the various structural units of the play as they occur; other translations totally ignore them perhaps to avoid confusing the uninformed reader. On occasion, confusion arises anyway because translators of the Greek texts seldom agree on where the specific divisions begin and end. For example, in the text of *Antigone* that you will read the exodos includes more than the final words of the chorus and the paean is not a monody at all but rather an exchange of dialogue between the chorus and the choral leader. Some scholars would call this final choral dialogue a *commus* instead of a paean. But whatever the passage is called it accomplishes its dramatic purpose. So, the best thing to do is to ignore the disagreement and enjoy the drama.

It is time now to consider what *Antigone* is about. In this play Sophocles is obviously not merely telling us the story of the Greek heroine. Why should he bother to do that when most if not all of his audience already knew the story? Besides, when the plot of the play unfolds, it becomes obvious that Antigone is not really the major character in the play at all; she plays the secondary role of the catalyst. What happens in the play seems to focus more upon Creon than anyone else and that is as it should be for this is actually Creon's tragedy. What happens to Creon illustrates and embodies the lesson of the play. Sophocles is obviously using the legend about Antigone and Creon to tell us or to demonstrate for us something he thinks is important.

The drama transpires in front of the palace of Creon, the king of Thebes, following a major catastrophe that has produced a state of chaos in the community. Often the Greek dramatist would provide a prologue character who would address the audience and give them the necessary expository information. It is to Sophocles credit as a playwright that the prologue of *Antigone*—and the prologues of most of his tragedies as well—is actively dramatized. In a dialogue between Antigone and her sister, Ismene, Sophocles allows the characters to tell us what we need to know. We are informed of the great battles that raged at the seven gates of Thebes and of the deaths of Polyneices and Eteocles—the brothers of the two girls and the sons of Oedipus. We are informed of Creon's decree that Eteocles shall receive an honorable burial as a hero of Thebes while Polyneices corpse must remain unburied and unmourned because he was a traitor to his native land. We are reminded of the curse of the house of Thebes; as Greek spectators we would know that the events of the battle and its aftermath are part of the working out of the curse.

The prologue provides us much more than plot exposition, however. As the two young women talk, we begin to perceive a difference in their characters. Ismene speaks with caution and reason expressing a typical Greek woman's point of view. But we begin to see Antigone, on the other hand, as a passionate woman of firm resolve. She has a strength of character and a sense of justice denied to Ismene. It is important that we see Antigone at this moment as a woman of passion, a woman to whom love matters—the love of country, the love of justice and honor, and the love of family. She is not a cold, calculating person. Later in the play, she will act because of her passionate loves; and this moment in the play helps us to understand and accept what she does. In other words, Sophocles is providing some important foreshadowing of character even in the prologue of his play.

Interestingly, both Antigone and Ismene are opposed to Creon's decree; but it is only Antigone who has the courage and determination to act. As she expresses that determination, at least two important themes or ideas are embodied in what she says. Through implication Antigone is telling us that the truly important thing is not what you say but what you do. Furthermore, she insists that there is, after all, something worse than death; she would rather be dead than live dishonorably. As she puts it: "Leave me my foolish plan:/ I am not afraid of the danger; if it means death,/ It will not be the worst of deaths—death without honour." Ismene provides a touching and persuasive summary for the prologue in her final words to her sister: "Go then, if you feel that you must./ You are unwise,/ But a loyal friend indeed to those who love you." Her emphasis on love is not accidental or gratuitous. The rest of the play will have much to say about the power of love.

By the end of the prologue events are already ripe for something of consequence to happen—which is, of course, a testimony to Sophocles's great artistic economy as a playwright. So much has already been accomplished while the exposition was being presented. We have heard, through the exposition, of Creon's decree; but we have seen through the activity of the prologue that Antigone is determined to take a course of action in opposition to her uncle. She is prepared to defy the laws of state to ensure that her brother, Polyneices, receives the honorable burial she is convinced he deserves. In short, she has pitted her will against Creon's; and now something is bound to happen. The incident that must transpire to trigger the action of the play, indeed, has occurred; the instigating action, or inciting incident, has taken place.

The chorus enters through the parodos singing an up-beat ode to the glorious sun shedding its comforting light and promising happier, brighter days following the suffering of the immediate past. The Greek audience, knowing the dire outcome of Antigone's declaration, would find a poignant irony in the choral passage as it again relates the unhappy events of the previous day. The closing lines in particular are rich in irony.

What follows in the episodes of the play is an enactment of the conflict between Antigone and Creon. But it is much more than that. The conflict will provide the basis of the plot; but the plot will imitate the working out of the action of the tragedy. In Creon's opening speech of the first episode, or Scene I, we learn some very important information. Creon is a ruler who sets the good of the state—or to put it another way, the laws of the land—above all else. And he is adamant in his belief that anyone who does not think as he does is a traitor to the state. In his unbending righteousness we get our first hints of his enormous pride—a chink in his armor, a flaw in his character, that will lead to his undoing. If we thought for a moment, as the chorus did in the parodos, that the chaos caused by the battle at the gates of Thebes has ended, we are very much mistaken. Chaos now reigns again in the clashing of Creon and Antigone. Creon stands steadfastly for the law and order of the state while Antigone firmly believes that there are certain inalienable rights from the gods which at times must supersede or share on an equal footing with temporal law. The only thing that can prevent a future catastrophe, then, is for the characters—or Man through implication—to find a practical, abiding and honorable compromise (a state of balance, if you will) between the rights of the state and the rights of the gods—between temporal laws and the rights of the human being. Creon, as the ruler of his people, must achieve that balance or all is lost. In other words, that is the major, profound deed he must accomplish; that is the action he must fulfill. That is the action imitated by the play *Antigone* embodying the lesson Sophocles has designed for us.

Little wonder, then, that *Antigone* has retained its popularity through the centuries and can still move audiences today. From Sophocles' time to the present day Man has struggled with that same issue of the conflict between state laws and human rights. The basic issue in the play is timeless. But let us see how the conflict works itself out in Sophocles's play.

At the outset of the play, we can sympathize quite readily with Antigone's point of view. Why is it, then, that Creon cannot see the validity of her position? The first episode of the play demonstrates the cause of his blindness. Listen to what he says and the manner in which he says it. Watch the workings of his mind. He is over-bearing in the statement of his position. He addresses the chorus disrespectfully as "doddering wrecks." He has no respect for sage advise because he is convinced in his own mind that he is right. He jumps to unwarranted conclusions that those who oppose him have taken bribes and have been corrupted by money. These are the words and deed of a stubborn, proud man.

Meanwhile, the Sentry in the first episode is providing us more evidence of Sophocles' skill as a dramatist. Notice, for example, the use of double motivation in the scene. The Sentry appears because events are fated by the gods to occur as they do; but he also arrives upon the scene for reasons of his own. He has come to save his own skin. He knows he is in dire trouble for permitting someone to bury the body of Polyneices. Notice, too, that Sophocles uses the Sentry to provide an interesting note of irony in the scene and to foreshadow what is to come. Near the end of the episode, the Sentry says to Creon: "How dreadful it is when the right judge judges wrong!" Creon is completely unaware that he has judged wrong, but the audience perceives the irony. Furthermore, subsequent events in the play will prove how dreadful deeds may transpire when one's judgment is in error. Creon's erroneous judgment will bring about the tragedy.

Creon has had much to say about the cunning machinations of men, especially those who would twist the laws of the land to suit their own ends. His words have implicated Antigone, the Sentry and even the chorus. It is fitting, then, for the chorus to discuss that very issue in its second stasimon. And it is interesting to encounter the subtle implications in the ode that Creon himself could possibly be guilty of the same crime. The chorus has effectively focused one of the major ideas of the play for the spectator.

The second episode begins with the revelation of Antigone's guilt. The contest is clearly stated, and the message of the play underscored, as she says to her uncle: "Your edict, King, was strong,/ But all your strength is weakness itself against/ The immortal unrecorded laws of God./ They are not merely now: they were, and shall be,/ Operative for ever, beyond man utterly." Again we see demonstrations of Creon's overweening pride, his unwavering belief in his own infallibility, as he fails to listen to Antigone's cool reason and, what is more, jumps to the conclusion that Ismene has been in league with her sister. We hear it again in his superiority toward the chorus when they ask: "Then she must die?" "You dazzle me," he replies, and we clearly hear his subtext: "You overwhelm me with your stupidity, you blockheads!" During the scene anger and tension mount. The scene begins relatively calmly with an exchange between the Sentry and the chorus; it builds a head of steam as Creon enters and confronts the Sentry. Tension mounts to even a higher pitch as Creon turns his wrath first on Antigone and then on Ismene. And the scene reaches a boiling climax as Creon pronounces the death sentence on the sisters.

As Antigone and Ismene are condemned to death by Creon, the chorus sings its second ode about the vengeance of the gods and the anger of heaven that destroys everything in its path. The chorus perceives in the actions of Creon the working out of the curse of the house of Thebes. Along with the chorus we have witnessed Creon committing disastrous errors of judgment because of his pride. It is fitting at this point for the chorus subtly to warn Creon (and the audience) of the sin of pride. "No pride on earth is free of the curse of heaven," they caution. The vengeance of the gods will be visited upon the proud man. The choral passage then focuses a major theme of the play while foreshadowing what is to come.

One of the most moving and brilliant scenes in all Greek drama occurs in the third episode of *Antigone* when Haimon comes to plead with his father. The young man speaks unfailing wisdom to Creon at the same time he indicates his profound love for Antigone. He pleads with his father not to be blind to the point of view of others. "Do not believe that you alone can be right," he urges. And then he forthrightly asserts, "You have no right to trample on God's right." But Creon is unbending even though Haimon pointedly tells him, "In flood time you can see how some trees bend,/ And because they bend, even their twigs are safe,/ While stubborn trees are torn up, roots and all."

Perhaps the most arresting aspect of the third episode is Sophocles's fascinating demonstration of Haimon's respect and love for his father in spite of everything and his immeasurable love for Antigone—a love for which he is willing to die. It is not surprising, then, that the third choral ode is devoted to a discussion of love and its power both to conquer and destroy. We will soon see Haimon wasted by love, Eurydice destroyed by love, and Creon made to suffer mightily through his love. If love were not a powerful element in the character relationships of *Antigone,* the final moments of the play would lose much of their tragic impact.

Tension mounts toward an even higher climactic peak as the fourth episode unfolds. The scene does not begin in tranquility, for the chorus is by now mightily distressed by the plight of Antigone. In the exchange between the chorus and the heroine, it becomes clear that Antigone is determined to pursue her path even to death; nothing can stop her. The conflict becomes even more vivid when Creon confronts Antigone for a final time and pronounces the death sentence. In the stasimon that follows, the chorus bewails the fate of Oedipus's daughter.

The crisis or turning point arrives in the fifth episode when the words of Teiresias and the intervention of the chorus finally persuade Creon that he could possibly be wrong. He recognizes that he is conceivably guilty of stubborn pride and changes his mind. "My mind misgives—" he says. "The laws of the gods are mighty, and a man must serve them/ To the last day of his life!" He has recognized the truth at last. But it is too late. The tragedy of Creon has begun. He must accept his guilt. He loses his beloved son. He is bereft of his wife. He pays a terrible price for his folly and suffers mightily. We hear his suffering in his final moment when he comes in bearing the body of Haimon. But in the final moments of the play, he has fulfilled the action, accomplished the mighty deed of the tragedy by realizing that there must be a proper balance between the laws of the land and human rights. Now that Creon—and Man through implication—perceives that majestic truth, order will once more return to the city of Thebes which is, after all, the world of this play.

Creon is led into the palace and the choral leader addresses the audience as he and the chorus depart from the orchestra. The choral leader's final words sum up the message of the tragedy; "There is no happiness where there is no wisdom;/ No wisdom but in submission to the gods./ Big words are always punished,/ And proud men in old age learn to be wise."

ANTIGONE

by *Sophocles*

Translated by Dudley Fitts and Robert Fitzgerald

Because of the curse that their father had laid upon them, ETEOCLES *and* POLYNEICES *quarreled about the royal power, and* POLYNEICES *was finally driven from Thebes. He took refuge in Argos and married the daughter of* KING ADRASTOS; *then, as one of seven captains whose commander was* ADRASTOS, *he marched upon Thebes to recover his throne. In the assault,* ETEOCLES *and* POLYNEICES *met at the Seventh Gate and killed each other in combat.* CREON *became king, and his first official act was to forbid, on pain of death, the burial of* POLYNEICES.

─────── DRAMATIS PERSONAE ───────

ANTIGONE	CREON	A SENTRY
ISMENE	HAIMON	A MESSENGER
EURYDICE	TEIRESIAS	CHORUS

─────── SCENE ───────

Before the palace of CREON, *King of Thebes. A central double door, and two lateral doors. A platform extends the length of the façade, and from this platform three steps lead down into the orchestra, or chorus-ground. Time: dawn of the day after the repulse of the Argive army from the assault on Thebes.*

PROLOGUE

[ANTIGONE *and* ISMENE *enter from the central door of the Palace.*

ANTIG. Ismenê, dear sister,
You would think that we had already suffered enough
For the curse on Oedipus:
I cannot imagine any grief
That you and I have not gone through. And now—
Have they told you the new decree of King Creon?

ISMENE. I have heard nothing: I know
That two sisters lost two brothers, a double death
In a single hour; and I know that the Argive army
Fled in the night; but beyond this, nothing.

| ANTIG. | I thought so. And that is why I wanted you
To come out here with me. There is something we must do. |
| --- | --- |
| ISMENE. | Why do you speak so strangely? |
| ANTIG. | Listen, Ismenê:
Creon buried our brother Eteoclês
With military honours, gave him a soldier's funeral,
And it was right that he should; but Polyneicês,
Who fought as bravely and died as miserably,—
They say that Creon has sworn
No one shall bury him, no one mourn for him,
But his body must lie in the fields, a sweet treasure
For carrion birds to find as they search for food.
That is what they say, and our good Creon is coming here
To announce it publicly; and the penalty—
Stoning to death in the public square!
                                    There it is,
And now you can prove what you are:
A true sister, or a traitor to your family. |
ISMENE.	Antigonê, you are mad! What could I possibly do?
ANTIG.	You must decide whether you will help me or not.
ISMENE.	I do not understand you. Help you in what?
ANTIG.	Ismenê, I am going to bury him. Will you come?
ISMENE.	Bury him! You have just said the new law forbids it.
ANTIG.	He is my brother. And he is your brother, too.
ISMENE.	But think of the danger! Think what Creon will do!
ANTIG.	Creon is not strong enough to stand in my way.
ISMENE.	Ah sister!
Oedipus died, everyone hating him
For what his own search brought to light, his eyes
Ripped out by his own hand; and Iocastê died,
His mother and wife at once: she twisted the cords
That strangled her life; and our two brothers died,
Each killed by the other's sword. And we are left:
But oh, Antigonê,
Think how much more terrible than these
Our own death would be if we should go against Creon
And do what he has forbidden! We are only women,
We cannot fight with men, Antigonê!
The law is strong, we must give in to the law
In this thing, and in worse. I beg the Dead
To forgive me, but I am helpless: I must yield
To those in authority. And I think it is dangerous business
To be always meddling.
ANTIG.	If that is what you think,
I should not want you, even if you asked to come.
You have made your choice, you can be what you want to be.

	But I will bury him; and if I must die,
	I say that this crime is holy: I shall lie down
	With him in death, and I shall be as dear
	To him as he to me.
	It is the dead,
	Not the living, who make the longest demands:
	We die for ever. . . .
	You may do as you like,
	Since apparently the laws of the gods mean nothing to you.
ISMENE.	They mean a great deal to me; but I have no strength
	To break laws that were made for the public good.
ANTIG.	That must be your excuse, I suppose. But as for me,
	I will bury the brother I love.
ISMENE.	Antigonê,
	I am so afraid for you!
ANTIG.	You need not be:
	You have yourself to consider, after all.
ISMENE.	But no one must hear of this, you must tell no one!
	I will keep it a secret, I promise!
ANTIG.	Oh tell it! Tell everyone!
	Think how they'll hate you when it all comes out
	If they learn that you knew about it all the time!
ISMENE.	So fiery! You should be cold with fear.
ANTIG.	Perhaps. But I am doing only what I must.
ISMENE.	But can you do it? I say that you cannot.
ANTIG.	Very well: when my strength gives out, I shall do no more.
ISMENE.	Impossible things should not be tried at all.
ANTIG.	Go away, Ismenê:
	I shall be hating you soon, and the dead will too,
	For your words are hateful. Leave me my foolish plan:
	I am not afraid of the danger; if it means death,
	It will not be the worst of deaths—death without honour.
ISMENE.	Go then, if you feel that you must.
	You are unwise,
	But a loyal friend indeed to those who love you.

[Exit into the Palace. ANTIGONE *goes off,* L. *Enters the* CHORUS.

PARODOS

CHORUS.	Now the long blade of the sun, lying	[STROPHE 1
	Level east to west, touches with glory	
	Thebes of the Seven Gates. Open, unlidded	
	Eye of golden day! O marching light	
	Across the eddy and rush of Dircê's stream,	
	Striking the white shields of the enemy	
	Thrown headlong backward from the blaze of morning!	

CHORAG. Polyneicês their commander
         Roused them with windy phrases,
         He the wild eagle screaming
         Insults above our land,
         His wings their shields of snow,
         His crest their marshalled helms.

CHORUS. Against our seven gates in a yawning ring   [ANTISTROPHE 1
         The famished spears came onward in the night;
         But before his jaws were sated with our blood,
         Or pinefire took the garland of our towers,
         He was thrown back; and as he turned, great Thebes—
         No tender victim for his noisy power—
         Rose like a dragon behind him, shouting war.

CHORAG. For God hates utterly
         The bray of bragging tongues;
         And when he beheld their smiling,
         Their swagger of golden helms,
         The frown of his thunder blasted
         Their first man from our walls.

CHORUS. We heard his shout of triumph high in the air   [STROPHE 2
         Turn to a scream; far out in a flaming arc
         He fell with his windy torch, and the earth struck him.
         And others storming in fury no less than his
         Found shock of death in the dusty joy of battle.

CHORAG. Seven captains at seven gates
         Yielded their clanging arms to the god
         That bends the battle-line and breaks it.
         These two only, brothers in blood,
         Face to face in matchless rage,
         Mirroring each the other's death,
         Clashed in long combat.

CHORUS. But now in the beautiful morning of victory   [ANTISTROPHE 2
         Let Thebes of the many chariots sing for joy!
         With hearts for dancing we'll take leave of war:
         Our temples shall be sweet with hymns of praise,
         And the long night shall echo with our chorus.

SCENE I

CHORAG. But now at last our new King is coming:
         Creon of Thebes, Menoiceus' son.
         In this auspicious dawn of his reign
         What are the new complexities
         That shifting Fate has woven for him?
         What is his counsel? Why has he summoned
         The old men to hear him?

[Enter CREON *from the Palace. He addresses the* CHORUS *from the top step.*

37

CREON. Gentlemen: I have the honour to inform you that our Ship of State, which recent storms have threatened to destroy, has come safely to harbour at last, guided by the merciful wisdom of Heaven. I have summoned you here this morning because I know that I can depend upon you: your devotion to King Laïos was absolute; you never hesitated in your duty to our late ruler Oedipus; and when Oedipus died, your loyalty was transferred to his children. Unfortunately, as you know, his two sons, the princes Eteoclês and Polyneicês, have killed each other in battle; and I, as the next in blood, have succeeded to the full power of the throne.

I am aware, of course, that no Ruler can expect complete loyalty from his subjects until he has been tested in office. Nevertheless, I say to you at the very outset that I have nothing but contempt for the kind of Governor who is afraid, for whatever reason, to follow the course that he knows is best for the State; and as for the man who sets private friendship above the public welfare,—I have no use for him, either. I call God to witness that if I saw my country headed for ruin, I should not be afraid to speak out plainly; and I need hardly remind you that I would never have any dealings with an enemy of the people. No one values friendship more highly than I; but we must remember that friends made at the risk of wrecking our Ship are not real friends at all.

These are my principles, at any rate, and that is why I have made the following decision concerning the sons of Oedipus: Eteoclês, who died as a man should die, fighting for his country, is to be buried with full military honours, with all the ceremony that is usual when the greatest heroes die; but his brother Polyneicês, who broke his exile to come back with fire and sword against his native city and the shrines of his fathers' gods, whose one idea was to spill the blood of his blood and sell his own people into slavery—Polyneicês, I say, is to have no burial: no man is to touch him or say the least prayer for him; he shall lie on the plain, unburied; and the birds and the scavenging dogs can do with him whatever they like.

This is my command, and you can see the wisdom behind it. As long as I am King, no traitor is going to be honoured with the loyal man. But whoever shows by word and deed that he is on the side of the State,—he shall have my respect while he is living, and my reverence when he is dead.

CHORAG. If that is your will, Creon son of Menoiceus,
You have the right to enforce it: we are yours.

CREON. That is my will. Take care that you do your part.

CHORAG. We are old men; let the younger ones carry it out.

CREON. I do not mean that: the sentries have been appointed.

CHORAG. Then what is it that you would have us do?

CREON. You will give no support to whoever breaks this law.

CHORAG. Only a crazy man is in love with death!

CREON. And death it is; yet money talks, and the wisest
Have sometimes been known to count a few coins too many.

[Enter SENTRY.

SENTRY. I'll not say that I'm out of breath from running, King, because every time I stopped to think about what I have to tell you, I felt like going back. And all the time a voice kept saying, 'You fool, don't you know you're walking straight into trouble?'; and then another voice: 'Yes, but if you let somebody else get the news to Creon first, it will be even worse than that for you!' But good sense won out, at least I hope it was good sense, and here I am with a story that makes no sense at all; but I'll tell it anyhow, because, as they say, what's going to happen's going to happen, and—

CREON.   Come to the point. What have you to say?

SENTRY.   I did not do it. I did not see who did it. You must not punish me for what someone else has done.

CREON.   A comprehensive defence! More effective, perhaps,
If I knew its purpose. Come: what is it?

SENTRY.   A dreadful thing . . . I don't know how to put it—
CREON.   Out with it!

SENTRY.   Well, then;
The dead man—
            Polyneicês—

[Pause. The SENTRY is overcome, fumbles for words. CREON
            waits impassively.

                    out there—
                        someone,—

New dust on the slimy flesh!

                [Pause. No sign from CREON.

Someone has given it burial that way, and
Gone . . .

        [Long pause. CREON finally speaks with deadly control:

CREON.   And the man who dared do this?

SENTRY.   I swear I
Do not know! You must believe me!
                        Listen:
The ground was dry, not a sign of digging, no,
Not a wheeltrack in the dust, no trace of anyone.
It was when they relieved us this morning: and one of them,
The corporal, pointed to it.
                        There it was,
The strangest—
            Look:
The body, just mounded over with light dust: you see?
Not buried really, but as if they'd covered it
Just enough for the ghost's peace. And no sign
Of dogs or any wild animal that had been there.

And then what a scene there was! Every man of us
Accusing the other: we all proved the other man did it,
We all had proof that we could not have done it.
We were ready to take hot iron in our hands,
Walk through fire, swear by all the gods,
It was not I!
I do not know who it was, but it was not I!

[CREON'S *rage has been mounting steadily, but the* SENTRY *is too intent upon his
            story to notice it.*

39

And then, when this came to nothing, someone said
A thing that silenced us and made us stare
Down at the ground: you had to be told the news,
And one of us had to do it! We threw the dice,
And the bad luck fell to me. So here I am,
No happier to be here than you are to have me:
Nobody likes the man who brings bad news.

CHORAG.   I have been wondering, King: can it be that the gods have done this?

[Furiously.

CREON.   Stop!
Must you doddering wrecks
Go out of your heads entirely? 'The gods!'
Intolerable!
The gods favour this corpse? Why? How had he served them?
Tried to loot their temples, burn their images,
Yes, and the whole State, and its laws with it!
Is it your senile opinion that the gods love to honour bad men?
A pious thought!—
             No, from the very beginning
There have been those who have whispered together,
Stiff-necked anarchists, putting their heads together,
Scheming against me in alleys. These are the men,
And they have bribed my own guard to do this thing.

[Sententiously.

Money!
There's nothing in the world so demoralising as money.
Down go your cities,
Homes gone, men gone, honest hearts corrupted,
Crookedness of all kinds, and all for money!

[To SENTRY:

                        But you—!
I swear by God and by the throne of God,
The man who has done this thing shall pay for it!
Find that man, bring him here to me, or your death
Will be the least of your problems: I'll string you up
Alive, and there will be certain ways to make you
Discover your employer before you die;
And the process may teach you a lesson you seem to have missed:
The dearest profit is sometimes all too dear.
That depends on the source. Do you understand me?
A fortune won is often misfortune.

SENTRY.   King, may I speak?

CREON.   Your very voice distresses me.

SENTRY.   Are you sure that it is my voice, and not your conscience?

CREON.   By God, he wants to analyse me now!

SENTRY.   It is not what I say, but what has been done, that hurts you.

CREON.   You talk too much.

SENTRY.	Maybe; but I've done nothing.
CREON.	Sold your soul for some silver: that's all you've done.
SENTRY.	How dreadful it is when the right judge judges wrong!
CREON.	Your figures of speech May entertain you now; but unless you bring me the man, You will get little profit from them in the end.

[Exit CREON *into the Palace.*

| SENTRY. | 'Bring me the man'—!
I'd like nothing better than bringing him the man!
But bring him or not, you have seen the last of me here.
At any rate, I am safe! |

[Exit SENTRY.

ODE I

| CHORUS. | Numberless are the world's wonders, but none | [STROPHE 1 |

Numberless are the world's wonders, but none
More wonderful than man; the stormgrey sea
Yields to his prows, the huge crests bear him high;
Earth, holy and inexhaustible, is graven
With shining furrows where his plows have gone
Year after year, the timeless labour of stallions.

[ANTISTROPHE 1

The lightboned birds and beasts that cling to cover,
The lithe fish lighting their reaches of dim water,
All are taken, tamed in the net of his mind;
The lion on the hill, the wild horse windy-maned,
Resign to him; and his blunt yoke has broken
The sultry shoulders of the mountain bull.

[STROPHE 2

Words also, and thought as rapid as air,
He fashions to his good use; statecraft is his,
And his the skill that deflects the arrows of snow,
The spears of winter rain: from every wind
He has made himself secure—from all but one:
In the late wind of death he cannot stand.

[ANTISTROPHE 2

O clear intelligence, force beyond all measure!
O fate of man, working both good and evil!
When the laws are kept, how proudly his city stands!
When the laws are broken, what of his city then?
Never may the anarchic man find rest at my hearth,
Never be it said that my thoughts are his thoughts.

SCENE II

[Re-enter SENTRY *leading* ANTIGONE.

| CHORAG. | What does this mean? Surely this captive woman
Is the Princess Antigonê. Why should she be taken? |
| SENTRY. | Here is the one who did it! We caught her
In the very act of burying him.—Where is Creon? |

41

CHORAG.	Just coming from the house.

[Enter CREON, *C.*

CREON.	What has happened? Why have you come back so soon?

[Expansively.

SENTRY.	O King, A man should never be too sure of anything: I would have sworn That you'd not see me here again: your anger Frightened me so, and the things you threatened me with; But how could I tell then That I'd be able to solve the case so soon? No dice-throwing this time: I was only too glad to come! Here is this woman. She is the guilty one: We found her trying to bury him. Take her, then; question her; judge her as you will. I am through with the whole thing now, and glad of it.
CREON.	But this is Antigonê! Why have you brought her here?
SENTRY.	She was burying him, I tell you!

[Severely.

CREON.	Is this the truth?
SENTRY.	I saw her with my own eyes. Can I say more?
CREON.	The details: come, tell me quickly!
SENTRY.	It was like this: After those terrible threats of yours, King, We went back and brushed the dust away from the body. The flesh was soft by now, and stinking, So we sat on a hill to windward and kept guard. No napping this time! We kept each other awake. But nothing happened until the white round sun Whirled in the centre of the round sky over us: Then, suddenly, A storm of dust roared up from the earth, and the sky Went out, the plain vanished with all its trees In the stinging dark. We closed our eyes and endured it. The whirlwind lasted a long time, but it passed; And then we looked, and there was Antigonê! I have seen A mother bird come back to a stripped nest, heard Her crying bitterly a broken note or two For the young ones stolen. Just so, when this girl Found the bare corpse, and all her love's work wasted, She wept, and cried on heaven to damn the hands That had done this thing And then she brought more dust And sprinkled wine three times for her brother's ghost.

We ran and took her at once. She was not afraid,
Not even when we charged her with what she had done.
She denied nothing.
                    And this was a comfort to me,
And some uneasiness: for it is a good thing
To escape from death, but it is no great pleasure
To bring death to a friend.
                    Yet I always say
There is nothing so comfortable as your own safe skin!

[Slowly, dangerously.

CREON.   And you, Antigonê,
You with your head hanging,—do you confess this thing?

ANTIG.   I do. I deny nothing.

[To SENTRY:

CREON.   You may go.

[Exit SENTRY.
[To ANTIGONE:

Tell me, tell me briefly:
Had you heard my proclamation touching this matter?

ANTIG.   It was public. Could I help hearing it?

CREON.   And yet you dared defy the law.

ANTIG.   I dared.
It was not God's proclamation. That final Justice
That rules the world below makes no such laws.

Your edict, King, was strong,
But all your strength is weakness itself against
The immortal unrecorded laws of God.
They are not merely now: they were, and shall be,
Operative for ever, beyond man utterly.

I knew I must die, even without your decree:
I am only mortal. And if I must die
Now, before it is my time to die,
Surely this is no hardship: can anyone
Living, as I live, with evil all about me,
Think Death less than a friend? This death of mine
Is of no importance; but if I had left my brother
Lying in death unburied, I should have suffered.
Now I do not.
                    You smile at me. Ah Creon,
Think me a fool, if you like; but it may well be
That a *fool* convicts me of *folly.*

CHORAG.   Like father, like daughter: both headstrong, deaf to reason!
She has never learned to yield.

CREON.   She has much to learn.
The inflexible heart breaks first, the toughest iron
Cracks first, and the wildest horses bend their necks
At the pull of the smallest curb.
                         Pride? In a slave?

This girl is guilty of a double insolence,
Breaking the given laws and boasting of it.
Who is the man here,
She or I, if this crime goes unpunished?
Sister's child, or more than sister's child,
Or closer yet in blood—she and her sister
Win bitter death for this!

[To servants:

              Go, some of you,
Arrest Ismenê. I accuse her equally.
Bring her: you will find her sniffling in the house there.

Her mind's a traitor: crimes kept in the dark
Cry for light, and the guardian brain shudders;
But how much worse than this
Is brazen boasting of barefaced anarchy!

ANTIG.   Creon, what more do you want than my death?

CREON.   Nothing.
That gives me everything.

ANTIG.   Then I beg you: kill me.
This talking is a great weariness: your words
Are distasteful to me, and I am sure that mine
Seem so to you. And yet they should not seem so:
I should have praise and honour for what I have done.
All these men here would praise me
Were their lips not frozen shut with fear of you.

[Bitterly.

Ah the good fortune of kings,
Licensed to say and do whatever they please!

CREON.   You are alone here in that opinion.

ANTIG.   No, *they* are with *me*. But they keep their tongues in leash.

CREON.   Maybe. But you are guilty, and they are not.

ANTIG.   There is no guilt in reverence for the dead.

CREON.   But Eteoclês—was he not your brother too?

ANTIG.   My brother too.

CREON.   And you insult his memory?

[Softly.

ANTIG.   The dead man would not say that I insult it.

CREON.   He would: for you honour a traitor as much as him.

ANTIG.   His own brother, traitor or not, and equal in blood.

CREON.   He made war on his country. Eteoclês defended it.

ANTIG.   Nevertheless, there are honours due all the dead.

CREON.   But not the same for the wicked as for the just.

ANTIG.   Ah Creon, Creon,
Which of us can say what the gods hold wicked?

CREON. An enemy is an enemy, even dead.

ANTIG. It is my nature to join in love, not hate.

[Finally losing patience.

CREON. Go join them, then; if you must have your love,
Find it in hell!

CHORAG. But see, Ismenê comes:

[Enter ISMENE, *guarded.*

Those tears are sisterly, the cloud
That shadows her eyes rains down gentle sorrow.

CREON. You too, Ismenê,
Snake in my ordered house, sucking my blood
Stealthily—and all the time I never knew
That these two sisters were aiming at my throne!
                                                Ismenê,
Do you confess your share in this crime, or deny it?
Answer me.

ISMENE. Yes, if she let me say so. I am guilty.

[Coldly.

ANTIG. No, Ismenê. You have no right to say so.
You would not help me, and I will not have you help me.

ISMENE. But now I know what you meant; and I am here
To join you, to take my share of punishment.

ANTIG. The dead man and the gods who rule the dead
Know whose act this was. Words are not friends.

ISMENE. Do you refuse me, Antigonê? I want to die with you:
I too have a duty that I must discharge to the dead.

ANTIG. You shall not lessen my death by sharing it.

ISMENE. What do I care for life when you are dead?

ANTIG. Ask Creon. You're always hanging on his opinions.

ISMENE. You are laughing at me. Why, Antigonê?

ANTIG. It's a joyless laughter, Ismenê.

ISMENE.   But can I do nothing?

ANTIG. Yes. Save yourself. I shall not envy you.
There are those who will praise you; I shall have honour, too.

ISMENE. But we are equally guilty!

ANTIG.   No, more, Ismenê.
You are alive, but I belong to Death.

CREON. *[To the* CHORUS:
Gentlemen, I beg you to observe these girls:
One has just now lost her mind; the other
It seems, has never had a mind at all.

ISMENE. Grief teaches the steadiest minds to waver, King.

45

CREON.	Yours certainly did, when you assumed guilt with the guilty!
ISMENE.	But how could I go on living without her?
CREON.	You are. She is already dead.
ISMENE.	But your own son's bride!
CREON.	There are places enough for him to push his plow. I want no wicked women for my sons!
ISMENE.	O dearest Haimon, how your father wrongs you!
CREON.	I've had enough of your childish talk of marriage!
CHORAG.	Do you really intend to steal this girl from your son?
CREON.	No; Death will do that for me.
CHORAG.	Then she must die?

CREON.   You dazzle me.
                    —But enough of this talk!

                    [*To* GUARDS:
You, there, take them away and guard them well:
For they are but women, and even brave men run
When they see Death coming.

              [*Exeunt* ISMENE, ANTIGONE, *and* GUARDS.

ODE II

                                                    [STROPHE 1

CHORUS.   Fortunate is the man who has never tasted God's vengeance!
          Where once the anger of heaven has struck, that house is shaken
          For ever: damnation rises behind each child
          Like a wave cresting out of the black northeast,
          When the long darkness under sea roars up
          And bursts drumming death upon the windwhipped sand.

                                                    [ANTISTROPHE 1
          I have seen this gathering sorrow from time long past
          Loom upon Oedipus's children: generation from generation
          Takes the compulsive rage of the enemy god.
          So lately this last flower of Oedipus' line
          Drank the sunlight! but now a passionate word
          And a handful of dust have closed up all its beauty.
                    What mortal arrogance   [STROPHE 2
                    Transcends the wrath of Zeus?
          Sleep cannot lull him, nor the effortless long months
          Of the timeless gods: but he is young for ever,
          And his house is the shining day of high Olympos.
                    All that is and shall be,
                    And all the past, is his.
          No pride on earth is free of the curse of heaven.

          The straying dreams of men   [ANTISTROPHE 2

May bring them ghosts of joy:
But as they drowse, the waking embers burn them;
Or they walk with fixed eyes, as blind men walk.
But the ancient wisdom speaks for our own time:
Fate works most for woe
With Folly's fairest show.
Man's little pleasure is the spring of sorrow.

SCENE III

CHORAG.   But here is Haimon, King, the last of all your sons.
Is it grief for Antigonê that brings him here,
And bitterness at being robbed of his bride?

[Enter HAIMON.

CREON.   We shall soon see, and no need of diviners.
                                                    —Son,
You have heard my final judgment on that girl:
Have you come here hating me, or have you come
With deference and with love, whatever I do?

HAIMON.   I am your son, father. You are my guide.
You make things clear for me, and I obey you.
No marriage means more to me than your continuing wisdom.

CREON.   Good. That is the way to behave: subordinate
Everything else, my son, to your father's will.
This is what a man prays for, that he may get
Sons attentive and dutiful in his house,
Each one hating his father's enemies,
Honouring his father's friends. But if his sons
Fail him, if they turn out unprofitably,
What has he fathered but trouble for himself
And amusement for the malicious?
                                      So you are right
Not to lose your head over this woman.
Your pleasure with her would soon grow cold, Haimon,
And then you'd have a hellcat in bed and elsewhere.
Let her find her husband in Hell!
Of all the people in this city, only she
Has had contempt for my law and broken it.

Do you want me to show myself weak before the people?
Or to break my sworn word? No, and I will not.
The woman dies.

I suppose she'll plead 'family ties.' Well, let her.
If I permit my own family to rebel,
How shall I earn the world's obedience?
Show me the man who keeps his house in hand,
He's fit for public authority.
                                   I'll have no dealings
With law-breakers, critics of the government:
Whoever is chosen to govern should be obeyed—
Must be obeyed, in all things, great and small,

Just and unjust! O Haimon,
The man who knows how to obey, and that man only,
Knows how to give commands when the time comes.
You can depend on him, no matter how fast
The spears come: he's a good soldier, he'll stick it out.

Anarchy, anarchy! Show me a greater evil!
This is why cities tumble and the great houses rain down,
This is what scatters armies!

No, no: good lives are made so by discipline.
We keep the laws then, and the lawmakers,
And no woman shall seduce us. If we must lose,
Let's lose to a man, at least! Is a woman stronger than we?

CHORAG. Unless time has rusted my wits,
What you say, King, is said with point and dignity.

[Boyishly earnest.

HAIMON. Father:
Reason is God's crowning gift to man, and you are right
To warn me against losing mine. I cannot say—
I hope that I shall never want to say!—that you
Have reasoned badly. Yet there are other men
Who can reason, too; and their opinions might be helpful.
You are not in a position to know everything
That people say or do, or what they feel:
Your temper terrifies them—everyone
Will tell you only what you like to hear.
But I, at any rate, can listen; and I have heard them
Muttering and whispering in the dark about this girl.
They say no woman has ever, so unreasonably,
Died so shameful a death for a generous act:
'She covered her brother's body. Is this indecent?
'She kept him from dogs and vultures. Is this a crime?
'Death?—She should have all the honour that we can give her!'

This is the way they talk out there in the city.

You must believe me:
Nothing is closer to me than your happiness.
What could be closer? Must not any son
Value his father's fortune as his father does his?
I beg you, do not be unchangeable:
Do not believe that you alone can be right.
The man who thinks that,
The man who maintains that only he has the power
To reason correctly, the gift to speak, the soul—
A man like that, when you know him, turns out empty.

It is not reason never to yield to reason!

In flood time you can see how some trees bend,
And because they bend, even their twigs are safe,
While stubborn trees are torn up, roots and all.
And the same thing happens in sailing:
Make your sheet fast, never slacken,—and over you go,
Head over heels and under: and there's your voyage.

48

	Forget you are angry! Let yourself be moved!
	I know I am young; but please let me say this:
	The ideal condition
	Would be, I admit, that men should be right by instinct;
	But since we are all too likely to go astray,
	The reasonable thing is to learn from those who can teach.
CHORAG.	You will do well to listen to him, King,
	If what he says is sensible. And you, Haimon,
	Must listen to your father.—Both speak well.
CREON.	You consider it right for a man of my years and experience
	To go to school to a boy?
HAIMON.	It is not right
	If I am wrong. But if I am young, and right,
	What does my age matter?
CREON.	You think it right to stand up for an anarchist?
HAIMON.	Not at all. I pay no respect to criminals.
CREON.	Then she is not a criminal?
HAIMON.	The City would deny it, to a man.
CREON.	And the City proposes to teach me how to rule?
HAIMON.	Ah. Who is it that's talking like a boy now?
CREON.	My voice is the one voice giving orders in this City!
HAIMON.	It is no City if it takes orders from one voice.
CREON.	The State is the King!
HAIMON.	Yes, if the State is a desert.

[Pause.

CREON.	This boy, it seems, has sold out to a woman.
HAIMON.	If you are a woman: my concern is only for you.
CREON.	So? Your 'concern'! In a public brawl with your father!
HAIMON.	How about you, in a public brawl with justice?
CREON.	With justice, when all that I do is within my rights?
HAIMON.	You have no right to trample on God's right.

[Completely out of control.

CREON.	Fool, adolescent fool! Taken in by a woman!
HAIMON.	You'll never see me taken in by anything vile.
CREON.	Every word you say is for her!

[Quietly, darkly.

HAIMON.	And for you.
	And for me. And for the gods under the earth.
CREON.	You'll never marry her while she lives.
HAIMON.	Then she must die.—But her death will cause another.

CREON.   Another?
            Have you lost your senses? Is this an open threat?

HAIMON.   There is no threat in speaking to emptiness.

CREON.   I swear you'll regret this superior tone of yours!
            You are the empty one!

HAIMON.   If you were not my father,
            I'd say you were perverse.

CREON.   You girlstruck fool, don't play at words with me!

HAIMON.   I am sorry. You prefer silence.

CREON.   Now, by God—!
            I swear, by all the gods in heaven above us,
            You'll watch it, I swear you shall!

                        [To the SERVANTS.

                                    Bring her out!
            Bring the woman out! Let her die before his eyes,
            Here, this instant, with her bridegroom beside her!

HAIMON.   Not here, no; she will not die here, King.
            And you will never see my face again.
            Go on raving as long as you've a friend to endure you.

                        [Exit HAIMON.

CHORAG.   Gone, gone.
            Creon, a young man in a rage is dangerous!

CREON.   Let him do, or dream to do, more than a man can.
            He shall not save these girls from death.

CHORAG.   These girls?
            You have sentenced them both?

CREON.   No, you are right.
            I will not kill the one whose hands are clean.

CHORAG.   But Antigonê?

                        [Sombrely.

CREON.   I will carry her far away
            Out there in the wilderness, and lock her
            Living in a vault of stone. She shall have food,
            As the custom is, to absolve the State of her death.
            And there let her pray to the gods of Hell:
            They are her only gods:
            Perhaps they will show her an escape from death,
            Or she may learn,
                        though late,
            That piety shown the dead is pity in vain.

                        [Exit CREON.

ODE III

CHORUS.   Love, unconquerable   [STROPHE
                Waster of rich men, keeper
                Of warm lights and all-night vigil
                In the soft face of a girl:
                Sea-wanderer, forest-visitor!
                Even the pure Immortals cannot escape you,
                And mortal man, in his one day's dusk,
                Trembles before your glory.

                Surely you swerve upon ruin   [ANTISTROPHE
                The just man's consenting heart,
                As here you have made bright anger
                Strike between father and son—
                And none has conquered but Love!
                A girl's glánce wórking the will of heaven:
                Pléasure to her alone who mocks us,
                Merciless Aphroditê.

SCENE IV

[As ANTIGONE *enters guarded.*

CHORAG.   But I can no longer stand in awe of this,
                Nor, seeing what I see, keep back my tears.
                Here is Antigonê, passing to that chamber
                Where all find sleep at last.

ANTIG.   Look upon me, friends, and pity me   [STROPHE 1
                Turning back at the night's edge to say
                Good-bye to the sun that shines for me no longer;
                Now sleepy Death
                Summons me down to Acheron, that cold shore:
                There is no bridesong there, nor any music.

CHORUS.   Yet not unpraised, not without a kind of honour,
                You walk at last into the underworld;
                Untouched by sickness, broken by no sword.
                What woman has ever found your way to death?

ANTIG.   How often I have heard the story of Niobê,   [ANTISTROPHE 1
                Tantalos' wretched daughter, how the stone
                Clung fast about her, ivy-close; and they say
                The rain falls endlessly
                And sifting soft snow; her tears are never done.
                I feel the loneliness of her death in mine.

CHORUS.   But she was born of heaven, and you
                Are woman, woman-born. If her death is yours,
                A mortal woman's, is this not for you
                Glory in our world and in the world beyond?

ANTIG.   You laugh at me. Ah, friends, friends,   [STROPHE 2
                Can you not wait until I am dead? O Thebes,
                O men many-charioted, in love with Fortune,

Dear springs of Dircê, sacred Theban grove,
Be witnesses for me, denied all pity,
Unjustly judged! and think a word of love
For her whose path turns
Under dark earth, where there are no more tears.

CHORUS. You have passed beyond human daring and come at last
Into a place of stone where Justice sits.
I cannot tell
What shape of your father's guilt appears in this.

ANTIG. You have touched it at last: that bridal bed   [ANTISTROPHE 2
Unspeakable, horror of son and mother mingling:
Their crime, infection of all our family!
O Oedipus, father and brother!
Your marriage strikes from the grave to murder mine.
I have been a stranger here in my own land:
All my life
The blasphemy of my birth has followed me.

CHORUS. Reverence is a virtue, but strength
Lives in established law: that must prevail.
You have made your choice,
Your death is the doing of your conscious hand.

ANTIG. Then let me go, since all your words are bitter,   [EPODE
And the very light of the sun is cold to me,
Lead me to my vigil, where I must have
Neither love nor lamentation; no song, but silence.

[CREON interrupts impatiently.

CREON. If dirges and planned lamentations could put off death,
Men would be singing for ever.

[To the SERVANTS.

Take her, go!
You know your orders: take her to the vault
And leave her alone there. And if she lives or dies,
That's her affair, not ours: our hands are clean.

ANTIG. O tomb, vaulted bride-bed in eternal rock,
Soon I shall be with my own again
Where Persephonê welcomes the thin ghosts underground:
And I shall see my father again, and you, mother,
And dearest Polyneicês—
dearest indeed
To me, since it was my hand
That washed him clean and poured the ritual wine:
And my reward is death before my time!

And yet, as men's hearts know, I have done no wrong,
I have not sinned before God. Or if I have,
I shall know the truth in death. But if the guilt
Lies upon Creon who judged me, then, I pray,
May his punishment equal my own.

CHORAG.   O passionate heart,
Unyielding, tormented still by the same winds!

CREON.   Her guards shall have good cause to regret their delaying.

ANTIG.   Ah! That voice is like the voice of death!

CREON.   I can give you no reason to think you are mistaken.

ANTIG.   Thebes, and you my fathers' gods.
           And rulers of Thebes, you see me now, the last
           Unhappy daughter of a line of kings,
           Your kings, led away to death. You will remember
           What things I suffer, and at what men's hands,
           Because I would not transgress the laws of heaven.

                    [To the GUARDS, *simply.*

           Come: let us wait no longer.

                    [Exit ANTIGONE, *L. guarded.*

ODE IV

CHORUS.   All Danaê's beauty was locked away   [STROPHE 1
           In a brazen cell where the sunlight could not come:
           A small room, still as any grave, enclosed her.
           Yet she was a princess too,
           And Zeus in a rain of gold poured love upon her.
           O child, child,
           No power in wealth or war
           Or tough sea-blackened ships
           Can prevail against untiring Destiny!

           And Dryas' son also, that furious king,   [ANTISTROPHE 1
           Bore the god's prisoning anger for his pride:
           Sealed up by Dionysos in deaf stone,
           His madness died among echoes.
           So at the last he learned what dreadful power
           His tongue had mocked:
           For he had profaned the revels,
           And fired the wrath of the nine
           Implacable Sisters that love the sound of the flute.

           And old men tell a half-remembered tale   [STROPHE 2
           Of horror done where a dark ledge splits the sea
           And a double surf beats on the grey shores:
           How a king's new woman, sick
           With hatred for the queen he had imprisoned,
           Ripped out his two sons' eyes with her bloody hands
           While grinning Arês watched the shuttle plunge
           Four times: four blind wounds crying for revenge,

           Crying, tears and blood mingled.—Piteously born,   [ANTISTROPHE 2
           Those sons whose mother was of heavenly birth!
           Her father was the god of the North Wind
           And she was cradled by gales,
           She raced with young colts on the glittering hills
           And walked untrammeled in the open light:
           But in her marriage deathless Fate found means
           To build a tomb like yours for all her joy.

SCENE V

[Enter blind TEIRESIAS, *led by a boy. The opening speeches of* TEIRESIAS *should be in singsong contrast to the realistic lines of* CREON.

TEIRES. This is the way the blind man comes, Princes, Princes,
Lock-step, two heads lit by the eyes of one.

CREON. What new thing have you to tell us, old Teiresias?

TEIRES. I have much to tell you: listen to the prophet, Creon.

CREON. I am not aware that I have ever failed to listen.

TEIRES. Then you have done wisely, King, and ruled well.

CREON. I admit my debt to you. But what have you to say?

TEIRES. This, Creon: you stand once more on the edge of fate.

CREON. What do you mean? Your words are a kind of dread.

TEIRES. Listen, Creon:
I was sitting in my chair of augury, at the place
Where the birds gather about me. They were all a-chatter,
As is their habit, when suddenly I heard
A strange note in their jangling, a scream, a
Whirring fury; I knew that they were fighting,
Tearing each other, dying
In a whirlwind of wings clashing. And I was afraid.
I began the rites of burnt-offering at the altar,
But Hephaistos failed me: instead of bright flame,
There was only the sputtering slime of the fat thigh-flesh
Melting: the entrails dissolved in grey smoke,
The bare bone burst from the welter. And no blaze!

This was a sign from heaven. My boy described it,
Seeing for me as I see for others.

I tell you, Creon, you yourself have brought
This new calamity upon us. Our hearths and altars
Are stained with the corruption of dogs and carrion birds
That glut themselves on the corpse of Oedipus' son.
The gods are deaf when we pray to them, their fire
Recoils from our offering, their birds of omen
Have no cry of comfort, for they are gorged
With the thick blood of the dead.
                      O my son,
These are no trifles! Think: all men make mistakes,
But a good man yields when he knows his course is wrong,
And repairs the evil. The only crime is pride.

Give in to the dead man, then: do not fight with a corpse—
What glory is it to kill a man who is dead?
Think, I beg you:
It is for your own good that I speak as I do.
You should be able to yield for your own good.

CREON. It seems that prophets have made me their especial province.
All my life long
I have been a kind of butt for the dull arrows
Of doddering fortune-tellers!
No, Teiresias:
If your birds—if the great eagles of God himself
Should carry him stinking bit by bit to heaven,
I would not yield. I am not afraid of pollution:
No man can defile the gods.
Do what you will,
Go into business, make money, speculate
In India gold or that synthetic gold from Sardis,
Get rich otherwise than by my consent to bury him.
Teiresias, it is a sorry thing when a wise man
Sells his wisdom, lets out his words for hire!

TEIRES. Ah Creon! Is there no man left in the world—

CREON. To do what?—Come, let's have the aphorism!

TEIRES. No man who knows that wisdom outweighs any wealth?

CREON. As surely as bribes are baser than any baseness.

TEIRES. You are sick, Creon! You are deathly sick!

CREON. As you say: it is not my place to challenge a prophet.

TEIRES. Yet you have said my prophecy is for sale.

CREON. The generation of prophets has always loved gold.

TEIRES. The generation of kings has always loved brass.

CREON. You forget yourself! You are speaking to your King.

TEIRES. I know it. You are a king because of me.

CREON. You have a certain skill; but you have sold out.

TEIRES. King, you will drive me to words that—

CREON. Say them, say them!
Only remember: I will not pay you for them.

TEIRES. No, you will find them too costly.

CREON. No doubt. Speak:
Whatever you say, you will not change my will.

TEIRES. Then take this, and take it to heart!
The time is not far off when you shall pay back
Corpse for corpse, flesh of your own flesh.
You have thrust the child of this world into living night,
You have kept from the gods below the child that is theirs:
The one in a grave before her death, the other,
Dead, denied the grave. This is your crime:
And the Furies and the dark gods of Hell
Are swift with terrible punishment for you.

Do you want to buy me now, Creon?

Not many days,

And your house will be full of men and women weeping,
And curses will be hurled at you from far
Cities grieving for sons unburied, left to rot before the walls of Thebes.

These are my arrows, Creon; they are all for you.

[To BOY:

But come, child: lead me home.
Let him waste his fine anger upon younger men.
Maybe he will learn at last
To control a wiser tongue in a better head.

[Exit TEIRESIAS.

CHORAG. The old man has gone, King, but his words
Remain to plague us. I am old, too,
But I can not remember that he was ever false.

CREON. That is true. . . . It troubles me.
Oh it is hard to give in! but it is worse
To risk everything for stubborn pride.

CHORAG. Creon: take my advice.

CREON. What shall I do?

CHORAG. Go quickly: free Antigonê from her vault
And build a tomb for the body of Polyneicês.

CREON. You would have me do this?

CHORAG. Creon, yes!
And it must be done at once: God moves
Swiftly to cancel the folly of stubborn men.

CREON. It is hard to deny the heart! But I
Will do it: I will not fight with destiny.

CHORAG. You must go yourself, you cannot leave it to others.

CREON. I will go.
—Bring axes, servants:
Come with me to the tomb. I buried her, I
Will set her free.
Oh quickly!
My mind misgives—
The laws of the gods are mighty, and a man must serve them
To the last day of his life!

[Exit CREON.

PÆAN

CHORAG. God of many names   [STROPHE 1
CHORUS.   O Iacchos
          son
of Cadmeian Sémelê
       O born of the Thunder!

                    Guardian of the West
                                Regent
                    of Eleusis' plain
                                O Prince of mænad Thebes
                    and the Dragon Field by rippling Ismenos:

CHORAG.   God of many names   [ANTISTROPHE 1
CHORUS.   the flame of torches
                    flares on our hills
                                the nymphs of Iacchos
                    dance at the spring of Castalia:
                    from the vine-close mountain
                                            come ah come in ivy:
                    Evohe evohe! sings through the streets of Thebes

CHORAG.   God of many names   [STROPHE 2
CHORUS.   Iacchos of Thebes
                    heavenly Child
                                of Sémelê bride of the Thunderer!
                    The shadow of plague is upon us:
                                                come
                    with clement feet
                                oh come from Parnasos
                    down the slopes
                                across the lamenting water

CHORAG.   Iô Fire! Chorister of the throbbing stars!   [ANTISTROPHE 2
                    O purest among the voices of the night!
                    Thou son of God blaze for us!

CHORUS.   Come with chronic rapture of circling Maenads
                    Who cry *Io Iacche!*
                                God of many names!

EXODOS

[Enter MESSENGER.

MESS.   Men of the line of Cadmos, you who live,
                    Near Amphion's citadel:
                                I cannot say
                    Of any condition of human life 'This is fixed,
                    This is clearly good, or bad.' Fate raises up,
                    And Fate casts down the happy and unhappy alike:
                    No man can foretell his Fate.
                                            Take the case of Creon:
                    Creon was happy once, as I count happiness:
                    Victorious in battle, sole governor of the land,
                    Fortunate father of children nobly born.
                    And now it has all gone from him! Who can say
                    That a man is still alive when his life's joy fails?
                    He is a walking dead man. Grant him rich,
                    Let him live like a king in his great house:
                    If his pleasure is gone, I would not give
                    So much as the shadow of smoke for all he owns.

CHORAG.   Your words hint at sorrow: what is your news for us?

57

MESS.	They are dead. The living are guilty of their death.
CHORAG.	Who is guilty? Who is dead? Speak!
MESS.	Haimon. Haimon is dead; and the hand that killed him Is his own hand.
CHORAG.	His father's? or his own?
MESS.	His own, driven mad by the murder his father had done.
CHORAG.	Teiresias, Teiresias, how clearly you saw it all!
MESS.	This is my news: you must draw what conclusions you can from it.
CHORAG.	But look: Eurydicê, our Queen: Has she overheard us?

[Enter EURYDICE *from the Palace, C.*

EURYD.	I have heard something, friends: As I was unlocking the gate of Pallas' shrine, For I needed her help today, I heard a voice Telling of some new sorrow. And I fainted There at the temple with all my maidens about me. But speak again; whatever it is, I can bear it: Grief and I are no strangers.
MESS.	Dearest Lady, I will tell you plainly all that I have seen. I shall not try to comfort you: what is the use, Since comfort could lie only in what is not true? The truth is always best. I went with Creon To the outer plain where Polyneicês was lying, No friend to pity him, his body shredded by dogs. We made our prayers in that place to Hecatê And Pluto, that they would be merciful. And we bathed The corpse with holy water, and we brought Fresh-broken branches to burn what was left of it, And upon the urn we heaped up a towering barrow Of the earth of his own land. When we were done, we ran To the vault where Antigonê lay on her couch of stone. One of the servants had gone ahead, And while he was yet far off he heard a voice Grieving within the chamber, and he came back And told Creon. And as the King went closer, The air was full of wailing, the words lost, And he begged us to make all haste. 'Am I a prophet?' He said, weeping, 'And must I walk this road, 'The saddest of all that I have gone before? 'My son's voice calls me on. Oh quickly, quickly! 'Look through the crevice there, and tell me 'If it is Haimon, or some deception of the gods!' We obeyed; and in the cavern's farthest corner We saw her lying: She had made a noose of her fine linen veil

And hanged herself. Haimon lay beside her,
His arms about her waist, lamenting her,
His love lost under ground, crying out
That his father had stolen her away from him.
When Creon saw him the tears rushed to his eyes
And he called to him: 'What have you done, child? Speak to me.
'What are you thinking that makes your eyes so strange?
'O my son, my son, I come to you on my knees!'
But Haimon spat in his face. He said not a word,
Staring—
          And suddenly drew his sword
And lunged. Creon shrank back, the blade missed; and the boy,
Desperate against himself, drove it half its length
Into his own side, and fell. And as he died
He gathered Antigonê close in his arms again,
Choking, his blood bright red on her white cheek.
And now he lies dead with the dead, and she is his
At last, his bride in the houses of the dead.

[Exit EURYDICE *into the Palace.*

CHORAG. She has left us without a word. What can this mean?

MESS. It troubles me, too; yet she knows what is best,
Her grief is too great for public lamentation,
And doubtless she has gone to her chamber to weep
For her dead son, leading her maidens in his dirge.

CHORAG. It may be so: but I fear this deep silence.

[Pause.

MESS. I will see what she is doing. I will go in.

[Exit MESSENGER *into the Palace.*

[Enter CREON *with attendants, bearing* HAIMON's *body.*

CHORAG. But here is the King himself: oh look at him,
Bearing his own damnation in his arms.

CREON. Nothing you say can touch me any more.
My own blind heart has brought me
From darkness to final darkness. Here you see
The father murdering, the murdered son—
And all my civic wisdom!
Haimon my son, so young, so young to die,
I was the fool, not you; and you died for me.

CHORAG. That is the truth; but you were late in learning it.

CREON. This truth is hard to bear. Surely a god
Has crushed me beneath the hugest weight of heaven,
And driven me headlong a barbaric way
To trample out the thing I held most dear.

The pains that men will take to come to pain!

[Enter MESSENGER *from the Palace.*

MESS. The burden you carry in your hands is heavy,
But it is not all: you will find more in your house.

59

CREON. What burden worse than this shall I find there?

MESS. The Queen is dead.

CREON. O port of death, deaf world,
Is there no pity for me? And you, Angel of evil,
I was dead, and your words are death again.
Is it true, boy? Can it be true?
Is my wife dead? Has death bred death?

MESS. You can see for yourself.

[The doors are opened, and the body of EURYDICE *is
disclosed within.*

CREON. Oh pity!
All true, all true, and more than I can bear!
O my wife, my son!

MESS. She stood before the altar, and her heart
Welcomed the knife her own hand guided,
And a great cry burst from her lips for Megareus dead,
And for Haimon dead, her sons; and her last breath
Was a curse for their father, the murderer of her sons.
And she fell, and the dark flowed in through her closing eyes.

CREON. O God, I am sick with fear.
Are there no swords here? Has no one a blow for me?

MESS. Her curse is upon you for the deaths of both.

CREON. It is right that it should be. I alone am guilty.
I know it, and I say it. Lead me in,
Quickly, friends.
I have neither life nor substance. Lead me in.

CHORAG. You are right, if there can be right in so much wrong.
The briefest way is best in a world of sorrow.

CREON. Let it come,
Let death come quickly, and be kind to me.
I would not ever see the sun again.

CHORAG. All that will come when it will; but we, meanwhile,
Have much to do. Leave the future to itself.

CREON. All my heart was in that prayer!

CHORAG. Then do not pray any more: the sky is deaf.

CREON. Lead me away. I have been rash and foolish.
I have killed my son and my wife.
I look for comfort; my comfort lies here dead.
Whatever my hands have touched has come to nothing.
Fate has brought all my pride to a thought of dust.

[As CREON *is being led into the house, the* CHORAGOS
advances and speaks directly to the audience.

CHORAG. There is no happiness where there is no wisdom;
No wisdom but in submission to the gods.
Big words are always punished,
And proud men in old age learn to be wise.

One variety of pageant wagon. From Leopold of Austria,
Compilatio de Astrorum Scientia. Augsburg: Erhard Ratdolt,
January 9, 1489. (Photo courtesy of The Rare Books' Room,
Pattee Library, Penn State University.)

A pageant wagon. Drawing by Jim Hoskins

CHAPTER III

The Medieval Experience

The Theatre of the Middle Ages

By the third century B.C. the influence and might of Rome was being felt throughout northern Africa, Asia Minor, and the Mediterranean coast of Europe. The Romans were profoundly impressed with the Greek drama and began to emulate it, alter it, and make it their own. When Greece was finally conquered by Rome at Carthage in 146 B.C., Carthage was burned and art treasures destroyed or carried to Rome. The glory that was Greece had ended and the long, sometimes bloody, sometimes brilliant seven centuries of the Roman Empire had begun.

In the area of tragedy, Seneca, writing in the first century A.D., is the only Roman playwright whose works have come down to us. While his nine extant plays are important in the legacy of dramatic literature, they cannot equal the tragic plays of Aeschylus or Sophocles. Seneca's dramas, by comparison with the Greeks, are static and rhetorical, and reveal an inability to employ the chorus effectively. The Romans were more successful in the area of comedy, particularly the playwright, Plautus, twenty-one of whose works survive. Roman comedy dealt with the well-to-do and centered on domestic situations. The plots were complex and farcical, usually involving mistaken identities, thwarted love affairs, and outrageous intrigues. Roman comedies present an array of character types—the clever slave, the solider who is both braggart and coward, the miserly father, the young lovers pitted against authority—all of whom we will meet later when we study the Italian comedy of the Renaissance, the *commedia dell'arte*.

While it is generally believed that the drama itself declined during the Roman Empire, the building of physical theatres (many of which stand today as a tribute to the great architectural and engineering skills of the Romans) flourished. The theatres became much larger than they had been in Greek times, more ornate, elaborate, and complex. No longer was the theatron carved out of the natural hillside but was built on level ground. The skene was massive and richly ornamented; the parados was covered over and incorporated into the building itself so that the skene and theatron became one architectural unit. As the proskenion became higher and more removed from the orchestra, the orchestra diminished in size and became a semi-circle instead of the full circle of the classical Greek period.

Perhaps the most striking feature of the Roman theatrical activity was its infinite variety. Besides their tragedies and comedies, the Romans performed short comic farces, mimes, circuses, acrobatics, dancing, chariot racing, gladiatorial combats, wild animal fights, and mock sea battles, for which the orchestras were flooded. Toward the end of the Empire, when excesses and decadence of all kinds prevailed, the theatre, too, fell prey to violence, corruption, and degradation. That

Christian women were raped and Christian men torn to bits by wild animals as the gathered throng cheered with delight is not an exaggeration. It is no wonder, then, that as the Romans slowly converted to Christianity and as the Church grew in importance and authority, the theatre was regarded as an evil to be crushed, as a representation of all that was crude, foul, and pagan.

By the year 400 A.D. barbaric tribes of Teutons, Vandals, and Visigoths from northern Europe began to swoop down on the Roman Empire looting, destroying, and burning whatever lay in their paths. The final defeat of Rome by these primitive and warring tribes in 476 A.D. marks the end of ancient history. The next five hundred years are known as the Dark Ages—the night-time of history. During this time the theatre was probably as feeble as it has ever been. Organized theatrical activity virtually disappeared but was somehow kept alive by the meager efforts of remnants of Roman mimes who took to the road, travelling minstrels, and itinerate performers who traveled about Europe. While the middle ages actually began with the fall of Rome in 476 A.D. and lasted until the fall of Constantinople to the Turks in 1453, a date generally assigned to the beginning of the Renaissance, the period beginning about 1000 A.D. is characterized by a great simplicity coupled with a groping toward enlightenment and understanding. It was a time when the theatre changed from a thing hated and shunned to a thing respected and integral to almost every person's way of life. Interestingly enough, the rebirth of drama as an organized and institutionalized entity occurred within the very walls of the Christian Church which had formerly decreed, "We are commanded to love no immodesty. By this means, therefore, we are cut off from the theatre, which is the private council chamber of immodesty."

Let us look for a moment at the background of medieval life. The people of Europe by 1000 A.D. were mostly hard-working serfs with simple lives and simple pleasures. Just as the Roman Empire had been fragmented by the barbarian invaders, so Europe was now divided into small feudal kingdoms with the lord of the land ruling his vassals from his mighty, fortified castle. The serfs, who worked the land and did the bidding of their feudal lords, arose and went to bed according to the sun, probably never traveled more than five miles from their homes, and could neither read nor write. They came to depend on the Church for all knowledge and understanding. Yet the Church's language was Latin; so even the knowledge of the Church was kept special and elitist. A life that was so hard offered little joy and pleasure; hope was not for this life but for the life hereafter. If one could simply lead a good and pure life, the reward could be Paradise. The great cathedrals with their spires rising to Heaven, built stone by stone with the labor of the serfs, were awesome and inspiring reminders of this fact. In church two extremes were presented to the simple peasants: paradise with harps and eternal peace, and hell in which the damned were burned.

Imagine for a moment that you are a youth living in the town of Winchester in England in the year 965 A.D. Down in the town square the jugglers, troubadours, and traveling players are peddling their humble wares along with the mountebanks and hawkers. These frivolities entice you away from your duties and away from your service to God. You would love to go to the square; but your fear of damnation is stronger, and you make your way to the cathedral. It is Easter Sunday, after all. You must forget the damp chill of the vast, vaulted cathedral, the fact that you have to stand all during the long mass which is recited in Latin. You cannot hear, see, or understand what goes on in church. But this particular Easter the Bishop of the cathedral has prepared a special event. At a certain point in the ceremony one of the priests, dressed to resemble an angel and carrying a palm leaf, approaches the sepulchre and sits quietly. From the back of the cathedral three more priests, with incense thuribles in their hands, step delicately as though looking for something. They approach the angel who asks them in dulcet voice, "Quem Quaeritis (Whom Do You Seek)?" The priests respond, "Ihesu Nazarem," and you begin to understand that they are the three Marys coming with spices to anoint the body of Christ. "Non est hic," the angel priest responds, "Surrexit sicut praedixerat. Ite, nuntiate quia surrexit a mortuis (He is not here, he is risen as was foretold. Go, proclaim that he is risen from the dead)." Anthems are sung, the angel priest invites the three Marys to examine the symbolic empty tomb. All sing out their gladness at the triumph of their Heavenly King in a Te Deum, and the cathedral bells ring out. Somehow you are moved. You understand a biblical moment as you have never understood it before. This small, probably crude, insertion into the mass called a trope has all of the elements of drama: setting (the tomb), action (the search of the Marys), dialogue (the questions and answers), characters (the three Marys and the angel), actors (the priests), and audience (the congregation).

We do not know whether or not this was the first dramatized trope or whether or not the Bishop of Winchester Cathedral was an innovator or an imitator, but he left a dated record of this Easter trope as evidence of the rebirth of institutionalized drama within the very walls of the Church that had discarded it in the early days of Christianity. These dramatic tropes became tremendously popular and varied, soon adding stories of the nativity, King Herod, Judgment Day, and the Harrowing of Hell; records indicate that they flourished throughout the Christian world.

For several hundred years, the tropes were performed in and associated strictly with the Church. The staging was extremely simple and consisted of two basic playing areas: mansions or platforms to suggest locales such as Herod's palace or the stable in which Christ was born; and the platea or acting area in front of or at the side of the mansions. The platea expanded the acting space available and could serve either as an extension of the place established by the mansion or as a neutral locale between mansions. Remembering that the cathedrals had no seats it is probable that the mansions were set up around the nave and that the audiences moved or adjusted their standing positions to see the playlets.

When we think of many mansions placed around a cathedral it becomes fairly obvious that the tropes were not only popular but were also extensive and numerous. About 1200 A.D. these brief plays began to be performed out-of-doors on the cathedral steps. Not only did this adjustment allow for larger audiences and probably better visibility and audibility than were possible within the church itself, but the change brought with it several important adjustments as well: first, the language of the plays was no longer Latin but was now the vernacular of the country; secondly, once out-of-doors, more and more secular material was introduced into the plays. While production of the playlets was still certainly under the auspices of the Church, both of these new features allowed for the involvement of townspeople as well as clergy. It may seem strange to contemporary audiences who think of church as serious and sanctimonious to realize how bawdy, earthy, and humorous these plays were. The major thrust involved humanizing, making real and believable the remote characters and events of the Bible. The Church had no qualms about poking fun at itself and in making the devils of hell vivid, graphic, and even lewd. In one of the plays, Mary has a difficult time initially convincing Joseph that he is not a cuckold and a fool. Also once out-of-doors the trade guilds became involved in producing the plays so that, as with the Greeks, we have an interesting combination of church and town government, professional and amateur working together to create the dramatic event.

By the beginning of the fourteenth century, several new features have been added to the production of the plays. First of all, great civic and religious festivals have supplanted many of the old pagan ones of the Romans and Teutons. Such a festival was the Feast of Corpus Christi, instituted by Pope Clement V in 1311, to honor Jesus in the sacrament of the Last Supper. These festivals included sumptuous processions in which elaborate scenic displays on wagons, very like our contemporary football floats, were pulled by horses through the towns. Soon the Biblical plays were also included in these festivals and, we believe, performed on specially built wagons in England, Italy, and Spain. Scholars disagree about how the wagons, called pageant wagons, were actually used. One theory is that the wagon served as the mansion and that either the ground in front of the wagon or a supplementary wagon placed in front of the mansion formed the platea. Critics reason that action played on the ground with a large crowd gathered around would be very difficult for the spectators to see.

By now the simple playlets that had once been performed in the churches and monasteries were grouped together into cycles. A cycle might tell the entire life of Christ from birth to resurrection, another might depict the Bible according to Genesis including the story of Adam and Eve and their expulsion from the Garden of Eden. Cycles were made up of many short plays, like the old tropes, each complete in itself, but each contributing to a larger story. These short plays were also called mysteries and miracles because of their Biblical subject matter. One cycle was reported to have forty-eight episodes; another to have taken forty days to perform. It is believed that the cycles were performed in association with religious holidays like Easter and Corpus Christi.

Once again we can imagine what performance days would have been like. At an appointed place, probably a field just outside the town, a large number of wagons, each with its own setting and ensemble of actors in appropriate costumes were made ready; then, as dawn broke, they were pulled one after the other to twelve or so stations in town. That is, the first wagon might perform at a given point at seven o'clock in the morning, after which it would move to a second location and perform the same play again, while by eight the second wagon is performing the second play at the original location. Recently this theory has been called into question: in the first place, many of the towns were relatively small, and it seems curious that they would have required twelve or so performance stations; secondly, we wonder how a group of actors might feel by the time they had performed a play twelve times on the same day; thirdly, assuming the plays were performed at approximately hour intervals, were people at the final station seeing their first play at six in the evening? It appears it would have been difficult with this arrangement to fit more than a few plays into the available daylight hours.

Certainly there is ample evidence to support the use of the pageant wagons themselves, but an increasing number of theatre historians are suggesting that perhaps only bits of the plays were performed at the stations along the road (just as today in a parade the bands actually play only at designated points on their march,) that all of the wagons were then drawn to the base of the cathedral or town square where the day's portion of the cycle was performed sequentially and in its entirety. The theory certainly answers some of our logistical questions and points to a more theatrical culmination of the day's activities. Certainly we know that in France the cycles were performed at one location as evidenced, for example, at Bourges in 1536 and Valenciennes in 1547. There, fixed stages, sometimes as long as two hundred feet, were constructed so that the mansions could be presented simultaneously while the audience moved from station to station. You can imagine a city block of a downtown district where mansions, instead of shops, lined the street. Just as passersby might pause at shop windows to admire decorations, so they would experience the individual plays of a cycle. These stages of the simultaneous scene, as they were called, often had enormous casts of actors, as many as twenty mansions, and required many days for the production of one complete cycle.

In discussing all of these theories of the medieval drama we must bear in mind that the entire period covered more than one thousand years. It is dangerous to generalize too much from the fragmentary evidence and documentation about a period of tremendous change and variety. We certainly know that the medieval people, however rustic themselves, had a great love of pomp, splendor, and effect, all of which was abundant in the mystery plays. Hell's Mouth, for example, was a graphic depiction of the Biblical jaws of hell. The entire mansion represented a huge, gaping monster's mouth with sharp teeth, open to admit its prey, capable of spewing smoke and uttering grotesque sounds. These scenic effects, often called secrets, were the domain of the craft guilds, societies of master craftsmen and their apprentices, who often had their own churches, supported their own guild halls, and maintained their own pageants or plays in a cycle. Probably the clergy or city government allocated the plays to the craft guilds in terms of appropriateness. For example, from the York, England cycle we know that The Creation was assigned to the plasterers, The Building of the Ark to the shipwrights, Noah and his Wife and The Flood to the fishers and mariners, Coming of the Kings and The Adoration to the goldsmiths, The Last Supper to the bakers, the Mortification of Christ and The Burial to the butchers, and The Resurrection to the carpenters. In one production of Noah, prepared by the shipbuilders guild, the ship was brought on stage in pieces and assembled by Noah during the early part of the play. In another at Mons in 1501 water was stored in barrels and then poured from the roofs of houses near the mansion, producing a rain storm that lasted five minutes.

Costumes were no less magnificent and lavish. Certainly when most of the roles were being acted by priests, the Church vestments provided opulent splendor. One contemporary record refers to Adam appearing in a red tunic and Eve in a robe of white with a white silk cloak. One need only look at the medieval concept of Christ, Mary, angels, and magi in paintings of the period to imagine the use of vibrant color, gold, jewels, and crowns. But the costumes that seemed to have captured the Medieval fancy most were the devils—toothed, winged, with tails, claws, and grotesque detail. There was no attempt at historical perspective in the costuming; all of the characters were conceived of and executed as medieval figures.

In the early days of the Church tropes, no doubt all of the acting was performed by the priests; once the plays had moved out-of-doors, however, we believe that townspeople and guild members also participated. By its final phase, when records indicate that a cycle involved three hundred performers, we can well imagine that clergy, townspeople, perhaps a noble or two, and professionals "jobbed in" for the event worked together to create a true communal event. Most of the performers were probably amateurs, more concerned with the joy of the occasion and service to God and community than with pay. A record of the Noah play of Hull, England in 1494 indicates that Thomas Sawyer playing God received ten pence and Noah's wife eight pence, while Jenkin Smith playing Noah received the astounding salary of one shilling.

While the cycles provided the dominant theatrical mode of the medieval period, three other types of plays were also popular. First of all, there were the morality plays which flourished from approximately 1400 to 1550 and offered moral lessons to the medieval people. The moralities were didactic and allegorical in their dramatization of the temptations of earthy existence, presenting the struggle between forces of good and evil for the possession of Man's soul. The most famous, *Everyman,* is no doubt typical in several features. It personifies abstract qualities such as good deeds, gluttony, arrogance, and the seven deadly sins; and it takes the form of a journey with man at the final judgment being forced to return to his life and correct the folly of his ways in order to achieve the kingdom of Heaven.

The final two dramatic forms represent the secular rather than the religious drama. Farces, such as the anonymous *Master Pierre Pathelin,* were probably performed in France and England for sheer entertainment. Their plots were simple and direct, their staging requirements were minimal, and their subject was the ridiculousness of man's behavior.

Pathelin is a lawyer near financial ruin. He nevertheless purchases a fine piece of cloth and then invites the merchant to come to his house for dinner and payment. When the trusting merchant arrives, Pathelin is in bed, feigns madness, beats the merchant, and drives him away without paying him. Soon after the crafty Pathelin agrees to defend a shepherd against a charge of sheep stealing. The lawyer instructs his client to answer only "baa" when examined by the prosecution, no matter what is asked him, thus pleading madness or slow-wittedness. In spite of mayhem in the court room caused by the appearance of the merchant, the simple shepherd is acquitted. When Pathelin tries to collect his fee, the shepherd answers "baa" and runs away. Justice has indeed been served on Pathelin and villainy is punished.

The final dramatic pieces of the period are called interludes, probably so named because they were performed by itinerate troupes of actors at the feudal castles between the courses of a banquet. In England these interludes—which included farces like John Heywood's *A Mery Play, between Johan Johan, the Husbande, Tyb, his wyfe, and Syr Johan, the Priest* or serious plays like Henry Medwell's *Nature*—formed a direct link with the Elizabethan period. Shakespeare employs an interlude in *Hamlet* when a troop of traveling players perform *The Murther of Gonzago* as a trap for King Claudius.

In Great Britain there was no clear end to the medieval drama. As the plays become increasingly secular and separate from the Church, they simply melded and evolved into that great period of English drama known as the Elizabethan. Surely the Elizabethan audiences inherited from their medieval ancestors a great love of pageantry and effect, a love of rustic good humor, word play and action, the supernatural, and finally a tremendous freedom and scope. After all, a drama that is free to encompass the entire story of the Bible from the creation to the resurrection, to move from location to location, to extend for forty days, and to involve a cast of three hundred establishes a precedent for drama that will be grand, bold, broad, and adventuresome.

Noah's Flood

It is sometimes naively assumed that during the Middle Ages all learning and culture faded until they ceased to exist. We have only to read *Noah's Flood* or many of the hundreds of mystery and miracle plays of the period to realize that drama, at least, was alive and well. True, the plays seem at times naive and stilted to us today, but a careful and sensitive reading of a medieval drama reveals that they were spirited, sometimes poignant, often earthy, meaningful and dramatic.

To understand the full meaning of *Noah's Flood*—to comprehend its action and perceive its message—we must remember that, while it is a concise and complete drama in and of itself, it was in reality one play in a large cycle of plays. All of the plays in a medieval cycle collectively conveyed one major deed that imitated the movement of the human psyche. The entire cycle presented the history of mankind as that story was interpreted for faithful Christians in the Bible. In fact, the cycle was employed by the Church to teach the biblical lesson to an illiterate congregation. The plays demonstrated the working out of God's will through the story of Christ and related biblical tales; and it illustrated the eternal conflict between good and evil. It may be said, then, that the action of *Noah's Flood* is to fulfil the will of God.

A series of plays presenting the entire story of man obviously will not have the conciseness and brevity of a Greek tragedy. The cycle will not deal with merely the climactic part of a legend because it is composed of as many as forty-eight playlets each with its own set of characters, its own climaxes and its own crisis. The cycle will obviously depict a much greater passage of time than a Greek play. In fact, while the entire story in a Greek play tended to transpire in less than one day, the cycle covered centuries of time. In *Noah's Flood* a minimum of forty-two days has to transpire even if we are willing to believe that Noah and his family built the ark in one day. Actually, the first four pages of the Noah play realistically encompass the passage of at least one full week. Still, the entire Noah play is shorter than a Greek tragedy. We may assume, then, that audiences of the medieval time were not disturbed by an unrealistic compression of time in a single play. Notice that the forty days and nights of the flood transpire in one crisp stage direction which instructs Noah to " . . . shut the window of the Ark, and for a little space within board he shall be silent, and afterwards opening the window and looking about. . . ." The foreshortening of time in each play permits the drama an incredible freedom of movement in time and space, a panoramic sweep as it were; and the narrowed focus of time also lends the play a tremendous vigor and rapid pace. There is no wasted time in *Noah's Flood*. It is crammed with vitality and activity. The panoramic movement in time and space permitted dramatists to relate tales of epic proportion spanning years in the lives of the characters and containing events that moved rapidly from one locale to the next. The practice established a convention in British theatre that was passed on to Shakespeare and his contemporaries who, consequently, wrote plays quite unlike the Greeks where structure is concerned.

The play opens with the appearance of God himself as a character; addressing the audience, he identifies himself for the spectators, states the intention of the play, and provides the necessary exposition for the action in the first two stanzas of his first speech. The opening moments of the play are remarkably like the prologue of a Greek tragedy. In the next three stanzas of God's prologue speech, he addresses Noah telling him precisely what he wants him to do. In other words, God himself states the action of the play and Noah's task is set for him. Noah accepts his obligation, after thanking God for his grace, and sets to work immediately. Meanwhile, the dramatist has established one of the conventions of the medieval drama; characters will address the audience directly at one moment and then speak to one another in relatively realistic dialogue the next moment. Obviously, audiences of the medieval period readily accepted the convention and were not disturbed by the mixture of realism and theatricalism. This explains, of course, why Shakespeare's audiences took in their stride the juxtaposition of realistic scenes and character portraits, poetry, direct address, asides and soliloquies.

The script of the play you are reading contains very few stage directions because they are really not needed; activity or stage business is implicit in practically every speech of the play. Imagine, for example, Noah's Wife, the sons, and their wives performing the deeds mentioned in their initial speeches. Shem, for example, apparently picks up his axe as he speaks his lines; Japheth's Wife gathers chips of wood. And after their sequence of speeches a stage direction indicates that the actors pantomime their work.

One of the most fascinating features of medieval drama is its treatment of character. An effort was obviously made, consciously or unconsciously, to depict the biblical character in terms that could be readily understood by the untutored commoner who saw the play. Each character tends to be, not the biblical, near-Eastern figure of scripture, but rather his contemporary counterpart. Noah is not Palestinian; he is unmistakably a patriarch of medieval England not unlike the noble lord of the district familiar to the playgoer. God may have enormous dignity in the play; but he is not austere and awesome. God was not a remote and frightening figure to the average man of the Middle Ages; so, he is depicted in the play as he might be seen in the imagination of the spectator.

Even more striking, however, is the treatment of Noah's Wife. Who was Noah's Wife in the Bible? What was she like? What did she think? What did she feel? No one knows because in the scriptures she is little more than a name. In the play, however, she emerges as a full-blown and delightful character not unlike a townswoman of Chester. She provides much of the conflict in the play by being recalcitrant. She is not about to bend to Noah's will; she even flaunts the will of God. She is shrewish and stubborn. Furthermore, she is a tippler who enjoys a nip or two with her chums. The dramatist provides her a believeable reason for not wanting to board the Ark: she cannot bear to leave her cronies or gossips. She even holds out to have them included in the cargo of the Ark, but to no avail. One of the comic highlights of the play is the moment when she is forcibly carried aboard the Ark by her sons. The stage direction says simply, "Then she shall go." But it does not take much imagination to figure out *how* she must go. The action is implicit in the dialogue. But one bit of business is pointedly set down in a stage direction; Noah's Wife, in a pique of contrariness, boxes his ears once she is on board. Again and again, Noah's Wife provides the play with delightful, broad, earthy humor.

The simplicity and naivete of the medieval theatre is apparent in the staging of the Noah play as it is implied in the script. Apparently, the play is staged on a double wagon with God appearing on the upper level; or he may simply have appeared on the roof of a one-story wagon. As the action of the play progresses it becomes obvious that the pageant wagon is the Ark itself and the characters are frequently performing on the street around the wagon or possibly on the additional one which may have been used. It is not inconceivable that the actors portraying the sons actually pursued the actor playing Noah's Wife around a portion of the town square or performance station as they attempted to force her to board the Ark. The procession of animals onto the Ark poses enormous production problems if the animals are actually portrayed by costumed actors. Where, for example, would they find the space on one wagon for all of the bodies required by the action? How, for that matter, could any one guild have afforded so many elaborate costumes? But, the production problem was so intelligently, imaginatively, and, neatly solved by the craftsmen of Chester. The stage directions tell us that the animals were painted on boards. It would seem that, as Noah and his family close the shutters on the windows of the Ark in preparation for sailing, images of various animals painted on the backs of the shutters were revealed to the spectators.

After the pageantry and the farcical humor, the play returns in its final moments to a more solemn tone as God reappears to thank Noah for his good efforts. In his final moments God promised to spare Mankind his wrath in the future. The action of the play has been completed as God's will has been fulfilled. The world of the play has been returned to a state of balance and order and the playlet ends.

NOAH'S FLOOD

Anonymous

edited by A. C. Cawley

―――――――――― CHARACTERS ――――――――――

GOD	NOAH'S WIFE
NOAH	SHEM'S WIFE
SHEM	HAM'S WIFE
HAM	JAPHETH'S WIFE
JAPHETH	GOSSIP

And first in some high place, or in the clouds if it may be, God speaketh unto Noah standing without the Ark with all his family.

GOD. I, God, that all the world have wrought,
    Heaven and earth, and all of nought,   *from nothing*
    I see my people, in deed and thought,
    Are set foully in sin.
5   My ghost shall not leng in man,
    That through fleshly liking is my fone,
    But till six score years be gone,
    To look if they will blin.

    Man that I made I will destroy,
10   Beast, worm, and fowl to fly;
    For on earth they do me noy,   *harm*
    The folk that are thereon.
    It harms me so heartfully,
    The malice now that can multiply,
15   That sore it grieveth me inwardly
    That ever I made man.

    Therefore, Noah, my servant free,   *noble*
    That righteous man art, as I see,
    A ship soon thou shalt make thee
20   Of trees dry and light.
    Little chambers therein thou make;
    And binding-slitch also thou take:
    Within and out thou ne slake
    To anoint it through all thy might.

5–8 My spirit shall remain in mankind, who are my foes because of their sensuality, only till six score years are gone, to see if they will stop [sinning].
10 Reptile, and bird flying.
13–14 The malice that now doth multiply wounds me deeply in my heart.

25	Three hundred cubits it shall be long,	
	And fifty of breadth, to make it strong;	
	Of height fifty. The met thou fong;	
	Thus measure it about.	*all round*
	One window work through thy wit,	
30	One cubit of length and breadth make it;	
	Upon the side a door shall sit,	*be placed*
	For to come in and out.	

Eating-places thou make also,
Three roofed chambers on a row;
35 For with water I think to flow   *drown*
  Man that I can make.   *did make*
  Destroyed all the world shall be,
  Save thou; thy wife, thy sons three,
  And all their wives also with thee
40 Shall saved be for thy sake.

  NOAH. Ah, Lord, I thank thee loud and still,   *at all times*
  That to me art in such will,
  And sparest me and my house to spill,
  As now I soothly find.
45 Thy bidding, Lord, I shall fulfil,
  And never more thee grieve ne grill,   *nor offend*
  That such grace has sent me till   *to me*
  Among all mankind.   *above*

               [To his family:

  Have done, you men and women all!
50 Help, for aught that may befall,
  To work this ship, chamber and hall,   *build*
  As God hath bidden us do.
  SHEM. Father, I am all ready boun: *prepared*
  An axe I have, by my crown,
55 As sharp as any in all this town,
  For to go thereto.   *to it*

  HAM. I have a hatchet wondrous keen
  To bite well, as may be seen;   *cut*
  A better grounden, as I ween,   *sharpened; think*
60 Is not in all this town.
  JAPHETH. And I can well make a pin,   *peg*
  And with this hammer knock it in;
  Go and work without more din,
  And I am ready boun.

22 *binding-slitch*, pitch used for stopping up the seams of a ship.
23–4 Do not slacken your efforts to anoint it inside and out with all your might.
27 Take the measurement yourself.
29 Make a window by your skill.
34 One on top of another.
42–3 That art so minded towards me, and refrainest from destroying me and my household.
50 Whatever happens.
54 *by my crown*, an asseveration.

65 *N's WIFE.* And we shall bring timber to,   *to this place*
    For we mun nothing else do;   *may*
    Women be weak to underfo   *undertake*
    Any great travail.   *labour*
  S's WIFE. Here is a good hackstock;   *chopping-block*
70   On this you may hew and knock;
    Shall none be idle in this flock,
    Ne now may no man fail.

  H's WIFE. And I will go to gather slitch,
    The ship for to caulk and pitch;
75   Anointed it must be every stitch,   *part*
    Board, tree, and pin.   *beam*
  J's WIFE. And I will gather chips here
    To make a fire for you in fere,   *you all*
    And for to dight your dinner,   *prepare*
80   Against you come in.

Then they make signs as if they were working with different tools.

NOAH. Now, in the name of God, I will begin
    To make the ship that we shall in,   *live in*
    That we be ready for to swim   *float*
    At the coming of the flood.
85   These boards I join here together,
    To keep us safe from the weather,
    That we may row both hither and thither,
    And safe be from this flood.

    Of this tree will I make the mast,
90   Tied with cables that will last,
    With a sail-yard for each blast,
    And each thing in their kind;
    With topcastle and bowsprit,
    With cords and ropes, I have all meet   *fit*
95   To sail forth at the next wet;   *downpour*
    This ship is at an end.   *finished*

Then Noah with all his family again make signs of working with different tools.

  Wife, in this castle we shall be kept;   *kept safe*
    My children and thou, I would, in leapt.
  N's WIFE. In faith, Noah, I had as lief thou slept.
100   For all thy frankish fare,
    I will not do after thy rede.
  NOAH. Good wife, do now as I thee bid.
  N's WIFE. By Christ, not ere I see more need,
    Though thou stand all the day and stare.

---

72 Nor may any one now fail [to do his part].
91 *sail-yard*, a yard-arm on which the sail is spread.
92 And every kind of thing [needed].
93 *topcastle*, a fortified platform at the mast-head.
97 *castle*, a raised structure on the deck of a ship.
98 I would like my children and you to hurry in.
99–101 I would as soon you slept. For all your polite behavior, I won't do as you advise.

105	*NOAH.* Lord, that women be crabbed ay,	*always perverse*
	And never are meek, that dare I say.	
	This is well seen by me to-day,	
	In witness of you each one.	
	Good wife, let be all this bere	*clamour*
110	That thou makes in this place here;	
	For all they ween thou art master—	
	And so thou art, by St. John!	

[*God speaks to Noah*]

	GOD. Noah, take thou thy meny,	*household*
	And in the ship hie that thou be;	
115	For none so righteous man to me	
	Is now on earth living.	
	Of clean beasts with thee thou take	
	Seven and seven, ere thou slake;	*by sevens; stop*
	He and she, make to make,	*mate*
120	Belive in that thou bring.	
	Of beasts unclean two and two,	*by twos*
	Male and female, without mo;	*and no more*
	Of clean fowls seven also,	*birds*
	The he and she together;	
125	Of fowls unclean two and no more,	
	As I of beasts said before,	
	That shall be saved through my lore,	*instruction*
	Against I send the weather.	*tempest*
	Of all meats that must be eaten	*food*
130	Into the ship look there be gotten,	
	For that no way may be forgotten;	
	And do all this bedene,	*at once*
	To sustain man and beast therein	
	Ay till the water cease and blin.	
135	This world is filled full of sin,	
	And that is now well seen.	*easy to see*
	Seven days be yet coming:	
	You shall have space them in to bring;	*time*
	After that it is my liking	*pleasure*
140	Mankind for to noy.	*harm*
	Forty days and forty nights	
	Rain shall fall for their unrights;	*iniquities*
	And that I have made through my mights	
	Now think I to destroy.	

108 As each of you (i.e. the audience) has witnessed.
111 *they,* i.e. the audience.
114–15 And hasten on board ship; for no man so righteous in my sight.
120 [See] that you quickly bring in.
131 For they must on no account be forgotten.
134 All the time till the flood-waters cease and come to an end.
143 And that which I made through my might.

145 *NOAH*. Lord, at your bidding I am bain;   *ready*
    Since no other grace will gain,
    It will I fulfil fain,   *gladly*
    For gracious I thee find.
    A hundred winters and twenty
150   This ship-making tarried have I,
    If through amendment any mercy
    Would fall unto mankind.

                             [To his family:

    Have done, you men and women all!
    Hie you lest this water fall,
155   That each beast were in his stall,
    And into the ship brought.
    Of clean beasts seven shall be,
    Of unclean two; this God bade me.
    This flood is nigh, well may we see;
160   Therefore tarry you nought.

    Then Noah shall go into the Ark with all his family, his wife except, and the
    Ark must be boarded round about, and on the boards all the beasts and fowls
    hereafter hearsed must be painted, that these words may agree with the pic-
    tures.

    SHEM. Sir, here are lions, leopards in,   *inside*
    Horses, mares, oxen, and swine;
    Goats, calves, sheep, and kine
    Here sitten thou may see.   *lying down*
165 *HAM*. Camels, asses men may find,
    Buck, doe, hart, and hind;
    And beasts of all manner kind
    Here be, as thinketh me.   *it seems to me*
    Japh. Take here cats and dogs too,
17   Otter, fox, fulmart also;   *polecat*
    Hares hopping gaily can go
    Have cole here for to eat.   *cabbage*
    N's WIFE. And here are bears, wolves set,   *lying*
    Apes, owls, marmoset,
175   Weasels, squirrels, and ferret;
    Here they eat their meat.

    S's WIFE. Yet more beasts are in this house:
    Here cats maken it full crouse;
    Here a ratton, here a mouse,   *rat*
180   They stand nigh together.
    H's WIFE. And here are fowls, less and more: *small and big*
    Herons, cranes, and bittor,   *bittern*
    Swans, peacocks; and them before
    Meat for this weather.

---

146 Since nothing else will win grace.
149–52 I have prolonged this shipbuilding for 120 years, [to see] if mankind would mend its ways and be
   granted mercy.
154–5 Hurry, lest the water pour down, so that each beast may be in its stall.
167 Of every sort and kind.
171 Hares which go hopping gaily.
178 Are having a lively time.
183–4 And in front of them is food for [them to eat during] the tempest.

185 *J's WIFE*. Here are cocks, kites, crows,
    Rooks, ravens, many rows,   *row upon row*
    Ducks, curlews, whoever knows
    Each one in his kind;
    And here are doves, digs, drakes,   *ducks*
190   Redshanks running through the lakes;
    And each fowl that leden makes   *song*
    In this ship men may find.

    NOAH. Wife, come in! Why stands thou there?
    Thou art ever froward, that dare I swear.   *perverse*
195 Come in, on God's half! Time it were,
    For fear lest that we drown.
    N's WIFE. Yea, sir, set up your sail,
    And row forth with evil hail,
    For, without any fail,   *doubt*
200   I will not out of this town.

    But I have my gossips every one,   *unless; friends*
    One foot further I will not gone;   *go*
    They shall not drown, by St. John,
    And I may save their life.   *if*
205 They loved me full well, by Christ;
    But thou wilt let them in thy chest,
    Else row forth, Noah, whither thou list,
    And get thee a new wife.

    NOAH. Shem, son, lo! thy mother is wrow: *angry*
210 Forsooth, such another I do not know.
    SHEM. Father, I shall fetch her in, I trow,   *think*
    Without any fail.   *[He goes to his mother.*
    Mother, my father after thee sent,
    And bids thee into yonder ship wend.   *go*
215 Look up and see the wind,
    For we be ready to sail.

    N's WIFE. Son, go again to him, and say
    I will not come therein to-day.
    NOAH. Come in, wife, in twenty devils way,
220   Or else stand there without.
    HAM. Shall we all fetch her in?
    NOAH. Yea, sons, in Christ's blessing and mine;   *with*
    I would you hied you betime,
    For of this flood I am in doubt.   *afraid*

225 *GOSSIP*. [*To Wife*] The flood comes fleeting in full fast   *flowing*
    On every side it spreads full far;
    For fear of drowning I am aghast;
    Good gossip, let us draw near.

    And let us drink ere we depart,

187–8 For anyone who knows each species.
195 Come in, for God's sake! It's high time.
198 With ill success, i.e. and bad luck to you
200 I will not leave this town.
206–7 Unless you will let them into your chest (i.e. the Ark), row away, Noah, where you like.
219 In the devil's name.
223 I would like you to hurry and waste no time.

76

230   For oft-times we have done so;
         For at a draught thou drink'st a quart,
         And so will I do ere I go.
     N's WIFE. Here is a pottle of Malmsey, good and strong;
         It will rejoice both heart and tongue;
235   Though Noah thinks us never so long,
         Yet we will drink alike.

     JAPH. Mother, we pray you altogether—
         For we are here your own childer—
         Come into the ship for fear of the weather,
240   For his love that you bought!
     N's WIFE. That will I not, for all your call,   *bidding*
         But I have my gossips all.
     SHEM. In faith, mother, yet you shall,
         Whether you will or nought.

                      Then she shall go.

245 *NOAH.* Welcome, wife, into this boat.
     N's WIFE. And have thou that for thy note!

     She boxes him on the ear.

     NOAH. Aha! marry, this is hot!
         It is good to be still.   *peaceful*
         Ah, children, methinks my boat removes;   *moves*
250   Our tarrying here hugely me grieves.
         Over the land the water spreads;
         God do as he will!

         Ah, great God that art so good,
         That works not thy will is wood.
255   Now all this world is on a flood,
         As I well see in sight.
         This window will I shut anon,
         And into my chamber will I gone,
         Till this water, so great one,
260   Be slaked through thy might.   *lessened*

     Then Noah shall shut the window of the Ark, and for a little space within board
        he shall be silent, and afterwards opening the window and looking round about,
        saying:

         Now forty days are fully gone,
         Send a raven I will anon,
         If aught-where earth, tree, or stone
         Be dry in any place;

233 *pottle,* a pot containing two quarts; *Malmsey,* a strong sweet wine.
236 i.e. a quart each.
240 For love of Him who redeemed you.
246 Have that for your trouble.
247 I'm catching it hot.
254 He who does not thy will is mad.
256 As I plainly see with my own eyes.
259 Till this flood, which is so great.
263 [To see] if anywhere.

265 And if this fowl come not again,
    It is a sign, sooth to sain,   *to speak truly*
    That dry it is on hill or plain,
    And God hath done some grace.   *granted*

    Then he shall send forth a raven; and taking a dove in his hand let him say:

    Ah, Lord, wherever this raven be,
270 Somewhere is dry, well I see;
    But yet a dove, by my lewty,   *faith*
    After I will send.
    Thou wilt turn again to me,
    For of all fowls that may flee,   *fly*
275 Thou art most meek and hend.   *gentle*

    Then he shall send forth a dove; and there shall be in the ship another dove bearing an olive-branch in her mouth, which Noah shall let down from the mast by a cord in his hand; and afterwards let Noah say:

    Ah, Lord, blessed be thou ay,
    That me hast comfort thus to-day;   *comforted*
    By this sight I may well say
    This flood begins to cease.
280 My sweet dove to me brought has
    A branch of olive from some place;
    This betokeneth God has done us some grace,
    And is a sign of peace.

    Ah, Lord, honoured must thou be!
285 All earth drys now, I see;
    But yet, till thou command me,
    Hence will I not hie.   *hasten*
    All this water is away;
    Therefore, as soon as I may,
290 Sacrifice I shall do, in fay,   *faith*
    To thee devoutly.

               [God speaks to Noah]

  GOD. Noah, take thy wife anon,
    And thy children every one;
    Out of the ship thou shalt gone,
295 And they all with thee.
    Beasts and all that can fly
    Out anon they shall hie,
    On earth to grow and multiply;
    I will that it so be.

300 *NOAH.* Lord, I thank thee through thy might;   *for*
    Thy bidding shall be done in hight,   *haste*
    And as fast as I may dight   *make ready*
    I will do thee honour,
    And to thee offer sacrifice;
305 Therefore come, in all wise,
    For of these beasts that be his,
    Offer I will this store.   *great number*

305 By all means. (Noah is addressing his family.)

Then going out of the Ark with all his family he shall take his animals and
birds and offer them in sacrifice.

Lord God in majesty,
That such grace hast granted me,
310   Where all was lorn, safe to be,   *lost*
Therefore now am I boun,   *ready*
My wife, my children, and my meny,   *household*
With sacrifice to honour thee;
Of beasts, fowls, as thou mayst see,
315   I offer here right soon.

[*God speaks to Noah*]

GOD. Noah, to me thou art full able,   *most compliant*
And thy sacrifice acceptable;
For I have found thee true and stable,   *because*
On thee now must I min:
320   Wary earth will I no more
For man's sin that grieves me sore;
For of youth man full yore
Has been inclined to sin.

You shall now grow and multiply,
325   And earth again you edify;   *shall build up*
Each beast, and fowl that may fly
Shall be afraid of you;
And fish in sea that may fleet   *float*
Shall sustain you, I you beheet;   *promise*
330   To eat of them you ne let
That clean be you may know.

Thereas you have eaten before   *whereas*
Grass and roots, since you were bore,   *born*
Of clean beasts now, less and more,
335   I give you leave to eat,
Save blood and flesh, both in fere,   *together*
Of wrong-dead carrion that is here;
Eat not of that in no manner,
For that ay you shall let.

340   Manslaughter also you shall flee,   *shun*
For that is not pleasant to me;   *pleasing*
That shedeth blood, he or she,
Aught-where amongst mankin,   *mankind*
That blood foully shed shall be
345   And vengeance have, that men shall see;
Therefore beware now all ye,
You fall not in that sin.

A forward, Noah, with thee I make,   *covenant*
And all thy seed for thy sake,

319–23 I must now be mindful of you: I will no more curse the earth because of man's sin that grieves me
    sorely; for from his youth man has long been inclined to sin.
330–1 Do not forbear to eat those that you know to be clean.
337 Wrongly dead, i.e. killed in an improper manner.
338–9 Do not eat that at all, for you must always leave that alone.
342 Whoever sheds blood.

350 Of such vengeance for to slake,
For now I have my will.
Here I beheet thee a hest
That man, woman, fowl ne beast,
With water, while the world shall last,
355 I will no more spill.   *destroy*

My bow between you and me   *rainbow*
In the firmament shall be,
By very token that you may see
That such vengeance shall cease,
360 That man ne woman never more
Be wasted by water, as is before;
But for sin that grieveth me sore,
Therefore this vengeance was.

Where clouds in the welkin been,
365 That ilk bow shall be seen,   *same*
In token that my wrath and teen   *anger*
Shall never thus worken be.   *wreaked*
The string is turned toward you,
And toward me is bent the bow,
370 That such weather shall never show;
And this beheet I thee.

My blessing now I give thee here,
To thee, Noah, my servant dear,
For vengeance shall no more appear;
375 And now farewell, my darling dear.

350 To lessen such vengeance, i.e. such vengeance as I have just taken.
352 Here I promise you.
358 As a true sign.
361 Shall be destroyed by water, as happened before.
364 Are in the sky.
370 [As a sign] that such bad weather shall never be seen.

Philip Benson as Oberon, Janice Benson as Titania, Frank M
Whiting as Bottom, Jan Thayer as Puck in *A Midsummer Night's
Dream,* University of Minnesota Theatre. Frank M Whiting,
director.

An Elizabethan playhouse. Drawing by Jim Hoskins

CHAPTER IV

The Age of Shakespeare

Shakespeare's Theatre

The fifteenth century was a time of extraordinary change: Guttenburg had invented movable type about 1440 so that the printing of books was possible for the first time in history; the Hundred Years' War in which England had battled for a claim to the French throne had ended in 1453; and in that same year the Turks had attacked Constantinople which, against the power of newly invented gunpowder, could not stand. So it was that in 1453 Constantinople—the last vestige of the Roman Empire—fell to the Mohammedans, forcing the center of learning and scholarship back to Europe. It was also an age of explorations with Diaz arriving at the Cape of Good Hope in 1486, Columbus landing in America in 1492, and Vasco da Gama discovering an all-water route to India in 1498.

Printing, advanced weaponry, and the compass thus lead to a new age: the Renaissance, or re-birth. It was primarily on the continent of Europe that the spirit of rediscovery asserted itself in a voracious desire to recapture the cultures of Greece and Rome, in great works of art by Michaelangelo and Raphael, the explorations of Magellan and Cortez, and the discovery of a solar system by Copernicus. For the first time, too, since the fall of Rome, there was a shift away from formal religion, the Holy Roman Church, toward an emphasis on individual and personal morality and conscience, the first person protesting against the authority of the pope being a German monk named Martin Luther in 1519. In 1531 Henry VIII of England also quarreled with Rome over his wish to divorce his first wife Catherine of Aragon, who had produced no male heir. When the pope declined the request, Henry issued the Act of Supremacy making himself head of the Church of England, thereby defying the absolute authority of the Catholic Church just as Luther had done and enabling himself legally to divorce his wife. Henry had in all six wives, three of whom he divorced.

Henry's only male issue died after a brief reign of six years, leaving Henry's two daughters as undesirable possible heirs to the English throne. The first of these, daughter of Catherine of Aragon, assumed the crown in a bloody coup, the object of which was the restoration of the Catholic Church in England. While Mary's husband, Philip II of Spain, conducted his own Inquisition abroad, Mary was earning herself the title of "Bloody Mary" for her violent torture and beheadings of Protestants at home.

When Mary died in 1558, her younger half-sister, Elizabeth, ascended the throne of England. Elizabeth had many strikes against her: her mother, Anne Boleyn, had been a commoner who was ultimately beheaded when Henry tired of her; Elizabeth was conceived out of wedlock; she was a mere twenty-five years old when she came to the throne and a woman at that; England was caught in a dizzy turn-over of monarchs and in a bewildering identity crisis over whether it was a Protestant or a Catholic nation. Elizabeth resolved all of these problems in no uncertain terms. She ruled for forty-five years; she never weakened her power by marrying; when she imprisoned and finally beheaded her popular relative, Mary Queen of Scots, in 1587 she suppressed the final Catholic threat to her throne; and in 1588, when Philip II of Spain sent the mighty Spanish Armada to take England for Spain, her famous victory established England once and for all as a world power. Elizabeth said, "I know I have the body of a weak, feeble woman; but I have the stomach of a king—and a king of England too; and think foul scorn that Parma or Spain or any Prince of Europe should dare to invade the borders of my realm." For the second time in the history of the theatre, great drama was born out of a tremendous sense of ascendancy as a world power, national pride, and prosperity.

Elizabeth, like her father before her, was a staunch Protestant who would tolerate no insubordination. Hence in 1559 she forbade all religious and political doctrine in the drama. That such laws had to be created at all is clear evidence of the health and popularity of the drama in Elizabeth's time. Some critics have argued that the English under Henry and Elizabeth were a backward and isolated people, insensitive to the great humanistic and classical exploration of the Renaissance on the continent. Certainly both Henry and his strong-willed daughter were intelligent and informed monarchs; if the drama in England took a different form than that of the continent, the fact was due more to individuality and lack of conformity than to ignorance. The development of school drama and classical study and drama in the English universities is ample evidence that England was neither cut off from nor ignorant of scholarship. The English merely elected to follow and secularize their own medieval tradition rather than to emulate Greek and Roman models. Finally, Elizabeth followed her father's path in her delight in dancing, pageantry, spectacle, pomp and show. She loved the theatre which flourished and prospered under her reign.

In spite of enjoying the theatre, Elizabeth was never willing to spend money for it and she kept an iron control over it. In the 1570s she created the office of Master of Revels whose duty it was to read all plays and license all acting companies. A company was not permitted to exist without noble patronage. One of Elizabeth's favorites, Robert Dudley, Earl of Leicester, became the enthusiastic patron of a group of actors who counted in their ranks a carpenter turned actor named James Burbage. In 1576 in the area of Shoreditch, northeast of London, Burbage erected the first building in England created solely for the performance of plays. Up to this time actors had traveled, seeking patronage in a noble home, performing on a village green, in a guild hall, or at country inns. Burbage probably would have opted for an accessible plot of land within the old walled City but London was virtually bursting her seams; besides, the location permitted Burbage freedom from the Puritan-minded London council.

We assume that in planning his structure, which was to be called simply The Theatre, Burbage combined the best features of two familiar buildings. From the popular innyards he took the concept of a simple booth stage set up at one end of the courtyard with standing space in front of the stage and additional viewing space established by a balcony that provided second story rooms access to the courtyard (just as one might see in a Holiday Inn today). From the amusement section in Southwark, Burbage took the circular configuration of the popular open-air bear pits, where audiences went on Sundays to gamble their money as a chained bear was set upon by wild dogs. In combining these two structures Burbage was establishing the prototype for all London public theatres to follow: an edifice that would provide both excellent audibility and visibility because of its circular or octagonal shape, one that was open to the elements, and that would seat between two and three thousand spectators while offering a degree of intimacy between performers and audience.

His colleagues must have thought Burbage was quite mad building a playhouse—and out of town at that. But James Burbage knew his Londoners; they came in droves. Almost immediately other playhouses were built, at first in Shoreditch and then on the marshy south bank of the Thames River just across London Bridge. Competition was healthy, and public theatres were money-making propositions. They proved that good theatre begets good theatre and that nothing succeeds like success, for London became a theatre-going town. Of the approximately 160,000 Londoners at the time, it is estimated that about 20,000 went to the theatre every week. There were probably about twenty licensed companies between 1558 and 1574.

Of the public playhouses of the time, perhaps the most important are The Swan (c. 1595), the Fortune, (1600), and The Globe (1599). The Swan is significant in that it provides our only concrete record of what these Elizabethan public playhouses actually looked like. A Dutch visitor, Johannes de Witt, both sketched and wrote a description of this theatre in 1596 indicating such features as a circular shape, a raised forestage, a canopy supported by pillars over that stage, and three tiers of galleries provided for the audiences. Yet there is no reason to assume that all of the theatres followed the same plan, housed an equal number, or were less diverse than theatres are today. The Fortune is important because its business manager, Philip Henslowe, father-in-law of its manager and leading actor, Edward Alleyn, kept excellent records including a contract with dimensions of that theatre. Although we have no such records of The Globe, it is the most important of all the Elizabethan theatres because Henslowe tells us it provided a model for The Fortune; it was the home of The Lord Chamberlain's Men, the company headed by James Burbage's sons, Cuthbert and Richard, and the company for which Shakespeare wrote. Piecing together what meager information exists, theatre scholars have tried to reconstruct what The Globe must have been like. Perhaps the most impressive research has been done by John C. Adams and C. Walter Hodges. Both argue for three roofed galleries, one above another, surrounding a yard or pit open to the sky. Into this yard jutted a forestage that was raised approximately four to six feet. Audience members either sat on benches in the galleries for two pence or stood in the pit in front of or at the sides of the stage for a penny. The pit was probably paved or covered with gravel, and while it was exposed to the sky and the frequent English rains, it provided close proximity to the forestage where most of the action occurred. The stage itself seems to have been covered with a roof called the heavens from which machinery and special effects could be operated and to have contained several trap doors in its floor for grave scenes or appearances of ghosts. Actors were sometimes flown or came out of trap doors in great clouds of smoke. Two doors led from the back stage space, called the tiring house, onto either side of the forestage.

But here agreement ends. Both Adams and Hodges believe there was some kind of discovery place at the back of the forestage. Adams suggests an inner-below, a curtained off recess where props and scenery could be placed, and a balcony area directly above this alcove called the inner-above. Hodges, however, believes that visibility in such an arrangement would have been negligible and argues for a pavilion of one or two stories (very like a medieval mansion) which was positioned at the back of the forestage and could be curtained around or exposed to provide visibility on three sides. Scholars further disagree as to whether or not this pavilion was permanent or temporary, used as a playing area in itself or merely as a way of setting the scene with all of the action played on the forestage. Some historians believe there was a third level, a musicians' gallery above any second story playing area.

While these theories about The Globe and other Elizabethan theatres may differ in detail, Shakespeare's plays themselves indicate a space that offers opportunity for flexibility, rapid change of scene, a variety of acting areas and entrances, and fast paced, fluid action. So it is that a play like *Othello* can move easily from a street with soldiers carousing, to a room in Othello's home, to Desdemona's bedroom.

There is evidence also that the theatres were not crude but sumptuous and ornate. Contemporary American reconstructions of Elizabethan theatres at The Folger Library in Washington, D.C. and The Oregon Shakespeare Theatre at Ashland, Oregon attest to the intimacy, flexibility, and practicality of Shakespeare's theatre. The theatrical experience was further enriched by ample use of music. Trumpets flourished before entrances, drums punctuated battle scenes, and background music underscored many episodes. It is believed that the musicians playing mainly brass and percussion instruments performed either from the stage or from the musicians' gallery on the third level of the theatre.

Not only were the theatres themselves richly decorated and embellished but many properties—trees, arbors, tents, altars, tombs, prisons, beds, thrones—were used. Elaborate set pieces rather than any kind of full scale scenery were standard on this flexible stage. Properties symbolized and suggested place rather than being a literal representation of it. Similarly, costumes were elegant, rich in color and detail, but there was no attempt to suggest any historical time beyond the Elizabethan. Perhaps as records suggest, there were some conventionalized costumes— a moor's coat, a Turkish bonnet, a Roman cloak—but generally speaking, theatrical attire reflected Elizabethan court dress. While the more prosperous theatres probably kept their own tailors, there is some evidence that the companies accepted used clothing from patrons and benefactors.

Besides these large open air theatres which performed on summer afternoons, we believe there were indoor theatres where Shakespeare's company acted for the court, aristocracy, and well-to-do during the winter months. That these theatres were called "private" seems to have more to do with the fact that they were enclosed than with their exclusiveness, however. Such a theatre was the Blackfriars which was built by James Burbage but used by a company of boy actors until 1610 when James I arranged for the King's Men, as Shakespeare's Company was now called, to perform there. Its advantages were its small size (approximately half that of The Globe), its convenient location, and the fact that it could be used in inclement weather. Since the companies moved freely from the out-of-door public theatres to the private ones, we assume that the staging was very similar in both.

The audience that attended these Elizabethan theatres was as diverse as it was enthusiastic. It is generally believed that for an extra fee seating—for those who went to the theatre as much to be seen in their finery as to see the plays—could be purchased on the edges of the forestage itself, that the galleries were crowded with women and people from all stations in life, and that the pit or yard was supported primarily by the working class audience of tradesmen, apprentices, servants and soldiers who were willing to stand for their afternoon's entertainment. While in *Hamlet* Shakespeare speaks of the groundlings, as this segment of the audience was called, as "capable of nothing but inexplicable dumb-shows and noise," they must have been a lively and spirited bunch. What theatre management today would not be delighted to have a large diversified audience willing to tolerate tired feet for several hours in rain or baking sun to see their favorite play and players?

Imagine for a moment what the occasion of going to one of the public theatres would have been like. You would walk through the crowded and dirty streets of London, across London Bridge, itself congested with shops and buildings, to the entertainment area on the south bank of the Thames River. There you would see several circular buildings clustered together. A flag flying from the hut or cupola at the top of the structure would indicate that there was a performance this afternoon. As you paid your penny and entered the theatre, you would guard your purse against pickpockets, order yourself a beer, or munch nuts and apples purchased from vendors who circulated among the crowds. Trumpets would signal curtain time, and soon the actors would appear.

It is difficult to know what it would have been like to be an actor in one of the great city companies like the Lord Chamberlain's Men. The fact that Shakespeare seems to have wandered down from Stratford-upon-Avon and joined a prestigious troupe makes it all seem very facile. Perhaps Shakespeare was lucky; perhaps there is much more to the story than we know. At any rate, acting was not an easy profession or one without tremendous competition and hardship. One could not study at the Royal Academy of Dramatic Art and then make a stage debut. There were no schools or training programs, so most of the actors were "trained up from childhood" by being apprenticed to an established company member just as they might be to a tailor or carpenter. Epidemics of plague frequently forced the theatres to close and the companies to tour the provinces. Pay was poor, probably about five pounds per year, plus allowances for food, light and fuel. Actors had to perform for the Queen and court on demand, and there were long periods of inactivity during the winter months.

London audiences also demanded much of their actors. Although we believe the acoustics to have been very good in the theatres, actors had to speak their lines, as Hamlet tells us, "trippingly on the tongue." They had to have sublime memories because the plays were performed in repertory, that is, in rotation with no play performed two days in a row. With the popularity of battles and sieges, athletic ability for falls and leaps was essential to the actor as was skill in stage fighting. A groundling would hardly pay his penny to see one actor make ineffectual stabs at another while declaring to fight to the death. Actors learned to handle a long, heavy rapier in one hand and a dagger for parrying in the other. On one occasion at The Swan, a fencer was run through the eye and died, an indication of the risks this sort of work involved even with trained, experienced fencers. Not being content with believeable fighting, the London audience also expected to see bloody deaths, and the Elizabethan theatre gave its audience real blood. Ox blood was considered too thick to run well, so sheep's blood was generally used. To stage a realistic stabbing, one actor would use a knife with a hollow handle into which the blade would retract when it was pressed home, and his fellow actor would be equipped with a bladder of blood inside his white jerkin. When the bladder was pricked, the blood spurted out in a terrible manner. This bit of stage magic was actually inherited from the medieval period and has remained unaltered to the present day. In one play of the Jacobean period, when James I was king and the plays became increasingly bloody and violent, there was a disemboweling scene for which the property man supplied three vials of blood and the liver, heart, and lungs of a sheep. To balance the bloodiness of the craft, the actors were expected to be excellent dancers. In fact, dancing became a national craze under Elizabeth, and London was full of dancing schools. Apart from the dances that were written into the actual texts of the plays, it was usual to end a performance with a dance by members of the company. Elizabethan dances were wonderfully intricate and acrobatic with leaps, dips and flourishes. Male dancers often padded the calves of their legs to make them appear more shapely.

In addition to all this, supporting actors were expected to handle several roles in an afternoon. The average company numbered between ten and twenty-five, and probably only ten of these were actors. In Henslowe's notes on Edward Alleyn's The Admiral's Men, a single actor played a Tartar nobleman, a priest, an attendant, a hostage, a ghost, a child, a captain, and a Persian. More than half the members of each troupe were "hired men" employed under a two-year contract at a salary equivalent to that earned by an unskilled laborer. In addition to acting, the hired men served as stage managers, prompters, wardrobe keepers and musicians. Apparently each company had strict rules of conduct. An actor could be fined one shilling for lateness to rehearsal, three shillings for lateness to a performance, ten for drunkenness during a performance, twenty for missing a performance, and forty for taking company property.

The leading companies balanced the rigors of the profession by providing incentives for actors. Companies such as The Admiral's Men and The Lord Chamberlain's Men were set up on a shareholder plan by which company members could be rewarded with a share of the profits. On still a higher level, actors could be made "householders" or part owners of the theatre building. It was through these two plans that we believe Shakespeare retired to Stratford-upon-Avon at the age of 48, a wealthy or certainly a very comfortable man. The shareholders formed a self-governing, democratic body, selecting and producing the plays given by the company. Each shareholder probably had some specific responsibility such as business management, supervising properties or costumes, or writing plays. A playwright was probably paid about six pounds for each play he wrote. Once he was paid, the script belonged to the company. Since, there was usually only one copy of a play, the actors used "sides"—just their own lines copied out by hand.

One of the most unique and puzzling aspects of the Elizabethan acting profession was the use of boy actors in the great women's roles. Older women, especially the comic ones like Mistress Quickly or Juliet's nurse, were probably played by the mature male actors. While one has no difficulty with the concept, for example, of the Japanese onnagata (men traditionally trained to play women's roles), it is difficult to imagine immature boys of fourteen or fifteen playing women's roles that have challenged even the most skilled actresses. Shakespeare makes an ironic comment on this convention when Cleopatra in *Antony and Cleopatra* says, "And I shall see some squeaking Cleopatra boy my greatness in the posture of a whore." Apparently these boys began apprenticeships between the ages of six and fourteen; they lived, studied with, and were supported by accomplished actors of the troupe who, in turn, were paid for their services by the company. Some of the apprentices continued careers as actors; others by the age of eighteen or twenty-one had left the theatre and taken up other professions or crafts.

Queen Elizabeth died in 1603 and James I of Scotland became king. In 1604 he tightened control of the theatre by ruling that nobles could no longer maintain acting troupes and that only members of the royal household could do so. Thus it was that the Lord Chamberlain's Men became the King's Men, no doubt a great honor for Shakespeare's company at the Globe.

Perhaps the most curious element of our entire discussion of Elizabethan theatre is how little we actually know. Philip Henslowe's records including a building contract for the Fortune and the deWitt sketch are virtually all that remain to tell us about one of the two greatest periods of theatrical activity. Fortunately, there is another source: the plays themselves which offer testimony of the freedom, fluidity, energy, pace, and dynamism of the Elizabethan theatre. Today's students should also be aware that both the Burbage family and Edward Alleyn were businessmen who went into theatre to please an audience and to make money. Apparently both objectives were accomplished.

William Shakespeare

If we know little about the Elizabethan threatre, we know even less about the man who claims the title of the greatest playwright who has ever lived. If you visit Shakespeare's birthplace on Henley Street in Stratford-upon-Avon, the cynical guide may tell you that there is nothing to prove that Shakespeare was not born there. Every few years an enthusiastic scholar will come up with a new theory: that Shakespeare was really Sir Francis Bacon or the Earl of Oxford. It bewilders us to imagine that a person of middle class parents with nothing beyond a grammar school education should be credited with thirty-eight extraordinary plays—comedies, histories, tragedies, and tragi-comedies—written in rapid succession within a span of less than twenty-five years. The very fact that we know so little about him intensifies both the mystery and our sense of wonder about the man.

Shakespeare's baptism at the Church of the Holy Trinity in Stratford was recorded on April 26, 1564. His birthday is generally accepted as April 23 in order to create a tidy parallel with the record of his death on April 23, 1616. He was the son of Mary Arden and John Shakespeare, who was by trade a glover or leatherworker. Apparently the elder Shakespeare became a prominent citizen of Stratford when he was selected as an alderman in 1565 and bailiff in 1568. It is likely that young William obtained his education at the local grammar school, but there is no record of a university education, a fact that caused Ben Jonson to say that Shakespeare possessed "small Latin and less Greek." The next known fact about the mercurial Bard of Avon is that he obtained a marriage license with Anne Hathaway, eight years older than he, and that their first child, a daughter named Susanna, was born six months later and christened on May 16, 1583. In 1585 twins named Hamnet and Judith were born to the couple. Hamnet, Shakespeare's only son, died eleven years later.

Nothing is known of Shakespeare beyond this point until his name appears in London theatre records. By 1595 he was a working member of The Lord Chamberlain's Men. Tradition assigns him two roles in his own plays: Adam in *As You Like It* and the ghost of Hamlet's father in *Hamlet*. How or why Shakespeare left Stratford and went to London to make his fortune as an actor is a matter of much conjecture. The fact remains, however, that he was a working man of the theatre. Historically, it is extremely rare when a man or woman writes plays from a study isolated from the working theatre. Almost all great playwrights have been actively involved in the day to day task of presenting plays. Shakespeare's dramas constantly reveal a keen awareness of the craft of the actor. Turning slowly from acting to playwriting, Shakespeare must have written about two plays annually. In 1597 the writer acquired New Place, a comfortable property in Stratford. By 1612 he is presumed to have given up the life of the theatre for a quiet and prosperous retirement in his native town.

Shakespeare's crafts must have been taken very much for granted in his own day. There is no evidence that his genius was felt either by his audiences or his theatrical colleagues. It was seven years after his death that two of his acting colleagues from The King's Men, John Heminge and Henry Condell, assembled thirty-six of his plays and published them in a first Folio. Besides writing plays that were imminently actable, Shakespeare possessed a divine gift for language and passion for dramatic tensions between characters. He was a master of character, of human psychology, of robust humor and agile wit. He knew history, geography, and classical literature; his sensitive and penetrating treatment of his subject matter—guilt, lust for power, hypocrisy, passion, and self-destruction—place him with the great humanists of the world. Perhaps it was fellow playwright Ben Jonson who first articulated Shakespeare's immortality when he wrote in the preface to the First Folio, "He was not of an age, but for all time!"

Shakespeare's *A Midsummer Night's Dream*

Drama, being dramatic rather than narrative, presents an image of the world in action. It is no mere accident or coincidence, then, that periods of great national drama tend to coincide with those moments in history when the nation is most actively and dynamically establishing its own identity in the world and accomplishing remarkable deeds politically, socially and economically. It should not be surprising that the nation in question is also making great strides artistically as well. For example, the American drama achieved world renown immediately following World War I when the United States was first taking its place as a major world power. Similarly, the magnificent Greek drama, particularly the tragedy, emerged in the Age of Pericles. It would seem inevitable, then, that the drama of Great Britain reached phenomenal heights of glory during the reign of Queen Elizabeth I as England was defeating the Spanish Armada and establishing herself as a dominant empire in Europe. We see the brilliance of that Elizabethan drama most vividly in the works of William Shakespeare.

During the reign of Elizabeth's father, Henry VIII, the spirit of the Renaissance stirred the British Isles. The fledgling universities, which were later to become great seats of learning, began to introduce into their curricula the study of Roman and Greek drama as exercises in the examination of classical literature and art. British scholars and students were thus introduced to the form of Greek drama as it had been adapted by the Romans. The new academic drama of Britain imitated the model of the Ancients in the use of a five-act structure, the employment of poetry in tragedy and prose in comedy, and the propensity to base new plays on the plots of old ones. But it is evident that the academicians in England—unlike those in France and many of their European followers—did not totally reject the medieval heritage for we still find in the university drama of Great Britain the panoramic freedom of time and place and the employment of multiple plots that we associate with the medieval cycle drama. As a new university plays containing classical influences melded with the popular theatre fare—the cycle plays, interludes, moralities and native farces—a vigorous new and distinctly English drama was born.

We see that blending of old and new traditions with striking clarity in Shakespeare's *A Midsummer Night's Dream* where the plot moves rather freely through a time period of two or three days (Shakespeare is somewhat unclear about the exact passage of time) while elaborating the complex plight of four sets of lovers (or six if we wish to include Titania and Bottom and also

Pyramus and Thisby). In the meantime the lovers, who appear to be based on models from classical drama and romances, collide with Homespuns right out of medieval native farce who perform a play drawn from Latin sources. And they all function within the environment of a court that is supposedly Greek while looking very British and a forest we are told is on the outskirts of Athens but, nonetheless, bears a remarkable resemblance to Arden Forest which has provided a setting for more than one Shakespearian comedy.

The Elizabethan age unquestionably created one of the most vital theatres and some of the greatest drama of all time. We sometimes tend to think of Shakespeare as the only real dramatist of that period. In reality, Shakespeare was only one of many superior playwrights contributing to the theatre of the day. Many of the new dramatists were university trained and employed their knowledge of the form and content of classical drama to the creation of new British plays. They were referred to as the University Wits; Shakespeare was not one of the group by virtue of the fact that he was not university trained. Still, Shakespeare was their superior in most respects. As great as he may have been, however, he was not one of the major innovators of the period. Christopher Marlowe had preceded Shakespeare in the creation of profound Renaissance blank verse tragedy in plays like *Doctor Faustus*. Robert Greene had already established romantic comedy as a popular form of theatrical entertainment. Thomas Kyd had established the form of the revenge play in *The Spanish Tragedy*. Ben Jonson, writing at the same time as Shakespeare for the same company of actors, actually outdid the Bard in realistic comedy in plays like *Everyman in his Humour* and *Volpone*. Beaumont and Fletcher, the first important writing team in the history of theatre, were writing tragi-comedies which outstripped Shakespeare's in popularity. There were many other writers as well—men such as Thomas Dekker, John Lyly, John Lodge, and George Peele—who were bringing audiences into the theatre with an array of interesting works.

In 1603, Elizabeth I died and James I, son of Mary of Scotland, assumed the throne of England. Scholars refer to the British drama written during the reign of James as Jacobean rather than Elizabethan; but essentially the same dramatists in addition to their followers and imitators were at work. We note, however, a gradual diminishing of power and splendor in the British drama during the Jacobean age characterized by the playwrights' growing preoccupation with violence and sensationalism. (The same might be said about the American drama from the 1970s forward.) After Shakespeare's death in 1616, in particular, the drama begins to decline. While Shakespeare was not a major innovator in British drama, he was unquestionably the greatest of the Elizabethan-Jacobean playwrights. If other dramatists beat him to the punch, as it were, in the creation of new forms and styles, he, for the most part, outdid all of his contemporaries in bringing those forms and styles to a full, shimmering realization. Little wonder, then, that he is now regarded as one of the greatest dramatists of all times equalled in brilliance only by Sophocles.

A Midsummer Night's Dream is a superior example of romantic comedy in which we are invited to laugh *with* the characters at a ridiculous world they inhabit rather than to laugh *at* the characters in a superior way because of their stupidities. Even when the courtiers are making fun of the theatrical efforts of the Homespuns they do it with a light and affectionate touch. *Dream* was probably written sometime around 1595 close to the time that *Romeo and Juliet* was first performed. Shakespeare seems to have been preoccupied at that time with the vicissitudes of young love, for, in a sense, *A Midsummer Night's Dream,* with its vision of young love thwarted by interference from the older generation, is the comic treatment of *Romeo and Juliet*. While *Dream* is one of the Bard's most popular comedies it is by no means his most accessible simply because it abounds in comedic riches. It is audaciously spontaneous and imaginative and lyrical. More than that, it is gloriously youthful. Those qualities—spontaneity, imagination, lyricism and youth—are guides to the play's style and meaning.

There are important clues in the play's title concerning the intentions of the dramatist. The major events in the play transpire on Midsummer Night—a very special time, specifically that time between sunset on June 23 and sunrise on June 24, the shortest night of the year. In Shakespeare's day this was a time of festival, a time to celebrate love and marriage. As it still is in our day, June was a time for brides and weddings and parties; June was a time to effect and celebrate the joining of lovers in wedlock. So the play concerns itself with those in love anticipating marriage. Theseus is about to marry Hippolyta; in fact, we have gathered to celebrate the wedding. The Homespuns are preparing a play as their contribution to the festivities. Hermia and Lysander wish to wed. Helena is in love with Demetrius and wishes to marry him. Oberon and Titania, king and queen of the fairies, are married but their marriage is non-functional at the moment. They will reunite during the course of the play. Titania, under a spell, is momentarily in love with Bottom. And in the play-within-a-play Pyramus and Thisby are lovers who wish nothing more than to be together. We are surrounded by lovers—royal ones, not-so-royal ones, young ones, older ones, real ones, mythical ones, even theatrical-comical ones.

In Shakespeare's day Midsummer's Eve was also regarded as a time of enchantment and witchcraft, a time when fairies walked the woods at night casting spells. For that reason it was an unsettling time for a people perhaps more superstitious than we are today. On this shortest night of the year the very air seemed to be so moon-drenched that sleep was near impossible; and that lent an air of restlessness and mystery and anxiety to the occasion. No wonder the various lovers are fretful and intolerant of delay. The impatience of lovers is focussed in the opening speeches of the play when Theseus bemoans the slow passage of time (" . . . how slow/This old moon wanes!") between the present moment and his anticipated wedding. He is comforted by Hippolyta who tells him, "Four Nights will quickly dream away the time." Despite Hippolyta's words of comfort, an air of restless, uneasy, and romantic anticipation prevails. It is a mood not unlike that surrounding many young lovers today during midsummer season. Why else would so many college students feel obliged to pursue a summer romance? And so in Shakespeare's play, because it is Midsummer's Eve, fairies materialize, magical spells are cast, and young lovers go blithely berserk.

Another useful clue to Shakespeare's intentions is to be found in the word "dream." The play is a dream—that dream which will "quickly dream away the time." Whose dream is it then? Theseus's dream? Possibly. The young lovers' dream? Maybe. The audience's dream? Most assuredly. Shakespeare even playfully suggests that it could be Bottom's dream for he has that character, in effect, sum up the play in the first scene of Act IV when he wakes from his spell, his sleep, and says: "I have had a most rare vision. I have had a dream, past the wit of man to say what dream it was . . ." Significantly, Bottom immediately goes on to say in his own fashion: " . . . man is but an ass, if he go about to expound this dream . . . it shall be called Bottom's Dream, because it has no bottom . . ." Shakespeare is saying with clarity and cleverness that the spectator (or reader) should not waste time attempting to explain what happens in the play in rational terms for the play is not a rational vision. It is a dream and, therefore, events may be oddly juxtaposed, may sometimes be confusing, and often transpire without logical motivation. It is a dream in which fanciful transformations can and do occur. It is a dream, and like all dreams it is airy imagination tangentially based on and derived from what has happened in reality or in everyday life. And, of course, it is one of the most gorgeously lyrical dreams that a creative mind has ever brought forth.

But, if Shakespeare's vision is a dream, it is also a play which means that it must embody an action. While the vision itself may be complex, the action is, by contrast, a simple one. For the world of this play to emerge from its state of chaos and achieve equilibrium one action must take place: *True lovers must be united.* In the first two acts of the play we are introduced to the various sets of lovers: Theseus and Hippolyta, Hermia and Lysander, Helena and Demetrius, Oberon and Titania. Mature, lofty, and lyric sentiments of love are expressed by the Duke of Athens and the Queen of the Amazons. The play ends with their marriage. Lovers are united.

We are introduced to more down-to-earth sentiments and youthful romanticism with the appearance of the quartet of young lovers. Propelled by their emotions they behave excessively, committing blunders, mistaking identities and intentions, being unconsciously cruel to one another. None of this is too serious, however, because the young lovers are under a spell. Initially, they are simply under the spell of love; later they are significantly under a magical spell induced by Puck and his fairy potion. Is Shakespeare perhaps telling us that young love is a magic spell? Interestingly enough, the young lovers, in spite of all of their excesses, remain sympathetic characters because we recognize that they are not entirely responsible for their behavior. Who is ever totally responsible when under the spell of blissful, romantic, summer love?

The young lovers are interesting characters, too, because the playwright somehow finds the time and the means to give each of them a distinct personality. The portraits are done with quick, broad strokes to be sure, but, nevertheless, done effectively. Lysander is gallant, gracious, handsome, respectful and somewhat put-upon. Hermia is short and dark, assertive, quietly willful and rebellious, and obviously in love with Lysander. When Theseus ventures to point out to her that Demetrius, the man her father has chosen to be her husband, should be given preference because he "is a worthy gentleman," she rather bluntly retorts: "So is Lysander." Furthermore, she suggests that her father should try seeing Lysander through her eyes. She is anything but the pallid, dutiful daughter. In her first scene she seems to want to know just one thing: what will happen to me if I tell my father to go to the devil? And she faithfully remains that kind of woman throughout the play. Characteristically, when she confronts her rival, Helena, in the woods, she is inclined to go after her with her fingernails. Helena, on the other hand, is tall and blond, vulnerable, insecure, self-effacing (she even doubts her own beauty), and tender. In her love-sickness she is prone to feel a bit sorry for herself and is prompted to inform Demetrius of Hermia's plans to elope, an understandable if not entirely trustworthy response. To the others she is "gentle Helena" and is consistently that through five acts. Demetrius, like Lysander, is handsome, gallant and in love. But he is also much more aggressive and a trifle less sensitive to others. In short, the young lovers are highly believable as flesh-and-blood creatures. And, as in the case of the older couple, young lovers are implicitly joined in matrimony at the end of the play.

Oberon and Titania are of another stamp entirely. As king and queen of the fairies, they are mythical creatures, and their emotions and actions are correspondingly somewhat excessive and larger than life. For this reason, Shakespeare gives them some of the most elegant poetic dialogue to speak. The dramatist also provides them with charming comic dimension by demonstrating that even fanciful creatures have very human problems. When they first meet, they are obviously estranged. They are, in Oberon's words, "Ill met by moonlight." Very shortly all lovers in the play will be ill met by moonlight. Titania finds herself, ironically like many women in everyday life, in love with an ass. Meanwhile Oberon has managerial problems; that is to say, he cannot entirely control his blundering and prankish servant—Puck, "the merry wanderer of the night." In spite of their trials, however, the mythical lovers are reconciled by the end of the play.

Superficially, all lovers are asleep and dreaming by the end of Act III. They awake and would seem to be united by the end of Act IV making Act V appear somewhat gratuitous. However, essential things happen in Act V which are designed to emphasize that the action of the play—the uniting of lovers—has truly been accomplished. For one thing all lovers are quite literally "out of the wood." Furthermore, the wedding festivities honoring Theseus and Hippolyta are in progress. The young lovers are present and their love has been accepted by the older generation. And the Homespuns stage their play. The performance of the play-within-a-play is delightfully, innocently, and comically inept and the source of much merriment for the courtiers. Shakespeare is obviously parodying many such ludicrous performances by local tradesmen he saw at fairs when he was younger. "The most lamentable comedy, and most cruel death of Pyramus and Thisby" as enacted by the Homespuns is such outrageous fun that the spectator or reader is apt to overlook its serious message, the same message one finds in *Romeo and Juliet:* parents should not intervene in the course of true love, for such intervention can have tragic consequences. Shakespeare keeps that message muted and totally within the spirit of comedy by making the performance so charmingly amateurish and amusing. Still, the play makes its point. True love must find fulfillment in marriage. In other words, true lovers must be united just as they are when the psychic action of *A Midsummer Night's Dream* is completed as Oberon and Titania arrive to jointly "sing and bless this place."

In 1935, Max Reinhardt, a German who at that time was perhaps the most famous director in the world, staged Shakespeare's comedy at the Hollywood Bowl in Los Angeles and then subsequently filmed his production for Warner Brothers Studio. The casting was outrageous. Lysander was played by Dick Powell, a popular crooner of the day, and Hermia was enacted by Olivia de Havilland who was much better a few years later as Melanie in *Gone With the Wind*. A very young Mickey Rooney appeared as Puck. The role of Bottom was entrusted to James Cagney, and Joe E. Brown, a film comic noted for his out-sized mouth, played Flute. Cellophane had just been invented, and Reinhardt used a veritable ton of it in the setting of the forest to capture that moondrenched quality of Midsummer's Eve. Unfortunately, the cellophane reflected, deflected and bounced so much uncontrollable light about the set that it was—and still is—impossible to recognize actors in the boggling blur of many of the scenes. Considering the quality of the acting in the movie, that was not entirely a bad thing. Still the film has its charm and is great fun to watch. All of which goes to say that not even a bad production can destroy the magic of *A Midsummer Night's Dream*.

A MIDSUMMER-NIGHT'S DREAM

———— DRAMATIS PERSONAE ————

THESEUS, Duke of Athens.
EGEUS, father to Hermia.
LYSANDER, } in love with Hermia.
DEMETRIUS, }
PHILOSTRATE, master of the revels to Theseus.
QUINCE, a carpenter.
SNUG, a joiner.
BOTTOM, a weaver.
FLUTE, a bellows-mender.
SNOUT, a tinker.
STARVELING, a tailor.

HIPPOLYTA, queen of the Amazons, betrothed to Theseus.
HERMIA, daughter to Egeus, in love with Lysander.
HELENA, in love with Demetrius.

OBERON, king of the fairies.
TITANIA, queen of the fairies.
PUCK, or Robin Goodfellow.
PEASEBLOSSOM,
COBWEB, } fairies.
MOTH,
MUSTARDSEED, }

Other fairies attending their King and Queen. Attendants on Theseus and Hippolyta.

———————— SCENE ————————

Athens, and a wood near it.

ACT I.
SCENE I.

Athens. The Palace of Theseus.

Enter THESEUS, HIPPOLYTA, PHILOSTRATE,
and ATTENDANTS.

THE. Now, fair Hippolyta, our nuptial hour
Draws on apace; four happy days bring in
Another moon: but, O, methinks, how slow
This old moon wanes! she lingers my desires,
Like to a step-dance or a dowager
Long withering out a young man's revenue.

HIP. Four days will quickly steep themselves in
    night;
Four nights will quickly dream away the time;
And then the moon, like to a silver bow
New-bent in heaven, shall behold the night
Of our solemnities.

THE. Go, Philostrate,
Stir up the Athenian youth to merriments;
Awake the pert and nimble spirit of mirth:
Turn melancholy forth to funerals;
The pale companion is not for our pomp.

[*Exit* PHILOSTRATE.

Hippolyta, I woo'd thee with my sword,
And won thy love, doing thee injuries;
But I will wed thee in another key,
With pomp, with triumph and with revelling.

Enter EGEUS, HERMIA, LYSANDER, *and*
DEMETRIUS.

EGE. Happy be Theseus, our renowned duke!

THE. Thanks, good Egeus: what's the news with
thee?

EGE. Full of vexation come I, with complaint
Against my child, my daughter Hermia.
Stand forth, Demetrius. My noble lord,
This man hath my consent to marry her.
Stand forth, Lysander: and, my gracious duke,
This man hath bewitch'd the bosom of my child:
Thou, thou, Lysander, thou hast given her rhymes
And interchanged love-tokens with my child:
Thou hast by moonlight at her window sung
With feigning voice verses of feigning love,
And stolen the impression of her fantasy
With bracelets of thy hair, rings, gawds, conceits,
Knacks, trifles, nosegays, sweetmeats, messengers
Of strong prevailment in unharden'd youth:
With cunning hast thou filch'd my daughter's heart,
Turn'd her obedience, which is due to me,
To stubborn harshness: and, my gracious duke,
Be it so she will not here before your grace
Consent to marry with Demetrius,
I beg the ancient privilege of Athens,
As she is mine, I may dispose of her:
Which shall be either to this gentleman
Or to her death, according to our law
Immediately provided in that case.

THE. What say you, Hermia? be advised, fair maid:
To you your father should be as a god;
One that composed your beauties, yea, and one
To whom you are but as a form in wax
By him imprinted and within his power
To leave the figure or disfigure it.
Demetrius is a worthy gentleman.

HER. So is Lysander.

THE. In himself he is;
But in this kind, wanting your father's voice,
The other must be held the worthier.

HER. I would my father look'd but with my eyes.

THE. Rather your eyes must with his judgement
look.

HER. I do entreat your grace to pardon me.
I know not by what power I am made bold,
Nor how it may concern my modesty,
In such a presence here to plead my thoughts;
But I beseech your grace that I may know
The worst that may befall me in this case,
If I refuse to wed Demetrius.

THE. Either to die the death or to abjure
For ever the society of men.
Therefore, fair Hermia, question your desires;
Know of your youth, examine well your blood,
Whether, if you yield not to your father's choice,
You can endure the livery of a nun,
For aye to be in shady cloister mew'd,
To live a barren sister all your life,
Chanting faint hymns to the cold fruitless moon.
Thrice-blessed they that master so their blood,
To undergo such maiden pilgrimage;
But earthlier happy is the rose distill'd,
Than that which withering on the virgin thorn
Grows, lives and dies in single blessedness.

HER. So will I grow, so live, so die, my lord,
Ere I will yield my virgin patent up
Unto his lordship, whose unwished yoke
My soul consents not to give sovereignty.

THE. Take time to pause; and, by the next new
moon—
The sealing-day betwixt my love and me,
For everlasting bond of fellowship—
Upon that day either prepare to die
For disobedience to your father's will,
Or else to wed Demetrius, as he would;
Or on Diana's altar to protest
For aye austerity and single life.

DEM. Relent, sweet Hermia: and, Lysander, yield
Thy crazed title to my certain right.

LYS. You have her father's love, Demetrius;
Let me have Hermia's: do you marry him.

EGE. Scornful Lysander! true, he hath my love,
And what is mine my love shall render him.
And she is mine, and all my right of her
I do estate unto Demetrius.

LYS. I am, my lord, as well derived as he,
As well possess'd; my love is more than his;
My fortunes every way as fairly rank'd,
If not with vantage, as Demetrius';
And, which is more than all these boasts can be,

I am beloved of beauteous Hermia;
Why should not I then prosecute my right?
Demetrius, I'll avouch it to his head,
Made love to Nedar's daughter, Helena,
And won her soul; and she, sweet lady, dotes,
Devoutly dotes, dotes in idolatry,
Upon this spotted and inconstant man.

THE. I must confess that I have heard so much,
And with Demetrius thought to have spoke thereof;
But, being over-full of self-affairs,
My mind did lose it. But, Demetrius, come;
And come, Egeus; you shall go with me,
I have some private schooling for you both.
For you, fair Hermia, look you arm yourself
To fit your fancies to your father's will;
Or else the law of Athens yields you up—
Which by no means we may extenuate—
To death, or to a vow of single life.
Come, my Hippolyta: what cheer, my love?
Demetrius and Egeus, go along:
I must employ you in some business
Against our nuptial and confer with you
Of something nearly that concerns yourselves.

EGE. With duty and desire we follow you.

[*Exeunt all but* LYSANDER *and* HERMIA.

LYS. How now, my love! why is your cheek so pale?
How chance the roses there do fade so fast?

HER. Belike for want of rain, which I could well
Beteem them from the tempest of my eyes

LYS. Ay me! for aught that I could ever read,
Could ever hear by tale or history,
The course of true love never did run smooth;
But, either it was different in blood,—

HER. O cross! too high to be enthrall'd to low.

LYS. Or else misgraffed in respect of years,—

HER. O spite! too old to be engaged to young.

LYS. Or else it stood upon the choice of friends,—

HER. O hell! to choose love by another's eyes.

LYS. Or, if there were a sympathy in choice,
War, death, or sickness did lay siege to it,
Making it momentany as a sound,
Swift as a shadow, short as any dream;
Brief as the lightning in the collied night,
That, in a spleen, unfolds both heaven and earth,
And ere a man hath power to say 'Behold!'
The jaws of darkness do devour it up:
So quick bright things come to confusion.

HER. If then true lovers have been ever cross'd,
It stands as an edict in destiny:
Then let us teach our trial patience,
Because it is a customary cross,
As due to love as thoughts and dreams and sighs,
Wishes and tears, poor fancy's followers.

LYS. A good persuasion: therefore, hear me, Hermia.
I have a widow aunt, a dowager
Of great revenue, and she hath no child:
From Athens is her house remote seven leagues;
And she respects me as her only son.
There, gentle Hermia, may I marry thee;
And to that place the sharp Athenian law
Cannot pursue us. If thou lovest me then,
Steal forth thy father's house to-morrow night;
And in the wood, a league without the town,
Where I did meet thee once with Helena,
To do observance to a morn of May,
There will I stay for thee.

HER.   My good Lysander!
I swear to thee, by Cupid's strongest bow,
By his best arrow with the golden head,
By the simplicity of Venus' doves,
By that which knitteth souls and prospers loves,
And by that fire which burn'd the Carthage queen,
When the false Troyan under sail was seen,
By all the vows that ever men have broke,
In number more than ever women spoke,
In that same place thou hast appointed me,
To-morrow truly will I meet with thee.

LYS. Keep promise, love. Look, here comes Helena.

Enter HELENA.

HER. God speed fair Helena! whither away?

HEL. Call you me fair? that fair again unsay.
Demetrius loves your fair: O happy fair!
Your eyes are lode-stars; and your tongue's sweet
  air
More tuneable than lark to shepherd's ear,
When wheat is green, when hawthorn buds appear.
Sickness is catching: O, were favour so,
Yours would I catch, fair Hermia, ere I go;
My ear should catch your voice, my eye your eye,
My tongue should catch your tongue's sweet melody.
Were the world mine, Demetrius being bated,
The rest I'd give to be to you translated.
O, teach me how you look, and with what art
You sway the motion of Demetrius' heart.

HER. I frown upon him, yet he loves me still.

HEL. O that your frowns would teach my smiles such
  skill!

HER. I give him curses, yet he gives me love.

HEL. O that my prayers could such affection move!

HER. The more I hate, the more he follows me.

HEL. The more I love, the more he hateth me.

HER. His folly, Helena, is no fault of mine.

HEL. None, but your beauty: would that fault were mine!

HER. Take comfort: he no more shall see my face;
Lysander and myself will fly this place.
Before the time I did Lysander see,
Seem'd Athens as a paradise to me:
O, then, what graces in my love do dwell,
That he hath turn'd a heaven unto a hell!

LYS. Helen, to you our minds we will unfold:
To-morrow night, when Phœbe doth behold
Her silver visage in the watery glass,
Decking with liquid pearl the bladed grass,
A time that lovers' flights doth still conceal,
Through Athens' gates have we devised to steal.

HER. And in the wood, where often you and I
Upon faint primrose-beds were wont to lie,
Emptying our bosoms of their counsel sweet,
There my Lysander and myself shall meet;
And thence from Athens turn away our eyes,
To seek new friends and stranger companies.
Farewell, sweet playfellow: pray thou for us;
And good luck grant thee thy Demetrius!
Keep word, Lysander: we must starve our sight
From lovers' food till morrow deep midnight.

LYS. I will, my Hermia.   [*Exit* HERMIA.
As you on him, Demetrius dote on you! Helena,
   adieu: [*exit*.

HEL. How happy some o'er other some can be!
Through Athens I am thought as fair as she.
But what of that? Demetrius thinks not so;
He will not know what all but he do know:
And as he errs, doting on Hermia's eyes,
So I, admiring of his qualities:
Things base and vile, holding no quantity,
Love can transpose to form and dignity:
Love looks not with the eyes, but with the mind;
And therefore is wing'd Cupid painted blind:
Nor hath Love's mind of any judgement taste;
Wings and no eyes figure unheedy haste:
And therefore is Love said to be a child,
Because in choice he is so oft beguiled.
As waggish boys in game themselves forswear,
So the boy Love is perjured every where:
For ere Demetrius look's on Hermia's eyne,
He hail'd down oaths that he was only mine;

And when this hail some heat from Hermia felt,
So he dissolved, and showers of oaths did melt.
I will go tell him of fair Hermia's flight:
Then to the wood will he to-morrow night
Pursue her; and for this intelligence
If I have thanks; it is a dear expense:
But herein mean I to enrich my pain,
To have his sight thither and back again.   [*exit*

SCENE II.

Athens. Quince's House.

Enter QUINCE, SNUG, BOTTOM, FLUTE, SNOUT, *and*
                    STARVELING.

QUIN. Is all our company here?

BOT. You were best to call them generally, man by man, according to the scrip.

QUIN. Here is the scroll of every man's name, which is thought fit, through all Athens, to play in our interlude before the duke and the duchess, on his wedding-day at night.

BOT. First, good Peter Quince, say what the play treats on, then read the names of the actors, and so grow to a point.

QUIN. Mary, our play is, The most lamentable comedy, and most cruel death of Pyramus and Thisby.

BOT. A very good piece of work, I assure you, and a merry. Now, good Peter Quince, call forth your actors by the scroll. Masters, spread yourselves.

QUIN. Answer as I call you. Nick Bottom, the weaver.

BOT. Ready. Name what part I am for, and proceed.

QUIN. You, Nick Bottom, are set down for Pyramus.

BOT. What is Pyramus? a lover, or a tyrant?

QUIN. A lover, that kills himself most gallant for love.

BOT. That will ask some tears in the true performing of it: if I do it, let the audience look to their eyes; I will move storms, I will condole in some measure. To the rest: yet my chief humour is for a tyrant: I could play Ercles rarely, or a part to tear a cat in, to make all split.
          The raging rocks
          And shivering shocks
          Shall break the locks
              Of prison gates;

And Phibbus' car
  Shall shine from far
  And make and mar
    The foolish Fates.
This was lofty! Now name the rest of the players. This is Ercles' vein, a tyrant's vein; a lover is more condoling.

QUIN. Francis Flute, the bellows-mender.

FLU. Here, Peter Quince.

QUIN. Flute, you must take Thisby on you.

FLU. What is Thisby? a wandering knight?

QUIN. It is the lady that Pyramus must love.

FLU. Nay, faith, let not me play a woman; I have a beard coming.

QUIN. That's all one: you shall play it in a mask, and you may speak as small as you will.

BOT. An I may hide my face, let me play Thisby too, I'll speak in a monstrous little voice, 'Thisne, Thisne'; 'Ah Pyramus, my lover dear! thy Thisby dear, and lady dear!'

QUIN. No, no; you must play Pyramus: and, Flute, you Thisby.

BOT. Well, proceed.

QUIN. Robin Starveling, the tailor.

STAR. Here, Peter Quince.

QUIN. Robin Starveling, you must play Thisby's mother. Tom Snout, the tinker.

SNOUT. Here, Peter Quince.

QUIN. You, Pyramus' father: myself, Thisby's father. Snug, the joiner; you, the lion's part: and, I hope, here is a play fitted.

SNUG. Have you the lion's part written? pray you, if it be, give it me, for I am slow of study.

QUIN. You may do it extempore, for it is nothing but roaring.

BOT. Let me play the lion too: I will roar, that I will do any man's heart good to hear me; I will roar, that I will make the duke say 'Let him roar again, let him roar again.'

QUIN. An you should do it too terribly, you would fright the duchess and the ladies, that they would shriek; and that were enough to hang us all.

ALL. That would hang us, every mother's son.

BOT. I grant you, friends, if that you should fright the ladies out of their wits, they would have no more discretion but to hang us: but I will aggravate my voice so that I will roar you as gently as any sucking dove; I will roar you an 'twere any nightingale.

QUIN. You can play no part but Pyramus; for Pyramus is a sweet-faced man; a proper man, as one shall see in a summer's day; a most lovely gentleman-like man: therefore you must needs play Pyramus.

BOT. Well, I will undertake it. What beard were I best to play it in?

QUIN. Why, what you will.

BOT. I will discharge it in either your straw-colour beard, your orange-tawny beard, your purple-in-grain beard, or your French-crown-colour beard, your perfect yellow.

QUIN. Some of your French crowns have no hair at all, and then you will play barefaced. But, masters, here are your parts: and I am to entreat you, request you and desire you, to con them by to-morrow night; and meet me in the palace wood, a mile without the town, by moonlight; there will we rehearse, for if we meet in the city, we shall be dogged with company, and our devices known. In the meantime I will draw a bill of properties, such as our play wants. I pray you, fail me not.

BOT. We will meet; and there we may rehearse most obscenely and courageously. Take pains; be perfect: adieu.

QUIN. At the duke's oak we meet.

BOT. Enough; hold or cut bow-strings.   [*exeunt.*

ACT II.

SCENE I.

A Wood Near Athens.

Enter, from opposite sides, a FAIRY, *and* PUCK.

PUCK. How now, spirit! whither wander you?

FAI. Over hill, over dale,
  Thorough bush, thorough brier,
Over park, over pale,
  Thorough flood, thorough fire.
I do wander every where,
Swifter than the moon's sphere;
And I serve the fairy queen,

To dew her orbs upon the green.
  The cowslips tall her pensioners be:
  In their gold coats spots you see;
  Those be rubies, fairy favours,
  In those freckles live their savours:
I must go seek some dewdrops here
And hang a pearl in every cowslip's ear.
Farewell, thou lob of spirits; I'll be gone:
Our queen and all her elves come here anon.

PUCK. The king doth keep his revels here to-night:
Take heed the queen come not within his sight;
For Oberon is passing fell and wrath,
Because that she as her attendant hath
A lovely boy, stolen from an Indian king;
She never had so sweet a changeling;
And jealous Oberon would have the child
Knight of his train, to trace the forests wild;
But she perforce withholds the loved boy,
Crowns him with flowers and makes him all her joy:
And now they never meet in grove or green,
By fountain clear, or spangled starlight sheen,
But they do square, that all their elves for fear
Creep into acorn-cups and hide them there.

FAI. Either I mistake your shape and making quite,
Or else you are that shrewd and knavish sprite
Call'd Robin Goodfellow: are not you he
That frights the maidens of the villagery;
Skim milk, and sometimes labour in the quern
And bootless make the breathless housewife churn;
And sometime make the drink to bear no barm;
Mislead night-wanderers, laughing at their harm?
Those that Hobgoblin call you and sweet Puck,
You do their work, and they shall have good luck:
Are not you he?

PUCK.   Thou speak'st aright;
I am that merry wanderer of the night.
I jest to Oberon and make him smile
When I a fat and bean-fed horse beguile,
Neighing in likeness of a filly foal:
And sometime lurk I in a gossip's bowl,
In very likeness of a roasted crab,
And when she drinks, against her lips I bob
And on her wither'd dewlap pour the ale.
The wisest aunt, telling the saddest tale,
Sometime for three-foot stool mistaketh me;
Then slip I from her bum, down topples she,
And 'tailor' cries, and falls into a cough;
And then the whole quire hold their hips and laugh,
And waxen in their mirth and neeze and swear
A merrier hour was never wasted there.
But, room, fairy! here comes Oberon.

FAI. And here my mistress. Would that he were
gone!

Enter, from one side, OBERON, *with his train;
from the other,* TITANIA, *with hers.*

OBE. Ill met by moonlight, proud Titania.

TITA. What, jealous Oberon! Fairies, skip hence:
I have forsworn his bed and company.

OBE. Tarry, rash wanton: am not I thy lord?

TITA. Then I must be thy lady: but I know
When thou hast stolen away from fairy land,
And in the shape of Corin sat all day,
Playing on pipes of corn and versing love
To amorous Phillida. Why art thou here,
Come from the farthest steppe of India?
But that, forsooth, the bouncing Amazon,
Your buskin'd mistress and your warrior love,
To Theseus must be wedded, and you come
To give their bed joy and prosperity.

OBE. How canst thou thus for shame, Titania,
Glance at my credit with Hippolyta,
Knowing I know thy love to Theseus?
Didst thou not lead him through the glimmering
  night
From Perigenia, whom he ravished?
And make him with fair Ægle break his faith,
With Ariadne and Antiopa?

TITA. These are the forgeries of jealousy:
And never, since the middle summer's spring,
Met we on hill, in dale, forest or mead,
By paved fountain or by rushy brook,
Or in the beached margent of the sea,
To dance our ringlets to the whistling wind,
But with thy brawls thou hast disturb'd our sport.
Therefore the winds, piping to us in vain,
As in revenge, have suck'd up from the sea
Contagious fogs; which falling in the land
Have every pelting river made so proud
That they have overborne their continents:
The ox hath therefore stretch'd his yoke in vain,
The ploughman lost his sweat, and the green corn
Hath rotted ere his youth attain'd a beard;
The fold stands empty in the drowned field,
And crows are fatted with the murrion flock;
The nine men's morris is fill'd up with mud,
And the quaint mazes in the wanton green
For lack of tread are undistinguishable:
The human mortals want their winter here;
No night is now with hymn or carol blest:
Therefore the moon, the governess of floods,
Pale in her anger, washes all the air,
That rheumatic diseases do abound:
And thorough this distemperature we see
The seasons alter: hoary-headed frosts
Fall in the fresh lap of the crimson rose,

And on old Hiems' thin and icy crown
An odorous chaplet of sweet summer buds
Is, as in mockery, set: the spring, the summer,
The childing autumn, angry winter, change
Their wonted liveries, and the mazed world,
By their increase, now knows not which is which:
And this same progeny of evils comes
From our debate, from our dissension;
We are their parents and original.

OBE. Do you amend it then; it lies in you:
Why should Titania cross her Oberon?
I do but beg a little changeling boy,
To be my henchman.

TITA.   Set your heart at rest:
The fairy land buys not the child of me.
His mother was a votaress of my order:
And, in the spiced Indian air, by night,
Full often hath she gossip'd by my side,
And sat with me on Neptune's yellow sands,
Marking the embarked traders on the flood,
When we have laugh'd to see the sails conceive
And grow big-bellied with the wanton wind;
Which she, with pretty and with swimming gait
Following,—her womb then rich with my young
   squire,—
Would imitate, and sail upon the land,
To fetch me trifles, and return again,
As from a voyage, rich with merchandise.
But she, being mortal, of that body did die;
And for her sake do I rear up her boy,
And for her sake I will not part with him.

OBE. How long within this wood intend you stay?

TITA. Perchance till after Theseus' wedding-day.
If you will patiently dance in our round
And see our moonlight revels, go with us;
If not, shun me, and I will spare your haunts.

OBE. Give me that boy, and I will go with thee.

TITA. Not for thy fairy kingdom. Fairies, away!
We shall chide downright, if I longer stay.
                    [*Exit* TITANIA *with her train.*

OBE. Well, go thy way: thou shalt not from this grove
Till I torment thee for this injury.
My gentle Puck, come hither. Thou rememberest
Since once I sat upon a promontory,
And heard a mermaid on a dolphin's back
Uttering such dulcet and harmonious breath
That the rude sea grew civil at her song
And certain stars shot madly from their spheres,
To hear the sea-maid's music.

PUCK.   I remember.

OBE. That very time I saw, but thou couldst not,
Flying between the cold moon and the earth,
Cupid all arm'd: a certain aim he took
At a fair vestal throned by the west,
And loosed his love-shaft smartly from his bow,
As it should pierce a hundred thousand hearts;
But I might see young Cupid's fiery shaft
Quench'd in the chaste beams of the watery moon,
And the imperial votaress passed on,
In maiden meditation, fancy-free.
Yet mark'd I where the bolt of Cupid fell:
It fell upon a little western flower,
Before milk-white, now purple with love's wound,
And maidens call it love-in-idleness.
Fetch me that flower; the herb I shew'd thee once:
The juice of it on sleeping eye-lids laid
Will make or man or woman madly dote
Upon the next live creature that it sees.
Fetch me this herb; and be thou here again
Ere the leviathan can swim a league.

PUCK. I'll put a girdle round about the earth
In forty minutes.   [*exit.*

OBE.   Having once this juice,
I'll watch Titania when she is asleep,
And drop the liquor of it in her eyes.
The next thing then she waking looks upon,
Be it on lion, bear, or wolf, or bull,
On meddling monkey, or on busy ape,
She shall pursue it with the soul of love:
And ere I take this charm from off her sight,
As I can take it with another herb,
I'll make her render up her page to me.
But who comes here? I am invisible;
And I will overhear their conference.

   Enter DEMETRIUS, HELENA *following him.*

DEM. I love thee not, therefore pursue me not.
Where is Lysander and fair Hermia?
The one I'll slay, the other slayeth me.
Thou told'st me they were stolen unto this wood;
And here am I, and wode within this wood,
Because I cannot meet my Hermia.
Hence, get thee gone, and follow me no more.

HEL. You draw me, you hard-hearted adamant;
But yet you draw not iron, for my heart
Is true as steel: leave you your power to draw,
And I shall have no power to follow you.

DEM. Do I entice you? do I speak you fair?
Or, rather, do I not in plainest truth
Tell you, I do not, nor I cannot love you?

HEL. And even for that do I love you the more.
I am your spaniel; and, Demetrius,
The more you beat me, I will fawn on you:
Use me but as your spaniel, spurn me, strike me,
Neglect me, lose me; only give me leave,
Unworthy as I am, to follow you.
What worser place can I beg in your love,—
And yet a place of high respect with me,—
Than to be used as you use your dog?

DEM. Tempt not too much the hatred of my spirit,
For I am sick when I do look on thee.

HEL. And I am sick when I look not on you.

DEM. You do impeach your modesty too much,
To leave the city and commit yourself
Into the hands of one that loves you not;
To trust the opportunity of night
And the ill counsel of a desert place
With the rich worth of your virginity.

HEL. Your virtue is my privilege; for that
It is not night when I do see your face,
Therefore I think I am not in the night;
Nor doth this wood lack worlds of company,
For you in my respect are all the world:
Then how can it be said I am alone,
When all the world is here to look on me?

DEM. I'll run from thee and hide me in the brakes,
And leave thee to the mercy of wild beasts.

HEL. The wildest hath not such a heart as you.
Run when you will, the story shall be changed:
Apollo flies, and Daphne holds the chase;
The dove pursues the griffin; the mild hind
Makes speed to catch the tiger; bootless speed,
When cowardice pursues and valour flies.

DEM. I will not stay thy questions; let me go:
Or, if thou follow me, do not believe
But I shall do thee mischief in the wood.

HEL. Ay, in the temple, in the town, the field,
You do me mischief. Fie, Demetrius!
Your wrongs do set a scandal on my sex;
We cannot fight for love, as men may do;
We should be woo'd and were not made to woo.

[*Exit* DEMETRIUS.

I'll follow thee and make a heaven of hell,
To die upon the hand I love so well. [*exit.*

OBE. Fare thee well, nymph; ere he do leave this
grove,
Thou shalt fly him and he shall seek thy love.

Re-enter PUCK.

Hast thou the flower there? Welcome, wanderer.

PUCK. Ay, there it is.

OBE.   I pray thee, give it me.
I know a bank where the wild thyme blows,
Where oxlips and the nodding violet grows,
Quite over-canopied with luscious woodbine,
With sweet musk-roses and with eglantine:
There sleeps Titania sometime of the night,
Lull'd in these flowers with dances and delight;
And there the snake throws her enamell'd skin,
Weed wide enough to wrap a fairy in:
And with the juice of this I'll streak her eyes,
And make her full of hateful fantasies.
Take thou some of it, and seek through this grove:
A sweet Athenian lady is in love
With a disdainful youth: anoint his eyes;
But do it when the next thing he espies
May be the lady: thou shalt know the man
By the Athenian garments he hath on.
Effect it with some care that he may prove
More fond on her than she upon her love:
And look thou meet me ere the first cock crow.

PUCK. Fear not, my lord, your servant shall do so.
[*exeunt.*

SCENE II.

Another Part of the Wood.

Enter TITANIA, *with her train.*

TITA. Come, now a roundel and a fairy song;
Then, for the third part of a minute, hence;
Some to kill cankers in the musk-rose buds,
Some war with rere-mice for their leathern wings,
To make my small elves coats, and some keep back
The clamorous owl that nightly hoots and wonders
At our quaint spirits. Sing me now asleep;
Then to your offices and let me rest.

The FAIRIES *sing.*

You spotted snakes with double tongue,
  Thorny hedgehogs, be not seen;
Newts and blind-worms, do no wrong,
  Come not near our fairy queen.
  Philomel, with melody
  Sing in our sweet lullaby;
Lulla, lulla, lullaby, lulla, lulla, lullaby:
    Never harm,
    Nor spell nor charm,
  Come our lovely lady nigh;
  So, good night, with lullaby.
Weaving spiders, come not here;

Hence, you long-legg'd spinners, hence!
Beetles black, approach not near;
Worm nor snail, do no offence
Philomel, with melody, etc.

A FAIRY. Hence, away! now all is well:
One aloof stand sentinel.
                    [*Exeunt* FAIRIES. TITANIA *sleeps.*

Enter OBERON, *and squeezes the flower on*
TITANIA'S *eyelids.*

OBE.   What thou seest when thou dost wake,
        Do it for thy true-love take,
        Love and languish for his sake:
        Be it ounce, or cat, or bear,
        Pard, or boar with bristled hair,
        In thy eye that shall appear
        When thou wakest, it is thy dear:
        Wake when some vile thing is near.
                            [*exit.*

Enter LYSANDER *and* HERMIA.

LYS. Fair love, you faint with wandering in the wood;
  And to speak troth, I have forgot our way:
We'll rest us, Hermia, if you think it good,
  And tarry for the comfort of the day.

HER. Be it so, Lysander: find you out a bed;
For I upon this bank will rest my head.

LYS. One turf shall serve as pillow for us both;
One heart, one bed, two bosoms and one troth.

HER. Nay, good Lysander; for my sake, my dear,
Lie further off yet, do not lie so near.

LYS. O, take the sense, sweet, of my innocence!
Love takes the meaning in love's conference.
I mean, that my heart unto yours is knit
So that but one heart we can make of it;
Two bosoms interchained with an oath;
So then two bosoms and a single troth.
Then by your side no bed-room me deny;
For lying so, Hermia, I do not lie.

HER. Lysander riddles very prettily:
Now much beshrew my manners and my pride,
If Hermia meant to say Lysander lied.
But, gentle friend, for love and courtesy
Lie further off; in human modesty,
Such separation as may well be said
Becomes a virtuous bachelor and a maid,
So far be distant; and, good night, sweet friend:
Thy love ne'er alter till thy sweet life end!

LYS. Amen, amen, to that fair prayer, say I;
And then end life when I end loyalty!
Here is my bed: sleep give thee all his rest!

HER. With half that wish the wisher's eyes be
press'd!

                        [*They sleep.*
            Enter PUCK.

PUCK.   Through the forest have I gone,
        But Athenian found I none,
        On whose eyes I might approve
        This flower's force in stirring love.
        Night and silence.—Who is here?
        Weeds of Athens he doth wear:
        This is he, my master said,
        Despised the Athenian maid;
        And here the maiden, sleeping sound,
        On the dank and dirty ground.
        Pretty soul! she durst not lie
        Near this lack-love, this kill-courtesy.
        Churl, upon thy eyes I throw
        All the power this charm doth owe.
        When thou wakest, let love forbid
        Sleep his seat on thy eyelid:
        So awake when I am gone;
        For I must now to Oberon.   [*exit.*

    Enter DEMETRIUS *and* HELENA, *running.*

HEL. Stay, though thou kill me, sweet Demetrius.

DEM. I charge thee, hence, and do not haunt me
thus.

HEL. O, wilt thou darkling leave me? do not so.

DEM. Stay, on they peril: I alone will go.   [*exit.*

HEL. O, I am out of breath in this fond chase!
The more my prayer, the lesser is my grace.
Happy is Hermia, wheresoe'er she lies;
For she hath blessed and attractive eyes.
How came her eyes so bright? Not with salt tears:
If so, my eyes are oftener wash'd than hers.
No, no, I am as ugly as a bear;
For beasts that meet me run away for fear:
Therefore no marvel though Demetrius
Do, as a monster, fly my presence thus.
What wicked and dissembling glass of mine
Made me compare with Hermia's sphery eyne?
But who is here? Lysander! on the ground!
Dead? or asleep? I see no blood, no wound.
Lysander, if you live, good sir, awake.

LYS. [*awaking.*] And run through fire I will for thy
  sweet sake.
Transparent Helena! Nature shows art,
That through thy bosom makes me see thy heart.
Where is Demetrius? O, how fit a word
Is that vile name to perish on my sword!

HEL. Do not say so, Lysander; say not so.
What though he love your Hermia? Lord, what
  though?
Yet Hermia still loves you: then be content.

LYS. Content with Hermia! No; I do repent
The tedious minutes I with her have spent.
Not Hermia but Helena I love:
Who will not change a raven for a dove?
The will of man is by his reason sway'd;
And reason says you are the worthier maid.
Things growing are not ripe until their season:
So I, being young, till now ripe not to reason;
And touching now the point of human skill,
Reason becomes the marshal to my will
And leads me to your eyes, where I o'erlook
Love's stories written in love's richest book.

HEL. Wherefore was I to this keen mockery born?
When at your hands did I deserve this scorn?
Is't not enough, is't not enough, young man,
That I did never, no, nor never can,
Deserve a sweet look from Demetrius' eye,
But you must flout my insufficiency?
Good troth, you do me wrong, good sooth, you do,
In such disdainful manner me to woo.
But fare you well: perforce I must confess
I thought you lord of more true gentleness.
O, that a lady, of one man refused,
Should of another therefore be abused!   [exit.

LYS. She sees not Hermia. Hermia, sleep thou there:
And never mayst thou come Lysander near!
For as a surfeit of the sweetest things
The deepest loathing to the stomach brings,
Or as the heresies that men do leave
Are hated most of those they did deceive,
So thou, my surfeit and my heresy,
Of all be hated, but the most of me!
And, all my powers, address your love and might
To honour Helen and to be her knight!   [exit.

HER. [awaking.] Help me, Lysander, help me! do
  thy best
To pluck this crawling serpent from my breast!
Ay me, for pity! what a dream was here!
Lysander, look how I do quake with fear:
Methought a serpent eat my heart away,
And you sat smiling at his cruel prey.
Lysander! what, removed? Lysander! lord!
What, out of hearing? gone? no sound, no word?
Alack, where are you? speak, an if you hear;
Speak, of all loves! I swoon almost with fear.
No? then I well perceive you are not nigh:
Either death or you I'll find immediately.   [exit.

ACT III.

SCENE I.

The Wood. Titania Lying Asleep.

Enter QUINCE, SNUG, BOTTOM, FLUTE, SNOUT,
  and STARVELING.

BOT. Are we all met?

QUIN. Pat, pat; and here's a marvellous convenient
place for our rehearsal. This green plot shall be
our stage, this hawthorn-brake our tiring-house;
and we will do it in action as we will do it before
the duke.

BOT. Peter Quince,—

QUIN. What sayest thou, bully Bottom?

BOT. There are things in this comedy of Pyramus
and Thisby that will never please. First, Pyramus
must draw a sword to kill himself; which the ladies
cannot abide. How answer you that?

SNOUT. By'r lakin, a parlous fear.

STAR. I believe we must leave the killing out, when
all is done.

BOT. Not a whit: I have a device to make all-well.
Write me a prologue; and let the prologue seem
to say, we will do no harm with our swords and
that Pyramus is not killed indeed; and, for the more
better assurance, tell them that I Pyramus am not
Pyramus, but Bottom the weaver: this will put
them out of fear.

QUIN. Well, we will have such a prologue; and it
shall be written in eight and six.

BOT. No, make it two more; let it be written in eight
and eight.

SNOUT. Will not the ladies be afeard of the lion?

STAR. I fear it, I promise you.

BOT. Masters, you ought to consider with yourselves: to bring in—God shield us!—a lion among
ladies, is a most dreadful thing; for there is not a
more fearful wild-fowl than your lion living; and
we ought to look to't.

SNOUT. Therefore another prologue must tell he is
not a lion.

BOT. Nay, you must name his name, and half his
face must be seen through the lion's neck: and he
himself must speak through, saying thus, or to the
same defect,—'Ladies,'—or 'Fair ladies,—I would

wish you,'—or 'I would request you,'—or 'I would entreat you,—not to fear, not to tremble: my life for yours. If you think I come hither as a lion, it were pity of my life: no, I am no such thing; I am a man as other men are'; and there indeed let him name his name, and tell them plainly he is Snug the joiner.

QUIN. Well, it shall be so. But there is two hard things; that is, to bring the moonlight into a chamber; for, you know, Pyramus and Thisby meet by moonlight.

SNOUT. Doth the moon shine that night we play our play?

BOT. A calendar, a calendar! look in the almanac; find out moonshine, find our moonshine.

QUIN. Yes, it doth shine that night.

BOT. Why, then may you leave a casement of the great chamber window, where we play, open, and the moon may shine in at the casement.

QUIN. Ay; or else one must come in with a bush of thorns and a lanthorn, and say he comes to disfigure, or to present, the person of Moonshine. Then, there is another thing: we must have a wall in the great chamber; for Pyramus and Thisby, says the story, did talk through the chink of a wall.

SNOUT. You can never bring in a wall. What say you, Bottom?

BOT. Some man or other must present Wall: and let him have some plaster, or some loam, or some rough-cast about him, to signify wall; and let him hold his fingers thus, and through that cranny shall Pyramus and Thisby whisper.

QUIN. If that may be, then all is well. Come, sit down, every mother's son, and rehearse your parts. Pyramus, you begin: when you have spoken your speech, enter into that brake: and so every one according to his cue.

Enter PUCK *behind.*

PUCK. What hempen home-spuns have we swaggering here,
So near the cradle of the fairy queen?
What, a play toward! I'll be an auditor;
An actor too perhaps, if I see cause.

QUIN. Speak, Pyramus. Thisby, stand forth.

BOT. Thisby, the flowers of odious savours sweet,—

QUIN. Odours, odours.

BOT. —odours savours sweet:
So hath thy breath, my dearest Thisby dear.
But hark, a voice! stay thou but here awhile,
And by and by I will to thee appear.   [*exit.*

PUCK. A stranger Pyramus than e'er played here.
[*exit.*

FLU. Must I speak now?

QUIN. Ay, marry, must you; for you must understand he goes but to see a noise that he heard, and is to come again.

FLU. Most radiant Pyramus, most lily-white of hue,
Of colour like the red rose on triumphant brier,
Most brisky juvenal and eke most lovely Jew,
As true as truest horse that yet would never tire,
I'll meet thee, Pyramus, at Ninny's tomb.

QUIN. 'Ninus' tomb.' man: why, you must not speak that yet; that you answer to Pyramus: you speak all your part at once, cues and all. Pyramus enter: your cue is past; it is, 'never tire.'

FLU. O,—As true as truest horse, that yet would never tire.

Re-enter PUCK, *and* BOTTOM *with an ass's head.*

BOT. If I were fair, Thisby, I were only thine.

QUIN. O monstrous! O strange! we are haunted. Pray, masters! fly, masters! Help!

[Exeunt QUINCE, SNUG, FLUTE, SNOUT, *and*
STARVELLING.

PUCK. I'll follow you, I'll lead you about a round,
Through bog, through bush, through brake, through brier:
Sometime a horse I'll be, sometime a hound,
A hog, a headless bear, sometime a fire;
And neigh, and bark, and grunt, and roar, and burn,
Like horse, hound, hog, bear, fire, at every turn.
[*exit.*

BOT. Why do they run away? this is a knavery of them to make me afeard.

Re-enter SNOUT.

SNOUT. O Bottom, thou art changed! what do I see on thee?

BOT. What do you see? you see an ass-head of your own, do you?   [*Exit* SNOUT.

Re-enter QUINCE.

QUIN. Bless thee, Bottom! bless thee! thou art translated.
[*exit.*

BOT. I see their knavery: this is to make an ass of
me: to fright me, if they could. But I will not stir
from this place, do what they can: I will walk up
and down here, and I will sing, that they shall hear
I am not afraid.   [sings.
          The ousel cock so black of hue,
              With orange-tawny bill,
          The throstle with his note so true,
              The wren with little quill,—

TITA. [awaking.] What angel wakes me from my
flowery bed?

BOT. [sings.]
          The finch, the sparrow and the lark,
              The plain-song cuckoo gray,
          Whose note full many a man doth mark,
              And dares not answer nay;—
for, indeed, who would set his wit to so foolish a bird?
who would give a bird the lie, though he cry
'cuckoo' never so?

TITA. I pray thee, gentle mortal, sing again:
Mine ear is much enamour'd of thy note;
So is mine eye enthralled to thy shape;
And thy fair virtue's force perforce doth move me
On the first view to say, to swear, I love thee.

BOT. Methinks, mistress, you should have little
reason for that: and yet, to say the truth, reason
and love keep little company together now-a-days;
the more the pity that some honest neighbours will
not make them friends. Nay, I can gleek upon occasion.

TITA. Thou art as wise as thou art beautiful.

BOT. Not so, neither: but if I had wit enough to get
out of this wood, I have enough to serve mine own
turn.

TITA. Out of this wood do not desire to go:
Thou shalt remain here, whether thou wilt or no.
I am a spirit of no common rate:
The summer still doth tend upon my state;
And I do love thee: therefore, go with me;
I'll give thee fairies to attend on thee,
And they shall fetch thee jewels from the deep,
And sing while thou on pressed flowers dost sleep:
And I will purge thy mortal grossness so
That thou shalt like an airy spirit go.
Peaseblossom! Coweb! Moth! and Mustardseed!

          Enter PEASEBLOSSOM, COBWEB, MOTH,
                  and MUSTARDSEED.

PEAS. Ready.

COB.   And I.

MOTH.   And I.

MUS.   And I.

ALL.   Where shall we go?

TITA. Be kind and courteous to this gentleman;
Hop in his walks and gambol in his eyes;
Feed him with apricocks and dewberries,
With purple grapes, green figs, and mulberries;
The honey-bags steal from the humble-bees,
And for night-tapers crop their waxen thighs
And light them at the fiery glow-worm's eyes,
To have my love to bed and to arise;
And pluck the wings from painted butterflies
To fan the moonbeams from his sleeping eyes:
Nod to him, elves, and do him courtesies.

PEAS. Hail, mortal!

COB. Hail!

MOTH. Hail!

MUS. Hail!

BOT. I cry your worships mercy, heartily: I beseech
your worship's name.

COB. Cobweb.

BOT. I shall desire you of more acquaintance, good
Master Cobweb: if I cut my finger, I shall make
bold with you. Your name, honest gentleman?

PEAS. Peaseblossom.

BOT. I pray you, commend me to Mistress Squash,
your mother, and to Master Peascod, your father.
Good Master Peaseblossom, I shall desire you of
more acquaintance too. Your name, I beseech you,
sir?

MUS. Mustardseed.

BOT. Good Master Mustardseed, I know your patience well: that same cowardly, giant-like ox-beef
hath devoured many a gentleman of your house:
I promise you your kindred hath made my eyes
water ere now. I desire your more acquaintance,
good Master Mustardseed.

TITA. Come, wait upon him; lead him to my bower.
The moon methinks looks with a watery eye;
And when she weeps, weeps every little flower,
Lamenting some enforced chastity.
Tie up my love's tongue, bring him silently.
                                              [exeunt.

SCENE II.

Another Part of the Wood.

Enter OBERON.

OBE. I wonder if Titania be awaked;
Then, what it was that next came in her eye,
Which she must dote on in extremity.

Enter PUCK.

Here comes my messenger.
                How now, mad spirit!
What night-rule now about this haunted grove?

PUCK. My mistress with a monster is in love.
Near to her close and consecrated bower,
While she was in her dull and sleeping hour,
A crew of patches, rude mechanicals,
That work for bread upon Athenian stalls,
Were met together to rehearse a play
Intended for great Theseus' nuptial-day.
The shallowest thick-skin of that barren sort,
Who Pyramus presented, in their sport
Forsook his scene and enter'd in a brake:
When I did him at this advantage take,
An ass's nole I fixed on his head:
Anon his Thisbe must be answered,
And forth my mimic comes. When they him spy,
As wild geese that the creeping fowler eye,
Or russet-pated choughs, many in sort,
Rising and cawing at the gun's report,
Sever themselves and madly sweep the sky,
So, at his sight, away his fellows fly;
And, at our stamp, here o'er and o'er one falls:
He murder cries and help from Athens calls.
Their sense thus weak, lost with their fears thus
    strong,
Made senseless things begin to do them wrong;
For briers and thorns at their apparel snatch;
Some sleeves, some hats, from yielders all things
    catch.
I led them on in this distracted fear,
And left sweet Pyramus translated there:
When in that moment, so it came to pass,
Titania waked and straightway loved an ass.

OBE. This falls out better than I could devise.
But hast thou yet latch'd the Athenian's eyes
With the love-juice, as I did bid thee do?

PUCK. I took him sleeping,—that is finish'd too,—
And the Athenian woman by his side;
That, when he waked, of force she must be eyed.

Enter HERMIA *and* DEMETRIUS.

OBE. Stand close: this is the same Athenian.

PUCK. This the woman, but not this the man.

DEM. O, why rebuke you him that loves you so?
Lay breath so bitter on your bitter foe.

HER. Now I but chide; but I should use thee worse,
For thou, I fear, hast given me cause to curse.
If thou hast slain Lysander in his sleep,
Being o'er shoes in blood, plunge in the deep,
And kill me too.
The sun was not so true unto the day
As he to me: would he have stolen away
From sleeping Hermia? I'll believe as soon
This whole earth may be bored and that the moon
May through the centre creep and so displease
Her brother's noontide with the Antipodes.
It cannot be but thou hast murder'd him;
So should a murderer look, so dead, so grim.

DEM. So should the murder'd look, and so should I,
Pierced through the heart with your stern cruelty:
Yet you, the murderer, look as bright, as clear,
As yonder Venus in her glimmering sphere.

HER. What's this to my Lysander? where is he?
Ah, good Demetrius, wilt thou give him me?

DEM. I had rather give his carcass to my hounds.

HER. Out, dog! out, cur! thou drivest me past the
    bounds
Of maiden's patience. Hast thou slain him, then?
Henceforth be never number'd among men!
O, once tell true, tell true, even for my sake!
Durst thou have look'd upon him being awake,
And hast thou kill'd him sleeping? O brave touch!
Could not a worm, an adder, do so much?
An adder did it; for with doubler tongue
Than thine, thou serpent, never adder stung.

DEM. You spend your passion on a misprised mood:
I am not guilty of Lysander's blood;
Nor is he dead, for aught that I can tell.

HER. I pray thee, tell me then that he is well.

DEM. An if I could, what should I get therefore?

HER. A privilege never to see me more.
And from thy hated presence part I so:
See me no more, whether he be dead or no. [*exit.*

DEM. There is no following her in this fierce vein;
Here therefore for a while I will remain.
So sorrow's heaviness doth heavier grow
For debt that bankrupt sleep doth sorrow owe;
Which now in some slight measure it will pay,
If for his tender here I make some stay.
                    [*lies down and sleeps.*

OBE. What hast thou done? thou hast mistaken quite
And laid the love-juice on some true-love's sight:
Of thy misprision must perforce ensue
Some true love turn'd and not a false turn'd true.

PUCK. Then fate o'er-rules, that, one man holding troth.
A million fail, confounding oath on oath.

OBE. About the wood go swifter than the wind,
And Helena of Athens look thou find:
All fancy-sick she is and pale of cheer,
With signs of love, that costs the fresh blood dear:
By some illusion see thou bring her here:
I'll charm his eyes against she do appear.

PUCK. I go, I go; look how I go,
Swifter than arrow from the Tatar's bow.　　[exit.

OBE.　　Flower of this purple dye,
Hit with Cupid's archery,
Sink in apple of his eye.
When his love he doth espy.
Let her shine as gloriously
As the Venus of the sky.
When thou wakest, if she be by,
Beg of her for remedy.

Re-enter PUCK.

PUCK.　　Captain of our fairy band,
Helena is here at hand;
And the youth, mistook by me,
Pleading for a lover's fee.
Shall we their fond pageant see?
Lord, what fools these mortals be!

OBE.　　Stand aside: the noise they make
Will cause Demetrius to awake.

PUCK.　　Then will two at once woo one;
That must needs be sport alone;
And those things do best please me
That befal preposterously.

Enter LYSANDER *and* HELENA.

LYS. Why should you think that I should woo in scorn?
Scorn and derision never come in tears:
Look, when I vow, I weep; and vows so born,
　In their nativity all truth appears.
How can these things in me seem scorn to you,
Bearing the badge of faith, to prove them true?

HEL. You do advance your cunning more and more.
　When truth kills truth, O devilish-holy fray!
These vows are Hermia's: will you give her o'er?
　Weigh oath with oath, and you will nothing weigh:
Your vows to her and me, put in two scales,
Will even weigh, and both as light as tales.

LYS. I had no judgement when to her I swore.

HEL. Nor none, in my mind, now you give her o'er.

LYS. Demetrius loves her, and he loves not you.

DEM. [*awaking.*] O Helen, goddess, nymph, perfect, divine!
To what, my love, shall I compare thine eyne?
Crystal is muddy. O, how ripe in show
Thy lips, those kissing cherries, tempting grow!
That pure congealed white, high Taurus' snow,
Fann'd with the eastern wind, turns to a crow
When thou hold'st up thy hand: O, let me kiss
This princess of pure white, this seal of bliss!

HEL. O spite! O hell! I see you all are bent
To set against me for your merriment:
If you were civil and knew courtesy,
You would not do me thus much injury.
Can you not hate me, as I know you do,
But you must join in souls to mock me too?
If you were men, as men you are in show,
You would not use a gentle lady so;
To vow, and swear, and superpraise my parts,
When I am sure you hate me with your hearts.
You both are rivals, and love Hermia;
And now both rivals, to mock Helena:
A trim exploit, a manly enterprise,
To conjure tears up in a poor maid's eyes
With your derision! none of noble sort
Would so offend a virgin and extort
A poor soul's patience, all to make you sport.

LYS. You are unkind, Demetrius; be not so;
For you love Hermia; this you know I know:
And here, with all good will, with all my heart,
In Hermia's love I yield you up my part;
And yours of Helena to me bequeath,
Whom I do love and will do till my death.

HEL. Never did mockers waste more idle breath.

DEM. Lysander, keep thy Hermia; I will none:
If 'er I loved her, all that love is gone.
My heart to her but as guest-wise sojourn'd,
And now to Helen is it home return'd,
There to remain.

LYS.　　　　　Helen, it is not so.

DEM. Disparage not the faith thou dost not know,
Lest, to thy peril, thou aby it dear.
Look, where thy love comes; yonder is thy dear.

Re-enter HERMIA.

HER. Dark night, that from the eye his function takes,
The ear more quick of apprehension makes;
Wherein it doth impair the seeing sense,

It pays the hearing double recompense.
Thou art not by mine eye, Lysander, found;
Mine ear, I thank it, brought me to thy sound.
But why unkindly didst thou leave me so?

LYS. Why should he stay, whom love doth press to
go?

HER. What love could press Lysander from my side?

LYS. Lysander's love, that would not let him bide,
Fair Helena, who more engilds the night.
Than all yon fiery oes and eyes of light.
Why seek'st thou me? could not this make thee
know,
The hate I bear thee made me leave thee so?

HER. You speak not as you think: it cannot be.

HEL. Lo, she is one of this confederacy!
Now I perceive they have conjoin'd all three
To fashion this false sport, in spite of me.
Injurious Hermia! most ungrateful maid!
Have you conspired, have you with these contrived
To bait me with this foul derision?
Is all the counsel that we two have shared,
The sisters' vows, the hours that we have spent,
When we have chid the hasty-footed time
For parting us,—O, is it all forgot?
All school-days' friendship, childhood innocence?
We, Hermia, like two artificial gods,
Have with our needles created both one flower,
Both on one sampler, sitting on one cushion,
Both warbling of one song, both in one key,
As if our hands, our sides, voices and minds,
Had been incorporate. So we grew together,
Like to a double cherry, seeming parted,
But yet an union in partition;
Two lovely berries moulded on one stem;
So, with two seeming bodies, but one heart;
Two of the first, like coats in heraldry,
Due but to one and crowned with one crest.
And will you rent our ancient love asunder,
To join with men in scorning your poor friend?
It is not friendly, 'tis not maidenly:
Our sex, as well as I, may chide you for it,
Though I alone do feel the injury.

HER. I am amazed at your passionate words.
I scorn you not: it seems that you scorn me.

HEL. Have you not set Lysander, as in scorn,
To follow me and praise my eyes and face?
And made your other love, Demetrius,
Who even but now did spurn me with his foot,
To call me goddess, nymph, divine and rare,
Precious, celestial? Wherefore speaks he this
To her he hates? and wherefore doth Lysander

Deny your love, so rich within his soul,
And tender me, forsooth, affection,
But by your setting on, by your consent?
What though I be not so in grace as you,
So hung upon with love, so fortunate,
But miserable most, to love unloved?
This you should pity rather than despise.

HER. I understand not what you mean by this.

HEL. Ay, do, persever, counterfeit sad looks,
Make mouths upon me when I turn my back;
Wink each at other; hold the sweet jest up:
This sport, well carried, shall be chronicled.
If you have any pity, grace, or manners,
You would not make me such an argument.
But fare ye well: 'tis partly my own fault;
Which death or absence soon shall remedy.

LYS. Stay, gentle Helena; hear my excuse:
My love, my life, my soul, fair Helena!

HEL. O excellent!

HER.   Sweet, do not scorn her so.

DEM. If she cannot entreat, I can compel.

LYS. Thou canst compel no more than she entreat:
Thy threats have no more strength than her weak
prayers.
Helen, I love thee; by my life, I do:
I swear by that which I will lose for thee,
To prove him false that says I love thee not.

DEM. I say I love thee more than he can do.

LYS. If thou say so, withdraw, and prove it too,

DEM. Quick, come!

HER.   Lysander, whereto tends all this?

LYS. Away, you Ethiope!

DEM.   No, no; he'll . . .
Seem to break loose; take on as you would follow,
But yet come not: you are a tame man, go!

LYS. Hang off, thou cat, thou burr! vile thing, let
loose,
Or I will shake thee from me like a serpent!

HER. Why are you grown so rude? What change is
this?
Sweet love,—

LYS.   Thy love! out, tawny Tarter,
out!
Out, loathed medicine! hated potion, hence!

HER. Do you not jest?

HEL. Yes, sooth; and so do you.

LYS. Demetrius, I will keep my word with thee.

DEM. I would I had your bond, for I perceive
A weak bond holds you: I'll not trust your word.

LYS. What, should I hurt her, strike her, kill her dead?
Although I hate her, I'll not harm her so.

HER. What, can you do me greater harm than hate?
Hate me! wherefore? O me! what news, my love!
Am not I Hermia? are not you Lysander?
I am as fair now as I was erewhile.
Since night you loved me; yet since night you left me:
Why, then you left me—O, the gods forbid!—
In earnest, shall I say?

LYS. Ay, by my life;
And never did desire to see thee more.
Therefore be out of hope, of question, of doubt;
Be certain, nothing truer; 'tis no jest
That I do hate thee and love Helena.

HER. O me! you juggler! you canker-blossom!
You thief of love! what, have you come by night
And stolen my love's heart from him?

HEL. Fine, i' faith!
Have you no modesty, no maiden shame,
No touch of bashfulness? What, will you tear
Impatient answers from my gentle tongue?
Fie, fie! you counterfeit, you puppet, you!

HER. Puppet? why so? ay, that way goes the game.
Now I perceive that she hath made compare
Between our statures; she hath urged her height;
And with her personage, her tall personage,
Her height, forsooth, she hath prevail'd with him.
And are you grown so high in his esteem,
Because I am so dwarfish and so low?
How low am I, thou painted maypole? speak;
How low am I? I am not yet so low
But that my nails can reach unto thine eyes.

HEL. I pray you, though you mock me, gentlemen,
Let her not hurt me: I was never curst;
I have no gift at all in shrewishness;
I am a right maid for my cowardice:
Let her not strike me. You perhaps may think,
Because she is something lower than myself,
That I can match her.

HER. Lower! hark, again.

HEL. Good Hermia, do not be so bitter with me.
I evermore did love you, Hermia,
Did ever keep your counsels, never wrong'd you;
Save that, in love unto Demetrius,
I told him of your stealth unto this wood.
He follow'd you; for love I follow'd him;
But he hath chid me hence and threaten'd me
To strike me, spurn me, nay, to kill me too:
And now, so you will let me quiet go,
To Athens will I bear my folly back
And follow you no further: let me go:
You see how simple and how fond I am.

HER. Why, get you gone: who is't that hinders you?

HEL. A foolish heart, that I leave here behind.

HER. What, with Lysander?

HEL. With Demetrius.

LYS. Be not afraid; she shall not harm thee, Helena,

DEM. No, sir, she shall not, though you take her part.

HEL. O, when she's angry, she is keen and shrewd!
She was a vixen when she went to school;
And though she be but little, she is fierce.

HER. 'Little' again! nothing but 'low' and 'little'!
Why will you suffer her to flout me thus?
Let me come to her.

LYS. Get you gone, you dwarf;
You minimus, of hindering knot-grass made;
You bead, you acorn.

DEM. You are too officious
In her behalf that scorns your services.
Let her alone: speak not of Helena;
Take not her part; for, if thou dost intend
Never so little show of love to her,
Thou shalt aby it.

LYS. Now she holds me not;
Now follow, if thou darest, to try whose right,
Of thine or mine, is most in Helena.

DEM. Follow! nay, I'll go with thee, cheek by jole.

[Exeunt LYSANDER and DEMETRIUS.

HER. You, mistress, all this coil is 'long of you:
Nay, go not back.

HEL. I will not trust you, I,
Nor longer stay in your curst company.
Your hands than mine are quicker for a fray,
My legs are longer though, to run away. [exit.

HER. I am amazed, and know not what to say.
[exit.

OBE. This is thy negligence: still thou mistakest,
Or else committ'st thy knaveries wilfully.

PUCK. Believe me, king of shadows, I mistook.
Did not you tell me I should know the man
By the Athenian garments he had on?
And so far blameless proves my enterprise,
That I have 'nointed an Athenian's eyes;
And so far am I glad it so did sort
As this their jangling I esteem a sport.

OBE. Thou see'st these lovers seek a place to fight:
Hie therefore, Robin, overcast the night;
The starry welkin cover thou anon
With drooping fog as black as Acheron,
And lead these testy rivals so astray
As one come not within another's way.
Like to Lysander sometime frame thy tongue,
Then stir Demetrius up with bitter wrong;
And sometime rail thou like Demetrius;
And from each other look thou lead them thus,
Till o'er their brows death-counterfeiting sleep
With leaden legs and batty wings doth creep:
Then crush this herb into Lysander's eye;
Whose liquor hath this virtuous property,
To take from thence all error with his might,
And make his eyeballs roll with wonted sight.
When they next wake, all this derision
Shall seem a dream and fruitless vision,
And back to Athens shall the lovers wend,
With league whose date till death shall never end.
Whiles I in this affair do thee employ,
I'll to my queen and beg her Indian boy;
And then I will her charmed eye release
From monster's view, and all things shall be peace.

PUCK. My fairy lord, this must be done with haste,
For night's swift dragons cut the clouds full fast,
And yonder shines Aurora's harbinger;
At whose approach, ghosts, wandering here and
  there,
Troop home to churchyards: damned spirits all,
That in crossways and floods have burial,
Already to their wormy beds are gone;
For fear lest day should look their shames upon,
They wilfully themselves exile from light
And must for aye consort with black-brow'd night.

OBE. But we are spirits of another sort:
I with the morning's love have oft made sport,
And, like a forester, the groves may tread, till the
  eastern gate, all fiery-red,
Opening on Neptune with fair blessed beams,
Turns into yellow gold his salt green streams.
But, notwithstanding, haste; make no delay:
We may effect this business yet ere day.   [*exit.*

PUCK.   Up and down, up and down,
             I will lead them up and down:
             I am fear'd in field and town:
             Goblin, lead them up and down.
Here comes one.

Re-enter LYSANDER.

LYS. Where art thou, proud Demetrius? speak thou
now.

PUCK. Here, villain; drawn and ready. Where art
thou?

LYS. I will be with thee straight.

PUCK.   Follow me, then,
To plainer ground.   [*Exit* LYSANDER,
                                 as following the voice.

Re-enter DEMETRIUS.

DEM.   Lysander! speak again:
Thou runaway, thou coward, art thou fled?
Speak! In some bush? Where dost thou hide thy
head?

PUCK. Thou coward, art thou bragging to the stars,
Telling the bushes that thou look'st for wars,
And wilt not come? Come, recreant; come, thou
child;
I'll whip thee with a rod: he is defiled
That draws a sword on thee.

DEM.   Yea, art thou there?

PUCK. Follow my voice; we'll try no manhood here.
                                          [*exeunt.*

Re-enter LYSANDER.

LYS. He goes before me and still dares me on:
When I come where he calls, then he is gone.
The villain is much lighter-heel'd than I:
I follow'd fast, but faster he did fly;
That fallen am I in dark uneven way,
And here will rest me. [*lies down.*] Come, thou
gentle day!
For if but once thou show me thy grey light,
I'll find Demetrius and revenge this spite. [*sleeps.*

Re-enter PUCK *and* DEMETRIUS.

PUCK. Ho, ho, ho! Coward, why comest thou not?

DEM. Abide me, if thou darest; for well I wot
Thou runn'st before me, shifting every place,
And darest not stand, nor look me in the face,
Where art thou now?

PUCK.   Come hither: I am here.

DEM. Nay, then, thou mock'st me. Thou shalt buy this dear,
If ever I thy face by daylight see:
Now, go thy way. Faintness constraineth me
To measure out my length on this cold bed.
By day's approach look to be visited.

[*lies down and sleeps.*

Re-enter HELENA.

HEL. O weary night, O long and tedious night,
  Abate thy hours! Shine comforts from the east,
That I may back to Athens by daylight,
  From these that my poor company detest:
And sleep, that sometimes shuts up sorrow's eye,
Stead me awhile from mine own company.

[*lies down and sleeps.*

PUCK. Yet but three? Come one more;
Two of both kinds makes up four.
Here she comes, curst and sad:
Cupid is a knavish lad,
Thus to make poor females mad.

Re-enter HERMIA.

HER. Never so weary, never so in woe,
  Bedabbled with the dew and torn with briers,
I can no further crawl, no further go;
  My legs can keep no pace with my desires.
Here will I rest me till the break of day.
Heavens shield Lysander, if they mean a fray!

[*lies down and sleeps.*

PUCK.   On the ground
Sleep sound:
I'll apply
To your eye,
Gentle lover, remedy
            [*squeezing the juice
            on* LYSANDER'S *eyes.*
When thou wakest,
Thou takest
True delight
In the sight
Of thy former lady's eye:
And the country proverb known,
That every man should take his own,
In your waking shall be shown:
Jack shall have Jill;
Nought shall go ill;
The man shall have his mare again,
and all shall be well.
                              [*exit.*

ACT IV.
SCENE I.

The Same. Lysander, Demetrius, Helena, and Hermia Lying Asleep.

Enter TITANIA *and* BOTTOM; PEASEBLOSSOM. COBWEB, MOTH, MUSTARDSEED, *and other* FAIRIES *attending;* OBERON *behind unseen.*

TITA. Come, sit thee down upon this flowery bed,
  While I thy amiable cheeks do coy,
And stick musk-roses in thy sleek smooth head,
  And kiss thy fair large ears, my gentle joy.

BOT. Where's Peaseblossom?

PEAS. Ready.

BOT. Scratch my head, Peaseblossom. Where's Mounsieur Cobweb?

COB. Ready.

BOT. Mounsieur Cobweb, good mounsieur, get you your weapons in your hand, and kill me a red-hipped humble-bee on the top of a thistle; and, good mounsieur, bring me the honey-bag. Do not fret yourself too much in the action, mounsieur; and, good mounsieur, have a care the honey-bag break not; I would be loath to have you overflown with a honey-bag, signior. Where's Mounsieur Mustardseed?

MUS. Ready.

BOT. Give me your neaf, Mounsieur Mustardseed. Pray you, leave your courtesy, good mounsieur.

MUS. What's your will?

BOT. Nothing, good mounsieur, but to help Cavalery Cobweb to scratch. I must to the barber's, mounsieur; for methinks I am marvellous hairy about the face; and I am such a tender ass, if my hair do but tickle me, I must scratch.

TITA. What, wilt thou hear some music, my sweet love?

BOT. I have a reasonable good ear in music. Let's have the tongs and the bones.

TITA. Or say, sweet love, what thou desirest to eat.

BOT. Truly, a peck of provender: I could munch your good dry oats. Methinks I have a great desire to a bottle of hay: good hay, sweet hay, hath no fellow.

TITA. I have a venturous fairy that shall seek The squirrel's hoard, and fetch thee new nuts.

BOT. I had rather have a handful or two of dried peas. But, I pray you, let none of your people stir me: I have an exposition of sleep come upon me.

TITA. Sleep thou, and I will wind thee in my arms. Fairies, be gone, and be all ways away. [*Exeunt* FAIRIES.
So doth the woodbine the sweet honeysuckle
Gently entwist; the female ivy so
Enrings the barky fingers of the elm.
O, how I love thee! how I dote on thee!
[*they sleep.*

Enter PUCK.

OBE. [*advancing.*] Welcome, good Robin. See'st thou this sweet sight?
Her dotage now I do begin to pity:
For, meeting her of late behind the wood,
Seeking sweet favours for this hateful fool,
I did upbraid her and fall out with her;
For she his hairy temples then had rounded
With coronet of fresh and fragrant flowers;
And that same dew, which sometime on the buds
Was wont to swell like round and orient pearls,
Stood now within the pretty flowerets' eyes
Like tears that did their own disgrace bewail.
When I had at my pleasure taunted her
And she in mild terms begg'd my patience,
I then did ask of her her changeling child;
Which straight she gave me, and her fairy sent
To bear him to my bower in fairy land.
And now I have the boy, I will undo
This hateful imperfection of her eyes:
And, gentle Puck, take this transformed scalp
From off the head of this Athenian swain;
That, he awaking when the other do,
May all to Athens back again repair
And think no more of this night's accidents
But as the fierce vexation of a dream.
But first I will release the fairy queen.
Be as thou wast wont to be;
See as thou wast wont to see:
Dian's bud o'er Cupid's flower
Hath such force and blessed power.
Now, my Titania; wake you, my sweet queen.

TITA. My Oberon! what visions have I seen!
Methought I was enamour'd of an ass.

OBE. There lies your love.

TITA.   How came these things to pass?
O, how mine eyes do loathe his visage now!

OBE. Silence awhile. Robin, take off his head.
Titania, music call; and strike more dead
Than common sleep of all these five the sense.

TITA. Music, ho! music, such as charmeth sleep!
[*Music, still.*

PUCK. Now, when thou wakest, with thine own fool's eyes peep.

OBE. Sound, music! Come, my queen, take hands with me,
And rock the ground whereon these sleepers be.
Now thou and I are new in amity
And will to-morrow midnight solemnly
Dance in Duke Theseus' house triumphantly
And bless it to all fair prosperity:
There shall the pairs of faithful lovers be
Wedded, with Theseus, all in jollity.

PUCK.   Fairy king, attend, and mark:
             I do hear the morning lark.

OBE.   Then, my queen, in silence sad,
             Trip we after night's shade:
             We the globe can compass soon,
             Swifter than the wandering moon.

TITA.   Come, my lord, and in our flight
             Tell me how it came this night
             That I sleeping here was found
             With these mortals on the ground.
[*exeunt.*
Horns winded within.

Enter THESEUS, HIPPOLYTA, EGEUS, *and train.*

THE. Go, one of you, find out the forester;
For now our observation is perform'd;
And since we have the vaward of the day
My love shall hear the music of my hounds.
Uncouple in the western valley; let them go:
Dispatch, I say, and find the forester.
[*Exit an* ATTENDANT.
We will, fair queen, up to the mountain's top
And mark the musical confusion
Of hounds and echo in conjunction.

HIP. I was with Hercules and Cadmus once,
When in a wood of Crete they bay'd the bear
With hounds of Sparta: never did I hear
Such gallant chiding; for, besides the groves
The skies, the fountains, every region near
Seem'd all one mutual cry: I never heard
So musical a discord, such sweet thunder.

THE. My hounds are bred out of the Spartan kind,
So flew'd, so sanded, and their heads are hung
With ears that sweep away the morning dew;
Crook-knee'd, and dew-lapp'd like Thessalian bulls;
Slow in pursuit, but match'd in mouth like bells,
Each under each. A cry more tuneable
Was never holla'd to, nor cheer'd with horn,

In Crete, in Sparta, nor in Thessaly:
Judge when you hear. But, soft! what nymphs are
  these?

EGE. My lord, this is my daughter here asleep;
And this, Lysander; this Demetrius is;
This Helena, old Nedar's Helena:
I wonder of their being here together.

THE. No doubt they rose up early to observe
The rite of May, and, hearing our intent,
Came here in grace of our solemnity.
But speak, Egeus; is not this the day
That Hermia should give answer of her choice?

EGE. It is, my lord.

THE. Go, bid the huntsmen wake them with their
  horns.

[*Horns and shout within.* LYSANDER, DEMETRIUS,
  HELENA, *and* HERMIA, *wake and start up.*

Good morrow, friends. Saint Valentine is past:
Begin these wood-birds but to couple now?

LYS. Pardon, my lord.

THE.   I pray you all, stand up.
I know you two are rival enemies:
How comes this gentle concord in the world,
That hatred is so far from jealousy,
To sleep by hate, and fear no enmity?

LYS. My lord, I shall reply amazedly,
Half sleep, half waking: but as yet, I swear,
I cannot truly say how I came here;
But, as I think,—for truly would I speak,
And now I do bethink me, so it is,—
I came with Hermia hither: our intent
Was to be gone from Athens, where we might,
Without the peril of the Athenian law.

EGE. Enough, enough, my lord; you have enough:
I beg the law, the law, upon his head.
They would have stolen away; they would, Deme-
  trius,
Thereby to have defeated you and me
You of your wife and me of my consent,
Of my consent that she should be your wife.

DEM. My lord, fair Helen told me of their stealth,
Of this their purpose hither to this wood;
And I in fury hither follow'd them,
Fair Helena in fancy following me.
But, my good lord, I wot not by what power,—
But by some power it is,—my love to Hermia,
Melted as the snow, seems to me now
As the remembrance of an idle gawd
Which in my childhood I did dote upon;

And all the faith, the virtue of my heart,
The object and the pleasure of mine eye,
Is only Helena. To her, my lord,
Was I betroth'd ere I saw Hermia:
But, like in sickness, did I loathe this food;
But, as in health, come to my natural taste,
Now I do wish it, love it, long for it,
And will for evermore be true to it.

THE. Fair lovers, you are fortunately met:
Of this discourse we more will hear anon.
Egeus, I will overbear your will;
For in the temple, by and by, with us
These couples shall eternally be knit:
And, for the morning now is something worn,
Our purposed hunting shall be set aside.
Away with us to Athens; three and three,
We'll hold a feast in great solemnity.
Come, Hippolyta.   [*Exeunt* THE., HIP., EGE.,
                                        and train.

DEM. These things seem small and undistinguishable, Like far-off mountains turned into clouds.

HER. Methinks I see these things with parted eye,
When every thing seems double

HEL.   So methinks:
And I have found Demetrius like a jewel,
Mine own, and not mine own.

DEM.   Are you sure
That we are awake? It seems to me
That yet we sleep, we dream. Do not you think
The duke was here, and bid us follow him?

HER. Yea; and my father.

HEL.   And Hippolyta.

LYS. And he did bid us follow to the temple.

DEM. Why, then, we are awake: let's follow him;
And by the way let us recount our dreams.
                                  [*exeunt.*

BOT. [*awaking.*] When my cue comes, call me, and
  I will answer: my next is, 'Most fair Pyramus.'
  Heigh-ho! Peter Quince! Flute, the bellows-
  mender! Snout, the tinker! Starveling! God's my
  life, stolen hence, and left me asleep! I have had
  a most rare vision. I have had a dream, past the
  wit of man to say what dream it was: man is but
  an ass, if he go about to expound this dream.
  Methought I was—there is no man can tell what.
  Methought I was,—and methought I had,—but
  man is but a patched fool, if he will offer to say
  what methought I had. The eye of man hath not
  heard, the ear of man hath not seen, man's hand
  is not able to taste, his tongue to conceive, nor his

heart to report, what my dream was. I will get Peter Quince to write a ballad of this dream: it shall be called Bottom's Dream, because it hath no bottom; and I will sing it in the latter end of a play, before the duke: peradventure, to make it the more gracious, I shall sing it at her death. [*exit.*

SCENE II.

Athens. Quince's House.

Enter QUINCE, FLUTE, SNOUT, *and* STARVELING.

QUIN. Have you sent to Bottom's house? is he come home yet?

STAR. He cannot be heard of. Out of doubt he is transported.

FLU. If he come not, then the play is marred: it goes not forward, doth it?

QUIN. It is not possible: you have not a man in all Athens able to discharge Pyramus but he.

FLU. No, he hath simply the best wit of any handicraft man in Athens.

QUIN. Yea, and the best person too; and he is a very paramour for a sweet voice.

FLU. You must say 'paragon': a paramour is, God bless us, a thing of naught.

Enter SNUG.

SNUG. Masters, the duke is coming from the temple, and there is two or three lords and ladies more married: if our sport had gone forward, we had all been made men.

FLU. O sweet bully Bottom! Thus hath he lost sixpence a day during his life; he could not have 'scaped sixpence a day: an the duke had not given him sixpence a day for playing Pyramus, I'll be hanged; he would have deserved it: sixpence a day in Pyramus, or nothing.

Enter BOTTOM.

BOT. Where are these lads? where are these hearts?

QUIN. Bottom! O most courageous day! O most happy hour!

BOT. Masters, I am to discourse wonders: but ask me not what; for if I tell you, I am no true Athenian. I will tell you every thing, right as it fell out.

QUIN. Let us hear, sweet Bottom.

BOT. Not a word of me. All that I will tell you is, that the duke hath dined. Get your apparel together, good strings to your beards, new ribbons to your pumps; meet presently at the palace; every man look o'er his part; for the short and the long is, our play is preferred. In any case, let Thisby have clean linen; and let not him that plays the lion pare his nails, for they shall hang out for the lion's claws. And, most dear actors, eat no onions nor garlic, for we are to utter sweet breath; and I do not doubt but to hear them say, it is a sweet comedy. No more words: away! go, away!

[*exeunt.*

ACT V.

SCENE I.

Athens, The Palace of Theseus.

Enter THESEUS, HIPPOLYTA, PHILOSTRATE, LORDS, *and* ATTENDANTS.

HIP. 'Tis strange, my Theseus, that these lovers speak of.

THE. More strange than true: I never may believe
These antique fables, nor these fairy toys.
Lovers and madmen have such seething brains,
Such shaping fantasies, that apprehend
More than cool reason ever comprehends.
The lunatic, the lover and the poet
Are of imagination all compact:
One sees more devils than vast hell can hold,
That is, the madman: the lover, all as frantic,
Sees Helen's beauty in a brow of Egypt:
The poet's eye, in a fine frenzy rolling,
Doth glance from heaven to earth, from earth to heaven;
And as imagination bodies forth
The forms of things unknown, the poet's pen
Turns them to shapes and gives to airy nothing
A local habitation and a name.
Such tricks hath strong imagination,
That, if it would but apprehend some joy,
It comprehends some bringer of that joy;
Or in the night, imagining some fear,
How easy is a bush supposed a bear!

HIP. But all the story of the night told over,
And all their minds transfigured so together,
More witnesseth than fancy's images
And grows to something of great constancy;
But, howsoever, strange and admirable.

THE. Here come the lovers, full of joy and mirth.

Enter LYSANDER, DEMETRIUS, HERMIA, *and*
HELENA.

Joy, gentle friends! joy and fresh days of love
Accompany your hearts!

LYS.   More than to us
Wait in your royal walks, your board, your bed!

THE. Come now; what masques, what dances shall
  we have,
To wear away this long age of three hours
Between our after-supper and bed-time?
Where is our usual manager of mirth?
What revels are in hand? Is there no play,
To ease the anguish of a torturing hour?
Call Philostrate.

PHIL.   Here, mighty Theseus.

THE. Say, what abridgement have you for this eve-
  ning?
What masque? what music? How shall we beguile
The lazy time, if not with some delight?

PHIL. There is a brief how many sports are ripe:
Make choice of which your highness will see first.
                          [*giving a paper.*

THE. [*reads.*] 'The battle with the Centaurs, to be
  sung
By an Athenian eunuch to the harp.'
We'll none of that: that have I told my love,
In glory of my kinsman Hercules.
[*reads.*] 'The riot of the tipsy Bacchanals,
Tearing the Thracian singer in their rage,'
That is an old device; and it was play'd
When I from Thebes came last a conqueror.
[*reads.*] 'The thrice three Muses mourning for the
  death
Of Learning, late deceased in beggary.'
That in some satire, keen and critical,
Not sorting with a nuptial ceremony.
[*reads.*] 'A tedious brief scene of young Pyramus
And his love Thisbe; very tragical mirth.'
Merry and tragical! tedious and brief!
That is, hot ice and wondrous strange snow.
How shall we find the concord of this discord?

PHIL. A play there is, my lord, some ten words long,
Which is as brief as I have known a play;
But by ten words, my lord, it is too long,
Which makes it tedious; for in all the play
There is not one word apt, one player fitted:
And tragical, my noble lord, it is;
For Pyramus therein doth kill himself.
Which, when I saw rehearsed, I must confess,
Made mine eyes water; but more merry tears
The passion of loud laughter never shed.

THE. What are they that do play it?

PHIL. Hard-handed men that work in Athens here,
Which never labour'd in their minds till now,
And now have toil'd their unbreathed memories
With this same play, against your nuptial.

THE. And we will hear it.

PHIL.   No, my noble lord;
It is not for you: I have heard it over,
And it is nothing, nothing in the world;
Unless you can find sport in their intents,
Extremely stretch'd and conn'd with cruel pain,
To do you service.

THE.   I will hear that play;
For never anything can be amiss,
When simpleness and duty tender it.
Go, bring them in: and take your places, ladies.
                          [*Exit* PHILOSTRATE

HIP. I love not to see wretchedness o'ercharged
And duty in his service perishing.

THE. Why, gentle sweet, you shall see no such thing.

HIP. He says they can do nothing in this kind.

THE. The kinder we, to give them thanks for nothing.
Our sport shall be to take what they mistake:
And what poor duty cannot do, noble respect
Takes it in might, not merit.
Where I have come, great clerks have purposed
To greet me with premeditated welcomes;
Where I have seen them shiver and look pale,
Make periods in the midst of sentences,
Throttle their practised accent in their fears
And in conclusion dumbly have broke off,
Not paying me a welcome. Trust me, sweet,
Out of this silence yet I pick'd a welcome;
And in the modesty of fearful duty
I read as much as from the rattling tongue
Of saucy and audacious eloquence.
Love, therefore, and tongue-tied simplicity
In least speak most, to my capacity.

Re-enter PHILOSTRATE.

PHIL. So please your grace, the Prologue is address'd.

THE. Let him approach.   [*Flourish of trumpets.*

Enter QUINCE *for the* PROLOGUE.

PRO. If we offend, it is with our good will.
    That you should think, we come not to offend,
But with good will. To show our simple skill,
    That is the true beginning of our end.
Consider then we come but in despite.
    We do not come as minding to content you,

Our true intent is. All for your delight
    We are not here. That you should here repent you,
The actors are at hand and by their show
You shall know all that you are like to know.

THE. This fellow doth not stand upon points.

LYS. He hath rid his prologue like a rough colt; he
    knows not the stop. A good moral, my lord: it is
    not enough to speak, but to speak true.

HIP. Indeed he hath played on his prologue like a
    child on a recorder; a sound, but not in govern-
    ment.

THE. His speech was like a tangled chain; nothing
    impaired, but all disordered. Who is next?

Enter PYRAMUS *and* THISBE, WALL, MOONSHINE,
and LION.

PRO. Gentles, perchance you wonder at this show;
    But wonder on, till truth make all things plain.
This man is Pyramus, if you would know;
    This beauteous lady Thisby is certain.
This man, with lime and rough-cast, doth present
    Wall, that vile Wall which did these lovers sunder;
And through Wall's chink, poor souls, they are con-
    tent
    To whisper. At the which let no man wonder.
This man, with lanthorn, dog, and bush of thorn,
    Presenteth Moonshine; for, if you will know,
By moonshine did these lovers think no scorn
    To meet at Ninus' tomb, there, there to woo.
This grisly beast, which Lion hight by name,
    The trusty Thisby, coming first by night,
Did scare away, or rather did affright;
And, as she fled, her mantle she did fall,
    Which Lion vile with bloody mouth did stain.
Anon comes Pyramus, sweet youth and tall,
    And finds his trusty Thisby's mantle slain:
Whereat, with blade, with bloody blameful blade,
    He bravely broach'd his boiling bloody breast;
And Thisby, tarrying in mulberry shade,
    His dagger drew, and died. For all the rest,
Let Lion, Moonshine, Wall, and lovers twain
At large discourse, while here they do remain.

[*Exeunt* PROLOGUE, PYRAMUS, THISBE,
    LION, *and* MOONSHINE.

THE. I wonder if the lion be to speak.

DEM. No wonder, my lord: one lion may, when many
    asses do.

WALL. In this same interlude it doth befall
That I, one Snout by name, present a wall;
And such a wall, as I would have you think,
That had in it a crannied hole or chink,

Through which the lovers, Pyramus and Thisby,
Did whisper often very secretly.
This loam, this rough-cast and this stone doth show
That I am that same wall; the truth is so:
And this the cranny is, right and sinister,
Through which the fearful lovers are to whisper.

THE. Would you desire lime and hair to speak
    better?

DEM. It is the wittiest partition that ever I heard
    discourse, my lord.

Re-enter PYRAMUS.

THE. Pyramus draws near the wall: silence!

PYR. O grim-look'd night! O night with hue so black!
    O night, which ever art when day is not!
O night, O night! alack, alack, alack,
    I fear my Thisby's promise is forgot!
And thou, O wall, O sweet, O lovely wall,
    That stand'st between her father's ground and
    mine!

Thou wall, O wall, O sweet and lovely wall,
    Show me thy chink, to blink through with mine
    eyne!
                    [WALL *holds up his fingers.*
Thanks, courteous wall: Jove shield thee well for this!
    But what see I? No Thisby do I see.
O wicked wall, through whom I see no bliss!
    Cursed be thy stones for thus deceiving me!

THE. The wall, methinks, being sensible, should
    curse again.

PYR. No, in truth, sir, he should not. 'Deceiving me'
    is Thisby's cue: she is to enter now, and I am to
    spy her through the wall. You shall see, it will fall
    pat as I told you. Yonder she comes.

Re-enter THISBE.

THIS. O wall, full often hast thou heard my moans,
    For parting my fair Pyramus and me!
My cherry lips have often kiss'd thy stones,
    Thy stones with lime and hair knit up in thee.

PYR. I see a voice: now will I to the chink,
To spy an I can hear my Thisby's face.
Thisby!

THIS. My love thou art, my love I think.

PYR. Think what thou wilt, I am thy lover's grace;
And, like Limander, am I trusty still.

THIS. And I like Helen, till the Fates me kill.

PYR. Not Shafalus to Procrus was so true.

THIS. As Shafalus to Procrus, I to you.

PYR. O, kiss me through the hole of this vile wall!

THIS. I kiss the wall's hole, not your lips at all.

PYR. Wilt thou at Ninny's tomb meet me straightway?

THIS. 'Tide life, 'tide death, I come without delay.

[*Exeunt* PYRAMUS *and* THISBE.

WALL. Thus have I, Wall, my part discharged so;
And, being done, thus Wall away doth go. [*exit.*

THE. Now is the mural down between the two neighbours.

DEM. No remedy, my lord, when walls are so wilful to hear without warning.

HIP. This is the silliest stuff that ever I heard.

THE. The best in this kind are but shadows; and the worst are no worse, if imagination amend them.

HIP. It must be your imagination then, and not theirs.

THE. If we imagine no worse of them than they of themselves, they may pass for excellent men. Here come two noble beasts in, a man and a lion.

Re-enter LION *and* MOONSHINE.

LION. You, ladies, you, whose gentle hearts do fear
    The smallest monstrous mouse that creeps on floor,
May now perchance both quake and tremble here,
    When lion rough in wildest rage doth roar.
Then know what I, one Snug the joiner, am
A lion-fell, nor else no lion's dam;
For, if I should as lion come in strife
Into this place, 'twere pity on my life.

THE. A very gentle beast, and of a good conscience.

DEM. The very best at a beast, my lord, that e'er I saw.

LYS. This lion is a very fox for his valour.

THE. True; and a goose for his discretion.

DEM. Not so, my lord; for his valour cannot carry his discretion; and the fox carries the goose.

THE. His discretion, I am sure, cannot carry his valour; for the goose carries not the fox. It is well: leave it to his discretion, and let us listen to the moon.

MOON. This lanthorn doth the horned moon present;—

DEM. He should have worn the horns on his head.

THE. He is no crescent, and his horns are invisible within the circumference.

MOON. This lanthorn doth the horned moon present;
Myself the man i' the moon do seem to be.

THE. This is the greatest error of all the rest: the man should be put into the lanthorn. How is it else the man i' the moon?

DEM. He dares not come there for the candle; for, you see, it is already in snuff.

HIP. I am aweary of this moon: would he would change!

THE. It appears, by his small light of discretion, that he is in the wane; but yet, in courtesy, in all reason, we must stay the time.

LYS. Proceed, Moon.

MOON. All that I have to say, is, to tell you that the lanthorn is the moon; I, the man in the moon; this thorn-bush, my thorn-bush; and this dog, my dog.

DEM. Why, all these should be in the lanthorn; for all these are in the moon. But, silence! here comes Thisbe.

Re-enter THISBE.

THIS. This is old Ninny's tomb. Where is my love?

LION. [*roaring.*] Oh— [THISBE *runs off.*

DEM. Well roared, Lion.

THE. Well run, Thisbe.

HIP. Well shone, Moon. Truly, the moon shines with a good grace. [*The* LION *shakes* THISBE'S *mantle, and exit.*

THE. Well moused, Lion.

LYS. And so the lion vanished.

DEM. And then came Pyramus.

Re-enter PYRAMUS.

PYR. Sweet Moon, I thank thee for thy sunny beams;
    I thank thee, Moon, for shining now so bright;
For, by the gracious, golden, glittering gleams,
    I trust to take of truest Thisby sight.
            But stay, O spite!
            But mark, poor knight,
        What dreadful dole is here!
            Eyes, do you see?
            How can it be?
        O dainty duck! O dear!
            Thy mantle good,
            What, stain'd with blood!

Approach, ye Furies fell!
  O Fates, come, come,
  Cut thread and thrum;
Quail, crush, conclude, and quell!

THE. This passion, and the death of a dear friend,
would go near to make a man look sad.

HIP. Beshrew my heart, but I pity the man.

PYR. O wherefore, Nature, didst thou lions frame?
  Since lion vile hath here deflower'd my dear:
Which is—no, no—which was the fairest dame
  That lived, that loved, that liked, that look'd with
  cheer.
      Come, tears, confound;
      Out, sword, and wound
    The pap of Pyramus;
      Ay, that left pap,
      Where heart doth hop: [*stabs himself.*
    Thus die I, thus, thus, thus.
      Now am I dead,
      Now am I fled;
    My soul is in the sky:
      Tongue, lose thy light;
      Moon, take thy flight:
            [*Exit* MOONSHINE.
    Now die, die, die, die, die.   [*dies.*

DEM. No die, but an ace, for him; for he is but one.

LYS. Less than an ace, man; for he is dead; he is
nothing.

THE. With the help of a surgeon he might yet recover, and prove an ass.

HIP. How chance Moonshine is gone before Thisbe
comes back and finds her lover?

THE. She will find him by starlight. Here she comes;
and her passion ends the play.

      Re-enter THISBE.

HIP. Methinks she should not use a long one for such
a Pyramus: I hope she will be brief.

DEM. A mote will turn the balance, which Pyramus, which Thisbe, is the better; he for a man,
God warrant us; she for a woman, God bless us.

LYS. She hath spied him already with those sweet
eyes.

DEM. And thus she means, videlicet:—

THIS.   Asleep, my love?
      What, dead, my dove?
    O Pyramus, arise!
      Speak, Speak. Quite dumb?
      Dead, Dead? A tomb
    Must cover thy sweet eyes.

    These lily lips,
    This cherry nose,
  These yellow cowslip cheeks,
    Are gone, are gone:
    Lovers, make moan:
  His eyes were green as leeks.
    O Sisters Three,
    Come, come to me,
  With hands as pale as milk;
    Lay them in gore,
    Since you have shore
  With shears his thread of silk.
    Tongue, not a word:
    Come, trusty sword;
  Come, blade, my breast imbrue:
            [*stabs herself.*
  And, farewell, friends;
    Thus Thisby ends:
  Adieu, adieu, adieu.   [*dies.*

THE. Moonshine and Lion are left to bury the dead.

DEM. Ay, and Wall too.

BOT. [*starting up.*] No, I assure you; the wall is down
that parted their fathers. Will it please you to see
the epilogue, or to hear a Bergomask dance between two of our company?

THE. No epilogue, I pray you; for your play needs
no excuse. Never excuse; for when the players are
all dead, there need none to be blamed. Marry, if
he that writ it had played Pyramus and hanged
himself in Thisbe's garter, it would have been a
fine tragedy: and so it is, truly; and very notably
discharged. But, come, your Bergomask: let your
epilogue alone.   [*A dance.*
The iron tongue of midnight hath told twelve:
Lovers, to bed; 'tis almost fairy time.
I fear we shall out-sleep the coming morn
As much as we this night have overwatch'd.
This palpable-gross play hath well beguiled
The heavy gait of night. Sweet friends, to bed.
A fortnight hold we this solemnity,
In nightly revels and new jollity   [*exeunt.*

      Enter PUCK.

PUCK.   Now the hungry lion roars,
      And the wolf behowls the moon;
    Whilst the heavy ploughman snores,
      All with weary task fordone.
    Now the wasted brands do glow,
      Whilst the screech-owl, screeching
    loud,
    Puts the wretch that lies in woe
      In remembrance of a shroud.

Now it is the time of night
    That the graves all gaping wide,
Every one lets forth his sprite,
    In the church-way paths to glide:
And we fairies, that do run
    By the triple Hecate's team,
From the presence of the sun,
    Following darkness like a dream,
Now are frolic: not a mouse
Shall disturb this hallow'd house:
I am sent with broom before,
To sweep the dust behind the door.

Enter OBERON *and* TITANIA *with their train.*

OBE.   Through the house give glimmering light,
    By the dead and drowsy fire:
Every elf and fairy sprite
    Hop as light as bird from brier;
And this ditty, after me,
Sing, and dance it trippingly.

TITA.   First, rehearse your song by rote,
    To each word a warbling note:
Hand in hand, with fairy grace,
Will we sing, and bless this place. [*Song
and dance.*

OBE.   Now, until the break of day,
Through this house each fairy stray.
To the best bride-bed will we,
Which by us shall blessed be;
And the issue there create
Ever shall be fortunate.
So shall all the couples three

Ever true in loving be;
And the blots of Nature's hand
Shall not in their issue stand;
Never mole, hare lip, nor scar,
Nor mark prodigious, such as are
Despised in nativity,
Shall upon their children be.
With this field-dew consecrate,
Every fairy take his gait;
And each several chamber bless,
Through this palace, with sweet peace;
And the owner of it blest
Ever shall in safety rest.
Trip away; make no stay;
Meet me all by break of day.
    [*Exeunt* OBERON, TITANIA, *and train.*

PUCK.   If we shadows have offended,
Think but this, and all is mended,
That you have but slumber'd here
While these visions did appear.
And this weak and idle theme,
No more yielding but a dream,
Gentles, do not reprehend:
If you pardon, we will mend:
And, as I am an honest Puck,
If we have unearned luck
Now to 'scape the serpent's tongue,
We will make amends ere long;
Else the Puck a liar call:
So, good night unto you all.
Give me your hands, if we be friends,
And Robin shall restore amends.   [*exit.*

A production of *The Miser*, Theatre Arts Department, Penn State University. Richard Edelman, director.

CHAPTER V

The Renaissance in Italy and France

The Theatre of the Renaissance

The same spirit of inquiry which fueled the great Elizabethan drama manifested itself on the continent of Europe as well, particularly in Italy and in France. In Italy, however, this sense of renewal did not evidence itself in drama as it had in England but in a love of beauty and inventiveness and in a return to the knowledge of the classical world. The center of this Renaissance culture was Florence, and the men who led the discovery, while amateurs where theatre was concerned, were aristocrats who formed small academies so that they might study a subject as exhaustively as they wished. So it was that in 1594 opera was created by such a group of scholars, the Camarata of Florence, who were attempting to recreate authentic Greek tragedy. With incomplete knowledge about the ancient Greek form, its use of music, dance, and the chorus, members of the Camarata, in writing *Dafne* (1594) failed to recreate tragedy but succeeded in creating a new genre that would be visually spectacular and would ultimately live far beyond its Renaissance beginnings to a full development during the Baroque period and popular success during the nineteenth century.

Just as opera was created by an incomplete understanding of the classical world, so the first major Renaissance threatre in Italy was created by a similar misinterpretation of data. In 1511 a ten volume masterpiece titled *De Architectura* by Roman architect Vitruvius had been published and had become a major source of information on the ancient Roman stage and auditorium. In 1585 the Teatro Olimpico was built in Vicenza. Begun by Andrea Palladio and completed by Vincenzo Scomozzi, the theatre—the oldest surviving Renaissance theatre—was an attempt to recreate a Greco-Roman structure. Again mistakes of interpretation resulted in the creation of something new rather than a recreation of something old. First of all, the Olimpico, unlike its Roman models, is an indoor theatre with painted clouds giving the illusion of open sky. With its small semi-circular orchestra and richly decorated skene pierced with three entrances and abutting paraskene with one entrance each, the Teatro Olimpico resembles a miniature Roman theatre brought indoors. But there are two unique features of this playhouse that are vitally important in the development of the Renaissance stage: first, the central entrance of the skene, conceived by Palladio as a kind of Roman triumphal arch, is far larger than it had been in Roman times, thus creating a kind of rudimentary proscenium arch; second, Scamozzi, who completed the structure, placed street scenes built in perspective, behind each of the entrances in the skene. Within the large central opening were three dead-end or blind vistas suggesting a merger of three city streets. Thus it was that an attempt to create a Roman theatre meshes with the Italian interest in perspective and serves to anticipate the proscenium arch theatre.

Scamozzi continued his experimentation in theatre architecture in the town of Sabbioneta where he was commissioned to build a small theatre seating only two hundred fifty as opposed to the three thousand of the Olimpico. Multiple doorways could not be accommodated in the miniature plan, and Scamozzi created, instead, a single vista that began at the very sides of the stage. Twenty miles away and just a few years later an architect named Giambattista Aleotti completed the first real proscenium theatre of the Renaissance with the Farnese Theatre at Parma (1618). A horseshoe of raised seats, with an open space in front for spectacle, accommodated three thousand five hundred audience members. Its stage was almost modern with a wide proscenium and deep stage. The Farnese has been reconstructed after its World War II bombing, so that these three theatres exist today as a living testimony to the research skill and inventiveness of Italian Renaissance acadamicians and aristocracy. Once the proscenium arch theatre—a prototype that was developed and continually refined until well into the twentieth century—was established, the extraordinary contribution of the Italian perspective scene painter became almost a creative necessity. Once a picture frame (the proscenium arch) has been created, something visually pleasing and effective must be placed behind that frame.

The art of perspective painting for the theatre had first been explored in a book by Sabastiano Serlio titled *Architteture* (1545.) Based on Vitruvius's descriptions, Serlio presented illustrations for tragic scenes (a palace), comic scenes (a street), and pastoral scenes (a woodland). More importantly, Serlio described how he built and painted scenery. In an effort to aid his forced perspective scenes, Serlio used a raked or slanted stage floor, lower toward the audience and slightly higher at the back of the stage, a feature which assisted in making the actor visible and has given us our modern stage terms, downstage and upstage. By the turn of the eighteenth century the techniques of perspective drawing initiated by Serlio reached their most technical and elaborate perfection in the works of members of the Bibiena family. Perspective techniques applied to large canvas backdrops and series of flat wings at either side of the stage, which masked the off stage space, became the perfect scenic backgrounds for the elaborate operas and spectacles presented before princes and kings.

Just as perspective scenery dominated the Italian Renaissance stage, so elaborate devices for quickly changing scenes and creating dramatic transformations became popular. Nicola Sabbattini's *Manual for Constructing Theatrical Scenes and Machines* (1638) provided a major source of material about machines and techniques for creating stage effects—descending clouds, rolling waves, flying gods, characters dancing in fire, collapse of buildings, sailing ships—all were perfected to unprecedented levels. It is perhaps interesting that, with the tremendous emphasis on scenic display and instantaneous scene shifts, the drama of the Italian Renaissance, as opposed to the English, was relatively undistinguished.

This complex series of innovations—amateur scholars inventing opera by trying to imitate Greek tragedy, the establishment of the convention of the modern picture frame (proscenium arch) stage, and architects and artists creating scenes and machines that are unsurpassed today for intricacy and ornateness—were equally balanced by the innovations of the professional and popular theatre of the Italian Renaissance: the *commedia dell'arte,* which flourished from approximately 1550 to 1750. Literally translated, the title means comedy of art; that is, the participants were professionals who made their living by performing and perfectionists who honed their craft to a high art. There has probably never been in the history of the theatre a form that so delights, amazes, and thrills audiences. The *commedia dell'arte* points back in time to Roman farces (fabula

Atellana) and forward to the works of Molière, Mozart, Marcel Marceau, Charlie Chaplin, the Marx Brothers, Second City, and Paul Sills's improvisational company. In the late 1960s when theatre students were seeking freedom, abandon, spontaneity and freshness, they turned for inspiration, as so many had done before them, to the wonders of the *commedia*. The home of the *commedia* was Italy but popular tours took them to France, Spain, northern Europe, and even England.

There were several features of the *commedia dell'arte* work that were as unique and innovative as anything that was being done in the elitist and erudite court theatre of Italy. First, they were professionals whose entire life was committed to perfecting their craft. Usually troupes were comprised of ten to twelve members, often belonging to one family. The troupes chose colorful names: I Accesi (The Inspired), I Confidenti (The Confident), I Gelosi (The Jealous), the latter being the most famous of all *commedia* troupes. Second, women—usually about three per company—were welcomed into the groups; hence, we have the first evidence of women acting professionally. Probably the most beloved of all *commedia* actors was a woman named Isabella Andreini (1562–1604), a poetess, a beauty, and a skilled actress who gave her name to the character of the young female lover. Third and most important, there were no scripts for the *commedia* plays. Scenarios, or outlines, were tacked up backstage, and the characters improvised or created on their feet during performance. There is ample evidence that the *commedia* actors memorized bits of business, gags, lines of dialogue, passages of contemporary literature, but the thrust was improvisation, spontaneity, and creativity in actual performance. Perhaps no form of dramatic endeavor demands more skill, mental agility, wit, daring, and tenacity than improvisation. The most beloved aspect of the *commedia* was the development of lazzi, or extended bits of humor and carefully developed sight gags. Balancing a glass of wine on the nose, battling with an insignificant house fly, wrestling with a plate of pasta—all could be developed, refined, and distilled into comic masterpieces. Two scenes from the Marx Brothers' *Night at the Opera* offer contemporary examples of lazzi. The contract scene developing the word play of "the party of the first part" and "the party of the second part" illustrates a verbal lazzo while the scene in which all of the characters crowd into a stateroom like the clowns in a circus car represents a physical lazzo. Perhaps more than any other comic, we can look to the art of Charlie Chaplin for the finest modern use of lazzi: the shaving scene and famous globe ballet of *The Great Dictator* or the shoe eating scene of *The Gold Rush* are prime illustrations. Lazzi reveal the comic art of seeing just how long, how far, and how imaginatively a gag can be extended.

The *commedia* plays were broad, farcical comedies based on stock situations; most often young lovers were thwarted by parental opposition and greed. The verbal humor was often bawdy and vulgar; the physical humor lusty and cruel. While focusing on ridiculing pretension and human foibles, the action of the *commedia* was fast paced and complex: characters eavesdropped, bribed, beat their servants, outwitted their masters, read one another's mail, disguised themselves, feigned death, and escaped danger by a hair. Stories began badly, became hopelessly complicated, resolved themselves, and ended happily.

Besides the use of stock situations, the *commedia dell'arte* utilized stock characters as well. Basically, there were three classifications of these characters: the lovers, the professionals, and the zanni, or clowns. The lovers, or innamorati, provided the norm against which the peculiarities of the other characters were seen. They were of good family, well dressed, well-brought-up, well-educated, witty and bright. If they had a failing, however, it was an excess of emotion, a single mindedness in their pursuit of love.

In the professional classification, there were three primary characters: Pantalone, Dottore, and Capitano. Pantalone, characterized by a pointed gray beard, a soft brimless hat, wisps of hair and a large nose, was an elderly merchant, guardian or father of one of the young lovers. He was depicted as miserly, paranoid, and often foolish where attractive young women are concerned. His traditional costume consisted of red vest, red breeches and stockings, soft slippers with pointed toes, and a black ankle length coat. Dottore, sometimes a medical doctor but more often a doctor of law, was characterized by his academic cap and gown. A friend of Pantalone, he was sometimes father of the other young lover. Cliches, old saws, proverbs, and pedantry represented this buffoon who showed off his learning but was easily duped. Third of the professionals was the beloved Capitano with his exaggerated uniform, sword, cape, and plumed hat. A type who clearly had his prototype in Roman drama, Capitano swaggered, bragged, and boasted but at the moment of crisis proved himself a fool and a coward.

The final category of characters was called the zanni or clowns. Usually there was a female clown: bright, perky, energetic, outspoken, bawdy, and good hearted. Her lover was often the most popular of all the clowns, Arlecchino, with his tradition black mask of a slave and suit of diamond tatters. Moody and volatile, Arlecchino was also witty, rogish, inventive, and clever. He had a cat-like agility to land on his feet and wriggle out of tight situations, and he possessed a natural un-schooled intelligence and common sense. Dramatically used to keep the plot moving, Arlecchino was also the most imaginative character of the drama, often carrying a slapstick which could become in an instant a weapon, a magic wand, a baby, a guitar or a phallus. Other clowns—Pulcinella with his hunched back, hooked nose and cruel humor is the ancestor to Mr. Punch of the violent Punch and Judy shows and Brighella, the intriguer—evolved over the several hundred years of the *commedia's* popularity. Although the characters were essentially fixed and predictable, each actor who played a role infused it with his or her own creativity, personality, and talent.

Because the *commedia dell'arte* troupes travelled from town to town, performing in market places and palaces, the staging was extremely simple. A platform placed on tressels created an acting space. Perhaps a simple curtain was hung at the back of the crude platform stage to mask entrances, to hide props and unused scenery. A grating held up could symbolize a prison, signs marked inns and roadways, upper windows were reached by stools, cloth walls were moved for eavesdropping. Disguises were only suggested by cloaks or turned down hat brims. The emphasis was on speed, mobility and imagination rather than on scenic illusion. Most of the players doubled as musicians playing drums, recorders, tamborines, and lutes. One of the interesting features of the *commedia* was that all of the characters, with the exception of the very conventional young lovers, wore masks. Each stock character had his stock mask. Most often these were half masks, made of leather lined with linen, that covered primarily the eyes and nose. The lower part of the face was exposed for freedom of expression and facility with dialogue.

In the eighteenth century, playwrights attempted to transcribe the *commedia* presentations into written plays. Once improvisation was gone from the art form, it was no longer vital and alive. Actors and theatre practitioners constantly look to the *commedia* for inspiration, finding in it the highest degree of skill an actor can achieve. Virtuosity, physical precision, economy, spontaneity, timing, imagination, freedom, vigor, belief, flexibility—these are just a few of the demands of improvisational acting. Add to these juggling, acrobatics, magic, singing, playing instruments, and developing the technique of using a mask, and we can easily comprehend why acting teachers have claimed that it is easier to train ten regular actors than one improvisational one. While not a drama of great depth or emotional intensity, the *commedia dell'arte* was an actor's theatre and still remains an actor's inspiration.

If the popular Italian drama represented all that was free and energetic in the theatre, the French drama of the Renaissance represented all that was ordered and controlled. The beginning of what became the golden age of French drama actually transpired in 1402 with the establishment of an amateur group of clerics, the Confrèrie de la Passion, who produced mystery plays for one hundred fifty years at the Hôtel de Bourgogne, actually the first public playhouse built since the fall of Rome. But the French did not open their second professional playhouse until 1634, did not respond to the Italian innovations in scenery and machines until 1641, and did not produce notable playwrights until the middle of the seventeenth century. The French had three excuses for their tardy development of the theatre: war, monopoly, and government restrictions.

From 1346 to 1450 France had been embroiled in battles with the English. For the next one hundred years, France fought—and none too successfully—with the pope, with Spain, with the Emperor Maximilian, and with Henry VIII of England. From 1562 to 1598 civil religious wars between the Huguenots (French protestants) and Catholics tore France apart internally. In 1610 Louis XIII ascended the throne, but he was always under the control of his advisors, particularly the powerful Cardinal Richelieu, who virtually controlled France from 1624 to 1642 and held power during the French involvement in the Thirty Years' War from 1631 to 1648. While generally not a strong financial administrator, Richelieu furthered the power of the royal bureaucracy. His true greatness, however, lay in restoring French influence abroad. It is no wonder in so unstable a time that little attention was paid to the drama. Since it was decreed in the Thirty Years' War that each country should have whatever religion its ruler professed, France was established as a powerful catholic nation.

Besides the draining effect of war on the art of the nation, a monopoly—namely the Confrèrie de la Passion—had enjoyed the exclusive privilege of presenting plays or licensing their productions in Paris for one hundred years. The confining atmosphere of monopoly proved as devastating to the theatre of France as the open spirit of free enterprise and competition had proved envigorating to the theatre of England.

Contributing further to the restrictive and controlled environment of the French theatre was the authority that Richelieu, as the King's representative, exerted over it. Richelieu himself wrote and produced plays. In one instance he wrote a plot and required five different playwrights to write each of the five acts of his drama. In 1635 Richelieu established the Académie française, a rigid institution created to establish and maintain standards of literary taste. Through the rulings of this august body, the French rules for tragedies were established and at least one writer brought to his knees in humiliation for not adhering strictly enough to these imposed dicta.

The playwright was Pierre Corneille and the play was *Le Cid* in 1637. Set in Spain with a complicated plot and a panoramic picture of patriotism and battles, the drama focuses on the conflict between love and honor. In a duel on behalf of his aging father, Rodrigue kills the father of the beloved Chimène, who is then duty-bound to seek revenge in spite of her love for Rodrigue. Corneille was brought under severe attack for his disregard for "rules," truth, decency, and artistry, and Richelieu brought *Le Cid* before the Académie who judged it guilty of severe flaws: that the setting was Spanish rather than classical, that the action was improbable, and the ending happy. Corneille acquiesced, and from that day forward subscribed to the "rules" of the Académie. It is interesting that in spite of the judgment against it, *Le Cid* has remained one of the most popular plays of the French theatre.

What were these so-called rules that the Académie française imposed upon the drama that sought to limit, order and control it? First of all, primarily as a result of a misinterpretation of Aristotle, they insisted on unities of time, place, and action. The time it takes the story to be performed should more or less conform to actual time; the setting should be single; and the action pure: no mingling of comic and tragic, no sub-plots, and no deviation from the clear, logical forward movement of the drama. The subject matter should present an avoidance of extremes, a preservation of decorum in which passion is pitted against reason, with the latter triumphant. There should be a relatively small number of characters, a five act structure, and—just in case these restrictions were not sufficiently limiting—the plays must be written Alexandrine verse (iambic hexameter) with six feet to the line in rhymed couplets. Corneille's younger contemporary, Jean Racine, seemed as comfortable with these regulations as Corneille had initially found them difficult. These dictates persisted in shaping—and stifling—French drama until 1830 when a young revolutionary named Victor Hugo defied the Académie in *Hernani,* causing Paris to divide into literary camps that literally fought in the streets.

With the restrictions remaining in force, the old patterns of war and monopoly began to subside with the ascension of the sun king, Louis XIV, at the age of five. Louis, who said "I am the state," remained on the throne for sixty two years and made France a center of artistic as well as political power. Money was no object in fashion, in the building of great palaces like Versailles, in the laying out of formal gardens, in fostering courtiers who were painters, writers, musicians, and intellectuals. Moreover, Louis loved the theatre and provided all manner of performances at court. He supported playwrights, foreign acting troupes, and charming small court theatres. In Louis's vast entourage was an upholsterer named Poquelin who had a son destined to become the greatest playwright France has ever known—a man who was able to write plays satirizing the aristocrats with whom Louis surrounded himself and yet remain in favor at court, and who was able to write the finest comedies the world has ever known. That man was Jean-Baptiste Poquelin who took the stage name of Molière, probably to save his father the disgrace of having an actor/ playwright for a son.

Molière

As a youth, Molière tried to follow in his father's footsteps as upholsterer and as valet in the royal court; he also studied law but was somehow attracted to the stage and joined an amateur company as an actor in 1643. The company, calling itself the Illustrious Theatre, struggled in the provinces for about thirteen years during which time Molière became the company's manager and also landed in jail for debts and had to be bailed out by his father.

The company grew in stature until on October 24, 1658 it was invited back to Paris to perform before the twenty year old king who had already established himself as the major force in the artistic world. Molière's group chose to perform Corneille's *Nicomede* which met with meager and only polite applause. It was obvious that the king was bored. Struggling to save the day, Molière stepped forward and asked permission to present a small diversion of his own titled *Le Docteur amoureux (The Love-Sick Doctor)*. The effect was electric: Molière's acting, his direction of the company, and his play were immediate successes. The king placed the players under the patronage of his brother, the Duc d'Orleans; they bore the title Le Troupe de Monsieur and were invited to perform in the king's own theatre. By 1662 Molière had married one of his actresses, Armande Bèjart, although it had long been rumored that Armande's mother was Molière's mistress.

Time and time again Molière's comedies were attacked for licentiousness, impiety, and assaults against the nobility. But Louis XIV staunchly supported Molière, making his troupe the Troupe du Roi in the summer of 1665 and granting it a royal subsidy. The greatest of Molière's difficulties arose over *Tartuffe* in 1664. This satire on religious hypocrisy was so pointedly aimed at courtiers and clergy that it created violent controversy which culminated in its being banned and Molière being branded as a devil. Only in 1669 did this comic masterpiece enjoy the success it deserved. The king remained stalwart in support of the comic genius. Not only did Louis recognize the playwright's talents, but he needed Molière to provide him entertainments at court. Molière wrote comedy-ballets and court spectacles in which he employed the vast machinery of the Italian stage.

Probably Molière's greatest achievements are his comedies of character: *The School for Wives* (1662), *Tartuffe* (1664), *The Misanthrope* (1668), *The Miser* (1668), and *The Learned Ladies* (1672). *The Miser* has been selected for inclusion here because of the strong influence of the *commedia dell'arte*. Molière's last comedy was *The Imaginary Invalid* (1673) in which, knowing he was dying, he wrote wittily of a man who imagines himself to be ill and of the quackery in the medical profession. During the fourth performance, Molière, who played the leading character himself, collapsed. Four hours later he was dead. Because he was an actor and because he had been a severe critic of court, he was denied Christian burial until Louis himself pleaded one last time for his friend. Molière was finally permitted burial but was denied a funeral. His grave is unmarked and unknown.

In an age of reason, Molière pleaded for a common sense view of life. He deplored excesses of all kinds and believed them fatal to society. His comedies are called social satires because they pit an individual's eccentricities against the established and accepted norm. His plays are also called comedies of character because of the brilliance of his broadly sketched but easily recognizable types. His characters are individuals with identifiable foibles and eccentricities whom Molière enlarges into believable universal types. Molière wrote, "The function of comedy is to correct the vices of mankind." His intellect and reason coexisted with his love of farce and buffoonery. In his fifty-one years, Molière staged approximately one hundred plays, most of which he acted in and thirty-one of which he had written.

In 1780 in Molière's honor, Louis XIV enacted his last great tribute to his favorite playwright by creating Le Théâtre Francais, also called La Maison de Molière. Now known as the Comédie-Française, this theatre was the first national theatre in the world—under government subsidy but also under government control. While the Comédie-Française has been a model for brilliant acting, high standards, and classical repertoire, it has also represented rigidity and traditionalism. With the establishment of the Comédie-Française, no one could question the power and the popularity of the French theatre nor question the importance of theatre itself in the make-up of a civilized nation.

Molière's The Miser

As Molière's *The Miser* will demonstrate, comedy, like tragedy, deals with the pursuit and fulfillment of an action or major deed. A striking difference between tragedy and comedy can be seen in the fact that the former deals with events and deeds of magnitude or universal significance while the latter tends to concern itself with everyday matters. It might be said that tragedy focuses upon Man's relationship to universal matters and the world at large while comedy centers its attention on Man's relationship to his fellow man and to the society in which they live. For that reason comedy tends to be the more topical of the two in its portrait of a contemporary, very recognizable time and place. And, therefore, comedy often seems to be dated and its point much less applicable to other ages than is the case in tragedy.

We have seen in the study of *Antigone* and *Othello* that the purpose of tragedy is the purging of negative emotions. A similar thing happens in the staging of comedy, for the audience is purged, too, but the catharsis has a different target. In the comedic form, the spectator is hopefully purged of negative, ridiculous, unproductive, potentially harmful social ideas. Comedy, in a sense, is designed to correct social ills by holding Man and his behavior up to close scrutiny and ridicule. At least, such is the case in what we call *classical* comedy where the audience is encouraged to laugh at the stupid and foolish behavior of the characters—and, through implication, at their own foolish and stupid behavior. This is not necessarily a gentle or kindly form of theatre, for the resulting catharsis can be scathing. We find such an approach to comedy in the plays of Aristophanes, Plautus, Terence, Ben Jonson and Molière. However, there is another form of comedy—epitomized by such plays as *A Midsummer Night's Dream, Twelfth Night* and *As You Like It* by Shakespeare—in which the approach is much gentler, where we, as spectators, are not asked to laugh *at* the characters but, rather, to laugh *with* them at the general ridiculousness of life.

Whether the comedy be classical or romantic, it will, like tragedy, present the efforts of the characters to achieve a state of equilibrium in a world that is off balance. Both genres show us a world ultimately brought to order out of a state of chaos. The difference between the two genres in this regard lies in the fact that the causal factors in the play which create the chaos at the outset are world-shattering in tragedy but merely socially distressing in comedy. In other words, in a tragedy the hero may have the horrendous task of re-establishing God's order in the realm while in comedy he may have little more to do than win the hand of the fair heroine in marriage. Consequently, in tragedy the hero generally has to be a man of spectacular gifts in order to accomplish his assignment whereas in comedy the hero, who has a much less demanding task, is often a comparatively average individual. Because that is the case, contemporary audiences can often enjoy a comedy from a past age (because they can recognize the characters as being relatively like themselves) even though the situations may be somewhat dated or foreign to them. Tragic characters of a past age often strike contemporary spectators as being somewhat stilted; but even then the spectators recognize and appreciate the universal problem confronting the hero as being similar in principle to the problems confronting them from time to time in their own lives.

In Molière's *The Miser* the present-day spectator (or reader) will find an instant delight in recognizing the characters as being very much like people they know even though the situations confronting Molière's characters—and the style in which the play is written—seem a bit unusual and, therefore, less believable by contemporary standards. In Cléante, Elise, Valère, and Mariane we find young lovers who have much the same needs, desires and problems as young people today have. Doubtlessly, more than one young man or woman today at one time or another has thought his or her father to be as unreasonably stingy and miserly as Harpagon even though the real father, hopefully, is not quite so comically extreme as the father in the play. To a large degree, Molière's comedy is about young people who find it necessary to out-wit and out-smart parental authority. Perhaps it is that element which lends the play a timelessness.

Harpagon is the epitome of avarice. His miserliness creates the problems in the play which produce the state of chaos or disbalance. If order is to prevail—if a social harmony is to be achieved—then the avaricious nature of the father must be overcome. In short, the action confronting the characters of this comedy is to defeat the forces of avarice as they are represented by Harpagon. The situation is made very clear to us in the exposition of Act One. As the play begins, we are informed of many facts in quick succession. Elise and Valère are in love and are secretly engaged. Valère has saved Elise's life at some point in the past. Valère is masquerading as a servant in Harpagon's household in order to be near the girl he loves. (This is a plot element which Molière borrows from Roman comedy and the *commedia dell'arte*.) Harpagon, Elise's father, is a miser who is afraid of losing his property. (That fact is neatly planted in the scene where Harpagon searches La Flèche while criticizing the extravagances of his children and voicing his suspicion that even his own son and daughter are stealing his money.) Valère has lost his parents. Cleante, Elise's brother, is also in love. Harpagon has buried large sums of money in his garden. Harpagon has plans to marry off Elise to an old man. Harpagon wants to marry a young woman. In general, the wishes of the children are at odds with the desires of the father which are all dictated by his avaricious nature. So, by the end of Act One the action is set. In order to achieve their own happiness and fulfillment, the children must defeat the miserliness of their father by out-smarting him.

Throughout the rest of the play we watch the seesaw battle of wits between the children and the father in which the younger generation make capital of Harpagon's comic flaws—his inordinate love of money and his foolish desire for a young wife. In Act One the welfare of the children is in jeopardy. In Act Two matters grow worse and the jeopardy deepens. By the third act the tables begin to turn for even though Harpagon still controls the situation, we have seen Cléante get the best of him and know that his defeat is possible. Events happen quickly in Act IV as Harpagon triumphs by disinheriting Cléante only to be dealt a resounding blow by the son at the close of the act which initiates a reversal of fortunes—very literally, in fact. In the final act of the play, the fortunes of the characters are reversed again as Harpagon seems on the threshold of success; but then, through a wild (and very deliberate) series of coincidences (and some events which are not at all coincidental) Harpagon goes down in defeat. But no one is seriously injured, however. This is a comedy after all. And Harpagon remains comically avaricious to the very end.

From beginning to end *The Miser* is an amusingly masterful demonstration of plot construction. Once the exposition is out of the way in Act One the plot builds quickly and consistently through a series of small climaxes toward a vivid moment of crisis at the end of Act Four. Each reversal along the way provides tension and suspense; and the tension is theatrically relieved from time to time by bits of "schtick" mostly borrowed from the *commedia dell'arte*. A peak of theatrical brilliance is reached at the climactic moment near the end of Act IV when Harpagon discovers he has been robbed. For a brief moment, the serious mental anguish of the protagonist steers the comedy toward something resembling tragedy. However, the dramatist expertly maintains the overall comedic tone by 1) subtly reminding us that the hero deserves his fate, 2) allowing

Harpagon to over-act his own passion in true comic fashion, and 3) letting Harpagon address the audience directly thereby involving them in the action of the scene—even implicating them in the theft of his fortune while seeking their assistance in apprehending the culprit—and cleverly reminding the spectators that it is, after all, only a play.

While Molière is treating us to a delightfully funny story, he is also taking full advantage of every opportunity in the play to criticize social behavior and attitudes in a most pointed and trenchant manner. As Elise and Valère declare their undying love for one another in Act One, Molière makes certain that the audience appreciates the silliness of their romantic posturings. The point is made remarkably clear to us when Elise romantically ponders whether or not she has sufficient right in the eyes of the world to love Valère. As Molière sees it, the young man has, after all, saved her life! What more right could she have? What more could any young woman want? Later, the playwright offers some sage advice on how to get ahead in seventeenth century France when he has Valère say very pointedly: "I have discovered that, to win men over, there is no better way than to . . . applaud everything they do. One need have no fear of overdoing complaisance. No matter how obviously you play on their feelings, the shrewdest men are always the greatest dupes when it comes to flattery."

Everyone and everything is subject to attack in a Molière comedy. In *The Miser* he takes on lawyers, money lenders, servants, children, parents, doctors and the theatre itself. It is not surprising to hear him attack doctors because he himself held them in great contempt. For most of his adult life he was afflicted with a cough for which no doctor he ever consulted found a cure. That is why Valère says in Act One: "Do doctors know anything about sickness? Come now, with doctors you can have any sickness you please, and they will find reasons for your having it, and tell you where it came from." But they will not cure you, according to Molière. (Interestingly, Harpagon has a cough. Molière wrote that detail into his character because the playwright created the role of Harpagon for himself and performed it many times.) Act Two contains a marvelously comic attack on the practices and principles (or lack thereof) of money-lenders. As the loan contract is discussed, the 'hidden costs" which send the interest rate sky-rocketing are skillfully exposed as are the many ridiculous "riders" designed to cheat the unsuspecting applicant. Loan companies today are indulging in similar disreputable practices even though their techniques may not be quite so blatant.

Students of theatre will readily perceive the influences of the *commedia dell' arte* on Molière's comedy. Molière admired the work of the *commedia* performers enormously; in fact, he personally trained with *commedia* actors and became very conversant with their techniques and materials which he borrowed and adapted to his own needs. In the four young lovers of the play we can detect elements of the Innamorati characters; Harpagon owes a great debt to Pantalone; and the Zannies can be seen in Molière's servant characters. Master Jacques in particular resembles the tricky servants of the *commedia* in his attempt to settle a personal score with Valère or, more obviously, in his scenes of "schtick" reminiscent of the lazzi of such characters as Brighella or Harlequin or Scapino. Notice especially the scene in which Jacques changes costumes in order to impersonate two different servants as well as the scene in which he is beaten by Harpagon and then again by Valère. The garbled communications and misrepresentations he perpetrates in Act Four when he acts as a go-between for Cleante and Harpagon are verbal lazzi adapted from the Italian improvised farces. And most certainly the events in Act Five with the appearance of Anselm and the reuniting of lost parents and children is plot material borrowed from any one of many *commedia* scenarios.

Spectators unfamiliar with the theatre of Molière may be somewhat dismayed, if not outrightly appalled, by his use of coincidences to resolve the action of the play in Act Five. Actually, Molière is acutely aware of every improbability and highly deliberate in its employment for he is having great fun at the audience's expense. Spectators of Molière's day readily accepted without question many such asinine, unmotivated, gratuitous events in plays. The discovery of long-lost children was a stock item in many plays. So, here is one of the playwright's most biting and daring bits of social criticism—an attack on the very audience attending *The Miser* for being willing to accept such nonsense.

Notice how Molière prepares us for that bit of nonsense; notice how skillfully he sets it up. As early as Act One Valère has dropped the clue that he has lost his parents. He does not tell us how or where or when. But he has foreshadowed that final moment in the play when long-lost parents and children are united. But, then, Molière carefully prepares us to accept everything that happens in his play. For example, La Flèche tells us, not once, but twice, how much it would delight him to steal something from the miserly Harpagon.

If the play seems to end in a highly theatrical way with a series of coincidences, it nonetheless remains, as most comedy must, a basically realistic picture of people and human behavior. As order is established out of chaos and a state of balance achieved at the end of the play, the balance is a rather comical and precarious one because Harpagon has not really changed. He has remained amazingly consistent. He is as avaricious in his final moment as he is in his first. His major concern is still his moneybox, and he is still demonstrating his skill at getting the monetary advantage over the next man. But, then, Anselm seems to be such a willing victim, such an exceedingly pleasant man, that all is well that ends well. Still, we are aware as we laugh at Harpagon—or any of the other characters, for that matter—that we are in essence laughing at ourselves, at our own foibles and short-comings, at our own ridiculous natures. Perhaps, while watching the play, we have been made conscious of our own need to change our ways. Certainly, it was Molière's intent to force the spectator to arrive at such an awareness.

THE MISER

by Molière

Adapted by Miles Malleson

───── DRAMATIS PERSONAE ─────

VALERE (*in love with Elise*)
ELISE (*Harpagon's daughter*)
CLEANTE (*Harpagon's son*)
HARPAGON (*the Miser*)
LA FLECHE (*Cleante's servant*)
MASTER SIMON (*a moneylender*)
FROSINE (*a scheming woman*)

JACQUES (*Harpagon's servant*)
1ST SERVANT
2ND SERVANT
MARIANE (*in love with Cleante*)
JUSTICE OF THE PEACE
CLERK TO THE JUSTICE
SEIGNEUR ANSELM

───── SYNOPSIS OF SCENES ─────

The action of the play passes during one day in the house of Monsieur Harpagon in Paris, in the year 1668.

───── ACT I ─────

SCENE 1.—A room in Harpagon's house. Morning.
SCENE 2.—The same. A little later.

───── ACT II ─────

SCENE 1.—The same. Afternoon.
SCENE 2.—The same. Early evening.

ACT I
SCENE 1

SCENE:—*A room in the house of* MONSIEUR HARPAGON *in Paris. The morning of a day in the year 1668.*

The setting is simple and formal. A backcloth depicts a large ornate fireplace C. *with windows* R. *and* L. *of it giving views of a garden. There are single wings* R. *and* L., *with exits above and below them. A plush upholstered settee with a high back, stands at an angle* R.C. *An armchair to match stands* L.C., *with a stool close to and* L. *of it. The furniture is shabby with the decorative fringes bedraggled and torn. Two heavy gilt chandeliers hang* R.C. *and* L.C.

When the CURTAIN *rises,* ELISE *is seated on the settee at the* R. *end of it. She is a beautiful girl in her early twenties.* VALERE, *about the same age, is kneeling* L. *of her, clasping her hand, and gazing into her eyes.*

VALERE. Then you'll marry me, you'll marry me, you will?

ELISE (*rising*). I will—I will.

VALERE (*rising; fervently*). My darling. My beautiful. My love. (*He takes her in his arms.*) Elise.

(ELISE *sighs deeply.*)

What a sigh. And at this moment. When you've made me the happiest man in the whole wide world. Why do you sigh? and so deeply?

ELISE (*breaking down* R.). I sigh, Valere, when I think of my father. (*She turns.*) How angry he'll be: demented. There'll be paroxysms of rage. I dare not imagine what he'll say or do. And my family: how they'll disapprove. And the world. The world, too, will censure me. When I think of these things, I sigh. (*She pauses.*) But I sigh *deeply* when I remember you'll not always love me as you do now.

VALERE (*breaking* L.C. *and turning*). That's true enough.

ELISE (*breaking* C.). Valere!

VALERE (*moving in quickly to* L. *of* ELISE). I shall love you more. And more, and more. Oh my dear, suspect me of anything you will, believe me capable of any crime—but not of that. Not of failing you. Never, never, never, of failing you.

ELISE. All men say such things.

VALERE. It's what we do that matters. You must believe me.

ELISE. I believe you. How easily we are persuaded by a lover. But I believe; you'll love me always, and will be faithful to me. And if I were told that would be a miracle, I would reply—I still believe—in miracles. So I'll not sigh—deeply; I'll just sigh.

VALERE. But why sigh at all?

ELISE. My dear, if only others knew you, as I know you. When I think of all you've done for me. Given up—everything, forsaken your country, your home, your fortune—

(VALERE *turns and moves up* L.)

—your parents—to take service in my father's house.

VALERE (*turning*). I left my country, true—but it can hardly be said I *left* my parents—I *lost* them.

ELISE. Still no news?

VALERE (*moving* C.). Well . . .

ELISE (*moving in quickly to* R. *of* VALERE). Valere! News? Good? Bad?

VALERE. Neither. Perhaps not even news. An old friend, who knew them well, and to whom I've given the charge of continuing the search, has sent me word. A hint—no more—that they may be yet alive.

ELISE. But, my dear, why didn't you tell me?

VALERE (*easing above the armchair* L.C.). I've been wondering . . .

ELISE. Yes?

VALERE (*turning*). Whether I ought not to—to go myself, and follow up this hint.

ELISE. And leave me?

VALERE. For the time being.

ELISE. Oh, my dear. (*She moves in to* R. *of* VALERE.). Valere, this friend—you can trust him?

VALERE. Absolutely.

ELISE. He can do everything that you could do?

VALERE. Yes.

ELISE. Don't go. Not till you have further word. (*She crosses below the armchair* L.C. *to* L. *of the stool, and turns.*) If you were to leave my father's service now, he'd never take you back. And then how could I be with you? Oh, stay here, close to me—and do your best to win my father's love.

VALERE. To win your father's love?

ELISE. Yes.

VALERE. Impossible.

ELISE. But, why?

VALERE. He has no love to win. (*He moves up* C.) No love for anything or anybody, but his money-bags.

(ELISE *sits on the stool, her back half turned to* VALERE.)

Forgive me, I have no right to speak to you so, of your father.

ELISE. But it's true. Only too horribly, ridiculously true—(*she turns and faces* VALERE) but how highly he thinks of *you*.

VALERE. And how easily his good opinion has been won. Oh yes (*he moves* C.) I'm learning quite a lot, in this rather unusual situation of mine. I'm learning that if you want a man to think well of you, all you have to do is to make him believe that you think as he thinks; feel as he feels—like what he likes. Especially, you have to applaud his stupidities and—follies; praise his shortcomings; and, above all, flatter. Flatter, flatter, flatter. At every turn, in every way, and all the time. You can't overdo flattery. The more outrageous it is, the more they like it. (*He pauses.*) The most cunning, the most suspicious are deceived by it. There's nothing so inappropriate, so far-fetched, that they won't swallow, with a dose of flattery. (*He pauses.*) Of course, one's own integrity may suffer somewhat; (*he moves below the settee*) but, even so, I flatter myself that the fault lies with the flatterer, not the flattered.

ELISE (*rising*). But, Valere, my dearest, (*she crosses below* VALERE *to* R. *of him*) why don't you seek the love of my brother?

VALERE (*turning and facing* L.). That's impossible, too.

ELISE (*crossing* L. *of* VALERE, *then turning and facing him*). Surely not?

VALERE. Your brother is so exactly the opposite to your father, in all he says, and does, and is. I couldn't manage the two of 'em. (*He pauses.*) But your idea's a good one. (*He pauses.*) Why don't *you* take him into your confidence; and tell him?

ELISE (L. *of* VALERE *and facing* R.). Of us?

VALERE (*looking off up* L.). Yes. Here he comes.

ELISE. I dare not. I haven't the courage.

VALERE. My dear, you would gain his sympathy, and *I* his help. I must go. (*He bows and kisses her hand.*) I have my work to do.

(*He turns abruptly, crosses above the settee and exits quickly up* R. *Simultaneously,* CLEANTE *enters excitedly up* L. *He is a year or so younger than* ELISE. *He is boyish, and impetuous, and just now is in a state of great excitement.*)

CLEANTE (*moving quickly to* ELISE *and clasping her in his arms*). Sister! Thank God, I've found you; and alone. (*He leads her below the settee.*) I want to talk to you. I've something to say to you. It's been on the tip of my tongue for days.

ELISE (R. *of* CLEANTE). Then why haven't you said it?

CLEANTE. I dared not. I hadn't the courage.

ELISE. Brother! (*She sits suddenly on the* R. *end of the settee.*) What is it you have to say?

CLEANTE. So much, so much, so much. (*He pauses.*) Yet, I can say it in one word—love.

ELISE. Cleante . . .

CLEANTE (*quickly*). Sister, I'm in love. But before I say another word, I want you to understand that I realize I can go no further in this without the full knowledge and consent of my father.

ELISE (*in amazement*). Cleante . . .

CLEANTE (*ignoring the interruption*). I'm dependent on him. (*He pauses.*) He gave me life; and therefore, everything. (*He pauses.*) After all, our parents are older than we are. We must always remember that. And, being older, they're beyond the clutches of passion. Their's is the cool judgement of reason. In this matter of marriage, our whole future is at stake; obviously, for our own sakes, we should allow them, out of their so much greater experience and wisdom, to choose for us; and abide by their decision, even when it's contrary to our own.

ELISE. Cleante . . .

CLEANTE. I'm saying all this to you, sister, to save you the trouble of saying it to me yourself—(*he moves to the stool* L.C.) because I don't propose to listen to a word of it.

ELISE. Brother!

CLEANTE. No, I've made up my mind. (*He sits on the stool.*) I mean to marry the lady I love; and nothing you can say can alter that.

ELISE. Am I, then, so utterly lacking in sympathy?

CLEANTE (*rising, moving to the settee and sitting on it* L. *of* ELISE). Oh no, no, no, no, no. (*He puts his right arm around her.*) But you're my sister—untouched by feelings like mine—

(ELISE *turns away from him.*)

—so cool, so sensible, so full of prudence.

ELISE. Oh Cleante! (*She gazes out over the audience.*) Even the most sensible of us can be imprudent, thank Heaven, at least once in our lives.

CLEANTE. What d'you mean by that?

ELISE. No matter! (*She turns and faces* CLEANTE.) It's *you* I'd hear about. Who is she?

CLEANTE (*rising*). Who is she! Oh, Elise! (*He is swept up on a rising tide of ecstasy. But there is no pose in his behaviour. He is just a very young man hopelessly in love for the first time, and completely uninhibited about it. He crosses quickly below* ELISE, *moves up* R. *of the settee, then to* C. *above it, turns and faces her.*) Her eyes! Her hair! Her mouth!

ELISE. Yes, but . . .

CLEANTE. So young! So fresh! So sweet!

ELISE. Yes, yes, but . . .

CLEANTE. Her voice! Her laugh!

ELISE. Yes, yes, yes, but . . .

CLEANTE (*moving up* L.C.). The way she moves! Her grace! Her modesty! Her charm!

ELISE. But who is she? Her name?

CLEANTE (*turning to face* ELISE). Her name! (*He pauses. Rapturously.*) Mariane—Mar-i-ane.

ELISE. Mariane.

CLEANTE (*moving to the settee and sitting on it* L. *of* ELISE). And she lives quite close to here: with her mother. They live alone together. Her mother's an invalid. And Mariane looks after her. And with what loving care! What tenderness! What sympathy! So patient! So long-suffering! So uncomplaining! (*He rises and moves down* L.) And they aren't well off.

ELISE. No?

CLEANTE. No. The father's dead; and now they've very little money. (*He sits on the stool* L.C.) Elise, can you imagine anything more maddening—here we are, by far the biggest house in the neighbourhood; everybody knows father's rolling in money. (*He pauses.*) I long to be able to help—if only to give the mother a few delicacies, and Mariane a few pleasures. But because we're not allowed a single penny for ourselves, I can't give Mariane even the slightest token of my affection.

ELISE (*rising and moving quickly to* CLEANTE). Poor Cleante! (*She kneels at his feet,* R. *of him.*)

CLEANTE (*almost in tears*). I'm desperate. I'm being driven to the most ridiculous subterfuges to try and borrow money—just to have something to spend on her. (*He pauses.*) But it can't go on like this. I mean to have it out with him.

ELISE (*after a pause*). With father?

CLEANTE. Yes.

ELISE. What will you say to him?

CLEANTE (*after a pause*).Tell him of my love; and more, my determination to get married—if he doesn't agree, if he refuses his consent, I shall—I shall—

ELISE. Yes?

CLEANTE. Do something desperate.

ELISE (*kneeling up to* CLEANTE). Oh, what?

CLEANTE (*rising*). I shall, I shall—leave this house.

ELISE. Where will you go?

CLEANTE (*with a magnificent gesture*). Away! Right away!

ELISE. And leave Mariane?

CLEANTE. No, no, no. I shall take her with me.

ELISE. And what will you live on?

CLEANTE. There you are. (*He crosses below* ELISE *to* R.C. *and stands with his back to her.*) I knew you'd make difficulties.

ELISE (*rising and moving in to* L. *of* CLEANTE'S *back*). Brother! My dear! I'm not *making* difficulties. (*She moves quickly above* CLEANTE *to* R. *of him and faces him.*) I'm pointing them out.

CLEANTE. I don't care, something's got to be done. It's *insufferable*—the way he keeps us both penniless. We have to bargain with the tradesmen for the very clothes on our backs.

HARPAGON (*off up* L.; *shouting*). Don't stand here, gaping—you great oaf—get along with you.

CLEANTE (*crossing below* ELISE *to* R. *of her and turning*). There he is.

HARPAGON (*off; shouting*). Out of my sight!

CLEANTE (*moving up* R.). Who's he shouting at? (*He moves up* R.C. *and looks off up* L.) My own servant! (*He turns to* ELISE.)

(ELISE *moves below the settee, then to* R. *of it.*)

Sister, we must join forces against him.

(*There is a loud racket off up* L., *and* HARPAGON'S *voice is heard uttering indistinct threats.*)

ELISE (*marching above the settee to* R. *of* CLEANTE *and shaking hands with him*). Agreed!

(CLEANTE *exits quickly up* R.C. ELISE *turns and quickly follows him off.* LA FLECHE, *who is* CLEANTE'S *servant, enters hurriedly up* L. *and backs to* L. *of the settee. He is followed on by* HARPAGON, *who stands up* L., *and shakes his stick at* LA FLECHE.)

HARPAGON. You gallows bird, you! That's what you are—a gallows bird!

LA FLECHE (*breaking down* R.; *muttering*). The wicked old skinflint! (*Behind his hand to the audience.*) He's so mean!

HARPAGON. What's that? (*He moves quickly to* R.C.). What are you muttering—grumbling to yourself? If you've got anything to say, say it. Speak out.

LA FLECHE (*turning to* HARPAGON). I want to know what it's all about. What are you turning me out for?

HARPAGON (*threatening* LA FLECHE *with his stick*). How dare you bandy words with me!

(LA FLECHE *dodges to* R. *of the settee.*)

(*He moves below the settee.*) Away with you! (*He chases* LA FLECHE *up* R. *of the settee.*) Out you go!

(LA FLECHE *runs across above the settee and arm-chair* L.C., *then down* L.)

(*He moves above the settee and then to* L. *of it.*) Out, out, out!

LA FLECHE (*moving* C.). Your son told me to wait for him here.

HARPAGON. Then go and wait for him in the street. Not in my house. I won't have you in the place— not a moment longer. (*He circles* LA FLECHE *as he speaks, first moving* R. *of him, then below him, and finishing down* L. *of him.*)

(LA FLECHE *follows* HARPAGON *with his eyes.*)

Hanging about all day and never doing a hand's turn; never moving; stock-still. (*He pauses.*) Like one of the door-posts. Only door-posts haven't got eyes. You have. And they follow me about, everywhere. Watching. Trying to see if there's anything you can steal.

LA FLECHE (*facing* HARPAGON). Steal! A fat chance anybody has to steal anything in this house. Everything under lock and key.

HARPAGON (*moving in close to* L. *of* LA FLECHE). You're spying on me—that's what you're doing. You know I've got things hidden away. (*He claps his hand quickly to his mouth and turns away, horrified at having said too much.*)

LA FLECHE (*quickly*). Have you?

HARPAGON (*turning to* LA FLECHE). What?

LA FLECHE. Got things hidden away?

HARPAGON. I didn't say so.

LA FLECHE. Yes, you did.

HARPAGON (*breaking down* L.C.). Oh, God forgive me—what am I saying? (*He turns to* LA FLECHE.) Get out!

(LA FLECHE *turns and runs up* R.)

Come back! (*He moves* C.)

What are you taking with you?

(LA FLECHE *stops, turns and moves to* L. *of the settee.*)

LA FLECHE. Thoughts.

HARPAGON. What have you got in your hand?

(LA FLECHE *holds out his right hand, empty.*)

The other one.

(LA FLECHE *holds out his left hand, empty.*)

Your pockets?

LA FLECHE. Come and see for yourself.

(HARPAGON *moves above* LA FLECHE, *and from behind him, feels and pats* LA FLECHE'S *trousers pockets.* LA FLECHE *giggles.*)

HARPAGON (*moving down* L. *of* LA FLECHE). And your breeches? (*He points with his stick to* LA FLECHE'S *breeches.*) Look at your breeches. There's enough room in 'em to carry away half my household. (*He crosses below* LA FLECHE *to the settee, puts his stick down on it, then bending a little, feels around the bottom edge of* LA FLECHE'S *breeches.*)

(LA FLECHE *smacks* HARPAGON, *who passes above him, then eases down* L.C.)

LA FLECHE. Have you quite finished? (*Behind his hand to the audience.*) A plague on all misers.

HARPAGON (*turning quickly to* LA FLECHE). What's that?

LA FLECHE (*moving in close to* R. *of* HARPAGON; *loudly*). A plague on all misers.

HARPAGON. And what d'you mean by that?

LA FLECHE. What I said.

HARPAGON. What did you say?

LA FLECHE (*loudly*). A plague on all misers.

HARPAGON. And *who* are you talking about?

LA FLECHE. *Them!*

HARPAGON. *Who?*

LA FLECHE. Misers! All misers—mean; dried up; terrified—they deserve all they're frightened of. Don't you agree?

HARPAGON (*after a pause*). You deserve a good beating. (*He crosses to the settee and picks up his stick.*)

LA FLECHE. Oh, no, master, you flatter me—that's more than I deserve.

(HARPAGON, *up* R. *of* LA FLECHE, *bends him over facing* L. *and raises his stick.*)

HARPAGON. You're going to get it.

LA FLECHE. Here's another pocket. You missed it. Want to see what's in it? (*He turns his hip pocket inside out.*) Nothing. (*He straightens up, breaks down* L. *and turns.*)

HARPAGON (*moving to the settee*). Oh, he's being too clever for me, I know he is. He's deceiving me. (*He sits on the settee at the* R. *end of it.*) Oh, my good fellow . . . My dear good fellow . . .

(LA FLECHE *crosses slowly to the settee and sits on it,* L. *of* HARPAGON.)

Be a good chap and give it up.

LA FLECHE. Give what up?

HARPAGON. What you've taken.

LA FLECHE. I tell you I've taken nothing. I've nothing in my hands. Nothing in my pockets. (*He rises.*) Nothing in my breeches except what's my own. So a very good day to you, dear master. (*He moves above the settee.*) And a plague on all misers.

(*He exits quickly up* R.)

HARPAGON. Thank God *he's* gone. (*He pauses.*) Although I don't know. As long as he was here, he couldn't take anything away with him. (*He pauses.*) Oh, what a misfortune—having so much money about the place. Happy the man who has all his money invested, and lives on the interest. But what investment's really safe? Of course, I might keep it in a bank. But I don't like banks. Banks aren't what they're said to be. Something happens to a bank—and then, where's your money? Yet it's so bewildering to find anywhere in the house. There's my strong box. But what's a strong box? Just bait for thieves. If thieves broke in, it would be the first thing they'd go for. (*He rises.*) It was (*he moves slowly up* L.C. *and looks off up* L.) a good idea of mine to bury it in the garden. (*He moves down* L.C. *and faces the audience.*) But *was* it?

(LA FLECHE *enters quietly up* R. *and listens.*)

People come and go in the garden, and I can't keep an eye on it, all the time. Ten thousand crowns! In the garden!

(LA FLECHE *crosses stealthily up stage and exits up* L.)

What misery! (*He moves to the chair* L.C.)

(ELISE *and* CLEANTE *enter up* R. *and stand silently hand in hand watching,* ELISE *below* CLEANTE.)

Was ever a man tortured by such anxieties— never a moment's peace. (*He sits in the chair* L.C., *and as he does so, sees* CLEANTE *and* ELISE). Hmm! How long have you been there? Come here.

(CLEANTE *moves* C.)

(*To* ELISE.) You too.

(ELISE *moves in close to* R. *of* CLEANTE, *and they again hold hands.*)

Did you hear what I was saying?

ELISE. No.

HARPAGON. You must have done.

ELISE. Indeed, no.

HARPAGON. You didn't hear me mention (*he whispers and glances up* L.) the garden?

ELISE. No.

HARPAGON. Nor ten thousand crowns?

CLEANTE. Ten thousand crowns!

HARPAGON (*quickly*). I didn't mean a word of it— not a word. I mean—I—I was just thinking aloud—how good it would be if I had ten thousand crowns—in the bank, in the garden—anywhere.

ELISE (*crossing below* CLEANTE *to* R. *of* HARPAGON). Father, Cleante and I want to speak to you.

(CLEANTE *breaks to* L. *of the settee.*)

HARPAGON. And don't you run away with the idea I meant anything else.

CLEANTE. Father . . .

HARPAGON. I could do with ten thousand crowns.

CLEANTE. But, Father, everyone knows you have ten thousand crowns.

HARPAGON. Ah! What a wretch I am—when my own children betray me.

CLEANTE. Betray you? (*He breaks down* R. *and turns.*) What's wrong with saying you have ten thousand crowns when everybody knows you have ten thousand crowns—ten thousand times over?

HARPAGON (*rising*). Aah! You'll be the death of me—one of these fine days. (*He crosses to* L. *of the settee and faces* CLEANTE.) Before I know where I am—I shall find myself here, in my own house, slit from top to toe—because you will go about telling people I'm made of money.

CLEANTE (*with a sharp step towards* HARPAGON). Father . . .

HARPAGON (*after a short pause*). Anyhow, even if it doesn't come to that, you'll be the ruin of me.

CLEANTE. Father, I want to . . . (*He breaks off.*) The ruin of you? How?

HARPAGON (*pointing to* CLEANTE *with his stick*). Well, look at you. Just look at you. Your clothes! Look at 'em. (*He moves to* CLEANTE *and circles him, touching his clothes.*) All these fiddle-faddles. Frills and furbelows and fancy knots—and all these bows. D'you want all that lot to keep your breeches up. (*He completes his circle of* CLEANTE *and stands up* L. *of him.*) There's a pretty penny there. And you've more underneath.

CLEANTE (*with a quick look at* HARPAGON). Of course.

HARPAGON. And as costly and extravagant as what I can see, I'll be bound—right thro' to your skin. Why, God bless my soul, if you were all added up as your stand there, I could buy quite a decent annuity with you. (*Suddenly.*) I never gave you the money for this get-up.

CLEANTE (*turning away*). Indeed you didn't.

HARPAGON (*with a quick step towards* CLEANTE). Then you've been robbing me.

CLEANTE (*turning to* HARPAGON). No.

HARPAGON. You must have.

CLEANTE. I've been to an old money . . .

ELISE. Ahem!

HARPAGON. Eh?

ELISE (*quickly*). He's been playing.

HARPAGON. Gambling?

CLEANTE. And lucky—winning, and spending it on clothes.

HARPAGON If you've been winning money, you ought to put it away for a rainy day.

ELISE. Father—Cleante and I—have something to say to you.

HARPAGON (*turning to* ELISE *and peering at her*). And I've something to say to you. (*He pauses and looks from one to another.*) Well, what it is? What have you to say? What's on your mind?

CLEANTE. Well—it's—I—you see . . .

HARPAGON. Come along—out with it.

ELISE (*after a short pause*). Father, we want to talk to you about . . . (*She breaks off.*)

CLEANTE (*after a short pause*). About . . .

ELISE. About—marriage.

(*They each laugh in succession,* CLEANTE *first, awkwardly,* ELISE *nervously, then* HARPAGON *cheerfully.*)

HARPAGON (*still laughing*). That's funny—very funny!

ELISE. Why?

HARPAGON (*after a short pause*). That's exactly what I want to talk to *you* about.

ELISE (*breaking down* L.). Oh!

HARPAGON. Eh? Why the "oh"? Frightened of the subject? A great girl like you. (*He moves to* R. *of* ELISE.) At your age! You ought to be more than ready for it. Then why the "oh"—eh?

(*There is a pause.* ELISE *can find no answer.*)

CLEANTE (*coming to* ELISE'S *rescue*). Father, I suppose we're both a little frightened that your ideas about marriage, and ours, mightn't be quite the same.

(HARPAGON *moves to* C. *and beckons* CLEANTE *and* ELISE *to him.* CLEANTE *moves cautiously to* L. *of him. He loops his left arm in* ELISE'S *right, his right arm in* CLEANTE'S *left, and draws them in close to him.*)

HARPAGON (*confidentially*). When I've told you what I have in mind, you'll have nothing to complain of—either of you. Now— to start with— d'you happen to have heard of a family, that have only recently moved into the neighbourhood; two of 'em—mother and daughter?

(CLEANTE *and* ELISE *are dumbfounded. There is a pause.* ELISE *finds her voice first.*)

ELISE. Yes, Father.

HARPAGON. Oh! You've heard of 'em. When?

ELISE (*after a pause*). Someone told me of her—of them—only today.

HARPAGON (*to* CLEANTE). And you—have *you* heard of 'em?

CLEANTE. Yes, Father.

HARPAGON. Only today?

CLEANTE. No, Father. I heard of them—some time ago.

HARPAGON. Have you *seen* 'em?

CLEANTE. Yes, Father.

HARPAGON. You don't *know* 'em?

(*There is a short pause.* CLEANTE *disengages his arm, breaks a little down* L.C. *and turns to face* HARPAGON. ELISE *disengages her arm and eases a little up* R.C.)

CLEANTE. Yes, Father.

HARPAGON. You *know* 'em! Well—this is very interesting. What do you think of her?

CLEANTE. The mother?

HARPAGON (*impatiently*). No—the daughter.

CLEANTE. What do I think of the daughter! (*Cautiously.*) Not unpleasing.

HARPAGON. Not unpleasing. And her looks?

CLEANTE (*still cautiously*). Not unsightly.

HARPAGON. Not unsightly. She's the kind of girl you'd look twice at, eh?

CLEANTE (*warmly*). Oh yes—indeed.

HARPAGON. And her manner?

CLEANTE. It becomes her.

HARPAGON. Not unpleasing—not unsightly—and her manner becomes her. Think she's a good housewife?

CLEANTE (*enthusiastically*). But of course. Look at the way she does everything for her mother.

HARPAGON. That's true enough. In fact, if (*he raises his stick and pokes* CLEANTE *in the chest with it*) you had her for a wife, you'd think you were a very lucky fellow, eh?

CLEANTE. If I . . . Oh yes, I would.

HARPAGON. She's no money.

CLEANTE. Oh, Father, with true love—what's money matter?

HARPAGON (*after a pause*). Well, I wouldn't go so far as that. But there *are* other ways of dealing with that side of it.

CLEANTE (*gripping* HARPAGON'S *right hand*). Oh, Father! Dear Father!

HARPAGON (*patting* CLEANTE). Well, my dear boy, I must say this is all very satisfactory.

(ELISE *excitedly grips* HARPAGON'S *left arm.*)

I'm glad you think so well of her, very glad; and that being so—we'll make her one of the family, eh?

CLEANTE ⎱ (*together; almost jumping up and*
ELISE ⎰ *down*). Father!

HARPAGON (*releasing himself and crossing below* CLEANTE *down* R.). Yes—I propose to marry her.

CLEANTE. You propose to marry her!

HARPAGON. That's what I said.

CLEANTE. You!

HARPAGON. Yes, me.

CLEANTE (*after a pause*). But—but—who to?

HARPAGON (*turning and facing* CLEANTE). *Who to?* I said I propose to marry her.

CLEANTE. But which?

HARPAGON. How which, which what?

CLEANTE. The mother or the daughter?

HARPAGON. Which d'you think?

CLEANTE (*after a short pause*). The mother?

HARPAGON. Then you're a bigger fool than I took you for.

CLEANTE (*after a pause; breaking* C.). But you *can't!*

(ELISE *runs above* CLEANTE *to* R. *of him.*)

HARPAGON. And why not, pray?

CLEANTE (*turning*). Because . . .

ELISE (*between* HARPAGON *and* CLEANTE; *interrupting in a composed voice*). Cleante . . .

HARPAGON. What's the matter with the boy?

ELISE. I fear he's not well. Cleante, dear brother, you're ill.

CLEANTE (*turning and striding up* C.). Faint! Very faint!

HARPAGON. Faint! Then run along into the kitchen, and get yourself a glass of cold water—

(CLEANTE *makes a move towards* HARPAGON. ELISE *stops him with a gesture.*)

—nothing stronger, mind.

ELISE. And lie down for a little. We can talk of this later.

CLEANTE. Yes—yes.

(*He stumbles up* R. *and exits.* ELISE *moves to the stool and sits.*)

HARPAGON (*easing* C. *and looking off after* CLEANTE). Lie down, indeed! Faint! I don't know what they're coming to. Overdressed! No stamina! All their strength goes into their fiddle-faddles. (*He pauses, glances at* ELISE, *then moves to the settee and sits.*) Well, my dear, now you know my plan to marry again. (*As he speaks, he takes a box of snuff from his pocket and takes a pinch.*) I can't have you two hanging about the place—so we must get you both married as well. I have a rich widow for your brother—a great stroke of luck; and for you—the good Seigneur Anselm.

ELISE (*after a pause; looking directly at* HARPAGON). Seigneur Anselm!

HARPAGON. Seigneur Anselm.

ELISE (*rising*). I'm obliged to you.

HARPAGON (*returning his snuff box to his pocket*). Don't mention it!

ELISE (*after a slight pause; pleasantly*). But, saving your presence, dear Father—(*with her back half turned to him, she curtsies*), I don't wish to marry him.

HARPAGON (*rising and casing up* C.). And, saving *your* presence, dear Daughter—(*he bows*) I wish that you should.

ELISE (*with her back to* HARPAGON). And begging your pardon, my *very* dear Father—(*she steps down* R.C., *and with her back still to him, gives a deep curtsy*) I don't mean to marry him.

HARPAGON (*moving a little down* C.). And, begging your pardon, my *very* dear Daughter—(*he bows*) I mean that you shall. (He *pauses.*) My dear girl, he's a wonderful match.

ELISE (*turning to face* HARPAGON). He's old.

HARPAGON. Old? How old d'you think he is? He's on the right side of fifty.

ELISE. He's nearer sixty.

HARPAGON. That's what I mean. (*He pauses and places his stick on the settee.*) You don't want to marry a young jackanapes like your brother. Fainting and lying down all over the place. (*He moves to* R. *of* ELISE.) You want a man in the prime of life. (*He turns and moves up* R.) And he's immensely rich, and quite kind.

ELISE. I share your regard for him . . .

HARPAGON (*turning and moving up* C.). Very well, then . . .

ELISE (*turning her back to him*). But I'll not marry him.

HARPAGON. Oh, yes you will.

ELISE. No, I won't.

HARPAGON (*moving to* R. *of* ELISE *and suddenly screaming violently at her*). You will, you will, you will. (*He pauses, turns and moves* C. *Quietly.*) And this evening.

ELISE (*turning suddenly and facing him*). This evening?

HARPAGON. This very evening.

ELISE. I'll not.

HARPAGON. You will.

ELISE. No.

HARPAGON. Yes.

ELISE. You'd force me?

HARPAGON. I'll force you.

ELISE (*breaking down* L.). I'd die rather.

HARPAGON (*shouting*). Very well then, die.

ELISE. And not marry him?

HARPAGON. Aah! (*As he speaks he stumps below the settee, up* R. *of it, then above it.*) The impudence of it! The wickedness! The folly. Any other girl would jump at him.

ELISE (*moving up* L.C.). Ask any other girl.

HARPAGON (*moving up* R.C.). Ask anybody.

ELISE. Very well. (*She turns sharply towards the exit up* L.) Here comes your new steward. Ask him.

HARPAGON. Valere?

ELISE (*turning*). Valere.

HARPAGON (*after a short pause*). Ah now, Valere's a good fellow, a sensible fellow. I know what he'd say.

ELISE (*after a short pause*). So do I.

HARPAGON. You mean you think he'd agree with *you*?

ELISE. I'm sure of it.

HARPAGON. You don't know what you're talking about.

ELISE (*after a short pause*). Father—if Monsieur Valere agrees with you, and thinks I should be obedient and marry the man you've chosen for me—then I'll acknowledge my impudence, ask your forgiveness, and marry Seigneur Anselm— this very evening. (*She moves to the stool and sits.*)

HARPAGON. Well, well, well.

(VALERE *enters up* L.)

Valere, come here.

(VALERE *moves to* L. *of* HARPAGON.)

My daughter and I are having a little disagreement—a little dispute—we want you to tell us which of us is in the right. (*He moves down* R.C.)

VALERE (*after a short pause and a glance at* ELISE). But, my dear master, there can be no doubt!

HARPAGON (*turning sharply*). What d'you mean by that?

VALERE (*flattering*). Master! The profound depths of your mature knowledge against the shallows of her youth and inexperience . . .

HARPAGON. Good. Very good. (*To* ELISE.) There you are, what did I tell you? He agrees with me.

ELISE. But he hasn't heard what we're talking about.

HARPAGON (*moving to the settee and sitting*). No. But he thinks I'm right.

ELISE. Please tell him. Monsieur Valere, please listen to what my father has to say.

VALERE (*bowing to* ELISE). At your service—(*he bows to* HARPAGON) and yours, master.

HARPAGON. Well, now—listen to this. You know the good Seigneur Anselm . . .

VALERE. The old gentleman who lives in the big house at the other end of the town?

HARPAGON. Well—yes—he lives in the big house at the other end of the town—a most worthy gentleman.

VALERE. So I have heard. Your judgement of him does you credit.

HARPAGON. Well, the good Seigneur proposed to me, that he should marry my daughter.

(*There is a long pause.* VALERIE *is taken aback and looks from* HARPAGON *to* ELISE.)

VALERE. Marry your daughter!

HARPAGON. You're surprised? (*To* ELISE.) He's surprised! So was I—quite taken aback, but of course I accepted. (*He pauses.*) And now the young baggage says she'll have none of it. Did you ever hear anything so outrageous?

VALERE (*with a very urgent sincerity*). No, no, never. I never heard anything so outrageous.

HARPAGON (*to* ELISE; *overjoyed*). What did I say?

VALERE (*with a step forward*). I can hardly believe my ears.

HARPAGON. He can hardly believe his ears. And he means it. You can hear it in his voice. Don't you?

VALERE. I do. I do. Indeed I do.

ELISE. Does Monsieur Valere really think I should obey you in this, and marry Seigneur Anselm? I'd hear it from his own lips.

HARPAGON. Very well, you shall. Go on. Tell her. Tell her. Plainly. In your own words.

ELISE (*rising*). Yes, Monsieur Valere. Plainly. In your own words. (*She pauses.*) And choose your words with care. (*She moves to* L. *of* VALERE.) For I have promised my father that if you think he is right—I will marry Seigneur Anselm—*this evening.*

VALERE (*after a short pause*). This evening!

HARPAGON. This evening. Now, young man. Let's hear you.

VALERE (*to* ELISE). Well, of course—as I've said— there can be no denying that your father must be right.

HARPAGON. He knows what he's talking about.

VALERE (*to* HARPAGON). Yet—at the same time— (*he eases a little to* L. *of the settee*) it might be said—in a kind of way—

(HARPAGON *looks sharply at* VALERE.)

—that your daughter is right, too.

(ELISE *eases in to* L. *of* VALERE.)

HARPAGON. My daughter is right, too! We can't *both* be right. Don't be a dam' fool.

VALERE. Well—she might, perhaps, say that you were going a little fast.

HARPAGON. Eh?

VALERE. Too fast for *her. Your* vision being so much finer and quicker in perception than hers, she has not (*to* ELISE) as yet, (*to* HARPAGON) that *certainty* that makes for unhesitating assent. (*He bends down a little towards* HARPAGON.) Whereas, given a little more *time* . . .

HARPAGON. Impossible. No time to spare. (*He leans towards* VALERE. *Confidentially.*) There's something about the offer that makes it unique. If he takes her at once, he takes her without a dowry.

VALERE. Without a dowry!

HARPAGON. I thought that 'ud take the wind out of your sails. I thought that 'ud rumple your feathers. Without a dowry!

VALERE. Why then—I must say . . .

HARPAGON. You see, there's nothing more to be said.

VALERE. Nothing!

HARPAGON. Nothing!

VALERE. Altho' she might perhaps say that marriage being a life-long affair, and her (*he moves above the settee, then behind it*) whole happiness or unhappiness for the rest of her life depending on it—

(ELISE *moves above the settee.*)

—and taking into consideration the great disparity in their ages . . .

HARPAGON. Without a dowry!

VALERE. Yes, of course—that's unanswerable. (*Unseen by* HARPAGON, *he gives* ELISE *a quick embrace.*)

HARPAGON. Right as usual, my dear Valere—unanswerable.

VALERE (*after a pause*). Though, of course, she might answer that there might be *some* fathers who would consider their daughter's happiness (*he eases to* R. *of the downstage end of the settee and leans over the back of it as he speaks*) rather than what they could save on them; who would shrink from sacrificing them to a bank balance; who might even desire for them—all the deep joy, the inner content, the peace of mind that only a successful marriage can bring.

HARPAGON. Without—a dowry.

VALERE (*easing up* R.). But it must be a marriage of love. (*Behind the settee, he holds* ELISE *in his arms as he speaks.*) Love—that unfolds and grows through the years, like a great tree—with its roots so deep that all the winds of misfortune may blow upon it, and only give it new vigour.

HARPAGON. Yes, yes, yes.

(VALERE *and* ELISE *break.*)

That's all very well. I know all that. But he's in a hurry. And we must make use of that. He wants immediate possession . . . (*He breaks off and listens for a moment.*) What's that?

VALERE. What's what?

HARPAGON (*rising*). In the garden—a noise—didn't you hear?

VALERE. No. I heard nothing.

HARPAGON. A dog barked—I may have imagined it. You didn't hear it?

VALERE. No.

HARPAGON. You are sure?

ELISE. I heard it distinctly.

HARPAGON. I thought so. (*He moves up* L.). That means there's someone in the garden. I *won't* have people in the garden. Excuse me. Stay here. I'll be back.

(*He exits quickly up* L.)

ELISE (*moving quickly down* C.). Valere, don't you realize that if you agree with my father, I shall be married this evening—to someone else.

VALERE (*moving quickly below the settee to* R. *of* ELISE). If I hadn't agreed with him, I should have been dismissed on the spot. As it is, here I am—to prevent it.

ELISE. How?

VALERE. We'll escape from this marriage, together—into our own. We'll run away. If your trust in me, and love, are enough.

ELISE. Need you ask? (*She throws her arms around his neck.*)

VALERE (*putting his arms around her*). Then let's thank God this has happened. (*He kisses her.*) My dear, my dear. (*He glances up* L. *as he hears* HARPAGON *returning. Loudly.*) My dear young woman (*he hastily releases himself from the embrace*) you ought to thank God—

(HARPAGON *enters up* L. *and stands watching them.*)

‑this has happened. (*He pushes* ELISE *to her knees.*) Down on your knees, my girl—and thank God that your future husband is such a man as he is, wanting you so much that he'll not wait a moment longer than he need. (*He looks up. To* HARPAGON.) Oh pardon, master, that I should talk to your daughter in this way. My feelings carried me away. (*He eases down* R.)

HARPAGON (*moving* C.). Oh, go on, go on, my boy. Don't mind me. Say what you like to her. Tell her exactly what you feel. (*He moves to* L. *of* ELISE.) And you—you wouldn't listen to *me*—perhaps you'll listen to *him*.

ELISE. Oh I *will*, Father—I will. (*She rises, moves to the settee and sits at the* R. *end of it.*) Never shall I forget what Monsieur Valere has just said to me.

HARPAGON. Splended—splendid. Well, I have to go and make the arrangement with the good Seigneur. Valere, I leave her in your charge.

VALERE. Monsieur Harpagon, I may have to be a little—familiar with her.

HARPAGON (*easing down* L.). As familiar as you wish.

VALERE. Very well. (*He moves to* ELISE *and takes her right hand in his left.*) Now, young lady, into the next room, if you please.

(ELISE *rises.*)

And I'll come with you. (*He moves* C., *passing* ELISE *across to* R. *of himself as he does so. To* HARPAGON.) She might try to run away.

HARPAGON. Run away!

VALERE (*half turning his back to* HARPAGON, *holding* ELISE *in front of him and looking at her*). Never fear. *I'll* take care of *that*. (*He draws her up* C.) I won't let her out of my sight. (*To* ELISE.) In you go.

(ELISE *turns, moves quickly above the settee and exits up* R. VALERE *follows her quickly off.*)

HARPAGON (*easing* C. *and looking off after them*). Strange how I've taken to that young fellow. Never argues; never contradicts. Always agrees with me. So *right*-minded! *Such* a comfort—(*he moves up* L.) such a comfort.

He exits up L. *as—*
the CURTAIN *falls.*

SCENE 2.

SCENE.—*The same. A little later.*

When the CURTAIN *rises, the stage is empty for a moment, then* LA FLECHE *enters stealthily up* L. *At the same time,* CLEANTE *enters stealthily up* R.

CLEANTE (*moving above the settee*). Hey! You! Where have *you* been? Didn't I tell you to wait for me here?

LA FLECHE (*crossing down* R.). That's right. You did. And I *was* waiting—till your father came. Master—that father of yours! Accused me of stealing; and wanted to beat me. So I didn't wait.

CLEANTE (*moving down* C.; *urgently*). How are things going? It's more urgent than ever now. You won't believe it, but since I saw you last, I've discovered my own father is my rival.

LA FLECHE. Your what?

CLEANTE. My rival.

LA FLECHE. What in?

CLEANTE. Love.

LA FLECHE. I don't believe it.

CLEANTE (*moving up* C.). I told you you wouldn't, but it's true.

LA FLECHE (*easing down* C.). The old scoundrel! What's he want with love? A high rate of interest? He's too old to take *any* interest. Did you tell him?

CLEANTE. What?

LA FLECHE. That you're rivals.

CLEANTE. Heavens, no. That would only have made matters worse. (*He moves down* R.) I nearly gave it away though—it was such a shock. (*He moves in to* R. *of* LA FLECHE.) But how are things going? Have you any news for me?

LA FLECHE. Oh, yes. I've news for you.

CLEANTE. Well?

LA FLECHE. It's an unkind world, master, for anyone who wants to borrow money.

CLEANTE. Why, aren't we going to get it?

LA FLECHE. Oh, yes, we shall get it—that old scamp of a go-between, that Master Simon, says he's working day and night for us—that's what he says;

145

and you'll be pleased to hear you've completely captivated him. Such a *charming* young man; such good looks, with such good manners—and a lot more nonsense of that sort.

CLEANTE. But are we going to get the money?

LA FLECHE. Oh, yes. We're going to get the money—on conditions.

CLEANTE. Did you meet the man who's actually lending it?

LA FLECHE. Did I *what?* Oh, no. It's not as simple as *that*. These things aren't carried on above-board in that fashion. No. They have to be wrapt in mystery. The man who's lending the money takes just as much care as you do to remain unknown. But you're to meet him this afternoon, at somebody else's house, and he's to learn from your own lips your name and security.

CLEANTE (*sitting on the settee*). My father's name; my mother's will. Security's all right. Nothing to worry about there.

LA FLECHE. No. Nothing to worry about there.

CLEANTE (*after a pause*). Then what *are* we worrying about?

LA FLECHE (*taking a document from his pocket*). Here are the conditions, which, I gather, our mysterious benefactor dictated, himself, to Master Simon—to be shown to you, before we go any further.

CLEANTE. Read them.

LA FLECHE (*reading with difficulty*). "Provided always that the lender is satisfied with the security—"

CLEANTE. He will be. Nothing wrong about that.

LA FLECHE. No. Nothing wrong with that.

CLEANTE (*after a pause*). Go on.

LA FLECHE (*reading*). "—then a good and exact bond shall be drawn up by an accredited notary."

CLEANTE. That's reasonable. Nothing to be said against that.

LA FLECHE. No. Nothing to be said against that.

CLEANTE. Go on.

LA FLECHE (*reading*). "In order not to burden his con-science—"

CLEANTE. His *what?*

LA FLECHE (*moving in to L. of CLEANTE and indicating the word in the document*). Con-science.

CLEANTE. Conscience.

LA FLECHE. Conscience. (*He reads.*) "—the lender does not intend to charge more than five and a half per cent."

CLEANTE. Five and a half! But *that's generous*. There's nothing to complain of in *that*.

LA FLECHE. No. There's nothing to complain of in that.

CLEANTE. Go on.

LA FLECHE (*reading*). "But, in consideration of the fact that the said lender has not, for the time being, in hand the said sum in question, and in consideration of the fact that the said lender is therefore compelled to borrow the said sum from another source, and at the rate of twenty per cent—"

CLEANTE (*rising; startled*). Twenty per cent?

LA FLECHE (*reading hastily*). "—it is hereby agreed that the said first borrower shall pay this interest in full and without prejudice to the rest, since it is only to oblige the said borrower that the said lender has himself to borrow the said money."

CLEANTE (*crossing below LA FLECHE to L.*). God in heaven! That makes over twenty-five per cent. What Arab, what Jew, what Turk, is this?

LA FLECHE. No, master, just French.

CLEANTE (*crossing angrily to R.*). Twenty-five and a half per cent. But what can I do? I must have the money. I need it desperately.

LA FLECHE. That's exactly what I told 'em.

(CLEANTE *turns quickly and looks sharply at* LA FLECHE.)

Shall I go on?

CLEANTE (*sitting on the settee*). Go on.

LA FLECHE (*reading*). "Of the fifteen thousand francs asked, the lender can only pay down half the amount."

CLEANTE (*rising quickly*). What's this? Only half— (*he slowly resumes his seat*) what about the other seven thousand odd?

LA FLECHE (*reading*). "In lieu of the remaining seven thousand, five hundred, the said borrower is requested to take various goods and chattels, as per the accompanying memorandum. Item—a four-poster bed with three posts, and an antique commode to match."

CLEANTE. Antique—commode!

LA FLECHE (*reading*). "Item—a large walnut dining table, with five well-turned legs—the sixth unfortunately missing." (*He pauses.*)

CLEANTE. What am I to do with it?

LA FLECHE (*reading*). "Item—three old-fashioned muskets, guaranteed quite harmless, but most picturesque, with three forks for them to stand on."

CLEANTE. Three forks!

LA FLECHE. But—quite harmless. (*He reads.*) "Item—a brick furnace—with two retorts, very handy for those who make a hobby of distilling. Item—a lute from Bologna, with all its strings—or nearly all. Item—a draught board and the game of Goose, very useful for passing the time when one has nothing better to do . . ."

CLEANTE (*rising and crossing below* LA FLECHE *to* L.). Stop! That's enough.

LA FLECHE. There's only one more. (*He reads.*) "A lizard skin, stuffed with hay, over three feet long."

CLEANTE. What?

LA FLECHE. Over three feet long. (*He reads.*) "A delightful curio for hanging on a wall. All the above-mentioned reduced by the good-will of the said lender to seven thousand, five hundred francs." (*He folds the document and replaces it in his pocket.*)

CLEANTE (*moving in to* L. *of* LA FLECHE). May his good-will choke him. The thief! You wait till I get my hands on him. (*He points up* L.). Take me to him now—at once.

LA FLECHE. But, master, I don't know who he is.

CLEANTE. Then take me to the go-between—this Master Simon. (*He turns up* L.)

LA FLECHE (*catching hold of* CLEANTE'S *arm*). You can't go out like that. (*He passes* CLEANTE *across to* R. *of himself.*)

CLEANTE. And why not, pray?

LA FLECHE. Master, when you want to borrow money, you've got to *look* well-off. Your hat, your stick, your cloak.

(CLEANTE, *followed by* LA FLECHE, *exits hurriedly up* R. *A moment later,* HARPAGON *enters up* L., *followed by* MASTER SIMON.)

HARPAGON (*moving* C.). And who is he—this young fellow?

SIMON (*moving to* R. *of* HARPAGON). A young man, Monsieur Harpagon, very badly in need of money, and who will agree to *almost* any terms that you care to impose.

HARPAGON. Wants money badly, eh? That's good. (*He sits in the armchair* L.C.) But the risk, Master Simon. Any risk?

SIMON (*moving in to* R. *of* HARPAGON). He was very highly recommended.

HARPAGON. His family?

SIMON (*after a short pause*). I've no doubt a very good one.

HARPAGON. Yes. But is it good for the money—that's what I want to know? If the father's rich, what's the boy want money for? Doesn't sound right to me.

SIMON (*poking* HARPAGON *in the ribs*). His servant assures me you'll be satisfied on every point when you meet him.

HARPAGON. But, so far, you don't know the name or the circumstances of this young client of yours.

SIMON. That you shall hear from his own lips. But I *do* know that the family's immensely rich. The mother's dead, and the father very old and decrepit. (*He again pokes* HARPAGON.) Indeed, the young man's more or less given his word that the father'll follow his poor dead wife before very long.

HARPAGON. Good. That's something. Well, if the poor young man's really in need of money, it behoves us to do what we can to help, eh, Master Simon? After all, there's pleasure—with profit—in helping the needy.

(CLEANTE *and* LA FLECHE *enter up* R. *and stand above the settee.*)

SIMON (*taking a document from his pocket*). Your part of the agreement. (*He hands the document to* HARPAGON.)

HARPAGON (*taking the document*). Ah! (*He studies it eagerly.*)

LA FLECHE. Eh! But there he is—Master Simon.

CLEANTE. Simon!

(SIMON, *hearing his name, turns and sees* CLEANTE *and* LA FLECHE.)

SIMON (*moving to* L. *of* CLEANTE *and taking hold of his left arm*). Well, I never expected to see *you* here. You're in a great hurry, aren't you? I'm sure I don't know how you found out . . .

CLEANTE. Found out?

SIMON (*leading* CLEANTE *down* R.). No matter, no matter. I don't see there's any great harm done—and now you *are* here, we can settle the whole business on the spot. (*He turns, and moves* R.C. *To* HARPAGON.) Monsieur.

HARPAGON (*looking up from the document*). Eh?

SIMON. Allow me to present my young client, of whom I've been telling you. (*He turns to* CLEANTE). And this, my dear young man, is the gentleman who is so generously ready to oblige us.

(CLEANTE *and* HARPAGON *glare at each other*.)

HARPAGON (*rising; to* SIMON). *Who* did you say this was?

CLEANTE (*to* SIMON). *Who's* this?

HARPAGON (*to* SIMON). Is *this* your young charming client?

SIMON (*moving to* CLEANTE). That's right, that's right—such a clever young fellow.

CLEANTE (*to* SIMON). And is *this* my generous benefactor?

SIMON (*moving to* HARPAGON *and tapping his right arm*). Up to any amount—such benevolence.

HARPAGON (*hitting* SIMON'S *hand with the document*). So!

(SIMON *eases up* C.)

CLEANTE. So!

HARPAGON. You!

CLEANTE. You!

HARPAGON. You—the young rascal in want of money, and trying to borrow it.

CLEANTE (*moving in to* R. *of* HARPAGON). You—the moneylender—at twenty-five and a half per cent.

(LA FLECHE *eases down* R.)

HARPAGON. And you ready to pay it. You'd have ruined me.

CLEANTE. A lot of worthless junk for seven thousand francs.

HARPAGON. And your father old and decrepit and about to die. Have you no moral principles?

(SIMON *eases down* L.)

CLEANTE. Moral principles!

HARPAGON. Yes—haven't you heard of 'em?

CLEANTE. Not in this house.

HARPAGON (*glaring into* CLEANTE'S *face; indignantly*). How can you hold up your head?

CLEANTE. How can you look me in the face?

HARPAGON. Look you in the face? I don't *want* to look you in the face. Out of my sight.

CLEANTE (*turning and moving up* R.). Gladly!

HARPAGON (*shouting after* CLEANTE). Aren't you ashamed . . . ?

CLEANTE (*stopping and turning*). Yes, I am—

HARPAGON (*moving up*, C.). I'm glad to hear it.

CLEANTE.—of *you!*

(*He turns abruptly and exits up* R. LA FLECHE *exits down* R.)

HARPAGON (*with a move as if to follow* CLEANTE). Aah! (*He changes his mind, stops and turns to* SIMON.) A nice mess you've made of it.

SIMON (*moving* C.; *heartbroken*). Monsieur!

HARPAGON (*moving to* SIMON *and giving him the document*). Here's your agreement. Take it. And never, never accept him as a client again. Borrowing money! I won't have it in my family. (*He moves slowly to the settee.*) Take care of that—or no more commission from *me*.

SIMON. Monsieur!

HARPAGON. That's enough! Go away.

SIMON. Monsieur . . .

HARPAGON. Go away.

SIMON. Monsieur!

HARPAGON (*sitting on the settee*). Go away!

(SIMON, *almost in tears, turns and exits sadly up* L. HARPAGON *takes out his snuff box and becomes engrossed in taking his pinch of snuff.* FROSINE *enters cautiously up* L., *unseen by* HARPAGON. *She moves stealthily up* L. *of the settee, is about to touch him on the shoulder, but changes her mind and coughs.*)

FROSINE. Ahem! Monsieur Harpagon . . .

HARPAGON (*looking up; startled*). What are you doing here?

FROSINE (*with a curtsy*). Come to see you.

HARPAGON. Why?

FROSINE. You told me to.

HARPAGON. Did I?

FROSINE. You know you did.

HARPAGON. Oh yes, of course. How did you get here?

FROSINE. Thro' the garden.

HARPAGON. Who told you to come thro' the garden?

FROSINE. You did. You said, "Don't come to the front door."

HARPAGON (*after a pause*). Oh—er—how's it looking?

FROSINE. What?

HARPAGON. The garden.

FROSINE. Lovely. Very bright. Very quiet.

HARPAGON. Quiet. Eh—good. Anybody about?

FROSINE. Only the gardener.

HARPAGON. What's he doing?

FROSINE. Digging.

HARPAGON. What for?

FROSINE. How should *I* know? It's what gardeners do, isn't it?

HARPAGON. Where's he digging?

FROSINE. Among the currant bushes.

HARPAGON (*rising suddenly*). Aaah! (*He moves quickly up* L., *speaking over his shoulder.*) Wait here. Want to see you. Back in a moment.

(*He exits hastily up* L. LA FLECHE *enters up* R. FROSINE *sits on the settee.*)

LA FLECHE (*moving* C.). What's he gone off for?

FROSINE. After his gardener—and the poor old wretch is half-dead with overwork already.

LA FLECHE. Half dead he may be, but he's in my way. I've got a bit of digging to do myself.

FROSINE. Digging—you?

LA FLECHE. Mm!

FROSINE. You're up to something.

LA FLECHE. Down to something more like. What are you up to in these parts?

FROSINE (*rising*). What I'm always up to. (*She moves to* LA FLECHE.) Living by my wits.

(LA FLECHE *kisses her.*)

The only thing I ever got for nothing was a little cunning, at my birth; and the only thing I ever acquired for myself, was a little skill in using it—which I do, whenever I can.

LA FLECHE. As best you can.

FROSINE. As often as I can.

LA FLECHE. Doing business with the master, eh?

FROSINE. From which I hope to pick up a little something for myself.

LA FLECHE. When you say—a little something, I presume you mean money.

FROSINE. What else?

LA FLECHE. What you pick up in this house won't make your arms ache.

FROSINE. There are some things the meanest of men will pay for. (*She takes a mirror from her handbag.*)

LA FLECHE (*glancing off* L.). We shall see. Old Harpagon *is* the meanest of men.

(*There is a short pause while* FROSINE *looks in her mirror.*)

FROSINE (*replacing the mirror in her bag*). I've done him a great service.

LA FLECHE (*moving slowly down* L.). Oh, and I daresay you'll be thanked for it. But thanks are words—they cost nothing. Even so, there's one word you'll never hear from him. The little verb—to give. I give—he's never learnt to say it.

(FROSINE *moves to* LA FLECHE *and links her left arm into his right.*)

He's so mean he won't even give you good morning—he'll lend it to you. (*He pauses.*) I'm no great philosopher—but I see what I see and tho' he never parts with a sou, he's the poorer for it.

FROSINE. Then it's *my* cunning against *his* meanness.

LA FLECHE. If you were half as cunning as he's mean, you'd own half France.

(*They stroll arm in arm to the settee and sit,* FROSINE L. *of* LA FLECHE.)

The very *sight* of anyone who he thinks is going to ask for money gives him the convulsions; and the *sound* of anyone asking for it—it's like a knife in his guts—agony. (*He kisses her, then glances up* L.) Here he comes. (*He rises quickly and moves behind the settee.*) I'm off. I'll share what you can get out of him. (*He leans over the back of the settee and kisses her, then moves to the exit down* R.) And I shan't bother to come back to collect it.

(*He exits quickly down* R. *as* HARPAGON *enters up* L.)

HARPAGON (*moving to the armchair* L.C.). I've sent him home. Given him a few days off. The poor old chap. He's getting on, y'know. Couldn't bear to see him digging all over the place. (*He is about to sit.*)

FROSINE (*rising; suddenly*). Monsieur Harpagon . . .

HARPAGON (*turning to her*). Yes?

FROSINE. Monsieur Harpagon . . .

HARPAGON. Well, what is it?

FROSINE (*moving* C.). You are the most remarkable man. Never have I seen you looking such a picture of health.

HARPAGON (*pleased*). Really? (*He sits in the armchair* L.C.)

FROSINE. Your complexion so clear, your eye so bright—altogether so spry; many a young man of twenty-five, I've seen looking older than you.

HARPAGON. Ah, these days the young ones are the old ones—fainting, and lying down all over the place. (*Something in him suddenly wilts.*) But for all that, you know, I've seen sixty.

FROSINE. What's sixty to a man of your age?

(*There is a short pause. There is something pathetic in* HARPAGON'S *wilting.*)

HARPAGON. I sometimes feel I could do with twenty years. I sometimes wish I was twenty years younger.

FROSINE. What rubbish! (*She crosses below* HARPAGON *to the stool.*) A man of your calibre, with your virility, lives to be a hundred.

HARPAGON. You think so?

FROSINE. I'm sure of it. (*She sits on the stool.*) Give me your hand. (*She takes* HARPAGON'S *left hand in her right, and studies it.*) Yes, here it is. What a line of life! Not a break in it—(*she turns his hand over*) and it goes on for ever. If they want to get rid of you, they'll have to put you to sleep. (*She pauses and again studies his palm.*) And I can tell you this—you'll bury your children, and your children's children. (*She releases his hand.*)

HARPAGON. I only hope you're right. And now, what have you got to report? How are things going?

FROSINE. How can you ask? I tell you, I've never undertaken anything that I haven't carried thro' to a successful conclusion. And match-making is my specialty. I began with a talk with the mother. I told her how her daughter had caught your eye as you sat at your window, as she passed by in the street—and how greatly the girl pleases you; and how you desire her in marriage.

HARPAGON. And what did she say?

FROSINE. She was overwhelmed—at your condescension. And when I told her that you wish her daughter to be present, here, tonight, in your house, on the occasion of your daughter's marriage, she willingly gave her consent.

HARPAGON. Yes—I *have* to give this supper tonight to the Seigneur; can't get out of it; and I thought it would be a good opportunity to have Mariane here—there's always too much to eat on these occasions, and a lot left over.

FROSINE (*to the audience*). A generous thought!

HARPAGON. Yes, but, look here—have you talked to the old lady about a dowry, eh?

(FROSINE *rises, crosses below* HARPAGON *to* C., *and takes a pencil and paper from her handbag.*)

She ought to make some effort to give her daughter *something.* A man doesn't marry a wife without anything to go with her, just for herself. It's unreasonable—not right—goes against my conscience. I doubt whether I ought to.

FROSINE (*turning to* HARPAGON). But she will.

HARPAGON. Will what?

FROSINE. Bring you something.

HARPAGON. Bring me what?

FROSINE. Five thousand crowns.

HARPAGON. Five thousand crowns! But this is the first I've heard of it. *What* a girl! What a *sweet* girl! I can hardly wait. (*Anxiously.*) There's no mistake?

FROSINE. There's no mistake—she eats only salads.

HARPAGON. Eh?

FROSINE. Occasionally a little cheese, perhaps, and an apple or so.

HARPAGON. What *are* you talking about?

FROSINE. None of your elaborate meals, your costly dishes. No. For years past she's been used to such a sparse diet that they wouldn't be good for her. Well, meal by meal, day by day, (*she writes some figures on the paper*) that mounts up; say five crowns a day—that's close on two thousand a year.

HARPAGON. Yes, but . . .

FROSINE. And she's used to very simple clothes; and takes great care of them; never buys any new ones; she'll be satisfied with what she's got.

HARPAGON. Ah, but will she? Will she?

FROSINE. A word from me, and she will. I can persuade her. If I were to tell her the simple style—the things she *has*—suit her best; that, with those she caught you, and with those she'll keep you; but that if she dresses up in a whole lot of silks and satins and velvets and fineries—

HARPAGON. Oh!

FROSINE. —then she'll be just like any other woman of society—one of many in your mind, and she'll lose you. (*She moves above* HARPAGON *to* L. *of him.*) Think what that means—(*she writes some figures on the paper*) another two thousand at least. Four thousand so far.

HARPAGON. Yes, but . . .

FROSINE. And then she's been very well brought up—she has a real horror of gambling.

HARPAGON. I should hope so.

FROSINE. Yes, but many young women of her age and class nowadays—most of 'em—play regularly and recklessly. (*She crosses below* HARPAGON *to* C.) I know a girl—not unlike Mariane to look at, same age, same background, lost four thousand last year. Four thousand! (*She writes some figures on the paper.*) Well, make it a quarter of that. There's another thousand for you; which makes up the five thousand. (*She hands the paper to* HARPAGON.) And that's quite a lot of money. (*She moves to the settee and sits.*)

HARPAGON (*momentarily impressed*). Yes, quite a lot. (*He pauses, then rises and moves* C. *Suddenly his voice runs crescendo up the scale of indignation.*) God Almighty! What's all this about? Are you mocking me? D'you expect me to give you (*he tears the paper in pieces*) a receipt for something I haven't had? What d'you take me for?

FROSINE. A wise man.

HARPAGON. Eh?

FROSINE. But you disappoint me.

HARPAGON (*moving to* FROSINE). Disappoint?

FROSINE. I can understand the ordinary man in the street, an ordinary business man—even a *good* business man—talking like that. But you, (*she rises*) Monsieur Harpagon: you, who have such an *immense*, (*she crosses below* HARPAGON *to* R.C.) almost *cosmic*, grasp of these things; who can look upon a balance sheet with the eye of a philosopher; who knows the innermost meaning—the ultimate significance—of debit and credit: that *you* should fail to realize that by marrying this girl, you're five thousand crowns better off than if you married anyone else.

HARPAGON. I'd be very much better off if I didn't marry at all. I know that. And yet I've set my heart on her. (*He pauses.*) You take me for a wise man—in your heart of hearts, d'you think I'm an old fool?

FROSINE. Monsieur!

HARPAGON. Do you?

FROSINE. Monsieur, I should only think you a fool if you were foolish enough to think so yourself.

HARPAGON (*breaking* R.; *bitterly*). But there *are* those who might think I'm—I'm a bit on the oldish side.

FROSINE. None that matter.

HARPAGON (*refusing to be comforted*). Oh, I don't know. There's the girl herself—*she* matters, I suppose, in this, in a way. Won't *she* think I'm too old?

FROSINE. Indeed no.

HARPAGON. Has she seen me?

FROSINE. No.

HARPAGON (*hopelessly*). Well, (*he sits on the settee, at the* R. *end of it*) there you are!

FROSINE. You can put all such fears right out of your head. (*She moves to* HARPAGON.) She doesn't *like* young men. She has an unconquerable aversion to them. She has no patience with them. She says they think of nothing but themselves. But older men—they have an understanding of the past—an appreciation of the present, and a design for the future—gifts that only the years can bring. (*She pauses.*) Youth she finds insipid. Age excites her by its very—maturity. Only a few weeks ago, she was contracted to be married . . .

HARPAGON (*alarmed*). Was she?

FROSINE. But on the very day of the marriage she broke it off when the bridegroom was able to sign the covenants without spectacles. She has no heart, she says, for a nose that doesn't wear specs.

HARPAGON (*doubtfully*). It all sounds a little unusual.

FROSINE. She's an unusual girl. (*She sits on the sofa,* L. *of* HARPAGON.) She has, in her room, a few—but very beautiful—engravings. And of whom? Of Adonis? Of Apollo? Of the youthful and god-like Paris? No! But of the *aged* Priam, King of Troy; of Nestor, *ancient* sage of Greece; of *blind* Homer; and the *bearded* Sophocles. So, you see, you have nothing to fear. Especially, as I've told you, I've never seen you looking so young.

HARPAGON (*anxiously*). Not too young?

FROSINE (*quickly*). No, no, no, just right. Let's have a look at you. Get up.

(HARPAGON *rises perkily.*)

Take a few steps.

(HARPAGON *braces himself and takes a few stiff steps to* C.)

What poise! What ease! I do believe you could still dance.

HARPAGON (*enthusiastically*). Why not? Why not?

(FROSINE *hums a tune. Thus encouraged,* HARPAGON *does a little dance, which finds him short of breath and brings on a fit of coughing.*)

Yes—there's nothing much wrong with me—except a touch of gout and this cough.

FROSINE (*rising and moving* R. *of* HARPAGON). Oh, but Monsieur, that only completes the picture—you cough so gracefully.

HARPAGON (*clapping his hand to his right hip and tottering to the armchair* L.C.). Well, I must say—(*he collapses into the chair*) it all sounds very satisfactory.

(FROSINE *moves in to* R. *of* HARPAGON.)

(*He pats her hand.*) And I'm sure I'm very much obliged to you.

(*They both laugh.*)

FROSINE (*laughing throughout the speech*). Don't mention it. To have had the privilege of being able to render you so great a service, has made me very happy.

HARPAGON. And I'm sure I'm very happy to have been able to afford—(*he winces at the word*) to afford you such happiness. (*He glances off, contemplating escape.*)

FROSINE (*interpreting the glance*). And now, Monsieur, the time has come . . .

HARPAGON. The time? (*He takes his watch from his pocket and glances at it.*) Goodness gracious me! (*He rises, crosses below* FROSINE *to* L. *of the settee and turns.*) I'd no idea it was so late. I must be getting along. (*He starts to move up* L.)

FROSINE (*intercepting him at* C.). Monsieur, d'you understand? I've striven so hard in your service, that the young woman you desire is all eagerness to meet you.

HARPAGON. I'm delighted to hear it. I'm sure I owe you a great deal.

FROSINE. Ah, you *do,* Monsieur. You *do.* On your behalf, I've devoted all my time, all my energies; yes, and all my money—and God knows, I'd little enough of that.

HARPAGON. Dear, dear, dear. Such devotion! Such a capacity for helping others! Really, I almost envy you. (*He crosses quickly below the stool to* L. *of it.*) Sorry I can't stay—

(FROSINE *moves above the armchair* L.C., *and intercepts* HARPAGON *up* L.)

—a little matter of business. (*He turns about and moves below the stool to* C.)

FROSINE (*turning and moving quickly above the armchair to* C.). Monsieur, for these last few weeks, I've more or less *lived* at their house. I've had to find excuses for going there so continuously. I took them little presents. (*She takes a bundle of receipts from a pocket in her petticoat and waves them at him.*) A succession of presents; and not such little ones. No. On several occasions, I took them out for a drive; or to dinner, or to the play. Monsieur, I've spared neither myself, nor anything that I own.

HARPAGON. And I've told you—I don't know how to thank you.

FROSINE (*after a pause*). It's not your thanks I want!

HARPAGON. Indeed! Oh well, of course, if you don't *want* to be thanked—there's no more to be said. (*He turns and moves below the settee to* R. *of it.*) A *little* matter of business did I say?

(FROSINE *moves quickly above the settee and intercepts* HARPAGON *up* R.)

Most important matter. (*He turns about and moves below the settee to* L. *of it.*) Several important matters.

FROSINE (*moving quickly above the settee and intercepting* HARPAGON, L. *of it*). Monsieur, you must listen. (*She pushes* HARPAGON *down on to the settee. Coarsely.*) Sit down! (*She pauses, then standing over* HARPAGON, *resumes in her normal voice.*) I've so filled her ears with your virtues, your uprightness, your good faith, your honour, your generosity . . .

HARPAGON. Yes, that's all very well—but I'm afraid you may have *overdone* it a bit.

(FROSINE *suddenly raises her voice to a shrill scream, and puts on an act to soften* HARPAGON'S *heart and loosen his purse-strings.*)

FROSINE. Overdone it! *Overdone it!* Yes, I have. Not for you. No. But for myself. Yes—there you are—with your bride-to-be so eager that she can hardly wait for the marriage to be fulfilled—and here am I—I who have brought this about—(*she goes down on to her knees at his feet*) without a sou left in the world—not a sou. Oh, Monsieur, can you accept such great happiness at these hands, (*she covers her face with her hands*)—

(HARPAGON *also covers his face with his hands.*)

—and see the owner of them starve? (*She peeps through her hands at* HARPAGON *to judge the effect of her act.*)

HARPAGON (*peeping through his hands at her; embarrassed and hesitating*). Er—well, of course—looked at like that. (*He rises.*) I *do* realize—(*he extends a hand to* FROSINE *and assists her to rise*) there's no doubt—I'm—I'm very much in your debt. (*He takes a purse from his pocket, fumbles in it, extracts a few coins and rattles them.*) Yes—very much. (*He pauses and looks at the coins.*) Good heavens! I never paid the gardener! I've only just enough here.

(FROSINE *makes a grab at the purse and money.*)

(*He quickly returns the coins and purse to his pocket, dodges* FROSINE, *and almost runs up* L.C.) Oh, what's to become of me, what's to become of me.

(FROSINE *runs after him, but he exits quickly up* L.)

FROSINE (*up* C.). Become of you! Become of you! May your body shrink to the size of your soul and be swept on to the floors of hell—a sizzling speck of dirt. (*She moves down* C.) So much for you. But I've not done with him yet—oh no—not by a long chalk. (*She pauses.*) Now, let me see, what next? Yes—I have to fetch Mariane, and bring her here, to the party. I don't envy her the first sight of him—but I *do* envy her his fortune. And when *that's* hers, I'll get my share of it.

She curtsies, turns and exits up L. *as— the* CURTAIN *falls.*

ACT II
SCENE 1

SCENE.—*The same. Afternoon.*

When the CURTAIN *rises, the stage is empty. After a moment,* HARPAGON *enters quickly down* L. *He carries a small sheet of paper on which he has noted the arrangements for the party.*

HARPAGON (*as he enters; calling*). Master Jacques. (*He crosses and calls off down* R.) Master Jacques. (*He turns, crosses and calls off up* L.) Master Jacques.

(JACQUES *enters down* R.)

JACQUES. Yes, master.

HARPAGON (*turning and moving* R.C.). Those two good-for-nothings—are they about?

JACQUES. Waiting for you.

HARPAGON. Fetch 'em in.

(JACQUES *exits down* R. *The* 1ST *and* 2ND SERVANTS *enter down* R. JACQUES *follows them on and remains standing down* R. *The* 1ST SERVANT *moves up* R. *of* HARPAGON, *the* 2ND SERVANT *moves* L. *of the settee.*)

Now then, come along. Come on in. (*He taps his paper.*) I want to give you your orders for the party this evening. You two have to look after the drinks—hand the glasses round. (*To the* 2ND SERVANT.) But don't go running at people every time you see an empty glass—or think they look thirsty. No, let 'em ask. And don't hear the first time. Let 'em ask again—keep on asking. (*To* JACQUES.) Master Jacques.

JACQUES. Yes, master?

HARPAGON. That rascally son of mine—do you know where he is?

JACQUES (*moving in down* C.). Shall I fetch him, master?

HARPAGON. Yes, tell him to come here at once.

(JACQUES *turns, runs below the settee, then towards the exit up* R.)

(*He calls.*) Master Jacques.

JACQUES (*stopping and turning*). Yes, master.

HARPAGON. And Monsieur Valere. Ask him if he'd be kind enough to step this way.

JACQUES. Yes, master.

(*He runs off up* R.)

1ST SERVANT. Shall we serve in our aprons, master, or without?

HARPAGON. I don't know. Let's have a look. Take 'em off.

(*The* 1ST *and* 2ND SERVANTS *remove their aprons.*)

Yes. That's better. Serve like that. Take care not to soil your liveries.

2ND SERVANT. Soil 'em, master! Look here. (*He indicates the front of his livery.*) There's a great black stain all down the front o' mine. Lamp oil. Been there for years. Can't get it off.

1ST SERVANT (*moving in to* R. *of* HARPAGON). And I've got a large hole in me breeches, behind. Saving your presence, they can see my . . .

HARPAGON (*quickly*). Hold your tongue. (*He pauses as he moves about the* 1ST SERVANT *and surveys him from behind.*) Oh yes, so they can. (*He moves down* C.) Well, you'll have to keep your backside to the wall, that's all. (*He turns to the* 2ND SERVANT.) And you can walk about in the middle of the room, with your tray in front of you. (*He demonstrates with his paper.*) So. Hide the stain. (*He moves down* L.C. *and turns.*) And keep a bucket of water handy—when a bottle's half empty—fill it up.

(CLEANTE *enters up* R., *and crosses below the* 1ST SERVANT *to* HARPAGON.)

(*To* CLEANTE.) What do you want?

CLEANTE. You sent for me.

HARPAGON. No, I didn't.

CLEANTE. Yes, you did.

HARPAGON. Did I? Ah, yes. (*He refers to his notes.*) When the young woman I'm going to marry comes to this house for the first time, be careful how you behave yourself.

CLEANTE. Careful, Father?

HARPAGON. Yes.

CLEANTE. Behave myself?

HARPAGON. Yes.

CLEANTE. What d'you mean?

(VALERE *enters up* R.)

HARPAGON. What I say. (*He pushes* CLEANTE *up* L.C.) Out of the way. (*To* VALERE.) Ah, there you are, Valere.

(CLEANTE *moves above the armchair, then down* L. VALERE *crosses below the* 1ST SERVANT *to* HARPAGON. JACQUES *enters up* R. *and moves down* R.)

Good of you to come.

CLEANTE. But—Father, why shouldn't I behave myself?

HARPAGON. Don't ask me. How should I know? But when a man remarries, his children are usually very unpleasant about it. And I won't have it. No sour looks! Give her a welcome. Look as if you were pleased to see her.

CLEANTE. I can't say, Father, that I'm overjoyed she's to be my step-mother; but, that I shall be pleased to see her—I can promise you that.

HARPAGON. Well, mind you are.

CLEANTE. And, Father . . .

HARPAGON. That's all. Make yourself scarce—all of you. I'm busy.

(VALERE *waves dismissal to the* 1ST *and* 2ND SERVANTS, *who exit up* R. CLEANTE *exits up* L.)

HARPAGON (*moving down* C.). Now, Master Jacques, *your* orders—and I've left you to the last.

(VALERE *moves to the stool and sits.*)

JACQUES (*moving in to* R. *of* HARPAGON). One moment, master. Are you speaking to your cook, or your coachman—for I'm both.

HARPAGON. I know that.

JACQUES. And which are you speaking to?

HARPAGON. I'm speaking to *you.*

JACQUES. Yes, master, but I should like to do this properly. Do you speak to me as cook or coachman?

HARPAGON. Cook.

JACQUES. Very good, master.

HARPAGON (*turning to* VALERE). Now, Valere—

(JACQUES *turns and exits quickly up* R.)

—I shall want your advice, if you'd be so good. (*He turns.*) Master Jacques . . . Hullo, where is he? Where's he gone to? (*He calls.*) Master Jacques.

(JACQUES *runs on up* R. *He wears a large white chef's cap, and is tying on a white apron.*)

What's all this?

JACQUES (*moving to* R. *of* HARPAGON). Your cook, master—awaiting orders.

HARPAGON. Well—I'm giving supper to some friends.

JACQUES. I've heard so. I could hardly believe my ears.

HARPAGON. Can you give us something good to eat?

JACQUES. I can, I can—indeed I can. Only give me the money to buy . . .

HARPAGON. Money, money, money. Why will everybody talk to me about money? That's what it always comes to. The only word in their mouths, the only thought in their heads.

JACQUES. Oh, but master—my dear master, that's not *fair*. Not *just*. If you want me to cook you a dinner, I must have the food to cook. And to get the food, I have to buy it; and to buy it, I must have money. Stands to reason. (*To* VALERE.) Doesn't it, master Steward?

VALERE. No, Master Jacques, it does *not*. Anybody can produce plenty of food with plenty of money. It takes the great cook—the real artist, to make a banquet out of nothing.

JACQUES. Nothing!

VALERE. Well, practically nothing.

HARPAGON (*turning to* VALERE). Ah, Valere, Valere—what wisdom! (*He shakes* VALERE *by the hand.*) Invaluable! Such a grasp of *essentials*.

JACQUES (*moving above the armchair* L.C. *to* L. *of* VALERE). Oh, well, if you know how to make a dinner without anything to cook, (*he removes his cap and plants it on* VALERE'S *head*) you do it yourself.

HARPAGON (*sitting in the armchair* L.C.). Don't be silly. Now, what shall we want?

JACQUES. Ask *him*. (*He moves above the armchair towards the exit up* R.) *He's* the magician in this house.

(VALERE *removes the cap and hands it to* HARPAGON.)

HARPAGON. Master Jacques!

(JACQUES *sulkily turns and moves to* R. *of* HARPAGON.)

What shall we want? (*He returns the cap to* JACQUES.)

JACQUES (*moving to* L. *of the settee; grudgingly*). How many are there to be? (*He puts on the cap, takes a small slate and pencil from his apron pocket and prepares to makes notes.*)

HARPAGON. Ten.

JACQUES (*writing*). Ten.

HARPAGON. But have enough for eight.

JACQUES (*writing*). Eight.

HARPAGON. If there's enough for eight, there's enough for ten.

VALERE. How true.

HARPAGON. Eh?

VALERE. I said—"how true".

HARPAGON. Oh, yes, of course. (*To* JACQUES.) Make it seven—to be on the safe side.

JACQUES (*writing*). Seven.

HARPAGON. Well, what shall we want?

JACQUES (*writing*). Well—we must begin with a tureen of soup.

HARPAGON. That's all right. Thick, filling soup—plenty of beans in it.

JACQUES. A good rich soup.

HARPAGON. Yes—no, not rich.

JACQUES (*writing*). And then, a roast.

HARPAGON (*in horror*). A roast!

JACQUES (*writing furiously; enthusiastically*). And then some pies—delicious game pies.

HARPAGON. Pies!

JACQUES. And various cheeses—and fruits.

HARPAGON. Cheese and fruits!

JACQUES. And several unusual dishes on the side.

HARPAGON (*rising*). No, no, no. (*To* VALERE.) Stop him. You must deal with this. This man'll cook me to death.

VALERE (*rising and crossing to* L. *of* JACQUES). Good master Jacques, (*he takes the slate from* JACQUES) you must realize that Monsieur Harpagon, out of the goodness of his heart, has asked his friends here to *enjoy* themselves.

(HARPAGON *eases down* L.)

The first requisite of enjoyment is—good health. And the greatest menace to good health is over-eating. Any doctor will tell you that. (*He eases* C.) To invite people to sit down to a table overladen with a plethora of food is little better than murder; the act of a culinary assassin. Now, good master Jacques, never must you forget the old saying— "we must eat to live—not live to eat".

HARPAGON (*moving in to* L. *of* VALERE *and putting his right hand on* VALERE'S *left shoulder*). Oh, beautiful, beautiful! What is it? "Eat to live; not live to eat." (*He eases down* R.C.) I'll have that engraved over my dining-room in letters of gold.

(VALERE *looks sharply at* HARPAGON.)

Well—that look like gold.

VALERE (*giving the slate to* JACQUES). There's no need for you to worry yourself about your supper party, Monsieur Harpagon. I'll see to all that. (*He moves above the armchair* L.C. *to* L. *of it.*)

HARPAGON. Good. Very good. Now—about getting the girl here. Do you think I ought to send the carriage for her?

JACQUES. Excuse me, master.

HARPAGON. *What* is it?

JACQUES. You wish to talk to your coachman?

HARPAGON. About the carriage . . .

JACQUES (*moving quickly up* R.). One moment, master.

(*He exits up* R.)

HARPAGON (*turning to* VALERE). What d'you think? Send the carriage? Might be a good thing—just for once. (*He sits in the armchair* L.C.)

(JACQUES *enters up* R. *He wears a battered top hat and carries a long whip.*)

JACQUES (*moving* C.). About the carriage? (*He cracks the whip.*)

HARPAGON. I want you to get it out, give it a clean.

JACQUES. Delighted.

HARPAGON. And the horses . . .

JACQUES. Impossible.

HARPAGON. Why?

JACQUES. Not fit to go out.

HARPAGON. Why shouldn't they be fit? What's wrong with 'em? They never do any work.

JACQUES. They never get anything to eat. I know— with us humans—the less you do, the more you eat; but, with the poor beasts, they'd rather do more work and get more food. (*He pauses.*) They get nothing. Except what I give 'em, myself—out of my own mouth, as you might say. I'm *fond* of 'em. I love 'em. (*He pauses.*) They're my best friends. It's hard to see your best friends starve.

VALERE (*to* HARPAGON). In any case, master, we shall want him in the kitchen. It's not far, I'll drive them myself.

JACQUES (*moving down* R.). Just as you please. And I'd sooner they died under *your* hand than mine.

VALERE. Master Jacques, you're a trouble-maker.

JACQUES. Master Steward, you are a busy-body.

HARPAGON (*rising; to* JACQUES). Be quiet!

JACQUES (*moving* R.C., *below the settee*). I won't!

HARPAGON (*moving* C.). You won't!

JACQUES (*moving in to* R. *of* HARPAGON). I won't!

HARPAGON. You answer me back?

JACQUES. I do!

HARPAGON. You dare!

JACQUES. I dare!

(*There is a pause as* HARPAGON *crosses below* JACQUES, *down* R.)

HARPAGON. Monstrous!

JACQUES (*following* HARPAGON *down* R.). For your own sake . . .

HARPAGON. Eh?

JACQUES. You know, really, master, I'm quite fond of you. God knows why—but I am. I like you better than anyone.

HARPAGON. Do you?

JACQUES. After the horses. And—(*he points to* VALERE *and whispers*) if you only knew the *truth*.

HARPAGON. The truth?

JACQUES. About him.

156

HARPAGON. About him?

VALERE (*taken by surprise; to the audience*). What's coming now? (*He moves above the armchair* L.C.)

JACQUES (*to* HARPAGON). How you're being deceived.

HARPAGON. Deceived?

JACQUES. That's what I said.

VALERE (*moving* C.). Master Jacques, be careful.

JACQUES (*moving to* R. *of* VALERE). I won't be careful. I've done with being careful. I'm going to tell—the truth.

VALERE (*angrily*). Get back to your kitchen.

JACQUES. Ah, you see. He's afraid. He knows I know.

HARPAGON. Know *what?*

JACQUES. The truth.

VALERE (*anxiously*). Master, is this necessary?

HARPAGON. Let him go on.

(VALERE *breaks down* L.)

JACQUES. Master! That man there.

(VALERE *moves up* L.)

Your new steward—whom you engaged only the other day; and already trust more than I've ever known you trust anyone; and treat better, too. If you only knew what he really is. He's not just a common servant—he's more than that. He's a . . .

VALERE (*in great agitation*). Master Jacques! (*He moves quickly up* C.) Can't you keep your mouth shut?

HARPAGON. Come along, out with it.

JACQUES. He's a fawning flatterer—that's all he is.

(VALERE *smiles, breaks up* L., *and mops his face with relief.*)

I know. *I* can see thro' him. And I know if *I* could do as he does, lie and flatter, and fawn, I should probably get double the wages and half the work. But *I* can't. No, I *like* the truth. I've a kind of *feeling* for it, if you know what I mean. I always tell it—(*he moves in to* L. *of* HARPAGON) and master, oh my *dear* master, when I hear the *lies* that he tells you—that you're good, and wise, and generous—not a word of truth in it—it breaks my heart. If you only knew what people really say about you.

HARPAGON. And what do people really say about me?

JACQUES. They say . . . (*He breaks off and pauses.*) No—you'd be terribly angry if I told you.

HARPAGON. I shall be terribly angry if you don't.

VALERE (*easing down* L.). Master, you won't listen to this impertinence.

JACQUES (*turning and moving* R.C.; *to* VALERE; *angrily*). And don't *you* come butting in—filling his ears with your dishonesty. Have you *no* respect for him? You know, as well as I do, he's known as the greatest scallywag in the town.

(HARPAGON *moves to* R. *of* JACQUES.)

The meanest old skinflint in all France. A thief; a usurer . . .

(HARPAGON *gives* JACQUES *a crack across the shins with his stick.*)

(*He yells.*) Wow!

HARPAGON. Usurer, eh? (*He kicks* JACQUES' *right shin.*)

JACQUES. Wow! (*He bends and rubs his shin.*)

HARPAGON (*kicking* JACQUES' *backside*). A thief!

JACQUES (*straightening up*). Wow!

HARPAGON (*kicking him again*). A skinflint!

JACQUES. Wow! (*He falls on his face, his head to* L., *his feet to* R.)

HARPAGON. Double wages and half the work, eh? From today, you get half wages and double the work. And next time you tell me the truth, out you go. (*He moves below* JACQUES, *faces up* L., *raises his foot to kick him, then pauses and gazes off.*) Who's that? (*He runs up* C. *and looks off up* L.) Someone in the garden. It's that rascally man of my rascally son. What's he doing? (*He calls.*) Hi! You! Come away from those currant bushes.

(*He exits quickly up* L. JACQUES *rises.*)

VALERE (*moving to* L. *of* JACQUES *and laughing kindly at him*). Oh, good master Jacques, (*he takes hold of* JACQUES' *left arm*) I'm afraid, once again, your devotion to truth hasn't done you a great deal of good.

JACQUES (*shaking himself free; furiously*). What right have you to laugh at me, eh? (*He picks up his whip.*) Laugh when you get a beating yourself, not when somebody else does.

VALERE (*contritely*). Oh, no, please, please. Don't take it to heart. (*He moves above* JACQUES *to* L. *of the settee.*) After all, the love of truth is a fine thing. And if the real truth were known, of the two of us, you're the better man.

JACQUES (*turning and easing down* L.; *muttering*). Polite, eh? I believe he's frightened of me. If I bully, he'll cringe—that 'ud make me feel a lot better. (*He turns, swaggers to* C. *with a great show of bluster and raises his voice.*) Now, master busy-body; (*he pokes* VALERE *in the ribs with the butt of his whip*) master know-all; master new broom.

VALERE (*moving in to* R. *of* JACQUES). But no, master Jacques, I mean it. I repeat—I respect you. I admire you.

JACQUES. So! You persist.

VALERE. Yes.

JACQUES. You—respect me?

VALERE. I do.

JACQUES. Do you?

VALERE. Very much indeed.

JACQUES. You—admire me! (*He pushes* VALERE, *suddenly and violently, in the chest.*) None of your silly flattery with me.

(VALERE, *surprised, gives way.*)

(*He drives* VALERE *backwards to the settee in a series of pushes as he talks.*) I'm sick of you. (*Push.*) Find something to do. (*Push.*) Paid more than any of us. (*Push.*) And do less. (*He pushes* VALERE *down on to the settee and stands over him.*) It's time you were taught a lesson. (*He whacks* VALERE *across the shins with the whip.*)

VALERE (*rising quickly and snatching the whip from* JACQUES). That's enough. You go too far. You forget yourself. After all, you're only a—coachman.

JACQUES (*cringing*). *And* a cook.

VALERE (*after a short pause*). *And* a fool. A great fool. (*He pushes* JACQUES *in the chest.*)

(JACQUES *gives way.*)

(*He drives* JACQUES *backwards to the armchair* L.C. *in a series of pushes as he talks.*) You have a passion for truth, eh? (*Push.*) But no reverence for it. (*Push.*) You babble it. (*Push.*) You blurt it out. (*He pushes* JACQUES *down into the armchair* L.C. *and stands over him.*)

(JACQUES *cringes.*)

And it's time *you* were taught—a lesson. (*He pauses, then hands the whip to* JACQUES, *turns and moves down* R.) There are times, master Jacques, when the truth is too naked to be seen, too sacred to be told, too brittle to be hammered. Gently does it, master Jacques, tact, discretion, manipulation. (*He laughs and demonstrates, making a gesture with the fingers of both his hands close together.*) Manipulation!

(*He turns and exits down* R.)

JACQUES (*rising and moving* C.). Very good, master Steward. (*He throws the whip angrily on to the floor down* R.) I've done with the truth. Done with it. But not with *you*—oh no, not with *you*. (*He stands gazing off* R.)

(FROSINE *enters quietly up* L., *moves to* L. *of* JACQUES *and taps him on shoulder.* JACQUES *turns, startled.*)

FROSINE. Is the old boy about?

JACQUES (*moving down* R. *and picking up the whip*). In the garden.

FROSINE. Be a good soul, and tell him I'm here, with his ladylove.

JACQUES. His *what*?

FROSINE (*moving below the settee*). You heard. Get along with you.

(MARIANE *enters up* L. *and moves* C. JACQUES, *with his eyes all the time on* MARIANE, *moves up* R., *crosses upstage, and exits up* L.)

MARIANE. Oh, Frosine, I'm so miserable.

(FROSINE *eases up* R.C.)

How I dread this meeting!

FROSINE. Oh, come now, my dear, it's not as bad as that.

MARIANE. I know, now, what it must have been like to be led to the rack. The first sight of it! (*She moves to the armchair* L.C.) And everybody around, eager to see one stretched in agony. (*She sits.*)

FROSINE (*moving to* R. *of* MARIANE). Well, of course, if you put it like that, old Harpagon isn't exactly the death I should choose. But look me in the eyes, girl. This sudden distress isn't so much because of the old man, but of the young man you've just told me about.

MARIANE. I can't deny it. I can't. Oh, Frosine, if you were bringing me to *his* house. If it were *he* who was to be my husband.

FROSINE. And you've no idea who he is?

MARIANE. No idea.

FROSINE. How often has he been to see you?

MARIANE. Not often enough.

FROSINE. Did he bring presents? Expensive ones?

MARIANE. No.

FROSINE. None?

MARIANE. None.

FROSINE. Then he's probably as poor as a church mouse. If you married him, he'd give you a baby—and that's about all you'd get out of *him*. But this old one—he'll die.

MARIANE. But I don't want him to die.

FROSINE. He's got to. It's in the contract.

MARIANE. In the contract?

FROSINE. Not in so many words, in black and white. But between the lines. Written, my dear, by the finger of time in invisible ink. And he'll leave you his fortune—and that *is* in the contract, and (*she moves quickly below the settee*)—

(HARPAGON *enters up* L. *and moves down to* L. *of the stool. He wears a pair of heavy horn-rimmed spectacles.*)

—here he comes.

MARIANE (*after a hasty glance at* HARPAGON). Oh! (*She closes her eyes and leans back in the chair.*)

HARPAGON. Ah, my dear.

MARIANE (*opening her eyes*). Ugh! (*She gazes at him in horror.*)

HARPAGON. I'm afraid I must ask you to excuse these spectacles. But the truth is, I'm not as young as I was.

(FROSINE *eases slowly up* C.)

I'm beginning to find these things useful—especially for signing contracts.

(MARIANE *glances at* FROSINE, *then resumes her gaze at* HARPAGON.)

Of course, (*he becomes embarrassed by her stare*) I know there's no need to wear spectacles to observe your beauty. No. But, on the other hand, one *does* wear them to look at the sun. (*He laughs nervously.*)

(MARIANE *looks in stricken silence at* FROSINE.)

(*He moves behind the armchair, then above* FRO-SINE *to* R. *of her.*) What's the matter with her? Why doesn't she answer? She doesn't seem pleased to see me.

FROSINE. Shy. She's shy. (*She raps* MARIANE *surreptitiously with her fan.*) A young girl hesitates to show her deepest feelings. (*She raps* MARIANE *again.*)

(ELISE *enters up* R. FROSINE *eases above the armchair, then to* L. *of it.*)

HARPAGON (*to* MARIANE). There's my daughter.

(MARIANE *rises.*)

Come to pay her respects. (*He moves to* ELISE.) Come along, child. (*He leads her* C.) Elise, this is Mariane. Mariane, my dear, this is Elise.

MARIANE (*with a curtsy*). So pleased.

ELISE (*with a curtsy*). Delighted.

MARIANE (*resuming her seat in the armchair* L.C.). I have to ask your pardon. I should have paid this visit before.

ELISE. On the contrary, I'm remiss. If I'd known sooner . . .

HARPAGON (*moving between* ELISE *and* MARIANE; *to* MARIANE, *indicating* ELISE). Big, isn't she? But rank weeds grow apace. (*He laughs nervously again.*)

(ELISE *eases below the settee.*)

MARIANE (*turning to* FROSINE). Detestable creature!

HARPAGON (*moving behind the armchair* L.C.; *to* FROSINE). What's she say?

(CLEANTE *enters up* R.)

FROSINE. She's overwhelmed. Now she's seen you, her feelings are even stronger than she expected.

HARPAGON (*moving down* L. *of the armchair; to* MARIANE). Oh, my dear; and I'm overwhelmed by your opinion of me. Ah, there's my son. (*He moves above the armchair to* R. *of it.*)

(MARIANE *turns and whispers to* FROSINE, *who is* L. *of her.* CLEANTE *eases* C.)

Come along, my boy, come along. (*He speaks out of the corner of his mouth to* CLEANTE.) Remember what I told you. (*To* MARIANE.) Mariane, my love—this is my son, Cleante.

(MARIANE, *with her eyes downcast, rises.*)

Cleante, my boy, this is Mariane.

(CLEANTE *bows.* MARIANE *gives a deep curtsy and as she does so, looks up and recognizes* CLEANTE. *Aghast and agape, she is unable to rise from her curtsy, and collapses gracefully into a sitting position on the floor.*)

MARIANE (*with a little cry*). Frosine!

FROSINE (*dropping to the floor* L. *of* MARIANE). What is it?

MARIANE (*speaking to* FROSINE *behind her fan*). It's he.

(CLEANTE *moves* R. *and with his back to* HARPAGON, *whispers with* ELISE. HARPAGON *looks anxiously from one pair to the other.*)

FROSINE. Who?

MARIANE. He!

FROSINE. No?

MARIANE. Yes!

FROSINE (*rising*). My God!

HARPAGON (*moving down* C.). What's this?

FROSINE. Nothing.

HARPAGON. Nothing?

FROSINE (*assisting* MARIANE *to rise*). She's a little upset.

HARPAGON. What about?

FROSINE. Your son.

HARPAGON. My son!

FROSINE. His size. He's so grown-up.

HARPAGON (*moving in to* R. *of* MARIANE). Oh, that's it, is it? Of course. Yes. I understand. My grown-up children. (*To* MARIANE.) But that's nothing to worry about, my dear. (*He takes her hand.*) All the easier to get rid of. (*He passes her in front of him to the armchair* L.C.)

(MARIANE *sits.*)

(*To* CLEANTE.) Now, my boy—give her your welcome. (*He eases below the stool.*)

(FROSINE *eases above the armchair* L.C.)

CLEANTE (*turning*). What can I say? How can I speak to her? Father, may I call this young lady—Mariane?

HARPAGON (*to* MARIANE). May he call you Mariane?

MARIANE (*looking at* HARPAGON). With all my heart.

FROSINE (*moving to* R. *of* MARIANE; *with a warning cough*). Ahem!

CLEANTE (*stepping to* C. *and facing* MARIANE). Mariane—Mar-i-ane! It doesn't need my father's bidding for me to tell you how pleased I am to see you.

(HARPAGON *looks sharply at* CLEANTE.)

Pleased—is too small a word. This room, this whole house, has changed since you entered it. (*He pauses.*) There are moments in our lives that live for ever. This is such a moment.

(HARPAGON *places the stool as close as possible to* MARIANE'S *chair.*)

For me, you will always be there, as you're there now—a loveliness, unfading, as long as I have memory to contain it.

HARPAGON. Not bad—not so bad. (*He bends to* MARIANE.) A bit flowery, perhaps—but not so bad.

CLEANTE (*violently*). But the thought of being your step-son, of having *you* for a step-mother, is not to be borne. (*He breaks down* R.C.) Unendurable! Too horrible for words! An outrage!

HARPAGON. What's this? The rascal!

MARIANE (*rising; pushing* HARPAGON *down on to the stool and taking a step to* C.). No, Monsieur. Let *me* answer him. (*Forcibly.*) Young man, please understand this—I feel as you do.

(CLEANTE *turns and faces* MARIANE.)

Exactly the same. Just as strongly.

(FROSINE *raps* MARIANE *with her fan.*)

(*She raps* FROSINE *with her fan.*) And, after hearing what you had to say, to have you for a step-son, to be your step-mother, would indeed be unendurable—not to be borne.

(FROSINE *fans herself furiously and moves up* L.)

HARPAGON (*rising and crossing below* MARIANE *to* L. *of* CLEANTE). Good, good, good! I like a young woman of spirit. (*To* CLEANTE.) You got as good as you gave. Now—say you're sorry.

(ELISE *eases behind the settee.*)

MARIANE. No. Please. I'm glad he spoke as he did. (*She glances over her shoulder at* FROSINE.) I'm deeply grateful. (*She curtsies.*) Now I know where I am with him. (*She eases down* L.C.)

HARPAGON. We'll make him change his tune.

CLEANTE (*striding up* C.). Never. (*He turns.*) I shall never change.

(ELISE *eases up* R. *of the settee.* FROSINE *eases down* L. *of the stool.*)

HARPAGON (*moving up* C. *to* L. *of* CLEANTE). I give you just one more chance. Now then.

CLEANTE. Very well, Father. I'll change my tune. I'll say this—if I were in your place, Father, I should consider I had found the perfect wife. (*He pauses.*) I should (*he moves slowly to* R. *of* MARIANE) want no further pleasure than to please her—I should see no beauty in the world but hers. (*He pauses.*) To call myself her husband would be the greatest honour I could covet; (*he kneels to* MARIANE) and to be a good one, the proudest of careers. (*He takes* MARIANE'S *hands in his.*) I should want no riches, except to see that *she* wanted nothing—counting myself the richest of men, possessing her. (*He pauses.*) Not only *I* would be wholly hers, every thought, every action; but everything I owned, every penny piece.

HARPAGON (*moving* R. *of* CLEANTE). Hey, hey, hey, that's enough—no good overdoing it. Now you're getting ridiculous.

(FROSINE *grips* MARIANE'S *left arm and swings her away down* L. ELISE *crosses slowly up stage to* L. CLEANTE *rises. As he does so,* HARPAGON *grips* CLEANTE'S *right arm and swings him away* R.C. CLEANTE *notices a ring* HARPAGON *is wearing and grips his right hand.*)

CLEANTE. Mariane! Have you ever seen a diamond more beautifully cut, or that sparkles more brilliantly, than this on my father's finger? (*He lifts* HARPAGON'S *hand.*)

(ELISE, *at a sign from* CLEANTE, *moves in close to* L. *of* HARPAGON.)

FROSINE. No indeed. It certainly seems to sparkle wonderfully.

CLEANTE. Seems to sparkle! But it *does*.

(CLEANTE *loops his left arm through* HARPAGON'S *right, and* ELISE *loops her right arm through his left, securing him between them.*)

And the setting—isn't it exquisite?

ELISE (*to* MARIANE). Can you see?

MARIANE (*crossing below* FROSINE *to* R. *of her*). Yes.

FROSINE. No, no, you can't.

ELISE. Of course you can't. Not properly.

CLEANTE. You must see more closely.

(ELISE *and* CLEANTE *bring* HARPAGON *down* R.C.)

HARPAGON (*under his breath to* CLEANTE). I got it for a bad debt, and it's worth a fortune.

(ELISE *pulls* HARPAGON *round to* L. *of her. As she does so,* CLEANTE *draws the ring off* HARPAGON'S *finger.*)

CLEANTE. My father wishes you to admire it. (*He holds the ring out to* MARIANE.)

(ELISE *breaks up* L.C. HARPAGON *moves above* CLEANTE *to* R. *of him, makes a grab at the ring and misses.*)

MARIANE. Indeed, it shines bright, (*she moves to* R. *of* CLEANTE) but so hard it looks—cruel.

(FROSINE *eases to* L. *of* MARIANE.)

CLEANTE (*slipping the ring on to* MARIANE'S *finger*). Not on this hand. Now see how soft and kind its light. (*He passes* MARIANE *across to* FROSINE.)

(FROSINE *passes* MARIANE *up* C. *to* ELISE, *then breaks down* L.)

HARPAGON (*grabbing* CLEANTE *and leading him down* R.; *whispering*). Don't be a fool, boy.

(MARIANE *moves to* R. *of the armchair,* L.C.)

(*He leads* CLEANTE *up* R., *behind the settee.*) Give it back—I won't have it. I won't have it. Back.

CLEANTE (*moving quickly above the settee to* L. *of it; to* MARIANE.) My father won't have it—back. He wishes you to keep it.

HARPAGON (*moving hastily down* R., *then below the settee*). Keep it!

CLEANTE. You hear. He wishes to make you a present of it.

(MARIANE *sits in the armchair* L.C.)

HARPAGON (*turning, moving below the settee, then up* R. *of it*). I shall go out of my mind. (*He is so distracted he does not hear* MARIANE'S *next remark.*)

MARIANE. Oh, no, no, no—please. (*She takes the ring from her finger.*) I couldn't dream of it. I won't accept it.

HARPAGON (*moving above the settee to* L. *of* CLEANTE *and hissing in his ear*). You young blackguard! (*He crosses below* CLEANTE *down* R.)

CLEANTE (*to* MARIANE). Keep it—keep it.

HARPAGON (*pacing up* R., *behind the settee and down again*). This is outrageous.

CLEANTE (*to* MARIANE). What did I say?

HARPAGON (*down* R.). Does she know what it's worth?

CLEANTE (*aside to* MARIANE). You don't know how you're hurting him.

HARPAGON (*moving in to* R. *of* CLEANTE *and hissing into his ear*). Thief, thief, thief. (*He breaks down* R.)

CLEANTE (*easing towards* MARIANE). He's getting desperate. Keep it.

FROSINE. Keep it—keep it.

MARIANE. Shall I?

(HARPAGON *paces up* R.)

ELISE. Keep it. You can give it back to him later.

FROSINE. But not now; we don't want him to have a fit.

ELISE. Keep it for now—keep it.

MARIANE. Very well. (*She replaces the ring on her finger.*)

CLEANTE (*turning and moving above the settee to* HARPAGON). She's so overcome, she has no words to thank you.

(HARPAGON *glowers at* CLEANTE, *who backs away up* C. VALERE *enters down* R.)

HARPAGON (*moving behind the settee to* VALERE *down* R.). I'm upset, Valere, almost beyond endurance. But I must pull myself together. I must be agreeable—yes—yes. (*He moves below the settee to* MARIANE *and takes her hands in his.*) My dear, my dear. (*The sight of the ring on her finger forces a groan from him.*) Ooh!

(VALERE *moves up* R., *then to* C., *where* CLEANTE *is standing with* ELISE.)

My dear, would you like to be shown over the house? We're to have a little supper later, when the Seigneur comes. I'm sorry we've nothing to offer you just now.

CLEANTE (*moving to* L. *of the settee*). Oh, but we have.

HARPAGON (*after a pause; turning to* CLEANTE). Have what?

CLEANTE. Something to offer.

HARPAGON. What?

CLEANTE. It's all set out in the next room.

HARPAGON. In the next room?

CLEANTE. Yes.

HARPAGON. What's set out?

CLEANTE. Ptarmigan, quail, peaches, pineapples, nectarines, grapes, sweetmeats from Tunis, and some of the choicest wines money can buy.

HARPAGON (*aghast*). Merciful God!

CLEANTE (*moving down* R.). You wanted her to have a real welcome, so I ordered them, and—had them put down to your account.

HARPAGON (*moving quickly up* R.). Put down to . . . Oh! Oh! (*He stops and turns.*) Valere, did you know about this? (*He grabs* VALERE.) Choice wines!

(*He turns and exits hurriedly up* R., *dragging* VALERE *off with him.*)

ELISE (*moving quickly to* MARIANE). Darling Mariane.

(MARIANE *rises.* FROSINE *moves above the armchair* L.C.)

My brother has told me. (*She leads* MARIANE *to the settee.*)

MARIANE. How kind you are. I hope you'll always be my friend, whatever happens. It will make—whatever happens, so much easier to bear

(*together*).

ELISE. I'm so happy to meet you; to make your acquaintance; to become friends; and alas, to tell you how sorry I am.

(MARIANE *and* ELISE *sit on the settee,* MARIANE *below* ELISE.)

CLEANTE. Whatever happens? But what *is* going to happen? What are we going to *do*?

MARIANE. What *can* we do?

CLEANTE. We must do *something!*

MARIANE. I'll do anything you ask; anything you tell me. Tell me what to do. I know you'll ask nothing dishonourable.

CLEANTE. Oh, if you're going to limit me like that . . .

MARIANE. Cleante, dear Cleante—in this, I'm thinking not so much of myself, or even of us, but of my mother. With me, she has practically nothing; without me, nothing at all. It was for *her* sake I agreed to this marriage.

FROSINE (*moving down* L.C.; *approvingly*). Spoken like a good girl.

CLEANTE (*with a step towards* FROSINE; *bitterly*). You got us into this.

FROSINE. Me?

MARIANE
ELISE   (*rising; together*). Yes.

(MARIANE *eases below* CLEANTE, ELISE *above him.*)

CLEANTE. Now get us out of it.

FROSINE. I like that! How did I know this was going to happen? Why didn't you tell me?

CLEANTE. We didn't know ourselves.

FROSINE. Then don't blame *me*.

ELISE (*moving above* FROSINE *to* L. *of her*). But you will help them.

(CLEANTE *eases up* R. *of* FROSINE, MARIANE *moves in to* R. *of her.*)

FROSINE. Oh, well, if there's anything I can do, I'll do it. Of course. (*She kisses* MARIANE.) I'm not hard. At least, I made myself hard. (*She turns and kisses* ELISE.) The good God made me soft—and His work is the better done. When I see true love, I melt, like ice before a flame. (*She moves between* CLEANTE *and* MARIANE *and turns.*) So— let's think. (*She links her left arm into* CLEANTE'S *right, and her right arm into* MARIANE'S *left.*) First of all, young man, (*she takes them slowly* R.C.) if your father gets wind of this—only a sniff of it—out you go, into the street; *and* without a penny. (*She releases their arms.*)

(*All three turn so that* CLEANTE *is down* R., FRO-SINE *up* L. *of him, and* MARIANE *up* L. *of* FRO-SINE.)

And what then? Of course, you could starve in each other's arms—there are worse deaths.

(ELISE *moves to* L. *of* MARIANE.)

But, as she says, there's her mother. *She* has only her memories—poor fare, at the best of times. No, it's your father, my lad, that's the trouble. (*To* MARIANE.) He's set his heart on you. (*She moves and sits on the settee.*) And I don't blame him.

(LA FLECHE *enters up* L. *and moves behind the armchair* L.C. *The others, pre-occupied, do not notice him.*)

But what to do?

ELISE (*easing up* L. *of the settee*). If we only had some bargaining power.

MARIANE (*crossing down* R.). Some hold over him.

CLEANTE (*moving below the settee, then up* R. *of it*). Some of his money.

(ELISE, MARIANE *and* CLEANTE *hang their heads in despair.* LA FLECHE *makes signs over the back of the armchair* L.C. *to* FROSINE. *He points first to himself, then towards the exit up* L.)

FROSINE. Little hope of that. He would . . . (*She sees* LA FLECHE *making signs and breaks off. Cautiously.*) I'm not so sure. (*She rises.*)

(LA FLECHE *ducks behind the armchair* L.C.)

I believe I know a man who might help.

CLEANTE. Help?

ELISE. In what?

LA FLECHE (*standing up and speaking over the back of the armchair* L.C.). In getting—pardon the in-trusion—in getting some of his money.

(CLEANTE, ELISE *and* MARIANE *move quickly and group around the armchair* L.C., *facing* LA FLECHE, CLEANTE *above it,* MARIANE *below it and* ELISE *kneeling on the seat.*)

And what's more—(*he winks at* FROSINE) I be-lieve I know a woman who might help that man.

FROSINE. The man would want paying.

LA FLECHE. The woman would do it for nothing.

FROSINE. I think not.

LA FLECHE. No? Twenty per cent.

(CLEANTE *eases up* L.)

FROSINE. No!

(ELISE *rises and breaks up* C.)

LA FLECHE. Twenty-five?

FROSINE. Oh, no!

LA FLECHE. And a half?

FROSINE (*moving above the armchair* L.C.). And the ring.

LA FLECHE. What ring?

MARIANE (*removing the ring from her finger*). This ring. (*She hands the ring to* LA FLECHE.)

CLEANTE. Isn't that rather a lot?

(LA FLECHE *gives the ring to* FROSINE.)

FROSINE (*moving* C. *and putting the ring in her handbag*). Think of the people you're dealing with. A human shark . . .

(MARIANE *moves up* R. *of the armchair* L.C. *to* R. *of* CLEANTE.)

LA FLECHE. A human jackdaw . . .

FROSINE. And the risk.

(CLEANTE *and* MARIANE *embrace.* LA FLECHE *crosses to* L. *of* FROSINE.)

(*To* CLEANTE.) For your father to lose his wife is one thing, but to lose his money . . .

(LA FLECHE *kisses* FROSINE *and takes her handbag from her.*)

Think of his rage. (*She takes her handbag from* LA FLECHE.) But he'll give up anything to get it back—even Mariane.

ELISE. Oh, Frosine!

CLEANTE (*gazing at* MARIANE). Oh, Mariane!

MARIANE (*gazing at* CLEANTE). Oh, Cleante!

FROSINE. Oh, you two!

LA FLECHE (*to* FROSINE). Oh, you beauty!

FROSINE. Oh, you wretch!

ELISE (*glancing off* R.). Oh, my goodness! There's a certain person coming.

FROSINE (*quickly*). Pretend to be dancing. (*She starts to hum a tune, grabs* LA FLECHE, *and dances him down* L.)

(ELISE *dances solo behind the settee, then down* R. CLEANTE *takes a step away from* MARIANE, *but doesn't leave go of her hand. For a moment*

he stands holding it and gazing at her in adoration, then he bows low over her hand and kisses it lovingly. As he does so, HARPAGON, *followed by* VALERE, *enters up* R.)

HARPAGON (*to* VALERE). What's this? My son kissing his future step-mother's hand.

(CLEANTE *quickly drops* MARIANE'S *hand, who turns to face* HARPAGON. LA FLECHE *exits unobtrusively down* L.)

VALERE. Very praiseworthy.

HARPAGON. Very queer—I must see into it. (*He moves to* R. *of* MARIANE.) Now, my dear—you want to see the house. (*He turns to* ELISE.) Elise.

ELISE. Yes, Father?

(CLEANTE *eases down* L.)

HARPAGON. Will you do the honours. And Valere—

VALERE. Yes, master?

HARPAGON. Will you go with Elise?

VALERE (*moving down* R. *to* ELISE). Certainly, master.

(MARIANE *crosses below* HARPAGON *and joins* ELISE *and* VALERE *down* R. CLEANTE *crosses below the armchair* L.C. *to follow them.*)

HARPAGON. And Cleante—

CLEANTE (*stopping* L. *of the settee*). Yes, Father?

HARPAGON. You stop here—I want to talk to you.

CLEANTE. Yes, Father.

(CLEANTE *and* FROSINE *exchange a look.*)

HARPAGON. Now then, the rest of you—what are you waiting for? Off you go—and Frosine, you too.

FROSINE (*crossing down* R.; *under her breath to* CLEANTE *as she passes him*). Be very careful—I think he saw.

(ELISE, MARIANE, FROSINE *and* VALERE *exit down* R.)

HARPAGON (*moving slowly to the stool and sitting*). And now, my boy. (*He pats his armchair, motioning* CLEANTE *to sit.*)

CLEANTE (*moving cautiously to the armchair*). Now what, Father? (*He sits.*)

HARPAGON (*after a pause*). What d'you think of her?

CLEANTE (*very cautiously*). Er—what do I think of her?

HARPAGON. Yes.

CLEANTE. Of Mariane?

HARPAGON. Of course.

CLEANTE. Er—oh—so, so!

HARPAGON. Eh? So-so. That's all?

CLEANTE. Well, (*he relaxes and turns to* HAR-PAGON) to tell the truth, Father, frankly, I was disappointed. Her figure is awkward; her pretti-ness ordinary; and her manner both coy and in-sipid. Mind you, I wouldn't say a word against her. As step-mothers go, I'd as soon her as anyone.

HARPAGON. But the things you said to her?

CLEANTE. Oh, trifles, my dear Father, trifles—thrown off more to please you than her.

HARPAGON. Then she doesn't attract you?

CLEANTE. Good heavens—no.

HARPAGON. Not in the least?

CLEANTE. No. Not in the least.

HARPAGON (*after a pause*). A pity. (*He rises and crosses to* C.) A great pity.

CLEANTE. A pity, Father?

HARPAGON (*over his shoulder*). I'm sorry.

CLEANTE. Sorry?

HARPAGON (*easing to* L. *of the settee*). Quite knocks it on the head.

CLEANTE. What on the head?

HARPAGON. An idea of mine.

CLEANTE. What idea?

HARPAGON (*sitting on the settee, at the* R. *end of it*). The fact is, when I saw her here in my house, face to face, I made up my mind to drop the whole thing. But then, as I'd offered my hand to the girl, given my word, I couldn't just put her out into the street, could I? No—I thought I'd give her to you.

CLEANTE (*rising suddenly*). Give her to me?

HARPAGON. Yes.

CLEANTE. In marriage?

HARPAGON. My dear boy, what d'you think? Yes, of course.

CLEANTE (*moving up* C. *and turning; after a pause*). Father, (*he pauses*) my dear Father, for *your* sake, and to please *you,* I'll marry her.

HARPAGON. Although she's—awkward, and—or-dinary, and—what was it coy and insipid? And she doesn't attract you. No—not in the least.

CLEANTE (*moving* C.). Out of my love for you, I'll make the sacrifice.

HARPAGON (*rising and moving to* R. *of* CLEANTE). Out of my love for you, I won't accept. (*He pauses.*) What d'you take me for? Forcing a child of mine against his will—'tisn't in my nature.

CLEANTE. But, perhaps, Father, after we're mar-ried, love may come. They say it does happen like that.

HARPAGON (*easing to the settee*). I won't risk it; couldn't have it on my conscience. As I say, it's a pity—but I must have her myself. (*He sits on the settee at the* R. *end of it.*)

CLEANTE (*moving to the settee and sitting* L. *of* HARPAGON). Father, I must open my heart to you.

HARPAGON (*half turned from* CLEANTE). Do, my boy, do; that's what I want.

CLEANTE. I love her. Desperately—ever since I first set eyes on her. I want to marry her; more than anything in the world. I was going to ask your con-sent to our marriage; but, when you told me of your plan, out of my great respect for you, I held my tongue.

HARPAGON. Have you known her for a long time?

CLEANTE. Not long.

HARPAGON. Have you been to her house?

CLEANTE. Oh, yes.

HARPAGON. Often?

CLEANTE. Very often; considering what a short time I've known her.

HARPAGON. Have you told her of your feeling for her?

CLEANTE. Yes.

HARPAGON. Does she return it?

CLEANTE. I believe she does. But, of course, she didn't know who I was. Just now she was com-pletely taken by surprise.

HARPAGON (*rising*). I see. (*He suddenly crosses below* CLEANTE *to* C. *and turns sharply to face him. His voice runs up the best part of an octave, into a screech.*) You young dog!

(CLEANTE *rises, startled.*)

Is there no devilry you're not capable of? A sink of lies and deception—that's what you are. God knows where you get it from!

CLEANTE. A sink of deception? I?—and you've deceived me into telling you.

HARPAGON. And I won't have you poaching on my preserves.

CLEANTE. Poaching! It's *you*—trespassing. I was there first.

HARPAGON. There first! You'd never have been there at all if it hadn't been for *me*.

CLEANTE (*angrily*). I'll never give her up.

HARPAGON (*raising both his hands threateningly over his head*). I can't keep my hands off you.

(JACQUES *enters up* R.)

CLEANTE
HARPAGON   (*together*).   You'd better . . .
                              I can't, I can't . . .

JACQUES (*running down between* CLEANTE *and* HARPAGON, *separating them*). Hey, hey, hey— what's this? My dear old master—my good young master.

HARPAGON (*crossing below* JACQUES *and* CLEANTE *to* R.). Good? There's nothing good about him; but he wants a good beating.

(CLEANTE *moves to* R. *of the armchair* L.C. *and turns.*)

JACQUES (*moving to* L. *of* HARPAGON). Oh, no, no. Beat me, Masters, if it'll do you any good; but not your own flesh and blood.

HARPAGON. If you knew what had happened— you'd condemn him, without another thought. You shall judge! I'll tell you; and you shall be the judge between us.

JACQUES. The judge between you!

CLEANTE (*moving to* L. *of* JACQUES). I agree to that.

JACQUES. As you will, dear master—as you will. Oh, master Cleante, don't stand there, looking so fierce. (*He pushes* CLEANTE *across to* L. *of the stool.*) A little further off, my good boy—a little further off, if I'm to be the judge. There—(*he turns and moves to* L. *of* HARPAGON) while I listen to what your father has to say.

(*During the next speech,* HARPAGON *takes hold of* JACQUES' *right arm with his left hand, and walks him around the settee, first below it, then up* R. *of it, then above it, and finishing* L. *of it.*)

HARPAGON. I decide to remarry; choose the lady; make the arrangements—and, if you please, along comes my son, and informs me he proposes to marry the lady himself.

JACQUES. Oh dear, dear, dear. No, no, no.

HARPAGON. Oh, dear, dear, dear. Yes, *yes,* YES! And he won't give way. No obedience. No respect. Just defiance. (*He sits on the settee.*) What d'you think of that?

JACQUES. Shocking. He can't be serious. (*He runs around the armchair* L.C., *then down* L. *of it to* L. *of* CLEANTE.) No, master Cleante.

(*During his next speech,* CLEANTE *takes hold of* JACQUES' *right arm with his left hand, and walks him around the armchair and stool, first below them, then up* C., *then above them, down* L. *of them, finishing below the stool.*)

CLEANTE. Jacques, in the town, I meet the loveliest young woman you've ever set eyes on. I bow; she smiles. I fall in love; and, miracle of miracles, she loves me—and now I find my father proposes to buy her for himself. What d'you think of that?

JACQUES. Oh, shocking, shocking, shocking. He must be joking.

CLEANTE (*sitting on the stool*). A very bad joke.

JACQUES (*crossing down* C.; *to the audience*). *Now what am I to do? There's only one thing I know— the truth's no good.* (*He moves to the settee and sits on it,* L. *of* HARPAGON.) Master—it's all a mistake. He says he doesn't want to marry the lady—if you'll find him someone else he can be happy with.

HARPAGON. If he'll give up Mariane, he can have anyone he chooses—anyone.

JACQUES (*rising*). Leave it to me. (*He crosses to the armchair and sits. To* CLEANTE.) Master, it's all a mistake. It's the way you behave makes him so angry. He'll let you marry the lady you love, if you'll only show him more respect.

CLEANTE. If he'll give me Mariane, my respect of him will be unbounded.

JACQUES (*rising*). Leave it to me. (*He crosses to* HARPAGON.) It's all arranged.

HARPAGON. Thank God for that!

JACQUES (crossing to CLEANTE). It's all fixed up.

CLEANTE. Heaven be praised!

JACQUES (moving C. and looking from CLEANTE to HARPAGON). There, my masters! Gently does it, gently—tact, discretion. (He moves down C. To the audience.) They were quarrelling all for the want of a little—(he demonstrates as VALERE did earlier in the Scene, making a gesture with the fingers of both his hands close together, but cannot remember the word) er—what he said.

CLEANTE (rising and easing down L.) Jacques— you're a good fellow.

(JACQUES moves in to R. of CLEANTE.)

(He takes a coin from his pocket.) You deserve something for yourself. (He gives the coin to JACQUES.) Take that.

JACQUES (taking the coin). Oh, thank you, master. (He gapes at the coin.) Thank you.

HARPAGON (rising). Jacques! And I, too. (He eases down R.)

(JACQUES crosses to HARPAGON and holds out his hand.)

I'm obliged to you. (He puts his hand in his trousers pocket.) You deserve a reward. I—all my life, (he brings an extremely dirty khaki hand-kerchief out of his pocket) I shall be in your debt. (He blows his nose.)

JACQUES. Thank you, master, thank you.

(He turns, moves up R. and exits. CLEANTE and HARPAGON at opposite sides of the stage, in mutual embarrassment, take side-long glances at each other.)

CLEANTE (after a pause). Father, (he pauses and takes a step towards C.) I must ask your— pardon—your forgiveness for my bad manners, and my bad temper.

HARPAGON (taking a step towards C.). Oh, that's all right, my boy, that's all right.

CLEANTE (taking another step). I can only say I'm very sorry.

HARPAGON (taking another step). And I—that I'm overjoyed to find you so reasonable, so under-standing, so considerate.

CLEANTE (taking another step). How generous of you to overlook all my faults.

HARPAGON (taking another step). Oh, it's easy enough to forgive the exuberance of youth, as long as it's realized that there is something due to our years.

CLEANTE (taking another step). Indeed, indeed, yes—I promise, never in my life, shall I forget this.

HARPAGON (moving in to R. of CLEANTE). And I promise—if ever there's anything you want, just ask me, (he puts his left arm over CLEANTE's right shoulder and kisses him French fashion on the right cheek) and you shall have it. (He kisses CLEANTE on the left cheek and pats his back with his left hand.)

CLEANTE (over HARPAGON's left shoulder). What more can there be to ask—now that you've given me Mariane?

HARPAGON (after a pause). I beg your pardon? (He breaks from CLEANTE.) I don't think I quite heard. Say that again.

CLEANTE. I was only saying, dear Father—what more can I want now you have given me Mariane?

HARPAGON. And who, dear Son—if I may ask—said anything about giving you Mariane?

CLEANTE. You.

HARPAGON. I?

CLEANTE. But, of course! Just this moment.

HARPAGON. But it was you, who renounced her.

CLEANTE. I?

HARPAGON. But of course! Just this moment.

CLEANTE. Most certainly not.

HARPAGON. Not?

CLEANTE. Never!

HARPAGON. What's this? You mean, in spite of all you've just said, in spite of having given me your solemn word, you're going back on it; within a few moments?

CLEANTE. As you're incapable of keeping a promise for more than ten seconds—yes. Yes. A thousand times yes.

(HARPAGON suddenly slaps CLEANTE's right cheek. There is a pause for a few moments as CLEANTE stands too surprised to speak or move, then he puts his hand to his cheek, crosses slowly below HARPAGON to R. and turns.)

HARPAGON (*turning furiously to* CLEANTE). Out you go! D'you hear? Out! Out of my house! Out!

(LA FLECHE *enters quietly down* L. *He carries a large casket-like box clasped in his arms. It is about all he can manage; and embarrassed by its weight, he makes violent and quite unintelligible signs behind* HARPAGON'S *back to* CLEANTE—*who stands staring, agape, at this surprising phenomenon.*)

(*Unaware of* LA FLECHE, *he continues without interruption.*) Out! I never want to see your face again. Never! I cast you forth. I disown you. I renounce you. I disinherit you—d'you hear?

(CLEANTE *continues to stare over* HARPAGON'S *shoulders at* LA FLECHE.)

You're renounced, disinherited, disowned, cast forth. (*He pauses.*) Confound it, boy, you might listen when I'm talking to you. (*He realizes that* CLEANTE *is staring agape, with eyes that are not focusing on him, but on something behind his back.*) *What* is it? What's the matter? What have you seen? What are you staring at?

(LA FLECHE, *still with the casket in his arms, exits quickly down* L.)

Something in the garden? (*He turns and looks up* L.) What was it? What did you see? (*He moves quickly up* C. *and looks off* L.) Something unusual? Something unusual in the garden? You must have done.

(*He exits hurriedly up* L. CLEANTE *watches him go and takes a few mystified steps after him.* LA FLECHE, *still with the casket, enters down* R.)

LA FLECHE (*calling*). Master!

CLEANTE (*turning to* LA FLECHE). Well, what is it? (*He moves to* L. *of* LA FLECHE.) What do you want?

LA FLECHE (*mysteriously*). Under the currant bushes!

CLEANTE. Currant bushes? What *is* all this? What are you talking about? What have you there?

HARPAGON (*off* L.; *calling*). Thieves! Thieves!

LA FLECHE. Listen.

HARPAGON (*off* L.; *calling*). Thieves! Help! Thieves!

LA FLECHE. Quick, master—out of his way.

(*He turns and exits quickly down* R., *followed by* CLEANTE, *as* HARPAGON *enters hurriedly up* L. *He is utterly distraught, and runs madly about the stage.*)

HARPAGON. Thieves! Thieves! Murder! Fire! I'm finished; I'm done for. (*He runs down* C.) I'm lost. I've been robbed. Robbed, robbed, robbed. (*He runs up* C.) My money! It's gone! It's not there! Somebody's taken it. Who can have taken it? Who? Who? Who, who, who, who, who, who, who? (*He sobs.*) Whooo, whooo? (*He moves to* L. *of the settee.*) Stolen! Stolen! Somebody's stolen it! Where have they gone? (*He moves above the armchair* L.C.) Where are they hiding? (*He moves up* C.) They must be somewhere! Of course they must. Somewhere. Oh, if I could lay my hands on 'em. (*He grips his left wrist with his right hand.*) My hands on 'em. Oooooh! Oooooh! Wowh! What's the matter? What's happening? (*He moves down* C.) Something's hurting! (*He looks at his hands.*) Oh, look. (*To the audience.*) I've got hold of myself! (*He waggles his left hand, the wrist still gripped.*) I've arrested myself. (*He releases his grip.*) I don't know where I am. I don't know what I'm doing. I can't believe it. I can't. Gone! All gone! Ten thousand crowns. (*He pauses.*) Ah, my money! My poor dear money—where are you now? They've taken you away from me. (*He moves to the settee and sits*). How lonely you must be. (*He pauses.*) There's nothing left—nothing. No more meaning in anything. No joy—no happiness—no purpose. My comfort; my consolation; my support—gone. I shall never get over it—never. I shall die—I'm dying. I'm dead. I'm buried. (*He rises.*) I don't know what I'm talking about. (*He moves* C.) Steady, steady, steady. I must be calm—I must keep control of myself. I must think. What can I *do*? That's it—what can I *do*? (*He sits in the armchair* L.C.) Do? Do? Do? *The police!* Of course. Fetch the police. They'll investigate. They'll find it. They'll get it back. (*He rises.*) Everybody in the house must be cross-examined—everybody. They must be *made* to confess; and if they won't, then put to the torture. No favouritism. The whole household. All the servants; my own children, my son and my daughter—and me, too, if necessary. (*He moves* C.) Now, which of 'em do I suspect? (*He pauses.*) I suspect 'em *all*. (*He sits again in the armchair* L.C.) As I think of each one, I'm sure they did it. (*He suddenly claps his hands over his ears.*) I can hear 'em laughing! They're laughing at me. Why? Why are they laughing? (*He rises.*)

Because they *all* did it. They've all taken my money. That's it. They've all got a share of it. (*He moves down* C.) Laugh, laugh, laugh away. But I'll be revenged. Wait. (*He moves to the armchair* L.C. *and holds on to it.*) Wait till I fetch the police—and the detectives and the inspectors and the superintendents; I'll fetch 'em all—and the magistrates, and the justices, and the judges and the hangman—with his gallows. I'll hang 'em all! I'll hang the whole world! And if that doesn't get my money back—(*he moves up* R.) I'll hang myself.

He exits up R. *as—*
the CURTAIN *falls.*

SCENE 2

SCENE.—*The same. Early evening.*

When the CURTAIN *rises, the stage is empty. Almost immediately, the* JUSTICE OF THE PEACE *enters up* R., *followed by* HARPAGON *and the* CLERK TO THE JUSTICE. *The* CLERK *carries a small folding stool, a note-book and pencil, and a sheaf of papers.*

JUSTICE (*as he enters; fussily*). You can leave it all to me, good Monsieur Harpagon, all to me. (*He moves to* R. *of the armchair* L.C. *and turns.*)

(*The* CLERK *moves up* C., *opens the stool, sits on it, and prepares to take notes.* HARPAGON *moves behind the settee, then down* R.)

No need to get excited. No need to get excited. Gracious goodness me, no. This isn't the first robbery I've had to deal with. Indeed, indeed, it isn't. I only wish I had a hundred gold pieces for every thief I've caused to be hung.

HARPAGON. And that's what you've to do now; hang the thief. Catch him and hang him.

JUSTICE. Hang him!

HARPAGON. And quickly. And if you can't, I'll find another Justice who can. Every Justice in the neighbourhood must concern himself over this.

JUSTICE (*moving up* C.). Over this!

HARPAGON (*sitting on the settee, at the* L. *end of it*). And if, together, they can't get my money back—

JUSTICE. Money back!

HARPAGON. —I'll have justice on the Justices.

JUSTICE. Justice on the Justices! (*He backs to the folding stool up* C., *and without looking behind him, sits. As the* CLERK *is already sitting on the stool, he sits on the* CLERK'S *knees.*) Dear, dear, dear. Irregular. Very irregular. No. We must follow the usual procedure. We must follow the usual procedure. (*He rises.*) Now—this missing casket. (*He eases to* R. *of the armchair* L.C.) What was in it?

HARPAGON. My money.

JUSTICE (*to the* CLERK). His money.

(*The* CLERK *makes a note.*)

JUSTICE (*to* HARPAGON). How much?

HARPAGON. Ten thousand crowns.

JUSTICE (*to the* CLERK). *Ten* thousand crowns.

CLERK (*making a note*). Ten thousand crowns.

HARPAGON. Ten thousand.

JUSTICE. Ten thousand.

CLERK. Ten thousand.

JUSTICE. Quite a robbery!

HARPAGON. That's what I'm telling you.

JUSTICE. Telling you!

HARPAGON. A terrible robbery. The blackest in the whole history of mankind. And if it goes unpunished, the most sacred things in Heaven and earth are sacred and safe no more.

JUSTICE (*after a short pause*). Um—d'you suspect anyone?

HARPAGON. Yes.

JUSTICE. Good. Who?

HARPAGON (*rising*). Everybody. (*He crosses down* L.) You must put the whole town under arrest—and most of the suburbs.

JUSTICE (*moving to* R. *of the* CLERK). Irregular. Very irregular. No. (*He snatches the papers from the* CLERK.) We must proceed in the usual way, quietly and carefully. (*He turns the papers over, mixes them and generally gets them into an untidy mess.*) First, sift the evidence, then collect and confirm the proofs, and then, (*he drops the papers to the floor*) seize our man.

(*The* CLERK *rises and gathers up the papers.*)

HARPAGON (*moving below the armchair* L.C.). I can't wait. Let's seize him first.

JACQUES (*off* R.; *calling*). Tie him up—tie him up! First, slit his throat—then hang him from the ceiling.

(*The* CLERK *runs behind the armchair, then hides behind* HARPAGON.)

Give his feet a good grilling and soak 'em in boiling water.

(*The* JUSTICE *crosses below* HARPAGON *and hides behind the* CLERK.)

HARPAGON (*to the* JUSTICE). D'you hear that? (*He runs up* L. *of the settee and looks off* R.) He's got him.

(*The* CLERK *and the* JUSTICE *creep to* HARPAGON, *and hide behind him.*)

He's caught the thief.

(JACQUES *enters up* R. *He carries a butcher's knife and steel, and wears his chef's cap.*)

Jacques has caught the thief.

JACQUES (*moving to* HARPAGON). Oh, master—such unexpected happenings—you could never guess—into my arms as it were, out of the blue.

(*The* CLERK *and the* JUSTICE *creep above the armchair* L.C., *the* CLERK *leading, the* JUSTICE *clinging on behind him.*)

HARPAGON (*easing* C.). Who is it?

JACQUES (*easing to* R. *of* HARPAGON). Who?

HARPAGON. Yes, who?

JACQUES. There's no who.

HARPAGON. No who?

JACQUES. Oh, master, the most divine little sucking pig.

HARPAGON. Sucking pig?

JACQUES. For the supper. I'm having it prepared in a special way of my own.

HARPAGON. Never mind about that now. (*He moves to* L. *of the* CLERK.) Never mind. This gentleman wants a word with you.

JACQUES (*after a pause; looking at the* CLERK). Is he coming to the supper?

HARPAGON (*pushing the* JUSTICE *towards* JACQUES). He wants to ask you some questions.

JACQUES. Questions? (*He sharpens his knife on the steel during the next speech.*)

JUSTICE (*nervously eyeing the knife*). Don't be alarmed, my man.

(HARPAGON *moves above the* JUSTICE *and* JACQUES *to* R. *of the settee. The* CLERK *sits on the stool up* C.)

Nothing to worry about. No need to be nervous—whatever you've done. I'll get it out of you.

JACQUES. Whatever I've done?

JUSTICE. Yes.

JACQUES. Well, as a matter of fact, it isn't.

JUSTICE. Isn't what?

JACQUES. Done. Not quite. But as soon as it is, you shall have it.

JUSTICE. You must keep nothing back.

JACQUES. No, Indeed, no. Why should I? But, if it isn't enough—well—if I hadn't the money—what could I do?

JUSTICE. Oh, so you hadn't the money, eh? What have you done with it?

JACQUES. Done with what?

JUSTICE. The money!

JACQUES. What money?

HARPAGON. The money you stole?

JACQUES (*turning to* HARPAGON). Stole?

HARPAGON. And if you don't give it back, I'll have you hanged.

JUSTICE (*moving above the settee to* HARPAGON). No, no, no, you mustn't say things like that.

(JACQUES *backs to* R. *of the armchair* L.C.)

You mustn't talk to him in that way. Most irregular. (*He glances at* JACQUES.) No. I can see by his face he's a truthful man. We shall get what we want out of him, without having to lock him up. (*He moves above the settee to* C. *To* JACQUES.) Now, my man, if you want to keep out of prison, all you have to do is confess. No harm'll come to you, and you'll be suitably rewarded.

HARPAGON. No—no!

JACQUES. Confess!

JUSTICE (*after a pause*). A large sum of money has been stolen. You're the only man who can know about it. Tell us all.

JACQUES (*breaking down* R.) Stolen! *Now* what am I to say? (*To the audience.*) Not the truth—even if I knew it.

(*The* JUSTICE *eases up* C. *to* R. *of the* CLERK.)

But what a chance to get my own back on that steward.

HARPAGON (*moving above the settee; to the* JUSTICE). What's he muttering about?

JUSTICE. Let him alone. He's making up his mind to confess. I told you he was a truthful man.

JACQUES (*turning to* HARPAGON). Master, if you must know—it was your steward.

HARPAGON (*after a pause*). My steward?

JACQUES. Yes.

HARPAGON. Valere! Monsieur Valere!

JACQUES. Yes.

HARPAGON. The only man I thought I could trust.

JACQUES. That's him. He did it.

JUSTICE. What makes you think so?

(HARPAGON *eases behind the settee, then down* R.)

JACQUES (*easing to* L. *of the settee*). Um? What—what makes me think so?

JUSTICE (*moving to* R. *of the armchair* L.C.). Yes. What makes you think so?

JACQUES. I think so, because—I think so!

JUSTICE. But you must have your reasons.

JACQUES. Oh, yes. I have my reasons.

JUSTICE. What reasons?

JACQUES. What reasons?

HARPAGON (*moving below the settee*). For instance, did you see him hanging round the place where I put it?

JACQUES. Yes, I did—where did you put it?

HARPAGON. In the garden.

JACQUES. That's right. (*To the* JUSTICE.) I saw him in the garden. (*To* HARPAGON.) Where did you keep it?

HARPAGON. In a casket.

JACQUES. That's right. (*To the* JUSTICE.) I saw him with a casket.

JUSTICE. The casket—what was it like?

JACQUES. What was what like?

JUSTICE (*moving in to* L. *of* JACQUES). The casket. (*To* HARPAGON.) We'll soon find out whether it was the missing one. (*To* JACQUES.) Well—what was it like?

JACQUES. What was it like?

JUSTICE. Yes—what was it like?

JACQUES. Well, (*he makes a vague gesture with both hands*) it was—it was like a casket.

JUSTICE. Of course, of course. But I want details. It's *size*—what about that? Was it large?

JACQUES (*looking from the* JUSTICE *to* HARPAGON). Er—small.

HARPAGON (*breaking down* R.). Oh, mine was large.

JACQUES (*to* HARPAGON). Oh—of course it was large—if you compare it to a snuff-box. I called it small because I was comparing it to the—town hall.

HARPAGON (*turning*). That's true enough. It would be small if you compared it to the town hall. (*He pauses.*) It sounds very like mine.

JUSTICE (*to* JACQUES). What colour was it?

JACQUES. Colour?

JUSTICE. Yes.

JACQUES. I'm not very good at colours.

(HARPAGON *moves in to* R. *of* JACQUES, *the* JUSTICE *moves in to* L. *to him.*)

It's difficult. (*To* HARPAGON.) How would you describe its colour?

HARPAGON. Me?

JUSTICE (*shouting suddenly*). Don't answer.

(HARPAGON *and* JACQUES, *startled, clutch each other.*)

JACQUES (*guessing*). A kind of—of red.

HARPAGON. Blue.

JACQUES (*blandly*). That's what I mean, a reddish-blue, or, (*he breaks below* HARPAGON *down* R.) as you might say, a blueish-red.

(*The* JUSTICE *breaks up* C. *to* L. *of the* CLERK.)

HARPAGON. That's right, it's mine, there's no doubt. (*He crosses to the armchair* L.C. *and sits.*) Oh, Valere, Valere! Who would have thought it? After this, I can believe I'm capable of robbing myself.

JACQUES (*looking off* R.). Here he comes. (*He runs up* R.) Master, if you want the truth, don't tell him what I said.

(VALERE *enters down* R.)

HARPAGON (*pointing at* VALERE). There he is!

(VALERE *moves below the settee to* C. *The* JUS-TICE, *then the* CLERK, *then* JACQUES, *all point accusing fingers at him.*)

The black-hearted scoundrel!

(VALERE *stops in surprise, looks from* HARPAGON *to* JACQUES, *then moves sharply towards the exit up* R. JACQUES *blocks the way.*)

(*He shouts.*) Hi, you! Come here! Come here!

(VALERE *turns and moves to* HARPAGON, *in speechless amazement.* JACQUES *eases behind the settee.*)

Well, what have you to say for yourself?

VALERE. My dear master . . .

HARPAGON. How dare you call me "my dear"!

VALERE. I beg your pardon?

HARPAGON. How dare you beg my pardon! There's only one thing for you to do now—confess, confess.

(VALERE *stares at him in silence.*)

Oh, how can you stand there and look me in the face, with the weight of your abominable crime on your conscience? What a betrayal! What treachery! I take you into my household; I trust you above all others; I treat you as one of the family—and this is my reward: this infamous, this utterly unspeakable theft.

JACQUES (*easing down* R.) Tsst, tsst, tsst!

(*There is a short pause as* VALERE *takes a step or two down* C., *then turns, and with his back almost to the audience, faces* HARPAGON.)

VALERE (*quietly*). Master—since, obviously, everything has been discovered, I'll make no attempt to deny it.

JACQUES (*moving below the settee*). My God! I've guessed right.

JUSTICE. What's this? You admit it?

VALERE (*after a short pause*). How can I do otherwise?

HARPAGON. You mean—you don't deny it?

VALERE. Why should I? For some days past, I've been meaning to discuss it with you.

HARPAGON. Discuss it?

VALERE. But now that you know, (*he takes a step towards* HARPAGON) I beg you not to be angry.

HARPAGON. Angry! Not to be angry! What d'you expect? D'you expect me to throw my arms around your neck and kiss you on both cheeks?

VALERE (*moving to* R. *of* HARPAGON *and holding on to the back of the armchair*). Monsieur Harpagon, that I've done you a great wrong, I admit.

(*The* CLERK *rises and moves slowly above the settee, writing.*)

HARPAGON. Oh, you do, do you? You go as far as that?

VALERE. But, after all, my offence is understandable.

HARPAGON (*rising and breaking down* L.). Understandable! You rob me of the most precious thing in all my house . . .

VALERE. I agree, I agree. Of course, I agree. But it isn't as if—your great treasure had fallen into bad hands.

HARPAGON (*turning*). Bad hands!

VALERE. It isn't as if I'd acted in any spirit of greed. No. From the very first moment that I entered your house, and my eyes fell—on the—object of my desire, I've been actuated only by love.

HARPAGON. Love—of my money!

VALERE. Oh, Monsieur Harpagon—no, no, no. I wouldn't have you think that—not for a moment. After all, what is money? I don't want a penny of your money—as long as you let me keep what I've got.

HARPAGON. Keep what you've got! (*He moves to* R. *of the armchair. To the* JUSTICE.) Did you hear that?

VALERE. Master, that of which I robbed you, *you* haven't lost. It's still *yours*. Nor can it ever again be taken from *me*.

HARPAGON (*crossing below* VALERE *to* L. *of* JACQUES). I'm going mad!

VALERE (*taking a step down* C.; *with deep feeling*). For never, Monsieur Harpagon, never again, in this life—whatever you may say, whatever you may do, can we be parted. Bound together, as we are, irrevocably—by a mutual passion which consumes, (*he pauses*) and illuminates us both.

HARPAGON. *He's* mad! The fear of the gallows has driven him out of his senses. (*He pauses.*)

(*The* JUSTICE *moves behind the armchair* L.C.)

(*With a sudden rush of fury, he raises his voice to a shout.*) What have you done with what you have taken?

VALERE (*looking from the* JUSTICE *to* HARPAGON). Done, master?

JUSTICE. Still in the house?

VALERE. Why, yes, of course.

HARPAGON. Intact?

VALERE. Master!

HARPAGON. You haven't *tampered,* in any way?

VALERE. Master, you insult me! (*He moves sharply in to face* HARPAGON.) You insult us both! You insult all three of us!

HARPAGON. *Three!*

(*The* JUSTICE *moves quickly down* L.)

VALERE. You insult me; you insult yourself—and you insult your daughter.

HARPAGON. What, in God's name, has my daughter to do with it?

(ELISE, MARIANE *and* FROSINE, *hand in hand, enter up* R., *cross and group up* C., MARIANE *is* R. *and* FROSINE *is* L. *of* ELISE.)

VALERE. I do assure you, Master, from the depths of my soul, she's in no way to blame.

HARPAGON. I should hope not, indeed.

VALERE. From the first, she's been modesty itself. (*He breaks to* R. *of the armchair.*) It's taken me all the time since I first came into your house, to gain her consent.

HARPAGON (*moving* C.). Her consent? What consent? Her consent to what?

VALERE. To the engagement.

HARPAGON. What engagement?

VALERE. *Our* engagement.

HARPAGON. *Ours?* Whose?

VALERE. Your daughter's—and mine.

HARPAGON. My daughter—and *you?* An engagement in marriage?

VALERE. What else?

HARPAGON (*with a great cry*). Oh, infamy, infamy, infamy! (*He suddenly grabs* ELISE.) Outrage upon outrage! Wretched girl! Wretched, wretched, wretched! (*He pulls her down* C.)

(ELISE *falls to her knees at* HARPAGON'S *feet,* L. *of him and facing* R. JACQUES *runs to* HARPAGON *and grabs hold of his coat.* MARIANE *runs behind* JACQUES *and holds on to him.* FROSINE *runs and holds on to* HARPAGON'S *left arm. The* JUSTICE *quickly hides behind the armchair* L.C.)

(*He stands threateningly over* ELISE.) I can scarce keep my fingers from your throat.

VALERE (*falling to his knees,* R. *of the armchair*). Master!

HARPAGON (*to* ELISE). I could throttle the life out of you.

(MARIANE, *almost fainting, clings to* JACQUES.)

VALERE. How can you speak so to your own daughter?

(JACQUES *turns and supports* MARIANE.)

HARPAGON (*to* ELISE). Give yourself to a servant, and a thief, would you?

(JACQUES *sits* MARIANE *on the settee.*)

(*He crosses below* ELISE *to* R. *of* VALERE.) Before you're a day older, you'll be swinging from a gallows.

(FROSINE *moves to* MARIANE *and assists* JACQUES *to bring her round. The* CLERK *leans over the back of the settee and fans* MARIANE *with his papers.*)

VALERE. Master, at least *listen* to me.

ELISE (*turning on her knees to face* HARPAGON). Father, I beg of you! (*She raises her clasped hands to him pleadingly.*) You'll look with kindlier eyes on my lover, I know you will, when you learn he's not what you think he is.

HARPAGON (*seizing her hands and throwing her to the floor*). I know that already, thank you! (*He turns and takes a step up* C.) Justice.

JUSTICE (*still on his knees behind the armchair*). Yes, Monsieur?

(VALERE *bends over* ELISE. MARIANE *rises and* FROSINE *leads her above, then behind the settee.* JACQUES *eases below the settee, then behind it.*)

HARPAGON. You heard this man confess—

(*The* JUSTICE *crawls above the armchair to* C.)

—on every count?

JUSTICE (*getting to his feet*). Yes, Monsieur.

HARPAGON. Do your duty—arrest him!

(VALERE *and* ELISE *rise to their feet.* ELISE *below* VALERE, *both facing* R.)

JUSTICE (*moving down* C. *to* R. *of* VALERE). Yes, Monsieur.

VALERE (*with tremendous ferocity*). Touch me, at your peril.

JUSTICE (*to* HARPAGON; *in terror*). I must fetch my men. (*He moves up* L.)

FROSINE (*glancing off* R.). Here's a to-do!

ALL. What?

FROSINE (*crossing up* L.C.). He's come to claim his bride.

ALL. Who?

FROSINE. Seigneur Anselm.

ALL. Anselm?

FROSINE. What's to happen now?

(ELISE *and* VALERE *cross quickly below the settee,* VALERE R. *of* ELISE. MARIANE *eases below* JACQUES, *behind the settee. The* CLERK *follows* FROSINE *across up* L. HARPAGON *stands* R. *of the armchair* L.C., *facing up* R. *The* SEIGNEUR ANSELM *enters up* R. *He is an upstanding silver-grey-haired elderly man of great distinction. He pauses for a·moment up* R.)

ANSELM (*moving* C.). My dear Harpagon. (*He shakes hands with him.*) What is it? What can be the matter? You look distraught—beside yourself.

HARPAGON. So would you be! (*He points to* VALERE.) See that fellow there—that one, with crime written all over him?

(*The* JUSTICE *moves up* C. *The* CLERK *eases behind the armchair* L.C. FROSINE *crosses below the* JUSTICE, *places herself between* VALERE *and* ELISE, *and keeps* VALERE *at arm's length.*)

He was planning to steal my daughter. He was planning to steal your wife. Well—there he stands, self-confessed. (*He eases a little down* L.) Take your revenge.

(*There is a pause.* ANSELM *treats* HARPAGON *with a slightly amused contempt. He eases a little down* R.C., *then speaks with unruffled dignity.*)

ANSELM. My good Harpagon, I assure you, I have no intention of marrying any woman against her will—

(FROSINE *sits on the settee, at the* R. *end of it.*)

—and, (*he moves to* ELISE *and takes her hand*) in particular, I would not dream of holding your daughter to any arrangement, (*he kisses* ELISE'S *hand*) if her heart (*he glances at* VALERE) is elsewhere. (*He still holds* ELISE'S *hand and speaks over his shoulder.*) But, for yourself, my dear Harpagon, if you've been wronged—why, to be sure, I'll protect your interests, as if they were my own. (*He gives* ELISE *a slight bow, releases her hand, moves to the armchair* L.C. *and sits.*)

(ELISE *moves in to* L. *of* VALERE.)

HARPAGON. Well said, well said. (*He moves* C., *points to* ANSELM, *and addresses* VALERE.) The Chief Magistrate of the Town. (*To* ANSELM.) You deal with him. (*He moves down* L.) Take over his case—and make it as black against him as you can.

VALERE (*crossing below* ELISE *to* R.C.; *angrily*). I must protest!

(MARIANE *moves to* R. *of* ELISE.)

Why should my affection, my love for your daughter be called a crime?

HARPAGON. Why—why! *You*—a rascally servant!

VALERE. True, in your eyes, I am a servant; nor can I blame you for that. It was part of my deception.

HARPAGON. Hark at him!

VALERE (*with growing dignity*). But I'd have you know, Monsieur Harpagon, I'd have you know—that in myself, I am of gentle, even noble, birth.

(*They all react.* JACQUES *eases up* R. FROSINE *rises and moves behind the settee, at the* R. *end of it. The* JUSTICE *moves behind the* L. *end of the settee. The* CLERK *crosses to* R. *of·the* JUSTICE. MARIANE *moves up* R. *of the settee, then above it.*)

HARPAGON (*sitting suddenly on the stool* L.C.). Rubbish! Stuff-and-nonsense!

VALERE (*to* HARPAGON; *indignantly*). You wrong me, Monsieur, indeed you do. Never would I make *any* claim to which I hadn't *every* right. I'll go further—there's no living *soul* throughout the whole great city of Naples, who couldn't bear witness to the truth of what I'm about to tell you.

ANSELM. Naples! Take care, young man. I know Naples.

VALERE. You know Naples?

ANSELM. Every stone of it.

VALERE. Then you've heard of the Count of Alberti?

(MARIANE *moves up* C.)

ANSELM (*leaning forward; completely taken by surprise*). The Count of Alberti?

VALERE. You've heard of him?

ANSELM. Why, yes, I've heard of him. Even, I might say, in a way, I knew him.

VALERE. You *knew* him?

ANSELM. No man better.

(*This time it is* VALERE'S *turn to be taken utterly by surprise. For a moment,* ANSELM *and* VALERE *stare at each other, then* HARPAGON *breaks in.*)

HARPAGON. What's all this? What's Naples to do with it? What do I care for Count What's-his-name? Or any count? Or anyone else?

ANSELM. Let him alone, good Harpagon, let him alone. Give him rope; and, if he goes on like this, in a few moments he'll be tied in a thousand knots. (*To* VALERE.) Well, young man, we're waiting. What more have you to tell us?

VALERE. That the Count of Alberti, of whom you've heard, and whom you profess to have known—was my father.

ANSELM. Your father!

VALERE. My father.

(ANSELM *regards* VALERE *for a moment, in utter amazement—then bursts into laughter. The* JUS-TICE, FROSINE *and* JACQUES *cross above* MAR-IANE *and group above the armchair* L.C., *the* JUSTICE *to* L. *of* FROSINE, JACQUES *to* R. *of her.*)

ANSELM (*laughing*). Really! This is too fantastic! You'll have to think of a better story than that. (*He slaps* HARPAGON'S *right knee and laughs heartily.*)

(*The* CLERK *moves* L. *of the settee and sits at the* R. *end of it.*)

VALERE (*with a step* C.; *livid with rage*). Stop that noise!

(*The laugh dies on* ANSELM'S *lips, as if he'd been struck.*)

ANSELM (*after a pause; almost whispering*). How dare you speak like that!

VALERE (*angrily*). How dare you doubt my words!

ANSELM (*rising angrily and taking a step towards* VALERE). And how dare such a claim pass your lips!

(*The* JUSTICE *moves behind the armchair* L.C., *then down* L.)

Your impudence, your audacity, are beyond bearing.

(HARPAGON *rises.*)

I suppose you made choice of such a parent— one of the wealthiest and noblest men of the city— because you knew he'd been dead some twenty years—and cannot be here, himself, to give you the lie.

VALERE (*stepping to* R. *of* ANSELM). Sixteen years ago, he was fleeing from the revolution in Naples; the ship in which he was making his escape struck on a rock and sank.

(HARPAGON *eases behind the armchair* L.C. *to* R. *of* FROSINE.)

ANSELM (*after a pause*). So! You know that much. Unfortunately for you, I can add to that. (*He turns to the* JUSTICE.) Olga—his wife, and his two children—his son and daughter; *his only son*—were with him on that ship; and perished with him, (*he turns to* VALERE) on that same night.

JUSTICE. Oh!

VALERE (*quietly*). The son was saved. I can remember those moments as if they were now. (*He pauses for a moment, and seems to look into the distance.*)

(*They are all intent on what* VALERE *is to say.*)

My father—the most honoured guest on the ship—was with the captain on his poop; I had just said good night to my little sister; my mother had taken her below to bed; they had just disappeared along the deck. I was standing by the ship's side, gazing down into the passing sea, in charge of a family servant. My hand was in his. (*He pauses.*) Below me, stars danced in the black water, above they filled the sky—the night was very still. Only the lap and swish of the sea, and the slow creaking of the ship—then a sudden grinding crash—and I found myself in the sea. I struck out; I felt an arm round me—it was the old servant; he supported me; gained a piece of wreckage; pulled me up beside him; and on it we drifted till morning. And when the dawn came, there was no sign of the ship, nor of any survivors. But before the next night fell we were picked up by a boat on its way to Spain. (*He pauses.*) Only recently, as I was at length making my way back to my native city, I saw Elise. (*He turns and moves in to* L. *of* ELISE.) From that moment, where she was, was home. (*He turns, takes a step or two up* R.C. *and with his back to the audience, looks at* HARPAGON.) I took service with her father, so as never to leave her side again.

MARIANE (*moving down* C. *a little and facing* VALERE). This old family servant whom you spoke of, and in whose charge you were—was his name—Pedro?

(ANSELM *looks startled.*)

VALERE. Why, yes of course! Old Pedro! But how d'you know? How can you possibly know?

MARIANE. I, and my mother, had hardly reached our cabin when the ship struck. (*She faces* ANSELM *and the group behind the armchair* L.C.) She seized me up, and was thrown into the sea, clasping me in her arms. Some sailors dragged us on to a raft; for days and nights we were on it; and were rescued by some fishing boats near to the coast of Africa. (*She turns to* VALERE.) How often have I heard it from my mother. My father on the poop with the captain—

(*The* CLERK *rises and with tears in his eyes, moves below the settee, then behind it.*)

—my brother on the deck with old Pedro.

VALERE. Your brother? (*He takes* MARIANE *in his arms and kisses her.*)

(*The* CLERK, *wiping his eyes, moves above the settee.*)

ANSELM (*after a pause; moving to* L. *of* VALERE *and* MARIANE). Have you any further proof of this strange story, in which you so strangely agree?

(ELISE *draws* VALERE'S *attention to the ring he is wearing.*)

VALERE (*holding out his hand to* ANSELM). My father's ring. He gave it to Pedro; and, on his deathbed, old Pedro gave it back to *me*.

(ANSELM *bends for a moment over* VALERE'S *outstretched hand to look at the ring, then stands upright.*)

ANSELM. The ways of God are mysterious. How well I remember giving that ring to old Pedro.

VALERE. You?

ANSELM. I, too, was saved! With the captain, I found myself in a small boat, but with a company of sailors whose one thought was home. They resisted every command, every entreaty to remain, even for a moment, on the scene of the wreck. They turned the boat towards home, and their oars dipped and pulled, pulled and dipped, till we beached on the shores of Italy. (*He pauses.*) Caring little whether I lived or died, I returned to Naples where I found my palace and my estates untouched—and there I have lived for sixteen years, mourning the loss of my wife and children. I came here under an assumed name to start life anew; and here, miracle of miracles, I find . . .

(MARIANE *runs to* ANSELM, *throws her arms around his neck and kisses him.* VALERE *clasps* ANSELM'S *hand, then reaches for* ELISE *and draws her to him.* MARIANE *breaks up* C.)

HARPAGON (*moving above the armchair* L.C., *then to* R. *of it and* L. *of* ANSELM). Here—hi—what's going on? Let me get hold of things—the right end of the stick. Are you saying this man is your son?

(*The* JUSTICE *moves up* L.)

ANSELM (*taking hold of* VALERE'S *left hand*). I am.

HARPAGON. Then I hold you responsible for all the money he's stolen from me—ten thousand crowns.

(ELISE *breaks down* R.)

ANSELM. Stolen money—my son?

VALERE. *I* steal your money?

HARPAGON (*moving below the armchair* L.C.). Well, you told me yourself . . .

VALERE. *I* told you?

HARPAGON. Yes—so did Jacques.

JACQUES (*moving quickly to* R. *of* VALERE). *Me?*

HARPAGON. Yes, you.

VALERE (*turning to* JACQUES *and drawing him down* C.; *quietly*). You told Monsieur Harpagon that I'd stolen his money? What were you thinking about? What have you to say for yourself?

(HARPAGON *sits on the stool* L.C.)

JACQUES. Nothing! I say nothing. (*He pauses and kneels at* VALERE'S *feet.*) Oh, good Monsieur Valere, it was you yourself taught me that truth was no good.

(LA FLECHE *enters up* L.)

Now I've found out for myself that lies are no better—so henceforth for the rest of my life I keep silent, I say nothing.

(LA FLECHE *and* FROSINE *confer in whispers behind the armchair* L.C. JACQUES *rises and eases behind the settee.*)

HARPAGON (*after a pause*). But this is terrible! If you didn't take my money, who did? I want my treasure back! I want—

FROSINE. You shall have your treasure back.

HARPAGON. —my money back.

LA FLECHE (*moving above the armchair to* C.). On one condition.

HARPAGON (*turning to face* LA FLECHE). A condition?

FROSINE (*aside*). Bait your hook with a man's weakness and watch the poor fish bite. (*She calls.*) Cleante!

ELISE (*turning and calling off* R.). Cleante!

LA FLECHE (*calling*). Master Cleante!

(CLEANTE *enters down* R. *and moves* C. FROSINE *takes the* JUSTICE'S *hand and leads him down* L. LA FLECHE *eases below the settee to* R. *of* ELISE.)

CLEANTE. It's all right, dear Father. I know where it is.

(VALERE *eases to* L. *of* ELISE.)

HARPAGON. You know?

CLEANTE. Yes, if you will give me Mariane. Now, make up your mind.

(MARIANE *moves to* R. *of* CLEANTE.)

HARPAGON. My casket—has it been opened?

CLEANTE. Yes.

HARPAGON. And the money gone?

CLEANTE. No, not a piece.

HARPAGON. How d'you know?

CLEANTE (*holding* MARIANE'S *left hand in his right*). You shall see for yourself—

(MARIANE *and* CLEANTE *kneel to* HARPAGON, CLEANTE *above* MARIANE.)

—the moment after you say—yes.

MARIANE (*to* CLEANTE). But, my dearest, your father's consent is no longer enough—for Heaven, in its great goodness, has restored me a father, too.

ANSELM (*moving to* R. *of* MARIANE *and helping her to rise*). And I'm quite sure Heaven hasn't restored you a father to forbid you to marry the man you love. (*He kisses her.*)

(CLEANTE *rises.*)

(*Between* MARIANE *and* VALERE.) So come, my dear Harpagon, agree, as I do, to this double marriage—your son to my daughter—

(CLEANTE *bows,* MARIANE *curtsies.*)

—and your daughter to my son.

(VALERE *bows,* ELISE *curtsies.* CLEANTE *and* MARIANE, *close together, ease a little up* L.C. VALERE *turns to* ELISE.)

HARPAGON (*crossing to* ANSELM *and tugging his coat*). I haven't got any money to give 'em.

ANSELM. Then it's fortunate I have.

HARPAGON. I shall want a new coat for the wedding—will you buy me a new coat?

ANSELM. With all my heart.

JUSTICE (*moving below the armchair* L.C.). And who's going to pay *me*?

(SIMON *enters up* L.)

FROSINE. And me?

CLERK. And me?

LA FLECHE. And me?

SIMON. And me?

(LA FLECHE *exits down* R.)

HARPAGON (*to the* JUSTICE). You! What do you want paying for? (*He moves to* C.) Hang Master Jacques for a false witness, and we'll think about it. (*He sits on the* CLERK'S *stool up* C.)

JUSTICE. Irregular!

JACQUES. Dear, oh dear! Beaten for telling the truth, hanged for telling lies, and my beautiful sucking pig burned to a cinder.

ANSELM (*easing down* L.C.). In which case, I propose we all repair to *my* house—where my chef will provide a wedding feast.

(*They all cheer.*)

Let the young couples lead the way.

VALERE (*taking* ELISE *by the hand*). Elise.

(*They run hand in hand up* L. *of the settee to up* R.)

CLEANTE (*taking* MARIANE *by the hand*). Mariane.

(*They run to* VALERE *and* ELISE, *and the four of them hand in hand dance off merrily up* R. *They are followed off by the* CLERK *and* SIMON. JACQUES *exits down* R. FROSINE *takes hold of the* JUSTICE'S *hand, leads him across and they exit down* R., *leaving* ANSELM *alone with* HARPAGON.)

ANSELM (*moving down* R.). Come along, old Harpagon, come along.

(*He exits down* R. HARPAGON *rises despondently and moves down* R. *As he is about to exit,* LA FLECHE *enters down* L. *He has the casket clasped in his arms. He moves* C. *and puts the casket down on the floor with a bang.* HARPAGON *turns, startled, and sees the casket.*)

HARPAGON (*with a loud screech*). Aaaah! (*He rushes to the casket.*)

(LA FLECHE, *scared, turns and runs hurriedly off* L.)

(*He falls on his knees beside the casket and embraces it.*) Oh, my own! My treasure! My precious! (*He opens the casket.*) Are you all there? Have you been ravaged? No—doesn't look like it. But how can I tell? They may have taken some from the bottom. Better find out. (*He picks out a handful of coins and starts to count.*) One—two—three . . . (*He hesitates, looks off* R., *then resumes counting.*)

The CURTAIN *falls, but rises almost at once.* HARPAGON *is surrounded by little piles of gold coins, and still counting furiously.*

CURTAIN

Patricia Raun and Christopher Howe as Mrs. Sullen and Archer
in *The Beaux' Stratagem,* Theatre Arts Department, Penn State
University. Helen Manfull, director.

The Restoration stage with pit, box, and gallery. Drawing by Jim
Hoskins

CHAPTER VI

The Restoration and the Eighteenth Century

The British Theatre of Charles II

Returning to England, we resume our story at a time when the theatre was as bleak as it had been in the days of the decaying Roman Empire. The English were not thoroughly comfortable with their reigning Stuart monarchs from Scotland. James I believed in the Divine Right of Kings and his son, Charles I, was even more autocratic. Meanwhile the Puritans had been steadily gaining in power until a series of civil wars erupted in England with the nation divided into Cavaliers (royalists) and Roundheads (parliamentarians and Puritans). The royalists prepared for battle by drinking and feasting; the Roundheads, lead by Oliver Cromwell, were well trained, earning them the title of Ironsides, and prepared for battle with devotions and prayer. In 1649 the king's army was defeated and Charles taken prisoner, a rump parliament ordering that he be brought to trial. He was sentenced to death and beheaded at Whitehall on January 30, 1649. His son, also Charles, fled to Scotland.

Cromwell took power and set up a commonwealth, a republican form of government, but under the title of Lord Protector of England, Scotland, and Ireland, he soon became a strict and rough, though profoundly religious, dictator. The Commonwealth proved a devastating time for the arts in England: statues in the great cathedrals were destroyed, paintings burned, and the theatres—considered dens of evil and corruption—were closed by an act of the puritan parliament in 1642. When Cromwell died in 1658, his less than able son, Richard, took over and the Commonwealth began to crumble. Charles II, who had fled from Scotland to France where he had lived in exile, was invited back to rule and entered London on May 29, 1660 amid cheering, rejoicing, and great celebration. A unique chapter in English history had ended: puritanism was defeated and the monarchy restored. England could now restore her theatre as well, and she did so with a glitter and brilliance that were dazzling.

Charles, in his French exile, had adopted French ways: he too could dress elegantly, keep mistresses, become an arbiter of taste, make himself a patron of the arts and of sciences, and foster the world of the mind. In spite of enormous difficulties early in his reign—the plague in London in 1665 and the great fire in 1666—Charles encouraged a lively, enthusiastic, and colorful resurgence of theatrical activity that suited the fancy of the restored English court. Two royal patents were issued: one to Thomas Killigrew, who had followed Charles into exile, and one to Sir William Davenant, who claimed to be Shakespeare's illegitimate son. Both of these men were staunch royalists.

Because the theatres had been closed from 1642–1660, there were no new nor innovative facilities for the performance of plays. At first, the two patent holders used converted tennis courts, relics of a once popular now discarded indoor sport. Killigrew moved his company, called The King's Players, to the Theatre Royal in 1663. When the building burned nine years later, the Theatre Royal at Drury Lane was built in 1674 by the famous architect Sir Christopher Wren. Davenant's group, the Duke of York's Players, performed first at Lincoln's Inn, then at Dorset Gardens, and finally at Covent Garden in 1732. These two theatres—Drury Lane and Covent Garden—remained the two licensed legitimate theatres until the beginning of the nineteenth century. The typical Restoration and eighteenth century playhouse had a large apron, comparable to the Elizabethan forestage, where most of the action took place. Two doors on either side of the apron, with a balcony above, provided playing areas similar to those of the Elizabethan playhouses. But the theatres were indoors, illuminated by candle light, and they employed the typical continental drop and wing sets.

There were three main seating areas for the lively, demanding, vocal, and highly visible audience. First of all there was the pit where the gentlemen and beaux sat on long benches—the orchestra of today's theatre. There were two tiers of galleries, the first attracting the ladies and elegant couples who went to the theatre as much to be seen and to gossip as to see the play. The uppermost gallery was held by the footmen, valets, and coachmen of the gentlemen as their own special province where they could be as noisy and rowdy as they wished. This gallery audience, however, was not treated contemptuously as these lines from a famous prologue indicate:

> To you, ye Gods! I make my last appeal
> You have a right to judge as well as feel.

The third area of seating was the boxes, the most expensive seats, reserved for king, nobles, perfumed and periwigged ladies of quality and their gallants. They nodded to actors on stage, frowned at vulgarities in the gallery, and flirted with the beaux in the pit below. And, finally, while not an extensive seating area, the Elizabethan tradition of a few select nobles and gallants placed on benches on either side of the stage persisted until well into the eighteenth century.

Adding to the color and new life to this active and intimate theatre setting was the fact that Charles II, a great fancier of the opposite sex himself, had decreed that women's parts should be played by women, a practice he had become accustomed to while living in France. The English actress became the darling of society, the object of much gossip, and the source of considerable intrigue. Audiences became passionate followers of the lives of performers, a tradition that has persisted to the present day. One of Charles's mistresses, Nell Gwynn, was a popular comedienne and a notorious personality. No less interesting were the first important women playwrights, of whom Aphra Behn was the most famous. *The Amorous Prince, The Dutch Lover,* and *The Rover*— all established her reputation as racy, witty, and entertaining.

The drama had not been so popular, so in demand, or so much a part of London life since Elizabethan times. There were flowery and elegant operas, epic and monumental heroic dramas, but most popular were the witty and brilliant reflections of high society: the restoration comedy or comedy of manners illustrated by Sir George Etherege's *The Man of Mode, or Sir Foppling Flutter,* William Wycherley's *The Country Wife* or William Congreve's *The Way of the World.* These plays, which mirrored London society, presented style, wit, and intelligence as the standards of behavior. The morals presented in the plays were relaxed by any standards; the only sin in a love affair was either getting caught or becoming too honestly involved. Pretenders to fashion, people who lived in the country, or witless dullards were the objects of ridicule in the game of love and marital intrigue. The plays demanded active, intelligent listening for the humor was verbal and intellectual; they also demanded an involved audience, addressed directly from the stage, flirted with and teased, and often made confidants in risque affairs and amours.

Taken by the upper classes and nobility as witty and bright, these comedies were interpreted by the middle classes as licentious and lewd. Perhaps still motivated by puritan ethics on the one hand and aware of changing attitudes in social decorum on the other, a preacher named Jeremy Collier wrote a pamphlet in 1698 titled, *A Short View of the Immorality and Profaneness of the English Stage*. What Collier argued for in the drama was the sentimental moralizing and conventional virtue that reflected the growing middle class taste and values. Two factions remained for some time in conflict: the supporters of the Restoration drama who saw in the comedies nothing more than an honest reflection of the taste and style of the aristocracy, and the reformers who sought a new drama to chronicle the public need for sentimental and moralistic dogma. Perhaps a parallel can be drawn with our own society in which we see the relaxed sexual codes of today's youth constantly under attack by the moral majority and fundamentalist groups. Many critics of the eighteenth century argued that platitudes and niceties were only facades which masked the seething undercurrents of the society. Such a critic was artist William Hogarth in whose trenchant and satiric prints we see the hypocrisy, the juxtaposition of vice and elegance, and the corruption that lurked beneath the surface of piety and respectability. We have chosen to illustrate this period by a play that represents the best features both of the Restoration and of the new eighteenth century drama: George Farquhar's 1707 comedy, *The Beaux' Stratagem*. Here the characters are witty and bright but they are also distinctly middle class in attitude and behavior.

As we look back on the drama of the eighteenth century, we are aware that it was vastly inferior to the brilliant British comedies of the Restoration. But a new audience was being heard. Attitudes were changing for a number of reasons. International trade and expansion was creating a new moneyed middle class with tremendous monetary power. James II who came to the throne in 1685 rekindled an old problem by his devout Catholicism and authoritarianism. In 1689 the Declaration of Rights, asserting the "true, ancient, and indubitable rights of the people of this realm," culminated in what is known as the Glorious Revolution. James's protestant daughter, Mary, and her husband William of Orange were invited to rule as constitutional rather than absolute monarchs. The will of the people was being heard in the real world, and the drama of the eighteenth century would second that voice.

Queen Anne, second child of James II, ascended the throne at the death of William III, and according to Sir Robert Walpole, "We are now arrived at the period in which the arts were sunk to the lowest ebb in Britain." During her reign, England and Scotland were united under the name of Great Britain, and upon her death in 1714, none of her seventeen children having survived her, the monarchy passed to the German house of Hanover and the first of three George's who dominated the eighteenth century. It was in the reign of George II that the power of the eighteenth century theatre was most keenly felt. While the two major patented theatre houses were absorbed in selling seats rather than offering quality drama, some interesting activity was going on in lesser houses. In 1728 John Gay's *The Beggar's Opera* was presented in John Rich's Lincoln's Inn Fields. This tremendously popular musical, employing popular ballads of the day with political satire in a low life, underworld setting, was so successful it was said to make "Gay rich and Rich gay." But the work made government officials nervous and a sequel to *The Beggar's Opera* was suppressed.

When the government finds it necessary to legislate control of the theatre, then we understand just how powerful an institution the theatre can be. This is exactly what happened in 1737 when parliament passed the famous Licensing Act dictating that all new plays must be submitted for approval to the Lord Chamberlain and that only the two legitimate patented houses—Covent Garden and Drury Lane—would be allowed to operate. Smaller theatres presumedly closed their doors; but enterprising entrepreneurs like Henry Giffard, who operated Goodman's Fields, found ways around the law so that they could claim their establishments really were not theatres at all. Giffard offered a concert for a price and at intermission presented "entertainments" free of charge. Others circumvented the law by serving food and free entertainment with the meal—the ancestor of today's dinner theatres. The Licensing Act of 1737 created a theatre of strict government control; censorship and sentimentality combined to make a drama that was mediocre. But public interest in the theatre and the dynamic influence of one of its personalities helped create a theatre that was exciting and filled with innovation.

Just as something quite extraordinary had happened with *The Beggar's Opera,* certainly the most popular production of the entire eighteenth century, something unique happened at Giffard's Goodman's Fields on October 19, 1741. A young actor named David Garrick, who came to London from Lichfield to be a wine merchant, made his debut in Shakespeare's *Richard III.* Garrick's acting was so natural, so subdued, and so seemingly effortless compared to the flamboyant histrionics in vogue that it prompted James Quin, the leading actor of the day to say, "If this young fellow be right, then I and all the rest of the players have been wrong." Quin further asserted that this upstart actor would prove a passing fancy—the Tiny Tim or Michael Jackson of his day. How wrong Quin was. David Garrick shaped a theatrical century; it was called the age of Garrick and one critic charged him, "A nation's taste depends on you." He was the first theatrical super star.

Managers of the two patented playhouses jealously had Goodman's Fields closed, and Garrick was quickly signed as an actor at Drury Lane. By 1747, at the age of thirty, Garrick raised £8,000 to buy one-half of the lease and patent to Drury Lane where he remained as actor-manager until he retired in 1775. Garrick made money at Drury Lane primarily because he believed this famous couplet written by Dr. Samuel Johnson:

> The drama's laws the drama's patrons give
> For we that live to please must please to live.

He created a popular theatre—and on his own terms. In an age that pigeon-holed its actors as to the types of roles they could play, Garrick alone was accepted in both comedy and tragedy. He revered Shakespeare, yet he bastardized the bard mercilessly. In *Hamlet,* for example, he cut Osric and the gravediggers, gave Gertrude a mad scene, added several duels, and gave Laertes's dying speech to Hamlet. In 1769 he was the primary force behind a Stratford Jubilee in honor of Shakespeare. But Garrick did not appreciate or foster the works of new playwrights, adding to public taste and censorship still another reason for the dearth of great writing in an age of tremendous theatrical innovation, much of which Garrick was personally responsible for.

The primary innovation with which we credit Garrick is his development of a more truthful, less flamboyant style of acting than had hitherto been popular. A contemporary critic wrote, "Mr. Garrick's easy and familiar, yet forcible style in speaking and acting, at first threw the critics into some hesitation concerning the novelty as well as propriety of his manner. They had been long accustomed to an elevation of the voice with a sudden mechanical depression of its tones, calculated to excite admiration, and to entrap applause." Of his great roles—Macbeth, Richard III,

Hamlet, and Lear—none was more celebrated than his Lear. A critic wrote that his movements were "slow and feeble, misery depicted in his countenance" that he had no "sudden starts, no violent gesticulation," and that he researched his role, using life models to observe and study.

Garrick encouraged other actors as well: the great comedienne, Kitty Clive; the celebrated tragic actress, Sarah Siddons who, after an unsuccessful debut, worked for six years in the provinces learning her craft, and then returned in triumph to her native city to become the greatest actress in the history of the British stage; and the perfecter of breeches roles (men's roles assigned by tradition to women), Peg Woffington. Of the male players, Garrick had no rival. Spranger Berry was the romantic hero, and the flamboyant Charles Macklin, who had been the star of Drury Lane before Garrick, continued to act until extreme old age, playing the role of Shylock in *The Merchant of Venice* when he was ninety-nine.

Besides his attempt to develop a more truthful acting style in himself and his colleagues, Garrick began to suggest historical costuming in his productions. Strange as it may seem, contemporary dress was the accepted attire whether the play being performed were *Romeo and Juliet* or *Julius Caesar*. Garrick began to change all that, to explore period costuming, and to stress that not all characters should appear in the fashion of the day. A friend of Garrick's brother journeyed from Lichfield to London to see Garrick in Ben Jonson's *The Alchemist*. Not understanding Garrick's costuming as the humble Abel Drugger, the friend reported, "Though he is your brother, Mr. Garrick, he is one of the shabbiest, meanest, most pitiful hounds I ever saw in the whole course of my life."

Perhaps the most important of Garrick's innovations, however, was his skill in conducting rehearsals. While some call him the first modern director, it can more appropriately be said that he anticipated the craft of the director. Up to this time there was no stage blocking or charting of movement. The actors simply moved as they chose, most often down stage center close to the audience. Rehearsals were minimal and began when it suited the stars to begin them. Garrick, however, made demands on his actors: there *were* rehearsals; moreover, they started on time and were guided by Garrick himself, who insisted on discipline and improved memorization. By 1765 Garrick replaced Drury Lane's chandeliers with new oil lamps from Paris that were used both as foot and as wing lights. In 1771 he brought German designer Philippe Jacques De Loutherbourg, an artist of great reputation on the continent, who ushered in a new era of spectacle with his complicated drop and wing sets which were enhanced with ground rows, rocks, mountains, fences, thus increasing naturalness and the illusion of space and distance. Under Garrick's supervision De Loutherbourg experimented with silk screens to control lighting, thus creating the first color and intensity effects in England. With all of this technical advancement, it was necessary that someone serve to direct and coordinate all of the activity.

Finally, Garrick's innovations extended to the audience whose behavior he judiciously sought to improve. In 1762 Garrick remodeled the auditorium of Drury Lane, increasing the seating capacity from 1,000 to 2,362 and doubling the profits. In doing so, Garrick irrevocably banished nobles, beaux and gallants from seating on the stage itself—a custom that had become increasingly problematic. Reports of Juliet being embraced in her tomb, Cordelia being lifted out of Lear's arms, or the head of a beaux appearing amid Caesar's assassins destroyed all sense of verisimilitude.

Garrick must have worked extremely hard. Of the thirty years that he managed Drury Lane and starred there, George II was king for thirteen of those years and George III for seventeen. Both the theatre and the company had to be ready to perform for the court at a moment's notice.

Garrick functioned as a contemporary producer, serving as his own press agent, planning and arranging seasons, programs, repertory, and supervising all elements of production, and guaranteeing the comfort and well-being of the audience.

As the century progressed, an average evening at old Drury consisted of a half-hour orchestra concert, a prologue or two spoken by one of the leading actors, a five act play, a short three act farce or afterpiece, of which Garrick wrote many, and entre-acte diversions which included pantomimes, masquerade dances, songs and pageants. All of these extra events appealed to the love of extravagance and spectacle of the ever-increasing middle class audience.

In 1776—probably the single most important year in American history—David Garrick retired and sold his share of the Drury Lane patent to a young man named Richard Brindsley Sheridan for the exorbitant sum of £35,000. In spite of Garrick's insistence that he had left Drury Lane in the hands of a Hercules, the fortunes of the theatre—and of Sheridan—declined rapidly. Although he had charm, wit and grace and was probably the finest playwright of the entire eighteenth century in England, Sheridan could not handle money and plunged the theatre more and more into debt. By the time he was twenty-nine, Sheridan had written three masterpieces—*The Rivals, The School for Scandal,* and *The Critic*—that returned much of the restoration wit and brilliance to the faltering and sentimental comedy of the eighteenth century, yet he declined ever to write for the theatre again. He sought a larger arena in the House of Commons, as a member of the Whig party. By 1783 Sheridan became Secretary of the Treasury, an ironic position for a man who was personally in debt and who could never manage the finances of Drury Lane. In 1809, Sheridan witnessed the devastation of Drury Lane by fire (just a year after Covent Garden had burned) and, broken in health and spirit, he gave up his share in the famous theatre. Sheridan died, heavily in debt, alone and forgotten in 1816. A theatrical era was ended. Both Drury Lane and Covent Garden were rebuilt, larger than ever. They continued to pander to a middle class taste that more and more wanted mindless spectacle. But many things had happened since Charles II had returned to London in great pomp and ceremony and established the Restoration theatre of wit and fashion. While the drama had declined woefully in eighteenth century England, acting had started to become a craft, scenery, lighting and costumes were becoming important in relation to the play itself, and, with them, the need of a person to unify and integrate the production. Most important of all, the theatre had changed from the plaything of the court to the plaything of the large middle classes and begins to reflect an interest and concern for the common man.

George Farquhar

George Farquhar was born in North Ireland in either 1677 or 1678. He attended Trinity College in Dublin with the intent of pursuing a church career. He left college, however, to become an amateur actor. When he was twenty, he accidentally stabbed and seriously injured a fellow actor in a stage duel, a fact which not only upset him greatly but also influenced his decision to abandon the acting profession.

By 1697, Farquhar had arrived in London to become a writer. His first play was titled *Love and a Bottle,* 1698, and he subsequently wrote a play approximately every year until his death in 1707 at the age of twenty-nine. His dramatic reputation rests primarily on his last two plays: *The*

Recruiting Officer in 1706, and *The Beaux' Stratagem* in 1707. The former was fashioned on his military duty in 1705 in which he held the rank of Captain. In the latter—his finest and final play—it is believed he drew heavily on his own 1703 marriage to a young woman from Yorkshire who led him incorrectly to believe she was an heiress to £700. Farquhar knew he was dying at the time he wrote *The Beaux' Stratagem*. Confined to his bed, he finished the play in six weeks in a valiant attempt to raise money to pay his persistent and nagging debts. The play opened on March 8, 1707 at the Queen's Theatre; Farquhar died after the third performance, an evening that had been planned as a benefit for the young author, his wife Margaret, and their two daughters. In the epilogue to the play Farquhar wrote:

> If to our play your judgment can't be kind,
> Let its expiring author pity find:
> Survey his mournful case with melting eyes,
> Nor let the bard be damned before he dies.
> Forbear, you fair, on his last scene to frown,
> But his true exit with a plaudit crown;
> Then shall the dying poet cease to fear
> The dreadful knell, while your applause he hears.

We cannot help but be amazed at the youthful high jinks of a dying playwright.

Farquhar was certainly less sophisticated than his Restoration contemporaries but he possessed an irrepressible spirit and vitality, an ability to shape a good story, characters who are vivid and alive, and an extraordinary comic sense. Yet he was somehow caught in a compromise between the sensibility of the Restoration and the new wave of sentimentality: the realistic and sardonic views contrasted with the idealistic and edifying.

The Beaux' Stratagem

George Farquhar's early eighteenth century comedy, while being a delightful romp as a theatre piece, is a highly interesting play precisely because it is so much of its own time while it also simultaneously looks back at the past and forward to the future. It represents an attempt on the part of the playwright to capture and retain the wit and audacity of the Restoration period just past as well as his endeavor honestly to reflect the growing sentiments of the rising Middle Class which would more and more dictate the direction of drama in England.

When Charles II resumed the throne of Great Britain in 1660, he brought home with him from his exile in France a taste for French drama, particularly the plays of Molière. In emulation of theatrical practices in France, Charles immediately gave his royal patents and patronage to only two theatres in the city of London and in effect dictated through his own taste and preference that the British dramatists should write plays of the French persuasion. It can be expected, then, that the classical comedies of Molière rather than the romantic comedies of Shakespeare became the models for the comedic drama of the Restoration theatres. Still, there was a remarkable and fundamental difference between the comedies that British dramatists produced and those of the French master.

As we have seen, Molière wrote social comedies in which he chastized, ridiculed and hoped to improve the social behavior of his largely aristocratic audiences. However, the theatre in London during the reign of Charles II was largely the province of the courtiers and aristocracy; commoners, usually of the same puritanical persuasion that had supported Cromwell, were distrustful of the theatre and, therefore, chose to shun it. Consequently, the British dramatists wisely wrote plays that appealed to the courtiers by dealing with a generally realistic depiction of life in the courtly circle. So, most of the plays, if not all of them, concern the romantic dalliances of the gallants of Charles's aristocracy. The aim of a Restoration gallant, if we are to believe the comedies, was to seduce as many women as possible before assuming the shackles of marriage. Marriage itself was regarded as purely a business proposition. The lady, on the other hand, sought to enjoy the favors of the gentleman without losing her virginity if she were single or without being caught if she were married.

The cardinal principle of the game was never to permit your genuine feelings to show. It was unsophisticated for the gallant to allow anyone to perceive that he might actually love the woman he was pursuing just as it was unseemly for the woman to allow anyone to know that she harbored sincere affection for the man she planned to marry. The game—and the artifice and pretense it entailed—was all. And, of course, the major weapon one possessed in maintaining the proper facade was wit. Wit, then, becomes a major component of the dialogue in scene after scene of supposedly artful banter. (Unfortunately, the wit of yesterday is not necessarily the wit of today. Consequently, much of the witty language of the Restoration comedy strikes the twentieth century spectator as peculiarly witless.) Just as the would-be sophisticate of America today tends to assume that the only suitable place to reside is New York City, the courtiers of the Restoration rather ardently believed that it was tantamount to sin to live any place other than London. After all, how could one expect to keep up with the latest fashions, the most recent cultural events or the hottest and newest gossip unless one resided where the action took place?

So, London was the only place to live, and the country outside the city was a boring desert inhabited by equally boring country relatives. One avoided one's country relatives at all cost. It is understandable then that country folk and the landed gentry become the butt of many jokes in the Restoration comedies. Merchants, trades people and the servant classes were similarly regarded with contempt primarily because they were uncultured and lacked aristocratic blood. It was little wonder, then, that the middle classes avoided the theatre and were suspicious of its morals.

Notice the subtle shift in the intention of the drama between Molière's comedies and those of the English Restoration. Molière was writing drama of social correction in which he sought to alter the behavior of all who saw his plays by underscoring the absurdity and unfairness of certain social behavior. The Restoration playwrights, on the other hand, were writing plays for a highly select audience of courtiers, plays that flattered their audiences by reaffirming their own opinions of their unquestioned superiority. In short, the Restoration comedy is designed to protect, support, comfort and flatter the in-group while excluding and demeaning the middle and lower classes. For all intents it is a highly precious drama whose one saving grace is its faithful and surprisingly realistic depiction of the behavior of the aristocratic society of the Restoration. It is truly centuries away from Shakespeare's theatre which existed for all.

By the beginning of the eighteenth century, when *The Beaux' Stratagem* was written, certain far-reaching social and economic changes were beginning to transpire in Great Britain and on the Continent. The aristocratic families which had controlled the country for centuries were reaching the ends of their inherited fortunes. The wealth of the nation was changing hands as the rising middle class, primarily the merchant segment, began to gain control of Britain's economy. The young gallant, if he were going to survive, could no longer fritter his time and money away in pursuit of pleasure; he had to think of earning a living. However, most aristocratic young gentlemen were woefully unprepared to enter the economic market place and forge a living. An easy answer to their economic plight, of course, was to seek the hand in marriage of the daughter of a wealthy member of the merchant class or the landed gentry. It would be a fair exchange of an aristocratic title for the merchant's daughter for the financial security the old man could provide. Enter Aimwell and Archer. What are these two young rakes up to? They have spent their fortunes, so they are scouring the English countryside for wealthy women to marry. Quite significantly, the action of the play takes place in the town of Lichfield, not in the city of London.

The aristocracy could no longer afford to offend the sensibilities of the middle class since they were now so fundamentally dependent on them in an economic sense. As the middle class citizen's economic status improves, he now has more time to devote to the pursuit of pleasure; consequently, he begins to attend the theatre—often in emulation of the behavior of his former social betters. The theatre, like the aristocracy, could not afford now to offend the new ticket buyer. So, the wise playwright and theatre manager began to present a drama that reflected the mores, tastes, interests and morality of the middle class. Rather swiftly, in a matter of the seven years between Congreve's *The Way of the World* (1700) and Farquhar's *The Beaux' Stratagem* (1707), those middle class characters who used to be the butt of the joke have taken center stage where they are accorded highly sympathetic treatment. Dorinda and Mrs. Sullen are daughters of the landed gentry; nonetheless, they are the heroines of Farquhar's play. Lady Bountiful is a true country gentlewoman who, while she may have a comic side, is decently big-hearted, virtuous and likable. Had Lady Bountiful appeared in a play by Congreve or Etherege, she would have been portrayed as the awkward and gauche country cousin who was the embarrassment of the aristocratic household. Now she is a woman to be admired and emulated for her generosity and goodness.

Even Cherry—the innkeeper's daughter who is a few rungs down the social ladder from Lady Bountiful—is treated with something approaching loving kindness. True, she is presented as only a rung or two above a common whore, still she is not without her redeeming virtues. Because of her undeniably low social status, she is by no stretch of the imagination a fit marriage partner for Archer. (There is, after all, a limit to social liberation and broad-mindedness even in eighteenth century England.) But what fundamental decency she possesses! For it is Cherry who warns Aimwell of the dire intentions of her father and his band of brigands; and it is Cherry who gallantly accepts the gulf in their social positions and releases Archer from all responsibility toward her where marriage might be concerned.

While Aimwell is pursuing a wealthy heiress, Dorinda, his friend Archer, like a true Restoration gallant, is engaged in a harmless dalliance with Cherry while at the same time attempting to seduce an attractive married woman, Mrs. Sullen, who, it would seem, is more than a little willing to be seduced. In any true Restoration comedy Archer would have succeeded brilliantly with his planned seduction. But such an act of gross immorality would now be an affront to the sensibilities of the middle class spectators in Farquhar's audience. Therefore, Mrs. Sullen's virtue, while being humorously threatened, remains firmly and unquestionably entact at the end of the play. However, Farquhar was daring enough to challenge his spectators on one taboo topic. Divorce was not a readily acceptable practice at the time, and yet Mrs. Sullen and her unpleasant and unsuitable husband openly discuss the obvious benefits of a symbolic divorce or legal separation which could conceivably make her available for at least a romantic involvement with Archer.

The behavior of Mrs. Sullen and Archer recall the cynical and witty conduct of lovers in Restoration comedies of decades before. The spectator is even left wondering somewhat about their ultimate sincerity. But, while Archer and Mrs. Sullen seem to be resurrecting the past drama, Aimwell and Dorinda are surely foreshadowing what is to come. Aimwell confesses to Dorinda that he has been pursuing her under false colors; he was, after all, initially attracted by her wealth. His courtship of her has been in essence a get-rich-quick scheme. But Dorinda not only forgives him; she agrees to marry him in spite of his admitted poverty. In their behavior Dorinda and Aimwell anticipate the conventional sentimental characters of the comedy that is to soon dominate the British stage.

The primary action of most Restoration comedies was fundamentally the same; the aristocratic courtiers of the plays wanted little more than to sustain the elegant facade of their lives. However, the basic action of *The Beaux' Stratagem* is different; and it is relatively simple and straight forward. The major characters are all concerned with making the right matrimonial match. To Aimwell and Archer the right and desirable marriage is one with a wealthy wife. It is interesting that Aimwell at least opts for true love along with money. To Dorinda, marriage must be an honorable love match. While Mrs. Sullen might pretend and profess otherwise, she is also primarily interested in a relationship with a man who deserves her and a man who is her equal. It is imperative, therefore, that Mrs. Sullen escape from her unpleasant marriage with Lady Bountiful's reprobate son—which she begins to accomplish at the end of the play and, significantly, with Lady Bountiful's genuine approval. While it is not firmly stated, it is nevertheless implicit that Mrs. Sullen and Archer will probably end up together one day. This comedy, like many of Shakespeare's romantic comedies, ends with the ritual of marriage. Aimwell and Dorinda achieve their most ardent wish in wedlock; Sullen and Mrs. Sullen approach the same happy state by ironically looking forward to desolving their marriage; and Archer and Mrs. Sullen will be free, hopefully, to think of marriage if they so desire. And thus the action of the play is fulfilled.

The Beaux' Stratagem may be seen as an interesting and necessary link between what Jeremy Collier regarded as the immoral comedy of the Restoration and the sentimental comedy that was to emerge fifteen years later in plays like Richard Steele's *The Conscious Lovers* (1722). The word "sentimental" in this context had little to do with the mockish attitudes we call sentimental today. In the eighteenth century to be sentimental meant to have a sincere and genuine regard and feeling for the welfare, wants, needs and feelings of others. That thing the characters of Restoration comedy lacked most was a genuine regard for others; they tended to be a very egocentric, self-absorbed and self-righteous lot. How remarkably different Farquhar's characters are. Lady Bountiful, even with her saving comic dimension, is all that is good and fine in a truly sentimental being. All four lovers ultimately demonstrate a genuine concern and regard for one another. Cherry gains a measure of sweet nobility through a profoundly sentimental act by surrendering all claim to Archer.

Here we are on the threshold of the goody-goody characters who will people the melodramatic drama of the late eighteenth century and the nineteenth century as well. And moving into the twentieth century, the heroines of many of the early silent movies are cut of the same cloth. By the time melodrama is born in the early part of the nineteenth century, the sentimental drama had definitely deteriorated into that mockish thing we think of today when we speak of sentimental dramatic fare. Thank heavens for the breath of fresh air that Ibsen ultimately introduces in his realistic drama, for Ibsen provides not only realism but reality.

THE BEAUX' STRATAGEM

By George Farquhar

edited by Nettleton and Case

———— DRAMATIS PERSONAE ————

MEN

[THOMAS] AIMWELL, } two gentlemen of broken
[FRANCIS] ARCHER, } fortune, the first as master, and the second as servant.

COUNT BELLAIR, a French officer, prisoner at Lichfield.

SULLEN, a country blockhead, brutal to his wife.

[SIR CHARLES] FREEMAN, a gentleman from London.

FOIGARD, a priest, chaplain to the French officers.

GIBBET, a highwayman.

HOUNSLOW, } his companions.
BAGSHOT, }

BONNIFACE, landlord of the inn.

SCRUB, servant to MR. SULLEN.

WOMEN

LADY BOUNTIFUL, an old, civil country gentlewoman, that cures all her neighbors of all distempers, and foolishly fond of her son, SULLEN.

DORINDA, LADY BOUNTIFUL'S daughter.

MRS. SULLEN, her daughter-in-law.

GIPSEY, maid to the ladies.

CHERRY, the landlord's daughter in the inn.

SCENE,

LICHFIELD.

PROLOGUE

SPOKEN BY MR. WILKS[1]

WHEN strife disturbs, or sloth corrupts an age,
Keen satire is the business of the stage.
When the Plain Dealer[2] writ, he lashed those crimes
Which then infested most—the modish times:
But now, when faction sleeps and sloth is fled,
And all our youth in active fields are bred;[3]
When through Great Britain's fair extensive round,
The trumps of fame the notes of Union[4] sound;
When Anna's sceptre points the laws their course,
And her example gives her precepts force:
There scarce is room for satire; all our lays
Must be, or songs of triumph, or of praise.
But as in grounds best cultivated, tares
And poppies rise among the golden ears;
Our products so, fit for the field or school,
Must mix with nature's favorite plant—a fool:
A weed that has to twenty summers ran,
Shoots up in stalk, and vegetates to man.
Simpling[5] our author goes from field to field,
And culls such fools as may diversion yield;
And, thanks to nature, there's no want of those,

For, rain or shine, the thriving coxcomb grows.
Follies tonight we show ne'er lashed before,
Yet such as nature shows you every hour;
Nor can the pictures give a just offence,
For fools are made for jests to men of sense.

ACT I
SCENE I

Scene, an inn.

Enter BONNIFACE, *running.*

BON. Chamberlain![6] maid! Cherry! daughter Cherry! all asleep? all dead?

Enter CHERRY, *running.*

CHER. Here, here! why d'ye bawl so, father? d'ye think we have no ears?

---

1. In the part of Archer.
2. Wycherley is here referred to by the title of his best-known play.
3. The War of the Spanish Succession had been in progress for more than five years.
4. The union of England and Scotland was finally brought about in 1707.
5. Gathering medicinal herbs.
6. The servant in charge of the bed-chambers.

BON. You deserve to have none, you young minx! The company of the Warrington[7] coach has stood in the hall this hour, and nobody to show them to their chambers.

CHER. And let 'em wait farther; there's neither redcoat in the coach, nor footman behind it.

BON. But they threaten to go to another inn tonight.

CHER. That they dare not, for fear the coachman should overturn them tomorrow.—Coming! coming!—Here's the London coach arrived.

Enter several people with trunks, bandboxes, and other luggage, and cross the stage.

BON. Welcome, ladies!

CHER. Very welcome, gentlemen!—Chamberlain, show the *Lion* and the *Rose*.[8]

Exit with the company.

Enter AIMWELL *in riding-habit,* ARCHER *as footman carrying a portmantle.*

BON. This way, this way, gentlemen!

AIM. [*to* ARCHER]. Set down the things; go to the stable, and see my horses well rubbed.

ARCH. I shall, sir. *Exit.*

AIM. You're my landlord, I suppose?

BON. Yes, sir, I'm old Will Bonniface, pretty well known upon this road, as the saying is.

AIM. O Mr. Bonniface, your servant!

BON. O sir!—What will your honor please to drink, as the saying is?

AIM. I have heard your town of Lichfield much famed for ale; I think I'll taste that.

BON. Sir, I have now in my cellar ten tun of the best ale in Staffordshire; 'tis smooth as oil, sweet as milk, clear as amber, and strong as brandy; and will be just fourteen year old the fifth day of next March, old style.[9]

AIM. You're very exact, I find, in the age of your ale.

BON. As punctual, sir, as I am in the age of my children. I'll show you such ale!—Here, tapster, broach number 1706,[10] as the saying is.—Sir, you shall taste my *Anno Domini*. I have lived in Lichfield, man and boy, above eight-and-fifty years, and, I believe, have not consumed eight-and-fifty ounces of meat.

AIM. At a meal, you mean, if one may guess your sense by your bulk.

BON. Not in my life, sir. I have fed purely upon ale; I have eat my ale, drank my ale, and I always sleep upon ale.

Enter Tapster with a bottle and glass.

Now, sir you shall see!—(*Filling it out.*) Your worship's health.—Ha! delicious, delicious!—fancy it burgundy, only fancy it, and 'tis worth ten shillings a quart.

AIM. (*drinks*). 'Tis confounded strong!

BON. Strong! It must be so, or how should we be strong that drink it?

AIM. And have you lived so long upon this ale landlord?

BON. Eight-and-fifty years, upon my credit, sir; but it killed my wife, poor woman, as the saying is.

AIM. How came that to pass?

BON. I don't know how, sir; she would not let the ale take its natural course, sir; she was for qualifying it every now and then with a dram,[11] as the saying is; and an honest gentleman that came this way from Ireland made her a present of a dozen bottles of usquebaugh[12]—but the poor woman was never well after. But, howe'er, I was obliged to the gentleman, you know.

AIM. Why, was it the usquebaugh that killed her?

BON. My Lady Bountiful said so. She, good lady, did what could be done; she cured her of three tympanies,[13] but the fourth carried her off. But she's happy, and I'm contented, as the saying is.

AIM. Who's that Lady Bountiful you mentioned?

BON. Ods my life, sir, we'll drink her health.— (*Drinks.*) My Lady Bountiful is one of the best of women. Her last husband, Sir Charles Bountiful,

---

7. A town about sixty miles north of Lichfield, on the road to Preston and Lancaster.
8. Rooms in inns were known by names, not numbers.
9. During the first half of the eighteenth century the English calendar was eleven days behind that of western Europe, which had adopted the 'new style' in 1582.
10. By this transparent 'code number' and the phrase '*Anno Domini*' Bonniface refers to the ale brewed in the preceding autumn (of 1706), which he proposes to palm off on the travellers in place of the fourteen-year-old ale of which he has boasted.
11. I.e., of spirituous liquor.
12. Whiskey.
13. Tumors.

left her worth a thousand pound a year; and, I believe, she lays out one-half on't in charitable uses for the good of her neighbors; she cures rheumatisms, ruptures, and broken shins in men; greensickness,[14] obstructions, and fits of the mother[15] in women; the king's evil,[16] chincough,[17] and chilblains in children: in short, she has cured more people in and about Lichfield within ten years than the doctors have killed in twenty; and that's a bold word.

AIM. Has the lady been any other way useful in her generation?

BON. Yes, sir; she has a daughter by Sir Charles, the finest woman in all our country, and the greatest fortune. She has a son too, by her first husband, Squire Sullen, who married a fine lady from London t'other day; if you please, sir, we'll drink his health.

AIM. What sort of a man is he?

BON. Why, sir, the man's well enough; says little, thinks less, and does—nothing at all, faith. But he's a man of a great estate, and values nobody.

AIM. A sportsman, I suppose?

BON. Yes, sir, he's a man of pleasure; he plays at whisk[18] and smokes his pipe eight and forty hours together sometimes.

AIM. And married, you say?

BON. Ay, and to a curious woman, sir.—But he's a—he wants it here, sir.

(Pointing to his forehead.)

AIM. He has it there, you mean.[19]

BON. That's none of my business; he's my landlord, and so a man, you know, would not—But—icod, he's not better than—Sir, my humble service to you.—(*Drinks*.) Though I value not a farthing what he can do to me; I pay him his rent at quarterday;[20] I have a good running-trade; I have but one daughter, and I can give her—but no matter for that.

AIM. You're very happy, Mr. Bonniface; pray, what other company have you in town?

BON. A power of fine ladies; and then we have the French officers.[21]

AIM. Oh, that's right, you have a good many of those gentlemen. Pray, how do you like their company?

BON. So well, as the saying is, that I could wish we had as many more of 'em; they're full of money, and pay double for everything they have: they know, sir, that we paid good round taxes for the taking of 'em, and so they are willing to reimburse us a little. One of 'em lodges in my house.

Enter ARCHER.

ARCH. Landlord, there are some French gentlemen below that ask for you.

BON. I'll wait on 'em—(*To* ARCHER.) Does your master stay long in town, as the saying is?

ARCH. I can't tell, as the saying is.

BON. Come from London?

ARCH. No.

BON. Going to London, mayhap?

ARCH. No.

BON. [*aside*]. An odd fellow this.—[*To* AIMWELL.] I beg your worship's pardon, I'll wait on you in half a minute.   *Exit.*

AIM. The coast's clear, I see.—Now, my dear Archer, welcome to Lichfield!

ARCH. I thank thee, my dear brother in iniquity.

AIM. Iniquity! prithee, leave canting; you need not change your style with your dress.

ARCH. Don't mistake me, Aimwell, for 'tis still my maxim, that there is no scandal like rags, nor any crime so shameful as poverty.

AIM. The world confesses it every day in its practice, though men won't own it for their opinion. Who did that worthy lord, my brother, single out of the side-box[22] to sup with him t'other night?

ARCH. Jack Handicraft, a handsome, well-dressed, mannerly, sharping rogue, who keeps the best company in town.

AIM. Right! And, pray, who married my lady Manslaughter t'other day, the great fortune?

---

14. An anemic disease of adolescence.
15. Hysteria.
16. Scrofula.
17. Whooping-cough.
18. Whist.
19. Bonniface meant that the squire was not very intelligent; Aimwell twists his remark to imply that the square bears the 'horns' of a cuckold on his forehead.
20. There were four recognized days for the payment of rent; in March, June, September and December.

21. Officers captured during the War of the Spanish Succession were liberated on parole in various parts of England.
22. The side-box at the theatre was a favorite place for the beaux.

ARCH. Why, Nick Marrabone,[23] a professed pick-pocket, and a good bowler; but he makes a handsome figure, and rides in his coach, that he formerly used to ride behind.

AIM. But did you observe poor Jack Generous in the Park[24] last week?

ARCH. Yes, with his autumnal periwig, shading his melancholy face, his coat older than anything but its fashion, with one hand idle in his pocket, and with the other picking his useless teeth; and though the Mall was crowded with company, yet was poor Jack as single and solitary as a lion in a desert.

AIM. And as much avoided, for no crime upon earth but the want of money.

ARCH. And that's enough. Men must not be poor; idleness is the root of all evil; the world's wide enough, let 'em bustle. Fortune has taken the weak under her protection, but men of sense are left to their industry.

AIM. Upon which topic we proceed, and, I think, luckily hitherto. Would not any man swear now that I am a man of quality, and you my servant, when if our intrinsic value were known—

ARCH. Come, come, we are the men of intrinsic value who can strike our fortunes out of ourselves, whose worth is independent of accidents in life, or revolutions in government; we have heads to get money, and hearts to spend it.

AIM. As to our hearts, I grant ye, they are as willing tits[25] as any within twenty degrees; but I can have no great opinion of our heads from the service they have done us hitherto, unless it be that they have brought us from London hither to Lichfield, made me a lord, and you my servant.

ARCH. That's more than you could expect already. But what money have we left?

AIM. But two hundred pound.

ARCH. And our horses, clothes, rings, etc.—Why, we have very good fortunes now for moderate people; and let me tell you, besides, that this two hundred pound, with the experience that we are now masters of, is a better estate than the ten [thousand] we have spent. Our friends, indeed, began to suspect that our pockets were low; but we came off with flying colors, showed no signs of want either in word or deed.

AIM. Ay, and our going to Brussels was a good pretence enough for our sudden disappearing; and, I warrant you, our friends imagine that we are gone a-volunteering.

ARCH. Why, faith, if this prospect fails, it must e'en come to that. I am for venturing one of the hundreds, if you will, upon this knight-errantry; but, in case it should fail, we'll reserve the t'other to carry us to some counterscarp, where we may die, as we lived, in a blaze.

AIM. With all my heart; and we have lived justly, Archer; we can't say that we have spent our fortunes, but that we have enjoyed 'em.

ARCH. Right! So much pleasure for so much money; we have had our pennyworths, and, had I millions, I would go to the same market again. O London! London! Well, we have had our share, and let us be thankful; past pleasures, for aught I know, are best, such as we are sure of: those to come may disappoint us.

AIM. It has often grieved the heart of me to see how some inhuman wretches murther their kind fortunes; those that, by sacrificing all to one appetite, shall starve all the rest. You shall have some that live only in their palates, and in their sense of tasting shall drown the other four. Others are only epicures in appearances, such who shall starve their nights to make a figure a-days, and famish their own to feed the eyes of others: a contrary sort confine their pleasures to the dark, and contract their specious acres to the circuit of a muffstring.

ARCH. Right! But they find the Indies[26] in that spot where they consume 'em, and I think your kind keepers[27] have much the best on't; for they indulge the most senses by one expense: there's the seeing, hearing, and feeling, amply gratified; and, some philosophers will tell you that from such a commerce there arises a sixth sense, that gives infinitely more pleasure than the other five put together.

---

23. A corruption of 'Marylebone,' the name of a district on the northern edge of London which was a fashionable gaming center. Bowling, in which there had been a revival of interest in 1706, was one of the games which served as a basis for wagering; see Lady Mary Wortley Montagu's *The Basset-table*, ll. 99–100:
At the Groom-Porter's battered bullies play,
Some dukes at Mary-bone bowl time away.

24. The reference to the Mall in Archer's next speech shows that St. James's Park is meant here.

25. Horses.

26. The source of their delights.

27. Of mistresses.

AIM. And to pass to the other extremity, of all keepers I think those the worst that keep their money.

ARCH. Those are the most miserable wights in being; they destroy the rights of nature, and disappoint the blessings of Providence. Give me a man that keeps his five senses keen and bright as his sword, that has 'em always drawn out in their just order and strength, with his reason as commander at the head of 'em; that detaches 'em by turns upon whatever party of pleasure agreeably offers, and commands 'em to retreat upon the least appearance of disadvantage or danger! For my part, I can stick to my bottle while my wine, my company, and my reason holds good; I can be charmed with Sappho's singing without falling in love with her face; I love hunting, but would not, like Actæon,[28] be eaten up by my own dogs; I love a fine house, but let another keep it; and just so I love a fine woman.

AIM. In that last particular you have the better of me.

ARCH. Ay, you've such an amorous puppy, that I'm afraid you'll spoil our sport; you can't counterfeit the passion without feeling it.

AIM. Though the whining part be out of doors in town, 'tis still in force with the country ladies; and let me tell you, Frank, the fool in that passion shall outdo the knave at any time.

ARCH. Well, I won't dispute it now; you command for the day, and so I submit.—At Nottingham, you know, I am to be master.

AIM. And at Lincoln, I again.

ARCH. Then, at Norwich I mount, which, I think, shall be our last stage; for, if we fail there, we'll imbark for Holland, bid adieu to Venus, and welcome Mars.

AIM. A match!

Enter BONNIFACE.

Mum!

BON. What will your worship please to have for supper?

AIM. What have you got?

BON. Sir, we have a delicate piece of beef in the pot, and a pig at the fire.

AIM. Good supper-meat, I must confess.—I can't eat beef, landlord.

ARCH. And I hate pig.

AIM. Hold your prating, sirrah! do you know who you are?

BON. Please to bespeak something else; I have everything in the house.

AIM. Have you any veal?

BON. Veal! Sir, we had a delicate loin of veal on Wednesday last.

AIM. Have you got any fish or wildfowl?

BON. As for fish, truly, sir, we are an inland town, and indifferently provided with fish, that's the truth on't; and then for wildfowl—we have a delicate couple of rabbits.

AIM. Get me the rabbits fricasseed.

BON. Fricasseed! Lard, sir, they'll eat much better smothered with onions.

ARCH. Pshaw! Damn your onions!

AIM. Again, sirrah!—Well, landlord, what you please. But hold, I have a small charge[29] of money, and your house is so full of strangers, that I believe it may be safer in your custody than mine; for when this fellow of mine gets drunk, he minds nothing.—Here, sirrah, reach me the strong-box.

ARCH. Yes, sir.—(*Aside.*) This will give us a reputation. (*Brings the box.*)

AIM. Here, landlord; the locks are sealed down both for your security and mine; it holds somewhat above two hundred pound; if you doubt it, I'll count it to you after supper; but be sure you lay it where I may have it at a minute's warning; for my affairs are a little dubious at present; perhaps I may be gone in half an hour, perhaps I may be your guest till the best part of that be spent; and pray order your ostler to keep my horses always saddled. But one thing above the rest I must beg, that you would let this fellow have none of your *Anno Domini*, as you call it; for he's the most insufferable sot.— Here, sirrah, light me to my chamber.

Exit, lighted by ARCHER.

BON. Cherry! Daughter Cherry!

Enter CHERRY.

CHER. D'ye call, father?

---

28. Actæon, who surprised Artemis bathing, was turned to a stag and torn to pieces by his dogs.

29. Burden, amount.

BON. Ay, child, you must lay by this box for the gentleman; 'tis full of money.

CHER. Money! all that money! Why, sure, father, the gentleman comes to be chosen parliament-man. Who is he?

BON. I don't know what to make of him; he talks of keeping his horses ready saddled, and of going perhaps at a minute's warning, or of staying perhaps till the best part of this be spent.

CHER. Ay, ten to one, father, he's a highwayman.

BON. A highwayman! Upon my life, girl, you have hit it, and this box is some new-purchased booty.— Now, could we find him out, the money were ours.

CHER. He don't belong to our gang?

BON. What horses have they?

CHER. The master rides upon a black.

BON. A black! ten to one the man upon the black mare; and since he don't belong to our fraternity, we may betray him with a safe conscience. I don't think it lawful to harbor any rogues but my own. Look ye, child, as the saying is, we must go cunningly to work; proofs we must have. The gentleman's servant loves drink,—I'll ply him that way; and ten to one loves a wench,—you must work him t'other way.

CHER. Father, would you have me give my secret for his?

BON. Consider, child, there's two hundred pound to boot.—(*Ringing without.*) Coming! coming!— Child, mind your business. [*Exit.*]

CHER. What a rogue is my father! My father! I deny it. My mother was a good, generous, freehearted woman, and I can't tell how far her good nature might have extended for the good of her children. This landlord of mine, for I think I can call him no more, would betray his guest, and debauch his daughter into the bargain—by a footman, too!

Enter ARCHER.

ARCH. What footman, pray, mistress, is so happy as to be the subject of your contemplation?

CHER. Whoever he is, friend, he'll be but little the better for't.

ARCH. I hope so, for I'm sure you did not think of me.

CHER. Suppose I had?

ARCH. Why, then you're but even with me; for the minute I came in, I was a-considering in what manner I should make love to you.

CHER. Love to me, friend!

ARCH. Yes, child.

CHER. Child! manners! If you kept a little more distance, friend, it would become you much better.

ARCH. Distance! Good-night, saucebox. (*Going.*)

CHER. [*aside*]. A pretty fellow! I like his pride.— [*Aloud.*] Sir, pray, sir, you see, sir, (ARCHER *returns*) I have the credit to be intrusted with your master's fortune here, which sets me a degree above his footman; I hope, sir, you an't affronted?

ARCH. Let me look you full in the face, and I'll tell you whether you can affront me or no.—'Sdeath, child, you have a pair of delicate eyes, and you don't know what to do with 'em!

CHER. Why, sir, don't I see everybody?

ARCH. Ay, but if some women had 'em, they would kill everybody. Prithee, instruct me, I would fain make love to you, but I don't know what to say.

CHER. Why, did you never make love to anybody before?

ARCH. Never to a person of your figure, I can assure you, madam; my addresses have been always confined to people within my own sphere; I never aspired so high before. (*A song.*)

But you look so bright,
And are dressed so tight,
[That a man would swear you're right,
As arm was e'er laid over.
Such an air
You freely wear
To ensnare,
As makes each guest a lover!

Since then, my dear, I'm your guest,
Prithee give me of the best
Of what is ready dressed:
Since then, my dear, etc.]

CHER. (*aside*). What can I think of this man?—Will you give me that song, sir?

ARCH. Ay, my dear, take it while 'tis warm.— (*Kisses her.*) Death and fire! her lips are honeycombs.

CHER. And I wish there had been bees too, to have stung you for your impudence.

ARCH. There's a swarm of Cupids, my little Venus, that has done the business much better.

CHER. (*aside*). This fellow is misbegotten as well as I.—What's your name, sir?

ARCH. (*aside*). Name! igad, I have forgot it.— [*Aloud*.] Oh! Martin.

CHER. Where were you born?

ARCH. In St. Martin's parish.

CHER. What was your father?

ARCH. St. Martin's parish.

CHER. Then, friend, good-night.

ARCH. I hope not.

CHER. You may depend upon't.

ARCH. Upon what?

CHER. That you're very impudent.

ARCH. That you're very handsome.

CHER. That you're a footman.

ARCH. That you're an angel.

CHER. I shall be rude.

ARCH. So shall I.

CHER. Let go my hand.

ARCH. Give me a kiss. (*Kisses her.*) (*Call without:* Cherry! Cherry!)

CHER. I'm-m—my father calls; you plaguy devil, how durst you stop my breath so? Offer to follow me one step, if you dare.   *Exit.*

ARCH. A fair challenge, by this light! This is a pretty fair opening of an adventure; but we are knight-errants, and so Fortune be our guide.   *Exit.*

ACT II
SCENE [I]

A gallery in LADY BOUNTIFUL'S *house.*

MRS. SULLEN *and* DORINDA, *meeting.*

DOR. Morrow, my dear sister; are you for church this morning?

MRS SUL. Anywhere to pray; for heaven alone can help me. But I think, Dorinda, there's no form of prayer in the liturgy against bad husbands.

DOR. But there's a form of law in Doctors-Commons;[30] and I swear, sister Sullen, rather than see you thus continually discontented, I would advise you to apply to that: for besides the part that I bear in your vexatious broils, as being sister to the husband, and friend to the wife, your example gives me such an impression of matrimony, that I shall be apt to condemn my person to a long vacation all its life. But supposing, madam, that you brought it to a case of separation, what can you urge against your husband? My brother is, first, the most constant man alive.

MRS. SUL. The most constant husband, I grant ye.

DOR. He never sleeps from you.

MRS. SUL. No, he always sleeps with me.

DOR. He allows you a maintenance suitable to your quality.

MRS. SUL. A maintenance! Do you take me, madam, for an hospital child,[31] that I must sit down, and bless my benefactors for meat, drink, and clothes? As I take it, madam, I brought your brother ten thousand pounds, out of which I might expect some pretty things, called pleasures.

DOR. You share in all the pleasures that the country affords.

MRS. SUL. Country pleasures! Racks and torments! dost think, child, that my limbs were made for leaping of ditches, and clamb'ring over stiles? or that my parents, wisely foreseeing my future happiness in country pleasures, had early instructed me in the rural accomplishments of drinking fat[32] ale, playing at whisk, and smoking tobacco with my husband? or of spreading of plasters, brewing of diet-drinks, and stilling[33] rosemary-water, with the good old gentlewoman, my mother-in-law?

DOR. I'm sorry, madam, that it is not more in our power to divert you; I could wish, indeed, that our entertainments were a little more polite, or your taste a little less refined. But, pray, madam, how came the poets and philosophers, that labored so much in hunting after pleasure, to place it at last in a country life?

MRS. SUL. Because they wanted money, child, to find out the pleasures of the town. Did you ever see a

30. The London society of lawyers learned in the civil law and entitled, among other things, to plead cases of separation or divorce in the ecclesiastical courts.
31. Inmate of an orphan asylum.
32. Full-bodied.
33. Distilling.

poet or philosopher worth ten thousand pound? If you can show me such a man, I'll lay you fifty pound you'll find him somewhere within the weekly bills.[34] Not that I disapprove rural pleasures, as the poets have painted them; in their landscape, every Phyllis has her Corydon, every murmuring stream, and every flow'ry mead, gives fresh alarms to love.—Besides, you'll find that their couples were never married.—But yonder I see my Corydon, and a sweet swain it is, heaven knows! Come, Dorinda, don't be angry, he's my husband, and your brother; and, between both, is he not a sad brute?

DOR. I have nothing to say to your part of him—you're the best judge.

MRS. SUL. O sister, sister! if ever you marry, beware of a sullen, silent sot, one that's always musing, but never thinks. There's some diversion in a talking blockhead; and since a woman must wear chains, I would have the pleasure of hearing 'em rattle a little. Now you shall see, but take this by the way. He came home this morning at his usual hour of four, wakened me out of a sweet dream of something else, by tumbling over the tea-table, which he broke all to pieces; after his man and he had rolled about the room, like sick passengers in a storm, he comes flounce into bed, dead as a salmon into a fishmonger's basket; his feet cold as ice, his breath hot as a furnace, and his hands and his face as greasy as his flannel night-cap. O matrimony! He tosses up the clothes with a barbarous swing over his shoulders, disorders the whole economy of my bed, leaves me half naked, and my whole night's comfort is the tuneable serenade of that wakeful nightingale, his nose! Oh, the pleasure of counting the melancholy clock by a snoring husband!—But now, sister, you shall see how handsomely, being a well-bred man, he will beg my pardon.

Enter SULLEN.

SUL. My head aches consumedly.

MRS. SUL. Will you be pleased, my dear, to drink tea with us this morning? It may do your head good.

SUL. No.

DOR. Coffee, brother?

SUL. Pshaw!

MRS. SUL. Will you please to dress, and go to church with me? The air may help you.

SUL. Scrub!

Enter SCRUB.

SCRUB. Sir.

SUL. What day o' th' week is this?

SCRUB. Sunday, an't please your worship.

SUL. Sunday! Bring me a dram; and d'ye hear, set out the venison-pasty, and a tankard of strong beer upon the hall-table; I'll go to breakfast. (*Going.*)

DOR. Stay, stay, brother, you shan't get off so; you were very naught[35] last night, and must make your wife reparation; come, come, brother, won't you ask pardon?

SUL. For what?

DOR. For being drunk last night.

SUL. I can afford it, can't I?

MRS. SUL. But I can't, sir.

SUL. Then you may let it alone.

MRS. SUL. But I must tell you, sir, that this is not to be borne.

SUL. I'm glad on't.

MRS. SUL. What is the reason, sir, that you use me thus inhumanely?

SUL. Scrub!

SCRUB. Sir.

SUL. Get things ready to shave my head.

Exit [followed by SCRUB].

MRS. SUL. Have a care of coming near his temples, Scrub, for fear you meet something there that may turn the edge of your razor.—Inveterate stupidity! did you ever know so hard, so obstinate a spleen as his? O sister, sister! I shall never ha' good of the beast till I get him to town: London, dear London, is the place for managing and breaking a husband.

DOR. And has not a husband the same opportunities there for humbling a wife?

MRS. SUL. No, no, child, 'tis a standing maxim in conjugal discipline, that when a man would enslave his wife, he hurries her into the country; and when a lady would be arbitrary with her husband,

34. Within the limits of the London parishes for which weekly bills of mortality (lists of deaths) were published.

35. Naughty.

she wheedles her booby up to town. A man dare not play the tyrant in London, because there are so many examples to encourage the subject to rebel. O Dorinda, Dorinda! a fine woman may do anything in London: o' my conscience, she may raise an army of forty thousand men.

DOR. I fancy, sister, you have a mind to be trying your power that way here in Lichfield; you have drawn the French count to your colors already.

MRS. SUL. The French are a people that can't live without their gallantries.

DOR. And some English that I know, sister, are not averse to such amusements.

MRS. SUL. Well, sister, since the truth must out, it may do as well now as hereafter; I think one way to rouse my lethargic, sottish husband is to give him a rival. Security begets negligence in all people, and men must be alarmed to make 'em alert in their duty: women are like pictures, of no value in the hands of a fool, till he hears men of sense bid high for the purchase.

DOR. This might do, sister, if my brother's understanding were to be convinced into a passion for you; but I fancy there's a natural aversion of his side; and I fancy, sister, that you don't come much behind him, if you dealt fairly.

MRS. SUL. I own it, we are united contradictions, fire and water. But I could be contented, with a great many other wives, to humor the censorious mob, and give the world an appearance of living well with my husband, could I bring him but to dissemble a little kindness to keep me in countenance.

DOR. But how do you know, sister, but that, instead of rousing your husband by this artifice to a counterfeit kindness, he should awake in a real fury?

MRS. SUL. Let him: if I can't entice him to the one, I would provoke him to the other.

DOR. But how must I behave myself between ye?

MRS. SUL. You must assist me.

DOR. What, against my own brother!

MRS. SUL. He's but half a brother, and I'm your entire friend. If I go a step beyond the bounds of honor, leave me; till then, I expect you should go along with me in everything; while I trust my honor in your hands, you may trust your brother's in mine. The count is to dine here today.

DOR. 'Tis a strange thing, sister, that I can't like that man.

MRS. SUL. You like nothing; your time is not come: love and death have their fatalities, and strike home one time or other. You'll pay for all one day, I warrant ye. But come, my lady's tea is ready, and 'tis almost church time. *Exeunt.*

SCENE [II]

The inn.

Enter AIMWELL *dressed, and* ARCHER.

AIM. And was she the daughter of the house?

ARCH. The landlord is so blind as to think so; but I dare swear she has better blood in her veins.

AIM. Why dost think so?

ARCH. Because the baggage has a pert *je ne sais quoi*,[36] she reads plays, keeps a monkey, and is troubled with vapors.

AIM. By which discoveries I guess that you know more of her.

ARCH. Not yet, faith; the lady gives herself airs; forsooth, nothing under a gentleman!

AIM. Let me take her in hand.

ARCH. Say one word more o' that, and I'll declare myself, spoil your sport there, and everywhere else; look ye, Aimwell, every man in his own sphere.

AIM. Right; and therefore you must pimp for your master.

ARCH. In the usual forms, good sir, after I have served myself.—But to our business. You are so well dressed, Tom, and make so handsome a figure, that I fancy you may do execution in a country church; the exterior part strikes first, and you're in the right to make that impression favorable.

AIM. There's something in that which may turn to advantage. The appearance of a stranger in a country church draws as many gazers as a blazing-star; no sooner he comes into the cathedral, but a train of whispers runs buzzing round the congregation in a moment: 'Who is he? Whence comes he? Do you know him?' Then I sir, tips me the verger with half a crown; he pockets the simony, and inducts me into the best pew in the church. I pull out my snuff-box; turn myself round, bow to the bishop, or the dean, if he be the commanding

36. An inexpressible something.

200

officer; single out a beauty, rivet both my eyes to hers, set my nose a-bleeding by the strength of imagination, and show the whole church my concern by my endeavoring to hide it; after the sermon, the whole town gives me to her for a lover, and by persuading the lady that I am a-dying for her, the tables are turned, and she in good earnest falls in love with me.

ARCH. There's nothing in this, Tom, without a precedent; but instead of riveting your eyes to a beauty, try to fix 'em upon a fortune; that's our business at present.

AIM. Pshaw! no woman can be a beauty without a fortune. Let me alone, for I am a marksman.

ARCH. Tom!

AIM. Ay.

ARCH. When were you at church before, pray?

AIM. Um—I was there at the coronation.[37]

ARCH. And how can you expect a blessing by going to church now?

AIM. Blessing! nay, Frank, I ask but for a wife.

Exit.

ARCH. Truly, the man is not very unreasonable in his demands. *Exit at the opposite door.*

Enter BONNIFACE *and* CHERRY.

BON. Well, daughter, as the saying is, have you brought Martin to confess?

CHER. Pray, father, don't put me upon getting anything out of a man; I'm but young, you know, father, and I don't understand wheedling.

BON. Young! why, you jade, as the saying is, can any woman wheedle that is not young? Your mother was useless at five and twenty. Not wheedle! would you make your mother a whore, and me a cuckold, as the saying is? I tell you his silence confesses it, and his master spends his money so freely, and is so much a gentleman every manner of way, that he must be a highwayman.

Enter GIBBET, *in a cloak.*

GIB. Landlord, landlord, is the coast clear?

BON. O Mr. Gibbet, what's the news?

GIB. No matter, ask no questions, all fair and honorable.—Here, my dear Cherry. (*Gives her a bag.*) Two hundred sterling pounds, as good as any that

ever hanged or saved a rogue; lay 'em by with the rest; and here—three wedding or mourning rings, 'tis much the same, you know.—Here, two silver-hilted swords; I took those from fellows that never show any part of their swords but the hilts. Here is a diamond necklace which the lady hid in the privatest place in the coach, but I found it out. This gold watch I took from a pawnbroker's wife; it was left in her hands by a person of quality—there's the arms upon the case.

CHER. But who had you the money from?

GIB. Ah! poor woman! I pitied her; from a poor lady just eloped from her husband. She had made up her cargo, and was bound for Ireland, as hard as she could drive; she told me of her husband's barbarous usage, and so I left her half a crown. But I had almost forgot, my dear Cherry, I have a present for you.

CHER. What is't?

GIB. A pot of ceruse,[38] my child, that I took out of a lady's under-pocket.

CHER. What! Mr. Gibbet, do you think that I paint?

GIB. Why, you jade, your betters do; I'm sure the lady that I took it from had a coronet upon her handkerchief. Here, take my cloak, and go, secure the premises.

CHER. I will secure 'em. *Exit.*

BON. But, hark ye, where's Hounslow and Bagshot?

GIB. They'll be here tonight.

BON. D'ye know of any other gentlemen o' the pad[39] on this road?

GIB. No.

BON. I fancy that I have two that lodge in the house just now.

GIB. The devil! How d'ye smoke[40] em?

BON. Why, the one is gone to church.

GIB. That's suspicious, I must confess.

BON. And the other is now in his master's chamber; he pretends to be servant to the other. We'll call him out and pump him a little.

GIB. With all my heart.

---

37. I.e., of Queen Anne, five years earlier.

38. A cosmetic compounded from white lead.
39. Highwaymen.
40. Come to suspect.

BON. [*calls.*] Mr. Martin! Mr. Martin!

Enter MARTIN, *combing a periwig and singing.*

GIB. The roads are consumed deep; I'm as dirty as Old Brentford at Christmas.[41]—A good pretty fellow that.—Whose servant are you, friend?

ARCH. My master's.

GIB. Really?

ARCH. Really.

GIB. That's much.—[*Aside to* BONNIFACE. The fellow has been at the bar by his evasions.—But pray, sir, what is your master's name?

ARCH. *Tall, all dall!* (*Sings and combs the periwig.*) This is the most obstinate curl—

GIB. I ask you his name.

ARCH. Name, sir—*tall, all dall!*—I never asked him his name in my life.—*Tall, all dall!*

BON. [*aside to* GIBBET]. What think you now?

GIB. [*aside to* BONNIFACE]. Plain, plain; he talks now as if he were before a judge.—But pray, friend, which way does your master travel?

ARCH. A-horseback.

GIB. [*aside*]. Very well again, an old offender, right.—But I mean, does he go upwards or downwards?

ARCH. Downwards, I fear, sir.—*Tall, all!*

GIB. I'm afraid my fate will be a contrary way.

BON. Ha, ha, ha! Mr. Martin, you're very arch. This gentleman is only travelling towards Chester, and would be glad of your company, that's all.—Come, Captain, you'll stay tonight, I suppose? I'll show you a chamber. Come, Captain.

GIB. Farewell, friend!

ARCH. Captain, your servant. [*Exeunt* BONNIFACE *and* GIBBET.]—Captain! a pretty fellow! 'Sdeath, I wonder that the officers of the army don't conspire to beat all scoundrels in red but their own.

Enter CHERRY.

CHER. (*aside*). Gone! and Martin here! I hope he did not listen; I would have the merit of the discovery all my own, because I would oblige him to love me.—Mr. Martin, who was that man with my father?

ARCH. Some recruiting sergeant, or whipped-out[42] trooper, I suppose.

CHER. [*aside*]. All's safe, I find.

ARCH. Come, my dear, have you conned over the catechise I taught you last night?

CHER. Come, question me.

ARCH. What is love?

CHER. Love is I know not what, it comes I know not how, and goes I know not when.

ARCH. Very well, an apt scholar.—(*Chucks her under the chin.*) Where does love enter?

CHER. Into the eyes.

ARCH. And where go out?

CHER. I won't tell ye.

ARCH. What are [the] objects of that passion?

CHER. Youth, beauty, and clean linen.

ARCH. The reason?

CHER. The two first are fashionable in nature, and the third at court.

ARCH. That's my dear.—What are the signs and tokens of that passion?

CHER. A stealing look, a stammering tongue, words improbable, designs impossible, and actions impracticable.

ARCH. That's my good child, kiss me.—What must a lover do to obtain his mistress?

CHER. He must adore the person that disdains him, he must bribe the chambermaid that betrays him, and court the footman that laughts at him.—He must, he must—

ARCH. Nay, child, I must whip you if you don't mind your lesson; he must treat his—

CHER. Oh, ay!—he must treat his enemies with respect, his friends with indifference, and all the world with contempt; he must suffer much, and fear more; he must desire much, and hope little; in short, he must embrace his ruin, and throw himself away.

ARCH. Had ever man so hopeful a pupil as mine!—Come, my dear, why is Love called a riddle?

CHER. Because, being blind, he leads those that see, and, though a child, he governs a man.

----

41. A proverbially muddy town and a proverbially muddy time of year are combined here.

42. Soldiers, for certain offenses, were flogged out of the army.

ARCH. Mighty well!—And why is Love pictured blind?

CHER. Because the painters out of the weakness or privilege of their act chose to hide those eyes that they could not draw.

ARCH. That's my dear little scholar, kiss me again.—And why should Love, that's a child, govern a man?

CHER. Because that a child is the end of love.

ARCH. And so ends love's catechism.—And now, my dear, we'll go in and make my master's bed.

CHER. Hold, hold, Mr. Martin! You have taken a great deal of pains to instruct me, and what d'ye think I have learnt by it?

ARCH. What?

CHER. That your discourse and your habit are contradictions, and it would be nonsense in me to believe you a footman any longer.

ARCH. 'Oons, what a witch it is!

CHER. Depend upon this, sir, nothing in this garb shall ever tempt me; for, though I was born to servitude, I hate it. Own your condition, swear you love me, and then—

ARCH. And then we shall go make the bed?

CHER. Yes.

ARCH. You must know, then, that I am born a gentleman, my education was liberal; but I went to London a younger brother, fell into the hands of sharpers, who stripped me of my money; my friends disowned me, and now my necessity brings me to what you see.

CHER. Then take my hand—promise to marry me before you sleep, and I'll make you master of two thousand pound.

ARCH. How!

CHER. Two thousand pound that I have this minute in my own custody; so, throw off your livery this instant, and I'll go find a parson.

ARCH. What said you? A parson!

CHER. What! do you scruple?

ARCH. Scruple! no, no, but—Two thousand pound, you say?

CHER. And better.

ARCH. [aside]. 'Sdeath, what shall I do?—[Aloud.] But hark'ee, child, what need you make me master of yourself and money, when you may have the same pleasure out of me, and still keep your fortune in your hands?

CHER. Then you won't marry me?

ARCH. I would marry you, but—

CHER. O sweet sir, I'm your humble servant! you're fairly caught: would you persuade me that any gentleman who could bear the scandal of wearing a livery would refuse two thousand pound, let the condition be what it would? No, no, sir. But I hope you'll pardon the freedom I have taken, since it was only to inform myself of the respect that I ought to pay you. (Going.)

ARCH. [aside]. Fairly bit, by Jupiter!—Hold! hold! And have you actually two thousand pound?

CHER. Sir, I have my secrets as well as you; when you please to be more open, I shall be more free, and be assured that I have discoveries that will match yours, be what they will—in the meanwhile, be satisfied that no discovery I make shall ever hurt you; but beware of my father! [Exit.]

ARCH. So! we're like to have as many adventures in our inn as Don Quixote had in his.[43] Let me see— two thousand pound! If the wench would promise to die when the money were spent, igad, one would marry her; but the fortune may go off in a year or two, and the wife may live—Lord knows how long. Then an innkeeper's daughter! ay, that's the devil—there my pride brings me off.
 For whatso'er the sages charge on pride,
 The angels' fall, and twenty faults beside,
 On earth, I'm sure, 'mong us of mortal calling,
 Pride saves man oft, and woman too, from falling.

Exit.

ACT III
[SCENE I

The gallery in LADY BOUNTIFUL'S *house.*]

Enter MRS. SULLEN, DORINDA.

MRS. SUL. Ha, ha, ha! my dear sister, let me embrace thee: now we are friends indeed; for I shall have a secret of yours as a pledge for mine—now you'll be good for something; I shall have you conversable[44] in the subjects of the sex.

---

43. See *Don Quixote,* III, ii–iii.
44. Disposed to converse.

DOR. But do you think that I am so weak as to fall in love with a fellow at first sight?

MRS. SUL. Pshaw! now you spoil all; why should not we be as free in our friendships as the men? I warrant you the gentleman has got to his confident already, has avowed his passion, toasted your health, called you ten thousand angels, has run over your lips, eyes, neck, shape, air, and everything, in a description that warms their mirth to a second enjoyment.

DOR. Your hand, sister, I an't well.

MRS. SUL. So—she's breeding already!—Come, child, up with it—hem a little—so—now tell me, don't you like the gentleman that we saw at church just now?

DOR. The man's well enough.

MRS. SUL. Well enough! is he not a demigod, a Narcissus, a star, the man i' the moon?

DOR. O sister, I'm extremely ill!

MRS. SUL. Shall I send to your mother, child, for a little of her cephalic plaster[45] to put to the soles of your feet, or shall I send to the gentleman for something for you?—Come, unlace your stays, unbosom yourself—the man is perfectly a pretty fellow; I saw him when he first came into church.

DOR. I saw him too, sister, and with an air that shone, methought, like rays about his person.

MRS. SUL. Well said, up with it!

DOR. No forward coquet behavior, no airs to set him off, no studied looks nor artful posture—but Nature did it all—

MRS. SULL. Better and better! One touch more—come!

DOR. But then his looks—did you observe his eyes?

MRS. SUL. Yes, yes, I did.—His eyes, well, what of his eyes?

DOR. Sprightly, but not wand'ring; they seemed to view, but never gazed on anything but me.—And then his looks so humble were, and yet so noble, that they aimed to tell me that he could with pride die at my feet, though he scorned slavery anywhere else.

MRS. SUL. The physic works purely![46]—How d'ye find yourself now, my dear?

DOR. Hem! much better, my dear.—Oh, here comes our Mercury!

Enter SCRUB.

Well, Scrub, what news of the gentleman?

SCRUB. Madam, I have brought you a packet of news.

DOR. Open it quickly, come.

SCRUB. In the first place I enquired who the gentleman was; they told me he was a stranger. Secondly, I asked what the gentleman was; they answered and said, that they never saw him before. Thirdly, I enquired what countryman he was; they replied, 'twas more than they knew. Fourthly, I demanded whence he came; their answer was, they could not tell. And, fifthly, I asked whither he went; and they replied, they knew nothing of the matter,—and this is all I could learn.

MRS. SUL. But what do the people say? Can't they guess?

SCRUB. Why, some think he's a spy, some guess he's a mountebank, some say one thing, some another; but for my own part, I believe he's a Jesuit.

DOR. A Jesuit. Why a Jesuit?

SCRUB. Because he keeps his horses always ready saddled, and his footman talks French.

MRS. SUL. His footman!

SCRUB. Ay, he and the count's footman were gabbering French like two intriguing ducks in a millpond; and I believe they talked of me, for they laughed consumedly.

DOR. What sort of livery has the footman?

SCRUB. Livery! Lord, madam, I took him for a captain, he's so bedizened with lace! And then he has tops to his shoes, up to his mid leg, a silverheaded cane dangling at his knuckles; he carries his hands in his pockets just so—(*walks in the French air*)—and has a fine long periwig tied up in a bag. Lord, madam, he's clear another sort of man than I!

MRS. SUL. That may easily be.—But what shall we do now, sister?

DOR. I have it. This fellow has a world of simplicity, and some cunning; the first hides the latter by abundance.—Scrub!

SCRUB. Madam!

DOR. We have a great mind to know who this gentleman is, only for our satisfaction.

---

45. A remedy for diseases of the head.
46. Finely.

204

SCRUB. Yes, madam, it would be a satisfaction, no doubt.

DOR. You must go and get acquainted with his footman, and invite him hither to drink a bottle of your ale, because you're butler today.

SCRUB. Yes, madam, I am butler every Sunday.

MRS. SUL. O brave, sister! O' my conscience, you understand the mathematics already—'tis the best plot in the world: your mother, you know, will be gone to church, my spouse will be got to the alehouse with his scoundrels, and the house will be our own—so we drop in by accident, and ask the fellow some questions ourselves. In the country, you know, any stranger is company, and we're glad to take up with the butler in a country-dance, and happy if he'll do us the favor.

SCRUB. Oh! Madam, you wrong me! I never refused your ladyship the favor in my life.

Enter GIPSEY.

GIP. Ladies, dinner's upon table.

DOR. Scrub, we'll excuse your waiting—go where we ordered you.

SCRUB. I shall.   *Exeunt.*

[SCENE II]

Scene changes to the inn.

Enter AIMWELL *and* ARCHER.

ARCH. Well, Tom, I find you're a marksman.

AIM. A marksman! who so blind could be, as not discern a swan among the ravens?

ARCH. Well, but hark'ee, Aimwell—

AIM. Aimwell! Call me Oroondates, Cesario, Amadis,[47] all that romance can in a lover paint, and then I'll answer. O Archer! I read her thousands in her looks, she looked like Ceres in her harvest: corn, wine, and oil, milk and honey, gardens, groves, and purling streams played on her plenteous face.

ARCH. Her face! her pocket, you mean; the corn, wine, and oil lies there. In short, she has ten thousand pound, that's the English on't.

AIM. Her eyes—

ARCH. Are demi-cannons, to be sure; so I won't stand their battery.   (*Going.*)

47. Well-known heroes of romance.

AIM. Pray excuse me; my passion must have vent.

ARCH. Passion! what a plague, d'ee think these romantic airs will do our business? Were my temper as extravagant as yours, my adventures have something more romantic by half.

AIM. Your adventures!

ARCH. Yes;

The nymph that with her twice ten hundred pounds,
With brazen engine[48] hot, and quoif[49] clear starched,
Can fire the guest in warming of the bed—

There's a touch of sublime Milton for you, and the subject but an innkeeper's daughter! I can play with a girl as an angler does with his fish; he keeps it at the end of his line, runs it up the stream, and down the stream, till at last he brings it to hand, tickles[50] the trout, and so whips it into his basket.

Enter BONNIFACE.

BON. Mr. Martin, as the saying is—yonder's an honest fellow below, my Lady Bountiful's butler, who begs the honor that you would go home with him and see his cellar.

ARCH. Do my *baise-mains*[51] to the gentleman, and tell him I will do myself the honor to wait on him immediately.   *Exit* BONNIFACE.

AIM. What do I hear?
Soft Orpheus play, and fair Toftida[52] sing!

ARCH. Pshaw! damn your raptures! I tell you, here's a pump going to be put into the vessel, and the ship will get into harbor, my life on't. You say there's another lady very handsome there?

AIM. Yes, faith.

ARCH. I am in love with her already.

AIM. Can't you give me a bill upon Cherry in the mean time?

ARCH. No, no, friend, all her corn, wine, and oil is ingrossed[53] to my market.—And once more I warn you to keep your anchorage clear of mine; for if you fall foul of me, by this light you shall go to

48. Warming-pan.
49. Cap.
50. Trout were 'tickled' by stroking them gently until they were quiet enough to permit the fisherman to close his hand upon them.
51. Hand-kissings: the phrase is equivalent to 'Pay my respects.'
52. Katherine Tofts, a famous contemporary soprano.
53. Bought up, monopolized.

205

the bottom! What! make prize of my little frigate, while I am upon the cruise for you!

AIM. Well, well, I won't.   *Exit* ARCHER.

Enter BONNIFACE.

Landlord, have you any tolerable company in the house? I don't care for dining alone.

BON. Yes, sir, there's a captain below, as the saying is, that arrived about an hour ago.

AIM. Gentlemen of his coat are welcome everywhere; will you make him a compliment from me, and tell him I should be glad of his company?

BON. Who shall I tell him, sir, would—

AIM. [*aside*]. Ha! that stroke was well thrown in!— [*Aloud.*] Ha! I'm only a traveller like himself, and would be glad of his company, that's all.

BON. I obey your commands, as the saying is.

Exit.

Enter ARCHER.

ARCH. 'Sdeath! I had forgot; what title will you give yourself?

AIM. My brother's, to be sure; he would never give me anything else, so I'll make bold with his honor this bout.—You know the rest of your cue.

ARCH. Ay, ay.   [*Exit.*]

Enter GIBBET.

GIB. Sir, I'm yours.

AIM. 'Tis more than I deserve, sir, for I don't know you.

GIB. I don't wonder at that, sir, for you never saw me before—(*aside*) I hope.

AIM. And pray, sir, how came I by the honor of seeing you now?

GIB. Sir, I scorn to intrude upon any gentleman— but my landlord—

AIM. O sir, I ask your pardon! You're the captain he told me of?

GIB. At your service, sir.

AIM. What regiment, may I be so bold?

GIB. A marching regiment, sir, an old corps.

AIM. (*aside*). Very old, if your coat be regimental.—[*Aloud.*] You have served abroad, sir?

GIB. Yes, sir—in the plantations;[54] 'twas my lot to be sent into the worst service. I would have quitted it indeed, but a man of honor, you know—besides, 'twas for the good of my country that I should be abroad. Anything for the good of one's country— I'm a Roman for that.

AIM. (*aside*). One of the first,[55] I'll lay my life.— You found the West Indies very hot, sir?

GIB. Ay, sir, too hot for me.

AIM. Pray, sir, han't I seen your face at Will's coffee-house?

GIB. Yes, sir, and at White's[56] too.

AIM. And where is your company now, captain?

GIB. They an't come yet.

AIM. Why, d'ye expect 'em here?

GIB. They'll be here tonight, sir.

AIM. Which way do they march?

GIB. Across the country.—[*Aside.*] The devil's in't, if I han't said enough to encourage him to declare; but I'm afraid he's not right; I must tack about.

AIM. Is your company to quarter in Lichfield?

GIB. In this house, sir.

AIM. What! all?

GIB. My company's but thin, ha, ha, ha! we are but three, ha, ha, ha!

AIM. You're merry, sir.

GIB. Ay, sir, you must excuse me, sir; I understand the world, especially the art of travelling; I don't care, sir, for answering questions directly upon the road—for I generally ride with a charge[57] about me.

AIM. (*aside*). Three or four, I believe.

GIB. I am credibly informed that there are highwaymen upon this quarter; not, sir, that I could suspect a gentleman of your figure—but truly, sir, I have got such a way of evasion upon the road, that I don't care for speaking truth to any man.

54. The audience is to understand that Gibbet's 'service' in the colonies was not as a soldier, but as a felon sentenced to transportation.
55. Gibbet's reference was to the Roman virtue of patriotism; Aimwell's aside, presumably, to the pillaging of Italy by the early Romans under Æneas.
56. Will's coffee house was the resort of literary men, White's of gamblers.
57. In the sense of 'sum of money'; Aimwell puns upon the word in the sense of loads of powder and shot for a pistol.

AIM. Your caution may be necessary.—Then I presume you're no captain?

GIB: Not I, sir; captain is a good travelling name, and so I take it; it stops a great many foolish inquiries that are generally made about gentlemen that travel; it gives a man an air of something, and makes the drawers obedient:—and thus far I am a captain, and no farther.

AIM. And pray, sir, what is your true profession?

GIB. O sir, you must excuse me!—Upon my word, sir, I don't think it safe to tell you.

AIM. Ha, ha, ha! upon my word, I commend you.

Enter BONNIFACE.

Well, Mr. Bonniface, what's the news?

BON. There's another gentleman below, as the saying is, that hearing you were but two, would be glad to make the third man, if you would give him leave.

AIM. What is he?

BON. A clergyman, as the saying is.

AIM. A clergyman! Is he really a clergyman? or is it only his travelling name, as my friend the captain has it?

BON. O sir, he's a priest, and chaplain to the French officers in town.

AIM. Is he a Frenchman?

BON. Yes, sir, born at Brussels.

GIB. A Frenchman, and a priest! I won't be seen in his company, sir; I have a value for my reputation, sir.

AIM. Nay, but captain, since we are by ourselves— Can he speak English, landlord?

BON. Very well, sir; you may know him, as the saying is, to be a foreigner by his accent, and that's all.

AIM. Then he has been in England before?

BON. Never, sir; but he's a master of languages, as the saying is—he talks Latin—it does me good to hear him talk Latin.

AIM. Then you understand Latin, Mr. Bonniface?

BON. Not I, sir, as the saying is; but he talks it so very fast, that I'm sure it must be good.

AIM. Pray, desire him to walk up.

BON. Here he is, as the saying is.

Enter FOIGARD.

FOI. Save you, gentlemens, both.

AIM. [*aside*]. A Frenchman!—[*To* FOIGARD.] Sir, your most humble servant.

FOI. Och, dear joy,[58] I am your most faithful shervant, and yours alsho.

GIB. Doctor, you talk very good English, but you have a mighty twang of the foreigner.

FOI. My English is very vel for the vords, but we foreigners, you know, cannot bring our tongues about the pronunciation so soon.

AIM. (*aside*). A foreigner! a downright Teague,[59] by this light!—Were you born in France, doctor?

FOI. I was educated in France, but I was borned at Brussels; I am a subject of the King of Spain, joy.

GIB. What King of Spain, sir? speak!

FOI. Upon my shoul, joy, I cannot tell you as yet.[60]

AIM. Nay, captain, that was too hard upon the doctor; he's a stranger.

FOI. Oh, let him alone, dear joy; I am of a nation that is not easily put out of countenance.

AIM. Come, gentlemen, I'll end the dispute.—Here, landlord, is dinner ready?

BON. Upon the table, as the saying is.

AIM. Gentlemen—pray—that door—

FOI. No, no, fait, the captain must lead.

AIM. No, doctor, the church is our guide.

GIB. Ay, ay, so it is. *Exit foremost, they follow.*

[SCENE III]

Scene changes to a gallery in LADY BOUNTIFUL'S *house.*

Enter ARCHER *and* SCRUB *singing, and hugging one another,* SCRUB *with a tankard in his hand,* GIPSEY *listening at a distance.*

SCRUB. *Tall, all dall!*—Come, my dear boy, let's have that song once more.

ARCH. No, no, we shall disturb the family.—But will you be sure to keep the secret?

---

58. A common term of friendly address among the Irish.
59. Irishman.
60. The War of the Spanish Succession had not yet settled this question.

SCRUB. Pho! upon my honor, as I'm a gentleman.

ARCH. 'Tis enough.—You must know, then, that my master is the Lord Viscount Aimwell; he fought a duel t'other day in London, wounded his man so dangerously that he thinks fit to withdraw till he hears whether the gentleman's wounds be mortal or not. He never was in this part of England before, so he chose to retire to this place, that's all.

GIP. [aside]. And that's enough for me. *Exit.*

SCRUB. And where were you when your master fought?

ARCH. We never know of our masters' quarrels.

SCRUB. No? If our masters in the country here receive a challenge, the first thing they do is to tell their wives; the wife tells the servants, the servants alarm the tenants, and in half an hour you shall have the whole county in arms.

ARCH. To hinder two men from doing what they have no mind for.—But if you should chance to talk now of my business?

SCRUB. Talk! ay, sir, had I not learned the knack of holding my tongue, I had never lived so long in a great family.

ARCH. Ay, ay, to be sure there are secrets in all families.

SCRUB. Secrets! ay;—but I'll say no more.—Come, sit down, we'll make an end of our tankard: here—

ARCH. With all my heart; who knows but you and I may come to be better acquainted, eh?—Here's your ladies' healths; you have three, I think, and to be sure there must be secrets among 'em.

[Drinks.]

SCRUB. Secrets! ay, friend. I wish I had a friend—

ARCH. Am not I your friend? Come, you and I will be sworn brothers.

SCRUB. Shall we?

ARCH. From this minute.—Give me a kiss—and now, brother Scrub—

SCRUB. And now, brother Martin, I will tell you a secret that will make your hair stand on end. You must know that I am consumedly in love.

ARCH. That's a terrible secret, that's the truth on't.

SCRUB. That jade, Gipsey, that was with us just now in the cellar, is the arrantest whore that ever wore a petticoat; and I'm dying for love of her.

ARCH. Ha, ha, ha!—Are you in love with her person or her virtue, brother Scrub?

SCRUB. I should like virtue best, because it is more durable than beauty; for virtue holds good with some women long and many a day after they have lost it.

ARCH. In the country, I grant ye, where no woman's virtue is lost, till a bastard be found.

SCRUB. Ay, could I bring her to a bastard, I should have her all to myself; but I dare not put it upon that lay,[61] for fear of being sent for a soldier.— Pray, brother, how do you gentlemen in London like that same Pressing Act?[62]

ARCH. Very ill, brother Scrub; 'tis the worst that ever was made for us. Formerly I remember the good days, when we could dun our masters for our wages, and if they refused to pay us, we could have a warrant to carry 'em before a justice; but now if we talk of eating, they have a warrant for us, and carry us before three justices.

SCRUB. And to be sure we go, if we talk of eating; for the justices won't give their own servants a bad example. Now this is my misfortune—I dare not speak in the house, while that jade Gipsey dings[63] about like a fury—once I had the better end of the staff.

ARCH. And how comes the change now?

SCRUB. Why, the mother of all this mischief is a priest.

ARCH. A priest!

SCRUB. Ay, a damned son of a whore of Babylon, that came over hither to say grace to the French officers, and eat up our provisions. There's not a day goes over his head without dinner or supper in this house.

ARCH. How came he so familiar in the family?

SCRUB. Because he speaks English as if he had lived here all his life; and tells lies as if he had been a traveller from his cradle.

ARCH. And this priest, I'm afraid, has converted the affections of your Gipsey.

SCRUB. Converted! ay, and perverted, my dear friend: for I'm afraid he has made her a whore and a papist!—But this is not all; there's the

---

61. I dare not take that line.
62. The act authorizing the impressment of men into the military service, passed two or three years earlier.
63. Flings.

French count and Mrs. Sullen, they're in the confederacy, and for some private ends of their own, to be sure.

ARCH. A very hopeful family yours, brother Scrub! I suppose the maiden lady has her lover too.

SCRUB. Not that I know. She's the best on 'em, that's the truth on't. But they take care to prevent my curiosity, by giving me so much business, that I'm a perfect slave. What d'ye think is my place in this family?

ARCH. Butler, I suppose.

SCRUB. Ah, Lord help you!—I'll tell you.—Of a Monday I drive the coach; of a Tuesday I drive the plough; on Wednesday I follow the hounds; a-Thursday I dun the tenants; on Friday I go to market; on Saturday I draw warrants; and a-Sunday I draw beer.

ARCH. Ha, ha, ha! if variety be a pleasure in life, you have enough on't, my dear brother.—But what ladies are those?

[SCRUB.] Ours, ours; that upon the right hand is Mrs. Sullen, and the other is Mrs. Dorinda.—Don't mind 'em; sit still, man.

Enter MRS. SULLEN *and* DORINDA.

MRS. SUL. I have heard my brother talk of my Lord Aimwell; but they say that his brother is the finer gentleman.

DOR. That's impossible, sister.

MRS. SUL. He's vastly rich, but very close, they say.

DOR. No matter for that; if I can creep into his heart, I'll open his breast, I warrant him. I have heard say, that people may be guessed at by the behavior of their servants; I could wish we might talk to that fellow.

MRS. SUL. So do I; for I think he's a very pretty fellow. Come this way, I'll throw out a lure for him presently.

(*They walk a turn towards the opposite side of the stage.*)

ARCH. [*aside*]. Corn, wine, and oil indeed! But, I think, the wife has the greatest plenty of flesh and blood; she should be my choice.—Ah, a, say you so!—(MRS. SULLEN *drops her glove*, ARCHER *runs, takes it up, and gives it to her.*) Madam—your ladyship's glove.

MRS. SUL. O sir, I thank you!—[*To* DORINDA.] What a handsome bow the fellow has!

DOR. Bow! why, I have known several footmen come down from London set up here for dancing-masters, and carry off the best fortunes in the country.

ARCH. (*aside*). That project, for aught I know, had been better than ours.—Brother Scrub, why don't you introduce me?

SCRUB. Ladies, this is the strange gentleman's servant that you see at church today; I understood he came from London, and so I invited him to the cellar, that he might show me the newest flourish in whetting my knives.

DOR. And I hope you have made much of him?

ARCH. Oh yes, madam, but the strength of your ladyship's liquor is a little too potent for the constitution of your humble servant.

MRS. SUL. What, then you don't usually drink ale?

ARCH. No, madam; my constant drink is tea, or a little wine and water. 'Tis prescribed me by the physician for a remedy against the spleen.

SCRUB. O la! O la! a footman have the spleen!

MRS. SUL. I thought that distemper had been only proper to people of quality.

ARCH. Madam, like all other fashions it wears out, and so descends to their servants; though in a great many of us I believe it proceeds from some melancholy particles in the blood, occasioned by the stagnation of wages.

DOR. [*aside to* MRS. SULLEN]. How affectedly the fellow talks!—How long, pray, have you served your present master?

ARCH. Not long; my life has been mostly spent in the service of the ladies.

MRS. SUL. And pray, which service do you like best?

ARCH. Madam, the ladies pay best; the honor of serving them is sufficient wages; there is a charm in their looks that delivers a pleasure with their commands, and gives our duty the wings of inclination.

MRS. SUL. [*aside*]. The flight was above the pitch of a livery.—And, sir, would not you be satisfied to serve a lady again?

ARCH. As a groom of the chamber, madam, but not as a footman.

MRS. SUL. I suppose you served as footman before.

ARCH. For that reason I would not serve in that post again; for my memory is too weak for the load of messages that the ladies lay upon their servants in London. My Lady Howd'ye, the last mistress I served, called me up one morning, and told me, 'Martin, go to my Lady Allnight with my humble service; tell her I was to wait on her ladyship yesterday, and left word with Mrs. Rebecca, that the preliminaries of the affair she knows of are stopped till we know the concurrence of the person that I know of, for which there are circumstances wanting which we shall accommodate at the old place; but that in the meantime there is a person about her ladyship that, from several hints and surmises, was accessary at a certain time to the disappointments that naturally attend things, that to her knowledge are of more importance—'

MRS. SUL., DOR. Ha, ha, ha! where are you going, sir?

ARCH. Why, I han't half done!—The whole howd'ye was about half an hour long; so I happened to misplace two syllables, and was turned off, and rendered incapable.

DOR. [aside]. The pleasantest fellow, sister, I ever saw!—But, friend, if your master be married, I presume you still serve a lady.

ARCH. No, madam, I take care never to come into a married family; the commands of the master and mistress are always so contrary, that 'tis impossible to please both.

DOR. (aside). There's a main point gained. My lord is not married, I find.

MRS. SUL. But I wonder, friend, that in so many good services you had not a better provision made for you.

ARCH. I don't know how, madam. I had a lieutenancy offered me three or four times; but that is not bread, madam—I live much better as I do.

SCRUB. Madam, he sings rarely.—I was thought to do pretty well here in the country till he came; but alack a day, I'm nothing to my brother Martin!

DOR. Does he?—Pray, sir, will you oblige us with a song?

ARCH. Are you for passion or humor?

SCRUB. Oh la! he has the purest ballad about a trifle—

MRS. SUL. A trifle! pray, sir, let's have it.

ARCH. I'm ashamed to offer you a trifle, madam; but since you command me—
(*Sings to the tune of Sir Simon the King.*)

A trifling song you shall hear,
Begun with a trifle and ended,
[All trifling people draw near,
And I shall be nobly attended.

Were it not for trifles a few,
That lately have come into play;
The men would want something to do,
And the women want something to say.

What makes men trifle in dressing?
Because the ladies (they know)
Admire, by often possessing,
That eminent trifle, a beau.

When the lover his moments has trifled,
The trifle of trifles to gain,
No sooner the virgin is rifled,
But a trifle shall part 'em again.

What mortal man would be able
At White's half an hour to sit?
Or who could bear a tea-table,
Without talking of trifles for wit?

The court is from trifles secure,
Gold Keys[64] are no trifles, we see;
White rods[65] are no trifles, I'm sure,
Whatever their bearers may be.

But if you will go to the place,
Where trifles abundantly breed,
The levee will show you his Grace
Makes promises trifles indeed.

A coach with six footmen behind,
I count neither trifle nor sin:
But, ye gods! how oft do we find
A scandalous trifle within?

A flask of champagne, people think it
A trifle, or something as bad:
But if you'll contrive how to drink it,
You'll find it no trifle, egad!

A parson's a trifle at sea,
A widow's a trifle in sorrow;
A peace is a trifle today,
Who knows what may happen tomorrow?

A black coat a trifle may cloak,
Or to hide [it], the red may endeavor:
But if once the army is broke,
We shall have more trifles than ever.

64. Symbols of office of the groom of the stole and the mistress of the robes.
65. Symbols of office of high-ranking cabinet ministers.

210

The stage is a trifle, they say,
The reason, pray carry along,
Because at ev'ry new play,
The house they with trifles so throng.

But with people's malice to trifle,
And to set us all on a foot:
The author of this is a trifle,
And his song is a trifle to boot.]

MRS. SUL. Very well, sir, we're obliged to you.—
Something for a pair of gloves.

(*Offering him money.*)

ARCH. I humbly beg leave to be excused: my master,
madam, pays me; nor dare I take money from any
other hand, without injuring his honor, and diso-
beying his commands   *Exit* [*with* SCRUB].

DOR. This is surprising! Did you ever see so pretty
a well-bred fellow?

MRS. SUL. The devil take him for wearing that livery!

DOR. I fancy, sister, he may be some gentleman, a
friend of my lord's, that his lordship has pitched
upon for his courage, fidelity, and discretion, to
bear him company in this dress, and who, ten to
one, was his second too.

MRS. SUL. It is so, it must be so, and it shall be so!—
for I like him.

DOR. What! better than the count?

MRS. SUL. The count happened to be the most
agreeable man upon the place; and so I chose him
to serve me in my design upon my husband.—But
I should like this fellow better in a design upon
myself.

DOR. But now, sister, for an interview with this lord
and this gentleman; how shall we bring that about?

MRS. SUL. Patience! You country ladies give no
quarter if once you be entered[66]—Would you
prevent[67] their desires, and give the fellows no
wishing-time?—Look ye, Dorinda, if my Lord
Aimwell loves you or deserves you, he'll find a way
to see you, and there we must leave it. My business comes now upon the tapis.—Have you prepared your brother?

DOR. Yes, yes.

MRS. SUL. And how did he relish it?

DOR. He said little, mumbled something to himself,
promised to be guided by me—but here he comes.

Enter SULLEN.

SUL. What singing was that I heard just now?

MRS. SUL. The singing in your head, my dear; you
complained of it all day.

SUL. You're impertinent.

MRS. SUL. I was ever so, since I became one flesh
with you.

SUL. One flesh! rather two carcasses joined unnaturally together.

MRS. SUL. Or rather a living soul coupled to a dead
body.

DOR. So, this is fine encouragement for me!

SUL. Yes, my wife shows you what you must do.

MRS. SUL. And my husband shows you what you
must suffer.

SUL. 'Sdeath, why can't you be silent?

MRS. SUL. 'Sdeath, why can't you talk?

SUL. Do you talk to any purpose?

MRS. SUL. Do you think to any purpose?

SUL. Sister, hark ye! (*Whispers.*) [*Aloud.*] I shan't
be home till it be late.   *Exit.*

MRS. SUL. What did he whisper to ye?

DOR. That he would go round the back way, come
into the closet, and listen as I directed him. But
let me beg you once more, dear sister, to drop this
project; for as I told you before, instead of awaking
him to kindness, you may provoke him to a rage;
and then who knows how far his brutality may
carry him?

MRS. SUL. I'm provided to receive him, I warrant
you. But here comes the count—vanish!

Exit DORINDA.

Enter COUNT BELLAIR.

Don't you wonder, monsieur le count, that I was not
at church this afternoon?

COUNT BEL. I more wonder, madam, that you go
dere at all, or how you dare to lift those eyes to
heaven that are guilty of so much killing.

MRS. SUL. If heaven, sir, has given to my eyes with
the power of killing the virtue of making a cure,
I hope the one may atone for the other.

66. Engaged in action.
67. Anticipate

COUNT BEL. Oh, largely, madam. Would your ladyship be as ready to apply the remedy as to give the wound? Consider, madam, I am doubly a prisoner—first to the arms of your general, then to your more conquering eyes. My first chains are easy—there a ransom may redeem me; but from your fetters I never shall get free.

MRS. SUL. Alas, sir! why should you complain to me of your captivity, who am in chains myself? You know, sir, that I am bound, nay, most be-tied up in that particular that might give you ease: I am like you, a prisoner of war—of war, indeed! I have given my parole of honor; would you break yours to gain your liberty?

COUNT BEL. Most certainly I would, were I a prisoner among the Turks; dis is your case: you're a slave, madam, slave to the worst of Turks, a husband.

MRS. SUL. There lies my foible, I confess; no fortifications, no courage, conduct, nor vigilancy can pretend to defend a place where the cruelty of the governor forces the garrison to mutiny.

COUNT BEL. And where de besieger is resolved to die before de place.—Here will I fix (*kneels*)—with tears, vows, and prayers assault your heart, and never rise till you surrender; or if I must storm—Love and St. Michael!—And so I begin the attack.—

MRS. SUL. Stand off!—(*Aside.*) Sure he hears me not! And I could almost wish he—did not! The fellow makes love very prettily.—[*Aloud.*] But, sir, why should you put such a value upon my person, when you see it despised by one that knows it so much better?

COUNT BEL. He knows it not, though he possesses it; if he but knew the value of the jewel he is master of, he would always wear it next his heart, and sleep with it in his arms.

MRS. SUL. But since he throws me unregarded from him—

COUNT BEL. And one that knows your value well comes by and takes you up, is it not justice?

(*Goes to lay hold of her.*)

Enter SULLEN *with his sword drawn.*

SUL. Hold, villain, hold!

MRS. SUL. (*presenting a pistol*). Do you hold!

SUL. What! murther your husband, to defend your bully!

MRS. SUL. Bully! for shame, Mr. Sullen. Bullies wear long swords, the gentleman has none; he's a prisoner, you know.—I was aware of your outrage, and prepared this to receive your violence; and, if occasion were, to preserve myself against the force of this other gentleman.

COUNT BEL. O madam, your eyes be bettre firearms than your pistol; they nevre miss.

SUL. What! court my wife to my face!

MRS. SUL. Pray, Mr. Sullen, put up; suspend your fury for a minute.

SUL. To give you time to invent an excuse!

MRS. SUL. I need none.

SUL. No, for I heard every syllable of your discourse.

COUNT BEL. Ah! and begar, I tink de dialogue was vera pretty.

MRS. SUL. Then I suppose, sir, you heard something of your own barbarity?

SUL. Barbarity! 'Oons, what does the [woman] call barbarity? Do I ever meddle with you?

MRS. SUL. No.

SUL. As for you, sir, I shall take another time.

COUNT BEL. Ah, begar, and so must I.

SUL. Look'ee, madam, don't think that my anger proceeds from any concern I have for your honor, but for my own, and if you can contrive any way of being a whore without making me a cuckold, do it and welcome.

MRS. SUL. Sir, I thank you kindly; you would allow me the sin but rob me of the pleasure.—No, no, I'm resolved never to venture upon the crime without the satisfaction of seeing you punished for't.

SUL. Then will you grant me this, my dear? Let anybody else do you the favor but that Frenchman, for I mortally hate his whole generation. *Exit.*

COUNT BEL. Ah, sir, that be ungrateful, for begar, I love some of yours.—Madam—

(*Approaching her.*)

MRS. SUL. No, sir.—

COUNT BEL. No, sir!—Garzoon, madam, I am not your husband!

212

MRS. SUL. 'Tis time to undeceive you, sir. I believed your addresses to me were no more than an amusement, and I hope you will think the same of my complaisance; and to convince you that you ought, you must know that I brought you hither only to make you instrumental in setting me right with my husband, for he was planted to listen by my appointment.

COUNT BEL. By your appointment?

MRS. SUL. Certainly.

COUNT BEL. And so, madam, while I was telling twenty stories to part you from your husband, begar, I was bringing you together all the while?

MRS. SUL. I ask your pardon, sir, but I hope this will give you a taste of the virtue of the English ladies.

COUNT BEL. Begar, madam, your virtue be vera great, but garzoon, your honeste be vera little.

Enter DORINDA.

MRS. SUL. Nay, now, you're angry, sir.

COUNT BEL. Angry!—*Fair Dorinda. (Sings 'Dorinda' the opera tune, and addresses to* DORINDA.) Madam, when your ladyship want a fool, send for me. *Fair Dorinda, Revenge, etc.*[68]   *Exit.*

MRS. SUL. There goes the true humor of his nation—resentment with good manners, and the height of anger in a song!—Well, sister, you must be judge, for you have heard the trial.

DOR. And I bring in my brother guilty.

MRS. SUL. But I must bear the punishment. 'Tis hard, sister.

DOR. I own it; but you must have patience.

MRS. SUL. Patience! the cant of custom—Providence sends no evil without a remedy—should I lie groaning under a yoke I can shake off, I were accessary to my ruin, and my patience were no better than self-murder.

DOR. But how can you shake off the yoke? Your divisions[69] don't come within the reach of the law for a divorce.

MRS. SUL. Law! what law can search into the remote abyss of nature? what evidence can prove the unaccountable disaffections of wedlock? Can a jury sum up the endless aversions that are rooted in our souls, or can a bench give judgment upon antipathies?

DOR. They never pretended, sister; they never meddle, but in case of uncleanness.

MRS. SUL. Uncleanness! O sister! casual violation is a transient injury, and may possibly be repaired, but can radical hatreds be ever reconciled?—No, no, sister, nature is the first lawgiver, and when she has set tempers opposite, not all the golden links of wedlock nor iron manacles of law can keep 'um fast.

Wedlock we own ordained by heaven's decree,
But such as heaven ordained it first to be—
Concurring tempers in the man and wife
As mutual helps to draw the load of life.
View all the works of Providence above,
The stars with harmony and concord move;
View all the works of Providence below,
The fire, the water, earth, and air, we know,
All in one plant agree to make it grow.
Must man, the chiefest work of art divine,
Be doomed in endless discord to repine?
No, we should injure heaven by that surmise;
Omnipotence is just, were man but wise.

ACT IV
[SCENE I]

Scene continues.

Enter MRS. SULLEN.

MRS. SUL. Were I born an humble Turk, where women have no soul nor property, there I must sit contented. But in England, a country whose women are its glory, must women be abused? where women rule, must women be enslaved? nay, cheated into slavery, mocked by a promise of comfortable society into a wilderness of solitude? I dare not keep the thought about me.—Oh, here comes something to divert me.

Enter a Country Woman.

WOM. I come, an't please your ladyships—you're my Lady Bountiful, an't ye?

MRS. SUL. Well, good woman, go on.

WOM. I have come seventeen long mail to have a cure for my husband's sore leg.

---

68. Stonehill suggests that the count combines snatches from Buononcini's opera *Camilla* (1706), with libretto by Stampiglio, translated by MacSwiney. In the first act Lavinia sings an air, 'Fair Dorinda, happy, happy, happy may'st thou ever be': in the second act an air sung by Camilla begins, 'Revenge, revenge I summon.'
69. Disagreements.

213

MRS. SUL. Your husband! what, woman, cure your husband!

WOM. Ay, poor man, for his sore leg won't let him stir from home.

MRS. SUL. There, I confess, you have given me a reason. Well, good woman, I'll tell you what you must do. You must lay your husband's leg upon a table, and with a chopping-knife you must lay it open as broad as you can; then you must take out the bone, and beat the flesh soundly with a rolling-pin; then take salt, pepper, cloves, mace, and ginger, some sweet herbs, and season it very well; then roll it up like brawn, and put it into the oven for two hours.

WOM. Heavens reward your ladyship!—I have two little babies too that are piteous bad with the graips, an't please ye.

MRS. SUL. Put a little pepper and salt in their bellies, good woman.

Enter LADY BOUNTIFUL.

I beg your ladyship's pardon for taking your business out of your hands; I have been a-tampering here a little with one of your patients.

LADY BOUN. Come, good woman, don't mind this mad creature; I am the person that you want, I suppose. What would you have, woman?

MRS. SUL. She wants something for her husband's sore leg.

LADY BOUN. What's the matter with his leg, goody?

WOM. It come first, as one might say, with a sort of dizziness in his foot, then he had a kind of a laziness in his joints, and then his leg broke out, and then it swelled, and then it closed again, and then it broke out again, and then it festered, and then it grew better, and then it grew worse again.

MRS. SUL. Ha, ha, ha!

LADY BOUN. How can you be merry with the misfortunes of other people?

MRS. SUL. Because my own make me sad, madam.

LADY BOUN. The worst reason in the world, daughter; your own misfortunes should teach you to pity others.

MRS. SUL. But the woman's misfortunes and mine are nothing alike; her husband is sick, and mine, alas! is in health.

LADY BOUN. What! would you wish your husband sick?

MRS. SUL. Not of a sore leg, of all things.

LADY BOUN. Well, good woman, go to the pantry, get your bellyful of victuals, then I'll give you a receipt of diet-drink for your husband—But d'ye hear, goody, you must not let your husband move too much.

WOM. No, no, madam, the poor man's inclinable enough to lie still. *Exit.*

LADY BOUN. Well, daughter Sullen, though you laugh, I have done miracles about the country here with my receipts.

MRS. SUL. Miracles indeed, if they have cured anybody; but I believe, madam, the patient's faith goes farther toward the miracle than your prescription.

LADY BOUN. Fancy helps in some cases; but there's your husband, who has as little fancy as anybody; I brought him from death's door.

MRS. SUL. I suppose, madam, you made him drink plentifully of ass's milk.

Enter DORINDA, *runs to* MRS. SULLEN.

DOR. News, dear sister! news! news!

Enter ARCHER, *running.*

ARCH. Where, where is my Lady Bountiful?—Pray, which is the old lady of you three?

LADY BOUN. I am.

ARCH. O madam, the fame of your ladyship's charity, goodness, benevolence, skill, and ability, have drawn me hither to implore your ladyship's help in behalf of my unfortunate master, who is this moment breathing his last.

LADY BOUN. Your master! where is he?

ARCH. At your gate, madam. Drawn by the appearance of your handsome house to view it nearer, and walking up the avenue within five paces of the court-yard, he was taken ill of a sudden with a sort of I know not what, but down he fell, and there he lies.

LADY BOUN. Here, Scrub! Gipsey! all run, get my easy chair down stairs, put the gentleman in it, and bring him in quickly, quickly!

ARCH. Heaven will reward your ladyship for this charitable act.

LADY BOUN. Is your master used to these fits?

ARCH. O yes, madam, frequently—I have known him have five or six of a night.

LADY BOUN. What's his name?

ARCH. Lord, madam, he's a-dying! a minute's care or neglect may save or destroy his life!

LADY BOUN. Ah, poor gentleman! Come, friend, show me the way; I'll see him brought in myself.
                                        Exit with ARCHER.

DOR. O sister, my heart flutters about strangely! I can hardly forbear running to his assistance.

MRS. SUL. And I'll lay my life he deserves your assistance more than he wants it; did not I tell you that my lord would find a way to come at you? Love's his distemper, and you must be the physician; put on all your charms, summon all your fire into your eyes, plant the whole artillery of your looks against his breast, and down with him.

DOR. O sister! I'm but a young gunner; I shall be afraid to shoot, for fear the piece should recoil and hurt myself.

MRS. SUL. Never fear, you shall see me shoot before you, if you will.

DOR. No, no, dear sister; you have missed your mark so unfortunately, that I shan't care for being instructed by you.

Enter AIMWELL *in a chair carried by* ARCHER *and* SCRUB; LADY BOUNTIFUL [*and*] GIPSEY. AIMWELL *counterfeiting a swoon.*

LADY BOUN. Here, here, let's see the hartshorn drops.—Gipsey, a glass of fair[70] water! His fit's very strong.—Bless me, how his hands are clinched!

ARCH. For shame, ladies, what d'ye do? why don't you help us?—(*To* DORINDA.) Pray, madam, take his hand and open it, if you can, whilst I hold his head.   (DORINDA *takes his hand.*)

DOR. Poor gentleman!—Oh!—he has got my hand within his, and squeezes it unmercifully—

LADY BOUN. 'Tis the violence of his convulsion, child.

ARCH. Oh, madam, he's perfectly possessed in these cases—he'll bite if you don't have a care.

DOR. Oh, my hand! my hand!

LADY BOUN. What's the matter with the foolish girl? I have got this hand open, you see, with a great deal of ease.

ARCH. Ay, but, madam, your daughter's hand is somewhat warmer than your ladyship's, and the heat of it draws the force of the spirits that way.

MRS. SUL. I find, friend, you're very learned in these sorts of fits.

ARCH. 'Tis no wonder, madam, for I'm often troubled with them myself; I find myself extremely ill at this minute. (*Looking hard at* MRS. SULLEN.)

MRS. SUL. (*aside*). I fancy I could find a way to cure you.

LADY BOUN. His fit holds him very long.

ARCH. Longer than usual, madam.—Pray, young lady, open his breast, and give him air.

LADY BOUN. Where did his illness take him first, pray?

ARCH. Today at church, madam.

LADY BOUN. In what manner was he taken?

ARCH. Very strangely, my lady. He was of a sudden touched with something in his eyes, which, at the first, he only felt, but could not tell whether 'twas pain or pleasure.

LADY BOUN. Wind, nothing but wind!

ARCH. By soft degrees it grew and mounted to his brain,—there his fancy caught it; there formed it so beautiful, and dressed it up in such gay, pleasing colors, that his transported appetite seized the fair idea, and straight conveyed it to his heart. That hospitable seat of life sent all its sanguine spirits forth to meet, and opened all its sluicy gates to take the stranger in.

LADY BOUN. Your master should never go without a bottle to smell to.—Oh—he recovers! The lavender-water—some feathers to burn under his nose—Hungary-water[71] to rub his temples.—Oh, he comes to himself!—Hem a little, sir, hem.—Gipsey! bring the cordial-water.

          (AIMWELL *seems to awake in amaze.*)

DOR. How d'ye, sir?

AIM. Where am I?   (*Rising.*)

> Sure I have passed the gulf of silent death,
> And now I land on the Elysian shore!—
> Behold the goddess of those happy plains,
> Fair Proserpine—let me adore thy bright divinity.

          (*Kneels to* DORINDA, *and kisses her hand.*)

70. Pure.

71. A mixture of spirit of wine and rosemary flowers.

MRS. SUL. So, so, so! I knew where the fit would end!

AIM. Eurydice perhaps—

How could thy Orpheus keep his word,
And not look back upon thee?
No treasure but thyself could sure have bribed him
To look one minute off thee.

LADY BOUN. Delirious, poor gentleman!

ARCH. Very delirious, madam, very delirious.

AIM. Martin's voice, I think.

ARCH. Yes, my lord.—How does your lordship?

LADY BOUN. Lord! did you mind that, girls?

AIM. Where am I?

ARCH. In very good hands, sir.—You were taken just now with one of your old fits, under the trees, just by this good lady's house; her ladyship had you taken in, and has miraculously brought you to yourself, as you see.

AIM. I am so confounded with shame, madam, that I can now only beg pardon—and refer my acknowledgments for your ladyship's care till an opportunity offers of making some amends.—I dare be no longer troublesome.—Martin! give two guineas to the servants. *(Going.)*

DOR. Sir, you may catch cold by going so soon into the air; you don't look, sir, as if you were perfectly recovered.

(Here ARCHER *talks to* LADY BOUNTIFUL *in dumb show.)*

AIM. That I shall never be, madam; my present illness is so rooted that I must expect to carry it to my grave.

MRS. SUL. Don't despair, sir; I have known several in your distemper shake it off with a fortnight's physic.

LADY BOUN. Come, sir, your survant has been telling me that you're apt to relapse if you go into the air.—Your good manners shan't get the better of ours—you shall sit down again, sir.—Come, sir, we don't mind ceremonies in the country—here, sir, my service t'ye. You shall taste my water; 'tis a cordial I can assure you, and of my own making—drink it off, sir.—(AIMWELL *drinks.*) And how d'ye find yourself now, sir?

AIM. Somewhat better—though very faint still.

LADY BOUN. Ay, ay, people are always faint after these fits.—Come girls, you shall show the gentleman the house.—'Tis but an old family building, sir; but you had better walk about and cool by degrees, than venture immediately into the air. You'll find some tolerable pictures.—Dorinda, show the gentleman the way, I must go to the poor woman below. *Exit.*

DOR. This way, sir.

AIM. Ladies, shall I beg leave for my servant to wait on you, for he understands pictures very well?

MRS. SUL. Sir, we understand originals[72] as well as he does pictures, so he may come along.

Exeunt DORINDA, MRS. SULLEN, AIMWELL, ARCHER. AIMWELL *leads* DORINDA.

Enter FOIGARD *and* SCRUB, *meeting.*

FOI. Save you, Master Scrub!

SCRUB. Sir, I won't be saved your way—I hate a priest, I abhor the French, and I defy the devil. Sir, I'm a bold Briton, and will spill the last drop of my blood to keep out popery and slavery.

FOI. Master Scrub, you would put me down in politics, and so I would be speaking with Mrs. Shipsey.

SCRUB. Good Mr. Priest, you can't speak with her; she's sick, sir, she's gone abroad, sir, she's—dead two months ago, sir.

Enter GIPSEY.

GIP. How now, impudence! how dare you talk so saucily to the doctor?—Pray, sir, don't take it ill; for the common people of England are not so civil to strangers, as—

SCRUB. You lie! you lie! 'Tis the common people that are civilest to strangers.

GIP. Sirrah, I have a good mind to—get you out, I say!

SCRUB. I won't.

GIP. You won't sauce-box!—Pray, doctor, what is the captain's name that came to your inn last night?

SCRUB. [*aside*]. The captain! Ah, the devil, there she hampers me again;—the captain has me on one side, and the priest on t'other:—so between the gown and the sword, I have a fine time on't.— But *cedunt arma togæ*.[73] *(Going.)*

GIP. What, sirrah, won't you march?

---

72. A pun on the word 'original' in its meaning of an odd or eccentric person.
73. 'Let arms yield to the gown.' (Cicero, *De Officiis*, I.22.)

SCRUB. No, my dear, I won't march—but I'll walk.—[*Aside.*] And I'll make bold to listen a little too.   (*Goes behind the side-scene and listens.*)

GIP. Indeed, doctor, the count has been barbarously treated, that's the truth on't.

FOI. Ah, Mrs. Gipsey, upon my shoul, now, gra,[74] his complainings would mollify the marrow in your bones, and move the bowels of your commiseration! He veeps, and he dances, and he fistles, and he swears, and he laughs, and he stamps, and he sings: in conclusion, joy, he's afflicted *à la fraçaise*, and a stranger would not know whider to cry or to laugh with him.

GIP. What would you have me do, doctor?

FOI. Noting, joy, but only hide the count in Mrs. Sullen's closet when it is dark.

GIP. Nothing! is that nothing? It would be both a sin and a shame, doctor.

FOI. Here is twenty louis d'ors, joy, for your shame; and I will give you an absolution for the shin.

GIP. But won't that money look like a bribe?

FOI. Dat is according as you shall tauk it.—If you receive the money beforehand, 'twill be *logicè*, a bribe; but if you stay till afterwards, 'twill be only a gratification.[75]

GIP. Well, doctor, I'll take it *logicè*.—But what must I do with my conscience, sir?

FOI. Leave dat wid me, joy; I am your priest, gra; and your conscience is under my hands.

GIP. But should I put the count into the closet—

FOI. Vel, is dere any shin for a man's being in a closhet? One may go to prayers in a closhet.

GIP. But if the lady should come into her chamber, and go to bed?

FOI. Vel, and is dere any shin in going to bed, joy?

GIP. Ay, but if the parties should meet, doctor?

FOI. Vel den—the parties must be responsible.—Do you be after putting the count in the closhet; and leave the shins wid themselves.—I will come with the count to instruct you in your chamber.

GIP. Well, doctor, your religion is so pure!—Methinks I'm so easy after an absolution, and can sin afresh with so much security, that I'm resolved to die a martyr to't.—Here's the key of the garden door, come in the back way when 'tis late, I'll be ready to receive you; but don't so much as whisper, only take hold of my hand; I'll lead you, and do you lead the count, and follow me.

Exeunt.

Enter SCRUB.

SCRUB. What witchcraft now have these two imps of the devil been a-hatching here?—There's twenty louis-d'ors; I heard that, and saw the purse. But I must give room to my betters.   [*Exit.*]

Enter AIMWELL, *leading* DORINDA, *and making love in dumb show;* MRS. SULLEN *and* ARCHER.

MRS. SUL. (*to* ARCHER). Pray, sir, how d'ye like that piece?

ARCH. Oh, 'tis Leda! You find, madam, how Jupiter comes disguised to make love—

MRS. SUL. But what think you there of Alexander's battles?

ARCH. We only want a Le Brun,[76] madam, to draw greater battles, and a greater general of our own.[77] The Danube,[78] madam, would make a greater figure in a picture than the Granicus;[79] and we have our Ramillies to match their Arbela.[80]

MRS. SUL. Pray, sir, what head is that in the corner there?

ARCH. O madam, 'tis poor Ovid in his exile.

MRS. SUL. What was he banished for?

ARCH. His ambitious love, madam.—(*Bowing.*) His misfortune touches me.

MRS. SUL. Was he successful in his amours?

ARCH. There he has left us in the dark. He was too much a gentleman to tell.

MRS. SUL. If he were secret, I pity him.

ARCH. And if he were successful, I envy him.

---

74. Dear.
75. Ie., a gratuity.

76. Charles Le Brun (1619–1690), court painter of Louis XIV; painter of murals, at Versailles and elsewhere, celebrating the deeds of his patron. He had also executed a series of murals depicting the exploits of Alexander the Great.
77. The Duke of Marlborough.
78. Blenheim, scene of the great victory (1704) of the English and the Austrians over the French and the Bavarians, was on the Danube.
79. A river in Asia Minor which was the scene of Alexander the Great's overwhelming defeat of the Persians in 344 B.C.
80. The first-named battle (1706) was a victory of the Allies over the French; the second (331. B.C.) one in which Alexander defeated Darius.

MRS. SUL. How d'ye like that Venus over the chimney?

ARCH. Venus! I protest madam, I took it for your picture; but now I look again, 'tis not handsome enough.

MRS. SUL. Oh, what a charm is flattery! If you would see my picture, there it is, over that cabinet.—How d'ye like it?

ARCH. I must admire anything, madam, that has the least resemblance of you.—But, methinks, madam—(*He looks at the picture and* MRS. SULLEN *three or four times, by turns.*) Pray, madam, who drew it?

MRS. SUL. A famous hand, sir.

Here AIMWELL *and* DORINDA *go off.*

ARCH. A famous hand, madam!—Your eyes, indeed, are featured there; but where's the sparkling moisture, shining fluid, in which they swim? The picture, indeed, has your dimples; but where's the swarm of killing Cupids that should ambush there? the lips too are figured out; but where's the carnation dew, the pouting ripeness, that tempts the taste in the original?

MRS. SUL. [*aside*]. Had it been my lot to have matched with such a man!

ARCH. Your breasts too—presumptuous man!—what, paint heaven!—Apropos, madam, in the very next picture is Salmoneus, that was struck dead with lightning, for offering to imitate Jove's thunder; I hope you served the painter so, madam?

MRS. SUL. Had my eyes the power of thunder, they should employ their lightning better.

ARCH. There's the finest bed in that room, madam! I suppose 'tis your ladyship's bedchamber.

MRS. SUL. And what then, sir?

ARCH. I think the quilt is the richest that ever I saw.—I can't at this distance, madam, distinguish the figures of the embroidery; will you give me leave, madam?—   [*Goes toward the door.*]

MRS. SUL. [*aside.*]. The devil take his impudence!—Sure, if I gave him an opportunity, he durst not offer it?—I have a great mind to try.—(*Going; returns.*) 'Sdeath, what am I doing?—And alone, too!—Sister! sister!   (*Runs out.*)

ARCH. I'll follow her close—
For where a Frenchman durst attempt to storm,
A Briton sure may well the work perform.

(*Going.*)

Enter SCRUB.

SCRUB. Martin! brother Martin!

ARCH. O brother Scrub, I beg your pardon, I was not a-going; here's a guinea my master ordered you.

SCRUB. A guinea! hi, hi, hi! a guinea! eh—by this light it is a guinea! But I suppose you expect one and twenty shillings in change.

ARCH. Not at all; I have another for Gipsey.

SCRUB. A guinea for her! Faggot and fire for the witch!—Sir, give me that guinea, and I'll discover a plot.

ARCH. A plot!

SCRUB. Ay, sir, a plot, and a horrid plot!—First, it must be a plot, because there's a woman in't; secondly, it must be a plot, because there's a priest in't; thirdly, it must be a plot, because there's French gold in't; and fourthly, it must be a plot, because I don't know what to make on't.

ARCH. Nor anybody else, I'm afraid, brother Scrub.

SCRUB. Truly, I'm afraid so too; for where there's a priest and a woman, there's always a mystery and a riddle. This I know, that here has been the doctor with a temptation in one hand and an absolution in the other; and Gipsey has sold herself to the devil; I saw the price paid down, my eyes shall take their oath on't.

ARCH. And is all this bustle about Gipsey?

SCRUB. That's not all; I could hear but a word here and there; but I remember they mentioned a count, a closet, a back door, and a key.

ARCH. The count!—Did you hear nothing of Mrs. Sullen?

SCRUB. I did hear some word that sounded that way; but whether it was Sullen or Dorinda, I could not distinguish.

ARCH. You have told this matter to nobody, brother?

SCRUB. Told! No, sir, I thank you for that; I'm resolved never to speak one word *pro* nor *con,* till we have a peace.

ARCH. You're i' the right, brother Scrub; here's a treaty afoot between the count and the lady: the priest and the chambermaid are the plenipotentiaries.—It shall go hard but I find a way to be included in the treaty.—Where's the doctor now?

SCRUB. He and Gipsey are this moment devouring my lady's marmalade in the closet.

AIM. (*from without*). Martin! Martin!

ARCH. I come, sir, I come.

SCRUB. But you forget the other guinea, brother Martin.

ARCH. Here, I give it with all my heart.

SCRUB. And I take it with all my soul.—Icod, I'll spoil your plotting, Mrs. Gipsey! and if you should set the captain upon me, these two guineas will buy me off.   [*Exeunt severally.*]

Enter MRS. SULLEN *and* DORINDA, *meeting.*

MRS. SUL. Well, sister!

DOR. And well, sister!

MRS. SUL. What's become of my lord?

DOR. What's become of his servant?

MRS. SUL. Servant! he's a prettier fellow, and a finer gentleman by fifty degrees than his master.

DOR. O' my conscience, I fancy you could beg that fellow at the gallows-foot![81]

MRS. SUL. O' my conscience I could, provided I could put a friend of yours in his room.

DOR. You desired me, sister, to leave you, when you transgressed the bounds of honor.

MRS. SUL. Thou dear censorious country girl! what dost mean? You can't think of the man without the bedfellow, I find.

DOR. I don't find anything unnatural in that thought; while the mind is conversant with flesh and blood, it must conform to the humors of the company.

MRS. SUL. How a little love and good company improves a woman! why, child, you begin to live—you never spoke before.

DOR. Because I was never spoke to.—My lord has told me that I have more wit and beauty than any of my sex; and truly I begin to think the man is sincere.

MRS. SUL. You're in the right, Dorinda; pride is the life of a woman, and flattery is our daily bread; and she's a fool that won't believe a man there, as much as she that believes him in anything else.—But I'll lay you a guinea that I had finer things said to me than you had.

DOR. Done!—What did your fellow say to ye?

MRS. SUL. My fellow took the picture of Venus for mine.

DOR. But my lover took me for Venus herself.

MRS. SUL. Common cant! Had my spark called me a Venus directly, I should have believed him a footman in good earnest.

DOR. But my lover was upon his knees to me.

MRS. SUL. And mine was upon his tiptoes to me.

DOR. Mine vowed to die for me.

MRS. SUL. Mine swore to die with me.

DOR. Mine spoke the softest moving things.

MRS. SUL. Mine had his moving things too.

DOR. Mine kissed my hand ten thousand times.

MRS. SUL. Mine has all that pleasure to come.

DOR. Mine offered marriage.

MRS. SUL. O Lard! D'ye call that a moving thing?

DOR. The sharpest arrow in his quiver, my dear sister!—Why, my ten thousand pounds may lie brooding here this seven years, and hatch nothing at last but some ill-natured clown like yours.
Whereas, if I marry my Lord Aimwell, there will be title, place, and precedence, the Park, the play, and the drawing-room, splendor, equipage, noise, and flambeaux.—'Hey, my Lady Aimwell's servants there!—Lights, lights to the stairs!—My Lady Aimwell's coach put forward!—Stand by, make room for her ladyship!'—Are not these things moving?—What! melancholy of a sudden?

MRS. SUL. Happy, happy sister! your angel has been watchful for your happiness, whilst mine has slept regardless of his charge.—Long smiling years of circling joys for you, but not one hour for me!
(*Weeps.*)

DOR. Come, my dear, we'll talk of something else.

MRS. SUL. O Dorinda! I own myself a woman, full of my sex, a gentle, generous soul—easy and yielding to soft desires; a spacious heart, where Love and all his train might lodge. And must the fair apartment of my breast be made a stable for a brute to lie in?

DOR. Meaning your husband, I suppose?

---

81. Occasionally a criminal condemned to death was reprieved upon the offer by a respectable woman to marry him if his life were spared. For an interesting instance of this custom see Narcissus Luttrell's diary for November, 1687.

MRS. SUL. Husband! no,—even husband is too soft a name for him.—But, come, I expect my brother here tonight or tomorrow; he was abroad when my father married me; perhaps he'll find a way to make me easy.

DOR. Will you promise not to make yourself easy in the meantime with my lord's friend?

MRS. SUL. You mistake me, sister. It happens with us as among the men, the greatest talkers are the greatest cowards; and there's a reason for it; those spirits evaporate in prattle, which might do more mischief if they took another course.—Though, to confess the truth, I do love that fellow;—and if I met him dressed as he should be, and I undressed as I should be—look ye, sister, I have no supernatural gifts—I can't swear I could resist the temptation; though I can safely promise to avoid it; and that's as much as the best of us can do.

Exeunt MRS. SULLEN *and* DORINDA.

[SCENE II]

[*The inn.*]

Enter AIMWELL *and* ARCHER, *laughing.*

ARCH. And the awkward kindness of the good motherly old gentlewoman—

AIM. And the coming easiness of the young one— 'Sdeath, 'tis pity to deceive her!

ARCH. Nay, if you adhere to those principles, stop where you are.

AIM. I can't stop; for I love her to distraction.

ARCH. 'Sdeath, if you love her a hair's breadth beyond discretion, you must go no farther.

AIM. Well, well, anything to deliver us from sauntering away our idle evenings at White's, Tom's, or Will's,[82] and be stinted to bear looking at our old acquaintance, the cards, because our impotent pockets can't afford us a guinea for the mercenary drabs.

ARCH. Or be obliged to some purse-proud cox-comb for a scandalous bottle, where we must not pretend to our share of the discourse, because we can't pay our club[83] o' th' reckoning. Damn it, I had rather sponge upon Morris,[84] and sup upon a dish of bohea[85] scored behind the door!

AIM. And there expose our want of sense by talking criticisms, as we should our want of money by railing at the government.

ARCH. Or be obliged to sneak into the sidebox, and between both houses steal two acts of a play,[86] and because we han't money to see the other three, we come away discontented, and damn the whole five.

AIM. And ten thousand such rascally tricks—had we outlived our fortunes among our acquaintance.—But now—

ARCH. Ay, now is the time to prevent all this.— Strike while the iron is hot.—This priest is the luckiest part of our adventure; he shall marry you, and pimp for me.

AIM. But I should not like a woman that can be so fond of a Frenchman.

ARCH. Alas, sir! Necessity has no law. The lady may be in distress; perhaps she has a confounded husband, and her revenge may carry her farther than her love.—Igad, I have so good an opinion of her, and of myself, that I begin to fancy strange things; and we must say this for the honor of our women, and indeed of ourselves, that they do stick to their men as they do to their *Magna Charta*. If the plot lies as I suspect, I must put on the gentleman.— But here comes the doctor.—I shall be ready.

Exit.

Enter FOIGARD.

FOI. Sauve you, noble friend,

AIM. O sir, your servant! Pray, doctor, may I crave your name?

FOI. Fat naam is upon me? My naam is Foigard, joy.

AIM. Foigard! a very good name for a clergyman.[87] Pray, Doctor Foigard, were you ever in Ireland?

FOI. Ireland! no, joy. Fat sort of plaace is dat saam Ireland? Dey say de people are catched dere when dey are young.

AIM. And some of 'em when they're old—as for example.—(*Takes* FOIGARD *by the shoulder.*) Sir, I arrest you as a traitor against the government; you're a subject of England, and this morning showed me a commission, by which you served as chaplain in the French army. This is death by our law, and your reverence must hang for't.

82. Fashionable London coffee-houses.
83. Share.
84. Presumably the owner of Morris's coffee-house in Essex Street, the Strand.
85. A kind of black tea.
86. The box-keeper collected the money for the performance after the second act.
87. It means 'defender of the faith.'

FOI. Upon my shoul, noble friend, dis is strange news you tell me! Fader Foigard a subject of England! de son of a burgomaster of Brussels a subject of England! ubooboo[88]—

AIM. The son of a bog-trotter in Ireland! Sir, your tongue will condemn you before any bench in the kingdom.

FOI. And is my tongue all your evidensh, joy?

AIM. That's enough.

FOI. No, no, joy, for I vil never spake English no more.

AIM. Sir, I have other evidence.—Here, Martin!

Enter ARCHER.

You know this fellow?

ARCH. (*in a brogue*). Saave you, my dear cussen, how does your health?

FOI. (*aside*). Ah! upon my shoul dere is my countryman, and his brogue will hang mine.—[*To* AIMWELL.] *Mynkeer, Ick wet neat watt hey zacht.* [*To* ARCHER.] *Ick universton ewe neat, sacramant!*[89]

AIM. Altering your language won't do, sir; this fellow knows your person, and will swear to your face.

FOI. Faace! fey, is dear a brogue upon my faash too?

ARCH. Upon my soulvation dere ish, joy!—But cussen Mackshane, vil you not put a remembrance upon me?

FOI. (*aside*). Mackshane! by St. Paatrick, dat is [my] naame, shure enough!

AIM. [*aside to* ARCHER]. I fancy, Archer, you have it.

FOI. The devil hang you, joy! By fat acquaintance are you my cussen?

ARCH. Oh, de devil hang yourshelf, joy! You know we were little boys togeder upon de school, and your foster-moder's son was married upon my nurse's chister, joy, and so we are Irish cussens.

FOI. De devil taak the relation! Vel, joy, and fat school was it?

ARCH. I tinks it vas—aay—'twas Tipperary.

FOI. No, no, joy; it vas Kilkenny.

AIM. That's enough for us—self-confession. Come, sir, we must deliver you into the hands of the next magistrate.

ARCH. He sends you to gaol, you're tried next assizes, and away you go swing into purgatory.

FOI. And is it so wid you, cussen?

ARCH. It vil be sho wid you, cussen, if you don't immediately confess the secret between you and Mrs. Gipsey.—Look'ee, sir, the gallows or the secret, take your choice.

FOI. The gallows! Upon my shoul I hate that saam gallow, for it is a diseash dat is fatal to our family.—Vel, den, dere is nothing, shentlemens, but Mrs. Shullen would spaak wid the count in her chamber at midnight, and dere is no haarm, joy, for I am to conduct the count to the plash, myshelf.

ARCH. As I guessed.—Have you communicated the matter to the count?

FOI. I have not sheen him since.

ARCH. Right again! Why then, doctor—you shall conduct me to the lady instead of the count.

FOI. Fat, my cussen to the lady! Upon my shoul, gra, dat is too much upon the brogue.

ARCH. Come, come, doctor; consider we have got a rope about your neck, and if you offer to squeak, we'll stop your windpipe, most certainly. We shall have another job for you in a day or two, I hope.

AIM. Here's company coming this way; let's into my chamber, and there concert our affairs farther.

ARCH. Come, my dear cussen, come along.

Exeunt.

Enter BONNIFACE, HOUNSLOW, *and* BAGSHOT *at one door,* GIBBET *at the opposite.*

GIB. Well, gentlemen, 'tis a fine night for our enterprise.

HOUN. Dark as hell.

BAG. And blows like the devil; our landlord here has showed us the window where we must break in, and tells us the plate stands in the wainscot cupboard in the parlor.

BON. Ay, ay, Mr. Bagshot, as the saying is, knives and forks, and cups and cans, and tumblers and tankards. There's one tankard, as the saying is,

88. Supposed to be a typical Irish interjection.
89. Foigard's speech, in 'Flemish' of his own invention, appears to mean, 'Sir, I don't know what he says.—I don't understand you, egad!'

221

that's near upon as big as me; it was a present to the squire from his godmother, and smells of nutmeg and toast like an East India ship.

HOUN. Then you say we must divide at the stairhead?

BON. Yes, Mr. Hounslow, as the saying is.—At one end of that gallery lies my Lady Bountiful and her daughter, and at the other Mrs. Sullen.—As for the squire—

GIB. He's safe enough, I have fairly entered[90] him, and he's more than half seas over already. But such a parcel of scoundrels are got about him now, that, igad, I was ashamed to be seen in their company.

BON. 'Tis now twelve, as the saying is—Gentlemen, you must set out at one.

GIB. Hounslow, do you and Bagshot see our arms fixed, and I'll come to you presently.

HOUN., BAG. We will.   *Exeunt.*

GIB. Well, my dear Bonny, you assure me that Scrub is a coward.

BON. A chicken, as the saying is.—You'll have no creature to deal with but the ladies.

GIB. And I can assure you, friend, there's a great deal of address and good manners in robbing a lady; I am the most a gentleman that way that ever travelled the road.—But, my dear Bonny, this prize will be a galleon, a Vigo business.[91]—I warrant you we shall bring off three or four thousand pound.

BON. In plate, jewels, and money, as the saying is, you may.

GIB. Why then, Tyburn,[92] I defy thee! I'll get up to town, sell off my horse and arms, buy myself some pretty employment in the household,[93] and be as snug and as honest as any courtier of 'um all.

BON. And what think you then of my daughter Cherry for a wife?

GIB. Look'ee, my dear Bonny—Cherry 'is the goddess I adore,' as the song goes; but it is a maxim that man and wife should never have it in their power to hang one another; for if they should, the Lord have mercy on 'um both!   *Exeunt.*

---

90. Started.
91. Referring to the capture or sinking of the Spanish treasure-ships by the allied fleet, in Vigo harbor, in northwestern Spain, in 1702.
92. The site of the gallows in London.
93. The royal household, the Court.

ACT V
[SCENE I]

Scene continues.

(*Knocking without.*)

Enter BONNIFACE.

BON. Coming! Coming!—A coach and six foaming horses at this time o'night! Some great man, as the saying is, for he scorns to travel with other people.

Enter SIR CHARLES FREEMAN.

SIR CHAS. What, fellow! a public house, and abed when other people sleep?

BON. Sir, I an't abed, as the saying is.

SIR CHAS. Is Mr. Sullen's family abed, think'ee?

BON. All but the squire himself, sir, as the saying is; he's in the house.

SIR CHAS. What company has he?

BON. Why, sir, there's the constable, Mr. Gage the exciseman, the hunchbacked barber, and two or three other gentlemen.

SIR CHAS. [*aside*]. I find my sister's letters gave me the true picture of her spouse.

Enter SULLEN, *drunk.*

BON. Sir, here's the squire.

SUL. The puppies left me asleep.—Sir!

SIR CHAS. Well, sir.

SUL. Sir, I'm an unfortunate man—I have three thousand pound a year, and I can't get a man to drink a cup of ale with me.

SIR CHAS. That's very hard.

SUL. Ay, sir; and unless you have pity upon me, and smoke one pipe with me, I must e'en go home to my wife, and I had rather go [to] the devil by half.

SIR CHAS. But I presume, sir, you won't see your wife tonight; she'll be gone to bed—you don't use to lie with your wife in that pickle?

SUL. What! not lie with my wife! Why, sir, do you take me for an atheist or a rake?

SIR CHAS. If you hate her, sir, I think you had better lie from her.

SUL. I think so too, friend.—But I'm a justice of peace, and must do nothing against the law.

222

SIR CHAS. Law! As I take it, Mr. Justice, nobody observes law for law's sake, only for the good of those for whom it was made.

SUL. But if the law orders me to send you to goal,[94] you must lie there, my friend.

SIR CHAS. Not unless I commit a crime to deserve it.

SUL. A crime? 'Oons, an't I married?

SIR CHAS. Nay, sir, if you call marriage a crime, you must disown it for a law.

SUL. Eh!—I must be acquainted with you, sir.—But, sir, I should be very glad to know the truth of this matter.

SIR CHAS. Truth, sir, is a profound sea, and few there be that dare wade deep enough to find out the bottom on't. Besides, sir, I'm afraid the line of your understanding mayn't be long enough.

SUL. Look'ee, sir, I have nothing to say to your sea of truth, but if a good parcel of land can intitle a man to a little truth, I have as much as any he in the country.

BON. I never heard your worship, as the saying is, talk so much before.

SUL. Because I never met with a man that I liked before.

BON. Pray, sir, as the saying is, let me ask you one question: are not man and wife one flesh?

SIR CHAS. You and your wife, Mr. Guts, may be one flesh, because ye are nothing else;—but rational creatures have minds that must be united.

SUL. Minds!

SIR CHAS. Ay, minds, sir; don't you think that the mind takes place of[95] the body?

SUL. In some people.

SIR CHAS. Then the interest of the master must be consulted before that of his servant.

SUL. Sir, you shall dine with me tomorrow!—'Oons, I always thought that we were naturally one.

SIR CHAS. Sir, I know that my two hands are naturally one, because they love one another, kiss one another, help one another in all the actions of life; but I could not say so much if they were always at cuffs.

SUL. Then 'tis plain that we are two.

SIR CHAS. Why don't you part with her, sir?

SUL. Will you take her, sir?

SIR CHAS. With all my heart.

SUL. You shall have her tomorrow morning, and a venison-pasty into the bargain.

SIR CHAS. You'll let me have her fortune too?

SUL. Fortune! Why, sir, I have no quarrel at her fortune. I only hate the woman, sir, and none but the woman shall go.

SIR CHAS. But her fortune, sir—

SUL. Can you play at whisk, sir?

SIR CHAS. No, truly, sir.

SUL. Nor at all-fours?[96]

SIR CHAS. Neither!

SUL. (aside). 'Oons! where was this man bred?— [Aloud.] Burn me, sir! I can't go home; 'tis but two o'clock.

SIR CHAS. For half an hour, sir, if you please. But you must consider 'tis late.

SUL. Late! that's the reason I can't go to bed.— Come, sir!   Exeunt.

Enter CHERRY, runs across the stage and knocks at AIMWELL'S chamber door. Enter AIMWELL in his nightcap and gown.

AIM. What's the matter? You tremble, child; you're frighted.

CHER. No wonder, sir.—But, in short, sir, this very minute a gang of rogues are gone to rob my Lady Bountiful's house.

AIM. How!

CHER. I dogged 'em to the very door, and left 'em breaking in.

AIM. Have you alarmed anybody else with the news?

CHER. No, no, sir, I wanted to have discovered the whole plot, and twenty other things, to your man Martin; but I have searched the whole house, and can't find him. Where is he?

AIM. No matter, child, will you guide me immediately to the house?

CHER. With all my heart, sir; my Lady Bountiful is my godmother, and I love Mrs. Dorinda so well—

---

94. An old spelling of 'gaol.'
95. Takes precedence of.

96. A two-handed card-game.

AIM. Dorinda! The name inspires me, the glory and the danger shall be all my own.—Come, my life, let me but get my sword. *Exeunt.*

[SCENE II]

Scene changes to a bedchamber in LADY BOUNTIFUL'S *house.*

Enter MRS. SULLEN, DORINDA *undressed; a table and lights.*

DOR. 'Tis very late, sister. No news of your spouse yet?

MRS. SUL. No, I'm condemned to be alone till towards four, and then perhaps I may be executed with his company.

DOR. Well, my dear, I'll leave you to your rest; you'll go directly to bed, I suppose?

MRS. SUL. I don't know what to do.—Heigh-ho!

DOR. That's a desiring sigh, sister.

MRS. SUL. This is a languishing hour, sister.

DOR. And might prove a critical minute, if the pretty fellow were here.

MRS. SUL. Here! What, in my bedchamber at two o'clock o' th' morning, I undressed, the family asleep, my hated husband abroad, and my lovely fellow at my feet!—O 'gad sister!

DOR. Thoughts are free, sister, and them I allow you.—So, my dear, good night.

MRS. SUL. A good rest to my dear Dorinda!—[*Exit* DORINDA.] Thoughts free! are they so? Why, then suppose him here, dressed like a youthful, gay, and burning bridegroom, (*here* ARCHER *steals out of the closet*) with tongue enchanting, eyes bewitching, knees imploring.—(*Turns a little o' one side and sees* ARCHER *in the posture she describes.*)—Ah!—(*Shrieks, and runs to the other side of the stage.*) Have my thoughts raised a spirit?—What are you, sir, a man or a devil?

ARCH. (*rising*). A man, a man, madam.

MRS. SUL. How shall I be sure of it?

ARCH. Madam, I'll give you demonstration this minute. (*Takes her hand.*)

MRS. SUL. What, sir! do you intend to be rude?

ARCH. Yes, madam, if you please.

MRS. SUL. In the name of wonder, whence came ye?

ARCH. From the skies, madam—I'm a Jupiter in love, and you shall be my Alcmena.[97]

MRS. SUL. How came you in?

ARCH. I flew in at the window, madam; your cousin Cupid lent me his wings, and your sister Venus opened the casement.

MRS. SUL. I'm struck dumb with admiration!

ARCH. And I—with wonder!

(*Looks passionately at her.*)

MRS. SUL. What will become of me?

ARCH. How beautiful she looks!—The teeming, jolly spring smiles in her blooming face, and when she was conceived, her mother smelt to roses, looked on lilies—

Lilies unfold their white, their fragrant charms,
When the warm sun thus darts into their arms.

(*Runs to her.*)

MRS. SUL. (*shrieks*). Ah!

ARCH. 'Oons, madam, what d'ye mean? you'll raise the house.

MRS. SUL. Sir, I'll wake the dead before I bear this!—What! approach me with the freedoms of a keeper! I'm glad on't, your impudence has cured me.

ARCH. If this be impudence—(*kneels*) I leave to your partial self; no panting pilgrim, after a tedious, painful voyage, e'er bowed before his saint with more devotion.

MRS. SUL. (*aside*). Now, now, I'm ruined if he kneels!—Rise, thou prostrate engineer, not all thy undermining skill shall reach my heart. Rise, and know I am a woman without my sex; I can love to all the tenderness of wishes, sighs, and tears—but go no farther. Still, to convince you that I'm more than woman, I can speak my frailty, confess my weakness even for you—but—

ARCH. (*going to lay hold on her*). For me!

MRS. SUL. Hold, sir! build not upon that; for my most mortal hatred follows if you disobey what I command you now. Leave me this minute.—(*Aside.*) If he denies, I'm lost.

ARCH. Then you'll promise—

MRS. SUL. Anything another time.

---

97. The mother of Hercules by Zeus, who assumed the form of her husband.

ARCH. When shall I come?

MRS. SUL. Tomorrow when you will.

ARCH. Your lips must seal the promise.

MRS. SUL. Pshaw!

ARCH. They must! they must!—(*Kisses her.*) Raptures and paradise!—And why not now, my angel? the time, the place, silence, and secrecy, all conspire. And the now conscious stars have preordained this moment for my happiness.
(*Takes her in [his] arms.*)

MRS. SUL. You will not! cannot, sure!

ARCH. If the sun rides fast, and disappoints not mortals of tomorrow's dawn, this night shall crown my joys.

MRS. SUL. My sex's pride assist me!

ARCH. My sex's strength help me!

MRS. SUL. You shall kill me first!

ARCH. I'll die with you. (*Carrying her off.*)

MRS. SUL. Thieves! thieves! murther!—

Enter SCRUB *in his breeches, and one shoe.*

SCRUB. Thieves! thieves! murther! popery!

ARCH. Ha! the very timorous stag will kill in rutting time. (*Draws, and offers to stab* SCRUB.)

SCRUB (*kneeling*). Oh pray, sir, spare all I have, and take my life!

MRS. SUL. (*holding* ARCHER'S *hand*). What does the fellow mean?

SCRUB. O madam, down upon your knees, your marrow-bones!—He's one of 'um.

ARCH. Of whom?

SCRUB. One of the rogues—I beg your pardon, sir, one of the honest gentlemen that just now are broke into the house.

ARCH. How!

MRS. SUL. I hope you did not come to rob me?

ARCH. Indeed I did, madam, but I would have taken nothing but what you might ha' spared; but your crying 'Thieves' has waked this dreaming fool, and so he takes 'em for granted.

SCRUB. Granted! 'tis granted, sir; take all we have.

MRS. SUL. The fellow looks as if he were broke out of Bedlam.

SCRUB. 'Oons, madam, they're broke into the house with fire and sword; I saw them, heard them; they'll be here this minute.

ARCH. What, thieves?

SCRUB. Under favor, sir, I think so.

MRS. SUL. What shall we do, sir?

ARCH. Madam, I wish your ladyship a good night.

MRS. SUL. Will you leave me?

ARCH. Leave you! Lord, madam, did not you command me to be gone just now, upon pain of your immortal hatred?

MRS. SUL. Nay, but pray, sir—
(*Takes hold of him.*)

ARCH. Ha, ha, ha! now comes my turn to be ravished. You see now, madam, you must use men one way or other; but take this by the way, good madam, that none but a fool will give you the benefit of his courage, unless you'll take his love along with it.—How are they armed, friend?

SCRUB. With sword and pistol, sir.

ARCH. Hush!—I see a dark lanthorn coming through the gallery.—Madam, be assured I will protect you, or lose my life.

MRS. SUL. Your life! No, sir, they can rob me of nothing that I value half so much; therefore, now, sir, let me intreat you to be gone.

ARCH. No, madam, I'll consult my own safety for the sake of yours; I'll work by stratagem. Have you courage enough to stand the appearance of 'em?

MRS. SUL. Yes, yes, since I have 'scaped your hands, I can face anything.

ARCH. Come hither, brother Scrub! don't you know me?

SCRUB. Eh! my dear brother, let me kiss thee.
(*Kisses* ARCHER.)

ARCH. This way—here—

(ARCHER *and* SCRUB *hide behind the bed.*)

Enter GIBBET, *with a dark lanthorn in one hand, and a pistol in t'other.*

GIB. Ay, ay, this is the chamber, and the lady alone.

MRS. SUL. Who are you, sir? what would you have? d'ye come to rob me?

GIB. Rob you! Alack-a-day, madam, I'm only a younger brother,[98] madam; and so, madam, if you make a noise, I'll shoot you through the head; but don't be afraid, madam.—(*Laying his lanthorn and pistol upon the table.*) These rings, madam— don't be concerned, madam, I have a profound respect for you, madam; your keys, madam—don't be frighted, madam, I'm the most of a gentleman.—(*Searching her pockets.*) This necklace, madam—I never was rude to a lady;—I have a veneration—for this necklace—

(*Here* ARCHER, *having come round and seized the* [*pistol*], *takes* GIBBET *by the collar, trips up his heels, and claps the pistol to his breast.*)

ARCH. Hold, profane villain, and take the reward of thy sacrilege!

GIB. Oh! pray, sir, don't kill me; I an't prepared.

ARCH. How many is there of 'em, Scrub?

SCRUB. Five-and-forty, sir.

ARCH. Then I must kill the villain, to have him out of the way.

GIB. Hold, hold, sir, we are but three, upon my honor.

ARCH. Scrub, will you undertake to secure him?

SCRUB. Not I, sir; kill him, kill him!

ARCH. Run to Gipsey's chamber, there you'll find the doctor; bring him hither presently.—(*Exit* SCRUB, *running.*) Come, rogue, if you have a short prayer, say it.

GIB. Sir, I have no prayer at all; the government has provided a chaplain to say prayers for us on these occasions.

MRS. SUL. Pray, sir, don't kill him. You fright me as much as him.

ARCH. The dog shall die, madam, for being the occasion of my disappointment.—Sirrah, this moment is your last.

GIB. Sir, I'll give you two hundred pound to spare my life.

ARCH. Have you no more, rascal?

GIB. Yes, sir, I can command four hundred, but I must reserve two of 'em to save my life at the sessions.

Enter SCRUB *and* FOIGARD.

ARCH. Here, doctor, I suppose Scrub and you between you may manage him.—Lay hold of him, doctor. (FOIGARD *lays hold of* GIBBET.)

GIB. What! turned over to the priest already!—Look ye, doctor, you come before your time; I an't condemned yet, I thank ye.

FOI. Come, my dear joy, I vill secure your body and your shoul too; I vill make you a good Catholic, and give you an absolution.

GIB. Absolution! can you procure me a pardon, doctor?

FOI. No, joy.

GIB. Then you and your absolution may go to the devil!

ARCH. Convey him into the cellar; there bind him. Take the pistol, and if he offers to resist, shoot him through the head—and come back to us with all the speed you can.

SCRUB. Ay, ay; come, doctor, do you hold him fast, and I'll guard him.

[*Exit* FOIGARD *and* SCRUB *with* GIBBET.]

MRS. SUL. But how came the doctor—

ARCH. In short, madam—(*shrieking without*). 'Sdeath! the rogues are at work with the other ladies. I'm vexed I parted with the pistol; but I must fly to their assistance. Will you stay here, madam, or venture yourself with me?

MRS. SUL. Oh, with you, dear sir, with you.

Takes him by the arm and exeunt.

[SCENE III]

Scene changes to another apartment in the same house.

Enter HOUNSLOW *dragging in* LADY BOUNTIFUL, *and* BAGSHOT *hauling in* DORINDA; *the rogues with swords drawn.*

[BAG.] Come, come, your jewels, mistress!

[HOUN.] Your keys, your keys, old gentlewoman!

Enter AIMWELL *and* CHERRY.

AIM. Turn this way, villains! I durst engage an army in such a cause. (*He engages 'em both.*)

DOR. O madam, had I but a sword to help the brave man!

---

98. A jesting reference to the fact that under the laws of primogeniture younger brothers had to make their living by any means that offered. Gibbet pretends to the rank of gentleman.

LADY BOUN. There's three or four hanging up in the hall; but they won't draw. I'll go fetch one, however. *Exit.*

Enter ARCHER *and* MRS. SULLEN.

ARCH. Hold, hold, my lord! every man his bird, pray.

(*They engage man to man; the rogues are thrown and disarmed.*)

CHER. [*aside*]. What! the rogues taken! then they'll impeach my father; I must give him timely notice. *Runs out.*

ARCH. Shall we kill the rogues?

AIM. No, no, we'll bind them.

ARCH. Ay, ay.—(*To* MRS. SULLEN, *who stands by him.*) Here, madam, lend me your garter.

MRS. SUL. (*aside*). The devil's in this fellow! he fights, loves, and banters, all in a breath.— [*Aloud.*] Here's a cord that the rogues brought with 'em, I suppose.

ARCH. Right, right, the rogue's destiny, a rope to hang himself.—Come, my lord.—This is but a scandalous sort of an office (*binding the rogues together*) if our adventures should end in this sort of hangman-work; but I hope there is something in prospect that—

Enter SCRUB.

Well, Scrub, have you secured your Tartar?

SCRUB. Yes, sir; I left the priest and him disputing about religion.

AIM. And pray carry these gentlemen to reap the benefit of the controversy.

Delivers the prisoners to SCRUB, *who leads 'em out.*

MRS. SUL. Pray, sister, how came my lord here?

DOR. And pray, how came the gentleman here?

MRS. SUL. I'll tell you the greatest piece of villainy— (*They talk in dumb show.*)

AIM. I fancy, Archer, you have been more successful in your adventures than the housebreakers.

ARCH. No matter for my adventure, yours is the principal. Press her this minute to marry you— now while she's hurried between the palpitation of her fear and the joy of her deliverance, now while the tide of her spirits are at high-flood. Throw yourself at her feet, speak some romantic nonsense or other—address her like Alexander in the height of his victory, confound her senses, bear down her reason, and away with her. The priest is in the cellar and dare not refuse to do the work.

Enter LADY BOUNTIFUL.

AIM. But how shall I get off without being observed?

ARCH. You a lover, and not find a way to get off!— Let me see—

AIM. You bleed, Archer.

ARCH. 'Sdeath, I'm glad on't; this wound will do the business.—I'll amuse the old lady and Mrs. Sullen about dressing my wound, while you carry off Dorinda.

LADY BOUN. Gentlemen, could we understand how you would be gratified for the services—

ARCH. Come, come, my lady, this is no time for compliments; I'm wounded, madam.

LADY BOUN., MRS. SUL. How! wounded!

DOR [*to* AIMWELL]. I hope, sir, you have received no hurt?

AIM. None but what you may cure—

(*Makes love in dumb show.*)

LADY BOUN. Let me see your arm, sir.—I must have some powder-sugar to stop the blood.—O me! an ugly gash, upon my word, sir! You must go into bed.

ARCH. Ay, my lady, a bed would do very well.— (*To* MRS. SULLEN.) Madam, will you do me the favor to conduct me to a chamber.

LADY BOUN. Do, do, daughter—while I get the lint and the probe and the plaster ready.

Runs out one way; AIMWELL *carries off* DORINDA *another.*

ARCH. Come, madam, why don't you obey your mother's commands?

MRS. SUL. How can you, after what is passed, have the confidence to ask me?

ARCH. And if you go to that, how can you, after what is passed, have the confidence to deny me? Was not this blood shed in your defence, and my life exposed for your protection? Look ye, madam, I'm none of your romantic fools, that fight giants and monsters for nothing; my valor is downright Swiss;[99] I'm a soldier of fortune, and must be paid.

99. The Swiss were famed for their services as mercenaries in the armies of foreign nations.

MRS. SUL. 'Tis ungenerous in you, sir, to upbraid me with your services!

ARCH. 'Tis ungenerous in you, madam, not to reward 'em.

MRS. SUL. How! at the expense of my honor?

ARCH. Honor! can honor consist with ingratitude? If you would deal like a woman of honor, do like a man of honor. D'ye think I would deny you in such a case?

Enter a Servant.

SERV. Madam, my lady ordered me to tell you that your brother is below at the gate.   [*Exit.*]

MRS. SUL. My brother! Heavens be praised!—Sir, he shall thank you for your services; he has it in his power.

ARCH. Who is your brother, madam?

MRS. SUL. Sir Charles Freeman. You'll excuse me, sir; I must go and receive him.   [*Exit.*]

ARCH. Sir Charles Freeman! 'Sdeath and hell! my old acquaintance. Now unless Aimwell has made good use of his time, all our fair machine goes souse into the sea like the Eddystone.[100]   *Exit.*

[SCENE IV]

Scene changes to the gallery in the same house.

Enter AIMWELL *and* DORINDA.

DOR. Well, well, my lord, you have conquered; your late generous action will, I hope, plead for my easy yielding; though I must own, your lordship had a friend in the fort before.

AIM. The sweets of Hybla[101] dwell upon her tongue!—Here, doctor—

Enter FOIGARD, *with a book.*

FOI. Are you prepared, boat?

DOR. I'm ready. But first, my lord, one word. I have a frightful example of a hasty marriage in my own family; when I reflect upon't, it shocks me. Pray, my lord, consider a little—

AIM. Consider! Do you doubt my honor or my love?

DOR. Neither. I do believe you equally just as brave; and were your whole sex drawn out for me to choose, I should not cast a look upon the multitude if you were absent. But, my lord, I'm a woman; colors, concealments may hide a thousand faults in me—therefore know me better first. I hardly dare affirm I know myself in anything except my love.

AIM. (*aside*). Such goodness who could injure! I find myself unequal to the task of villain; she has gained my soul, and made it honest like her own. I cannot, cannot hurt her.—Doctor, retire.— (*Exit* FOIGARD.) Madam, behold your lover and your proselyte, and judge of my passion by my conversion! I'm all a lie, nor dare I give a fiction to your arms; I'm all counterfeit, except my passion.

DOR. Forbid it, heaven! a counterfeit!

AIM. I am no lord, but a poor needy man, come with a mean, a scandalous design to prey upon your fortune. But the beauties of your mind and person have so won me from myself that, like a trusty servant, I prefer the interest of my mistress to my own.

DOR. Sure I have had the dream of some poor mariner, a sleepy image of a welcome port, and wake involved in storms!—Pray, sir, who are you?

AIM. Brother to the man whose title I usurped, but stranger to his honor or his fortune.

DOR. Matchless honesty!—Once I was proud, sir, of your wealth and title, but now am prouder that you want it; now I can show my love was justly levelled, and had no aim but love.—Doctor, come in.

Enter FOIGARD *at one door,* GIPSEY *at another, who whispers* DORINDA.

[*To* FOIGARD.] Your pardon, sir, we sha'not [want] you now.—[*To* AIMWELL.] Sir, you must excuse me. I'll wait on you presently. *Exit with* GIPSEY.

FOI. Upon my shoul, now, dis is foolish.

Exit.

AIM. Gone! and bid the priest depart!—It has an ominous look.

Enter ARCHER.

ARCH. Courage, Tom! Shall I wish you joy?

AIM. No.

ARCH. 'Oons, man, what ha' you been doing?

AIM. O Archer! my honesty, I fear, has ruined me.

---

100. The 'great storm' of 1703 destroyed the first Eddystone lighthouse, an engineering marvel of its day.
101. Mt. Hybla, in Sicily, was famous for its honey.

228

ARCH. How?

AIM. I have discovered myself.

ARCH. Discovered! and without my consent? What! have I embarked my small remains in the same bottom with yours, and you dispose of all without my partnership?

AIM. O Archer! I own my fault.

ARCH. After conviction—'tis then too late for pardon. You may remember, Mr. Aimwell, that you proposed this folly—as you begun, so end it. Henceforth I'll hunt my fortune single. So farewell!

AIM. Stay, my dear Archer, but a minute.

ARCH. Stay! what, to be despised, exposed, and laughed at! No, I would sooner change conditions with the worst of the rogues we just now bound, than bear one scornful smile from the proud knight that once I treated as my equal.

AIM. What knight?

ARCH. Sir Charles Freeman, brother to the lady that I had almost—but no matter for that; 'tis a cursed night's work, and so I leave you to make the best on't. *(Going.)*

AIM. Freeman!—One word, Archer. Still I have hopes; methought she received my confession with pleasure.

ARCH. 'Sdeath! who doubts it?

AIM. She consented after to the match; and still I dare believe she will be just.

ARCH. To herself, I warrant her, as you should have been.

AIM. By all my hopes, she comes, and smiling comes!

Enter DORINDA, *mighty gay.*

DOR. Come, my dear lord—I fly with impatience to your arms. The minutes of my absence was a tedious year. Where's this tedious priest?

Enter FOIGARD.

ARCH. 'Oons, a brave girl!

DOR. I suppose, my lord, this gentleman is privy to our affairs?

ARCH. Yes, yes, madam, I'm to be your father.

DOR. Come, priest, do your office.

ARCH. Make haste, make haste, couple 'em any way.—(*Takes* AIMWELL'S *hand.*) Come, madam, I'm to give you—

DOR. My mind's altered; I won't.

ARCH. Eh!—

AIM. I'm confounded!

FOI. Upon my shoul, and sho is myshelf.

ARCH. What's the matter now, madam?

DOR. Look ye, sir, one generous action deserves another. This gentleman's honor obliged him to hide nothing from me; my justice engages me to conceal nothing from him. In short, sir, you are the person that you thought you counterfeited; you are the true Lord Viscount Aimwell, and I wish your lordship joy.—Now, priest, you may be gone; if my lord is pleased now with the match, let his lordship marry me in the face of the world.

AIM., ARCH. What does she mean?

DOR. Here's a witness for my truth.

Enter SIR CHARLES FREEMAN *and* MRS. SULLEN.

SIR CHAS. My dear Lord Aimwell, I wish you joy.

AIM. Of what?

SIR CHAS. Of your honor and estate. Your brother died the day before I left London; and all your friends have writ after you to Brussels; among the rest I did myself the honor.

ARCH. Hark ye, sir knight, don't you banter now?

SIR CHAS. 'Tis truth, upon my honor.

AIM. Thanks to the pregnant stars that formed this accident!

ARCH. Thanks to the womb of time that brought it forth!—away with it!

AIM. Thanks to my guardian angel that led me to the prize! (*Taking* DORINDA'S *hand.*)

ARCH. And double thanks to the noble Sir Charles Freeman.—My Lord, I wish you joy,—My Lady, I wish you joy.—Igad, Sir Freeman, you're the honestest fellow living!—'Sdeath, I'm grown strange airy upon this matter!—My lord, how d'ye?—A word, my lord; don't you remember something of a previous agreement, that entitles me to the moiety of this lady's fortune, which, I think, will amount to five thousand pound?

AIM. Not a penny, Archer; you would ha' cut my throat just now, because I would not deceive this lady.

ARCH. Ay, and I'll cut your throat again, if you should deceive her now.

AIM. That's what I expected; and to end the dispute, the lady's fortune is ten thousand pound; we'll divide stakes: take the ten thousand pound or the lady.

DOR. How! is your lordship so indifferent?

ARCH. No, no, no, madam! his lordship knows very well that I'll take the money; I leave you to his lordship, and so we're both provided for.

Enter COUNT BELLAIR.

COUNT BEL. *Mesdames et messieurs,* I am your servant trice humble! I hear you be rob here.

AIM. The ladies have been in some danger, sir.

COUNT BEL. And, begar, our inn be rob too!

AIM. Our inn! by whom?

COUNT BEL. By the landlord, begar! Garzoon, he has rob himself and run away!

ARCH. Robbed himself!

COUNT BEL. Ay, begar, and me too of a hundre pound.

ARCH. A hundred pound?

COUNT BEL. Yes, that I owed him.

AIM. Our money's gone, Frank.

ARCH. Rot the money! my wench is gone.— (*To* COUNT BELLAIR.] *Savez-vous quelque chose de Mademoiselle Cherry?*[102]

(*Enter a Fellow with a strong-box and a letter.*)

FELL. Is there one Martin here?

ARCH. Ay, ay—who wants him?

FELL. I have a box here and letter for him.

ARCH. (*taking the box*). Ha, ha, ha! what's here? Legerdemain!—By this light, my lord, our money again!—But this unfolds the riddle.—(*Opening the letter, reads*) Hum, hum, hum!—Oh, 'tis for the public good, and must be communicated to the company. [*Reads.*]

MR. MARTIN,

My father being afraid of an impeachment by the rogues that are taken tonight, is gone off; but if you can procure him a pardon, he will make great discoveries that may be useful to the country. Could I have met you instead of your master tonight, I would have delivered myself into your hands, with a sum that much exceeds that in your strong-box,

which I have sent you, with an assurance to my dear Martin that I shall ever be his most faithful friend till death.

CHERRY BONNIFACE.

There's a billet-doux for you! As for the father, I think he ought to be encouraged; and for the daughter—pray, my lord, persuade your bride to take her into her service instead of Gipsey.

AIM. I can assure you, madam, your deliverance was owing to her discovery.

DOR. Your command, my lord, will do without the obligation. I'll take care of her.

SIR CHAS. This good company meets opportunely in favor of a design I have in behalf of my unfortunate sister. I intend to part her from her husband—gentlemen, will you assist me?

ARCH. Assist you! 'Sdeath, who would not?

COUNT BEL. Assist! Garzoon, we all assest!

Enter SULLEN.

SUL. What's all this?—They tell me, spouse, that you had like to have been robbed.

MRS. SUL. Truly, spouse, I was pretty near it—had not these two gentlemen interposed.

SUL. How came these gentlemen here?

MRS. SUL. That's his way of returning thanks, you must know.

COUNT BEL. Garzoon, the question be apropos for all dat.

SIR CHAS. You promised last night, sir, that you would deliver your lady to me this morning.

SUL. Humph!

ARCH. Humph! what do you mean by humph? Sir, you shall deliver her!—in short, sir, we have saved you and your family; and if you are not civil, we'll unbind the rogues, join with 'um, and set fire to your house.—What does the man mean? not part with his wife!

COUNT BEL. Ay, garzoon, de man no understan common justice.

MRS. SUL. Hold, gentlemen, all things here must move by consent; compulsion would spoil us. Let my dear and I talk the matter over, and you shall judge it between us.

SUL. Let me know first who are to be our judges.— Pray, sir, who are you?

102. Do you know anything about Miss Cherry?

230

SIR CHAS. I am Sir Charles Freeman, come to take away your wife.

SUL. And you, good sir?

AIM. [Thomas], Viscount Aimwell, come to take away your sister.

SUL. And you, pray, sir?

ARCH. Francis Archer, esquire, come—

SUL. To take away my mother, I hope.—Gentlemen, you're heartily welcome; I never met with three more obliging people since I was born!—And now, my dear, if you please, you shall have the first word.

ARCH. And the last, for five pound!

MRS. SUL. Spouse!

SUL. Rib!

MRS. SUL. How long have we been married?

SUL. By the almanac, fourteen months—but by my account, fourteen years.

MRS. SUL. 'Tis thereabout by my reckoning.

COUNT BEL. Garzoon, their account will agree.

MRS. SUL. Pray, spouse, what did you marry for?

SUL. To get an heir to my estate.

SIR CHAS. And have you succeeded?

SUL. No.

ARCH. The condition fails of his side.—Pray, madam, what did you marry for?

MRS. SUL. To support the weakness of my sex by the strength of his, and to enjoy the pleasures of an agreeable society.

SIR CHAS. Are your expectations answered?

MRS. SUL. No.

COUNT BEL. A clear case! a clear case!

SIR CHAS. What are the bars to your mutual contentment?

MRS. SUL. In the first place, I can't drink ale with him.

SUL. Nor can I drink tea with her.

MRS. SUL. I can't hunt with you.

SUL. Nor can I dance with you.

MRS. SUL. I hate cooking and racing.

SUL. And I abhor ombre and piquet.

MRS. SUL. Your silence is intolerable

SUL. Your prating is worse.

MRS. SUL. Have we not been a perpetual offence to each other? a gnawing vulture at the heart?

SUL. A frightful goblin to the sight?

MRS. SUL. A porcupine to the feeling?

SUL. Perpetual wormwood to the taste?

MRS. SUL. Is there on earth a thing we could agree in?

SUL. Yes—to part.

MRS. SUL. With all my heart.

SUL. Your hand.

MRS. SUL. Here.

SUL. These hands joined us, these shall part us. Away!

MRS. SUL. North.

SUL. South.

MRS. SUL. East.

SUL. West—far as the poles asunder.

COUNT BEL. Begar, the ceremony be vera pretty!

SIR CHAS. Now, Mr. Sullen, there wants only my sister's fortune to make us easy.

SUL. Sir Charles, you love your sister, and I love her fortune; every one to his fancy.

ARCH. Then you won't refund—

SUL. Not a stiver.

ARCH. Then I find, madam, you must e'en go to your prison again.

COUNT BEL. What is the portion?

SIR CHAS. Ten thousand pound, sir.

COUNT BEL. Garzoon, I'll pay it, and she shall go home wid me.

ARCH. Ha, ha, ha! French all over.—Do you know, sir, when ten thousand pound English is?

COUNT BEL. No begar, not *justement*.[103]

ARCH. Why, sir, 'tis a hundred thousand livres.

COUNT BEL. A hundre tousand livres! Ah, garzoon! me canno' do't; your beauties and their fortunes are both too much for me.

103. Exactly.

ARCH. Then I will.—This night's adventure has proved strangely lucky to us all—for Captain Gibbet in his walk had made bold, Mr. Sullen, with your study and escritoire, and had taken out all the writings of your estate, all the articles of marriage with his lady, bills, bonds, leases, receipts to an infinite value. I took 'em from him, and I deliver them to Sir Charles.

(*Gives him a parcel of papers and parchments.*)

SUL. How, my writings!—my head aches consumedly.—Well gentlemen, you shall have her fortune, but I can't talk. If you have a mind, Sir Charles, to be merry, and celebrate my sister's wedding and my divorce, you may command my house—but my head aches consumedly.—Scrub, bring me a dram.

ARCH. (*to* MRS. SULLEN). Madam, there's a country dance to the trifle that I sung today; your hand, and we'll lead it up.   (*Here a dance.*)

ARCH. 'Twould be hard to guess which of these parties is the better pleased, the couple joined or the couple parted; the one rejoicing in hopes of an untasted happiness, and the other in their deliverance from an experienced misery.

Both happy in their several states we find,
Those parted by consent, and those conjoined.
Consent, if mutual, saves the lawyer's fee—
Consent is law enough to set you free.

AN EPILOGUE

DESIGNED TO BE SPOKE IN 'THE BEAUX' STRATAGEM.'

If to our play your judgment can't be kind,
Let its expiring author pity find:[104]
Survey his mournful case with melting eyes,
Nor let the bard be damned before he dies.
Forbear, you fair, on his last scene to frown,
But his true exit with a plaudit crown;
Then shall the dying poet cease to fear
The dreadful knell, while your applause he hears.
At Leuctra so the conqu'ring Theban died,[105]
Claimed his friends' praises, but their tears denied:
Pleased in the pangs of death he greatly thought
Conquest with loss of life but cheaply bought.
The difference this, the Greek was one would fight,
As brave, though not so gay, as Sergeant Kite;[106]
Ye sons of Will's, what's that to those who write?
To Thebes alone the Grecian owed his bays,
You may the bard above the hero raise,
Since yours is greater than Athenian praise.

104. Farquhar lay on his death-bed when *The Beaux' Stratagem* was produced.
105. Epaminondas actually died at the battle of Mantineia, nine years after his victory over the Spartans at Leuctra.
106. The recruiting officer in Farquhar's play of the same name.

Peter Moore and Sarah Rush in the final scene of *A Doll House,*
Theatre Arts Department, Penn State University. Marc Field,
director.

CHAPTER VII

Ibsen and Realism in the Nineteenth Century

The Beginning of the Modern Theatre

In the year 1879, a young woman named Nora closed the front door of her home leaving her husband and three children and going off in search of herself. The play was *A Doll House,* the playwright a Norwegian named Henrik Ibsen, and the action, "the door slam heard round the world." *A Doll House* marks the real beginning of modern drama, and Ibsen is undisputably the first of the great modern, realistic playwrights.

At the end of the eighteenth century we saw English sentimental comedies of no particular distinction flourishing in a theatre of innovation and change. Interestingly enough it was the very pandering to middle class taste in the drama coupled with the innovations begun by Garrick that helped shape the phenomenal activity in the second half of the nineteenth century. What lead to the excitement, energy, new ideas, and unsurpassed creative achievement of the period?

First of all, we must consider the socio-economic and political forces at work in nineteenth century Europe. The industrial revolution had begun in 1769 with James Watt's invention of the steam engine. The power loom followed in 1785, Fulton's steamboat in 1807, the locomotive in 1812, and the first railway line in 1825. Samuel F. B. Morse's development of the first practical electrical telegraph in 1832 added to the dizzying mechanical and technological advancements. As the potential of these achievements became evident, two major occurances manifested themselves: factories sprang up in the major cities of Europe, and in order to work in these factories people began to cluster together in large urban pockets. Urbanization brought slums, overcrowding, sub-standard working conditions, disease, and poverty.

With all of this change from hand labor to mechanized industrialization, it became very difficult for monarchs of major European countries to distinguish between mob violence and legitimate demands for social reform. The American Revolution had began in 1776 when colonists proclaimed that "Taxation without representation is tyranny" and renounced their king. Just a few years later in 1789, the French populace with cries of "Liberty, equality, fraternity" rebelled against king and nobles in one of the longest and bloodiest revolutions of all time. More and more the cry went up throughout Europe, "All men are created free and equal." The lower classes, who most needed help, became more and more dependent on the benevolence of those who governed, and those in power were terrified that concessions to the working classes would mean new demands and ultimately rebellion and bloodshed. It is not surprising, therefore, that this inability to communicate eventually led to the very thing rulers most feared—new revolutions. The Belgian revolution occurred in 1830; the abdication of Napoleon's successor, Louis Phillipe of France, the

Italian War of Independence, the Revolution in the Hapsburg Dominions, and the German Revolution against King Frederick William—all occured in 1848 and made it painfully obvious that new democratic systems were needed and that the will of the people would be known.

The increased awareness of man's plight fostered romanticism—the first major dramatic form of the nineteenth century. Felt first in the German *Sturm und Drang* (Storm and Stress) drama of Johann Wolfgang von Goethe and Friedrich Schiller, romanticism emphasized the essential goodness of human beings. The romantic dramatists throughout Europe were democratic and humanistic in their sympathies. Their heroes were often rebels against the king, and power was often seen as corrupt. As revolutionary as the content of the romantic plays was the fact that they rejected the neo-classical unities which had fettered the French drama for over one hundred years. A dramatic revolution occured in Paris on the stage of the Comédie-Française on February 25, 1830 with *Hernani* by Victor Hugo. When Hugo dared to reject the alexandrine verse form, dared to break the unities of time and place, dared to mix the comic and the tragic, and finally dared to show acts of violence on stage, riots broke out in the theatre and in the streets. Romanticism ultimately triumphed over the intellectual restraints of neo-classicism. Yet the principle thrust of romanticism—the glory of the human spirit and its ability to survive all hardships—must have seemed as remote as Europe's downtrodden working class as the far away settings and exotic names of the characters.

Following hard upon Romanticism came that form which proved the most popular drama in both Europe and America in the nineteenth century: melodrama. Originally melodrama meant drama with musical accompaniment as evidenced, for example, in the silent films in the first decades of the twentieth century. In offering audiences conventional and moral modes of behavior, melodrama was a continuation of the tradition of the eighteenth century sentimental comedies. Melodrama seemed on the surface to be more realistic than romanticism; at least the characters existed in the present and were recognizable and identifiable types. But they were cardboard characters of dastardly wrong-doing or of simpering rightousness. Audiences were offered escape from the drabness of their daily lives; they were offered an opiate in which happy endings prevailed, in which evil was punished and virtue rewarded. The appeal was to the heart strings, and, as Eric Bentley tells us, melodrama asks for more of an emotional response from the audience than the material itself warrants. Throughout Europe and America—whether it was *Black-Ey'd Susan, The London Assurance,* or *Uncle Tom's Cabin*—melodrama audiences from the middle and lower classes flocked into oversized theatres to satisfy their taste for thrills and excitement. But just as romanticism offered false assertions about the dignity and ability of human beings, so melodrama offered predictable moral platitudes that were fundamentally dishonest and frustrating. What could a man or woman living in a dank slum in London or Paris, working from dawn to dusk for a few pennies, and suffering from malnutrition, care about the glories of the human spirit or mythical rewards for endurance of hardships? They needed help not hollow sham or facile answers.

By the middle of the nineteenth century traditional attitudes had been pushed aside by a number of revolutionary thinkers and reformers. August Compte became the founder of Positivism, a type of social physics, that argued that the scientific method of observation, hypothesis, and analysis could be applied to social phenomena. To Compte and to Herbert Spencer, who interpreted society in terms of principles derived from mechanics, science and technology seemed to be the panaceas for all of man's problems. John Stuart Mill wrote his *Principles of Political*

Economy in 1848, expressing a sympathetic view of human suffering, and in the same year *The Communist Manifesto* by Karl Marx and Friedrich Engles marked the advent of "scientific socialism."

Perhaps no theory was as important as that of Charles Darwin in *Origin of Species* (1859). Darwin spent twenty years collecting his data and proving his hypothesis that species evolve through variation and natural selection of those best suited to their environments—"survival of the fittist." Darwin felt that behavior could be attributed to two major factors: heredity, those characteristics transmitted to an individual genetically, and environment, those characteristics transmitted after birth.

The implication of Darwin's theory was, of course, staggering, for it reduced the role of God in the shaping of human destiny. In particular, the biblical story of creation was challenged by Darwin's view. Man had merely evolved from lower forms of animals; he had not been created in a divine and purposeful scheme. Moreover, with no control over either his heredity or his environment, man was a victim of circumstances rather than the architect of his own fate. A person could scarcely be blamed for his or her actions when those actions were determined by forces over which he or she had no control. Criminals, mental patients, social deviants were not villains, they were victims, and a vast array of social reforms sprang into being.

Darwin's theory, the most important in modern biology, not only caused violent reactions among religious factions—reactions that are still going on—but also contributed much to the idea of progress. If animals could be made better, the implications to education, cultural development, and scientific thought were staggering. Soon new branches of learning—sociology, physchology, anthropology—sprang into being. Yet in spite of all mankind's new knowledge and understanding, conditions did not dramatically improve. Poverty, hardship, crime, ignorance, and disease continued to plague the poor, and optimism about the potential of science and technology as a panaceas gave way to pessimism. It was a profound search for answers and for a new set of values that most informed the drama in the second half of the nineteenth century. It was the new emphasis on heredity and environment that created the genre we refer to as realism.

Realism in drama may be defined as a probing attempt to create the illusion of life on stage. In creating this illusion, the dramatist must first and foremost be truthful, presenting an honest interpretation of life, action, character, dialogue and motivation. He presents human experiences and recognizable people who, like members of the audience, are intricate mixtures of heredity, environment, psychological complexities, subtleties, and flaws. The realistic play presents a slice-of-life, as though the fourth wall of the room were removed and we, the observers, were allowed to eavesdrop on the characters' lives. George Jean Nathan, American theatre critic once said, "Where there is no honesty, there can be no genuine realism." One hundred years of the so-called modern drama still finds us submerged in realism. Plays like Eugene O'Neill's *Long Day's Journey into Night,* Lanford Wilson's *Fifth of July,* or David Mamet's *Glengarry Glen Ross* attest to the contemporary strength of the realistic play.

It is incredible to us now, when so many of the early realistic plays seem tame, to think of the outrage they created in their own day. In the decades of the 70s and 80s, Ibsen, for example, literally scandalized Europe. He was branded as evil, degenerate, and immoral. It is interesting that almost any new direction in drama, either toward or away from realism, is usually met with cries of indignation. Non-realistic movements such as expressionism, surrealism, or absurdism are initially branded as avante garde mumbo jumbo foisted off on a gullible public, while trends toward greater realism are usually declared obscene, primarily because previously taboo subjects—nudity, homosexuality, drug addiction, incest, for example—are brought onto the stage. It has always seemed curious that multiple murders in *Hamlet* fail to shock whereas a four-letter word or homosexual kiss will send audience members stomping angrily out of theatres demanding censorship. From our vantage point today, we may smile to think of the furor that was created by subjects such as divorce, double standards in marriage, or venereal disease. Yet audiences today can find difficulty in dealing with plays that take an honest look at A.I.D.S. (*The Normal Heart, As Is*) or the right of the individual to take his or her own life (*Whose Life Is It Anyway?*). It is this very ability of drama to be in the forefront of progressive thought that is so powerful. Ironically, that the issues now seem tame, attests to the influence the plays had on audiences of their own day.

Let us take, as an example, Alexander Dumas *fils* play, *Camille,* written in 1849 but too scandalous to be produced until 1852. Drawing on an actual case history, Dumas deals with the plight of the "kept" woman in society, espousing his belief that no woman should be judged by her past life. This perennially appealing story, a novel before it was a play, became the basis for Verdi's *La Traviata* and was ultimately made into one of the most popular films of all time starring Greta Garbo and Robert Taylor. Dumas *fils* wrote about other social outcasts: the illegitimate child, the unwed mother, the philandering husband. Emile Augier, another French playwright, dealt with such problems as divorce and the power of the newspaper. One of his major works, *Olympe's Marriage* (1855), deals with a courtesan who marries an aristocrat, becomes bored by the life she lives, spreads malicious gossip out of boredom which nearly wreck's her husband's life. Finally, her father-in-law shoots her in order to save his family and then later commits suicide as the final curtain falls. Both Dumas *fils* and Augier were concerned with social problems, with moral issues, and with believable pictures of life-like people who were victims of life and of society. Today, we are aware that these plays which abound with curtains falling at climactic moments, with deathbed rescues of heroines, and with motifs of self-sacrifice had not progressed much beyond sheer melodrama. Their subject matter, however, was controversial and their stand on issues progressive and enlightened.

A third playwright, one who must have had a significant influence on Henrik Ibsen and one we associate with well-contrived plots, was Eugène Scribe (1791–1861). Scribe was incredibly prolific, writing to please a vast audience. A typical year for him included writing about one hundred plays, ten each month with a two month vacation—or, so we are told. He could manage this output working with numerous collaborators and by developing a fool proof dramatic technique we call the well-made play. Scribe concentrated on action, on what happened, and his plots were meticulously constructed. Background exposition was firmly plotted and gotten out of the way early in the drama (usually by two servants in the first scene), all important events (or props) were planted and prepared for, scenes were carefully built toward climaxes paying particular attention to cause-and-effect relationships between events, and ended with effective curtain lines to sustain interest and suspense between acts (a device we refer to as "the cliff-hanger"). The denouement had to be brief and explicit. Ridiculous as Scribe's well-made plays may seem today, they provided writers like Dumas *fils* and Ibsen with a basic dramatic, quasi-scientific technique.

Besides the evolution of the drama itself—from romanticism, through melodrama, to the social-reform plays—there were many events in the theatre itself that prepared the public for the realistic drama that was to astound Europe and America in the second half of the nineteenth century. Emphasis on a more subdued mode of acting and efforts toward historic costuming continued. With the increasing need for domestic interiors, the box set with three walls and a ceiling began to replace the drop and wing set. While it is impossible to say when the box set appeared, the first steps were probably taken in the late eighteenth century. There are references to "rooms with real walls" as early as 1811. It was a French actress-manager, however, Mme. Lucia Vestris, who is generally credited with developing the first real box set in London in 1832. By 1841 the concept had won complete favor, and critics wrote of Mme. Vestris's production of Dion Boucicault's play, *The London Assurance,* as correct and realistic in the depiction of the rooms. Finally, gaslight arrived on the London stage in 1817. While the number of theatre fires mounted critically with this new improvement, it also meant that light could be dimmed and brightened easily, that theatres could be darkened and attention directed toward the stage. Such lighting supported the illusion that the audience, seated in the dark, was observing life on the stage through a window or even a peep-hole in the fourth wall.

Even more important than any of these theatrical innovations, however, was the pioneering work of Georg II, the Duke of Saxe-Meiningen and his troupe called the Meiningen Players. Relatively unknown until it played Berlin in 1874, the troupe had been personally taken over by the head of the small German duchy in 1866. Not only had the Duke of Saxe-Meiningen been educated in the great cities of Europe, but he had studied art and seen the finest acting companies of London, Paris, and Vienna. While Georg himself acted as producer, he hired several directors, one of whom—Ludwig Chronegk—contributed richly to the vitality of the Meiningen Players. They worked together beautifully as a team: the Duke had the ideas and Chronegk the practical knowledge to make those dreams a reality. From 1874–1890 the Meiningen Players were the most admired company in the world. As Garrick had anticipated the art of stage direction, Meiningen (with Chronegk) actually achieved it. The Duke was a strict disciplinarian; as both head of state and head of the theatre, he could demand and gain strict obedience. Besides being a strict task master, Georg II enforced a number of extraordinary theatrical innovations. First, he demanded and involved himself in exhaustive research for the designs of costumes, settings, and properties. Second, he demanded unity and illusion in the design concept of his productions to an unprecedented degree. Third, he abolished the star system and perceived of all actors in his company as equal. He payed attention to the ensemble acting, planning and sketching each precise movement of even the most insignificant member of the crowd. Fourth, Meiningen insisted on a series of innovative rehearsal techniques, including rehearsing a play until he believed it was ready to open, and providing full setting, furniture, and properties at the first rehearsal. Here was the first modern director, creating illusion, dictating autocratic control, striving toward fine ensemble playing, and demanding accurate detail. It was Meiningen who emphasized the unified production and the importance of the director's concept that has become paramount in today's theatre.

It will be remembered that theatres like Drury Lane and Covent Garden had been repeatedly enlarged in an attempt to draw larger and more diversified audiences. When the entertainments in these houses became little more than spectacles and extravaganzas, it occurred to serious writers and managers that small subscription houses would offer a far greater degree of artistic freedom than the oversized theatres provided. Just as off or off-off Broadway has become a playwrights' theatre in direct opposition to the commercialization of Broadway, so these small independent theatres shaped the course of realism and paved the way for the avante garde and experimental plays that were subsequently written in rejection of the literal nature of realism. In fact, we might point to three pioneers who followed the unique contribution of the Duke of Saxe-Meiningen: Andre Antoine and the Théâtre Libre in Paris, Otto Brahm and the Freie Bühne in Berlin, and J. T. Grein and the Independent Theatre in London, which not only championed Ibsen but also introduced Ireland and England's master realist, George Bernard Shaw. A fourth, and perhaps the greatest theatre of all, Russia's Moscow Art Theatre, will be treated separately in connection with Anton Chekhov.

Andre Antoine took the lead and set the tone for the entire independent theatre movement. An army veteran and a clerk for the Paris Gas Company, Antoine joined a small amateur theatre group for diversion. When his suggestion of performing plays by new and untried playwrights failed to rally support, he rented a hall, borrowed furniture from his mother, and staged the plays, doing most of the work himself. He called his group the Théâtre Libre or Free Theatre. His first production got such a cool reception that Antoine wanted to give up, but friends persuaded him to try a second venture, which met with success. Antoine's commitment to new plays resembles that, for example, of Ellen Stewart at the famous La Mama Experimental Theatre Club in New York. The Théâtre Libre performed a total of one hundred eighty-four plays and introduced the most important playwrights in the European theatre.

Like Meiningen, whose work he saw and admired, Antoine was a pioneer. He learned how to circumvent censors by playing to private audiences; he learned how to raise capital by selling subscriptions; he taught the world the value of doing plays that would not interest commercial producers; and he encouraged amateur actors "to live" and not "to act." Antoine wanted each play to have its own detailed environment and its own truth to such a degree that his name and his theatre became synonymous with the realistic movement.

Two years after the founding of the Théâtre Libre, a Free Theatre (Freie Bühne) was founded in Berlin by Otto Brahm. The German theatre was patterned after the French prototype and opened in 1889 with a controversial production of *Ghosts* by Henrik Ibsen, whom Brahm believed to be the "pathfinder of the new dramatic art." Similarly the London Independent Theatre became a major producer of Ibsen's new and startling work a few years later.

Literally hundreds of outstanding playwrights saw their work produced by the independent theatres, making the final decades of the nineteenth century one of the most dynamic and exciting periods in the entire history of the theatre: new ideas, new techniques, and a new respect for the theatre. It is vitally important that the finest playwrights of the period—Ibsen, Strindberg, Chekhov, Gorki, Becque, Brieux, Wedekind, Hauptmann, Shaw and Synge—found their audience with small independent theatres. It is repeatedly in such rarified environments that the important drama and the trail-blazing playwrights find their voices. Rarely is theatrical history made in the great commercial houses like those of Broadway. While it seems incredible, titles like *Cats, Annie,* or *Hello, Dolly* may fade into obscurity while the works of Sam Shepard, who has never had a play on Broadway, or David Mamet, whose work is associated with the Goodman Theatre of Chicago, may well prove to be the real voices of our contemporary theatre.

Henrik Ibsen

Henrik Ibsen was born on March 20, 1828 in the small trading town of Skein on the east coast of Norway. When Ibsen was six years old, his father experienced financial difficulties, gave up his home, and took his family of four children to a small country house in Venstop. As a child Ibsen was reticent and shy, enjoying his own puppet theatre, amateur magic, and ventriloquism. Ibsen left school when he was fifteen to become an apothecary's apprentice in Grimstad where he was to remain for six years. In 1846, Ibsen became involved with a twenty-eight year old servant at the apothecary's house and fathered an illegitimate son whom he would support until the boy was fourteen.

By the time he was twenty, Ibsen was deeply interested in politics and wanted to attend the University of Christiania (now Oslo) to pursue a career in medicine. But he failed his matriculation exams and while permitted to attend lectures, Ibsen was never fully admitted to the University. At this time he wrote his first play, *Cataline,* in 1850. He also wrote poems, dabbled in politics and journalism, and painted (a hobby he seriously considered making his life work). Attracting the attention of the devout Norwegian nationalist, Ole Bull, Ibsen was offered the job of poet and stage manager at the Norwegian National Theatre in Bergen, a job he was to hold for six years. Although Ibsen was dismayed at finding the theatre fifty years behind his time, he gained a profound knowledge of his craft and wrote five plays—all romantic histories extoling Norway's past.

In August of 1857 Ibsen moved to the Norwegian Theatre of Christiania as stage instructor and artistic supervisor. At the end of his first year at Christiania, Ibsen married Suzanna Thoreson and had his first modest success with *The Vikings of Helgeland* (1858). But the theatre filed for bankruptcy in 1862, and Ibsen was blamed for the failure. He began to apply for grants to travel and write, finally obtaining one from a small scholarly society. Ibsen left Norway, not to return there for ten years and not to live there for a further seventeen. By now father of a small son, Sigurd, Ibsen traveled first to Rome and later to Dresden and wrote a series of plays which the Scandinavian scholar Alrik Gustafson calls Ibsen's plays of indignation—plays in which he expressed his deep disappointment with his native country. *Brand* (1866) is the story of an unrelenting idealist, whereas *Peer Gynt* (1867) depicts a dreamer, a ne'er-do-well who thinks only of himself. Peer epitomizes what Ibsen considered to be the Norwegian national temperament. The playwright said, "Brand is myself in my best moments and Peer Gynt is myself at my worst."

The next major phase of Ibsen's dramaturgy began in 1877 with *The Pillars of Society* when Ibsen was fifty years old. The play marks the beginning of modern drama and of realism as well as the beginning of the great phase of the playwright's career. From this point on he wrote a play methodically almost every two years for the remainder of his writing life. In 1879 *A Doll House* brought international attention and critical scorn. How dare a playwright say that a wife be right in leaving her husband and children? Two years after *A Doll House,* Ibsen answered his critics in *Ghosts,* in which a wife stays with her husband, lives a lie, and remains inhibited by the conventions of her times. Again branded as a perpetrator of filth, Ibsen thumbed his nose at the critics with *An Enemy of the People* (1883), in which his leading character proclaims that the man is strongest who stands most alone.

Ibsen was by now the master of the realistic form. He wrote:

> Before I write one word, I must know the character through and through, I must penetrate into the last wrinkle of his soul. I always proceed from the individual; the stage setting, the dramatic ensemble, all that comes naturally and causes me no worry, as soon as I am certain of the individual in every aspect of his humanity. But I have his exterior in mind also, down to the last button, how he stands and walks, how he bears himself, what his voice sounds like. Then I do not let him go until his fate is fulfilled.

But now the center of gravity in his thinking may be said gradually to shift from purely social and ethical preoccupations to a new, essentially objective psychological and symbolic approach to problems. Once he had mastered realism, he found it too limiting and moved quickly to an interest in the study of the sub-conscious. Hence his next and perhaps his finest group of plays can be labelled the symbolic and psychological plays: *The Wild Duck* (1884), *Rosmersholm* (1886), *Lady from the Sea* (1888), and *Hedda Gabler* (1890).

The final phase of Ibsen's career, the late autobiographical plays, begin in 1892 with *The Master Builder* in which Ibsen expresses his fear that he will be superceded by a younger genius. The artist must strive to express his finest self, Ibsen tells us, in an ultimate achievement of art even if it means self-destruction. Near the end of his career Ibsen wrote *John Gabriel Borkman* (1896), a guilt ridden study of emotional bankruptcy—perhaps a last personal statement about the relationshp between career and personal happiness.

Ibsen suffered a series of strokes in 1900. He told his wife that it was strange that he, quite a playwright, had to learn to write the alphabet again. He was never to fully recover and died on May 22, 1906. His last word, "Tvetimod" meaning "on the contrary" was an ironic reinforcement of his independent, progressive, and revolutionary career as the father of modern drama. Ibsen stands with Sophocles, Shakespeare, Molière, and Strindberg as one of the true giants of the theatre.

A Doll House

Ibsen and the realistic drama he championed in such plays as *A Doll House* were perhaps inevitable products of the nineteenth century. As scientific knowledge and technology created an Industrial Revolution which forever changed the way man lived, so scientific thought drastically altered the drama of the period with profound and lasting effect. If the drama was to keep pace with its time, it became essential that playwrights apply the scientific method to drama. The well-made-play formula, as it was created by Eugène Scribe and honed to perfection by Victorien Sardou, was little more than the dramatist's attempt to be scientific regarding the *form* of the play. Naturalism, as it was conceived by Emile Zola, demanded a scientific *content* in which character behavior was believably motivated by heredity, environment and moment (what happened to a person in a moment of time). Objectively observed Truth should be the sole subject of the drama in an unmanipulated "slice of life".

A major part of Ibsen's genius was his ability to take the scientific form of the well-made-play, give it a sense of truth by adding the scientific content of Naturalism, and then breathing real theatrical life into his drama by insisting on the artist's right to be creative. Ibsen was as perceptive and diligent in his *observation* of life as Zola. But, unlike Zola, he demanded his right as an artist to depart from the slavish depiction of reality by offering in his play a thoughtful *selection* of detail from real life. Then Ibsen, departing again from the rules of Naturalism, produced an artful and purposeful *arrangement* of those details in order to provide his own insightful *interpretation* of life phenomenon. In Ibsen's dramatic masterpieces the shallow well-made-play and the stultifying naturalistic drama become a work of art once more. In his plays the form works like a finely tuned machine with carefully structured events and a highly logical progression of the action. And all the while his characters are consistently motivated by heredity, environment and moment.

In *A Doll House,* one of Ibsen's earlier realistic dramas of social reform, we can readily perceive his use of the well-made-play formula. The formula itself held that the plot was the most essential part of the play and, therefore, had to be constructed with great care. The plot, as in the Greek drama, should deal only with those events immediately surrounding the climactic moment of a story. That is to say the play should have a late point of attack—the story being "attacked" late in its development at a point near the climax. Certainly, Ibsen begins his play with a late point of attack. In fact, he improves on Scribe by employing a technique which has been called "ripe circumstance"—that is, attacking the action of the play at that point where the circumstances are ripe for things to happen. Helmer (Torvald) has gotten his promotion and Krogstad is demanding payment of his loan. Something is bound to happen.

In Scribe's formula, the episodes or occurrences of the plot were strung together in a hopefully flawless cause-effect chain of events moving logically and quickly toward the climax of the play. The episodes should move rapidly and contain sufficient interest and suspense to sustain the attention of the spectator. No one could fault Ibsen here. His plot is so logical and moves with such dexterity that there is an air of inevitability and pending doom in the play. Interest and suspense could often be achieved by centering the plot around a central misunderstanding of some sort and withholding key pieces of information from certain characters or by providing well-timed interruptions or unexpected arrival. When all else failed, the playwright could resort to accidents such as losing or mislaying a vital document or by sudden unexpected changes of plans. Ibsen is too intelligent to stoop to accidents in *A Doll House,* but notice how the plot does turn on a central misunderstanding and withheld information; Helmer is not aware of Nora's loan and Nora is certainly unaware of the true nature of her husband's character. If there is a well-made-play gimmick in Ibsen's play, it is Krogstad's letter, for much of the play does revolve around a vital document. There is even a sudden change of plans when Krogstad decides not to demand payment of his note; but notice how skillfully that is employed by Ibsen to set off the final confrontation between Nora and Helmer.

Since a late point of attack essentially meant that much of the story had already occurred, it became essential for the well-made playwright to fill in the important and necessary past details—the exposition—with great skill so that the spectators would know who the characters were, where they were, and what had previously happened to them. According to Scribe, the first act of the play had to be devoted to exposition; the actual action of the play would not begin until the last page of Act One. In short, Act One was the set-up. *All* necessary details had to be presented with clarity and with dispatch. In order to accomplish this, Scribe often began his play with a homecoming so that it would be logical for one character to tell the returning character all that had transpired in his absence. Frequently, Scribe began his plays in another way with servants on stage gossiping about what had been going on in the household of late. It was not uncommon for Scribe to use both techniques simultaneously.

We can really appreciate Ibsen's genius when we examine the way he handles exposition. He obviously found Scribe's techniques crude, unrealistic, mechanical and boring. Ibsen devised his own technique which we call *retrospective analysis*. Essentially, he felt that audiences were not so stupid that they needed all the facts presented to them at the outset of a play. Furthermore, he reasoned that exposition, after all, was merely past history. And how does past history function in real life? Man only solves the problems of the moment by calling on all that he has learned and experienced in the past. Ibsen, therefore, reasoned that exposition could and should be introduced in the play at those moments when the characters need information from the past to accomplish something in the present. Notice how we learn about the loan. We are *not* told about it by gossiping servants; Nora herself tells us all about it but only because Mrs. Linde has had the poor taste to refer to Nora as an indulged and pampered woman who knows nothing of the world of reality. Nora, smarting from the attack, defends herself by telling Mrs. Linde just how wrong she is. The facts of the loan come out not because an uninvolved servant is gossiping but because the heroine is under attack and has to set the record straight. Similarly, an important bit of expository information in the play concerns the fact that Dr. Rank is in love with Nora and, consequently, is not the person she could go to for help without compromising herself. Again, we are not told that fact by servants "dishing the dirt"; we discover the fact as Nora discovers it—when she flirts naively but outrageously with the man and learns from his responses that he loves her. Even more daring perhaps is Ibsen's structuring of the exposition about the former relationship between Mrs. Linde and Krogstad which is fated to have a decisive impact on the outcome of the play. We are not told the facts until the beginning of the third act of the play at just the time when we need to know the information. Notice how easily and unobtrusively Ibsen introduces the information by simply providing the two characters a moment alone together where they can respond privately to one another.

In order for the events of a well-made-play to appear highly logical Scribe felt it was necessary then to prepare the audience for what was to come—even for the ultimate outcome of the plot—by carefully planting certain bits of information or hints in the exposition of the first act. (Remember the example in the introductory chapter of the revolver in the desk drawer which the heroine uses at the last moment to save herself from the villain.) As might be expected, Ibsen is much more subtle in his use of pointers and planters. If we are alert, we begin to suspect in Act One that there is a significant relationship between Mrs. Linde and Krogstad when Mrs. Linde asks some rather pointed questions about the man. Why is she interested in him? But you do have to be alert to pick up the hints Ibsen provides; and that makes his plays all the more exciting to read or see.

Whatever the arrangement of events, the plot of the skillfully crafted well-made-play always focused on a battle of wits between two formidable and well-matched opponents. It then became necessary for those two contenders to face one another for an inevitable showdown. This was the scene the playwright was obliged to write; consequently we call it the "obligatory scene." If there is one area where critics have real problems analyzing Ibsen's *A Doll House,* it relates to that obligatory scene. The action of the play is the educating of Nora so that she might function meaningfully in life. Another way of saying it is that Nora must find out who she is and fulfill her human potential by educating herself for life. This is not a play about a forged loan then. If it were, the two dynamic opponents in the battle of wits would be Nora and Krogstad. This is a play about Nora's education to become a complete woman. Her opponent in this regard is her husband Torvald (Helmer). So the true obligatory scene in the battle of wits comes, not when Torvald learns of the loan, but after that when Nora learns that the "miracle" is not going to happen. And the climax of the battle arrives with the slam of the door—one of the grandest climactic moments in all drama.

Once the action of the play was completed, Scribe felt that the dramatist had an obligation to wind things up with great dispatch. The denouement—or tying up of the loose thread of the play—should require no more than a half of a page of dialogue. Scribe at times was adamant on this score. He felt that the denouement, or the last few minutes of the play were so vital to the success of the structure that he often began with his denouement and wrote his play backwards. Scribe would have been proud of Ibsen for the Norwegian playwright accomplishes the entire denouement in one brief speech by Helmer Torvald after Nora walks out the door. In fact, depending on the way you want to interpret the final moment of the play, the climax possibly comes as Nora leaves the room; then Torvald's speech is, indeed, the denouement. However, since the slam of the door follows Torvald's final speech, the play may be said to have no denouement whatsoever.

Scribe felt that characters were after all merely the logical beings to perform the deeds of the play. Consequently, most of his characters are merely dull cardboard figures when compared to the well-rounded people Ibsen created. Notice the wealth of detail in Nora's character—her childish deceitfulness (nicely portrayed in her harmless snitching of macaroons), her keen intelligence (she knows how to get what she wants from Torvald by playing the little "squirrel" to please him), her naivete (she flirts rather outrageously with Dr. Rank without understanding the implications of her behavior), her strength (she has, after all, taken hold of a dire situation and possibly saved her husband's life), her romantic nature (she clings rather desperately to an unrealistic image of Torvald and her dream that the "miracle" will happen), her conscientiousness (she is dutifully paying installments on her loan through her secret work project). We could go on and on for Nora is enormously complex and real. She is so real and so well defined that you can actually imagine and predict how she might behave in situations other than those in the play. It might be said that she is so real that she has a life outside the play which is more than can be said for any character in a Scribe play.

Of course, one of Ibsen's crowning achievements was his depth of character portrayed. In this he owes a partial debt at least to Zola and the Naturalists who concluded that all human behavior was predicated on the interaction of heredity, environment and moment. Notice the enormous amount of attention that is paid in the play to the possible impact of heredity. Nora may have inherited a certain relaxed or impaired moral fiber from her father; and there is the danger, certainly in Torvald's eyes, that their children could have inherited some of their mother's weakness. If she is a thief, her children may become thieves, too, if not through heredity then through being exposed to her in the home environment. That environment is impressively important in the play as well. It is precisely because Nora was raised in an environment where she was treated as a child that she is so ill-prepared to face the realities of life. And moment plays an important role

245

in what the characters do. It is because Torvald has been given a promotion that Krogstad begins to apply pressure for advancement. It is because Krogstad has demanded payment on his loan that Nora is under extreme pressure and is in danger of being exposed. It is because Nora learns that Dr. Rank is in love with her that she cannot possibly go to him for help in her plight. It is because Mrs. Linde renews her affair with Krogstad that the actual loan ceases to be an issue. Notice that the working out of the logical chain of events in the play is largely a manipulation of the aspect of moment.

Where dialogue was concerned, Scribe felt that it should simply be suitable to character and situation and nothing more. At all cost, it had to be subservient to the plot. Consequently his dialogue is flat and devoid of literary merit. Of course, we cannot truly appreciate Ibsen's dialogue unless we can read his plays in the original Norwegian. In fact, Ibsen's language has suffered enormously from the lack of talent on the part of his translators—especially William Archer who makes Ibsen sound like a very dull and prissy Victorian. Still, scholars who do know the Norwegian language tell us that Ibsen's dialogue is one of his truly brilliant achievements and one of his greatest assets. Apparently, in the original language the speech *sounds* very realistic but is actually highly theatrical. He says what has to be said, but he says it beautifully and effectively. Furthermore, he says it *affectively*—he says what has to be said in a way that moves the spectators' emotions. In other words, it is the difference between hearing a character say "I love ya," and hearing Romeo declare his love for Juliet.

We see in Ibsen's *A Doll House* a skillful blend of well-made-play techniques in its form and the scientific analysis of Naturalism in its content. But we also see the playwright transcend the limitations of both influences through highly creative and imaginative vision. Ibsen refused to depict life slavishing in his content just as he refused to be mechanical and formularistic in the structure of his play. He had, after all, the poet's voice, the artist's soul and the artist's vision of the world. Furthermore, he had something important to say about woman's—and man's—right to personal fulfillment and he could not permit static formula or slavish reality to get in his way. The play's plot had to be carefully and specifically structured and the characters had to be portrayed in tremendous detail in order to make that message viable and believable. He knew his audience for the most part would not accept what he was saying. So, in order to reach their reluctant ears, he had to make his play as truthful and logical and, at the same time, as theatrically exciting as possible. He succeeded so incredibly well that *A Doll House* is not only still dynamically alive today, it is a play for all time.

A DOLL HOUSE

By Henrik Ibsen

Translated By Rolf Fjelde

———— THE CHARACTERS ————

TORVALD HELMER, a lawyer
NORA, his wife
DR. RANK
MRS. LINDE
NILS KROGSTAD, a bank clerk
THE HELMERS' THREE SMALL CHILDREN
ANNE-MARIE, their nurse
HELENE, a maid
A DELIVERY BOY

The action takes place in HELMER'S *residence.*

ACT ONE

A comfortable room, tastefully but not expensively furnished. A door to the right in the back wall leads to the entryway; another to the left leads to HELMER'S *study. Between these doors, a piano. Midway in the left-hand wall a door, and further back a window. Near the window a round table with an armchair and a small sofa. In the right-hand wall, toward the rear, a door, and nearer the foreground a porcelain stove with two armchairs and a rocking chair beside it. Between the stove and the side door, a small table. Engravings on the walls. An* etagère *with china figures and other small art objects; a small bookcase with richly bound books; the floor carpeted; a fire burning in the stove. It is a winter day.*

A bell rings in the entryway; shortly after we hear the door being unlocked. NORA *comes into the room, humming happily to herself; she is wearing street clothes and carries an armload of packages, which she puts down on the table to the right. She has left the hall door open; and through it a* DELIVERY BOY *is seen, holding a Christmas tree and a basket, which he gives to the* MAID *who let them in.*

NORA. Hide the tree well, Helene. The children mustn't get a glimpse of it till this evening, after it's trimmed. (*To the* DELIVERY BOY, *taking out her purse.*) How much?

DELIVERY BOY. Fifty, ma'am.

NORA. There's a crown. No, keep the change. (*The* BOY *thanks her and leaves.* NORA *shuts the door. She laughs softly to herself while taking off her street things. Drawing a bag of macaroons from her pocket, she eats a couple, then steals over and listens at her husband's study door.*) Yes, he's home. (*Hums again as she moves to the table right.*)

HELMER (*from the study*). Is that my little lark twittering out there?

NORA (*busy opening packages*). Yes, it is.

HELMER. Is that my squirrel rummaging around?

NORA. Yes!

HELMER. When did my squirrel get in?

NORA. Just now. (*Putting the macaroon bag in her pocket and wiping her mouth.*) Do come in, Torvald, and see what I've bought.

HELMER. Can't be disturbed. (*After a moment he opens the door and peers in, pen in hand.*) Bought, you say? All that there? Has the little spendthrift been out throwing money around again?

NORA. Oh, but Torvald, this year we really should let ourselves go a bit. It's the first Christmas we haven't had to economize.

HELMER. But you know we can't go squandering.

NORA. Oh yes, Torvald, we can squander a little now. Can't we? Just a tiny, wee bit. Now that you've got a big salary and are going to make piles and piles of money.

HELMER. Yes—starting New Year's. But then it's a full three months till the raise comes through.

NORA. Pooh! We can borrow that long.

HELMER. Nora! (*Goes over and playfully takes her by the ear.*) Are your scatterbrains off again? What if today I borrowed a thousand crowns, and you squandered them over Christmas week, and then on New Year's Eve a roof tile fell on my head, and I lay there—

NORA (*putting her hand on his mouth*). Oh! Don't say such things!

HELMER Yes, but what if it happened—then what?

NORA. If anything so awful happened, then it just wouldn't matter if I had debts or not.

HELMER. Well, but the people I'd borrowed from?

NORA. Them? Who cares about them! They're strangers.

HELMER. Nora, Nora, how like a woman! No, but seriously, Nora, you know what I think about that. No debts! Never borrow! Something of freedom's lost—and something of beauty, too—from a home that's founded on borrowing and debt. We've made a brave stand up to now, the two of us; and we'll go right on like that the little while we have to.

NORA (*going toward the stove*). Yes, whatever you say, Torvald.

HELMER (*following her*). Now, now, the little lark's wings mustn't droop. Come on, don't be a sulky squirrel. (*Taking out his wallet.*) Nora, guess what I have here.

NORA (*turning quickly*). Money!

HELMER. There see. (*Hands her some notes.*) Good grief, I know how costs go up in a house at Christmastime.

NORA. Ten—twenty—thirty—forty. Oh, thank you, Torvald; I can manage no end on this.

HELMER. You really will have to.

NORA. Oh yes, I promise I will! But come here so I can show you everything I bought. And so cheap! Look, new clothes for Ivan here—and a sword. Here a horse and a trumpet for Bob. And a doll and a doll's bed here for Emmy; they're nothing much, but she'll tear them to bits in no time anyway. And here I have dress material and handkerchiefs for the maids. Old Anne-Marie really deserves something more.

HELMER. And what's in that package there?

NORA (*with a cry*). Torvald, no! You can't see that till tonight!

HELMER. I see. But tell me now, you little prodigal, what have you thought of for yourself?

NORA. For myself? Oh, I don't want anything at all.

HELMER. Of course you do. Tell me just what—within reason—you'd most like to have.

NORA. I honestly don't know. Oh, listen, Torvald—

HELMER. Well?

NORA. (*fumbling at his coat buttons, without looking at him*). If you want to give me something, then maybe you could—you could—

HELMER. Come on, out with it.

NORA. (*hurriedly*). You could give me money, Torvald. No more than you think you can spare; then one of these days I'll buy something with it.

HELMER. But Nora—

NORA. Oh, please, Torvald darling, do that! I beg you, please. Then I could hang the bills in pretty gilt paper on the Christmas tree. Wouldn't that be fun?

HELMER. What are those little birds called that always fly through their fortunes?

NORA. Oh yes, spendthrifts; I know all about that. But let's do as I say, Torvald; then I'll have time to decide what I really need most. That's very sensible, isn't it?

HELMER (*smiling*). Yes, very—that is, if you actually hung onto the money I give you, and you actually used it to buy yourself something. But it goes for the house and for all sorts of foolish things, and then I only have to lay out some more.

NORA. Oh, but Torvald—

HELMER. Don't deny it, my dear Little Nora. (*Putting his arm around her waist.*) Spendthrifts are sweet, but they use up a frightful amount of money. It's incredible what it costs a man to feed such birds.

NORA. Oh, how can you say that! Really, I save everything I can.

HELMER (*laughing*). Yes, that's the truth. Everything you can. But that's nothing at all.

NORA (*humming, with a smile of quiet satisfaction*). Hm, if you only knew what expenses we larks and squirrels have, Torvald.

HELMER. You're an odd little one. Exactly the way your father was. You're never at a loss for scaring up money; but the moment you have it, it runs right out through your fingers; you never know what you've done with it. Well, one takes you as you are. It's deep in your blood. Yes, these things are hereditary, Nora.

NORA. Ah, I could wish I'd inherited many of Papa's qualities.

HELMER. And I couldn't wish you anything but just what you are, my sweet little lark. But wait; it seems to me you have a very—what should I call it?—a very suspicious look today—

NORA. I do?

HELMER. You certainly do. Look me straight in the eye.

NORA (*looking at him*). Well?

HELMER (*shaking an admonitory finger*). Surely my sweet tooth hasn't been running riot in town today, has she?

NORA No. Why do you imagine that?

HELMER. My sweet tooth really didn't make a little detour through the confectioner's?

NORA. No, I assure you, Torvald—

HELMER. Hasn't nibbled some pastry?

NORA. No, not at all.

HELMER. Not even munched a macaroon or two?

NORA. No, Torvald, I assure you, really—

HELMER. There, there now. Of course I'm only joking.

NORA (*going to the table, right*). You know I could never think of going against you.

HELMER. No, I understand that; and you *have* given me your word. (*Going over to her.*) Well, you keep your little Christmas secrets to yourself, Nora darling. I expect they'll come to light this evening, when the tree is lit.

NORA. Did you remember to ask Dr. Rank?

HELMER. No. But there's no need for that; it's assumed he'll be dining with us. All the same, I'll ask him when he stops by here this morning. I've ordered some fine wine. Nora, you can't imagine how I'm looking forward to this evening.

NORA. So am I. And what fun for the children, Torvald!

HELMER. Ah, it's so gratifying to know that one's gotten a safe, secure job, and with a comfortable salary. It's a great satisfaction, isn't it?

NORA. Oh, it's wonderful!

HELMER. Remember last Christmas? Three whole weeks before, you shut yourself in every evening till long after midnight, making flowers for the Christmas tree, and all the other decorations to surprise us. Ugh, that was the dullest time I've ever lived through.

NORA. It wasn't at all dull for me.

HELMER (*smiling*). But the outcome *was* pretty sorry, Nora.

NORA. Oh, don't tease me with that again. How could I help it that the cat came in and tore everything to shreds.

HELMER. No, poor thing, you certainly couldn't. You wanted so much to please us all, and that's what counts. But it's just as well that the hard times are past.

NORA. Yes, it's really wonderful.

HELMER. Now I don't have to sit here alone, boring myself, and you don't have to tire your precious eyes and your fair little delicate hands—

NORA (*clapping her hands*). No, is it really true, Torvald, I don't have to? Oh, how wonderfully lovely to hear! (*Taking his arm.*) Now I'll tell you just how I've thought we should plan things. Right after Christmas—(*The doorbell rings.*) Oh, the bell. (*Straightening the room up a bit.*) Somebody woud have to come. What a bore!

HELMER. I'm not at home to visitors, don't forget.

MAID (*from the hall doorway*). Ma'am, a lady to see you—

NORA. All right, let her come in.

MAID (*to* HELMER). And the doctor's just come too.

HELMER. Did he go right to my study?

MAID. Yes, he did.

(HELMER *goes into his room. The* MAID *shows in* MRS. LINDE, *dressed in traveling clothes, and shuts the door after her.*)

MRS. LINDE (*in a dispirited and somewhat hesitant voice*). Hello, Nora.

NORA. (*uncertain.*) Hello—

MRS. LINDE. You don't recognize me.

NORA. No, I don't know—but wait, I think—(*Exclaiming.*) What! Kristine! Is it really you?

MRS. LINDE. Yes, it's me.

NORA. Kristine! To think I didn't recognize you. But then, how could I? (*More quietly.*) How you've changed, Kristine!

MRS. LINDE. Yes, no doubt I have. In nine—ten long years.

NORA. Is it so long since we met! Yes, it's all of that. Oh, these last eight years have been a happy time, believe me. And so now you've come in to town, too. Made the long trip in the winter. That took courage.

MRS. LINDE. I just got here by ship this morning.

NORA. To enjoy yourself over Christmas, of course. Oh, how lovely! Yes, enjoy ourselves, we'll do that. But take your coat off. You're not still cold? (*Helping her.*) There now, let's get cozy here by the stove. No, the easy chair there! I'll take the rocker here. (*Seizing her hands.*) Yes, now you have your old look again; it was only in that first moment. You're a bit more pale, Kristine—and maybe a bit thinner.

MRS. LINDE. And much, much older, Nora.

NORA. Yes, perhaps a bit older; a tiny, tiny bit; not much at all. (*Stopping short; suddenly serious.*) Oh, but thoughtless me, to sit here, chattering away. Sweet, good Kristine, can you forgive me?

MRS. LINDE. What do you mean, Nora?

NORA (*softy*). Poor Kristine, you've become a widow.

MRS LINDE. Yes, three years ago.

NORA. Oh, I knew it, of course; I read it in the papers. Oh, Kristine, you must believe me; I often thought of writing you then, but I kept postponing it, and something always interfered.

MRS. LINDE. Nora dear, I understand completely.

NORA. No, it was awful of me, Kristine. You poor thing, how much you must have gone through. And he left you nothing?

MRS. LINDE. No.

NORA. And no children?

MRS. LINDE. No.

NORA. Nothing at all, then?

MRS. LINDE. Not even a sense of loss to feed on.

NORA (*looking incredulously at her*). But Kristine, how could that be?

MRS. LINDE (*smiling wearily and smoothing her hair*). Oh, sometimes it happens, Nora.

NORA. So completely alone. How terribly hard that must be for you. I have three lovely children. You can't see them now; they're out with the maid. But now you must tell me everything—

MRS. LINDE. No, no, no, tell me about yourself.

NORA. No, you begin. Today I don't want to be selfish. I want to think only of you today. But there *is* something I must tell you. Did you hear of the wonderful luck we had recently?

MRS. LINDE. No, what's that?

NORA. My husband's been made manager in the bank, just think!

MRS. LINDE. Your husband? How marvelous!

NORA. Isn't it? Being a lawyer is such an uncertain living, you know, especially if one won't touch any cases that aren't clean and decent. And of course Torvald would never do that, and I'm with him completely there. Oh, we're simply delighted, believe me! He'll join the bank right after New Year's and start getting a huge salary and lots of commissions. From now on we can live quite differently—just as we want. Oh, Kristine, I feel so light and happy! Won't it be lovely to have stacks of money and not a care in the world?

MRS. LINDE. Well, anyway, it would be lovely to have enough for necessities.

NORA. No, not just for necessities, but stacks and stacks of money!

MRS. LINDE (*smiling*). Nora, Nora, aren't you sensible yet? Back in school you were such a free spender.

NORA (*with a quiet laugh*). Yes, that's what Torvald still says. (*Shaking her finger.*) But "Nora, Nora" isn't as silly as you all think. Really, we've been in no position for me to go squandering. We've had to work, both of us.

MRS. LINDE. You too?

NORA. Yes, at odd jobs—needlework, crocheting, embroidery, and such—(*Casually,*) and other things too. You remember that Torvald left the department when we were married? There was no chance of promotion in his office, and of course he needed to earn more money. But that first year he drove himself terribly. He took on all kinds of extra work that kept him going morning and night. It wore him down, and then he fell deathly ill. The doctors said it was essential for him to travel south.

MRS. LINDE. Yes, didn't you spend a whole year in Italy?

NORA. That's right. It wasn't easy to get away, you know. Ivar had just been born. But of course we had to go. Oh, that was a beautiful trip, and it saved Torvald's life. But it cost a frightful sum, Kristine.

MRS. LINDE. I can well imagine.

NORA. Four thousand, eight hundred crowns it cost. That's really a lot of money.

MRS. LINDE. But it's lucky you had it when you needed it.

NORA. Well, as it was, we got it from Papa.

MRS. LINDE I see. It was just about the time your father died.

NORA. Yes, just about then. And, you know, I couldn't make that trip out to nurse him. I had to stay here, expecting Ivar any moment, and with my poor sick Torvald to care for. Dearest Papa, I never saw him again, Kristine. Oh, that was the worst time I've known in all my marriage.

MRS. LINDE. I know how you loved him. And then you went off to Italy?

NORA. Yes. We had the means now, and the doctors urged us. So we left a month after.

MRS. LINDE. And your husband came back completely cured?

NORA. Sound as a drum!

MRS. LINDE. But—the doctor?

NORA. Who?

MRS. LINDE. I thought the maid said he was a doctor, the man who came in with me.

NORA. Yes, that was Dr. Rank—but he's not making a sick call. He's our closest friend, and he stops by at least once a day. No, Torvald hasn't had a sick moment since, and the children are fit and strong, and I am, too. (*Jumping up and clapping her hands.*) Oh, dear God, Kristine, what a lovely thing to live and be happy! But how disgusting of me—I'm talking of nothing but my own affairs. (*Sits on a stool close by* KRISTINE, *arms resting across her knees.*) Oh, don't be angry with me! Tell me, is it really true that you weren't in love with your husband? Why did you marry him, then?

MRS. LINDE. My mother was still alive, but bedridden and helpless—and I had my two younger brothers to look after. In all conscience, I didn't think I could turn him down.

NORA. No, you were right there. But was he rich at the time?

MRS. LINDE. He was very well off, I'd say. But the business was shaky, Nora. When he died, it all fell apart, and nothing was left.

NORA. And then—?

MRS. LINDE. Yes, so I had to scrape up a living with a little shop and a little teaching and whatever else I could find. The last three years have been like one endless workday without a rest for me. Now it's over, Nora. My poor mother doesn't need me, for she's passed on. Nor the boys, either; they're working now and can take care of themselves.

NORA. How free you must feel—

MRS. LINDE. No—only unspeakably empty. Nothing to live for now. (*Standing up anxiously.*) That's why I couldn't take it any longer out in that desolate hole. Maybe here it'll be easier to find something to do and keep my mind occupied. If I could only be lucky enough to get a steady job, some office work—

NORA. Oh, but Kristine, that's so dreadfully tiring, and you already look so tired. It would be much better for you if you could go off to a bathing resort.

MRS. LINDE (*going toward the window*). I have no father to give me travel money, Nora.

NORA (*rising*). Oh, don't be angry with me.

MRS. LINDE (*going to her*). Nora dear, don't you be angry with me. The worst of my kind of situation is all the bitterness that's stored away. No one to work for, and yet you're always having to snap up your opportunities. You have to live; and so you grow selfish. When you told me the happy change in your lot, do you know I was delighted less for your sakes than for mine?

NORA. How so? Oh, I see. You think maybe Torvald could do something for you.

MRS. LINDE. Yes, that's what I thought.

NORA. And he will, Kristine! Just leave it to me; I'll bring it up so delicately—find something attractive to humor him with. Oh, I'm so eager to help you.

MRS. LINDE. How very kind of you, Nora, to be so concerned over me—doubly kind, considering you really know so little of life's burdens yourself.

NORA. I—? I know so little—?

MRS. LINDE (*smiling*). Well, my heavens—a little needlework and such—Nora, you're just a child.

NORA (*tossing her head and pacing the floor*). You don't have to act so superior.

MRS. LINDE. Oh?

NORA. You're just like the others. You all think I'm incapable of anything serious—

MRS. LINDE. Come now—

NORA. That I've never had to face the raw world.

MRS. LINDE. Nora dear, you've just been telling me all your troubles.

NORA. Hm! Trivia! (*Quietly.*) I haven't told you the big thing.

MRS. LINDE. Big thing? What do you mean?

NORA. You look down on me so, Kristine, but you shouldn't. You're proud that you worked so long and hard for your mother.

MRS. LINDE. I don't look down on a soul. But it *is* true: I'm proud—and happy, too—to think it was given to me to make my mother's last days almost free of care.

NORA. And you're also proud thinking of what you've done for your brothers.

MRS. LINDE. I feel I've a right to be.

NORA. I agree. But listen to this, Kristine—I've also got something to be proud and happy for.

MRS. LINDE. I don't doubt it. But whatever do you mean?

NORA. Not so loud. What if Torvald heard! He mustn't, not for anything in the world. Nobody must know, Kristine. No one but you.

MRS. LINDE. But what is it, then?

NORA. Come here. (*Drawing her down beside her on the sofa.*) It's true—I've also got something to be proud and happy for. I'm the one who saved Torvald's life.

MRS. LINDE. Saved—? Saved how?

NORA. I told you about the trip to Italy. Torvald never would have lived if he hadn't gone south—

MRS. LINDE. Of course; your father gave you the means—

NORA (*smiling*). That's what Torvald and all the rest think, but—

MRS. LINDE. But—?

NORA. Papa didn't give us a pin. I was the one who raised the money.

MRS. LINDE. You? That whole amount?

NORA. Four thousand, eight hundred crowns. What do you say to that?

MRS. LINDE. But Nora, how was it possible? Did you win the lottery?

NORA (*disdainfully*). The lottery? Pooh! No art to that.

MRS. LINDE. But where did you get it from then?

NORA (*humming, with a mysterious smile*). Hmm, tra-la-la-la.

MRS. LINDE. Because you couldn't have borrowed it.

NORA. No? Why not?

MRS. LINDE. A wife can't borrow without her husband's consent.

NORA (*tossing her head*). Oh, but a wife with a little business sense, a wife who knows how to manage—

MRS. LINDE. Nora, I simply don't understand—

NORA. You don't have to. Whoever said I *borrowed* the money? I could have gotten it other ways. (*Throwing herself back on the sofa.*) I could have gotten it from some admirer or other. After all, a girl with my ravishing appeal—

MRS. LINDE. You lunatic.

NORA. I'll bet you're eaten up with curiosity, Kristine.

MRS. LINDE. Now listen here, Nora—you haven't done something indiscreet?

NORA. (*sitting up again*). Is it indiscreet to save your husband's life?

MRS. LINDE. I think it's indiscreet that without his knowledge you—

NORA. But that's the point; he mustn't know! My Lord, can't you understand? He mustn't ever know the close call he had. It was to *me* the doctors came to say his life was in danger—that nothing could save him but a stay in the south. Didn't I try strategy then! I began talking about how lovely it would be for me to travel abroad like other young wives; I begged and cried; I told him please to remember my condition, to be kind and indulge me; and then I dropped a hint that he could easily take out a loan. But at that, Kristine, he nearly exploded. He said I was frivolous, and it was his duty as man of the house not to indulge me in whims and fancies—as I think he called them. Aha, I thought, now you'll just have to be saved—and that's when I saw my chance.

MRS. LINDE. And your father never told Torvald the money wasn't from him?

NORA. No, never. Papa died right about then. I'd considered bringing him into my secret and begging him never to tell. But he was too sick at the time—and then, sadly, it didn't matter.

MRS. LINDE. And you've never confided in your husband since?

NORA. For heaven's sake, no! Are you serious? He's so strict on that subject. Besides—Torvald, with all his masculine pride—how painfully humiliating for him if he ever found out he was in debt to me. That would just ruin our relationship. Our beautiful, happy home would never be the same.

MRS. LINDE. Won't you ever tell him?

NORA (*thoughtfully, half smiling*). Yes—maybe sometime, years from now, when I'm no longer so attractive. Don't laugh! I only mean when Torvald loves me less than now, when he stops enjoying my dancing and dressing up and reciting for him. Then it might be wise to have something in reserve— (*Breaking off.*) How ridiculous! That'll never happen— Well, Kristine, what do you think of my big secret? I'm capable of something too, hm? You can imagine, of course, how this thing hangs over me. It really hasn't been easy meeting the payments on time. In the business world there's what they call quarterly interest and what they call amortization, and these are always so terribly hard to manage. I've had to skimp a little here and there, wherever I could, you know. I could hardly spare anything from my house allowance, because Torvald has to live well. I couldn't let the children go poorly dressed; whatever I got for them, I felt I had to use up completely—the darlings!

MRS. LINDE. Poor Nora, so it had to come out of your own budget, then?

NORA. Yes, of course. But I was the one most responsible, too. Every time Torvald gave me money for new clothes and such, I never used more than half; always bought the simplest, cheapest outfits. It was a godsend that everything looks so well on me that Torvald never noticed. But it did weigh me down at times, Kristine. It *is* such a joy to wear fine things. You understand.

MRS. LINDE. Oh, of course.

NORA. And then I found other ways of making money. Last winter I was lucky enough to get a lot of copying to do. I locked myself in and sat writing every evening till late in the night. Ah, I was tired so often, dead tired. But still it was wonderful fun, sitting and working like that, earning money. It was almost like being a man.

MRS. LINDE. But how much have you paid off this way so far?

NORA. That's hard to say, exactly. These accounts, you know, aren't easy to figure. I only know that I've paid out all I could scrape together. Time and again I haven't known where to turn. (*Smiling.*) Then I'd sit here dreaming of a rich old gentleman who had fallen in love with me—

MRS. LINDE. What! Who is he?

NORA. Oh, really! And that he'd died, and when his will was opened, there in big letters it said, "All my fortune shall be paid over in cash, immediately, to that enchanting Mrs. Nora Helmer."

MRS. LINDE. But Nora dear—who *was* this gentlemen?

NORA. Good grief, can't you understand? The old man never existed; that was only something I'd dream up time and again whenever I was at my wits' end for money. But it makes no difference now; the old fossil can go where he pleases for all I care; I don't need him or his will—because now I'm free. (*Jumping up.*) Oh, how lovely to think of that, Kristine! Carefree! To know you're carefree, utterly carefree; to be able to romp and play with the children, and to keep up a beautiful, charming home—everything just the way Torvald likes it! And think, spring is coming, with big blue skies. Maybe we can travel a little then. Maybe I'll see the ocean again. Oh yes, it *is* so marvelous to live and be happy!

(*The front doorbell rings.*)

MRS. LINDE (*rising*). There's the bell. It's probably best that I go.

NORA. No, stay. No one's expected. It must be for Torvald.

MAID (*from the hall doorway*). Excuse me, ma'am—there's a gentleman here to see Mr. Helmer, but I didn't know—since the doctor's with him—

NORA. Who is the gentleman?

KROGSTAD (*from the doorway*). It's me, Mrs. Helmer.

(MRS. LINDE *starts and turns away toward the window.*)

NORA (*stepping toward him, tense, her voice a whisper*). You? What is it? Why do you want to speak to my husband?

KROGSTAD. Bank business—after a fashion. I have a small job in the investment bank, and I hear now your husband is going to be our chief—

NORA. In other words, it's—

KROGSTAD. Just dry business, Mrs. Helmer. Nothing but that.

NORA. Yes, then please be good enough to step into the study. (*She nods indifferently as she sees him out by the hall door, then returns and begins stirring up the stove.*)

MRS. LINDE. Nora—who was that man?

NORA. That was a Mr. Krogstad—a lawyer.

MRS. LINDE. Then it really was him.

NORA. Do you know that person?

MRS. LINDE. I did once—many years ago. For a time he was a law clerk in our town.

NORA. Yes, he's been that.

MRS. LINDE. How he's changed.

NORA. I understand he had a very unhappy marriage.

MRS. LINDE. He's a widower now.

NORA. With a number of children. There now, it's burning. (*She closes the stove door and moves the rocker a bit to one side.*)

MRS. LINDE. They say he has a hand in all kinds of business.

NORA. Oh? That may be true; I wouldn't know. But let's not think about business. It's so dull.

(DR. RANK *enters from* HELMER'S *study.*)

RANK (*still in the doorway*). No, no, really—I don't want to intrude, I'd just as soon talk a little while with your wife.
(*Shuts the door, then notices* MRS. LINDE.) Oh, beg pardon. I'm intruding here too.

NORA. No, not at all. (*Introducing him.*) Dr. Rank, Mrs. Linde.

RANK. Well now, that's a name much heard in this house. I believe I passed the lady on the stairs as I came.

MRS. LINDE. Yes, I take the stairs very slowly. They're rather hard on me.

RANK. Uh-hm, some touch of internal weakness?

MRS. LINDE. More overexertion, I'd say.

RANK. Nothing else? Then you're probably here in town to rest up in a round of parties?

MRS. LINDE. I'm here to look for work.

RANK. Is that the best cure for overexertion?

MRS. LINDE. One has to live, Doctor.

RANK. Yes, there's a common prejudice to that effect.

NORA. Oh, come on, Dr. Rank—you really do want to live yourself.

RANK. Yes, I really do. Wretched as I am, I'll gladly prolong my torment indefinitely. All my patients feel like that. And it's quite the same, too, with the morally sick. Right at this moment there's one of those moral invalids in there with Helmer—

MRS. LINDE (*softly*). Ah!

NORA. Who do you mean?

RANK. Oh, it's a lawyer, Krogstad, a type you wouldn't know. His character is rotten to the root—but even he began chattering all-importantly about how he had to *live*.

NORA. Oh? What did he want to talk to Torvald about?

RANK. I really don't know. I only heard something about the bank.

NORA. I didn't know that Krog—that this man Krogstad had anything to do with the bank.

RANK. Yes, he's gotten some kind of berth down there. (*To* MRS. LINDE.) I don't know if you also have, in your neck of the woods, a type of person who scuttles about breathlessly, sniffing out hints of moral corruption, and then maneuvers his victim into some sort of key position where he can keep an eye on him. It's the healthy these days that are out in the cold.

MRS. LINDE. All the same, it's the sick who most need to be taken in.

RANK (*with a shrug*). Yes, there we have it. That's the concept that's turning society into a sanatorium.

(NORA, *lost in her thoughts, breaks out into quiet laughter and claps her hands.*)

RANK. Why do you laugh at that? Do you have any real idea of what society is?

NORA. What do I care about dreary old society? I was laughing at something quite different—something terribly funny. Tell me, Doctor—is everyone who works in the bank dependent now on Torvald?

RANK. Is that what you find so terribly funny?

NORA (*smiling and humming*). Never mind, never mind! (*Pacing the floor.*) Yes, that's really immensely amusing: that we—that Torvald has so much power now over all those people. (*Taking the bag out of her pocket.*) Dr. Rank, a little macaroon on that?

RANK. See here, macaroons! I thought they were contraband here.

NORA. Yes, but these are some that Kristine gave me.

MRS. LINDE. What? I—?

NORA. Now, now, don't be afraid. You couldn't possibly know that Torvald had forbidden them. You see, he's worried they'll ruin my teeth. But hmp! Just this once! Isn't that so, Dr. Rank? Help yourself! (*Puts a macaroon in his mouth.*) And you too, Kristine. And I'll also have one, only a little one—or two, at the most. (*Walking about again.*) Now I'm really tremendously happy. Now there's just one last thing in the world that I have an enormous desire to do.

RANK. Well! And what's that?

NORA. It's something I have such a consuming desire to say so Torvald could hear.

RANK. And why can't you say it?

NORA. I don't dare. It's quite shocking.

MRS. LINDE. Shocking?

RANK. Well, then it isn't advisable. But in front of us you certainly can. What do you have such a desire to say so Torvald could hear?

NORA. I have such a desire to say—to hell and be damned!

RANK. Are you crazy?

MRS. LINDE. My goodness, Nora!

RANK. Go on, say it. Here he is.

NORA (*hiding the macaroon bag*). Shh, shh, shh!

(HELMER *comes in from his study, hat in hand, overcoat over his arm.*)

NORA (*going toward him*). Well, Torvald dear, are you through with him?

HELMER. Yes. He just left.

NORA. Let me introduce you—this is Kristine, who's arrived here in town.

HELMER. Kristine—? I'm sorry, but I don't know—

NORA. Mrs. Linde, Torvald dear. Mrs. Kristine Linde.

HELMER. Of course. A childhood friend of my wife's, no doubt?

MRS. LINDE. Yes, we knew each other in those days.

NORA. And just think, she made the long trip down here in order to talk with you.

HELMER. What's this?

MRS. LINDE. Well, not exactly—

NORA. You see, Kristine is remarkably clever in office work, and so she's terribly eager to come under a capable man's supervison and add more to what she already knows—

HELMER. Very wise, Mrs. Linde.

NORA. And then when she heard that you'd become a bank manager—the story was wired out to the papers—then she came in as fast as she could and—Really, Torvald, for my sake you can do a little something for Kristine, can't you?

HELMER. Yes, it's not at all impossible. Mrs. Linde, I suppose you're a widow?

MRS. LINDE. Yes.

HELMER. Any experience in office work?

MRS. LINDE. Yes, a good deal.

HELMER. Well, it's quite likely that I can make an opening for you—

NORA (clapping her hands). You see, you see!

HELMER. You've come at a lucky moment, Mrs. Linde.

MRS. LINDE. Oh, how can I thank you?

HELMER. Not necessary. (Putting his overcoat on.) But today you'll have to excuse me—

RANK. Wait, I'll go with you. (He fetches his coat from the hall and warms it at the stove.)

NORA. Don't stay out long, dear.

HELMER. An hour; no more.

NORA. Are you going too, Kristine?

MRS. LINDE (putting on her winter garments). Yes, I have to see about a room now.

HELMER. Then perhaps we can all walk together.

NORA (helping her). What a shame we're so cramped here, but it's quite impossible for us to—

MRS. LINDE. Oh, don't even think of it! Good-bye, Nora dear, and thanks for everything.

NORA. Good-bye for now. Of course you'll be back this evening. And you too, Dr. Rank. What? If you're well enough? Oh, you've got to be! Wrap up tight now.

(In a ripple of small talk the company moves out into the hall; children's voices are heard outside on the steps.)

NORA. There they are! There they are! (She runs to open the door. The children come in with their nurse, ANNE-MARIE.) Come in, come in! (Bends down and kisses them.) Oh, you darlings—! Look at them, Kristine. Aren't they lovely!

RANK. No loitering in the draft here.

HELMER. Come, Mrs. Linde—this place is unbearable now for anyone but mothers.

(DR. RANK, HELMER, and MRS. LINDE go down the stairs. ANNE-MARIE goes into the living room with the children. NORA follows, after closing the hall door.)

NORA. How fresh and strong you look. Oh, such red cheeks you have! Like apples and roses. (The children interrupt her throughout the following.) And it was so much fun? That's wonderful. Really? You pulled both Emmy and Bob on the sled? Imagine, all together! Yes, you're a clever boy, Ivar. Oh, let me hold her a bit, Anne-Marie. My sweet little doll baby! (Takes the smallest from the nurse and dances with her.) Yes, yes, Mama will dance with Bob as well. What? Did you throw snowballs? Oh, if I'd only been there! No, don't bother, Anne-Marie—I'll undress them myself. Oh yes, let me. It's such fun. Go in and rest; you look half frozen. There's hot coffee waiting for you on the stove. (The nurse goes into the room to the left. NORA takes the children's winter things off, throwing them about, while the children talk to her all at once.) Is that so? A big dog chased you? But it didn't bite? No, dogs never bite little, lovely doll babies. Don't peek in the packages, Ivar! What is it? Yes, wouldn't you like to know. No, no, it's an ugly something. Well? Shall we play? What shall we play? Hide-and-seek? Yes, let's play hide-and-seek. Bob must hide first. I must? Yes, let me hide first. (Laughing and shouting, she and the children play in and out of the living room and the adjoining room to the right. At last NORA hides under the table. The children come storming in, search, but cannot find her, then hear her muffled laughter, dash over to the table, lift the cloth up and find her. Wild shouting. She creeps forward as if to scare them. More shouts. Mean-

while, a knock at the hall door; no one has noticed it. Now the door half opens, and KROGSTAD *appears. He waits a moment; the game goes on.*)

KROGSTAD. Beg pardon, Mrs. Helmer—

NORA (*with a strangled cry, turning and scrambling to her knees*). Oh! What do you want?

KROGSTAD. Excuse me. The outer door was ajar; it must be someone forgot to shut it—

NORA (*rising*). My husband isn't home, Mr. Krogstad.

KROGSTAD. I know that.

NORA. Yes—then what do you want here?

KROGSTAD. A word with you.

NORA. With—? (*To the children, quietly.*) Go in to Anne-Marie. What? No, the strange man won't hurt Mama. When he's gone, we'll play some more. (*She leads the children into the room to the left and shuts the door after them. Then, tense and nervous:*) You want to speak to me?

KROGSTAD. Yes, I want to.

NORA. Today? But it's not yet the first of the month—

KROGSTAD. No, it's Christmas Eve. It's going to be up to you how merry a Christmas you have.

NORA. What is it you want? Today I absolutely can't—

KROGSTAD. We won't talk about that till later. This is something else. You do have a moment to spare, I suppose?

NORA. Oh yes, of course—I do, except—

KROGSTAD. Good. I was sitting over at Olsen's Restaurant when I saw your husband go down the street—

NORA. Yes?

KROGSTAD. With a lady.

NORA. Yes. So?

KROGSTAD. If you'll pardon my asking: wasn't that lady a Mrs. Linde?

NORA. Yes.

KROGSTAD. Just now come into town?

NORA. Yes, today.

KROGSTAD. She's a good friend of yours?

NORA. Yes, she is. But I don't see—

KROGSTAD. I also knew her once.

NORA. I'm aware of that.

KROGSTAD. Oh? You know all about it. I thought so. Well, then let me ask you short and sweet: is Mrs. Linde getting a job in the bank?

NORA. What makes you think you can cross-examine me, Mr. Krogstad—you, one of my husband's employees? But since you ask, you might as well know—yes, Mrs. Linde's going to be taken on at the bank. And I'm the one who spoke for her, Mr. Krogstad. Now you know.

KROGSTAD. So I guessed right.

NORA (*pacing up and down*). Oh, one does have a tiny bit of influence, I should hope. Just because I am a woman, don't think it means that— When one has a subordinate position, Mr. Krogstad, one really ought to be careful about pushing somebody who—hm—

KROGSTAD. Who has influence?

NORA. That's right.

KROGSTAD (*in a different tone*). Mrs. Helmer, would you be good enough to use your influence on my behalf?

NORA. What? What do you mean?

KROGSTAD. Would you please make sure that I keep my subordinate position in the bank?

NORA. What does that mean? Who's thinking of taking away your position?

KROGSTAD. Oh, don't play the innocent with me. I'm quite aware that your friend would hardly relish the chance of running into me again; and I'm also aware now whom I can thank for being turned out.

NORA. But I promise you—

KROGSTAD. Yes, yes, yes, to the point: there's still time, and I'm advising you to use your influence to prevent it.

NORA. But Mr. Krogstad, I have absolutely no influence.

KROGSTAD. You haven't? I thought you were just saying—

NORA. You shouldn't take me so literally. I! How can you believe that I have any such influence over my husband?

KROGSTAD. Oh, I've known your husband from our student days. I don't think the great bank manager's more steadfast than any other married man.

NORA. You speak insolently about my husband, and I'll show you the door.

KROGSTAD. The lady has spirit.

NORA. I'm not afraid of you any longer. After New Year's, I'll soon be done with the whole business.

KROGSTAD (*restraining himself*). Now listen to me, Mrs. Helmer. If necessary, I'll fight for my little job in the bank as if it were life itself.

NORA. Yes, so it seems.

KROGSTAD. It's not just a matter of income; that's the least of it. It's something else— All right, out with it! Look, this is the thing. You know, just like all the others, of course, that once, a good many years ago, I did something rather rash.

NORA. I've heard rumors to that effect.

KROGSTAD. The case never got into court; but all the same, every door was closed in my face from then on. So I took up those various activities you know about. I had to grab hold somewhere; and I dare say I haven't been among the worst. But now I want to drop all that. My boys are growing up. For their sakes, I'll have to win back as much respect as possible here in town. That job in the bank was like the first rung in my ladder. And now your husband wants to kick me right back down in the mud again.

NORA. But for heaven's sake, Mr. Krogstad, it's simply not in my power to help you.

KROGSTAD. That's because you haven't the will to— but I have the means to make you.

NORA. You certainly won't tell my husband that I owe you money?

KROGSTAD. Hm—what if I told him that?

NORA. That would be shameful of you. (*Nearly in tears.*) This secret—my joy and my pride—that he should learn it in such a crude and disgusting way—learn it from you. You'd expose me to the most horrible unpleasantness—

KROGSTAD. Only unpleasantness?

NORA (*vehemently*). But go on and try. It'll turn out the worse for you, because then my husband will really see what a crook you are, and then you'll *never* be able to hold your job.

KROGSTAD. I asked if it was just domestic unpleasantness you were afraid of?

NORA. If my husband finds out, then of course he'll pay what I owe at once, and then we'd be through with you for good.

KROGSTAD (*a step closer*). Listen, Mrs. Helmer— you've either got a very bad memory, or else no head at all for business. I'd better put you a little more in touch with the facts.

NORA. What do you mean?

KROGSTAD. When your husband was sick, you came to me for a loan of four thousand, eight hundred crowns.

NORA. Where else could I go?

KROGSTAD. I promised to get you that sum—

NORA. And you got it.

KROGSTAD. I promised to get you that sum, on certain conditions. You were so involved in your husband's illness, and so eager to finance your trip, that I guess you didn't think out all the details. It might just be a good idea to remind you. I promised you the money on the strength of a note I drew up.

NORA. Yes, and that I signed.

KROGSTAD. Right. But at the bottom I added some lines for your father to guarantee the loan. He was supposed to sign down there.

NORA. Supposed to? He did sign.

KROGSTAD. I left the date blank. In other words, your father would have dated his signature himself. Do you remember that?

NORA. Yes, I think—

KROGSTAD. Then I gave you the note for you to mail to your father. Isn't that so?

NORA. Yes.

KROGSTAD. And naturally you sent it at once—because only some five, six days later you brought me the note, properly signed. And with that, the money was yours.

NORA. Well, then; I've made my payments regularly, haven't I?

KROGSTAD. More or less. But—getting back to the point—those were hard times for you then, Mrs. Helmer.

NORA. Yes, they were.

KROGSTAD. Your father was very ill, I believe.

NORA. He was near the end.

KROGSTAD. He died soon after?

NORA. Yes.

KROGSTAD. Tell me, Mrs. Helmer, do you happen to recall the date of your father's death? The day of the month, I mean.

NORA. Papa died the twenty-ninth of September.

KROGSTAD. That's quite correct; I've already looked into that. And now we come to a curious thing— (*Taking out a paper.*) which I simply cannot comprehend.

NORA. Curious thing? I don't know—

KROGSTAD. This is the curious thing: that your father co-signed the note for your loan three days after his death.

NORA. How—? I don't understand.

KROGSTAD. Your father died the twenty-ninth of September. But look. Here your father dated his signature October second. Isn't that curious, Mrs. Helmer? (NORA *is silent.*) Can you explain it to me? (NORA *remains silent.*) It's also remarkable that the words "October second" and the year aren't written in your father's hand, but rather in one that I think I know. Well, it's easy to understand. Your father forgot perhaps to date his signature, and then someone or other added it, a bit sloppily, before anyone knew of his death. There's nothing wrong in that. It all comes down to the signature. And there's no question about *that*, Mrs. Helmer. It really *was* your father who signed his own name here, wasn't it?

NORA (*after a short silence, throwing her head back and looking squarely at him*). No, it wasn't. *I* signed Papa's name.

KROGSTAD. Wait, now—are you fully aware that this is a dangerous confession?

NORA. Why? You'll soon get your money.

KROGSTAD. Let me ask you a question—why didn't you send the paper to your father?

NORA. That was impossible. Papa was so sick. If I'd asked him for his signature, I also would have had to tell him what the money was for. But I couldn't tell him, sick as he was, that my husband's life was in danger. That was just impossible.

KROGSTAD. Then it would have been better if you'd given up the trip abroad.

NORA. I couldn't possibly. The trip was to save my husband's life. I couldn't give that up.

KROGSTAD. But didn't you ever consider that this was a fraud against me?

NORA. I couldn't let myself be bothered by that. You weren't any concern of mine. I couldn't stand you, with all those cold complications you made, even though you knew how badly off my husband was.

KROGSTAD. Mrs. Helmer, obviously you haven't the vaguest idea of what you've involved yourself in. But I can tell you this: it was nothing more and nothing worse that I once did—and it wrecked my whole reputation.

NORA. You? Do you expect me to believe that you ever acted bravely to save your wife's life?

KROGSTAD. Laws don't inquire into motives.

NORA. Then they must be very poor laws.

KROGSTAD. Poor or not—if I introduce this paper in court, you'll be judged according to law.

NORA. This I refuse to believe. A daughter hasn't a right to protect her dying father from anxiety and care? A wife hasn't a right to save her husband's life? I don't know much about laws, but I'm sure that somewhere in the books these things are allowed. And you don't know anything about it—you who practice the law? You must be an awful lawyer, Mr. Krogstad.

KROGSTAD. Could be. But business—the kind of business we two are mixed up in—don't you think I know about that? All right. Do what you want not. But I'm telling you *this:* if I get shoved down a second time, you're going to keep me company. (*He bows and goes out through the hall.*)

NORA (*pensive for a moment, then tossing her head*). Oh, really! Trying to frighten me! I'm not so silly as all that. (*Begins gathering up the children's clothes, but soon stops.*) But—? No, but that's impossible! I did it out of love.

THE CHILDREN (*in the doorway, left*). Mama, that strange man's gone out the door.

NORA. Yes, yes, I know it. But don't tell anyone about the strange man. Do you hear? Not even Papa!

THE CHILDREN. No, Mama. But now will you play again?

NORA. No, not now.

THE CHILDREN. Oh, but Mama, you promised.

. Yes, but I can't now. Go inside; I have too much to do. Go in, go in, my sweet darlings. (*She herds them gently back in the room and shuts the door after them. Settling on the sofa, she takes up a piece of embroidery and makes some stitches, but soon stops abruptly.*) No! (*Throws the work aside, rises, goes to the hall door and calls out.*) Helene! Let me have the tree in here. (*Goes to the table, left, opens the table drawer, and stops again.*) No, but that's utterly impossible!

MAID (*with the Christmas tree*). Where should I put it, ma'am?

NORA. There. The middle of the floor.

MAID. Should I bring anything else?

NORA. No, thanks. I have what I need.

(*The* MAID, *who has set the tree down, goes out*).

NORA (*absorbed in trimming the tree*). Candles here—and flowers here. That terrible creature! Talk, talk, talk! There's nothing to it at all. The tree's going to be lovely. I'll do anything to please you, Torvald, I'll sing for you, dance for you—

(HELMER *comes in from the hall, with a sheaf of paper under his arm.*)

NORA. Oh! You're back so soon?

HELMER. Yes. Has anyone been here?

NORA. Here? No.

HELMER. That's odd. I saw Krogstad leaving the front door.

NORA. So? Oh yes, that's true. Krogstad was here a moment.

HELMER. Nora, I can see by your face that he's been here, begging you go put in a good word for him.

NORA. Yes.

HELMER. And it was supposed to seem like your own idea? You were to hide it from me that he'd been here. He asked you that, too, didn't he?

NORA. Yes, Torvald, but—

HELMER. Nora, Nora, and you could fall for that? Talk with that sort of person and promise him anything? And then in the bargain, tell me an untruth.

NORA. An untruth—?

HELMER. Didn't you say that no one had been here? (*Wagging his finger.*) My little songbird must never do that again. A songbird needs a clean beak to warble with. No false notes. (*Putting his arm about her waist.*) That's the way it should be, isn't it? Yes, I'm sure of it. (*Releasing her.*) And so, enough of that. (*Sitting by the stove.*) Ah, how snug and cozy it is here. (*Leafing among his papers.*)

NORA (*busy with the tree, after a short pause*). Torvald!

HELMER. Yes.

NORA. I'm so much looking forward to the Stenborgs' costume party, day after tomorrow.

HELMER. And I can't wait to see what you'll surprise me with.

NORA. Oh, that stupid business!

HELMER. What?

NORA. I can't find anything that's right. Everything seems so ridiculous, so inane.

HELMER. So my little Nora's come to *that* recognition?

NORA (*going behind his chair, her arms resting on its back*). Are you very busy, Torvald?

HELMER. Oh—

NORA. What papers are those?

HELMER. Bank matters.

NORA. Already?

HELMER. I've gotten full authority from the retiring management to make all necessary changes in personnel and procedure. I'll need Christmas week for that. I want to have everything in order by New Year's.

NORA. So that was the reason this poor Krogstad—

HELMER. Hm.

NORA (*still leaning on the chair and slowly stroking the nape of his neck*). If you weren't so very busy, I would have asked you an enormous favor, Torvald.

HELMER. Let's hear. What is it?

NORA. You know, there isn't anyone who has your good taste—and I want so much to look well at the costume party. Torvald, couldn't you take over and decide what I should be and plan my costume?

HELMER. Ah, is my stubborn little creature calling for a lifeguard?

NORA. Yes, Torvald, I can't get anywhere without your help.

HELMER. All right—I'll think it over. We'll hit on something.

NORA. Oh, how sweet of you. (*Goes to the tree again. Pause.*) Aren't the red flowers pretty—? But tell me, was it really such a crime that this Krogstad committed?

HELMER. Forgery. Do you have any idea what that means?

NORA. Couldn't he have done it out of need?

HELMER. Yes, or thoughtlessness, like so many others. I'm not so heartless that I'd condemn a man categorically for just one mistake.

NORA. No, of course not, Torvald!

HELMER. Plenty of men have redeemed themselves by openly confessing their crimes and taking their punishment.

NORA. Punishment—?

HELMER. But now Krogstad didn't go that way. He got himself out by sharp practices, and that's the real cause of his moral breakdown.

NORA. Do you really think that would—?

HELMER. Just imagine how a man with that sort of guilt in him has to lie and cheat and deceive on all sides, has to wear a mask even with the nearest and dearest he has, even with his own wife and children. And with the children, Nora—that's where it's most horrible.

NORA. Why?

HELMER. Because that kind of atmosphere of lies infects the whole life of a home. Every breath the children take in is filled with the germs of something degenerate.

NORA (*coming closer behind him*). Are you sure of that?

HELMER. Oh, I've seen it often enough as a lawyer. Almost everyone who goes bad early in life has a mother who's a chronic liar.

NORA. Why just—the mother?

HELMER. It's usually the mother's influence that's dominant, but the father's works in the same way, of course. Every lawyer is quite familiar with it. And still this Krogstad's been going home year in, year out, poisoning his own children with lies and pretense; that's why I call him morally lost. (*Reaching his hands out toward her.*) So my sweet little Nora must promise me never to plead his cause. Your hand on it. Come, come, what's this? Give me your hand. There, now. All settled. I can tell you it'd be impossible for me to work alongside of him. I literally feel physically revolted when I'm anywhere near such a person.

NORA (*withdraws her hand and goes to the other side of the Christmas tree*). How hot it is here! And I've got so much to do.

HELMER (*getting up and gathering his papers*). Yes, and I have to think about getting some of these read through before dinner. I'll think about your costume, too. And something to hang on the tree in gilt paper. I may even see about that. (*Putting his hand on her head.*) Oh you, my darling little songbird. (*He goes into his study and closes the door after him.*)

NORA (*softly, after a silence*). Oh, really! it isn't so. It's impossible. It must be impossible.

ANNE-MARIE (*in the doorway, left*). The children are begging so hard to come in to Mama.

NORA. No, no, no, don't let them in to me! You stay with them, Anne-Marie.

ANNE-MARIE. Of course, ma'am. (*Closes the door.*)

NORA (*pale with terror*). Hurt my children—! Poison my home? (*A moment's pause; then she tosses her head.*) That's not true. Never. Never in all the world.

ACT TWO

Same room. Beside the piano the Christmas tree now stands stripped of ornament, burned-down candle stubs on its ragged branches. NORA'S *street clothes lie on the sofa.* NORA, *alone in the room, moves restlessly about; at last she stops at the sofa and picks up her coat.*

NORA (*dropping the coat again*). Someone's coming! (*Goes toward the door, listens.*) No— there's no one. Of course—nobody's coming today, Christmas Day—or tomorrow, either. But maybe—(*Opens the door and looks out.*) No, nothing in the mailbox. Quite empty. (*Coming forward.*) What nonsense! He won't do anything serious. Nothing terrible could happen. It's impossible. Why, I have three small children.

(ANNE-MAIRE, *with a large carton, comes in from the room to the left.*)

ANNE-MARIE. Well, at last I found the box with the masquerade clothes.

NORA. Thanks. Put it on the table.

ANNE-MARIE (*does so*). But they're all pretty much of a mess.

NORA. Ahh! I'd love to rip them in a million pieces!

ANNE-MARIE. Oh, mercy, they can be fixed right up. Just a little patience.

NORA. Yes, I'll go get Mrs. Linde to help me.

ANNE-MARIE. Out again now? In this nasty weather? Miss Nora will catch cold—get sick.

NORA. Oh, worse things could happen— How are the children?

ANNE-MARIE. The poor mites are playing with their Christmas presents, but—

NORA. Do they ask for me much?

ANNE-MARIE. They're so used to having Mama around, you know.

NORA. Yes, but Anne-Marie, I *can't* be together with them as much as I was.

ANNE-MARIE. Well, small children get used to anything.

NORA. You think so? Do you think they'd forget their mother if she was gone for good?

ANNE-MARIE. Oh, mercy—gone for good!

NORA. Wait, tell me, Anne-Marie—I've wondered so often—how could you ever have the heart to give your child over to strangers?

ANNE-MARIE. But I had to, you know, to become little Nora's nurse.

NORA. Yes, but how could you *do* it?

ANNE-MARIE. When I could get such a good place? A girl who's poor and who's gotten in trouble is glad enough for that. Because that slippery fish, he didn't do a thing for me, you know.

NORA. But your daughter's surely forgotten you.

ANNE-MARIE. Oh, she certainly has not. She's written to me, both when she was confirmed and when she was married.

NORA (*clasping her about the neck*). You old Anne-Marie, you were a good mother for me when I was little.

ANNE-MARIE. Poor little Nora, with no other mother but me.

NORA. And if the babies didn't have one, then I know that you'd— What silly talk (*Opening the carton*). Go in to them. Now I'll have to— Tomorrow you can see how lovely I'll look.

ANNE-MARIE. Oh, there won't be anyone at the party as lovely as Miss Nora. (*She goes off into the room, left.*)

NORA (*begins unpacking the box, but soon throws it aside*). Oh, if I dared to go out. If only nobody would come. If only nothing would happen here while I'm out. What craziness—nobody's coming. Just don't think. This muff—needs a brushing. Beautiful gloves, beautiful gloves. Let it go. Let it go! One, two, three, four, five, six—(*With a cry.*) Oh, there they are! (*Poises to move toward the door, but remains irresolutely standing.* MRS. LINDE *enters from the hall, where she has removed her street clothes.*)

NORA. Oh, it's you, Kristine. There's no one else out there? How good that you've come.

MRS. LINDE. I hear you were up asking for me.

NORA. Yes, I just stopped by. There's something you really can help me with. Let's get settled on the sofa. Look, there's going to be a costume party tomorrow evening at the Stenborgs' right above us, and now Torvald wants me to go as a Neapolitan peasant girl and dance the tarantella that I learned in Capri.

MRS. LINDE. Really, you are giving a whole performance?

NORA. Torvald says yes, I should. See, here's the dress. Torvald had it made for me down there; but now it's all so tattered that I just don't know—

MRS. LINDE. Oh, we'll fix that up in no time. It's nothing more than the trimmings—they're a bit loose here and there. Needle and thread? Good, now we have what we need.

NORA. Oh, how sweet of you!

MRS. LINDE (*sewing*). So you'll be in disguise tomorrow, Nora. You know what? I'll stop by then for a moment and have a look at you all dressed up. But listen, I've absolutely forgotten to thank you for that pleasant evening yesterday.

NORA (*getting up and walking about*). I don't think it was as pleasant as usual yesterday. You should have come to town a bit sooner, Kristine— Yes, Torvald really knows how to give a home elegance and charm.

MRS. LINDE. And you do, too, if you ask me. You're not your father's daughter for nothing. But tell me, is Dr. Rank always so down in the mouth as yesterday?

NORA. No, that was quite an exception. But he goes around critically ill all the time—tuberculosis of the spine, poor man. You know, his father was a disgusting thing who kept mistresses and so on—and that's why the son's been sickly from birth.

MRS. LINDE (*lets her sewing fall to her lap*). But my dearest Nora, how do you know about such things?

NORA (*walking more jauntily*). Hmp! When you've had three children, then you've had a few visits from—from women who know something of medicine, and they tell you this and that.

MRS. LINDE (*resumes sewing; a short pause*). Does Dr. Rank come here every day?

NORA. Every blessed day. He's Torvald's best friend from childhood, and *my* good friend, too. Dr. Rank almost belongs to this house.

MRS. LINDE. But tell me—is he quite sincere? I mean, doesn't he rather enjoy flattering people?

NORA. Just the opposite. Why do you think that?

MRS. LINDE. When you introduced us yesterday, he was proclaiming that he'd often heard my name in this house; but later I noticed that your husband hadn't the slightest idea who I really was. So how could Dr. Rank—?

NORA. But it's all true, Kristine. You see, Torvald loves me beyond words, and, as he puts it, he'd like to keep me all to himself. For a long time he'd almost be jealous if I even mentioned any of my old friends back home. So of course I dropped that. But with Dr. Rank I talk a lot about such things, because he likes hearing about them.

MRS. LINDE. Now listen, Nora; in many ways you're still like a child. I'm a good deal older than you, with a little more experience. I'll tell you something: you ought to put an end to all this with Dr. Rank.

NORA. What should I put an end to?

MRS. LINDE. Both parts of it, I think. Yesterday you said something about a rich admirer who'd provide you with money—

NORA. Yes, one who doesn't exist—worse luck. So?

MRS. LINDE. Is Dr. Rank well off?

NORA. Yes, he is.

MRS. LINDE. With no dependents?

NORA. No, no one. But—

MRS. LINDE. And he's over here every day?

NORA. Yes, I told you that.

MRS. LINDE. How can a man of such refinement be so grasping?

NORA. I don't follow you at all.

MRS. LINDE. Now don't try to hide it, Nora. You think I can't guess who loaned you the forty-eight hundred crowns?

NORA. Are you out of your mind? How could you think such a thing! A friend of ours, who comes here every single day. What an intolerable situation that would have been!

MRS. LINDE. Then it really wasn't him.

NORA. No, absolutely not. It never even crossed my mind for a moment— And he had nothing to lend in those days; his inheritance came later.

MRS. LINDE. Well, I think that was a stroke of luck for you, Nora dear.

NORA. No, it never would have occurred to me to ask Dr. Rank— Still, I'm quite sure that if I had asked him—

MRS. LINDE. Which you won't, of course.

NORA. No, of course not. I can't see that I'd ever need to. But I'm quite positive that if I talked to Dr. Rank—

MRS. LINDE. Behind your husband's back?

NORA. I've got to clear up this other thing; *that's* also behind his back. I've *got* to clear it all up.

MRS. LINDE. Yes, I was saying that yesterday, but—

NORA (*pacing up and down*). A man handles these problems so much better than a woman—

MRS. LINDE. One's husband does, yes.

NORA. Nonsense. (*Stopping.*) When you pay everything you owe, then you get your note back, right?

MRS. LINDE. Yes, naturally.

NORA. And can rip it into a million pieces and burn it up—that filthy scrap of paper!

MRS. LINDE (*looking hard at her, laying her sewing aside, and rising slowly*). Nora, you're hiding something from me.

NORA. You can see it in my face?

MRS. LINDE. Something's happened to you since yesterday morning. Nora, what is it?

NORA (*hurrying toward her*). Kristine! (*Listening.*) Shh! Torvald's home. Look, go in with the children a while. Torvald can't bear all this snipping and stitching. Let Anne-Marie help you.

MRS. LINDE (*gathering up some of the things*). All right, but I'm not leaving here until we've talked this out. (*She disappears into the room, left, as* TORVALD *enters from the hall.*)

NORA. Oh, how I've been waiting for you, Torvald dear.

HELMER. Was that the dressmaker?

NORA. No, that was Kristine. She's helping me fix up my costume. You know, it's going to be quite attractive.

HELMER. Yes, wasn't that a bright idea I had?

NORA. Brilliant! But then wasn't I good as well to give in to you?

HELMER. Good—because you give in to your husband's judgment? All right, you little goose, I know you didn't mean it like that. But I won't disturb you. You'll want to have a fitting, I suppose.

NORA. And you'll be working?

HELMER. Yes. (*Indicating a bundle of papers.*) See. I've been down to the bank. (*Starts toward his study.*)

NORA. Torvald.

HELMER (*stops*). Yes.

NORA. If your little squirrel begged you, with all her heart and soul, for something—?

HELMER. What's that?

NORA. Then would you do it?

HELMER. First, naturally, I'd have to know what it was.

NORA. Your squirrel would scamper about and do tricks, if you'd only be sweet and give in.

HELMER. Out with it.

NORA. Your lark would be singing high and low in every room—

HELMER. Come on, she does that anyway.

NORA. I'd be a wood nymph and dance for you in the moonlight.

HELMER. Nora—don't tell me it's that same business from this morning?

NORA (*coming closer*). Yes, Torvald, I beg you, please!

HELMER. And you actually have the nerve to drag that up again?

NORA. Yes, yes, you've got to give in to me; you *have* to let Krogstad keep his job in the bank.

HELMER. My dear Nora, I've slated his job for Mrs. Linde.

NORA. That's awfully kind of you. But you could just fire another clerk instead of Krogstad.

HELMER. This is the most incredible stubbornness! Because you go and give an impulsive promise to speak up for him, I'm expected to—

NORA. That's not the reason, Torvald. It's for your own sake. That man does writing for the worst papers; you said it yourself. He could do you any amount of harm. I'm scared to death of him—

HELMER. Ah, I understand. It's the old memories haunting you.

NORA. What do you mean by that?

HELMER. Of course, you're thinking about your father.

NORA. Yes, all right. Just remember how those nasty gossips wrote in the papers about Papa and slandered him so cruelly. I think they'd have had him dismissed if the department hadn't sent you up to investigate, and if you hadn't been so kind and open-minded toward him.

HELMER. My dear Nora, there's a notable difference between your father and me. Your father's official career was hardly above reproach. But mine is; and I hope it'll stay that way as long as I hold my position.

NORA. Oh, who can ever tell what vicious minds can invent? We could be so snug and happy now in our quiet, carefree home—you and I and the children, Torvald! That's why I'm pleading with you so—

HELMER. And just by pleading for him you make it impossible for me to keep him on. It's already known at the bank that I'm firing Krogstad. What if it's rumored around now that the new bank manager was vetoed by his wife—

NORA. Yes, what then——?

HELMER. Oh yes—as long as our little bundle of stubbornness gets her way—! I should go and make myself ridiculous in front of the whole office—give people the idea I can be swayed by all kinds of outside pressure. Oh, you can bet I'd feel the effects of that soon enough! Besides—there's something that rules Krogstad right out at the bank as long as I'm the manager.

NORA. What's that?

HELMER. His moral failings I could maybe overlook if I had to—

NORA. Yes, Torvald, why not?

HELMER. And I hear he's quite efficient on the job. But he was a crony of mine back in my teens—one of those rash friendships that crop up again and again to embarrass you later in life. Well, I might as well say it straight out: we're on a first-name basis. And that tactless fool makes no effort at all to hide it in front of others. Quite the contrary—he thinks that entitles him to take a familiar air around me, and so every other second he comes booming out with his "Yes, Torvald!" and "Sure thing, Torvald!" I tell you, it's been excruciating for me. He's out to make my place in the bank unbearable.

NORA. Torvald, you can't be serious about all this.

HELMER. Oh no? Why not?

NORA. Because these are such petty considerations.

HELMER. What are you saying? Petty? You think I'm petty!

NORA. No, just the opposite, Torvald dear. That's exactly why—

HELMER. Never mind. You call my motives petty; then I might as well be just that. Petty! All right! We'll put a stop to this for good. (*Goes to the hall door and calls.*) Helene!

NORA. What do you want?

HELMER (*searching among his papers*). A decision. (*The* MAID *comes in.*) Look here; take this letter; go out with it at once. Get hold of a messenger and have him deliver it. Quick now. It's already addressed. Wait, here's some money.

MAID. Yes, sir. (*She leaves with the letter.*)

HELMER (*straightening his papers*). There, now, little Miss Willful.

NORA (*breathlessly*). Torvald, what was that letter?

HELMER. Krogstad's notice.

NORA. Call it back, Torvald! There's still time. Oh, Torvald, call it back! Do it for my sake— for your sake, for the children's sake! Do you hear, Torvald; do it! You don't know how this can harm us.

HELMER. Too late.

NORA. Yes, too late.

HELMER. Nora dear, I can forgive you this panic, even though basically you're insulting me. Yes, you are! Or isn't it an insult to think that *I* should be afraid of a courtroom hack's revenge? But I forgive you anyway, because this shows so beautifully how much you love me. (*Takes her in his arms.*) This is the way it should be, my darling Nora. Whatever comes, you'll see: when it really counts, I have strength and courage enough as a man to take on the whole weight myself.

NORA (*terrified*). What do you mean by that?

HELMER. The whole weight, I said.

NORA (*resolutely*). No, never in all the world.

HELMER. Good. So we'll share it, Nora, as man and wife. That's as it should be. (*Fondling her.*) Are you happy now? There, there, there—not these frightened dove's eyes. It's nothing at all but empty fantasies— Now you should run through your tarantella and practice your tambourine. I'll go to the inner office and shut both doors, so I won't hear a thing; you can make all the noise you like. (*Turning in the doorway.*) And when Rank comes, just tell him where he can find me. (*He nods to her and goes with his papers into the study, closing the door.*)

NORA (*standing as though rooted, dazed with fright, in a whisper*). He really could do it. He will do it. He'll do it in spite of everything. No, not that, never, never! Anything but that! Escape! A way out— (*The doorbell rings.*) Dr. Rank! Anything but that! *Anything*, whatever it is! (*Her hands pass over her face, smoothing it; she pulls herself together, goes over and opens the hall door.* DR. RANK *stands outside, hanging his fur coat up. During the following scene, it begins getting dark.*)

NORA. Hello, Dr. Rank. I recognized your ring. But you mustn't go in to Torvald yet; I believe he's working.

RANK. And you?

NORA. For you, I always have an hour to spare— you know that. (*He has entered, and she shuts the door after him.*)

RANK. Many thanks. I'll make use of these hours while I can.

NORA. What do you mean by that? While you can?

RANK. Does that disturb you?

NORA. Well, it's such an odd phrase. Is anything going to happen?

RANK. What's going to happen is what I've been expecting so long—but I honestly didn't think it would come so soon.

NORA (*gripping his arm*). What is it you've found out? Dr. Rank, you have to tell me!

RANK (*sitting by the stove*). It's all over with me. There's nothing to be done about it.

NORA (*breathing easier*). Is it you—then—?

RANK. Who else? There's no point in lying to one's self. I'm the most miserable of all my patients, Mrs. Helmer. These past few days I've been auditing my internal accounts. Bankrupt! Within a month I'll probably be laid out and rotting in the churchyard.

NORA. Oh, what a horrible thing to say.

RANK. The thing itself is horrible. But the worst of it is all the other horror before it's over. There's only one final examination left; when I'm finished with that, I'll know about when my disintegration will begin. There's something I want to say. Helmer with his sensitivity has such a sharp distaste for anything ugly. I don't want him near my sickroom.

NORA. Oh, but Dr. Rank—

RANK. I won't have him in there. Under no condition. I'll lock my door to him— As soon as I'm completely sure of the worst, I'll send you my calling card marked with a black cross, and you'll known then the wreck has started to come apart.

NORA. No, today you're completely unreasonable. And I wanted you so much to be in a really good humor.

RANK. With death up my sleeve? And then to suffer this way for somebody else's sins. Is there any justice in that? And in every single family, in some way or another, this inevitable retribution of nature goes on—

NORA (*her hands pressed over her ears*). Oh, stuff! Cheer up! Please—be gay!

RANK. Yes, I'd just as soon laugh at it all. My poor, innocent spine, serving time for my father's gay army days.

NORA (*by the table, left*). He was so infatuated with asparagus tips and *pate de foie gras,* wasn't that it?

RANK. Yes—and with truffles.

NORA. Truffles, yes. And then with oysters, I suppose?

RANK. Yes, tons of oysters, naturally.

NORA. And then the port and champagne to go with it. It's so sad that all these delectable things have to strike at our bones.

RANK. Especially when they strike at the unhappy bones that never shared in the fun.

NORA. Ah, that's the saddest of all.

RANK (*looks searchingly at her*). Hm.

NORA (*after a moment*). Why did you smile?

RANK. No, it was you who laughed.

NORA. No, it was you who smiled, Dr. Rank!

RANK (*getting up*). You're even a bigger tease than I'd thought.

NORA. I'm full of wild ideas today.

RANK. That's obvious.

NORA (*putting both hands on his shoulders*). Dear, dear Dr. Rank, you'll never die for Torvald and me.

RANK. Oh, that loss you'll easily get over. Those who go away are soon forgotten.

NORA (*looks fearfully at him*). You believe that?

RANK. One makes new connections, and then—

NORA. Who makes new connections?

RANK. Both you and Torvald will when I'm gone. I'd say you're well under way already. What was that Mrs. Linde doing here last evening?

NORA. Oh, come—you can't be jealous of poor Kristine?

RANK. Oh yes, I am. She'll be my successor here in the house. When I'm down under, that woman will probably—

NORA. Shh! Not so loud. She's right in there.

RANK. Today as well. So you see.

NORA. Only to sew on my dress. Good gracious, how unreasonable you are. (*Sitting on the sofa.*) Be nice now, Dr. Rank. Tomorrow you'll see how beautifully I'll dance; and you can imagine then that I'm dancing only for you—yes, and of course for Torvald, too—that's understood. (*Takes various items out of the carton.*) Dr. Rank, sit over here and I'll show you something.

RANK (*sitting*). What's that?

NORA. Look here. Look.

RANK. Silk stockings.

NORA. Flesh-colored. Aren't they lovely? Now it's so dark here, but tomorrow— No, no, no, just look at the feet. Oh well, you might as well look at the rest.

RANK. Hm—

NORA. Why do you look so critical? Don't you believe they'll fit?

RANK. I've never had any chance to form an opinion on that.

NORA (*glancing at him a moment*). Shame on you. (*Hits him lightly on the ear with the stockings.*) That's for you. (*Puts them away again.*)

RANK. And what other splendors am I going to see now?

NORA. Not the least bit more, because you've been naughty. (*She hums a little and rummages among her things.*)

RANK (*after a short silence*). When I sit here together with you like this, completely easy and open, then I don't know— I simply can't imagine— whatever would have become of me if I'd never come into this house.

NORA (*smiling*). Yes, I really think you feel completely at ease with us.

RANK (*more quietly, staring straight ahead*). And then to have to go away from it all—

NORA. Nonsense, you're not going away.

RANK (*his voice unchanged*). —and not even be able to leave some poor show of gratitude behind, scarcely a fleeting regret—no more than a vacant place that anyone can fill.

NORA. And if I asked you now for—? No—

RANK. For what?

NORA. For a great proof of your friendship—

RANK. Yes, yes?

NORA. No, I mean—for an exceptionally big favor—

RANK. Would you really, for once, make me so happy?

NORA. Oh, you haven't the vaguest idea what it is.

RANK. All right, then tell me.

NORA. No, but I can't, Dr. Rank—it's all out of reason. It's advice and help, too—and a favor—

RANK. So much the better. I can't fathom what you're hinting at. Just speak out. Don't you trust me?

NORA. Of course. More than anyone else. You're my best and truest friend, I'm sure. That's why I want to talk to you. All right, then, Dr. Rank: there's something you can help me prevent. You know how deeply, how inexpressibly dearly Torvald loves me; he'd never hesitate a second to give up his life for me.

RANK (*leaning close to her*). Nora—do you think he's the only one—

NORA (*with a slight start*). Who—?

RANK. Who'd gladly give up his life for you.

NORA (*heavily*). I see.

RANK. I swore to myself you should know this before I'm gone. I'll never find a better chance. Yes, Nora, now you know. And also you know now that you can trust me beyond anyone else.

NORA (*rising, natural and calm*). Let me by.

RANK (*making room for her, but still sitting*). Nora—

NORA (*in the hall doorway*). Helene, bring the lamp in. (*Goes over to the stove.*) Ah, dear Dr. Rank, that was really mean of you.

RANK (*getting up*). That I've loved you just as deeply as somebody else? Was *that* mean?

NORA. No, but that you came out and told me. That was quite unnecessary—

RANK. What do you mean? Have you known—?

(*The* MAID *comes in with the lamp, sets it on the table, and goes out again.*)

RANK. Nora—Mrs. Helmer—I'm asking you: have you known about it?

NORA. Oh, how can I tell what I know or don't know? Really, I don't know what to say— Why did you have to be so clumsy, Dr. Rank! Everything was so good.

RANK. Well, in any case, you now have the knowledge that my body and soul are at your command. So won't you speak out?

NORA (*looking at him*). After that?

RANK. Please, just let me know what it is.

NORA. You can't know anything now.

RANK. I have to. You mustn't punish me like this. Give me the chance to do whatever is humanly possible for you.

NORA. Now there's nothing you can do for me. Besides, actually, I don't need any help. You'll see— it's only my fantasies. That's what it is. Of course! (*Sits in the rocker, looks at him, and smiles.*) What a nice one you are, Dr. Rank. Aren't you a little bit ashamed, now that the lamp is here?

RANK. No, not exactly. But perhaps I'd better go— for good?

NORA. No, you certainly can't do that. You must come here just as you always have. You know Torvald can't do without you.

RANK. Yes, but *you*?

NORA. You know how much I enjoy it when you're here.

RANK. That's precisely what threw me off. You're a mystery to me. So many times I've felt you'd almost rather be with me than with Helmer.

NORA. Yes—you see, there are some people that one loves most and other people that one would almost prefer being with.

RANK. Yes, there's something to that.

NORA. When I was back home, of course I loved Papa most. But I always thought it was so much fun when I could sneak down to the maid's quarters, because they never tried to improve me, and it was always so amusing, the way they talked to each other.

RANK. Aha, so it's *their* place that I've filled.

NORA (*jumping up and going to him*). Oh, dear, sweet Dr. Rank, that's not what I meant at all. But you can understand that with Torvald it's just the same as with Papa—

(*The* MAID *enters from the hall.*)

MAID. Ma'am—please! (*She whispers to* NORA *and hands her a calling card.*)

NORA (*glancing at the card*). Ah! (*Slips it into her pocket.*)

RANK. Anything wrong?

NORA. No, no, not at all. It's only some—it's my new dress—

RANK. Really? But—there's your dress.

NORA. Oh, that. But this is another one—I ordered it—Torvald mustn't know—

RANK. Ah, now we have the big secret.

NORA. That's right. Just go in with him—he's back in the inner study. Keep him there as long as—

RANK. Don't worry. He won't get away. (*Goes into the study.*)

NORA (*to the* MAID). And he's standing waiting in the kitchen?

MAID. Yes, he came up by the back stairs.

NORA. But didn't you tell him somebody was here?

MAID. Yes, but that didn't do any good.

NORA. He won't leave?

MAID. No, he won't go till he's talked with you, ma'am.

NORA. Let him come in, then—but quietly. Helene, don't breathe a word about this. It's a surprise for my husband.

MAID. Yes, yes, I understand— (*Goes out.*)

NORA. This horror—it's going to happen. No, no, no, it can't happen, it mustn't. (*She goes and bolts* HELMER's *door. The* MAID *opens the hall door for* KROGSTAD *and shuts it behind him. He is dressed for travel in a fur coat, boots, and a fur cap.*)

NORA (*going toward him*). Talk softly. My husband's home.

KROGSTAD. Well, good for him.

NORA. What do you want?

KROGSTAD. Some information.

NORA. Hurry up, then. What is it?

KROGSTAD. You know, of course, that I got my notice.

NORA. I couldn't prevent it, Mr. Krogstad. I fought for you to the bitter end, but nothing worked.

KROGSTAD. Does your husband's love for you run so thin? He knows everything I can expose you to, and all the same he dares to—

NORA. How can you imagine he knows anything about this?

KROGSTAD. Ah, no—I can't imagine it either, now. It's not at all like my fine Torvald Helmer to have so much guts—

NORA. Mr. Krogstad, I demand respect for my husband!

KROGSTAD. Why, of course—all due respect. But since the lady's keeping it so carefully hidden, may I presume to ask if you're also a bit better informed than yesterday about what you've actually done?

NORA. More than you ever could teach me.

KROGSTAD. Yes, I *am* such an awful lawyer.

NORA. What is it you want from me?

KROGSTAD. Just a glimpse of how you are, Mrs. Helmer. I've been thinking about you all day long. A cashier, a night-court scribbler, a—well, a type like me also has a little of what they call a heart, you know.

NORA. Then show it. Think of my children.

KROGSTAD. Did you or your husband ever think of mine? But never mind. I simply wanted to tell you that you don't need to take this thing too seriously. For the present, I'm not proceeding with any action.

NORA. Oh no, really! Well—I knew that.

KROGSTAD. Everything can be settled in a friendly spirit. It doesn't have to get around town at all; it can stay just among us three.

NORA. My husband must never know anything of this.

KROGSTAD. How can you manage that? Perhaps you can pay me the balance?

NORA. No, not right now.

KROGSTAD. Or you know some way of raising the money in a day or two?

NORA. No way that I'm willing to use.

KROGSTAD. Well, it wouldn't have done you any good, anyway. If you stood in front of me with a fistful of bills, you still couldn't buy your signature back.

NORA. Then tell me what you're going to do with it.

KROGSTAD. I'll just hold onto it—keep it on file. There's no outsider who'll even get wind of it. So if you've been thinking of taking some desperate step—

NORA. I have.

KROGSTAD. Been thinking of running away from home—

NORA. I have!

KROGSTAD. Or even of something worse—

NORA. How could you guess that?

KROGSTAD. You can drop those thoughts.

NORA. How could you guess I was thinking of *that*?

KROGSTAD. Most of us think about *that* at first. I thought about it too, but I discovered I hadn't the courage—

NORA (*lifelessly*). I don't either.

KROGSTAD (*relieved*). That's true, you haven't the courage? You too?

NORA. I don't have it—I don't have it.

KROGSTAD. It would be terribly stupid, anyway. After that first storm at home blows out, why, then— I have here in my pocket a letter for your husband—

NORA. Telling everything?

KROGSTAD. As charitably as possible.

NORA (*quickly*). He mustn't ever get that letter. Tear it up. I'll find some way to get money.

KROGSTAD. Beg pardon, Mrs. Helmer, but I think I just told you—

NORA. Oh, I don't mean the money I owe you. Let me know how much you want from my husband, and I'll manage it.

KROGSTAD. I don't want any money from your husband.

NORA. What do you want, then?

KROGSTAD. I'll tell you what. I want to recoup, Mrs. Helmer; I want to get on in the world—and there's where your husband can help me. For a year and a half I've kept myself clean of anything disreputable—all that time struggling with the worst conditions; but I was satisfied, working my way up step by step. Now I've been written right off, and I'm just not in the mood to come crawling back. I tell you, I want to move on. I want to get back in the bank—in a better position. Your husband can set up a job for me—

NORA. He'll never do that!

KROGSTAD. He'll do it. I know him. He won't dare breathe a word of protest. And once I'm in there together with him, you just wait and see! Inside of a year, I'll be the manager's right-hand man. It'll be Nils Krogstad, not Torvald Helmer, who runs the bank.

NORA. You'll never see the day!

KROGSTAD. Maybe you think you can—

NORA. I have the courage now—for *that*.

KROGSTAD. Oh, you don't scare me. A smart, spoiled lady like you—

NORA. You'll see; you'll see!

KROGSTAD. Under the ice, maybe? Down in the freezing, coal-black water? There, till you float up in the spring, ugly, unrecognizable, with your hair falling out—

NORA. You don't frighten me.

KROGSTAD. Nor do you frighten me. One doesn't do these things, Mrs. Helmer. Besides, what good would it be? I'd still have him safe in my pocket.

NORA. Afterwards? When I'm no longer—?

KROGSTAD. Are you forgetting that *I'll* be in control then over your final reputation? (NORA *stands speechless, staring at him.*) Good; now I've warned you. Don't do anything stupid. When Helmer's read my letter, I'll be waiting for his reply. And bear in mind that it's your husband himself who's forced me back to my old ways. I'll never forgive him for that. Good-bye, Mrs. Helmer. (*He goes out through the hall.*)

NORA (*goes to the hall door, opens it a crack, and listens*). He's gone. Didn't leave the letter. Oh no, no, that's impossible too! (*Opening the door more and more.*) What's that? He's standing outside— not going downstairs. He's thinking it over? Maybe he'll—? (*A letter falls in the mailbox; then* KROGSTAD'S *footsteps are heard, dying away down a flight of stairs.* NORA *gives a muffled cry and runs over toward the sofa table. A short pause.*) In the mailbox. (*Slips warily over to the hall door.*) It's lying there. Torvald, Torvald—now we're lost!

MRS. LINDE (*entering with the costume from the room, left*). There now, I can't see anything else to mend. Perhaps you'd like to try—

NORA (*in a hoarse whisper*). Kristine, come here.

MRS. LINDE (*tossing the dress on the sofa*). What's wrong? You look upset.

NORA. Come here. See that letter? *There!* Look— through the glass in the mailbox.

MRS. LINDE. Yes, yes, I see it.

NORA. That letter's from Krogstad—

MRS. LINDE. Nora—it's Krogstad who loaned you the money!

NORA. Yes, and now Torvald will find out every-thing.

MRS. LINDE. Believe me, Nora, it's best for both of you.

NORA. There's more you don't know. I forged a name.

MRS. LINDE. But for heaven's sake—?

NORA. I only want to tell you that, Kristine, so that you can be my witness.

MRS. LINDE. Witness? Why should I—?

NORA. If I should go out of my mind—it could easily happen—

MRS. LINDE. Nora!

NORA. Or anything else occurred—so I couldn't be present here—

MRS. LINDE. Nora, Nora, you aren't yourself at all!

NORA. And someone should try to take on the whole weight, all of the guilt, you follow me—

MRS. LINDE. Yes, of course, but why do you think—?

NORA. Then you're the witness that it isn't true, Kristine. I'm very much myself; my mind right now is perfectly clear; and I'm telling you: nobody else has known about this; I alone did everything. Remember that.

MRS. LINDE. I will. But I don't understand all this.

NORA. Oh, how could you ever understand it? It's the miracle now that's going to take place.

MRS. LINDE. The miracle?

NORA. Yes, the miracle. But it's so awful, Kristine. It mustn't take place, not for anything in the world.

MRS. LINDE. I'm going right over and talk with Krogstad.

NORA. Don't go near him; he'll do you some terrible harm!

MRS. LINDE. There was a time once when he'd gladly have done anything for me.

NORA. He?

MRS. LINDE. Where does he live?

NORA. Oh, how do I know? Yes. (*Searches in her pocket.*) Here's his card. But the letter, the letter—!

HELMER (*from the study, knocking on the door*). Nora!

NORA (*with a cry of fear*). Oh! What is it? What do you want?

HELMER. Now, now, don't be so frightened. We're not coming in. You locked the door—are you trying on the dress?

NORA. Yes, I'm trying it. I'll look just beautiful, Torvald.

MRS. LINDE (*who has read the card*). He's living right around the corner.

NORA. Yes, but what's the use? We're lost. The letter's in the box.

MRS. LINDE. And your husband has the key?

NORA. Yes, always.

MRS. LINDE. Krogstad can ask for his letter back unread; he can find some excuse—

NORA. But it's just this time that Torvald usually—

MRS. LINDE. Stall him. Keep him in there. I'll be back as quick as I can. (*She hurries out through the hall entrance.*)

NORA (*goes to* HELMER's *door, opens it, and peers in*). Torvald!

HELMER (*from the inner study*). Well—does one dare set foot in one's own living room at last? Come on, Rank, now we'll get a look— (*In the doorway.*) But what's this?

NORA. What, Torvald dear?

HELMER. Rank had me expecting some grand masquerade.

RANK (*in the doorway*). That was my impression, but I must have been wrong.

NORA. No one can admire me in my splendor—not till tomorrow.

HELMER. But Nora dear, you look so exhausted. Have you practiced too hard?

NORA. No, I haven't practiced at all yet.

HELMER. You know, it's necessary—

NORA. Oh, it's absolutely necessary, Torvald. But I can't get anywhere without your help. I've forgotten the whole thing completely.

HELMER. Ah, we'll soon take care of that.

NORA. Yes, take care of me, Torvald, please! Promise me that? Oh, I'm so nervous. That big party— You must give up everything this evening for me. No business—don't even touch your pen. Yes? Dear Torvald, promise?

HELMER. It's a promise. Tonight I'm totally at your service—you little helpless thing. Hm—but first there's one thing I want to— (*Goes toward the hall door.*)

NORA. What are you looking for?

HELMER. Just to see if there's any mail.

NORA. No, no, don't do that, Torvald!

HELMER. Now what?

NORA. Torvald, please. There isn't any.

HELMER. Let me look, though. (*Starts out.* NORA, *at the piano, strikes the first notes of the tarantella.* HELMER, *at the door, stops.*) Aha!

NORA. I can't dance tomorrow if I don't practice with you.

HELMER (*going over to her*). Nora dear, are you really so frightened?

NORA. Yes, so terribly frightened. Let me practice right now; there's still time before dinner. Oh, sit down and play for me, Torvald. Direct me. Teach me, the way you always have.

HELMER. Gladly, if it's what you want. (*Sits at the piano.*)

NORA (*snatches the tambourine up from the box, then a long, varicolored shawl, which she throws around herself, whereupon she springs forward and cries out:*) Play for me now! Now I'll dance!

(HELMER *plays and* NORA *dances.* RANK *stands behind* HELMER *at the piano and looks on.*)

HELMER (*as he plays*). Slower. Slow down.

NORA. Can't change it.

HELMER. Not so violent, Nora!

NORA. Has to be just like this.

HELMER (*stopping*). No, no, that won't do at all.

NORA (*laughing and swinging her tambourine*). Isn't that what I told you?

RANK. Let me play for her.

HELMER (*getting up*). Yes, go on. I can teach her more easily then.

(RANK *sits at the piano and plays;* NORA *dances more and more wildly.* HELMER *has stationed himself by the stove and repeatedly gives her directions; she seems not to hear them; her hair loosens and falls over her shoulders; she does not notice, but goes on dancing.* MRS. LINDE *enters.*)

MRS. LINDE (*standing dumbfounded at the door*). Ah—!

NORA. (*still dancing*). See what fun, Kristine!

HELMER. But Nora darling, you dance as if your life were at stake.

NORA. And it is.

HELMER. Rank, stop! This is pure madness. Stop it, I say!

(RANK *breaks off playing, and* NORA *halts abruptly*).

HELMER (*going over to her*). I never would have believed it. You've forgotten everything I taught you.

NORA (*throwing away the tambourine*). You see for yourself.

HELMER. Well, there's certainly room for instruction here.

NORA. Yes, you see how important it is. You've got to teach me to the very last minute. Promise me that, Torvald?

HELMER. You can bet on it.

NORA. You mustn't, either today or tomorrow, think about anything else but me; you mustn't open any letters—or the mailbox—

HELMER. Ah, it's still the fear of that man—

NORA. Oh yes, yes, that too.

HELMER. Nora, it's written all over you—there's already a letter from him out there.

NORA. I don't know. I guess so. But you mustn't read such things now; there mustn't be anything ugly between us before it's all over.

RANK (*quietly to* HELMER). You shouldn't deny her.

HELMER (*putting his arm around her*). The child can have her way. But tomorrow night, after you've danced—

NORA. Then you'll be free.

MAID (*in the doorway, right*). Ma'am, dinner is served.

NORA. We'll be wanting champagne, Helene.

MAID. Very good, ma'am. (*Goes out.*)

HELMER. So—a regular banquet, hm?

NORA. Yes, a banquet—champagne till daybreak! (*Calling out.*) And some macaroons, Helene. Heaps of them—just this once.

HELMER (*taking her hands*). Now, now, now—no hysterics. Be my own little lark again.

NORA. Oh, I will soon enough. But go on in—and you, Dr. Rank. Kristine, help me put up my hair.

RANK (*whispering as they go*). There's nothing wrong—really wrong, is there?

HELMER. Oh, of course not. It's nothing more than this childish anxiety I was telling you about. (*They go out, right.*)

NORA. Well?

MRS. LINDE. Left town.

NORA. I could see by your face.

MRS. LINDE. He'll be home tomorrow evening. I wrote him a note.

NORA. You shouldn't have. Don't try to stop anything now. After all, it's a wonderful joy, this waiting here for the miracle.

MRS. LINDE. What is it you're waiting for?

NORA. Oh, you can't understand that. Go in to them; I'll be along in a moment.

(MRS. LINDE *goes into the dining room.* NORA *stands a short while as if composing herself; then she looks at her watch.*)

NORA. Five. Seven hours to midnight. Twenty-four hours to the midnight after, and then the tarantella's done. Seven and twenty-four? Thirty-one hours to live.

HELMER (*in the doorway, right*). What's become of the little lark?

NORA (*going toward him with open arms*). Here's your lark!

ACT THREE

Same scene. The table, with chairs around it, has been moved to the center of the room. A lamp on the table is lit. The hall door stands open. Dance music drifts down from the floor above. MRS. LINDE *sits at the table, absently paging through a book, trying to read, but apparently unable to focus her thoughts. Once or twice she pauses, tensely listening for a sound at the outer entrance.*

MRS. LINDE (*glancing at her watch*). Not yet—and there's hardly any time left. If only he's not— (*Listening again.*) Ah, there he is. (*She goes out in the hall and cautiously opens the outer door. Quiet footsteps are heard on the stairs. She whispers:*) Come in. Nobody's here.

KROGSTAD (*in the doorway*). I found a note from you at home. What's back of all this?

MRS. LINDE. I just *had* to talk to you.

KROGSTAD. Oh? And it just *had* to be here in this house?

MRS. LINDE. At my place it was impossible; my room hasn't a private entrance. Come in; we're all alone. The maid's asleep, and the Helmers are at the dance upstairs.

KROGSTAD (*entering the room*). Well, well, the Helmers are dancing tonight? Really?

MRS. LINDE. Yes, why not?

KROGSTAD. How true—why not?

MRS. LINDE. All right, Krogstad, let's talk.

KROGSTAD. Do we two have anything more to talk about?

MRS. LINDE. We have a great deal to talk about.

KROGSTAD. I wouldn't have thought so.

MRS. LINDE. No, because you've never understood me, really.

KROGSTAD. Was there anything more to understand—except what's all too common in life? A calculating woman throws over a man the moment a better catch comes by.

MRS. LINDE. You think I'm so thoroughly calculating? You think I broke it off lightly?

KROGSTAD. Didn't you?

MRS. LINDE. Nils—is that what you really thought?

KROGSTAD. If you cared, then why did you write me the way you did?

MRS. LINDE. What else could I do? If I had to break off with you, then it was my job as well to root out everything you felt for me.

KROGSTAD (*wringing his hands*). So that was it. And this—all this, simply for money!

MRS. LINDE. Don't forget I had a helpless mother and two small brothers. We couldn't wait for you, Nils; you had such a long road ahead of you then.

KROGSTAD. That may be; but you still hadn't the right to abandon me for somebody else's sake.

MRS. LINDE. Yes—I don't know. So many, many times I've asked myself if I did have that right.

KROGSTAD (*more softly*). When I lost you, it was as if all the solid ground dissolved from under my feet. Look at me; I'm a half-drowned man, now, hanging onto a wreck.

MRS. LINDE. Help may be near.

KROGSTAD. It was near—but then you came and blocked it off.

MRS. LINDE. Without my knowing it, Nils. Today for the first time I learned that it's you I'm replacing at the bank.

KROGSTAD. All right—I believe you. But now that you know, will you step aside?

MRS. LINDE. No, because that wouldn't benefit you in the slightest.

KROGSTAD. Not "benefit" me, hm! I'd step aside anyway.

MRS. LINDE. I've learned to be realistic. Life and hard, bitter necessity have taught me that.

KROGSTAD. And life's taught me never to trust fine phrases.

MRS. LINDE. Then life's taught you a very sound thing. But you do have to trust in actions, don't you?

KROGSTAD. What does that mean?

MRS. LINDE. You said you were hanging on like a half-drowned man to a wreck.

KROGSTAD. I've good reason to say that.

MRS. LINDE. I'm also like a half-drowned woman on a wreck. No one to suffer with; no one to care for.

KROGSTAD. You made your choice.

MRS. LINDE. There wasn't any choice then.

KROGSTAD. So—what of it?

MRS. LINDE. Nils, if only we two shipwrecked people could reach across to each other.

KROGSTAD. What are you saying?

MRS. LINDE. Two on one wreck are at least better off than each on his own.

KROGSTAD. Kristine!

MRS. LINDE. Why do you think I came into town?

KROGSTAD. Did you really have some thought of me?

MRS. LINDE. I have to work to go on living. All my born days, as long as I can remember, I've worked, and it's been my best and my only joy. But now I'm completely alone in the world; it frightens me to be so empty and lost. To work for yourself—there's no joy in that. Nils, give me something—someone to work for.

KROGSTAD. I don't believe all this. It's just some hysterical feminine urge to go out and make a noble sacrifice.

MRS. LINDE. Have you ever found me to be hysterical?

KROGSTAD. Can you honestly mean this? Tell me—do you know everything about my past?

MRS. LINDE. Yes.

KROGSTAD. And you know what they think I'm worth around here.

MRS. LINDE. From what you were saying before, it would seem that with me you could have been another person.

KROGSTAD. I'm positive of that.

MRS. LINDE. Couldn't it happen still?

KROGSTAD. Kristine—you're saying this in all seriousness? Yes, you are! I can see it in you. And do you really have the courage, then—?

MRS. LINDE. I need to have someone to care for; and your children need a mother. We both need each other. Nils, I have faith that you're good at heart—I'll risk everything together with you.

KROGSTAD (gripping her hands). Kristine, thank you, thank you— Now I know I can win back a place in their eyes. Yes—but I forgot—

MRS. LINDE (listening). Shh! The tarantella. Go now! Go on!

KROGSTAD. Why? What is it?

MRS. LINDE. Hear the dance up there? When that's over, they'll be coming down.

KROGSTAD. Oh, then I'll go. But—it's all pointless. Of course, you don't know the move I made against the Helmers.

MRS. LINDE. Yes, Nils, I know.

KROGSTAD. And all the same, you have the courage to—?

MRS. LINDE. I know how far despair can drive a man like you.

KROGSTAD. Oh, if I only could take it all back.

MRS. LINDE. You easily could—your letter's still lying in the mailbox.

KROGSTAD. Are you sure of that?

MRS. LINDE. Positive. But—

KROGSTAD (looks at her searchingly). Is that the meaning of it, then? You'll save your friend at any price. Tell me straight out. Is that it?

MRS. LINDE. Nils—anyone who's sold herself for somebody else once isn't going to do it again.

KROGSTAD. I'll demand my letter back.

MRS. LINDE. No, no.

KROGSTAD. Yes, of course. I'll stay here till Helmer comes down; I'll tell him to give me my letter again—that it only involves my dismissal—that he shouldn't read it—

MRS. LINDE. No, Nils, don't call the letter back.

KROGSTAD. But wasn't that exactly why you wrote me to come here?

MRS. LINDE. Yes, in that first panic. But it's been a whole day and night since then, and in that time I've seen such incredible things in this house. Helmer's got to learn everything; this dreadful secret has to be aired; those two have to come to a full understanding; all these lies and evasions can't go on.

KROGSTAD. Well, then, if you want to chance it. But at least there's one thing I can do, and do right away—

MRS. LINDE (*listening*). Go now, go, quick! The dance is over. We're not safe another second.

KROGSTAD. I'll wait for you downstairs.

MRS. LINDE. Yes, please do; take me home.

KROGSTAD. I can't believe it; I've never been so happy. (*He leaves by way of the outer door; the door between the room and the hall stays open.*)

MRS. LINDE (*straightening up a bit and getting together her street clothes*). How different now! How different! Someone to work for, to live for—a home to build. Well, it is worth the try! Oh, if they'd only come! (*Listening.*) Ah, there they are. Bundle up. (*She picks up her hat and coat.* NORA's *and* HELMER's *voices can be heard outside; a key turns in the lock, and* HELMER *brings* NORA *into the hall almost by force. She is wearing the Italian costume with a large black shawl about her; he has on evening dress, with a black domino open over it.*)

NORA (*struggling in the doorway*). No, no, no, not inside! I'm going up again. I don't want to leave so soon.

HELMER. But Nora dear—

NORA. Oh, I beg you, please, Torvald. From the bottom of my heart, *please*—only an hour more!

HELMER. Not a single minute, Nora darling. You know our agreement. Come on, in we go; you'll catch cold out here. (*In spite of her resistance, he gently draws her into the room.*)

MRS. LINDE. Good evening.

NORA. Kristine!

HELMER. Why, Mrs. Linde—are you here so late?

MRS. LINDE. Yes, I'm sorry, but I did want to see Nora in costume.

NORA. Have you been sitting here, waiting for me?

MRS. LINDE. Yes. I didn't come early enough; you were all upstairs; and then I thought I really couldn't leave without seeing you.

HELMER (*removing* NORA's *shawl*). Yes, take a good look. She's worth looking at, I can tell you that, Mrs. Linde. Isn't she lovely?

MRS. LINDE. Yes, I should say—

HELMER. A dream of loveliness, isn't she? That's what everyone thought at the party, too. But she's horribly stubborn—this sweet little thing. What's to be done with her? Can you imagine, I almost had to use force to pry her away.

NORA. Oh, Torvald, you're going to regret you didn't indulge me, even for just a half hour more.

HELMER. There, you see. She danced her tarantella and got a tumultuous hand—which was well earned, although the performance may have been a bit too naturalistic—I mean it rather overstepped the proprieties of art. But never mind—what's important is, she made a success, an overwhelming success. You think I could let her stay on after that and spoil the effect? Oh no; I took my lovely little Capri girl—my capricious little Capri girl, I should say—took her under my arm; one quick tour of the ballroom, a curtsy to every side, and then—as they say in novels—the beautiful vision disappeared. An exit should always be effective, Mrs. Linde, but that's what I can't get Nora to grasp. Phew, it's hot in here. (*Flings the domino on a chair and opens the door to his room.*) Why's it dark in here? Oh yes, of course. Excuse me. (*He goes in and lights a couple of candles.*)

NORA (*in a sharp, breathless whisper*). So?

MRS. LINDE (*quietly*). I talked with him.

NORA. And—?

MRS. LINDE. Nora—you must tell your husband everything.

NORA (*dully*). I knew it.

MRS. LINDE. You've got nothing to fear from Krogstad, but you have to speak out.

NORA. I won't tell.

MRS. LINDE. Then the letter will.

NORA. Thanks, Kristine. I know now what's to be done. Shh!

HELMER (*reentering*). Well, then, Mrs. Linde—have you admired her?

MRS. LINDE. Yes, and now I'll say good night.

HELMER. Oh, come, so soon? Is this yours, this knitting?

MRS. LINDE. Yes, thanks. I nearly forgot it.

HELMER. Do you knit, then?

MRS. LINDE. Oh yes.

HELMER. You know what? You should embroider instead.

MRS. LINDE. Really? Why?

HELMER. Yes, because it's a lot prettier. See here, one holds the embroidery so, in the left hand, and then one guides the needle with the right—so—in an easy, sweeping curve—right?

MRS. LINDE. Yes, I guess that's—

HELMER. But, on the other hand, knitting—it can never be anything but ugly. Look, see here, the arms tucked in, the knitting needles going up and down—there's something Chinese about it. Ah, that was really a glorious champagne they served.

MRS. LINDE. Yes, good night, Nora, and don't be stubborn anymore.

HELMER. Well put, Mrs. Linde!

MRS. LINDE. Good night, Mr. Helmer.

HELMER (*accompanying her to the door*). Good night, good night. I hope you get home all right. I'd be very happy to—but you don't have far to go. Good night, good night. (*She leaves. He shuts the door after her and returns.*) There, now, at last we got her out the door. She's a deadly bore, that creature.

NORA. Aren't you pretty tired, Torvald?

HELMER. No, not a bit.

NORA. You're not sleepy?

HELMER. Not at all. On the contrary. I'm feeling quite exhilarated. But you? Yes, you really look tired and sleepy.

NORA. Yes, I'm very tired. Soon now I'll sleep.

HELMER. See! You see! I was right all along that we shouldn't stay longer.

NORA. Whatever you do is always right.

HELMER (*kissing her brow*). Now my little lark talks sense. Say, did you notice what a time Rank was having tonight?

NORA. Oh, was he? I didn't get to speak with him.

HELMER. I scarcely did either, but it's a long time since I've seen him in such high spirits. (*Gazes at her a moment, then comes nearer her.*) Hm—it's marvelous, though, to be back home again—to be completely alone with you. Oh, you bewitchingly lovely young woman!

NORA. Torvald, don't look at me like that!

HELMER. Can't I look at my richest treasure? At all that beauty that's mine, mine alone—completely and utterly.

NORA (*moving around to the other side of the table*). You mustn't talk to me that way tonight.

HELMER (*following her*). The tarantella is still in your blood, I can see—and it makes you even more enticing. Listen. The guests are beginning to go. (*Dropping his voice.*) Nora—it'll soon be quiet through this whole house.

NORA. Yes, I hope so.

HELMER. You do, don't you, my love? Do you realize—when I'm out at a party like this with you—do you know why I talk to you so little, and keep such a distance away; just send you a stolen look now and then—you know why I do it? It's because I'm imagining then that you're my secret darling, my secret young bride-to-be, and that no one suspects there's anything between us.

NORA. Yes, yes; oh, yes, I know you're always thinking of me.

HELMER. And then when we leave and I place the shawl over those fine young rounded shoulders—over that wonderful curving neck—then I pretend that you're my young bride, that we're just coming from the wedding, that for the first time I'm bringing you into my house—that for the first time I'm alone with you—completely alone with you, your trembling young beauty! All this evening I've longed for nothing but you. When I saw you turn and sway in the tarantella—my blood was pounding till I couldn't stand it—that's why I brought you down here so early—

NORA. Go away, Torvald! Leave me alone. I don't want all this.

HELMER. What do you mean? Nora, you're teasing me. You will, won't you? Aren't I your husband—?

(*A knock at the outside door.*)

NORA (*startled*). What's that?

HELMER (*going toward the hall*). Who is it?

RANK (*outside*). It's me. May I come in a moment?

HELMER (*with quiet irritation*). Oh, what does he want now? (*Aloud.*) Hold on. (*Goes and opens the door.*) Oh, how nice that you didn't just pass us by!

RANK. I thought I heard your voice, and then I wanted so badly to have a look in. (*Lightly glancing about.*) Ah, me, these old familiar haunts. You have it snug and cozy in here, you two.

HELMER. You seemed to be having it pretty cozy upstairs, too.

RANK. Absolutely. Why shouldn't I? Why not take in everything in life? As much as you can, anyway, and as long as you can. The wine was superb—

HELMER. The champagne especially.

RANK. You noticed that too? It's amazing how much I could guzzle down.

NORA. Torvald also drank a lot of champagne this evening.

RANK. Oh?

NORA. Yes, and that always makes him so entertaining.

RANK. Well, why shouldn't one have a pleasant evening after a well-spent day?

HELMER. Well spent? I'm afraid I can't claim that.

RANK (slapping him on the back). But I can, you see!

NORA. Dr. Rank, you must have done some scientific research today.

RANK. Quite so.

HELMER. Come now—little Nora talking about scientific research!

NORA. And can I congratulate you on the results?

RANK. Indeed you may.

NORA. Then they were good?

RANK. The best possible for both doctor and patient—certainty.

NORA (quickly and searchingly). Certainty?

RANK. Complete certainty. So don't I owe myself a gay evening afterwards?

NORA. Yes, you're right, Dr. Rank.

HELMER. I'm with you—just so long as you don't have to suffer for it in the morning.

RANK. Well, one never gets something for nothing in life.

NORA. Dr. Rank—are you very fond of masquerade parties?

RANK. Yes, if there's a good array of odd disguises—

NORA. Tell me, what should we two go as at the next masquerade?

HELMER. You little featherhead—already thinking of the next!

RANK. We two? I'll tell you what: you must go as Charmed Life—

HELMER. Yes, but find a costume for *that*!

RANK. Your wife can appear just as she looks every day.

HELMER. That was nicely put. But don't you know what you're going to be?

RANK. Yes, Helmer, I've made up my mind.

HELMER. Well?

RANK. At the next masquerade I'm going to be invisible.

HELMER. That's a funny idea.

RANK. They say there's a hat—black, huge—have you never heard of the hat that makes you invisible? You put it on, and then no one on earth can see you.

HELMER (suppressing a smile). Ah, of course.

RANK. But I'm quite forgetting what I came for. Helmer, give me a cigar, one of the dark Havanas.

HELMER. With the greatest pleasure. (Holds out his case.)

RANK. Thanks. (Takes one and cuts off the tip.)

NORA (striking a match). Let me give you a light.

RANK. Thank you. (She holds the match for him; he lights the cigar.) And now good-bye.

HELMER. Good-bye, good-bye, old friend.

NORA. Sleep well, Doctor.

RANK. Thanks for that wish.

NORA. Wish me the same.

RANK. You? All right, if you like—Sleep well. And thanks for the light. (He nods to them both and leaves.)

HELMER (his voice subdued). He's been drinking heavily.

NORA (absently). Could be. (HELMER takes his keys from his pocket and goes out in the hall.) Torvald—what are you after?

HELMER. Got to empty the mailbox; it's nearly full. There won't be room for the morning papers.

NORA. Are you working tonight?

HELMER. You know I'm not. Why—what's this? Someone's been at the lock.

NORA. At the lock—?

HELMER. Yes, I'm positive. What do you suppose—? I can't imagine one of the maids—? Here's a broken hairpin. Nora, it's yours—

NORA (*quickly*). Then it must be the children—

HELMER. You'd better break them of that. Hm, hm—well, opened it after all. (*Takes the contents out and calls into the kitchen.*) Helene! Helene, would you put out the lamp in the hall. (*He returns to the room, shutting the hall door, then displays the handful of mail.*) Look how it's piled up. (*Sorting through them.*) Now what's this?

NORA (*at the window*). The letter! Oh, Torvald, no!

HELMER. Two calling cards—from Rank.

NORA. From Dr. Rank?

HELMER (*examining them*). "Dr. Rank, Consulting Physician." They were on top. He must have dropped them in as he left.

NORA. Is there anything on them?

HELMER. There's a black cross over the name. See? That's a gruesome notion. He could almost be announcing his own death.

NORA. That's just what he's doing.

HELMER. What! You've heard something? Something he's told you?

NORA. Yes. That when those cards came, he'd be taking his leave of us. He'll shut himself in now and die.

HELMER. Ah, my poor friend! Of course I knew he wouldn't be here much longer. But so soon— And then to hide himself away like a wounded animal.

NORA. If it has to happen, then it's best it happens in silence—don't you think so, Torvald?

HELMER (*pacing up and down*). He'd grown right into our lives. I simply can't imagine him gone. He with his suffering and loneliness—like a dark cloud setting off our sunlit happiness. Well, maybe it's best this way. For him, at least. (*Standing still.*) And maybe for us too, Nora. Now we're thrown back on each other, completely. (*Embracing her.*) Oh you, my darling wife, how can I hold you close enough? You know what, Nora—time and again I've wished you were in some terrible danger, just so I could stake my life and soul and everything, for your sake.

NORA (*tearing herself away, her voice firm and decisive*). Now you must read your mail, Torvald.

HELMER. No, no, not tonight. I want to stay with you, dearest.

NORA. With a dying friend on your mind?

HELMER. You're right. We've both had a shock. There's ugliness between us—these thoughts of death and corruption. We'll have to get free of them first. Until then—we'll stay apart.

NORA (*clinging about his neck*). Torvald—good night! Good night!

HELMER (*kissing her on the cheek*). Good night, little songbird. Sleep well, Nora. I'll be reading my mail now. (*He takes the letters into his room and shuts the door after him.*)

NORA (*with bewildered glances, groping about, seizing* HELMER'*s domino, throwing it around her, and speaking in short, hoarse, broken whispers*). Never see him again. Never, never. (*Putting her shawl over her head.*) Never see the children either—them, too. Never, never. Oh, the freezing black water! The depths—down— Oh, I wish it were over— He has it now; he's reading it—now. Oh no, no, not yet. Torvald, good-bye, you and the children— (*She starts for the hall; as she does,* HELMER *throws open his door and stands with an open letter in his hand.*)

HELMER. Nora!

NORA (*screams*). Oh—!

HELMER. What is this? You know what's in this letter?

NORA. Yes, I know. Let me go! Let me out!

HELMER (*holding her back*). Where are you going?

NORA (*struggling to break loose*). You can't save me, Torvald!

HELMER (*slumping back*). True! Then it's true what he writes? How horrible! No, no, it's impossible—it can't be true.

NORA. It *is* true. I've loved you more than all this world.

HELMER. Ah, none of your slippery tricks.

NORA (*taking one step toward him*). Torvald—!

HELMER. What *is* this you've blundered into!

NORA. Just let me loose. You're not going to suffer for my sake. You're not going to take on my guilt.

HELMER. No more playacting. (*Locks the hall door.*) You stay right here and give me a reckoning. You understand what you've done? Answer! You understand?

NORA (*looking squarely at him, her face hardening*). Yes. I'm beginning to understand everything now.

HELMER (*striding about*). Oh, what an awful awakening! In all these eight years—she who was my pride and joy—a hypocrite, a liar—worse, worse—a criminal! How infinitely disgusting it all is! The shame! (NORA *says nothing and goes on looking straight at him. He stops in front of her.*) I should have suspected something of the kind. I should have known. All your father's flimsy values— Be still! All your father's flimsy values have come out in you. No religion, no morals, no sense of duty— Oh, how I'm punished for letting him off! I did it for your sake, and you repay me like this.

NORA. Yes, like this.

HELMER. Now you've wrecked all my happiness—ruined my whole future. Oh, it's awful to think of. I'm in a cheap little grafter's hands; he can do anything he wants with me, ask for anything, play with me like a puppet—and I can't breathe a word. I'll be swept down miserably into the depths on account of a featherbrained woman.

NORA. When I'm gone from this world, you'll be free.

HELMER. Oh, quit posing. Your father had a mess of those speeches too. What good would that ever do me if you were gone from this world, as you say? Not the slightest. He can still make the whole thing known; and if he does, I could be falsely suspected as your accomplice. They might even think that I was behind it—that I put you up to it. And all that I can thank you for—you that I've coddled the whole of our marriage. Can you see now what you've done to me?

NORA (*icily calm*). Yes.

HELMER. It's so incredible, I just can't grasp it. But we'll have to patch up whatever we can. Take off the shawl. I said, take it off! I've got to appease him somehow or other. The thing has to be hushed up at any cost. And as for you and me, it's got to seem like everything between us is just as it was—to the outside world, that is. You'll go right on living in this house, of course. But you can't be allowed to bring up the children; I don't dare trust you with them— Oh, to have to say this to someone I've loved so much! Well, that's done with. From now on happiness doesn't matter; all that matters is saving the bits and pieces, the appearance—(*The doorbell rings.* HELMER *starts.*) What's that? And so late. Maybe the worst—? You think he'd—? Hide, Nora! Say you're sick. (NORA *remains standing motionless.* HELMER *goes and opens the door.*)

MAID (*half dressed, in the hall*). A letter for Mrs. Helmer.

HELMER. I'll take it. (*Snatches the letter and shuts the door.*) Yes, it's from him. You don't get it; I'm reading it myself.

NORA. Then read it.

HELMER (*by the lamp*). I hardly dare. We may be ruined, you and I. But—I've got to know. (*Rips open the letter, skims through a few lines, glances at an enclosure, then cries out joyfully.*) Nora! (NORA *looks inquiringly at him.*) Nora! Wait—better check it again—Yes, yes, it's true. I'm saved. Nora, I'm saved!

NORA. And I?

HELMER. You too, of course. We're both saved, both of us. Look. He's sent back your note. He says he's sorry and ashamed—that a happy development in his life—oh, who cares what he says! Nora, we're saved! No one can hurt you. Oh, Nora, Nora—but first, this ugliness all has to go. Let me see—(*Takes a look at the note*). No, I don't want to see it; I want the whole thing to fade like a dream. (*Tears the note and both letters to pieces, throws them into the stove and watches them burn.*) There—now there's nothing left—He wrote that since Christmas Eve you—Oh, they must have been three terrible days for you Nora.

NORA. I fought a hard fight.

HELMER. And suffered pain and saw no escape but— No, we're not going to dwell on anything unpleasant. We'll just be grateful and keep on repeating: it's over now, it's over! You hear me, Nora? You don't seem to realize—it's over. What's it mean—that frozen look? Oh, poor little Nora, I understand. You can't believe I've forgiven you. But I have, Nora; I swear I have. I know that what you did, you did out of love for me.

NORA. That's true.

HELMER. You loved me the way a wife ought to love her husband. It's simply the means that you couldn't judge. But you think I love you any the less for not knowing how to handle your affairs?

No, no—just lean on me; I'll guide you and teach you. I wouldn't be a man if this feminine helplessness didn't make you twice as attractive to me. You mustn't mind those sharp words I said—that was all in the first confusion of thinking my world had collapsed. I've forgiven you, Nora; I swear I've forgiven you.

NORA. My thanks for your forgiveness. (*She goes out through the door, right.*)

HELMER. No, wait— (*Peers in.*) What are you doing in there?

NORA (*inside*). Getting out of my costume.

HELMER (*by the open door*). Yes, do that. Try to calm yourself and collect your thoughts again, my frightened little songbird. You can rest easy now; I've got wide wings to shelter you with. (*Walking about close by the door.*) How snug and nice our home is, Nora. You're safe here; I'll keep you like a hunted dove I've rescued out of a hawk's claws. I'll bring peace to your poor, shuddering heart. Gradually it'll happen, Nora; you'll see. Tomorrow all this will look different to you; then everything will be as it was. I won't have to go on repeating I forgive you; you'll feel it for yourself. How can you imagine I'd ever conceivably want to disown you—or even blame you in any way? Ah, you don't know a man's heart, Nora. For a man there's something indescribably sweet and satisfying in knowing he's forgiven his wife—and forgiven her out of a full and open heart. It's as if she belongs to him in two ways now: in a sense he's given her fresh into the world again, and she's becoming his wife and his child as well. From now on that's what you'll be to me—you little, bewildered, helpless thing. Don't be afraid of anything, Nora; just open your heart to me, and I'll be conscience and will to you both—(NORA *enters in her regular clothes.*) What's this? Not in bed? You've changed your dress?

NORA. Yes, Torvald, I've changed my dress.

HELMER. But why now, so late?

NORA. Tonight I'm not sleeping.

HELMER. But Nora dear—

NORA (*looking at her watch*). It's still not so very late. Sit down, Torvald; we have a lot to talk over. (*She sits at one side of the table.*)

HELMER. Nora—what is this? That hard expression—

NORA. Sit down. This'll take some time. I have a lot to say.

HELMER (*sitting at the table directly opposite her*). You worry me, Nora. And I don't understand you.

NORA. No, that's exactly it. You don't understand me. And I've never understood you either—until tonight. No, don't interrupt. You can just listen to what I say. We're closing our accounts, Torvald.

HELMER. How do you mean that?

NORA (*after a short pause*). Doesn't anything strike you about our sitting here like this?

HELMER. What's that?

NORA. We've been married now eight years. Doesn't it occur to you that this is the first time we two, you and I, man and wife, have ever talked seriously together?

HELMER. What do you mean—seriously?

NORA. In eight whole years—longer even—right from our first acquaintance, we've never exchanged a serious word on any serious thing.

HELMER. You mean I should constantly go and involve you in problems you couldn't possibly help me with?

NORA. I'm not talking of problems. I'm saying that we've never sat down seriously together and tried to get to the bottom of anything.

HELMER. But dearest, what good would that ever do you?

NORA. That's the point right there: you've never understood me. I've been wronged greatly, Torvald—first by Papa, and then by you.

HELMER. What! By us—the two people who've loved you more than anyone else?

NORA (*shaking her head*). You never loved me. You've thought it fun to be in love with me, that's all.

HELMER. Nora, what a thing to say!

NORA. Yes, it's true now, Torvald. When I lived at home with Papa, he told me all his opinions, so I had the same ones too; or if they were different I hid them, since he wouldn't have cared for that. He used to call me his doll-child, and he played with me the way I played with my dolls. Then I came into your house—

HELMER. How can you speak of our marriage like that?

NORA (*unperturbed*). I mean, then I went from Papa's hands into yours. You arranged everything to your own taste, and so I got the same taste as you—or I pretended to; I can't remember. I guess a little of both, first one, then the other. Now when I look back, it seems as if I'd lived here like a beggar—just from hand to mouth. I've lived by doing tricks for you, Torvald. But that's the way you wanted it. It's a great sin what you and Papa did to me. You're to blame that nothing's become of me.

HELMER. Nora, how unfair and ungrateful you are! Haven't you been happy here?

NORA. No, never. I thought so—but I never have.

HELMER. Not—not happy!

NORA. No, only lighthearted. And you've always been so kind to me. But our home's been nothing but a playpen. I've been your doll-wife here, just as at home I was Papa's doll-child. And in turn the children have been my dolls. I thought it was fun when you played with me, just as they thought it fun when I played with them. That's been our marriage, Torvald.

HELMER. There's some truth in what you're saying—under all the raving exaggeration. But it'll all be different after this. Playtime's over; now for the schooling.

NORA. Whose schooling—mine or the children's?

HELMER. Both yours and the children's, dearest.

NORA. Oh, Torvald, you're not the man to teach me to be a good wife to you.

HELMER. And you can say that?

NORA. And I—how am I equipped to bring up children?

HELMER. Nora!

NORA. Didn't you say a moment ago that that was no job to trust me with?

HELMER. In a flare of temper! Why fasten on that?

NORA. Yes, but you were so very right. I'm not up to the job. There's another job I have to do first. I have to try to educate myself. You can't help me with that. I've got to do it alone. And that's why I'm leaving you now.

HELMER (*jumping up*). What's that?

NORA. I have to stand completely alone, if I'm ever going to discover myself and the world out there. So I can't go on living with you.

HELMER. Nora, Nora!

NORA. I want to leave right away. Kristine should put me up for the night—

HELMER. You're insane! You've no right! I forbid you!

NORA. From here on, there's no use forbidding me anything. I'll take with me whatever is mine. I don't want a thing from you, either now or later.

HELMER. What kind of madness is this!

NORA. Tomorrow I'm going home—I mean, home where I came from. It'll be easier up there to find something to do.

HELMER. Oh, you blind, incompetent child!

NORA. I must learn to be competent, Torvald.

HELMER. Abandon your home, your husband, your children! And you're not even thinking what people will say.

NORA. I can't be concerned about that. I only know how essential this is.

HELMER. Oh, it's outrageous. So you'll run out like this on your most sacred vows.

NORA. What do you think are my most sacred vows?

HELMER. And I have to tell you that! Aren't they your duties to your husband and children?

NORA. I have other duties equally sacred.

HELMER. That isn't true. What duties are they?

NORA. Duties to myself.

HELMER. Before all else, you're a wife and a mother.

NORA. I don't believe in that anymore. I believe that, before all else, I'm a human being, no less than you—or anyway, I ought to try to become one. I know the majority thinks you're right, Torvald, and plenty of books agree with you, too. But I can't go on believing what the majority says, or what's written in books. I have to think over these things myself and try to understand them.

HELMER. Why can't you understand your place in your own home? On a point like that, isn't there one everlasting guide you can turn to? Where's your religion?

NORA. Oh, Torvald, I'm really not sure what religion is.

HELMER. What—?

NORA. I only know what the minister said when I was confirmed. He told me religion was this thing and that. When I get clear and away by myself, I'll go into that problem too. I'll see if what the minister said was right, or, in any case, if it's right for me.

HELMER. A young woman your age shouldn't talk like that. If religion can't move you, I can try to rouse your conscience. You do have some moral feeling? Or, tell me—has that gone too?

NORA. It's not easy to answer that, Torvald. I simply don't know. I'm all confused about these things. I just know I see them so differently from you. I find out, for one thing, that the law's not at all what I'd thought—but I can't get it through my head that the law is fair. A woman hasn't a right to protect her dying father or save her husband's life! I can't believe that.

HELMER. You talk like a child. You don't know anything of the world you live in.

NORA. No, I don't. But now I'll begin to learn for myself. I'll try to discover who's right, the world or I.

HELMER. Nora, you're sick; you've got a fever. I almost think you're out of your head.

NORA. I've never felt more clearheaded and sure in my life.

HELMER. And—clearheaded and sure—you're leaving your husband and children?

NORA. Yes.

HELMER. Then there's only one possible reason.

NORA. What?

HELMER. You no longer love me.

NORA. No. That's exactly it.

HELMER. Nora! You can't be serious!

NORA. Oh, this is so hard, Torvald—you've been so kind to me always. But I can't help it. I don't love you anymore.

HELMER (*struggling for composure*). Are you also clearheaded and sure about that?

NORA. Yes, completely. That's why I can't go on staying here.

HELMER. Can you tell me what I did to lose your love?

NORA. Yes, I can tell you. It was this evening when the miraculous thing didn't come—then I knew you weren't the man I'd imagined.

HELMER. Be more explicit; I don't follow you.

NORA. I've waited now so patiently eight long years—for, my Lord, I know miracles don't come every day. Then this crisis broke over me, and such a certainty filled me: *now* the miraculous event would occur. While Krogstad's letter was lying out there, I never for an instant dreamed that you could give in to his terms. I was so utterly sure you'd say to him: go on, tell your tale to the whole wide world. And when he'd done that—

HELMER. Yes, what then. When I'd delivered my own wife into shame and disgrace—!

NORA. When he'd done that, I was so utterly sure that you'd step forward, take the blame on yourself and say: I am the guilty one.

HELMER. Nora—!

NORA. You're thinking I'd never accept such a sacrifice from you? No, of course not. But what good would my protests be against you? That was the miracle I was waiting for, in terror and hope. And to stave that off, I would have taken my life.

HELMER. I'd gladly work for you day and night, Nora—and take on pain and deprivation. But there's no one who gives up honor for love.

NORA. Millions of women have done just that.

HELMER. Oh, you think and talk like a silly child.

NORA. Perhaps. But you neither think nor talk like the man I could join myself to. When your big fright was over—and it wasn't from any threat against me, only for what might damage you—when all the danger was past, for you it was just as if nothing had happened. I was exactly the same, your little lark, your doll, that you'd have to handle with double care now that I'd turned out so brittle and frail. (*Gets up.*) Torvald—in that instant it dawned on me that for eight years I've been living here with a stranger, and that I'd even conceived three children—oh, I can't stand the thought of it! I could tear myself to bits.

HELMER (*heavily*). I see. There's a gulf that's opened between us—that's clear. Oh, but Nora, can't we bridge it somehow?

NORA. The way I am now, I'm no wife for you.

HELMER. I have the strength to make myself over.

NORA. Maybe—if your doll gets taken away.

HELMER. But to part! To part from you! No, Nora, no—I can't imagine it.

NORA (*going out, right*). All the more reason why it has to be. (*She reenters with her coat and a small overnight bag, which she puts on a chair by the table.*)

HELMER. Nora, Nora, not now! Wait till tomorrow.

NORA. I can't spend the night in a strange man's room.

HELMER. But couldn't we live here like brother and sister—

NORA. You know very well how long that would last. (*Throws her shawl about her.*) Good-bye, Torvald. I won't look in on the children. I know they're in better hands than mine. The way I am now, I'm no use to them.

HELMER. But someday, Nora—someday—?

NORA. How can I tell? I haven't the least idea what'll become of me.

HELMER. But you're my wife, now and wherever you go.

NORA. Listen, Torvald—I've heard that when a wife deserts her husband's house just as I'm doing, then the law frees him from all responsibility. In any case, I'm freeing you from being responsible. Don't feel yourself bound, any more than I will. There has to be absolute freedom for us both. Here, take your ring back. Give me mine.

HELMER. That too?

NORA. That too.

HELMER. There it is.

NORA. Good. Well, now it's all over. I'm putting the keys here. The maids know all about keeping up the house—better than I do. Tomorrow, after I've left town, Kristine will stop by to pack up everything that's mine from home. I'd like those things shipped up to me.

HELMER. Over! All over! Nora, won't you ever think about me?

NORA. I'm sure I'll think of you often, and about the children and the house here.

HELMER. May I write you?

NORA. No—never. You're not to do that.

HELMER. Oh, but let me send you—

NORA. Nothing. Nothing.

HELMER. Or help you if you need it.

NORA. No. I accept nothing from strangers.

HELMER. Nora—can I never be more than a stranger to you?

NORA (*picking up the overnight bag*). Ah, Torvald—it would take the greatest miracle of all—

HELMER. Tell me the greatest miracle!

NORA. You and I both would have to transform ourselves to the point that— Oh, Torvald, I've stopped believing in miracles.

HELMER. But I'll believe. Tell me! Transform ourselves to the point that—?

NORA. That our living together could be a true marriage. (*She goes out down the hall.*)

HELMER (*sinks down on a chair by the door, face buried in his hands*). Nora! Nora! (*Looking about and rising.*) Empty. She's gone. (*A sudden hope leaps in him.*) The greatest miracle—?

(*From below, the sound of a door slamming shut.*)

The three sisters, Masha, Olga, and Irene, in a Penn State Theatre Department production of *The Three Sisters*. Richard Edelman, director.

CHAPTER VIII

Chekhov and the Moscow Art Theatre

Of all the independent theatres that emerged in Europe in the second half of the nineteenth century, one stands out as both the most unique and the most important: the Moscow Art Theatre of Russia. Not only did this enterprise nurture Anton Chekhov as one of the greatest modern realistic playwrights, but the theatre itself under the leadership of Vladimir Nemirovich-Danchenko and Constantin Stanislavsky created a superlative model for ensemble work and a modern system of acting based on truth and motivation. While the story of this perfect union of playwright and theatre is fascinating, it is so clouded by myth and emotion that truth is difficult to separate from fiction.

If the theatre on the continent of Europe seemed antiquated at the middle of the nineteenth century, the theatre of Russia seemed downright primitive. While it is true that the Russians had produced some superior dramas—Gogol's *The Inspector-General* in 1836, Ostrovsky's *The Thunderstorm* in 1860, and Turgenev's *A Month in the Country* in 1869, for example—the theatre itself was steeped in tawdry tradition: conventionalized painted backdrops were used repeatedly no matter how unsuitable to the play, acting was declamatory, stilted and artificial. Elements of historic costuming, attention to accurate detail, unity of production concept simply did not exist. Given these conditions, the tours of the Meiningen Players to Moscow in 1885 and in 1890 must have seemed revolutionary to practitioners in the Russian theatre. We know this to be true, for two young men—Constantin Stanislavsky and Vladamir Nemirovich-Danchenko—met in a Moscow restaurant, The Slavyanski Bazaar, in June of 1897, and, after conversing from ten o'clock one morning until three o'clock the following morning (a total of seventeen hours), they emerged with a working plan for what they would call The Moscow Art and Popular Theatre. Nemirovich-Danchenko—writer of comedies and novels, critic, stage director, and teacher—was named literary and managing director and Stanislavsky—son of a wealthy merchant, amateur actor and director—was named artistic director. These two young idealists outlined their dream for the future of the Russian theatre based on the Duke of Saxe-Meiningen's model: all players would be equal and would play both large and small roles; there would be a devoted ensemble that would grow and develop through working together; and there would be a noble commitment both to the work of the playwright and to the ideals of the ensemble.

For over a year the two impresarios honed their plan and assembled their company which included Stanislavsky's wife, a former pupil of Nemirovich-Denchenko's named Olga Knipper, and a vital young intellectual named Vsevelod Meyerhold. The company rented a barn on an estate near Pushkino and began long and intense rehearsals which culminated in their opening production, *Tsar Fyodor Ivanovich* by Aleksey Tolstoy, performed at the Hermitage Theatre in Moscow, October 14, 1898. While the audiences loved the historical accuracy of the 1600s—reproduction of the old Kremlin, robes, jewels and weapons of the period—Stanislavsky remained dissatisfied with the production and the acting. Three other productions followed, and the theatre might have drifted into obscurity had it not been for a tenacious determination on the part of Nemirovich-Danchenko to perform the work of a gifted young playwright and short story writer named Anton Chekhov (1860–1904).

Chekhov's third full length play, *The Sea Gull*, was produced at the Imperial Alexandrinsky Theatre in St. Petersburg on October 17, 1896. Rehearsed for only a few days, melodramatically acted, and performed with a conventional drop and wing set, it is no wonder the delicate play was a disaster. Chekhov, by now no stranger to failure, fled the theatre and resolved never to write for the stage again. The playwright wrote:

> I walked the streets. I couldn't just dismiss that performance from my mind, could I? If I live for another hundred years, I shall not give another play to the theatre. In that sphere I am unlucky. That's the end. I shall write no more plays. As I was leaving the theatre last night, hiding my face in the turned-up collar of my overcoat, I heard one man say to another, 'That's literature and not drama'; and the other added, 'And bad literature at that.' A third one asked, 'Who's this Chekhov? Where did he spring from?' And as I was going out I overheard a shortish gentleman say indignantly, 'I can't understand how the administration of the theatre allows such plays to be performed. To put on such plays is an insult!'

In spite of its disasterous premier, Nemirovich-Danchenko wrote Chekhov on May 5, 1898 requesting permission to perform *The Sea Gull*. Chekhov responded politely that he would not risk another failure and that surely the theatre had other playwrights to choose from. Nemirovich-Danchenko responded forcefully on May 12, "If you don't give me your play you will ruin me, for *The Sea Gull* is the only modern play that appeals to me strongly as a producer and you are the only modern writer who is of any interest to a theatre with a decent repertoire." Finally, on May 16, Chekhov capitulated and admitted, "You can't imagine how much I want to see you, and for the pleasure of seeing you and talking things over with you, I will gladly give you all my plays."

There were only twenty-six rehearsals for the production which opened on December 17, 1898. Although Chekhov had attended several rehearsals, he was not present at the opening. A victim of tuberculosis, he was convalescing in sunny Yalta. Stanislavsky, who played the writer Trigorin in that fateful production wrote:

> There was a gravelike silence. Olga Knipper fainted on stage. All of us could hardly keep our feet. In the throes of despair we began moving to our dressing rooms. Suddenly there was a roar in the auditorium, and a shreik of joy or fright on the stage. The curtain was lifted, fell, was lifted again, showing the whole auditorium our amazed and astounded immovability. It fell again, it rose; it fell, it rose, and we could not gather sense enough to bow. Then there were congratulations and embraces like those of Easter night, and ovations to Lilina, who played Masha, and who had broken the ice with her last words, which tore themselves from her heart, moans washed with tears. This it was that held the audience mute for a time before it began to roar and thunder in mad ovation.

Nemirovich-Danchenko telegraphed Chekhov news of the triumph and asked permission to stage *Uncle Vanya*, another of Chekhov's previous failures. From that time forward the Moscow Art Theatre and Anton Chekhov were not parted until the playwright's untimely death in 1904.

The theatre and its directors had found a subtle realistic playwright who served the detailed, truthful acting they were fostering, and Chekhov—although he staunchly maintained that Stanislavsky made his plays too sad and brooding—found the ensemble that understood and could present his delicate gentle vision of life. When the company moved to its new quarters in 1902, the curtain, the tickets, the posters, the stationery—all bore the seagull as emblem and symbol of the Moscow Art Theatre.

Equally as remarkable as the relationship between Chekhov and the MAT was the system of acting devised by Stanislavsky that has become the cornerstone of acting in the twentieth century. Perhaps only one person before Stanislavsky, the French teacher, Francois Delsarte, had seriously attempted to develop and codify a system of acting. Delsarte essentially sought to apply the scientific method to acting. He subdivided the human body into zones and developed rules for using each to express basic human emotions. He believed that there was a characteristic external gesture or mode of expression for every internal emotion. Delsarte's system dominated actor training in Europe and in America until Stanislavsky's teachings took hold.

Stanislavsky wrote copiously; *My Life in Art* was released in 1924 and *An Actor Prepares* in 1936. Two other major books by Stanislavsky, *Building a Character* and *Creating a Role* did not appear in America until 1949 and 1961 respectively. As brilliant as these acting texts are, the Stanislavsky system has frequently caused confusion and bewilderment for the simple reasons that we must read his works in translation—especially difficult where technical material and a particular vocabulary are demanded—and the fact that Stanislavsky himself was constantly altering and modifying his method. Besides these extraordinary texts, the Moscow Art Company toured the United States in 1923–1924, and several of Stanislavsky's desciples—Mikhail Chekhov, nephew of the famous playwright, and Richard Boleslavsky, for example—remained in America to spread the master's teachings. Culminating in the 1950s with the work of Lee Strasberg at the Actors' Studio, the "method" produced such super stars as Geraldine Page, Marilyn Monroe and Marlon Brando. By the 1960s, however, with a new interest in nonrealistic drama and the classics, the method as advocated by the Actors' Studio appeared too limited. In America, devotees of the Stanislavsky system too often emphasized the emotional and psychological aspects of the work without paying equal attention to the need for technique, movement, and vocal training—a fact that surely would have met with Stanislavsky's disapproval. No matter how criticized or limited, however, the Stanislavsky system remains the single most concrete, workable, reasoned, and solid approach for actors.

Stanislavsky would no doubt be surprised at the impact of his method on the American actor. He doggedly maintained that he created nothing new in his approach, and that—concerned with his own limitations as an actor—he was seeking to understand and distill what all great actors since the beginning of time have advocated and practiced. Since many fine books explore the Stanislavsky system in great depth, we must content ourselves with only a brief summary here. Above all, Stanislavsky urged the actor to avoid theatrical posturing and forcing of emotion. He wanted truth and honesty that could result only from careful, detailed, painstaking analysis of the given circumstances of the play in connection with the character's psychological make-up, motives, drives, and needs. Besides urging concentration, relaxation, and discipline, Stanislavsky urged careful observation of human behavior, yet he encouraged the actor to free the self through use of what he called "the magic if"; in the quest for honest behavior the actor was admonished to ask, "What would I do if I were in this character's place?"

Stanislavsky taught the actor to work in small units of the play, which we call beats, thus avoiding general acting. Plays are carefully structured, the master teacher believed, with each character possessing what is called the super-objective. Yet as characters go through their daily lives they must fulfill a myriad of smaller objectives in order to approach that major goal. In fulfilling these objectives we *do* things; we *act*. For example, a character's super-objective might be to go to college. In order to do that the character must graduate from high school and secure the money to pay tuition. Now the character is faced with a series of smaller objectives that relate specifically to the super-objective: to secure the tuition, the character must get a job, refrain from frivolous spending, create a budget, discipline the self. The hypothetical situation can be broken down even more. In the specific scene that represents the job interview, the character may employ a series of actions, "doings," or intentions to get the job. He may try to answer all questions in a way pleasing to the interviewer, try to keep his hands from shaking, try to crack jokes, try to impress, and try to ingratiate himself with the interviewee. All this he does because he wants the job in order to go to college.

If, Stanislavsky advocated, the character will concentrate on what he does to get what he wants, then general, forced, or result-oriented acting will be avoided. A situation may result in our being sad, but we do not and should not play the quality of sadness. Suppose a character wants his loved one to go away with him. He may tease, scold, cajole, beg, and plead. When he fails to achieve his objective, he may be sad as a result of that failure but he need never concentrate on the sadness. Playing quality, mood, or the result of the scene is a trap Stanislavsky warned against; actors need to learn to make strong, positive choices to fulfill their character needs.

Still other techniques to emphasize specific, honest stage behavior involve substitution, the process of finding events in the actor's own life and understanding to use in a dramatic situation, remembering emotions and sensory experiences, finding the sub-text or meaning behind the spoken lines, learning to listen, working to play a scene moment to moment rather than leaping to the results, trusting and working with fellow actors, doing everything truthfully and for a purpose. Besides all of these techniques, Stanislavsky taught the actor to work slowly and with great detail yet to be selective and to avoid anything extraneous. He emphasized the look of the character, the importance of the clothes, the make-up, and the props. But above all, Stanislavsky taught that acting was not about falsehood and emotion but about truth and positive action. It is a system that the conscientious actor spends a lifetime learning and assimilating and perhaps never completely mastering.

Even before the Stanislavsky approach to acting had been tried outside Russia, there were detractors who argued that the system was too limiting, too linked with realism and social drama. Stanislavsky and Nemirovich-Danchenko established a series of studios connected with the MAT whose purpose was experimentation and development of nonrealistic styles. The first of these was headed by Stanislavsky's pupil, Vsevelod Meyerhold. Too radical for Stanislavsky's taste, Meyerhold was dismissed but went on to distinguish himself as one of the major creative forces of the twentieth century. Meyerhold believed that the actor and the script should be subjugated to the will of the director. Anti-realistic and anti-illusionistic, he was keenly interested in the theatricality of the *commedia del 'arte* and the ancient Oriental theatre.

In the last phase of his career, Meyerhold developed his theory of *biomechanics,* his approach to the training of actors as gymnasts, circus performers, ballet dancers in order to make them as efficient as complex machines. Meyerhold replaced Stanislavsky's emphasis on motivation and internal life with one of physical responsiveness. Meyerhold also developed his theory of *construc-*

tivism involving the creation of a non-illusionistic space in which the actor could work. By creating platforms, ramps, step units, wheels, levers, and pulleys, Meyerhold made bold strides in rejecting the limited world of the realistic play. A tireless experimentor and innovator, Meyerhold refused to conform to political ideology and subsequently "disappeared" during the Stalin purges of 1939.

Anton Chekhov

Anton Chekhov (1860–1904) was the third of five children of an ex-serf in Taganrog. His father, a struggling grocer, was tyranical and despotic. Chekhov wrote, "As a little boy I was treated with so little kindness that now, having grown up, I accept kindness as something unusual, something of which I have had little experience." Chekhov was extremely bright and decided upon a career as a medical doctor, completing his studies in 1884. He often practiced among the peasants without charging a fee and even journeyed to Eastern Siberia to investigate conditions of the Russian prison camps. However, as a student at the University of Moscow, Chekhov contracted tuberculosis, a disease which caused his premature death at the age of forty-four.

As a young doctor, Chekhov started supplementing his meager income by writing short stories. He said, "Medicine is my lawful wife and literature my mistress. When I get tired of one I spend a night with the other. That may not be quite respectable, but at any rate it isn't boring, and, besides, neither of them loses anything from my unfaithfulness." In 1887, Chekhov composed his first full-length drama, *Ivanov,* the tragedy of a provincial character whose unconventional marriage proves a failure. Although the play failed in production, Chekhov worked over a year on a second play, titled *The Wood Demon* and later reworked under the title of *Uncle Vanya.* Putting the manuscript aside as a second failure, Chekhov returned to short stories and short farce plays of which "The Bear" and "The Marriage Proposal" exist as classic examples.

Then in December of 1898, the Moscow Art Theatre produced *The Sea Gull* and Chekhov's position as playwright was firmly established. After a successful production of *Uncle Vanya* in 1899, Chekhov wrote *The Three Sisters* expressly for the MAT and for his future wife, the actress Olga Knipper. It opened on January 31, 1901 and was, in Nemirovitch-Danchenko's opinion, the best production ever given at the MAT.

Two years before his death, Chekhov and Olga Knipper were married in Moscow. He wrote his bride on April 19, 1901, "If you give me your word that not a single soul in Moscow will know of our wedding till it is over, then I shall be ready to marry you on the very first day of my arrival. I don't know why, but I am simply terrified of the wedding ceremony, and the congratulations and the glass of champagne you have to hold in your hand at the same time smiling vaguely." Chekhov added prophetically, "I have everything in order, everything except one small trifle—my health."

Although the couple were married on May 25, 1901, they were destined to spend only two years as man and wife. In 1904 Chekhov completed his final masterpiece for the MAT. *The Cherry Orchard,* written for Olga Knipper as the aristocratic Madame Ranevsky, anticipated the coming Russian revolution and depicted a Russia in transition between the fading aristocracy and a new energetic breed of young working class men and women. Chekhov progressed slowly on the play, writing only a few sentences a day in great pain. It is said that Chekhov coughed uncontrollably on opening night. He died in the German spa of Badenweiler on July 1, 1904. Chekhov's young colleague at the Moscow Art Theatre, playwright Maxim Gorki said, "I think that in Anton Chekhov's presence everyone involuntarily felt in himself a desire to be simple, more truthful, more oneself."

The Three Sisters

Lionel Trilling once wrote that "*The Three Sisters* is surely one of the saddest works in all literature. It is also one of the most saddening." Because the play deals with each character's failure to achieve happiness or fulfillment, it does seem drenched in sadness. But the play also concerns the inescapable disparity between dreams and reality. By the end of the play we know that even if the three sisters could return to Moscow—the symbol of happiness and fulfillment for them—their lot in life would be no better. The sisters live in a time of change when the old aristocracy is crumbling and a new order is about to assert itself. This is not a time conducive to personal happiness.

While Chekhov's play may have its air of sadness, it is by no means gloomy. In reflecting the dramatist's own ironic view of life, it is rich with humor at times. As Chekhov saw it, life could be both amusing and sad, harsh and gentle, at one and the same time. And man could be both pitiable and laughable in one moment; the most insignificant man could have his moment of importance, and the most important man could be insignificant at times. Often the man can be noble and absurd at one and the same moment. If you are inclined to laugh at the Chekhovian character at that moment when he is being most serious or when life is being cruelest to him, you are probably right. That is what the playwright intended. Furthermore, Chekhov's plays are notable for their blend of gaiety, tenderness, and sadness and notable as well for their absence of bitterness, anger and coarseness. In *The Three Sisters,* as in Chekhov's other major plays, there is a mood of nostalgic sorrow for that which is forever lost which plays in counterpoint to an equally prevalent mood of gentle and persistent hope that the future will be a happy one. The interplay of moods imparts a poetic quality to the drama.

Perhaps it is because of the unique view of life in his plays that Chekhov, possibly more than any other dramatist, has suffered at the hands of translators, directors and actors who misunderstand his intentions, his humor, and his form. It is often thought that nothing seems to happen in his plays. Nothing could be farther from the truth. A great deal is going on in terms of the pursuit of the major action of the play—to achieve happiness and fulfillment; but it all happens in a subtle, understated manner in what has been called Chekhov's "indirect approach." Characters become engaged, have affairs, suffer losses, fight duels, win jobs and earn honors, fail at life, depart never to return again and even die. Life, in short, passes on the stage. However, the playwright consistently suggests more than he tells; so each event in the plays is ripe with potential and possibility. Major events are not treated as world-shaking beginnings or ends as they are in most plays; they occur as they do in life—as passages from one moment to the next.

Much of what happens in a Chekhov play happens *inside* the characters as the dramatist suggests more than he tells. We do not know all there is to know about anyone, and yet we are given tantalizing glimpses of many different facets of one character. Kulygin, for example, is a stuffed-shirt and a bore, and yet he loves Masha with a depth of human understanding and tenderness that few men ever achieve. Chebutykin may seem like a drunken, old fool at times and yet we know the depth of his disappointment with himself. Vershinin is the romantic lover but he is also something of a wind-bag when he begins talking about his children or his philosophy of life. All of this, of course, makes for superb and complex character delineation. Chekhov treats every character with enormous sympathy; no one is totally revolting, nor is he totally sympathetic. What the character does is no more important than what he thinks and feels. And so there are many moments in the play when the character seems to wander off into a soliloquy which reveals the depth and complexity of his inner being. These are reflective characters who seem to live in the past much of the time. But as they lose themselves in the past, Chekhov is providing us with a rich supply of vital and interestingly delivered exposition. Interestingly, the dramatist is fascinated equally by each and every character. So there are no single heroes or heroines in his major plays. Perhaps this accounts for the fact that actors love to play Chekhov. After all, there are no bit parts. But, for this reason, if we are to understand the play, we must pay careful heed to what every single character says or feels and to how he reacts at every moment.

Because of Chekhov's indirect approach his dialogue is rather unique. Characters do not talk to one another in order to advance the plot as happens in most plays. Often, they seem to talk in what appears to be a series of soliloquies which are designed to reveal their inner natures. For this reason, the dialogue occasionally seems to consist of inanities as the characters talk *past* one another rather than *to* one another. They pick up ideas from each other and then wander off on their own tangents just as people do in everyday life. In those moments they are most often speaking of what is closest to their hearts; and so they inadvertently reveal their souls to us. Perhaps it is because of this penchant on the part of the characters that they seem so often to be making furtive attempts to reach one another or to touch life or truth. And sometimes they seem also to be avoiding one another as well.

Just as the profound characters of Chekhovian drama are major assets and rewarding experiences, so is the Russian playwright's incredible sense of humor. We tend to miss the humor in Chekhov because we have been preconditioned to think of the plays as direly serious (largely because they are performed that way outside of Russia by actors and directors who do not sufficiently understand what the playwright intends). In *The Three Sisters* it is very important to pay attention to *how* a thing is said as well as *what* is said; it is necessary also to take into account everything else that might be happening in the background of a scene when something is said. For example, at the end of Act II, the heartbreak of Irene desperately longing for Moscow is nicely undercut when we realize that, in the background, Natasha is trying, not too subtly, to sneak away for an assignation with her lover. In the last act Natasha boldly has her lover in the house with her; but before anyone can feel too sorry for her husband Andrey—who is pushing the baby-buggy on the terrace—it becomes evident that the lover is not enjoying the favors of his mistress but, rather, baby-sitting indoors. Furthermore, the absurdity of old Chebutykin singing "Tarara-boom-di-ay . . . I'm sitting on a tomb-di-ay" is given a heart-wrenching edge by our awareness that tragedy is about to strike Tusenbach.

It is necessary to read a Chekhov play very carefully paying particular attention to every detail of character, thought, action, and plot. It is necessary, too, to allow our mind full play with each and every suggestion or implication in the play. However, in order to accomplish all that, it is sometimes equally necessary to keep a pencil on hand with which to jot down the many variations on character names that occur so that you know precisely who is speaking or being spoken about. It is helpful also to note the relationships between characters—father, mother, sister, brother, uncle, aunt, lover, friend, rival, servant. In short, it takes a little effort to read a Chekhov play; you cannot expect to absorb it passively as you might the weekly installment of a favorite television sitcom. You have to become an active participant in the creative experience when you approach Chekhov. But all of the effort is richly rewarded, for *The Three Sisters*—as well as all of Chekhov's major works—is one of the most stimulating, delightful, moving, and insightful plays of the entire modern drama.

THE THREE SISTERS

by *Anton Chekhov*

translated by David Magarshack

———— CHARACTERS ————

ANDREY SERGYEEVICH PROZOROV
NATASHA (NATALIE IVANOVNA), *his fiancee, afterwards his wife*
OLGA
MASHA (MARIA) } *his sisters*
IRINA
FYODOR ILYICH KULYGIN, *secondary school teacher, Masha's husband*
ALEXANDER IGNATYEVICH VERSHININ, *lieutenant colonel, battery commander*
NIKOLAI (NICHOLAS) LVOVICH TUSENBACH, *Baron, lieutenant*
VASILY VASILYEVICH SOLYONY, *subaltern*
IVAN ROMANOVICH CHEBUTYKIN, *army doctor*
ALEXEY PETROVICH FEDOTIK, *second lieutenant*
VLADIMIR KARLOVICH RODE, *second lieutenant*
FERAPONT, *an old District Council porter*
ANFISA, *a nurse, an old woman of eighty*
TWO ARMY OFFICERS
TWO MUSICIANS
A SOLDIER
A MAID

The action takes place in a provincial capital.

ACT ONE

A drawing room in the Prozorovs' house, separated from a large ballroom by a row of columns. Noon; it is a bright, sunny day. In the ballroom the table is being laid for lunch.
OLGA, *wearing the dark-blue regulation dress of a secondary school mistress, is correcting her pupils' exercise books, standing or walking about the room;* MASHA, *in a black dress, is sitting reading a book, her hat on her lap;* IRINA, *in white, stands lost in thought.*

OLGA. It is just a year since Father died, on this very day, the fifth of May—your birthday, Irina. It was dreadfully cold; it was snowing then. I felt as though I'd never be able to live through it, and you were lying in a dead faint. But now a whole year has gone by and the thought of it no longer troubles us. You're wearing a white dress again; you look so radiant. [*The clock strikes twelve.*] Then, too, the clock struck twelve. [*Pause.*] I remember the military band playing at Father's funeral, and they fired a salute at the cemetery. Though Father was a general and a brigade commander, there were not many people at his funeral. It is true, it was raining then. Pouring with rain, and snowing.

294

IRINA. Why must you talk about it?

In the ballroom, behind the columns, BARON TUS-ENBACH, CHEBUTYKIN, *and* SOLYONY *appear near the table.*

OLGA. It is warm today—the windows can be opened wide—but the birch trees have not opened up yet. It is eleven years since Father was given his brigade and left Moscow with us, and I distinctly remember it, the flowers were in bloom in Moscow just at this time—the beginning of May. Oh, it was so warm then, and everything was drenched in sunlight. Eleven years have passed, but I can remember everything just as if we had left Moscow only yesterday. My goodness! When I woke up this morning and saw the bright sunshine, saw the spring, my heart leapt for joy, and I felt such a passionate longing to be back home!

CHEBUTYKIN. The devil you did!

TUSENBACH. It's all nonsense, of course!

MASHA, *daydreaming over her book, whistles a tune softly.*

OLGA. Don't whistle, Masha. How can you? [*Pause.*] I suppose it's because I'm at school all day and giving private lessons in the evenings that I'm getting these constant headaches and these thoughts, just as if I were old already. And really, all these four years while I've been working at school, I've felt as though my strength and my youth were draining out of me drop by drop. And one's longing only grows stronger and stronger—

IRINA. To go to Moscow. Sell the house, finish with everything here, and leave for Moscow.

OLGA. Yes! To Moscow, as soon as possible.

CHEBUTYKIN *and* TUSENBACH *laugh.*

IRINA. I expect Andrey will get a professorship soon, and anyway, he's not going to live here much longer. The only difficulty is poor old Masha.

OLGA. Masha could come to Moscow every year and stay with us the whole summer.

MASHA *continues whistling her tune softly.*

IRINA. Let's hope everything will turn out all right. [*Looking through the window.*] Oh, what a beautiful day! I don't know why I'm feeling so calm and serene. This morning I remembered that it was my birthday, and suddenly, I felt so happy. I remembered our childhood, when Mother was still alive, and such wonderful, exciting thoughts kept flashing through my mind. Oh, what wonderful thoughts!

OLGA. You look so radiant today, more beautiful than ever. Masha, too, is beautiful. Andrey would have been quite good-looking if he had not put on so much weight. It doesn't suit him at all. As for me, I've grown old and a lot thinner. I suppose it must be because I get so irritable with the girls at school. Today I'm free, I'm at home, I haven't got a headache, and I feel much younger than I did yesterday. After all, I'm only twenty-eight, except that . . . Everything's all right, everything's as God wills, but I can't help thinking that if I'd got married and stayed at home all day, things would be much better. [*Pause.*] I'd have loved my husband.

TUSENBACH [*to* SOLYONY]. What nonsense you talk. I'm sick of listening to you. [*Going into the drawing room.*] I forgot to tell you: Vershinin, our new battery commander, will be calling on you today. [*Sits down at the piano.*]

OLGA. Will he? He'll be very welcome.

IRINA. Is he old?

TUSENBACH. No, not really. Forty—forty-five at most. [*Plays quietly.*] An excellent fellow by all accounts. Not a fool by any means, that's certain. He talks too much, though.

IRINA. Is he an interesting man?

TUSENBACH. Yes, I should say so, only, you see, he's got a wife, a mother-in-law, and two little girls. You see, it's his second wife. He calls on people and tells everybody that he has a wife and two little girls. He's sure to tell you all about it too. His second wife, I'm sorry to say, does not seem to be altogether in her right mind. She wears a long plait like a girl, uses very grandiloquent language, philosophizes, and every now and again tries to commit suicide. Apparently, to annoy her husband. I'd have left a woman like that long ago, but he puts up with it. Just keeps on complaining.

SOLYONY [*enters the drawing room with* CHEBU-TYKIN]. I can only lift half a hundredweight with one hand, but with two I can lift a hundredweight and more. From which I infer that two men are not only twice but three or even more times as strong as one.

CHEBUTYKIN [*reads a newspaper while he comes in*]. For falling hair: one hundred and thirty grains of naphthalene in half a bottle of spirits. Dissolve and apply daily. [*Writes it down in his notebook.*] Let's make a note of it. [*To* SOLYONY.] Well, as I was saying, you put a cork into the bottle and pass a glass tube through the cork. . . . Then you take a pinch of ordinary powdered alum—

IRINA. Doctor, dear Doctor . . .

CHEBUTYKIN. What is it, child? What is it, my sweet?

IRINA. Tell me, why am I so happy today? I feel as if I were sailing under a wide blue sky and great white birds were flying above me. Why is it? Why?

CHEBUTYKIN [*kissing both her hands, tenderly*]. My lovely white bird . . .

IRINA. When I awoke this morning, got up, and washed, I suddenly felt as if everything in the world had become clear to me and I knew how one ought to live. Dear Doctor, I do know everything. Man must work, work by the sweat of his brow, whoever he might be. That alone gives a meaning and a purpose to his life, his happiness, his success. Oh, how wonderful it must be to be a laborer who gets up with the sun and breaks stones by the roadside, or a shepherd, or a schoolmaster teaching children, or a driver of a railway engine. Why, dear Lord, better be an ox or a horse and go on working than a young woman who wakes up at twelve, drinks her coffee in bed, then takes two hours dressing. . . . Oh, how dreadful! Just as one is sometimes dying for a drink of water on a hot day, so I'm dying to do some work. Why, if I don't get up early and do some real work, don't count me among your friends any more, Doctor.

CHEBUTYKIN [*tenderly*]. I won't. . . . I won't. . . .

OLGA. Father trained us to get up at seven o'clock. That is why Irina always wakes up at seven and lies in bed at least till nine thinking about all sorts of things. How serious she looks! [*Laughs.*]

IRINA. You're so used to looking on me as a little girl that it seems strange to you when I look serious.

TUSENBACH. Dear Lord, how well I understand this craving for work. I've never done a stroke of work in my life. I was born in Petersburg, a cold and idle city. My family never knew what work or worry meant. I remember when I came home from the military academy, a valet would pull off my boots while I swore at him. My mother looked at me with adoring eyes and was genuinely surprised when people looked differently at me. I was carefully guarded against work. But they did not succeed in shielding me from it. Not now, at any rate. The time is coming when something huge is about to overwhelm us. A mighty hurricane is on the way; it is quite near already, and soon, very soon, it will sweep away from our society idleness, complacency, prejudice against work, and effete boredom. I shall work and in another twenty-five or thirty years everyone will work—everyone!

CHEBUTYKIN. I won't work.

TUSENBACH. You don't count.

SOLYONY. In twenty-five years you won't be alive, thank goodness. In a couple of years you will die of a stroke or I'll lose my temper and put a bullet through your head, dear fellow. [*Takes a perfume bottle from his pocket and sprinkles the perfume over his chest and hands.*]

CHEBUTYKIN [*laughs*]. It's quite true, I have never done a stroke of work in my life. As soon as I left the university, I never lifted a finger or opened a book. I only read newspapers. [*Takes another newspaper out of his pocket.*] Here. . . . I know from the papers that we had—er—a critic by the name of Dobrolyubov, but I'm hanged if I know what he wrote about. [*Somebody is heard knocking on the floor from downstairs.*] There. . . . Somebody wants to see me downstairs. They're calling me to come down. I'll be back in a moment. I won't be long. [*Goes out hurriedly, stroking his beard.*]

IRINA. He's up to something.

TUSENBACH. I think so too. He's gone out looking very solemn. I expect he's gone to fetch your present.

IRINA. Oh, how I hate it!

OLGA. Yes, it is dreadful. He's always doing something silly.

MASHA. "For he on honey-dew had fed, and drunk the milk of Paradise . . . and drunk the milk of Paradise" . . . * [*Gets up, humming quietly.*]

---

*The first two lines from Pushkin's epilogue to *Ruslan and Lyudmila,* which Masha repeats once in Act One and twice in Act Four, are full of magic and mystery. But this is only apparent in the original and can only be perceived by a Russian audience familiar with those lines from childhood. When translated—"A green oak tree grows at the bay/A golden chain is on that oak tree"—they are meaningless. To convey this feeling, I have chosen two lines from Coleridge's "Kubla Khan," which are not only similar but which also help us to understand Masha's sudden attraction to the idealist Vershinin, the man who fits most closely the two lines of Coleridge's poem. It must be remembered that Masha knew English and would most certainly have read "Kubla Khan" in the original—not that it matters, since the important thing is to convey Masha's feeling and mood to an English-speaking audience [D.M.].

OLGA. You're not very cheerful today, Masha. [MASHA *puts on her hat, humming.*] Where are you off to?

MASHA. Home.

IRINA. Strange!

TUSENBACH. Leave a birthday party!

MASHA. What does it matter? I'll be back this evening. Good-bye, darling. [*Kisses* IRINA.] Let me wish you again good health and happiness. In the old days, when Father was alive, we always used to have thirty or forty army officers at our birthday parties—such noisy parties—but today we've only got a man and a half, and it's quiet as a desert. I'm going home. I'm in a terribly melancholy mood today. I'm not feeling particularly cheerful, so you'd better not listen to me. [*Laughing through tears.*] We'll have a good talk later; good-bye for now, my darling. I'll just go somewhere, anywhere.

IRINA [*displeased*]. Really, Masha . . .

OLGA [*tearfully*]. I understand you, Masha.

SOLYONY. If a man philosophizes, it is philosophistry or, if you like, sophistry, but if a woman or a couple of women start philosophizing, it's all a lot of nonsense.

MASHA. What do you mean by that, you frightfully terrible man?

SOLYONY. Nothing. "He had barely time to catch his breath before the bear was hugging him to death."

MASHA [*to* OLGA, *crossly*]. Don't howl.

Enter ANFISA *and* FERAPONT *with a cake.*

ANFISA. This way, my good man. Come in, your boots are clean. [*To* IRINA.] From the District Council, my dear, from Mr. Protopopov, Mikhail Ivanovich, a cake.

IRINA. Thank you. Please give my thanks to Mr. Protopopov. [*Accepts the cake.*]

FERAPONT. Beg pardon, miss?

IRINA [*louder*]. Thank Mr. Protopopov.

OLGA. Nanny, let him have some pie. Go to the kitchen, Ferapont. They'll give you some pie there.

FERAPONT. Beg pardon, miss?

ANFISA. Come along, my dear, come along. [*Goes out with* FERAPONT.]

MASHA. I don't like this Protopopov, this Mikhail Potapych or Ivanych.* I don't think we ought to invite him.

IRINA. I didn't invite him.

MASHA. Good!

Enter CHEBUTYKIN, *followed by a* SOLDIER *carrying a silver samovar; murmurs of astonishment and displeasure.* OLGA *covers her face.*

OLGA. A samovar! This is awful. [*Goes through to the ballroom and stands by the table.*]

IRINA. Oh, dear Doctor, what are you doing?

TUSENBACH [*laughs*]. I told you so.

MASHA. Really, Doctor, you ought to be ashamed of yourself!

CHEBUTYKIN. My dear sweet darlings, you're all I have, you're all I hold most dear in the world. I shall soon be sixty. I'm an old man, a lonely, worthless old man. There's nothing good about me except my love for you. But for you I'd have been dead long ago. [*To* IRINA.] My darling, my dear child, I've known you ever since you were born. . . . I used to carry you about in my arms. . . . I loved your mother. . . .

IRINA. But why such expensive presents?

CHEBUTYKIN [*through tears, crossly*]. Expensive presents! Don't talk such nonsense. [*To his orderly.*] Take the samovar to the other room. [*In a mocking voice.*] Expensive presents!

The orderly carries off the samovar to the ballroom.

ANFISA [*crossing the drawing room*]. My dears, a strange colonel's just arrived. He's taken off his coat and he's coming here now. Irina, darling, be nice and polite to him. [*Going out.*] Lunch should have been served long ago. Dear, oh dear. [*Goes out.*]

TUSENBACH. I expect it must be Vershinin. [*Enter* VERSHININ.] Lieutenant Colonel Vershinin!

*The Russian folk name for a bear is Mishka, a pet name for Mikhail. Sometimes the patronymic Potapych is added. Protopopov's name is also Mikhail, but his patronymic is Ivanovich or Ivanych. Coming so quickly after Solyony's quotation from Krylov's fable *The Peasant and the Bear*, the indirect implication is that the bear Protopopov will, in the end, bring about the ruin of the three sisters [D.M.].

VERSHININ [to MASHA and IRINA]. Allow me to introduce myself: Vershinin. I'm very glad, very glad indeed, that I'm here at last. Good heavens, how you've grown!

IRINA. Please be seated. We're very pleased to meet you, Colonel.

VERSHININ [gaily]. I'm so glad, so glad! But surely there are three of you, three sisters. I remember three little girls. I don't remember their faces, but I do remember that your father, Colonel Prozorov, had three little girls. I remember it very well. I saw them myself. How time flies! Dear me, how time flies!

TUSENBACH. The Colonel comes from Moscow.

IRINA. Moscow? Are you from Moscow?

VERSHININ. Yes, I'm from Moscow. Your father was a battery commander there, and I served in the same brigade. [To MASHA.] I seem to remember your face a little.

MASHA. I'm afraid I don't remember you.

IRINA. Olga! Olga! [Shouts into the ballroom.] Olga! Do come! [OLGA comes in from the ballroom.] Lieutenant Colonel Vershinin, it seems, comes from Moscow.

VERSHININ. So you're Olga, the eldest sister. And you are Maria. And you are Irina, the youngest.

OLGA. You are from Moscow?

VERSHININ. Yes. I went to school in Moscow and began my service in Moscow. I served there a long time and, at last, was put in command of the battery here. Moved over here, as you see. I do not really remember you. All I remember is that there were three sisters. I remember your father very well. I have only to shut my eyes to see him just as if he were alive. I used to visit you in Moscow.

OLGA. I thought I remembered everybody, and suddenly—

VERSHININ. My Christian name is Alexander.

IRINA. Alexander Vershinin, and you are from Moscow. What a surprise!

OLGA. You see, we're going to live there.

IRINA. Yes, we hope to be there by autumn. It's our home town. We were born there, in Old Basmanny Street.

OLGA and IRINA laugh happily.

MASHA. Meeting a fellow townsman so unexpectedly . . . [With animation.] Now I remember! Do you remember, Olga, there was someone we used to call "the lovesick major"? You were only a lieutenant then and you were in love with some girl, and for some reason, we all nicknamed you, teasingly, the major.

VERSHININ [laughs]. That's it! That's it! The lovesick major. Yes, that's true.

MASHA. In those days you only had a mustache. Oh, you look so much older! [Through tears.] So much older!

VERSHININ. Yes, when I was known as the lovesick major, I was still a young man. I was in love then. It's different now.

OLGA. But you haven't got a single gray hair. You've grown older, but you're not an old man.

VERSHININ. I shall soon be forty-three all the same. How long have you been away from Moscow?

IRINA. Eleven years. What are you crying for, Masha? You funny girl! [Through tears.] You're making me cry, too.

MASHA. I'm all right. And where did you live?

VERSHININ. In Old Basmanny Street.

OLGA. We lived there, too.

VERSHININ. At one time I lived in German Street. I used to walk from there to the barracks. I had to cross a gloomy bridge on the way; the water rushed so noisily under it. It made me feel so sad when walking over it by myself. [Pause.] But here you have such a fine river, such a wonderful river!

OLGA. Yes, only it's very cold. It's very cold here and lots of mosquitoes.

VERSHININ. You can't mean it! Here you have such a good, healthy climate, a real Russian climate. Forest, river . . . and also birch trees. Dear, modest birch trees. I love them more than any other trees. It's nice living here. The only trouble is that the railway is fifteen miles from the town. Nobody seems to know why.

SOLYONY. I know why. [Everyone looks at him.] Because, you see, if the railway station had been near, it wouldn't have been far, and if it's far, it's because it is not near.

An awkward silence.

TUSENBACH. He likes his little joke, our subaltern does.

OLGA. Now I've remembered you, too. Yes, I remember you.

VERSHININ. I knew your mother.

CHEBUTYKIN. She was a good woman, God rest her soul.

IRINA. Mother was buried in Moscow.

OLGA. At the Novo-Devichy Monastery.

MASHA. I'm afraid I'm already beginning to forget what she looked like. I suppose people will forget us, too, in the same way. They'll forget us.

VERSHININ. Yes, they'll forget us. Such is our fate. There's nothing we can do about it. The things that seem great, significant, and very important to us now will no more seem to be important with time. [Pause.] It's certainly an interesting fact that we cannot possibly know today what in the future will be considered great and important or just pitiful and ridiculous. Didn't the discoveries of Copernicus, or, let's say, Columbus appear to be useless and ridiculous at the time, while some utter drivel, written by some crank, seemed to be a great truth? It is quite likely that our present life, to which we are so reconciled, will in time appear to be odd, uncomfortable, stupid, not particularly clean and, perhaps, even immoral.

TUSENBACH. Who knows? Perhaps our life will be considered to have been noble and will be remembered with respect. We no longer have tortures, public executions, or invasions, and yet there's still so much suffering.

SOLYONY [in a high-pitched voice]. Cluck, cluck, cluck . . . No need to scatter corn for the Baron; just give him a chance to philosophize.

TUSENBACH. Leave me alone, will you? [Changes his place.] It's getting rather boring.

SOLYONY [in a high-pitched voice]. Cluck, cluck, cluck.

TUSENBACH [to VERSHININ]. The suffering that we can observe today—and there's so much of it—still shows a certain degree of moral uplift already achieved by our society.

VERSHININ. Yes, yes, of course.

CHEBUTYKIN. You've said just now, Baron, that our present life may be called great, but people are rather small all the same. [Gets up.] Look how small I am. It's to console me that one should say my life is noble. That, I think, is clear enough.

A violin is played offstage.

MASHA. It's our brother, Andrey, playing the violin.

IRINA. He's our scholar. We hope he's going to be a professor one day. Father was a soldier, but his son has chosen an academic career.

MASHA. It was Father's wish.

OLGA. We've been teasing him today. We think he's a little in love.

IRINA. With a local girl. She'll be calling on us today, most probably.

MASHA. Heavens, how she dresses! It isn't that her clothes are not pretty or fashionable—they are just pathetic. Some sort of bright-yellow frock with a cheap-looking fringe and a red blouse. Her cheeks, too, are so thoroughly scrubbed! Andrey's not in love with her. I just can't believe it, for after all, he has got some taste. I think he's simply doing it to tease us. It's his way of playing the fool. I was told yesterday that she was going to marry Protopopov, the chairman of our District Council. And an excellent thing, too! [Calls through the side door.] Andrey, come here! Just for a moment, dear!

Enter ANDREY.

OLGA. This is my brother, Andrey.

VERSHININ. Vershinin.

ANDREY. Prozorov. [Wipes the perspiration from his face.] Are you our new battery commander?

OLGA. Just imagine! Colonel Vershinin comes from Moscow.

ANDREY. Oh? Well, I congratulate you. Now my sisters won't give you any peace.

VERSHININ. I'm afraid your sisters must be getting bored with me already.

IRINA. Look what a lovely picture frame Andrey gave me today for a present. [Shows him the frame.] Andrey made it himself.

VERSHININ [looks at the picture frame and is at a loss for what to say]. Well, yes, er—it's—er—very nice.

IRINA. And the little frame over the piano, he made that too.

ANDREY *waves his hand deprecatingly and walks off.*

OLGA. He's our scholar, he plays the violin, and he's very clever with a fret saw. In fact, he can turn his hand to anything. Andrey, don't go. He has a habit of always walking away. Come here!

MASHA *and* IRINA *take* ANDREY *by the arms and, laughing, lead him back.*

MASHA. Come on, come on!

ANDREY. Leave me alone, please.

MASHA. You are funny! We used to call Colonel Vershinin the lovesick major, and he was never cross.

VERSHININ. Not a bit!

MASHA. I'd like to call you the lovesick fiddler!

IRINA. Or the lovesick professor.

OLGA. He's fallen in love. Our little Andrey has fallen in love. [*Clapping her hands.*] Bravo, bravo! Encore! Our little brother is in love!

CHEBUTYKIN [*walks up behind* ANDREY *and puts his arms round* ANDREY'S *waist*]. It's for love alone that nature has created us. [*Bursts out laughing, still holding his newspaper in his hand.*]

ANDREY. All right, that'll do, that'll do. [*Wipes his face.*] I didn't sleep a wink last night, and I'm not in top form now, as they say. I read till four o'clock and then went to bed. But it was no use. I kept thinking of one thing and another, and before I knew it, it was dawn and the sun was simply pouring into the bedroom. I'd like to translate a book from the English during the summer while I'm here.

VERSHININ. Do you read English?

ANDREY. Yes. Father, may he rest in peace, inflicted education upon us. This may sound silly and ridiculous, but I must confess all the same that since he died, I've been putting on weight. Indeed, in one year I've put on so much weight that it is as if my body had burst its bonds. But thanks to Father, my sisters and I know French, German, and English, and Irina knows Italian too. But at what a cost!

MASHA. To speak three languages in this town is an unnecessary luxury. Why, it isn't even a luxury, just a sort of useless appendage, like a sixth finger. We know a lot that is of no use to us.

VERSHININ. Good heavens! [*Laughs.*] You know a lot that is of no use to you. Well, I can't help thinking there's no town so dull and depressing that an intelligent, educated man would be superfluous in it. Let's assume that among the hundred thousand people in this town, who, I admit, are rather backward and coarse, there are only three people

like you. It stands to reason that you won't be able to convert the uneducated mass of people around you. In the course of your life you will have to make some concessions till, little by little, you'll get lost among these hundred thousand people. Life will stifle you, but nevertheless, you'll not be lost entirely. Neither will you be gone without having exerted some influence. Six people like you will perhaps emerge after you, then twelve, and so on, until the majority of people will have become like you. In two or three hundred years life on earth will become incredibly beautiful and marvelous. Man must have a life like that. If it isn't here yet, he must be able to anticipate it, to wait for it, to dream about it, and to prepare himself for it. To make sure of it, he must be able to see and know more than his father and grandfather did. [*Laughs.*] And you're complaining that you know a lot that's of no use to you.

MASHA [*takes off her hat*]. I'm staying to lunch.

IRINA [*with a sigh*]. Really, someone should have written it all down.

ANDREY *has left the room, unnoticed.*

TUSENBACH. You say that many years later life on earth will be beautiful, marvelous. That's true. But to take part in it now, even at a distance, one has to prepare for it, one has to work for it.

VERSHININ [*gets up*]. Yes, indeed. What a lot of flowers you have here! [*Looks round.*] And what a wonderful place you have here! I envy you. All my life I've lived in lodgings with two chairs, a sofa, and a stove which invariably smoked. What I missed most in my life were just such flowers. [*Rubs his hands.*] Oh, well, what's the use? . . .

TUSENBACH. Yes, we must work. I expect you must be thinking: That German has grown sentimental all of a sudden. But I assure you, I'm a Russian. I don't speak a word of German. My father was Greek Orthodox.

Pause.

VERSHININ [*walks up and down the stage*]. I often wonder what it would be like if we were to start our life all over again. Consciously, I mean. If our first life had been, as it were, only a rough copy and our second, a fair one. In that case, I believe, every one of us would first of all do his utmost not to repeat himself. At lest he would create a different environment for himself. He would, for instance, get himself a place like this, with flowers and full of light. I have a wife and two little girls.

My wife, I'm sorry to say, always complains of being poorly, and so on and so forth. Well, if I had to start my life all over again, I wouldn't get married. . . . No, certainly not.

Enter KULYGIN, *wearing his schoolmaster's uniform.*

KULYGIN [*walks up to* IRINA]. Congratulations, dear sister. Many happy returns. I wish you good health and everything a girl of your age ought to have. Let me, finally, present you with this book. [*Hands her a book.*] It's the history of our school for the last fifty years. I wrote it myself. Not a very important book, I admit. I wrote it in my spare time, having nothing better to do, but you should read it all the same. Good morning, ladies and gentlemen. [*To* VERSHININ.] Let me introduce myself: Kulygin, a master at the secondary school here, civil servant of the seventh rank. [*To* IRINA.] In this book you'll find a list of all the pupils who've completed their course of studies at our school during the last fifty years. *Feci, quod potui, faciant meliora potentes.* [*Kisses* MASHA.]

IRINA. But you gave me this book as a present last Easter!

KULYGIN [*laughs*]. Impossible! In that case, you'd better give it back to me, or, no, better give it to the Colonel. Please take it, Colonel. You may read it one day when you've nothing better to do.

VERSHININ. Thank you. [*Is about to leave.*] I'm very glad to have made your acquaintance.

OLGA. You're not going, are you? Please don't.

IRINA. You must stay and have lunch with us. Please!

OLGA. Please do.

VERSHININ [*bows*]. I seem to have dropped in on your birthday party. I'm sorry, I didn't know. I didn't offer you my congratulations.

He goes into the ballroom with OLGA.

KULYGIN. Today, ladies and gentlemen, is Sunday, a day of rest. Let us, therefore, rest. Let us make merry, each in accordance with his age and position in life. The carpets will have to be taken up for the summer and put away till the winter. Must sprinkle them first with Persian powder or naphthalene. The Romans were healthy because they knew how to work and how to rest. They had *mens sana in corpore sano*. Their life ran according to well-established forms. Our headmaster says the main thing in life is form. Anything that loses its form is finished. It's the same in our everyday life. [*Takes* MASHA *by the waist, laughing.*] Masha loves me. My wife loves me. The curtains, too, will have to be put away with the carpets. . . . Today I'm happy. I'm in excellent spirits. [*To* MASHA.] At four o'clock, my dear, we have to be at the headmaster's. An outing has been arranged for the teachers and their families.

MASHA. Sorry, I'm not going.

KULYGIN [*chagrined*]. My dear Masha, why not?

MASHA. We'll talk about it later. . . . [*Crossly.*] Oh, very well, I'll come. Only leave me alone, please. [*Walks away.*]

KULYGIN. Afterwards, we'll spend the evening at the headmaster's. Though in bad health, that man is doing his best to be sociable above all. A fine man, a man of irreproachable conduct. A most excellent man! After the staff meeting yesterday he said to me: "I'm tired, my dear fellow, I'm tired!" [*Looks at the clock, then at his watch.*] Your clock is seven minutes fast. Yes, he said: "I'm tired."

Someone is playing a violin offstage.

OLGA. Please, gentlemen, lunch is served. We're having a pie!

KULYGIN. My dear, dear Olga, yesterday I began work in the morning and I went on working till eleven o'clock at night. I felt tired, but now I feel happy. [*Goes into the ballroom to the table.*] Dear Olga!

CHEBUTYKIN [*puts the newspaper in his pocket and combs his beard*]. A pie! Excellent!

MASHA [*to* CHEBUTYKIN, *sternly*]. Mind, no drinking today. Do you hear? It's bad for you.

CHEBUTYKIN. Don't worry. That's all in the past. Haven't had a real drinking bout for two years. [*Impatiently.*] Good Lord, my dear woman, does it really matter so much?

MASHA. All the same, don't you dare to drink. Don't you dare! [*Crossly, but trying not to be overheard by her husband.*] Damnation, another boring evening at the headmaster's.

TUSENBACH. If I were you, I wouldn't go. Very simple.

CHEBUTYKIN. Don't go, my dear.

MASHA. Don't go, indeed! A damnable, unbearable life! [*Goes into the ballroom.*]

CHEBUTYKIN [*goes after her*[. Oh, well!

SOLYONY [*crossing into the ballroom*]. Cluck, cluck, cluck.

TUSENBACH. Chuck it, my dear sir, chuck it!

SOLYONY. Cluck, cluck, cluck . . .

KULYGIN [*gaily*]. Your health, Colonel. I'm a schoolmaster and quite at home here. I'm Masha's husband. She's a good woman, a very good woman.

VERSHININ. I'll have some of that dark brandy. [*Drinks.*] Your health! [*To* OLGA.] I feel so happy here.

Only IRINA *and* TUSENBACH *remain in the drawing room.*

IRINA. Masha's in a bad mood today. She got married when she was eighteen. At the time, her husband seemed the most intelligent man in the world to her. It's quite different now. He's the most good-natured but not the most intelligent of men.

OLGA [*impatiently*]. Andrey, are you coming?

ANDREY [*offstage*]. One moment. [*Comes in and goes to the table.*]

TUSENBACH. What are you thinking about?

IRINA. Oh, I don't know. I don't like that Solyony of yours. I'm afraid of him. He says such stupid things.

TUSENBACH. He's a strange fellow. I'm both sorry for him and annoyed by him. Mostly sorry, though. I think he's shy. When I'm alone with him, he's very intelligent and friendly, but in company he's coarse, a bully. Don't go in there yet, not before they've taken their places at the table. Stay with me a little longer. What are you thinking about? [*Pause.*] You're twenty, and I'm not yet thirty. Think of the years we still have ahead of us. A long succession of days, each one full of my love for you.

IRINA. Please don't talk to me about love.

TUSENBACH [*not listening*]. I've such a passionate yearning for life, for work, to strive for a better life. This yearning has, somehow, become mingled with my love for you, Irina. And as luck would have it, you are beautiful, and life also seems to be so beautiful to me. What are you thinking about?

IRINA. You say life is beautiful. Yes, but what if it only seems so? Our life, I mean the lives of us three sisters, has not been particularly beautiful so far. Life has stifled us like a weed. I'm sorry, I'm

crying. I mustn't. [*Quickly dries her eyes and smiles.*] We must work, work! We are so unhappy and we have so gloomy a view of life because we don't know the meaning of work. We're the children of people who despised work.

NATASHA *enters wearing a pink dress with a green belt.*

NATASHA. Good heavens, they've gone in to lunch already. . . . I'm late. . . . [*Throws a quick glance at herself in the mirror and tidies herself up.*] My hair's all right, I think. [*Catches sight of* IRINA.] Dear Irina, congratulations. [*Gives her a hearty and drawn-out kiss.*] You've got such a lot of visitors. . . . I feel quite shy. . . . Good morning, Baron.

OLGA [*enters the drawing room*]. Ah, here you are, Natasha. How are you, my dear? [*They kiss.*]

NATASHA. Congratulations. You've such a lot of people. I'm so shy.

OLGA. It's all right, they're all old friends. [*Lowering her voice, startled.*] My dear, you're wearing a green belt. That's not nice.

NATASHA. Is it unlucky?

OLGA. No, it simply doesn't suit you and—er—it looks a little out of place.

NATASHA [*in a tearful voice*]. Does it? It isn't really green, you know. It's not shiny. [*Follows* OLGA *into the ballroom.*]

They are all seated at the table now. The drawing room is empty.

KULYGIN. I wish you a good husband, Irina. It's time you got married.

CHEBUTYKIN. I wish you a nice fiancé too, Natasha.

KULYGIN. Natasha has one already, I believe.

MASHA [*strikes her plate with a fork*]. Let's have a glass of vodka! Oh, life is sweet! What the hell!

KULYGIN. You get Unsatisfactory for conduct.

VERSHININ. The brandy's excellent. What is it made of?

SOLYONY. Cockroaches!

IRINA [*tearfully*]. Ugh! How disgusting!

OLGA. We're having roast turkey for dinner tonight and an apple turnover for dessert. Thank goodness I'm at home all day today. At home this evening, too. Please, you must all come this evening.

VERSHININ. I'd like to come this evening if you don't mind.

IRINA. Please do.

NATASHA. They don't stand on ceremony here.

CHEBUTYKIN. It's for love alone that nature has created us. [Laughs.]

ANDREY [crossly]. Do stop it, please. Haven't you had enough?

FEDOTIK and RODE come in with a large basket of flowers.

FEDOTIK. We're late. They're having lunch.

RODÉ [in a loud voice and speaking with a burr]. Are they? Good Lord, yes, so they are!

FEDOTIK. One moment, please. [Takes a snapshot.] One! One moment. [Takes another snapshot.] Two! That's all!

They pick up the basket and go into the ballroom, where they get a noisy reception.

RODÉ [in a loud voice]. Congratulations! I wish you all the best. Gorgeous weather today. Simply marvelous! I spent the morning with some schoolboys. I'm a gym teacher, you see.

FEDOTIK. You can move now, Irina, if you want to. [Taking a snapshot.] You look lovely today. [Takes a humming top out of his pocket.] Here, by the way, is a top. It's got a marvelous hum.

IRINA. It's lovely!

MASHA. "For he on honey-dew hath fed, and drunk the milk of Paradise . . . and drunk the milk of Paradise." [Tearfully.] Why do I go on saying this? Can't get these lines out of my head.

KULYGIN. Thirteen at table!

RODE [in a loud voice]. Surely you're not superstitious, are you?

Laughter.

KULYGIN. When there are thirteen at table, it means that some of them are in love. It isn't you, Doctor, by any chance?

Laughter.

CHERBUTYKIN. I'm an old sinner, but why Natasha should look so embarrassed, I simply fail to understand.

Loud laughter; NATASHA runs out of the ballroom into the drawing room. ANDREY follows her.

ANDREY. Please don't pay any attention to them. Don't go, I beg you.

NATASHA. I feel so ashamed. I don't know what I've done wrong, and they're just laughing at me. I know it wasn't nice to leave the table like that, but I couldn't help it. [Covers her face with her hands.]

ANDREY. Oh, my dear, I beg you, I implore you, don't be upset. I assure you, they're only joking. They don't mean to be unkind. My dear, my dear, my beautiful one! They're all nice, kindly people, and they're fond of us both. Come over to the window. They won't be able to see us there. [Looks round.]

NATASHA. I'm so unaccustomed to being with people!

ANDREY. Oh, you're so young, so beautifully, so splendidly young. My dear, my darling, don't be upset. Do believe me. Believe me. I'm so happy, my heart is so full of love, of ecstasy. . . . No, they can't see us from here, they can't! Why, why did I fall in love with you? When did I fall in love with you? Oh, I don't understand anything. My darling, my beautiful darling, my pure one, be my wife! I love you, I love you as I've never loved anyone before.

A kiss.

TWO ARMY OFFICERS come in, and seeing the kissing couple, stop dead in amazement.

Curtain.

ACT TWO

The scene is the same as in Act One.

It is eight o'clock in the evening. Offstage, in the street, the sound of an accordion can be heard faintly. The stage is dark. Enter NATASHA in a dressing gown, carrying a candle; she walks across the stage and stops at the door leading to ANDREY'S room.

NATASHA. What are you doing, Andrey dear? Reading? Never mind, I just . . . [Goes to another door, opens it, looks into the room, and shuts it again.] Must make sure there's no light left burning.

ANDREY [comes in with a book in his hand]. What's the matter, Natasha?

NATASHA. I'm just making sure no one's left a light burning. It's Shrovetide—carnival time. The servants are all excited, and you have to make sure that nothing goes wrong. About twelve o'clock last night I walked through the dining room and there was a candle burning on the table. I just couldn't find out who lit it. [*Puts the candle down.*] What's the time?

ANDREY [*glancing at the clock*]. A quarter past eight.

NATASHA. Olga and Irina are out. Not back yet. Still hard at work, poor darlings. Olga at her staff meeting and Irina at the telegraph office. [*Sighs.*] Only this morning I said to your sister: "You must take more care of yourself, Irina darling." But she won't listen to me. A quarter past eight, did you say? I'm afraid our Bobby isn't at all well. Why is he so cold? Yesterday he had a temperature. But today he's quite cold. I'm so worried.

ANDREY. Don't worry, Natasha. The boy's well enough.

NATASHA. All the same I think we ought to be more careful about his diet. I'm worried. I'm told, dear, that after nine o'clock some carnival dancers are expected to come. I wish they weren't coming. Andrey dear.

ANDREY. Well, I don't know. They've been invited, you see.

NATASHA. This morning our little darling woke up, looked at me, and suddenly smiled. He must have recognized me. "Good morning, Bobby," I said. "Good morning, darling." He laughed. Little children understand, oh, they understand everything. You don't mind, Andrey dear, if I tell the servants not to let the dancers in, do you?

ANDREY [*hesitatingly*]. But you see, it depends on my sisters. It's their house.

NATASHA. Yes, it's their house, too, I suppose. I'll tell them. They're so kind. [*Going.*] I've ordered sour milk for supper. The doctor says you ought to eat nothing but sour milk. Otherwise you won't lose weight. [*Stops.*] Bobby is so cold. I'm afraid his room is too cold. We'll have to find him another room. At least till the warm weather. Now, Irina's room is just right for a baby. It's dry and it gets the sun all day long. I must tell her. She could share Olga's room for the time being. She isn't at home during the day, anyway. She only sleeps here. [*Pause.*] Darling, why don't you say anything?

ANDREY. Oh, I was thinking. . . . There's nothing really I can say, is there?

NATASHA. Now, what is it I wanted to tell you? Oh, yes. Ferapont from the District Council is here. He wants to see you about something.

ANDREY [*yawns*]. Tell him to come in. [NATASHA *goes out.* ANDREY, *bending over the candle she has left behind, is reading his book. Enter* FERAPONT. *He wears a shabby old overcoat with a turned-up collar. His ears are muffled.*] Hello, old man. What have you got to tell me?

FERAPONT. The chairman, sir, sent you this register and a document. Here. [*Hands him the book and the document.*]

ANDREY. Thanks. That's all right. But why are you so late? It's past eight o'clock.

FERAPONT. Beg pardon, sir?

ANDREY [*louder*]. I said you've come too late. It's after eight.

FERAPONT. That's right, sir. When I came here, it was still daylight, but they wouldn't let me in. "The master's busy," they said. Well, I thought to myself, if he's busy, he's busy. I'm in no hurry. [*Thinking that* ANDREY *has asked him about something.*] Beg pardon, sir?

ANDREY. Nothing. [*Turning over the pages of the book.*] Tomorrow's Friday. There's no Council meeting, but I'll go to the office just the same. Do some work. It's boring at home. [*Pause.*] My dear old fellow, how strangely everything changes, how life deceives us! Today I picked up this book (I was bored, you see, had nothing else to do), my old university lectures, and I couldn't help laughing. Good Lord, I am the secretary of the District Council, the Council of which Protopopov is chairman. I am a secretary, and the most I can hope for is to become a member of the Council. A member of a District Council! I, who used to dream every night that I was a professor of Moscow University, a famous scholar of whom the whole of Russia was proud.

FERAPONT. Afraid I don't know, sir. Don't hear very well.

ANDREY. If you could hear properly, I might not be talking to you like this. I must talk to someone. My wife does not understand me, and for some reason I'm afraid of my sisters. I'm afraid they will ridicule me, make me feel ashamed of myself. . . . I don't drink and I don't like going to pubs, but, my dear fellow, you can't imagine how I'd love to spend some time in Moscow at Testov's or at The Great Moscow Restaurant.

FERAPONT. Did you say Moscow, sir? A contractor was telling us at the office the other day about some businessmen who were eating pancakes in Moscow. One of them who ate forty pancakes apparently died. Was it forty or fifty? Don't remember.

ANDREY. You sit in a big dining room of a restaurant in Moscow—you know no one, no one knows you, but you don't feel you're a stranger. Here, you know everyone and everyone knows you, but you're a stranger, a stranger. . . . A stranger and all alone.

FERAPONT. Beg pardon, sir? [*Pause.*] The same contractor said—he may be lying for all I know—that a rope is stretched right across the whole of Moscow.

ANDREY. Whatever for?

FERAPONT. Don't know, sir. The contractor said so.

ANDREY. Nonsense! [*Reads his book.*] Have you ever been to Moscow?

FERAPONT [*after a pause*]. No, sir. It wasn't God's will that I should go there, I suppose. [*Pause.*] Can I go now, sir?

ANDREY. You can go. Good-bye. [FERAPONT *goes out.*] Good-bye. [*Reads.*] Come and take the papers tomorrow morning. You can go now. [*Pause.*] He's gone. [*A bell rings.*] Yes, that's how it is. . . . [*Stretches and goes back to his room unhurriedly.*]

Offstage the nurse is heard singing while rocking the baby to sleep. Enter MASHA *and* VERSHININ. *While they talk, a maid lights a lamp and candles.*

MASHA. I don't know. [*Pause.*] I don't know. Habit's very important, of course. For instance, after Father died, it took us a long time to get accustomed to the idea that we no longer had any orderlies. But quite apart from habit, it seems to me that what I said was only fair. It may be different somewhere else, but in our town the military are the most well-bred and well-educated people.

VERSHININ. I'm thirsty. I'd love some tea.

MASHA [*glancing at the clock*]. They'll bring it in presently. I was married off when I was eighteen. I was afraid of my husband because he was a schoolmaster and I had only just left school. He seemed to me frightfully learned, clever, and distinguished. Now, I'm sorry to say, it's quite different.

VERSHININ. Yes, I see.

MASHA. But I'm not discussing my husband. I've got used to him. You see, there are so many coarse, ill-bred, uneducated people among the civilians. Coarseness upsets and offends me. I suffer physically in the presence of a man who is not sufficiently well-bred, not sufficiently delicate or courteous. I suffer agonies in the company of schoolmasters, my husband's colleagues.

VERSHININ. Well, yes, but I should have thought that in a town like this there was nothing to choose between a civilian and an army officer. It really makes no difference. Listen to any educated person here, civilian or army officer, and he'll tell you that he's sick and tired of his wife or his family or his estate or his horses. A Russian is particularly susceptible to high thinking, but tell me, why does he aim so low in life? Why?

MASHA. Why?

VERSHININ. Why is he sick and tired of his children, sick and tired of his wife, and why are his wife and children sick and tired of him?

MASHA. You're not in a very good mood today, are you?

VERSHININ. Perhaps not. I haven't had any lunch today. I haven't had anything to eat since morning. One of my daughters is not very well, and when my little girls are not well, I'm worried. You see, I can't help thinking that it's my fault they have such a mother. Oh, if you'd seen her today—what a nonentity! We started quarreling at seven o'clock and at nine I walked out, slamming the door behind me. [*Pause.*] I never talk about it to anyone, and curiously enough, it's to you alone that I complain. [*Kisses her hand.*] Don't be angry with me. I've no one but you. No one.

MASHA. Listen to that noise in the chimney! Before Father died the wind howled in the chimney just like that. Exactly like that.

VERSHININ. You're not superstitious, are you?

MASHA. Yes, I am.

VERSHININ. That's strange. [*Kisses her hand.*] You're a magnificent, wonderful woman. Magnificent, wonderful! It's dark here, but I can see your eyes gleaming.

MASHA [*sits down on another chair*]. There's more light here.

VERSHININ. I love you, I love you, I love you! I love your eyes, your movements. I dream about them. Magnificent, wonderful woman!

MASHA [*laughing softly*]. When you talk to me like that, I somehow cannot help laughing, though I'm terrified. Don't say it again, I beg you. [*In an undertone.*] Yes, yes, do go on. [*Covers her face with her hands.*] I don't mind. Someone's coming. Talk about something else.

IRINA *and* TUSENBACH *come in through the ballroom.*

TUSENBACH. I have a triple-barreled name: Baron Tusenbach-Krone-Altschauer, but I'm a Russian, a Greek Orthodox like you. There's little of the German left in me, except perhaps patience and the obstimacy with which I'm boring you. I see you home every night.

IRINA. I'm so tired!

TUSENBACH. And I'll go on coming to the telegraph office and seeing you home every day for ten or twenty years if necessary, until you drive me away. [*Catching sight of* MASHA *and* VERSHININ, *joyfully.*] Is it you? Good evening.

IRINA. At home at last. [*To* MASHA.] A woman came to the telegraph office an hour or so ago. She wanted to send a telegram to her brother in Saratov to tell him that her son had died today, but she just couldn't remember the address. So I sent on the telegram without an address. Simply to Saratov. She was crying. I was rude to her. I don't know why. "I'm sorry," I said, "I'm in a hurry." It was so stupid. We are having the carnival dancers in today, aren't we?

MASHA. Yes.

IRINA [*sits down in an armchair*]. Must rest. Awfully tired.

TUSENBACH [*with a smile*]. Every time you come back from the office, you look so young, so unhappy.

Pause.

IRINA. I'm tired. I'm afraid I don't like the telegraph office. Don't like it at all.

MASHA. You've grown thinner. [*Whistles a tune.*] And you look younger. You look like a boy.

TUSENBACH. That's because of the way she does her hair.

IRINA. I'll have to find another job. This one doesn't suit me. It isn't what I was looking for, what I was dreaming of. Work without poetry, without thought. [*A knock on the floor from below.*] The Doctor's knocking. [*To* TUSENBACH.] Please be an angel and answer him. I can't. I'm tired. [TUSENBACH *knocks on the floor.*] He'll be here in a moment. We must do something. Yesterday the Doctor and Andrey went to the club and lost at cards again. Apparently, Andrey lost two hundred rubles.

MASHA [*with indifference*]. It's a little late to do anything about it.

IRINA. Two weeks ago he lost; in December he lost. I wish he'd hurry up and lose everything he's got. Perhaps we'd leave for Moscow then. Dear Lord, every night I dream of Moscow. I'm going quite off my head. [*Laughs.*] We shall be going there in June, but before June there's still—February, March, April, May—nearly half a year!

MASHA. We must make sure Natasha doesn't find out about his losses.

IRINA. I don't think she cares.

CHEBUTYKIN, *who has only just got out of bed— he had a nap after dinner—enters the ballroom combing his beard. He sits down at the table and takes a newspaper out of his pocket.*

MASHA. Just look at him! Has he paid his rent?

IRINA [*laughs*]. Good Lord, no. Not a penny for the last eight months. Forgotten all about it, I daresay.

MASHA [*laughs*]. How importantly he sits!

They all laugh; pause.

IRINA. Why so silent, Colonel?

VERSHININ. Don't know. I'm dying for a cup of tea. Half a life for a cup of tea! Haven't had a bite since morning.

CHEBUTYKIN. Irina, my dear.

IRINA. What is it?

CHEBUTYKIN. Please come here. *Venez ici.* [IRINA *goes over and sits at the table.*] You must help me.

IRINA *lays out the cards for a game of patience.*

VERSHININ. Well, if we can't have any tea, let's at least have a talk.

TUSENBACH. Let's. What about?

VERSHININ. What about? Let's just—er—imagine what life will be like after we're gone—er—say, in two or three hundred years.

TUSENBACH. Well, I suppose after us, people will fly about in balloons, wear a different cut of coat, perhaps discover and develop a sixth sense, but life will still remain the same as ever: a hard life, a life full of all sorts of mysteries and . . . a happy life. A thousand years hence, man will still be sighing: "Oh, life is hard!" At the same time he'll be just as afraid of death, just as unwilling to die as he is now.

VERSHININ. [*thinking it over*]. Now, how shall I put it? I can't help thinking that everything on earth must change little by little. Indeed it is already changing before our very eyes. In two hundred, three hundred, or even a thousand years—the actual time doesn't matter—a new and happy life will begin. We shan't take part in it, of course, but we're living for it now . . . working and . . . well . . . suffering for it, creating it. . . . This alone is the goal of our existence and, if you like, our happiness.

MASHA *laughs quietly.*

TUSENBACH. What's the matter?

MASHA. Don't know. I've been laughing all day today. Ever since morning.

VERSHININ. I went to the same school as you. I did not go to the Military Academy. I read a lot, but I don't know what books to choose. I shouldn't be at all surprised if I read all the wrong books. Yet the longer I live, the more I want to know. My hair's turning gray, I'm almost an old man, but I know little—oh, how little! Nevertheless, I think I know what matters most now. I'm certain of that. What I'd most like to prove to you is that there is no such thing as happiness, that there must not be, and that it will not be for us. All we must do is work, work, and work. Happiness is for our distant descendants. [*Pause.*] If not for me, then at least for the descendants of my descendants.

FEDOTIK *and* RODE *come into the ballroom; they sit down and sing softly, strumming a guitar.*

TUSENBACH. According to you, one oughtn't even to dream of happiness. But what if I am happy!

VERSHININ. You're not.

TUSENBACH. [*flinging up his hands and laughing*]. I'm afraid we don't understand one another. How am I to convince you? [MASHA *laughs quietly. He points a finger at her.*] Laugh! [*To* VERSHININ.] Life will be the same, not only in two or three hundred years, but in a million years. It never changes, it remains constant. It follows its own laws regardless of us. At least those laws will always remain a mystery to you. Migrant birds, cranes for instance, fly and fly, and whatever thoughts—great or little—might be drifting through their heads, they will go on flying without knowing where or why. They'll fly and go on flying, however many philosophers may be born among them. Indeed, let them philosophize as much as they like so long as they go on flying.

MASHA. But there must be some meaning, mustn't there?

TUSENBACH. A meaning . . . Look, it's snowing. What meaning is there in that?

Pause.

MASHA. It seems to me that a man must be either religious or seeking some religion. Otherwise, his life is empty, empty. To live and not to know why cranes fly, why children are born, why there are stars in the sky . . . You must either know what you live for or else nothing matters any more. It's all meaningless nonsense.

Pause.

VERSHININ. All the same, it is a pity that I'm no longer young.

MASHA. Gogol says: "It's a boring world, my friends."

TUSENBACH. And I say: "It's difficult to agree with you, my friends." Let's drop the subject.

CHEBUTYKIN [*reading his paper*]. Balzac was married in Berdichev. [IRINA *hums softly.*] In a hole like Berdichev! I think I'll make a note of that. [*Writes down in his notebook.*] Balzac was married in Berdichev. [*Reads his paper.*]

IRINA [*laying out patience, reflectively*]. Balzac was married in Berdichev.

TUSENBACH. The die is cast. I've sent in my resignation. Did you know that, Masha?

MASHA. Yes, I did. I must say, I can't see anything good about it. I don't like civilians.

TUSENBACH. Makes no difference. [*Gets up.*] I'm not handsome—what sort of a soldier am I? Well, anyway, it makes no difference, I'll work. . . . Spend at least one day of my life working so hard that when I come home in the evening, I'll fall on my bed dead tired and go to sleep at once. [*Going into the ballroom.*] I expect workers sleep soundly.

FEDOTIK [*to* IRINA]. I've just bought some colored pencils for you at Pyzhikov's in the Moscow Road. And this penknife.

IRINA. You still go on treating me like a child. You forget I'm a grown-up woman. [*Accepts pencils and penknife joyfully.*] They're lovely!

FEDOTIK. I bought a knife for myself. Have a look: one blade, another blade, a third for scooping out your ears, a fourth for cleaning your nails—

RODÉ [*loudly*]. Doctor, how old are you?

CHEBUTYKIN. Me? Thirty-two.

Laughter.

FEDOTIK. Let me show you another game of patience. [*Lays out the cards.*]

A samovar is put on the table. ANFISA *is busy at the samovar. A little later* NATASHA *comes in and also busies herself at the table. Enter* SOLYONY, *who, after greeting everybody, sits down at the table.*

VERSHININ. What a wind, though!

MASHA. Yes. I'm tired of winter. I've already forgotten what summer's like.

IRINA. I can see it's working out. We shall be in Moscow.

FEDOTIK. It's not working out. See! The eight has to cover the two of spades. [*Laughs.*] Which means, you won't be in Moscow.

CHEBUTYKIN [*reads his paper*]. Tsitsihar. Smallpox is raging here.

ANFISA [*going up to* MASHA]. Masha, tea, darling. [*To* VERSHININ.] Please, sir. I'm sorry I've forgotten your name.

MASHA. Bring it here, Nanny. I'm not going over there.

IRINA. Nanny!

ANFISA. Coming, dear.

NATASHA [*to* SOLYONY]. Little babies understand very well. "Good morning, Bobby," I said. "Good morning, darling!" He gave me a knowing look. You think it's the mother in me speaking, don't you? It isn't. Believe me, it isn't! It's quite an extraordinary child.

SOLYONY. If it was my child, I'd roast him in a frying pan and eat him. [*Goes into the drawing room with his glass of tea and sits down in a corner.*]

NATASHA [*covering her face with her hands*]. What a coarse, ill-bred fellow!

MASHA. Anyone who doesn't notice whether it's summer or winter now is a happy man. I can't help thinking that if I were in Moscow, I'd be indifferent to the weather.

VERSHININ. The other day I read the diary of a French Cabinet Minister. He wrote it in prison. He'd been sentenced for the Panama affair. With what rapturous delight does he mention the birds he sees through the prison window, the birds he never noticed before when he was a Minister. Of course, now that he's been released, he doesn't notice the birds any more. Neither will you notice Moscow when living there. Happiness doesn't exist. It cannot exist! We merely desire it.

TUSENBACH [*takes a chocolate box from the table*]. Where are the chocolates?

IRINA. Solyony's eaten them.

TUSENBACH. All of them?

ANFISA. [*serving tea*]. Here's a letter for you, sir.

VERSHININ. For me? [*Takes the letter.*] From my daughter. [*Reads.*] Yes, of course. . . . Excuse me, Masha, I'll slip out quietly. I won't have any tea. [*Gets up, excitedly.*] Always the same thing.

MASHA. What is it? It's not a secret, is it?

VERSHININ [*in a low voice*]. My wife's taken poison again. I must go. I'll go out unobserved. Terribly unpleasant, all this. [*Kisses* MASHA's *hand.*] My dear one, you're so good, so sweet. . . . I'll go this way . . . quietly. [*Goes out.*]

ANFISA. Where is he off to? I've just given him tea. Well, I must say . . .

MASHA [*angrily*]. Leave me alone! Pestering me! Not a moment's peace! [*Goes to the table with her cup of tea.*] I'm tired of you, old woman!

ANFISA. Why are you so cross, my dear?

ANDREY [*offstage*]. Anfisa!

ANFISA [*mimicking*]. Anfisa! Sitting there . . . [*Goes out.*]

MASHA [*in the ballroom, crossly*]. Let me sit down, will you? [*Mixing up the cards on the table.*] Sprawling all over the place with your cards. Why don't you drink your tea?

IRINA. You've got a foul temper, Masha.

MASHA. Don't talk to me if I've a foul temper. Leave me alone!

CHEBUTYKIN [*laughing*]. Leave her alone, leave her alone—

MASHA. You're sixty, but you're always talking some damned nonsense as if you were a silly little boy.

NATASHA [*sighs*]. My dear Masha, why must you use such language? I assure you that with your attractive appearance you'd be simply bewitching in any refined society if it were not for your language. *Je vous prie, pardonnez-moi, Marie, mais vous avez des manieres un peu grossieres.*

TUSENBACH [*restraining his laughter*]. Please . . . please . . . pass me. . . . There's some brandy, I think.

NATASHA. *Il parait que mon Bobby deja ne dort pas*—he's awake. I'm afraid he isn't well today. I'd better go and see. Excuse me. [*Goes out.*]

IRINA. And where has the Colonel gone?

MASHA. Home. He's having some trouble with his wife again.

TUSENBACH. [*goes up to* SONYONY *with a decanter of brandy*]. You always sit alone thinking, goodness knows what about. Come, let's make it up. Let's have some brandy. [*They drink.*] I expect I'll have to play the piano all night—all sorts of rubbish. . . . Oh, well!

SOLYONY. Why make it up? We haven't quarreled, have we?

TUSENBACH. You always make me feel as if something's happened between us. You're a strange character, I must say.

SOLYONY [*declaiming*]. I am strange. Who isn't? Do not be angry, Aleko!

TUSENBACH. What's Aleko got to do with it?

Pause.

SOLYONY. When I'm alone with someone, I'm all right. I'm just like the rest. But in company I feel depressed, I'm shy and . . . and I talk a lot of nonsense. But all the same I'm a damn sight better and more honest than a lot of other people. And I can prove it.

TUSENBACH. I'm often angry with you, you continually pick on me when we're in company, but I like you for all that. I don't know why. Anyway, I'm going to get drunk tonight. Let's have another drink!

SOLYONY. Let's. [*They drink.*] I've never had anything against you, Baron. But my character is like Lermontov's. [*In a low voice.*] I even look a little like Lermontov. So I'm told. [*Takes a perfume bottle from his pocket and sprinkles his hands.*]

TUSENBACH. I've sent in my resignation. I've had enough. I've been thinking about it for five years, and I've made up my mind at last. I shall work.

SOLYONY [*declaiming*]. Do not be angry, Aleko . . . . Forget, forget your dreams. . . .

While they are talking, ANDREY *enters quietly with a book and sits down by the candle.*

TUSENBACH. I shall work.

CHEBUTYKIN [*going into the drawing room with* IRINA]. And the food was genuinely Caucasian: onion soup and for a roast—mutton, chekhartma.

SOLYONY. Cheremsha isn't meat at all; it's a plant, something like our onion.

CHEBUTYKIN. No, sir. No, my angel. Chekhartma isn't an onion; it's roast mutton.

SOLYONY. And I'm telling you cheremsha is an onion.

CHEBUTYKIN. And I'm telling you chekhartma is mutton.

SOLYONY. And I'm telling you cheremsha is an onion.

CHEBUTYKIN. What's the use of arguing with you? You've never been to the Caucasus, and you've never eaten chekhartma.

SOLYONY. Haven't eaten it because I can't stand it. Cheremsha reeks like garlic.

ANDREY [*imploringly*]. Enough, gentlemen. Please!

TUSENBACH. When will the carnival dancers come along?

IRINA. They promised to be here by nine, which means any moment now.

TUSENBACH [*embraces* ANDREY]. "Oh, my bright, my beautiful hallway, my beautiful new hall- way . . ."*

ANDREY [*dances and sings*]. "My maple-wood hall . . ."

CHEBUTYKIN [*dances*]. "My latticed hall . . ."

Laughter.

---

*A traditional Russian folk song and dance [D.M.].

309

TUSENBACH [kisses ANDREY]. Hang it all, let's drink! Andrey, my dear fellow, let's drink to our friendship. I'll come to Moscow with you, to the university.

SOLYONY. Which one? There are two universities in Moscow.

ANDREY. There's only one university in Moscow.

SOLYONY. And I tell you there are two.

ANDREY. Three, if you like. So much the better.

SOLYONY. There are two universities in Moscow. [Murmurs of protest and booing.] There are two universities in Moscow: the old and the new. But if you don't want to listen to me, if my words annoy you, I'll shut up. I can even go to another room. [Goes out through one of the doors.]

TUSENBACH. Bravo, bravo! [Laughs.] Let's start, ladies and gentlemen. I'm sitting down at the piano. Funny fellow, that Solyony. [Sits down at the piano and plays a waltz.]

MASHA [dances by herself]. The Baron's drunk, the Baron's drunk, the Baron's drunk.

Enter NATASHA.

NATASHA [to CHEBUTYKIN]. Doctor . . . [Speaks to CHEBUTYKIN, then goes out quietly.]

CHEBUTYKIN *touches* TUSENBACH *on the shoulder and whispers something to him.*

IRINA. What is it?

CHEBUTYKIN. Time we were going. Good-bye.

TUSENBACH. Good night. It's time we were off.

IRINA. Wait a minute. What about the carnival dancers?

ANDREY [greatly embarrassed]. There won't be any. You see, my dear, Natasha says that Bobby isn't very well, and that's why. . . . Anyway, I don't know. . . . I don't care a damn. . . .

IRINA [shrugging]. Bobby isn't well!

MASHA. Oh, all right! If they're kicking us out, we'd better go. [To IRINA.] It isn't Bobby who's ill, it's she herself. . . . Here! [Taps her forehead.] The stupid, selfish, trivial creature!

ANDREY *goes to his room through the right-hand door.* CHEBUTYKIN *follows him. In the ballroom they are saying good-bye.*

FEDOTIK. What a shame! I counted on spending the evening here, but of course, if the baby's ill . . . I'll bring him some toys tomorrow.

RODE [in a loud voice]. I had a good sleep after lunch because I thought I was going to dance all night. Why, it's only nine o'clock!

MASHA. Let's go outside. We can talk there. We'll decide what to do.

Voices saying "Good-bye" and "Good night" can be heard. TUSENBACH *is heard laughing gaily. All go out.* ANFISA *and a maid clear the table, put out the lights. The nurse is heard singing a lullaby.* ANDREY, *wearing an overcoat and a hat, and* CHEBUTYKIN *enter quietly.*

CHEBUTYKIN. I never managed to get married because my life flashed by like a streak of lightning. Also because I was madly in love with your mother, a married woman.

ANDREY. One shouldn't marry. One shouldn't because it's so boring.

CHEBUTYKIN. That may be so, but what about the loneliness? Say what you like, but loneliness, my dear fellow, is a terrible thing. Although, as a matter of fact . . . I mean, it makes absolutely no difference, does it?

ANDREY. Let's get out quickly.

CHEBUTYKIN. What's the hurry? Plenty of time.

ANDREY. I'm afraid my wife may stop me.

CHEBUTYKIN. Oh!

ANDREY. I won't gamble today. I'll just sit and watch. Don't feel too well. . . . What am I to do for my asthma, Doctor?

CHEBUTYKIN. Why ask me? I can't remember, dear boy. Don't know.

ANDREY. Let's go through the kitchen.

They go out. The doorbell rings twice; voices and laughter are heard.

IRINA [comes in]. What's that?

ANFISA [in a whisper]. The mummers!

The doorbell rings.

IRINA. Tell them, Nanny, there's no one at home. Say we're sorry.

ANFISA *goes out.* IRINA *paces the room pensively; she's upset. Enter* SOLYONY.

SOLYONY [bewildered]. No one here. Where's everybody?

IRINA. Gone home.

SOLYONY. Strange. Are you alone here?

IRINA. Yes. [*Pause.*] Good-bye.

SOLYONY. I'm sorry I behaved rather tactlessly a short while ago . . . forgot myself. But you're not like the rest. You're high-minded and pure. You see the truth. . . . You alone can understand me. I love you; I love you deeply, passionately—

IRINA. Good-bye. Please go away.

SOLYONY. I can't live without you. [*Going after her.*] Oh, my joy! [*Through tears.*] Oh, my happiness! Lovely, exquisite, wonderful eyes, eyes unlike those of any other woman I've ever known.

IRINA [*coldly*]. Don't, please.

SOLYONY. It's the first time I've spoken to you of my love, and I feel as though I'm not on earth but on another planet. [*Rubs his forehead.*] Oh, never mind. I can't force you to love me, of course. But I shall not put up with any successful rivals. I shan't. I swear to you by all that I hold sacred that I shall kill my rival. Oh, my wonderful one!

NATASHA *enters carrying a candle.*

NATASHA [*glances into one room, then into another, and passes the door leading into her husband's room*]. Andrey's there. Let him read. [*To* SOLONY.] I'm sorry. I didn't know you were here. Excuse my dressing gown.

SOLYONY. Don't mind me. Good-bye. [*Goes out.*]

NATASHA. You look tired, darling. Oh, you poor child! [*Kisses* IRINA.] You ought to go to bed earlier.

IRINA. Is Bobby asleep?

NATASHA. Yes, he is. But he's very restless. By the way, my dear, I've been wanting to say something to you, but either you've been out or I've been too busy. I can't help thinking that the nursery is too cold and damp for Bobby. Your room is just what a baby wants. Darling, don't you think you could move into Olga's room? Just for a short time.

IRINA [*not understanding*]. Where?

The harness bells of a troika can be heard as it drives up to the house.

NATASHA. You and Olga will share one room, for the time being, I mean, and Bobby will have your room. He's such a darling! Today I said to him: "Bobby, you're mine! Mine!" And he looked at me with his sweet little eyes. [*The doorbell rings.*] Must be Olga. She is late! [*The maid goes up to* NATASHA *and whispers in her ear.*] Protopopov? What a funny man! Protopopov asks me to go for a drive with him in his troika. [*Laughs.*] These men are strange, aren't they? [*The doorbell rings.*] Somebody's come. I suppose I could go for a drive for a quarter of an hour. [*To the maid.*] Tell him I shan't be long. [*The doorbell rings.*] The doorbell again. That must be Olga. [*Goes out.*]

The maid runs off; IRINA *sits lost in thought; enter* KULYGIN *and* OLGA, *followed by* VERSHININ.

KULYGIN. How do you like that? I was told they'd be having a party.

VERSHININ. I must be off. I left not so long ago, half an hour ago to be precise, and they were expecting carnival dancers.

IRINA. They've all gone.

KULYGIN. Masha gone too? What's Protopopov waiting for outside in a troika? Who is he waiting for?

IRINA. Don't ask me. I'm tired.

KULYGIN. Oh, you naughty child!

OLGA. The staff meeting has only just ended. I'm dead tired. Our headmistress is ill and I'm deputizing for her. Oh, my head! My head's aching! [*Sits down.*] Andrey lost two hundred rubles at cards yesterday. The whole town is talking about it.

KULYGIN. Yes, our staff meeting has made me tired too. [*Sits down.*]

VERSHININ. My wife's taken it into her head to frighten me. She nearly poisoned herself. Everything's all right, I'm glad to say. I'm no longer worried, thank goodness. I suppose we must go, mustn't we? Well, in that case, I wish you all the best. What about coming with me, Kulygin? I can't stay at home, I simply can't. Come on!

KULYGIN. Too tired. Sorry I can't go with you. [*Get's up.*] Too tired. Has my wife gone home?

IRINA. I suppose so.

KULYGIN [*kisses* IRINA's *hand*]. Good-bye. I shall take it easy all day tomorrow and the day after tomorrow. All the best. [*Going.*] I'd love a cup of tea. Counted on spending the evening in pleasant company and—O, *fallacem hominum spem!* The accusative case in exclamations!

VERSHININ. Oh, well, I'll be going somewhere by myself.

Goes out with KULYGIN, *whistling.*

OLGA. My head, my head aches. . . . Andrey lost . . . The whole town's talking. I'll go and lie down. [*Going.*] Tomorrow I'm free. Goodness, that really is lovely! Free tomorrow, free the day after tomorrow. My head aches . . . my head . . . [*Goes out.*]

IRINA [*alone*]. All gone. No one's left.

The sound of an accordian from the street; the nurse sings a lullaby.

NATASHA [*walks across the ballroom in a fur coat, followed by the maid*]. I'll be back in half an hour. Just going out for a little drive. [*Goes out.*]

IRINA [*alone, longingly*]. To Moscow! To Moscow! To Moscow!

Curtain.

ACT THREE

OLGA's *and* IRINA's *room. Screened-off beds on the right and the left. It is past two o'clock in the morning. Offstage a fire alarm bell is ringing on account of a fire that started a long time before. It is clear that no one in the house has yet gone to bed.* MASHA *is lying on a sofa, dressed, as usual, in black.* OLGA *and* ANFISA *come in.*

ANFISA. They're downstairs, sitting under the staircase. "Please," I says to them, "come upstairs. You can't carry on like that." But they go on crying. "We don't know where Daddy is," they says. "He's probably been burnt in the fire." The things they think of! In the yard, too, there are some people . . . also in their night clothes.

OLGA [*takes dresses out of the wardrobe*]. Take this gray one . . . this one too . . . also this blouse. And this frock, too, Nanny. Goodness me, how awful! The entire Kirsanov Lane seems to have burned down. . . . Take this too . . . and this. [*Throws clothes into* ANFISA's *hands.*] The poor Vershinins! They were terrified. Their house nearly burned down. Let them spend the night here. They mustn't be allowed to go home. Poor old Fedotik lost everything in the fire. Nothing left.

ANFISA. I think I'd better call Ferapont, dear. I can't carry it all.

OLGA [*rings*]. They never answer. [*Calls through the door.*] Anyone there? Come here, please. [*Through the open door a window, red with the glow of the fire, can be seen; a fire engine can be heard passing the house.*] Oh, the horror of it! And what a mess it is! [*Enter* FERAPONT.] Take all this downstairs. You'll find the Kolotilin girls under the staircase. Give it to them. And this . . .

FERAPONT. Yes'm. In 1812 Moscow was also burnt down. Dear, oh dear, weren't the French surprised!

OLGA. Go on. Hurry up.

FERAPONT. Yes'm. [*Goes out.*]

OLGA. Nanny dear, give everything away. We don't want anything. Give it all away. I'm dead tired. Can hardly stand on my feet. We mustn't let the Vershinins go back home. The girls can sleep in the drawing room, and the Colonel, downstairs with the Baron. Fedotik can also stay with the Baron or else in the ballroom. The Doctor would get drunk, dead drunk, just now, and we can't let anyone go into his room. Vershinin's wife, too, in the drawing room.

ANFISA [*in a tired voice*]. Don't turn me out of the house, Olga dear. Please don't turn me out.

OLGA. Don't talk nonsense, Nanny. No one is turning you out.

ANFISA [*puts her head on* OLGA's *bosom*]. My darling child, my precious, you know I work as hard as I can. But as soon as I grows too weak for work, they're all sure to say: Out with her! Where could I go? I'm in my eighties. Nearly eighty-two.

OLGA. You'd better sit down, Nanny. You're tired, poor dear. [*Makes her sit down.*] Rest a while, dear. You're so pale.

NATASHA *enters.*

NATASHA. They're saying we ought to form a committee as soon as possible to raise funds for the people made homeless by the fire. Well, why not? It's an excellent idea. Anyway, it's the duty of the rich to help the poor. Bobby and little Sophie are peacefully asleep. The little darlings are asleep as if nothing had happened. There are people everywhere; the house is full of them, whichever way you turn. There's a flu epidemic in town. I'm afraid the children might catch it.

OLGA [*not listening to her*]. We can't see the fire in this room. It's quiet here.

NATASHA. Yes. . . . I must be an awful sight. [*Stands in front of the mirror.*] People say I've got fat—it just isn't true! I'm no fatter. Masha's asleep. She's tired out, poor girl. [*To* ANFISA, *coldly.*] Don't you dare sit down in my presence!

Get up! Get out of here! [ANFISA *goes out; pause.*] I simply can't understand why you keep the old woman!

OLGA [*taken aback*]. I'm sorry, but I don't understand—

NATASHA. She's quite useless in the house. She's a peasant and she ought to live in the country. Spoiling her, aren't you? I like order in the house. There should be no superfluous people in the house. [*Strokes* OLGA's *cheek.*] Oh, you poor thing! You're tired. Our headmistress is tired. When my little Sophie grows up and goes to school, I'll be afraid of you.

OLGA. I shan't be a headmistress.

NATASHA. They're going to appoint you, dearest. It's settled.

OLGA. I'll refuse. I couldn't. . . . It's beyond me. [*Drinks water.*] You treated Nanny so abominably just now. I'm sorry, but I can't bear it. It made me feel quite faint.

NATASHA [*excitedly*]. I'm sorry, Olga, I'm sorry. I didn't want to upset you.

MASHA *gets up, picks up a pillow, and walks out angrily.*

OLGA. Please understand, my dear. We may have been brought up in a rather peculiar way, but I can't bear this sort of thing. Such an attitude cuts me to the quick. It makes me ill. . . . I simply lose heart.

NATASHA. I'm sorry, I'm sorry. . . . [*Kisses her.*]

OLGA. Any rudeness, however slight, any harsh word, upsets me.

NATASHA. I admit I often say things I shouldn't, but, my dear, you must agree that there's no reason why she shouldn't live in the country.

OLGA. She's been with us for thirty years.

NATASHA. But she can't do any work now! Either I don't understand or you don't want to understand me. She's incapable of doing any work. All she does is sleep or sit about.

OLGA. Well, let her sit about.

NATASHA [*in surprise*]. Let her sit about? But she's a servant, isn't she? [*Through tears.*] I don't understand you, Olga. I have a nanny, I have a wet nurse, we have a maid, a cook; whatever do we want this old woman for? What for?

Fire alarm offstage.

OLGA. I've aged ten years tonight.

NATASHA. We must come to an understanding, Olga. You're at school; I'm at home. You've got your teaching; I've got to run the house. And if I talk about it, I know what I'm talking about. I know what I'm talk-ing a-bout! By tomorrow I want that old thief, that old hag, out of my house. [*Stamps her foot.*] The old witch! Don't you dare exasperate me! Don't you dare! [*Recollecting herself.*] Really, Olga, if you don't move downstairs, we'll always be quarreling. This is dreadful!

Enter KULYGIN.

KULYGIN. Where's Masha? Time we went home. They say the fire is subsiding. [*Stretching.*] Only one block has burned down. There was a strong wind, though, and it did seem at first that the whole town was on fire. [*Sits down.*] Oh, I'm tired, dear Olga. I often think that if it hadn't been for Masha, I'd have married you, dear. You're so good. . . . Oh, I'm exhausted. [*Listens.*]

OLGA. What is it?

KULYGIN. The Doctor is on one of his drinking sprees. It would happen just now. Terribly drunk. [*Gets up.*] I believe he's coming here. Listen! Yes, he's coming here. [*Laughs.*] What a man! Really! I'd better hide myself. [*Goes toward the wardrobe and stands in the corner.*] What a bandit!

OLGA. He hasn't been drinking for two years, and now, all of a sudden, he goes and gets drunk.

OLGA *retires, with* NATASHA, *to the back of the room. Enter* CHEBUTYKIN; *he walks across the room without swaying, just as if he were sober, looks round, goes up to the washstand, and starts washing his hands.*

CHEBUTYKIN [*morosely*]. To hell with all of them! To blazes with them! They think I'm a doctor, that I can treat any illness. The truth is, I know absolutely nothing, forgotten everything I ever knew, remember nothing, absolutely nothing. [OLGA *and* NATASHA *go out, unnoticed by him.*] To hell with it! Last Wednesday I attended a woman in Zasyp. She died, and it was my fault that she died. Yes. . . . Twenty-five years ago I knew something or other, but I don't remember a damn thing now. Not a damn thing. Perhaps I'm not a human being at all but merely imagine that I have hands and feet and a head; perhaps I don't exist at all but merely imagine that I walk, eat, and sleep.

[*Weeps.*] Oh, if only I did not exist! [*Stops weeping; morosely.*] Oh, hell! Day before yesterday they were talking at the club. . . . Heard them say: "Shakespeare," "Voltaire . . ." Never read them, not a single word, but I did my best to look as if I had. The others did the same. The vulgarity of it! The baseness! But then I remembered the woman I killed on Wednesday—remembered everything—and I felt dirty, nasty, loathsome. . . . I went and got drunk.

Enter IRINA, VERSHININ, *and* TUSENBACH. TUSENBACH *is wearing a new, fashionable suit.*

IRINA. Let's sit down. No one will come in here.

VERSHININ. If it weren't for the soldiers, the whole town would have burned down. Stout fellows! [*Rubs his hands with pleasure.*] What splendid people! Fine men, every one of them!

KULYGIN [*going up to them*]. What's the time?

TUSENBACH. After three. It's getting light.

IRINA. Everyone's sitting in the ballroom. No one thinks of going home. Your Solyony's there too. [*To* CHEBUTYKIN.] You'd better go to bed, Doctor.

CHEBUTYKIN. Never mind me, thank you. [*Combs his beard.*]

KULYGIN [*laughs*]. Sozzled, eh, Doctor? [*Slaps him on the shoulder.*] Good lad! *In vitro veritas,* the ancients used to say.

TUSENBACH. Everyone's asking me to organize a concert in aid of the homeless.

IRINA. But who—

TUSENBACH. It could be arranged if we tried. If you ask me, Masha plays the piano beautifully.

KULYGIN. She plays wonderfully.

IRINA. She's forgotten how to. She hasn't played for three years . . . or four.

TUSENBACH. There's absolutely no one in this town who appreciates music, not a soul, but I do, and I assure you that Masha plays wonderfully, almost like a concert pianist.

KULYGIN. You're quite right, Baron. I love Masha very much. She's a dear.

TUSENBACH. To be able to play so splendidly and to know all the time that there's no one to appreciate you—no one!

KULYGIN [*sighs*]. Yes, but do you think it would be the correct thing for her to take part in a concert? [*Pause.*] I know nothing about such matters, of course. It may be all right. I must say our headmaster is a decent fellow, a very decent fellow indeed, and very intelligent too, but he has—er—well, views. . . . Of course, it isn't his business, but all the same, I might perhaps have a talk with him.

CHEBUTYKIN *picks up a porcelain clock and examines it.*

VERSHININ. I got so filthy at the fire. I look like nothing on earth. [*Pause.*] I heard a rumor yesterday that our brigade is to be transferred somewhere very far away. Some say to Poland, others to Chita.

TUSENBACH. I heard it too. Yes, well, I suppose the town will be quite deserted then.

IRINA. We shall be gone, too!

CHEBUTYKIN [*drops the clock, which breaks*]. Smashed to bits!

Pause; everyone looks upset and embarrassed.

KULYGIN [*picking up the pieces*]. Break an expensive thing like that! Oh, Doctor, Doctor, zero minus for conduct!

IRINA. That was Mother's clock.

CHEBUTYKIN. Possibly. So it was your mother's clock. Perhaps I didn't smash it, but it just seems as though I did. Perhaps we only imagine that we exist, but we don't really exist at all. I don't know anything. Nobody knows anything. [*Stops at the door.*] What are you staring at? Natasha is having a disgusting affair with Protopopov, and you don't see it. You're just sitting about here and don't see anything, while Natasha is having her disgusting affair with Protopopov. [*Sings.*] Won't you accept this little present from me? [*Goes out.*]

VERSHININ. Well, well . . . [*Laughs.*] As a matter of fact, the whole thing is rather odd. [*Pause.*] When the fire broke out, I hurried off home. I got there. . . . Our house wasn't damaged and wasn't in danger, but my two little girls were standing at the front door in their night clothes; their mother wasn't there, people were rushing about, horses galloping past, dogs—and the girls looked upset, frightened, appealing. I don't know what else. My heart sank when I saw their faces. Good Lord, I thought, what else will these girls have to experience during a long life? I snatched them up, started running, and all the time kept thinking one and the same thing: What else would they have to experience in this world? [*Fire alarm; pause.*] I come here, their mother's here . . . angry, shouting.

MASHA *enters with a pillow and sits down on the sofa.*

VERSHININ. When my little girls were standing at the front door in their night clothes and the street was red with the glow of the fire and the noise around was terrifying, the thought occurred to me that something like it must have happened many years ago when an enemy made a sudden raid, looted, burned. . . . And yet, what a difference between what was happening now and what had happened before. When a little more time has passed, say, in two or three hundred years, people will look upon our present life, too, with horror and contempt. Everything we accept now will seem to them clumsy and dreadful, extremely uncomfortable and strange. I'm sure of it! Oh, what a wonderful life it will be, what a life! [*Laughs.*] I'm sorry, I'm off again! Please, let me continue. I'd really like to go on airing my views. I'm in the mood for it now. [*Pause.*] They all seem to be asleep. So, as I was saying, what a wonderful life it will be. You can just imagine it. . . . There are only three like you in the town now, but in the generations to come there will be more and more and more, and the time will come when everything will change as you would have it—people will live as you do now—and then you, too, will become antiquated. People will be born who will be better than you. . . . [*Laughs.*] I'm in a curious kind of mood. Damn it, I want to live and live! [*Sings.*] "To love all ages are in thrall, her impulses are good for all."* [*Laughs.*]

MASHA. Tram-tum-tum.

VERSHININ. Tam-tam.

MASHA. Tra-ra-ra.

VERSHININ. Tra-ta-ta. . . . [*Laughs.*]

Enter FEDOTIK.

FEDOTIK [*dances*]. Burnt down! Burnt down! To the last cinder!

IRINA. You're joking! Everything burned?

FEDOTIK [*laughs*]. Everything to the last cinder. Nothing left. My guitar, my camera, and all my letters.

Enter SOLYONY.

IRINA [*to* SOLYONY]. Please go away. You can't come in here.

SOLYONY. Why can the Baron and I can't?

VERSHININ. We really ought to go. How's the fire?

SOLYONY. Dying down, I'm told. But I really can't see why the Baron can and I can't. [*Takes out a perfume bottle and sprinkles himself.*]

VERSHININ. Tram-tam-tam.

MASHA. Tam-tam.

VERSHININ [*laughs; to* SOLYONY]. Let's go to the ballroom.

SOLYONY. Very well. We'll make a note of that. "I could make my tale much more clear, but that may irritate the geese, I fear."* [*Looking at* TUSENBACH.] Cluck-cluck-cluck.

SOLYONY *goes out with* VERSHININ *and* FEDOTIK.

IRINA. What a stink Solyony's left behind him. [*Bewildered.*] The Baron's asleep! Baron! Baron!

TUSENBACH [*waking*]. Sorry, I'm terribly tired. . . . The brickworks . . . I'm not talking in my sleep. I really will start work at a brickworks soon. Start work . . . I've discussed it already. [*Tenderly, to* IRINA.] You are so pale, so beautiful, so fascinating. Your pallor, it seems to me, irradiates the dark air like a shaft of light. You're sad, you're dissatisfied with life. Oh, come away with me! Come away and let's work together.

MASHA. Go away, Baron.

TUSENBACH [*laughing*]. You here? I can't see. [*Kisses* IRINA's *hand.*] Good-bye, I'm going. I look at you now and it comes back to me how a long time ago, on your birthday, you were so bright and cheerful and talked of the joys of life. At the time I, too, looked forward to a happy life. Where is it? [*Kisses her hand.*] There are tears in your eyes. You ought to go to bed. It's getting light, the day's dawning. Oh, if only I were allowed to give my life for you!

MASHA. Go away! Well, really! . . .

TUSENBACH. I'm going. [*Goes out.*]

MASHA [*lying down*]. Are you asleep, Fyodor?

KULYGIN. Eh?

---

*The old general's aria from *Eugene Onegin* [D.M.].

*A quotation from Krylov's fable *Geese* [D.M.].

MASHA. Why don't you go home?

KULYGIN. My dear Masha, my darling Masha—

IRINA. She's tired. Let her have a rest.

KULYGIN. I'll go in a minute. My wife's a good, nice woman. I love you, my only one.

MASHA [*angrily*]. *Amo, amas, amat, amamus, amatis, amant.*

KULYGIN [*laughs*]. Isn't she wonderful? I've been married to you for seven years, but it seems as if we only left the church yesterday. On my word of honor! You really are a wonderful woman. I'm content, content, content.

MASHA. I'm bored, bored, bored. [*Sits up.*] I can't get it out of my head. It's simply disgraceful. It preys on my mind. I can't keep silent. I mean about Andrey. He's mortgaged the house to a bank, and his wife's grabbed all the money, but the house doesn't belong to him alone, does it? It belongs to all four of us. He should have known that if he's an honest man.

KULYGIN. Why should you worry, Masha? What do you care? Andrey's up to his neck in debt. Well, let him do what he likes.

MASHA. It's disgraceful, however you look at it. [*Sits down.*]

KULYGIN. You and I aren't poor. I work, I teach at the high school, I give private lessons, I'm an honest man. A plain man. *Omnia mea mecum porto,* as they say.

MASHA. I don't want anything, but I can't bear injustice. [*Pause.*] Go home, Fyodor.

KULYGIN [*kisses her*]. You're tired. Rest for half an hour. I'll sit and wait for you downstairs. Try to sleep. [*Going.*] I'm content, content, content. [*Goes out.*]

IRINA. Our Andrey really has degenerated, gone to seed and grown old beside that woman. Once upon a time he was thinking of becoming a professor; yesterday he was boasting of having at last been a member of the local Council. He's a member of the Council, while Protopopov is chairman. The whole town's talking and laughing about it. He alone doesn't see or know anything. Here's everyone rushing off to the fire, but he sits in his room as if nothing were happening. Just plays his fiddle. [*Distractedly.*] Oh, it's awful, awful, awful! [*Weeps.*] I can't, I can't bear it any longer. I can't,

I can't. [OLGA *comes in and starts tidying up things on her bedside table.* IRINA *sobs loudly.*] Throw me out, throw me out. I can't bear it any longer!

OLGA [*frightened*]. What's the matter? What is it, darling?

IRINA [*sobbing*]. Where, where has it all gone to? Where is it? Oh, God; oh, God! I've forgotten everything, forgotten. . . . It's got all mixed up in my head. I can't remember the Italian for *window* or for *ceiling.* I'm forgetting everything, every day I'm forgetting, and life's passing and will never return, never! We'll never go to Moscow. I can see that we'll never go.

OLGA. Darling, darling . . .

IRINA [*controlling herself*]. I'm so unhappy. I can't work. I won't work. I've had enough, thank you. I worked as a telegraphist; now I've got a job at the Town Council, and I hate and despise everything I have to do there. I'm twenty-three. I've worked for a long time and my brain's dried up. I'm growing thin. I'm losing my looks. I'm getting old, and there's nothing, nothing I can look forward to, no satisfaction out of life I can hope for. Time's flying past, and I seem to be getting further and further away from real life, from a life that is beautiful, and heading for some horrible disaster. I'm in despair and I simply can't understand how I go on living, how I haven't killed myself before now.

OLGA. Don't cry, darling. I can't bear to see you cry.

IRINA. I'm not crying. I'm not crying. I've stopped now. See? I'm not crying any more. I've stopped. I've stopped.

OLGA. Darling, I'm talking to you as your sister, as your friend. If you take my advice, you'll marry the Baron! [IRINA *cries softly.*] You do respect him, don't you? You think highly of him. It's true he's not handsome, but he's such an honest, decent man. After all, people don't marry for love but to do their duty. At least I think so. I wouldn't hesitate to marry a man I didn't love. I would marry anyone who asked me, provided he was a decent man. I'd even marry an old man.

IRINA. I was always waiting until we moved to Moscow, where I hoped to meet the right man for me, the man I've dreamed of, the man I'd love. . . . But, as it turned out, it was all nonsense . . . all nonsense.

OLGA [*embraces her sister*]. My dear, my sweet sister, I understand, I understand everything. When the Baron left the army and came to see us in civilian clothes, I thought he looked so unprepossessing that I even started crying. He asked me why I was crying, but I couldn't tell him that, could I? But I'd be very happy if he married you. That's quite a different matter, quite different.

NATASHA, *carrying a lighted candle, walks across the stage in silence from the door on the right to the door on the left.*

MASHA. She walks as if she had set the town on fire herself.

OLGA. You're silly, Masha. You're the silliest in our family. I'm sorry.

MASHA. I'd like to confess to you, dear sisters. My heart is heavy. Let me confess to you and never to anyone again, never again. I'll tell you now. [*Softly.*] It's my secret, but you must know everything. I can't be silent any more. [*Pause.*] I love him, I love him, I love that man. You've just seen him. Well, why conceal it? I love Vershinin.

OLGA [*goes behind the screen*]. Don't. I'm not listening anyway.

MASHA. What am I to do? [*Clutches at her head.*] At first I thought him rather strange, then I began to pity him, and then I fell in love with him. . . . I fell in love with his voice, his talk, his misfortunes, his two little daughters.

OLGA [*behind the screen*]. I'm telling you I'm not listening. You can say any stupid thing you like; I'm not listening.

MASHA. Oh, you are stupid, Olga. I love him. Well, you can't do anything about it, can you? It's happened. It's fate. He loves me, too. It's terrible, isn't it? It's not nice, is it? [*Draws* IRINA *to her by her hand.*] Oh, my dear, what's to become of us? What's our life going to be like? When you read some love story, it all seems so old and so obvious, but when you fall in love yourself, you realize that no one knows anything and that everyone has to decide for himself. My dear, dear sisters . . . I've told you everything and now I shall be silent. I shall be like Gogol's madman—silence . . . silence . . .

Enter ANDREY, *followed by* FERAPONT.

ANDREY [*crossly*]. What do you want? I don't understand.

FERAPONT [*in the doorway, impatiently*]. I've told you a dozen times already.

ANDREY. Sir!

FERAPONT. Sir. The firemen, sir, are asking for permission to drive down to the river through your garden. Otherwise they has to drive all the way round, which, they says, sir, is a terrible nuisance.

ANDREY. Oh, all right. Tell them it's all right. [FERAPONT *goes out.*] Fed up! Where's Olga? [OLGA *comes out from behind the screen.*] I've come to ask you for the key to the cupboard. I've lost mine. You've got it. The little key. [OLGA *gives him the key in silence.* IRINA *goes behind the screen in her part of the room. Pause.*] What a terrific fire! It's dying down now. Damn that Ferapont! He made me furious and made me say something silly. Sir! [*Pause.*] Why are you so silent, Olga? [*Pause.*] It's time you dropped this nonsense and stopped sulking like this without rhyme or reason. You're here, Masha, and so are you, Irina. Excellent! Let's have a frank talk—once and for all. What have you got against me? What?

OLGA. Leave it, Andrey dear. We'll have our talk tomorrow. [*Agitatedly.*] What an awful night!

ANDREY [*looking very embarrassed*]. Don't get excited. I'm perfectly calm and I'm asking you what you've got against me. Tell me straight.

VERSHININ [*offstage*]. Tram-tam-tam.

MASHA [*gets up; loudly*]. Tra-ta-ta! [*To* OLGA.] Good-bye, Olga. God bless. [*Goes behind the screen and kisses* IRINA.] Sleep well. Good-bye, Andrey. Go away now. They're tired. Talk it over tomorrow. [*Goes out.*]

OLGA. Really, Andrey dear, why not put if off till tomorrow? [*Goes behind the screen to her part of the room.*] Time to go to bed.

ANDREY. Let me say what's on my mind and I'll go at once. To begin with, you've got something against Natasha, my wife. I've noticed it ever since the first day of our marriage. Natasha's a fine and honest person, straightforward and honorable— that's my opinion. I love and respect my wife, understand?—respect—and I demand that others should also respect her. I repeat, she's an honest and decent person, and, I'm sorry to say, the reason why you resent her so much is because you're so eager to find fault with her. [*Pause.*] Secondly, you seem to be angry with me because I'm not a professor and because I've given up my studies. But I work at the District Council and I'm a member of its board. I regard my service there as honorable and as important as service to science. I'm a member of the board of the District Council and I'm proud of it if you want to know. [*Pause.*] Thirdly . . . there's one thing more I'd like to say. I've mortgaged the house without your consent. It was wrong of me—yes. I'm sorry; I was driven to it by my debts . . . thirty-five thousand. I've given up gambling for some time now, but the chief thing I have to say to justify myself is that you girls, you get Father's pension, while I . . . haven't anything—I mean, any income. [*Pause.*]

KULYGIN [*at the door*]. Isn't Masha here? [*Anxiously.*] Where is she? That's funny. . . . [*Goes out.*]

ANDREY. They're not listening. Natasha's an excellent, honest person. [*Paces the stage in silence and then stops dead.*] When I got married, I thought we'd be happy, all of us happy. But, my God . . . [*Weeps.*] My dear sisters, my darling sisters, don't believe me, don't believe . . . [*Goes out.*]

KULYGIN [*at the door; anxiously*]. Where's Masha? Isn't Masha here? Extraordinary business! [*Goes out.*]

Fire alarm; then stage is empty.

IRINA [*behind the screen*]. Olga, who's knocking on the floor?

OLGA. It's the Doctor. He's drunk.

IRINA. What a restless night! [*Pause.*] Olga! [*Looks out from behind the screen.*] Have you heard? The brigade's been ordered to leave. It's being transferred somewhere far away.

OLGA. It's only a rumor.

IRINA. We shall be left all alone then. . . . Olga!

OLGA. Well?

IRINA. Oh, my dear, my darling, I respect the Baron. I think a lot of him. He's a fine man. I will marry him. I agree. Only, let's go to Moscow. Please, please let's go. There's no place like Moscow in the whole world. Let's go, Olga. Let's go!

Curtain.

ACT FOUR

The old garden of the Prozorov's house. A long avenue of firs, with a river at the end of it. On the other side of the river, a forest. On the right, a veranda; empty bottles and glasses on a table make it obvious that champagne has just been drunk. It is midday. Passers-by occasionally walk through the garden on their way to the river from the street; five soldiers march past rapidly.

CHEBUTYKIN, *in a good-humored frame of mind which doesn't desert him throughout the whole of the act, is sitting in an easy chair in the garden waiting to be called; he is wearing his army cap and holding a walking stick.* IRINA, KULYGIN, *with a decoration round his neck and with his mustache shaved off, and* TUSENBACH, *standing on the veranda, are seeing off* FEDOTIK *and* RODE, *who are coming down the steps; both officers are in field dress.*

TUSENBACH [*exchanging kisses with* FEDOTIK]. You're a good fellow. We got on well together. [*Exchanging kisses with* RODE]. Again . . . good-bye, dear friend.

IRINA. *Au revoir.*

FEDOTIK. Not *au revoir*, but good-bye. We shall never meet again.

KULYGIN. Who knows? [*Wipes his eyes, smiles.*] Look at me—crying!

IRINA. We shall meet one day.

FEDOTIK. In ten or fifteen years? But we'll hardly know each other then. Exchange cold greetings. [*Takes a snapshot.*] Stand still, please . . . for the last time.

RODE [*embraces* TUSENBACH]. We shan't meet again. [*Kisses* IRINA*'s hand.*] Thanks for everything, for everything!

FEDOTIK [*annoyed*]. Wait!

TUSENBACH. Let's hope we shall meet. Write to us. Be sure to write.

RODE [*glancing round the garden*]. Good-bye, trees! [*Shouts.*] Ho-ho! [*Pause.*] Good-bye, echo!

KULYGIN. For all we know you may get married there—in Poland. Your Polish wife will throw her arms around you and say: *"Kochany!"* [*Laughs.*]

FEDOTIK [*glancing at his watch*]. There's less than an hour left. Solyony is the only one from our battery who's going on the barge. The rest of us are marching with the troops. Three batteries are leaving today, another three tomorrow—the town will be quiet and peaceful at last.

TUSENBACH. And terribly boring.

RODE. Where's Masha?

KULYGIN. In the garden.

FEDOTIK. Must say good-bye to her.

RODE. Good-bye. We must go or I'll burst into tears. [*Embraces quickly* TUSENBACH *and* KULYGIN, *and kisses* IRINA's *hand.*] We've had a lovely time here.

FEDOTIK [*to* KULYGIN]. Here's something to remember me by—a notebook with a pencil. We'll go down to the river from here.

They go away, both looking round several times.

RODE [*shouts*]. Ho-ho!

KULYGIN [*shouts*]. Good-bye!

At the back of the stage FEDOTIK *and* RODE *meet* MASHA *and take leave of her;* MASHA *goes off with them.*

IRINA. They've gone. [*Sits down on the bottom step of the veranda.*]

CHEBUTYKIN. They forgot to say good-bye to me.

IRINA. What about you?

CHEBUTYKIN. Well, yes, I too forgot, somehow. Still, I shall be seeing them soon. I'm leaving tomorrow. Yes . . . one more day. In another year I shall be put on the retired list. I shall come back here and spend the rest of my life near you. There's only one more year left before I qualify for a pension. [*Puts a newspaper in his pocket and takes out another.*] I'll come back to you here and change my way of life drastically. I shall become a very quiet, well-behaved, decent little man.

IRINA. You jolly well have to change your way of life, dear Doctor. You really must.

CHEBUTYKIN. Yes, I feel it. [*Sings softly.*] Tara-ra boom di-ay . . . I'm sitting in a room di ay. . . .

KULYGIN. The Doctor's incorrigible. Incorrigible!

CHEBUTYKIN. Why don't you give me a few lessons? I'd become a reformed character then.

IRINA. Fyodor's shaved off his mustache. I can't bear to look at him.

KULYGIN. Why not?

CHEBUTYKIN. I could tell you what your face looks like, only I wouldn't like to.

KULYGIN. Ah, well! I'm afraid it's the accepted thing, the *modus vivendi*. Our headmaster has shaved off his mustache and so have I now that I have become second master. No one likes it, but I don't care. I'm content. Whether with or without a mustache, I'm content. [*Sits down.*]

At the back of the stage ANDREY *is wheeling a pram with a sleeping baby.*

IRINA. Dear Doctor, I'm terribly worried. You were out on the boulevard yesterday. Be a darling and tell me what happened there.

CHEBUTYKIN. What happened? Nothing. Nothing at all. [*Reads his newspaper.*] It's of no importance.

KULYGIN. I'm told Solyony and the Baron met yesterday on the boulevard near the theatre—

TUSENBACH. Do shut up! Really! [*Waves his hand and goes into the house.*]

KULYGIN. . . . near the theatre. Solyony began picking a quarrel with the Baron, and the latter lost his temper and said something offensive.

CHEBUTYKIN. Don't know. It's all nonsense.

KULYGIN. In some seminary a teacher wrote "nonsense" in Russian on an essay, and the pupil thought it was written in Latin but couldn't find the word in a dictionary. [*Laughs.*] Terribly funny. They say that Solyony's in love with Irina and that he's grown to hate the Baron. Well, that's understandable. Irina's a very nice girl. She's very like Masha, just as given to daydreaming. Except that your character, Irina, is more gentle. Though I must say, Masha, too, has a very good character. I love her. I love my Masha.

At the back of the stage someone shouts: "Coo-ee! Hey!"

IRINA [*shudders*]. Everything seems to startle me today for some reason. [*Pause.*] I've got everything packed. I'm sending my things off after lunch. The Baron and I are getting married tomorrow. We're leaving for the brickworks tomorrow, and the day after I shall be at the school. A new life will begin. May God help me! When I was sitting for my teacher's diploma, I cried for you, so conscious was I of the importance of the career I was about to embark on. [*Pause.*] The cart will be here in a moment for my things.

KULYGIN. Yes, that's how it is. And yet, it doesn't seem to be serious. All this, I mean. It's all just fine ideas, nothing very serious. Still, I wish you every success with all my heart.

CHEBUTYKIN [*deeply moved*]. My sweet child, my good, my precious girl. . . . You've gone so far ahead of me that I shall never catch up with you. I've been left behind, an old migrant bird that can't fly. Fly, my dear one, fly, and God bless you. [*Pause.*] You shouldn't have shaved off your mustache, Kulygin.

KULYGIN. Drop it for goodness' sake. [*Sighs.*] The soldiers will be gone today, and everything will go on as before. Whatever people may say, Masha's a good, honest woman. I love her very much and I thank my fate. Everyone's fate is different. A certain Kozyryov, an excise officer, was at school with me. He was expelled from the eighth grade because he seemed quite unable to understand *ut consecutivum*. He's terribly hard up now and in bad health too. Every time I meet him I say to him: "How d'you do, *ut consecutivum*!" "Yes, indeed, that's just it: *consecutivum*," he replies, and starts coughing. But I've been lucky all my life. I'm happy, have even been awarded the order of Stanislav, second class, and am now myself teaching others the *ut consecutivum*. Of course, I'm a clever man, much cleverer than most people, but that's no guarantee of happiness.

"The Maiden's Prayer" is being played on the piano in the house.

IRINA. Tomorrow night, thank goodness, I shan't have to listen to "The Maiden's Prayer," shan't have to meet Protopopov. [*Pause.*] Protopopov's sitting there in the drawing room. He's here today, too. . . .

KULYGIN. The headmistress hasn't arrived yet, has she?

IRINA. No. We've sent for her. Oh, if only you knew how difficult it is for me to live here by myself, without Olga. She lives at the school; she's the headmistress, she's busy all day, while I'm alone here. I'm bored, I have nothing to do, and I hate the room I live in. So what I've decided is that if I'm not going to live in Moscow, then I must make the best of it. I suppose it's fate and there's nothing to be done about it. It's all the will of God—that's clear. The Baron proposed to me. Well, I thought it over and decided to accept. He's a good man, it's really quite extraordinary how good he is. It

was then that my soul, as it were, suddenly grew a pair of wings. I felt cheerful again, lighthearted, and once more I wanted to work, work. Only something happened yesterday, and some kind of awful uncertainty seems to hang over me.

CHEBUTYKIN. Nonsense!

NATASHA [*through the window*]. The headmistress!

KULYGIN. The headmistress has arrived. Let's go.

He goes with IRINA *into the house.*

CHEBUTYKIN [*reads his papers, humming a tune*]. Tara-ra-boom-di-ay . . . I'm sitting in a room-di-ay. . . .

MASHA *walks up; at the back of the stage* ANDREY *is wheeling the pram.*

MASHA. There he sits, enjoying himself.

CHEBUTYKIN. And why not?

MASHA [*sits down*]. Oh, nothing. [*Pause.*] Were you in love with my mother?

CHEBUTYKIN. Yes, very much.

MASHA. Was she in love with you?

CHEBUTYKIN [*after a pause*]. That, I'm afraid, I don't remember.

MASHA. Is my man here? That's what our cook Marfa used to call her policeman, "my man." Is he here?

CHEBUTYKIN. No, not yet.

MASHA. When you have to snatch your happiness piecemeal, in little bits, and then lose it as I've lost it, you gradually become coarse and bitter. [*Pointing to her breast.*] I feel it seething here. [*Looking at her brother,* ANDREY, *who is wheeling the pram.*] There's old Andrey, our darling brother. All our hopes have perished. Thousands of people were raising a bell, much money and labor was spent on it, and then it suddenly fell and got smashed to bits. That is Andrey!

ANDREY. When are they going to be quiet in the house? Such a noise!

CHEBUTYKIN. Soon. [*Looks at his watch.*] This is a very old watch. It chimes. [*Winds his watch, which chimes.*] The first, second, and fifth battery will be leaving at exactly one o'clock. [*Pause.*] I'm leaving tomorrow.

ANDREY. For good?

CHEBUTYKIN. Don't know. I may return in about a year. Damned if I know. . . . It makes no difference. . . .

Somewhere far away a harp and a violin can be heard being played.

ANDREY. The town will be deserted, just as if a bell glass had been put over it. [*Pause.*] Something happened outside the theatre yesterday. Everyone's talking about it, but I don't know anything.

CHEBUTYKIN. Nothing much. Solyony began picking a quarrel with the Baron, who lost his temper and insulted him. In the end, of course, Solyony was obliged to challenge him to a duel. [*Looks at his watch.*] I think it's time. . . . At half past twelve, in the forest there, on the other side of the river. You can see it from here. Bang-bang! [*Laughs.*] Solyony imagines he's a second Lermontov. He even writes poetry. Joking apart, though, it's his third duel.

MASHA. Whose third duel?

CHEBUTYKIN. Solyony's.

MASHA. And the Baron's?

CHEBUTYKIN. What about the Baron?

MASHA. I'm all confused. Anyway, they shouldn't be allowed to fight. He might wound the Baron, or even kill him.

CHEBUTYKIN. The Baron is an excellent fellow, but one Baron more or less—what difference does it make? Let them! It makes no difference. [*Beyond the garden somebody shouts: "Coo-ee! Hollo!"*] That's Skvortsov shouting, one of the seconds. He's waiting in the boat. Let him wait.

Pause.

ANDREY. If you ask me, it's simply immoral to fight a duel or to be present at one as a doctor.

CHEBUTYKIN. It only seems so. We don't exist, nothing exists in the world. It only seems that we exist. Besides, what difference does it make?

MASHA. They just talk, talk all day long. [*Going.*] You live in a climate where it may start snowing any moment, and here they go on talking. [*Stopping.*] I won't go into the house. I can't go there. Please tell me when Vershinin comes. [*Walks off along the avenue.*] The birds are already flying away. [*Looks upward.*] Swans or geese. Oh, my dear, my happy birds! . . . [*Goes out.*]

ANDREY. There'll be no one left in the house. The army officers will go, you will go, my sister will get married, and I'll be left alone.

CHEBUTYKIN. What about your wife?

FERAPONT *comes in with papers.*

ANDREY. A wife's a wife. My wife's an honest, decent woman and—well, yes!—a kind woman, but for all that there's something in her that brings her down to the level of a mean, blind animal, a sort of horrible, rough-skinned animal. In any case, she's not a human being. I'm telling you this as a friend, for you're the only person to whom I can open up my heart. I love Natasha, that's quite true. But sometimes she strikes me as extraordinarily vulgar, and then I feel completely lost; I don't understand why—for what reason—I love her so much or, anyway, did love her.

CHEBUTYKIN [*gets up*]. Well, my dear fellow, I'm going away tomorrow, and we may never meet again, so here's my advice to you: Put on your hat, take your walking stick in your hand, and go away—go away and go on walking without looking back. The farther you go the better.

SOLYONY *walks across the back of the stage with* TWO ARMY OFFICERS; *seeing* CHEBUTYKIN, *he turns toward him; the* OFFICERS *go on.*

SOLYONY. It's time, Doctor. Half past twelve already. [*Exchanges greetings with* ANDREY.]

CHEBUTYKIN. One moment, please. Oh, I'm sick of the lot of you. [*To* ANDREY.] I say, my dear fellow, if anyone should ask for me, tell him I'll be back presently. [*Sighs.*] Dear, oh dear!

SOLYONY. "He had barely time to catch his breath before the bear was hugging him to death." [*Goes with him.*] What are you groaning about, old man?

CHEBUTYKIN. Well!

SOLYONY. How do you feel?

CHEBUTYKIN [*angrily*]. Fit as a fiddle.

SOLYONY. There's nothing to be upset about, old man. I shan't go too far. I'll only wing him like a woodcock. [*Takes out a perfume bottle and sprinkles his hands.*] I've emptied a whole bottle on my hands today and still they smell—smell like a corpse. [*Pause.*] Yes, sir. . . . Remember Lermontov's lines? "And he, the rebel, the raging tempest seeks, as though peace in tempests could be found."

CHEBTUYKIN. Yes. "He had barely time to catch his breath before the bear was hugging him to death."

They go out. Shouts of "Coo-ee! Hollo!" are heard. ANDREY *and* FERAPONT *come in.*

FERAPONT. Papers to sign, sir.

ANDREY [*nervously*]. Leave me alone, will you? Leave me alone. Please! [*Goes off with the pram.*]

FERAPONT. What's papers for if not to be signed? [*Goes off to the back of the stage.*]

Enter IRINA *and* TUSENBACH *in a straw hat.* KULYGIN *walks across the stage shouting: "Coo-ee, Masha, coo-ee!"*

TUSENBACH. He seems to be the only person in town who's glad the soldiers are going away.

IRINA. That's understandable. [*Pause.*] Our town will be deserted.

TUSENBACH. Darling, I'll be back presently.

IRINA. Where are you going?

TUSENBACH. I've something to see to in town. Then I must . . . see off all my colleagues.

IRINA. It's not true. Nicholas, why are you so preoccupied today? [*Pause.*] What happened outside the theatre yesterday?

TUSENBACH [*making an impatient movement*]. I'll be back in an hour and I'll be with you again. [*Kisses her hand.*] My dearest darling . . . [*Gazes into her eyes.*] It's five years since I fell in love with you, and I still can't get used to it. You seem more and more beautiful to me. What lovely, wonderful hair! What lovely eyes! I'm going to take you away tomorrow. We shall work. We shall be rich. My dreams will come true. You will be happy, darling. Only one thing, one thing only, worries me: You don't love me!

IRINA. I can't help that. I shall be your wife, your true and faithful wife, but I don't love you. We can't do anything about it. [*Weeps.*] I've never been in love and, oh, how I dreamed of love, dreamed of it for years and years, night and day, but my heart is like an expensive grand-piano that is locked and the key is lost. [*Pause.*] You look troubled.

TUSENBACH. I didn't sleep last night. There's nothing in my life I'm afraid of; it's only the lost key I'm worried about. Say something to me. [*Pause.*] Say something to me.

IRINA. What? What do you want me to say? What?

TUSENBACH. Just something.

IRINA. Don't fret, dear. Don't please.

Pause.

TUSENBACH. It is strange how sometimes little things, mere stupid trifles, suddenly, without rhyme or reason, become important in our life. One laughs at them, as one always does, one considers them of no importance, but one goes on all the same, and one hasn't got the strength to stop. Oh, don't let's talk about it! I feel fine! I feel as though I were seeing those firs, maples, and birch trees for the first time in my life, as though they were all looking curiously at me and . . . waiting. How beautiful these trees are and how beautiful life ought really to be near them. [*There is a shout: "Coo-ee! Hollo!"*] I must go. It's time. This tree here is dead, but it goes on swaying in the wind with the others. So I, too, can't help feeling that if I should die, I'd go on taking part in life one way or another. Good-bye, darling. [*Kisses her hands.*] The papers that you gave me are on my desk under the calendar.

IRINA. I'm coming with you.

TUSENBACH [*uneasily*]. No, no! [*Walks away quickly but stops in the avenue.*] Irina!

IRINA. What?

TUSENBACH [*not knowing what to say*]. I haven't had my coffee today. Please tell them to get it ready for me. [*Goes off quickly.*]

IRINA *stands, lost in thought, then walks off to the back of the stage and sits down on a swing. Enter* ANDREY *with the pram;* FERAPONT *appears.*

FERAPONT. The papers, sir, belong to the office. They're not mine, sir. I didn't make 'em.

ANDREY. Oh, where's my past? Where's it gone to? Where's the time when I was young, gay, clever, when my dreams and thoughts were so exquisite? When the present and the future were so bright with hope? Why is it that before we even begin to live, we become dull, drab, uninteresting, lazy, indifferent, useless, unhappy? Our town's been in existence for two hundred years, it has a hundred thousand inhabitants, and yet not one of them is different from the others. Not one saint—now or in the past—not one scholar, not one artist. Not one fairly outstanding man who could arouse envy or a passionate desire to emulate him. They just eat, drink, sleep, then die. Others are born and they, too, eat, drink, sleep, or, to avoid lapsing into complete idiocy out of sheer boredom, try to introduce some variety into their lives by nasty gossip, drink, cards, or malicious litigation. The wives deceive their husbands; the husbands tell lies, pretend not to see anything, not to hear anything; and their profoundly vulgar influence has so crushing an effect on their children that the divine spark in them is extinguished and they become just as pitiable corpses, and as like to one another, as their fathers and mothers. . . . [*To* FERAPONT, *crossly.*] What do you want?

FERAPONT. Beg pardon, sir. The papers to sign, sir.

ANDREY. I'm sick and tired of you.

FERAPONT [*handing him the papers*]. The porter of the Tax Collector's Office was telling me just now, sir, that there was two hundred degrees of frost in Petersburg this winter.

ANDREY. The present is hateful, but whenever I think of the future, everything becomes so wonderful! I feel so lighthearted, so unconfused. In the distance I can discern a glimmer of light, I can see freedom, I can see my children becoming free from idleness, from kvass, from geese with cabbage stuffing, from after-dinner naps, from a life of mean sponging.

FERAPONT. He was saying, sir, that two thousand people was frozen to death. Frightened to death, they was. In Petersburg or Moscow—can't remember rightly.

ANDREY [*in an excess of tenderness*]. My dear, dear sisters! My wonderful sisters! [*Through tears.*] Masha, my sister . . .

NATASHA [*at the window*]. Who's talking so loudly out there? Is that you, Andrey dear? You'll wake little Sophie. *Il ne faut pas faire du bruit, la Sophie est dormee deja. Vous etes un ours.* [*Getting angry.*] If you must talk, give the pram with the child to someone else. Ferapont, take the pram from the master.

FERAPONT. Yes'm. [*Takes the pram.*]

ANDREY [*embarrassed*]. I was talking quietly.

NATASHA [*behind the window, carressing her little boy*]. Bobby darling! Naughty Bobby! Bad Bobby!

ANDREY [*glancing through the papers*]. All right, I'll go through them, sign if necessary, and you can take them back to the office.

ANDREY *goes into the house, reading the papers;* FERAPONT *is pushing the pram at the back of the stage.*

NATASHA [*behind the window*]. Darling Bobby, what's your Mummy's name? You sweet little darling! And who's this? It's Auntie Olga. Say to your auntie: Good morning, Olga.

Two street musicians, a man and a girl, play on a violin and a harp; VERSHININ, OLGA, *and* ANFISA *come out of the house and stand listening for a moment in silence;* IRINA *comes up to them.*

OLGA. Our garden's like a public thoroughfare. Everyone walks and drives through it. Give something to the musicians, Nanny.

ANFISA [*gives some money to the* MUSICIANS]. Get along with you, my dears. [*The* MUSICIANS *bow and go out.*] Poor wretches! You don't play music in the street on a full stomach. [*To* IRINA.] How are you, my darling? [*Kisses her.*] Well, my little one, I'm having a lovely time now. A lovely time! Living with dear Olga in her flat at school. The Lord has been good to me, dear, in my old age. I've never lived so comfortably before, sinner that I am. It's a large apartment, no rent to pay, and I've got a room to myself and a lovely bed. Nothing to pay. I wakes up at night and—oh, dear God, holy Mother of God, there's no one happier than me.

VERSHININ [*glancing at his watch*]. We shall be leaving soon, Olga. It's time I went. [*Pause.*] I wish you all the best, all the best. Where's Masha?

IRINA. She's somewhere in the garden. I'll go and look for her.

VERSHININ. Thank you. I *am* in a hurry.

ANFISA. I'll go and look for her, too. [*Shouts.*] Masha, coo-ee! [*They go together to the back of the garden.*] Coo-ee! Coo-ee

VERSHININ. Everything comes to an end. We, too, must part. [*Looks at his watch.*] The town gave us a sort of farewell lunch; we drank champagne, the mayor made a speech, I ate and listened, but in spirit I was here with you. [*Looking round the garden.*] I've got used to you.

OLGA. Shall we ever meet again?

VERSHININ. I don't suppose we shall. [*Pause.*] My wife and my two little girls will be staying here for another two months. Please, if anything happens, if they should need anything—

OLGA. Of course, of course. You needn't worry. [*Pause.*] There won't be a single soldier left in the town tomorrow; it will be all a memory, and of course, a new life will begin for us. [*Pause.*]

Nothing happens as we want it to. I didn't want to be a headmistress and yet I'm one now. So we shan't be in Moscow. . . .

VERSHININ. Oh, well, thank you for everything. Forgive me if things haven't turned out exactly as—er . . . I'm afraid I've been talking a lot. Too much, indeed. Please forgive me for that too. Don't think too badly of me.

OLGA [*wipes her tears*]. Why isn't Masha coming?

VERSHININ. What else can I tell you before leaving? Any more views to air? [*Laughs.*] Life is hard. To many of us it seems dull and hopeless, but we must admit nevertheless that it is getting brighter and easier, and I should say that the time is not far off when it will be quite bright. [*Looks at his watch.*] It's time, high time, I went. Before, mankind was busy making war. Its whole existence was taken up with campaigns, invasions, and victories; but now all that is out of date. It's left a huge vacuum behind it, which we don't seem to know how to fill. Mankind is passionately looking for something to fill it with and will, I have no doubt, find it one day. Oh, if only we hadn't to wait too long! [*Pause.*] You know, if only we could add education to diligence and diligence to education. . . . [*Looks at his watch.*] I'm afraid I simply must go. . . .

OLGA. Here she comes!

Enter MASHA.

VERSHININ. I've come to say good-bye.

OLGA *walks away a little so as not to interfere with them.*

MASHA [*gazes at his face*]. Good-bye.

A prolonged kiss.

OLGA. There . . . there . . .

MASHA *sobs bitterly.*

VERSHININ. Write to me. Don't forget me. Let me go now—it's time. Olga, please take her. I have to go. . . . I'm late as it is. [*Deeply moved, he kisses OLGA's hands, then embraces MASHA again, and goes out quickly.*]

OLGA. There, there, darling. Don't, don't. . . .

Enter KULYGIN.

KULYGIN [*embarrassed*]. Never mind, let her cry, let her. My good Masha, my sweet Masha. . . . You're my wife and I'm happy, whatever may have happened. I'm not complaining, I don't reproach

you. . . . I don't. Olga's my witness. Let's live again as we used to. You won't hear a word from me, not a hint.

MASHA [*suppressing her sobs*]. "For he on honey-dew hath fed, and drunk the milk of Paradise . . . and drunk the milk of Paradise" . . . I'm going mad. . . . "On honey-dew hath fed . . ."

OLGA. Take hold of yourself, Masha. Take hold of yourself. . . . Give her some water.

MASHA. I'm not crying any more.

KULYGIN. She's not crying. . . . She's good. . . .

A dull report of a distant shot is heard.

MASHA. "For he on honey-dew hath fed, and drunk the milk of Paradise" . . . "singing of Mount Abora." . . . I'm getting all mixed up. [*Drinks water.*] My life's a failure. . . . I don't want anything any more now. . . . I'll be all right in a moment. . . . It doesn't matter. . . . Honey-dew . . . what's honey-dew? Why can't I get this word out of my head? My thoughts are all in a muddle.

IRINA comes in.

OLGA. Compose yourself, Masha. That's right . . . . Clever girl. . . . Let's go indoors.

MASHA [*angrily*]. I'm not going into that house. [*Sobs but stops immediately.*] I won't go into that house again—never again!

IRINA. Let's sit down together and, please, don't let's talk. I'm going away tomorrow.

Pause.

KULYGIN. Yesterday I took this false beard and mustache away from a boy in the sixth grade. [*Puts on the false beard and mustache.*] I look like our German master, don't I? [*Laughs.*] Those boys are funny beggars.

MASHA. You do look like you're German.

OLGA [*laughs*]. Yes.

MASHA *cries.*

IRINA. Stop it, Masha.

KULYGIN. I certainly look like him.

Enter NATASHA.

NATASHA [*to the maid*]. What? Mr. Protopopov will sit with little Sophie and let your master take out Bobby in the pram. Children are such a bother! [*To IRINA.*] You're leaving tomorrow, aren't you, Irina? What a pity! Why don't you stay here another week? [*Gives a little scream on catching sight of* KULYGIN, *who laughs and takes off the beard and mustache.*] Good heavens, you frightened me to death! [*To* IRINA.] I've got so used to you that it won't be so easy for me to part from you. I'll tell Andrey to move into your room with his fiddle—let him saw away there—and I'll put darling Sophie in his room. Oh, she's such a lovely child! Such a darling little girl! Today she looked at me with such big eyes and said: "Mummy!"

KULYGIN. A lovely child—that's true!

NATASHA. So it seems I shall be alone here tomorrow. [*Sighs.*] First of all, I shall have this avenue of trees cut down, then that maple—it's so unsightly in the evening. [*To* IRINA.] My dear, that belt doesn't suit you at all. It's such bad taste. You ought to get something bright and shiny. And here I shall have flowers, flowers, flowers everywhere, and there'll be such a lovely smell. . . . [*Suddenly.*] Why's this fork left lying about on the seat? [*On the way back to the house, to the maid.*] Why's this fork left lying about on the seat? I asked you. [*Screams.*] Don't answer me back!

KULYGIN. There she goes again!

A march is played offstage; they all listen.

OLGA. They're going away.

CHEBUTYKIN *comes in.*

MASHA. Our friends are going away. Well . . . happy journey to them. [*To her husband.*] We must go home. Where's my hat and cape?

KULYGIN. I left them indoors. I'll fetch them at once.

CHEBUTYKIN. I say, Olga . . .

OLGA. What is it? [*Pause.*] What?

CHEBUTYKIN. Oh, nothing. I don't know how to tell you. . . . [*Whispers in her ear.*]

OLGA [*aghast*]. It can't be!

CHEBUTYKIN. Yes. Too bad. . . . I'm awfully tired—exhausted. I'm not going to say another word. [*Vexed.*] Still, it makes no difference!

MASHA. What's happened?

OLGA [*embraces* IRINA]. What a dreadful day! I don't know how to tell you, my dear.

IRINA. What is it? Tell me quickly; what? For God's sake! [*Bursts into tears.*]

CHEBUTYKIN. The Baron has just been killed in a duel.

IRINA [*cries quietly*]. I knew . . . I knew. . . .

CHEBUTYKIN [*sits down on a garden seat at the back of the stage*]. Tired out . . . [*Takes a newspaper out of his pocket.*] Let her have a good cry. [*Sings softly.*] Tara-ra-boom-di-ay . . . I'm sitting in a room-di-ay. . . . What difference does it make?

The three sisters are standing, clinging to each other.

MASHA. Oh, how gay the music sounds! They're going away from us—one has gone already, gone forever—and we shall be left alone to start our life anew. We must live. . . . We must live.

IRINA [*lays her head on* OLGA's *breast*]. The time will come when there will be no more secrets, when all that is now hidden will be made plain, and when all will know what these sufferings are for. Till then we must live. We must work, just work! Tomorrow I shall go away alone; I shall teach in a school, and I shall give my life to those who may need it. . . . It is autumn now. It will be winter soon, and everything will be covered with snow. But I shall be working. . . . I shall be working. . . .

OLGA [*embraces her two sisters*]. The music is so cheerful and gay, and I want to live. Dear God! Time will pass and we shall be gone forever. We shall be forgotten, and people will no longer remember our voices or our faces or how many of us there were. But our sufferings will pass into joy for those who live after us. . . . Peace and happiness will reign on earth, and we who live now will be remembered with gratitude and will be blessed. Oh, my dear, dear sisters, our lives are not finished yet. Let us live! The music is so gay, so joyful, and it almost seems that in a little while we shall know why we live and why we suffer. Oh, if only we knew . . . if only we knew!

The music is growing fainter and fainter; KULYGIN, *looking happy and smiling, comes in carrying the hat and cape.* ANDREY *is wheeling the pram, in which Bobby is sitting.*

CHEBUTYKIN [*sings softly*]. Tara-ra-boom-di-ay . . . I'm sitting in a room-di-ay. . . . [*Reads his newspaper.*] It makes no difference! It makes no difference!

OLGA. If only we knew . . . if only we knew!

Curtain.

Robert Breuler and Karen Shallo as Hummel and the Mummy in
The Ghost Sonata, Theatre Arts Department, Penn State
University. Lowell L. Manfull, director.

CHAPTER IX

Strindberg and Expressionism

No sooner had realism been established as the most important dramatic mode of the nineteenth century than artists and playwrights began to feel constrained by the photographic literalness of the genre. The limitations of the box set, the constraints of consistently life-like speech, and cause-and-effect behavior and relationships began to hamper the artist. Ibsen in his mature work had moved beyond realism to a preoccupation with human psychology and symbolism. The developing scientific knowledge that had seemed a panacea to all the evils of the world now proved inadequate. Just how far the scientific method extended to the theatre is evidenced by the theory of naturalism propounded by Emile Zola (1840–1902) in France. Zola taught that the scientific method must be applied to drama and that the dramatist was not a creative talent but a recorder of human behavior. As evidenced in his own plays like *Thérèse Raquin* (1873), Zola believed that drama was nothing more nor less than life under a microcscope, that human beings were mere products of their heredity and environment. What the dramatist created on the stage was a slice of life, essentially unedited with all of the ugliness and sordidness of life exposed. The playwright was an impartial observer who took no sides in the drama, merely presented it. The dramatist in his search for truth merely observed, recorded, and presented with the scientist's detachment.

One of the young dramatists in the forefront of the avant garde, quick to support Zola's tenets, was an explosive Swedish writer named August Strindberg (1849–1912). Strindberg himself maintained that he was born without an epidermis; similarly one critic said of him that no playwright ever found a shorter route from blood to ink. Although Strindberg had begun his writing career with historical and romantic dramas, he came under the influence of Zola in the 1880s and began to write naturalistic dramas. His first major attempt, *The Father* (1887) deals with an army captain and his wife who quarrel over the education of their daughter, Bertha. In the wife's quest to win this battle, she plants in the Captain's mind the doubt that he is really Bertha's father, thus sending him on a collision course to madness. In the final scene of the play, the Captain is taken off in a straight jacket. Zola found fault with Strindberg's script, noting that the Captain did not even have a name but was only addressed by his military rank, that the writer's sentiments were clearly with the father and against the mother, and that Strindberg's language was too explosive and poetic to represent the speech of everyday life. Hurt by Zola's response, Strindberg determined to write the perfect naturalistic play in *Miss Julie* (1888) which was based on an actual case in Sweden. Strindberg depicts a conflict of wills between a young aristocratic woman and her father's man servant whom she allows to seduce her under the hypnotic excitement of midsummer's eve on their country estate. The action, which culminates in Julie's suicide, is seemingly random and spontaneous; the time sequence of the play directly parallels real time, and the characters are products of their heredity and the environment. In his famous introduction to the play, Strindberg wrote:

> I do not believe in simple characters on stage. . . . My souls are conglomerations from past and present stages of civilization, they are excerpts from books and newspapers, scraps of humanity, pieces torn from festive garments which have become rags—just as the soul itself is a piece of patchwork.

Again Strindberg commented on his naturalistic techniques:

> I have avoided the mathematically symmetrical construction of French dialogue and let people's brains work irregularly as they do in actual life, where no topic of conversation is drained to the dregs but one brain receives haphazard from the other a cog to engage with. Consequently my dialogue too wanders about, providing itself in the earlier scenes with material which is afterwards worked up, admitted, repeated, developed, and built up, like the theme in a musical composition.

Miss Julie exists as one of the greatest of all naturalistic plays.

At this time in his life, however, Strindberg was already precariously close to madness. Between 1894 and 1896, after the failure of his second marriage, Strindberg suffered what we would call today a nervous breakdown, a severe mental and spiritual crisis which he recorded in his powerful autobiography, *Inferno.* During the darkest period of this breakdown Strindberg had been absorbed with scientific experiments—trying to manufacture gold, exploring the nature of sulfur, and attempting to prove that plants have a nervous system—which culminated in frenzied activity and badly burned and infected hands. He was placed, for a time, in a charity hospital in Paris and then settled in a small hotel, a sanctuary for monks and students, where he heard nails being pounded into the plaster over his bed and where he believed his enemies were trying to kill him by sending electric shocks through the walls. Ultimately Strindberg fled and placed himself in the hands of a Dr. Anders Eliasson, who not only diagnosed Strindberg's extreme mental disorder but helped him begin to put the pieces of his shattered life back together again.

On March 8, 1898, Strindberg sent Gustaf af Geijerstam, his editor at Gernandt's publishing firm the manuscript of a new play accompanied by a short note:

> Herewith a play, of whose value I haven't the faintest idea. If you find it good, throw it into the theatre. If you find it impossible, hide it in Gernandt's safe. But the manuscript remains my possession. It is my only savings bank.

The manuscript for the play, *To Damascus,* was published and marks the beginning of a kind of drama referred to as expressionism.

During his period of mental crisis, Strindberg had come to believe that he had sinned against wives, children, colleagues, God, and humanity. Suffering, he believed, was God's judgment upon the sins of humanity. We must repent and atone for our sins, we must accept this mortal life as a hell. Through suffering, repentence, and atonement for our sins will come—not hope, not peace—but acceptance and resignation. In seeking to give form to the world of madness with its bizarre interplay of the real and the imagined, Strindberg had rejected all existing dramatic forms. There are only three main characters in *To Damascus,* The Unknown One (Strindberg himself), The Lady (his second wife, Frieda Uhl), and the Unseen One (God), who actually never appears. In the first half of the play, the Unknown one is proud and spiteful as he sins against his fellow beings; in the second half of the play he is forced to retrace his steps with repentence until he begins to understand the ways of the Unseen One.

The struggle is primarily one within the Unknown One himself. There is almost no plot here but the power of the play lies in its terrifying half-reality, the extraordinary blending of the world of reality with the world of a dream. The play takes the form of a journey, the second half repeating the pattern of the first. Although he was never to abandon realism as in *The Dance of Death* (1901), Strindberg was to continue his expressionistic masterpieces in *The Dream Play* (1902) and the play we have chosen for discussion, *The Ghost Sonata* (1907).

Strindberg did not consciously set out to create a new genre. He simply recorded life with a new perception and a new awareness of what, in fact, constituted truth for a human being: not what the eye perceived but what the psyche and the soul experienced. Expressionism, then, is the attempt of artists and writers to capture the inner reality of the human being. As Strindberg explained:

> Anything can happen; everything is possible and probable. Time and Space do not exist; on an insignificant groundwork of reality, imagination spins and weaves new patterns made up of memories, experiences, unrestrained fancies, absurdities and improvisations. The characters split, double and multiply; they evaporate, crystallize, scatter and converge. But a single consciousness holds sway over them all—that of the dreamer. For him there are no secrets, no incongruities, no scruples and no law. He neither condemns nor acquits, only relates, and since on the whole there is more pain than pleasure in the dream, a tone of melancholy, and of compassion for all living things, runs through the swaying narrative.

Expressionism, then, rejects realism's emphasis on externals and is subjective rather than objective in its depiction of truth.

The expressionists' major devices are these: (1) Plot is virtually absent and is replaced by an emphasis on structure. Notice that *The Ghost Sonata* takes a musical structure: allegro (introduction of theme), largo (slow development of theme), and andante (quiet emergence of principle theme). (2) Just as structure is more important than plot, so theme or idea—the pitiable condition of humanity, the need for spiritual values in a mechanized society—gives the plays the feel of modern moralities. (3) Time and place are suspended as in a dream; rather than occuring in a room, an expressionistic play might take place in a symbolic environment like a prison or a wasteland, in a distorted room—collapsed, pinched, twisted—and in a non-existant, fragmentary, or non-progressive time frame. The play really transpires inside the head of the dramatist. (4) Characters may be nameless, universal, abstract or symbols of an idea, as the Cook in *The Ghost Sonata* is a symbol of the vampire who lives by sucking the blood from others. (5) Symbols abound—in language, setting, idea as well as character. *The Ghost Sonata*'s very title is symbolic of this grotesque collection of dead, about to die, or living-dead creatures. (6) The expressionist consistently seeks theatrical devices to externalize inner states such as pain, anguish and suffering. In order to illuminate some thematic point, distortion or bizarre effects are employed: walls may move inward to suggest oppression, branches of trees may appear as clutching fingers, characters may move or speak mechanically to indicate dehumanization. (6) Sharp contrasts are omnipresent; dialogue may alternate between poetry and prose, obscenity and idealized speech, short stoccato speeches and lengthy monologues. (7) The works are permeated with a sense of fantasy, sometimes peaceful, sometimes frightening. (8) The plays often take the guise of a journey or quest as in *The Ghost Sonata* we move from the outside of the apartment building into its darkest secrets as an X-Ray sees within the human body. The overall impression is one of allegory, clothed in a nightmare or vision. Think as you read *The Ghost Sonata* of the macabre forms of your dreams and you will be freer to respond to the emotions and ideas of the play.

It is interesting that these developments in the drama coexist with similar movements in art. Certainly painters like Van Gogh and Edvard Munch were trying to capture the torture, pain and anguish of the human condition. Psychology was gaining importance as the study of behavior and although the two men did not know each other, much of Strindberg's perception parallels that of the famous Austrian psychoanalyst, Sigmund Freud. Later, in Germany around 1910, expressionism took root as a theatrical movement in the works of playwrights like Georg Kaiser and Ernst Toller. Their plays, however, became social and political rather than personal and psychological as they depicted the little person at odds with the corruption and injustices of the world.

August Strindberg freed the modern drama for new modes of creation. Critics often refer to him as the father of experimental drama. So much of the theatre that developed in the twentieth century—surrealism, theatre of cruelty, absurdism—owes a debt to this tormented genius's adventure into the unknown. Individual artists of the theatre openly acknowledge their debt to Strindberg: for example, Eugene O'Neill—one of America's greatest playwrights of the twentieth century and avid experimentor—and the remarkable contemporary Swedish film director, Ingmar Bergman, both cite Strindberg as their mentor. Irish playwright Sean O'Casey wrote, "Strindberg, Strindberg, Strindberg, the greatest of them all! . . . Ibsen can sit serenely in his Doll's House, while Strindberg is battling with his heaven and his hell."

August Strindberg

Johan August Strindberg was born in Stockholm, Sweden on January 22, 1849. He just missed illegitimacy, his parents marrying shortly before his birth. His father's bankruptcy when he was four, his mother's death when he was thirteen, his father's remarriage and his subsequent sense of rejection, and his pietistic, strict upbringing—all profoundly affected this hypersensitive child.

Yet Strindberg was a brilliant student—when it suited him to be brilliant. At Upsalla University, where he studied intermittently, he quarreled with professors and despised equally the formal intellectual discipline and the easy-going student life. In 1869 Strindberg auditioned as an actor at the Royal Dramatic Academy in Stockholm. Humiliated by his failure, he took an overdose of opium in a half-hearted attempt to kill himself. Instead, he dreamed in dialogue form, wakened, and recorded his dream. While no longer extant, *A Name's Day Gift,* written in four hours, was Strindberg's first play.

After a series of odd jobs—as school teacher and editor of an insurance newspaper—Strindberg became Assistant Royal Librarian in 1875. Here Strindberg disciplined himself, became a serious scholar, learned Chinese, and organized the library's vast Chinese holdings. A new social world opened to the young man. He met a Baron Carl Wrangel, Captain of the King's Guards, and his charming actress wife, Siri von Essen, who in 1877 after divorcing the Baron, became the first of Strindberg's three wives. Strindberg and Siri von Essen had three children before their marriage ended in a sordid and painful divorce in 1891.

Strindberg moved to Berlin, began drinking heavily, grew his hair long and wild, and cultivated the association of bohemian artists at a bar called the Black Swine. His nights were devoted to evil, he said, and his days to his scientific experiments. In January of 1893 Strindberg met a young German journalist by the name of Frieda Uhl. As soon as he received legal proof of his divorce, they were married. In 1893, Uhl's sister wrote to her husband about Strindberg:

> I can never shake off the fear of seeing him suddenly go insane. At the same time he more and more impresses me as a great genius. . . . It is terribly strenuous listening to him talk. You almost see how his thoughts work and rush ahead, and he can't catch up with his speech and suffers martyrdom. Half of what he says you must really guess. He also paints; there, too, he is a law unto himself, naturalistic symbolism he calls it. He finishes a picture in two or three days, he paints surprisingly well considering that he never learnt to paint. He is so full of talent that he doesn't seem to know what to do with it. But his is not a joyful way of creating. It is more like the savage impulse driving a murderer to his crime.

After less than three months of marriage the couple parted. In spite of the birth of a daughter and attempts at reconciliation, the marriage was dissolved in 1894, and Strindberg plummeted into the mental crisis described earlier in this chapter.

Strindberg was to marry a third time in 1901: an exotic young actress named Harriet Bosse who was to create several of Strindberg's greatest roles—Indra's Daughter in *The Dream Play* and Eleanora in *Easter*. Their daughter, Anne-Marie, was a joy to Strindberg in his declining years, and although the couple separated in 1902 they remained friends.

At the time Strindberg wrote *The Ghost Sonata* in 1907, he was suffering from stomach cancer. His view of life as hell and of people as evil contrasts with the serenity he seemed to achieve in his personal existence. He worked tirelessly on a world religion which would draw from all great religious teachings and on the development of an international language. Writer of four autobiographies, over sixty plays including histories and children's plays, essays, scientific and philosophical papers, poems, short stories, novels—Strindberg was a genius and a visionary. Just as Ibsen and Chekhov perfected the realistic play so Strindberg pushed beyond it into uncharted and dark realms.

The Ghost Sonata

Strindberg wrote *The Ghost Sonata* as a chamber play in 1907 specifically for performance in his own intimate theatre. A chamber drama, according to the dramatist, related to the rest of the drama as chamber music relates to the rest of music. Its plot was to be reduced to basic simplicity; its props and scenic effects were to be minimal. The entire impact of the play was to be subtle, restrained, lyrical and quiet as it was performed in a small theatre where the audience sat in close proximity to the actors. While he wrote the play quickly and under much pressure and obviously in a cynical mood, he nonetheless produced a masterpiece of macabre, bizarre and brutal drama peopled with some of his most monstrous characters. The title of the play (which, by the way, was originally titled *Kama-Loka,* meaning essentially the world beyond life) can be as aptly translated as *The Spook Sonata* in tribute to that strange cast of characters.

While the play is a masterpiece of expressionistic writing, its nihilistic message is vividly clear: life is vile, miserable and rotten. The action of the play unmistakably concerns escaping the destruction caused by all the evil, sin and corruption of life. The play would have us believe that most of the horrible misery and evil of life is not the result of crimes on a grand scale but rather the ultimate result of the piling up of the ordinary sins and corruptions of everyday life.

With the exception of the Student and possibly the Hyacinth Girl, all of the characters are vile to one degree or another. The Student is unique in being healthy and decent; but through him we see that even the vigor and vitality of youth are inadequate defenses in a corrupt, decaying world. Most of the characters are "old" and "done with." Bengtsson describes them quite accurately to Johansson in scene two when he says, "They look like ghosts. And they've kept this up for twenty years, always the same people saying the same things or saying nothing at all for fear of being found out . . . when people stay a long time together and torment each other they go mad. . . ." People, according to this play, are bound together in intricate, almost unfathomable patterns of relationships created by mutually shared crimes against humanity. As the Mummy puts it: "Crimes and secret guilts bind us together."

The characters are a fascinatingly disreputable lot. Bengtsson and Johansson are more than mere servants; they are criminals blackmailed into being slaves who would willingly enslave others at the first opportunity. The Aristocrat is a jewel thief and an adulterer who married a woman for money and is now being bought off by her. The Woman in Black is his pregnant mistress and the illegitimate daughter of The Caretaker's Wife who is the Consul's (Dead Man's) mistress. The Consul, a truly despicable human being, offers to help the needy only if his act will be well publicized and enhance his reputation. He appears as the ultimate expression of human vanity when he returns from the dead to see if the flag is flying at half-mast in his honor. The Fiancée, who has had numerous affairs, now spends her time spying on the rest of the world with the aid of her window mirror. The Colonel, who has stolen his rank and title, is a rotten seducer and a liar.

But they are not alone. The Mummy is married to the Colonel but has had an illegitimate child by Hummel. Still, she is somewhat unique in the play for she does not wholly give herself over to evil. She regrets the wrong she has done and is attempting to do good by exposing Hummel. At one point she says, ". . . if we could only die," expressing her wish to escape the sordidness of life. Unlike the other characters, she possesses some pity for her fellowman and represents a feeble hope for the basic goodness of the human race when she says, ". . . in our souls we are better than we seem because we hate our sins." Hummel, of course, is the most vile character of all for he is a vampire who steals life from everyone and takes what he wants regardless of who might suffer. He has to possess the Hyacinth Girl for she represents continued life and youth to him. He delights in destroying others. The Milkmaid is one of his victims. Now he would destroy the Student by stealing his vitality. The vampire theme is reiterated in the Cook who also survives by sucking the vitality from others.

There are really only two decent people in the play. The Student is the only character with a healthy soul. As a Sunday child he is hypersensitive to the suffering of the world and, therefore, must save the Hyacinth Girl. But even the student is no match for the evil in the house. The Hyacinth Girl, despite his help, dies because goodness and decency, which she represents, cannot survive in a corrupt world.

As the play deals with the exposing of evil, a central symbol emerges in the removing of facades. As the play progresses, the true nature of characters and deeds is revealed when surfaces are stripped away so that we can perceive the underlying evil, terror and pain of life. False faces are removed, and we see the real person beneath. (It is no accident that the Colonel has false teeth, false moustache and a wig to go along with his false titles and his false stories.) Ironically, Hummel comes to the house to expose others and ends up being exposed himself. The play as a whole is constructed with an architectonic structure in which the arrangement of the four scenes becomes a key to the play's meaning. Each scene represents the penetration of a facade. In the beginning we are in the street in front of a grand and beautiful house. Scene Two takes us into the round room or parlor we can see through the windows in the first scene where all is not as beautiful as it seems. The third scene goes even deeper into the house and deeper into the evil as we move into a room behind the parlor. And then, finally, we move through implication into the world beyond as the final moment of the play focuses upon a picture of Bocklin's "Isle of the Dead" hanging on the wall and we actually hear music coming from the island.

The Ghost Sonata is unquestionably one of the most successful and effective expressionistic plays ever written. Its full impact demands staging for it is undeniably a theatre piece. Interestingly, many of its effects could be tellingly enhanced by cinema techniques. In fact, it would make an incredible movie. Audiences, largely through the impact of post-war films, are only now fully receptive to the ideas, devices, symbols, and images to be found in Strindberg's chamber play. He was eighty years, at least, ahead of his time.

THE GHOST SONATA

by August Strindberg

Translated by Evert Sprinchorn

———— CHARACTERS ————

THE OLD MAN, Mr. Hummel
THE STUDENT, Arkenholz
THE MILKMAID, an apparition
THE SUPERINTENDENT'S WIFE
THE SUPERINTENDENT
THE DEAD MAN, formerly a consul
THE WOMAN IN BLACK, daughter of The Dead Man and The Superintendent's Wife
THE COLONEL
THE MUMMY, The Colonel's wife
THE YOUNG LADY, The Colonel's daughter, actually The Old Man's daughter
BARON SKANSKORG, engaged to The Woman in Black
JOHANSSON, Hummel's servant
BENGTSSON, The Colonel's manservant
THE FIANCEE, Hummel's former fiancée, now a white-haired old woman
[THE COOK*]
BEGGARS
A HOUSEMAID

———— SCENE ————

Stockholm

[1]

The first two floors of a facade of a new house on a city square. Only the corner of the house is visible, the ground floor terminating in a round room, the second floor in a balcony with a flagpole.

When the curtains are drawn and the windows opened in the round room, one can see a white marble statue of a young woman surrounded by palms and bathed in sunlight. On the windowsill farthest to the left are pots of hyacinths—blue, white, pink.

Hanging on the railing of the balcony on the second story are a blue silk bedspread and two white bed pillows. The windows to the left are covered with white sheets signifying a death in the house. It is a bright Sunday morning.

A green park bench is downstage toward the left.

Downstage right is a drinking fountain with a long-handled drinking cup hanging at its side. To the left a kiosk, plastered with advertisements. A telephone booth is also onstage.

*Not included in Strindberg's list of characters.

The main entrance to the house is at the left. Through the door can be seen the hall and the staircase with marble steps and balustrade of mahogany and brass. On the sidewalk on both sides of the entryway are tubs with small laurels.

The corner of the house with the round room also faces a side street that runs upstage.

On the first floor to the left of the entryway is a window with a special mirror, quite common in Sweden around the turn of the century, which enables those inside to view the passing scene without sticking their heads out the window.

At the rise of the curtain, the bells of several churches can be heard ringing in the distance.

The double doors in the entryway are wide open. The Woman in Black stands motionless in the doorway.

The Superintendent's Wife is sweeping the vestibule. Having finished that, she polishes the brass on the door and then waters the laurels.

Sitting in a wheelchair near the kiosk is The Old Man, reading a newspaper. He has white hair and beard and is wearing glasses.

The Milkmaid comes in from around the corner, carrying a wire basket filled with bottles. She is wearing a summer dress, with brown shoes, black stockings, and white cap. She takes off her cap and hangs it on the drinking fountain; wipes the sweat from her brow; takes a drink from the cup; washes her hands; arranges her hair, using the water in the fountain as a mirror.

The ringing of a steamship bell is heard, and now and then the silence is broken by the deep notes of the organs in the nearby churches.

After a few moments of silence, and after The Milkmaid has finished arranging her hair, The Student enters from the left. He is unshaven and looks haggard from lack of sleep. He goes directly to the drinking fountain.

Pause.

THE STUDENT. Could I borrow the cup, please?

The Milkmaid hugs the cup to herself.

Aren't you through using it?

The Milkmaid stares at him in terror.

THE OLD MAN (*to himself*). Who on earth is he talking to?—I don't see anyone!—Is he crazy? (*He continues to stare at them in amazement.*)

THE STUDENT. What are you looking at? Do I look so awful?—Well, I haven't slept a wink all night. I suppose you think that I've been out doing the town. . . .

The Milkmaid still stares at him in terror.

Think I've been drinking, don't you?—Do I smell like it?

The Milkmaid as before.

I haven't had a chance to shave. . . . Come on, let me have a drink of water. After last night, I think I've earned it. (*Pause.*) Must I tell you the whole story? I've spent the night caring for the injured. I've bound up their wounds. You see, I was there when the house collapsed last night. I was there. . . . Well, that's it.

The Milkmaid rinses the cup and offers him a drink of water.

Thanks!

The Milkmaid does not move.

(*The Student continues, slowly*): I wonder if you would do me a great favor? (*Pause.*) The thing is, my eyes are inflamed, as you can see—but I've had my hands on wounds and on corpses—so I don't want to risk using my hands to wash my eyes. . . . Would you take this clean handkerchief, dip it in that fresh water, and bathe my sore eyes with it?—Would you do that?—Will you be my Good Samaritan?

The Milkmaid hesitates for a moment before doing as asked.

That's very kind of you. And here's something for your trouble—(*He has taken his wallet out and is about to offer her some money. The Milkmaid makes a gesture of refusal.*) I'm sorry. Forgive me. I'm still in a daze. . . .

* * *

THE OLD MAN (*to The Student*). Forgive my speaking to you, but I could not help hearing you say you were in on that terrible accident yesterday evening. I was just sitting here reading about it in the paper.

THE STUDENT. Is it already in the paper?

THE OLD MAN. The whole story! And they've got a picture of you too. But they regret they were unable to obtain the name of the courageous young student. . . .

THE STUDENT (*looking at the paper*). So that's me! What do you know!

THE OLD MAN. Who . . . who was that you were talking to just now?

THE STUDENT. Didn't you see?

Pause

THE OLD MAN. I suppose I'm being nosey, but would you do me the honor of giving me your name?

THE STUDENT. Why do you want to know that? I don't care for publicity. First they build you up, then they tear you down. The insult now ranks among the fine arts—and the ranker the finer. Besides I'm not looking for any reward.

THE OLD MAN. Rich, I suppose?

THE STUDENT. Not at all! I haven't got a dime to my name.

THE OLD MAN. It's strange . . . but I can't help thinking that I've heard your voice before. . . . When I was a young man I had a friend who couldn't pronounce window, he always said winder. I've only met one person who said that, and that was him. The other is you, of course. Is it possible that you are related to Arkenholz, the wholesale dealer?

THE STUDENT. He was my father.

THE OLD MAN. Isn't fate strange? Then I saw you when you were a child—under very trying circumstances.

THE STUDENT. I suppose so. I understand I came into the world right in the middle of bankruptcy proceedings.

THE OLD MAN. Exactly!

THE STUDENT. May I ask what your name is?

THE OLD MAN. My name is Hummel.

THE STUDENT. Hummel? Then you're—. Yes, I remember. . . .

THE OLD MAN. You've heard my name mentioned in your family?

THE STUDENT. Yes.

THE OLD MAN. And mentioned, perhaps, with a certain antipathy?

The Student remains silent.

I can well imagine!. . . No doubt you heard that I was the man who ruined your father? . . . Everyone who is ruined by stupid speculations comes to realize sooner or later that he was actually ruined by someone he couldn't fool. (*Pause.*)

The truth of the matter is that your father fleeced me of seventeen thousand crowns, every cent I had saved up at the time.

THE STUDENT. It's remarkable how the same story can be told in two exactly opposite ways.

THE OLD MAN. Surely you don't think I'm being untruthful?

THE STUDENT. What do you think? My father didn't lie.

THE OLD MAN. That's true, a father never lies. . . . But I too am a father, and consequently. . . .

THE STUDENT. What're you getting at?

THE OLD MAN. I saved your father from the worst possible misery, and he repaid me with all the terrible hatred of a man who feels obliged to be grateful. He taught his family to speak ill of me.

THE STUDENT. Maybe you made him ungrateful. The help you gave him was probably poisoned with unnecessary humiliations.

THE OLD MAN. My dear young man, all help is humiliating.

THE STUDENT. What do you want of me?

THE OLD MAN. Don't worry, I'm not asking for the money back. But if you would render me a few small services, I would consider myself well repaid. You see that I'm a cripple—some say it's my own fault—others blame my parents—personally I blame it all on life itself, with all its traps—in avoiding one you fall right into the next one. Anyway, I can't run up and down stairs—can't even pull bell cords. And so I ask you: help me!

THE STUDENT. What can I do?

THE OLD MAN. Well, first of all you might give my chair a push so that I can read the posters. I want to see what's playing tonight.

THE STUDENT (*pushing the wheelchair*). Don't you have a man who takes care of you?

THE OLD MAN. He's off on an errand. . . . Be right back. . . . Are you a medical student?

THE STUDENT. No, I'm studying languages. But I really don't know what I want to be.

THE OLD MAN. Ah ha!—How are you at mathematics?

THE STUDENT. Fairly good.

THE OLD MAN. Good! Good!—Would you possibly be interested in a job?

THE STUDENT. Sure, why not?

THE OLD MAN Splendid! (*Reading the posters.*) They're giving *Die Walkure* at the matinee. . . . That means that the colonel will be there with his daughter. And since he always sits on the aisle in the sixth row, I'll put you next to him. . . . You go into that telephone booth over there and order a ticket for seat number eighty-two in the sixth row.

THE STUDENT. An afternoon at the opera!

THE OLD MAN. That's right! Just do as I tell you and you won't regret it. I want to see you happy—rich, respected. Your debut last night as the courageous rescuer is the beginning of your fame. From now on your name is your fortune.

THE STUDENT (*going toward the telephone booth*). All right! Sounds like fun. Let's see what happens.

THE OLD MAN. You're a good sport, aren't you?

THE STUDENT. Suppose so. That's my misfortune.

THE OLD MAN. No more. This will make your fortune.

He picks up his newspaper and starts to read. In the meantime The Lady in Black has come out on the sidewalk and is talking with The Superintendent's Wife. The Old Man listens furtively, but the audience hears nothing. The Student returns.

All set?

THE STUDENT. It's all taken care of.

THE OLD MAN. Take a look at that house.

THE STUDENT. I have already looked at it—very carefully. . . . I went by here yesterday, when the sun was glittering on the panes—and dreaming of all the beauty and luxury there must be in that house, I said to my friend, "Imagine having an apartment there, four flights up, and a beautiful wife, and two pretty kids, and twenty thousand crowns in dividends every year."

THE OLD MAN. Did you now? Did you say that? Well, well! I too am very fond of that house. . . .

THE STUDENT. Do you speculate in houses?

THE OLD MAN. Mmm—yes! But not in the way you think. . . .

THE STUDENT. Do you know the people who live there?

THE OLD MAN. Every single one. At my age you know everyone, including their fathers and their grandfathers—and you always find you're related

to them somehow. I've just turned eighty. . . . But no one knows me, not really. . . . I take a great interest in human destinies. . . .

The curtains in the round room are drawn up. The Colonel is seen inside, dressed in civilian clothes. After having looked at the thermometer, he moves away from the window and stands in front of the marble statue.

Look, there's the colonel! You'll sit next to him this afternoon.

THE STUDENT. Is that him—the colonel? I don't understand anything that's going on. It's like a fairy tale.

THE OLD MAN. My whole life, my dear young man, is like a book of fairy tales. But although the stories are different, one thread ties them all together and the same leitmotif recurs constantly.

THE STUDENT. Who is that marble statue in there?

THE OLD MAN. That's his wife, naturally. . . .

THE STUDENT. Was she so wonderful? Did he love her so much?

THE OLD MAN. Hmm yes . . . yes, of course. . . .

THE STUDENT. Well, tell me!

THE OLD MAN. Come now, you know we can't judge other people. . . . Suppose I were to tell you that she left him, that he beat her, that she came back again and married him again, and that she is sitting in there right now like a mummy, worshiping her own statue. You would think I was crazy.

THE STUDENT. I can't understand it!

THE OLD MAN. That doesn't surprise me!—And over there we have the hyacinth window. That's where his daughter lives. She's out horseback riding, but she'll be home soon. . . .

THE STUDENT. Who's the lady in black talking to the caretaker?

THE OLD MAN. Well, that's a little complicated. But it's connected with the dead man upstairs, there where you see the white sheets.

THE STUDENT. And who was he?

THE OLD MAN. A human being, like the rest of us. The most conspicuous thing about him was his vanity. . . . Now if you were a Sunday child, you would soon see him come out of that very door just to look at the consulate flag at half-mast for himself. Yes, you see, he was a consul. Liked nothing better than coronets and lions, plumed hats and colored ribbons.

THE STUDENT. Sunday child, did you say? I was actually born on a Sunday, so I'm told.

THE OLD MAN. Really! Are you—! I should have guessed it. I could tell by the color of your eyes. . . . But—then you can see . . . what others can't see, haven't you noticed that?

THE STUDENT. I don't know what others see. But sometimes—. Well, there are some things you don't talk about!

THE OLD MAN. I knew it, I knew it! But you can talk to me about it. I understand—things like that . . .

THE STUDENT. Yesterday, for example. . . . I was drawn to that little side street where the house collapsed afterward. . . . I walked down the street and stopped in front of a house that I had never seen before. . . . Then I noticed a crack in the wall. I could hear the floor beams snapping in two. I leaped forward and grabbed up a child that was walking under the wall. . . . The next moment the house collapsed. . . . I escaped—but in my arms—where I thought I had the child—there wasn't anything. . . .

THE OLD MAN. Remarkable. Remarkable. . . . I always knew that. . . . But tell me something: why were you making all those gestures just now at the fountain? And why were you talking to yourself?

THE STUDENT. Didn't you see the milkmaid I was talking to?

THE OLD MAN (in horror). Milkmaid?!

THE STUDENT. Yes, of course. She handed me the cup.

THE OLD MAN. Indeed? . . . So that's the way it is? . . . Very well, I may not have second sight, but I have other powers . . .

A white-haired woman sits down at the window with the mirror.

Look at the old lady in the window! Do you see her? . . . Good, good! That was my fiancée—once upon a time—sixty years ago. . . . I was twenty. Don't be afraid, she doesn't recognize me. We see each other every day, but it doesn't mean a thing to me—although we once vowed to love each other forever. Forever!

THE STUDENT. How foolish you were in those days! Nowadays we don't tell girls things like that.

THE OLD MAN. Forgive us, young man. We didn't know any better! . . . But can you see that that old woman was once young and beautiful?

THE STUDENT. No, I can't. . . . Well, maybe. I like the way she tilts her head. . . . I can't see her eyes.

The Superintendent's Wife comes out carrying a basket of spruce greens, which she strews on the sidewalk, in accordance with Swedish custom at funerals.

THE OLD MAN. Ah ha, the wife of the superintendent! The lady in black is her daughter by the dead man upstairs. That's why her husband got the job as superintendent. . . . But the lady in black has a lover—very aristocratic and waiting to inherit a fortune. Right now he's in the process of getting a divorce—from his present wife, who is giving him a town house just to get rid of him. The aristocratic lover is the son-in-law of the dead man, and you see his bedclothes being aired on the balcony up there.—Complicated, wouldn't you say?

THE STUDENT. It's damned complicated!

THE OLD MAN. Yes, indeed it is, both on the inside and the outside, although it all looks so simple.

THE STUDENT. But then who is the dead man?

THE OLD MAN. You just asked me and I told you. If you could look around the corner where the service entrance is, you'd see a pack of poor people whom he used to help—when he felt like it.

THE STUDENT. Then I suppose he was a kind and charitable man?

THE OLD MAN. Oh, yes—sometimes.

THE STUDENT. Not always?

THE OLD MAN. No, that's how people are!—Listen, will you give me a little push over there into the sun? I'm so terribly cold. When you never get to move around, the blood congeals. I'm going to die soon, I know that. But before I do, there are a few things I want to take care of.—Feel my hand, just feel how cold I am.

THE STUDENT. My god! It's unbelievable! (*He tries to free his hand, but The Old Man holds on to it.*)

THE OLD MAN. Don't leave me, I beg you—I'm tired, I'm lonely—but it hasn't always been this way, I tell you.—I have an infinitely long life behind me— infinitely long—I've made people unhappy and people have made me unhappy, the one cancels out the other. But before I die, I want to make you happy. . . . Our destinies are tangled together through your father—and other things.

THE STUDENT. Let go, let go of my hand—you are drawing all my strength from me—you're turning my blood to ice—what do you want of me?

THE OLD MAN. Patience. You'll soon see and understand. . . . There she comes—

THE STUDENT. The colonel's daughter?

THE OLD MAN. Yes! *His* daughter! Just look at her!—Have you ever seen such a masterpiece?

THE STUDENT. She looks like the marble statue in there.

THE OLD MAN. She should. That's her mother!

THE STUDENT. Incredibly beautiful! "Thou art fairer than the evening air, clad in the beauty of a thousand stars."

THE OLD MAN. Yes, indeed. "And happy he who on her lips shall press the bridegroom's greeting."—I see you appreciate her beauty. Not everyone recognizes it. . . . Well, then, it is ordained!

* * *

The Young Lady enters from the left dressed in a riding habit like a modern English horsewoman, and, without taking notice of anyone, crosses slowly over to the door of the house. Before entering, she stops and says a few words to The Superintendent's Wife. The Student covers his eyes with his hands.

Are you crying?

THE STUDENT. When I see how far beyond my reach my happiness is, what can I feel but despair?

THE OLD MAN. But I can open doors—and hearts—if only I can find an arm to do my will. Serve me, and you shall be a lord of creation!

THE STUDENT. A devil's bargain? You want me to sell my soul?

THE OLD MAN. Sell nothing!—Don't you understand, all my life I have *taken, taken*! Now I crave to give, to give! But nobody will take what I have to offer. I'm a rich man, very rich—and without any heirs. —Oh, yes, I have a good-for-nothing son who torments the life out of me. . . . You could become my son, become my heir while I'm still alive, enjoy life while I'm here to see it—at least from a distance.

THE STUDENT. What do you want me to do?

THE OLD MAN. First: go an hear *Die Walkure*!

THE STUDENT. That's already been taken care of. What else?

THE OLD MAN. This evening you shall be sitting in there—in the round room!

THE STUDENT: How do you expect me to get in?

THE OLD MAN. By way of *Die Walkure*!

THE STUDENT. Why did you pick me for your—your medium? Did you know me before?

THE OLD MAN. Of course, of course! I've had my eye on you for a long time. . . . Ah! Look up there, on the balcony, where the maid is raising the flag to half-mast for the consul—and now she's turning over the bedclothes. . . . Do you see that blue quilt? It was made for two to sleep under, and now it covers only one. . . .

The Young Lady, in a change of clothes, appears at the window to water the hyacinths.

There's my dear little girl. Look at her, just look at her! . . . She's talking to the flowers now. Isn't she just like a blue hyacinth herself? She gives them water to drink, the purest water, and they transform the water into color and perfume. — Here comes the colonel with a newspaper. . . . Now he's pointing to your picture! She's reading about your heroic deed. —It's starting to cloud over. Suppose it starts to rain? I'll be in a pretty mess if Johansson doesn't come back soon.

It grows cloudy and dark. The Old Woman at the window mirror closes her window.

I see my fiancée is closing up shop. . . . Seventy-nine years. . . . That window mirror is the only mirror she ever uses. That's because she can't see herself in it, only the outside world and from two directions at once. But the world can see her. She doesn't realize that. . . . All the same, not bad-looking for an old woman.

The Dead Man, wrapped in a winding sheet, is seen coming out of the main door.

THE STUDENT: Oh my god, what—?

THE OLD MAN. What do you see?

THE STUDENT. Don't *you* see? Don't you see, in the doorway, the dead man?

THE OLD MAN. No, I don't see anything. But I'm not surprised. Tell me exactly what—

THE STUDENT. He's stepping out into the street. . . . (*Pauses.*) Now he's turning his head and looking up at the flag.

THE OLD MAN. What did I tell you? Watch, he will count every wreath and read every calling card. I pity whoever is missing!

341

THE STUDENT. Now he's turning the corner. . . .

THE OLD MAN. He's gone to count the poor people at the service entrance. The poor add such a nice touch to an obituary: "Received the blessings of the populace!" Yes, but he won't receive my blessing!—Just between us, he was a big scoundrel.

THE STUDENT. But benevolent.

THE OLD MAN. A benevolent scoundrel. Always thinking of his own magnificent funeral. . . . When he could feel his end was near, he embezzled fifty thousand crowns from the state. . . . Now his daughter is running around with another woman's husband and wondering about the will. . . . The scoundrel can hear every word we're saying. I hope he gets an earful! —Here's Johansson.

Johansson enters from the left.

Report!

Johannson speaks to The Old Man, but the audience cannot hear what he says.

What do you mean, not at home? You're an ass! —What about the telegram? —Not a word! . . . Go on, go on! . . . Six o'clock this evening? That's good! —An extra edition? —With all the details about him? . . . Arkenholz, student . . . born . . . his parents. . . . Splendid! . . . It's beginning to rain, I think. . . . And what did he say? . . . Really, really! —He didn't *want* to? Well, he's going to have to! —Here comes the baron, or whatever he is! —Push me around the corner, Johansson. I want to hear what the poor people are saying. —And Arkenholz! Don't go away. Do you understand? —Well, come on, come on, what are you waiting for!

Johansson pushes the wheelchair around the corner.

* * *

The Student has turned to look at The Young Lady, who is loosening the earth in hyacinth pots.

* * *

Dressed in mourning, Baron Skanskorg enters and speaks to The Lady in Black, who has been walking up and down the sidewalk.

BARON SKANSKORG. What can we do about it? We simply have to wait.

LADY IN BLACK (*intensely*). But I can't wait, don't you understand?

BARON SKANSKORG. Well, if that's the way it is, you'll have to go to the country.

LADY IN BLACK. I don't want to do that!

BARON SKANSKORG. Come over here. Otherwise they'll hear what we're saying.

They move over toward the kiosk and continue their conversation unheard by the audience.

* * *

Johansson enters from the right.

JOHANSSON (*to The Student*). My master asks you not to forget that other matter . . .

THE STUDENT (*warily*). Just a minute—I want to know something first. Tell me, exactly who is Hummel? What is he?

JOHANSSON. What can I say? He's so many things, and he's been everything.

THE STUDENT. Is he in his right mind?

JOHANSSON. Who is? All his life he's been looking for a Sunday child. That's what he says—but he might be making it up . . .

THE STUDENT. What's he after? Money?

JOHANSSON. Power. —All day long he rides around in his chariot like the great god Thor. . . . He keeps his eye on houses, tears them down, opens up streets, builds up city squares. But he also breaks into houses, sneaks in through the windows, ravages human lives, kills his enemies, and forgives nothing and nobody. . . . Can you imagine that that little cripple was once a Don Juan? But no woman would ever stick with him.

THE STUDENT. Sounds inconsistent.

JOHANSSON. Oh, no. You see, he was so sly that he knew how to get the women to leave when he got bored with them. But that was a long time ago. Now he's more like a horse thief at a slave market. He steals people—in more ways than one. . . . He literally stole me out of the hands of the law. I made a little mistake—that's all—and he was the only one who knew about it. But instead of putting me in jail, he made me his slave. I slave for him just for my food—which isn't the best in the world.

THE STUDENT. What's he got up his sleeve? What's he want to do in this house?

JOHANSSON. I wouldn't want to say! I wouldn't even know where to begin!

THE STUDENT. I think I'd better get out while the getting is good.

JOHANSSON. Look at the young lady! She's dropped her bracelet out of the window.

The bracelet has fallen off The Young Lady's arm and through the open window. The Student crosses over slowly, picks up the bracelet, and hands it to The Young Lady, who thanks him stiffly. The Student goes back to Johansson.

I thought you said you were leaving. It isn't as easy as you think once *he* has slipped his net over your head. . . . And he's afraid of nothing between heaven and earth—yes, one thing—or rather one person.

THE STUDENT. I bet I know.

JOHANSSON. How can you know?

THE STUDENT. Just guessing! Could it be . . . he's afraid of a little milkmaid?

JOHANSSON. He turns his head away whenever he sees a milk wagon. . . . Sometimes he talks in his sleep. He must have been in Hamburg once . . .

THE STUDENT. Can I depend on him?

JOHANSSON. You can depend on him—to do anything and everything!

THE STUDENT. What's he up to around the corner?

JOHANSSON. Eavesdropping on the poor. . . . Planting a word here and there, chipping away at one stone at a time—until the whole house falls—metaphorically speaking. Oh yes, I've had an education. And I used to be a bookseller. . . . Are you leaving or staying?

THE STUDENT. I don't like to be ungrateful. This man once saved my father, and all he's asking for now is a little favor in return.

JOHANSSON. What's that?

THE STUDENT. He wants me to go and see *Die Walkure.*

JOHANSSON. That's beyond me. . . . He's always got something up his sleeve. . . . Look at him, he's talking to the policeman. He's always in with the police. He makes use of them, gets them involved in his business, ties them hand and foot with false promises of future possibilities. And all the while,

he's pumping them, pumping them. —Mark my words, before the night is over he'll be received in the round room.

THE STUDENT. What does he want in there? What's he got to do with the colonel?

JOHANSSON. I'm not sure, but I've got my ideas. You'll be able to see for yourself when you go there!

THE STUDENT. I'll never get in there . . .

JOHANSSON. That depends on you! Go to *Die Walkure.*

THE STUDENT. Is that the way?

JOHANSSON. If he said so, it is! —Look at him, just look at him! Riding his war chariot, drawn in triumph by the beggars, who don't get a cent for it, just a hint that something might come their way at his funeral!

The Old Man enters, standing in his wheelchair, drawn by one of the Beggars and followed by the others.

THE OLD MAN. Let us hail the noble youth, who risked his own life to save so many in yesterday's disaster! Hail Arkenholz!

The Beggars bare their heads but do not cheer. The Young Lady, standing in the window, waves her handkerchief. The Colonel looks at the scene from his window. The Fiancee stands up at her window. The Housemaid on the balcony raises the flag to the top.

Hail the hero, my fellow citizens! I know indeed it is Sunday, but the ass in the pit and the ears of corn in the field absolve us. And though I may not be a Sunday child, I can see into the future and I can heal the sick. I have even brought a drowned soul back to life. . . . That happened in Hamburg, yes, on a Sunday morning, just like this—

The Milkmaid enters, seen only by The Student and The Old Man. She stretches her arms above her head like a drowning person and stares fixedly at The Old Man.

* * *

The Old Man sits down and shrivels up in terror.

Get me out of here, Johansson! Quick! —Arkenholz, don't you forget *Die Walkure*!

THE STUDENT. What is all this?

JOHANSSON. We shall see! We shall see!

In the round room. At the back of the stage a stove of white glazed porcelain, its mantel decorated with a mirror, a pendulum clock, and candelabra. At the right side of the stage a hallway can be seen and through it a view of a green room with mahogany furniture. At the left of the stage stands the statue in the shadow of the palm trees, and with a curtain that can be drawn to conceal it. In the rear wall to the left of the stove is the door to the hyacinth room, where The Young Lady is seen reading. The Colonel's back can be seen in the green room, where he is writing at his desk.

The Colonels' valet, Bengtsson, wearing livery, enters from the hall, accompanied by Johansson, wearing the formal attire of a waiter.

BENGTSSON. Now, Johansson, you'll have to wait on the table while I take care of the coats. Have you done this before?

JOHANSSON. During the day I push that war chariot, as you know, but in the evenings I work as a waiter at receptions. It's always been my dream to get into this house. . . . They're peculiar people, aren't they?

BENGTSSON. Well, yes, I think one might say that they're a little strange.

JOHANSSON. Are we going to have a musicale this evening? Or what is the occasion?

BENGTSSON. Just the ordinary ghost supper, as we call it. They drink tea, without saying a word, or else the colonel talks all by himself. And they chomp their biscuits and crackers all at once and all in unison. They sound like a pack of rats in an attic.

JOHANSSON. Why do you call it the ghost supper?

BENGTSSON. They all look like ghosts. . . . This has been going on for twenty years—always the same people, always saying the same things. Or else keeping silent to avoid being embarrassed.

JOHANSSON. Where's the lady of the house? Isn't she around?

BENGTSSON. Oh, yes. But she's crazy. She keeps herself shut up in a closet because her eyes can't stand the light. She's sitting in there right now. (*He points to a wallpapered door.*)

JOHANSSON. In there?

BENGTSSON. I told you they were a little peculiar.

JOHANSSON. What on earth does she look like?

BENGTSSON. Like a mummy. Do you want to see her? (*He opens the papered door.*) There she sits!

JOHANSSON. Je-sus!

* * *

THE MUMMY (*babbling*). Why do you open the door? Didn't I tell you to keep it closed?

BENGTSSON (*as if talking to a baby*). Ta, ta, ta, ta, ta! —Is little chickadee going to be nice to me? Then little chickadee will get something good! — Pretty Polly!

THE MUMMY (*like a parrot*). Pretty Polly! Are you there, Jacob? Jacob? Cluck, cluck!

BENGTSSON. She thinks she's a parrot—and maybe she is. (*To The Mummy.*) Come on, Polly, whistle for us!

The Mummy whistles.

JOHANSSON. I thought I had seen everything, but this tops it all.

BENGTSSON. Well, when a house grows old, it turns moldy and rotten, and when people are together too much and torment each other too long, they go crazy. Take the lady in this house—shut up, Polly! —This mummy has been sitting here for forty years—the same husband, same furniture, same relatives, same friends. . . . (*Closing the door on The Mummy.*) And imagine what's gone on in this house! Even I don't know the whole story. . . . Look at this statue. That's the lady of the house as a young girl!

JOHANSSON. Oh my god! —Is that the mummy?

BENGTSSON. Yes. It's enough to make one cry! But this lady—carried away by her imagination or something—has acquired certain peculiarities, as babbling parrots do. She can't stand cripples, for instance—or sick people. She can't even stand the sight of her own daughter because she's sick.

JOHANSSON. Is that young girl sick?

BENGTSSON. Yes. Didn't you know?

JOHANSSON. No. . . . What about the colonel? Who is he?

BENGTSSON. Wait awhile and you'll see!

JOHANSSON (*looking at the statue*). It's terrifying to realize that—. How old is the lady now?

BENGTSSON. Who knows? But I've heard it said that when she was thirty-five she looked like she was nineteen. —And she convinced the colonel that she was . . . here in this house. . . . Do you know what that black Japanese screen by the couch is for? It's called a death screen, and when somebody's going to die, it's placed around them, same as in a hospital.

JOHANSSON. What a horrible house. . . . That poor student thought that when he entered this house he would be entering paradise.

BENGTSSON. Which student? Oh, yes, of course! The one that's coming here tonight. The colonel and his daughter met him at the opera and were captivated by him. . . . Hm. . . . But let me ask you a couple of questions. Who's your master? The financier in the wheelchair?

JOHANSSON (*nodding*). Yes, that's right. —Is he coming here too?

BENGTSSON. He's not invited.

JOHANSSON. He'll come uninvited—if he has to.

The Old Man appears in the hallway dressed in frock coat and high hat. He creeps silently forward on his crutches and eavesdrops on the servants.

BENGTSSON. I'll bet he's a real mean old one.

JOHANSSON. A perfect specimen!

BENGTSSON. He looks like the devil incarnate!

JOHANSSON. And he's a black magician, I tell you. He can go through locked doors—

* * *

THE OLD MAN (*coming forward and grabbing Johansson by the ear*). Fool! Hold your tongue! (*To Bengtsson.*) Announce me to the colonel.

BENGTSSON. But we're expecting company here.

THE OLD MAN. I know you are! My visit is not unexpected—although undesired.

BENGTSSON. I see. What was the name? Mr. Hummel?

THE OLD MAN. That's right! Precisely!

Bengtsson goes down the hall into the green room and closes the door.

* * *

THE OLD MAN (*to Johansson*). Disappear!

Johansson hesitates.

Vanish!

Johansson vanishes down the hall.

* * *

The Old Man inspects the room. Stops in front of the statue. Much amazed.

THE OLD MAN. Amelia! . . . It is she! . . . Amelia! (*He roams about the room fingering objects. Stops in front of the mirror to adjust his wig. Returns to the statue.*)

THE MUMMY (*from within the closet*). Pretty Polly!

THE OLD MAN (*startled*). What on earth? Sounded like a parrot in the room. But I don't see any.

THE MUMMY. You there, Jacob?

THE OLD MAN. Place is haunted.

THE MUMMY. Jacob!

THE OLD MAN. It's enough to frighten one! . . . So that's the kind of secrets they keep in this house. (*With his back to the closet, he studies a portrait on the wall.*) There he is! —The old colonel himself!

* * *

THE MUMMY (*coming out of the closet, goes up to The Old Man from behind and gives his wig a pull*). Coo, coo, coo! Cuckoo, cuckoo!

THE OLD MAN (*frightened out of his skin*). Oh my God in heaven! —Who are you?

THE MUMMY (*speaking in her normal voice*). Is that you, Jacob?

THE OLD MAN. Yes. My name is Jacob.

THE MUMMY (*movingly*). And my name is Amelia!

THE OLD MAN. Oh no. . . . No, no. . . . Oh my God!

THE MUMMY. Yes, this is how I look! —And that's how I did look once upon a time. Life gives one a great education. Most of my life I've spent in the closet, so that I won't have to see—or be seen. . . . But you, Jacob, what are you looking for here?

THE OLD MAN. My child! Our child!

THE MUMMY. She's sitting in there.

THE OLD MAN. Where?

THE MUMMY. In there, in the hyacinth room.

THE OLD MAN (*looking at The Young Lady*). Yes, there she is! (*Pause.*) And what does her father think of her—I mean, the colonel—your husband?

THE MUMMY. I had a quarrel with him once, and told him everything. . . .

THE OLD MAN. And. . . ?

THE MUMMY. He didn't believe me. He said, "That's what all women say when they want to murder their husbands." . . . All the same it was a terrible crime. His whole life has been falsified, including his family tree. When I look at his family record in the peerage, I say to myself she's no better than a runaway servant girl with a false birth certificate, and girls like that are sent to the reformatory.

THE OLD MAN. A lot of people forge their birth certificates. I seem to remember that even you falsified the date of your birth.

THE MUMMY. It was my mother who put me up to it. I'm not to blame for that! . . . And furthermore, you played the biggest part in our crime.

THE OLD MAN. Not true! Your husband started it all when he stole my fiancée from me! I was born unable to forgive until I have punished. I've always looked upon it as an imperative duty. And I still do!

THE MUMMY. What do you expect to find in this house? What do you want here? And how did you get in? —Does your business concern my daughter? Keep your hands off her, I warn you, or you'll die!

THE OLD MAN. I wish her nothing but the best!

THE MUMMY. And you must have consideration for her father, too!

THE OLD MAN. Never!

THE MUMMY. Then you must die. In this room. Behind that screen.

THE OLD MAN. Be that as it may. But I'm a bulldog. I never let go.

THE MUMMY. You want to marry her to that student. Why? He has nothing; he is nothing.

THE OLD MAN. He'll be a rich man, thanks to me.

THE MUMMY. Are you one of the invited guests tonight?

THE OLD MAN. No. I've decided to invite myself to this ghost supper!

THE MUMMY. Do you know who'll be here?

THE OLD MAN. Not entirely.

THE MUMMY. The baron—who lives upstairs, and whose father-in-law was buried this afternoon—

THE OLD MAN. Yes, the baron—who is getting a divorce in order to marry the daughter of the superintendent's wife. The baron—who was once—your lover!

THE MUMMY. And then there'll be your former fiancée—whom my husband seduced. . . .

THE OLD MAN. A very select gathering. . . .

THE MUMMY. Oh God, why can't we die? If only we could die!

THE OLD MAN. Then why do you keep seeing one another?

THE MUMMY. Our crimes and our secrets and our guilt bind us together! We have split up and gone our separate ways an infinite number of times. But we're always drawn back together again. . . .

THE OLD MAN. I believe the colonel is coming.

THE MUMMY. Then I'll go in to Adele. . . . (*Pause.*) Jacob, don't do anything foolish! Be considerate toward him . . .

A pause. She leaves.

* * *

THE COLONEL (*enters, cold and reserved*). Please sit down.

The Old Man takes his time seating himself. A pause. The Colonel stares at him.

Did you write this letter?

THE OLD MAN. I did.

THE COLONEL. And your name is Hummel?

THE OLD MAN. It is.

Pause.

THE COLONEL. Since it's clear that you have bought up all my outstanding promissory notes, it follows that I'm completely at your mercy. Now what do you want?

THE OLD MAN. I want to be paid—in one way or another.

THE COLONEL. In what way?

THE OLD MAN. A very simple way. Don't let's talk about money. Allow me to come and go in your house—as a guest.

THE COLONEL. If that's all it takes to satisfy you—

THE OLD MAN. Thank you!

THE COLONEL. And what else?

THE OLD MAN. Dismiss Bengtsson!

THE COLONEL. Why? Bengtsson is my devoted servant. He's been with me during my whole career. The army awarded him a medal for faithful service. Why should I dismiss him?

THE OLD MAN. I have no doubt he's a very fine man in your eyes. But he's not the man he seems to be!

THE COLONEL. Who is?

THE OLD MAN (*taken aback*). True! —But Bengtsson must go!

THE COLONEL. Are you going to give orders in my house?

THE OLD MAN. Yes! Since I own everything that you can lay your eyes on—furniture, curtains, dinner service, linen . . . and other things . . .

THE COLONEL. What other things?

THE OLD MAN. Everything. I own it all. Everything that you see here is mine!

THE COLONEL. I can't dispute that. But my family honor, my coat of arms, and my good name are things you cannot take from me!

THE OLD MAN. Yes, I can. They don't belong to you. (*Pause.*) You are not a nobleman.

THE COLONEL. I shall give you the opportunity of withdrawing those words!

THE OLD MAN (*producing a piece of paper*). If you will take the trouble to read this extract from the standard book of genealogy, you will see that the family whose name you have assumed has been extinct for over a century.

THE COLONEL (*reading*). Of course I've heard rumors like this before. But it was my father's name before it was mine. . . . (*Reading on.*) I can't deny it. You are quite right. . . . I am not a nobleman! Not even that. . . . Therefore I shall take this signet ring off my hand. —Oh, but of course, excuse me: it belongs to you. There you are.

THE OLD MAN (*putting the ring in his pocket*). Let us continue.—You are not a colonel either!

THE COLONEL. Am I not?

THE OLD MAN. No! You held a temporary commission as a colonel in the American Volunteers, but at the end of the Spanish-American War and the reorganization of the army, all such titles were abolished.

THE COLONEL. Is that true?

THE OLD MAN (*reaching into his pocket*). Do you want to see for yourself?

THE COLONEL. No, it won't be necessary. . . . Who are you? What gives you the right to sit there and strip me naked in this way?

THE OLD MAN. Patience, my good man! And as far as stripping is concerned—do you really want to know who you are?

THE COLONEL. Have you no decency?

THE OLD MAN. Take off that wig of yours and have a look at yourself in the mirror. And while you're at it, take out those false teeth and shave off that moustache and let Bengtsson unlace your metal corset, and then we shall see if a certain valet who shall be nameless won't recognize himself—the cupboard lover who flirted with the maids so he could scrounge in the kitchen.

The Colonel reaches for the bell on the table. The Old Man stops him, saying:

I wouldn't touch that if I were you. If you call Bengtsson I'll order him arrested. . . . I believe your guests are arriving. Now let us be calm and go on playing our old roles for a while longer.

THE COLONEL. Who are you? I've seen your eyes and heard your voice before.

THE OLD MAN. Never mind that. Be silent and do as you're told!

* * *

THE STUDENT (*enters and bows to The Colonel*). How do you do, sir!

THE COLONEL. Welcome to my house, young man! Your heroism at that terrible accident has brought your name to everybody's lips. I deem it an honor to receive you in my house.

THE STUDENT. You're very kind, sir. It's a great honor for me, sir. I've never expected—well, my humble birth—and your illustrious name and your noble birth . . .

THE COLONEL. Mr. Hummel, may I introduce Mr. Arkenholz, who is a student at the university. The ladies are in there, Mr. Arkenholz—if you care to join them. I have a few more things I want to say to Mr. Hummel.

The Colonel shows The Student into the hyacinth room, where he remains visible to the audience, engaged in shy conversation with The Young Lady.

* * *

THE COLONEL. An excellent young man—musical, sings, writes poetry. . . . If it weren't for his birth and social position I certainly wouldn't have anything against—my . . .

THE OLD MAN. Against what?

THE COLONEL. Having my daughter—

THE OLD MAN. *Your* daughter! . . . Apropos of her, why does she always sit in that room?

THE COLONEL. She feels she has to sit in the hyacinth room whenever she's in the house. A peculiarity of hers. . . . Here comes Miss Beatrice von Holsteinkrona. Charming woman.—Very distinguished family, but hasn't a cent to her name. All she's got goes to the nursing home.

THE OLD MAN (*to himself*). My fiancée!

* * *

The Fiancee enters, white-haired and giving every appearance of being crazy.

THE COLONEL. Miss Holsteinkrona—Mr. Hummel.

The Fiancee curtsies and takes a seat.

* * *

Baron Skanskorg enters next—dressed in mourning and with a strange look on his face—and sits down.

THE COLONEL. Baron Skanskorg—

THE OLD MAN (*in an aside, without rising.*). A jewel thief, if ever I saw one. (*To The Colonel.*) Now let the mummy in, and the party can begin.

THE COLONEL (*in the doorway to the hyacinth room*). Polly!

* * *

THE MUMMY (*enters*). Coo, coo! Cuckoo, cuckoo!

THE COLONEL. Shall we invite the young people, too?

THE OLD MAN. No! Not the young people! They shall be spared.

They seat themselves in a circle. Silence.

* * *

THE COLONEL. Shall I ring for tea?

THE OLD MAN. Why bother? No one cares for tea. Why play games?

Pause.

THE COLONEL. Then perhaps we should start a conversation?

THE OLD MAN (*slowly, deliberately, and with frequent pauses*). About the weather? Which we know. Ask one another how we're feeling? Which we also know. I prefer silence . . . in which one can hear thoughts and see the past. Silence cannot hide anything—which is more than you can say for words. I read the other day that the differences in languages originated among the primitive savages, who sought to keep their secrets from other tribes. Languages are therefore codes, and he who finds the key can understand all the languages of the world. But that doesn't mean that secrets cannot be discovered without a key. Especially in those cases where paternity must be proved. Legal proof is of course a different matter. Two false witnesses provide complete proof of whatever they agree to say. But in the kind of escapades I have in mind, one doesn't take witnesses along. Nature herself has planted in man a blushing sense of shame, which seeks to hide what should be hidden. But we slip into certain situations without intending to, and chance confronts us with moments of revelation, when the deepest secrets are revealed, the mask is ripped from the imposter and the villain stands exposed . . .

Pause. All look at one another in silence.

Extraordinary, how silent you all are! (*Long silence.*) Take this house, for example. In this estimable house, in this elegant house, where beauty, wealth, and culture are united. . . . (*Long silence.*) All of us sitting here, we know who we are, don't we? . . . I don't have to tell you. . . . And you know me, although you pretend ignorance. . . . Sitting in that room is my daughter, yes mine, you know that too. . . . She had lost all desire to live, without knowing why. . . . She was withering away because of the air in this house, which reeks of crime, deception, and lies of every kind. . . . That is why I had to find a friend for her, a friend from whose very presence she would apprehend the warmth and light radiated by a noble deed. . . . (*Long silence.*) That was my mission in this house. To pull up the weeds, to expose the crimes, to settle the accounts, so that these young people might make a new beginning in this home, which is my gift to them! (*Long silence.*) Listen to the ticking of the clock, like a deathwatch beetle in the wall! Listen to what it's saying: "time's-up, time's-up! . . ." When it strikes—in just a few moments—your time is up. Then you may go—not before.

The clock can be heard preparing to strike the hour.

Hear! The hammer draws back, the wheels whir. It's warning you: "clocks can strike!" —And I can strike too! (*He strikes the table with his crutch.*) Do you understand?

Silence.

THE MUMMY (*goes over to the clock and stops its pendulum. In her normal voice, speaking purposefully*). But I can stop time in its course. I can wipe out the past, and undo what is done. Not with bribes, not with threats—but through suffering and repentance. (*Approaching The Old Man.*) We are poor miserable creatures, we know that. We have erred, we have transgressed, we, like all the rest. We are not what we seem to be. At bottom we are better than ourselves, since we abhor and detest our misdeeds. But when you, Jacob Hummel, with your false name, come here to sit in judgment over us, that proves that you are more contemptible than we! And you are not the one you seem to be! You are a slave trader, a stealer of souls! You once stole me with false promises. You murdered the consul who was buried today; you strangled him with debts. You have stolen the student and shackled him with an imaginary debt of his father's, who never owed you a penny . . .

The Old Man has tried to rise and speak but has collapsed in his chair and shriveled up and, like a dying insect, he shrivels up more and more during the following dialogue.

But there is one dark spot in your life, which I'm not sure about—although I have my suspicions. . . . I think that Bengtsson might help us. (*She rings the bell on the table.*)

THE OLD MAN. No! Not Bengtsson! Not him!

THE MUMMY. Then it is true? He does know! (*She rings again.*)

The Milkmaid appears in the door to the hall, unseen by all except The Old Man, who shies in terror. The Milkmaid disappears when Bengtsson enters.

Bengtsson, do you know this man?

BENGTSSON. Yes, I know him, and he knows me. Life has its ups and downs, as we all know, and I have been in his service, and once he was in mine. To be exact, he was a sponger in my kitchen for two whole years. Since he had to be out of the house by three o'clock, dinner had to be ready at two, and those in the house had to eat the warmed-up food left by that ox. Even worse, he drank up the pure soup stock and the gravy, which then had to be diluted with water. He sat there like a vampire, sucking all the marrow out of the house, and turned us all into skeletons. And he nearly succeeded in putting us into prison, when we accused the cook of being a thief. . . . Later I met this man in Hamburg under another name. He had become a usurer or bloodsucker. And it was there that he was accused of having lured a young girl out onto the ice in order to drown her, for she was the only witness to a crime that he was afraid would come to light . . .

THE MUMMY (*passes her hand over The Old Man's face*). That is the real you! Now empty your pockets of the notes and the will!

Johansson appears in the door to the hall and watches The Old Man intently, knowing that his slavery is coming to an end. The Old Man produces a bundle of papers, which he throws on the table.

The Mummy strokes The Old Man's back.

> Little Polly Parrot
> Sat in the garret,
> Eating toast and tea.

THE OLD MAN (*like a parrot*).

> Polly put the kettle on,
> Polly put the kettle on,
> We'll all have tea.
> Jack and Jill, Jack and Jill!

THE MUMMY. Can—clocks—strike?

THE OLD MAN (*making clucking sounds*). Clocks can strike! (*He imitates a cuckoo clock.*) Coo-coo! Coo-coo! Coo-coo!

THE MUMMY (*opening the jib door to the closet*). Now the clock has struck! Stand up and enter the closet where I have sat for twenty years, crying over our misdeeds. You'll find a rope in there. It can stand for the one you strangled the consul with—for the one you intended to strangle your benefactor with. . . . Go in!

The Old Man goes into the closet. The Mummy closes the door.

THE MUMMY. Bengtsson! Put up the screen. The death screen.

Bengtsson places the screen in front of the door.

It is finished. —May God have mercy on his soul!

ALL. Amen!

Long silence.

* * *

In the hyacinth room, The Young Lady can be seen sitting at a harp on which she accompanies The Student. After a prelude played by The Young Lady, The Student recites.

THE STUDENT:
I saw the sun
And from its blaze
There burst on me
The deepest truth:

Man reaps as he sows;
Blessed is he
Who sows the good.

For deeds done in anger
Kindness alone
Can make amends.

Bring cheer to those
Whom you have hurt,
And kindness reaps
Its own rewards.

The pure in heart
Have none to fear.
The harmless are happy.
The guileless are good.

[3]

A room decorated in a bizarre style, predominantly oriental. A profusion of hyacinths in all colors fills the room. On the porcelain tile stove sits a large Buddha with a bulb of a shallot (allium ascalonicum) in its lap. The stem of the shallot rises from the bulb and bursts into a spherical cluster of white, starlike flowers. In the rear to the right, a door leads to the round room. The Colonel and The Mummy can be seen in there sitting motionless and silent. A part of the death screen is also visible. To the left in the rear, a door to the pantry and the kitchen. The Student and The Young Lady (Adele) are near a table, she seated at her harp, he standing beside her.

THE YOUNG LADY. Now you must sing a song to my flowers!

THE STUDENT. Is this the flower of your soul?

THE YOUNG LADY. The one and only! Don't you love the hyacinth?

THE STUDENT. I love it above all other flowers—its stem rising straight and slender, like a young maiden, from the round bulb, which floats on water and sends its white rare roots down into clear, colorless nothingness. I love it for its colors: the snow-white, innocent and pure—the golden yellow, sweet as honey—the shy pink, the ripe red—but above all the blue ones—blue as morning mist, deep-eyed blue, ever-faithful blue. I love them all—more than gold and pearls. Have loved them ever since I was a child, have worshiped them because they possess all the virtues I lack. . . . But still—

THE YOUNG LADY. What?

THE STUDENT. My love is not returned. These beautiful blossoms hate and detest me.

THE YOUNG LADY. How?

THE STUDENT. Their fragrance—as strong and clear as the first winds of spring, sweeping down from the fields of melting snow—confuses my senses— they deafen me, blind me, drive me out of my mind—impale me with their poisonous arrows that stab my heart and set my head afire! . . . Don't you know the story behind that flower?

THE YOUNG LADY. No. Tell me.

THE STUDENT. First you have to interpret it. The bulb is the earth, whether floating on water or buried deep in black humus. Here the stalk shoots up, straight as the axis of the world, and here at its upper end are gathered together the six-pointed star flowers.

THE YOUNG LADY. Above the earth, the stars! How sublime! How did you know that? Where did you discover that?

THE STUDENT. I don't know. Let me think. —In your eyes! . . . So you see, it's an image of the whole cosmos. That's why Buddha sits there with the bulb of the earth in his lap, watching it constantly to see it shoot up and burst forth and be transformed into a heaven. This poor earth shall become a heaven! That is what Buddha is waiting for!

THE YOUNG LADY. Of course! I see that now! —And don't the snowflakes have six points like the hyacinth?

THE STUDENT. Exactly! Then snowflakes are falling stars—

THE YOUNG LADY. And the snowdrop is a snow-star—growing out of the snow.

THE STUDENT. And Sirius, the largest and most beautiful of all the stars in the firmament, golden-red Sirius is the narcissus with its golden-red chalice and its six white rays—

THE YOUNG LADY. Have you seen the shallot burst into bloom?

THE STUDENT. Yes, of course I have! It hides its blossoms in a ball—a globe just like the celestial globe, strewn with white stars.

THE YOUNG LADY. How heavenly! Wonderful! Whose idea was it?

THE STUDENT. Yours!

THE YOUNG LADY. Yours!

THE STUDENT. Ours. We have given birth to something together. We are wedded . . .

THE YOUNG LADY. No, not yet . . .

THE STUDENT. Why not? What else?

THE YOUNG LADY. Time—testing—patience.

THE STUDENT. Very well! Put me to the test! (*Pause.*) So silent? . . . Why do your parents sit in there, silent, without saying a single word?

THE YOUNG LADY. Because they have nothing to say to each other, since they don't believe what the other says. My father explains it this way: he says, "What good does talking do, we can't pull the wool over our eyes."

THE STUDENT. It makes me sick to hear things like that . . .

THE YOUNG LADY. The cook is coming this way. . . . Look at her, how big and fat she is . . .

THE STUDENT. What does she want?

THE YOUNG LADY. She wants to ask me about dinner. I've been managing the house during my mother's illness.

THE STUDENT. What have we got to do with the kitchen?

THE YOUNG LADY. We have to eat, don't we? . . . Look at her, look at her. I can't bear to . . .

THE STUDENT. Who is that bloated monster?

THE YOUNG LADY. She belongs to the Hummel family of vampires. She's eating us up . . .

THE STUDENT. Why don't you fire her?

THE YOUNG LADY. She won't leave! We can't control her. We got her because of our sins. . . . Don't you see that we're wasting away, withering?

THE STUDENT. Don't you get enough food to eat?

THE YOUNG LADY. We get course after course, but all the strength is gone from the food. She boils the beef until there's nothing left of it and serves us the sinews swimming in water while she herself drinks the stock. And when we have a roast, she cooks all the juice out of it and drinks it and eats the gravy. Everything she touches loses its flavor. It's as if she sucked it up with her very eyes. We get the grounds when she has finished her coffee. She drinks the wine and fills up the bottles with water.

THE STUDENT. Get rid of her!

THE YOUNG LADY. We can't!

THE STUDENT. Why not?

THE YOUNG LADY. We don't know! She won't leave! No one can control her. . . . She has taken all our strength from us.

THE STUDENT. Let me get rid of her for you.

THE YOUNG LADY. Oh, no! I guess this is how it's supposed to be. . . . Here she is! She'll ask me what we're having for dinner—I'll tell her this and that—she'll make objections—and finally we'll have what she says.

THE STUDENT. Then let her decide in the first place!

THE YOUNG LADY. She won't do that.

THE STUDENT. What a strange house! It's haunted, isn't it?

THE YOUNG LADY. Yes. —She's turning back now. She saw you!

* * *

THE COOK (*in the doorway*). Ha, that ain't why! (*Grinning so that all her teeth show.*)

THE STUDENT. Get out!

THE COOK. When I feel like it I will! (*Pause.*) Now I feel like it!

She vanishes.

THE YOUNG LADY. Don't lose your temper. Learn to be patient. She's part of the trials and tribulations we have to go through in this home. And we've got a housemaid, too! Whom we have to clean up after!

THE STUDENT. I can feel myself sinking into the earth! —*Cor in aethere*! —Let's have music!

THE YOUNG LADY. Wait!

THE STUDENT. No! Music now!

THE YOUNG LADY. Patience! —This room is called the testing room. It's beautiful to look at, but it's full of imperfections.

THE STUDENT. I don't believe it. But if it's true, we'll just have to ignore them. It's beautiful, but a little cold. Why don't you start the fire?

THE YOUNG LADY. Because it smokes up the room.

THE STUDENT. Can't you have the chimney cleaned?

THE YOUNG LADY. It doesn't help! . . . Do you see that writing table?

THE STUDENT. What an extraordinarily handsome piece!

THE YOUNG LADY. But it wobbles. Every day I lay a piece of cork under that foot, but the housemaid takes it away when she sweeps, and I have to cut a new piece. The penholder is covered with ink every morning, and so is the inkstand, and I have to clean them up after her, as regularly as the sun goes up. (*Pause.*) What do you hate most to do?

THE STUDENT. To sort the week's wash! (*Grimaces in disgust.*)

THE YOUNG LADY. That's what I have to do! (*Grimacing in disgust.*)

THE STUDENT. What else?

THE YOUNG LADY. To be awakened in the middle of the night, to have to get up and close the banging window—which the housemaid forgot to close.

THE STUDENT. Go on.

THE YOUNG LADY. To climb up on a ladder and fix the damper on the stovepipe after the maid broke off the cord.

THE STUDENT. Go on.

THE YOUNG LADY. To sweep up after her, to dust after her, and to start the fire in the stove after her—all she does is bring in the wood! To adjust the damper, to dry the glasses, to set the table *over* and *over* again, to pull the corks out of the bottles, to open the windows and air the rooms, to make and remake my bed, to rinse the water bottle when it's green with sediment, to buy matches and soap, which we're always out of, to wipe the chimneys and trim the wicks to keep the lamps from smoking—and to keep the lamps from going out, I have to fill them myself when we have company. . . .

THE STUDENT. Let's have music!

THE YOUNG LADY. You have to wait! —First comes the drudgery, the drudgery of keeping oneself above the dirt of life.

THE STUDENT. But you're well off. You've got two servants.

THE YOUNG LADY. Doesn't make any difference! Even if we had three! Living is such a nuisance, and I get so tired at times. . . . Imagine, if on top of it all one had a nursery and a baby crib.

THE STUDENT. The dearest of joys!

THE YOUNG LADY. The dearest in more ways than one. . . . Is life really worth so much trouble?

THE STUDENT. I suppose that depends on the reward you expect for all your troubles. . . . There's nothing I wouldn't do to win your hand.

THE YOUNG LADY. Don't say that! You can never have me!

THE STUDENT. Why not?

THE YOUNG LADY. You mustn't ask.

Pause.

THE STUDENT. You dropped your bracelet out the window. . . .

THE YOUNG LADY. Because my hand has grown so thin.

Pause. The Cook appears with a Japanese bottle in her hand.

She's the one who's eating me—and all the rest of us.

THE STUDENT. What is she holding in her hand?

THE YOUNG LADY. It's a bottle of coloring matter. It's got letters on it that look like scorpions. It's filled with soy sauce—which takes the place of gravy, which is transformed into soup, which serves as stock for cooking cabbage in, which is used to make mock turtle soup . . .

THE STUDENT. Get out!

THE COOK. You suck the sap from us and we from you. We take the blood and give you back water—with coloring added. This is the coloring! —I'm leaving now, but you won't ever be rid of me.

She leaves.

THE STUDENT. Why was Bengtsson given a medal?

THE YOUNG LADY. Because of his great merits.

THE STUDENT. Has he no faults?

THE YOUNG LADY. Yes, many great ones. But you don't get medals for them.

They smile at each other.

* * *

THE STUDENT. You have a great many secrets in this house.

THE YOUNG LADY. As in all houses. Permit us to keep ours.

Pause.

THE STUDENT. Do you admire frankness?

THE YOUNG LADY. Yes, within moderation.

THE STUDENT. Sometimes there comes over me a crazy desire to say everything I'm thinking. But I know the world would collapse completely if we were completely honest. (*Pause.*) I went to a funeral the other day. . . . In church. . . . Very solemn, very beautiful.

THE YOUNG LADY. Mr. Hummel's funeral?

THE STUDENT. Yes, my false benefactor's. At the head of the coffin stood an old friend of the deceased. He carried the mace. The priest impressed me especially, his dignified manner and his moving words. I cried. We all cried. And afterward we went to a restaurant. . . . And there I learned that the macebearer had been in love with the dead man's son.

The Young Lady looks at him to catch his meaning.

Yes. And the dead man had borrowed money from his son's lover. . . . (*Pause.*) The day after that, they arrest the priest for embezzling church funds! It's a pretty story isn't it?

The Young Lady turns her head away in disgust. Pause.

Do you know what I think of you now?

THE YOUNG LADY. You must not tell me or I'll die!

THE STUDENT. But I must or I'll die!

THE YOUNG LADY. In an asylum they say whatever they feel like.

THE STUDENT. Exactly right! That's where my father ended up—in a madhouse.

THE YOUNG LADY. Was he ill?

THE STUDENT. No, he was quite healthy. But he was crazy! It just came over him. Let me tell you how it happened. . . . Like all of us, he had his circle of acquaintances, whom for convenience' sake he called his friends. Of course they were a pretty sorry bunch of good-for-nothings—like most people. But he had to have some acquaintances, he couldn't just sit alone. Now one doesn't tell a person what one really thinks of him, not in ordinary conversation anyway—and my father didn't either. He knew how false they were. He saw through their deceitfulness right to the bottom of their souls. But he was an intelligent man, brought up to behave properly, and so he was always polite. But one day he gave a big party. It was evening, he was tired after a day's work, and under the strain of forcing himself to hold his tongue half the time and of bullshitting with his guests the other half . . .

The Young Lady glances at him reproachfully.

Well, whatever the reason, at the dinner table he rapped for silence, raised his glass, and began to make a speech. . . . Then something loosed the trigger, and in a long oration he stripped naked every single person there, one after another. Told them of all their deceits. And at the end, exhausted, he sat down right in the middle of the table and told them all to go straight to hell!

The Young Lady moans.

I was there and heard it all. I'll never forget what happened afterward. . . . Father and Mother began to fight, the guests rushed for the door— and my father was taken off to the madhouse, where he died! (*Pause.*) If you keep silent too long, things begin to rot. Stagnant, stinking pools begin to form. That's what's happening in this house. Something's rotting here. And I thought it was paradise when I saw you come in here for the first time. . . . It was a Sunday morning, and I stood looking into these rooms. I saw a colonel who wasn't a colonel. I had a magnanimous benefactor who turned out to be a bandit and had to hang himself. I saw a mummy who wasn't one, and a maiden who—speaking of which, where can one find virginity? Where is beauty to be found? In nature, and in my mind when it's all dressed up in its Sunday clothes. Where do honor and faith exist? In fairy tales and plays for children. Where can you find anything that fulfills its promise? Only in one's imagination! . . . Now your flowers have poisoned me, and I have passed the poison back. I begged you to become my wife in my home. We played and we sang. We created poetry together.

And then came the cook. . . . *Sursum corda!* Try just once again to pluck fire and brightness from the golden harp! Please try! I beg you, I implore you on my knees! . . . Very well. Then I shall do it myself. (*He takes the harp, but no sound comes from the strings.*) It is silent and deaf. Tell me, why are beautiful flowers so poisonous, and the most beautiful the most deadly? Why? The whole creation, all of life, is cursed and damned. . . . Why would you not become my bride? Because you are sick, infected at the very core of life. . . . Now I can feel that vampire in the kitchen beginning to suck the blood from me. She must be one of those lamias that suck the blood of suckling babes. It's always in the kitchen that the children are nipped in the bud. And if not there, then in the bedroom. . . . There are poisons that seal the eyes and poisons that open them. I must have been born with the latter kind in my veins, because I cannot see what is ugly as beautiful and I cannot call what is evil good. I cannot. They say that Christ harrowed hell. What they really meant was that He descended to earth, to this madhouse, jailhouse, charnel house. And the inmates crucified Him when He tried to free them. But the robber they let go. Robbers always win sympathy. . . . Woe! Woe to all of us! Saviour of the World, save us! We are perishing!

The Young Lady has collapsed during this speech. She is obviously dying. She rings the bell. Bengtsson enters.

THE YOUNG LADY. Bring the screen. Quickly! I'm dying.

Bengtsson returns with the screen, opens it, and places it in front of The Young Lady.

THE STUDENT. Your redeemer is coming! Welcome, pale and gentle one. . . . And you, my darling, you beautiful, innocent, lost soul who suffers for no fault of your own, sleep, sleep a dreamless sleep. And when you wake again . . . may you be greeted by a sun that doesn't scorch, in a home without dust, by friends without faults, and by a love without flaw. . . . Buddha, wise and gentle Buddha, sitting there waiting for a heaven to grow out of the earth, grant us the purity of will and the patience to endure our tribulations that hope will not come to shame.

The harp strings begin to move and hum. Pure white light pours into the room.

> I saw the sun
> And from its blaze
> There burst on me
> The deepest truth:
>
> Man reaps as he sows;
> Blessed is he
> Who sows the good.
>
> For deeds done in anger
> Kindness alone
> Can make amends.
>
> Bring cheer to those
> Whom you have hurt,
> And kindness reaps
> Its own rewards.
>
> The pure in heart
> Have none to fear.
> The harmless are happy.
> The guileless are good.

A moaning is heard from behind the screen.

You poor little child! Child of this world of illusion and guilt and suffering and death—this world of eternal change and disappointment and never-ending pain! May the Lord of Heaven have mercy on you as you journey forth . . .

The room vanishes. In the distance Boecklin's The Island of the Dead *appears. Music—soft, pleasant, and melancholy—is heard coming from the island.*

CURTAIN

A scene from Brecht's *Fear and Misery of the Third Reich,*
University of Minnesota, directed by Arthur H. Ballet. (Photo
courtesy of the Theatre Department, University of Minnesota.)

CHAPTER X

Brecht and Epic Theatre

With Ibsen, Chekhov and Strindberg, we have been looking at naturalism, realism, and expressionism—the cornerstones of the modern drama. In the next three chapters we examine three kinds of drama—epic theatre, theatre of cruelty, and theatre of the absurd—that represent both natural evolution of these dominant forms and at the same time strong reactions against them.

Our story of epic theatre begins, perhaps erroneously, with a young German playwright named Bertolt Brecht (1898–1956). Brecht was a Marxist and a political activist who selected the theatre as his arena of social reform. He wanted a theatre of action which would provide incentives for a new society. Brecht rejected the realistic play with its cause-and-effect plot development and need of the audience to identify with the characters. The illusion of life represented by realism, Brecht argued, involved the spectators for two hours and then left them exhausted and full of vague recollections and vaguer hopes.

Brecht knew the theatre well, for he had served as an assistant with the great German director, Max Reinhardt, at the Deutsches Theatre from 1924–1926. In 1927 Brecht came to work with a revolutionary German director, Edwin Piscator. Much of what we credit to Brecht in fact reflected the views and methods of his lesser known mentor. Piscator called his theatre "epic" and developed a series of startlingly theatrical techniques: use of choral groups to achieve the effect of mass forces in modern society; use of captions, film strips, cartoons and slides as production devices; the employment of theatrical staging, exposed lighting instruments, unadorned platforms and scaffoldings as acting areas; and theatrical intermingling of actors and audience in the audience space. Brecht was no doubt impressed with Piscator's major work, *The Good Soldier Schweik,* and one year later, in 1928, in collaboration with Kurt Weill, wrote his first major success, *The Three Penny Opera,* based on John Gay's eighteenth century British ballad opera, *The Beggar's Opera.* It is interesting that Brecht almost never dealt with original stories; he reworked fables, history, Oriental tales, newspaper accounts to present his own political and analytical vision of the world. The satire in *The Three Penny Opera* is biting and ironical. Thieves, whores, and beggars ape the manners and values of the middle and upper classes. With grotesque irony Brecht attacks the hypocrisy and resignation of the lower classes who simply accept their lot in life. The musical has traditionally been successful: its premiere production ran for 400 performances; in New York in the 1950s a version arranged by Marc Blitzstein ran for almost fifteen years, establishing a record for the long off-Broadway run; a more recent production starring Raul Julia and directed by Richard Foreman won critical acclaim at the Vivian Beaumont Theatre of Lincoln Center.

Once his reputation was established, Brecht continued to write a series of powerful political plays: *Fear and Misery in the Third Reich* (1935–1938), *Galileo* (1937–38), *Mother Courage* (1939), *The Good Woman of Setzuan* (1938–1940), *The Resistible Rise of Arturo Ui* (1941),

357

and his last major play, *The Caucasian Chalk Circle* (1944–45). Perhaps the greatest of these is *Mother Courage* set in Europe during the Thirty Years' War in the 1600s. Anna Fierling is an enterprising capitalist who lives by selling necessities to soldiers, irregardless of whether they are on the Lutheran or Catholic side. She lives off the war. At the beginning of the play three children—Eilif, Swiss Cheese, and Kattrin—help her pull her wagon full of begged, bargained for, or stolen goods. Her eldest son is seduced into enlisting while Courage haggles over the price of a belt. He is later executed for doing in peacetime what he was praised for doing in wartime. Her second son, Swiss Cheese, sweet of temperament but slow of wit, tries to protect a regimental cash box when the camp is suddenly overrun by the opposing army. Courage is given the chance to buy him back after he is taken prisoner, but she haggles over the price and her son is executed. In a scene of incredible tension, the body of Swiss Cheese is placed in front of Mother Courage, who looks at her dead son with a silent, internal scream, and then tells the soldiers she never saw him before. Courage's third child, Kattrin—plain and unable to speak—dreams of being loved and having children. She, too, is sacrificed to the war, shot when she frantically beats her drum from a rooftop to warn the children of the town of the coming military attack. At the end of the play, Courage pulls her wagon by herself as she doggedly follows the army. She has lost everything to the war; she has learned nothing. Brecht's characters never denigrate the war; on the contrary they consistently praise it, making an ironic anti-war statement.

In all of his major works, Brecht was developing his concept of epic theatre, so called because it possessed the sweep, the grandeur, and the scope of the classic epic tales. Brecht permitted the use of narrative in his dramas through a commentator, story teller, or legend flashed on a screen. He explored history, fable, and foreign settings, believing that social content and context may change but that fundamental human nature does not. Finally, Brecht perceived of epic theatre as episodic, avoiding progressive order, a culminative story, cause and effect relationships, anything that smacked of the conventional, realistic theatre or, as he perceived it, expressionistic hocus-pocus.

Brecht, like Piscator, was an iconoclast of the theatre. He wanted to do away with the gilt and plush of the auditorium; he wanted to do away with the uncomfortable black tie and formal dress of the spectator. The theatre, he argued, should be like a sports arena where the audience members smoke and are comfortably dressed, where they think and are active, anticipating events and calculating strategies. Above all, Brecht did not want the audience to become conventionally involved, sucked into the story, purged or released emotionally. The audience should be kept in a state of tension, active, inquisitive, animated, and surprised.

How would this lack of conventional involvement, this state of tension be achieved? Brecht developed what is referred to as the alienation or strange-making effect (*verfremdungs effekt*). No attempt should be made to create a total empathic response in the audience or to give them the illusion of witnessing natural, unrehearsed events. Brecht wanted his audience to think, not to feel. It was wrong, he reasoned, when they "stare rather than see, listen rather than hear." The *verfremdungs effekt,* therefore, was designed to jar or interrupt the audience just as it was becoming involved in the story. To do this Brecht used many of Piscator's devices: interjection of song and straight-forward speeches to the audience; the use of poetry, ballad, or sharp prose; the use of placcards or narrator that tell the audience exactly what is going to happen in the scene, hence preventing an element of suspense; presentational or theatrical style, not only openly acknowledging the existence of the audience but also employing deliberate theatricality in the use of masks, slapstick humor, vaudeville, cabaret, and music hall routines; theatrical use of platforms, screens, bare white light, exposed lighting instruments; the use of slides, projections, and motion picture sequences; the employment of music, always very important to Brecht, with an orchestra on stage, pretty melodies accompanied by hard-hitting lyrics, dissonance, cheap cabaret instruments, heavy percussion, and tacks in untuned pianos; and finally the use of short, fast changing scenes. The whole effect is one of distancing, of making strange. Brecht believed that the audience, the actors, the playwrights and the directors were so conditioned to the realistic play of pity, illusion, and suspense that distance could only be achieved by such drastic methods.

Ironically, Brecht's strange-making technique can generate moments of supreme artistic quality. Precisely because of our human impulse to identify and empathize, the efforts to inhibit involvement produce a tension, a tug-of-war, and a disequilibrium between opposing tendencies: intellect and emotion, detachment and passion, attraction and repulsion.

In all of this alienation, Brecht rejected Aristotle's catharsis through fear and pity, emotions he believed were achieved only when we surrender to stage illusion and identify ourselves with the characters. When we are thoroughly purged, Brecht reasoned, there is no longer any necessity to take action against the evils we have witnessed or against the injustices of the world. Epic theatre requires decision of the audience. With his pixie grin, the playwright thumbed his nose at Aristotle.

In relation to acting, Brecht declared himself to be anti-Stanislavsky. Yet he demanded the same attention to detail that Stanislavsky did. A delightful sketch Brecht wrote about the meticulous care with which an actor chose the right hat for a supporting character in *The Three Penny Opera* illustrates the importance of external detail or what Brecht referred to as "quotable gestures." While he manipulated his characters to make them serve his didactic purposes, Brecht wanted his actors to perform a dual role: to both be the character in the play and to remain the actor performing the role. He said that the actors "should not squander all their art on the single trick of pretending to *be* the characters they are portraying." Actors, Brecht believed, should not completely feel their roles. They should be cool, not mannered, accomplished and subtle, but not ostentatious and artificial. Anyone who has studied acting, of course, realizes that Brecht is only speaking common sense. Most actors are aware of themselves both as performer and as character. Moreover, Brecht's own alienation techniques served to prevent the actors' complete identification with their characters.

Brecht himself wrote prolifically about the theatre and his theory of epic drama. Much of his doctrine has been misunderstood and misinterpreted, but it remains that Brecht, along with Meyerhold and Piscator, made audiences aware of theatre as theatre, aware of the artificiality of pretending that the stage represents life, aware of the power of theatre as a political platform. In one sense epic theatre—with its presentationalism, inclusion of narration and great freedom in time and place—freed the drama from too narrow constraints; on the other hand, the extensive use of narration, long didactic speeches, and the fragmented episodes of the genre have too often become a crutch, taking us further and further away from Aristotle's conception of the drama as an imitation of an action. Nevertheless, Brecht's influence in both political content and theatrical modes of presentation has been profound. One need only think of the works of Britain's Edward Bond, Peter Shaffer, or Caryl Churchill to realize the impact of Brecht's concepts.

Bertolt Brecht

Bertolt Brecht was born in 1898 into a middle class family in the provincial Bavarian town of Augsburg, where his father was the managing director of a paper mill. A precocious student, Brecht decided upon a career as a doctor and enthusiastically joined the medical corps in World War I. From his medical training Brecht developed trenchant wit and objectivity, often using his pen as a surgeon might use a scalpel. But in the service Brecht's views began to change; he saw men sent back to the fields before their wounds were healed; he saw needless amputations to free more hospital beds. He became convinced that the working classes were being ruthlessly sacrificed, the pawns of the rich and powerful who had influenced the Kaiser to perpetrate the war for their advantage. When the war was over, Brecht dropped out of society, affected his famous crew cut and big cigar, wore scraggy clothes, and supported himself by singing protest songs in the cabarets of Berlin. It was at this time that Brecht became an active Marxist, dedicated to justice for the worker and the poor.

In 1928, the year *The Three Penny Opera* was performed, Brecht married Helene Weigel, an actress and political colleague. By 1933, appalled by the growing power of Hitler and the Nazi regime, Brecht emigrated first to Denmark, then to Finland, to the Soviet Union, and finally to the United States of America where he was to live from 1941 until his return to East Germany in 1947. This period of self-imposed exile was the most productive of Brecht's playwriting career. In 1947 Brecht was one of a group of screen writers, directors, and producers who were called before the House Un-American Activities Committee because of alleged communist party membership. While the other ten witnesses went to prison for contempt of Congress, Brecht managed to appease the committee. His airline ticket back to East Germany was in his pocket at the time of the hearings.

The final phase of Brecht's career, from 1947 until his death by a heart attack in August of 1956, was a time of testing his plays in production. He and Helene Weigel established the Berliner Ensemble and in 1949 offered a spectacular production of *Mother Courage* which featured Weigel in the title role and made Brecht's company the outstanding theatre group in post-war Europe.

It is interesting that Brecht did not always practice what he preached. Once Brecht had failed to intercede for his mistress, Carola Neher, when she was arrested in the Soviet Union; during the HUAC hearings Brecht perjured himself to get out of the United States; and when he returned to East Berlin he held a generous subsidy from the government, a car, several residences, and a Swiss bank account. Ironically, Brecht found the freedom to write as he wished in the United States, not in Europe. Ironically, too, Brecht gained the admiration of the West, the middle classes, and the establishment he professed to hold in contempt. Nevertheless, Bertolt Brecht established a unique form of staging, developed one of the world's great ensemble theatres, and evolved a theory of drama that has profoundly affected the theatre of the second half of the twentieth century.

Fear and Misery in the Third Reich

While *Fear and Misery in the Third Reich* (or *The Private Life of the Master Race,* as it is sometimes called) is not one of Brecht's best known plays, it is nevertheless a typical and superior example of his epic theatre. In his anti-Aristotelian, non-empathetic approach Brecht focuses his play on a socio-political message rather than on the telling of a story. There is a chronological ordering of scenes in the play but not for the purposes of laying out a logically ordered plot; the intention behind the chronology is to demonstrate methodically through a series of episodic sketches the beginnings, the rising menace, and the ultimate destructive force of Nazism. But even though the play may be anti-Aristotelian in its lack of a clearly ordered plot line, it still possesses a very clear action or major deed which is intricately linked to the message of the play. Obviously, Brecht is bent on exposing the insidiousness of Nazism hoping that through his critical attack the spectator may become more aware of how such a hideous thing can happen and how devastating such a thing truly can be for only then can we hope to avoid or avert the repetition of such moral, spiritual and physical catastrophe. The play has a profound lesson to teach and it teaches it forcefully and matter-of-factly.

A pronounced didactic purpose—to teach a lesson—is a characteristic feature of epic theatre and is readily apparent in every episode of Brecht's play. The episodic structure itself enables the playwright to pile up data in scene after scene to support his thesis without the necessity of motivating and justifying everything the character says or does. For this reason, dialogue in the play often gives way to didacticism as characters depart from realistic speech in order to explain a political issue or event at length. Notice, for example, in one of the episodes—"The Chalk Cross"— the scene revolves around two lengthy jokes which are rigged and extended by the dramatist to make his point. In short, the jokes are not related as one man might relate a joke to another, but they are carefully spun out to underscore the political message. And in the process, in this scene and every other, a major theme is reiterated—Nazism has pitted friend against friend, child against parents, husband against wife, one political or social group against another.

The episodic structure is, of course, one of the major characteristics of epic theatre allowing the dramatist a free and uninhibited movement in time and space. The action of this play begins in 1933 and ends sometime possibly in 1938 with each of the eighteen scenes transpiring at a different time. The various scenes take place in different locales as well as we move from Breslau to Berlin and on to Oranienburg, Leipzig, Essen, Gottingen, Frankfurt, Augsburg (Brecht's own hometown), Cologne, back to Berlin, Wurttemberg, Landsberg, Dresden, Schwetzingen (in Bavaria), Karlsbuhe, Lubeck, Hamburg, and even somewhere in Russia. The multiplicity of locales gives the play the sweep and grandeur of an epic legend; but, more importantly, it tells us very vividly, without the playwright having to make a particular point of it, that the plague of Nazism is infesting all of Germany and all of Europe as well.

Fear and Misery in the Third Reich is particularly interesting in its obvious demonstration of Brecht's use of alienation effects to focus the spectator's attention on his political message. In one version of the play, a narrator intervenes between each scene to underscore the political point of the preceding scene or to anticipate the point of the coming scene. (In some versions of the text the narrator is referred to as "The Voice"; in others, as in the text provided here, the lines at the opening of each scene are unassigned. For that reason, those lines could be printed on placards and displayed above the stage if the director of the production so desired.) In one setting of the play, Brecht's message is reinforced by the use of song in which the lyrics focus on political messages. It is obvious that the military sounding music itself is not realistically or logically motivated in any scene; nothing happens to justify the appearance of a military band. The music is simply superimposed on the play. But, interestingly, Brecht chooses to employ the "Horst Wessel Song"— one of the anthems of the Nazi Party—to provide the melody line for his trenchant lyrics. The song, then, serves as a constant reminder of the Nazi threat while the lyrics are making ironically anti-Nazi statements. Since the point of each scene is given away, as it were, by the narrator and the song, suspense is undercut if not entirely destroyed. Or, at least, that is the intention of the dramatist. Consequently, the spectator is prepared to concentrate on the important meaning of the scene rather than on its story or character development. The song and the narrator's speeches function as printed legends function in other plays by Brecht.

Just as the above elements interrupt the flow of the play and hopefully prevent the audience from becoming too emotionally involved, so do the signs that set the various locations and the dramatic image and, in one setting of the play, the sound of the panzer. The elements reappear between every scene as the "Poland" sign, for example, suddenly appears out of darkness and the Panzer is heard in the blackout. It is obviously Brecht's intention at these moments to destroy the spectator's empathic responses and emotional identifications with what is happening in scenes. For this purpose he also instructed his actors—as part of their epic acting technique—to step aside from the character they were enacting and comment upon that character. How exactly this was to be accomplished is anyone's guess; but obviously Brecht did not want his actors to become emotionally involved with their characters and forget to stress the message of the scene. This was one way of forcefully reminding the spectator at all times that he was in the theatre watching a play with a message. Notice that his use of fragmentary scenery in many scenes has the effect of telling us that this is not a real place but, rather, a stage setting. Look, for instance, at the setting of the first scene ("Betrayal") which calls for nothing more than a doorway, a staircase and a sign reading "Breslau—1933."

But what actually was the result of these alienation effects in actual production? Occasionally, the results are rather startling as when the actors seem to step out of character and preach to the spectator. Such instances occur in at least half of the scenes in *Fear and Misery in the Third Reich*. And we as spectators are caught up short; we are distanced from the story at that moment, and we do attend to the message. On the other hand, the effects of the song, the titles, the narrator's speeches and especially the sights and sounds of the panzer have quite a different and startling impact in actual production. Far from alienating the spectator and destroying his emotional involvement these techniques have precisely the opposite effect at times, for his emotions are stirred tremendously. Ironically, most of Brecht's alienation effects are such tried-and-true theatrical hokum that they frequently produce a result diametrically opposed to the dramatist's stated intention. (But one may suspect that they are totally in keeping with Brecht's aims as a director in the theatre for he simply could not pass up an opportunity for a spectacular theatrical moment.)

Whatever its strength and weaknesses as an example of Epic Theatre, *Fear and Misery in the Third Reich* remains wonderfully effective drama. It contains at least two of Brecht's most stunning scenes—"The Jewish Wife" and "The Informer"—and many, many moments of superior writing. The first scene, for example, is a masterpiece of playwrighting. It is composed entirely of only ten speeches and yet it completely sets the tone, the style, the mood and the message of the play with its vivid emphasis on guilt, distrust and fear. The second scene ("The Chalk Cross") has an added theatrical excitement because it operates on two levels simultaneously; it is a game people are playing and at the same time it is a frightening reality. "Prisoners Mix Cement"—the third scene—has a marvelously contrasting brevity but it still conveys with an enormous theatrical thrust the idea that political factions are being pitted one against the other. "The Box" lasts for little more than a page and yet it has incredible dramatic impact. Even "In Search of Justice"— which in its unnecessary length is the most clumsily and unimaginatively structured episode with its awkward, arbitrary entrances and exits of characters and its blunt, bald statement of issues— makes a devastating point when we realize that the judge is not really seeking justice at all but is trying desperately to discover which political faction his judgment must please if he is going to survive. "The Old Nazi" is remarkable for its economic, but shattering, demonstration of quiet, but emphatic, defiance. One of the last episodes "Children's Shoes" is particularly noteworthy for its subtle indictment of the Hitler Youth program. Here the playwright is content to suggest more than he tells. Notice, for example, that a healthy summer in the country is not a gift that the Nazi party gives to the youth of Germany; they have to pay for it with pennies their families cannot afford. Furthermore, the summer they get may not be really so healthy after all, for there are at least two hints that the farmers sexually abuse the young girls. The play ends, too, on a wonderfully understated note. The German troops are about to invade Vienna and are experiencing what seems to be a major triumph. But there are those who see that Germany stands potentially on the brink of destruction—the destruction of all moral fiber and human decency. But the hope the final scene holds out is feeble indeed. Brecht's message to the world is lucid and emphatic!

FEAR AND MISERY IN THE THIRD REICH

By Bertolt Brecht

English Version by Eric Bentley
Scenes from German Life, 1933–1938

These scenes have been produced and published in Britain and the United States under the title of *The Private Life of the Master Race*. However, Brecht's original title was *Fear and Misery in the Third Reich,* and this title seems better, now that the episodes are a matter of history, and the idea of a Master Race is no longer current.

Bertolt Brecht twice provided his scenes with a topical framework: once, before World War II and, the second time, during that War. In each case the framework brought the material up to the moment but by that token both frameworks are now out of date. Neither is included here. It does not follow, however, that in future productions, scene should follow scene without any further comment. The present adaptor's suggestion would be that headlines of the day be used to bring home the idea of each scene to a particular audience. These could be augmented by news pictures and quotations from the recent speeches of statesmen.

The play has relevance whenever a great nation is preparing for war.

E. B.
January 1, 1962

SCENE ONE

When the lights go up, we see a staircase. Above the scene is written in large black letters: BRESLAU 1933.

THE BETRAYAL

(*A man and a woman stand listening. They are very pale.*)

WOMAN. Now they're downstairs.

MAN. Not yet.

WOMAN. They've smashed the banister. He was already unconscious when they dragged him out of the apartment.

MAN. But the only thing I said was that the radio with the broadcasts from Russia wasn't in *our* apartment.

WOMAN. That wasn't the *only* thing you said.

MAN. Yes it was.

WOMAN. Don't look at me like that. It serves them right. Why must they be Communists?

MAN. But they didn't have to tear his jacket for him. None of us are *that* well off.

WOMAN. The jacket has nothing to do with it.

MAN. They didn't have to tear his jacket for him.

SCENE TWO

When the lights go up, we see the kitchen of a well-to-do house. Above the scene is written in black letters: BERLIN 1933.

THE CHALK CROSS

(*An* S.A. MAN, *a* PARLOR-MAID, *a* COOK, *and a* CHAUFFEUR *are talking.*)

PARLOR MAID. Have you really only half an hour?

S.A. MAN. Night drill.

COOK. Why are you always drilling?

S.A. MAN. Top secret.

COOK. Is it a raid?

S.A. MAN. Wouldn't you like to know? Nobody will get anything out of me. Start fishing if you want: you'll catch nothing. I'm as deep as a well.

PARLOR MAID. And you still have to go to Reinickendorf?

S.A. MAN. Reinickendorf or Rummelsburg or maybe Lichterfelde, huh?

PARLOR MAID. (*rather bewildered*). Won't you have something to eat before you leave?

S.A. MAN. Sure, wheel in the field kitchen, I wouldn't like to disappoint you. (*The* COOK *brings a tray.*) There'll be no blabbing. Always surprise the enemy! Always come at him when he sees no cloud on the horizon! Just watch the Führer when *he* prepares to strike! Impenetrable! Beforehand you don't know a thing. Maybe beforehand he doesn't know, himself. And then it comes. Lickety-split. Colossal things! That's what makes them all fear us. (*He has tucked the napkin in at the neck and taken up his knife and fork.*) Sure the boss won't blow in, Anna? And me with my mouth full of high-class mayonnaise? (*Speaks as if with his mouth full, in an exaggerated way.*) Heil Hitler!

PARLOR MAID. No, they'd ring for the car first. Am I right, Herr Franke?

CHAUFFEUR. Beg pardon? Oh, sure.

(*The* S.A. MAN, *reassured, busies himself with the food.*)

PARLOR MAID (*sitting next to him*). Aren't you tired?

S.A. MAN. Terrifically.

PARLOR MAID. But you still have Friday free?

S.A. MAN. If nothing happens in between.

PARLOR MAID. Look, I paid four marks fifty to have the watch repaired.

S.A. MAN. It's a scandal.

PARLOR MAID. The whole watch only cost twelve.

S.A. MAN. Is the boy in the drugstore still making passes?

PARLOR MAID. Oh heavens!

S.A. MAN. You've only to tell me.

PARLOR MAID. I tell you everything. Have you got your new boots on?

S.A. MAN (*listlessly*). Yes, why?

PARLOR MAID. Minna, have you seen Theo's new boots?

COOK. No.

PARLOR MAID. Show them to her, Theo. That's what they get in the S.A. now. (*The S.A. Man, still chewing, stretches out his leg for inspection.*) Lovely, aren't they? (*The S.A. Man looks around inquisitively.*)

COOK. Something missing?

S.A. MAN. It's a bit dry.

PARLOR MAID. Want some beer? I'll get some. (*She runs out*)

COOK. She'd run the legs off her body for you, Herr Theo!

S.A. MAN. With me things gotta go lickety-split.

COOK. You fellows may be taking too many liberties.

S.A. MAN. Women like it! (*As the Cook takes up a heavy kettle*) Why wear yourself out like that? It's my business. (*He carries the kettle for her.*)

COOK. That's good of you. You always find something to take off my hands. They're not all so obliging. (*With a glance at the Chauffeur*)

S.A. MAN. Oh, we're glad to do it.

(*There is a knock at the back door.*)

COOK. That's my brother. He's bringing the radio tube. (*She lets in her brother, a* WORKER.) My brother.

S.A. MAN AND CHAUFFEUR. Heil Hitler!

(*The worker murmurs something which could be interpreted as "Heil Hitler".*)

COOK. You have the tube?

WORKER Yes.

COOK. Want to put it in now?

(*They both go out.*)

S.A. MAN. Who's he?

CHAUFFEUR. Unemployed.

S.A. MAN. Comes here often?

CHAUFFEUR (*shrugs his shoulders*). I'm not around much.

S.A. MAN. Well, the fat lady is okay. Heart of gold—in the patriotic sense.

CHAUFFEUR. Right.

S.A. MAN. At that, the brother may be another story.

CHAUFFEUR. Any grounds for suspicion?

S.A. MAN. Me? Never. I'm never suspicious. Suspicion is practically the same thing as certainty. And then things start moving.

CHAUFFEUR (mumbles). Lickety-split.

S.A. MAN. Exactly. (He leans back and closes one eye.) Did you understand what he was muttering just now? (He imitates the WORKER'S "Heil Hitler".) Could be interpreted as "Heil Hitler". Doesn't have to be. These fellows appeal to me. (He laughs loudly.) (The Cook and the Worker return)

COOK. My brother is so clever with radios. But he hardly ever cares to listen. If I'd time I'd always be turning it on. (To the Worker) And you do have time, Franz.

S.A. MAN. Really? You have a radio and don't turn it on?

WORKER. Music. Now and then.

COOK. He knocked together a wonderful radio out of nothing.

S.A. MAN. How many tubes?

WORKER (with a challenging stare). Four.

S.A. MAN. Tastes differ, I see. (To the Chauffeur) Right?

CHAUFFEUR. Beg your pardon? Oh, sure.

(The Parlor Maid comes in with the beer.)

PARLOR MAID. It's been on ice!

S.A. MAN (he lays a friendly hand on hers). My, you're quite out of breath, my girl. You didn't have to run like that. I could have waited.

(She fills glass from the bottle.)

PARLOR MAID. That's all right. (She shakes hands with the Worker) Have you brought the tube? Why don't you sit down for a minute? You've walked all this way again! (To the S.A. Man) He's living in Moabit.

S.A. MAN. Hey, where's my beer? Someone's taken it! (To the Chauffeur) Have you been drinking my beer?

CHAUFFEUR. I certainly have not! What gives you that idea? Has it gone?

PARLOR MAID. But I just poured it out.

S.A. MAN (to the Cook). So you've been taking a quick one! (He laughs loudly) Well, don't get excited. That's what we learn in the S.A. A little trick. Drinking beer without anyone noticing. (To the Worker) You wanted to say something?

WORKER. An old trick.

S.A. MAN. Maybe you'd like to pull it, too.

(He fills glass from the bottle)

WORKER. Sure. Now: here is the beer. (He holds up the glass.) Now comes the trick.

(Quite calmly and with evident enjoyment he drinks the beer)

COOK. But everybody can see that.

WORKER (wiping his mouth). Really? It must have gone wrong.

(The Chauffeur roars with laughter.)

S.A. MAN. Think that's so funny?

WORKER. You couldn't have done it any other way. How did you do it?

S.A. MAN. How can I show you when you've finished the beer?

WORKER. Correct. You can't do the trick without beer. Know any other tricks? You fellows must know more than one trick.

S.A. MAN. What do you mean, "you fellows"?

WORKER. You young fellows.

S.A. MAN. Yeah.

PARLOR MAID. But Herr Lincke was only joking, Theo.

WORKER. (he judges it better to smooth things over) You won't take offence?

COOK (to S.A. Man). I'll bring you another beer.

S.A. MAN. Not necessary. I had enough to wash my food down.

COOK. Herr Theo understands a joke.

S.A. MAN (to the worker). Why not sit down? We don't eat people.

(The Worker sits down.)

S.A. MAN. Live and let live. And why not a joke now and then? We're only strict about political convictions.

COOK. You got to be strict about *them!*

WORKER. How *are* convictions these days?

S.A. MAN. They're fine. Or don't you agree?

WORKER. All I mean is: nobody tells you what he thinks.

S.A. MAN. How's that? They tell *me.*

WORKER. Really?

S.A. MAN. Of course they don't come to you to *explain* what they think. You go to them.

WORKER. Where?

S.A. MAN. Well, let's say in the breadline. In the morning we're in the breadline.

WORKER. Yeah, there's still some grumbling, that's correct.

S.A. MAN. Right.

WORKER. But that way you make one catch, and you're known. And they won't talk any more.

S.A. MAN. Known, am I? Shall I show you why they *don't* know me? You're interested in tricks. It won't do any harm to show you *one,* we have so many. And what I always say is this. As soon as they realize what we have on the ball, as soon as they realize they won't get by in any circumstances whatsoever—why, maybe they'll give up.

PARLOR MAID. Yes, Theo, tell us how you do it.

S.A. MAN. Fine. Let's assume we are in the breadline on Munz Street. Let's say (*he looks at the Worker*) you're next in front of me. But first, I must make a few minor preparations. (*He goes out*)

WORKER. (*winks at the Chauffeur*). Well, let's see how they do it.

COOK. The Reds will all be found out. Subversive activities will have to stop.

WORKER. Well.

(*The S.A. Man returns.*)

S.A. MAN. Naturally I'm in civvies. (*To the Worker*) Okay, start grumbling.

WORKER. What about?

S.A. MAN. Oh, skip it. There's always some chip on your shoulder.

WORKER. On mine? No.

S.A. MAN. You'd put up with anything. You surely can't claim everything's perfect already?

WORKER. Why not?

S.A. MAN. Listen, this won't work. If you won't co-operate, it won't work.

WORKER. Okay, I'll shoot off my mouth for once. (*He starts acting.*) They let you stand around here as if your time meant nothing. It takes me two hours to come in from Rummelsburg. Then the waiting starts.

S.A. MAN. Aw, that's nothing. Rummelsburg is no farther away under the Third Reich than under the Weimar Republic.

COOK. Try again. It's only play-acting, Franz. We know what you say now isn't what you really believe.

PARLOR MAID. You're only kind of pretending to be a grumbler. You can trust Theo not to take it wrong. He only wants to show us.

WORKER. Good. This is what I say then: you can take the whole goddamned S.A. and shove it. I'm *for* the Reds and I'm *for* the Jews!

COOK (*shocked*). Franz!

PARLOR MAID. That's going too far, Herr Lincke.

S.A. MAN (*laughing*). Man, I'd have you arrested by the next cop. Haven't you any imagination? You must say something you can turn around later, something somebody might really say.

WORKER. Then do me a favor: provoke me.

S.A. MAN. That doesn't work any more. Suppose I say: Our Führer is the greatest man that ever moved upon the surface of the earth, greater than Jesus Christ and Napoleon put together. You reply at the most: quite right. Then I try it the other way and say: they are great talkers. All propaganda. They're masters of that. Know the joke of Goebbels and the two lice? No? Very well: two lice make a bet—which could get from one corner of Goebbels' mouth to the other first. They say the winner was the one that ran around the back of his head. They say it's shorter that way.

CHAUFFEUR. Oh.

(*They all laugh*)

S.A. MAN (*to the Worker*). Well, pull yourself together and talk.

WORKER. What can I say to such baloney? It's a joke. But you could still be an informer.

PARLOR MAID. That's correct, Theo.

S.A. MAN. You people are yellow. I'm through with you. No one will risk saying a thing.

WORKER. Do you really mean that? Or is it just for the breadline?

S.A. MAN. For the breadline *as well*.

WORKER. If you're saying that for the breadline, then I'm saying to you on the breadline: discretion is the better part of valor. I'm scared. I have no revolver.

S.A. MAN. I'll tell you something, my friend, since you're so careful to be careful, you can go on being careful till you wake up in the Voluntary Labour Corps.

WORKER. And if you're not careful?

S.A. MAN. You end up in the Labour Corps just the same. I'll grant you that. The *Voluntary* Labor Corps.

WORKER. Now listen. Suppose you S.A. men are standing near the breadline looking at one of us. The man you're looking at with your blue German eyes is a pretty daring fellow and he gives you a piece of his mind about the Voluntary Labour Corps. Now, what could a man in his position say? Maybe something like this, "Fifteen more left yesterday. I often wonder how they get them to go. After all it's voluntary. In camp they need more to eat, but they get no more for doing something there than for doing nothing here." Then there's the story of Dr. Ley and the cat. It made everything clear to me, of course. Do you people know the story?

S.A. MAN. No, we don't.

WORKER. Okay. Dr. Ley is on a little business trip for *Kraft durch Freude* and he meets one of the old bosses from the Weimar Republic. I'm not sure of the name and maybe it was in a concentration-camp, but, no, that's impossible, Dr. Ley, he has too much sense, well, the first thing the boss said was: "The workers sit down under it now. In the old days they'd never stand for all this. How do you do it?" Dr. Ley points at a cat lying in the sun and says: "Suppose you want the cat to take a good dose of mustard whether she likes it or not. How would you go about it?" The boss takes the mustard and smears the cat's mouth with it. The cat spits the mustard right back in his face. The cat

swallows nothing, the boss is scratched all over for his trouble. "No man," says Dr. Ley in his most winning manner, "that's not the way. Watch me." He sweeps the mustard off the table and in a split second daubs it all over the cat's ass-hole. (*To the ladies*) Pardon me, but it belongs to the story. The cat is stunned and dizzy. The pain is terrible. So she starts licking off all the mustard. "You see, my dear fellow," says Dr. Ley in triumph. "Now she's eating it! And voluntarily at that!"

(*They laugh*)

Yes, it's very funny.

S.A. MAN. Now we're getting somewhere. Voluntary Labour Corps. A favorite subject. (*He starts acting again*) The worst thing is, no one has the guts to fight back any more. They could give us dirt to eat and we'd say "Thank You."

WORKER. No, that's not true either. The other day I was standing on the Alexanderplatz wondering whether to join the Voluntary Labour Corps on my own steam or wait till they shove me in. Out of the grocery store on the corner came a little, thin woman, obviously the wife of a proletarian. "Wait," I said. "Since when are there proletarians in the Third Reich, where all Germans are brothers, even Fritz Thyssen not excluded?" "Look," says she. "Margarine is going up like a rocket. From fifty pfennings to a mark. D'you mean to tell me we're all brothers?" "Mother," I said, "you'd better be careful what you say. I'm a Nazi to my very bones." "Bones," she said, "and no meat—and bran in the bread. That's what they're using now." It took my breath away and I mumbled: "Why don't you buy butter, it's healthier? But don't cut down on food, it saps the people's health, and we can't afford that, because we're encircled by enemies, even our big shots live surrounded by enemies. We've been warned to be on our guard." "Oh no," she said. "We're all Nazis till our last breath, which can be soon, what with wars and rumors of wars. The other day," she went on, "I was going to give my best sofa to the Winter Relief, 'cause I heard Goering had to sleep on bare boards, with all the trouble they're having over raw materials. At the office they said to me: 'We'd rather've had a piano for *Kraft durch Freude*, you know.' There's no real flour now. I took my sofa back from the Winter Relief and went straight to the second-hand shop 'round the corner. I'd been wanting a half pound of butter for a long time. In the butter shop they said: "No butter today, Fellow German, would you like a cannon?"

"Sure, give me one," I said . . ."
I interrupted her: "What's that? Why a cannon, mother? On an empty stomach?"
"No," she said. "If I have to starve I'll shoot up the whole damn show, the whole filthy gang, and let Hitler lead the way. . . ."
"What's this," I said. "What's this," I shouted in her ear. . . ."
"Let Hitler lead the way and we'll conquer France too," she said. "Why, already we make wool out of gasoline!"
"And the wool?" I said.
"The wool," she said. "We make it from gasoline nowadays, and we need wool too. But if a real good piece from the good old days finds its way into the Winter Relief, the big boys grab it for themselves," she said. " 'If only Hitler knew it,' they say. He knows nothing. They tell me he didn't even go through high school." Well, I was speechless at such subversive talk.
"Young woman," I said, "wait here a minute. I'm off to the Gestapo!" But do you know, when I came back with a Gestapo man, she hadn't waited for us! . . . (*He abandons the game*) Well, what do you say?

S.A. MAN. Me? Oh yes, what do I say? Maybe I give you a disapproving look. (*He takes up the game again.*) Maybe I say: "To go running to the Gestapo! Nobody'll dare open his mouth when you're around!"

WORKER. You're right. Not when I'm around. If they confide in me they're done for. I know my duty as a German. If my own mother whispered something in my ear about margarine going up I'd go straight to the S.S. I'd betray my own brother if he grumbled about the Voluntary Labour Corps. And as for my girl, if she wrote me they've got her pregnant in the Labour Camp with their "Heil Hitler" I'd take out after her. And no abortion! If we won't take a stand against our own flesh and blood, the Third Reich which we cherish above all things would cease to exist . . . There, is that better? Satisfied with me?

S.A. MAN. Yes. I guess that'll do. (*He takes up the game again.*) Now you can go and get your card stamped. I understood you, we all understood you, didn't we, boys? But you can rely on me, my friend, whatever you tell me, I'll be as silent as the grave. (*He slaps him on the shoulder and stops acting*) Okay, and now go to the employment-board and they'll arrest you—pronto.

WORKER. Even if *you* don't leave the line and follow me?

S.A. MAN. Right.

WORKER. Without you winking at anyone? That would put me on my guard.

S.A. MAN. Without any winking.

WORKER. How do you do it?

S.A. MAN. Yeah, wouldn't you like to know? Stand up a minute and show me your back. (*He takes him by the shoulder and turns him around so that all can see his back. Then to the Parlor Maid*) See that?

PARLOR MAID. Heavens, it's a cross, a white cross!

COOK. Right on the shoulder.

CHAUFFEUR. It's a fact.

S.A. MAN. And how did it get there? (*he shows the palm of his hand*) Well there's the little white chalk cross on his shoulder in life-size reproduction.

(*The Worker takes off his jacket and studies the cross*)

WORKER. Neat job.

S.A. MAN. Pretty good, huh? I always have the chalk on me. Yes, you need a head on your shoulders. Instructions aren't always enough. (*Satisfied with himself*) And now for Reinickendorf. (*He corrects himself*) I've an aunt there.—Well, you don't show much enthusiasm? (*To the Parlor Maid*) Why are you looking so silly, Anna? Didn't you understand?

PARLOR MAID. What do you think? I'm not *that* stupid.

S.A. MAN. (*as if the joke were now spoilt for him, he holds out his hand to her*) Wipe it off.

(*She wipes his hand with a towel.*)

COOK. We gotta use these methods if they try to upset everything our Führer has built up, everything that makes us "the envy of other nations!"

CHAUFFEUR. Beg your pardon? Oh. Yes. (*He takes out his watch.*) I'll go wash the car. Heil Hitler! (*He goes out*)

S.A. MAN. What's wrong with that guy?

PARLOR MAID. He's all right. Just not interested in politics.

WORKER (*getting up*). Yes, Minna, I must be on my way too. (*To the S.A. Man*) And don't be sore about the beer. I'm glad you convinced me once again that if people plot against the Third Reich, they won't get away with it. That's quite a comfort. As for me I never come in contact with subversive elements, though of course I'd be glad to give them what they deserve. Only I'm not as quick on the trigger as you. Okay, Minna, thanks a lot. (*Clearly and distinctly*) And Heil Hitler!

THE OTHERS. Heil Hitler!

S.A. MAN. If I can give you a good piece of advice: don't play it too innocent. It attracts attention. You can give yourself a little leeway with me. I understand a joke. Well, Heil Hitler!

(*The Worker leaves*)

They left in a bit of a hurry, those two. It must have struck home. I shouldn't have said that about Reinickendorf. They're on the lookout like a couple of watchdogs.

PARLOR MAID. I had something to ask you, Theo.

S.A. MAN. Fire away.

COOK. I'll go sort out the linen. I was young once.

(*Cook goes out*)

S.A. MAN. What is it?

PARLOR MAID. But I'll only say it if you'll not get sore at me again. If you're sore, I won't say a thing.

S.A. MAN. Sounds pretty bad.

PARLOR MAID. Then I won't say it. You're talking the wrong way.

S.A. MAN. Come on, out with it.

PARLOR MAID. It's only that . . . But I really don't like to say it . . . I need some of the money. Twenty marks.

S.A. MAN. Twenty marks?

PARLOR MAID. Look, you *are* taking it the wrong way.

S.A. MAN. Twenty marks from our savings account at the bank. I don't like to hear it. What do you want twenty marks for?

PARLOR MAID. I'd rather not say.

S.A. MAN. So you don't want to tell? Seems funny to me.

PARLOR MAID. I know you don't agree with me and that's why I'd rather not tell you, Theo.

S.A. MAN. If you don't trust me . . .

PARLOR MAID. But I do trust you.

S.A. MAN. Then you mean we should drop our joint account.

PARLOR MAID. How can you think that? When I take out the twenty, I still have ninety-seven left.

S.A. MAN. You don't have to give me the figures, I know how much we have. I'm beginning to wonder if you're planning to break with me. Maybe you're flirting with someone else. Maybe you want *him* to look over the books.

PARLOR MAID. I don't flirt with anybody.

S.A. MAN. Then tell me what the money's for.

PARLOR MAID. But you won't give it to me.

S.A. MAN. How do I know it's not for something bad? I regard myself as responsible.

PARLOR MAID. It's nothing bad, but if I didn't need it, I wouldn't ask for it, you know that.

S.A. MAN. I know nothing. I only know the whole thing sounds screwy to me. What would you suddenly need twenty marks for? That's big money. Are you pregnant?

PARLOR MAID. No.

S.A. MAN. Are you sure?

PARLOR MAID. Yes.

S.A. MAN. If I heard you intended something illegal, if I got wind of anything like that, I'd be through, I can tell you that. You may have heard that meddling with the seeds of life is the worst crime you can commit. If the German people doesn't multiply, it's all over with our historic mission!

PARLOR MAID. But Theo, I haven't a clue what you're talking about. It's nothing of *that* sort. I wouldn't have kept a thing like that to myself. After all it would have concerned you. But if that's what you believe, I'll tell you the truth. I want to help Frieda buy a winter coat. That's all.

S.A. MAN. How is it your sister can't buy a coat herself?

PARLOR MAID. She can't make it on a sick pension of 26.80 a month.

S.A. MAN. How about the Winter Relief? But I see what the trouble is. You've no confidence in the National Socialist State. I can tell that from the talk in this kitchen. Think I didn't notice your reaction to my experiment just now?

PARLOR MAID. How do you mean?

S.A. MAN. Very cool. Just like those two fellows who suddenly left.

PARLOR MAID. If you want my honest opinion, I don't like that kind of thing.

S.A. MAN. What kind of thing don't you like?

PARLOR MAID. The way you set traps for those poor devils with tricks and pretending and all that. My father's unemployed, too.

S.A. MAN. That's just what I wanted to hear. Anyway I had my suspicions, talking with that Lincke.

PARLOR MAID. You mean you'll round him up for that? He did it to please you and we all egged him on.

S.A. MAN. I'm not saying a thing, as I said before. And if you've anything against what I'm doing in the way of duty, you can read in *Mein Kampf* that the Führer himself wasn't too good to try out the temper of the people. As a matter of fact that was his job for a long time when he worked for the Reichswehr. And just look at the consequences for Germany!

PARLOR MAID. Oh, how you talk, Theo! Tell me, can I have the twenty marks or not?

S.A. MAN. I can only say I'm not in the mood to shell out.

PARLOR MAID. What do you mean "shell out?" Is it my money or yours?

S.A. MAN. You've started talking in a very funny way about *our* money. Maybe we've driven the Jews out of the nation's life to have our blood sucked by fellow Germans?

PARLOR MAID. You can't say that just because of twenty marks!

S.A. MAN. I've enough expenses already. The boots alone cost me twenty-seven marks.

PARLOR MAID. They were provided, weren't they?

S.A. MAN. Well, we thought so. That's why I took the better brand, the ones with the leggings. Then they came for the money. There was nothing we could do.

PARLOR MAID. Twenty-seven marks just for some boots? And what other expenses do you have?

S.A. MAN. *What* other expenses?

PARLOR MAID. You said there were expenses.

S.A. MAN. I don't remember. What's more, don't ask questions. You can rest assured I won't deceive you. As for the twenty marks, I'll think it over.

PARLOR MAID. Theo, it surely isn't possible you'd say the money was in order and then it wouldn't be? I don't know what to think any more. There must be twenty marks left in the bank out of all that money!

S.A. MAN (*tapping her on the shoulder*). But who says we've nothing left in the bank? No, no. You can rely on me. Trust me with something, it's as good as locked in a safe. Now do you trust Theo again?

(*She weeps without replying.*)

S.A. MAN. It's just nerves—you're overworked. Well, I'll be going to my night drill. Come for you Friday. Heil Hitler! (*He goes out.*)

(*The Parlor Maid tries to stop crying and walks up and down the kitchen in despair. The Cook returns with a laundry basket.*)

COOK. What's the matter? You been quarrelling? Theo is such a fine person. We could do with more like him. It can't be anything serious?

PARLOR MAID. (*still weeping*). Minna, couldn't you go to your brother and advise him to be careful?

COOK. What for?

PARLOR MAID. Well, I just thought . . .

COOK. Because of this evening? You can't mean that? Theo wouldn't act that way!

PARLOR MAID. I don't know what to think any more, Minna. He's so changed. They've ruined him. He's not keeping good company. We've been going together four years and now it's just like . . . I'd almost want to ask you to look at *my* shoulder and see if there's a cross there!

SCENE THREE

When the lights go up we see a concentration camp. Above the scene is written in large black letters: ORANIENBURG 1934.

PRISONERS MIX CEMENT

(*Four prisoners are digging below a dam.*)

A SOCIAL DEMOCRAT (*quietly to a non-political man*). Keep away from Dietz, he's not kosher.

THE NON-POLITICAL MAN (*loudly*). Dietz, Lettner says to keep away from you, you're not kosher.

THE SOCIAL DEMOCRAT. Swine!

A COMMUNIST. You say that, you Judas! How did Karl get into the bunker?

THE SOCIAL DEMOCRAT. Are you suggesting I had anything to do with it? Have I ever gotten cigarettes from who knows where?

THE COMMUNIST. When have I gotten cigarettes?

A PASTOR. Look out!

(*An S.S. Guard walks along the dam above.*)

THE S.S. GUARD. There was talking here. Who was talking? (*No one replies*) If it happens again, the bunker for everyone, understand? I'd like to know what you have to say that's so important. Start singing!

(*The prisoners sing the first stanza of "Song of the Bog Brigades"*)*

> As we march we look around us
> Heath and bog on ev'ry hand
> Not a bird to break the silence
> Withered, bare, the oak trees stand.
>> We are the bog brigades and
>> We're marching with our spades
>> To the bog.

(*The S.S. Guard walks on.*)

THE PASTOR. Why are you men forever quarrelling?

THE NON-POLITICAL MAN. Never you worry, Little Minister, you wouldn't understand. It's about the question whether the united front against the Nazis should have come from above or below.

THE PASTOR. What do you mean "below?"

THE COMMUNIST. Without the bosses.

THE SOCIAL DEMOCRAT. That is, without *your* bosses.

THE NON-POLITICAL MAN (*to The Pastor*). The Social Democrats suspected the Communists of trying to steal their members, understand?

THE PASTOR (*to the Non-Political Man*). What were you?

THE NON-POLITICAL MAN. I stayed outside.

THE COMMUNIST. And now you're inside—this concentration camp.

---

*The story behind this song was fully told by Eric Bentley in the magazine Sing Out! August–September, 1966. This story includes two versions of the melody, one of which has been much reprinted and recorded.

THE PASTOR. Look out!

(*the S.S. Guard appears again. He notices them. The Social Democrat begins slowly to sing the second stanza of the song:*)

> Up and down the guards are pacing
> No one, no one can get by
> Walls and wire all round the fortress
> Try to flee and you will die.
>> We are the bog brigades and
>> We're marching with our spades
>> To the bog.

(*The S.S. Guard walks on.*)

THE SOCIAL DEMOCRAT (*throwing down his spade*). When I think I have to be here because you people made a united front impossible I could break your skull.

THE COMMUNIST. Go ahead.

THE SOCIAL DEMOCRAT. If your crowd hadn't been baiting us, Hitler would never have come to power. You were responsible.

THE COMMUNIST. You even *wanted* to let him get to power so he'd discredit himself.

THE SOCIAL DEMOCRAT. You can't call a general strike if the workers are unemployed.

THE COMMUNIST. Your crowd can't. You betrayed the people!

THE SOCIAL DEMOCRAT. (*He furiously seizes the spade and lifts it to strike the Communist, who already holds his own spade.*) I'll show you!

THE PASTOR. Look out!

(*The Non-Political Man starts to sing the last stanza of the song.*)

> But away with desperation
> After drought will come the rain
> One day comes our liberation
> And our homeland's ours again
> We are the bog brigades and
> We're marching with our spades
> To the bog.

(*As they sing, the S.S. Guard appears and makes a sign to a second S.S. Guard to come over.*)

S.S. GUARD (*with quiet asperity*). You people have learnt nothing. Who was it shouted "You betrayed the people," just now?

(*Nobody answers*)

THE S.S. GUARD (*to the Pastor*). What was it?

(*The pastor is silent.*)

THE S.S. GUARD (*to the Social Democrat*). Who was it?

(*The Social Democrat is silent*)

THE S.S. GUARD. We'll shove you in the bunker till you pass out. I'll give you five seconds. Then . . . the bunker!

(*The prisoners stare in front of them without a word.*)

SCENE FOUR

When the lights go up, we see a Foreman's booth in a factory. Above the scene is written in large black letters: LEIPZIG 1934.

THE WORKING MAN ON THE AIR

(*A Radio announcer with a microphone is holding a conversation with a middle-aged Worker, an Old Worker, and a Woman Worker. In the background are a Gentleman from the Office and a thickset person in S.A. Uniform.*)

THE ANNOUNCER. We are standing in the midst of the bustle of power wheels and driving belts, surrounded by our cheerful and industrious working folk, compatriots who are doing their bit to provide our beloved Fatherland with everything it needs. This morning we are in the textile works of The Fuchs Company. And although the work is hard, and every muscle is strained to the breaking point, we see around us only perfectly contented and gay faces. But we want to have our fellow Germans speak for themselves.

(*To The Old Worker*)

You have been employed here twenty-one years, Herr . . .

THE OLD WORKER. Sedelmeier.

THE ANNOUNCER. Herr Sedelmeier. Well, Herr Sedelmeier, how does it happen that we see here only such joyous and cheerful faces?

THE OLD WORKER (*after reflecting*). They always make cracks about things.

THE ANNOUNCER (*suspiciously*). Oh. Yes, and thus with lively words of jest, the work goes on apace, does it not? Pessimism is hostile to life itself, and

National Socialism has no room for it, you mean? It wasn't like this in the old days, was it?

THE OLD WORKER (*non-committally*). Oh no.

THE ANNOUNCER. Under the Weimer System there was nothing for the workers to laugh at, you mean? Then they said, "What are we working for?"

THE OLD WORKER. Well, there are still a few who say that.

THE ANNOUNCER. I beg your pardon? Oh, I see, you refer to grumblers. They crop up occasionally, though, of course, they're getting fewer all the time because they realize they'd get nowhere. They realize that in the Third Reich, now we have a firm hand at the helm, we're going steadily forward. That's what you

(*Turning to the Woman Worker*)

are trying to say, isn't it, Fraulein . . .

WOMAN WORKER. Schmidt.

THE ANNOUNCER. Fraulein Schmidt. Which of our giants of steel do you work at?

WOMAN WORKER (*reciting by rote*). And then there is the work at the beautification of the workroom which affords us much joy. The Führer's picture was purchased by means of voluntary subscriptions and how proud we are of that. We are also proud of the geranium plants which bring the magic of color into the grey workroom, an inspiration of Fraulein Kinze.

THE ANNOUNCER. And so you beautify the workroom with flowers, the lovely children of the field? And a good many other things in the factory have been different, haven't they, since Germany's destiny took a new turn?

GENTLEMAN FROM THE OFFICE (*prompting*). Wash rooms.

WOMAN WORKER. The wash rooms were the idea of Herr Direktor Bauchle himself, for which we would like to offer our heartfelt thanks. Whoever wishes may wash in the beautiful wash rooms (*Adding an afterthought of her own*) if there aren't too many, and no pushing.

THE ANNOUNCER. Yes, everyone wants to be there first, isn't that so? Always merrily jostling each other?

WOMAN WORKER. Only six faucets for five hundred and fifty-two workers. There's always a squabble. Some of them are awful.

THE ANNOUNCER. But everything proceeds with perfect smoothness! And now, Herr . . . what is his name again . . . wishes to speak to us.

THE WORKER. Mahn.

THE ANNOUNCER. Yes, Mahn. Herr Mahn. Now tell us, Herr Mahn, have the numerous newcomers to the factory affected the temper of their fellow workers?

THE WORKER. What do you mean by that?

THE ANNOUNCER. Well, do you all rejoice that every wheel is turning again and every hand has work to do?

THE WORKER. Oh yes.

THE ANNOUNCER. And that every man can take his pay envelope home at weekends? We wouldn't like to forget that either.

THE WORKER. No.

THE ANNOUNCER. It certainly was not always the case. Under the Weimar System many a German had to suffer the indignity of public relief—had to solace himself with alms!

THE WORKER. Eighteen marks, fifty. No deductions.

THE ANNOUNCER (with a forced laugh). Ha! ha! ha! Wonderful joke! There wasn't much to deduct from!

THE WORKER. No. Now there's more.

(The Gentleman from the Office steps forward. So does the thickset man in S.A. Uniform)

THE ANNOUNCER. Yes, in this way, everyone is getting bread and employment once more, in the Third Reich. You are quite right, Herr . . . what was your name again? . . . Our wheels are no longer still, our arms need no longer go to rust in the Germany of Adolf Hitler.

(With a brutal gesture he pushes the worker from the microphone.)

Those who work with their brains and those who work with their hands, advance together in joyful co-operation to rebuild our beloved Fatherland. Heil Hitler!

SCENE FIVE

When the lights go up we see a worker's living room. Above the scene is written in large black letters: ESSEN 1934.

THE BOX

(*A woman and two Children are in the room. A Young Worker and his Wife are paying a visit. The Woman is crying. The sound of footsteps is heard on the stairs. The door is open.*)

THE WOMAN. But he only said they pay starvation wages. And it's true. Our eldest has a spot on the lung and we can't afford milk. But they can't have done anything to him.

(*Two S.A. Men come in, bringing a big box, which they place on the floor.*)

ONE OF THE S.A. MEN. Now don't make a song and dance. Anyone can get pneumonia. There are the papers! Everything in perfect order. Now don't do anything silly.

(*The S.A. Men leave.*)

THE CHILD. Mother, is father in there?

THE WORKER. (*He has walked over to the box*) It's made of zinc.

THE CHILD. Can't we open it up?

THE WORKER (*furiously*). Yes we can. Where's your tool box? (*He looks for tools. His young wife tries to stop him.*)

THE YOUNG WIFE. Don't open it, Hans! They'll come for you too.

THE WORKER. I want to see what they've done with him. They're afraid of anyone seeing or they wouldn't have used zinc. Let me alone!

THE YOUNG WIFE. I won't let you alone. Didn't you hear them?

THE WORKER. We can surely take a look at him, can't we?

THE WOMAN (*she takes her children by the hand and goes to the zinc box*). I still have a brother they could come for, Hans. And they could come for you too. The box can stay shut. We needn't see him. We shall not forget him.

SCENE SIX

When the lights go up we see a room in an Institute of Physics. Above the scene is written in large black letters: UNIVERSITY OF GOETTINGEN 1935.

PHYSICISTS

(Two scientists, X and Y, are talking together. Y has just come in. He has a conspirational look.)

Y. I have it!

X. What?

Y. The answer to the questions we sent to Mikowsky in Paris.

X. About the gravitation waves?

Y. Yes.

X. Well?

Y. The letter gives exactly the information we need. Do you know who wrote it?

X. Who?

(Y writes a name on a scrap of paper and hands it to X. When X has read it, Y takes the scrap of paper back, tears it in very small pieces, and throws it into the stove.)

Y. The questions we sent to Mikowsky. He handed them on to *him.* Here's the reply.

X *(He grabs it greedily).* Give it to me! *(He suddenly restrains himself.)* But suppose we get caught through corresponding with him . . .

Y. We mustn't. On no account.

X. We can't get any further without writing. Please give it to me.

Y. You can't read it. I wrote it in my own shorthand system. It's safer that way. I'll read it out loud.

X. You have to be careful!

Y. Is Rollkopf in the lab? *(He points off to the right.)*

X *(pointing to the left).* No, but Reinhardt is. Come and sit *here.*

Y *(reading).* It has to do with two arbitrary counter-variant vectors, phi and nu, and a counter-variant vector t. With the help of these the component parts of a mixed tensor of the second degree are formed and their structure is $Elr = \dfrac{C^l}{h^i}$ . . . *(He continues in an undertone.)*

X *(Who has been taking it down, suddenly signals him to stop).* Just a moment!

(He stands up and walks on tiptoe to the wall at the left. He apparently hears nothing suspicious and returns. Y goes on reading, but is occasionally interrupted in the same manner. Then they examine the telephone, quickly open the door, and so on.)

Y. For static incoherent matter, without any interaction of tension, $T = \mu$ is the only component of the tensorial density of energy which is different from 0. Consequently a static factor of proportionality 8π is added gives $\Delta f = 4\pi \chi\mu$. If the coordinates of space are rightly selected the deviation of $c^2 dt^2$ is very small . . .

(Whenever a door is heard closing they start to hide their notes. Then it seems hardly necessary. They get deeper and deeper into the material and seem to forget the danger of their undertaking.)

Y *(reading on).* . . . . on the other hand the masses in question are very small in relation to the static masses which produce the fields, and consequently the movement of the body drawn in the field of gravitation is given by a geodetic world-line in this static field of gravitation. This is as such sufficient for the principle of variation. $ds = 0$ whereby the ends of the fragment of the world-line in question remain fixed.

X. What does Einstein say about . . .

(Y is horrified. X realizes what he has said and sits rigid with horror. Y snatches the notes he has just written out of his hand and puts all the papers in his pocket.)

Y *(facing the left wall, speaking very loudly).* Yes, typical Jewish sophistry! What has that to do with physics?

(Feeling relieved, they take up their notes again and silently proceed with their work, with the utmost caution.)

SCENE SEVEN

When the lights go up we see a comfortable, bourgeois bedroom. Above the scene is written in large black letters: FRANKFURT 1935.

THE JEWISH WIFE

(It is evening. A woman is packing. She is picking out the things she wants to take with her. Sometimes she takes an article out of the bag again and puts it back in its place so that she can pack something else. She hesitates a long time over a large picture of her husband which is on the dressing-table. In the end she leaves it where it is. Getting tired of packing, she sits for a few moments on a suitcase, her head propped on her hand. Then she goes to the telephone.)

THE WIFE. Judith Keith speaking. Is that you doctor? Good evening.—I just wanted to call and say you'll have to be looking for a new bridge partner. Yes, I'm going away.—No, not for very long, but not less than a couple of weeks. I'm going to Amsterdam.—Yes, they say the spring is lovely there.—I have friends there.—No, friends, in the plural, unbelievable as it sounds.—How can you play bridge now? But we haven't played for two weeks.—Certainly, Fritz had a cold too. When it gets so cold, bridge is impossible, I said so too.—Oh no, doctor, how could I?—Thekla had to accommodate her mother.—I know.—How should I suppose *that*?—No, it really didn't come suddenly at all, it's just that I kept putting it off, but now I must. . . .Yes, we'll have to call off our movie date. Say hello to Thekla for me.—Perhaps you'll call him sometimes on Sundays? So long then.—Well, gladly, of course.—Good-bye.

(She hangs up and calls another number.)

Judith Keith speaking. I'd like to speak to Frau Shoeck.—Lotte?—I wanted to say a quick good-bye, I'm going away for a time.—No, I'm quite well, I just want to see a couple of new faces.—Yes, what I wanted to say was that Fritz is bringing the professor here for the evening next Tuesday, and perhaps you could come too. As I said, I'm leaving tonight.—Yes Tuesday.—No, I only wanted to say I'm leaving tonight, that has nothing to do with it, I thought you could come then too.—All right, let's say: although I'm not there, O.K.?—Of course I know you're not like that and, even if

you were, these are troubled times, and everybody's careful. You'll come then?—If Max can? Oh, he will be able to, the professor'll be here, tell him.—I must hang up now. Fine. Good-bye.

(She hangs up and calls another number.)

Is that you Gertrude? This is Judith. Sorry to disturb you.—Thanks. I wanted to ask you if you can look after Fritz, I'm going away for a couple of months.—I think that you as his sister . . . Why wouldn't you like to?—But there's no likelihood of that, not in Fritz's case. Naturally he knows that—er—you and I didn't get on too well together, but . . . Then *he'll* call *you* if you wish it.—Yes, I'll tell him.—It's all pretty much in order though the apartment's a bit too big.—His study? Oh, Ida knows how to look after it, just leave that to her.—I find her quite intelligent, and he's used to her.—And another thing, please don't misunderstand me, he doesn't like to talk before dinner, would you remember that? I've always avoided it.—I don't want to discuss it now, my train leaves soon and I've not finished packing, you see.—Look after his suits and remind him he has to go to the tailor—he's ordered a coat—and take care that his bedroom's well heated, he always sleeps with an open window and it's too cold.—I don't believe he should "become inured" to it, but now I must stop.—Thank you so much, Gertrude, and we'll write to each other.—Good-bye.

(She hangs up and calls another number.)

Anna? This is Judith. Look, I'm leaving right away.—No, it has to be, it's getting too difficult—too difficult! Yes, no, Fritz *doesn't* want it, he knows nothing. I simply packed.—I don't think so.—I don't think he'll say much.—It's simply too hard for him, I mean, too many technicalities.—We never discussed it.—We never even spoke about it, never.—No, he was *not* different, on the contrary—I want you to be good to him a little at first.—Yes, especially Sundays, and advise him to move.—The apartment is too big for him.—I'd like to say goodbye to you, but you know—the superintendant?—Good-bye then. No, don't come to the station, by no means. Good-bye, I'll write.—Surely.

(She hangs up and calls no more numbers. She has been smoking. She now burns the little book in which she looked up the telephone numbers. She walks up and down a couple of times. Then she begins to speak. She is trying out the little speech which she wishes to make to her husband. One sees that he is supposed to be sitting in a certain chair.)

Yes, I'm going now, Fritz. Perhaps I've stayed too long already, you must forgive me, but. . . .

(*She stands thinking and then tries again.*)

Fritz, you shouldn't keep me any longer, you can't . . . It's clear that I'll be your undoing. I know you're not cowardly, you're not afraid of the police—but there are worse things than the police. They won't take you to a concentration camp but—to-morrow or the next day—they'll exclude you from the clinic. You won't say anything then, but you'll be sick. I won't see you sitting around here turning the pages of magazines. I'm going out of pure selfishness and nothing else. Don't say anything.

(*She stops again. And tries again.*)

Don't say you're not changed. You are! Last week you found—"quite objectively"—that the percentage of Jewish scientists is after all not so great. It always begins with objectivity. And why are you always telling me I was "never such a nationalist as today". Naturally! It's so catching! Oh Fritz, what has happend to us?

(*She pauses.*)

I didn't tell you I wanted to go, and *have* wanted to go a long time, because I can't talk when I look at you, Fritz. Talking seems so futile. They've fixed everything. What's wrong with them? What do they want actually? What do I do to them? I've never meddled in politics. Was I for Thaelmann? No, I'm thoroughly bourgeois, a housewife with servants and so forth, and now suddenly only blondes can do this sort of thing. I've often thought lately how you said years ago: "There are valuable people and less valuable people. The valuable people get insulin when they have sugar in the blood, the less valuable don't." I agreed with you. Well, now they've made new categories of this sort, and I belong to the less valuable. It serves me right.

(*Another pause.*)

Yes, I'm packing. You mustn't act as if you hadn't noticed it in the last few days . . . Fritz, everything is tolerable except one thing: that we're not looking each other in the eyes during the last hour that remains to us. That they shall not achieve—the liars who set everyone lying. Ten years ago when somebody thought no one could tell I was Jewish you quickly said: "Oh, yes, they can tell." And I liked that. It was clear-headed. Why evade the issue now? I'm packing because otherwise they'll take away your position as chief surgeon at the clinic. And because they already cut you there to your face and because already you can't sleep at night. I don't want you to tell me not to go. I'm going in a hurry because I don't want to have you tell me I *should* go. It's a question of time. Character is a question of time. It lasts for a certain length of time, just like a glove. There are good ones that last a long time. But they don't last forever. Incidentally, I'm not angry. And yet: I am. Why should I always be so understanding? What's wrong with the shape of my nose and the color of my hair? They want me to leave the town where I was born lest they should need to give me butter. What kind of men are you all? What kind of a man are you? You people discover the quantum theory and let yourselves be bossed by half-savages; you have to conquer the world, but you're not allowed to have the wife you want. Artificial respiration and every shot a hit! You're monsters or the bootlickers of monsters. Yes, this is unreasonable of me, but what use is reason in such a world? There you sit, watching your wife pack and you say nothing. The walls have ears, don't they? And you all say nothing? One lot listen and the other lot hold their tongues. God! I should hold my tongue too. If I loved you, I'd hold my tongue. I love you, really. Give me that underwear. Those have sex appeal, I'll need them. I'm thirty-six, that's not too old, but I can't do much more experimenting. It mustn't be this way in the next country I come to. The next man I get must be allowed to keep me. And don't say you'll send money, you know you can't. And you shouldn't act as if it were for four weeks. This business doesn't last a mere four weeks. You know it and I know it. So don't say, "Well, it's only for a couple of weeks," as you hand me the fur coat I won't need till winter. And let's not talk about misfortune. Let's talk about shame. Oh, Fritz!

(*She stops. A door is heard opening. She hastily puts herself to rights. Her Husband comes in.*)

THE HUSBAND. What are you doing, tidying up?

THE WIFE. No.

THE HUSBAND. Why are you packing?

THE WIFE. I want to get away.

THE HUSBAND. What do you mean?

THE WIFE. We've talked sometimes about my going away for a time. Things are not too good here these days.

THE HUSBAND. That's a lot of nonsense.

THE WIFE. Shall I stay then?

THE HUSBAND. Where do you intend to go?

THE WIFE. To Amsterdam. Away from here.

THE HUSBAND. But you have no one there.

THE WIFE. No.

THE HUSBAND. Why don't you stay here then? You certainly mustn't go on my account.

THE WIFE. No.

THE HUSBAND. You know I've not changed, don't you, Judith?

THE WIFE. Yes.

(*He embraces her. They stand, silent, between the bags.*)

THE HUSBAND. And there's nothing else to make you go?

THE WIFE. You know the answer to that.

THE HUSBAND. Perhaps it isn't so stupid. You need a breather. It's stifling here. I'll bring you back. Two days on the other side of the frontier, and I'd feel much better.

THE WIFE. Yes, by all means.

THE HUSBAND. This business here can't last too long. A complete change will come—from somewhere. All this will calm down again like an inflammation. It's really a misfortune.

THE WIFE. It certainly is. Did you meet Shoeck?

THE HUSBAND. Yes, that is, only on the stairs. I believe he's sorry again they cut us. He was quite embarrassed. In the long run they can't hold us intellectuals down like this, however much they hate us. Nor can they make war with completely spineless wrecks. These people are not so unresponsive if one confronts them boldly. When do you want to leave?

THE WIFE. Quarter past nine.

THE HUSBAND. And where shall I send the money?

THE WIFE. General delivery, Amsterdam, perhaps.

THE HUSBAND. I'll get myself a special permit. My God, I can't send my wife away with ten marks a month! What a mess everything is in. I feel awful about it.

THE WIFE. When you come for me, it'll do you good.

THE HUSBAND. To read a paper for once that has something in it!

THE WIFE. I called Gertrude. She'll look after you.

THE HUSBAND. Quite unnecessary—for a couple of weeks.

THE WIFE. (*she has begun to pack*). Hand me the fur coat now, will you?

THE HUSBAND (*he gives it to her*). After all, it's only for a couple of weeks.

SCENE EIGHT

When the lights go up we see the Council Chamber of a Court of Justice. Above the scene is written in large black letters: AUGSBURG 1935.

IN SEARCH OF JUSTICE

(*The haze of a January morning is seen through the window. A round gas lamp is still burning. Judge A is just putting on his robe. There is a knock at the door.*)

JUDGE A. Come in.

(*A Police Inspector comes in.*)

INSPECTOR. Good morning, Judge.

JUDGE A. Good morning, Herr Tallinger. I asked you to come and see me about the case Haebele, Schuent, and Gaunitzer. I frankly admit the matter is not entirely clear to me.

(*The Inspector does not answer.*)

JUDGE A. I gather from the records that the scene of the affair was Arndt's jewelery store. Arndt is Jewish, isn't he?

(*Again the Inspector does not answer.*)

JUDGE A. And Haebele, Schuent, and Gaunitzer are still members of Storm Troop Seven in the S.A.?

(*The Inspector nods.*)

JUDGE A. Which means that the S.A. have seen no need to discipline these three men on their own account?

(*The Inspector shakes his head.*)

JUDGE A. In view of the sensation the affair has created in the neighbourhood one can assume that the S.A. have held an investigation?

(*The Inspector shrugs his shoulders.*)

JUDGE A. I'd be grateful, Tallinger, if you could give me a summary of the whole business before the trial. Can you do that now?

INSPECTOR (*Speaking mechanically*). Last year on the second of December at quarter past eight in the morning three S.A. men, Haebele, Schuent, and Gaunitzer, broke into Arndt's jewelry store in Sletov Street, exchanged a few words, and wounded Arndt, who is fifty-four years old, on the back of his head. It involved also material damages in the region of 11,834 marks. Police investigations made on December 7 of last year revealed. . . .

JUDGE A. My dear Tallinger, that's all in the records. (*Annoyed, he points to the indictment which consists of a single sheet of paper.*) The indictment is the thinnest and sloppiest I've ever seen in my life, and I haven't been spoiled in the last few months either. Nevertheless all that's in it. I hoped you might be in a position to explain something of the background of the case.

INSPECTOR. Certainly, your honor.

JUDGE A. Well?

INSPECTOR. There's no background to the case at all, your honour.

JUDGE A. Tallinger, are you really going to maintain that this case is quite straightforward?

INSPECTOR (*grinning*). Why no, of course not.

JUDGE A. It's said that some jewelry got lost during the incident. Has it been recovered since?

INSPECTOR. Not that I know of.

(*The Judge looks hard at the Inspector.*)

INSPECTOR. I have a family, your honour.

JUDGE A. So have I, Tallinger.

INSPECTOR. Yes.

(*There is a pause.*)

INSPECTOR. Arndt is a Jew, don't you see?

JUDGE A. As the name indicates.

INSPECTOR. Right. And there's a rumour going round in the neighbourhood. A case of racial pollution.

(*The Judge appears to begin to understand.*)

JUDGE A. Aha. Who was involved?

INSPECTOR. Arndt's daughter. Nineteen. Supposed to be pretty.

JUDGE A. Has the matter been officially gone into?

INSPECTOR (*reluctantly*). Not exactly. The rumour died out again.

JUDGE A. Who spread it then?

INSPECTOR. The owner of the building. A Herr von Miel.

JUDGE A. He wanted to get the Jewish store out of his building?

INSPECTOR. So we thought. But then apparently he went back on it.

JUDGE A. But anyway this would explain why there was some ill feeling against Arndt in the neighbourhood? And the young fellows acted out of a sort of patriotic excitement.

INSPECTOR (*he answers with decision*). I don't think so, your honour.

JUDGE A. What don't you think?

INSPECTOR. That Haebele, Schuent, and Gaunitzer will make much of this pollution business.

JUDGE A. Why not?

INSPECTOR. The name of the Aryan concerned was never mentioned in the records. God knows who he is. He could be wherever there's a crowd of Aryans, couldn't he? Well, and where are there crowds of Aryans? In short, the S.A. doesn't want it brought into the discussion.

JUDGE A (*impatiently*). Then why do you tell me?

INSPECTOR. Because you said you had a family. So that *you* won't bring it into the discussion. All the same some witness from that part of town might start in.

JUDGE A. I understand. But aside from this I don't understand very much.

INSPECTOR. Between ourselves: the less you understand the better.

JUDGE A. It's easy for you to talk. But I have to render a verdict.

INSPECTOR (*vaguely*). Well, yes.

JUDGE A. The only other possibility is direct provocation of the three S.A. men by Arndt himself. Otherwise the episode cannot be explained.

INSPECTOR. Just what *I* think, your honour.

JUDGE A. In that case how were the S.A. men provoked?

INSPECTOR. According to their own deposition they were provoked both by Arndt himself and by an unemployed laborer who shoveled snow for Arndt. Evidently they were going to have a drink and as they passed the store, Wagner, the laborer, and Arndt himself called them names.

JUDGE A. But you haven't got a witness for that, have you?

INSPECTOR. Yes. The owner of the house, this Herr von Miel, declared that he saw Wagner provoke the S.A. men. He saw it through his window. And Arndt's partner, one Herr Stau, visited S.A. headquarters the same afternoon and in the presence of Haebele, Schuent, and Gaunitzer admitted that Arndt had always spoken contemptuously of the S.A.

JUDGE A. So Arndt has a partner? Aryan?

INSPECTOR. Obviously. Do you think he'd choose a Jew to represent him?

JUDGE A. But then his partner wouldn't make a statement against him?

INSPECTOR (*cunningly*). I'm not so sure.

JUDGE A (*irritated*). What do you mean? The store can't sue for damages if it's proved that Arndt provoked the attack of Haebele, Schuent, and Gaunitzer.

INSPECTOR. How do you know Stau has any interest in damages?

JUDGE A. I don't understand. He's a partner, isn't he?

INSPECTOR. Exactly.

(*The Judge looks puzzled.*)

INSPECTOR. We have established that Stau comes and goes at S.A. headquarters—not officially, I mean, but sub rosa—and that's probably why Arndt made him his partner. Stau was once involved in a strange affair: the S.A. took someone for a ride but it turned out to be the wrong man, and it was quite a job to fix everything up afterwards. Of course I wouldn't go so far as to say that Stau himself in the present case . . . Anyway, you may have to be careful with him. You spoke just now about your family: I know I can trust you to keep this confidential.

JUDGE A (*shaking his head*). What I don't see is this. How can it be to the interest of Herr Stau that the store should lose over eleven thousand marks?

INSPECTOR. Yes, the jewelry is certainly gone. I mean Haebele, Schuent, and Gaunitzer don't have it anyway. And they haven't sold it either.

JUDGE A. I see.

INSPECTOR. Naturally Stau can't be expected to keep Arndt on as his partner after Arndt has been proven guilty of provocation. As for the losses which Arndt has incurred, he'll have to make them good to Stau. Is that clear?

JUDGE A. Certainly that is quite clear. (*Thoughtfully, he looks at The Inspector for a moment. The Inspector looks straight in front of him, expressionless and entirely official.*) Yes, and it will boil down to this: Arndt provoked the S.A. men. Apparently he has made himself unpopular everywhere. Didn't you say he gave the owner of the building cause for complaint through the scandalous goings-on of his family? Yes, yes, I know the affair must not be brought into the discussion, but one can readily imagine he won't mind if someone moves out in the near future. Thanks very much, Tallinger. You've done me a real service.

(*Judge A gives The Inspector a cigar. The Inspector goes out. In the doorway he meets the Junior Prosecutor who is just coming in.*)

PROSECUTOR (*to Judge A*). Can I speak to you a minute?

JUDGE A (*he is now peeling an apple for his lunch*). You can.

PROSECUTOR. In concerns the case of Haebele, Schuent, and Gaunitzer.

JUDGE A (*busy with the apple*). Yes.

PROSECUTOR. The case is somewhat straightforward as far as . . .

JUDGE A. Yes. To be quite frank, I don't in the least understand why your prosecutor's office has opened proceedings.

PROSECUTOR. But why? The case has attracted attention rather disagreeably in the neighbourhood. Even party members wanted an investigation.

JUDGE A. I see it as merely an obvious case of Jewish provocation and nothing else.

PROSECUTOR. Oh nonsense, Goll! Our indictments may be somewhat laconic these days, but they deserve your closer attention, believe me. Don't be so naive about it; you have to see a little further than your nose. And take care not to make mistakes or before you know it you'll be a country judge in Eastern Pomerania. It's not too cozy there nowadays.

JUDGE A (*he is perplexed, and stops eating the apple*). I don't understand. You don't mean to say you intend to let the Jew Arndt go?

PROSECUTOR (*on his dignity*). And if I do? The man did not intend provocation. You think he can't get justice in a court of the Third Reich because he's a Jew? Now listen: you're developing extremely strange opinions, Goll.

JUDGE A (*he is annoyed*). I'm developing no opinions. I merely considered that Haebele, Schuent, and Gaunitzer were acting under provocation.

PROSECUTOR. They were not provoked by Arndt but by the unemployed laborer, what was his name—er—Wagner.

JUDGE A. There's not a word of it in your indictment, my dear Spitz.

PROSECUTOR. Of course not. All the prosecutor's office heard was that The S.A. men had attacked Arndt. And then we intervened as a matter of duty. But if for example the witness von Miel says in court that Arndt was never on the street during the whole episode but that, on the contrary, it was the laborer—what was his name—er—Wagner who called them names, somehow we have to take that into account.

JUDGE A. Von Miel is going to make a statement of that sort? But he's the owner of the building. He wants to get Arndt out of the place. He won't make a statement in his favor.

PROSECUTOR. What on earth do you have against von Miel? Why shouldn't he tell the truth under oath? Perhaps you don't know that von Miel is not only in the S.S., he has highly influential contacts in the Department of Justice? I would advise you to regard him as a respectable citizen, my dear Goll.

JUDGE A. So I do. After all you don't have to respect a man less these days for not wanting a Jewish store in his house.

PROSECUTOR (*magnanimously*). As long as the man pays the rent. . . .

JUDGE A (*diplomatically*). I'm given to understand that he once gave information against Arndt concerning. . . .

PROSECUTOR So you know that. But aren't you wrong in assuming von Miel was trying to get Arndt out of the building? The more so since the accusation was withdrawn. Wouldn't one rather assume they had come to a somewhat satisfactory understanding? My dear Goll, please don't be so naive.

JUDGE A (*he is now getting really annoyed*). My dear Spitz, it is not so simple. His own partner whom I expected to protect him wants to indict him, and the owner of the building who indicted him wants to protect him. And we have to reach a decision.

PROSECUTOR. What are we paid for?

JUDGE A. A frightfully involved affair. Would you care for a Havana?

(*The Prosecutor takes a Havana and they smoke in silence. Then Judge A continues, with gloomy reflectiveness.*)

JUDGE A. But if it is established in the court that Arndt was not guilty of provocation he can immediately bring an action for damages against the S.A.

PROSECUTOR. In the first place he can't bring an action against the S.A. but at best only against Haebele, Schuent, and Gaunitzer, who haven't a penny—unless he were to get his money out of the unemployed laborer—er—what's his name—er—Wagner. (*with emphasis*): In the second place he will think twice before indicting the S.A. men.

JUDGE A. Where is he at the moment?

PROSECUTOR. In hospital.

JUDGE A. And Wagner?

PROSECUTOR. In a concentration camp.

JUDGE A (*he is now somewhat at ease again*). Well, well, in view of the circumstances, it's true, Arndt will hardly wish to accuse the S.A. And Wagner will not bank too much on his innocence. But the S.A. will scarcely be content if the Jew gets off scot free.

PROSECUTOR. But the court will confirm the fact that the S.A. men were provoked. It doesn't matter to them whether it was the Jew or the Communist.

JUDGE A (*he is still in doubt*). That's not quite true. After all, during the argument between Wagner and the S.A. men the jewelry store was damaged. To a certain extent the S.A. is still implicated.

PROSECUTOR. Well, you can't have it every way, and you can't do right by everybody. But your patriotic feelings must tell you, my dear Goll, whom you *should* do right by. I must stress one thing: I'm advised—and the advice comes from the highest circles in the S.A.—that by now somewhat more backbone is expected from German judges.

JUDGE A (*sighing*). In any case it isn't easy to know what *is* just, my dear Spitz. You must admit that.

PROSECUTOR. By all means. But our Minister of Justice made an excellent remark which might give you something to hold on to: "Whatever's useful to the German Folk is just."

JUDGE A (*apathetically*). Yes, of course.

PROSECUTOR. But cheer up. (*He stands up.*) Now you know the background, it shouldn't be hard. I'll see you later, my dear Goll.

(*He leaves the room. Judge A is very uneasy. He stands for a time at the window. Then absentmindedly, he thumbs through the records. Finally he rings. An attendant comes in.*)

JUDGE A. Please bring Inspector Tallinger in again from the witness room. And don't be obtrusive about it.

(*The Attendant leaves. The Inspector comes in again.*)

JUDGE A. Tallinger, it's lucky I didn't take your advice when you told me to regard it as a case of provocation by Arndt. I hear that Herr von Miel is ready to give evidence under oath that it was the laborer Wagner who was guilty of provocation, and not Arndt.

INSPECTOR (*impenetrably*). That's correct, your honor.

JUDGE A. "That's correct?" *Now* what do you mean?

INSPECTOR. That Wagner was the one who called names.

JUDGE A. And isn't that true?

INSPECTOR (*he is offended*). Your Honor: whether it's true or not we can't. . . .

JUDGE A (*decisively*). Listen a moment, man. You're in a German court of Justice. Has Wagner confessed or has he not confessed?

INSPECTOR. Your honor, I wasn't in the concentration camp in person, if that's what you want to know. In the report of the official investigation—

Wagner is reported to have kidney trouble—it says he confessed. Only. . . .

JUDGE A. Well then, he confessed. What d'you mean by "only?"

INSPECTOR. He's a World War veteran and, in fact, was shot in the neck, and, according to Stau, who, as you know gave evidence as Arndt's partner, is incapable of speaking out loud. That von Miel on the second floor should be able to hear him shouting at the S.A. men is not wholly. . . .

JUDGE A. Oh well, it may of course be said you don't need a voice to tell someone to shove it. A simple gesture would do the job. I have gotten the impression throughout that the Prosecutor's Office wishes to leave a loophole for the S.A. More correctly stated: that is *precisely* what they wish.

INSPECTOR. Yes, your honor.

JUDGE A. What does Arndt say?

INSPECTOR. That he definitely was not there and got the wound in the head by falling on the stairs. You can't get anything more out of him.

JUDGE A. The man is probably quite innocent and got into this accidentally.

INSPECTOR (*he gives it up*). Yes, your honor.

JUDGE A. And the S.A. will be satisfied if their own people get off?

INSPECTOR. Yes, your honor.

JUDGE A. Stop saying, "Yes, your honor" like a nutcracker.

INSPECTOR. Yes, your honor.

JUDGE A. What do you wish to imply? Please don't misunderstand me, Tallinger. You should realize that I am somewhat nervous. I'm quite aware you're a man of honor, but when you gave me advice you must surely have had something in mind?

INSPECTOR (*goodnaturedly, he pulls himself together*). Haven't you ever wondered if the Prosecutor isn't simply after your job and that's why he leads you up the garden path? Such cases are not uncommon nowadays. Let's suppose, your honor, you certify that the Jew is innocent. He didn't provoke those fellows. Wasn't even there. Got that hole in the back of his head quite accidentally in a fight between other people. And so after a time he returns to the store. Stau can't stop him. And the store has been damaged to the tune of eleven thousand marks. But now Stau shares the losses since he can't demand the eleven thousand marks from Arndt. And so Stau, if I know the type, will apply to the S.A. for compensation for the lost jewels. Naturally he won't go to them himself since he's the associate of a Jew and therefore "a lackey of the Jews", but he'll have other people on hand. Then it'll be said that the S.A. in its patriotic enthusiasm grabs jewelry! You can imagine what the S.A. will think of your verdict then. The general run of people won't understand it anyway. For in the Third Reich how can a Jew put the S.A. in the wrong?

(*For some time there has been a noise in the rear. Now it gets rather loud.*)

JUDGE A. What's that frightful noise? One moment, Tallinger. (*He rings and the Attendant comes in.*) What's all the row about?

ATTENDANT. The court-roorm is full. And they're jammed so close together in the aisles no one can get through. And there are some S.A. men saying they have to get through, they're under orders to attend the trial.

(*The Attendant leaves, while Judge A merely looks frightened.*)

INSPECTOR (*continuing*). You'll get it in the neck from those people, you know. I strongly advise you to concentrate on Arndt and leave the S.A. in peace.

JUDGE A (*he sits down, brokenly, his head in his hands. He is very tired*). Very good, Tallinger, I'll have to think it over.

INSPECTOR. You'll be well advised to do just that, your honor.

(*He goes out. Judge A stands up with difficulty, and noisily rings the bell. The Attendant comes in.*)

JUDGE A. Go over to Judge Fey and ask him if he could come over and see me for a few minutes.

(*The Attendant leaves. Judge A's Housemaid comes in with a lunchbag.*)

THE MAID. You'd forget your head, your honor. It's really dreadful. Look what you've forgotten today. Think hard for a moment: the main thing! (*She hands the bag over to him*) Your lunchbag! And then you'd have to buy those warm rolls and you'd get stomach ache like last week. All because you don't take care of yourself.

JUDGE A. Very well, Mary.

THE MAID. I could hardly get through. The whole building is full of S.A. men on account of the trial. But today it's coming to them, isn't it, your honor? At the butcher's, people were saying: "It's good there's some justice left in the world." Knocking down a respectable man of business! The whole neighbourhood knows half the S.A. are former criminals. Except for the judges and the courts they'd run off with the cathedral. They did it for the rings. One of them—Haebele—is marrying a girl who was on the streets till six months ago. And they assaulted Wagner, the laborer with a wound in the neck, while he was shovelling snow. Everybody saw it. They do it quite openly. They're terrorising the whole neighbourhood. And if anyone says anything, they wait for him after dark and when they hit him he doesn't get up again.

JUDGE A. Very well, Mary. Now run along.

THE MAID. I said in the butcher's: "Judge Goll will give them what they deserve." Am I right? You have the decent people on your side, that's a fact, your honour. Only don't eat your lunch too quickly, it's bad for you. It's so unhealthy, and now I'm going. I won't be keeping you any longer. You have to go into court and don't let it excite you or you may as well eat now. You don't need more than a minute or two, and that won't make any difference. But you can't eat on an excited stomach. Now take care of yourself. Your health is the best thing you have. Now I'm going. I can see you're eager to go into court, you know you are, and I must get to the grocery store.

(*The Maid leaves. Judge B, and elderly judge and friend of A, comes in.*)

JUDGE B. What's the matter?

JUDGE A. I wanted to talk something out with you if you have a few minutes to spare. This afternoon I have a rather dreadful case to deal with.

JUDGE B (*he sits down*). Yes, the S.A. affair.

JUDGE A (*he suddenly stands still*). Who told *you* about it?

JUDGE B. It was discussed over there yesterday afternoon. A nasty case.

(*Judge A begins to pace up and down.*)

JUDGE A. What do they say?

JUDGE B. Nobody envies you. (*Inquisitively*): What are you going to do?

JUDGE A. I don't know. Moreover, I didn't know the case was so well known.

JUDGE B (*he is surprised*). Really?

JUDGE A. They say this partner is quite a dangerous type.

JUDGE B. He certainly is. But this von Miel is also no philanthropist.

JUDGE A. What is known about him?

JUDGE B. Enough. He has contacts.

(*There is a pause.*)

JUDGE A. Highly influential contacts?

JUDGE B. Highly influential.

(*Another Pause*)

JUDGE B (*cautiously*). If you leave the Jew out of it and acquit Haebele, Schuent, and Gaunitzer on the grounds that they were provoked by the laborer who then ran back into the store, won't the S.A. be satisfied? In any case Arndt won't bring charges against the S.A.

JUDGE A (*he is troubled*). You forget Arndt's partner. He'll go to the S.A. to claim the valuables. And then I'll have the whole leadership of the S.A. at my throat, Fey.

JUDGE B (*after he has considered this argument, which apparently surprises him*). But if you leave the Jew out of it, von Miel will most certainly break your neck. Perhaps you don't know about the bills of exchange at his bank? He's clutching at Arndt as a drowning man clutches at a straw.

JUDGE A (*he is appalled*). Bills of exchange!

(*There is a knock at the door.*)

JUDGE B. Come in.

ATTENDANT. Your honor, I really don't know how I can reserve seats for the Senior Prosecutor and the President of the District Court. If you gentlemen would only let me know in time!

JUDGE B (*since Judge A is silent*). Keep two seats free and don't disturb us in here.

(*The Attendant leaves*)

JUDGE A. That's the last straw.

JUDGE B. Von Miel cannot in any circumstance abandon Arndt and allow him to be ruined. He needs him.

JUDGE A (*annihilated*). As a milch cow.

JUDGE B. I said nothing of the kind, my dear Goll! I don't understand how you can think it of me! I really don't! I must insist that I said *nothing* against Herr von Miel. I'm sorry this is necessary, Goll.

JUDGE A (*getting excited*). But you can't take it that way, Fey. Remember our relationship!

JUDGE B. What d'you mean "our relationship"? I cannot meddle in your cases. Whether you want to be in with the Minister of Justice or the S.A. you must do it yourself. In these days, after all *everyone* must look out for himself.

JUDGE A. I *am* looking out for myself! Only I don't know what advice to give myself!

(*He stands in the doorway listening to the noise outside.*)

JUDGE B. A bad business.

JUDGE A. My God, I'm willing to do anything, please understand me. You've changed completely. I decide this and I decide that as they require but at least I must know *what* they require. When you don't know that, there's no justice left.

JUDGE B. If I were you, I wouldn't be shouting there's no justice left, Goll!

JUDGE A. Now what have I said again? I didn't mean that! I only mean . . . if such contradictions exist. . . .

JUDGE B. We consider ourselves a "people of brothers".

JUDGE A. Yes, of course. I never said anything different. Please don't weigh every word I say!

JUDGE B. Why not? I'm a judge.

JUDGE A (*sweating*). My dear Fey, if one weighed every word of every judge. I am quite willing to examine the whole case in the most rigorous and conscientious manner but I *must* be told which decision is in the interest of the higher authorities. If I let the Jew stay in the store, I naturally make the owner of the building angry. . . . No, not the owner, I mean the partner . . . I'm getting hopelessly confused. And if the laborer was the source of provocation, the owner—what's his name?—von Miel wants. . . . They can't transfer me to Eastern Pomerania, I have a rupture, and I want nothing to do with the S.A. After all I have a family, Fey. It's easy for my wife to say I should merely find out what really happened: I'd wake up in hospital. Am I to speak of an attack? Am I to speak of provocation? What do they want of me?

Naturally I don't sentence the S.A. but either the Jew or the unemployed laborer. But which? How am I to choose between the laborer and the Jew? Between the partner and the landlord? In any case I won't go to Pomerania, that's out of the question, Fey. I'd rather go to a concentration camp. Don't look at me like that: I'm not the accused. I'm willing to do *anything*.

JUDGE B. Willingness is not everything, my friend. (*He stands up*)

JUDGE A. Who is to decide, then?

JUDGE B. In general, a judge's conscience tells him that, Herr Goll. Remember. Good-bye.

JUDGE A. Yes, of course. "According to his knowledge and his conscience." But in this case: *what* am I to choose? What, Fey?

(*Judge B has left. Speechless, Judge A stands looking after him. The telephone rings.*)

JUDGE A (*he picks up the receiver*). Yes?—Emmy?—They can't come to what? The bowling party? Who called you up?—Attorney Priesnitz?—Who told him?—What do I mean? I have to pronounce a verdict.

(*He hangs up. The Attendant comes in. The noise of the crowd is loud again.*)

ATTENDANT. Haebele, Schuent, and Gaunitzer, your honor.

JUDGE A (*gathering up his documents*). Coming.

ATTENDANT. I found a seat for the President of the District Court at the press table. He was quite satisfied. But the Senior Prosecutor refused to sit at the judge's table. Then you'd have to conduct the trial from the dock, your honor. (*He laughs absurdly at his joke.*)

JUDGE A. I won't do that in any circumstances!

ATTENDANT. Here's the door, your honor. Where did you put your brief case with the indictment in it?

JUDGE A (*absolutely bewildered*). Yes, that's what I want. Or else I won't know who is accused, will I? What shall we do with the Senior Prosecutor?

ATTENDANT. Now you've put your address book under your arm, your honor. Here's your brief case. (*He stuffs it under the Judge's arms.*)

(*Distracted and wiping the sweat from his brow, Judge A goes into the court.*)

SCENE NINE

When the lights go up we see a living-room. Above the scene is written in large black letters: COLOGNE 1935.

THE INFORMER

(*It is a rainy Sunday afternoon. A Husband, his Wife, and their Boy have just finished lunch. A Maid enters.*)

MAID. Herr and Frau Klimbtsch want to know if you're at home, sir.

HUSBAND (*snapping*). We're not.

(*The Maid goes out.*)

WIFE. You should have gone to the telephone yourself. They know we couldn't possibly have gone out yet.

HUSBAND. Why couldn't we have gone out?

WIFE. Because it's raining.

HUSBAND. That's not a reason.

WIFE. What would we have gone out for? They'll certainly wonder about that now.

HUSBAND. There are plenty of places to go to.

WIFE. Then why don't we go?

HUSBAND. Where should we go to?

WIFE. If only it weren't raining.

HUSBAND. And where on earth should we go if it weren't raining?

WIFE. In the old days you could at least arrange to meet somebody.

(*There is a pause.*)

WIFE. It was a mistake not to go to the phone. Now they know we don't want them here.

HUSBAND. What if they do?

WIFE. Why, then it means we're dropping them just when everybody's dropping them. I don't like it.

HUSBAND. We're not dropping them.

WIFE. Then why shouldn't they come here?

HUSBAND. Because this Klimbtsch fellow bores me stiff.

WIFE. In the old days he didn't bore you.

HUSBAND. "In the old days!" Don't keep saying that. You make me nervous.

WIFE. At any rate you wouldn't have cut him in the old days just because his case is being looked into by the school-inspectors.

HUSBAND. Are you suggesting I'm a coward?

(*There is a pause.*)

HUSBAND. All right. Call them and say we've just come back because of the rain.

(*The Wife remains seated.*)

WIFE. Shall we ask the Lemkes if they want to come over?

HUSBAND. So they can tell us we're not keen enough on Civil Defense?

WIFE (*to the Boy*). Klaus-Heinrich! Leave the radio alone.

(*The Boy turns to the newspapers.*)

HUSBAND. It's certainly a catastrophe to have rain today. You just can't live in a country where it's a castastrophe when it rains.

WIFE. Is it wise to throw remarks like that around?

HUSBAND. Within my own four walls I can make whatever remarks I please. In my own home I can say what I. . . .

(*He is interrupted. The Maid comes in with the coffee things. There is silence while she is in the room.*)

HUSBAND. Must we have a maid whose father is Block Warden?

WIFE. I think we've talked about that enough. Last time you said it had it's advantages.

HUSBAND. I've said a lot of things. Only say something of the sort to your mother and we'll be in a wonderful mess.

WIFE. What I say to my mother . . . !

(*The maid interrupts them again as she brings in the coffee.*)

WIFE. Leave it now, Erna, you can go. I'll look after this.

MAID. Thanks very much, gnädige Frau. (She goes out.)

BOY (*looking up from the paper*). Do all priests do this, Papa?

HUSBAND. What?

BOY. What it says here.

HUSBAND. What is it you're reading?

(*He snatches the paper out of his hand.*)

BOY. Our Group Leader told us we could all know what it says in *this* paper.

HUSBAND. I don't care what the Group Leader said. I decide what you can read and what you can't.

WIFE. Here's ten cents, Klaus-Heinrich, go buy yourself something.

BOY. But it's raining.

(*He hangs around near the window, undecided.*)

HUSBAND. If these reports of the priest trials don't stop, I won't order this paper any more.

WIFE. And which one *will* you subscribe to? It's in all of them.

HUSBAND. If all the papers carry filth like that, I'll read none. I couldn't know less of what's going on in the world.

WIFE. A house cleaning doesn't hurt once in a while.

HUSBAND. House cleaning! That's just politics.

WIFE. Anyway it's no concern of ours: we're Lutherans.

HUSBAND. It's not a matter of indifference for our people if they can't think of a church without also thinking of such abominations.

WIFE. Then what should they do if such things happen?

HUSBAND. What should they do? Maybe they might look to their own affairs. It may not all be as clean as it might be in their own Brown House, so I hear.

WIFE. But that goes to prove our people has recovered its health, Karl.

HUSBAND. If that's what health looks like, give me disease.

WIFE. You're nervous today. Did anything happen at school?

HUSBAND. What should happen at school? And please stop telling me I'm nervous. That's what makes me so.

WIFE. We shouldn't always be quarrelling, Karl. In the old days. . . .

HUSBAND. I was waiting for it: "in the old days!" I didn't want my child's mind poisoned in the old days and I don't want it poisoned now!

WIFE. Where is he anyway?

HUSBAND. How do I know?

WIFE. Did you see him leave?

HUSBAND. No.

WIFE. I don't understand where he can have gone. (*Shouting*) Klaus-Heinrich!

(*She runs out and is heard shouting. She returns.*)

WIFE. Well, he's out.

HUSBAND. Why on earth shouldn't he be out?

WIFE. Why, because it's simply pouring.

HUSBAND. Why are you so nervous if the boy goes out once in a while?

WIFE. What have you been saying?

HUSBAND. What's that got to do with it?

WIFE. You're so uncontrolled these days.

HUSBAND. I certainly am not uncontrolled these days, but, even if I were, what has that got to do with the boy being out?

WIFE. Oh, you know they listen.

HUSBAND. So what?

WIFE. So what? What if he tells tales? You know what's drummed into them at the Hitler Youth. They're under orders to report *everything*. Strange he left so quietly.

HUSBAND. Nonsense!

WIFE. Didn't you notice it, when he'd left?

HUSBAND. He was at the window quite a while.

WIFE. I wonder what he overheard.

HUSBAND. He knows what happens to people who're denounced.

WIFE. What of the boy the Schmulkes told about? His father must be in the concentration camp still. If only we knew how long he was in the room.

HUSBAND. Oh, that's all nonsense.

(*He goes through the other room and shouts for the Boy.*)

WIFE. I can't believe he'd just go off without saying a word. He isn't like that.

HUSBAND. Maybe he's at some school-friends.

WIFE. In that case he can only be at the Mummermann's. I'll phone.

(*She phones.*)

HUSBAND. I regard the whole thing as a false alarm.

WIFE (*at the phone*). This is Frau Furcke. Good afternoon, Frau Mummermann. Is Klaus-Heinrich at your place?—He isn't?—Then I just can't think where the boy is.—Tell me, Frau Mummermann, is the club room of the Hitler Youth open Sunday afternoon?—It is?—Thanks, I'll try them.

(*She hangs up. The couple sit in silence.*)

HUSBAND. What can he have heard after all?

WIFE. You talked about the paper. You shouldn't have said that about the Brown House. He's such a nationalist.

HUSBAND. And *what* may I have said about the Brown House?

WIFE. You can hardly have forgotten: that it's not clean!

HUSBAND. That can't be interpreted as an attack. To say: it's not clean, or rather as I more moderately put it, not *quite* clean, which certainly makes a difference, a considerable difference, why, that's more of a jocular observation, idiomatic and popular, one might almost say a colloquialism. It means little more than that probably, even there, something is not always, and under all circumstances, as the Führer wishes it. I intentionally indicated the merely probable character of my allegation by using the expression: "it *may* not all be *quite*"—quite in the mildest sense—"clean". This was my formulation of the matter. *May* be! Not: *is!* I can't say that anything there *is* not clean, there's no proof. But wherever there are men, there are imperfections. I never suggested anything more than that, and that only in the mildest form. The Führer himself on a certain occasion said much the same thing a good deal more sharply!

WIFE. I don't understand. You don't have to talk this way to me.

HUSBAND. I wish I didn't. I'm not sure what you yourself say, in the way of gossip, about the things you've heard between these four walls, insignificant things, probably only said in a moment of excitement. Naturally I'm far from accusing you of spreading frivolous tales against your husband and I don't for a moment assume the boy would do anything against his father. But unfortunately there is an important distinction between *doing* wrong and *knowing* you do it.

WIFE. Now please stop! Watch *your* tongue! You said one can't live in Hitler Germany. All along I've been trying to remember whether you said that before or after what you said about the Brown House.

HUSBAND. I didn't say it at all.

WIFE. You go on as if I were the police! What can the boy have heard? That's what tortures me.

HUSBAND. The expression "Hitler Germany" is not in my vocabulary.

WIFE. And about the Block Warden and about the papers being full of lies and what you said recently about Civil Defense—the boy hears nothing positive at all! That certainly isn't good for a young mind. Youth can only be perverted by such talk. The Führer always stresses: "Germany's youth is Germany's future." The boy doesn't run off and turn informer. He isn't made that way. I feel bad.

HUSBAND. He's revengeful.

WIFE. What can he take revenge *for?*

HUSBAND. God knows. There's always something. Maybe because I took his green frog away from him.

WIFE. That was a week ago.

HUSBAND. He remembers.

WIFE. Why did you take it?

HUSBAND. Because he caught no flies for it. Just let it starve.

WIFE. He really has too much to do, though.

HUSBAND. That's not the frog's fault!

WIFE. But he never said anything about that. And just now I gave him ten cents. Why, he gets everything he wants.

HUSBAND. Bribery!

WIFE. What do you mean?

HUSBAND. They'll say we tried to bribe him to keep his mouth shut.

WIFE. What do you think they can do to you?

HUSBAND. Oh, everything. There are no limits to what they can do. Good God! "Educator of the youth!" I fear them. To be a teacher in such circumstances!

WIFE. But there's nothing against you.

HUSBAND. There's something against everyone. All are suspect. If suspicion exists, one is suspected. Suspicion need only exist.

WIFE. A child is not a reliable witness. A child has no idea what he's saying.

HUSBAND. That's *your* opinion. Since when have *they* needed a witness for anything?

WIFE. Can't we figure out what you must have meant by your remarks? I mean: then it will be clear he misunderstood.

HUSBAND. What could I have said? I can't remember. It's the fault of the damned rain. . . . It makes you disgruntled. After all I'd be the last to say anything against the spiritual revival the German people have experienced! I saw it coming in 1932.

WIFE. Karl, we haven't time to talk. We must straighten everything out at once. We haven't a moment to lose.

HUSBAND. I can't think it of Klaus-Heinrich.

WIFE. Now: first this matter of the Brown House and the filth.

HUSBAND. I said nothing about filth.

WIFE. You said the paper is full of filth and you intend to cancel your subscription.

HUSBAND. Yes, the paper, not the Brown House.

WIFE. Mightn't you have said you disapprove of such filth in the churches? And you think it's quite possible the very men now on trial invented the atrocity stories about the Brown House and *they* said that it wasn't clean? Therefore, *they* should have looked to their own affairs? Above all, you told the boy to leave the radio and read the paper instead because you take the stand that youth in the Third Reich should note with open eyes what is going on?

HUSBAND. All this wouldn't help in the least.

WIFE. Karl, don't let your courage fail you. You must be strong, as the Führer always . . . !

HUSBAND. I can't stand in the dock with my own flesh and blood in the witness-box giving evidence against me!

WIFE. You mustn't take it this way.

HUSBAND. It is unpardonably careless to have anything to do with the Klimbtsches!

WIFE. Why? Nothing's happened to him yet.

HUSBAND. But an investigation is pending.

WIFE. An investigation is pending for a lot of people. What would happen if they were all in despair?

HUSBAND. Do you think the Block Warden has anything against us?

WIFE. You mean if enquiries are made? He got a box of cigarettes on his birthday and a splendid tip at New Year's.

HUSBAND. The Gauffs next door gave *fifteen* marks!

WIFE. They read Vorwärts as late as '32 and in May '33 they put out the black-white-and-red flag.

(*The telephone rings.*)

HUSBAND. The telephone!

WIFE. Shall I go?

HUSBAND. I don't know.

WIFE. Who can it be?

HUSBAND. Wait a while. If it rings again, you can answer it.

(*They wait. It does not ring again*)

HUSBAND. This isn't living.

WIFE. Karl!

HUSBAND. You bore me a Judas. He sits at table listening while he drinks the soup we place before him! He commits to memory the conversation of his own parents! He's an informer!

WIFE. You mustn't say that!

(*There is a pause.*)

WIFE. Do you think we should make preparations?

HUSBAND. Do you think they'll come with him *now*?

WIFE. It's quite impossible.

HUSBAND. Maybe I should put on my Iron Cross?

WIFE. By all means, Karl.

(*He brings the cross and puts it on with trembling fingers.*)

WIFE. There's nothing against you at school?

HUSBAND. How should I know? I'm willing to teach everything they want taught. But what *do* they want taught? If only I ever knew! How do I know *how* they want Bismarck to have been if they're so slow bringing out the new textbooks? Can't you give the maid another ten marks? *She's* always listening too.

WIFE (*nods*). And the picture of Hitler. Shall we hang it over your desk? It'll look better.

HUSBAND. Yes, do that.

(*The wife begins to move the pictures.*)

HUSBAND. But if the boy says we hung it specially, it'll all end in "consciousness of guilt."

(*She puts the picture back where it was.*)

HUSBAND. Wasn't that the door?

WIFE. I heard nothing.

HUSBAND. There!

WIFE. Karl!

(*She throws her arms around him.*)

HUSBAND. Don't lose your nerve. Pack me some underwear.

(*The door is heard opening. Husband and Wife stand close together, petrified, in the corner of the room. The door opens and in comes The Boy, a bag of chocolates in his hand. There is a silence.*)

BOY. What's the matter?

WIFE. Where've you been?

(*The Boy points to the bag of chocolates.*)

WIFE. Have you only been buying chocolate?

BOY. Sure. What do you think?

(*He walks, munching, across the room and out. His parents look after him searchingly.*)

HUSBAND. Do you think he's telling the truth?

(*The Wife shrugs her shoulders.*)

SCENE TEN

When the lights go up we see a room in a worker's house. Above the scene is written in large black letters: BERLIN 1936.

THE MAN THEY RELEASED

(*A Sunday morning. A man and his Wife are talking. From the distance military music is heard.*)

MAN. He'll be here any time now.

THE WIFE. Does he look very different?

THE MAN. Not very.

THE WIFE. Do you think he's coming here because he wants to work again with you and the others?

THE MAN. Probably.

THE WIFE. And do you want him to?

THE MAN. Not right away.

THE WIFE. Do you know anything against him?

THE MAN. No. We only know he's been released from the concentration camp.

THE WIFE. Then why do you distrust him?

THE MAN. Too much has happened. They put too much pressure on them.

THE WIFE. But how is he going to prove to you he's still the same?

THE MAN. Oh, we can find out where he stands.

THE WIFE. That can take time.

THE MAN. Yes.

THE WIFE. But he may be absolutely loyal.

THE MAN. He may be.

THE WIFE. In that case it'll be terrible for him when he sees everyone distrusts him.

THE MAN. He knows it's necessary.

THE WIFE. All the same.

THE MAN. I can hear something now. Stay here while we talk.

(*The bell rings. The man opens the door. The Released Man comes in.*)

THE MAN. 'llo, Max.

(*The Released Man shakes hands with The Man and The Wife.*)

THE WIFE. Will you have a cup of coffee? We were just going to have some.

RELEASED MAN. If it's no trouble.

(*There is a pause.*)

RELEASED MAN. You have a new cupboard.

THE WIFE (*on her guard*). It's really second hand. Got it for eleven marks fifty. The other fell to pieces.

RELEASED MAN. I see.

THE MAN. Anything going on outside?

RELEASED MAN. They're taking up a collection. For the Winter Relief, I guess.

THE WIFE. We could use a suit for Willi.

THE MAN. But I'm working.

THE WIFE. We could use a suit for you at that.

THE MAN. Don't talk nonsense.

RELEASED MAN. Work or no work, we could all use something, couldn't we? They pay such wages.

THE MAN. Have you found work yet?

RELEASED MAN. I expect to.

THE MAN. At Siemens'?

RELEASED MAN. Or some other place.

THE MAN. It's not hard nowadays.

RELEASED MAN. No.

(*There is a pause.*)

RELEASED MAN. What are you doing at Borsig's now?

THE MAN. All sorts.

RELEASED MAN (*nods*). Rearmament?

THE MAN (*vaguely*). Don't know. How long were you in?

RELEASED MAN. Six months.

THE MAN. Did you meet anyone?

RELEASED MAN. I didn't know anyone. (*He pauses*) They always take them to different camps now. They might have taken them to Bavaria.

THE MAN. I see.

RELEASED MAN. The world outside hasn't changed much.

THE MAN. Not specifically.

THE WIFE. We're keeping to ourselves, you know, quite quietly. Willi hardly ever meets any of his old friends now, isn't that so, Willi?

THE MAN. Yes. We don't have much company.

RELEASED MAN. You still haven't gotten rid of the garbage cans out in the hall?

THE WIFE. Oh, you remember that? Yes, the super says he has no other place for them.

RELEASED MAN. (*As The Wife pours him a cup of coffee*). Just half a cup. I can't stay.

THE MAN. Doing anything?

RELEASED MAN. Selma told me you two looked after her when she was sick. Thanks very much.

THE WIFE. Don't mention it. We'd have told her to come over sometimes of an evening, but we don't even have a radio.

THE MAN. Anyway, what you hear on the radio is in the paper too.

RELEASED MAN. There's not much in the *Mottenpost*.

THE WIFE. As much as in their *Volkischer Beobachter*.

RELEASED MAN. And there's as much in the *Volkischer* as in the *Mottenpost*, right?

THE MAN. I don't read much in the evening. Too tired.

THE WIFE. What's wrong with your hand? It's all shrivelled. And two fingers gone!

RELEASED MAN (*evasively*). I fell.

THE WIFE (*She is hurt by the evasivenes*). Listen. . . .

THE MAN (*interrupts her*). Good thing it's the left.

RELEASED MAN. Yes, that was lucky. (*In a changed tone.*) I'd like to have talked with you, Willi. No offense, Frau Mahn.

THE WIFE. Yes, sure. I must clean up the stove.

(*She busies herself with the stove. The Released Man looks at her, a slight smile on his lips. He understands.*)

THE MAN. Is Selma all right again?

RELEASED MAN. Her hip isn't. She can't do any washing. Tell me, is Karl . . . couldn't I . . . .

(*He stops and looks at them both. They look at him. He does not finish the sentence.*)

THE MAN (*hoarsely*). Should we go out on the Alexanderplatz and see the crowd?

THE WIFE (*relieved*). We could, couldn't we?

RELEASED MAN. Sure.

(*Pause*)

RELEASED MAN (*he speaks quietly as The Wife carries out the coffee things*). Willi, listen, I'm still the same.

THE MAN (*lightly*). Of course. Maybe there's music on the Alex. Get yourself ready, Anna. We've had coffee. I'll just run a comb through my hair.

(*The Man and Wife go into the next room. The Released Man remains seated. He has taken his hat. He whistles. The couple come back dressed for going out.*)

THE MAN. Come on, Max.

THE RELEASED MAN. Okay. I want to tell you one thing: I think it's right.

THE MAN. Let's go then.

(*They go together.*)

SCENE ELEVEN

When the lights go up we see a town-square. Above the scene is written in large Black Letters: CALW, WÜRTTEMBERG, 1936.

THE OLD NAZI

A number of small stores. In the background is a butcher shop; In the foreground, a dairy. It is a dark winter's morning. The butcher shop is still closed; but the dairy is already lit up and several customers are waiting.

THE TRADESMAN. No butter again today, hm?

THE WOMAN. There should be as much as I can buy with the money *he* earns.

THE YOUNG FELLOW. What's all this grumbling about? Germany needs cannons, not butter! He made it quite plain.

THE WOMAN (*timidly*). That's true too.

(*There is silence.*)

THE YOUNG FELLOW. Think we could have occupied the Rhineland with butter? Everyone was for it once it was done, but no one wants to make sacrifices.

THE SECOND WOMAN. Take it easy. We're all making sacrifices.

THE YOUNG FELLOW (*distrustfully*). How do you mean?

THE SECOND WOMAN (*she speaks to The First Woman*). You give something when there's a collection, don't you?

(*The First Woman nods.*)

THE SECOND WOMAN. Very well then. She gives. And we give too. Voluntarily.

THE YOUNG FELLOW. You hang on to every penny whenever the Führer needs what you might call support for his great undertakings. They give nothing but rags to the Winter Relief. They'd like to just give their moths. We know them. The factory owner at Number 11 actually donated a pair of wornout riding boots.

THE TRADESMAN. Some people are careless.

(*The Dairy Woman comes out of the dairy wearing a white apron.*)

THE DAIRY WOMAN. We're nearly ready.

(*She speaks to the Second Woman.*)

Good morning, Frau Ruhl. Have you heard last night they came for young Lettner from next door?

THE SECOND WOMAN. The Butcher?

THE DAIRY WOMAN. Yes, the son.

THE SECOND WOMAN. But wasn't he in the S.A.?

THE DAIRY WOMAN. He was. The old man has been in the party since '29. Yesterday he happened to be out of town at a cattle auction or they'd have taken him too.

THE SECOND WOMAN. But what have they done?

THE DAIRY WOMAN. Put the price of meat up. He didn't get any lately and had to let his customers go. And then they say he bought on the black market. From a Jew, the story goes.

THE YOUNG FELLOW. You think they shouldn't have come for him then?

THE DAIRY WOMAN. He was always one of the most enthusiastic. He rounded up old Zeisler from Number 17 for not subscribing to the *Volkischer Beobachter*. He's an old Nazi.

THE SECOND WOMAN. When he comes back it'll be quite a surprise for him.

THE DAIRY WOMAN. *If* he comes back.

THE TRADESMAN. Some people are careless.

THE SECOND WOMAN. They don't seem to be opening at all today.

THE DAIRY WOMAN. A wise move. The police take one look at a place like that and they find something, don't you see? Everything's so hard to get now. We get our things from our co-op. So far there've been no difficulties. (*She calls out*) No cream today!

(*There is a general murmur of disappointment.*)

They say the Lettners have a mortgage on the house. They figured it would be cancelled or something.

THE TRADESMAN. But they can't cancel mortgages. That's asking a bit too much.

THE SECOND WOMAN. Young Lettner was quite a nice person.

THE DAIRY WOMAN. Old Lettner was always the wild one. He simply shoved the boy into S.A. He'd rather have gone out with a girl, of course.

THE YOUNG FELLOW. What do you mean by the "wild one"?

THE DAIRY WOMAN. Did I say "wild one"? Well, he always got wild whenever they said anything against the Theory. Before '33. He always talked about the Theory and against the selfishness of the individual.

THE TRADESMAN. They *are* opening up.

THE SECOND WOMAN. After all, they have to live.

(*A fat woman comes out of the butcher's, which is now partly lit. She stays on the sidewalk and looks inquiringly down the street. Then she turns to The Dairy Woman.*)

THE BUTCHER'S WIFE. Good morning, Frau Schlichter. Have you seen our Richard? He should have been here long ago, with the meat.

(*The Dairy Woman does not reply. They all just stare at her. She understands and quickly goes back into the store.*)

THE DAIRY WOMAN (*she acts as if nothing had happened*). Things came to a head the day before yesterday when the old man made such a row he was heard screaming all over the square. They chalked that up to his score.

THE SECOND WOMAN. I didn't hear a thing about it, Frau Schlichter.

THE DAIRY WOMAN. Really? Well, he refused to display the fake cardboard hams they brought him. He'd ordered them earlier because they required it and he hadn't hung anything in his window for a week but price lists. "I've nothing left for the window," he said. Later when they came with the fake hams—there was even half a calf quite like a real one—he roared out that he wouldn't hang things in his window just for show and a great deal else that isn't repeatable. It was all against the government, and then he threw the things out on the street. They had to pick 'em out of the mud.

THE SECOND WOMAN. You don't say!

THE TRADESMAN. Some people are careless.

THE SECOND WOMAN. How can men go off the handle like that? How can they?

THE DAIRY WOMAN. And crafty men at that.

(*At this moment another light is switched on in the butcher's.*)

THE DAIRY WOMAN. Look!

(*She points excitedly to the window.*)

THE SECOND WOMAN. There's something in the window.

THE DAIRY WOMAN. It's old Lettner. In his top coat. But what's he standing on? (*She shouts suddenly*) Frau Lettner!

THE BUTCHER'S WIFE. (*she comes out of the store*). What's the matter?

(*The Dairy Woman points at the window, unable to speak. The Butcher's Wife looks in for a second, cries out, and falls in a faint. The Second Woman and The Dairy Woman run over to her.*)

THE SECOND WOMAN. He's hanged himself in the window!

THE TRADESMAN. There's a board round his neck.

THE FIRST WOMAN. It's the price list. There's something written on it.

THE SECOND WOMAN. It says: "I VOTED FOR HITLER!"

SCENE TWELVE

When the lights go up we see the yard of a prison. Above the scene is written in large black letters: LANDSBERG 1936.

TWO BAKERS

(*The prisoners walk around in a circle. Each time they pass, two Bakers speak to each other.*)

FIRST BAKER. You're a baker too, newcomer?

SECOND BAKER. Yes, Are you?

FIRST BAKER. Yes. What did they get *you* for?

SECOND BAKER. Look out!

(*The circle revolves once.*)

SECOND BAKER. Because I didn't put bran and potatoes in the bread. And you? How long have you been here?

FIRST BAKER. Two years.

SECOND BAKER. And why are *you* here? Look out!

(*The circle revolves again.*)

FIRST BAKER. Because I did put bran in the bread. Two years ago that was still a crime.

SECOND BAKER. Look out!

SCENE THIRTEEN

When the lights go up we see the kitchen of a working-class house. Above the scene is written in large black letters: DRESDEN 1936.

CHILDREN'S SHOES

(*A mother is peeling potatoes. Her daughter, thirteen years old, is doing her homework.*)

DAUGHTER. Mother, do I get the two pennies?

MOTHER. For the Hitler Youth?

DAUGHTER. Yes.

MOTHER. I have no money to spare.

DAUGHTER. But if I don't hand in two pennies a week I can't go to the country in the summer. And the teacher said "Hitler wants town and country to know each other." The town people should come closer to the farmers. But I have to give the two pennies.

MOTHER. I'll be thinking how I can let you have them.

DAUGHTER. That's wonderful, mother. I'll help you peel the potatoes too. It's wonderful in the country, isn't it? You can eat till you're full. In the gym the teacher said I had a potbelly.

MOTHER. Oh no, you haven't.

DAUGHTER. No, not now. Last year I had. But not so very.

MOTHER. Maybe I can get a bit of tripe.

DAUGHTER. Oh, I get rolls at school. *You* don't get rolls. Bertha said there was goose fat on the bread when she was in the country. And sometimes meat. Isn't that wonderful?

THE MOTHER. Very.

THE DAUGHTER. And the good air.

THE MOTHER. But didn't she have to work too?

THE DAUGHTER. Oh yes. But a lot to eat. The farmer was rude to her, she said.

THE MOTHER. What?

THE DAUGHTER. Oh nothing. Only he wouldn't leave her alone.

THE MOTHER. Ah.

THE DAUGHTER. But Bertha was bigger than me. A year older.

THE MOTHER. Get on with your homework.

(*There is a pause.*)

THE DAUGHTER. I don't have to wear the old black shoes from the Führer's Charity Chest, do I?

THE MOTHER. No, you don't need to. You still have the other pair.

THE DAUGHTER. But there's a hole in one of them.

THE MOTHER. And the weather's wet now.

THE DAUGHTER. I'll put some paper in them. That should do it.

THE MOTHER. No, it won't. When they come through, they have to be soled.

THE DAUGHTER. It costs so much.

THE MOTHER. Why don't you like the shoes from the Charity Chest?

THE DAUGHTER. I can't stand them.

THE MOTHER. Because they're so big?

THE DAUGHTER. Look, you think so too!

THE MOTHER. It's just because they're old.

THE DAUGHTER. Do I have to wear them?

THE MOTHER. You don't *have* to wear them if you can't stand them.

THE DAUGHTER. I'm not vain, am I?

THE MOTHER. No. Just getting bigger.

(*There is a pause.*)

THE DAUGHTER. Can I have the two pennies, mother? I want to go to the country.

THE MOTHER (*slowly*). I have no money for that.

SCENE FOURTEEN

When the lights go up, we see a farmyard. Above the scene is written in large black letters: SCHWETZINGEN, BAVARIA, 1937.

A FARMER FEEDS HIS SOW

(*The scene is a farm at night. In front of the pigsty a Farmer is instructing his Wife and two Children.*)

THE FARMER. I never wanted to drag you into this, but you worried it out of me and now you'll have to keep your mouth shut or your father'll be in the Landsberg prison for life. If we feed our animals when they are hungry, we're doing nothing wrong. It's not the will of God that any creature should go hungry. And when they're hungry they scream and I can't listen to a sow screaming with hunger on my own farm. And we aren't allowed to feed them. It's against the law. I'm feeding them just the same. If I don't feed them they'll die and no one's going to make good the loss.

THE FARMER'S WIFE. I think so too. Our grain is *our* grain. Those bastards can't lay down the law to us. They've sent those Jews away, but the Government is the biggest Jew. And the pastor said: "Thou shalt not muzzle the ox that treadeth out the corn." That's how he dropped the hint that we should go ahead and feed our cattle. *We* didn't make their Four Year Plan for them. We weren't consulted.

THE FARMER. That's right. They're not for the farmers and the farmers are not for them. I have to hand over my grain and then buy fodder for more, so that super bum can buy cannon!

THE FARMER'S WIFE. The parson says: "Blessed are the peacemakers." That's in the Bible.

THE FARMER. Stand at the fence, Tony. And Mary, go out in the meadow, and as soon as anyone comes, let us know.

(*The children take up their positions. The Farmer mixes fodder and carries it, looking around nervously, to the pig-sty. His Wife also peers around nervously.*)

THE FARMER (*he pours out the fodder for the sow*). Go ahead and eat, Lena. Heil Hitler! When God's creatures are hungry, there *is* no Government.

SCENE FIFTEEN

When the lights go up, we see a poorly furnished room. Above the scene is written in large black letters: KARLSRUHE 1937.

WINTER RELIEF

(*Two S.A. Men bring a package from the Winter Relief to an old woman who is standing at the table with her Daughter.*)

FIRST S.A. MAN. Here, mother, the Führer sends you this.

SECOND S.A. MAN. So you can't say he doesn't care for you.

THE OLD WOMAN. Thank you, thank you. Potatoes, Erna. And a woolen sweater. And apples.

FIRST S.A. MAN. And a letter from the Führer with something in it. Just you see.

THE OLD WOMAN (*she opens the letter*). Twenty-five marks! Now what do you say, Erna?

SECOND S.A. MAN. Winter Relief!

OLD WOMAN. You must have an apple, young man, and you as well, for bringing the package and up all those stairs too. I don't have anything else at present. And I'll eat one myself.

(*She takes a bite of an apple. They all start eating apples except The Young Woman.*)

OLD WOMAN. Now do eat an apple, Erna. Don't just stand around. You see now, what your husband says isn't true.

FIRST S.A. MAN. What does he say?

YOUNG WOMAN. He says nothing. The old lady's rambling.

THE OLD WOMAN. Oh, what he says is only talk. Nothing bad, you know. Only what they all say. The prices have gone up a bit recently. (*She points with her apple at the Young Woman.*) And she figured out from her housekeeping books that she needed 123 marks more for food this year than last. Didn't you, Erna?

(*She sees that the S.A. Men don't seem to like this.*) But that's only because of rearmament, isn't it? What's the matter? What have I said?

FIRST S.A. MAN. Where do you keep the household accounts, young woman?

SECOND S.A. MAN. And who do you show it all to?

YOUNG WOMAN. It's at home. I show it to nobody.

OLD WOMAN. You can't find fault with her for keeping accounts, can you?

FIRST S.A. MAN. Or for spreading atrocity stories, either, I suppose?

SECOND S.A. MAN. And I didn't notice she said "Heil Hitler" any too loud when we came in, did you?

OLD WOMAN. But she *did* say "Heil Hitler". And I say it too. "Heil Hitler!"

SECOND S.A. MAN. A nice nest of Communists, Albert. We must take a closer look at those accounts. Take us where you live. And get moving.

(*He seizes the young woman by the arm.*)

OLD WOMAN. But she's three months gone! You can't. . . . And after they brought the package and took the apples, Erna! She did say, "Heil Hitler." What shall I do? Heil Hitler! Heil Hitler!

(*She vomits up the apple. The S.A. Men lead her daughter off.*)

OLD WOMAN (*continues to vomit*). Heil Hitler!

SCENE SIXTEEN

When the lights go up, we see the kitchen of a fisherman. Above the scene is written in large black letters: LÜBECK 1937.

THE SERMON ON THE MOUNT

(*A fisherman lies dying. At his bedside are his wife and his son in S.A. Uniform. A pastor is also there.*)

DYING MAN. Tell me, is there really something afterwards?

PASTOR. Are you troubled with doubt?

WIFE. In the last few days he's been saying: "There's so much talking and promising, you don't know what to believe." Please don't be sore at him, pastor.

PASTOR. After death, life is eternal.

DYING MAN. And that's better?

PASTOR. Yes.

DYING MAN. It must be.

WIFE. He's been fretting so much, you understand.

PASTOR. God knows it, believe me.

DYING MAN. You think so? Up above, can you say what you want again?

PASTOR (*he's somewhat disturbed*). It is written: "Faith can remove Mountains." Only believe. It will be easier for you.

THE WIFE. You can't mean he's lacking in faith, pastor. He's taken communion.

(*To the dying man,* compelling.)

The pastor thinks you don't believe. But you do believe, don't you?

DYING MAN. Yes. . . .

(*There is a silence.*)

DYING MAN. There's nothing else, I suppose.

PASTOR. What do you mean, there's nothing else?

DYING MAN. Well, there's nothing else, is there? I mean, if there *had* been something. . . .

PASTOR. But what *could* there have been?

DYING MAN. Something.

PASTOR. Well, you had your dear wife and your son.

WIFE. Yes, you had us, didn't you?

DYING MAN. Yes. . . .

(*There is a longer silence.*)

DYING MAN. I mean, if there'd *ever* been anything in life. . . .

PASTOR. Perhaps I don't quite understand you. You don't mean you only believe because your life has all been toil and trouble?

DYING MAN (*he looks searchingly around till he sees his son*). And will it be better for them now?

PASTOR. You mean for the young people? Yes, we hope so.

DYING MAN. If only we had a motorboat to fish with. . . .

WIFE. Don't trouble yourself now.

PASTOR. You shouldn't be thinking about such things.

DYING MAN. I have to.

WIFE. We'll come through.

DYING MAN. But maybe there'll be war?

WIFE. Don't talk about it now. (*To the Pastor*) Lately he's always been talking to the boy about war. And they always got to quarrelling about it.

(*Pastor looks at the son.*)

SON. He has no faith in the future of the movement.

DYING MAN. Tell me, is it the Lord's will that there be war?

PASTOR. It is written, "Blessed are the Peacemakers."

DYING MAN. But if there's a war. . . .

SON. The Führer does not want war.

(*The dying man brushes this aside with a gesture.*)

DYING MAN. As I said, if there's a war. . . .

(*The son tries to speak.*)

WIFE. Be quiet now.

DYING MAN (*he points to his son and addresses the Pastor*). Say that about the Peacemakers to him!

PASTOR. We are all in God's hands, don't forget that.

DYING MAN. Say it to him!

WIFE. Please be reasonable. The Pastor can't do anything against war. You can't talk about such things in these times, can you, Pastor?

DYING MAN. Yes, you know they're all swindlers. I can't buy a motor for my boat. They make motors for their airplanes. For war, for slaughter. And I can't get back to shore in bad weather because I've not got a motor. The swindlers! They *want* war!

(*He sinks back exhausted.*)

WIFE (*frightened, she brings a dish of water and wipes off his sweat with a cloth. Addresses Pastor*). You mustn't hear this. He doesn't know what he's saying any more.

PASTOR. Calm yourself now, Herr Claasen.

DYING MAN. Will you say that about the peacemakers to him?

PASTOR (*pauses*). He can read it himself. It's from the Sermon on The Mount.

DYING MAN. He says a Jew wrote all that and it doesn't count.

WIFE. Don't start in again. He doesn't really think so. That's only what he hears from his party comrades.

DYING MAN. Yes. (*To Pastor*) Does it really not count?

WIFE (*looks anxiously at her son*). Don't get the Pastor into trouble, Hannes.

(*To the Dying Man*)

You shouldn't ask him that.

SON. Why not?

DYING MAN. Does it count or doesn't it?

PASTOR. It's in the Bible.

(*The Son leaves without speaking. Frightened, the Pastor watches him go.*)

WIFE. You shouldn't have said that.

PASTOR. Maybe not.

WIFE (*to her husband*). Why did you have to ask him that?

SCENE SEVENTEEN

When the lights go up, a woman is on stage. Above the scene is written in large black letters: BERLIN 1945.

A MOTHER SINGS

And the Woman sings:

Song of a German Mother*

My son, I gave you the jackboots,
    And your brown shirt came from me
But had I known what I now know
    I'd have hanged myself from a tree.

And when I saw your arm, son,
    Raised high in the Hitler salute
I did not know all those arms, son,
    Would wither at the root.

*Sheet music for this song, and others that might be used between the scenes of this play, is available in The Brecht Eisler Song Book, as distributed today (1988) by Music Sales Corporation,
  24 East 22nd Street
  New York, New York, 10010.
The songs can be heard on records or tapes distributed for Folkways by Rounder Records
    One Camp Street
    Cambridge, Mass. 02140

And then I saw you march off, son,
    Following in Hitler's train
And I did not know all those marchers
    Would never come back again.

I saw you wear your brown shirt
    And did not complain or entreat
For I did not know what I now know:
    It was your winding sheet.

SCENE EIGHTEEN

When the lights go up we see a working-class kitchen. Above the scene is written in large block letters: HAMBURG, March 13, 1938.

PLEBISCITE

(*Two Workers and a Woman are listening to a radio. The little room is divided in two by a flag-pole. From the radio, cheering, the ringing of bells, and the noise of planes are heard. A voice says, "And now the Führer enters Vienna."*)

WOMAN. It's like an ocean.

OLDER WORKER. Yes. He conquers and conquers.

YOUNGER WORKER. And we are conquered.

WOMAN. That's how it is.

YOUNGER WORKER. Listen! The way they shout! Like they were getting something out of it.

OLDER WORKER. They are: an army of invasion.

YOUNGER WORKER. It'a a plebiscite. "One Folk, one Reich, one Führer! Do you want this, Germans?" And at this plebiscite we can't even give out a leaflet. Here in Hamburg, the workers' city.

WOMAN. Why can't we?

YOUNGER WORKER. Too dangerous.

OLDER WORKER. Now they've even caught Karl. How are we going to get the addresses?

YOUNGER WORKER. And we've no one to *write* the leaflet.

WOMAN (*she points to the radio*). He had a hundred thousand men for his attack. We need one. Wonderful. If he has what he needs, naturally he can't lose.

YOUNGER WORKER (*angrily*). In that case we won't need Karl.

WOMAN. If that's how we feel, we may as well break up right now.

OLDER WORKER. Comrades, it's no use pretending. It *is* getting more difficult to bring out a leaflet, that's true. We can't act as if we simply didn't hear the roar of victory. (*He points to the radio. He turns to the Woman.*) You must admit anyone hearing stuff like that might feel they are getting stronger all the time. Doesn't it really sound like one Folk?

WOMAN. It sounds like twenty thousand people drunk on someone else's money.

YOUNGER WORKER. Maybe we're the only ones who say that?

WOMAN. Yes. We and others like us.

(*The Woman smooths out a small, crumpled piece of paper.*)

OLDER WORKER. What's that?

WOMAN. It's the copy of a letter. While the noise is on I can read it to you. (*She reads it.*)

My Dear Son,

Tomorrow I shall not be alive. Executions are usually at six in the morning. I am writing because I want you to know that my opinions have not changed. Since I have done nothing wrong I have not asked for mercy. I have only served my class. Even if it looks as if I achieved nothing that is really not the truth. Our watchword must be, "Each man to his post!" To free mankind from its oppressors, our task is very hard but it is the greatest of all tasks. Until it is completed life has no value. If we do not always keep it in view the human race will sink into barbarism. As yet you are very small, but that can't hurt you if you always remember which side you are on. Be true to your class, and your father will not have met his hard fate in vain. It isn't easy. And take care of mother and the family. You are the oldest. You must be intelligent. My best wishes to all of you.

Your loving father.

OLDER WORKER. Maybe we're not so few.

YOUNGER WORKER. What shall we put in our leaflet for the plebiscite?

WOMAN (*thinking*). A single word would be best: NO!

The whore (Gina Nagy) biting the hand of God (Todd Beadle),
Theatre 100 Company. George Brown, Director. Photo by Dave
Reifsnyder

CHAPTER XI

Artaud and Theatre of Cruelty

While Bertolt Brecht was writing his plays and dramatic theory in Berlin, a young aristocrat named Antonin Artaud (1896–1948) had come to Paris to find work as an actor and scenic designer. Artaud first associated himself with the surrealists—writers obsessed with dreams, symbols, Freudian psychology, and the power of our unconscious—and went on to become one of the most profound theorists of twentieth century theatre. It is interesting that Artaud was rejected by the surrealists, that he failed at sustaining his own experimental theatre, that his attempt at staging Shelley's *The Cenci* in 1935 met with ridicule and lasted only seventeen performances, that his theory was virtually ignored until shortly before his death, and that many people dismissed him as a mad and impractical dreamer.

In 1931 Artaud saw a Balinese theatre troupe at the Colonial Exposition in Paris. In this performance, the young artist found a unique synthesis of all that he thought theatre should embrace: dance, drama, art, folklore, possession and trance, masquerade and religious ceremony. Artaud wrote:

> In a spectacle like that of Balinese theatre there is something that has nothing to do with entertainment. . . . The Balinese productions . . . have in them something of the ceremonial quality of a religious rite in the sense that they extirpate from the mind of the onlooker all idea of pretence, of cheap imitations of reality. . . . The thought it aims at, the spiritual state it seeks to create, the mystic solutions it proposes are aroused and attained without delay or circumlocutions.

This statement focuses a major element of Artaud's theory: the need to return to the primitive and ritualistic basis of drama, to fundamental problems of human existence.

In 1938 Artaud's extensive writings were collected under the title of *The Theatre and its Double*. The double, of course, refers to the human experience or life itself. The term, Theatre of Cruelty, comes from Artaud's belief that the cruelest thing imaginable was to make people aware of the pain of human existence. Artaud sought to reach a large, indeed a mass, audience. Theatre must not, he argued, become a museum where texts, masterpieces, and playwrights' dead ideas and words are worshipped. We need a theatre, Artaud said, "which does not numb us with ideas for the intellect but stirs us to feeling by stirring up pain."

Like so many young artists after the "war to end all wars," Artaud suffered disillusion and despair and perceived of humanity as corrupt and evil. He saw the theatre as one of the few hopes for humankind. The theatre could cleanse; it could provide true communication and purgation. There the audience must confront itself as it witnesses on the stage acts of moral, physical, and psychic cruelty. One goes to the theatre to experience all of the chaos, torment, evil, corruption, and decay of our ugly society. "The audience," Artaud explained, "should leave the theatre intact, but exhausted, involved, perhaps transformed."

Expounding his ideas still further, Artaud argued that the theatre experience should be analogous to times of plague when order collapses, authority crumbles, anarchy and fear prevail, and humans give free reign to all the disordered, primitive, negative impulses that lie dormant within them. "For impelling men to see themselves as they are, the theatre causes the mask to fall, reveals the lie, the slackness, baseness, hypocricy of the world."

Within the theatre, Artaud not only exposed the ugly boils of the world but symbolically allowed the infected pus to ooze through graphic depictions of corruption, filth, and evil. The theatre has been created, he wrote, to drain the abcesses of the world. Once man has suffered in the theatre, Artaud said, "I defy that spectator to give himself up, once outside the theatre, to ideas of war, riot, and blatant murder." When one experiences the physical and psychological agony of plague, one must either die or recover. Artaud's ideal theatre would produce a frenzied response. It would rely not on words as much as on an overwhelming assault on the audience's senses and emotions. Artaud also sought a new language for the stage. Since we are no longer affected by words, we must find the cries, grunts, moans of human anguish. We must assault the audience with visual explosions and with violent, physical action.

So much of what Artaud wanted led him to explore new techniques and devices for the theatre. Establishment theatres were taboo to him. Focus must not be on the decor of the theatre but on the experience itself. Artaud might be considered the first environmental director, for he chose places like airplane hangars, factories, and barns as his theatres, and he wanted to rethink the usual audience-actor relationship by placing actors in corners, above the audience, by surrounding the action with spectators or the spectators with action.

Artaud experimented with puppets thirty feet tall—just as Peter Schumann did in the 1960s with his famous and radical Bread and Puppet Theatre. He experimented with light, trying to achieve remarkable effects of color, vibration, patterns, illusions of fog, dust, and blood. Similarly, he explored the potential of sound by inventing an electrical device that anticipates the Moog synthesizer. He described shrill, stacatto effects, overpowering volume, abrupt changes in volume, and non-verbal human sounds creating harmonies and disonance out of yelps, barks, screams, groans, and sighs. Artaud's theatre was visceral, ritualistic, powerful, theatrical, frightening, and overwhelming. Music, media, sound, dance, art, ritual, gesture, chanting, incantation, and visual shapes—all united to create "a poetry of space."

Artaud wanted to free the theatre from the playwright and the word. He wanted to assault the audience, to break down its resistence, to purge it morally and spiritually. He wanted the spectator to confront himself, to cleanse himself and find harmony with his fellow man. Artaud was an idealist who saw the theatre as the salvation of mankind. People recognized his dark torment but scoffed at his vision.

In the 1960s, however, British director Peter Brook began to see in Artaud's writings a concept for the theatre of our troubled contemporary world. Not only did Brook help to popularize Artaud's teachings, but he put them into practice both in his production of Artaud's own brief play, *Spurt of Blood,* but also with his history-making production of Peter Weiss's *The Persecution and Assassination of Jean-Paul Marat as Performed by the Inmates of the Asylum of Charenton Under the Direction of the Marquis de Sade* (*Marat/Sade*) for the Royal Shakespeare Company in 1964. One is aware of the fact that the play involves a group of actors in relation to a particular audience during the futile and lengthy Viet Nam War; but the actual setting of the play is a mental institution where the patients—each with his or her particular aberration—have been coerced into acting out scenes of the violent and murderous French revolution. As scenes of murder, indiscriminate beheadings at the guillotine are acted out, the patients become anxious and over-excited until the mental institution itself erupts into chaos and anarchy. One is constantly reminded that

> We only show these people massacred because this indisputably occurred
> Please calmly watch these barbarous displays which could not happen nowadays
> The men of that time most now demised were primitive we are more civilized

The play makes a powerful statement against the bloodiness, futility, and horror of all war.

While it was Brook who first brought Artaud's teachings international attention, many others have been profoundly influenced by his theories. The whole spirit of the experimental theatre movement of the 1960s owes a debt to Artaud. The Happenings of 1959, under the direction of Allen Kapprow, gave a new freedom to art and theatrical endeavor. Spontaneous, chaotic, drawing from all the materials at the artist's disposal, the happenings commented on contemporary society and involved audience as both spectator and participant. After the new freedom established by happenings, groups like the Living Theatre, founded by Julian Beck and Judith Molina, combined radical politics with radical theatre techniques. Like Artaud, they de-emphasized the written word; in fact, their productions were collective creations, often without text or story line. Less radical than the Living Theatre was Joseph Chaikin's Open Theatre, established by a small group who broke away from the anarchy and radicalism of the Becks' theatre. The Open Theatre made bold statements about Viet Nam in such productions as *The Serpent*. Their work was collaborative, highly visceral and sensual, and concentrated frequently on dreams and meditation. Similarly the so-called environmentalists—particularly Richard Schechner with his Performance Group—used ritual, unique environments, audience involvement to create theatrical events.

Perhaps the most important experimental theatre that reflected Artaud's teachings was not in America but in Poland: the Polish Laboratory Theatre under the leadership of Jerzy Grotowski. Attempting to redefine the nature of theatrical experience, Grotowski labelled his theatre "a poor theatre," stripped to essential ingredients of actor and audience and free from theatrical elements of scenery, costumes, and lighting. Similarly, his theatre was a temple or sacred place—"a holy theatre," an event akin to religious experience. Unlike Artaud, Grotowski strictly limited the size and scope of his audiences, but like his predecessor he obliterated original text in favor of what he labelled the "dialectic of apotheosis and derision": a montage of scenes which juxtapose classics, myths and traditional beliefs with mockery, self-parody and nightmare. In his pioneering work, Grotowsky placed tremendous emphasis on the actors' continual and intense vocal and physical exploration. Grotowski's actors of the 1960s did not acquire skills; on the contrary, they worked intensely through a system of exercises designed to eradicate learned behavior that blocked pure impulses. Appeal to the audience senses, new ways of perceiving audience and actor relationships, reflections of the chaos and violence of contemporary society, emphasis on ritual and theatre as a near holy experience, a de-emphasis of text and written word—all of these experimental techniques were rooted in the extraordinary theory of Artaud.

As his playwriting legacy, Artaud leaves us very little. Moreover if we look for clear-cut examples of contemporary theatre of cruelty, they simply do not exist. Yet writers from Gunter Grass to the absurdists to contemporary British playwrights like Edward Bond and Howard Brenton have melded the models of Brecht and Artaud into their eclectic and political dramas. Finally, perhaps the most profound violence of the impact of Theatre of Cruelty exists in the American film. Beginning in the 1960s with *Bonnie and Clyde,* continuing in the works like *The Wild Bunch* by film maker Sam Peckinpah, and culminating in the contemporary works of Stanley Kubrick, *Clockwork Orange* and more recently *Full Metal Jacket,* the art of the cinema has encouraged us to look closely at the ugliness, violence, and chaos of our lives—at the pain of human existence.

Antonin Artaud

Born in Marseilles in 1895, Artaud spent much of his youth as an invalid. Not only did he suffer meningitis, but trouble with his teeth caused doctors to prescribe morphine, and Artaud became dependent on drugs. By 1915 he had already suffered his first periods of severe mental illness, a problem that was to plague him throughout his lifetime. By 1921, after coming to Paris, Artaud designed sets for a production of Calderon's *Life Is a Dream.* Artaud also developed some reputation as an actor, and audiences today can see his work as Jean Paul Marat in the Abel Gance film classic, *Napoleon.* In 1926, Artaud and several colleagues founded the Théâtre Alfred Jarry and planned an ambitious bill including Strindberg's *A Dream Play,* but the theatre was not successful and did not survive two seasons.

Apparently a major turning point occurred with the aforementioned experience of seeing a group of Balinese dancers. Artaud then began to wander the world in search of authentic primitive rituals and experiences. His journeys took him to Bali, to Mexico and to the Aran Islands of Ireland. Everywhere he went, Artaud felt hunted and pursued by mysterious dark forces. Apparently, he became excited and interrupted a performance at the famous Abbey Theatre in Dublin, was taken back to France, and committed to a psychiatric hospital in 1938, the very year that his writings were collected and published as *The Theatre and Its Double.* Artaud was institutionalized until just two years before his death by cancer in 1948. He was fifty-three years old. Photographs of Artaud shortly before his death reveal on the surface a wasted, toothless, wrinkled old man and underneath the suffering, pain, addiction, and illness that haunted his life.

Spurt of Blood

For all of its brevity *Spurt of Blood* is a remarkable demonstration of Theatre of Cruelty tenets and techniques. Reading it, one is aware of the play's limited appeal for a mass audience which may explain why it has been staged only once since its original production in Paris in 1925; it received a production by the Royal Shakespeare Company under the direction of Peter Brook in 1963. The script displays a preoccupation with nightmarish dreams and violent images of the subconscious and unconscious states which are thrown together frantically and haphazardly in a disjointed sequence almost denying logic patterns or reasonable interpretation. It comes across to the reader, as it must to the viewer, as a kind of surrealistic horror film—an illogical, insane blend of "The Cabinet of Dr. Caligari" and "Whatever Happened to Baby Jane?"

In approaching *Spurt of Blood* or any Theatre of Cruelty play for the first time it is important and necessary to free one's mind. Readers, or viewers, should not strive to find meanings or to understand images and ideas as the play progresses. Rather, readers should surrender themselves completely to the emotional and visceral impact produced by the script. Experience the play first through your five senses and then seek to understand what it means not in its specific moments but in its totality.

Read the play now. Then come back to this essay.

What did you make of it? Can you verbalize the impression it made on you?

Notice that the play begins in a tranquil moment of romantic, innocent love between the Young Man and the Young Girl. There is an emphasis on beauty and fulfillment through love—romantic love or even sexual love. Then almost immediately, as their voices lower and darken and then become exalted and high-pitched, the innocent love of the two characters seems to be tainted with the perversity of sexual passion as beauty is tainted with ugliness. Beauty co-exists with ugliness, goodness with evil.

Suddenly, and for no apparent reason, chaos descends and the two young lovers are separated as stars collide, wheels turn in the air, a hurricane strikes and a hideous debris of human limbs, vile insects, and architectural scraps rain down from the heavens. Are the lovers destroyed by the devastating forces of nature and Man-made society which we cannot control? In any event, everything disintegrates as the world recoils in madness. The Young Man cries out, "The sky has gone mad!" as he hastily exits pushing the Young Girl before him.

As abruptly as the chaos descended, a kind of specious order seems to return. We move back in time as the Knight and Wet Nurse enter. They are quickly identified as male and female, man and wife, father and mother; and the cycle of life goes on. However, the family—the basic unit of all human society—is plunged into moral corruption. The children are committing incest, the father is a pimp, and the mother has become a mid-wife. The Knight-Father, impervious to the corruption around him, demands his own selfish gratifications; his gluttony is at once expressed in terms of physical hunger and excessive, perverse sexual appetite as Man and Wife hurl vicious insults at one another. They seemed to be locked into a kind of love-hate relationship that reflects a Strindbergian vision of the world.

The scene again changes abruptly and we are with the Young Man on a street inhabited by an assortment of characters representing many aspects of life—divine and temporal, rich and poor, good and bad, legal and illegal, just and unjust. The Young Man seems to be searching for love ("I've lost her. Give her back to me.") Significantly, the Beadle—symbolic of a legal system or a system of order and justice—will not and does not help him. The Priest should help him; however, the priest seems preoccupied (as most priests in confessional booths seem to be) with the salacious reports of the young man's perverse and adolescent sexual behavior. The Young Man's spiritual, metaphysical reply is beyond the priest's comprehension and only confuses him. The voice of the priest's vengeful god only speaks in natural disasters sent to punish Man. And the world of the play again descends into chaos in a moment replete with images of storms, fires and destruction. Life is meaningless.

The Bawd, the whore of the world, now appears in all of her hideous nakedness. When she is chastized by the vindictive god—The Huge Hand/Huge Voice—she rejects him by biting his wrist. And immediately the world is engulfed in blood. (This scenic effect alone would challenge any scene designer.) At that moment the innocence of the Young Man is betrayed and seduced by the Bawd as the Wet-Nurse/Mid Wife returns bearing the body of the Young Girl—the symbol of pure, innocent, decent love. The Young Girl is not only dead, she is entirely deflated. As in the case of the Hyacinth Girl in *The Ghost Sonata,* her innocence and decency cannot survive in our corrupt and meaningless world.

The gluttonous Knight returns still in quest of the Swiss cheese. The young man, totally incapacitated now by the evil around him, can only make the feeblest, puppet-like gestures in defense of his mother. And then, in one of the most gross moments in all drama, The Wet Nurse (who, we must remember, is also wife and mother), raises her skirt and we actually see her give birth to all of the disease, evil, corruption and vileness of the earth. The Young Man, stripped of all sanity and intelligence, runs off "as though lobotomized." The Young Girl revives momentarily to comment on the absurdity, meaninglessness and insanity of it all.

Now read the brief play again.

Did it make any more sense to you? Did you understand it to any deeper degree? Did it emotionally move you a second time?

If the above interpretation does not gibe with your own in its detail, it is still probably safe to say that our emotional responses to the images and the activities are very similar. Unquestionably those images and activities convey the horror and pain of human existence. We are left with a sense of the cruelty and meaninglessness of human experience. If our intellect has not been satisfied, certainly our emotions have been painfully stirred.

Artaud's strongest critics have asserted that he is guilty of turning the theatre into something it was not intended to be under the false notion that he is returning it to its original, primitive roots in religious ritual—roots that some critics will argue never truly existed in the way Artaud interprets them. He has been guilty then of indulging himself in a kind of psychotic experience that he seeks to dignify by the name of theatre. In a sense, they are saying this is not theatre at all but rather personal and highly public self-indulgence.

Critics, too, have been quick to point out that Artaud has deluded himself on another score. He says, "I defy that spectator to give himself up, once outside the theatre, to ideas of war, riot, and blatant murder." The playwright is arguing an efficacy for this kind of theatre in that it will purge society of its penchant for violence, corruption and murder. But, say some of the critics, quite the opposite has happened. Once audiences have been shown horrendous violence on the stage they first become perversely attracted to it and then immune to its reality. Consequently, spectators may go forth from the theatre and commit even more hideous acts of violence simply because of their potential for satisfying the fundamental need for violence in human nature. They offer the atrocities of the Vietnamese war, the multiple acts of assassination in recent years, the horror of terroristic acts, the nightmare of serial murders, the bloody political clashes in South Africa and the Mid East and even the corruptions of Watergate and the Iran-Contra scandals as ample evidence of the inhuman excesses we not only tolerate but enjoy because our theatre, film, and television drama (and our highly theatrical news media) have made them so commonplace and acceptable to us. The theatre of the past taught man to triumph over his animal nature. The present-day Theatre of Cruelty may be inadvertently encouraging man to revel in his basic bestiality.

If Artaud is indeed guilty of making something more of theatre than theatre, perhaps his sternest critics are equally guilty of making more of his negative impact than is truly warranted. Whatever the case, when we consider Artaud's Theatre of Cruelty, we must be open-minded enough to see that it—along with Strindberg's Expressionism and the Theatre of the Absurd—has freed the twentieth century drama of the shackles of slavish Realism. So perhaps Artaud has pumped some much needed life into our present-day drama.

JET OF BLOOD

By Antonin Artaud

Translated by George E. Wellwarth.

—————— CHARACTERS ——————

THE YOUNG MAN
THE YOUNG GIRL
THE KNIGHT
THE NURSE
THE PRIEST
THE SHOEMAKER
THE SEXTON
THE WHORE
THE JUDGE
THE STREET PEDDLER
A THUNDEROUS VOICE

THE YOUNG MAN. I love you, and everything is beautiful.

THE YOUNG GIRL (*with a strong tremolo in her voice*). You love me, and everything is beautiful.

THE YOUNG MAN. (*in a deep voice*). I love you, and everything is beautiful.

THE YOUNG GIRL (*in an even deeper voice than his*). You love me, and everything is beautiful.

THE YOUNG MAN (*leaving her abruptly*). I love you. (*Pause.*) Turn around and face me.

THE YOUNG GIRL (*she turns to face him*). There!

THE YOUNG MAN (*in a shrill and exalted voice*). I love you, I am big, I am shining, I am full, I am solid.

THE YOUNG GIRL (*in the same shrill tone*). We love each other.

THE YOUNG MAN We are intense. Ah, how well ordered this world is!

A pause. Something that sounds like an immense wheel turning and blowing out air is heard. A hurricane separates the two. At this moment two stars crash into each other, and we see a number of live pieces of human bodies falling down: hands, feet, scalps, masks, colonnades, porches, temples, and alembics, which, however, fall more and more slowly, as if they were falling in a vacuum. Three scorpions fall down, one after the other, and finally a frog and a beetle, which sets itself down with a maddening, vomit-inducing slowness.

(*Shouting as loud as he can.*) The sky has gone mad! (*He looks at the sky.*) Let's get out of here. (*He pushes The Young Girl out before him.*)

Enter a knight of the Middle Ages in an enormous suit of armor, followed by a nurse holding her breasts in both hands and puffing and wheezing because they are both very swollen.

THE KNIGHT. Leave your breasts alone. Give me my papers.

THE NURSE (*crying shrilly*). Ah! Ah! Ah!

407

THE KNIGHT. Shit, what's the matter with you?

THE NURSE. Look! Our daughter—there—with him!

THE KNIGHT. Bah! There's no girl there!

THE NURSE. I tell you, they're screwing each other.

THE KNIGHT. What the hell do I care if they're screwing each other?

THE NURSE. Incest.

THE KNIGHT. Old woman.

THE NURSE (*plunges her hands into her pockets, which are as large as her breasts*): Pimp! (*She throws the papers at him.*)

THE KNIGHT. Bitch! Let me eat.

The Nurse runs off. The Knight gets up again and pulls an enormous slice of Gruyere cheese out of each paper. Suddenly he coughs and chokes.

(*His mouth full.*) Ehp! Ehp! Show me your breasts. Show me your breasts. Where did she go to?

He runs off.

THE YOUNG MAN (*re-enters*). I have seen, I have learned, I have understood. Here are the public square, the priest, the cobbler, the street peddlers, the threshold of the church, the red light of the whorehouse, the scales of justice. I can't any more!

A Priest, a Shoemaker, a Sexton, a Whore, a Judge, and a Street Peddler enter like shadows.

I have lost her. . . . Give her back to me.

ALL (*in various tones*). Who, who, who, who?

THE YOUNG MAN. My wife.

THE SEXTON (*very sexton-like*). Your wife . . . Phooey! Clown!

THE YOUNG MAN. Clown! You're talking about *your* wife, maybe!

THE SEXTON (*tapping his forehead*). That may be true.

He runs off. The Priest leaves the group and puts his arm round The Young Man's neck.

THE PRIEST (*in a confessional tone*). To what part of your body would you say you refer most often?

THE YOUNG MAN. To God.

The Priest, put out of countenance by this answer, immediately starts talking with a Swiss accent.

THE PRIEST (*with a Swiss accent*). But that doesn't go any more. We don't listen to that sort of thing any more. It's necessary to ask such things of volcanoes and earthquakes. We others feed ourselves on the dirty little stories we hear in the confessional. And that's all there is—that's life!

THE YOUNG MAN (*very impressed*). Ah, yes, there we are, that's life! Oh, well, it all goes down the drain sooner or later.

THE PRIEST (*still with his Swiss accent*). But of course.

Night suddenly falls. Earthquake. Thunder shakes the air, and lightning zigzags in all directions. In the intermittent flashes of lightning one sees people running around in panic, embracing each other, falling down, getting up again, and running around like madmen.

At a given moment an enormous hand seizes The Whore's hair, which bursts into ever-widening flames.

A THUNDEROUS VOICE. Bitch, look at your body!

The Whore's body appears completely nude and hideous under her dress, which suddenly becomes transparent.

THE WHORE. Leave me, God.

She bites God's wrist. An immense jet of blood shoots across the stage, and we can see The Priest making the sign of the cross during a flash of lighting that lasts longer than the others.

When the lights come up again, all the characters are dead and their bodies lie scattered over the ground. Only The Young Man and The Whore are left. They are eating each other's eyes.

The Whore falls into The Young Man's arms.

THE WHORE (*with a sigh as if she were at the point of orgasm*). Tell me how this happened to you.

The Young Man hides his face in his hands.

The Nurse comes back carrying The Young Girl in her arms like a parcel. The Young Girl is dead. The Nurse lets her fall to the ground, where she is crushed flat as a pancake.

The Nurse no longer has any breasts. Her front is completely flat. At this moment The Knight comes out and throws himself on The Nurse, shaking her violently.

THE KNIGHT (*in a threatening voice*). Where have you put it? Give me my Gruyère!

THE NURSE (*cheerfully*). Here you are. (*She lifts her dress. The Young Man tries to flee but freezes at the sight like a petrified marionette.*)

THE YOUNG MAN (*as if suspended in mid-air and with the voice of a ventriloquist's dummy*). Don't hurt Mummy.

THE KNIGHT. Accursed woman! (*He covers his face in horror.*)

An army of scorpions comes out from under The Nurse's dress and swarms over his sex, which swells up and bursts, becoming glassy and shining like the sun. The Young Man and The Whore flee.

THE YOUNG GIRL (*reviving as if dazzled*). The virgin! Ah, that's what he was looking for.

CURTAIN

Bill Gabelhausen in a presentation of *Act Without Words* for the
Introduction to Theatre classes at Penn State University. George
Brown, director.

CHAPTER XII

Theatre of the Absurd

As with both epic theatre and theatre of cruelty, theatre of the absurd was never a clearly defined movement but rather a point of view reflected in the works of a number of playwrights in the period following World War II. The absurdists had their roots in Europe, particularly in France, and their influence spread throughout the Continent, Britain, America, and the Eastern European countries. In recent years there has been a tendency to romanticize the 1950s as a time of prosperity and the good life. We have celebrated the era—in America at any rate—in shallow musicals like *Grease,* and we recall with nostalgia the complacency of the post-war decade. The truth of the fifties was, in fact, very different from these cliches. We understood what power was more poignantly than at any previous time in history. After all, just a few years before, a madman named Adolph Hitler had almost succeeded in taking over the world. We had seen the devastating films and testimonies of concentration camp prisoners and were made painfully aware that six million Jews at these camps had been lured into showers, administered poison gas, and thrown into open pit graves. On August 6, 1945, an atomic bomb, secretly prepared by British and American scientists, had been dropped on the Japanese city of Hiroshima, obliterating more than half of that city and shocking the entire world. It was now undeniably clear that whole populations could literally be destroyed with a mere push of a button. By 1950, just five years after the end of World War II, the United Nations sent troops into Korea as a policing action to control the aggression of the Red Chinese; similarly in Europe, from the signing of the peace agreements after World War II, the Soviet Union—so recently an ally—was now an enemy of the West in the so-called cold war. As Europe watched, this difficult relationship led to political witch-hunts in the United States that surpassed anything that had occurred in Salem in 1692. The House Un-American Activities Committee began its investigations in 1947 in Hollywood and continued on into the 1950s until virtually hundreds of artists in film, theatre and radio had been blacklisted and denied the right to work in their chosen fields. HUAC's cause was taken up by Joseph McCarthy, a junior senator from Wisconsin, and the accusations of communist infiltration into the upper echelons of the American government approached a kind of national hysteria. On both sides of the Atlantic where were the hopes and dreams of peace and normalcy? That troubled time seemed dominated by an air of disillusion and futility.

Traditional values seemed somehow incapable of coping with such monumental and irrational events and realizations. New questions or ones that had been asked before by the existentalists like Camus and Sartre—questions creating their own disequilibrium—were being pondered. Is there a god? If so, what is God? What does it mean to exist? What matters to us? What are our fundamental human values? To explore some of these questions came the absurdists.

It would be unfair to suggest that the absurdist writers simply appeared on the scene to speak to the problems of the post-war decade without crediting at least one writer who prepared the way for the absurdists. After all, in his expressionistic plays Strindberg raised most of the issues that were later to concern the absurdists. Furthermore, an Italian dramatist, Luigi Pirandello, almost forgotten at the time he received the Nobel Peace Prize in 1934, not only anticipated absurdist drama but stands today as one of the profoundly great playwrights of the twentieth century. In such extraordinary works as *Six Characters in Search of an Author* (1921) and *Henry VI* (1922), Pirandello not only explored the dynamic potential of drama itself but questioned the very nature of reality. Pirandello's wife was mentally ill and subject to wild and painful aberrations. It became increasingly clear to Pirandello, however, that no matter how false his wife's fantasies were, they created firm reality for her. His plays are complex and darkly pessimistic but they profoundly explore human concerns about truth and character, about, as Pirandello himself said, "the need to deceive ourselves constantly by creating a reality."

Although many critics find the root of the label, "Absurdism" in *The Myth of Sisyphus* (1942) by Camus, others trace it to this statement by absurdist writer Eugene Ionesco: "Cut off from his religious, metaphysical, and transcendental roots, man is lost; all of his actions become senseless, absurd, useless." Two major works mark the beginning of absurdism. In 1950 Rumanian born Ionesco's *The Bald Soprano* was produced in Paris. In this nonsensical one-act play, Ionesco articulates some of the themes that were to dominate his work: the disintegration of language as a means of communication, the stultifying effect of middle-class life with its meaningless rituals and habitual patterns of behavior, the loneliness and isolation of the individual, and finally—because Ionesco had lived under Nazi control—the power struggles that dominate our existence.

The year before Ionesco wrote *The Bald Soprano,* Samuel Beckett had written a play in French called *En Attendant Godot* which did not reach the stage until three years later. On January 5, 1953, Beckett's masterpiece opened at the Théâtre de Babylone in Paris and ran for over four-hundred performances. On August 3, 1955 the play, translated into English by Beckett himself, opened at the Arts Theatre Club in London. Ronald Harwood in *All the World's a Stage* says, "It helped to change not only the face of the theatre, but also its heart and soul." Audiences were bewildered by *Godot;* some labelled it a hoax that was being perpetrated against the audiences, others saw it as the play that most accurately articulated the despair, hopelessness, and futility of contemporary life. Very few agreed about its meaning, and Beckett himself refused to enlighten his audiences, insisting that his play make its own statement. But no matter what spectators thought of *Godot,* they came in droves to see it and the play was produced in every major city in the world. One of the most famous productions occurred in America when the San Francisco Actor's Workshop produced the play before an enthusiastic audience of inmates at San Quentin Prison who had little difficulty in understanding a play about man's eternal wait, the aimlessness, inarticulateness, and hopelessness of that condition. One prisoner named Rick Cluchey was so affected by that production that he formed a drama group within the prison and, after his release, founded a company that specializes in interpreting Beckett's work. Cluchey's own *Godot,* in which he plays Pozzo, has toured Europe and has attracted the support and attention of Beckett himself.

The characteristics of Theatre of the Absurd remind one of the major elements of Expressionism. There is little story and certainly the realists' emphasis on cause-and-effect relationships or the well-made play's structure—exposition, complication, and denoument—do not exist. Rather than telling a story in a linear way, absurdist plays tend to be circular; that is, instead of presenting a situation with a beginning, a middle, and an end, the plays examine a condition—being trapped, isolated, or lost, for example—from a multiplicity of viewpoints. In *Waiting for Godot,* the two tramps, Estragon and Vladimir, fill their time with meaningless banter, feeble attempts at suicide, arguments, attacks on one another, games, and empty rituals. Beckett, then, examines the condition of contemporary life far more than he tells a progressive story.

Characters in the plays are symbols or representations of universal types. They become every man or every woman and, as such, reflect the pain of the human condition. Lucky and Pozzo in *Godot,* for example, reflect the master-slave relationship, the interdependence of the mind and the body, and the fact that those who move about frantically are just as trapped as those who stand still. Similarly, in Ionesco's *The Chairs,* the old man and old woman become at once parents, children, lovers, and antagonists; they represent all human relationships that can be shared by a man and a woman.

Settings, too, are highly symbolised. Wastelands, deserts, circular rooms without windows become the environments of absurdist drama. One of the most unique settings occurs in Beckett's *Happy Days,* in which the leading character, Winnie, is buried in sand up to her waist in Act I and up to her neck in Act II. Similarly, time and logical sequence or chronology often possess a bizarre dream-like quality or simply do not exist at all. For instance, in the work of British playwright, Harold Pinter—often linked with absurdism—characters confuse time, chronology, and even have faulty memories about sequences or events, causing a kind of mysterious ambiguity and confusion. In *Old Times,* for example, each of the three characters in a love triangle, remembers the past in a remarkably different way. Anna says, "There are some things one remembers even though they may never have happened. There are things I remember which may never have happened, but as I recall them so they take place."

Certainly one of the most characteristic features of Theatre of the Absurd is the consistent downgrading of language. The absurdists, like Artaud, were firm in their belief that language had lost any real ability to communicate. In some of his plays, Beckett has abandoned language altogether, but it is typical of all the absurdists that language is meaningless, distorted, incomprehensible, petty, or exaggerated to sheer mechanics. In *Happy Days,* Winnie babbles aimlessly. Whole pages of dialogue consist of speech fragments like these: "I used to think—I say I used to think—that all these things—put back into the bag—if too soon—put back too soon—could be taken out again—if necessary—if needed—and so on—indefinitely—back into the bag—back out of the bag—until the bell—went."

One aspect of absurdist drama has become a major characteristic of much subsequent contemporary drama and that is the bold theatricalism and eclecticism, the fact that traditional distinctions of dramatic forms cease to exist. Just as an absurdist play veers from outrageous Buster Keaton-esque comedy to tragic implications or from broad vaudeville routines to Chekhovian realistic dialogue, so plays of our contemporary theatre not strictly associated with absurdism retain this eclectic theatricalism. One example will suffice. In Peter Barnes's play, *Red Noses,* produced by the Royal Shakespeare Company in London, the leading character, Father Flote, organizes a troupe of clowns to help dispel the fear of the plague in France in 1348. The audience is brought up short when Flote in the first scene of the play begins to sing, "Life Is Just a Bowl of Cherries," or in a later scene when a character speaks of a tinman, scarecrow, and lion looking for a little girl with ruby slippers.

The subject of the absurdist plays was invariably the same: humanity's entrapment in an illogical, hostile, impersonal, and indifferent world. And therein we have perhaps the greatest problem with absurdist drama: how many times and in how many ways can playwrights tell us that truth is unknowable, the world is irrational, and life is futile? In some regards, watching absurdist plays is like seeing the same play over and over again. Do we not already understand the pain of the human condition and look to our playwrights to offer some help, some insight, some hope for humankind? Ultimately, no matter how much the absurdist dramatists rejected logic, they remained intellectual, always conceptualising about the plight of humanity. The plays are often obscure, remote, difficult to understand, but they are exciting to audiences and actors because of the freedom offered in interpreting them, opportunities for exploration, and the intellectual challenges they present.

Besides Beckett and Ionesco, there was a third great absurdist writing in French: Jean Genet, the one playwright whose whole life reflected the absurdist point of view. One critic said of Genet that he had the fascination of a hunch-back turned ballet-dancer. Born in 1910, an illegitimate child abandoned by his mother, Genet was first imprisoned for theft at the age of ten. At thirty, after ten imprisonments on charges of theft, smuggling, and male prostitution, Genet was declared an habitual, incurable criminal by the French courts. He began writing seriously in prison and depicted the inhabitants of a world he knew and understood: whores, pimps, murderers, rapists, and opportunists. Reality for Genet consisted of illusion piled upon illusion. When all these layers are stripped away, nothing is left but nothingness, a great void. The very structure of society, he argued, is meaningless; when all of the facades of life are stripped away, saint and sinner are at heart just the same. In 1948 when imprisoned for life, the great French literary figures appealed to President Charles DeGaulle on Genet's behalf and he was released. His great plays include *The Maids, Deathwatch, The Balcony, The Blacks,* and *The Screens.*

France was not the only scene of absurdist writing. Its major practitioners include in Russia Arthur Adamov, in England Harold Pinter whose work has far surpassed the narrow limitations of absurdism, in Spain Fernando Arrabal, and in America Edward Albee whose *Who's Afraid of Virginia Wolfe, Tiny Alice,* and *The Delicate Balance* are masterpieces. If we think of today's theatre as making its impact through stark, unforgettable imagery, through bold and eclectic theatricalism, through striking portraits of the pain of human experience, then we acknowledge our debt to the three major antecedents of our theatre today: epic theatre, theatre of cruelty, and theatre of the absurd.

Samuel Beckett

Samuel Beckett was born in Foxrock, a suburb of Dublin, Ireland in 1906. An excellent scholar and athlete, he graduated from Trinity College, Dublin. In 1928 Beckett became a reader in English at the Ecole Normale Supérieure in Paris, at which time he translated for and was influenced by his famous compatriot, James Joyce. In 1930, Beckett returned briefly to Dublin as a teacher after which he traveled widely and restlessly before settling permanently in Paris in 1937. The following year, Beckett published *Murphy,* his first novel.

Although an established literateur, Beckett did not achieve an international reputation until director Roger Blin's production of *Waiting for Godot.* Fortunately, because of his facility in both languages, Beckett writes his plays in French and translates them into English himself. His dramatic successes continued with *Endgame* (1957), *Krapp's Last Tape* (1959), and *Happy Days* (1961). As Beckett's stature as a dramatist has continued to grow, the length of his work has decreased in almost direct proportion. Plays like *Not I, Act without Words, That Time,* and *Come and Go* evidence unique sparcity, compression, and economy. In 1969 Samuel Beckett was awarded the Nobel Prize for Literature. A tireless experimentor, Beckett has also written for radio, television, and film.

The theatrical world was dealt a sad blow when, in 1985, the director Beckett chose to oversee all of his American productions, Alan Schneider, was killed crossing a street in London. In 1986 Beckett directed his own play, *Rockabye,* which enjoyed a successful run off-Broadway in New York. His plays continue to live in productions throughout the world. A private and introspective individual, Beckett possesses penetrating eyes and a deeply lined, chiseled face. The same themes continue to pervade his work: human isolation, entrapment, and hopelessness; but his tireless experimentation, his brilliant imagery and poetic prose, his remarkable minimalism, his intellectual facility and depth, and his dynamic theatricalism—all contribute to the critical recognition of him as the world's greatest living playwright. On April 13, 1986 the international theatrical community paid him tribute on his eightieth birthday.

Act Without Words

Where theatre of the absurd dramas are concerned, the uninitiated and unsophisticated theatre-goer has often been heard to complain that the plays are senseless, meaningless, and confusing. Prior to the 1950s when theatre of the absurd became widely known, play-goers had been accustomed to linearly developed plots that proceded along logical lines to inevitable conclusions and told coherent stories about recognizably believable people. The absurdists, however, were not interested in telling stories. They were determined to confront the spectator with a vivid and often painful awareness of the critical state of human existence in the present-day world. In the past half-century our world has become a rather hostile and alien environment to practically everyone who inhabits the earth. So, the absurdist cares little for creating believable individual characters; he wants, instead, to create in his protagonist a symbol that stands for all human beings.

Act Without Words is just such a play. If the script seems to lack an immediate coherent meaning, that is as it should be. Ironically, the lack of meaning is the message. This play, like every worthwhile play, deals with the accomplishment of a major action or deed which requires the concentrated psychic energies of the protagonist. The major deed is simple—in fact, it is absurdly simple: to reach a carafe of water. More generally, it might be said that the deed is to accomplish one purposeful and meaningful action. Symbolically, the man (the single character in the play) is striving to accomplish one deed that would sustain his life and give it meaning. As the play procedes, the spectators discover, as the character does, that meaningful action is apparently beyond us. The message becomes painfully obvious—and the play comes full circle—when we discover that the character is no better off at the end of the play than he was at the beginning.

He has not progressed; he is back where he began. The circularity of the simple story is characteristic of the plays of the absurd. What better way to demonstrate the impossibility of achieving meaningful action than to leave the characters at the end of the play in the exact state they were found in the beginning?

Perhaps what disturbs audiences most about Beckett's plays, and those of other absurdists as well, is the manner in which the message is presented. Theatre-goers, after all, are usually more than content to sit back passively and allow the playwright to deliver his message. But the absurdists will have none of this passivity on the part of the spectator. Rather than imbedding the message in a story, absurdists create an atmosphere and situation in their plays which force the audience to experience and feel the message of meaninglessness. In other words, instead of telling the spectator in logical arguments that the world is illogical, the absurdist playwrights confront the spectator with scenes, dialogue, characters and character behavior which are entirely illogical. Consequently, the spectator is forced to *experience* illogicality just as the characters—metaphors for us all—are experiencing it. The spectator cannot remain passive, for he is at once engaged in the search for meaning in the play just as the characters are engaged in a search for meaning in their existence. The *form* of the play (its episodes, activities, characters, dialogue, settings, props) is doing precisely what the *content* (themes, theses, ideas, observations on life) is doing. In other words, the form says exactly what the content says. Certainly, that is the case in *Act Without Words*. In this regard, the absurdists have provided us with the first drama since the days of the Greeks in which form and content are inseparably one. This alone is a remarkable achievement that more than justifies the existence of the theatre of the absurd.

As we have said numerous times before in this text, the best plays contain a carefully constructed plot that imitates the working out or accomplishment of an action. The plot of *Antigone,* you will remember, concerns the effort to achieve the rational and sane balance between the laws of the land and human rights. Approaching Beckett's *Act Without Words* requires some adjustment on the part of the reader, however. There is no plot here in the traditional sense of a story or a series of logically constructed episodes. In fact, little seems to happen in the play in terms of major events when it is compared to *Othello* or *The Three Sisters.* Beckett makes no attempt to structure a storyline; he seeks instead to create a moment in time, a feeling, a human experience, a state of being. *Act Without Words* does not tell a story; it creates a state of mind.

The fact that the play centers on a state of mind accounts for the circular progression we referred to a moment ago. No real time elapses in the course of the play. Nothing of any great moment is accomplished; the character ends up where he began. In this manner the structure of the play tells us two things: first, that we are observing a moment of perception in the mind of the man when he realizes the purposelessness of his own life and his own endeavors, and, secondly, that the life condition is a hopeless one because life's patterns have been meaninglessly repeated without progress or achievement of any sort.

In spite of what we have just said, it might be argued, on the other hand, that *Act Without Words* does contain a faint and rather simple plotline. The play does, after all, encapsulate the entire history of the man's civilization. Man was created and was placed on this earth; or perhaps he evolved from lower species. Whatever the case, he came into being. He subsequently learned the necessity of protecting himself from the elements. He engaged in problem solving to answer the needs of life and to better his condition. But through the centuries he failed rather miserably to learn his lessons and improve his lot. Still, this is scarcely a fully wrought storyline. It remains a dramatized moment of perception in the history of man.

Since the play does deal with a state of being, perhaps this is a clue that the reader should not approach the play initially seeking a story or logically ordered arguments and meaning. As in the case of the theatre of cruelty, the reader should ideally allow himself to experience the play in its totality—to live it empathically, to surrender to its emotional impact—on first reading. There will be time later to ponder the significant meanings of the play on an intellectual level. So, perhaps at this point, as in the last chapter, you should read the play, respond to it, and then return to this discussion realizing that what follows is merely one perception of the meaning of the text, a guide along one path through the play. You may find other, deeper meanings for yourself. You may find no meaning whatsoever. Surely, if you were to watch the play in performance, a director and an actor, as well as designers of costumes, setting and properties, would inescapably provide meanings of their own in the process of interpreting the playwright's work. Read and visualize as you go. That will be necessary, for the script is merely a description of what the dramatist wants to have happen on stage.

As the play opens, we see a desert under dazzling light. The implication is obvious. This is a barren, forlorn space—a wasteland devoid of habitation or vegetation. Life is an ominous, empty desert in which everything is laid bare and is exposed under the relentless glare of light. Is this the sun or the light of knowledge and awareness? Suddenly, the man is literally flung onstage just as humans are rudely and abruptly thrust from the womb and into the world. His first responses are mere reflex actions. He hears a whistle from the right and responds almost automatically to its call only to be flung back again into the barrenness of the stage area. He hears a whistle from the right, and the business is repeated. However, at the third whistle, he reflects a moment and decides not to respond. Man has learned his first lesson even though it may be more of a conditioned reflex than a truly reasoned response. Nonetheless, he has learned an important fact: there is no escape from this existence.

If the character's behavior in the opening moment of the play causes you to think of the vaudeville routine in which the comic repeatedly slips on a banana peel—or, for that matter, the delightfully inane behavior of Donald O'Connor in the "Make 'em Laugh" sequence of *Singin' in the Rain*—that is all to the good. The business of life often has no more meaning or sense than the brainless behavior of vaudeville or music hall comics. Since the play is, indeed, a mime piece without words, the behavior of the man may instantly recall the silent behavior of Charlie Chaplin or Harpo Marx. In this regard, the play demonstrates the influence of vaudeville, silent movies and music hall on the absurdist movement. At the same time, the script is also demonstrating another aspect of absurdism: the devaluation of language. The absurdists assert that our language—a supposedly logical structure—is devoid of any real meaning. Words have long since lost the ability to communicate thought. To demonstrate this fact, many plays of the absurd feature incoherent and meaningless dialogue. In *Act Without Words* language significantly has been eliminated entirely.

The only important sound one hears in the play is a whistle. At least, this is the only sound that seems to produce any impact at all; it is a sound that does cause a behavioral response. But what does it truly mean? Is this the vague and commanding voice of God? Or, is this the dim inner voice of the man occasionally jarring him into awareness and prompting him to act?

As the play progresses, the man discovers a palm branch and takes shelter in its shade just as humankind, growing more civilized, began to seek or build shelter against the elements. A pair of scissors appears. There could scarcely be a more common, simple and direct symbol for the kind of tools man has created to help him control his environment. Is there a message in the fact that this particular man—a symbol for all humankind—can find little more to do with the scissors than trim his nails? While he is engaged in this mundane routine—repeating the kind of empty, vacuous ritual with which we all clutter our lives—a potential catastrophe occurs. The palm branch closes up leaving the man dangerously exposed to the elements once more.

Given that the man is abandoned now in an arid desert under the blazing sun, the sudden appearance of a carafe of water takes on profound significance. Man cannot exist without water. Our protagonist seems at least vaguely aware of this fact for he now devotes his energies to gaining possession of the carafe. Through implication this is a fight for life. Notice how he uses his past experience, knowledge and education in his problem solving. Like a child playing with blocks, he learns by trial and error to stack one cube on top of another to build a tower or platform by which he might reach the distant carafe of water that would sustain his life. But it stubbornly remains out of his grasp. A kindly God (or is it the man-made achievements of a scientific, technological society?) provides him with additional tools and building materials that he might use to accomplish his purpose. Still, he blunders on. While contemplating how he might use a combination of building blocks of various confusing sizes, scissors, and a rope, his opportunity to act passes him by as the boughs of the palm tree collapse umbrella-like down against the trunk of the tree.

At this point, the man is back where he began. He must learn the lesson of life all over again. For a brief second, he seems to contemplate suicide only to learn his very first lesson for a second time. There is no escape from this life. He is flung back on the stage once more and begins to repeat the same old patterns. Eventually, he ceases trying altogether. Even when the carafe is tantalizingly lowered a few feet away from him, he makes no attempt to retrieve it. His experience of life has produced a paralyzing state of inertia. He is ultimately left staring at his hands in an ending which tells us that he is back where he began while also telling us that in the end man is all that man has in this life. There is no meaning, no design, no great purpose. Man exists, and that is all.

But perhaps not all is lost. After all, man has not been destroyed by his experience in the play. He still emphatically exists. Perhaps there is hope. Perhaps man, at last realizing that there is no profound order or universal plan imparting meaning to human existence, is free to create his own meaning. As our protagonist sits looking at his hands at the end of the play, he still seems to be dumbly contemplating what he can do with them.

Interestingly enough, the play has not surrendered its meaning readily to the viewer. As the character of man sits throughout the play and contemplates the meaning of his existence, the spectator sits throughout the performance and contemplates the exact meaning of the play. In other words, the search for meaning that engages the protagonist is the very thing demanded of the theatre-goer as he watches the play. We are not told the meaning of the play. It is not set down for us in logical language and logically ordered scenes that present a rational argument to us. We are forced to experience the meaning of the play in our muscles and mind and five senses. This is precisely the great gift of the absurdists to the development of our drama: providing a form that makes us experience the content.

Fortunately, our drama has never been quite the same since the absurdists. At times out of boredom, confusion, irritation, familiarity, or indifference we may wish to dismiss the absurdists' vision. However, if we think for a moment we discover how much richer our theatre is for their efforts. For example, one of the finest of all contemporary American plays is Arthur Kopit's *Wings* in which the dramatist tells the story of a woman who suffers the devastation of a stroke and must struggle to become a functioning human being once more or, failing that, escape her critical impairment. Before the advent of the absurdist drama *Wings* in all probability would have been a fairly realistic and straight-forward account of the woman's struggle. But thanks to the influence of the absurdists upon Kopit his play becomes a vivid and painful recreation of the *experience* of a stroke. The audience shares the confusion, mental derangement, terror and anguish of the patient. Films—such as *Bonnie and Clyde, The Wild Bunch, Brazil, Aliens, Dr. Strangelove, Empire of the Sun* and many many more—often contain moments when the audience is forced to experience the pain, absurdity and senselessness of the human condition. In *The Spook Sonata* Strindberg tells us how evil and corruption are destroying us. In many of the films listed above we are forced to feel the impact of evil and corruption and, therefore, know for ourselves that they are indeed a threat to human existence.

In a very real sense, then, the absurdists have replaced that theatre in which we are told stories with the theatre in which we experience life.

ACT WITHOUT WORDS

by Samuel Beckett

Desert. Dazzling light.

The man is flung backwards on stage from right wing. He falls, gets up immediately, dusts himself, turns aside, reflects.

Whistle from right wing.

He reflects, goes out right.

Immediately flung back on stage he falls, gets up immediately, dusts himself, turns aside, reflects.

Whistle from left wing.

He reflects, goes out left.

Immediately flung back on stage he falls, gets up immediately, dusts himself, turns aside, reflects.

Whistle from left wing.

He reflects, goes towards left wing, hesitates, thinks better of it, halts, turns aside, reflects.

A little tree descends from flies, lands. It has a single bough some three yards from ground and at its summit a meager tuft of palms casting at its foot a circle of shadow.

He continues to reflect.

Whistle from above.

He turns, sees tree, reflects, goes to it, sits down in its shadow, looks at his hands.

A pair of tailor's scissors descends from flies, comes to rest before tree, a yard from ground.

He continues to look at his hands.

Whistle from above.

He looks up, sees scissors, takes them and starts to trim his nails.

The palms close like a parasol, the shadow disappears.

He drops scissors, reflects.

A tiny carafe, to which is attached a huge label inscribed WATER, descends from flies, comes to rest some three yards from ground.

He continues to reflect.

Whistle from above.

He looks up, sees carafe, reflects, gets up, goes and stands under it, tries in vain to reach it, renounces, turns aside, reflects.

A big cube descends from flies, lands.

He continues to reflect.

Whistle from above.

He turns, sees cube, looks at it, at carafe, reflects, goes to cube, takes it up, carries it over and sets it down under carafe, tests its stability, gets up on it, tries in vain to reach carafe, renounces, gets down, carries cube back to its place, turns aside, reflects.

A second smaller cube descends from flies, lands.

He continues to reflect.

Whistle from above.

He turns, sees second cube, looks at it, at carafe, goes to second cube, takes it up, carries it over and sets it down under carafe, tests its stability, gets up on it, tries in vain to reach carafe, renounces, gets down, takes up second cube to carry it back to its place, hesitates, thinks better of it, sets it down, goes to big cube, takes it up, carries it over and puts it on small one, tests their stability, gets up on them, the cubes collapse, he falls, gets up immediately, brushes himself, reflects.

He takes up small cube, puts it on big one, tests their stability, gets up on them and is about to reach carafe when it is pulled up a little way and comes to rest beyond his reach.

He gets down, reflects, carries cubes back to their place, one by one, turns aside, reflects.

A third still smaller cube descends from flies, lands.

He continues to reflect.

Whistle from above.

He turns, sees third cube, looks at it, reflects, turns aside, reflects.

422

The third cube is pulled up and disappears in flies.

Beside carafe a rope descends from flies, with knots to facilitate ascent.

He continues to reflect.

Whistle from above.

He turns, sees rope, reflects, goes to it, climbs up it and is about to reach carafe when rope is let out and deposits him back on ground.

He reflects, looks around for scissors, sees them, goes and picks them up, returns to rope and starts to cut it with scissors.

The rope is pulled up, lifts him off ground, he hangs on, succeeds in cutting rope, falls back on ground, drops scissors, falls, gets up again immediately, brushes himself, reflects.

The rope is pulled up quickly and disappears in flies.

With length of rope in his possession he makes a lasso with which he tries to lasso carafe.

The carafe is pulled up quickly and disappears in flies.

He turns aside, reflects.

He goes with lasso in his hand to tree, looks at bough, turns and looks at cubes, looks again at bough, drops lasso, goes to cubes, takes up small one, carries it over and sets it down under bough, goes back for big one, takes it up and carries it over under bough, makes to put it on small one, hesitates, thinks better of it, sets it down, takes up small one and puts it in big one, tests their stability, turns aside and stoops to pick up lasso.

The bough folds down against trunk.

He straightens up with lasso in his hand, turns and sees what has happened.

He drops lasso, turns aside, reflects.

He carries back cubes to their place, one by one, goes back for lasso, carries it over to cubes and lays it in a neat coil on small one.

He turns aside, reflects.

Whistle from right wing.

He reflects, goes out right.

Immediately flung back on stage he falls, gets up immediately, brushes himself, turns aside, reflects.

Whistle from left wing.

He does not move.

He looks at his hands, looks around for scissors, sees them, goes and picks them up, starts to trim his nails, stops, reflects, runs his finger along blade of scissors, goes and lays them on small cube, turns aside, opens his collar, frees his neck and fingers it.

The small cube is pulled up and disappears in flies, carrying away rope and scissors.

He turns to take scissors, sees what has happened.

He turns aside, reflects.

He goes and sits down on big cube.

The big cube is pulled from under him. He falls. The big cube is pulled up and disappears in flies.

He remains lying on his side, his face toward auditorium, staring before him.

The carafe descends from flies and comes to rest a few feet from his body.

He does not move.

Whistle from above.

He does not move.

The carafe descends further, dangles and plays about his face.

He does not move.

The carafe is pulled up and disappears in flies.

The bough returns to horizontal, the palms open, the shadow returns.

Whistle from above.

He does not move.

The tree is pulled up and disappears in flies.

He looks at his hands.

CURTAIN

Jim Caldwell as Mr. DePinna, Marian Baer as Penelope Sycamore
in *You Can't Take It With You*. University Resident Theatre
Company, Penn State University. David Dannenbaum, director.

CHAPTER XIII

American Theatre: Beginnings to Maturity

As we approach the enormous scope of our own cultural heritage, that theatre that we know best, several problems emerge. On the one hand, it is important that our discussion not be merely a listing of names and dates; on the other in avoiding a detailed treatment, many important and revered names, institutions, and plays will not be mentioned. What follows is not a history of the American theatre so much as an introduction to some of its highlights.

Prior to the American Revolution, dramatic activity in the colonies was, to say the least, meager. Perhaps a lack of national pride or native roots on the part of the colonists prevented dramatic endeavors, but it is more likely that the important business of living occupied so much of the colonial individual's time and energy that there was insufficient leisure time to pursue entertainment. It must be remembered, too, that many of our forebearers were Puritans who considered the theatre a den of evil and blasphemy. Nevertheless, the first recorded production of a play in the new land seems to have been *Ye Bare and Ye Cubb* in 1665. This work is not extant, but official documents in Virginia indicated that three young men were summoned to court for acting in this amateur play and found not guilty.

While theatrical activity was meager during the days of colonization, it proved almost non-existent during the Revolutionary War. When in 1774, the Continental Congress decreed that it would "discountenance and discourage every species of extravagance and dissipation, especially all horseracing, and all kinds of gaming, cock-fighting, exhibitions of shews, plays, and other expensive diversions and entertainments," dramatic activity virtually ceased.

After the Revolution, however, the first important American play was produced. Royall Tyler's *The Contrast* (1787) was also the first American comedy to be acted professionally. Though modelled on Richard Brinsley Sheridan's British comedies, *The Contrast* introduced a novel character, Jonathan, who proved to be the archetype of the popular and distinctly American yankee character. The appearance of this shrewd and yet uncultivated New Englander marked the real beginnings of a native drama in America; he has remained a stage favorite and in our own time is perhaps best realized in the film work of Frank Capra and in the persona of Jimmy Stewart.

It is possible to leap forward almost sixty years to name another drama of major importance: *Fashion* in 1845 by Anna Cora Mowatt. A leading drama critic of the day, Edgar Allan Poe, was reserved in his praise of *Fashion:* "Compared with the generality of modern dramas, it is a good play—compared with most American dramas it is a very good one—estimated by the natural principles of dramatic art, it is altogether unworthy of notice." In spite of Poe's criticism, the play was extremely popular and has been repeatedly revived. Its characters—especially the social-climber and butcherer of the French language, Mrs. Tiffany, and the droll Yankee type, Adam Truman—are colorful and amusing. It is worthy of note that Mowatt is America's first successful woman playwright.

Unlike the period of the Revolutionary War, the Civil War era was one of great energy and activity, if not of quality. Melodramas, such as *East Lynne* and *Ten Nights in a Barroom,* were popular dramatic fare. Probably the most celebrated play of the period, and indeed for about fifty years afterwards, was George L. Aiken's stage adaptation of Harriet Beecher Stowe's novel, *Uncle Tom's Cabin.* Aiken's version ran for three hundred performances in New York, and, thereby, set the pattern of the long run on Broadway. Minstrel shows—vaudevilles in black face—employed companies of as many as forty men, and showboats, the first of which was Chapman's Floating Theatre in 1831, flourished before and after the Civil War. A group of English ladies called The British Blondes inaugurated a type of entertainment in the United States that eventually came to be known as burlesque. Closely related was vaudeville, then called variety. It began about 1826 and developed until, by the Civil War, it brought a series of acts—acrobats, musical turns, juggling, topical songs, ethnic and "off-color" jokes—to noisy but appreciative family audiences.

It was during this period, too, that the first musical extravaganza was presented to American audiences. There is a delightful story that a New York theatre burned down, leaving a group of imported French ballet dancers unemployed. An enterprising producer named William Wheatley decided to help all one hundred young ladies by integrating their dances with the mediocre melodrama he was presenting. The result was *The Black Crook* (1866) which ran 475 performances at Niblo's Gardens in New York and became, as many critics feel, the forerunner of the American musical. One need only think of the Ziegfeld Follies that ran yearly from 1907 until 1924 and periodically until 1942 to realize the impact of this new form.

With the end of the Civil War in 1865, America was again unified, and a new era was beginning. The first transcontinental railroad was constructed, and with its operation came a great surge of industrial development. Factories, mines, and railroads multiplied. Old urban centers grew, and new ones appeared. The population of the country expanded, partly through natural increase and partly through the sudden and abundant influx of immigrants. The ever-increasing foreign population contributed to a change in the character of the American scene. As American playwright Elmer Rice said, "For one thing, the new arrivals were mostly young, vigorous and adventuresome enough to risk the uncertainties of life in an alien country, and they gave the American bloodstream a new infusion of vitality, enterprise and optimism." While the theatre scene was still dominated by melodrama, America was beginning to produce some noteworthy dramatists: James A. Herne who wrote social drama in the style of Ibsen, Edward Harrigan and Charles Hoyt who explored ethnic characters, David Balasco who worked in naturalism with highly authentic settings, and William Vaughn Moody who developed tragedies of American life. All of them were making honest attempts to deal with American subjects, themes and characters.

One writer, perhaps, should be singled out because of his contribution to the beginnings of American musical comedy: George M. Cohan who wrote his first play in 1897 and his last in 1936. His most typical works—*Forty-Five Minutes from Broadway* (1906), *Get Rich Quick Wallingford* (1910), and *Broadway Jones* (1912)—combined the elements of melodrama with musical comedy. Characteristic throughout his writing career was a peculiar mixture of impudence, breeziness, sentiment, and optimism. His character types, though hardly more than sketched in, were recognizable, contemporary, and unmistakable American figures, the people and the speech that he heard on his beloved Broadway. Life to Cohan was a fairy tale, a success story, worked out by formula: if one were smart and substantially honest, if his heart were in the right place, and if he got the right girl, everything would turn out happily in the end. Cohan lost popularity when he sided with producers in the great Actors' Equity strike of 1919, in which members of the actors' union fought hard for decent working conditions and pay. But late in his career Cohan distinguished himself as an actor, playing the leading role in Rodgers and Hart's *I'd Rather Be Right* and as the father in Eugene O'Neill's *Ah, Wilderness!* His statue stands on Duffy Square in the very center of Broadway's theatre district.

In the first few decades of the twentieth century, dramatic activity flourished. In 1915, for example, two important theatre groups came into being. The first of these was The Provincetown Players who devoted themselves to the production of new American plays and are known largely for their introduction and fostering of the work of the playwright many critics believe to be America's greatest, Eugene O'Neill. The group began in Cape Cod and then moved to a stable in Greenwich Village in New York. In the eight years of its existence it produced, besides O'Neill, plays by Theodore Dreiser, Susan Glaspell, and Edna St. Vincent Millay.

The second group, known as The Washington Square Players, formed a dedicated art theatre devoted mainly to the production of fine European plays. After just two years, The Washington Square Players dissolved only to re-form as the powerful Theatre Guild in 1919. During the period of the 1920s the Theatre Guild attracted the work of outstanding young designers like Robert Edmund Jones and Lee Simonson, America's greatest playwrights like Eugene O'Neill, Sidney Howard, and S. N. Behrman, and distinguished producers like Theresa Helpburn and Lawrence Langner.

These two theatrical groups fought commercialism in the theatre just as George Pierce Baker fought it in the colleges in which he taught playwriting. Baker first taught at Radcliff; he went to Harvard in 1905 and to Yale in 1924. In his class, English 47 Workshop, he treated drama as a contemporary phenomenon deserving academic consideration. He did not offer his students a formula but rather encouraged them to make use of their individual talents to express themselves in dramatic form. Almost all of the talented young playwrights to emerge after World War I had studied with George Pierce Baker. He gave them ideals, encouraged their individuality, and gave them confidence to put pen to paper. If his students had one thing in common, it was their interest in American themes and characters, no matter what the treatment or form.

There are many critics who believe that immediately after World War I American drama reached maturity and that the amount and quality of dramatic work in the 1920s and 1930s remains unsurpassed. Certainly, America emerged as a world power after the war, and while Europe had been devastated by the losses and destruction of battle, America had not. The U.S. had only been in the war for one year and emerged with a sense of importance but with an enormous reserve of energy and vitality. That vitality was certainly reflected in the fact that as many as 260 plays opened on Broadway in the 1925–26 season, thirty more than had been seen in any previous year.

Similarly, the musical theatre flourished. One particular work stands as a major milestone: *Showboat* (1927) by Jerome Kern and Oscar Hammerstein II. Adapted from Edna Ferber's 1926 novel of the same name, *Showboat* moves sharply away from the slight musical comedies of the past. The action centers on a showboating family and the rigors of their life on the Mississippi River. Cap'n Andy Hawks daughter, Magnolia, falls in love with a handsome man addicted to gambling. Julie, the leading lady of the company who has black blood in her veins but who passes for white, is not only forced to leave the troupe but is ostracized because her mixed marriage is considered unlawful. Julie develops a serious drinking problem and the action ends unhappily for both couples—certainly not the typical sugar-coated musical comedy story; moreover, the book was integrated with the music, the songs grew out of the action and reflected the characters who sang them. *Showboat* prepared the way for the musical drama or play or as it has come to be known the integrated musical.

Quite apart from the flourishing musical theatre, the decades of the 1920s and 30s were dominated by the outstanding work of one playwright: Eugene O'Neill (1888–1953), son of a popular American actor, James O'Neill. After attending Baker's playwriting classes, O'Neill worked with the Provincetown Players where his one-act plays about life at sea were performed. He arrived on Broadway in 1920 with his Pulitzer Prize winning play, *Beyond the Horizon.* O'Neill went on to write approximately twenty-five full length plays for the theatre. He was a great experimentor who began as a realist, moved into expressionism in plays like *The Emperor Jones* (1920), *The Hairy Ape* (1922), and *The Great God Brown* (1926), exploration of the subconscious in *Strange Interlude* (1928), reinterpretation of Greek myth in his massive trilogy, *Mourning Becomes Electra* (1931) and ultimately returned to realism in his late masterpieces, *The Iceman Cometh (1939), Moon for the Misbegotten* (1943), and perhaps his finest work, the boldly autobiographical *Long Day's Journey into Night* (1939–41). O'Neill saw humanity as adrift in a materialistic world that had lost its faith. His plays exude passion and raw emotion, subsequently seeming at times old-fashioned and melodramatic. But O'Neill was prolific, bold, fearless, and varied in his dramatic output for which he won the Nobel Prize for Literature in 1936, after his reputation had waned but, ironically, before he had completed his greatest work.

O'Neill was profoundly influenced by August Strindberg and their lives were parallel in many ways. O'Neill, like Strindberg, felt passionately, suffered precarious mental health, married unhappily three times, felt alienated from his children, and wrote intensely autobiographical plays. *Ah, Wilderness!,* written in 1933, is an autobiographical comedy about O'Neill's youth; *Long Day's Journey into Night* is the tragedy. It was so personal and so revealing—about his brother's alcoholism, his mother's drug addiction, his father's miserliness, his own sense of rejection—that O'Neill placed it in a sealed envelope that was not to be opened until twenty-five years after his death. He further stated that he never wanted the play performed. His widow, Carlotta Monterey, disregarded his wishes, however, and the play was produced in 1956. In it O'Neill summarizes his own pain and anguish, "It was a great mistake, my being born a man, I would have been much more successful as a sea gull or a fish. As it is, I will always be a stranger who never feels at home, who does not really want and is not really wanted, who can never belong, who must always be a little in love with death!"

After the prolific activity of the 1920's which included the work of O'Neill and many others like high comedy writers Philip Barry and S. N. Behrman, expressionist Elmer Rice, realist Sidney Howard, and writer of social comedies George Kelly, the stock market crash of 1929 brought about significant changes in the theatre, the most important innovation being America's solitary attempt at a national theatre with the creation of the Federal Theatre Project in 1935. The project was a part of Franklin D. Roosevelt's WPA (Works Projects Administration) designed to get a nation back to work during the devastating depression years. The Federal Theatre Project, under the leadership of Hallie Flanagan, who had been a professor at Vassar College, produced 1,200 shows and provided work for 12,000 theatre artists. There were five regional centers and forty states involved. The organization produced children's plays, dance plays, classics, new plays, plays out-of-doors, black productions, folk plays, and musicals. Shows toured by truck and reached areas of the country that had never seen theatre before. One of the most innovative of the units of the project was one called the Living Newspaper in which daily news events like the dust bowl, the plight of the farmer, and housing conditions were explored and dramatized in highly presentational, Brechtian modes. The Federal Theatre Project, however, was destined to last only four years. Just as it had been created by an act of Congress in 1935, rumors of leftist involvement and domination caused it to be destroyed by Congress in 1939. Hallie Flanagan tells the incredible story of this unique chapter in American theatre in her moving book, *Arena.* It remains, perhaps, one of the reasons why the United States is the only major country in the world which does not have a government supported national theatre.

In addition to the Federal Theatre Project, the 1930s produced an extraordinary producing organization in The Group Theatre. It actually began informally in 1928 when a group of young artists got together to work on plays in their spare time. The first season of The Group occurred in 1931 and it lasted until 1940. There were two main principles which governed their activity: ensemble work based on the teachings of Constantin Stanislavsky, and emphasis on American social drama by young playwrights. Both principles were realized richly in the ten years of The Group's existence. Morris Carnovsky, Lee Strasberg, Harold Clurman, and Sanford Meisner were principle directors and acting teachers. They remain to this date the masters of the Stanislavsky system in America and the backbone of our approach to acting. Actors included Stella and Luther Adler, Elia Kazan, John Garfield, and Lee J. Cobb. They lived together as a company, grew by working together, and were paid equally. Their playwrights included Paul Green, John Howard Lawson, Sidney Kingsley, and Clifford Odets.

Unfortunately, as Harold Clurman writes in his story of The Group, *The Fervent Years,* dissension about the Stanislavsky system, the lure of Hollywood and commercialism, debts and political strife undermined the objectives of the idealistic young company. Nevertheless, the Group Theatre may well have been the most important theatrical force in the country during its ten years of existence. It fostered the work of young, socially minded American playwrights and directors, and it represented the high level of acting that was to set standards and establish models for generations to come.

There are those critics who maintain that the energy and commitment to theatre evidenced in the twenties and thirties have never been surpassed in America. As we look at this first chapter of our own dramatic heritage, we choose a play from the year 1936, a play that speaks of hope even in the darkest days of the Depression. With unmistakable American spirit, humor, and flavor it is also a play that takes a clear and critical (however light-hearted) look at American values and character types.

George S. Kaufman and Moss Hart

It is interesting that our only collaboration in the anthology reflects the united effort of two men, both of Jewish background, both without college educations, and both literally self-taught in the machinations of the American professional theatre. Of the two, George S. Kaufman was the older. Born in Pittsburgh in 1889, Kaufman was already an established and successful playwright when he began work with Hart, fifteen years his junior, on *Once in A Lifetime* (1930).

It has been said that Hart brought the plots and that Kaufman with sharpened pencils poised like scalpels brought, as Rhoda-Gale Pollack says, "the flashes of wit, fast-paced dialogue, jibes at potentates of business and government, volleys of wisecracks, observations on details of daily life, and an overall satiric tone." Kaufman graduated from Pittsburgh's Central High School in

431

1907. An attack of pleurisy interrupted his first semester at Western University of Pennsylvania (now Pitt), so the tall, lanky and shy youth began a series of odd jobs with Pennsylvania firms and county agencies until he was offered a job as a ribbon salesman at his father's newly acquired business in Patterson, New Jersey. Kaufman began to write plays, served briefly as a humor columnist for the *Washington Post,* and in 1913 accepted a job as cub reporter for the *New York Tribune.* Living in New York, Kaufman became increasingly interested in the theatre and in playwriting. He took an extension course at Columbia University and in 1917 almost simultaneously married Beatrice Bakrow and became drama editor of the *New York Times,* a post he would hold until 1930.

In 1919 Kaufman met his first major collaborator, Marc Connelly, with whom he wrote a series of Broadway successes: *Dulcy* (1921), *To the Ladies!* and *Merton of the Movies* (1922) and *Beggar on Horseback* (1924). He collaborated with Edna Ferber on *Minick* (1924) and *Royal Family* (1927). In 1928 Kaufman began a second career, that of theatrical director, when he staged the hit production of Hecht and MacArthur's *The Front Page*; he remained a highly successful, precise, and demanding director for thirty years.

Moss Hart (1904–1960) was born into humble surroundings in the Bronx where his father was a cigar maker. Working after school when he was twelve took him on an errand to Manhattan where he saw Times Square for the first time. Hart was hopelessly stage struck from this time forward. He worked in a fur storage vault and at seventeen became an office boy for a theatrical producer named Augustus Pitou, and it was there that he began reading the hundreds of scripts that would pass through Pitou's office. For a number of years he directed community theatre in the winter and worked as a social director in the Catskills during the summers.

Hart had written many scripts, all quite amateurish, until he drafted in three weeks a play titled *Once in a Lifetime* about the panic in Hollywood over the advent of sound. The play came to the attention of director, Jed Harris, and producer, Sam Harris, who recognized its possibilities but realized that it needed help. Enter George S. Kaufman. Hart smoked cigars, a habit Kaufman despised; Kaufman maintained a Spartan schedule, much to Hart's dismay. Kaufman was merciless with his pencils, rewriting, cutting, rewriting again. "Cut it to the bone," Kaufman told Hart. "Then we can see the good stuff left and build from there." When the play opened, Kaufman insisted that Hart have top billing, and on opening night he went in front of the curtain to say, "I would like this audience to know that eighty percent of this play is Moss Hart."

Both artists continued to work separately and with others, Kaufman winning the Pulitzer Prize with Morrie Ryskind, George and Ira Gershwin for *Of Thee I Sing,* Hart going off with the Cole Porters to write *Jubilee* and writing the book for several Irving Berlin musicals. But the famous team was to collaborate seven more times: *Merrily We Roll Along* (1934), *You Can't Take It with You* (1936), *I'd Rather Be Right* (1937) with Richard Rodgers and Lorenz Hart, *The Fabulous Invalid* (1938), *The American Way* (1939), *The Man Who Came to Dinner* (1939), and *George Washington Slept Here* (1940). A couple of these were flops; several have achieved the status of American classic.

It has been said that Hart became too dependent upon Kaufman, that he became afraid he could not write without his older collaborator. For whatever reason the two were never to work together again. Hart became deeply involved in analysis, which culminated in *Lady in the Dark* with Kurt Weill. In 1959 Hart wrote a loving tribute to Kaufman in his enchanting memoir, *Act*

One. Hart wrote a number of plays on his own: *Light up the Sky* and *The Climate of Eden* and the film version of *A Star Is Born* for Judy Garland. He married the charming actress, Kitty Carlyle, and distinguished himself as a director of musicals with *My Fair Lady* and *Camelot*.

In 1945 Kaufman's wife and Moss Hart's dear friend, Beatrice Kaufman, died. Kaufman married the British actress and writer, Leueen MacGrath in 1949. After he had suffered several strokes MacGrath divorced him in 1957. He continued to direct after his collaboration with Hart ended, to doctor other writers plays, and to collaborate on such works as *The Late George Apley, The Solid Gold Cadillac,* and *Silk Stockings.* But his work never matched the wit, polish, and style that he had mastered with Hart. George S. Kaufman—director, drama editor, wit, producer, play doctor, collaborator—died in 1961. Even though Hart was fifteen years his junior, within six months Moss Hart, too, had died of a heart attack. Not only were they a remarkable team, but American comedy has rarely before or since experienced the technical skill, wit, and vibrancy that their plays achieved.

YOU CAN'T TAKE IT WITH YOU

In the 1919–1920 Broadway theatre season the American drama emphatically established itself as one of the most lively, significant, artistic and committed dramas of the world beginning with the up-town Broadway production of Eugene O'Neill's *Beyond the Horizon.* Within a year a dozen or so talented and productive playwrights with something worthwhile to say appeared rather spectacularly on the theatrical scene each one contributing in a particular and profound way to the establishment of an important American drama. One such contributor was George Kaufman who specialized in popular comedy enhanced by superior wit.

As the decade of the Twenties drew to a close, Kaufman entered a partnership with Moss Hart; together they became one of the most successful writing teams in the history of the American theatre. As the younger member of the team Moss Hart contributed a sure skill in plot construction and a gift for creating interesting characters. Kaufman was noted for a superior sense of what really worked in the theatre. He was also regarded as one of the outstanding wits of his day. Theater-goers and readers alike can appreciate his remarkable talents for witty dialogue in the brilliant one-liners and epigrams in *You Can't Take It With You* which are always skillfully expressed in speech ideally suiting a specific character. In other words, these are not comic lines for the sake of laughs; these are unique expressions from the mouths of unique individuals. And they are all the more humorous for that reason.

Within a year of Kaufman and Hart's first collaborative effort the country was plunged into the Great Depression of the Thirties. Since comedy is most often rooted in the contemporary scene, it is understandable that their plays of the Thirties took on a slightly darker hue as they reflected the hard times inflicted upon the nation by a sickly economy. It is impossible to read *You Can't Take It With You* without sensing the presence of that depressed economy. But, in spite of that fact, the play strikes a universal chord somewhere that has helped it to transcend its own time and to speak to generations of another time.

There has to be a reason why *You Can't Take It With You* has remained one of the most enduring and popular comedies of the American theatre. In recent years, through revival after revival, it has become the mainstay of our regional theatres. It has undergone at least two outstanding television productions. Frank Capra's film version won an academy award in 1938 as best picture of the year; it can still be seen as a staple on the television movie channels. In fact, considering its popularity, one wonders how it has escaped being transformed into a musical version—the inevitable fate of most popular plays. One hopes that fate never befalls the script because music would surely add nothing to enhance the play. Music would only truncate the play's extravagant wackiness, interrupt its breathtaking speed, and romanticize its zany characters.

When Kaufman and Hart's comedy opened on Broadway on the night of December 14, 1936 at the very height of the Depression, it was generously welcomed by most critics who regarded it as a much needed tonic for hard times. However, there were a few critics at the time—and some since—who found the play's message shallow and sentimental and even a bit dangerous. They were quick to point out that the play would seem to encourage irresponsible behavior and escapism as viable answers to the problem of survival in 1936. One such critic, John Gassner, found the play highly entertaining but was apparently alarmed by its tendency "to pour balm on all wounds with the madcap, philosophical plea to let life slide." He went on to say that most Americans at the time could not afford to "let life slide." Other critics, responding to the same element in the play, found Kaufman and Hart's view bordering on something almost dangerously un-American. After all, we Americans face our problems head-on and defeat them by that Puritan ethic of self-sacrifice and hard work. But, then, critics have an innate talent for finding what they want to find in a play. One has to have a rather perverse sense of humor to twist the positive message of the play into something as negative as letting life slide.

It is impossible to miss one of the dominate and very positive themes of the play couched in the dramatists' advise to the audience—a message particularly appropriate to sufferers of the Depression. Money does not guarantee happiness. While a lack of monetary funds may not be a blessing, you do not have to let it destroy your life. After all, as the play tells us, true happiness comes from doing those things which make you feel fulfilled. Life becomes bearable, even joyous, when it is lived with imagination. So, in the play we are introduced to a set of characters who (to take the clue in the opening stage directions) go "about the business of living in the fullest sense of the word." This is the lesson Grandpa understands so well; this is the lesson which Mr. Kirby has to learn. But this is more than a mere lesson in the play; it is the essential psychic action of the comedy: to achieve fulfillment in life by living with imagination. As Grandpa says to Mr. Kirby, "The world's not so crazy. . . . It's the people *in* it. Life's pretty simple if you just relax."

The enactment of the basic thrust of the play, then, requires a "brood" of characters devoted to doing what makes them happy. Kaufman and Hart provide us with an entire array of seemingly eccentric characters who are actually not so eccentric at all; they are merely doing those things which give them pleasure. Penny writes plays when she is not painting. Essie is devoted to ballet dancing. Paul is an enthusiastic tinker who plays with an erector set or creates magical fireworks in the basement. Mr. DePinna is his creative assistant who comes up with the idea of attaching balloons to sky rockets. Ed is a xylophonist and a part-time composer who loves to run a printing press. Then there is Grandpa who more than anyone else lives creatively. Added to this menage is an assortment of hangers-on—a cook who is treated like one of the family, the cook's lover, a couple of displaced Russian aristocrats and an alcoholic actress. (The last three characters had a special appeal because they were precisely the kind of quaint individuals one would likely encounter on the streets of New York in 1936. America had become a place of refuge for countless Russian aristocrats escaping the Communists. And, of course, one can always find more unemployed than employed actors in New York City. This was genuine local color.)

All one needs for conflict in the play is to bring a few relatively "normal" individuals into close contact with such zanies. Therefore, the plot revolves around the "normal" daughter Alice and her attempts to avoid the inevitable clashes between her "normal" love and his "normal" parents on the one hand and her outrageous family and friends on the other. The plot, indeed, is little more than a dramatization of every girl's nightmare. All the things that could conceivably go wrong when the family of the prospective bride meets the family of the prospective groom actually happen in this play. The play reaches a peak of marvelous hysteria when the two families collide.

In all honesty it must be admitted that the playwrights stack the deck in favor of the zany individualists. The Vanderhof family has one tremendously endearing trait. They sincerely and profoundly love one another and are highly tolerant of each other's individual idiosyncracies. For example, it would not occur to Essie and Ed to have a child without the approval of Grandpa and everyone else in the household. In fact, the thought of having a child apparently does not even occur to them; it is Penny, Essie's mother, who suggests the idea. They care deeply for one another and take care of anyone who enters their space. Mr. DePinna is a case in point: he arrived one day eight years ago to deliver the ice and was so warmly received that he stayed on and on and on. And he was not alone. A milkman predating Mr. DePinna had remained as a welcomed guest in the bosom of this family for five years. Kolenkhov consistently shows up at mealtime as does Donald. At the end of the play we can assume that the Grand Duchess Olga Katrina, cousin of the Czar, will be a frequent visitor in the future. So will Mr. Kirby probably with his saxophone in tow.

In this family of riotous individualists it is significant that the one thing that dampens the ardor with which the various members live is the thought that they have made someone they love unhappy. This is a family held together by love. The entire family shares a sense of guilt over Alice's unhappiness. This is a comedy, however; so the unhappiness is temporary and life goes on its merry way. In this comedy love conquers all. But, thank heavens, it is not the usual boy-meets-girl love. This is the love of true caring, one individual's love and respect for another. This is the kind of family that we all wish in our heart of hearts was our own. This is the kind of family in which there is time for everything but unkindness and unpleasantness. In fact, there does not seem to be time for much else. As Ed remarks when asked what time it is: "It was about five o'clock a couple of hours ago." Who watches a clock when you're enjoying life?

There is an entire philosophy of life in *You Can't Take It With You* nicely summed up on two occasions when Grandpa offers Grace before dinner. He prays: "Well, Sir, we've been getting along pretty good for quite a while now, and we're certainly much obliged. Remember, all we ask is just to go along and be happy in our own sort of way. Of course we want to keep our health, but as far as anything else is concerned, we'll leave it to You. Thank You." By the time the prayer is voiced, we know only too well what Grandpa means by "our own sort of way." It is a very magnanimous, loving and caring sort of way. That simple message of regard for your fellow man seemed a very viable one to audiences in 1936; and it seems to have remained a very viable one. In these days of the 1990s it is more than a viable message. It's a vital one.

YOU CAN'T TAKE IT WITH YOU

By Moss Hart and George S. Kaufman

―――― CAST OF CHARACTERS ――――

"You Can't Take It With You" was produced at the Booth Theatre, New York City, Monday night, December 14th, 1936, by Sam. H. Harris.

PENELOPE SYCAMORE
ESSIE
RHEBA
PAUL SYCAMORE
MR. DE PINNA
ED
DONALD
MARTIN VANDERHOF
ALICE
HENDERSON
TONY KIRBY
BORIS KOLENKHOV
GAY WELLINGTON
MR. KIRBY
MRS. KIRBY
THREE MEN
OLGA

The Scene Is the Home of Martin Vanderhof, New York.

ACT I
A Wednesday Evening
During this act the curtain is lowered to denote the passing of several hours.

ACT II
A Week Later

ACT III
The Next Day

ACT ONE
SCENE I

The home of MARTIN VENDERHOF—*just around the corner from Colombia University, but don't go looking for it. The room we see is what is customarily described as a living room, but in this house the term is something of an understatement. The every-man-for-himself room would be more like it. For here meals are eaten, plays are written, snakes collected, ballet steps practiced, xylophones played, printing presses operated—if there were room enough there would probably be ice skating. In short, the brood presided over by* Martin Vanderhof *goes on about the business of living in the fullest sense of the word. This is a house where you do as you like, and no questions asked.*

At the moment, GRANDPA VENDERHOF'S *daughter,* MRS. PENELOPE SYCAMORE, *is doing what she likes more than anything else in the world. She is writing a play—her eleventh. Confortably ensconced in what is affectionately known as Mother's Corner, she is pounding away on a typewriter perched precariously on a rickety card table. Also on the table is one of those plaster-paris skulls ordinarily used as an ash tray, but which serves* PENELOPE *as a candy jar. And, because* PENNY *likes companionship, there are two kittens on the table, busily lapping at a saucer of milk.*

PENELOPE VENDERHOF SYCAMORE *is a round little woman in her early fifties, comfortable looking, gentle, homey. One would not suspect that under that placid exterior there surges the Divine Urge—but it does, it does.*

After a moment her fingers lag on the keys; a thoughtful expression comes over her face. Abstractedly she takes a piece of candy out of the skull, pops it into her mouth. As always, it furnishes the needed inspiration—with a furious burst of speed she finishes a page and whips it out of the machine. Quite mechanically, she picks up one of the kittens, adds the sheet of paper to the pile underneath, replaces the kitten.

As she goes back to work, ESSIE CARMICHAEL, MRS. SYCAMORE'S *eldest daughter, comes in from the kitchen. A girl of about twenty-nine, very slight, a curious air of the pixie about her. She is wearing ballet slippers—in fact, she wears them throughout the play.*

ESSIE (*fanning herself*). My that kitchen's hot.

PENNY (*finishing a bit of typing*). What Essie?

ESSIE. I say the kitchen's awful hot. That new candy I'm making—it just won't ever get cool.

PENNY. Do you have to make candy today, Essie? It's such a hot day.

ESSIE. Well, I got all those new orders. Ed went out and got a bunch of new orders.

PENNY. My, if it keeps on I suppose you'll be opening up a store.

ESSIE. That's what Ed was saying last night, but I said No, I want to be a dancer. (*Bracing herself against the table, she manipulates her legs, ballet fashion.*)

PENNY. The only trouble with dancing is, it takes so long. You've been studying such a long time.

ESSIE (*slowly drawing a leg up behind her as she talks*). Only—eight—years. After all, mother, you've been writing plays for eight years. We started about the same time, didn't we?

PENNY. Yes, but you shouldn't count my first two years, because I was learning to type. (*From the kitchen comes a colored maid named* RHEBA—*a very black girl somewhere in her thirties. She carries a white tablecloth, and presently starts to spread it over the table.*)

RHEBA (*as she enters*). I think the candy's hardening up now, Miss Essie.

ESSIE. Oh, thanks, Rheba. I'll bring some in, mother—I want you to try it. (*She goes into the kitchen.*)

(PENNY *returns to her work as* RHEBA *busies herself with the table.*)

RHEBA. Finish the second act, Mrs. Sycamore?

PENNY. Oh, no, Rheba. I've just got Cynthia entering the monastery.

RHEBA. Monastery? How'd she get there? She was at the El Morocco, wasn't she?

PENNY. Well, she gets tired of the El Morocco, and there's this monastery, so she goes there.

RHEBA. Do they let her in?

PENNY. Yes, I made it Visitors' Day, so of course anybody can come.

RHEBA. Oh.

PENNY. So she arrives on Visitors' Day, and—just stays.

RHEBA. All night?

PENNY. Oh, yes. She stays six years.

RHEBA (*as she goes into the kitchen*). Six years? My, I bet she busts that monastery wide open.

PENNY (*half to herself, as she types.*) "Six Years Later.". . . (PAUL SYCAMORE *comes up from the cellar. Mid-fifties, but with a kind of youthful air. His quiet charm and mild manner are distinctly engaging.*)

PAUL (*turning back as he comes through the door.*) Mr. De Pinna! (*A voice from below. "Yah?"*) Mr. De Pinna, will you bring up one of those new sky rockets, please? I want to show them to Mrs. Sycamore. (*An answering monosyllable from the cellar as he turns toward* PENNY.) Look, Penny— what do you think of these little fire crackers? Ten strings for a nickel. Listen. (*He puts one down on the center table and lights it. It goes off with a good bang.*) Nice, huh?

PENNY. Paul, dear, were you ever in a monastery?

PAUL (*quite calmly*). No, I wasn't. . . . Wait till you see the new rockets. Gold stars, then blue stars, then some bombs, and then a balloon. Mr. De Pinna thought of the balloon.

PENNY. Sounds lovely. Did you do all that today?

PAUL. Sure. We made up—oh, here we are. (MR. DE PINNA *comes up from the cellar. A bald-headed little man with a serious manner, and carrying two*

good-sized sky rockets.) Look, Penny. Cost us eighteen cents to make and we sells 'em for fifty. How many do you figure we can make before the Fourth, Mr. De Pinna?

DE PINNA. Well, we've got two weeks yet—what day you going to take the stuff up to Mount Vernon?

PAUL. Oh, I don't know—about a week. You know, we're going to need a larger booth this year—got a lot of stuff made up.

DE PINNA (*examining the rocket in his hand*). Look, Mr. Sycamore, the only thing that bothers me is, I'm afraid the powder chamber is just a little bit close to the balloon.

PAUL. Well, we've got the stars and the bombs in between.

DE PINNA. But that don't give the balloon time enough. A balloon needs plenty of time.

PAUL. Want to go down in the cellar and try it?

DE PINNA. All right.

PAUL (*as he disappears through the cellar door*). That's the only way you'll really tell.

PENNY (*halting* DE PINNA *in the cellar doorway*). Mr. De Pinna, if a girl you loved entered a monastery, what would you do?

DE PINNA (*he wasn't expecting that one*). Oh I don't know, Mrs. Sycamore—it's been so long. (*He goes.*)

(RHEBA *returns from the kitchen, bringing a pile of plates.*)

RHEBA. Miss Alice going to be home to dinner tonight, Mrs. Sycamore?

PENNY (*deep in her thinking*). What? I don't know, Rheba. Maybe.

RHEBA. Well, I'll set a place for her, but she's only been home one night this week. (*She puts down a plate or two.*) Miss Essie's making some mighty good candy today. She's doing something new with cocoanuts. (*More Plates.*) Let's see—six, and Mr. De Pinna, and if Mr. Kolenkhov comes that makes eight, don't it? (*At which point a muffled crack, reminiscent of the Battle of the Marne, comes up from the cellar. It is the sky rocket, of course. The great preliminary hiss, followed by a series of explosions.* PENNY *and* RHEBA, *however, don't even notice it.* RHEBA *goes right on.*) Yes, I'd better set for eight.

PENNY. I think I'll put this play away for a while, Rheba, and go back to the war play.

RHEBA. Oh, I always liked that one—the war play. (ESSIE *returns from the kitchen, carrying a plate of freshly made candy.*)

ESSIE. They'll be better when they're harder, mother, but try one—I want to know what you think.

PENNY. Oh, they look awfully good. (*She takes one.*) What do you call them?

ESSIE. I think I'll call 'em Love Dreams.

PENNY. Oh, that's nice....I'm going back to my war play, Essie. What do you think?

ESSIE. Oh, are you mother?

PENNY. Yes, I sort of got myself into a monastery and I can't get out.

ESSIE. Oh, well, it'll come to you, mother. Remember how you got out of that brothel. . . . Hello, boys. (*This little greeting is idly tossed toward the snake solarium, a glass structure looking something like a goldfish aquarium, but containing, believe it or not, snakes.*) The snakes look hungry. Did Rheba feed them?

PENNY (*as* RHEBA *re-enters*). I don't know. Rheba, did you feed the snakes yet?

RHEBA. No, Donald's coming and he always brings flies with him.

PENNY. Well, try to feed them before Grandpa gets home. You know how fussy he is about them.

RHEBA. Yes'm.

PENNY (*handing her the kittens*). And take Groucho and Harpo into the kitchen with you. . . . I think I'll have another Love Dream. (MR. SYCAMORE *emerges from the cellar again.*)

PAUL. Mr. De Pinna was right about the balloon. It was too close to the powder.

ESSIE (*practicing a dance step*). Want a Love Dream, father? They're on the table.

PAUL. No, thanks. I gotta wash.

PENNY. I'm going back to the war play, Paul.

PAUL. Oh, that's nice. We're putting some red stars after the blue stars, then come the bombs, and *then* the balloon. That ought to do it. (*He goes up the stairs.*)

ESSIE (*another dance step.*) Mr. Kolenkhov says I'm his most promising pupil.

PENNY (*absorbed in her own troubles*). You know, with forty monks and one girl, something ought to happen. (ED CARMICHAEL *comes down the stairs. A nondescript young man in his mid-thirties. In shirtsleeves at the moment.*)

ED. Listen! (*He hums a snatch of melody as he heads for the far corner of the room—the xylophone corner. Arriving there, he picks up the sticks and continues the melody on the xylophone. Immediately* ESSIE *is up on her toes, performing intricate ballet steps to* ED'S *accompaniment.*)

ESSIE (*dancing*). I like that, Ed. Yours?

ED (*shakes his head*). Beethoven.

ESSIE (*never coming down off her toes*). Lovely. Got a lot of *you* in it. . . . I made those new candies this afternoon, Ed.

ED (*playing away*). Yah?

ESSIE. You can take 'em around tonight.

ED. All right. . . . Now, here's the finish. This is me. (*He works up to an elaborate crescendo, but* ESSIE *keeps pace with him right to the finish.*)

ESSIE. That's fine. Remember it when Kholenkhov comes, will you?

PENNY (*who has been busy with her papers*). Ed, dear, why don't you and Essie have a baby? I was thinking about it just the other day.

ED. I don't know—we could have one if you wanted us to. What about it, Essie? Do you want to have a baby?

ESSIE. Oh, I don't care. I'm willing if Grandpa is.

ED. Let's ask him. (ESSIE *goes into the kitchen as* PENNY *goes back to her manuscripts.*)

PENNY (*running through the pile*). Labor play . . . religious play . . . sex play. I know it's here some place. (ED *meanwhile, has transferred his attention from the xylophone to a printing press that stands handily by and now gives it a preliminary workout.*) (MR. DE PINNA *comes out of the cellar, bound for the kitchen to wash up.*)

DE PINNA. I was right about the balloon. It was too close to the powder.

ED. Anything you want printed, Mr. De Pinna? How about some more calling cards?

DE PINNA (*as he passes into the kitchen*). No thanks. I've still got the *first* thousand.

ED (*calling after him*). Well, call on somebody, will you? (*He then gives his attention to* RHEBA, *who is busy with the table again.*) What have we got for dinner, Rheba? I'm ready to print the menu.

RHEBA. Cornflakes, watermelon, some of those candies Miss Essie made and some kind of meat—I forget.

ED. I think I'll set it up in boldface Cheltenham tonight. (*He starts to pick out the letters.*) If I'm going to take those new candies around I'd better print up some descriptive matter after dinner.

PENNY. Do you think anybody reads those things, Ed—that you put in the candy boxes? . . . Oh here it is. (*She pulls a manuscript out of a pile.*) "Poison Gas." (*The door bell sounds.*) I guess that's Donald. (*As* RHEBA *breaks into a broad grin.*) Look at Rheba smile.

ED. The boy friend, eh, Rheba?

PENNY (*as* RHEBA *disappears into the hallway*). Donald and Rheba are awfully cute together. Sort of like Porgy and Bess. (RHEBA *having opened the door, the gentleman named* DONALD *now looms up in the doorway—darkly. He is a colored man of no uncertain hue.*)

DONALD. Good evening, everybody!

ED. Hi, Donald! How have you been?

DONALD. I'm pretty good, Mr. Ed. How you been, Mrs. Sycamore?

PENNY. Very well, thank you. (*she looks at him, appraisingly.*) Donald, were you ever in a monastery?

DONALD. No-o. I don't go no place much. I'm on relief.

PENNY. Oh, yes, of course.

DONALD (*pulling a bottle out of each side pocket*). Here's the flies, Rheba. Caught a big mess of them today.

RHEBA (*taking the jars*). You sure did.

DONALD. I see you've been working, Mrs. Sycamore.

PENNY. Yes, indeed, Donald.

DONALD. How's Grandpa?

PENNY. Just fine. He's over at Columbia this afternoon. The Commencement exercises.

DONALD. My, the years certainly do roll 'round.

ED (*with his typesetting*). M—E—A—T. . . . What's he go there for all the time, Penny?

PENNY. I don't know, It's so handy—just around the corner. (PAUL *comes downstairs.*)

PAUL. Oh Donald! Mr. De Pinna and I are going to take the fireworks up to Mount Vernon next week. Do you think you could give us a hand?

DONALD. Yes, sir, only I can't take no money for it this year, because if the Government finds out I'm working they'll get sore.

PAUL. Oh! . . . Ed, I got a wonderful idea in the bathroom just now. I was reading Trotzky. (*He produces a book from under his arm.*) It's yours, isn't it?

ED. Yah, I left it there.

PENNY. *Who* is it?

PAUL. *You* know, Trotzky. The Russian Revolution.

PENNY. Oh.

PAUL. Anyhow, it struck me it was a great fireworks idea. Remember "The Last Days of Pompeii"?

PENNY. Oh, yes. Palisades Park. (*With a gesture of her arms she loosely describes a couple of arcs, indicative of the eruption of Mt. Vesuvius.*) That's where we met.

PAUL. Well, I'm going to do the Revolution! A full hour display.

DONALD. Say!

PENNY. Paul, that's wonderful!

ED. The red fire is the flag, huh?

PAUL. Sure! And the Czar, and the Cossacks!

DONALD. And the freeing of the slaves?

PAUL. No, no, Donald—(*The sound of the front door slamming. A second's pause, and then* GRANDPA *enters the living room.* GRANDPA *is about 75, a wiry little man whom the years have treated kindly. His face is youthful, despite the lines that sear it; his eyes are very much alive. He is a man who made his peace with the world long, long ago, and his whole attitude and manner are quietly persuasive of this.*)

GRANDPA (*surveying the group*). Well, sir, you should have been there. That's all I can say—you should have been there.

PENNY. Was it a nice Commencement, Grandpa?

GRANDPA. Wonderful. They get better every year. (*He peers into the snake solarium.*) You don't know how lucky you are you're snakes.

ED. Big class this year Grandpa? How many were there?

GRANDPA. Oh, must have been two acres. *Everybody* graduated. And much funnier speeches than they had last year.

DONALD. You want to listen to a good speech you go up and hear Father Divine.

GRANDPA. I'll wait—they'll have him at Columbia.

PENNY. Donald, will you tell Rheba Grandpa's home now and we won't wait for Miss Alice.

DONALD. Yes'm . . . (*As he goes through the kitchen door.*) Rheba, Grandpa's home—we can have dinner.

PAUL. Got a new sky rocket today, Grandpa. Wait till you see it . . . Wonder why they don't have fireworks at Commencements.

GRANDPA. Don't make enough noise. You take a good Commencement orator and he'll drown out a whole carload of fireworks. And say just as much, too.

PENNY. Don't the graduates ever say anything?

GRANDPA. No, they just sit there in cap and nightgown, get their diplomas, and then along about forty years from now they suddenly say, "Where am I?" (ESSIE *comes in from the kitchen, bringing a plate of tomatoes for the evening meal.*)

ESSIE. Hello, Grandpa. Have a nice day?

GRANDPA (*watching* ESSIE *as she puts the tomatoes on the table*). Hello-have-a-nice-day. (*Suddenly he roars at the top of his voice.*) Don't I even get kissed?

ESSIE (*kissing him*). Excuse me, Grandpa.

GRANDPA. I'll take a tomato, too. (ESSIE *passes the plate;* GRANDPA *takes one and sits with it in his hand, solemnly weighing it.*) You know, I could have used a couple of these this afternoon. . . . Play something, Ed.

(ED *at once obliges on the xylophone—something on the dreamy side. Immediately* ESSIE *is up on her toes again, drifting through the mazes of a toe dance.*)

ESSIE (*after a moment*). There was a letter came for you, Grandpa. Did you get it?

GRANDPA. Letter for me? I don't know anybody.

ESSIE. It was for you, though. Had your name on it.

GRANDPA. That's funny. Where is it?

ESSIE. I don't know. Where's Grandpa's letter, mother?

PENNY (*who has been deep in her work*). What, dear?

ESSIE (*dancing dreamily away*). Where's that letter that came for Grandpa last week?

PENNY. I don't know. (*Then, brightly.*) I remember seeing the kittens on it.

GRANDPA. Who was it from? Did you notice?

ESSIE. Yes, it was on the outside.

GRANDPA. Well, who was it?

ESSIE (*first finishing the graceful flutterings of the Dying Swan*). United States Government.

GRANDPA. Really? Wonder what *they* wanted.

ESSIE. There was one before that, too, from the same people. There was a couple of them.

GRANDPA. Well, if any more come I wish you'd give them to me.

ESSIE. Yes, Grandpa. (*A fresh flurry of dancing; the xylophone grows a little louder.*)

GRANDPA. I think I'll go to Westchester tomorrow and do a little snake-hunting.

PAUL (*who has settled down with his book some time before this*). "God is the State; the State is God."

GRANDPA. What's that?

PAUL. "God is the State; the State is God."

GRANDPA. Who says that?

PAUL. Trotzky.

GRANDPA. Well, that's all right—I thought *you* said it.

ED. It's nice for printing, you know. Good and short. (*He reaches into the type case.*) G—O—D— space—I—S—space—T—H—E (*The sound of the outer door closing, and* ALICE SYCAMORE *enters the room. A lovely, fresh young girl of about twenty-two. She is plainly* GRANDPA'S *grand-daughter, but there is something that sets her apart from the rest of the family. For one thing, she is in daily contact with the world; in addition, she seems to have escaped the tinge of mild insanity that pervades the rest of them. But she is a Sycamore for all that, and her devotion and love for them are plainly apparent. At the moment she is in a small nervous flutter, but she is doing her best to conceal it.*)

ALICE (*as she makes the rounds, kissing her grandfather, her father, her mother*). And so the beautiful princess came into the palace, and kissed her mother, and her father, and her grandfather—hi, Grandpa—and what do you think? They turned into the Sycamore family. Surprised?

ESSIE (*examining* ALICE'S *dress*). Oh, Alice, I like it. It's new, isn't it?

PENNY. Looks nice and summery.

ESSIE. Where'd you get it?

ALICE. Oh, I took a walk during lunch hour.

GRANDPA. You've been taking a lot of walks lately. That's the second new dress this week.

ALICE. Oh, I just like to brighten up the office once in a while. I'm known as the Kay Francis of Kirby & Co. . . . Well, what's new around here? In the way of plays, snakes, ballet dancing or fireworks. Dad, I'll bet you've been down in that cellar all day.

PAUL. Huh?

PENNY. I'm going back to the war play, Alice.

ESSIE. Ed, play Alice that Beethoven thing you wrote. Listen, Alice. (*Like a shot* ED *is at the xylophone again,* ESSIE *up on her toes.*)

(GRANDPA, *meanwhile, has unearthed his stamp album from under a pile of oddments in the corner, and is now busy with his magnifying glass.*)

GRANDPA. Do you know that you can mail a letter all the way from Nicaragua for two pesetos?

PENNY (*meanwhile dramatically reading one of her own deathless lines*). "Kenneth, my virginity is a priceless thing to me."

ALICE (*finding it hard to break through all this*). Listen, people. . . . Listen. (*A break in the music; she gets scattered sort of attention.*) I'm not home to dinner. A young gentleman is calling for me.

ESSIE. Really? Who is it?

PENNY. Well isn't that nice?

ALICE (*with quiet humor*). I did everything possible to keep him from coming here, but he's calling for me.

PENNY. Why don't you both stay for dinner?

ALICE. No, I want him to take you in easy doses. I've tried to prepare him a little, but don't make it any worse than you can help. Don't read him any plays, mother, and don't let any snakes bite him, Grandpa, because I like him. And I wouldn't dance for him, Essie, because we're going to the Monte Carlo ballet tonight.

GRANDPA. Can't do *anything*. Who *is* he—President of the United States?

ALICE. No, he's vice-president of Kirby & Co. Mr. Anthony Kirby, Jr.

ESSIE. The Boss' son?

PENNY. Well!

ALICE. The Boss' son. Just like in the movies.

ESSIE. That explains the new dresses.

ED. And not being home to dinner for three weeks.

ALICE. Why, you're wonderful!

PENNY (*all aglow*). Are you going to marry him?

ALICE. Oh, of course. Tonight! Meanwhile I have to go up and put on my wedding dress.

ESSIE. Is he good-looking?

ALICE (*vainly consulting her watch*). Yes, in a word. Oh dear! What time is it?

PAUL. Mr. De Pinna might know.

ED. It was about five o'clock a couple of hours ago.

ALICE. Oh I ought to know better that to ask you people . . . Will you let me know the minute he comes, please?

PENNY. Of course, Alice.

ALICE. Yes, I know, but I mean the *minute* he comes.

PENNY. Why, of course. (ALICE *looks apprehensively from one to the other; then disappears up the stairs.*) Well, what do you think of that?

GRANDPA. She seems to like him, if you ask me.

ESSIE. I should say so. She's got it bad.

PENNY. Wouldn't it be wonderful if she married him? We could have the wedding right in this room.

PAUL. Now wait a minute, Penny. This is the first time he's ever called for the girl.

PENNY. You only called for me once.

PAUL. Young people are different nowadays.

ESSIE. Oh, I don't know. Look at Ed and me. He came to dinner *once* and just stayed.

PENNY. Anyhow, I think it's wonderful. I'll bet he's crazy about her. It must be he that's been taking her out every night. (*The door bell rings*). There he is! Never mind, Rheba, I'll answer it. (*She is fluttering to the door.*) Now remember what Alice said, and be *very* nice to him.

GRANDPA (*rising*). All right—let's take a look at him.

PENNY (*at the front door, milk and honey in her voice*). Well! Welcome to our little home! I'm Alice's mother. Do come right in! Here we are! (*She reappears in the archway, piloting the stranger.*) This is Grandpa, and that's Alice's father, and Alice's sister, and her husband, Ed Carmichael. (*The family all give courteous little nods and smiles as they are introduced.*) Well now give me your hat and make yourself right at home.

THE MAN. I'm afraid you must be making a mistake.

PENNY. How's that?

THE MAN. My card.

PENNY (*reading*). "Wilbur C. Henderson. Internal Revenue Department."

HENDERSON. That's right.

GRANDPA. What can we do for you?

HENDERSON. Does a Martin Vanderhof live here?

GRANDPA. Yes, sir. That's me.

HENDERSON (*all milk and honey*). Well, Mr. Vanderhof, the Government wants to talk to you about a little matter of income tax.

PENNY. Income tax?

HENDERSON. Do you mind if I sit down?

GRANDPA. No, no. Just go right ahead.

HENDERSON (*settling himself*). Thank you. (*From above stairs the voice of* ALICE *floats down.*)

ALICE. Mother! Is that Mr. Kirby?

PENNY (*going to the stairs*). No. No, it isn't darling. It's—an internal something or other. (*to Mr. Henderson.*) Pardon me.

HENDERSON (*pulling a sheaf of papers from his pocket*). We've written you several letters about this, Mr. Vanderhof, but you have not had any reply.

GRANDPA. Oh, that's what those letters were.

ESSIE. I told you they were from the government. (MR. DE PINNA *comes up from the cellar, bearing a couple of giant firecrackers. He pauses as he sees a stranger.*)

DE PINNA. Oh, pardon me.

PAUL. Yes, Mr. De Pinna?

DE PINNA. These things are not going off, Mr. Sycamore. Look. (*He prepares to apply a match to one of them, as a startled income tax man nearly has a connniption fit. But* PAUL *is too quick for him.*)

PAUL. Ah—not here, Mr. De Pinna. Grandpa's busy.

DE PINNA. Oh. (MR. DE PINNA *and* PAUL *hurry into the hall with their firecrackers.*)

HENDERSON (*now that order has been restored*). According to our records, Mr. Vanderhof, you have never paid an income tax.

GRANDPA. That's right.

HENDERSON. Why not?

GRANDPA. I don't believe in it.

HENDERSON. Well—you own property, don't you?

GRANDPA. Yes, sir.

HENDERSON. And you receive a yearly income from it?

GRANDPA. I do.

HENDERSON. Of—(*He consults his records.*)—between three and four thousand dollars.

GRANDPA. About that.

HENDERSON. You've been receiving it for years.

GRANDPA. I have. 1901, if you want the exact date.

HENDERSON. Well, the Government is only concerned from 1914 on. That's when the income tax started.

GRANDPA. Well?

HENDERSON. Well—it seems, Mr. Vanderhof, that you owe the Government twenty-two years' back income tax.

ED. Wait a minute! You can't go back that far—that's outlawed.

HENDERSON (*calmly regarding him*). What's *your* name?

ED. What difference does that make?

HENDERSON. Ever file an income tax return?

ED. No, sir.

HENDERSON. What was your income last year?

ED. Ah—twenty-eight dollars and fifty cents, wasn't it Essie? (ESSIE *gives a quick assent; the income tax man dismisses the whole matter with an impatient wave of the hand and returns to bigger game.*)

HENDERSON. Now, Mr. Vanderhof, you know there's quite a penalty for not filing an income tax return.

PENNY. Penalty?

GRANDPA. Look, Mr. Henderson, let me ask you something.

HENDERSON. Well?

GRANDPA. Suppose I pay you this money—mind you, I don't say I'm going to do it—but just for the sake of argument—what's the Government going to do with it?

HENDERSON. How do you mean?

GRANDPA. Well, what do I get for my money? If I go into Macy's and buy something, there it *is*—I see it. What's the government give me?

HENDERSON. Why, the Government gives you everything. It protects you.

GRANDPA. What from?

HENDERSON. Well—invasion. Foreigners that might come over here and take everything you've got.

GRANDPA. Oh, I don't think they're going to do that.

HENDERSON. If you didn't pay an income tax, they would. How do you think the Government keeps up the Army and Navy? All those battleships . . .

GRANDPA. Last time we used battleships was in the Spanish-American War, and what did we get out of it? Cuba—and we gave that back. I wouldn't mind paying if it were something sensible.

HENDERSON (*beginning to get annoyed*). Well, what about Congress, and the Supreme Court, and the President? We've got to pay *them*, don't we?

GRANDPA (*ever so calmly*). Not with my money—no, sir.

HENDERSON (*furious*). Now wait a minute! I'm not here to argue with you. All I know is that you haven't paid an income tax and you've got to pay it!

GRANDPA. They've got to show me.

HENDERSON (*furious*). We *don't* have to show you! I just told you! All those buildings down in Washington, and Interstate Commerce, and the Constitution!

GRANDPA. The Constitution was paid for long ago. And Interstate Commerce—what *is* Interstate Commerce, anyhow?

HENDERSON (*with murderous calm*). There are forty-eight states—see? And if there weren't Interstate Commerce, nothing could go from one state to another. See?

GRANDPA. Why not? They got fences?

HENDERSON. No, they haven't got fences! They've got *laws!* . . . My God, I never came across anything like this before!

GRANDPA. Well, I might pay about seventy-five dollars, but that's all it's worth.

HENDERSON. You'll pay every cent, like everybody else!

ED (*who has lost interest*). Listen, Essie—listen to this a minute. (*The xylophone again;* ESSIE *goes into her dance.*)

HENDERSON (*going right ahead, battling against the music*). And let me tell you something else! You'll go to jail if you don't pay, do you hear that? There's a law, and if you think you're bigger than the law, you've got another think coming! You'll hear from the United States Government, that's all I can say! (*He is backing out of the room.*)

GRANDPA (*quietly*). Look out for those snakes.

HENDERSON (*jumping*). Jesus! (*Out in the hall, and not more than a foot or two behind* MR. HENDERSON, *the firecracker boys are now ready to test that little bomber. It goes off with a terrific detonation, and* MR. HENDERSON *jumps a full foot. He wastes no time at all in getting out of there.*)

PAUL (*coming back into the room*). How did that sound to you folks?

GRANDPA (*quite judicially*). I liked it.

PENNY. My goodness, he was mad, wasn't he?

GRANDPA. Oh, it wasn't his fault. It's just that the whole thing is so silly.

PENNY (*suddenly finding herself with a perfectly good Panama in her hand*). He forgot his hat.

GRANDPA. What size is it?

PENNY (*Peering into its insides*). Seven and an eighth.

GRANDPA. Just right for me.

DE PINNA. Who was that fellow, anyhow? (*Again the door bell.*)

PENNY. This *must* be Mr. Kirby.

PAUL. Better make sure this time.

PENNY. Yes, I will. (*She disappears.*)

ESSIE. I hope he's good-looking.

PENNY (*heard at the door*). How do you do?

A MAN'S VOICE. Good evening.

PENNY (*taking no chances*). Is this Mr. Anthony Kirby, Jr.?

TONY. Yes.

PENNY (*giving her all*). Well, Mr. Kirby, come right in! We've been expecting you. Come right in! (*They come into sight;* PENNY *expansively addresses the family.*) This is *really* Mr. Kirby! Now, I'm Alice's mother, and that's *Mr.* Sycamore, and Alice's grandfather, and her sister Essie, and Essie's husband. (*There are a few mumbled greetings.*) There! Now you know *all* of us, Mr. Kirby. Give me your hat and make yourself right at home. (TONY KIRBY *comes a few steps into the room. He is a personable young man, not long out of Yale, and, as we will presently learn, even more recently out of Cambridge. Although he fits all the physical requirements of a Boss' son, his face has something of the idealist in it. All in all, a very nice young man.*)

TONY. How do you do? (*Again the voice of the vigilant* ALICE *floats down from upstairs.* "Is that Mr. Kirby, mother?")

PENNY (*shouting up the stairs*). Yes, Alice. He's lovely!

ALICE (*Aware of storm signals*). I'll be right down.

PENNY. Do sit down, Mr. Kirby.

TONY. Thank you. (*A glance at the dinner table.*) I hope I'm not keeping you from dinner?

GRANDPA. No, no. Have a tomato?

TONY. No, thank you.

PENNY (*producing the candy-filled skull*). How about a piece of candy?

TONY (*eyeing the container*). Ah—no, thanks.

PENNY. Oh, I forgot to introduce Mr. De Pinna. This is Mr. De Pinna, Mr. Kirby. (*An exchange of "How do you do's?"*)

DE PINNA. Wasn't I reading about your father in the newspaper the other day? Didn't he get indicted or something?

TONY (*smiling*). Hardly that. He just testified before the Securities Commission.

DE PINNA. Oh.

PENNY (*sharply*). Yes, of course. I'm sure there was nothing crooked about it, Mr. De Pinna. As a matter of fact—(*She is now addressing* TONY.)— Alice has often told us what a lovely man your father is.

TONY. Well, I know father couldn't get along without Alice. She knows more about the business than any of us.

ESSIE. You're awful young, Mr. Kirby, aren't you, to be vice-president of a big place like that.

TONY. Well, you know what that means, vice-president. All I have is a desk with my name on it.

PENNY. Is that all? Don't you get any salary?

TONY (*with a laugh*). Well, a little. More than I'm worth, I'm afraid.

PENNY. Now you're just being modest.

GRANDPA. Sounds kind of dull to me—Wall Street. Do you like it?

TONY. Well, the hours are short. And I haven't been there very long.

GRANDPA. Just out of college, huh?

TONY. Well, I knocked around for a while first. Just sort of had fun.

GRANDPA. What did you do? Travel?

TONY. For a while. Then I went to Cambridge for a year.

GRANDPA (*nodding*). England.

TONY. That's right.

GRANDPA. Say, what's the English commencement like? Did you see any?

TONY. Oh, very impressive.

GRANDPA. They are, huh?

TONY. Anyhow, now the fun's over, and—I'm facing the world.

PENNY. You've certainly got a good start, Mr. Kirby. Vice-president, and a rich father.

TONY. Well, that's hardly my fault.

PENNY (*brightly*). So now I suppose you're all ready to settle down and—get married.

PAUL. Come now, Penny, I'm sure Mr. Kirby knows his own mind.

PENNY. I wasn't making up his mind for him—was I Mr. Kirby?

TONY. That's quite all right, Mrs. Sycamore.

PENNY (*to the others*). You see?

ESSIE. You musn't rush him, mother.

PENNY. Well, all I meant was he's bound to get married, and suppose the wrong girl gets him? (*The descending* ALICE *mercifully comes to* TONY'S *rescue at this moment. Her voice is heard from the stairs.*)

ALICE. Well, here I am, a vision in white. (*She comes into the room—and very lovely indeed.*) Apparently you've had time to get acquainted.

PENNY. Oh, yes, indeed. We were just having a delightful talk about love and marriage.

ALICE. Oh, dear. (*She turns to* TONY.) I'm sorry. I came down as fast as I could.

RHEBA (*bringing a platter of sliced watermelon*). God damn those flies in the kitchen. . . . Oh, Miss Alice, you look beautiful. Where you going?

ALICE (*making the best of it*). I'm going out, Rheba.

RHEBA (*noticing* TONY). Stepping, huh? (*The door bell sounds.*)

ESSIE. That must be Kolenkhov.

ALICE (*uneasily*). I think we'd better go, Tony.

TONY. All right. (*Before they can escape, however,* DONALD *emerges from the kitchen, bearing a tray.*)

DONALD. Grandpa, you take cream on your corn-flakes? I forget.

GRANDPA. Half and half, Donald. (*The voice of* BORIS KOLENKHOV *booms from the outer door.*)

KOLENKHOV. Ah, my little Rhebishka!

RHEBA (*with a scream of laughter*). Yassuh, Mr. Kolenkhov!

KOLENKHOV. I am so hungry I could even eat my little Rhebishka! (*He appears in the archway, his great arm completley encircling the delighted* RHEBA. MR. KOLENKHOV *is one of* RHEBA'S *pets, and if you like Russians he might be one of yours. He is enormous, hairy, loud, and very, very Russian. His appearance in the archway still further traps* ALICE *and* TONY.) Grandpa, what do you think? I have had a letter from Russia! The Second Five Year Plan is a failure! (*He lets out a laugh that shakes the rafters.*)

ESSIE. I practiced today, Mr. Kolenkhov!

KOLENKHOV (*with a deep Russian bow*). My Pavlowa! (*another bow.*) Madame Sycamore! . . . My little Alice! (*He kisses her hand.*) Never have I seen you look so magnificent.

ALICE. Thank you, Mr. Kolenkhov. Tony, this is Mr. Kolenkhov, Essie's dancing teacher. Mr. Kirby.

TONY. How do you do? (*A click of the heels and a bow from* KOLENKHOV.)

ALICE (*determined, this time*). And now we really *must* go. Excuse me, Mr. Kolenkhov—we're going to the Monte Carlo ballet.

KOLENKHOV (*at the top of his tremendous voice*). The Monte Carlo ballet! It *stinks!*

ALICE (*panicky now*). Yes. . . . Well—goodbye, everybody. Goodbye.

TONY. Goodbye. I'm so glad to have met you all. (*A chorus of answering "Good-byes" from the family. The young people are gone.*)

KOLENKHOV (*still furious*). The Monte Carlo ballet!

PENNY. Isn't Mr. Kirby lovely? . . . Come on, everybody! Dinner's ready!

ED (*pulling up a chair*). I thought he was a nice fellow, didn't you?

ESSIE. Mm. And so good-looking.

PENNY. And he had such nice manners. Did you notice, Paul? Did you notice his manners?

PAUL. I certainly did. You were getting pretty personal with him.

PENNY. Oh, now Paul . . . Anyhow, he's a very nice young man.

DE PINNA (*as he seats himself*). He looks like a cousin of mine.

KOLENKHOV. Bakst! Diaghlieff! *Then* you had the *ballet!*

PENNY. I think if they get married here I'll put the altar right where the snakes are. You wouldn't mind, Grandpa, would you?

ESSIE. Oh, they'll want to get married in a church. His family and everything.

GRANDPA (*tapping on a plate for silence*). Quiet, everybody! Quiet! (*They are immediately silent—Grace is about to be pronounced.* GRANDPA *pauses a moment for heads to bow, then raises his eyes heavenward. He clears his throat and proceeds to say Grace.*) Well, Sir, we've been getting along pretty good for quite a while now, and we're certainly much obliged. Remember, all we ask is just to go along and be happy in our own sort of way. Of course we want to keep our health, but as far as anything else is concerned, we'll leave it to You. Thank You. (*The heads come up as* RHEBA *comes through the door with a steaming platter.*) So the Second Five Year Plan is a failure, eh, Kolenkhov?

KOLENKHOV (*booming*). Catastrophic! (*He reaches across the table and spears a piece of bread. The family, too, is busily plunging in.*)

THE CURTAIN IS DOWN

SCENE II

Late the same night. The house is in darkness save for a light in the hall.

Somewhere in the back regions an accordion is being played. Then quiet. Then the stillness of the night is suddenly broken by a good loud BANG! from the cellar. Somewhere in the nether regions, one of the Sycamore's is still at work.

Once more all is quiet, then the sound of a key in the outer door. The voices of ALICE *and* TONY *drift through.*

ALICE. I could see them dance every night of the week. I think they're marvelous.

TONY. They are, aren't they? But of course just walking inside *any* theatre gives *me* a thrill.

ALICE (*as they come into sight in the hallway*). It's been *so* lovely, Tony. I hate to have it over.

TONY. Oh, is it over? Do I have to go right away?

ALICE. Not if you don't want to.

TONY. I don't.

ALICE. Would you like a cold drink.

TONY. Wonderful.

ALICE (*pausing to switch on the light*). "I'll see what's in the ice-box. Want to come along?

TONY. I'd follow you to the ends of the earth.

ALICE. Oh, just to the kitchen is enough. (*They go out. A pause, a ripple of laughter from the kitchen, then they return.* ALICE *is carrying a couple of glasses,* TONY *brings two bottles of ginger ale and an opener.*) Lucky you're not hungry, Mr. K. An ice-box full of cornflakes. That gives you a rough idea of the Sycamores.

TONY (*walking away with the opener*). Of course, why they make these bottle openers for Singer midgets I never *was* able to—ah! (*As the bottle opens.*) All over my coat.

ALICE. I'll take mine in a glass, if you don't mind.

TONY (*pouring*). There you are. A foaming beaker.

ALICE. Anyhow, it's cold.

TONY (*pouring his own*). Now if you'll please be seated, I'd like to offer a toast.

ALICE (*settling herself*). We are seated.

TONY. Miss Sycamore—(*He raises his glass on high.*)—to you.

ALICE. Thank you, Mr. Kirby. (*Lifting her own glass.*) To you. (*They both drink.*)

TONY (*happily*). I wouldn't trade one minute of this evening for—all the rice in China.

ALICE. Really?

TONY. Cross my heart.

ALICE (*a little sigh of contentment. Then shyly*). Is there much rice in China?

TONY. Terrific. Didn't you read "The Good Earth?" (*She laughs. They are silent for a moment.*) I suppose I ought to go.

ALICE. Is it very late?

TONY (*looks at his watch*). Very. (ALICE *gives a little nod. Time doesn't matter.*) I don't want to go.

ALICE. I don't want you to.

TONY. All right, I won't. (*Silence again.*) When do you get your vacation?

ALICE. Last two weeks in August.

TONY. I might take mine then, too.

ALICE. Really?

TONY. What are you going to do?

ALICE. I don't know. I hadn't thought much about it.

TONY. Going away, do you think?

ALICE. I might not. I like the city in the summer time.

TONY. I do too.

ALICE. But you always go up to Maine, don't you?

TONY. Why—yes, but I'm sure I *would* like the city in the summer time. That is, I'd like it if—Oh, you know what I mean, Alice. I'd love it if *you* were here.

ALICE. Well—it'd be nice if you were here, Tony.

TONY. You know what you're saying, don't you?

ALICE. What?

TONY. That you'd rather spend the summer with me than anybody else.

ALICE. It looks that way, doesn't it?

TONY. Well, if it's true about the summer, how would you feel about—the winter?

ALICE (*seeming to weigh the matter*). Yes, I'd like that, too.

TONY (*tremulous*). Then comes spring—and autumn. If you could—see your way clear about those, Miss Sycamore. . . .

ALICE (*again a little pause*). Yes.

TONY. I guess that's the whole year. We haven't forgot anything, have we?

ALICE. No.

TONY. Well, then—(*Another pause; their eyes meet. And at this moment,* PENNY *is heard from the stairway.*)

PENNY. Is that you, Alice? What time is it? (*She comes into the room, wrapped in a bathrobe.*) Oh! (*In sudden embarrassment.*) Excuse me, Mr. Kirby. I had no idea—that is, I—(*She senses the situation.*) I didn't mean to interrupt anything.

TONY. Not at all, Mrs. Sycamore.

ALICE (*quietly*). No, mother.

PENNY. I just came down for a manuscript—(*Fumbling at her table.*)—then you can go right ahead. Ah, here it is. "Sex Takes a Holiday." Well—good-night, Mr. Kirby.

TONY. Good-night, Mrs. Sycamore.

PENNY. Oh, I think you can call me Penny, don't you, Alice? At least I hope so. (*With a little laugh she vanishes up the stairs.*) (*Before* PENNY'S *rippling laugh quite dies, BANG! from the cellar.* TONY *jumps.*)

ALICE (*quietly*). It's all right, Tony. That's father.

TONY. This time of night?

ALICE (*ominously*). *Any* time of night. Any time of day. (*She stands silent. In the pause,* TONY *gazes at her fondly.*)

TONY. You're more beautiful, more lovely, more adorable than anyone else in the whole world.

ALICE (*as he starts to embrace her*). Don't, Tony. I can't.

TONY. What?

ALICE. I can't, Tony.

TONY. My dear, just because your mother—all mothers are like that, Alice, and Penny's a darling. You see, I'm even calling her Penny.

ALICE. I don't mean that. (*She faces him squarely*.) Look, Tony. This is something I should have said a long time ago, but I didn't have the courage. I let myself be swept away because—because I loved you so.

TONY. Darling!

ALICE. No, wait, Tony. I want to make it clear to you. You're of a different world—a whole different kind of people. Oh, I don't mean money or socially—that's too silly. But your family and mine—it just wouldn't work, Tony. It just wouldn't work. (*Again an interruption. This time it is* ED *and* ESSIE, *returning from the neighborhood movie. We hear their voices at the door, deep in an argument.* ED: "*All right, have it your way. She can't dance. That's why they pay her all that money—because she can't dance.*" *And then* ESSIE: "*Well, I don't call that dancing, what she does.*") (*They come into sight.*)

ESSIE. Oh, hello. (*There is an exchange of greetings, a note of constraint in* ALICE'S *voice. But* ESSIE *goes right ahead.*) Look! What do *you* think? Ed and I just saw Fred Astaire and Ginger Rogers. Do you think she can dance, Mr. Kirby?

TONY (*mildly taken aback by this*). Why yes—I always thought so.

ESSIE. What does she do, anyhow? Now look— you're Fred Astaire and I'm Ginger Rogers. (*She drapes herself against* TONY, *a la Ginger Rogers.*)

ALICE. Essie, please.

ESSIE. I just want to use him for a minute. . . . Look, Mr. Kirby—(*Her arms go round his neck, her cheek against his.*)

ALICE (*feeling that it's time to take action*). Essie, you're just as good as Ginger Rogers. We all agree.

ESSIE (*triumphantly*). You see, Ed?

ED. Yeh. . . . Come on, Essie—we're butting in here.

ESSIE. Oh, they've been together all evening. . . . Good night, Mr. Kirby. (*An exchange of goodnights—it looks as though the* CARMICHAELS *are really going upstairs before the whole thing gets too embarrassing. Then* ED *turns casually to* ESSIE *in the doorway.*)

ED. Essie, did you ask Grandpa about us having a baby?

ESSIE (*as they ascend the stairs*). Yes—he said go right ahead.

ALICE (*when they are gone*). You see? That's what it would be like, always.

TONY. But I didn't mind that. Besides, darling, we're not going to live with our families. It's just you and I.

ALICE. No, it isn't—it's never quite that. I love them, Tony—I love them deeply. Some people could cut away, but I couldn't. I know they do rather strange things—I never know what to expect next—but they're gay, and they're fun, and—I don't know— there's a kind of nobility about them. That may sound silly, but I mean—the way they just don't care about things that other people give their whole lives to. They're—really wonderful, Tony.

TONY. Alice, you talk as though only you could understand them. That's not true. Why, I fell in love with them tonight.

ALICE. But your family, Tony. I'd want *you* and everything about you, everything about *me*, to be— one. I couldn't start out with a part of me that you didn't share, and part of you that I didn't share. Unless we were all one—you, and *your* mother and father—I'd be miserable. And they never can be, Tony—I know it. They couldn't be.

TONY. Alice, every family has got curious little traits. What of it? My father raises orchids at ten thousand dollars a bulb. Is that sensible? My mother believes in spiritualism. That's just as bad as your mother writing plays, isn't it?

ALICE. It goes deeper, Tony. Your mother believes in spiritualism because it's fashionable. And your father raises orchids because he can afford to. My mother writes plays because eight years ago a typewriter was delivered here by mistake.

TONY. Darling, what *of* it?

ALICE. And look at Grandpa. Thirty-five years ago he just quit business one day. He started up to his office in the elevator and came right down again. He just stopped. He could have been a rich man, but he said it took too much time. So for thirty-five years he's just collected snakes and gone to circuses and commencements. It never occurs to any of them—(*As if to prove her point, they are suddenly interupted at this moment by the entrance of* DONALD *from the kitchen. It is a* DONALD *who has plainly not expected to encounter midnight visitors, for he is simply dressed in a long nightgown and a somewhat shorter bathrobe—a costume that permits a generous expanse of white nightshirt down around the legs, and, below that, a couple of very black shins. His appearance, incidentally, explains where all that music has been coming from, for an accordion is slung over his shoulder.*)

DONALD (*surprised, but not taken aback*). Oh, excuse me. I didn't know you folks was in here.

ALICE (*resigned*). It's all right, Donald.

DONALD. Rheba kind of fancied some candy, and— (*His gaze is roaming the room.*)—oh, there it is. (*He picks up* PENNY'S *skull, if you know what we mean.*) You-all don't want it, do you?

ALICE. No, Donald. Go right ahead.

DONALD. Thanks. (*He feels that the occasion calls for certain amenities.*) Have a nice evening?

ALICE. Yes, Donald.

DONALD. Nice dinner?

ALICE (*restraining herself*). Yes, Donald.

DONALD. The ballet nice?

ALICE (*entirely too quietly*). Yes, Donald.

DONALD (*summing it all up*). That's nice. (*He goes—and* ALICE *bursts forth.*)

ALICE. Now! Now do you see what I mean? Could you explain Donald to your father? Could you explain Grandpa? You couldn't, Tony, you couldn't! I should have known! I did know! I love you, Tony, but I love them too! And it's no use, Tony! It's no use! (*She is weeping now in spite of herself.*)

TONY (*quietly*). There's only one thing you've said that matters—that makes any sense at all. You love me.

ALICE. But, Tony, I know so well . . .

TONY. My darling, don't you think other people have had the same problem? Everybody's got a family.

ALICE (*through her tears*). But not like mine.

TONY. That doesn't stop people who love each other. . . . Darling! Darling, won't you trust me, and go on loving me, and forget everything else?

ALICE. How can I?

TONY. Because nothing can keep us apart. You know that. You must know it. Just as I know it. (*He takes her in his arms.*) They want you to be happy, don't they? They *must*.

ALICE. Of course they do. But they can't change, Tony. I wouldn't want them to change.

TONY. They won't have to change. They're charming, lovable people, just as they are. You're worrying about something that may never come up.

ALICE. Oh, Tony, am I?

TONY. All that matters right now is that we love each other. That's right, isn't it?

ALICE (*whispering*). Yes.

TONY. Well, then!

ALICE (*in his arms*). Tony, Tony!

TONY. Now! I'd like to see a little gayety around here. Young gentleman calling, and getting engaged and everything.

ALICE (*smiling up into his face*). What do I say?

TONY. Well, first you thank the young man for getting engaged to you.

ALICE. Thank you, Mr. Kirby, for getting engaged to me.

TONY. And then you tell him what it was about him that first took your girlish heart.

ALICE. The back of your head.

TONY. Huh?

ALICE. Uh-huh. It wasn't your charm, and it wasn't your money—it was the back of your head. I just happened to like it.

TONY. What happened when I turned around?

ALICE. Oh, I got used to it after a while.

TONY. I see . . . Oh, Alice, think of it. We're pretty lucky, aren't we?

ALICE. I know that *I* am. The luckiest girl in the world.

TONY. I'm not exactly unlucky myself.

ALICE. It's wonderful, isn't it?

TONY. Yes . . . Lord, but I'm happy.

ALICE. Are you, Tony?

TONY. Terribly . . . And now—good-night, my dear. Until tomorrow.

ALICE. Good-night.

TONY. Isn't it wonderful we work in the same office? Otherwise I'd be hanging around *here* all day.

ALICE. Won't it be funny in the office tomorrow—seeing each other and just going on as though nothing had happened?

TONY. Thank God I'm vice-president. I can dictate to you all day. "Dear Miss Sycamore: I love you, I love you, I love you."

ALICE. Oh darling! You're such a fool.

TONY (*an arm about her as he starts toward the hallway*). Why don't you meet me in the drugstore in the morning—before you go up to the office? I'll have millions of things to say to you by then.

ALICE. All right.

TONY. And then lunch, and then dinner tomorrow night.

ALICE. Oh, Tony! What will people say?

TONY. It's got to come out some time. In fact, if you know a good housetop, I'd like to do a little shouting. (*She laughs—a happy little ripple. They are out of sight in the hallway by this time; their voices become inaudible.*)

(PAUL, *at this point, decides to call it a day down in the cellar. He comes through the door, followed by* MR. DE PINNA. *He is carrying a small metal container, filled with powder.*)

PAUL. Yes, sir, Mr. De Pinna, we did a good day's work.

DE PINNA. That's what. Five hundred Black Panthers, three hundred Willow Trees, and eight dozen Junior Kiddie Bombers. (ALICE *comes back from the hallway, still under the spell of her love.*)

PAUL. Why, hello, Alice. You just come in?

ALICE (*softly*). No. No, I've been home quite a while.

PAUL. Have a nice evening? Say, I'd like you to take a look at this new red fire we've got.

ALICE (*almost singing it*). I had a beautiful evening, father.

PAUL. Will you turn out the lights, Mr. De Pinna? I want Alice to get the full effect.

ALICE (*who hasn't heard a word*). What, father?

PAUL. Take a look at this new red fire. It's beautiful. (MR. DE PINNA *switches the lights out,* PAUL *touches a match to the powder. The red fire blazes, shedding a soft glow over the room.*) There! What do you think of it? Isn't it beautiful?

ALICE (*radiant; her face aglow, her voice soft*). Yes, father. Everything is beautiful. It's the most beautiful red fire in the world! (*She rushes to him and throws her arms about him, almost unable to bear her own happiness.*)

CURTAIN

ACT TWO

A week later, and the family has just risen from the dinner table. Two or three of them have drifted out of the room, but GRANDPA *and* PAUL *still sit over their coffee cups. There is, however, a newcomer in the room. Her name is* GAY WELLINGTON, *and, as we will presently guess, she is an actress, a nymphomaniac, and a terrible souse. At the moment she sits with a gin bottle in one hand and a glass in the other, and is having a darned good time. Hovering over her, script in hand, is a slightly worried* PENNY. ED *is watching the proceedings from somewhere in the vicinice of the printing press, and* DONALD *, leisurely clearing the table, has paused to see if* MISS WELLINGTON *can really swallow that one more drink of gin that she is about to tackle. She does, and another besides.* PENNY *finally decides to make a try.*

PENNY. I'm ready to read the play now, Miss Wellington, if you are.

GAY WELLINGTON. Just a minute, dearie—just a minute. (*The gin again.*)

PENNY. The only thing is—I hope you won't mind my mentioning this, but—you don't drink when you're acting, do you, Miss Wellington? I'm just asking, of course.

GAY. I'm glad you brought it up. Once a play opens, I never touch a drop. Minute I enter a stage door, this bottle gets put away till intermission.

GRANDPA (*who plainly has his doubts*). Have you been on the stage a long time, Miss Wellington?

GAY. All my life. I've played everything. Ever see "Peg o' my Heart"?

GRANDPA. Yes, indeed.

GAY (*with that fine logic for which the inebriated brain is celebrated*). I saw it too. Great show. (*She staggers backwards a bit, but recovers herself just in time.*) My! Hot night, ain't it?

DONALD (*ever helpful*). Want me to open a window, Miss Wellington?

GAY. No, the hell with the weather. (*She takes a second look at the dusky DONALD.*) Say, he's cute. (RHEBA, *who has entered just in time to overhear this, gives* GAY *a look that tells her in no uncertain terms to keep out of Harlem on dark nights. Then she stalks back into the kitchen,* DONALD *close on her heels.*)

DONALD (*trying to explain it all*). She's just acting, Rheba. She don't mean anything.

PENNY. Well, any time you're ready, we can go up to my room and start. I thought I'd read the play up in my room.

GAY. All right, dearie, just a minute. (*She starts to pour one more drink, then suddenly her gaze becomes transfixed. She shakes her head as though to dislodge the image, then looks again, receives verification, and starts to pour the gin back into the bottle.*) When I see snakes it's time to lay down. (*She makes for a couch in the corner, and passes right out—cold.*)

PENNY. Oh, but those are real, Miss Wellington. They're Grandpa's. . . . Oh, dear! I hope she's not going to—(*Shaking her*). Miss Wellington! Miss Wellington!

ED. She's out like a light.

PAUL. Better let her sleep it off.

DONALD (*carrying the news into the kitchen*). Rheba, Miss Wellington just passed out. (*From the nether recesses we hear* RHEBA'S *reaction—an emphatic "Good!"*)

PENNY. Do you think she'll be all right?

GRANDPA. Yes, but I wouldn't cast her in a religious play.

PENNY. Well, I suppose I'll just have to wait. I wonder if I shouldn't cover her up.

GRANDPA. Next time you meet an actress on the top of a bus, Penny. I think I'd *send* her the play, instead of bringing her home to read it.

ESSIE (*as* ED *starts in with the printing press*). Ed, I wish you'd stop printing and take those Love Dreams around. They're in the kitchen.

ED. I will. I just want to finish up these circulars.

ESSIE. Well, do that later, can't you? You've got to get back in time to play for me when Kolenkhov comes.

GRANDPA. Kolenkhov coming tonight?

ESSIE. Yes, tomorrow night's his night, but I had to change it on account of Alice.

GRANDPA. Oh! . . . Big doings around here tomorrow night, huh?

PENNY. Isn't it exciting? You know, I'm so nervous—you'd think it was me he was engaged to, instead of Alice.

ESSIE. What do you think they'll *be* like—his mother and father? . . . Ed, what are you doing *now*?

ED. Penny, did you see the new mask I made last night? (*He reveals a new side of his character by suddenly holding a homemade mask before his face.*) Guess who it is.

PENNY. Don't tell me now, Ed. Wait a minute . . . Cleopatra.

ED (*furious*). It's Mrs. Roosevelt. (*He goes into the kitchen.*)

(PAUL, *meanwhile, has gone to a table in the corner of the room, from which he now brings a steel-like boat model, two or three feet high, puts it down on the floor, and proceeds to sit down beside it. From a large cardboard box, which he has also brought with him, he proceeds to take out additional pieces of steel and fit them into the model.*)

PAUL. You know, the nice thing about these Erector Sets, you can make so many different things with them. Last week it was the Empire State Building.

GRANDPA. What is it this week?

PAUL. The Queen Mary.

PENNY (*looking it over*). Hasn't got the right hat on. (ED *comes in from the kitchen, bringing a pile of about a dozen candy boxes, neatly wrapped, and tied together for purposes of delivery.*)

ED (as MR. DE PINNA comes in from the hall). Look. Mr. De Pinna, would you open the door and see if there's a man standing in front of the house?

ESSIE. Why, what for?

ED. Well, the last two days, when I've been out delivering, I think a man's been following me.

ESSIE. Ed, you're crazy.

ED. No, I'm not. He follows me, and he stands and watches the house.

DE PINNA. Really? (Striding out.) I'll take a look and see.

GRANDPA. I don't see what anybody would follow you for, Ed.

PENNY. Well, there's a lot of kidnapping going on, Grandpa.

GRANDPA. Yes, but not of Ed.

ED (as MR. DE PINNA returns from the hall).

DE PINNA. There's nobody out there at all.

ED. You're sure?

DE PINNA. Positive. I just saw him walk away.

ED. You see? I told you.

ESSIE. Oh, it might have been anybody, walking along the street. Ed, will you hurry and get back?

ED (picking up his boxes). Oh, all right.

DE PINNA. Want to go down now, Mr. Sycamore, and finish packing up the fireworks?

PAUL (putting the Queen Mary back on the table). Yeh, we've got to take the stuff up to Mt. Vernon in the morning. (They go into the cellar. Simultaneously the voice of ALICE, happily singing, is heard as she descends the stairs.)

ALICE. Mother, may I borrow some paper? I'm making out a list for Rheba tomorrow night.

PENNY. Yes, dear. Here's some.

ALICE (as she sights MISS WELLINGTON). Why, what happened to your actress friend? Is she giving a performance?

PENNY. No, she's not acting, Alice. She's really drunk.

ALICE. Essie, you're going to give Rheba the kitchen all day tomorrow, aren't you? Because she'll need it.

ESSIE. Of course, Alice. I'm going to start some Love Dreams now, so I'll be way ahead. (She goes into the kitchen.)

ALICE. Thanks, dear . . . Look, mother, I'm coming home at three o'clock tomorrow. Will you have everything down in the cellar by that time? The typewriter, and the snakes, and the xylophone, and the printing press . . .

GRANDPA. And Miss Wellington.

ALICE. And Miss Wellington. That'll give me time to arrange the table, and fix the flowers.

GRANDPA. The Kirbys are certainly going to get the wrong impression of this house.

ALICE. You'll do all that, won't you, mother?

PENNY. Of course, dear.

ALICE. And I think we'd better have cocktails ready by seven-fifteen, in case they happen to come a little early. . . . I wonder if I ought to let Rheba cook the dinner. What do you think, Grandpa?

GRANDPA. Now, Alice, I wouldn't worry. From what I've seen of the boy I'm sure the Kirbys are very nice people, and if everything isn't so elaborate tomorrow night, it's all right too.

ALICE. Darling, I'm not trying to impress them, or pretend we're anything that we aren't. I just want everything to—to go off well.

GRANDPA. No reason why it shouldn't, Alice.

PENNY. We're all going to do everything we can to make it a nice party.

ALICE. Oh, my darlings, I love you. You're the most wonderful family in the world, and I'm the happiest girl in the world. I didn't know anyone could be so happy. He's so wonderful, Grandpa. Why, just seeing him—you don't know what it does to me.

GRANDPA. Just seeing him. Just seeing him for lunch, and dinner, and until four o'clock in the morning, and at nine o'clock next morning you're at the office again and there he is. You just see him, huh?

ALICE. I don't care! I'm in love. (She swings open the kitchen door.) Rheba! Rheba! (She goes into the kitchen.)

GRANDPA. Nice, isn't it? Nice to see her so happy.

PENNY. I remember when I was engaged to Paul— how happy I was. And you know, I still feel that way.

GRANDPA. I know . . . Nice the way Ed and Essie get along too, isn't it?

PENNY. And Donald and Rheba, even though they're *not* married . . . Do you suppose Mr. De Pinna will every marry anyone, Grandpa?

GRANDPA (*a gesture toward the couch*). Well, there's Miss Wellington.

PENNY. Oh, dear, I *wish* she'd wake up. If we're going to read the play tonight—(MR. DE PINNA *comes up from the cellar, bringing along a rather large-sized unframed painting.*)

DE PINNA. Mrs. Sycamore, look what I found! (*He turns the canvas around, revealing a portrait of a somewhat lumpy discus thrower, in Roman costume—or was it Greek?*) Remember?

PENNY. Why, of course. It's my painting of you as The Discus Thrower. Look, Grandpa.

GRANDPA. I remember it. Say, you've gotten a little bald, haven't you, Mr. De Pinna?

DE PINNA (*running a hand over his completely hairless head*). Is it very noticeable?

PENNY. Well, it was a long time ago—just before I stopped painting. Let me see—that's eight years.

DE PINNA. Too bad you never finished it, Mrs. Sycamore.

PENNY. I always meant to finish it, Mr. De Pinna, but I just started to write a play one day and that was that. I never painted again.

GRANDPA. Just as well, too. *I* was going to have to strip next.

DE PINNA (*meditatively*). Who would have thought, that day I came to deliver the ice, that I was going to stay here for eight years?

GRANDPA. The milkman was here for five, just ahead of you.

DE PINNA. Why did he leave, anyhow? I forget.

GRANDPA. He didn't leave. He died.

PENNY. He was such a nice man. Remember the funeral, Grandpa? We never knew his name and it was kind of hard to get a certificate.

GRANDPA. What was the name we finally made up for him?

PENNY. Martin Vanderhof. We gave him *your* name.

GRANDPA. Oh, yes, I remember.

PENNY. It was a lovely night, because otherwise he never would have got all those flowers.

GRANDPA. Certainly was. And it didn't hurt *me* any. Not bothered with mail anymore, and I haven't had a telephone call from that day to this. (*He catches an unwary fly and drops it casually into the snake solarium.*)

PENNY. Yes, it was really a wonderful idea.

DE PINNA (*with the picture*). I wish you'd finish this sometime, Mrs. Sycamore. I'd kind of like to have it.

PENNY. You know what, Mr. De Pinna? I think I'll do some work on it. Right tonight.

DE PINNA. Say! Will you? (*The door bell rings.*)

PENNY (*peering at the prostrate* GAY). I don't think she's going to wake up anyhow. . . . Look, Mr. De Pinna! You go down in the cellar and bring up the easel and get into your costume. Is it still down there?

DE PINNA (*excited*). I think so! (*He darts into the cellar.*)

PENNY. Now, where did I put my palette and brushes? (*She dashes up the stairs as the voice of* KOLENKHOV *is heard at the door, booming, of course.*)

KOLENKHOV. Rhebishka! My little Rhebishka!

RHEBA (*delighted, as usual*). Yassuh, Mr. Kolenkhov!

PENNY (*as she goes up the stairs*). Hello, Mr. Kolenkhov. Essie's in the kitchen.

KOLENKHOV. Madame Sycamore, I greet you! (*His great arm again encircling* RHEBA, *as he drags her protestingly into the room.*) Tell me, Grandpa—what should I do about Rhebishka! I keep telling her she would make a great toe dancer, but she laughs only!

RHEBA (*breaking away*). No, suh! I couldn't get up on my toes, Mr. Kolenkhov! I got corns! (*She goes into the kitchen.*)

KOLENKHOV (*calling after her*). Rhebishka, you could wear diamonds! (*Suddenly he sights the portrait of* MR. DE PINNA.) What is that?

GRANDPA (*who has taken up his stamp album again*). It's a picture of Mr. De Pinna. Penny painted it.

KOLENKHOV (*summing it up*). It stinks.

GRANDPA. I know. (*He indicates the figure on the couch.*) How do you like that?

KOLENKHOV (*peering over*). What is *that?*

GRANDPA. She's an actress. Friend of Penny's.

KOLENKHOV. She is drunk—no?

GRANDPA. She is drunk—yes . . . How are *you*, Kolenkhov?

KOLENKHOV. Magnificent! Life is chasing me around inside of me, like a squirrel.

GRANDPA. 'Tis, huh? . . . What's new in Russia? Any more letters from your friend in Moscow?

KOLENKHOV. I have just heard from him. I saved for you the stamp. (*He hands it over.*)

GRANDPA (*receiving it with delight*). Thanks, Kolenkhov.

KOLENKHOV. They have sent him to Siberia.

GRANDPA. That so? How's he like it?

KOLENKHOV. He has escaped and gone back to Moscow. He will get them yet, if they do not get him. The Soviet Government! I could take the whole Soviet Government and—grrah! (*He crushes Stalin and all in one great paw, just as* ESSIE *comes in from the kitchen.*)

ESSIE. I'm sorry I'm late, Mr. Kolenkhov. I'll get into my dancing clothes right away.

KOLENKHOV. Tonight you will really work, Pavlowa. (*As* ESSIE *goes up the stairs.*) Tonight we will take something new.

GRANDPA. Essie making any progress, Kolenkhov?

KOLENKHOV (*first making elaborately sure that* ESSIE *is gone.*) Confidentially, she stinks.

GRANDPA. Well, as long as she's having fun. . . . (DONALD *ambles in from the kitchen, chuckling.*)

DONALD. You sure do tickle Rheba, Mr. Kolenkhov. She's laughing her head off out there.

KOLENKHOV. She is a great woman. . . . Donald, what do you think of the Soviet Government?

DONALD. The what, Mr. Kolenkhov?

KOLENKHOV. I withdraw the question. What do you think of *this* government?

DONALD. Oh, I like it fine. I'm on relief, you know.

KOLENKHOV. Oh, yes. And you like it?

DONALD. Yassuh, it's fine. Only thing is you got to go round to the place every week and collect it, and sometimes you got to stand in line pretty near half an hour. Government ought to be run better than that—don't you think, Grandpa?

GRANDPA (*as he fishes an envelope out of his pocket*). Government ought to stop sending me letters. Want me to be at the United States Marshal's office Tuesday morning at ten o'clock.

KOLENKHOV (*peering at the letter*). Ah! Income tax! They have got you, Grandpa.

GRANDPA. Mm. I'm supposed to give 'em a lot of money so as to keep Donald on relief.

DONALD. You don't say, Grandpa? You going to pay it now?

GRANDPA. That's what they want.

DONALD. You mean I can come right *here* and get it instead of standing in that line?

GRANDPA. No, Donald. You will have to waste a full half hour of your time every week.

DONALD. Well, I don't like it. It breaks up my week. (*He goes into the kitchen.*)

KOLENKHOV. He should have been in Russia when the Revolution came. Then he would have stood in line—a bread line. (*He turns to* GRANDPA.) Ah, Grandpa, what they have done to Russia. Think of it! The Grand Duchess Olga Katrina, a cousin of the Czar, she is a waitress in Child's restaurant! I ordered baked beans from her only yesterday. It broke my heart. A crazy world, Grandpa.

GRANDPA. Oh, the world's not so crazy, Kolenkhov. It's the people *in* it. Life's pretty simple if you just relax.

KOLENKHOV. How can you relax in times like these?

GRANDPA. Well, if they'd relaxed there wouldn't *be* times like these. That's just my point. Life is simple and kind of beautiful if you let it come to you. But the trouble is, people forget that. I know I did. I was right in the thick of it—fighting, and scratching, and clawing. Regular jungle. One day it just kind of struck me. I wasn't having any fun.

KOLENKHOV. So you did what?

GRANDPA. Just relaxed. Thirty-five years ago, that was. And I've been a happy man ever since. (*From somewhere or other* GRANDPA *has brought one of those colored targets that one buys at Schwartz's.*

He now hangs it up on the cellar door, picks up a handful of feathered darts, and carefully throws one at the target.)

(*At the same time* ALICE *passes through the room, en route from kitchen to the upstairs region.*)

ALICE. Good evening, Mr. Kolenkhov.

KOLENKHOV (*bowing low over her hand*). Ah, Miss Alice! I have not seen you to present my congratulations. May you be very happy and have many children. That is my prayer for you.

ALICE. Thank you, Mr. Kolenkhov. That's quite a thought. (*Singing gayly, she goes up the stairs.*)

KOLENKHOV (*looking after her*). Ah, love! That is all that is left in the world, Grandpa.

GRANDPA. Yes, but there's plenty of that.

KOLENKHOV. And soon Stalin will take that away, too. I tell you Grandpa—(*He stops as* PENNY *comes down the stairs—a living example of what the well-dressed artist should wear. She has on an artist's smock over her dress, a flowing black tie, and a large black velvet tam-o'-shanter, worn at a rakish angle. She carries a palette and an assortment of paints and brushes.*)

PENNY. Seems so nice to get into my art things again. They still look all right, don't they, Grandpa?

GRANDPA. Yes, indeed.

KOLENKHOV. You are a breath of Paris, Madame Sycamore.

PENNY. Oh, thank you, Mr. Kolenkhov.

DONALD (*coming in from the kitchen*). I didn't know you was working for the WPA.

PENNY. Oh, no, Donald. You see, I used to paint all the time, and then one day—(*The outer door slams and* ED *comes in.*)

ED (*in considerable excitement*). It happened again! There was a fellow following me every place I went!

PENNY. Nonsense, Ed. It's your imagination.

ED. No, it isn't. It happens every time I go out to deliver candy.

GRANDPA. Maybe he wants a piece of candy.

ED. It's all right for you to laugh, Grandpa, but he keeps following me.

KOLENKHOV (*somberly*). You do not know what following is. In Russia *everybody* is followed. I was followed right out of Russia.

PENNY. Of course. You see Ed—the whole thing is just imagination. (MR. DE PINNA *comes up from the cellar, ready for posing. He wears the traditional Roman costume, and he certainly cuts a figure. He is carrying* PENNY'S *easel, a discus, and a small platform for posing purposes.*) Ah here we are! . . . Right here, Mr. De Pinna.

DONALD (*suddenly getting it*). Oh, is that picture supposed to be of Mr. De Pinna?

PENNY (*sharply*). Of course it is, Donald. What's it look like—me?

DONALD (*studying the portrait*). Yes, it does—a little bit.

PENNY. Nonsense! What would I be doing with a discus?

KOLENKHOV. Ed, for tonight's lesson we use the first movement of Scheherazade.

ED. Okay.

DE PINNA (*about to mount the platform*). I hope I haven't forgot how to pose. (*He takes up the discus and strikes the classic pose of the Discus Thrower. Somehow, it is not quite convincing.*)

DONALD. What's he going to do with that thing? Throw it?

PENNY. No, no, Donald. He's just posing. . . . Mr. De Pinna, has something happened to your figure during these eight years?

DE PINNA (*pulling in his stomach*). No, I don't think it's any different. (*With a sudden snort,* GAY WELLINGTON *comes to.*)

PENNY (*immediately alert*). Yes, Miss Wellington? (*For answer,* GAY *peers first at* PENNY, *then at* MR. DE PINNA. *Then, with a strange snort, she just passes right out again.*)

PENNY. Oh, dear. (ESSIE *comes tripping down the stairs—very much the ballet dancer. She is in full costume—ballet skirt, tight white satin bodice, a garland of roses in her hair.*)

ESSIE. Sorry, Mr. Kolenkhov, I couldn't find my slippers.

KOLENKHOV (*having previously removed his coat, he now takes off his shirt, displaying an enormous hairy chest beneath his undershirt*). We have a hot night for it, my Pavlowa, but art is only achieved through perspiration.

PENNY. Why, that's wonderful, Mr. Kolenkhov. Did you hear that, Grandpa—art is only achieved through perspiration.

GRANDPA. Yes, but it helps if you've got a little talent with it. (*He returns to his dart throwing.*) Only made two bull's-eyes last night. Got to do better than that. (*He hurls a dart at the board, then his eye travels to* MISS WELLINGTON, *whose posterior offers an even easier target.*) Mind if I use Miss Wellington, Penny?

PENNY. What, Grandpa?

GRANDPA (*shakes his head*). Never mind. . . . Too easy. (GRANDPA *throws another dart at the target.*)

KOLENKHOV. You are ready? We begin! (*With a gesture he orders the music started; under* KO-LENKHOV'S *critical eye* ESSIE *begins the mazes of the dance.*) Foutte temp el levee. (ESSIE *obliges with her own idea of foutte temp el levee.*) Pirouette! . . . Come, come! You can't do that! It's eight years now. Pirouette! . . . At last . . . Entre chat . . . Entre chat! (ESSIE *leaps into the air, her feet twirling.*) No, Grandpa, you cannot relax with Stalin in Russia. The Czar relaxed, and what happened to *him?*

GRANDPA. He was too late.

ESSIE (*still leaping away*). Mr. Kolenkhov! Mr. Kolenkhov!

KOLENKHOV. If he had not relaxed the Grand Duchess Olga Katrina would not be selling baked beans today.

ESSIE (*imploringly*). Mr. Kolenkhov!

KOLENKHOV. I am sorry. (*The door bell rings.*) We go back to the pirouette.

PENNY. Could you pull in your stomach, Mr. De Pinna? . . . That's right.

KOLENKHOV. A little freer. A little freer with the hands. The whole body must work. Ed, help us with the music. The music must be free, too. (*By way of guiding* ED, KOLENKHOV *hums the music at the pace that it should go. He is even pirouetting a bit himself.*)

(*From the front door comes the murmur of voices, not quite audible over the music. Then the stunned figure of* RHEBA *comes into the archway, her eyes popping.*)

RHEBA. Mrs. Sycamore. . . . Mrs. Sycamore. (*With a gesture that has a grim foreboding in it, she motions toward the still invisible reason for her panic.*)

(*There is a second's pause, and then the reason is revealed in all its horror. The* KIRBY'S *in full evening dress, stand in the archway. All three of them.* MR. *and* MRS. KIRBY, *and* TONY.)

(PENNY *utters a stifled gasp; the others are too stunned even to do that. Their surprise at seeing the* KIRBYS, *however, is no greater that of the* KIRBYS *at the sight that is spread before them.*)

(GRANDPA, *alone of them all, rises to the situation. With a kind of old world grace, he puts away his darts and makes the guests welome.*)

GRANDPA. How do you do?

KIRBY (*uncertainly*). How do you do? (*Not that it helps any, but* MR. DE PINNA *is squirming into his bathrobe,* KOLENKHOV *is thrusting his shirt into his trousers, and* ED *is hastily getting into his coat.*)

TONY. Are we too early?

GRANDPA. No, no. It's perfectly all right—we're glad to see you.

PENNY (*getting rid of the smock and tam*). Why—yes. Only—we thought it was to be tomorrow night.

MRS. KIRBY. Tomorrow night!

KIRBY. What!

GRANDPA. Now, it's perfectly all right. Please sit right down and make yourselves at home. (*His eyes still on the* KIRBYS, *he gives* DONALD *a good push toward the kitchen, by way of a hint.* DONALD *goes, promptly, with a quick little stunned whistle that sums up* HIS *feelings.*)

KIRBY. Tony, how could you possibly—

TONY. I—I don't know. I thought—

MRS. KIRBY. Really, Tony! This is most embarrassing.

GRANDPA. Not at all. Why, we weren't doing a thing.

PENNY. Just spending the evening at home.

GRANDPA. That's all. . . . Now don't you let it bother you. This is Alice's mother, Mrs. Sycamore . . . Alice's sister, Mrs. Carmichael . . . *Mr.* Carmichael. . . . Mr. Kolenkhov. . . . (*At this point* MR. DE PINNA *takes an anticipatory step forward, and* GRANDPA *is practically compelled to perform the introduction.*) And—Mr. De Pinna. Mr. De Pinna, would you tell Mr. Sycamore to come right up? Tell him that Mr. and Mrs. Kirby are here.

PENNY (*her voice a heavy whisper*). And be sure to put his pants on.

DE PINNA (*whispering right back*). All right. . . . Excuse me. (*He vanishes—discus and all.*)

GRANDPA. Won't you sit down?

PENNY (*first frantically trying to cover the prostrate* GAY WELLINGTON). I'll tell Alice that you're—(*She is at the foot of the stairs.*)—Alice! Alice, dear! (*The voice of* ALICE *from above, "What is it?"*) Alice, will you come down, dear? We've got a surprise for you. (*She comes down into the room, summoning all her charm.*) Well!

GRANDPA. Mrs. Kirby, may I take your wrap?

MRS. KIRBY Well—thank you. If you're perfectly sure that we're not—(*Suddenly she sees the snakes and lets out a scream.*)

GRANDPA. Oh, don't be alarmed, Mrs. Kirby. They're perfectly harmless.

MRS. KIRBY (*edging away from the solarium*). Thank you. (*She sinks into a chair, weakly.*)

GRANDPA. Ed, take 'em into the kitchen. (ED *at once obeys.*)

PENNY. Of course, we're so used to them around the house—

MRS. KIRBY. I'm sorry to trouble you, but snakes happen to be the one thing—

KIRBY. I feel very uncomfortable about this. Tony, how could you have done such a thing?

TONY. I'm sorry, Dad. I thought it was tonight.

KIRBY. It was very careless of you. *Very!*

GRANDPA. Now, now Mr. Kirby—we're delighted.

PENNY. Oh, anybody can get mixed up, Mr. Kirby.

GRANDPA. Penny, how about some dinner for these folks? They've come for dinner, you know.

MRS. KIRBY. Oh, please don't bother. We're not really hungry at all.

PENNY. But it's not a bit of bother. Ed!—(*Her voice drops to a loud whisper.*) Ed, tell Donald to run down to the A. and P. and get a half dozen bottles of beer, and—ah—some canned salmon—(*Her voice comes up again.*)—do you like canned salmon, Mr. Kirby?

KIRBY. Please don't trouble, Mrs. Sycamore. I have a little indigestion, anyway.

PENNY. Oh, I'm sorry . . . How about you, Mrs. Kirby? Do you like canned salmon?

MRS. KIRBY (*you just know that she hates it*). Oh, I'm very fond of it.

PENNY. You can have frankfurters if you'd rather.

MRS. KIRBY (*regally*). Either one will do.

PENNY (*to* ED *again*). Well, make it frankfurters, and some canned corn, and Campbell's Soup.

ED (*going out the kitchen door*). Okay!

PENNY (*calling after him*). And tell him to hurry! (PENNY *again addresses the* KIRBYS.) The A. and P. is just at the corner, and frankfurters don't take *any* time to boil.

GRANDPA (*as* PAUL *comes through the cellar door*). And this is Alice's father, *Mr.* Sycamore. Mr. and Mrs. Kirby.

THE KIRBYS. How do you do?

PAUL. I hope you will forgive my appearance.

PENNY. This is Mr. Sycamore's busiest time of the year. Just before the Fourth of July—(*And then* ALICE *comes down. She is a step into the room before she realizes what has happened; then she fairly freezes in her tracks.*)

ALICE. Oh!

TONY. Darling, will you ever forgive me? I'm the most dull-witted person in the world. I thought it was tonight.

ALICE (*staggered*). Why, Tony, I thought you—(*To the* KIRBYS.)—I'm so sorry—I can't imagine—why, I wasn't—have you all met each other?

KIRBY. Yes, Indeed.

MRS. KIRBY. How do you do, Alice?

ALICE (*not even yet in control of herself*). How do you do, Mrs. Kirby? I'm afraid I'm not very—presentable.

TONY. Darling, you look lovely.

KIRBY. Of course she does. Don't let this upset you, my dear—we've all just met each other a night sooner, that's all.

MRS. KIRBY. Of course.

ALICE. But I was planning such a nice party tomorrow night . . .

KIRBY (*being the good fellow*). Well, we'll come again tomorrow night.

TONY. There you are, Alice. Am I forgiven?

ALICE. I guess so. It's just that I—we'd better see about getting you some dinner.

PENNY. Oh, that's all done, Alice. That's all been attended to. (DONALD, *hat in hand, comes through the kitchen door; hurries across the room and out the front way. The* KIRBYS *graciously pretend not to see.*)

ALICE. But mother—what are you—what did you send out for? Because Mr. Kirby suffers from indigestion—he can only eat certain things.

KIRBY. Now, it's quite all right.

TONY. Of course it is, darling.

PENNY. I asked him what he wanted, Alice.

ALICE (*doubtfully*). Yes, but—

KIRBY. Now, now, it's not as serious as all that. Just because I have a little indigestion.

KOLENKHOV (*helping things along*). Perhaps it is not indigestion at all, Mr. Kirby. Perhaps you have stomach ulcers.

ALICE. Don't be absurd, Mr. Kolenkhov!

GRANDPA. You mustn't mind Mr. Kolenkhov, Mr. Kirby. He's a Russian, and Russians are inclined to look on the dark side.

KOLENKHOV. All right, I am a Russian. But a friend of mine, a Russian, *died* from stomach ulcers.

KIRBY. Really, I—

ALICE (*desperately*). Please, Mr. Kolenkhov! Mr. Kirby has indigestion and that's all.

KOLENKHOV (*with a Russian shrug of the shoulders*). All right. Let him wait.

GRANDPA (*leaping into the breach*). Tell me, Mr. Kirby, how do you find business conditions? Are we pretty well out of the depression?

KIRBY. What? . . . Yes, yes, I think so. Of course, it all depends.

GRANDPA. But you figure that things are going to keep improving?

KIRBY. Broadly speaking, yes. As a matter of fact, industry is now operating at sixty-four per cent. of full capacity, as against eighty-two per cent. in 1925. Of course in 1929, a peak year—(*Peak year or no peak year,* GAY WELLINGTON *chooses this moment to come to life. With a series of assorted*

snorts, she throws the cover back and pulls herself to a sitting position, blinking uncertainly at the assemblage. Then she rises, and weaves unsteadily across the room. The imposing figure of MR. KIRBY *intrigues her.*)

GAY (*playfully rumpling* MR. KIRBY'S *hair as she passes him.*) Hello, Cutie. (*And with that she lunges on her way—up the stairs.*)

(*The* KIRBYS, *of course, are considerably astounded by this exhibition; the* SYCAMORES *have watched it with varying degrees of frozen horror.* ALICE, *in particular, is speechless; it is* GRANDPA *who comes to her rescue.*)

GRANDPA. That may seem a little strange to you, but she's not quite accountable for her actions. A friend of Mrs. Sycamore's. She came to dinner and was overcome by the heat.

PENNY. Yes, some people feel it, you know, more than others. Perhaps I'd better see if she's all right. Excuse me, please. (*She goes hastily up the stairs.*)

ALICE. It *is* awfully hot. (*A fractional pause.*) You usually escape all this hot weather, don't you, Mrs. Kirby? Up in Maine?

MRS. KIRBY (*on the frigid side*). As a rule. I had to come down this week, however, for the Flower Show.

TONY. Mother wouldn't miss that for the world. That blue ribbon is the high spot of her year.

ESSIE. I won a ribbon at a Flower Show once. For raising onions. Remember?

ALICE (*quickly*). That was a Garden Show, Essie.

ESSIE. Oh, yes. (PENNY *comes bustling down the stairs again.*)

PENNY. I'm so sorry, but I think she'll be all right now. . . . Has Donald come back yet?

ALICE. No, he hasn't.

PENNY. Well, he'll be right back, and it won't take any time at all. I'm afraid you must be starved.

KIRBY. Oh, no. Quite all right. (*Pacing the room, he suddenly comes upon* PAUL'S *Erector Set.*) Hello! What's this? I didn't know there were little children in the house.

PAUL. Oh, no. That's mine.

KIRBY. Really? Well, I suppose every man has his hobby. Or do you use this as a model of some kind?

PAUL. No, I just play with it.

KIRBY. I see.

TONY. Maybe you'd be better off if *you* had a hobby like that, Dad. Instead of raising orchids.

KIRBY (*indulgently*). Yes, I wouldn't be surprised.

ALICE (*leaping on this as a safe topic*). Oh, do tell us about your orchids, Mr. Kirby. (*She addresses the others.*) You know, they take six years before they blossom. Think of that!

KIRBY (*warming to his subject*). Oh, some of them take longer than that. I've got one coming along now that I've waited ten years for.

PENNY (*making a joke*). Believe it or not, I was waiting for an orchid.

KIRBY. Ah—yes. Of course during that time they require the most scrupulous care. I remember a bulb that I was very fond of—(DONALD *suddenly bulges through the archway, his arms full. The tops of beer bottles and two or three large cucumbers peep over the edge of the huge paper bags.*)

PENNY. Ah, here we are! Did you get everything, Donald?

DONALD. Yes'm. Only the frankfurters didn't look very good, so I got pickled pigs' feet. (MR. KIRBY *blanches at the very idea.*)

ALICE (*taking command*). Never mind, Donald—just bring everything into the kitchen. (*She turns at the kitchen door.*) Mr. Kirby, please tell them *all* about the orchids—I know they'd love to hear it. And—excuse me. (*She goes.*)

GRANDPA. Kind of expensive hobby, isn't it, Mr. Kirby—raising orchids?

KIRBY. Yes, it is, but I feel that if a hobby gives one sufficient pleasure, it's never expensive.

GRANDPA. That's very true.

KIRBY. You see, I need something to relieve the daily nerve strain. After a week in Wall Street I'd go crazy if I didn't have something like that. Lot of men I know have yachts—just for that very reason.

GRANDPA (*mildly*). Why don't they give up Wall Street?

KIRBY. How's that?

GRANDPA. I was just joking.

MRS. KIRBY. I think it's necessary for everyone to have a hobby. Of course it's more to me than a hobby, but my great solace is—spiritualism.

PENNY. Now Mrs. Kirby, don't tell me you fell for that. Why everybody knows it's a fake.

MRS. KIRBY (*freezing*). To me, Mrs. Sycamore, spiritualism is—I would rather not discuss it, Mrs. Sycamore.

PAUL. Remember, Penny, you've got one or two hobbies of your own.

PENNY. Yes, but not silly ones.

GRANDPA (*with a little cough*). I don't think it matters what the hobby is—the important thing is to have one.

KOLENKHOV. To be ideal, a hobby should improve the body as well as the mind. The Romans were a great people! Why! What was their hobby? Wrestling. In wrestling you have to think quick with the mind and act quick with the body.

KIRBY. Yes, but I'm afraid wrestling is not very practical for most of us. (*He gives a depreciating little laugh.*) I wouldn't make a very good showing as a wrestler.

KOLENKHOV. You could be a *great* wrestler. You are built for it. Look! (*With a startling quick movement* KOLENKHOV *grabs* MR. KIRBY'S *arms, knocks his legs from under him with a quick movement of a foot, and presto!* MR. KIRBY *is flat on his whatsis. Not only that, but instantaneously* KOLENKHOV *is on top of him.*)

(*Just at this moment* ALICE *re-enters the room—naturally, she stands petrified. Several people, of course, rush immediately to the rescue,* TONY *and* PAUL *arriving at the scene of the battle first. Amidst the general confusion they help* MR. KIRBY *to his feet.*)

ALICE. Mr. Kirby! Are you—hurt?

TONY. Are you all right, father?

KIRBY (*pulling himself together*). I—I—uh–(*He blinks, uncertainly.*)—where are my glasses?

ALICE. Here they are, Mr. Kirby. . . . Oh, Mr. Kirby, they're broken.

KOLENKHOV (*full of apology*). Oh, I am sorry. But when you wrestle again, Mr. Kirby, you will of course not wear glasses.

KIRBY (*coldly furious*). *I* do not intend to wrestle again, Mr. Kolenkhov. (*He draws himself up, stiffly, and in return gets a sharp pain in the back. He gives a little gasp.*)

TONY. Better sit down, father.

ALICE. Mr. Kolenkhov, how could you do such a thing? Why didn't somebody stop him?

MRS. KIRBY. I think, if you don't mind, perhaps we had better be going.

TONY. Mother!

ALICE (*close to tears*). Oh, Mrs. Kirby—please! Please don't go! Mr. Kirby—please! I—I've ordered some scrambled eggs for you, and—plain salad—Oh, please don't go!

KOLENKHOV. I am sorry if I did something wrong. And I apologize.

ALICE. I can't tell you how sorry I am, Mr. Kirby. If I'd been here—

KIRBY (*from a great height*). That's quite all right.

TONY. Of course it is. It's all right, Alice. We're not going. (*The KIRBYS reluctantly sit down again.*)

(*A moment of silence—no one knows quite what to say.*)

PENNY (*brightly*). Well! That was exciting for a minute, wasn't it?

GRANDPA (*quickly*). You were talking about your orchids, Mr. Kirby. Do you raise many different varieties?

KIRBY (*still unbending*). I'm afraid I've quite forgotten about my orchids. (*More silence, and everyone very uncomfortable.*)

ALICE. I'm—awfully sorry, Mr. Kirby.

KOLENKHOV (*exploding*). What did I do that was so terrible? I threw him on the floor! Did it kill him?

ALICE. Please, Mr. Kolenkhov. (*An annoyed gesture from KOLENKHOV; another general pause.*)

PENNY. I'm sure dinner won't be any time at all now. (*A pained smile from MRS. KIRBY.*)

ESSIE. Would you like some candy while you're waiting? I've got some freshly made.

KIRBY. My doctor does not permit me to eat candy. Thank you.

ESSIE. But these are nothing, Mr. Kirby. Just cocoanut and marshmallow fudge.

ALICE. Don't, Essie. (*RHEBA appears in the kitchen doorway, beckoning violently to ALICE.*)

RHEBA (*in a loud whisper*). Miss Alice! Miss Alice! (*ALICE quickly flies to RHEBA'S side.*) The eggs fell down the sink.

ALICE (*desperately*). Make some more! Quick!

RHEBA. I ain't got any.

ALICE. Send Donald out for some!

RHEBA (*disappearing*). All right.

ALICE (*calling after her*). Tell him to run! (*She turns back to the KIRBY'S.*) I'm so sorry. There'll be a little delay, but everything will be ready in just a minute. (*At this moment DONALD fairly shoots out of the kitchen door and across the living room, beating the Olympic record for all time.*)

(*PENNY tries to ease the situation with a gay little laugh. It doesn't quite come off, however.*)

TONY. I've certainly put you people to a lot of trouble, with my stupidity.

GRANDPA. Not at all, Tony.

PENNY. Look! Why don't we play a game of some sort while we're waiting?

TONY. Oh, that'd be fine.

ALICE. Mother, I don't think Mr. and Mrs. Kirby—

KOLENKHOV. *I* have an idea. I know a wonderful trick with a glass of water. (*He reaches for a full glass that stands on the table.*)

ALICE (*quickly*). No, Mr. Kolenkhov.

GRANDPA (*shaking his head*). No-o.

PENNY. But I'm sure Mr. and Mrs. Kirby would love this game. It's perfectly harmless.

ALICE. Please, mother. . . .

KIRBY. I'm not very good at games, Mrs. Sycamore.

PENNY. Oh, but *any* fool could play this game, Mr. Kirby. (*She is bustling around, getting paper and pencil.*) All you do is write your name on a piece of paper—

ALICE. But mother, Mr. Kirby doesn't want—

PENNY. Oh, he'll love it! (*Goes right on.*) Here you are, Mr. Kirby. Write your name on this piece of paper. And Mrs. Kirby, you do the same on this one.

ALICE. Mother, what *is* this game?

PENNY. I used to play it at school. It's called Forget-Me-Not. Now, I'm going to call out five words—just anything at all—and as I say each word, you're to put down the first thing that comes into your mind. Is that clear? For instance, if I say "grass," you might put down "green"—just whatever you think of, see? Or if I call out "chair," you might put down "table." It shows the reactions people have to different things. You see how simple it is, Mr. Kirby?

TONY. Come on, father! Be a sport!

KIRBY (*stiffly*). Very well. I shall be happy to play it.

PENNY. You see, Alice? He *does* want to play.

ALICE (*uneasily*). Well—

PENNY. Now, then! Are we ready?

KOLENKHOV. Ready!

PENNY. Now, remember—you must play fair. Put down the first thing that comes into your mind.

KIRBY (*pencil poised*). I understand.

PENNY. Everybody ready?. . . The first word is "potatoes." (*She repeats it.*) "Potatoes." . . . Ready for the next one? . . . "Bathroom." (ALICE *shifts rather uneasily, but seeing that no one else seems to mind, she relaxes again.*) Got that?

KOLENKHOV. Go ahead.

PENNY. All ready? . . . "Lust."

ALICE. Mother, this is not exactly what you—

PENNY. Nonsense, Alice—that word's all right.

ALICE. Mother, it's *not* all right.

MRS. KIRBY (*unexpectedly*). Oh, I don't know. It seems to me that's a perfectly fair word.

PENNY (*to* ALICE). You see? Now, you musn't interrupt the game.

KIRBY. May I have the last word again, please?

PENNY. "Lust," Mr. Kirby.

KIRBY (*writing*). I've got it.

GRANDPA. This is quite a game.

PENNY. Sssh, Grandpa . . . All ready? . .. "Honeymoon." (ESSIE *snickers a little, which is all it takes to start* PENNY *off. Then she suddenly remembers herself.*) Now, Essie! . . . All right. The last word is "sex."

ALICE (*under her breath*). Mother!

PENNY. Everybody got "sex?" . . . All right—now give me the papers.

GRANDPA. What happens now?

PENNY. Oh, this is the best part. Now I read out your reactions.

KIRBY. I see. It's really quite an interesting game.

PENNY. I knew you'd like it. I'll read your paper first, Mr. Kirby. (*To the others.*) I'm going to read Mr. Kirby's paper first. Listen, everybody! This is Mr. Kirby. . . . "Potatoes—steak." That's very good. See how they go together? Steak and potatoes?

KIRBY (*modestly, but obviously pleased with himself*). I just happened to think of it.

PENNY. It's *very* good. . . . "Bathroom—toothpaste." Uh-huh. "Lust—unlawful." Isn't that nice? "Honeymoon—trip." Yes. And "sex—male." Yes, of course . . . That's really a wonderful paper, Mr. Kirby.

KIRBY (*taking a curtain call*). Thank you . . . It's more than just a game, you know. It's sort of an experiment in psychology, isn't it?

PENNY. Yes, it is—it shows just how your *mind* works . . . Ready? . . . This is *Mrs.* Kirby . . ."Potatoes—starch." I know just what you mean, Mrs. Kirby. . . . "Bathroom—Mr. Kirby."

KIRBY. What's that?

PENNY. "Bathroom—Mr. Kirby."

KIRBY (*turning to his wife*). I don't quite follow that, my dear.

MRS. KIRBY. I don't know—I just thought of you in connection with it. After all, you *are* in there a good deal, Anthony. Bathing, and shaving—well, you *do* take a long time.

KIRBY. Indeed? I hadn't realized that I was being selfish in the matter. . . . Go on, Mrs. Sycamore.

ALICE (*worried*). I think it's a very silly game and we ought to stop it.

KIRBY. No, no. Please go on, Mrs. Sycamore.

PENNY. Where was I . . . Oh, yes . . . "Lust—human."

KIRBY. Human? (*Thin—lipped.*) Really!

MRS. KIRBY. I just meant, Anthony, that lust is after all a—human emotion.

KIRBY. I don't agree with you, Miriam. Lust is not a human emotion. It is depraved.

MRS. KIRBY. Very well, Anthony. I'm wrong.

ALICE. Really, it's the most pointless game. Suppose we play Twenty Questions?

KIRBY. No, I find this game rather interesting. Will you go on, Mrs. Sycamore? What was the next word?

PENNY (*reluctantly*). Honeymoon.

KIRBY. Oh, yes. And what was Mrs. Kirby's answer?

PENNY. Ah—"Honeymoon—dull."

KIRBY (*murderously calm*). Did you say—dull?

MRS. KIRBY. What I meant, Anthony, was that Hot Springs was not very gay that season. All those old people sitting on the porch all afternoon, and—nothing to do at night.

KIRBY. That was not your reaction at the time, as I recall it.

TONY. Father, this is only a *game*.

KIRBY. A very illuminating game. Go on, Mrs. Sycamore!

PENNY (*brightly, having taken a look ahead*). This one's all right, Mr. Kirby. "Sex—Wall Street."

KIRBY. Wall Street? What do you mean by that, Miriam?

MRS. KIRBY (*nervously*). I don't know what I meant, Anthony. Nothing.

KIRBY. But you must have meant something, Miriam, or you wouldn't have put it down.

MRS. KIRBY. It was just the first thing that came into my head, that's all.

KIRBY. But what does it mean? Sex—Wall Street.

MRS. KIRBY (*annoyed*). Oh, I don't know what it means, Anthony. It's just that you're always talking about Wall Street, even when—(*She catches herself.*) I don't know what I meant . . . Would you mind terribly, Alice, if we didn't stay for dinner? I'm afraid this game has given me a headache.

ALICE (*quietly*). I understand, Mrs. Kirby.

KIRBY (*clearing his throat*). Yes, possibly we'd better postpone the dinner, if you don't mind.

PENNY. But you're coming tomorrow night, aren't you?

MRS. KIRBY (*quickly*). I'm afraid we have an engagement tomorrow night.

KIRBY. Perhaps we'd better postpone the whole affair a little while. This hot weather, and—ah—

TONY (*smoldering*). I think we're being very ungracious, father. Of *course* we'll stay to dinner—tonight.

MRS. KIRBY (*unyielding*). I have a very bad headache, Tony.

KIRBY. Come, come, Tony, I'm sure everyone understands.

TONY (*flaring*). Well, I don't. I think we ought to stay to dinner.

ALICE (*very low*). No, Tony.

TONY. What?

ALICE. We were fools, Tony, ever to think it would work. It won't. Mr. Kirby, I won't be at the office tomorrow. I—won't be there at all any more.

TONY. Alice, what are you talking about?

KIRBY (*to* ALICE). I'm sorry, my dear—very sorry . . . Are you ready, Miriam?

MRS. KIRBY (*with enormous dignity*). Yes, Anthony.

KIRBY. It's been very nice to have met you all. Are you coming, Anthony?

TONY. No, father. I'm not.

KIRBY. I see . . . Your mother and I will be waiting for you at home. . . . Good night. (*With* MRS. KIRBY *on his arm, he sweeps toward the outer door.*)

(*Before the* KIRBY'S *can take more than a step toward the door, however, a new* FIGURE *looms up in the archway. It is a quiet and competent-looking individual with a steely eye, and two more just like him loom up behind him.*)

THE MAN (*very quietly*). Stay right where you are, everybody. (*There is a little scream from* MRS. KIRBY, *and exclamation from* PENNY.) Don't move.

PENNY. Oh, good heavens!

KIRBY. How dare you? Why, what does this mean?

GRANDPA. What *is* all this?

KIRBY. I demand an explanation!

THE MAN. Keep your mouth shut, you! (*He advances slowly into the room, looking the group over. Then he turns to one of his men.*) Which one is it?

ANOTHER MAN (*goes over and puts a hand on* ED'S *shoulder.*) This is him.

ESSIE. Ed!

ED (*terrified*). Why, what do you mean?

ALICE. Grandpa, what is this?

KIRBY. This is an outrage!

THE MAN. Shut up! (*He turns to* ED.) What's your name?

ED. Edward—Carmichael. I haven't done anything.

THE MAN. You haven't, huh?

GRANDPA (*not at all scared*). This seems rather high-handed to me. What's this all about?

THE MAN. Department of Justice.

PENNY. Oh, my goodness! J-men!

ESSIE. Ed, what have you done?

ED. I haven't done anything.

GRANDPA. What's the boy done, Officer?

ALICE. What is it? What's this all about?

THE MAN (*taking his time and surveying the room*). That door lead to the cellar?

PENNY. Yes, it does.

PAUL. Yes.

THE MAN (*ordering a man to investigate*). Mac . . . (MAC *goes into the cellar.*) . . . Jim!

JIM. Yes, sir.

THE MAN. Take a look upstairs and see what you find.

JIM. Okay. (JIM *goes upstairs.*)

ED (*panicky*). I haven't done anything!

THE MAN. Come here, you! (*He takes some slips of paper out of his pocket.*) Ever see these before?

ED (*gulping*). They're my—circulars.

THE MAN. You printing this stuff, huh?

ED. Yes, sir.

THE MAN. And you put 'em into boxes of candy to get 'em into people's homes.

ESSIE. The Love Dreams!

ED. But I didn't mean anything!

THE MAN. You didn't, huh? (*He reads the circulars.*) "Dynamite the Capitol!" "Dynamite the White House!" "Dynamite the Supreme Court!" "God is the State; the State is God!"

ED. But I didn't mean that. I just like to print. Don't I, Grandpa? (DONALD *returns with the eggs at this point, and stands quietly watching the proceedings.*)

GRANDPA. Now, Officer, the government's in no danger from Ed. Printing is just his hobby, that's all. He prints anything.

THE MAN. He does, eh?

PENNY. I never heard of such nonsense.

KIRBY. I refuse to stay here and—(MR. DE PINNA, *at this point, is shoved through the cellar door, by* MAC, *protesting as he comes.*)

DE PINNA. Hey, let me get my pipe, will you? Let me get my pipe!

MAC. Shut up, you! . . . We were right, Chief. They've got enough gun powder down there to blow up the whole city.

PAUL. But we only use that—

THE MAN. Keep still! . . . Everybody in this house is under arrest.

KIRBY. What's that?

MRS. KIRBY. Oh, good heavens!

GRANDPA. Now look here, Officer—this is all nonsense.

DE PINNA. You'd better let me get my pipe. I left it—

THE MAN. Shut up, all of you!

KOLENKHOV. It seems to me, Officer—

THE MAN. Shut up! (*from the stairs comes the sound of drunken singing—"There was a young lady," etc.* GAY WELLINGTON *wrapped in* PENNY'S *negligee, is being carried down the stairway by a somewhat bewildered* G-MAN.)

THE G-MAN. Keep still, you! Stop that! Stop it!

THE LEADER (*after* GAY *has been persuaded to quiet down*). Who's that?

GRANDPA (*pretty tired of the whole business*). That—is my mother. (*And then, suddenly, we hear from the cellar.* MR. DE PINNA *seems to have been right about his pipe, to judge from the sounds below. It is a whole year's supply of fireworks—bombs, big crackers, little crackers, sky rockets, pin wheels, everything. The house is fairly rocked by the explosion.*)

(*In the room, of course, pandemonium reigns.* MRS. KIRBY *screams; the* G-MAN *drops* GAY *right where he stands and dashes for the cellar, closely followed by* MR. DE PINNA *and* PAUL; PENNY *dashes for her manuscripts and* ED *rushes to save his xylophone.* KOLENKHOV *waves his arms wildly and dashes in all directions at once; everyone is rushing this way and that.*)

(*All except one. The exception, of course, is* GRANDPA, *who takes all things as they come.* GRANDPA *just says "Well, well, well!"—and sits down. If a lot of people weren't in the way, in fact, you feel like he'd like to throw a few darts.*)

CURTAIN

ACT THREE

The following day.

RHEBA *is in the midst of setting the table for dinner, pausing occasionally in her labors to listen to the Edwin C. Hill of the moment—*DONALD. *With intense interest and concentration, he is reading aloud from a newspaper.*

DONALD. ". . . for appearance in the West Side Court this morning. After spending the night in jail, the defendants, thirteen in all, were brought before Judge Callahan and given suspended sentences for manufacturing fireworks without a permit."

RHEBA. Yah. Kept me in the same cell with a strip teaser from a burlesque show.

DONALD. I was in the cell with Mr. Kirby. My, he was mad!

RHEBA. Mrs. Kirby and the strip teaser—they were fighting all night.

DONALD. Whole lot about *Mr.* Kirby here. (*Reading again.*) "Anthony W. Kirby, head of Kirby & Co., 62 Wall Street, who was among those apprehended, declared he was in no way interested in the manufacture of fireworks, but refused to state why he was on the premises at the time of the raid. Mr. Kirby is a member of the Union Club, the Racquet Club, the Harvard Club, and the National Geographic Society." My, he certainly is a joiner!

RHEBA. All those rich men are Elks or something.

DONALD (*looking up from his paper*). I suppose, after all this, Mr. Tony ain't ever going to marry Miss Alice, huh?

RHEBA. No, suh, and it's too bad, too. Miss Alice sure loves that boy.

DONALD. Ever notice how white folks always getting themselves in trouble?

RHEBA. Yassuh, I'm glad I'm colored. (*She sighs, heavily.*) I don't know what I'm going to do with all that food out in the kitchen. Ain't going to be no party tonight, that's sure.

DONALD. Ain't we going to eat it anyhow?

RHEBA. Well, I'm cooking it, but I don't think anybody going to have an appetite.

DONALD. *I'm* hungry.

RHEBA. Well, *they* ain't. They're all so broke up about Miss Alice.

DONALD. What's she want to go 'way for? Where's she going?

RHEBA. I don't know—mountains some place. And she's *going*, all right, no matter what they say. I know Miss Alice when she gets that look in her eye.

DONALD. Too bad, ain't it?

RHEBA. Sure is. (MR. DE PINNA *comes up from the cellar, bearing the earmarks of previous day's catastrophe. There is a small bandage around his head and over one eye, and another around his right hand. He also limps slightly.*)

DE PINNA. Not even a balloon left. (*He exhibits a handful of exploded firecrackers.*) Look.

RHEBA. How's your hand, Mr. De Pinna? Better?

DE PINNA. Yes, it's better. (*A step toward the kitchen.*) Is there some more olive oil out there?

RHEBA (*nods*). It's in the salad bowl.

465

DE PINNA. Thanks. (*He goes into the kitchen door as* PENNY *comes down the stairs. It is a new and rather subdued* PENNY.)

PENNY (*with a sigh*). Well, she's going. Nothing anybody said could change her.

RHEBA. She ain't going to stay away long, is she, Mrs. Sycamore?

PENNY. I don't know, Rheba. She won't say.

RHEBA. My, going to be lonesome around here without her. (*She goes into the kitchen.*)

DONALD. How *you* feel, Mrs. Sycamore?

PENNY. Oh, I'm all right, Donald. Just kind of upset. (*She is at her desk.*) Perhaps if I do some work maybe I'll feel better.

DONALD. Well, I won't bother you then, Mrs. Sycamore. (*He goes into the kitchen.*)

(PENNY *puts a sheet of paper into the typewriter; stares at it blankly for a moment; types in desultory fashion, gives it up. She leans back and sits staring straight ahead.*)

(PAUL *comes slowly down the stairs; stands surveying the room a moment; sighs. He goes over to the Erector Set; absentmindedly pulls out the flag. Then, with another sigh, he drops into a chair.*)

PAUL. She's going, Penny.

PENNY. Yes. (*She is quiet for a moment; then she starts to weep, softly.*)

PAUL (*going to her*). Now, now, Penny.

PENNY. I can't help it, Paul. Somehow I feel it's our fault.

PAUL. It's mine more than yours, Penny. All these years I've just been—going along, enjoying myself, when maybe I should have been thinking more about Alice.

PENNY. Don't say that, Paul, You've been a wonderful father. And husband, too.

PAUL. No, I haven't. Maybe if I'd gone ahead and been an architect—I don't know—something Alice could have been proud of. I felt that all last night, looking at Mr. Kirby.

PENNY. But we've been so happy, Paul.

PAUL. I know, but maybe that's not enough. I used to think it was, but—I'm kind of all mixed up now.

PENNY (*after a pause*). What time is she going?

PAUL. Pretty soon. Train leaves at half past seven.

PENNY. Oh, if only she'd see Tony. I'm sure he could persuade her.

PAUL. But she won't, Penny. He's been trying all day.

PENNY. Where is he now?

PAUL. I don't know—I suppose walking around the block again. Anyhow, she won't talk to him.

PENNY. Maybe Tony can catch her as she's leaving.

PAUL. It won't help, Penny.

PENNY. No, I don't suppose so. . . . I feel so sorry for Tony, too. (GRANDPA *comes down the stairs—unsmiling, but not too depressed by the situation.*) (*Anxiously.*) Well?

GRANDPA. Now, Penny, let the girl alone.

PENNY. But, Grandpa—

GRANDPA. Suppose she *goes* to the Adirondacks? She'll be back. You can take just so much Adirondacks, and then you come home.

PENNY. Oh, but it's all so terrible, Grandpa.

GRANDPA. In a way, but it has its bright side, too.

PAUL. How do you mean?

GRANDPA. Well, Mr. Kirby getting to the patrol wagon, for one thing, and the expression on his face when he and Donald had to take a bath together. I'll never forget that if I live to be a hundred, and I warn you people I intend to. If I can have things like that going on.

PENNY. Oh, it was even worse with Mrs. Kirby. When the matron stripped her. There was a burlesque dancer there and she kept singing a strip song while Mrs. Kirby undressed.

GRANDPA. I'll bet you Bar Harbor is going to seem pretty dull to the Kirbys for the rest of the summer. (*With a determined step,* ALICE *comes swiftly down the stairs. Over her arm she carries a couple of dresses. Looking neither to right nor left, she heads for the kitchen.*)

GRANDPA. Need any help, Alice?

ALICE (*in a strained voice*). No, thanks, Grandpa. Ed is helping with the bags. I'm just going to press these.

PENNY. Alice, dear—

GRANDPA. Now, Penny. (ED *has appeared in the hallway with a couple of hatboxes,* ESSIE *behind him.*)

ED. I'll bring the bag down as soon as you're ready, Alice.

ESSIE. Do you want to take some candy along for the train, Alice?

ALICE. No thanks, Essie.

PENNY. Really, Alice, you could be just as alone here as you could in the mountains. You could stay right in you room all the time.

ALICE (*quietly*). No, mother, I want to be by myself—away from everybody. I love you all—you know that. But I just have to go away for a while. I'll be all right. . . . Father, did you 'phone for a cab?

PAUL. No, I didn't know you wanted one.

PENNY. Oh, I told Mr. De Pinna to tell you, Paul. Didn't he tell you?

ED. Oh, he told *me,* but I forgot.

ALICE (*the final straw*). Oh, I wish I lived in a family that didn't always forget *everything.* That—that behaved the way *other* people's families do. I'm sick of cornflakes, and—Donald, and—(*Unconsciously, in her impatience, she has picked up one of* GRANDPA'S *darts; is surprised to find it suddenly in her hand.*)—everything! (*She dashes the dart to the floor.*) Why can't we be like other people? Roast beef, and two green vegatables, and—doilies on the table, and—a place you could bring your friends to—without—(*unable to control herself further, she bursts out of the room, into the kitchen.*)

ESSIE. I'll see if I can do anything. (*She goes into the kitchen.*)

(*The others look at each other for a moment, helplessly.* PENNY, *with a sigh, drops into her chair again.* PAUL *also sits.* GRANDPA *mechanically picks up the dart from the floor; smooths out the feathers.* ED, *with a futile gesture, runs his fingers idly over the xylophone keys. He stops quickly as every head turns to look at him.*)

(*The sound of the door opening and* TONY *appears in the archway. A worried and disheveled* TONY.)

PENNY (*quickly*). Tony, talk to her! She's in the kitchen!

TONY. Thanks. (*He goes immediately into the kitchen.*)

(*The family, galvanized, listen intently.*)

(*Almost immediately,* ALICE *emerges from the kitchen again, followed by* TONY. *She crosses the living room and starts quickly up the stairs.*) Alice, won't you listen to me? Please!

ALICE (*not stopping*). Tony, it's no use.

TONY (*following her*). Alice, you're not being fair. At least let me talk to you. (*They are both gone—up the stairs.*)

PENNY. Perhaps if I went upstairs with them . . .

GRANDPA. Now, Penny. Let them alone. (ESSIE *comes out of the kitchen.*)

ESSIE. Where'd they go? (ED, *with a gesture, indicates the upstairs region.*) She walked out the minute he came in. (MR. DE PINNA *also emerges from the kitchen.*)

MR. DE PINNA. Knocked the olive oil right out of my hand. I'm going to smell kind of fishy.

GRANDPA. How're you feeling, Mr. De Pinna? Hand still hurting you?

MR. DE PINNA. No, it's better.

PAUL. Everything burnt up, huh? Downstairs?

DE PINNA (*nodding, sadly*). Everything. And my Roman costume, too.

GRANDPA (*to* PENNY). I told you there was a bright side to everything. All except my twenty-two years back income tax. (*He pulls an envelope out of his pocket.*) I get another letter every day.

DE PINNA. Say, what are you going to do about that, Grandpa?

GRANDPA. Well, I had a kind of idea yesterday. It may not work, but I'm trying it, anyhow.

DE PINNA (*eagerly*). What is it? (*Suddenly* KOLENKHOV *appears in the doorway.*)

KOLENKHOV (*everybody is subdued*). Good evening, everybody!

PENNY. Why, Mr. Kolenkhov!

GRANDPA. Hello, Kolenkhov.

KOLENKHOV. Forgive me. The door was open.

GRANDPA. Come on in.

KOLENKHOV. You will excuse my coming today. I realize you are—upset.

PENNY. That's all right, Mr. Kolenkhov.

ESSIE. I don't think I can take a lesson, Mr. Kolenkhov. I don't feel up to it.

KOLENKHOV (*uncertainly*). Well, I—ah—

PENNY. Oh, but do stay to dinner, Mr. Kolenkhov. We've got all that food out there, and somebody's got to eat it.

KOLENKHOV. I will be happy to, Madame Sycamore.

PENNY. Fine.

KOLENKHOV. Thank you. . . . Now, I wonder if I know you well enough to ask a great favor.

PENNY. Why, of course, Mr. Kolenkhov. What is it?

KOLENKHOV. You have heard me talk about my friend the Grand Duchess Olga Katrina.

PENNY. Yes?

KOLENKHOV. She is a great woman, the Grand Duchess. Her cousin was the Czar of Russia, and today she is a waitress in Childs' Restaurant. Columbus Circle.

PENNY. Yes, I know. If there's anything at all that we can do, Mr. Kolenkhov . . .

KOLENKHOV. I tell you. The Grand Duchess Olga Katrina has not had a good meal since before the Revolution.

GRANDPA. She must be hungry.

KOLENKHOV. And today the Grand Duchess not only has her day off—Thursday—but it is also the anniversary of Peter the Great. A remarkable man!

PENNY. Mr. Kolenkhov, if you mean you'd like the Grand Duchess to come to dinner, why, we'd be honored.

ESSIE. Oh, yes!

KOLENKHOV (*with a bow*). In the name of the Grand Duchess, I thank you.

PENNY. I can hardly wait to meet her. When will she be here?

KOLENKHOV. She is outside in the street, waiting. I bring her in. (*And he goes out.*)

GRANDPA. You know, if this keeps on I want to live to be a hundred and *fifty*.

PENNY (*feverishly*). Ed, straighten your tie. Essie, look at your dress. How do *I* look? All right? (KOLENKHOV *appears in the hallway and stands at rigid attention.*)

KOLENKHOV (*his voice booming*). The Grand Duchess Olga Katrina! (*And the* GRAND DUCHESS OLGA KATRINA, *wheat cakes and maple syrup out*

of her life for a few hours, sweeps into the room. She wears a dinner gown that has seen better days, and the whole is surmounted by an extremely tacky-looking evening wrap, trimmed with bits of ancient and moth-eaten fur. But once a Grand Duchess, always a Grand Duchess. She rises above everything—Childs', evening wrap, and all.) Your Highness, permit me to present Madame Sycamore—(PENNY, *having seen a movie or two in her time, knows just what to do. She curtsies right to the floor, and catches hold of a chair just in time.*) Madame Carmichael—(ESSIE *does a curtsey that begins where all others leave off. Starting on her toes, she merges the Dying Swan with an extremely elaborate genuflection.*) Grandpa—

GRANDPA (*with a little bow*). Madame.

KOLENKHOV. Mr. Sycamore, Mr. Carmichael, and Mr. De Pinna. (PAUL *and* ED *content themselves with courteous little bows, but not so the social-minded* MR. DE PINNA. *He bows to the floor—and stays there for a moment.*)

GRANDPA. All right now, Mr. De Pinna. (MR. DE PINNA *gets to his feet again.*)

PENNY. Will you be seated, Your Highness?

THE GRAND DUCHESS. Thank you. You are most kind.

PENNY. We are honored to receive you, Your Highness.

THE GRAND DUCHESS. I am most happy to be here. What time is dinner?

PENNY (*a little startled*). Oh, it'll be quite soon, Your Highness—very soon.

THE GRAND DUCHESS. I do not mean to be rude, but I must be back at the restaurant by eight o'clock. I am substituting for another waitress.

KOLENKHOV. I will make sure you are on time, Your Highness.

DE PINNA. You know, Highness, I think you waited on me in Childs' once. The Seventy-Second Street place?

THE GRAND DUCHESS. No, no. That was my sister.

KOLENKHOV. The Grand Duchess Natasha.

THE GRAND DUCHESS. *I* work in Columbus Circle.

GRANDPA. Quite a lot of your family living over here now, aren't there?

THE GRAND DUCHESS. Oh, yes—many. My uncle, the Grand Duke Sergei—he is an elevator man at

Macy's. A very nice man. Then there is my cousin, Prince Alexis. He will not speak to the rest of us because he works at Hattie Carnegie's. He has cards printed Prince Alexis of Hattie Carnegie. Bah!

KOLENKHOV. When he was selling Eskimo Pies at Luna Park he was willing to talk to you.

THE GRAND DUCHESS. Ah, Kolenkhov, our time is coming. My sister Natasha is studying to be a manicure, Uncle Sergei they have promised to make floor-walker, and next month I get transferred to the Fifth Avenue Childs'. From there it is only a step to Schraffts' and *then* we will see what Prince Alexis says!

GRANDPA (*nodding*). I think you've got him.

THE GRAND DUCHESS. You are telling *me?* (*She laughs a triumphant Russian laugh in which* KOLENKHOV *joins*).

PENNY. Your Highness—did you know the Czar? Personally, I mean.

THE GRAND DUCHESS. Of course—he was my cousin. It was terrible, what happened, but perhaps it was for the best. Where could he get a job now?

KOLENKHOV. That is true.

THE GRAND DUCHESS (*philosophically*). Yes. And poor relations are poor relations. It is the same in every family. My cousin, the King of Sweden—he was very nice to us for about ten years, but then he said, I just cannot go on. I am not doing so well, either. . . . I do not blame him.

PENNY. No, of course not . . . Would you excuse me for just a moment? (*She goes to the foot of the stairs and stands peering up anxiously, hoping for news of* ALICE.)

DE PINNA (*the historian at heart*). Tell me, Grand Duchess, is it true what they say about Rasputin?

THE GRAND DUCHESS. Everyone wants to know about Rasputin. . . . Yes, my dear sir, it is true. In spades.

DE PINNA. You don't say?

KOLENKHOV. Your Highness, we have to watch the time.

THE GRAND DUCHESS. Yes, I must not be late. The manager does not like me. He is a Communist.

PENNY. We'll hurry things up. Essie, why don't you go out in the kitchen and give Rheba a hand?

THE GRAND DUCHESS (*rising*). I will help, too. I am a very good cook.

PENNY Oh, but Your Highness! Not on your day off!

THE GRAND DUCHESS. I do not mind. Where is your kitchen?

ESSIE. Right through here, but you're the guest of honor, Your Highness.

THE GRAND DUCHESS. But I love to cook! Come, Kolenkhov! If they have got sour cream and pot cheese I will make you some blintzes!

KOLENKHOV. Ah! Blintzes! . . . Come, Pavlowa! We show you something! (*With* ESSIE, *he goes into the kitchen*.)

DE PINNA. Say! The Duchess is all right, isn't she? Hey Duchess! Can I help? (*And into the kitchen*.)

PENNY. Really, she's a very nice woman, you know. Considering she's a Grand Duchess.

GRANDPA. Wonderful what people go through, isn't it? And still keep kind of gay, too.

PENNY. Mm. She made me forget about everything for a minute (*She returns to the stairs and stands listening*.)

PAUL. I'd better call that cab, I suppose.

PENNY. No, wait, Paul. I think I hear them. Maybe Tony has— (*She stops as* ALICE'S *step is heard on the stair. She enters—dressed for traveling.* TONY *looms up behind her*.)

ALICE. Ed, will you go up and bring my bag down?

TONY (*quickly*). Don't you do it, Ed! (ED *hesitates, uncertain*.)

ALICE. Ed, please!

TONY (*a moment's pause; then he gives up*). All right, Ed. Bring it down. (ED *goes up the stairs as* TONY *disconsolately stalks across the room. Then he faces the Sycamores*.) Do you know that you've got the stubbornest daughter in all forty-eight states? (*The door bell rings*.)

ALICE. That must be the cab (*She goes to the door*.)

GRANDPA. If it is, it's certainly wonderful service. (*To the considerable surprise of everyone, the voice of* MR. KIRBY *is heard at the front door*.)

KIRBY. Is Tony here, Alice?

ALICE. Yes. Yes, he is. (MR. KIRBY *comes in*.)

KIRBY (*uncomfortably*). Ah—good afternoon. Forgive my intruding . . . Tony, I want you to come home with me. Your mother is very upset.

TONY (*he looks at* ALICE). Very well, father . . . Good-bye, Alice.

ALICE. (*very low*). Good-bye, Tony.

KIRBY (*trying to ease the situation*). I need hardly say that this is as painful to Mrs. Kirby and myself as it is to you people. I—I'm sorry, but I'm sure you understand.

GRANDPA. Well, yes—and in a way, no. Now, I'm not the kind of person tries to run other people's lives, but the fact is, Mr. Kirby, I don't think these two young people have got as much sense as—ah—you and I have.

ALICE (*tense*). Grandpa, will you please not do this?

GRANDPA (*disarmingly*). I'm just talking to Mr. Kirby. A cat can look at a king, can't he? (ALICE, *with no further words, takes up the telephone and dials a number. There is finality in her every movement.*)

PENNY. You—you want me to do that for you, Alice?

ALICE. No, thanks, mother.

PAUL. You've got quite a while before the train goes, Alice.

ALICE (*into the phone*). Will you send a cab to 761 Claremont, right away, please? . . . That's right, thank you. (*She hangs up.*)

KIRBY. And now if you'll excuse us . . . are you ready, Tony?

GRANDPA. Mr Kirby, I suppose after last night you think this family is crazy, don't you?

KIRBY. No, I would not say that, although I am not accustomed to going out to dinner and spending the night in jail.

GRANDPA. Well, you've got to remember, Mr. Kirby, you came on the wrong night. Now tonight, I'll bet you, nothing'll happen at all. (*There is a great burst of Russian laughter from the kitchen—the mingled voices of* KOLENKHOV *and the* GRAND DUCHESS. GRANDPA *looks off in the direction of the laughter, then decides to play safe.*) Maybe.

KIRBY. Mr. Vanderhof, it was not merely last night that convinced Mrs. Kirby and myself that this engagement would be unwise.

TONY. Father, I can handle my own affairs. (*He turns to* ALICE.) Alice, for the last time, will you marry me?

ALICE. No, Tony. I know exactly what your father means, and he's right.

TONY. No, he's *not*, Alice.

GRANDPA. Alice, you're in love with this boy, and you're not marrying him because we're the kind of people we are.

ALICE. Grandpa—

GRANDPA. I know. You think the two families wouldn't get along. Well, maybe they wouldn't—but who says they're right and we're wrong?

ALICE. I didn't say that, Grandpa. I only feel—

GRANDPA. Well, *what I* feel is that Tony's too nice a boy to wake up twenty years from now with nothing in his life but stocks and bonds.

KIRBY. How's that?

GRANDPA (*turning to* MR. KIRBY). Yes. Mixed up and unhappy, the way you are.

KIRBY (*outraged*). I beg your pardon, Mr. Vanderhof, I am a very happy man.

GRANDPA. Are you?

KIRBY. Certainly I am.

GRANDPA. I don't think so. What do you think you get your indigestion from? Happiness? No, sir. You get it because most of your time is spent in doing things you don't want to do.

KIRBY. I don't do anything I don't want to do.

GRANDPA. Yes, you do. You said last night that at the end of a week in Wall Street you're pretty near crazy. Why do you keep on doing it?

KIRBY. Why do I keep on—why, that's my *business*. A man can't give up his business.

GRANDPA. Why not? You've got all the money you need. You can't take it with you.

KIRBY. That's a very easy thing to say, Mr. Vanderhof. But I have spent my entire life building my business.

GRANDPA. And what's it got you? Same kind of mail every morning, same kind of deals, same kind of meetings, same dinners at night, same indigestion. Where does the fun come in? Don't you think there ought to be something *more*, Mr. Kirby? You must have wanted more than that when you started out. We haven't got too much time, you know—any of us.

KIRBY. What do you expect me to do? Live the way *you* do? Do nothing?

GRANDPA. Well, I have a lot of fun. Time enough for everything—read, talk, visit the zoo now and then, practice my darts, even have time to notice when spring comes around. Don't see anybody I don't want to, don't have six hours of things I *have* to do every day before I get *one* hour to do what I like in—and I haven't taken bicarbonate soda in thirty-five years. What's the matter with that?

KIRBY. The matter with that? But suppose we *all* did it? A fine world we'd have, everybody going to zoos. Don't be ridiculous, Mr. Vanderhoff. Who would do the work?

GRANDPA. There's always people that like to work—you can't *stop* them. Inventions, and they fly the ocean. There're always people to go down to Wall Street, too—because they *like* it. But from what I've seen of you, I don't think you're one of them. I think you're missing something.

KIRBY. I am not aware of missing anything.

GRANDPA. I wasn't either, till I quit. I used to get down to that office nine o'clock sharp, no matter how I felt. Lay awake nights for fear I wouldn't get that contract. Used to worry about the world, too. Got *all* worked up about whether Cleveland or Blaine was going to be elected President—seemed awful important at the time, but who cares now? What I'm trying to say, Mr. Kirby, is that I've had thirty-five years that nobody can take away from me, no matter what they do to the world. See?

KIRBY. Yes, I do see. And it's a very dangerous philosophy, Mr. Vanderhoff. It's—it's unAmerican. And it's exactly why I'm opposed to this marriage. I don't want Tony to come under its influence.

TONY (*a gleam in his eye*). What's the matter with it, father?

KIRBY. Matter with it? Why, it's—it's downright Communism, that's what it is.

TONY. You didn't always think so.

KIRBY. I most certainly did. What are you talking about?

TONY. I'll tell you what I'm talking about. You didn't always think so, because there was a time when you wanted to be a trapeze artist.

KIRBY. Why—why, don't be an idiot, Tony.

TONY. Oh, yes, you did. I came across those letters you wrote to grandfather. Do you remember those?

KIRBY. NO! . . . How dared you read those letters? How dared you?

PENNY. Why, isn't that wonderful? Did you wear tights, Mr. Kirby?

KIRBY. Certainly not! The whole thing is absurd. I was fourteen years old at the time.

TONY. Yes, but at *eighteen* you wanted to be a saxophone player, didn't you?

KIRBY. Tony!

TONY. And at twenty-one you ran away from home because grandfather wanted you to go into the business. It's all down there in black and white. You didn't *always* think so.

GRANDPA. Well, well, well!

KIRBY. I may have had silly notions in my youth, but thank God my father knocked them out of me. I went into the business and forgot about them.

TONY. Not altogether, father. There's still a saxophone in the back of your clothes closet.

GRANDPA. There is?

KIRBY (*quietly*). That's enough, Tony. We'll discuss this later.

TONY. No, I want to talk about it *now*. I think Mr. Vanderhof is right—dead right. I'm never going back to that office. I've always hated it, and I'm not going on with it. And I'll tell you something else. I didn't make a mistake last night. I knew it was the wrong night. I brought you here on purpose.

ALICE. Tony!

PENNY. Well, for heaven's—

TONY. Because I wanted to wake you up. I wanted you to see a real family—as they really *were*. A family that loved and understood each other. You don't understand *me*. You've never had time. Well, I'm not going to make *your* mistake. I'm clearing out.

KIRBY. Clearing out? What do you mean?

TONY. I mean I'm not going to be pushed into the business just because I'm your son. I'm getting out while there's still time.

KIRBY (*stunned*). Tony, what are you going to do?

TONY. I don't know. Maybe I'll be a bricklayer, but at least I'll be doing something I want to do. (*Whereupon the door bell rings.*)

PENNY. That must be the cab.

GRANDPA. Ask him to wait, Ed.

ALICE. Grandpa!

GRANDPA. Do you mind, Alice? . . . You know, Mr. Kirby, Tony is going through just what you and I did when we were his age. I think, if you listen hard enough, you can hear yourself saying the same things to *your* father twenty-five years ago. We all did it. And we were right. How many of us would be willing to settle when we're young for what we eventually get? All those plans we make . . . what happens to them? It's only a handful of the lucky ones that can look back and say that they even come close. (GRANDPA *has hit home.* MR. KIRBY *turns slowly and looks at his son, as though seeing him for the first time.* GRANDPA *continues.*) So . . . before they clean out that closet, Mr. Kirby, I think I'd get in a few good hours on that saxophone. (*A slight paue, then* THE GRAND DUCHESS, *apron over her evening dress, comes in from the kitchen.*)

THE GRAND DUCHESS. I beg your pardon, but before I make the blintzes, how many will there be for dinner?

PENNY. Why, I don't know—ah—

GRANDPA. Your Highness, may I present Mr. Anthony Kirby, and Mr. Kirby, Junior? The Grand Duchess Olga Katrina.

KIRBY. How's that?

THE GRAND DUCHESS. How do you do? Before I make the blintzes, how many will there be to dinner?

GRANDPA. Oh, I'd make quite a stack of them, Your Highness. Can't ever tell.

THE GRAND DUCHESS. Good! The Czar always said to me, Olga, do not be stingy with the blintzes. (*She returns to the kitchen, leaving a somewhat stunned* MR. KIRBY *behind her.*)

KIRBY. Ah—who did you say that was, Mr. Vanderhof?

GRANDPA (*very offhand*). The Grand Duchess Olga Katrina, of Russia. She's cooking the dinner.

KIRBY. Oh!

GRANDPA. And speaking of dinner, Mr. Kirby, why don't you and Tony both stay?

PENNY. Oh, please do, Mr. Kirby. We've got all that stuff we were going to have last night, I mean to-night.

GRANDPA. Looks like a pretty good dinner, Mr. Kirby, and'll kind of give us a chance to get acquainted. Why not stay?

KIRBY. Why—I'd like to very much. (*He turns to* TONY, *with some trepidation.*) What do you say, Tony? Shall we stay to dinner?

TONY. Yes, father. I think that would be fine. If— (*His eyes go to* ALICE.)—if Alice will send away that cab.

GRANDPA. How about it, Alice? Going to be a nice crowd. Don't you think you ought to stay for dinner?

ALICE. Mr. Kirby—Tony—oh, Tony! (*And she is in his arms.*)

TONY. Darling!

ALICE. Grandpa, you're wonderful!

GRANDPA. I've been telling you that for years. (*He kisses her.*)

(ESSIE *enters from the kitchen, laden with dishes.*)

ESSIE. Grandpa, here's a letter for you. It was in the ice-box.

GRANDPA (*looks at the envelope*). The Government again.

TONY (*happily*). Won't you step into the office, Miss Sycamore? I'd like to do a little dictating.

GRANDPA (*with his letter*). Well, well, well!

PENNY. What is it, Grandpa?

GRANDPA. The United States Government apologizes. I don't owe 'em a nickel. It seems I died eight years ago.

ESSIE. Why, what do they mean, Grandpa?

GRANDPA. Remember Charlie, the milkman? Buried under my name?

PENNY. Yes.

GRANDPA. Well, I just told them they made a mistake and I was Martin Vanderhof, Jr. So they're very sorry and I may even get a refund.

ALICE. Why, Grandpa, you're an old crook.

GRANDPA. Sure!

KIRBY (*interested*). Pardon me, how did you say you escaped the income tax, Mr. Vanderhof?

KOLENKHOV (*bursting through the kitchen door, bringing a chair with him*). Tonight, my friends, you are going to eat . . . (*He stops short as he catches sight of* KIRBY.)

KIRBY (*heartily*). Hello, there!

KOLENKHOV (*stunned*). How do you do?

KIRBY. Fine! Fine! Never was better.

KOLENKHOV (*to* GRANDPA). What has happened?

GRANDPA. He's relaxing. (ED *strikes the keys of the xylophone.*) That's right. Play something, Ed. (*He starts to play.* ESSIE *is immediately up on her toes.*)

THE GRAND DUCHESS (*entering from the kitchen*). Everything will be ready in a minute. You can sit down.

PENNY. Come on everybody. Dinner! (*They start to pull up chairs.*) Come on, Mr. Kirby!

KIRBY (*still interested in the xylophone*). Yes, yes, I'm coming.

PENNY. Essie, stop dancing and come to dinner.

KOLENKHOV. You will like Russian food, Mr. Kirby.

PENNY. But you must be careful of your indigestion.

KIRBY. Nonsense! I haven't got any indigestion.

TONY. Well, Miss Sycamore, how was your trip to the Adirondacks?

ALICE. Shut your face, Mr. Kirby!

KOLENKHOV. In Russia, when they sit down to dinner . . .

GRANDPA (*tapping on his plate*). Quiet! Everybody! Quiet! (*Immediately the talk ceases. All heads are lowered as* GRANDPA *starts to say Grace.*) Well, Sir, here we are again. We want to say thanks once more for everything You've done for us. Things seem to be going fine. Alice is going to marry Tony, and it looks as if they're going to be very happy. Of course the fireworks blew up, but that was Mr. De Pinna's fault, not Yours. We've all got our health and as far as anything else is concerned, we'll leave it to You. Thank You. (*The heads come up again.* RHEBA *and* DONALD *come through the kitchen door with stacks and stacks of blintzes. Even the Czar would have thought there were enough.*)

CURTAIN

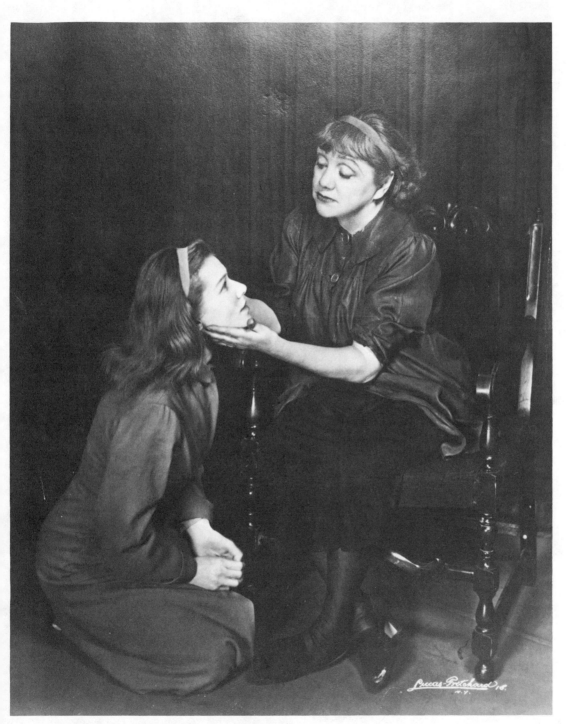

Julie Haydon and Laurette Taylor in the original Broadway
production of *The Glass Menagerie,* 1945. Used with permission.
Billy Rose Theatre Collection, The New York Public Library at
Lincoln Center, Astor, Lenox and Tilden Foundations.

CHAPTER XIV

American Theatre After World War II

If the period of the 1920s and 1930s evidenced the maturation of the theatre in America, then the period immediately following World War II offered the very pinnacle of that achievement. During the war years there had been some interesting propaganda or patriotic endeavors, and a sprinkling of good plays, but nothing of any profound significance—save one theatrical event that would change the course of musical theatre from that time forward.

It will be remembered that *Showboat* in 1927 was singled out as a work that anticipated musical drama. During the 1930s composers like Irving Berlin and Cole Porter had written pleasing, light musicals with marvelous songs and lyrics; George Gershwin, with lyrics by his brother Ira, had certainly advanced the sophistication of the musical scores; and the musical comedy team of Richard Rodgers and Lorenz Hart had perfected the union of music and lyrics. Rodgers and Hart had begun with frivolous musicals like *Betsy* (1926), which Burns Mantle summarizes glibly: "Louie, Joseph and Moe Kitzel want to get married, but Mama Kitzel won't let them until they have found a husband for their older sister Betsy. They try to sell Bet to a youthful pigeon fancier, Archie, but he loves her younger sister Ruth. And so it goes until 11 o'clock when things just naturally right themselves." But by 1940, the team was exploring far richer and darker material from John O'Hara's *New Yorker* short stories in a work titled *Pal Joey*. Here was a sordid tale about tawdry Chicago night club life, blackmail, a self-serving opportunist as hero and an equally self-centered, middle-aged, married matron as leading lady. Although Brooks Atkinson in the *New York Times* wrote, "Can you draw sweet water from a foul well?" other critics applauded the three-dimensional characters and unity of the work. But the world was not quite ready for *Pal Joey*. Only when it was revived in 1952 was it thoroughly successful. Hart, who believed that he and his partner had contributed something significant to the world of musical theatre, was despondent. Already deeply troubled by his alcohol addiction, Hart retreated more and more from work. By 1943, Rodgers had lost confidence in his brilliant colleague's ability to work and had Oscar Hammerstein II, lyricist and librettist from *Showboat,* waiting in the wings. When the Theatre Guild approached Rodgers and Hart with the idea of turning an American folk play by Lynn Riggs into a musical, Hart was disinterested, stating that his milieu was the world of New York not that of the American frontier. As Lorenz Hart sat at the opening of *Oklahoma!*, cheering and applauding, he must have suffered deeply to see twenty years of collaboration and work surpassed in a moment. He died within the year.

The story of *Oklahoma!* is a fascinating one. Hammerstein had had a number of failures since *Showboat* over fifteen years before, and the theatre public knew and loved Rodgers and Hart, not Rodgers and Hammerstein. The new collaborators decided they would open the musical with a woman alone on stage churning butter; they would delay the use of the chorus and then use it only when it served the story at a party or gathering; they would depict a villainous bully and present his murder on stage; there would be a dream ballet; and a choreographer from the ballet world, Agnes DeMille, would be hired to stage the dances. When tryouts in New Haven were not successful, people joked, "No gags, no girls, no chance." They needed $83,000 to produce the show and had enormous difficulty raising that sum. The rest is history. *Oklahoma!* ran on Broadway for 2,248 performances, grossed millions of dollars, and has been more praised and lauded than any musical in the history of the American theatre. Much of that praise is justified. The strong orchestral score, the directness and simplicity of the book, the depiction of real people from America's past, the seriousness of the tone, and the unity achieved between book, lyric, and score are commendable. However, the integrated musical had been on its way for a long time; besides *Pal Joey,* Gershwin's *Porgy and Bess,* Kurt Weill and Ira Gershwin's *Lady in the Dark* and many others had prepared the way. The fact remains, however, that once *Oklahoma!* had found its way into the hearts of the American theatre-goers, they would never be content with froth again.

Rodgers and Hammerstein continued their phenomenal success with *Carousel, South Pacific, The King and I, The Sound of Music* and many others. Through the 1950s and 1960s, the integrated musical prospered with such works, for example, as Frank Loesser's *Most Happy Fella,* a musical version of Sidney Howard's play, *They Knew What They Wanted;* Lerner and Loewe's *My Fair Lady,* a musical telling of George Bernard Shaw's *Pygmalion;* Leonard Bernstein and Stephen Sondheim's *West Side Story,* a modern *Romeo and Juliet* depicting the gang warfare of New York's west side; Jerry Bock and Sheldon Harnick's *Fiddler on the Roof,* derived from Yiddish tales of Sholom Aleichem, and John Kander and Fred Ebb's *Cabaret,* drawn from John Van Druten's *I Am a Camera* which, in turn, had been adapted from Christopher Isherwood's Berlin stories.

More compelling than any innovation in the area of musical theatre, however, was the appearance after the second world war of two immensely talented young playwrights: Arthur Miller and Tennessee Williams. To compare the two is both impossible and inappropriate. Miller, much more of a social realist than Williams, is the obvious decendent of Ibsen. Williams, always concerned with psychology and the survival of decency and humanity in a cruel world, is the natural offspring of Strindberg. Both made an incredible impact on post-war drama.

Miller was born in New York City in 1915 and got his first experience as a playwright working with the Federal Theatre Project. During the war, he had worked as a steamfitter in the Brooklyn Navy Yard. He had also been assigned to the infantry to gather material for Ernie Pyle's film on the G.I. experience, a project which resulted in his own book, *Situation Normal* (1944). Miller had been deeply impressed by the aims and creativity of The Group Theatre, and Elia Kazan—closely associated with The Group—agreed to direct Miller's first play, *All My Sons* (1947). Today the play seems old-fashioned and contrived, but its plot—about an airplane manufacturer whose faulty equipment causes the death of many young airmen, including possibly his own son—with its implicit criticism of American capitalism was explosive and controversial.

Miller's masterpiece came two years later with *Death of A Salesman,* also directed by Kazan. Again Miller attacks the American emphasis on material possessions and on false dreams of success and getting ahead. Its leading character, Willy Loman, is an overweight, dime-a-dozen, blustering salesman, who pins his hopes on his two sons, Biff and Happy. The younger boy, Happy, accepts his father's values, but Biff rejects them. In many ways, Biff Loman anticipates the youthful rebellion against middle class values that was to come in the 1960s. In the climactic scene of the play, Biff says:

> Willy! I ran down eleven flights with a pen in my hand today. And suddenly I stopped, you hear me? In the middle of that office building, do you hear this? I stopped in the middle of that building and I saw—the sky. I saw the things that I love in this world. The work and the food and time to sit and smoke. And I looked at the pen and said to myself, what the hell am I grabbing this for? Why am I trying to become what I don't want to be? What am I doing in an office, making a contemptuous, begging fool of myself, when all I want is out there, waiting for me the minute I say I know who I am! Why can't I say that, Willy?

In *Salesman,* Miller abandoned a straightforward realistic style in favor of an interesting mixture of realism, the filmic technique of flashbacks and even flashbacks within flashbacks, and an expressionistic character, Willy's brother Ben, who exists only in Willy's imagination. The setting, too, was unique in that designer Jo Mielziner presented the Loman house in Brooklyn in its entirety: the structural outline of the facade; the suggestions of whole rooms, allowing free play between one part of the house and another; a prevailing atmosphere of doom, the humble house overpowered by the huge apartment buildings that crowd in upon it; and finally the use of scrims and projections that could radically alter the mood, color, and atmosphere of whole scenes.

If we look at Miller's social awareness and affiliation with the Federal Theatre and members of The Group it is not surprising that in the early 1950s, Miller came under the attack of Joseph McCarthy and the House Un-American Activities Committee. In 1953, Miller expressed his dismay about the hysteria surrounding McCarthy's accusations and character assassinations by turning to a similar time in American history: the Salem witch trials of 1692. The resulting play, *The Crucible,* continues to be one of Miller's most popular and frequently performed works.

Concerns about the hearings also informed Miller's next play, *A View from the Bridge* (1955–56), in which a Brooklyn longshoreman, Eddie Carbone, is killed by his former friends when he turns informer against an illegal alien who has fallen in love with his niece. Again, the play has continued to enjoy revivals and positive-re-evaluations. After a long break with the theatre during which he wrote for Hollywood films, Miller resumed his playwriting career with *After the Fall* (1964), an autobiographical epic about the HUAC hearings and his marriage to the tragic superstar, Marilyn Monroe, and *Incident at Vichy* (1964). While neither of these plays met with the success of his former work, Miller did enjoy critical acclaim with *The Price* in 1968, a drama about two middle-aged brothers—one a policeman and one a lawyer—who meet to dispose of their dead father's possessions and are forced to assess their relationship to one another and to their father.

While Arthur Miller was absorbed with the conflict between material and personal values, Tennessee Williams was obsessed with the person—most often a woman—who was alienated from society. Williams's first success came with the play we have chosen for discussion, *The Glass Menagerie* (1945), and his masterpiece is considered by many to be *A Streetcar Named Desire* (1947). It is interesting that the first play returned to stardom a forgotten actress of the 1920s, Laurette Taylor, and the second brought stardom to a charismatic young actor named Marlon Brando who played the role of Stanley Kowalski. *Streetcar* is representative of all of William's plays in its sympathetic, profoundly insightful portrait of a lost soul, a social misfit, a person—like Chekhov's characters—born out of his or her own time. Yet his plays are imbued with such poetry, compassion, and insight that we not only understand the suffering of these victims but we learn truths about ourselves through them. Blanche Dubois, the leading character of *Streetcar Named Desire,* has lied, put on airs, snared young boys sexually, and lost her job on morals charges; but she has also cared for the sick and dying; tried to hold together a bankrupt estate, taught children about poetry and literature, and loved deeply. She tells her sister, Stella:

> . . . Maybe we are a long way from being made in God's image, but Stella— my sister—there has been *some* progress since then! Such things as art—as poetry and music—such kinds of new light have come into the world since then! In some kinds of people some tenderer feelings have had some little beginning! That we have got to make *grow!* And *cling* to, and hold as our flag! In this dark march toward whatever it is we're approaching. . . . *Don't—don't hang back with the brutes!*

Williams's lost souls—the artist, the non-conformist, the idealist—are also flawed creatures: self-destructive, tortured, psychotic, addictive, or sexually deviant and obsessive. They are often too vulnerable to face the truth of our hard, crass, crude, materialistic, dog-eat-dog world. As Williams struggled with his own vulnerability and mental and physical fragility, his plays became more and more sensational and obscure. No subject—cannibalism, castration, rape, violence, the ravages of addiction—was taboo to him; yet it was not sensationalism for its own sake but rather the mad poet's vision of the sensitive individual lost in a corrupt and destructive world.

Streetcar, like *Death of a Salesman,* was directed by Elia Kazan with sets by Jo Mielziner. Both artists evidenced the integrity which the crafts of directing and design had come to represent. Kazan, as an indirect disciple of Stanislavsky, helped actors explore the psychological depth of their characters, every facet of their make-up and behavior. His productions were beautifully orchestrated with the subtle and explosive dynamics of every moment of the action carefully attended to. It was with the work of Kazan that the director's shaping of and imprint on a production— so evident in today's theatre—began to be felt. Similarly, Jo Mielziner may well be the finest designer of the American theatre. Influenced by the pioneering work of two European designers, Adolphe Appia and Gordon Craig, Mielziner emphasized mood, unity of all elements of the production, the importance of the actor, the creation of an evocative environment, and the collaborative spirit demanded of all the artists and craftspeople of the theatre.

At the same time that the quality of productions and the direction of fine plays seemed to peak, the theatre on Broadway was experiencing a decline. Only fifty-nine new productions were mounted in the 1949–50 season; by 1956 there were only thirty playhouses left on The Great White Way. For one thing, it was becoming increasingly expensive to mount a play on Broadway because of high union rates required by performers and theatre practitioners, the cost of renting the theatres, and the prohibitive costs of materials. Moreover, the theatre now had a second rival; just as movies had once lured audiences away from live productions, it was now possible via television to attend a theatrical event without ever leaving the confines of one's living room. The theatre in Ameria was changing.

The League of Off-Broadway Theatres had been formed in 1949, and by the mid-1950s off-Broadway was a flourishing answer to high costs and safe, commercial properties. One of the striking early off-Broadway productions was the Circle in the Square 1952 revival of Tennessee

Williams's *Summer and Smoke,* directed by Jose Quintero and starring Geraldine Page. Off-Broadway theatres were intimate, permitted a more experimental, off-beat, or risky repertoire, and made simpler, less expensive demands on the scenic artists. Summer theatre festivals were also gaining prominence in the 1950s. Tyrone Guthrie established the famous Shakespeare Festival at Stratford, Ontario in 1953 opening it with a stunning production of *Oedipus Rex,* which attracted vast numbers of American theatre-goers. The following year Joseph Papp created the New York Shakespeare Festival which, besides its regular offerings and encouragement of new playwrights, has offered plays free of charge in Central Park since 1957.

In addition to the beginning of the now popular festivals, the post-war years produced the beginning of the regional theatre movement. Theatre 47 in Dallas, Texas was launched by Margo Jones in 1947, the same year the Alley Theatre in Houston was begun by Nina Vance; the Arena Stage in Washington, D.C., under the leadership of Zelda Fischandler and Edward Mangum, opened its doors in 1949. It is interesting that all three of these pioneering regional theatres were the accomplishments of women. Building on his Stratford experiment, Tyrone Guthrie sought to establish a major regional theatre outside the confines of New York and chose the seemingly remote mid-western city of Minneapolis, Minnesota. Perhaps more than any other, The Guthrie Theatre which opened in 1963, proved that first-rate professional theatre demanding the talents of the finest artists in the English-speaking world could exist outside New York City. As early as 1961, the Theatre Communications Group (TCG) had been established as a network for the growing professional theatrical activity across the country. The regional theatre movement was underway.

Tennessee Williams

Born in Columbus, Mississippi, in 1914, Thomas Lanier Williams was the son of a lady of Southern gentility and a shoe salesman, Cornelius Coffin Williams, who disapproved of the sensitive and effeminate boy, disparagingly nicknaming him "Miss Nancy." Williams attended the University of Missouri for two years, after which he worked as a clerk in the shoe company that employed his father. He wrote in his spare time and returned to university studies in 1936, attending the University of Washington and graduating from Iowa, where he studied writing, in 1938. A series of odd jobs—everything from bellhop to nightclub waiter—took the young Williams around the country, gathering material, characters, and incidents for his work. After some success with one-act plays, Williams achieved his first critical acclaim with *The Glass Menagerie* (1945), his largely autobiographical "memory play," and *A Streetcar Named Desire* in 1947. Play followed play, each time the critics lamenting that Williams did not sustain the promise of *Menagerie* or *Streetcar.* In retrospect, however, the canon is enormously impressive: *Rose Tattoo* (1951), *Camino Real* (1952), *Cat on a Hot Tin Roof* (1954), *Orpheus Descending* (1957), *Sweet Bird of Youth* (1959), and *Night of the Iguana* (1961). In 1969, Williams, like so many of his characters, suffered a severe mental and physical breakdown. Although his later plays did not win the approval of either audiences or critics, Williams did achieve a degree of recognition with *Small Craft Warnings* in 1972. Plagued by poor health, alcoholism, and the loneliness and rejection he felt as a homosexual, Tennessee Williams died in a New York hotel room in 1983 at the age of sixty-nine.

The Glass Menagerie

A favorite pastime of theatre critics and scholars, and theater-goers in general for that matter, is finding the proper pigeon-hole in which to file a play with the assumption that a convenient descriptive category will explain the play and unlock its meaning. But most great plays have a stubborn way of resisting precise categorizing. *The Glass Menagerie* is just such a play. It has been labelled "Expressionism," "Romantic Expressionism" (whatever that may be), Realism, Poetic Drama, Lyrical Character Drama, and many more such things. Williams himself refers to it as a "memory play"; since he is the author, perhaps we should take his word for it and let it go at that.

The fact is *The Glass Menagerie* is all those things and something more, for as a play it undeniably and remarkably transcends any shallow pigeon-holing. It is fundamentally realistic in form but it tempers stultifying Realism with stunning poetic vision. The sensitivity of character portraiture is certainly beyond that found in run-of-the-mill realistic drama. Its dialogue is hardly the speech of everyday life; Tennessee Williams's language is beautifully and unobtrusively poetic. Williams's characters not only say what they have to say, they say it affectively. We understand their world not simply by attending to what they say but by being sensitive to how they say it. Perhaps in this regard, Williams is the true inheritor of the mantle of Anton Chekhov.

Furthermore, the particular form of the play is itself a non-realistic, highly poetic vision. Here Williams undoubtedly owes a debt to Eugene O'Neill for the freedom of form his works guaranteed to the American dramatist. Even more obviously, he owes a debt to Thornton Wilder and the free-wheeling dramatic form he popularized in such plays as *Our Town* and *The Skin of Our Teeth*. Like the Stage Manager in Wilder's play, Williams's protagonist is in part a narrator who sets the scenes and introduces the other characters. The presence of the narrator in effect sets the play back in time. We are talking about and dealing with the past in memory.

The realistic frame of the play is further shattered—or perhaps we should say stretched—by the inclusion of screen projections, music, and special lighting for certain theatrical effects. Williams himself tells us in his introduction to the production manuscript that the music "is used to give emotional emphasis to suitable passages." The images and legends, which are to be projected on a section of the wall between the dining room and living room areas, were intended by the playwright "to give accent to certain values in each scene." Williams did not want his intention in various scenes to become lost in the episodic narrative line of the play. So, he designed the images and legends to "strengthen the effect of what is merely allusion in the writing and allow the primary point to be made more simply and lightly than if the entire responsibility were on the spoken lines." Williams also insisted that "The lighting in the play is not realistic." He even goes so far as to specify that "The light upon Laura should be distinct from the others, having a peculiar pristine clarity such as light used in early religious portraits of female saints or madonnas." No other playwright has more emphatically said that his play is a stage piece and not a piece of literature. The meaning and intention of Williams's play is controlled and fulfilled by the staging. This is definitely not a play that anyone can understand fully simply be reading it. If the reader cannot visualize what is *suggested* on the printed page, he will miss the fundamental meaning that is there.

When Williams informs us that *The Glass Menagerie* is a "memory play," he tips his hand that it is essentially autobiographical. He, very much like August Strindberg, has tilled the fertile soil of his own past to harvest a masterpiece. Anyone who is familiar with the playwright's life instantly recognizes that Amanda and Laura are thinly veiled portraits of his own mother and sister and that he himself is Tom. His own sister, like Laura, was a gentle social misfit who suffered from mental disturbances and, unlike Laura, was eventually lobotomized. His mother had strong emotional ties to the Antebellum South as has Amanda; and, if we are to believe Williams, she was also something of the gentle, well-meaning nag. In his own youth Tennessee Williams realized that if he did not escape the emotionally crippling ties of his home he would not survive in the world. And so Tom, like Williams himself, must free himself of the past in order to live meaningfully in the present and future. The spiritual and psychological pain the playwright's escape cost him is summed up brilliantly in Tom's last lines:

> I didn't go to the moon, I went much further—for time is the longest distance between two places. . . . I traveled around a great deal. . . . I would have stopped, but I was pursued by something. It always came upon me unawares. . . . Oh, Laura, Laura, I tried to leave you behind me, but I am more faithful than I intended to be! I reach for a cigarette, I cross the street, I run into the movies or a bar, I buy a drink, I speak to the nearest stranger—anything that can blow your candles out! . . .—for nowadays the world is lit by lightning! Blow out your candles, Laura—and so goodbye. . . .

In the final moment of the play the protagonist triumphantly fulfills the major action and escapes the pull of the past that would ultimately destroy him.

At first glance, *The Glass Menagerie*, like *The Show-Off*, seems like such a simple, straightforward domestic play. But in its action the play embraces universal truths that give it a philosophical weight, social significance, and dramatic substance that far out-strip most plays of its time. Williams may be writing about socially and emotionally damaged human beings who find it impossible to survive in the contemporary world—characters like Amanda, Laura, Blanche (in *Streetcar Named Desire*) and Alma (in *Summer and Smoke*). But more importantly he is writing about the real world of Post World War II—a time of vital, inevitable transition when our set of values and our very way of life would be called into question and tested. The world has become a cruel and sometimes alien place in which to live. Much of great worth and beauty, including human decency and human dignity, is passing from existence. Crassness, vulgarity, and deceit are triumphing in a world devoid of integrity. It is a time not unlike that depicted in Chekhov's plays. It is a time when only the very strong and healthy will survive "for nowadays the world is lit by lightning." The Lauras of the world are doomed. But the Toms may triumph yet if they can strengthen themselves for the future and escape the enervating impact of the past. Hopefully, in the process Mankind will not lose all touch with what was valuable in the past; hopefully, Mankind, like Tom, will still retain its love of beauty, dignity, decency, and integrity.

As has been stated earlier, the works of Tennessee Williams and Arthur Miller mark the fruition of the great American drama which began in 1920 with the advent in the Broadway theatre of the plays of Eugene O'Neill. At the time of his death, Williams was hailed by more than one critic as disputedly our greatest dramatist. If that is the truth, and it certainly well may be, then *The Glass Menagerie* can safely be called one of the finest masterpieces of the American theatre. It assuredly has very few equals.

THE GLASS MENAGERIE

Tennessee Williams

-------- CHARACTERS --------

AMANDA WINGFIELD (*the mother*), *a little woman of great but confused vitality clinging frantically to another time and place. Her characterization must be carefully created, not copied from type. She is not paranoiac, but her life is paranoia. There is much to admire in Amanda, and as much to love and pity as there is to laugh at. Certainly she has endurance and a kind of heroism, and though her foolishness makes her unwittingly cruel at times, there is tenderness in her slight person.*

LAURA WINGFIELD (*her daughter*). *Amanda, having failed to establish contact with reality, continues to live vitally in her illusions, but Laura's situation is even graver. A childhood illness has left her crippled, one leg slightly shorter than the other, and held in a brace. This defect need not be more than suggested on the stage. Stemming from this, Laura's separation increases till she is like a piece of her own glass collection, too exquisitely fragile to move from the shelf.*

TOM WINGFIELD (*her son and the narrator of the play*). *A poet with a job in a warehouse. His nature is not remorseless, but to escape from a trap he has to act without pity.*

JIM O'CONNOR (*the gentleman caller*), *a nice, ordinary, young man.*

-------- SCENE --------

An Alley in St. Louis.

-------- TIME --------

Now and the Past.

The Glass Menagerie was first produced at the Civic Theater, Chicago, Illinois, on December 26, 1944, and then at the Playhouse Theater, New York City, on March 31, 1945.

SCENE ONE

The Wingfield apartment is in the rear of the building, one of those vast hive-like conglomerations of cellular living-units that flower as warty growths in overcrowded urban centers of lower middle-class population and are symptomatic of the impulse of this largest and fundamentally enslaved section of American society to avoid fluidity and differentiation and to exist and function as one interfused mass of automatism.

The apartment faces an alley and is entered by a fire-escape, a structure whose name is a touch of accidental poetic truth, for all of these huge build-ings are always burning with the slow and implacable fires of human desperation. The fire-escape is included in the set—that is, the landing of it and steps descending from it.

The scene is memory and is therefore nonrealistic. Memory takes a lot of poetic license. It omits some details; others are exaggerated, according to the emotional value of the articles it touches, for memory is seated predominantly in the heart. The interior is therefore rather dim and poetic.

At the rise of the curtain, the audience is faced with the dark, grim rear wall of the Wingfield tenement. This building, which runs parallel to the footlights, is flanked on both sides by dark, narrow alleys which run into murky canyons of tangled clotheslines, garbage cans and the sinister lattice-work of neighboring fire-escapes. It is up and down these side alleys that exterior entrances and exits are made, during the play. At the end of TOM'S *opening commentary, the dark tenement wall slowly reveals (by means of a transparency) the interior of the ground floor Wingfield apartment.*

Downstage is the living room, which also serves as a sleeping room for LAURA, *the sofa unfolding to make her bed. Upstage, center, and divided by a wide arch or second proscenium with transparent faded portieres (or second curtain), is the dining room. In an old-fashioned whatnot in the living room are seen scores of transparent glass animals. A blown-up photograph of the father hangs on the wall of the living room, facing the audience, to the left of the archway. It is the face of a very hand-some young man in a doughboy's First World War cap. He is gallantly smiling, ineluctably smiling, as if to say, "I will be smiling forever."*

The audience hears and sees the opening scene in the dining room through both the transparent fourth wall of the building and the transparent gauze portieres of the dining-room arch. It is during this revealing scene that the fourth wall slowly ascends, out of sight. This transparent exterior wall is not brought down again until the very end of the play, during TOM'S *final speech.*

The narrator is an undisguised convention of the play. He takes whatever license with dramatic convention as is convenient to his purposes.

TOM *enters dressed as a merchant sailor from alley, stage left, and strolls across the front of the stage to the fire-escape. There he stops and lights a cigarette. He addresses the audience.*

TOM. Yes, I have tricks in my pocket, I have things up my sleeve. But I am the opposite of a stage magician. He gives you illusion that has the appearance of truth. I give you truth in the pleasant disguise of illusion.

To begin with, I turn back time. I reverse it to that quaint period, the thirties, when the huge middle class of America was matriculating in a school for the blind. Their eyes had failed them, or they had failed their eyes, and so they were having their fingers pressed forcibly down on the fiery Braille alphabet of a dissolving economy.

In Spain there was revolution. Here there was only shouting and confusion.

In Spain there was Guernica. Here there was disturbances of labor, sometimes pretty violent, in otherwise peaceful cities such as Chicago, Cleveland, Saint Louis. . . .

This is the social background of the play. (*Music*)

The play is memory.

Being a memory play, it is dimly lighted, it is sentimental, it is not realistic.

In memory everything seems to happen to music. That explains the fiddle in the wings.

I am the narrator of the play, and also a character in it.

The other characters are my mother, Amanda, my sister, Laura, and a gentleman caller who appears in the final scenes.

He is the most realistic character in the play, being an emissary from a world of reality that we were somehow set apart from.

But since I have a poet's weakness for symbols, I am using this character also as a symbol; he is the long delayed but always expected something that we live for.

There is a fifth character in the play who doesn't appear except in this larger-than-life-size photograph over the mantel.

This is our father who left us a long time ago.

He was a telephone man who fell in love with long distances; he gave up his job with the telephone company and skipped the light fantastic out of town. . . .

The last we heard of him was a picture post-card from Mazatlan, on the Pacific coast of Mexico, containing a message of two words—

"Hello—Good-bye!" and no address.

I think the rest of the play will explain itself. . . .

(AMANDA'S *voice becomes audible through the portieres.* LEGEND ON SCREEN: "OU SONT LES NEIGES?"[1] *He divides the portieres and enters the upstage area.* AMANDA *and* LAURA *are seated at a drop-leaf table. Eating is indicated by gestures without food or utensils.* AMANDA *faces the audience,* TOM *and* LAURA *are seated in profile. The interior has lit up softly and through the scrim we see* AMANDA *and* LAURA *seated at the table in the upstage area.*)

AMANDA (*calling*). Tom?

TOM. Yes, Mother.

AMANDA. We can't say grace until you come to the table!

TOM. Coming, Mother. (*He bows slightly and withdraws, reappearing a few moments later in his place at the table.*)

---

1. "Where are the snows of yesteryear?"—the famous tribute to beautiful women written by the fifteenth-century lyric poet François Villon.

AMANDA (*to her son*). Honey, don't *push* with your *fingers*. If you have to push with something, the thing to push with is a crust of bread. And chew—chew! Animals have sections in their stomachs which enable them to digest food without mastication, but human beings are supposed to chew their food before they swallow it down. Eat food leisurely, son, and really enjoy it. A well-cooked meal has lots of delicate flavors that have to be held in the mouth for appreciation. So chew your food and give your salivary glands a chance to function!

(TOM *deliberately lays his imaginary fork down and pushes his chair back from the table.*)

TOM. I haven't enjoyed one bite of this dinner because of your constant directions on how to eat it. It's you that make me rush through meals with your hawk-like attention to every bite I take. Sickening—spoils my appetite—all this discussion of—animals' secretion—salivary glands—mastication!

AMANDA (*lightly*). Temperament like a Metropolitan star! (*He rises and crosses downstage*) You're not excused from the table.

TOM. I'm getting a cigarette.

AMANDA. You smoke too much.

(LAURA *rises.*)

LAURA. I'll bring in the blanc mange.

(*He remains standing with his cigarette by the portieres during the following.*)

AMANDA (*rising*). No, sister, no, sister—you be the lady this time and I'll be the darky.

LAURA. I'm already up.

AMANDA. Resume your seat, little sister—I want you to stay fresh and pretty—for gentlemen callers!

LAURA. I'm not expecting any gentlemen callers.

AMANDA (*crossing out to kitchenette. Airily*). Sometimes they come when they are least expected! Why, I remember one Sunday afternoon in Blue Mountain (*Enters kitchenette.*)

TOM. I know what's coming!

LAURA. Yes. But let her tell it.

TOM. Again?

LAURA. She loves to tell it.

(AMANDA *returns with bowl of dessert.*)

AMANDA. One Sunday afternoon in Blue Mountain—your mother received—*seventeen!*—gentlemen callers! Why, sometimes there weren't chairs enough to accommodate them all. We had to send the nigger over to bring in folding chairs from the parish house.

TOM (*remaining at portieres*). How did you entertain those gentlemen callers?

AMANDA. I understood the art of conversation!

TOM. I bet you could talk.

AMANDA. Girls in those days *knew* how to talk, I can tell you.

TOM. Yes?

(IMAGE: AMANDA AS A GIRL ON A PORCH, GREETING CALLERS.)

AMANDA. They knew how to entertain their gentlemen callers. It wasn't enough for a girl to be possessed of a pretty face and a graceful figure—although I wasn't slighted in either respect. She also needed to have a nimble wit and a tongue to meet all occasions.

TOM. What did you talk about?

AMANDA. Things of importance going on in the world! Never anything coarse or common or vulgar. (*She addresses* TOM *as though he were seated in the vacant chair at the table though he remains by portieres. He plays this scene as though he held the book*) My callers were gentlemen—all! Among my callers were some of the most prominent young planters of the Mississippi Delta—planters and sons of planters! (TOM *motions for music and a spot of light on* AMANDA. *Her eyes lift, her face glows, her voice becomes rich and elegiac.* SCREEN LEGEND: "OU SONT LES NEIGES?")

There was young Champ Laughlin, who later became vice-president of the Delta Planters Bank.

Hadley Stevenson, who was drowned in Moon Lake and left his widow one hundred and fifty thousand in Government bonds.

There were the Cutrere brothers, Wesley and Bates. Bates was one of my bright particular beaux! He got in a quarrel with that wild Wainwright boy. They shot it out on the floor of Moon Lake Casino. Bates was shot through the stomach. Died in the ambulance on his way to Memphis. His widow was also well-provided for, came into eight or ten thousand acres, that's all. She married him on the rebound—never lover her—carried my picture on him the night he died!

And there was that boy that every girl in the Delta had set her cap for! That beautiful, brilliant young Fitzhugh boy from Greene County!

TOM. What did he leave his widow?

AMANDA. He never married! Gracious, you talk as though all of my old admirers had turned up their toes to the daisies!

TOM. Isn't this the first you've mentioned that still survives?

AMANDA. That Fitzhugh boy went North and made a fortune—came to be known as the Wolf of Wall Street! He had the Midas touch, whatever he touched turned to gold!

And I could have been Mrs. Duncan J. Fitzhugh, mind you! But—I picked your *father!*

LAURA (*rising*). Mother, let me clear the table.

AMANDA. No, dear, you go in front and study your typewriter chart. Or practice your shorthand a little. Stay fresh and pretty!—It's almost time for our gentlemen callers to start arriving. (*She flounces girlishly toward the kitchenette*) How many do you suppose we're going to entertain this afternoon?

(TOM *throws down the paper and jumps up with a groan.*)

LAURA (*alone in the dining room*). I don't believe we're going to receive any, Mother.

AMANDA (*reappearing, airily*). What? No one—not one? You must be joking! (LAURA *nervously echoes her laugh. She slips in a fugitive manner through the half-open portieres and draws them gently behind her. A shaft of very clear light is thrown on her face against the faded tapestry of the curtains.* MUSIC: "THE GLASS MENAGERIE" UNDER FAINTLY. *Lightly*) Not one gentleman caller! It can't be true! There must be a flood, there must have been a tornado!

LAURA. It isn't a flood, it's not a tornado, Mother. I'm just not popular like you were in Blue Mountain. . . . (TOM *utters another groan.* LAURA *glances at him with a faint, apologetic smile. Her voice catching a little*) Mother's afraid I'm going to be an old maid.

(*The Scene Dims Out with "Glass Menagerie" Music.*)

SCENE TWO

LEGEND. "LAURA, HAVEN'T YOU EVER LIKED SOME BOY?"

On the dark stage the screen is lighted with the image of blue roses. Gradually LAURA'S *figure becomes apparent and the screen goes out. The music subsides.*

LAURA *is seated in the delicate ivory chair at the small clawfoot table.*

She wears a dress of soft violet material for a kimono—her hair tied back from her forehead with a ribbon.

She is washing and polishing her collection of glass.

AMANDA *appears on the fire-escape steps. At the sound of her ascent,* LAURA *catches her breath, thrusts the bowl of ornaments away and seats herself stiffly before the diagram of the typewriter keyboard as though it held her spellbound.*

Something has happened to AMANDA. *It is written in her face as she climbs to the landing: a look that is grim and hopeless and a little absurd.*

She has on one of those cheap or imitation velvety-looking cloth coats with imitation fur collar. Her hat is five or six years old, one of those dreadful cloche hats that were worn in the late twenties and she is clasping an enormous black patent-leather pocketbook with nicked clasps and initials. This is her full-dress outfit, the one she usually wears to the D.A.R.[2]

Before entering she looks through the door.

She purses her lips, opens her eyes very wide, rolls them upward and shakes her head.

Then she slowly lets herself in the door. Seeing her mother's expression LAURA *touches her lips with a nervous gesture.*

LAURA. Hello, Mother, I was— (*She makes a nervous gesture toward the chart on the wall.* AMANDA *leans against the shut door and stares at* LAURA *with a martyred look.*)

AMANDA. Deception? Deception? (*She slowly removes her hat and gloves, continuing the sweet suffering stare. She lets the hat and gloves fall on the floor—a bit of acting.*)

---

2. The Daughters of the American Revolution, an organization of American women whose ancestors fought in the American Revolution.

LAURA (*shakily*). How was the D.A.R. meeting? (AMANDA *slowly opens her purse and removes a dainty white handerchief which she shakes out delicately and delicately touches to her lips and nostrils*) Didn't you go to the D.A.R. meeting, Mother?

AMANDA (*faintly, almost inaudibly*). —No.—No. (*Then more forcibly*) I did not have the strength— to go to the D.A.R. In fact, I did not have the courage! I wanted to find a hole in the ground and hide myself in it forever! (*She crosses slowly to the wall and removes the diagram of the typewriter keyboard. She holds it in front of her for a second, staring at it sweetly and sorrowfully— then bites her lips and tears it in two pieces.*)

LAURA (*faintly*). Why did you do that, Mother? (AMANDA *repeats the same procedure with the chart of the Gregg Alphabet*[3]) Why are you—

AMANDA. Why? Why? How old are you, Laura?

LAURA. Mother, you know my age.

AMANDA. I thought that you were an adult; it seems that I was mistaken. (*She crosses slowly to the sofa and sinks down and stares at* LAURA.)

LAURA. Please don't stare at me, Mother.

(AMANDA *closes her eyes and lowers her head. Count ten.*)

AMANDA. What are we going to do, what is going to become of us, what is the future?

(*Count ten.*)

LAURA. Has something happened, Mother? (AMANDA *draws a long breath and takes out the handkerchief again. Dabbing process*) Mother, has—something happened?

AMANDA. I'll be all right in a minute, I'm just bewildered—(*Count five*)—by life. . . .

LAURA. Mother, I wish that you would tell me what's happened!

AMANDA. As you know, I was supposed to be inducted into my office at the D.A.R. this afternoon. (IMAGE: A SWARM OF TYPEWRITERS) But I stopped off at Rubicam's Business College to speak to your teachers about your having a cold and ask them what progress they thought you were making down there.

LAURA. Oh. . . .

AMANDA. I went to the typing instructor and introduced myself as your mother. She didn't know who you were. Wingfield, she said. We don't have any such student enrolled at the school!

I assured her she did, that you had been going to classes since early in January.

"I wonder," she said, "if you could be talking about that terribly shy little girl who dropped out of school after only a few days' attendance?"

"No," I said, "Laura, my daughter, has been going to school every day for the past six weeks!"

"Excuse me," she said. She took the attendance book out and there was your name, unmistakably printed, and all the dates you were absent until they decided that you had dropped out of school.

I still said, "No, there must have been some mistake! There must have been some mix-up in the records!"

And she said, "No—I remember her perfectly now. Her hands shook so that she couldn't hit the right keys! The first time we gave a speed-test, she broke down completely—was sick at the stomach and almost had to be carried into the wash-room! After that morning she never showed up any more. We phoned the house but never got any answer"— while I was working at Famous and Barr, I suppose, demonstrating those—Oh!

I felt so weak I could barely keep on my feet!

I had to sit down while they got me a glass of water!

Fifty dollars' tuition, all of our plans—my hopes and ambitions for you—just gone up the spout, just gone up the spout like that. (LAURA *draws a long breath and gets awkwardly to her feet. She crosses to the victrola and winds it up*) What are you doing?

LAURA. Oh! (*She releases the handle and returns to her seat.*)

AMANDA. Laura, where have you been going when you've gone out pretending that you were going to business college?

LAURA. I've just been going out walking.

AMANDA. That's not true.

LAURA. It is. I just went walking.

AMANDA. Walking? Walking? In winter? Deliberately courting pneumonia in that light coat? Where did you walk to, Laura?

LAURA. All sorts of places—mostly in the park.

AMANDA. Even after you'd started catching that cold?

---

3. A commonly used shorthand alphabet.

LAURA. It was the lesser of two evils, Mother. (IMAGE: WINTER SCENE IN PARK) I couldn't go back up. I—threw up—on the floor!

AMANDA. From half past seven till after five every day you mean to tell me you walked around in the park, because you wanted to make me think that you were still going to Rubicam's Business College?

LAURA. It wasn't as bad as it sounds. I went inside places to get warmed up.

AMANDA. Inside where?

LAURA. I went in the art museum and the bird-houses at the Zoo. I visited the penguins every day! Sometimes I did without lunch and went to the movies. Lately I've been spending most of my afternoons in the Jewel-box, that big glass house where they raise the tropical flowers.

AMANDA. You did all this to deceive me, just for deception? (LAURA looks down) Why?

LAURA. Mother, when you're disappointed, you get that awful suffering look on your face, like the picture of Jesus' mother in the museum!

AMANDA. Hush!

LAURA. I couldn't face it.

(Pause. A whisper of strings. LEGEND: "THE CRUST OF HUMILITY.")

AMANDA (hopelessly fingering the huge pocket-book). So what are we going to do the rest of our lives? Stay home and watch the parades go by? Amuse ourselves with the glass menagerie, darling! Eternally play those worn-out phonograph records your father left as a painful reminder of him?
We won't have a business career—we've given that up because it gave us nervous indigestion! (Laughs wearily) What is there left but dependency all our lives? I know so well what becomes of unmarried women who aren't prepared to occupy a position. I've seen such pitiful cases in the South—barely tolerated spinsters living upon the grudging patronage of sister's husband or brother's wife!—stuck away in some little mouse-trap of a room—encouraged by one in-law to visit another—little birdlike women without any nest—eating the crust of humility all their life!
Is that the future that we've mapped out for ourselves?
I swear it's the only alternative I can think of!
It isn't a very pleasant alternative, is it?
Of course—some girls do marry. (LAURA twists

Of course—some girls do marry. (LAURA twists her hands nervously) Haven't you ever liked some boy!

LAURA. Yes. I liked one once. (Rises) I came across his picture a while ago.

AMANDA (with some interest). He gave you his picture?

LAURA. No, it's in the year-book.

AMANDA (disappointed). Oh—a high-school boy. (SCREEN IMAGE: JIM AS HIGH-SCHOOL HERO BEARING A SILVER CUP.)

LAURA. Yes. His name was Jim. (LAURA lifts the heavy annual from the claw-foot table) Here he is in The Pirates of Penzance.

AMANDA (absently). The what?

LAURA. The operetta the senior class put on. He had a wonderful voice and we sat across the aisle from each other Mondays, Wednesdays and Fridays in the Aud. Here he is with the silver cup for debating! See his grin?

AMANDA (absently). He must have had a jolly disposition.

LAURA. He used to call me—Blue Roses.

(IMAGE: BLUE ROSES.)

AMANDA. Why did he call you such a name as that?

LAURA. When I had that attack of pleurosis—he asked me what was the matter when I came back. I said pleurosis—he thought that I said Blue Roses! So that's what he always called me after that. Whenever he saw me, he'd holler, "Hello, Blue Roses!" I didn't care for the girl that he went out with. Emily Meisenbach. Emily was the best-dressed girl at Soldan. She never struck me, though, as being sincere. . . . It says in the Personal Section—they're engaged. That's—six years ago! They must be married by now.

AMANDA. Girls that aren't cut out for business careers usually wind up married to some nice man. (Gets up with a spark of revival) Sister, that's what you'll do!

(LAURA utters a startled, doubtful laugh. She reaches quickly for a piece of glass.)

LAURA. But, Mother—

AMANDA. Yes? (Crossing to photograph.)

LAURA (in a tone of frightened apology). I'm—crippled!

(IMAGE: SCREEN.)

AMANDA. Nonsense! Laura, I've told you never, never to use that word. Why, you're not crippled, you just have a little defect—hardly noticeable, even! When people have some slight disadvantage like that, they cultivate other things to make up for it—develop charm—and vivacity—and—*charm!* That's all you have to do! (*She turns again to the photograph*) One thing your father had *plenty of*—was *charm!*

(TOM *motions to the fiddle in the wings.*)

(*The Scene Fades Out with Music.*)

SCENE THREE

LEGEND ON SCREEN: "AFTER THE FIASCO—"
TOM *speaks from the fire-escape landing.*

TOM. After the fiasco at Rubicam's Business College, the idea of getting a gentleman caller for Laura began to play a more and more important part in Mother's calculations.
It became an obsession. Like some archetype of the universal unconscious, the image of the gentleman caller haunted our small apartment.

. . . (IMAGE: YOUNG MAN AT DOOR WITH FLOWERS)
An evening at home rarely passed without some allusion to this image, this spectre, this hope. . . .
Even when he wasn't mentioned, his presence hung in Mother's preoccupied look and in my sister's frightened, apologetic manner—hung like a sentence passed upon the Wingfields!
Mother was a woman of action as well as words.
She began to take logical steps in the planned direction.
Late that winter and in the early spring—realizing that extra money would be needed to properly feather the nest and plume the bird—she conducted a vigorous campaign on the telephone, roping in subscribers to one of those magazines for matrons called *The Homemaker's Companion,* the type of journal that features the serialized sublimations of ladies of letters who think in terms of delicate cuplike breasts, slim, tapering waists, rich, creamy thighs, eyes like wood-smoke in autumn, fingers that soothe and caress like strains of music, bodies as powerful as Etruscan sculpture.

(SCREEN IMAGE: GLAMOR MAGAZINE COVER. AMANDA *enters with phone on long extension cord. She is spotted in the dim stage.*)

AMANDA. Ida Scott? This is Amanda Wingfield!
We *missed* you at the D.A.R. last Monday!
I said to myself: She's probably suffering with that sinus condition! How is that sinus condition?
Horrors! Heaven have mercy!—You're a Christian martyr, yes, that's what you are, a Christian martyr!
Well, I just now happened to notice that your subscription to the *Companion's* about to expire! Yes, it expires with the next issue, honey!—just when that wonderful new serial by Bessie Mae Hopper is getting off to such an exciting start. Oh, honey, it's something that you can't miss! You remember how *Gone With the Wind* took everybody by storm? You simply couldn't go out if you hadn't read it. All everybody *talked* was Scarlett O'Hara. Well, this is a book that critics already compare to *Gone With the Wind*. It's the *Gone With the Wind* of the post-World War generation!—What?—Burning?—Oh, honey, don't let them burn, go take a look in the oven and I'll hold the wire! Heavens—I think she's hung up!

Dim Out

(LEGEND ON SCREEN: "YOU THINK I'M IN LOVE WITH CONTINENTAL SHOEMAKERS?" *Before the stage is lighted, the violent voices of* TOM *and* AMANDA *are heard. They are quarreling behind the portieres. In front of them stands* LAURA *with clenched hands and panicky expression. A clear pool of light on her figure throughout this scene.*)

TOM. What in Christ's name am I—

AMANDA (*shrilly*). Don't you use that—

TOM. Supposed to do!

AMANDA. Expression! Not in my—

TOM. Ohhh!

AMANDA. Presence! Have you gone out of your senses?

TOM. I have, that's true, *driven* out!

AMANDA. What is the matter with you, you—big—big—IDIOT!

TOM. Look!—I've got *no thing,* no single thing—

AMANDA. Lower your voice!

TOM. In my life here that I can call my own! Everything is—

AMANDA. Stop that shouting!

TOM. Yesterday you confiscated my books! You had the nerve to—

AMANDA. I took that horrible novel back to the library—yes! That hideous book by that insane Mr. Lawrence. (TOM *laughs wildly*) I cannot control the output of diseased minds or people who cater to them—(TOM *laughs still more wildly*) BUT I WON'T ALLOW SUCH FILTH BROUGHT INTO MY HOUSE! No, no, no, no, no!

TOM. House, house! Who pays rent on it, who makes a slave of himself to—

AMANDA (*fairly screeching*). Don't you DARE to—

TOM. No, no, *I* mustn't say things! *I've* got to just—

AMANDA. Let me tell you—

TOM. I don't want to hear any more! (*He tears the portieres open. The upstage area is lit with a turgid smoky red glow.*)

(AMANDA'S *hair is in metal curlers and she wears a very old bathrobe, much too large for her slight figure, a relic of the faithless Mr. Wingfield. An upright typewriter and a wild disarray of manuscripts is on the dropleaf table. The quarrel was probably precipitated by* AMANDA'S *interruption of his creative labor. A chair lying overthrown on the floor. Their gesticulating shadows are cast on the ceiling by the fiery glow.*)

AMANDA. You *will* hear more, you—

TOM. No, I won't hear more, I'm going out!

AMANDA. You come right back in—

TOM. Out, out, out! Because I'm—

AMANDA. Come back here, Tom Wingfield! I'm not through talking to you!

TOM. Oh, go—

LAURA (*desperately*). —Tom!

AMANDA. You're going to listen, and no more insolence from you! I'm at the end of my patience!

(*He comes back toward her.*)

TOM. What do you think I'm at? Aren't I supposed to have any patience to reach the end of, Mother? I know, I know. It seems unimportant to you, what I'm *doing*—what I *want* to do—having a little *difference* between them! You don't think that—

AMANDA. I think you've been doing things that you're ashamed of. That's why you act like this. I don't believe that you go every night to the movies. Nobody goes to the movies night after night. Nobody in their right minds goes to the movies as often as you pretend to. People don't go

to the movies at nearly midnight, and movies don't let out at two A.M. Come in stumbling. Muttering to yourself like a maniac! You get three hours' sleep and then go to work. Oh, I can picture the way you're doing down there. Moping, doping, because you're in no condition.

TOM (*wildly*). No, I'm in no condition!

AMANDA. What right have you got to jeopardize your job? Jeopardize the security of us all? How do you think we'd manage if you were—

TOM. Listen! You think I'm crazy *about the warehouse*? (*He bends fiercely toward her slight figure*) You think I'm in love with the Continental Shoemakers? You think I want to spend fifty-five *years* down there in that—*celotex interior!* with —*fluorescent*—*tubes!* Look! I'd rather somebody pick up a crowbar and battered out my brains— than go back mornings! I *go!* Every time you come in yelling that God damn *"Rise and Shine!"* *"Rise and Shine!* I say to myself, "How *lucky dead* people are!" But I get up. I *go!* For sixty-five dollars a month I give up all that I dream of doing and being ever! And you say self—*self's* all I ever think of. Why, listen, if self is what I thought of, Mother, I'd be where he is—GONE! (*Pointing to father's picture*) As far as the system of transportation reaches! (*He starts past her. She grabs his arm*) Don't grab at me, Mother!

AMANDA. Where are you going?

TOM. I'm going to the *movies!*

AMANDA. I don't believe that lie!

TOM (*crouching toward her, overtowering her tiny figure. She backs away, gasping*): I'm going to opium dens! Yes, opium dens, dens of vice and criminals' hang-outs, Mother. I've joined the Hogan gang,[4] I'm a hired assassin, I carry a tommy-gun in a violin case! I run a string of cathouses in the Valley! They call me Killer, Killer Wingfield, I'm leading a double-life, a simple, honest warehouse worker by day, by night a dynamic *czar* of the *underworld, Mother.* I go to gambling casinos, I spin away fortunes on the roulette table! I wear a patch over one eye and a false mustache, sometimes I put on green whiskers. On those occasions they call me—*El Diablo!* Oh, I could tell you things to make you sleepless! My enemies plan to dynamite this place. They're going to blow us all sky-high some night! I'll be glad,

4. "Dapper Danny" Hogan was the leader of the underworld in St. Paul, Minnesota, during the 1920s.

491

very happy, and so will you! You'll go up, up on a broomstick, over Blue Mountain with seventeen gentlemen callers! You ugly—babbling old—witch. . . . (*He goes through a series of violent, clumsy movements, seizing his overcoat, lunging to the door, pulling it fiercely open. The women watch him, aghast. His arm catches in the sleeve of the coat as he struggles to pull it on. For a moment he is pinioned by the bulky garment. With an outraged groan he tears the coat off again, splitting the shoulder of it, and hurls it across the room. It strikes against the shelf of* LAURA'S *glass collection, there is a tinkle of shattering glass.* LAURA *cries out as if wounded.* MUSIC. LEGEND: "THE GLASS MENAGERIE.")

LAURA (*shrilly*). *My glass!*—menagerie. . . . (*She covers her face and turns away.*)

(*But* AMANDA *is still stunned and stupefied by the "ugly witch" so that she barely notices this occurrence. Now she recovers her speech.*)

AMANDA (*in an awful voice*). I won't speak to you—until you apologize!

(*She crosses through portieres and draws them together behind her.* TOM *is left with* LAURA. LAURA *clings weakly to the mantel with her face averted.* TOM *stares at her stupidly for a moment. Then he crosses to shelf. Drops awkwardly on his knees to collect the fallen glass, glancing at* LAURA *as if he would speak but couldn't.*)

(*"The Glass Menagerie" steals in as The Scene Dims Out.*)

SCENE FOUR

The interior is dark. Faint light in the alley.

A deep-voiced bell in a church is tolling the hour of five as the scene commences.

TOM *appears at the top of the alley. After each solemn boom of the bell in the tower, he shakes a little noise-maker or rattle as if to express the tiny spasm of man in contrast to the sustained power and dignity of the Almighty. This and the unsteadiness of his advance make it evident that he has been drinking.*

As he climbs the few steps to the fire-escape landing light steals up inside. LAURA *appears in night-dress, observing* TOM'S *empty bed in the front room.*

TOM *fishes in his pockets for door-key, removing a motley assortment of articles in the search, including a perfect shower of movie-ticket stubs and an empty bottle. At last he finds the key, but just as he is about to insert it, it slips from his fingers. He strikes a match and crouches below the door.*

TOM (*bitterly*). One crack—and it falls through!

(LAURA *opens the door.*)

LAURA. Tom, Tom, what are you doing?

TOM. Looking for a door-key.

LAURA. Where have you been all this time?

TOM. I have been to the movies.

LAURA. All this time at the movies?

TOM. There was a very long program. There was a Garbo[5] picture and a Mickey Mouse and a travelogue and a newsreel and a preview of coming attractions. And there was an organ solo and a collection for the milkfund simultaneously—which ended up in a terrible fight between a fat lady and an usher!

LAURA (*innocently*). Did you have to stay through everything?

TOM. Of course! And, oh, I forgot! There was a big stage show! The headliner on this stage show was Malvolio the Magician. He performed wonderful tricks, many of them, such as pouring water back and forth between pitchers. First it turned to wine and then it turned to beer and then it turned to whiskey. I know it was whiskey it finally turned into because he needed somebody to come up out of the audience to help him, and I came up—both shows! It was Kentucky Straight Bourbon. A very generous fellow, he gave souvenirs. (*He pulls from his back pocket a shimmering rainbow-colored scarf*) He gave me this. This is his magic scarf. You can have it, Laura. You wave it over a canary cage and you get a bowl of gold-fish. You wave it over the gold-fish bowl and they fly away canaries. . . . But the wonderfullest trick of all was the coffin trick. We nailed him into a coffin and he got out of the coffin without removing one nail. (*He has come inside*) There is a trick that would come in handy for me—get me out of this 2 by 4 situation! (*Flops onto bed and starts removing shoes.*)

5. Greta Garbo (1905–1990), an American motion picture actress of Swedish descent, achieved great popularity in the 1930s for her roles in *Camille* and *Anna Karenina.*

LAURA. Tom—Shhh!

TOM. What're you shushing me for?

LAURA. You'll wake up Mother.

TOM. Goody, goody! Pay 'er back for all those "Rise an' Shines." (*Lies down, groaning*) You know it don't take much intelligence to get yourself into a nailed-up coffin, Laura. But who in hell ever got himself out of one without removing one nail?

(*As if in answer, the father's grinning photograph lights up.*) Scene Dims Out

(*Immediately following: The church bell is heard striking six. At the sixth stroke the alarm clock goes off in* AMANDA'S *room, and after a few moments we hear her calling: "Rise and Shine! Rise and Shine! Laura, go tell your brother to rise and shine!"*)

TOM (*sitting up slowly*). I'll rise—but I won't shine.

(*The light increases.*)

AMANDA. Laura, tell your brother his coffee is ready.

(LAURA *slips into front room.*)

LAURA. Tom!—It's nearly seven. Don't make Mother nervous. (*He stares at her stupidly. Beseechingly*) Tom, speak to Mother this morning. Make up with her, apologize, speak to her!

TOM. She won't to me. It's her that started not speaking.

LAURA. If you just say you're sorry she'll start speaking.

TOM. Her not speaking—is that such a tragedy?

LAURA. Please—please!

AMANDA (*calling from kitchenette*). Laura, are you going to do what I asked you to do, or do I have to get dressed and go out myself?

LAURA. Going, going—soon as I get on my coat! (*She pulls on a shapeless felt hat with nervous, jerky movement, pleadingly glancing at* TOM. *Rushes awkwardly for coat. The coat is one of* AMANDA'S, *inaccurately made-over, the sleeves too short for* LAURA) Butter and what else?

AMANDA (*entering upstage*). Just butter. Tell them to charge it.

LAURA. Mother, they make such faces when I do that.

AMANDA. Sticks and stones can break our bones, but the expression on Mr. Garfinkel's face won't harm us! Tell your brother his coffee is getting cold.

LAURA (*at door*). Do what I asked you, will you, will you, Tom?

(*He looks sullenly away.*)

AMANDA. Laura, go now or just don't go at all!

LAURA (*rushing out*). Going—going! (*A second later she cries out.* TOM *springs up and crosses to door,* AMANDA *rushes anxiously in.* TOM *opens the door.*)

TOM. Laura?

LAURA. I'm all right. I slipped, but I'm all right.

AMANDA (*peering anxiously after her*). If anyone breaks a leg on those fire-escape steps, the landlord ought to be sued for every cent he possesses!

(*She shuts door. Remembers she isn't speaking and returns to other room.*)

(*As* TOM *enters listlessly for his coffee, she turns her back to him and stands rigidly facing the window on the gloomy gray vault of the areaway. Its light on her face with its aged but childish features is cruelly sharp, satirical as a Daumier[6] print.* MUSIC UNDER: "AVE MARIA."

TOM *glances sheepishly but sullenly at her averted figure and slumps at the table. The coffee is scalding hot; he sips it and gasps and spits it back in the cup. At his gasp,* AMANDA *catches her breath and half turns. Then catches herself and turns back to window.*

TOM *blows on his coffee, glancing sidewise at his mother. She clears her throat.* TOM *clears his. He starts to rise. Sinks back down again, scratches his head, clears his throat again.* AMANDA *coughs.* TOM *raises his cup in both hands to blow on it, his eyes staring over the rim of it at his mother for several moments. Then he slowly sets the cup down and awkwardly and hesitantly rises from the chair.*)

TOM (*hoarsely*). Mother, I—I apologize, Mother. (AMANDA *draws a quick shuddering breath. Her face works grotesquely. She breaks into childlike tears*) I'm sorry for what I said, for everything that I said, I didn't mean it.

AMANDA (*sobbingly*). My devotion has made me a witch and so I make myself hateful to my children!

6. Honoré Daumier (1808–1879) was a French caricaturist and painter. His famous lithographs hold the foibles of a bourgeois society up to ridicule.

TOM. No, you *don't*.

AMANDA. I worry so much, don't sleep, it makes me nervous!

TOM (*gently*). I understand that.

AMANDA. I've had to put up a solitary battle all these years. But you're my right-hand bower![7] Don't fall down, don't fail!

TOM (*gently*). I'll try Mother.

AMANDA (*with great enthusiasm*). Try and you will SUCCEED! (*The notion makes her breathless*) Why, you—you're just *full* of natural endowments! Both my children—they're *unusual* children! Don't you think I know it? I'm so—*proud!* Happy and—feel I've—so much to be thankful for but—Promise me one thing, Son!

TOM. What, Mother?

AMANDA. Promise, son, you'll—never be a drunkard!

TOM (*turns to her grinning*). I will never be a drunkard, Mother.

AMANDA. That's what frightened me so, that you'd be drinking! Eat a bowl of Purina!

TOM. Just coffee, Mother.

AMANDA. Shredded wheat biscuit?

TOM. No. No, Mother, just coffee.

AMANDA. You can't put in a day's work on an empty stomach. You've got ten minutes—don't gulp! Drinking too-hot liquids makes cancer of the stomach. . . . Put cream in.

TOM. No, thank you.

AMANDA. To cool it.

TOM. No! No, thank you, I want it black.

AMANDA. I know, but it's not good for you. We have to do all that we can to build ourselves up. In these trying times we live in, all that we have to cling to is—each other. . . . That's why it's so important to—Tom, I—I sent out your sister so I could discuss something with you. If you hadn't spoken I would have spoken to you. (*Sits down.*)

TOM (*gently*). What is it, Mother, that you want to discuss?

AMANDA. *Laura!*

(TOM *puts his cup down slowly.* LEGEND ON SCREEN: "LAURA." MUSIC: "THE GLASS MENAGERIE.")

TOM. —Oh.—Laura. . . .

AMANDA (*touching his sleeve*). You know how Laura is. So quiet but—still water runs deep! She notices things and I think she—broods about them. (TOM *looks up*) A few days ago I came in and she was crying.

TOM. What about?

AMANDA. You.

TOM. Me?

AMANDA. She has an idea that you're not happy here.

TOM. What gave her that idea?

AMANDA. What gives her any idea? However, you do act strangely. I—I'm not criticizing, understand *that!* I know your ambitions do not lie in the warehouse, that like everybody in the whole wide world—you've had to—make sacrifices, but—Tom—Tom—life's not easy, it calls for—Spartan endurance! There's so many things in my heart that I cannot describe to you! I've never told you but I—*loved* your father. . . .

TOM (*gently*). I know that, Mother.

AMANDA. And you—when I see you taking after his ways! Staying out late—and—well, you *had* been drinking the night you were in that—terrifying condition! Laura says that you hate the apartment and that you go out nights to get away from it! Is that true, Tom?

TOM. No. You say there's so much in your heart that you can't describe to me. That's true of me, too. There's so much in my heart that I can't describe to *you!* So let's respect each other's—

AMANDA. But, why—*why,* Tom—are you always so *restless?* Where do you *go* to, nights?

TOM. I—go to the movies.

AMANDA. Why do you go to the movies so much, Tom?

TOM. I go to the movies because—I like adventure. Adventure is something I don't have much of at work, so I go to the movies.

AMANDA. But, Tom, you go to the movies *entirely* too *much!*

TOM. I like a lot of adventure.

7. In the card games of euchre and five hundred, the highest card, the jack of trumps, is called the right bower.

(AMANDA *looks baffled, then hurt. As the familiar inquisition resumes he becomes hard and impatient again.* AMANDA *slips back into her querulous attitude toward him.* IMAGE ON SCREEN: SAILING VESSEL WITH JOLLY ROGER.[8])

AMANDA. Most young men find adventure in their careers.

TOM. Then most young men are not employed in a warehouse.

AMANDA. The world is full of young men employed in warehouses and offices and factories.

TOM. Do all of them find adventure in their careers?

AMANDA. They do or they do without it! Not everybody has a craze for adventure.

TOM. Man is by instinct a lover, a hunter, a fighter, and none of those instincts are given much play at the warehouse!

AMANDA. Man is by instinct! Don't quote instinct to me! Instinct is something that people have got away from! It belongs to animals! Christian adults don't want it!

TOM. What do Christian adults want, then, Mother?

AMANDA. Superior things! Things of the mind and the spirit! Only animals have to satisfy instincts! Surely your aims are somewhat higher than theirs! Than monkeys—pigs—

TOM. I reckon they're not.

AMANDA. You're joking! However, that isn't what I wanted to discuss.

TOM (*rising*). I haven't much time.

AMANDA (*pushing his shoulders*). Sit down.

TOM. You want me to punch in red at the warehouse, Mother?

AMANDA. You have five minutes. I want to talk about Laura.

(LEGEND: "PLANS AND PROVISIONS.")

TOM. All right! What about Laura?

AMANDA. We have to be making some plans and provisions for her. She's older than you, two years, and nothing has happened. She just drifts along doing nothing. It frightens me terribly how she just drifts along.

TOM. I guess she's the type that people call home girls.

AMANDA. There's no such type, and if there is, it's a pity! That is unless the home is hers, with a husband!

TOM. What?

AMANDA. Oh, I can see the handwriting on the wall as plain as I see the nose in front of my face! It's terrifying!

More and more you remind me of your father! He was out all hours without explanation!—Then *left? Good-bye!*

And me with the bag to hold. I saw that letter you got from the Merchant Marine. I know what you're dreaming of. I'm not standing here blindfolded.

Very well, then. Then *do* it!

But not till there's somebody to take your place.

TOM. What do you mean?

AMANDA. I mean that as soon as Laura has got somebody to take care of her, married, a home of her own, independent—why, then you'll be free to go wherever you please, on land, on sea, whichever way the wind blows you!

But until that time you've got to look out for your sister. I don't say me because I'm old and don't matter! I say for your sister because she's young and dependent.

I put her in business college—a dismal failure! Frightened her so it made her sick at the stomach.

I took her over to the Young People's League at the church. Another fiasco. She spoke to nobody, nobody spoke to her. Now all she does is fool with those pieces of glass and play those worn-out records. What kind of a life is that for a girl to lead?

TOM. What can I do about it?

AMANDA. Overcome selfishness!

Self, self, self is all that you ever think of! (TOM *springs up and crosses to get his coat. It is ugly and bulky. He pulls on a cap with earmuffs*) Where is your muffler? Put your wool muffler on! (*He snatches it angrily from the closet and tosses it around his neck and pulls both ends tight*) Tom! I haven't said what I had in mind to ask you.

TOM. I'm too late to—

AMANDA (*catching his arm—very importunately. Then shyly*). Down at the warehouse, aren't there some—nice young men?

TOM. No!

8. A black pirate flag with white skull and crossbones.

AMANDA. There *must* be—*some*. . . .

TOM. Mother—(*Gesture.*)

AMANDA. Find out one that's clean-living—doesn't drink and—ask him out for sister!

TOM. What?

AMANDA. For *sister!* To *meet!* Get *acquainted!*

TOM (*stamping to door*). Oh, my *go-osh!*

AMANDA. Will you? (*He opens door. Imploringly*) Will you? (*He starts down*) Will you? *Will* you, dear?

TOM (*calling back*). YES!

(AMANDA *closes the door hesitantly and with a troubled but faintly hopeful expression.* SCREEN IMAGE: GLAMOR MAGAZINE COVER. *Spot* AMANDA *at phone.*)

AMANDA. Ella Cartwright? This is Amanda Wing-field!

How are you, honey?

How is that kidney condition? (*Count five*)

Horrors! (*Count five*)

You're a Christian martyr, yes, honey, that's what you are, a Christian martyr!

Well, I just now happened to notice in my little red book that your subscription to the *Companion* has just run out! I knew that you wouldn't want to miss out on the wonderful serial starting in this new issue. It's by Bessie Mae Hopper, the first thing she's written since *Honeymoon for Three.*

Wasn't that a strange and interesting story? Well, this one is even lovelier, I believe. It has a sophisticated, society background. It's all about the horsey set on Long Island!

(*Fade Out.*)

SCENE FIVE

LEGEND ON SCREEN: "ANNUNCIATION."[9] *Fade with music.*

It is early dusk of a spring evening. Supper has just been finished in the Wingfield apartment. AMANDA *and* LAURA *in light-colored dresses are removing dishes from the table, in the upstage area, which is shadowy, their movements formalized almost as a dance or ritual, their moving forms as pale and silent as moths.*

9. The actual moment of the Incarnation, when the angel announced to the Virgin Mary that God the Son was to be born to her (Luke 1:26–28).

TOM, *in white shirt and trousers, rises from the table and crosses toward the fire-escape.*

AMANDA (*as he passes her*). Son, will you do me a favor?

TOM. What?

AMANDA. Comb your hair! You look so pretty when your hair is combed! (TOM *slouches on a sofa with evening paper. Enormous caption "Franco Triumphs"*) There is only one respect in which I would like you to emulate your father.

TOM. What respect is that?

AMANDA. The care he always took of his appearance. He never allowed himself to look untidy. (*He throws down the paper and crosses to fire-escape*) Where are you going?

TOM. I'm going out to smoke.

AMANDA. You smoke too much. A pack a day at fifteen cents a pack. How much would that amount to in a month? Thirty times fifteen is how much, Tom? Figure it out and you will be astounded at what you could save. Enough to give you a night-school course in accounting at Washington U! Just think what a wonderful thing that would be for you, Son!

(TOM *is unmoved by the thought.*)

TOM. I'd rather smoke. (*He steps out on landing, letting the screen door slam.*)

AMANDA (*sharply*). I know! That's the tragedy of it. . . . (*Alone, she turns to look at her husband's picture.*)

(DANCE MUSIC: "ALL THE WORLD IS WAITING FOR THE SUNRISE!")

TOM (*to the audience*). Across the alley from us was the Paradise Dance Hall. On evenings in spring the windows and doors were open and the music came outdoors. Sometimes the lights were turned out except for a large glass sphere that hung from the ceiling. It would turn slowly about and filter the dusk with delicate rainbow colors. Then the orchestra played a waltz or a tango, something that had a slow and sensuous rhythm. Couples would come outside, to the relative privacy of the alley. You could see them kissing behind ash-pits and telephone poles.

This was the compensation for lives that passed like mine, without any change or adventure.

Adventure and change were imminent in this year. They were waiting around the corner for all these kids.

Suspended in the mist over Berchtesgaden, caught in the folds of Chamberlain's umbrella— In Spain there was Guernica!

But here there was only hot swing music and liquor, dance halls, bars, and movies, and sex that hung in the gloom like a chandelier and flooded the world with brief, descriptive rainbows. . . .

All the world was waiting for bombardments!

(AMANDA *turns from the picture and comes outside.*)

AMANDA (*sighing*). A fire-escape landing's a poor excuse for a porch. (*She spreads a newspaper on a step and sits down, gracefully and demurely as if she were settling into a swing on a Mississippi veranda*) What are you looking at?

TOM. The moon.

AMANDA. Is there a moon this evening?

TOM. It's rising over Garfinkel's Delicatessen.

AMANDA. So it is! A little silver slipper of a moon. Have you made a wish on it yet?

TOM. Um-hum.

AMANDA. What did you wish for?

TOM. That's a secret.

AMANDA. A secret, huh? Well, I won't tell mine either. I will be just as mysterious as you.

TOM. I bet I can guess what yours is.

AMANDA. Is my head so transparent?

TOM. You're not a sphinx.

AMANDA. No, I don't have secrets. I'll tell you what I wished for on the moon. Success and happiness for my precious children! I wish for that whenever there's a moon, and when there isn't a moon, I wish for it, too.

TOM. I thought perhaps you wished for a gentleman caller.

AMANDA. Why do you say that?

TOM. Don't you remember asking me to fetch one?

AMANDA. I remember suggesting that it would be nice for your sister if you brought home some nice young man from the warehouse. I think that I've made that suggestion more than once.

TOM. Yes, you have made it repeatedly.

AMANDA. Well?

TOM. We are going to have one.

AMANDA. *What?*

TOM. A gentleman caller!

(THE ANNUNCIATION IS CELEBRATED WITH MUSIC. AMANDA *rises*. IMAGE ON SCREEN: CALLER WITH BOUQUET.)

AMANDA. You mean you have asked some nice young man to come over?

TOM. Yep. I've asked him to dinner.

AMANDA. You really did?

TOM. I did!

AMANDA. You did, and did he—*accept?*

TOM. He did!

AMANDA. Well, well—well, well! That's—lovely!

TOM. I though that you would be pleased.

AMANDA. It's definite, then?

TOM. Very definite.

AMANDA. Soon?

TOM. Very soon.

AMANDA. For heaven's sake, stop putting on and tell me some things, will you?

TOM. What things do you want me to tell you?

AMANDA. *Naturally* I would like to know when he's *coming!*

TOM. He's coming tomorrow.

AMANDA. *Tomorrow?*

TOM. Yep. Tomorrow.

AMANDA. But, Tom!

TOM. Yes, Mother?

AMANDA. Tomorrow gives me no time!

TOM. Time for what?

AMANDA. Preparations! Why didn't you phone me at once, as soon as you asked him, the minute that he accepted? Then, don't you see, I could have been getting ready!

TOM. You don't have to make any fuss.

AMANDA. Oh, Tom, Tom, Tom, of course I have to make a fuss! I want things nice, not sloppy! Not thrown together. I'll certainly have to do some fast thinking, won't I?

TOM. I don't see why you have to think at all.

AMANDA. You just don't know. We can't have a gentleman caller in a pigsty! All my wedding silver has to be polished, the monogrammed table linen ought to be laundered! The windows have to be washed and fresh curtains put up. And how about clothes! We have to *wear* something, don't we?

TOM. Mother, this boy is no one to make a fuss over!

AMANDA. Do you realize he's the first young man we've introduced to your sister?

It's terrible, dreadful, disgraceful that poor little sister has never received a single gentleman caller! Tom, come inside! (*She opens the screen door.*)

TOM. What for?

AMANDA. I want to ask you some things.

TOM. If you're going to make such a fuss, I'll call it off, I'll tell him not to come!

AMANDA. You certainly won't do anything of the kind. Nothing offends people worse than broken engagements. It simply means I'll have to work like a Turk! We won't be brilliant, but we will pass inspection. Come on inside. (TOM *follows, groaning*) Sit down.

TOM. Any particular place you would like me to sit?

AMANDA. Thank heavens I've got that new sofa! I'm also making payments on a floor lamp I'll have sent out! And put the chintz covers on, they'll brighten things up! Of course I'd hoped to have these walls re-papered. . . . What is the young man's name?

TOM. His name is O'Connor.

AMANDA. That, of course, means fish—tomorrow is Friday! I'll have that salmon loaf—with Durkee's dressing! What does he do? He works at the warehouse?

TOM. Of course! How else would I—

AMANDA. Tom, he—doesn't drink?

TOM. Why do you ask me that?

AMANDA. Your father *did!*

TOM. Don't get started on that!

AMANDA. He *does* drink, then?

TOM. Not that I know of!

AMANDA. Make sure, be certain! The last thing I want for my daughter's a boy who drinks!

TOM. Aren't you being a little bit premature? Mr. O'Connor has not yet appeared on the scene!

AMANDA. But will tomorrow. To meet your sister, and what do I know about his character? Nothing! Old maids are better off than wives of drunkards!

TOM. Oh, my God!

AMANDA. Be still!

TOM (*leaning forward to whisper*). Lots of fellows meet girls whom they don't marry!

AMANDA. Oh, talk sensibly, Tom—and don't be sarcastic! (*She has gotten a hairbrush.*)

TOM. What are you doing?

AMANDA. I'm brushing that cow-lick down!

What is this young man's position at the warehouse?

TOM (*submitting grimly to the brush and the interrogation*). This young man's position is that of a shipping clerk, Mother.

AMANDA. Sounds to me like a fairly responsible job, the sort of a job *you* would be in if you just had more *get-up.*

What is his salary? Have you any idea?

TOM. I would judge it to be approximately eighty-five dollars a month.

AMANDA. Well—not princely, but—

TOM. Twenty more than I make.

AMANDA. Yes, how well I know! But for a family man, eighty-five dollars a month is not much more than you can just get by on. . . .

TOM. Yes, but Mr. O'Connor is not a family man.

AMANDA. He might be, mightn't he? Some time in the future?

TOM. I see. Plans and provisions.

AMANDA. You are the only young man that I know of who ignores the fact that the future becomes the present, the present the past, and the past turns into everlasting regret if you don't plan for it!

TOM. I will think that over and see what I can make of it.

AMANDA. Don't be supercilious with your mother! Tell me some more about this—what do you call him?

TOM. James D. O'Connor. The D. is for Delaney.

AMANDA. Irish on *both* sides! *Gracious!* And doesn't drink?

TOM. Shall I call him up and ask him right this minute?

AMANDA. The only way to find out about those things is to make discreet inquiries at the proper moment. When I was a girl in Blue Mountain and it was suspected that a young man drank, the girl whose attentions he had been receiving, if any girl *was,* would sometimes speak to the minister of his church, or rather her father would if her father was living, and sort of feel him out on the young man's character. That is the way such things are discreetly handled to keep a young woman from making a tragic mistake!

TOM. Then how did you happen to make a tragic mistake?

AMANDA. That innocent look of your father's had everyone fooled!
He *smiled*—the world was *enchanted!*
No girl can do worse than put herself at the mercy of a handsome appearance!
I hope that Mr. O'Connor is not too good-looking.

TOM. No, he's not too good-looking. He's covered with freckles and hasn't too much of a nose.

AMANDA. He's not right-down homely, though?

TOM. Not right-down homely. Just medium homely, I'd say.

AMANDA. Character's what to look for in a man.

TOM. That's what I've always said, Mother.

AMANDA. You've never said anything of the kind and I suspect you would never give it a thought.

TOM. Don't be so suspicious of me.

AMANDA. At least I hope he's the type that's up and coming.

TOM. I think he really goes in for self-improvement.

AMANDA. What reason have you to think so?

TOM. He goes to night school.

AMANDA (*beaming*). Splendid! What does he do, I mean study?

TOM. Radio engineering and public speaking!

AMANDA. Then he has visions of being advanced in the world!
Any young man who studies public speaking is aiming to have an executive job some day!
And radio engineering? A thing for the future!
Both of these facts are very illuminating. Those are the sort of things that a mother should know concerning any young man who comes to call on her daughter. Seriously or—not.

TOM. One little warning. He doesn't know about Laura. I didn't let on that we had dark ulterior motives. I just said, why don't you come and have dinner with us? He said okay and that was the whole conversation.

AMANDA. I bet it was! You're eloquent as an oyster.
However, he'll know about Laura when he gets here. When he sees how lovely and sweet and pretty she is, he'll thank his lucky stars he was asked to dinner.

TOM. Mother, you mustn't expect too much of Laura.

AMANDA. What do you mean?

TOM. Laura seems all those things to you and me because she's ours and we love her. We don't even notice she's crippled any more.

AMANDA. Don't say crippled! You know that I never allow that word to be used!

TOM. But face facts, Mother. She is and—that's not all—

AMANDA. What do you mean "not all"?

TOM. Laura is very different from other girls.

AMANDA. I think the difference is all to her advantage.

TOM. Not quite all—in the eyes of others—strangers—she's terribly shy and lives in a world of her own and those things make her seem a little peculiar to people outside the house.

AMANDA. Don't say peculiar.

TOM. Face the facts. She is.

(THE DANCE-HALL MUSIC CHANGES TO A TANGO THAT HAS A MINOR AND SOMEWHAT OMINOUS TONE.)

AMANDA. In what way is she peculiar—may I ask?

TOM (*gently*). She lives in a world of her own—a world of—little glass ornaments, Mother. . . . (*Gets up.* AMANDA *remains holding brush, looking at him, troubled*) She plays old phonograph records and —that's about all—(*He glances at himself in the mirror and crosses to door.*)

AMANDA (*sharply*). Where are you going?

TOM. I'm going to the movies. (*Out screen door.*)

AMANDA. Not to the movies, every night to the movies! (*Follows quickly to screen door*) I don't believe you always go to the movies! (*He is gone,* AMANDA *looks worriedly after him for a moment.*

Then vitality and optimism return and she turns from the door. Crossing to portieres) Laura! Laura! (LAURA *answers from kitchenette.*)

LAURA. Yes, Mother.

AMANDA. Let those dishes go and come in front! (LAURA *appears with dish towel. Gaily*) Laura, come here and make a wish on the moon!

(SCREEN IMAGE: MOON.)

LAURA (*entering*). Moon—moon?

AMANDA. A little silver slipper of a moon.
Look over your left shoulder, Laura, and make a wish! (LAURA *looks faintly puzzled as if called out of sleep.* AMANDA *seizes her shoulders and turns her at an angle by the door*)
Now!
Now, darling, *wish!*

LAURA. What shall I wish for, Mother?

AMANDA (*her voice trembling and her eyes suddenly filling with tears*). Happiness! Good fortune!

(*The violin rises and the stage dims out.*)

(*The curtain Falls.*)

SCENE SIX

IMAGE: HIGH SCHOOL HERO.

TOM. And so the following evening I brought Jim home to dinner. I had known Jim slightly in high school. In high school Jim was a hero. He had tremendous Irish good nature and vitality with the scrubbed and polished look of white chinaware. He seemed to move in a continual spotlight. He was a star in basketball, captain of the debating club, president of the senior class and the glee club and he sang the male lead in the annual light operas. He was always running or bounding, never just walking. He seemed always at the point of defeating the law of gravity. He was shooting with such velocity through his adolescence that you would logically expect him to arrive at nothing short of the White House by the time he was thirty. But Jim apparently ran into more interference after his graduation from Soldan. His speed had definitely slowed. Six years after he left high school he was holding a job that wasn't much better than mine. (IMAGE: CLERK)

He was the only one at the warehouse with whom I was on friendly terms. I was valuable to him as someone who could remember his former glory, who had seem him win basketball games and the silver cup in debating. He knew of my seret practice of retiring to a cabinet of the washroom to work on poems when business was slack in the warehouse. He called me Shakespeare. And while the other boys in the warehouse regarded me with suspicious hostility, Jim took a humorous attitude toward me. Gradually his attitude affected the others, their hostility wore off and they also began to smile at me as people smile at an oddly fashioned dog who trots across their path at some distance.

I knew that Jim and Laura had known each other at Soldan, and I had heard Laura speak admiringly of his voice. I didn't know if Jim remembered her or not. In high school Laura had been as unobtrusive as Jim had been astonishing. If he did remember Laura, it was not as my sister, for when I asked him to dinner, he grinned and said, "You know, Shakespeare, I never thought of you as having folks!"

He was about to discover that I did. . . .

(LIGHT UP STAGE. LEGEND ON SCREEN: "THE ACCENT OF A COMING FOOT." *Friday evening. It is about five o'clock of a late spring evening which comes "scattering poems in the sky." A delicate lemony light is in the Wingfield apartment.* AMANDA *has worked like a Turk in preparation for the gentleman caller. The results are astonishing. The new floor lamp with its rose-silk shade is in place, a colored paper lantern conceals the broken light fixture in the ceiling, new billowing white curtains are at the windows, chintz covers are on chairs and sofa, a pair of new sofa pillows make their initial appearance. Open boxes and tissue paper are scattered on the floor.* LAURA *stands in the middle with lifted arms while* AMANDA *crouches before her, adjusting the hem of the new dress, devout and ritualistic. The dress is colored and designed by memory. The arrangement of* LAURA'S *hair is changed; it is softer and more becoming. A fragile, unearthly prettiness has come out in* LAURA: *she is like a piece of translucent glass touched by light, given a momentary radiance, not actual, not lasting.*)

AMANDA (*impatiently*). Why are you trembling?

LAURA. Mother, you've made me so nervous!

AMANDA. How have I made you nervous?

LAURA. By all this fuss! You make it seem so important!

AMANDA. I don't understand you, Laura. You couldn't be satisfied with just sitting home, and yet whenever I try to arrange something for you, you seem to resist it. (*She gets up*)

Now take a look at yourself.

No, wait! Wait just a moment—I have an idea!

LAURA. What is it now??

(AMANDA *produces two powder puffs which she wraps in handkerchiefs and stuffs in* LAURA'S *bosom.*)

LAURA. Mother, what are you doing?

AMANDA. They call them "Gay Deceivers"!

LAURA. I won't wear them!

AMANDA. You will!

LAURA. Why should I?

AMANDA. Because, to be painfully honest, your chest is flat.

LAURA. You made it seem like we were setting a trap.

AMANDA. All pretty girls are a trap, a pretty trap, and men expect them to be. (LEGEND: "A PRETTY TRAP")

Now look at yourself, young lady. This is the prettiest you will ever be!

I've got to fix myself now! You're going to be surprised by your mother's appearance! (*She crosses through portieres, humming gaily.*)

(LAURA *moves slowly to the long mirror and stares solemnly at herself. A wind blows the white curtains inward in a slow, graceful motion and with a faint, sorrowful sighing.*)

AMANDA (*off stage*). It isn't dark enough yet. (LAURA *turns slowly before the mirror with a troubled look.*)

(LEGEND ON SCREEN: "THIS IS MY SISTER: CELEBRATE HER WITH STRINGS!" MUSIC.)

AMANDA (*laughing, off*). I'm going to show you something. I'm going to make a spectacular appearance!

LAURA. What is it, Mother?

AMANDA. Possess your soul in patience—you will see!

Something I've resurrected from that old trunk! Styles haven't changed so terribly much after all. . . . (*She parts the portieres*)

Now just look at your mother! (*She wears a girlish frock of yellowed voile with a blue silk sash. She carries a bunch of jonquils—the legend of her youth is nearly revived. Feverishly*)

This is the dress in which I led the cotillion. Won the cakewalk twice at Sunset Hill, wore one spring to the Governor's ball in Jackson!

See how I sashayed around the ballroom, Laura? (*She raises her skirt and does a mincing step around the room*)

I wore it on Sundays for my gentlemen callers! I had it on the day I met your father—

I had malaria fever all that spring. The change of climate from East Tennessee to the Delta—weakened resistance—I had a little temperature all the time—not enough to be serious—just enough to make me restless and giddy!—Invitations poured in—parties all over the Delta!—"Stay in bed," said Mother, "you have fever!"—but I just wouldn't.—I took quinine but kept on going, going! Evenings, dances!—Afternoons, long, long rides! Picnics—lovely!—So lovely, that country in May.—All lacy with dogwood, literally flooded with jonquils!—That was the spring I had the craze for jonquils. Jonquils became an absolute obsession. Mother said, "Honey, there's no more room for jonquils." And still I kept on bringing in more jonquils. Whenever, wherever I saw them, I'd say, "Stop! Stop! I see jonquils!" I made the young men help me gather the jonquils! It was a joke, Amanda and her jonquils! Finally there were no more vases to hold them, every available space was filled with jonquils. No vases to hold them? All right, I'll hold them myself! And then I—(*She stops in front of the picture.* MUSIC) met your father!

Malaria fever and jonquils and then—this—boy. . . . (*She switches on the rose-colored lamp*)

I hope they get here before it starts to rain. (*She crosses upstage and places the jonquils in bowl on table*)

I gave your brother a little extra change so he and Mr. O'Connor could take the service car home.

LAURA (*with altered look*). What did you say his name was?

AMANDA. O'Connor.

LAURA. What is his first name?

AMANDA. I don't remember. Oh, yes, I do. It was—Jim!

(LAURA *sways slightly and catches hold of a chair.* LEGEND ON SCREEN: "NOT JIM!")

LAURA (*faintly*). Not—Jim!

AMANDA. Yes, that was it, it was Jim! I've never known a Jim that wasn't nice!

(MUSIC: OMINOUS.)

LAURA. Are you sure his name is Jim O'Connor?

AMANDA. Yes. Why?

LAURA. Is he the one that Tom used to know in high school?

AMANDA. He didn't say so. I think he just got to know him at the warehouse.

LAURA. There was a Jim O'Connor we both knew in high school—(*Then, with effort*) If that is the one that Tom is bringing to dinner—you'll have to excuse me, I won't come to the table.

AMANDA. What sort of nonsense is this?

LAURA. You asked me once if I'd ever liked a boy. Don't you remember I showed you this boy's picture?

AMANDA. You mean the boy you showed me in the year book?

LAURA. Yes, that boy.

AMANDA. Laura, Laura, were you in love with that boy?

LAURA. I don't know, Mother. All I know is I couldn't sit at the table if it was him!

AMANDA. It won't be him! It isn't the least bit likely. But whether it is or not, you will come to the table. You will not be excused.

LAURA. I'll have to be, Mother.

AMANDA. I don't intend to humor your silliness, Laura. I've had too much from you and your brother, both!

So just sit down and compose yourself till they come. Tom has forgotten his key so you'll have to let them in, when they arrive.

LAURA (*panicky*). Oh, Mother,—*you* answer the door!

AMANDA (*lightly*). I'll be in the kitchen—busy!

LAURA. Oh, Mother, please answer the door, don't make me do it!

AMANDA (*crossing into kitchenette*). I've got to fix the dressing for the salmon. Fuss, fuss—silliness!—over a gentleman caller!

(*Door swings shut.* LAURA *is left alone.* LEGEND: "TERROR!" *She utters a low moan and turns off the lamp—sits stiffly on the edge of the sofa, knotting her fingers together.* LEGEND ON SCREEN: "THE OPENING OF A DOOR!" TOM *and* JIM *appear on the fire-escape steps and climb to landing. Hearing their approach,* LAURA *rises with a panicky gesture. She retreats to the portieres. The doorbell.* LAURA *catches her breath and touches her throat. Low drums.*)

AMANDA (*calling*). Laura, sweetheart! The door!

(LAURA *stares at it without moving.*)

JIM. I think we just beat the rain.

TOM. Uh-huh. (*He rings again, nervously.* JIM *whistles and fishes for a cigarette.*)

AMANDA (*very, very gaily*). Laura, that is your brother and Mr. O'Connor! Will you let them in, darling?

(LAURA *crosses toward kitchenette door.*)

LAURA (*breathlessly*). Mother—you go to the door!

(AMANDA *steps out of kitchenette and stares furiously at* LAURA. *She points imperiously at the door.*)

LAURA. Please, please!

AMANDA (*in a fierce whisper*). What is the matter with you, you silly thing?

LAURA (*desperately*). Please, you answer it, *please!*

AMANDA. I told you I wasn't going to humor you, Laura. Why have you chosen this moment to lose your mind?

LAURA. Please, please, please, you go!

AMANDA. You'll have to go to the door because I can't!

LAURA (*despairingly*). I can't either!

AMANDA. *Why?*

LAURA. I'm *sick!*

AMANDA. I'm sick, too—of your nonsense! Why can't you and your brother be normal people? Fantastic whims and behavior! (TOM *gives a long ring*)

Preposterous goings on! Can you give me one reason—(*Calls out lyrically*) COMING! JUST ONE SECOND!—why you should be afraid to open a door? Now you answer it Laura!

LAURA. Oh, oh, oh . . . (*She returns through the portieres. Darts to the victrola and winds it frantically and turns it on.*)

AMANDA. Laura Wingfield, you march right to that door!

LAURA. Yes—yes, Mother!

(*A faraway, scratchy rendition of "Dardanella" softens the air and gives her strength to move through it. She slips to the door and draws it cautiously open.* TOM *enters with the caller,* JIM O'CONNOR.)

TOM. Laura, this is Jim, this is my sister, Laura.

JIM (*stepping inside*). I didn't know that Shakespeare had a sister!

LAURA (*retreating still and trembling from the door*). How—how do you do?

JIM (*heartily extending his hand*). Okay!

(LAURA *touches it hesitantly with hers.*)

JIM. Your hand's *cold,* Laura!

LAURA. Yes, well—I've been playing the victrola. . . .

JIM. Must have been playing classical music on it! You ought to play a little hot swing music to warm you up!

LAURA. Excuse me—I haven't finished playing the victrola. . . .

(*She turns awkwardly and hurries into the front room. She pauses a second by the victrola. Then catches her breath and darts through the portieres like a frightened deer.*)

JIM (*grinning*). What was the matter?

TOM. Oh—with Laura? Laura is—terribly shy.

JIM. Shy, huh? It's unusual to meet a shy girl nowadays. I don't believe you ever mentioned you had a sister.

TOM. Well, now you know. I have one. Here is the *Post Dispatch.* You want a piece of it?

JIM. Uh-huh.

TOM. What piece? The comics?

JIM. Sports! (*Glances at it*) Ole Dizzy Dean is on his bad behavior.

TOM (*disinterest*). Yeah? (*Lights cigarette and crosses back to fire-escape door.*)

JIM. Where are *you* going?

TOM. I'm going out on the terrace.

JIM (*goes after him*). You know, Shakespeare—I'm going to sell you a bill of goods!

TOM. What goods?

JIM. A course I'm taking.

TOM. Huh?

JIM. In public speaking! You and me, we're not the warehouse type.

TOM. Thanks—that's good news. But what has public speaking got to do with it?

JIM. It fits you for—executive positions!

TOM. Awww.

JIM. I tell you it's done a helluva lot for me.

(IMAGE: EXECUTIVE AT DESK.)

TOM. In what respect?

JIM. In every! Ask yourself what is the difference between you an' me and men in the office down front? Brains?—No!—Ability?—No! Then what? Just one little thing—

TOM. What is that one little thing?

JIM. Primarily it amounts to—social poise! Being able to square up to people and hold your own on any social level!

AMANDA (*off stage*). Tom?

TOM. Yes, Mother?

AMANDA. Is that you and Mr. O'Connor?

TOM. Yes, Mother.

AMANDA. Well, you must make yourselves comfortable in there.

TOM. Yes, Mother.

AMANDA. Ask Mr. O'Connor if he would like to wash his hands.

JIM. Aw, no—no—thank you—I took care of that at the warehouse. Tom—

TOM. Yes?

JIM. Mr. Mendoza was speaking to me about you.

TOM. Favorably?

JIM. What do you think?

TOM. Well—

JIM. You're going to be out of a job if you don't wake up.

TOM. I am waking up—

JIM. You show no signs.

TOM. The signs are interior.

TOM. I'm planning to change. (*He leans over the rail speaking with quiet exhilaration. The incandescent marquees and signs of the first-run movie houses light his face from across the alley. He looks like a voyager*) I'm right at the point of committing myself to a future that doesn't include the warehouse and Mr. Mendoza or even a night-school course in public speaking.

JIM. What are you gassing about?

TOM. I'm tired of the movies.

JIM. Movies!

TOM. Yes, movies! Look at them— (*A wave toward the marvels of Grand Avenue*) All of those glamorous people—having adventures—hogging it all, gobbling the whole thing up! You know what happens? People go to the *movies* instead of *moving!* Hollywood characters are supposed to have all the adventures for everybody in America, while everybody in America sits in a dark room and watches them have them! Yes, until there's a war. That's when adventure becomes available to the masses! *Everyone's* dish, not only Gable's! Then the people in the dark room come out of the dark room to have some adventures themselves—Goody, goody!—It's our turn now, to go to the South Sea Islands—to make a safari—to be exotic, far-off!— But I'm not patient. I don't want to wait till then. I'm tired of the *movies* and I am *about* to *move!*

JIM (*incredulously*). Move?

TOM. Yes.

JIM. When?

TOM. Soon!

JIM. Where? Where?

(THEME THREE MUSIC SEEMS TO ANSWER THE QUESTION, WHILE TOM THINKS IT OVER. HE SEARCHES AMONG HIS POCKETS.)

TOM. I'm starting to boil inside. I know I seem dreamy, but inside—well, I'm boiling!—Whenever I pick up a shoe, I shudder a little thinking how short life is and what I am doing!—Whatever that means, I know it doesn't mean shoes—except as something to wear on a traveler's feet! (*Finds paper*) Look—

JIM. What?

TOM. I'm a member.

JIM (*reading*). The Union of Merchant Seamen.

TOM. I paid my dues this month, instead of the light bill.

JIM. You will regret it when they turn the lights off.

TOM. I won't be here.

JIM. How about your mother?

TOM. I'm like my father. The bastard son of a bastard! See how he grins? And he's been absent going on sixteen years!

JIM. You're just talking, you drip. How does your mother feel about it?

TOM. Shhh!—Here comes Mother! Mother is not acquainted with my plans!

AMANDA (*enters portieres*). Where are you all?

TOM. On the terrace, Mother.

(*They start inside. She advances to them.* TOM *is distinctly shocked at her appearance. Even* JIM *blinks a little. He is making his first contact with girlish Southern vivacity and in spite of the night-school course in public speaking is somewhat thrown off the beam by the unexpected outlay of social charm. Certain responses are attempted by* JIM *but are swept aside by* AMANDA'S *gay laughter and chatter.* TOM *is embarrassed but after the first shock* JIM *reacts very warmly. Grins and chuckles, is altogether won over.* IMAGE: AMANDA AS A GIRL.)

AMANDA (*coyly smiling, shaking her girlish ringlets*). Well, well, well, so this is Mr. O'Connor. Introductions entirely unnecessary. I've heard so much about you from my boy. I finally said to him, Tom—good gracious!—why don't you bring this paragon to supper? I'd like to meet this nice young man at the warehouse!—Instead of just hearing him sing your praises so much!

I don't know why my son is so stand-offish— that's not Southern behavior!

Let's sit down and—I think we could stand a little more air in here! Tom, leave the door open. I felt a nice fresh breeze a moment ago. Where has it gone to?

Mmm, so warm already! And not quite summer, even. We're going to burn up when summer really gets started.

However, we're having—we're having a very light supper. I think light things are better fo' this time of year. The same as light clothes are. Light clothes an' light food are what warm weather calls fo'. You know our blood gets so thick during th' winter—it takes a while fo' us to *adjust* ou'-selves!—when the season changes. . . .

It's come so quick this year. I wasn't prepared. All of a sudden—heavens! Already summer!—I ran to the trunk an' pulled out this light dress—Terribly old! Historical almost! But feels so good—so good an' co-ol, y' know. . . .

TOM. Mother—

AMANDA. Yes, honey?

TOM. How about—supper?

AMANDA. Honey, you go ask Sister if supper is ready! You know that Sister is in full charge of supper!

Tell her you hungry boys are waiting for it. (*To* JIM) Have you met Laura?

JIM. She—

AMANDA. Let you in? Oh, good, you've met already! It's rare for a girl as sweet an' pretty as Laura to be domestic! But Laura is, thank heavens, not only pretty but also very domestic. I'm not at all. I never was a bit. I never could make a thing but angel-food cake. Well, in the South we had so many servants. Gone, gone, gone. All vestige of gracious living! Gone completely! I wasn't prepared for what the future brought me. All of my gentlemen callers were sons of planters and so of course I assumed that I would be married to one and raise my family on a large piece of land with plenty of servants. But man proposes—and woman accepts the proposal!—To vary that old, old saying a little bit—I married no planter! I married a man who worked for the telephone company!—That gallantly smiling gentleman over there! (*Points to the picture*) A telephone man who—fell in love with long-distance!—Now he travels and I don't even know where!—But what am I going on for about my—tribulations?

Tell me yours—I hope you don't have any! Tom?

TOM (*returning*). Yes, Mother?

AMANDA. Is supper nearly ready?

TOM. It looks to me like supper is on the table.

AMANDA. Let me look— (*She rises prettily and looks through portieres*) Oh, lovely!—But where is Sister?

TOM. Laura is not feeling well and she says that she thinks she'd better not come to the table.

AMANDA. What?—Nonsense!—Laura? Oh, Laura!

LAURA (*off stage, faintly*). Yes, Mother.

AMANDA. You really must come to the table. We won't be seated until you come to the table!

Come in, Mr. O'Connor. You sit over there, and I'll—

Laura? Laura Wingfield!

You're keeping us waiting, honey! We can't say grace until you come to the table!

(*The back door is pushed weakly open and* LAURA *comes in. She is obviously quite faint, her lips trembling, her eyes wide and staring. She moves unsteadily toward the table,* LEGEND: "TERROR!" *Outside a summer storm is coming abruptly. The white curtains billow inward at the windows and there is a sorrowful murmur and deep blue dusk.* LAURA *suddenly stumbles—she catches at a chair with a faint moan.*)

TOM. Laura!

AMANDA. Laura! (*There is a clap of thunder.* LEGEND: "AH!" *Despairingly*) Why, Laura, you *are* sick, darling! Tom, help your sister into the living room, dear!

Sit in the living room, Laura—rest on the sofa. Well! (*To the gentleman caller*)

Standing over the hot stove made her ill!—I told her that it was just too warm this evening, but—(TOM *comes back in.* LAURA *is on the sofa*)

Is Laura all right now?

TOM. Yes.

AMANDA. What *is* that? Rain? A nice cool rain has come up! (*She gives the gentleman caller a frightened look*)

I think we may—have grace—now. . . . (TOM *looks at her stupidly*)

Tom, honey—you say grace!

TOM. Oh . . .

"For these and all thy mercies—" (*They bow their heads,* AMANDA *stealing a nervous glance at* JIM. *In the living room* LAURA, *stretched on the sofa, clenches her hand to her lips, to hold back a shuddering sob*)

God's Holy Name be praised—

(*The Scene Dims Out.*)

SCENE SEVEN

A souvenir.

Half an hour later. Dinner is just being finished in the up-stage area which is concealed by the drawn portieres.

As the curtain rises, LAURA *is still huddled upon the sofa, her feet drawn under her, her head resting on a pale blue pillow, her eyes wide and mysteriously watchful. The new floor lamp with its shade of rose-colored silk gives a soft, becoming light to her face, bringing out the fragile, unearthly prettiness which usually escapes attention. There is a steady murmur of rain, but it is slackening and stops soon after the scene begins; the air outside becomes pale and luminous as the moon breaks out.*

A moment after the curtain rises, the lights in both rooms flicker and go out.

JIM. Hey, there, Mr. Light Bulb!

(AMANDA *laughs nervously.* LEGEND: "SUSPENSION OF A PUBLIC SERVICE.")

AMANDA. Where was Moses when the lights went out? Ha-ha. Do you know the answer to that one, Mr. O'Connor?

JIM. No, Ma'am, what's the answer?

AMANDA. In the dark! (JIM *laughs appreciatively*) Everybody sit still. I'll light the candles. Isn't it lucky we have them on the table? Where's a match? Which of you gentlemen can provide a match?

JIM. Here.

AMANDA. Thank you, sir.

JIM. Not at all, Ma'am!

AMANDA. I guess the fuse has burnt out. Mr. O'Connor, can you tell a burnt-out fuse? I know I can't and Tom is a total loss when it comes to mechanics. (SOUND: GETTING UP: VOICES RECEDE A LITTLE TO KITCHENETTE) Oh, be careful you don't bump into something. We don't want our gentleman caller to break his neck. Now wouldn't that be a fine howdy-do?

JIM. Ha-ha! Where is the fuse-box?

AMANDA. Right here next to the stove. Can you see anything?

JIM. Just a minute.

AMANDA. Isn't electricity a mysterious thing? Wasn't it Benjamin Franklin who tied a key to a kite? We live in such a mysterious universe, don't we? Some people say that science clears up all the mysteries for us. In my opinion it only creates more! Have you found it yet?

JIM. No Ma'am. All these fuses look okay to me.

AMANDA. Tom!

TOM. Yes, Mother?

AMANDA. That light bill I gave you several days ago. The one I told you we got the notices about?

(LEGEND: "HA!")

TOM. Oh.—Yeah.

AMANDA. You didn't neglect to pay it by any chance?

TOM. Why, I—

AMANDA. Didn't! I might have known it!

JIM. Shakespeare probably wrote a poem on that light bill, Mrs. Wingfield.

AMANDA. I might have known better than to trust him with it! There's such a high price for negligence in this world!

JIM. Maybe the poem will win a ten-dollar prize.

AMANDA. We'll just have to spend the remainder of the evening in the nineteenth century, before Mr. Edison made the Mazda lamp!

JIM. Candlelight is my favorite kind of light.

AMANDA. That shows you're romantic! But that's no excuse for Tom. Well, we got through dinner. Very considerate of them to let us get through dinner before they plunged us into everlasting darkness, wasn't it, Mr. O'Connor?

JIM. Ha-ha!

AMANDA. Tom, as a penalty for your carelessness you can help me with the dishes.

JIM. Let me give you a hand.

AMANDA. Indeed you will not!

JIM. I ought to be good for something.

AMANDA. Good for something? (*Her tone is rhapsodic*)

You! Why, Mr. O'Connor, nobody, *nobody's* given me this much entertainment in years—as you have!

JIM. Aw, now, Mrs. Wingfield!

AMANDA. I'm not exaggerating, not one bit! But Sister is all by her lonesome. You go keep her company in the parlor!

I'll give you this lovely old candelabrum that used to be on the altar at the church of the Heavenly Rest. It was melted a little out of shape when the church burnt down. Lightning struck it one spring. Gypsy Jones was holding a revival at the time and he intimated that the church was destroyed because the Episcopalians gave card parties.

JIM. Ha-ha!

AMANDA. And how about you coaxing Sister to drink a little wine? I think it would be good for her! Can you carry both at once?

JIM. Sure. I'm Superman!

AMANDA. Now, Thomas, get into this apron!

(*The door of kitchenette swings closed on* AMANDA'S *gay laughter; the flickering light approaches the portieres.* LAURA *sits up nervously as he enters. Her speech at first is low and breathless from the almost intolerable strain of being alone with a stranger.* THE LEGEND: "I DON'T SUPPOSE YOU REMEMBER ME AT ALL!" *In her first speeches in this scene, before* JIM'S *warmth overcomes her paralyzing shyness,* LAURA'S *voice is thin and breathless as though she has just run up a steep flight of stairs.* JIM'S *attitude is gently humorous. In playing this scene it should be stressed that while the incident is apparently unimportant, it is to* LAURA *the climax of her secret life.*)

JIM. Hello, there, Laura.

LAURA (*faintly*). Hello. (*She clears her throat.*)

JIM. How are you feeling now? Better?

LAURA. Yes. Yes, thank you.

JIM. This is for you. A little dandelion wine. (*He extends it toward her with extravagant gallantry.*)

LAURA. Thank you.

JIM. Drink it—but don't get drunk! (*He laughs heartily.* LAURA *takes the glass uncertainly; laughs shyly*) Where shall I set the candles?

LAURA. Oh—oh, anywhere. . . .

JIM. How about here on the floor? Any objections?

LAURA. No.

JIM. I'll spread a newspaper under to catch the drippings. I like to sit on the floor. Mind if I do?

LAURA. Oh, no.

JIM. Give me a pillow?

LAURA. What?

JIM. A pillow!

LAURA. Oh . . . (*Hands him one quickly.*)

JIM. How about you? Don't you like to sit on the floor?

LAURA. Oh—yes.

JIM. Why don't you, then?

LAURA. I—will.

JIM. Take a pillow! (LAURA *does. Sits on the other side of the candelabrum.* JIM *crosses his legs and smiles engagingly at her*) I can't hardly see you sitting way over there.

LAURA. I can—see you.

JIM. I know, but that's not fair, I'm in the limelight. (LAURA *moves her pillow closer*) Good! Now I can see you! Comfortable?

LAURA. Yes.

JIM. So am I. Comfortable as a cow! Will you have some gum?

LAURA. No, thank you.

JIM. I think that I will indulge, with your permission. (*Musingly unwraps it and hold it up*) Think of the fortune made by the guy that invented the first piece of chewing gum. Amazing, huh? The Wrigley Building is one of the sights of Chicago.—I saw it summer before last when I went up to the Century of Progress. Did you take in the Century of Progress?

LAURA. No, I didn't.

JIM. Well, it was quite a wonderful exposition. What impressed me most was the Hall of Science. Gives you an idea of what the future will be in America, even more wonderful than the present time is! (*Pause. Smiling at her*) Your brother tells me you're shy. Is that right, Laura?

LAURA. I—don't know.

JIM. I judge you to be an old-fashioned type of girl. Well, I think that's a pretty good type to be. Hope you don't think I'm being too personal—do you?

LAURA (*hastily, out of embarrassment*). I believe I *will* take a piece of gum, if you—don't mind. (*Clearing her throat*) Mr. O'Connor, have you—kept up with your singing?

JIM. Singing? Me?

LAURA. Yes. I remember what a beautiful voice you had.

JIM. When did you hear me sing?

(VOICE OFF STAGE IN THE PAUSE.)

VOICE (*off stage*).

> O blow, ye winds, heigh-ho,
> A-roving I will go!
> I'm off to my love
> With a boxing glove—
> Ten thousand miles away!

JIM. You say you've heard me sing?

LAURA. Oh, yes! Yes, very often. . . . I—don't suppose—you remember me—at all?

JIM (*smiling doubtfully*). You know I have an idea I've seen you before. I had that idea soon as you opened the door. It seemed almost like I was about to remember your name. But the name that I started to call you—wasn't a name! And so I stopped myself before I said it.

LAURA. Wasn't it—Blue Roses?

JIM (*springs up. Grinning*). Blue Roses!—My gosh, yes—Blue Roses!
That's what I had on my tongue when you opened the door!
Isn't it funny what tricks your memory plays? I didn't connect you with high school somehow or other.
But that's where it was; it was high school. I didn't even know you were Shakespeare's sister!
Gosh, I'm sorry.

LAURA. I didn't expect you to. You—barely knew me!

JIM. But we did have a speaking acquaintance, huh?

LAURA. Yes, we—spoke to each other.

JIM. When did you recognize me?

LAURA. Oh, right away!

JIM. Soon as I came in the door?

LAURA. When I heard your name I thought it was probably you. I knew that Tom used to know you a little in high school. So when you came in the door—
Well, then I was—sure.

JIM. Why didn't you *say* something, then?

LAURA (*breathlessly*). I didn't know what to say, I was—too surprised!

JIM. For goodness' sakes! You know, this sure is funny!

LAURA. Yes! Yes, isn't it, though. . . .

JIM. Didn't we have a class in something together?

LAURA. Yes, we did.

JIM. What class was that?

LAURA. It was—singing—Chorus!

JIM. Aw!

LAURA. I sat across the aisle from you in the Aud.

JIM. Aw.

LAURA. Mondays, Wednesdays and Fridays.

JIM. Now I remember—you always came in late.

LAURA. Yes, it was so hard for me, getting upstairs. I had that brace on my leg—it clumped so loud!

JIM. I never heard any clumping.

LAURA (*wincing at the recollection*). To me it sounded like—thunder!

JIM. Well, well, well, I never even noticed.

LAURA. And everybody was seated before I came in. I had to walk in front of all those people. My seat was in the back row. I had to go clumping all the way up the aisle with everyone watching!

JIM. You shouldn't have been self-conscious.

LAURA. I know, but I was. It was always such a relief when the singing started.

JIM. Aw, yes, I've placed you now! I used to call you Blue Roses. How was it that I got started calling you that?

LAURA. I was out of school a little while with pleurosis. When I came back you asked me what was the matter. I said I had pleurosis—you thought I said Blue Roses. That's what you always called me after that!

JIM. I hope you didn't mind.

LAURA. Oh, no—I liked it. You see, I wasn't acquainted with many—people. . . .

JIM. As I remember you sort of stuck by yourself.

LAURA. I—I—never have had much luck at—making friends.

JIM. I don't see why you wouldn't

LAURA. Well, I—started out badly.

JIM. You mean being—

LAURA. Yes, it sort of—stood between me—

JIM. You shouldn't have let it!

LAURA. I know, but it did, and—

JIM. You were shy with people!

LAURA. I tried not to be but never could—

JIM. Overcome it?

LAURA. No, I—I never could!

JIM. I guess being shy is something you have to work out of kind of gradually.

LAURA (sorrowfully). Yes I guess it—

JIM. Takes time!

LAURA. Yes.

JIM. People are not so dreadful when you know them. That's what you have to remember! And everybody has problems, not just you, but practically everybody has got some problems.

You think of yourself as having the only problems, as being the only one who is disappointed. But just look around you and you will see lots of people as disappointed as you are. For instance, I hoped when I was going to high school that I would be further along at this time, six years later, than I am now— You remember that wonderful write-up I had in *The Torch?*

LAURA. Yes! (*She rises and crosses to table.*)

JIM. It said I was bound to succeed in anything I went into! (LAURA *returns with the annual*) Holy Jeez! *The Torch!* (*He accepts it reverently. They smile across it with mutual wonder.* LAURA *crouches beside him and they begin to turn through it.* LAURA'S *shyness is dissolving in his warmth.*)

LAURA. Here you are in *The Pirates of Penzance!*

JIM (*wistfully*). I sang the baritone lead in that operetta.

LAURA (*raptly*). So—beautifully!

JIM (*protesting*). Aw—

LAURA. Yes, yes—beautifully—beautifully!

JIM. You heard me?

LAURA. All three times!

JIM. No!

LAURA. Yes!

JIM. All three performances?

LAURA (*looking down*). Yes.

JIM. Why?

LAURA. I—wanted to ask you to—autograph my program.

JIM. Why didn't you ask me to?

LAURA. You were always surrounded by your own friends so much that I never had a chance to.

JIM. You should have just—

LAURA. Well, I—thought you might think I was—

JIM. Thought I might think you was—what?

LAURA. Oh—

JIM (*with reflective relish*). I was beleaguered by females in those days.

LAURA. You were terribly popular!

JIM. Yeah—

LAURA. You had such a—friendly way—

JIM. I was spoiled in high school.

LAURA. Everybody—liked you!

JIM. Including you?

LAURA. I—yes, I—I did, too— (*She gently closes the book in her lap.*)

JIM. Well, well, well!—Give me that program, Laura. (*She hands it to him. He signs it with a flourish*) There you are—better late than never!

LAURA. Oh, I—what a—surprise!

JIM. My signature isn't worth very much right now. But some day—maybe—it will increase in value! Being disappointed is one thing and being discouraged is something else. I am disappointed but I am not discouraged.

I'm twenty-three years old.

How old are you?

LAURA. I'll be twenty-four in June.

509

JIM. That's not old age!

LAURA. No, but—

JIM. You finished high school?

LAURA (*with difficulty*). I didn't go back.

JIM. You mean you dropped out?

LAURA. I made bad grades in my final examinations. (*She rises and replaces the book and the program. Her voice strained*) How is—Emily Meisenbach getting along?

JIM. Oh, that kraut-head!

LAURA. Why do you call her that?

JIM. That's what she was.

LAURA. You're not still—going with her?

JIM. I never see her.

LAURA. It said in the Personal Section that you were—engaged!

JIM. I know, but I wasn't impressed by that—propaganda!

LAURA. It wasn't—the truth?

JIM. Only in Emily's optimistic opinion!

LAURA. Oh—

(LEGEND: "WHAT HAVE YOU DONE SINCE HIGH SCHOOL?" JIM *lights a cigarette and leans indolently back on his elbows smiling at* LAURA *with a warmth and charm which lights her inwardly with altar candles. She remains by the table and turns in her hands a piece of glass to cover her tumult.*)

JIM (*after several reflective puffs on a cigarette*). What have you done since high school? (*She seems not to hear him*) Huh? (LAURA *looks up*) I said what have you done since high school, Laura?

LAURA. Nothing much.

JIM. You must have been doing something these six long years.

LAURA. Yes.

JIM. Well, then, such as what?

LAURA. I took a business course at business college—

JIM. How did that work out?

LAURA. Well, not very—well—I had to drop out, it gave me—indigestion—

(JIM *laughs gently.*)

JIM. What are you doing now?

LAURA. I don't do anything—much. Oh, please don't think I sit around doing nothing! My glass collection takes up a good deal of time. Glass is something you have to take good care of.

JIM. What did you say—about glass?

LAURA. Collection I said—I have one— (*She clears her throat and turns away again, acutely shy.*)

JIM (*abruptly*). You know what I judge to be the trouble with you?

Inferiority complex! Know what that is? That's what they call it when someone low-rates himself!

I understand it because I had it, too. Although my case was not so aggravated as yours seems to be. I had it until I took up public speaking, developed my voice, and learned that I had an aptitude for science. Before that time I never thought of myself as being outstanding in any way whatsoever!

Now I've never made a regular study of it, but I have a friend who says I can analyze people better than doctors that make a profession of it. I don't claim that to be necessarily true, but I can sure guess a person's psychology. Laura! (*Takes out his gum*) Excuse me, Laura. I always take it out when the flavor is gone. I'll use this scrap of paper to wrap it in. I know how it is to get it stuck on a shoe.

Yep—that's what I judge to be your principal trouble. A lack of confidence in yourself as a person. You don't have the proper amount of faith in yourself. I'm basing that fact on a number of your remarks and also on certain observations I've made. For instance, that clumping you thought was so awful in high school. You say that you even dreaded to walk into class. You see what you did? You dropped out of school, you gave up an education because of a clump, which as far as I know was practically non-existent! A little physical defect is what you have. Hardly noticeable even! Magnified thousands of times by imagination!

You know what my strong advice to you is? Think of yourself as *superior* in some way!

LAURA. In what way would I think?

JIM. Why, man alive, Laura! Just look about you a little. What do you see? A world full of common people! All of 'em born and all of 'em going to die!

Which of them has one-tenth of your good points! Or mine! Or anyone else's, as far as that goes— Gosh!

Everybody excels in some one thing. Some in many! (*Unconsciously glances at himself in the mirror*)

All you've got to do is discover in *what!*

Take me, for instance. (*He adjusts his tie at the mirror*)

My interest happens to lie in electro-dynamics. I'm taking a course in radio engineering at night school, Laura, on top of a fairly responsible job at the warehouse. I'm taking that course and studying public speaking.

LAURA. Ohhhh.

JIM. Because I believe in the future of television! (*Turning back to her*) I wish to be ready to go up right along with it. Therefore I'm planning to get in on the ground floor. In fact I've already made the right connections and all that remains is for the industry itself to get under way! Full steam— (*His eyes are starry*)

Knowledge—Zzzzzp! Money—Zzzzzzp!—Power! That's the cycle democracy is built on! (*His attitude is convincingly dynamic.* LAURA *stares at him, even her shyness eclipsed in her absolute wonder. He suddenly grins*)

I guess you think I think a lot of myself!

LAURA. No—o-o-o, I—

JIM. Now how about you? Isn't there something you take more interest in than anything else?

LAURA. Well, I do—as I said—have my—glass collection—

(*A peal of girlish laughter from the kitchen.*)

JIM. I'm not right sure I know what you're talking about.

What kind of glass is it?

LAURA. Little articles of it, they're ornaments mostly!

Most of them are little animals made out of glass, the tiniest little animals in the world. Mother calls them a glass menagerie!

Here's an example of one, if you'd like to see it! This one is one of the oldest. It's nearly thirteen. (MUSIC: "THE GLASS MENAGERIE." *He stretches out his hand*) Oh, be careful—if you breathe, it breaks!

JIM. I'd better not take it. I'm pretty clumsy with things.

LAURA. Go on, I trust you with him! (*Places it in his palm*)

There now—you're holding him gently!

Hold him over the light, he loves the light! You see how the light shines through him?

JIM. It sure does shine!

LAURA. I shouldn't be partial, but he is my favorite one.

JIM. What kind of a thing is this one supposed to be?

LAURA. Haven't you noticed the single horn on his forehead?

JIM. A unicorn, huh?

LAURA. Mmm-hmmm!

JIM. Unicorns, aren't they extinct in the modern world?

LAURA. I know!

JIM. Poor little fellow, he must feel sort of lonesome.

LAURA (*smiling*). Well, if he does he doesn't complain about it. He stays on a shelf with some horses that don't have horns and all of them seem to get along nicely together.

JIM. How do you know?

LAURA (*lightly*). I haven't heard any arguments among them!

JIM (*grinning*). No arguments, huh? Well, that's a pretty good sign! Where shall I set him?

LAURA. Put him on the table. They all like a change of scenery once in a while!

JIM (*stretching*). Well, well, well, well—
Look how big my shadow is when I stretch!

LAURA. Oh, oh, yes—it stretches across the ceiling!

JIM (*crossing to door*). I think it's stopped raining. (*Opens fire-escape door*) Where does the music come from?

LAURA. From the Paradise Dance Hall across the alley.

JIM. How about cutting the rug a little, Miss Wingfield?

LAURA. Oh, I—

JIM. Or is your program filled up? Let me have a look at it. (*Grasps imaginary card*) Why, every dance is taken! I'll just have to scratch some out. (WALTZ MUSIC: "LA GOLONDRINA") Ahhh, a waltz! (*He executes some sweeping turns by himself then holds his arms toward* LAURA.)

LAURA (*breathlessly*). I—can't dance!

JIM. There you go, that inferiority stuff!

LAURA. I've never danced in my life!

JIM. Come on, try!

LAURA. Oh, but I'd step on you!

JIM. I'm not made out of glass.

LAURA. How—how—how do we start?

JIM. Just leave it to me. You hold your arms out a little.

LAURA. Like this?

JIM. A little bit higher. Right. Now don't tighten up, that's the main thing about it—relax.

LAURA (*laughing breathlessly*). It's hard not to.

JIM. Okay.

LAURA. I'm afraid you can't budge me.

JIM. What do you bet I can't. (*He swings her into motion.*)

LAURA. Goodness, yes, you can!

JIM. Let yourself go, now, Laura, just let yourself go.

LAURA. I'm—

JIM. Come on!

LAURA. Trying!

JIM. Not so stiff—Easy does it!

LAURA. I know but I'm—

JIM. Lossen th' backbone! There now, that's a lot better.

LAURA. Am I?

JIM. Lots, lots better! (*He moves her about the room in a clumsy waltz.*)

LAURA. Oh, my!

JIM. Ha-ha!

LAURA. Oh, my goodness!

JIM. Ha-ha-ha! (*They suddenly bump into the table. JIM stops*) What did we hit on?

LAURA. Table.

JIM. Did something fall off it? I think—

LAURA. Yes.

JIM. I hope it wasn't the little glass horse with the horn!

LAURA. Yes.

JIM. Aw, aw, aw. Is it broken?

LAURA. Now it is just like all the other horses.

JIM. It's lost its—

LAURA. Horn!
It doesn't matter. Maybe it's a blessing in disguise.

JIM. You'll never forgive me. I bet that was your favorite piece of glass.

LAURA. I don't have favorites much. It's no tragedy, Freckles. Glass breaks so easily. No matter how careful you are. The traffic jars the shelves and things fall off them.

JIM. Still I'm awfully sorry that I was the cause.

LAURA (*smiling*). I'll just imagine he had an operation.
The horn was removed to make him feel less—freakish! (*They both laugh*)
Now he will feel more at home with the other horses, the ones that don't have horns. . . .

JIM. Ha-ha, that's very funny! (*Suddenly serious*)
I'm glad to see that you have a sense of humor. You know—you're—well—very different!
Surprisingly different from anyone else I know! (*His voice becomes soft and hesitant with a genuine feeling*)
Do you mind me telling you that? (LAURA *is abashed beyond speech*) I mean it in a nice way. . . . (LAURA *nods shyly, looking away*)
You make me feel sort of—I don't know how to put it!
I'm usually pretty good at expressing things, but—
This is something that I don't know how to say! (LAURA *touches her throat and clears it—turns the broken unicorn in her hands. Even softer*) Has anyone ever told you that you were pretty? (PAUSE: MUSIC. LAURA *looks up slowly, with wonder, and shakes her head*)
Well, you are! In a very different way from anyone else.
And all the nicer because of the difference, too. (*His voice becomes low and husky.* LAURA *turns away, nearly faint with the novelty of her emotions*)
I wish that you were my sister. I'd teach you to have some confidence in yourself. The different people are not like other people, but being different is nothing to be ashamed of. Because other people are not such wonderful people. They're one hundred times one thousand. You're one times one!

They walk all over the earth. You just stay here. They're common as—weeds, but—you—well, you're—*Blue Roses!* (IMAGE ON SCREEN: BLUE ROSES. MUSIC CHANGES.)

LAURA. But blue is wrong for—roses. . . .

JIM. It's right for you!—You're—pretty!

LAURA. In what respect am I pretty?

JIM. In all respects—believe me! Your eyes—your hair—are pretty! Your hands are pretty! (*He catches hold of her hand*)

You think I'm making this up because I'm invited to dinner and have to be nice. Oh, I could do that! I could put on an act for you, Laura, and say lots of things without being very sincere. But this time I am. I'm talking to you sincerely. I happened to notice you had this inferiority complex that keeps you from feeling comfortable with people. Somebody needs to build your confidence up and make you proud instead of shy and turning away and—blushing—

Somebody—ought to—

Ought to—*kiss* you, Laura! (*His hand slips slowly up her arm to her shoulder.* MUSIC SWELLS TUMULTUOUSLY. *He suddenly turns her about and kisses her on the lips. When he releases her,* LAURA *sinks on the sofa with a bright, dazed look.* JIM *backs away and fishes in his pocket for a cigarette.* LEGEND ON SCREEN: "SOUVENIR")

Stumble-john! (*He lights the cigarette, avoiding her look. There is a peal of girlish laughter from* AMANDA *in the kitchen.* LAURA *slowly raises and opens her hand. It still contains the little broken glass animal. She looks at it with a tender, bewildered expression*)

Stumble-john!

I shouldn't have done that—That was way off the beam. You don't smoke, do you?

(*She looks up, smiling, not hearing the question. He sits beside her a little gingerly. She looks at him speechlessly—waiting. He coughs decorously and moves a little farther aside as he considers the situation and senses her feelings, dimly, with perturbation. Gently*) Would you—care for a—mint? (*She doesn't seem to hear him but her look grows brighter even*)

Peppermint—Life-Saver?

My pocket's a regular drug store—wherever I go. . . . (*He pops a mint in his mouth. Then gulps and decides to make a clean breast of it. He speaks slowly and gingerly*)

Laura, you know, if I had a sister like you, I'd do the same thing as Tom. I'd bring out fellows and—introduce her to them. The right type of boys of a type to—appreciate her.

Only—well—he made a mistake about me.

Maybe I've got no call to be saying this. That may not have been the idea in having me over. But what if it was?

There's nothing wrong about that. The only trouble is that in my case—I'm not in a situation to—do the right thing.

I can't take down your number and say I'll phone.

I can't call up next week and—ask for a date.

I thought I had better explain the situation in case you—misunderstood it and—hurt your feelings. . . .

(*Pause. Slowly, very slowly,* LAURA'S *look changes, her eyes returning slowly from his to the ornament in her palm.* AMANDA *utters another gay laugh in the kitchen.*)

LAURA (faintly). You—won't—call again?

JIM. No, Laura, I can't. (*He rises from the sofa*)

As I was just explaining. I've—got strings on me.

Laura, I've—been going steady!

I go out all the time with a girl named Betty. She's a homegirl like you, and Catholic, and Irish, and in a great many ways we—get along fine.

I met her last summer on a moonlight boat trip up the river to Alton, on the *Majestic*.

Well—right away from the start it was—love! (LEGEND: LOVE! LAURA *sways slightly forward and grips the arm of the sofa. He fails to notice, now enrapt in his own comfortable being*)

Being in love has made a new man of me! (*Leaning stiffly forward, clutching the arm of the sofa,* LAURA *struggles visibly with her storm. But* JIM *is oblivious, she is a long way off*)

The power of love is really pretty tremendous!

Love is something that—changes the whole world, Laura! (*The storm abates a little and* LAURA *leans back. He notices her again*)

It happened that Betty's aunt took sick, she got a wire and had to go to Centralia. So Tom—when he asked me to dinner—I naturally just accepted the invitation, not knowing that you—that he—that I—(*He stops awkwardly*)

Huh—I'm a stumble-john! (*He flops back on the sofa. The holy candles in the altar of* LAURA'S *face have been snuffed out. There is a look of almost infinite desolation.* JIM *glances at her uneasily*)

I wish that you would—say something. (*She bites her lip which was trembling and then bravely smiles. She opens her hand again on the broken glass ornament. Then she gently takes his hand and raises it level with her own. She carefully places the unicorn in the palm of his hand, then pushes his fingers closed upon it*) What are you— doing that for? You want me to have him?— Laura? (*She nods*) What for?

LAURA. A—souvenir. . . . (*She rises unsteadily and crouches beside the victrola to wind it up.* LEGEND ON SCREEN: "THINGS HAVE A WAY OF TURNING OUT SO BADLY!" OR IMAGE: "GENTLEMAN CALLER WAVING GOOD-BYE!—GAILY." *At this moment* AMANDA *rushes brightly back in the front room. She bears a pitcher of fruit punch in an old-fashioned cut-glass pitcher and a plate of macaroons. The plate has a gold border and poppies painted on it.*)

AMANDA. Well, well, well! Isn't the air delightful after the shower? I've made you children a little liquid refreshment. (*Turns gaily to the gentleman caller*)
Jim, do you know that song about lemonade?

> "Lemonade, lemonade
> Made in the shade and stirred with a spade—
> Good enough for any old maid!"

JIM (*uneasily*). Ha-ha! No—I never heard it.

AMANDA. Why, Laura! You look so serious!

JIM. We were having a serious conversation.

AMANDA. Good! Now you're better acquainted!

JIM (*uncertainly*). Ha-ha! Yes.

AMANDA. You modern young people are much more serious-minded than my generation. I was so gay as a girl!

JIM. You haven't changed, Mrs. Wingfield.

AMANDA. Tonight I'm rejuvenated! The gaiety of the occasion, Mr. O'Connor! (*She tosses her head with a peal of laughter. Spills lemonade*) Oooo! I'm baptizing myself!

JIM. Here—let me—

AMANDA (*setting the pitcher down*). There now. I discovered we had some maraschino cherries. I dumped them in, juice and all!

JIM. You shouldn't have gone to that trouble, Mrs. Wingfield.

AMANDA. Trouble, trouble? Why, it was loads of fun!

Didn't you hear me cutting up in the kitchen? I bet your ears were burning! I told Tom how out-done with him I was for keeping you to himself so long a time! He should have brought you over much, much sooner! Well, now that you've found your way, I want you to be a very frequent caller! Not just occasional but all the time.
Oh, we're going to have a lot of gay times to-gether! I see them coming!
Mmm, just breathe that air! So fresh, and the moon's so pretty!
I'll skip back out—I know where my place is when young folks are having a—serious conver-sation!

JIM. Oh, don't go out, Mrs. Wingfield. The fact of the matter is I've got to be going.

AMANDA. Going, now? You're joking! Why, it's only the shank of the evening, Mr. O'Connor!

JIM. Well, you know how it is.

AMANDA. You mean you're a young workingman and have to keep workingmen's hours. We'll let you off early tonight. But only on the condition that next time you stay later.
What's the best night for you? Isn't Saturday night the best night for you workingmen?

JIM. I have a couple of time-clocks to punch, Mrs. Wingfield. One at morning, another one at night!

AMANDA. My, but you *are* ambitious! You work at night, too?

JIM. No, Ma'am, not work but—Betty! (*He crosses deliberately to pick up his hat. The band at the Paradise Dance Hall goes into a tender waltz.*)

AMANDA. Betty? Betty? Who's—Betty?

(*There is an ominous cracking sound in the sky.*)

JIM. Oh, just a girl. The girl I go steady with! (*He smiles charmingly. The sky falls.*)

(LEGEND: "THE SKY FALLS.")

AMANDA (*a long-drawn exhalation*). Ohhhh. . . . It is a serious romance, Mr. O'Connor?

JIM. We're going to be married the second Sunday in June.

AMANDA. Ohhhh—how nice!
Tom didn't mention that you were engaged to be married.

JIM. The cat's not out of the bag at the warehouse yet.

You know how they are. They call you Romeo and stuff like that.

(*He stops at the oval mirror to put on his hat. He carefully shapes the brim and the crown to give a discreetly dashing effect*)

It's been a wonderful everning, Mrs. Wingfield. I guess this is what they mean by Southern hospitality.

AMANDA. It really wasn't anything at all.

JIM. I hope it don't seem like I'm rushing off. But I promised Betty I'd pick her up at the Wabash depot, an' by the time I get my jalopy down there her train'll be in. Some women are pretty upset if you keep 'em waiting.

AMANDA. Yes, I know— The tyranny of women! (*Extends her hand*)
Good-bye, Mr. O'Connor.
I wish you luck—and happiness—and success! All three of them, and so does Laura!—Don't you, Laura?

LAURA. Yes!

JIM (*taking her hand*). Good-bye, Laura. I'm certainly going to treasure that souvenir. And don't you forget the good advice I gave you. (*Raises his voice to a cheery shout*)
So long, Shakespeare!
Thanks again, ladies— Good night! (*He grins and ducks jauntily out. Still bravely grimacing,* AMANDA *closes the door on the gentleman caller. Then she turns back to the room with a puzzled expression. She and* LAURA *don't dare to face each other.* LAURA *crouches beside the victrola to wind it.*)

AMANDA (*faintly*). Things have a way of turning out so badly.
I don't believe that I would play the victrola.
Well, well—well—
Our gentleman caller was engaged to be married!
Tom!

TOM (*from back*). Yes, Mother?

AMANDA. Come in here a minute. I want to tell you something awfully funny.

TOM (*enters with macaroon and a glass of the lemonade*). Has the gentleman caller gotten away already?

AMANDA. The gentleman caller has made an early departure.
What a wonderful joke you played on us!

TOM. How do you mean?

AMANDA. You didn't mention that he was engaged to be married.

TOM. Jim? Engaged?

AMANDA. That's what he just informed us.

TOM. I'll be jiggered! I didn't know about that.

AMANDA. That seems very peculiar.

TOM. What's peculiar about it?

AMANDA. Didn't you call him your best friend down at the warehouse?

TOM. He is, but how did I know?

AMANDA. It seems extremely peculiar that you wouldn't know your best friend was going to be married!

TOM. The warehouse is where I work, not where I know things about people!

AMANDA. You don't know things anywhere! You live in a dream; you manufacture illusions! (*He crosses to door*) Where are you going?

TOM. I'm going to the movies.

AMANDA. That's right, now that you've had us make such fools of ourselves. The effort, the preparations, all the expense! The new floor lamp, the rug, the clothes for Laura! All for what? To entertain some other girl's fiancé!
Go to the movies, go! Don't think about us, a mother deserted, an unmarried sister who's crippled and has no job! Don't let anything interfere with your selfish pleasure!
Just go, go, go—to the movies!

TOM. All right, I will! The more you shout about my selfishness to me the quicker I'll go, and I won't go to the movies!

AMANDA. Go, then! Then go to the moon—you selfish dreamer!

(TOM *smashes his glass on the floor. He plunges out on the fire-escape, slamming the door.* LAURA *screams—cut by door. Dance-hall music up.* TOM *goes to the rail and grips it desperately, lifting his face in the chill white moonlight penetrating the narrow abyss of the alley.* LEGEND ON SCREEN: "AND SO GOOD-BYE . . ." TOM'S *closing speech is timed with the interior pantomime. The interior scene is played as though viewed through soundproof glass.* AMANDA *appears to be making a comforting speech to* LAURA, *who is huddled upon the sofa. Now that we cannot hear the mother's speech, her silliness is gone and she has dignity and tragic beauty.* LAURA'S *dark hair hides her face until at the end of the speech she lifts it to smile at her mother.* AMANDA'S *gestures are slow and graceful, almost dance-like, as she comforts the daughter. At the end of her speech she glances a moment at the father's picture—then withdraws through the portieres. At close of* TOM'S *speech,* LAURA *blows out the candles, ending the play.*)

TOM. I didn't go to the moon, I went much further—for time is the longest distance between two places—

Not long after that I was fired for writing a poem on the lid of a shoe-box.

I left Saint Louis. I descended the steps of this fire-escape for a last time and followed, from then on, in my father's footsteps, attempting to find in motion what was lost in space—

I traveled around a great deal. The cities swept about me like dead leaves, leaves that were brightly colored but torn away from the branches.

I would have stopped, but I was pursued by something.

It always came upon me unawares, taking me altogether by surprise. Perhaps it was a familiar bit of music. Perhaps it was only a piece of transparent glass—

Perhaps I am walking along a street at night, in some strange city, before I have found companions. I pass the lighted window of a shop where perfume is sold. The window is filled with pieces of colored glass, tiny transparent bottles in delicate colors, like bits of a shattered rainbow.

Then all at once my sister touches my shoulder. I turn around and look into her eyes. . . .

Oh, Laura, Laura, I tried to leave you behind me, but I am more faithful than I intended to be!

I reach for a cigarette, I cross the street, I run into the movies or a bar, I buy a drink, I speak to the nearest stranger—anything that can blow your candles out! (LAURA *bends over the candles*)—for nowadays the world is lit by lightning! Blow out your candles, Laura—and so good-bye. . . .

(*She blows the candles out.*)

(*The Scene Dissolves.*)

James Earl Jones as Troy Maxson in *Fences*. Lloyd Richards,
director. (Photo courtesy of Ron Scherl, copyright 1987.)

CHAPTER XV

Black Theatre in America

Looking at our theatre today, we are aware of the enormous contribution of black Americans to our theatrical heritage. One need only think of some of the more successful shows of the past decade—musicals like *Bubblin' Brown Sugar, The Wiz, Ain't Misbehavin',* and *Dream Girls,* and plays like *Ma Rainey's Black Bottom, The Colored Museum, The Soldiers' Play,* and *For Colored Girls Who Have Considered Suicide When the Rainbow is Enough*—to recognize just how rich that contribution has been. However, the struggle for acknowledgement of black playwrights and performers and the acceptance of a Black Theatre as an integral part of our native drama was not easily won, and as we tell this story it is not one we can be proud of.

The stage stereotyping of blacks first appeared in Isaac Bickerstaffe's play *The Padlock,* written in 1768, in which a West Indian slave named Mungo became a comic character in a role that was relished by many of America's first important white actors. In 1828, a white performer named Thomas Dartmouth Rice succeeded in creating the character of Jim Crow as a result of observing a slave who worked in the stable across the street from the Louisville theatre where Rice was performing. Jim Crow, who had taken his master's name, was deformed with a stiff-legged limp and one shoulder higher than the other; in spite of this he performed a curious little jig and song as he worked:

> Wheel about, turn about,
> Do jis so,
> An' every time I wheel about
> I jump Jim Crow.

Apparently Louisville and subsequent audiences were delighted with Rice's comic imitation on the old black slave, and the stereotype of Jim Crow was created on the American stage.

Another stereotype was firmly established in 1843 when Daniel Emmett, composer of "Dixie," took his group called the Virginia Minstrels to New York for a successful engagement. The minstrel shows, which continued in popularity until the 1920s, possessed a fairly rigid format: there were at least seventeen costumed men with faces darkened by burnt cork seated in a semi-circle; at the center of this semi-circle was the interlocutor or master of ceremonies, not in black face, who provided transitions and acted as the straight man for the comic's jokes; at either end of the line sat Mr. Bones and Mr. Tambo, the stand-up comics of the event; and the show consisted of dances, dialogue, ballads, jokes and comic songs. Musical accompaniment was provided by banjos, tambourines, and fiddles. The minstrel shows were similar to vaudeville; but they provided white man's humor and frivolity at the black man's expense. Probably the most famous group was the

Christy Minstrels who played one hall for ten years and made E. P. Christy a rich man. In *The Negro in the American Theatre,* Sterling Brown says this of the minstrel tradition:

> It succeeded in fixing one stereotype deeply in the American consciousness: the shiftless, lazy, improvident, loud-mouthed, flashily dressed Negro, with kinky hair and large lips, over-addicted to the eating of watermelon and chicken . . . the shooting of dice and the twisting of the language into ludicrous malformations.

Just after the Civil War a few black groups decided to get on the minstrel bandwagon. A black man named Charles Hicks organized the Georgia Minstrels in 1865. By 1882 they had changed their name to Callender's Consolidated Spectacular Colored Minstrels. Even these troupes followed white patterns by blackening their faces and enlarging their lips with rouge. They became an imitation of an imitation, a stereotype of a stereotype.

It was not until the twentieth century that the minstrel form lost its popularity, waning as vaudeville waned, giving way to more commercial and unified musical comedies. Perhaps black comics like George Walker and Bert Williams helped make the public aware of the injustice of the stage stereotype when they billed themselves as "Two Real Coons." Yet how degrading for Burt Williams to have to dress as Jim Crow in the *Ziegfeld Follies,* present himself as the head-scratching, shuffling bungler, and sing songs like

> Bon Bon Buddie, the chocolate drop,
> That's me, that's me
> Bon Bon Buddie, the chocolate drop,
> That's all I want to be!

A black comic could entertain, as long as he did not offend white sensibilities—and as long as he used the service elevator.

At approximately the same time that Jim Crow was titilating audiences in Louisville, a black man named James Hewlett established the first serious black theatre in America. Opening in 1831 and primarily interested in producing Shakespeare, the African Grove Theatre, was doomed almost from its inception. Although it performed for mixed audiences, the press was hostile to the African Grove, and soon their performances were disrupted by white hecklers. The management posted a sign saying that whites had to sit at the rear of the theatre because they did not know "how to behave themselves at entertainment designed for ladies and gentlemen of Colour." Violence erupted and the police closed the African Grove Theatre—and in so doing ended James Hewlett's career.

It was over fifty years before there would be another attempt at a serious black theatre. This time it was to be in Harlem where it would be supported by the black community. The Lafayette Players, established in 1912, was the outstanding black producing agency until after World War I. Then a series of groups emerged: the Negro Unit of the Federal Theatre Project, the Rose McClendon Players, the American Negro Theatre, and the Negro Playwrights Company. Although some of these were short-lived, they provided the seeds of the major black or minority companies to emerge after the civil rights movement of the 1960s. Woodie King, Jr., director and producer, established the New Federal Theatre at the Henry Street Settlement in New York, named in honor of the spirit of the Federal Theatre Project and its concern for minority interests and issues. The New Lafayette Company was established in 1967 and operated until 1973. Besides serving as a cultural mecca in Harlem and an information center on black theatre, the company encouraged and fostered the works of black playwrights. Most successful, however, is the Negro Ensemble Company, which was established in 1968 and is highly successful today. Douglas Turner Ward, one of its co-founders, remains artistic director and has consistently encouraged and fostered the work of black actors and playwrights. In spite of outstanding productions like *The River Niger* (1972) by Joseph A. Walker and *A Soldier's Play* (1982) by Charles Fuller, Ward still does not feel that acclaimed plays and performances insure an individual writer or actor's success. "The joke is," he writes, "if we could only rent our reviews out to white actors, they would be millionaires."

The American theatre scene has certainly never been an easy path for black actors. Beginning with the distinguished Ira Aldridge (1807–1867), casting, ability to secure roles, and acceptance have been stumbling blocks to success. Although Aldridge was born and spent his childhood in New York, he found it necessary to go to Europe in order to escape prejudice and to find stage work. As early as 1833, he played *Othello* at London's Covent Garden and attracted the attention of the great Edmund Kean who engaged him to play Othello to Kean's Iago. Other Shakespearean roles, which he played in white face, included Lear, Shylock, and Macbeth. Aldridge never returned to America and died on tour in Poland. A Russian critic said of his work, ". . . such is the power of his spirit, such is the might of his art, that you surrender to him from the very first minute; you understand what he says, you apprehend all that he feels, you listen to every beat of his heart . . . every stage of human passion. . . . In my imagination I saw the history of a whole people."

Aldridge's plight, being unable to pursue his art in his native land, might indeed be regarded as tragic. But similarly unfortunate was the experience of another great black actor of the 1920s who became completely identified with a single major role during his career and simply never had the opportunity to grow in his craft by exploring beyond that part. Charles Gilpin played the title role in Eugene O'Neill's *The Emperor Jones*, becoming the first black actor to play a leading role in a serious American play on Broadway. When the New York Drama League planned a dinner to honor those who had made an outstanding contribution to the theatre in 1921 and it was learned that Gilpin was a leading contender, some members objected to inviting a black man to the affair. Many distinguished writers, including O'Neill himself, persuaded the bigots of the League membership to retreat. Gilpin was honored, and although he had intended only to put in an appearance, he said he, "stayed four hours and had the time of his life. No, it didn't take much nerve to go and face the crowd. I could count on the artists treating me fairly, and I didn't care a hang about the others. They could sit there and stare at me as though I were some kind of a prize monkey and it wouldn't disturb me at all." Gilpin played 204 performances of *The Emperor Jones,* two seasons on the road, and periodic revivals. But after 1923, his life was a constant struggle. He battled drink and the boredom and self-indulgence of too long an association with a single role. Director Moss Hart, who once created a revival of *The Emperor Jones* for Gilpin, wrote that the actor seemed to possess a resignation and disenchantment about his work but that when he extended himself, "He had an inner violence and a maniacal power that engulfed the spectator. . . . Had he not been a Negro . . . he would have been one of the great actors of his time." Gilpin died in 1930, in poverty, on his small farm in New Jersey. Eugene O'Neill said in 1946, "As I look back now on all my work, I can honestly say there was only one actor who carried out every notion of a character I had in mind. That actor was Charles Gilpin. . . ."

A third distinguished black actor was also rejected in his own country. Paul Robeson graduated Phi Beta Kappa from Rutgers, earned a law degree from Columbia, was an all-American athlete, a distinguished singer, and an extraordinary actor. He had played the leading role in the

London production of *The Emperor Jones* and had created the role of the young husband in O'Neill's *All God's Chillun Got Wings.* With his rich, powerful bass voice, he had immortalized the Jerome Kern song, "Ol' Man River" from *Showboat,* and his portrayal of Othello in the Margaret Webster production during World War II won him great critical acclaim. But Robeson was caught in the red-baiting scare of the late 1940s and 50s, was blacklisted, and was forced to work, like Ira Aldridge one hundred years before, in Europe and the Soviet Union. Writing of being a black actor, Robeson said, "From an early age I had come to accept and follow a certain protective tactic of Negro life in America, and I did not fully break with the pattern until many years later. Even while demonstrating that he is really equal (and, strangely, the proof must be superior performance!) the Negro must never appear to be challenging white superiority. Climb up if you can—but don't act 'uppity.' "

One likes to believe that the example of the fourth and final actor on our list is different. James Earl Jones became a distinguished actor when he played in South African playwright, Athol Fugard's *Blood Knot,* and a star when he created the role of boxer, Jack Johnson, in *The Great White Hope,* first at the Arena Stage and later on Broadway. Jones was admired for his *Othello* on Broadway, and then, in 1987, he won the coveted Antoinette Perry Award as the Outstanding Actor of the New York season for his performance of Troy Maxson in August Wilson's *Fences.* Of the many superb black actors in America today, one can only hope that more of them will have the kind of success Jones has earned. As Lloyd Richards, black director and dean of the Yale Drama School observes, those opportunities depend to a large extent on the encouragement and development of black playwrights.

The first known play by a black author—although probably never staged—was *Escape; or a Leap to Freedom* by William Wells Brown in 1858. In 1910, a white playwright Edward Sheldon, made a sincere attempt to deal with racial discrimination in *The Nigger.* Ironically, black actors were not accepted on Broadway, and the roles were played by black-faced white actors. In the 1920s there were a number of sincere attempts to treat black characters honestly and sympathetically, but all of the works were by white playwrights: O'Neill's *All God's Chillun Got Wings,* Paul Green's *In Abraham's Bosom,* DuBose and Dorothy Heyward's *Porgy,* which served as the basis for George Gershwin's great folk opera, *Porgy and Bess,* and in 1930 Marc Connelly's *Green Pastures.*

It was not until the 1950s that black America found its own playwright in a young black woman named Lorraine Hansberry. Unfortunately, Hansberry died of cancer at the age of thirty four and left only a few full length plays, the best of which was *Raisin in the Sun* which opened on Broadway in 1959 under the direction of Lloyd Richards. The cast reads like a Who's Who in black theatre: Sidney Portier, Claudia McNeil, Ruby Dee, and Diana Sands. The well-made realistic play evolves around the Younger family in Chicago and their struggle to achieve a better life. Even as dreams are shattered, love and a sense of pride and purpose are achieved. In many ways this first important American play by a black playwright prepared the way for the fervor, commitment, and anger that fueled the revolutionary black playwrights of the 1960s.

Of these revolutionary playwrights—Ed Bullins, Charles Gordone, Ronald Milner, and Imamu Amiri Baraka (LeRoi Jones)—the last offers an example of the rage and passion that surrounded the Civil Rights movement of the 1960s. Baraka's play, *Dutchman,* (1964) represents his finest work. The play takes place in a subway car, symbol of the underbelly of the city and a place where modern myths are created. A young black man, Clay, minding his own business, is teased, tempted, tormented, goaded, and finally enraged by a white woman named Lulu. She needles Clay about all the things that mark him as middle class, as "Uncle Tom," indeed for his failure to live up to her notion of the debased person she thinks a black man should be. When he is finally provoked to violence, and what she considers his primitive instincts, she murders him. As the play ends, Lulu systematically crosses Clay's name off her list. She will no doubt move on to other prey. Lulu represents, in Baraka's view, the tendency of whites to categorize blacks, to hate them for assuming white middle class values and decorum, to humiliate and insult them, and then to use any sign of resentment or rage as an excuse to destroy them. An angry and provocative play, *Dutchman* won an Obie Award as the best off-Broadway play of 1964. It is interesting that Pulitzer Prize winner playwright, August Wilson, says that black playwrights today could not write as they do, with the freedom to explore black America, had it not been for the revolutionary writers of the 1960s.

One final playwright must be mentioned here, a man who is neither black nor American but who has acted on Broadway himself and whose plays have been extraordinarily successful and popular in American productions both on Broadway and in the regional theatres: Athol Fugard, one of the truly great playwrights of the English-speaking world today. In *Blood Knot* (1961), *Boesman and Lena* (1969), *Sizwe Bansi is Dead* (1972), *A Lesson from Aloes* (1978), and *'Master Harold' . . . and the Boys* (1982), to name just a few, Fugard speaks eloquently for understanding, compassion and enlightenment in a time when racial strife has literally torn South Africa apart. In *'Master Harold',* a play about a lonely white boy and his relationship with his surrogate black father, Fugard develops one of the most idyllic and moving metaphors in modern dramatic literature in which Sam, a black man, sees the world as a ballroom where "accidents don't happen and everyone knows the steps,"—a world without collisions.

While there has been much improvement for black playwrights and actors in the past twenty years, many feel that the passion and promise of the 1960s has not been realized. Nevertheless we see the fine attempts of organizations like Joseph Papp's New York Shakespeare Festival to explore non-traditional casting. (In 1986, Actors' Equity sponsored a symposium on nontraditional casting, encouraging theatres to explore ways of expanding opportunities for black, Hispanic, Asian-American and native American actors.) We must admire the fine work of Douglas Turner Ward at the Negro Ensemble Company and Lloyd Richards at the Yale Repertory Theatre for encouraging and promoting the work of black playwrights. More and more we see other repertory theatres following their lead. It is a part of our on-going dream, or as actor Ossie Davis said, "What sustains us in this mad adventure is the feeling that, from the inside, there is a light at the end of the tunnel."

August Wilson

Fulfillment of the dream of how fine black American drama can be has come with the work of playwright August Wilson, winner of the 1987 Pulitzer Prize for drama with *Fences,* which also received a Tony Award as the best play of the 1986–87 Broadway season. Wilson's previous successes have been *Ma Rainey's Black Bottom,* which ran on Broadway in 1984–85, and *Joe Turner's Come and Gone* which became a popular success in the 1987–88 Broadway season. Apparently Wilson plans a series of plays, each independent, that chronicle the story of black Americans through the twentieth century. *Joe Turner* deals with a man who fights to regain his dignity after seven years of forced labor in the early 1900s, and Ma Rainey deals with a jazz singer in the 1920s who is queen only within the confines of the recording studio and even then is manipulated and controlled by white producers, agents, and business men. In both *Ma Rainey* and *Fences,* Wilson says he is dealing with two avenues traditionally open to blacks in America, jazz and sports, and showing how—at points in our history—even these areas fail the characters.

August Wilson was born in Pittsburgh, Pennsylvania in 1946. He dropped out of school at the age of fifteen and feels that had his talent for words not manifested itself, his own sense of justice might have taken him in another, and less positive, direction. He writes, "After I turned 20, I spent the next 10 to 15 years hanging out on streetcorners, following old men around, working odd jobs. There was this place called Pat's Cigar Store in Pittsburgh. It was the same place that Claude McKay mentioned in his book *Home to Harlem.* When I found out about that, I said, 'This is a part of history,' and I ran down there to where all the old men in the community would congregate."

As co-founder of Pittsburgh's Black Horizons Theatre, Wilson wrote one-act plays at the height of the black revolution "to politicize the community and raise consciousness." But he really considered himself a poet early in his career and believes that his work as a poet has helped him as a playwright. In the early 1970s Wilson moved to St. Paul, Minnesota where he worked as a script writer for the local science museum's childrens' theatre and began sending scripts to the Eugene O'Neill Playwrights' Conference, where the work of aspiring playwrights is read and developed. When he submitted his play, *Jitney,* to the Minneapolis Playwrights' Center, Wilson won a Jerome Foundation Fellowship, which was then followed by many others including Rockefeller, McKnight, and Guggenheim Awards. Wilson continues to live and work in the Twin Cities. Wilson openly acknowledges his debt to Lloyd Richards who has directed his plays and allowed Wilson to develop them through rehearsal, tryout, and pre-Broadway productions. His plays are a poetic melding of African and Western imagery, his dialogue is brilliant, and his characters powerful and real. As critic Hilary Devries concludes, "Indeed, the theme that surges through Wilson's work is the need for black Americans to forge anew their identity, an identity that is at once African and American."

Fences

Like *The Glass Menagerie,* August Wilson's *Fences,* can, at a first superficial glance, appear to be a simple, straight-forward, realistic domestic play. It is, after all, a play about family conflicts—a father who opposes the wishes of his son, a son who is misunderstood by his parent, a husband who cheats on his wife, a long-suffering wife who strives to make the best of an unhappy situation. But all of this is merely the plot on which the dramatist hangs his highly perceptive and sensitive view of American life in one time and place.

Perhaps the most out-spoken and least compromising drama critic in America today is John Simon who writes for *New York Magazine.* (Here is a man who lost his job for bluntly, and aptly, using a choice four-letter word to describe the calibre of Pulitzer Prize winning play a few seasons ago.) Simon, our most demanding critic, says of Wilson's play:

Fences is an eloquent play . . . a comedy-drama that is well-nigh flawless . . . Life, in all its bittersweetness, fills the stage . . . pain and anger are balanced by humor and common sense, and both passion and compassion are played on a muted trumpet that insinuates rather than insists. *Fences* marks a long step forward for Wilson's dramaturgy.

Simon was not alone in his praise of the play. Howard Kissel, writing for the New York Daily News called it: "A blockbuster piece of theater, a major American play passionately performed." And Clive Barnes, of the New York Post, said: "What makes *Fences* so engrossing, so embracing, so simply powerful, is Wilson's startling ability to tell a story, reveal feeling, paint emotion."

The critical acclaim suggests that the play goes far beyond mere story-telling. While the play does deal with material recognizable and, therefore, interesting to the theater-goer, it achieves a level of superiority in character delineation. The leading character, Troy Maxson, is a giant figure who dominates the play. He is an enormously complex man—incredibly more complex than any hero of a television sit-com; he is as complex as any real man in real life. In some regards, he is specifically Black; in other respects, he is without race or color. For that reason, what he thinks, feels, says and does can speak to all of us. He is, to be sure, a bundle of contradictions, and that fact may cause some concern to the superficial viewer or reader. He is a man with an enormous sense of responsibility toward his family. Still, he destroys his son's possible chances to succeed in a world where he himself was not allowed to succeed. He is a devoted husband, and yet he has an adulterous affair with another woman. He is a stickler for what he knows to be the truth but that does not prevent him from being an incredible exaggerater and story-teller. He is a man of undeniable strength; but still he is a highly vulnerable man. Troy is not an easy character for the near-sighted viewer to accept. After all, he behaves in ways that we would superficially find nonsympathetic. That, of course, is the intention of the playwright. Wilson is not asking you to love Troy in this play; he could not care less whether or not you love his protagonist. What the dramatist demands is that you come to *understand* Troy Maxson as a black man at a particular time in this country's history.

Other characters in the play share Troy's wonderful complexity as human portraits. Rose is the epitome of the indulgent, supporting wife at times; still, she possesses a considerable strength of character on her own. She is not all-forgiving; she is human. She speaks wonderfully levelheaded wisdom throughout the play. In her simple, unassuming way, she has a clarity of vision that other characters lack. For this reason, she becomes an invaluable tool for the playwright, for it is through Rose's eyes most often that we perceive the clearest, most humane, most sensible view of events. It is Rose who, in the end of the play, is able to make her son Cory—and the audience as well—understand Troy Maxson. Rose has understood Troy, and, if she cannot entirely forgive him, at least she can accept him. Cory must learn to do the same before he can free himself of resentment, disappointment and hatred in order to function as a mature adult in a not-too-perfect world.

Cory is one of the victims of the play, the young man of blighted promise. In that regard, he painfully symbolizes a vast segment of the black population of America in the 1950s and 1960s. His half-brother Lyons, on the other hand, represents a less positive image of other young blacks. Devoid of any real purpose in life, he is content to fool himself about his musical talents and allow others to support him. There is even a hint in the play that he has set himself up as a pimp in order to profit from others. He consistently seeks the easy life—something his father, Troy, never permitted himself to do.

One of the most fascinating characters in the play is Gabriel—Troy's mentally impaired brother. Ironically, Gabriel's impairment is a result of his service to his country during World War II for which he, like many blacks, was never fully compensated. But what makes him especially interesting as a dramatic character is the manner in which he occasionally breaks the realistic frame of the play. We can accept him for the most part as a simple-minded, gentle soul. Still, there is something about him that constantly reminds us that he is in touch with something beyond the present realistic moment. It is not that he is a religious mystic. There is little that is mystical about Gabriel; he quite literally believes he is Saint Peter's helper. In some manner or another, Gabriel, more than any other character in the play, constantly reminds us of the black man's strong ties to Christian faith as well as his roots in something deeper, darker and perhaps even more profound through his African heritage.

One element of the play which imparts to the characters a breath-taking reality is the language they speak. The dialogue of Wilson's play requires a bit of patience, for it first strikes the ear as odd, even a bit foreign. The dialogue is, of course, an attempt to capture the authenticity of black speech—especially that spoken in Wilson's native Pittsburgh; but the language quickly transcends realistic speech. From black speech the dramatist has extracted musicality, imagery, simplicity, humor and gusto which he has brilliantly shaped into a kind of stage poetry. (It must be remembered that August Wilson was an established poet before he was a recognized playwright.) Once the spectator has become accustomed to it, Wilson's language strikes the ear, stirs the muscles, and touches the heart like fine music. Here is language specifically designed for the theatre not the street corner or even the classroom, for it achieves the ends of poetry without once losing its firm grounding in everyday speech of a particular kind. If Wilson accomplishes nothing else as a playwright, he certainly brings a much-needed poetry back into our theatre.

For all of its superficially realistic situations, characters and speech, August Wilson's *Fences* is not an easy play to grasp with one equally superficial reading. The tendency is to be misled by the seemingly obvious reality of the play into thinking that this is the usual domestic drama. Because of that, Troy tends to emerge for the most part as an unsympathetic character—an adulterous husband and a harsh father. The reader and the viewer have to keep in mind that Wilson is not simply telling a story. His real intention is to create a highly comprehensive image of a typical black caught at a particular time in our history. As Wilson himself says in an interview in *American Theatre Magazine:* "I'm taking each decade and looking back at one of the most important questions that blacks confronted in that decade and writing a play about it. Put them all together and you have a history." Troy, then, represents the American black population between 1957 and 1965—in other words, on the brink of the civil rights movement. Here is a man who has learned to accept responsibility for himself and others but a man who has not been permitted by his society to fulfill his own very real, god-given potential, a man who is asked to serve his country but is denied many of the rewards of true citizenship, a man who has fought very hard for his respectability in a world that will not recognize him, a man who is proud, strong, fundamentally decent, loving, selfish, disappointed, hurt, resentful, self-protective, wrong and right. In a way, too, he is an unfinished man because all that he has striven for and worked to be has not yet come to fruition.

But all of this is about to change as the civil rights movement begins to have its impact. The change will be slow and sporadic but inevitable. It is Gabriel, the symbol of simple-minded faith in the play, who focuses the final moments for us. In his simple way he has believed throughout the play that he will open the golden gates by blowing his horn. Perhaps Wilson is saying that only a simple soul can believe that his actions will open the gates to the golden future for all blacks. Significantly, it is not his trumpet (without a mouthpiece) that finally moves the gates any more than it is Man's Christian faith that moves mountains. When his trumpet fails to produce the needed sound, Gabriel ". . . begins to dance. A slow, strange dance, eerie and life-giving. A dance of atavistic signature and ritual. . . . He begins to howl in what is an attempt at song, or perhaps a song turning back into itself in an attempt at speech." Gabriel's behavior instantly recalls primitive man's first efforts, in a time before sophisticated speech, to alter and control the course of events in his environment through religious ritual. It is no mere accident that "the gates of heaven stand open as wide as God's closet" once Gabriel taps all the resources of his black heritage. In the final image of the play Wilson is telling us so much. Only a simple fool would believe that the mere legislation of the civil rights movement would open the gates to magnificent changes. Changes will come only through the diligent efforts of the blacks who must remain faithful to their racial heritage, for that is the major source of their strength.

So much is said in the last moment of the play. The human story of a family conflict finally resolves itself through Rose's disarming wisdom when she says to Cory: "Whatever was between you and your daddy . . . the time has come to put it aside. Just take it and set it over there on the shelf and forget about it. Disrespecting your daddy ain't gonna make you a man, Cory. You got to find a way to come to that on your own." And in Gabriel's dance—and his final words, "That's the way that go!"—the larger issues of the play resolve themselves in a clear vision of the world of the blacks in America at one crucial time in our recent past.

Fences has so much to teach, but, like a truly fine play, it gives you its didactic lesson in purely dramatic terms. Rather than preaching to you, August Wilson sets a series of interesting, well-chosen events and excitingly complex characters in motion toward the accomplishment of a major deed. As in all fine plays, you learn your lesson in *Fences* by having your sensibilities and emotions engaged in addition to having your brain stimulated. Because the play deals so intelligently with social issues and is so insightful in its character portraiture, it has deep and special meaning to blacks. Because it deals so tellingly with a time in our history and embraces so many universal issues in its domestic scenes, *Fences* has interest and meaning for all people.

FENCES

by August Wilson

When the sins of our fathers visit us
We do not have to play host.
We can banish them with forgiveness
As God, in His Largeness and Laws.
—August Wilson

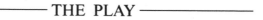

CHARACTERS

TROY MAXSON

JIM BONO   TROY'S *friend*

ROSE   TROY'S *wife*

LYONS   TROY'S *oldest son by previous marriage*

GABRIEL   TROY'S *brother*

CORY   TROY'S *and* ROSE'S *son*

RAYNELL   TROY'S *daughter*

SETTING

The setting is the yard which fronts the only entrance to the MAXSON household, an ancient two-story brick house set back off a small alley in a big-city neighborhood. The entrance to the house is gained by two or three steps leading to a wooden porch badly in need of paint.

A relatively recent addition to the house and running its full width, the porch lacks congruence. It is a sturdy porch with a flat roof. One or two chairs of dubious value sit at one end where the kitchen window opens onto the porch. An old-fashioned icebox stands silent guard at the opposite end.

The yard is a small dirt yard, partially fenced, except for the last scene, with a wooden sawhorse, a pile of lumber, and other fence-building equipment set off to the side. Opposite is a tree from which hangs a ball made of rags. A baseball bat leans against the tree. Two oil drums serve as garbage receptacles and sit near the house at right to complete the setting.

THE PLAY

Near the turn of the century, the destitute of Europe sprang on the city with tenacious claws and an honest and solid dream. The city devoured them. They swelled its belly until it burst into a thousand furnaces and sewing machines, a thousand butcher shops and bakers' ovens, a thousand churches and hospitals and funeral parlors and money-lenders. The city grew. It nourished itself and offered each man a partnership limited only by his talent, his guile, and his willingness and capacity for hard work. For the immigrants of Europe, a dream dared and won true.

The descendants of African slaves were offered no such welcome or participation. They came from places called the Carolinas and the Virginias, Georgia, Alabama, Mississippi, and Tennessee. They came strong, eager, searching. The city rejected them and they fled and settled along the river-banks and under bridges in shallow, ramshackle houses made of sticks and tar-paper. They collected rags and wood. They sold the use of their muscles and their bodies. They cleaned houses and washed clothes, they shined shoes, and in quiet desperation and vengeful pride, they stole, and lived in pursuit of their own dream. That they could breathe free, finally, and stand to meet life with the force of dignity and whatever eloquence the heart could call upon.

By 1957, the hard-won victories of the European immigrants had solidified the industrial might of America. War had been confronted and won with new energies that used loyalty and patriotism as its fuel. Life was rich, full, and flourishing. The Milwaukee Braves won the World Series, and the hot winds of change that would make the sixties a turbulent, racing, dangerous, and provocative decade had not yet begun to blow full.

ACT ONE
SCENE ONE

It is 1957. TROY *and* BONO *enter the yard, engaged in conversation.* TROY *is fifty-three years old, a large man with thick, heavy hands; it is this large-ness that he strives to fill out and make an accommodation with. Together with his blackness, his largeness informs his sensibilities and the choices he has made in his life.*
Of the two men, BONO *is obviously the follower. His commitment to their friendship of thirty-odd years is rooted in his admiration of* TROY'S *honesty, capacity for hard work, and his strength, which* BONO *seeks to emulate.*

It is Friday night, payday, and the one night of the week the two men engage in a ritual of talk and drink. TROY *is usually the most talkative and at times he can be crude and almost vulgar, though he is capable of rising to profound heights of expression. The men carry lunch buckets and wear or carry burlap aprons and are dressed in clothes suitable to their jobs as garbage collectors.*

BONO. Troy, you ought to stop that lying!

TROY. I ain't lying! The nigger had a watermelon this big.
   (*He indicates with his hands.*)
   Talking about . . . "What watermelon, Mr. Rand?" I liked to fell out! "What watermelon, Mr. Rand?" . . . And is sitting there big as life.

BONO. What did Mr. Rand say?

TROY. Ain't said nothing. Figure if the nigger too dumb to know he carrying a watermelon, he wasn't gonna get much sense out of him. Trying to hide that great big old watermelon under his coat. Afraid to let the white man see him carry it home.

BONO. I'm like you . . . I ain't got no time for them kind of people.

TROY. Now what he look like getting mad cause he see the man from the union talking to Mr. Rand?

BONO. He come to me talking about . . . "Maxson gonna get us fired." I told him to get away from me with that. He walked away from me calling you a troublemaker. What Mr. Rand say?

TROY. Ain't said nothing. He told me to go down the Commissioner's office next Friday. They called me down there to see them.

BONO. Well, as long as you got your complaint filed, they can't fire you. That's what one of them white fellows tell me.

TROY. I ain't worried about them firing me. They gonna fire me cause I asked a question? That's all I did. I went to Mr. Rand and asked him, "Why?" Why you got the white mens driving and the colored lifting? Told him, "what's the matter, don't I count? You think only white fellows got sense enough to drive a truck. That ain't no paper job! Hell, anybody can drive a truck. How come you got all whites driving and the colored lifting? He told me "take it to the union." Well, hell, that's what I done! Now they wanna come up with this pack of lies.

BONO. I told Brownie if the man come and ask him any questions . . . just tell the truth! It ain't nothing but something they done trumped up on you cause you filed a complaint on them.

TROY. Brownie don't understand nothing. All I want them to do is change the job description. Give everybody a chance to drive the truck. Brownie can't see that. He ain't got that much sense.

BONO. How you figure he be making out with that gal be up at Taylors' all the time . . . that Alberta gal?

TROY. Same as you and me. Getting just as much as we is. Which is to say nothing.

BONO. It is, huh? I figure you doing a little better than me . . . and I ain't saying what I'm doing.

TROY. Aw, nigger, look here . . . I know you. If you had got anywhere near that gal, twenty minutes later you be looking to tell somebody. And the first one you gonna tell . . . that you gonna want to brag to . . . is gonna be me.

BONO. I ain't saying that. I see where you be eyeing her.

TROY. I eye all the women. I don't miss nothing. Don't never let nobody tell you Troy Maxson don't eye the women.

BONO. You been doing more than eyeing her. You done bought her a drink or two.

TROY. Hell yeah, I bought her a drink! What that mean? I bought you one, too. What that mean cause I buy her a drink? I'm just being polite.

BONO. It's alright to buy her one drink. That's what you call being polite. But when you wanna be buying two or three . . . that's what you call eyeing her.

TROY. Look here, as long as you known me . . . you ever known me to chase after women?

BONO. Hell yeah! Long as I done known you. You forgetting I knew you when.

TROY. Naw, I'm talking about since I been married to Rose?

BONO. Oh, not since you been married to Rose. Now, that's the truth, there. I can say that.

TROY. Alright then! Case closed.

BONO. I see you be walking up around Alberta's house. You supposed to be at Taylors' and you be walking up around there.

TROY. What you watching where I'm walking for? I ain't watching after you.

BONO. I seen you walking around there more than once.

TROY. Hell, you liable to see me walking anywhere! That don't mean nothing cause you see me walking around there.

BONO. Where she come from anyway? She just kinda showed up one day.

TROY. Tallahassee. You can look at her and tell she one of them Florida gals. They got some big healthy women down there. Grow them right up out the ground. Got a little bit of Indian in her. Most of them niggers down in Florida got some Indian in them.

BONO. I don't know about that Indian part. But she damn sure big and healthy. Woman wear some big stockings. Got them great big old legs and hips as wide as the Mississippi River.

TROY. Legs don't mean nothing. You don't do nothing but push them out of the way. But them hips cushion the ride!

BONO. Troy, you ain't got no sense.

TROY. It's the truth! Like you riding on Goodyears!

(ROSE *enters from the house. She is ten years younger than* TROY, *her devotion to him stems from her recognition of the possibilities of her life without him: a succession of abusive men and their babies, a life of partying and running the streets, the Church, or aloneness with its attendant pain and frustration. She recognizes* TROY'S *spirit as a fine and illuminating one and she either ignores or forgives his faults, only some of which she recognizes. Though she doesn't drink, her presence is an integral part of the Friday night rituals. She alternates between the porch and the kitchen, where supper preparations are under way.*)

ROSE. What you all out here getting into?

TROY. What you worried about what we getting into for? This is men talk, woman.

ROSE. What I care what you all talking about? Bono, you gonna stay for supper?

BONO. No, I thank you, Rose. But Lucille say she cooking up a pot of pigfeet.

TROY. Pigfeet! I'm going home with you! Might even stay the night if you got some pigfeet. You got something in there to top them pigfeet, Rose?

ROSE. I'm cooking up some chicken. I got some chicken and collard greens.

TROY. Well, go on back in the house and let me and Bono finish what we was talking about. This is men talk. I got some talk for you later. You know what kind of talk I mean. You go on and powder it up.

ROSE. Troy Maxson, don't you start that now!

TROY (*Puts his arm around her.*) Aw, woman . . . come here. Look here, Bono . . . when I met this woman . . . I got out that place, say, "Hitch up my pony, saddle up my mare . . . there's a woman out there for me somewhere. I looked here. Looked there. Saw Rose and latched on to her." I latched on to her and told her—I'm gonna tell you the truth—I told her, "Baby, I don't wanna marry, I just wanna be your man." Rose told me . . . tell him what you told me, Rose.

ROSE. I told him if he wasn't the marrying kind, then move out the way so the marrying kind could find me.

TROY. That's what she told me. "Nigger, you in my way. You blocking the view! Move out the way so I can find me a husband." I thought it over two or three days. Come back—

ROSE. Ain't no two or three days nothing. You was back the same night.

TROY. Come back, told her . . . "Okay, baby . . . but I'm gonna buy me a banty rooster and put him out there in the backyard . . . and when he see a stranger come, he'll flap his wings and crow . . ." Look here, Bono, I could watch the front door by myself . . . it was that back door I was worried about.

ROSE. Troy, you ought not talk like that. Troy ain't doing nothing but telling a lie.

TROY. Only thing is . . . when we first got married . . . forget the rooster . . . we ain't had no yard!

BONO. I hear you tell it. Me and Lucille was staying down there on Logan Street. Had two rooms with the outhouse in the back. I ain't mind the outhouse none. But when that goddamn wind blow through there in the winter . . . that's what I'm talking about! To this day I wonder why in the hell I ever stayed down there for six long years. But see, I didn't know I could do no better. I thought only white folks had inside toilets and things.

ROSE. There's a lot of people don't know they can do no better than they doing now. That's just something you got to learn. A lot of folks still shop at Bella's.

TROY. Ain't nothing wrong with shopping at Bella's. She got fresh food.

ROSE. I ain't said nothing about if she got fresh food. I'm talking about what she charge. She charge ten cents more than the A&P.

TROY. The A&P ain't never done nothing for me. I spends my money where I'm treated right. I go down to Bella, say, "I need a loaf of bread, I'll pay for Friday." She give it to me. What sense that make when I got money to go and spend it somewhere else and ignore the person who done right by me? That ain't in the Bible.

ROSE. We ain't talking about what's in the Bible. What sense it make to shop there when she overcharge?

TROY. You shop where you want to. I'll do my shopping where the people been good to me.

ROSE. Well, I don't think it's right for her to overcharge. That's all I was saying.

BONO. Look here . . . I got to get on. Lucille going be raising all kind of hell.

TROY. Where you going, nigger? We ain't finished this pint. Come here, finish this pint.

BONO. Well, hell, I am . . . if you ever turn the bottle loose.

TROY (*Hands him the bottle.*) The only thing I say about the A&P is I'm glad Cory got that job down there. Help him take care of his school clothes and things. Gabe done moved out and things getting tight around here. He got that job. . . . He can start to look out for himself.

ROSE. Cory done went and got recruited by a college football team.

TROY. I told that boy about that football stuff. The white man ain't gonna let him get nowhere with that football. I told him when he first come to me with it. Now you come telling me he done went and got more tied up in it. He ought to go and get recruited in how to fix cars or something where he can make a living.

ROSE. He ain't talking about making no living playing football. It's just something the boys in school do. They gonna send a recruiter by to talk to you. He'll tell you he ain't talking about making no living playing football. It's a honor to be recruited.

TROY. It ain't gonna get him nowhere. Bono'll tell you that.

BONO. If he be like you in the sports . . . he's gonna be alright. Ain't but two men ever played baseball as good as you. That's Babe Ruth and Josh Gibson. Them's the only two men ever hit more home runs than you.

TROY. What it ever get me? Ain't got a pot to piss in or a window to throw it out of.

ROSE. Times have changed since you was playing baseball, Troy. That was before the war. Times have changed a lot since then.

TROY. How in hell they done changed?

ROSE. They got lots of colored boys playing ball now. Baseball and football.

BONO. You right about that, Rose. Times have changed, Troy. You just come along too early.

TROY. There ought not never have been no time called too early! Now you take that fellow . . . what's that fellow they had playing right field for the Yankees back then? You know who I'm talking about, Bono. Used to play right field for the Yankees.

ROSE. Selkirk?

TROY. Selkirk! That's it! Man batting .269, understand? .269. What kind of sense that make? I was hitting .432 with thirty-seven home runs! Man batting .269 and playing right field for the Yankees! I saw Josh Gibson's daughter yesterday. She walking around with raggedy shoes on her feet. Now I bet you Selkirk's daughter ain't walking around with raggedy shoes on her feet! I bet you that!

ROSE. They got a lot of colored baseball players now. Jackie Robinson was the first. Folks had to wait for Jackie Robinson.

TROY. I done seen a hundred niggers play baseball better than Jackie Robinson. Hell, I know some teams Jackie Robinson couldn't even make! What you talking about Jackie Robinson. Jackie Robinson wasn't nobody. I'm talking about if you could play ball then they ought to have let you play. Don't care what color you were. Come telling me I come along too early. If you could play . . . then they ought to have let you play.

(TROY takes a long drink from the bottle.)

ROSE. You gonna drink yourself to death. You don't need to be drinking like that.

TROY. Death ain't nothing. I done seen him. Done wrassled with him. You can't tell me nothing about death. Death ain't nothing but a fastball on the outside corner. And you know what I'll do to that! Lookee here, Bono . . . am I lying? You get one of them fastballs, about waist high, over the outside corner of the plate where you can get the meat of the bat on it . . . and good god! You can kiss it goodbye. Now, am I lying?

BONO. Naw, you telling the truth there. I seen you do it.

TROY. If I'm lying . . . that 450 feet worth of lying!

(Pause.)

That's all death is to me. A fastball on the outside corner.

ROSE. I don't know why you want to get on talking about death.

TROY. Ain't nothing wrong with talking about death. That's part of life. Everybody gonna die. You gonna die, I'm gonna die. Bono's gonna die. Hell, we all gonna die.

ROSE. But you ain't got to talk about it. I don't like to talk about it.

TROY. You the one brought it up. Me and Bono was talking about baseball . . . you tell me I'm gonna drink myself to death. Ain't that right, Bono? You know I don't drink this but one night out of the week. That's Friday night. I'm gonna drink just enough to where I can handle it. Then I cuts it loose. I leave it alone. So don't you worry about me drinking myself to death. 'Cause I ain't worried about Death. I done seen him. I done wrestled with him.

Look here, Bono . . . I looked up one day and Death was marching straight at me. Like Soldiers on Parade! The Army of Death was marching straight at me. The middle of July, 1941. It got real cold just like it be winter. It seem like Death himself reached out and touched me on the shoulder. He touch me just like I touch you. I got cold as ice and Death standing there grinning at me.

ROSE. Troy, why don't you hush that talk.

TROY. I say . . . What you want, Mr. Death? You be wanting me? You done brought your army to be getting me? I looked him dead in the eye. I wasn't fearing nothing. I was ready to tangle. Just like I'm ready to tangle now. The Bible say be ever vigilant. That's why I don't get but so drunk. I got to keep watch.

ROSE. Troy was right down there in Mercy Hospital. You remember he had pneumonia? Laying there with a fever talking plumb out of his head.

TROY. Death standing there staring at me . . . carrying that sickle in his hand. Finally he say, "You want bound over for another year?" See, just like that . . . "You want bound over for another year?" I told him, "Bound over hell! Let's settle this now!"

It seem like he kinda fell back when I said that, and all the cold went out of me. I reached down and grabbed that sickle and threw it just as far as I could throw it . . . and me and him commenced to wrestling.

We wrestled for three days and three nights. I can't say where I found the strength from. Every time it seemed like he was gonna get the best of me, I'd reach way down deep inside myself and find the strength to do him one better.

ROSE. Every time Troy tell that story he find different ways to tell it. Different things to make up about it.

TROY. I ain't making up nothing. I'm telling you the facts of what happened. I wrestled with Death for three days and three nights and I'm standing here to tell you about it.

(*Pause.*)

Alright. At the end of the third night we done weakened each other to where we can't hardly move. Death stood up, throwed on his robe . . . had him a white robe with a hood on it. He throwed on that robe and went off to look for his sickle. Say, "I'll be back." Just like that. "I'll be back." I told him, say, "Yeah, but . . . you gonna have to find me!" I wasn't no fool. I wasn't going looking for him. Death ain't nothing to play with. And I know he's gonna get me. I know I got to join his army . . . his camp followers. But as long as I keep my strength and see him coming . . . as long as I keep up my vigilance . . . he's gonna have to fight to get me. I ain't going easy.

BONO. Well, look here, since you got to keep up your vigilance . . . let me have the bottle.

TROY. Aw hell, I shouldn't have told you that part. I should have left out that part.

ROSE. Troy be talking that stuff and half the time don't even know what he be talking about.

TROY. Bono know me better than that.

BONO. That's right. I know you. I know you got some Uncle Remus in your blood. You got more stories than the devil got sinners.

TROY. Aw hell, I done seen him too! Done talked with the devil.

ROSE. Troy, don't nobody wanna be hearing all that stuff.

(LYONS *enters the yard from the street. Thirty-four years old,* TROY'S *son by a previous marriage, he sports a neatly trimmed goatee, sport coat, white shirt, tieless and buttoned at the collar. Though he fancies himself a musician, he is more caught up in the rituals and "idea" of being a musician than in the actual practice of the music. He has come to borrow money from* TROY, *and while he knows he will be successful, he is uncertain as to what extent his lifestyle will be held up to scrutiny and ridicule.*)

LYONS. Hey, Pop.

TROY. What you come "Hey, Popping" me for?

LYONS. How you doing, Rose?

(*He kisses her.*)

Mr. Bono. How you doing?

BONO. Hey, Lyons . . . how you been?

TROY. He must have been doing alright. I ain't seen him around here last week.

ROSE. Troy, leave your boy alone. He come by to see you and you wanna start all that nonsense.

TROY. I ain't bothering Lyons.

(*Offers him the bottle.*)

Here . . . get you a drink. We got an understanding. I know why he come by to see me and he know I know.

LYONS. Come on, Pop . . . I just stopped by to say hi . . . see how you was doing.

TROY. You ain't stopped by yesterday.

ROSE. You gonna stay for supper, Lyons? I got some chicken cooking in the oven.

LYONS. No, Rose . . . thanks. I was just in the neighborhood and thought I'd stop by for a minute.

TROY. You was in the neighborhood alright, nigger. You telling the truth there. You was in the neighborhood cause it's my payday.

LYONS. Well, hell, since you mentioned it . . . let me have ten dollars.

TROY. I'll be damned! I'll die and go to hell and play blackjack with the devil before I give you ten dollars.

BONO. That's what I wanna know about . . . that devil you done seen.

LYONS. What . . . Pop done seen the devil? You too much, Pops.

TROY. Yeah, I done seen him. Talked to him too!

ROSE. You ain't seen no devil. I done told you that man ain't had nothing to do with the devil. Anything you can't understand, you want to call it the devil.

TROY. Look here, Bono . . . I went down to see Hertzberger about some furniture. Got three rooms for two-ninety-eight. That what it say on the radio. "Three rooms . . . two-ninety-eight." Even made up a little song about it. Go down there . . . man tell me I can't get no credit. I'm working every day and can't get no credit. What to do? I got an empty house with some raggedy furniture in it. Cory ain't got no bed. He's sleeping on a pile of rags on the floor. Working every day and can't get no credit. Come back here—Rose'll tell you—madder than hell. Sit down . . . try to figure what I'm gonna do. Come a knock on the door. Ain't been living here but three days. Who know I'm here? Open the door . . . devil standing there bigger than life. White fellow . . . got on good clothes and everything. Standing there with a clipboard in his hand. I ain't had to say nothing. First words come out of his mouth was . . ."I understand you need some furniture and can't get no credit." I liked to fell over. He say "I'll give you all the credit you want, but you got to pay the interest on it." I told him, "Give me three rooms worth and charge whatever you want." Next day a truck pulled up here and two men unloaded them three rooms. Man what drove the truck give me a book. Say send ten dollars, first of every month to the address in the book and everything will be alright. Say if I miss a payment the devil was coming back and it'll be hell to pay. That was fifteen years ago. To this day . . . the first of the month I send my ten dollars, Rose'll tell you.

ROSE. Troy lying.

TROY. I ain't never seen that man since. Now you tell me who else that could have been but the devil? I ain't sold my soul or nothing like that, you understand. Naw, I wouldn't have truck with the devil about nothing like that. I got my furniture and pays my ten dollars the first of the month just like clockwork.

BONO. How long you say you been paying this ten dollars a month?

TROY. Fifteen years!

BONO. Hell, ain't you finished paying for it yet? How much the man done charged you.

TROY. Aw hell, I done paid for it. I done paid for it ten times over! The fact is I'm scared to stop paying it.

ROSE. Troy lying. We got that furniture from Mr. Glickman. He ain't paying no ten dollars a month to nobody.

TROY. Aw hell, woman. Bono know I ain't that big a fool.

LYONS. I was just getting ready to say . . . I know where there's a bridge for sale.

TROY. Look here, I'll tell you this . . . it don't matter to me if he was the devil. It don't matter if the devil give credit. Somebody has got to give it.

ROSE. It ought to matter. You going around talking about having truck with the devil . . . God's the one you gonna have to answer to. He's the one gonna be at the Judgment.

LYONS. Yeah, well, look here, Pop . . . let me have that ten dollars. I'll give it back to you. Bonnie got a job working at the hospital.

TROY. What I tell you, Bono? The only time I see this nigger is when he wants something. That's the only time I see him.

LYONS. Come on, Pop, Mr. Bono don't want to hear all that. Let me have the ten dollars. I told you Bonnie working.

TROY. What that mean to me? "Bonnie working." I don't care if she working. Go ask her for the ten dollars if she working. Talking about "Bonnie working." Why ain't you working?

LYONS. Aw, Pop, you know I can't find no decent job. Where am I gonna get a job at? You know I can't get no job.

TROY. I told you I know some people down there. I can get you on the rubbish if you want to work. I told you that the last time you came by here asking me for something.

LYONS. Naw, Pop . . . thanks. That ain't for me. I don't wanna be carrying nobody's rubbish. I don't wanna be punching nobody's time clock.

TROY. What's the matter, you too good to carry people's rubbish? Where you think that ten dollars you talking about come from? I'm just supposed to haul people's rubbish and give my money to you cause you too lazy to work. You too lazy to work and wanna know why you ain't got what I got.

ROSE. What hospital Bonnie working at? Mercy?

LYONS. She's down at Passavant working in the laundry.

TROY. I ain't got nothing as it is. I give you that ten dollars and I got to eat beans the rest of the week. Naw . . . you ain't getting no ten dollars here.

LYONS. You ain't got to be eating no beans. I don't know why you wanna say that.

TROY. I ain't got no extra money. Gabe done moved over to Miss Pearl's paying her the rent and things done got tight around here. I can't afford to be giving you every payday.

LYONS. I ain't asked you to give me nothing. I asked you to loan me ten dollars. I know you got ten dollars.

TROY. Yeah, I got it. You know why I got it? Cause I don't throw my money away out there in the streets. You living the fast life . . . wanna be a musician . . . running around in them clubs and things . . . then, you learn to take care of yourself. You ain't gonna find me going and asking nobody for nothing. I done spent too many years without.

LYONS. You and me is two different people, Pop.

TROY. I done learned my mistake and learned to do what's right by it. You still trying to get something for nothing. Life don't owe you nothing. You owe it to yourself. Ask Bono. He'll tell you I'm right.

LYONS. You got your way of dealing with the world . . . I got mine. The only thing that matters to me is the music.

TROY. Yeah, I can see that! It don't matter how you gonna eat . . . where your next dollar is coming from. You telling the truth there.

LYONS. I know I got to eat. But I got to live too. I need something that gonna help me to get out of the bed in the morning. Make me feel like I belong in the world. I don't bother nobody. I just stay with my music cause that's the only way I can find to live in the world. Otherwise there ain't no telling what I might do. Now I don't come criticizing you and how you live. I just come by to ask you for ten dollars. I don't wanna hear all that about how I live.

TROY. Boy, your mama did a hell of a job raising you.

LYONS. You can't change me, Pop. I'm thirty-four years old. If you wanted to change me, you should have been there when I was growing up. I come by to see you . . . ask for ten dollars and you want to talk about how I was raised. You don't know nothing about how I was raised.

ROSE. Let the boy have ten dollars, Troy.

TROY (To LYONS.) What the hell you looking at me for? I ain't got no ten dollars. You know what I do with my money.
(To ROSE.)
Give him ten dollars if you want him to have it.

ROSE. I will. Just as soon as you turn it loose.

TROY (Handing ROSE the money.) There it is. Seventy-six dollars and forty-two cents. You see this, Bono? Now, I ain't gonna get but six of that back.

ROSE. You ought to stop telling that lie. Here, Lyons.

(She hands him the money.)

LYONS. Thanks, Rose. Look . . . I got to run . . . I'll see you later.

TROY. Wait a minute. You gonna say, "thanks, Rose" and ain't gonna look to see where she got that ten dollars from? See how they do me, Bono?

LYONS. I know she got it from you, Pop. Thanks. I'll give it back to you.

TROY. There he go telling another lie. Time I see that ten dollars . . . he'll be owing me thirty more.

LYONS. See you, Mr. Bono.

BONO. Take care, Lyons!

LYONS. Thanks, Pop. I'll see you again.

(LYONS exits the yard.)

TROY. I don't know why he don't go and get him a decent job and take care of that woman he got.

BONO. He'll be alright, Troy. The boy is still young.

TROY. The boy is thirty-four years old.

ROSE. Let's not get off into all that.

BONO. Look here . . . I got to be going. I got to be getting on. Lucille gonna be waiting.

TROY (Puts his arm around ROSE.) See this woman, Bono? I love this woman. I love this woman so much it hurts. I love her so much . . . I done run out of ways of loving her. So I got to go back to basics. Don't you come by my house Monday morning talking about time to go to work . . . 'cause I'm still gonna be stroking!

ROSE. Troy! Stop it now!

BONO. I ain't paying him no mind, Rose. That ain't nothing but gin-talk. Go on, Troy. I'll see you Monday.

TROY. Don't you come by my house, nigger! I done told you what I'm gonna be doing.

(The lights go down to black.)

ACT ONE
SCENE TWO

The lights come up on ROSE *hanging up clothes. She hums and sings softly to herself. It is the following morning.*

ROSE. (*Sings*) Jesus, be a fence all around me every day

Jesus, I want you to protect me as I travel on my way.

Jesus, be a fence all around me every day.

(*Troy enters from the house*)

ROSE (*continued*). Jesus, I want you to protect me As I travel on my way.

(*To* TROY)

Morning. You ready for breakfast? I can fix it soon as I finish hanging up these clothes?

TROY. I got the coffee on. That'll be alright. I'll just drink some of that this morning.

ROSE. That 651 hit yesterday. That's the second time this month. Miss Pearl hit for a dollar . . . seem like those that need the least always get lucky. Poor folks can't get nothing.

TROY. Them numbers don't know nobody. I don't know why you fool with them. You and Lyons both.

ROSE. It's something to do.

TROY. You ain't doing nothing but throwing your money away.

ROSE. Troy, you know I don't play foolishly. I just play a nickel here and a nickel there.

TROY. That's two nickels you done thrown away.

ROSE. Now I hit sometimes . . . that makes up for it. It always comes in handy when I do hit. I don't hear you complaining then.

TROY. I ain't complaining now. I just say it's foolish. Trying to guess out of six hundred ways which way the number gonna come. If I had all the money niggers, these Negroes, throw away on numbers for one week—just one week—I'd be a rich man.

ROSE. Well, you wishing and calling it foolish ain't gonna stop folks from playing numbers. That's one thing for sure. Besides . . . some good things come from playing numbers. Look where Pope done bought him that restaurant off of numbers.

TROY. I can't stand niggers like that. Man ain't had two dimes to rub together. He walking around with his shoes all run over bumming money for cigarettes. Alright. Got lucky there and hit the numbers . . .

ROSE. Troy, I know all about it.

TROY. Had good sense, I'll say that for him. He ain't throwed his money away. I seen niggers hit the numbers and go through two thousand dollars in four days. Man brought him that restaurant down there . . . fixed it up real nice . . . and then didn't want nobody to come in it! A Negro go in there and can't get no kind of service. I seen a white fellow come in there and order a bowl of stew. Pope picked all the meat out the pot for him. Man ain't had nothing but a bowl of meat! Negro come behind him and ain't got nothing but the potatoes and carrots. Talking about what numbers do for people, you picked a wrong example. Ain't done nothing but make a worser fool out of him than he was before.

ROSE. Troy, you ought to stop worrying about what happened at work yesterday.

TROY. I ain't worried. Just told me to be down there at the Commissioner's office on Friday. Everybody think they gonna fire me. I ain't worried about them firing me. You ain't got to worry about that.

(*Pause.*)

Where's Cory? Cory in the house? (*Calls.*) Cory?

ROSE. He gone out.

TROY. Out, huh? He gone out 'cause he know I want him to help me with this fence. I know how he is. That boy scared of work.

(GABRIEL *enters. He comes halfway down the alley and, hearing Troy's voice, stops.*)

TROY (*continues*). He ain't done a lick of work in his life.

ROSE. He had to go to football practice. Coach wanted them to get in a little extra practice before the season start.

TROY. I got his practice . . . running out of here before he get his chores done.

ROSE. Troy, what is wrong with you this morning? Don't nothing set right with you. Go on back in there and go to bed . . . get up on the other side.

TROY. Why something got to be wrong with me? I ain't said nothing wrong with me.

ROSE. You got something to say about everything. First it's the numbers . . . then it's the way the man runs his restaurant . . . then you done got on Cory. What's it gonna be next? Take a look up there and see if the weather suits you . . . or is it gonna be how you gonna put up the fence with the clothes hanging in the yard.

TROY. You hit the nail on the head then.

ROSE. I know you like I know the back of my hand. Go on in there and get you some coffee . . . see if that straighten you up. 'Cause you ain't right this morning.

(TROY *starts into the house and sees* GABRIEL. GABRIEL *starts singing.* TROY'S *brother, he is seven years younger than* TROY. *Injured in World War II, he has a metal plate in his head. He carries an old trumpet tied around his waist and believes with every fiber of his being that he is the Archangel Gabriel. He carries a chipped basket with an assortment of discarded fruits and vegetables he has picked up in the strip district and which he attempts to sell.*)

GABRIEL (*Singing.*)
    Yes, ma'am, I got plums
    You ask me how I sell them
    Oh ten cents apiece
    Three for a quarter
    Come and buy now
    'Cause I'm here today
    And tomorrow I'll be gone

(GABRIEL *enters.*)

    Hey, Rose!

ROSE. How you doing, Gabe?

GABRIEL. There's Troy . . . Hey, Troy!

TROY. Hey, Gabe.

(*Exit into kitchen.*)

ROSE (*To* GABRIEL.) What you got there?

GABRIEL. You know what I got, Rose. I got fruits and vegetables.

ROSE (*Looking in basket.*) Where's all these plums you talking about?

GABRIEL. I ain't got no plums today, Rose. I was just singing that. Have some tomorrow. Put me in a big order for plums. Have enough plums tomorrow for St. Peter and everybody.

(TROY *re-enters from kitchen, crosses to steps.*)
(*To* ROSE.)

    Troy's mad at me.

TROY. I ain't mad at you. What I got to be mad at you about? You ain't done nothing to me.

GABRIEL. I just moved over to Miss Pearl's to keep out from in your way. I ain't mean no harm by it.

TROY. Who said anything about that? I ain't said anything about that.

GABRIEL. You ain't mad at me, is you?

TROY. Naw . . . I ain't mad at you, Gabe. If I was mad at you I'd tell you about it.

GABRIEL. Got me two rooms. In the basement. Got my own door too. Wanna see my key?

(*He holds up a key.*)

    That's my own key! Ain't nobody else got a key like that. That's my key! My two rooms!

TROY. Well, that's good, Gabe. You got your own key . . . that's good.

ROSE. You hungry, Gabe? I was just fixing to cook Troy his breakfast.

GABRIEL. I'll take some biscuits. You got some biscuits? Did you know when I was in heaven . . . every morning me and St. Peter would sit down by the gate and eat some big fat biscuits? Oh, yeah! We had us a good time. We'd sit there and eat us them biscuits and then St. Peter would go off to sleep and tell me to wake him up when it's time to open the gates for the judgment.

ROSE. Well, come on . . . I'll make up a batch of biscuits.

(ROSE *exits into the house.*)

GABRIEL. Troy . . . St. Peter got your name in the book. I seen it. It say . . . Troy Maxson. I say . . . I know him! He got the same name like what I got. That's my brother!

TROY. How many times you gonna tell me that, Gabe?

GABRIEL. Ain't got my name in the book. Don't have to have my name. I done died and went to heaven. He got your name though. One morning St. Peter was looking at his book . . . marking it up for the judgment . . . and he let me see your name. Got it in there under M. Got Rose's name . . . I ain't seen it like I seen yours . . . but I know it's in there. He got a great big book. Got everybody's name what was ever been born. That's what he told me. But I seen your name. Seen it with my own eyes.

TROY. Go on in the house there. Rose going to fix you something to eat.

GABRIEL. Oh, I ain't hungry. I done had breakfast with Aunt Jemimah. She come by and cooked me a whole mess of flapjacks. Remember how we used to eat them flapjacks?

TROY. Go on in the house and get you something to eat now.

GABRIEL. I got to go sell my plums. I done sold some tomatoes. Got me two quarters. Wanna see?

(*He shows* TROY *his quarters.*)

I'm gonna save them and buy me a new horn so St. Peter can hear me when it's time to open the gates.

(GABRIEL *stops suddenly. Listens.*)

Hear that? That's the hellhounds. I got to chase them out of here. Go on get out of here! Get out!

(GABRIEL *exits singing.*)

Better get ready for the judgment
Better get ready for the judgment
My Lord is coming down

(ROSE *enters from the house.*)

TROY. He gone off somewhere.

GABRIEL. (*Offstage*)
Better get ready for the judgment
Better get ready for the judgment morning
Better get ready for the judgment
My God is coming down

ROSE. He ain't eating right. Miss Pearl say she can't get him to eat nothing.

TROY. What you want me to do about it, Rose? I done did everything I can for the man. I can't make him get well. Man got half his head blown away . . . what you expect?

ROSE. Seem like something ought to be done to help him.

TROY. Man don't bother nobody. He just mixed up from that metal plate he got in his head. Ain't no sense for him to go back into the hospital.

ROSE. Least he be eating right. They can help him take care of himself.

TROY. Don't nobody wanna be locked up, Rose. What you wanna lock him up for? Man go over there and fight the war . . . messin' around with them Japs, get half his head blown off . . . and they give him a lousy three thousand dollars. And I had to swoop down on that.

ROSE. Is you fixing to go into that again?

TROY. That's the only way I got a roof over my head . . . cause of that metal plate.

ROSE. Ain't no sense you blaming yourself for nothing. Gabe wasn't in no condition to manage that money. You done what was right by him. Can't nobody say you ain't done what was right by him. Look how long you took care of him . . . till he wanted to have his own place and moved over there with Miss Pearl.

TROY. That ain't what I'm saying, woman! I'm just stating the facts. If my brother didn't have that metal plate in his head . . . I wouldn't have a pot to piss in or a window to throw it out of. And I'm fifty-three years old. Now see if you can understand that!

(TROY *gets up from the porch and starts to exit the yard.*)

ROSE. Where you going off to? You been running out of here every Saturday for weeks. I thought you was gonna work on this fence?

TROY. I'm gonna walk down to Taylors'. Listen to the ball game. I'll be back in a bit. I'll work on it when I get back.

(*He exits the yard. The lights go to black.*)

ACT ONE
SCENE THREE

The lights come up on the yard. It is four hours later. ROSE *is taking down the clothes from the line.* CORY *enters carrying his football equipment.*

ROSE. Your daddy like to had a fit with you running out of here this morning without doing your chores.

CORY. I told you I had to go to practice.

ROSE. He say you were supposed to help him with this fence.

CORY. He been saying that the last four or five Saturdays, and then he don't never do nothing, but go down to Taylors'. Did you tell him about the recruiter?

ROSE. Yeah, I told him.

CORY. What he say?

ROSE. He ain't said nothing too much. You get in there and get started on your chores before he gets back. Go on and scrub down them steps before he gets back here hollering and carrying on.

CORY. I'm hungry. What you got to eat, Mama?

ROSE. Go on and get started on your chores. I got some meat loaf in there. Go on and make you a sandwich . . . and don't leave no mess in there.

(CORY *exits into the house.* ROSE *continues to take down the clothes.* TROY *enters the yard and sneaks up and grabs her from behind.*)

Troy! Go on, now. You liked to scare me to death. What was the score of the game? Lucille had me on the phone and I couldn't keep up with it.

TROY. What I care about the game? Come here, woman.

(*He tries to kiss her.*)

ROSE. I thought you went down Taylors' to listen to the game. Go on, Troy! You supposed to be putting up this fence.

TROY. (*Attempting to kiss her again.*) I'll put it up when I finish with what is at hand.

ROSE. Go on, Troy. I ain't studying you.

TROY. (*Chasing after her.*) I'm studying you . . . fixing to do my homework!

ROSE. Troy, you better leave me alone.

TROY. Where's Cory? That boy brought his butt home yet?

ROSE. He's in the house doing his chores.

TROY. (*Calling.*) Cory! Get your butt out here, boy!

(ROSE *exits into the house with the laundry.* TROY *goes over the pile of wood, picks up a board, and starts sawing.* CORY *enters from the house.*)

TROY. You just now coming in here from leaving this morning?

CORY. Yeah, I had to go to football practice.

TROY. Yeah, what?

CORY. Yessir.

TROY. I ain't but two seconds off you noway. The garbage sitting in there overflowing . . . you ain't done none of your chores . . . and you come in here talking about "Yeah."

CORY. I was just getting ready to do my chores now, Pop . . .

TROY. Your first chore is to help me with this fence on Saturday. Everything else come after that. Now get that saw and cut them boards.

(CORY *takes the saw and begins cutting the boards.* TROY *continues working. There is a long pause.*)

CORY. Hey, Pop . . . why don't you buy a TV?

TROY. What I want with a TV? What I want one of them for?

CORY. Everybody got one. Earl, Ba Bra . . . Jesse!

TROY. I ain't asked you who had one. I say what I want with one?

CORY. So you can watch it. They got lots of things on TV. Baseball games and everything. We could watch the World Series.

TROY. Yeah . . . and how much this TV cost?

CORY. I don't know. They got them on sale for around two hundred dollars.

TROY. Two hundred dollars, huh?

CORY. That ain't that much, Pop.

TROY. Naw, it's just two hundred dollars. See that roof you got over your head at night? Let me tell you something about that roof. It's been over ten years since that roof was last tarred. See now . . . the snow come this winter and sit up there on that roof like it is . . . and it's gonna seep inside. It's just gonna be a little bit . . . ain't gonna hardly notice it. Then the next thing you know, it's gonna be leaking all over the house. Then the wood rot from all that water and you gonna need a whole new roof. Now, how much you think it cost to get that roof tarred?

CORY. I don't know.

TROY. Two hundred and sixty-four dollars . . . cash money. While you thinking about a TV, I got to be thinking about the roof . . . and whatever else go wrong around here. Now if you had two hundred dollars, what would you do . . . fix the roof or buy a TV?

CORY. I'd buy a TV. Then when the roof started to leak . . . when it needed fixing . . . I'd fix it.

TROY. Where you gonna get the money from? You done spent it for a TV. You gonna sit up and watch the water run all over your brand new TV.

CORY. Aw, Pop. You got money. I know you do.

TROY. Where I got it at, huh?

CORY. You got it in the bank.

TROY. You wanna see my bankbook? You wanna see that seventy-three dollars and twenty-two cents I got sitting up in there.

CORY. You ain't got to pay for it all at one time. You can put a down payment on it and carry it on home with you.

TROY. Not me. I ain't gonna owe nobody nothing if I can help it. Miss a payment and they come and snatch it right out your house. Then what you got? Now, soon as I get two hundred dollars clear, then I'll buy a TV. Right now, as soon as I get two hundred and sixty-four dollars, I'm gonna have this roof tarred.

CORY. Aw . . . Pop!

TROY. You go on and get your two hundred dollars and buy one if ya want it. I got better things to do with my money.

CORY. I can't get no two hundred dollars. I ain't never seen two hundred dollars.

TROY. I'll tell you what . . . you get you a hundred dollars and I'll put the other hundred with it.

CORY. Alright, I'm gonna show you.

TROY. You gonna show me how you can cut them boards right now.

(CORY *begins to cut the boards. There is a long pause.*)

CORY. The Pirates won today. That makes five in a row.

TROY. I ain't thinking about the Pirates. Got an all-white team. Got that boy . . . that Puerto Rican boy . . . Clemente. Don't even half-play him. That boy could be something if they give him a chance. Play him one day and sit him on the bench the next.

CORY. He gets a lot of chances to play.

TROY. I'm talking about playing regular. Playing every day so you can get your timing. That's what I'm talking about.

CORY. They got some white guys on the team that don't play every day. You can't play everybody at the same time.

TROY. If they got a white fellow sitting on the bench . . . you can bet your last dollar he can't play! The colored guy got to be twice as good before he get on the team. That's why I don't want you to get all tied up in them sports. Man on the team and what it get him? They got colored on the team and don't use them. Same as not having them. All them teams the same.

CORY. The Braves got Hank Aaron and Wes Covington. Hank Aaron hit two home runs today. That makes forty-three.

TROY. Hank Aaron ain't nobody. That's what you supposed to do. That's how you supposed to play the game. Ain't nothing to it. It's just a matter of timing . . . getting the right follow-through. Hell, I can hit forty-three home runs right now!

CORY. Not off no major-league pitching, you couldn't.

TROY. We had better pitching in the Negro leagues. I hit seven home runs off of Satchel Paige. You can't get no better than that!

CORY. Sandy Koufax. He's leading the league in strike-outs.

TROY. I ain't thinking of no Sandy Koufax.

CORY. You got Warren Spahn and Lew Burdette. I bet you couldn't hit no home runs off of Warren Spahn.

TROY. I'm through with it now. You go on and cut them boards.

(*Pause.*)

Your mama tell me you done got recruited by a college football team? Is that right?

CORY. Yeah. Coach Zellman say the recruiter gonna be coming by to talk to you. Get you to sign the permission papers.

TROY. I thought you supposed to be working down there at the A&P. Ain't you suppose to be working down there after school?

CORY. Mr. Stawicki say he gonna hold my job for me until after the football season. Say starting next week I can work weekends.

TROY. I thought we had an understanding about this football stuff? You suppose to keep up with your chores and hold that job down at the A&P. Ain't been around here all day on a Saturday. Ain't none of your chores done . . . and now you telling me you done quit your job.

CORY. I'm gonna be working weekends.

TROY. You damn right you are! And ain't no need for nobody coming around here to talk to me about signing nothing.

CORY. Hey, Pop . . . you can't do that. He's coming all the way from North Carolina.

TROY. I don't care where he coming from. The white man ain't gonna let you get nowhere with that football noway. You go on and get your book-learning so you can work yourself up in that A&P or learn how to fix cars or build houses or something, get you a trade. That way you have something can't nobody take away from you. You go on and learn how to put your hands to some good use. Besides hauling people's garbage.

CORY. I get good grades, Pop. That's why the recruiter wants to talk with you. You got to keep up your grades to get recruited. This way I'll be going to college. I'll get a chance . . .

TROY. First you gonna get your butt down there to the A&P and get your job back.

CORY. Mr. Stawicki done already hired somebody else 'cause I told him I was playing football.

TROY. You a bigger fool than I thought . . . to let somebody take away your job so you can play some football. Where you gonna get your money to take out your girlfriend and whatnot? What kind of foolishness is that to let somebody take away your job?

CORY. I'm still gonna be working weekends.

TROY. Naw . . . naw. You getting your butt out of here and finding you another job.

CORY. Come on, Pop! I got to practice. I can't work after school and play football too. The team needs me. That's what Coach Zellman say . . .

TROY. I don't care what nobody else say. I'm the boss . . . you understand? I'm the boss around here. I do the only saying what counts.

CORY. Come on, Pop!

TROY. I asked you . . . did you understand?

CORY. Yeah . . .

TROY. What?!

CORY. Yessir.

TROY. You go on down there to that A&P and see if you can get your job back. If you can't do both . . . then you quit the football team. You've got to take the crookeds with the straights.

CORY. Yessir.

(*Pause.*)

Can I ask you a question?

TROY. What the hell you wanna ask me? Mr. Stawicki the one you got the questions for.

CORY. How come you ain't never liked me?

TROY. Liked you? Who the hell say I got to like you? What law is there say I got to like you? Wanna stand up in my face and ask a damn fool-ass question like that. Talking about liking somebody. Come here, boy, when I talk to you.

(CORY *comes over to where* TROY *is working. He stands slouched over and* TROY *shoves him on his shoulder.*)

Straighten up, goddammit! I asked you a question . . . what law is there say I got to like you?

CORY. None.

TROY. Well, alright then! Don't you eat every day?

(*Pause.*)

Answer me when I talk to you! Don't you eat every day?

CORY. Yeah.

TROY. Nigger, as long as you in my house, you put that sir on the end of it when you talk to me!

CORY. Yes . . . sir.

TROY. You eat every day.

CORY. Yessir!

TROY. Got a roof over your head.

CORY. Yessir!

TROY. Got clothes on your back.

CORY. Yessir.

TROY. Why you think that is?

CORY. Cause of you.

TROY. Aw, hell I know it's 'cause of me . . . but why do you think that is?

CORY. (*Hesitant.*) Cause you like me.

TROY. Like you? I go out of here every morning . . . bust my butt . . . putting up with them crackers every day . . . cause I like you? You about the biggest fool I ever saw.

(*Pause.*)

It's my job. It's my responsibility! You understand that? A man got to take care of his family. You live in my house . . . sleep you behind on my bedclothes . . . fill you belly up with my food . . .

cause you my son. You my flesh and blood. Not 'cause I like you! Cause it's my duty to take care of you. I owe a responsibility to you! Let's get this straight right here . . . before it go along any further . . . I ain't got to like you. Mr. Rand don't give me my money come payday cause he likes me. He gives me cause he owe me. I done give you everything I had to give you. I gave you your life! Me and your mamma worked that out between us. And liking your black ass wasn't part of the bargain. Don't you try and go through life worrying about if somebody like you or not. You best be making sure they doing right by you. You understand what I'm saying, boy?

CORY. Yessir.

TROY. Then get the hell out of my face, and get on down to that A&P.

(ROSE *has been standing behind the screen door for much of the scene. She enters as* CORY *exits.*)

ROSE. Why don't you let the boy go ahead and play football, Troy? Ain't no harm in that. He's just trying to be like you with the sports.

TROY. I don't want him to be like me! I want him to move as far away from my life as he can get. You the only decent thing that ever happened to me. I wish him that. But I don't wish him a thing else from my life. I decided seventeen years ago that boy wasn't getting involved in no sports. Not after what they did to me in the sports.

ROSE. Troy, why don't you admit you was too old to play in the major leagues? For once . . . why don't you admit that?

TROY. What do you mean too old? Don't come telling me I was too old. I just wasn't the right color. Hell, I'm fifty-three years old and can do better than Selkirk's .269 right now!

ROSE. How's was you gonna play ball when you were over forty? Sometimes I can't get no sense out of you.

TROY. I got good sense, woman. I got sense enough not to let my boy get hurt over playing no sports. You been mothering that boy too much. Worried about if people like him.

ROSE. Everything that boy do . . . he do for you. He wants you to say "Good job, son." That's all.

TROY. Rose, I ain't got time for that. He's alive. He's healthy. He's got to make his own way. I made mine. Ain't nobody gonna hold his hand when he get out there in that world.

ROSE. Times have changed from when you was young, Troy. People change. The world's changing around you and you can't even see it.

TROY. (*Slow, methodical.*) Woman . . . I do the best I can do. I come in here every Friday. I carry a sack of potatoes and a bucket of lard. You all line up at the door with your hands out. I give you the lint from my pockets. I give you my sweat and my blood. I ain't got no tears. I done spent them. We go upstairs in that room at night . . . and I fall down on you and try to blast a hole into forever. I get up Monday morning . . . find my lunch on the table. I go out. Make my way. Find my strength to carry me through to the next Friday.

(*Pause.*)

That's all I got, Rose. That's all I got to give. I can't give nothing else.

(TROY *exits into the house. The lights go down to black.*)

ACT ONE
SCENE FOUR

It is Friday. Two weeks later. CORY *starts out of the house with his football equipment. The phone rings.*

CORY. (*Calling.*) I got it!

(*He answers the phone and stands in the screen door talking.*)

Hello? Hey, Jesse. Naw . . . I was just getting ready to leave now.

ROSE. (*Calling.*) Cory!

CORY. I told you, man, them spikes is all tore up. You can use them if you want, but they ain't no good. Earl got some spikes.

ROSE. (*Calling.*) Cory!

CORY. (*Calling to Rose.*) Mam? I'm talking to Jesse.

(*Into phone.*)

When she say that? (*Pause.*) Aw, you lying, man. I'm gonna tell her you said that.

ROSE. (*Calling.*) Cory, don't you go nowhere!

CORY. I got to go to the game, Ma!

(*Into the phone.*)

Yeah, hey, look, I'll talk to you later. Yeah, I'll meet you over Earl's house. Later. Bye, Ma.

(CORY *exits the house and starts out the yard.*)

ROSE. Cory, where you going off to? You got that stuff all pulled out and thrown all over your room.

CORY. (*In the yard.*) I was looking for my spikes. Jesse wanted to borrow my spikes.

ROSE. Get up there and get that cleaned up before your daddy get back in here.

CORY. I got to go to the game! I'll clean it up *when I get back*.

(CORY *exits*.)

ROSE. That's all he need to do is see that room all messed up.

(ROSE *exits into the house.* TROY *and* BONO *enter the yard.* TROY *is dressed in clothes other than his work clothes.*)

BONO. He told him the same thing he told you. Take it to the union.

TROY. Brownie ain't got that much sense. Man wasn't thinking about nothing. He wait until I confront them on it . . . then he wanna come crying seniority.

(*Calls.*)

Hey, Rose!

BONO. I wish I could have seen Mr. Rand's face when he told you.

TROY. He couldn't get it out of his mouth! Liked to bit his tongue! When they called me down there to the Commissioner's office . . . he thought they was gonna fire me. Like everybody else.

BONO. I didn't think they was gonna fire you. I thought they was gonna put you on the warning paper.

TROY. Hey, Rose!

(*To* BONO.)

Yeah, Mr. Rand like to bit his tongue.

(TROY *breaks the seal on the bottle, takes a drink, and hands it to* BONO.)

BONO. I see you run right down to Taylors' and told that Alberta gal.

TROY. (*Calling.*) Hey Rose! (*To* BONO.) I told everybody. Hey, Rose! I went down there to cash my check.

ROSE. (*Entering from the house.*) Hush all that hollering, man! I know you out here. What they say down there at the Commissioner's office?

TROY. You supposed to come when I call you, woman. Bono'll tell you that.

(*To* BONO.)

Don't Lucille come when you call her?

ROSE. Man, hush your mouth. I ain't no dog . . . talk about "come when you call me."

TROY. (*Puts his arm around* ROSE.) You hear this, Bono? I had me an old dog used to get uppity like that. You say, "C'mere, Blue!" . . . and he just lay there and look at you. End up getting a stick and chasing him away trying to make him come.

ROSE. I ain't studying you and your dog. I remember you used to sing that old song.

TROY. (*He sings.*) Hear it ring! Hear it ring! I had a dog his name was Blue.

ROSE. Don't nobody wanna hear you sing that old song.

TROY. (*Sings.*) You know Blue was mighty true.

ROSE. Used to have Cory running around here singing that song.

BONO. Hell, I remember that song myself.

TROY. (*Sings.*) You know Blue was a good old dog.
    Blue treed a possum in a hollow log.

   That was my daddy's song. My daddy made up that song.

ROSE. I don't care who made it up. Don't nobody wanna hear you sing it.

TROY. (*Makes a song like calling a dog.*) Come here, woman.

ROSE. You come in here carrying on. I reckon they ain't fired you. What they say down there at the Commissioner's office?

TROY. Look here, Rose . . . Mr. Rand called me into his office today when I got back from talking to them people down there . . . it comes from up top . . . he called me in and told me they was making me a driver.

ROSE. Troy, you kidding!

TROY. No I ain't. Ask Bono.

ROSE. Well, that's great, Troy. Now you don't have to hassle them people no more.

(LYONS *enters from the street.*)

TROY. Aw hell, I wasn't looking to see you today. I thought you was in jail. Got it all over the front page of the *Courier* about them raiding Sefus' place . . . where you be hanging out with all them thugs.

LYONS. Hey, Pop . . . that ain't got nothing to do with me. I don't go down there gambling. I go down there to sit in with the band. I ain't got nothing to do with the gambling part. They got some good music down there.

TROY. They got some rogues . . . is what they got.

LYONS. How you been, Mr. Bono? Hi, Rose.

BONO. I see where you playing down at the Crawford Grill tonight.

ROSE. How come you ain't brought Bonnie like I told you. You should have brought Bonnie with you, she ain't been over in a month of Sundays.

LYONS. I was just in the neighborhood . . . thought I'd stop by.

TROY. Here he come . . .

BONO. Your daddy got a promotion on the rubbish. He's gonna be the first colored driver. Ain't got to do nothing but sit up there and read the paper like them white fellows.

LYONS. Hey, Pop . . . if you knew how to read you'd be alright.

BONO. Naw . . . naw . . . you mean if the nigger knew how to *drive* he'd be all right. Been fighting with them people about driving and ain't even got a license. Mr. Rand know you ain't got no driver's license?

TROY. Driving ain't nothing. All you do is point the truck where you want it to go. Driving ain't nothing.

BONO. Do Mr. Rand know you ain't got no driver's license? That's what I'm talking about. I ain't asked if driving was easy. I asked if Mr. Rand know you ain't got no driver's license.

TROY. He ain't got to know. The man ain't got to know my business. Time he find out, I have two or three driver's licenses.

LYONS. (*Going into his pocket.*) Say, look here, Pop . . .

TROY. I knew it was coming. Didn't I tell you, Bono? I know what kind of "Look here, Pop" that was.

The nigger fixing to ask me for some money. It's Friday night. It's my payday. All them rogues down there on the avenue . . . the ones that ain't in jail . . . and Lyons is hopping in his shoes to get down there with them.

LYONS. See, Pop . . . if you give somebody else a chance to talk sometime, you'd see that I was fixing to pay you back your ten dollars like I told you. Here . . . I told you I'd pay you when Bonnie got paid.

TROY. Naw . . . you go ahead and keep that ten dollars. Put it in the bank. The next time you feel like you wanna come by here and ask me for something . . . you go on down there and get that.

LYONS. Here's your ten dollars, Pop. I told you I don't want you to give me nothing. I just wanted to borrow ten dollars.

TROY. Naw . . . you go on and keep that for the next time you want to ask me.

LYONS. Come on, Pop . . . here go your ten dollars.

ROSE. Why don't you go on and let the boy pay you back, Troy?

LYONS. Here you go, Rose. If you don't take it I'm gonna have to hear about it for the next six months.

(*He hands her the money.*)

ROSE. You can hand yours over here too, Troy.

TROY. You see this, Bono. You see how they do me.

BONO. Yeah, Lucille do me the same way.

(GABRIEL *is heard singing offstage. He enters.*)

GABRIEL. Better get ready for the Judgment! Better get ready for . . . Hey! . . . Hey! . . . There's Troy's boy!

LYONS. How you doing, Uncle Gabe?

GABRIEL. Lyons . . . The King of the Jungle! Rose . . . hey, Rose. Got a flower for you.

(*He takes a rose from his pocket.*)

Picked it myself. That's the same rose like you is!

ROSE. That's right nice of you, Gabe.

LYONS. What you been doing, Uncle Gabe?

GABRIEL. Oh, I been chasing hellhounds and waiting on the time to tell St. Peter to open the gates.

LYONS. You been chasing hellhounds, huh? Well . . . you doing the right thing, Uncle Gabe. Somebody got to chase them.

GABRIEL. Oh, yeah . . . I know it. The devil's strong. The devil ain't no pushover. Hellhounds snipping at everybody's heels. But I got my trumpet waiting on the judgment time.

LYONS. Waiting on the Battle of Armageddon, huh?

GABRIEL. Ain't gonna be too much of a battle when God get to waving that Judgment sword. But the people's gonna have a hell of a time trying to get into heaven if them gates ain't open.

LYONS. (*Putting his arms around* GABRIEL.) You hear this, Pop. Uncle Gabe, you alright!

GABRIEL. (*Laughing with* LYONS.) Lyons! King of the Jungle.

ROSE. You gonna stay for supper, Gabe. Want me to fix you a plate?

GABRIEL. I'll take a sandwich, Rose. Don't want no plate. Just wanna eat with my hands. I'll take a sandwich.

ROSE. How about you, Lyons? You staying? Got some short ribs cooking.

LYONS. Naw, I won't eat nothing till after we finished playing.

(*Pause.*)

You ought to come down and listen to me play, Pop.

TROY. I don't like that Chinese music. All that noise.

ROSE. Go on in the house and wash up, Gabe . . . I'll fix you a sandwich.

GABRIEL. (*To* LYONS, *as he exits.*) Troy's mad at me.

LYONS. What you mad at Uncle Gabe for, Pop.

ROSE. He thinks Troy's mad at him cause he moved over to Miss Pearl's.

TROY. I ain't mad at the man. He can live where he want to live at.

LYONS. What he move over there for? Miss Pearl don't like nobody.

ROSE. She don't mind him none. She treats him real nice. She just don't allow all that singing.

TROY. She don't mind that rent he be paying . . . that's what she don't mind.

ROSE. Troy, I ain't going through that with you no more. He's over there cause he want to have his own place. He can come and go as he please.

TROY. Hell, he could come and go as he please here. I wasn't stopping him. I ain't put no rules on him.

ROSE. It ain't the same thing, Troy. And you know it.

(GABRIEL *comes to the door.*)

Now, that's the last I wanna hear about that. I don't wanna hear nothing else about Gabe and Miss Pearl. And next week . . .

GABRIEL. I'm ready for my sandwich, Rose.

ROSE. And next week . . . when that recruiter come from that school . . . I want you to sign that paper and go on and let Cory play football. Then that'll be the last I have to hear about that.

TROY. (*To* ROSE *as she exits into the house.*) I ain't thinking about Cory nothing.

LYONS. What . . . Cory got recruited? What school he going to?

TROY. That boy walking around here smelling his piss . . . thinking he's grown. Thinking he's gonna do what he want, irrespective of what I say. Look here, Bono . . . I left the Commissioner's office and went down to the A&P . . . that boy ain't working down there. He lying to me. Telling me he got his job back . . . telling me he working weekends . . . telling me he working after school . . . Mr. Stawicki tell me he ain't working down there at all!

LYONS. Cory just growing up. He's just busting at the seams trying to fill out your shoes.

TROY. I don't care what he's doing. When he get to the point where he wanna disobey me . . . then it's time for him to move on. Bono'll tell you that. I bet he ain't never disobeyed his daddy without paying the consequences.

BONO. I ain't never had a chance. My daddy came on through . . . but I ain't never knew him to see him . . . or what he had on his mind or where he went. Just moving on through. Searching out the New Land. That's what the old folks used to call it. See a fellow moving around from place to place . . . woman to woman . . . called it searching out the New Land. I can't say if he ever found it. I come along, didn't want no kids. Didn't know if I was gonna be in one place long enough to fix on them right as their daddy. I figured I was going searching too. As it turned out I been hooked up with Lucille near about as long as your daddy been with Rose. Going on sixteen years.

TROY. Sometimes I wish I hadn't known my daddy. He ain't cared nothing about no kids. A kid to him wasn't nothing. All he wanted was for you to learn how to walk so he could start you to working. When it come time for eating . . . he ate first. If there was anything left over, that's what you got. Man would sit down and eat two chickens and give you the wing.

LYONS. You ought to stop that, Pop. Everybody feed their kids. No matter how hard times is . . . everybody care about their kids. Make sure they have something to eat.

TROY. The only thing my daddy cared about was getting them bales of cotton in to Mr. Lubin. That's the only thing that mattered to him. Sometimes I used to wonder why he was living. Wonder why the devil hadn't come and got him. "Get them bales of cotton in to Mr. Lubin" and find out he owe him money. . .

LYONS. He should have just went on and left when he saw he couldn't get nowhere. That's what I would have done.

TROY. How he gonna leave with eleven kids? And where he gonna go? He ain't knew how to do nothing but farm. No, he was trapped and I think he knew it. But I'll say this for him . . . he felt a responsibility toward us. Maybe he ain't treated us the way I felt he should have . . . but without that responsibility he could have walked off and left us . . . made his own way.

BONO. A lot of them did. Back in those days what you talking about . . . they walk out their front door and just take on down one road or another and keep on walking.

LYONS. There you go! That's what I'm talking about.

BONO. Just keep on walking till you come to something else. Ain't you never heard of nobody having the walking blues? Well, that's what you call it when you just take off like that.

TROY. My daddy ain't had them walking blues! What you talking about? He stayed right there with his family. But he was just as evil as he could be. My mamma couldn't stand him. Couldn't stand that evilness. She run off when I was about eight. She sneaked off one night after he had gone to sleep. Told me she was coming back for me. I ain't never seen her no more. All his women run off and left him. He wasn't good for nobody.

When my turn come to head out, I was fourteen and got to sniffling around Joe Canewell's daughter. Had us an old mule we called Greyboy.

My daddy sent me out to do some plowing and I tied up Greyboy and went to fooling around with Joe Canewell's daughter. We done found us a nice little spot, got real cozy with each other. She about thirteen and we done figured we was grown anyway . . . so we down there enjoying ourselves . . . ain't thinking about nothing. We didn't know Greyboy had got loose and wandered back to the house and my daddy was looking for me. We down there by the creek enjoying ourselves when my daddy come up on us. Surprised us. He had them leather straps off the mule and commenced to whupping me like there was no tomorrow. I jumped up, mad and embarrassed. I was scared of my daddy. When he commenced to whupping on me . . . quite naturally I run to get out of the way.

(*Pause.*)

Now I thought he was mad cause I ain't done my work. But I see where he was chasing me off so he could have the gal for himself. When I see what the matter of it was, I lost all fear of my daddy. Right there is where I become a man . . . at fourteen years of age.

(*Pause.*)

Now it was my turn to run him off. I picked up them same reins that he had used on me. I picked up them reins and commenced to whupping on him. The gal jumped up and run off . . . and when my daddy turned to face me, I could see why the devil had never come to get him . . . cause he was the devil himself. I don't know what happened. When I woke up, I was laying right there by the creek, and Blue . . . this old dog we had . . . was licking my face. I thought I was blind. I couldn't see nothing. Both my eyes were swollen shut. I layed there and cried. I didn't know what I was gonna do. The only thing I knew was the time had come for me to leave my daddy's house. And right there the world suddenly got big. And it was a long time before I could cut it down to where I could handle it.

Part of that cutting down was when I got to the place where I could feel him kicking in my blood and knew that the only thing that separated us was the matter of a few years.

(GABRIEL *enters from the house with a sandwich.*)

LYONS. What you got there, Uncle Gabe?

GABRIEL. Got me a ham sandwich. Rose gave me a ham sandwich.

TROY. I don't know what happened to him. I done lost touch with everybody except Gabriel. But I hope he's dead. I hope he found some peace.

LYONS. That's a heavy story, Pop. I didn't know you left home when you was fourteen.

TROY. And didn't know nothing. The only part of the world I knew was the forty-two acres of Mr. Lubin's land. That's all I knew about life.

LYONS. Fourteen's kinda young to be out on your own. (*Phone rings.*) I don't even think I was ready to be out on my own at fourteen. I don't know what I would have done.

TROY. I got up from the creek and walked on down to Mobile. I was through with farming. Figured I could do better in the city. So I walked two hundred miles to Mobile.

LYONS. Wait a minute . . . you ain't walked no two hundred miles, Pop. Ain't nobody gonna walk no two hundred miles. You talking about some walking there.

BONO. That's the only way you got anywhere back in them days.

LYONS. Shhh. Damn if I wouldn't have hitched a ride with somebody!

TROY. Who you gonna hitch it with? They ain't had no cars and things like they got now. We talking about 1918.

ROSE. (*Entering.*) What you all out here getting into?

TROY. (*To* ROSE.) I'm telling Lyons how good he got it. He don't know nothing about this I'm talking.

ROSE. Lyons, that was Bonnie on the phone. She say you supposed to pick her up.

LYONS. Yeah, okay, Rose.

TROY. I walked on down to Mobile and hitched up with some of them fellows that was heading this way. Got up here and found out . . . not only couldn't you get a job . . . you couldn't find no place to live. I thought I was in freedom. Shhh. Colored folks living down there on the riverbanks in whatever kind of shelter they could find for themselves. Right down there under the Brady Street Bridge. Living in shacks made of sticks and tarpaper. Messed around there and went from bad to worse. Started stealing. First it was food. Then I figured, hell, if I steal money I can buy me some food. Buy me some shoes too! One thing led to another. Met your mama. I was young and anxious to be a man. Met your mama and had you. What I do for that? Now I got to worry about feeding you and her. Got to steal three times as much. Went out one day looking for somebody to rob . . .

that's what I was, a robber. I'll tell you the truth. I'm ashamed of it today. But it's the truth. Went to rob this fellow . . . pulled out my knife . . . and he pulled out a gun. Shot me in the chest. It felt just like somebody had taken a hot branding iron and laid it on me. When he shot me I jumped at him with my knife. They told me I killed him and they put me in the penitentiary and locked me up for fifteen years. That's where I met Bono. That's where I learned how to play baseball. Got out that place and your mama had taken you and went on to make life without me. Fifteen years was a long time for her to wait. But that fifteen years cured me of that robbing stuff. Rose'll tell you. She asked me when I met her if I had gotten all that foolishness out of my system. And I told her, "Baby, it's you and baseball all what count with me." You hear me, Bono? I meant it too. She say, "Which one comes first?" I told her, "Baby, ain't no doubt it's baseball . . . but you stick and get old with me and we'll both outlive this baseball." Am I right, Rose? And it's true.

ROSE. Man, hush your mouth. You ain't said no such thing. Talking about, "Baby, you know you'll always be number one with me." That's what you was talking.

TROY. You hear that, Bono. That's why I love her.

BONO. Rose'll keep you straight. You get off the track, she'll straighten you up.

ROSE. Lyons, you better get on up and get Bonnie. She waiting on you.

LYONS. (*Gets up to go.*) Hey, Pop, why don't you come on down to the Grill and hear me play?

TROY. I ain't going down there. I'm too old to be sitting around in them clubs.

BONO. You got to be good to play down at the Grill.

LYONS. Come on, Pop . . .

TROY. I got to get up in the morning.

LYONS. You ain't got to stay long.

TROY. Naw, I'm gonna get my supper and go on to bed.

LYONS. Well, I got to go. I'll see you again.

TROY. Don't you come around my house on my payday.

ROSE. Pick up the phone and let somebody know you coming. And bring Bonnie with you. You know I'm always glad to see her.

LYONS. Yeah, I'll do that, Rose. You take care now. See you, Pop. See you, Mr. Bono. See you, Uncle Gabe.

GABRIEL. Lyons! King of the Jungle!

(LYONS *exits.*)

TROY. Is supper ready, woman? Me and you got some business to take care of. I'm gonna tear it up too.

ROSE. Troy, I done told you now!

TROY. (*Puts his arm around* BONO.) Aw hell, woman . . . this is Bono. Bono like family. I done known this nigger since . . . how long I done know you?

BONO. It's been a long time.

TROY. I done known this nigger since Skippy was a pup. Me and him done been through some times.

BONO. You sure right about that.

TROY. Hell, I done know him longer than I known you. And we still standing shoulder to shoulder. Hey, look here, Bono . . . a man can't ask for no more than that.

(*Drinks to him.*)

I love you, nigger.

BONO. Hell, I love you too . . . but I got to get home see my woman. You got yours in hand. I got to go get mine.

(BONO *starts to exit as* CORY *enters the yard, dressed in his football uniform. He gives* TROY *a hard, uncompromising look.*)

CORY. What you do that for, Pop?

(*He throws his helmet down in the direction of* TROY.)

ROSE. What's the matter? Cory . . . what's the matter?

CORY. Papa done went up to the school and told Coach Zellman I can't play football no more. Wouldn't even let me play the game. Told him to tell the recruiter not to come.

ROSE. Troy . . .

TROY. What you Troying me for. Yeah, I did it. And the boy know why I did it.

CORY. Why you wanna do that to me? That was the one chance I had.

ROSE. Ain't nothing wrong with Cory playing football, Troy.

TROY. The boy lied to me. I told the nigger if he wanna play football . . . to keep up his chores and hold down that job at the A&P. That was the conditions. Stopped down there to see Mr. Stawicki . . .

CORY. I can't work after school during the football season, Pop! I tried to tell you that Mr. Stawicki's holding my job for me. You don't never want to listen to nobody. And then you wanna go and do this to me!

TROY. I ain't done nothing to you. You done it to yourself.

CORY: Just cause you didn't have a chance! You just scared I'm gonna be better than you, that's all.

TROY. Come here.

ROSE. Troy . . .

(CORY *reluctantly crosses over to* TROY.)

TROY. Alright! See. You done made a mistake.

CORY. I didn't even do nothing!

TROY. I'm gonna tell you what your mistake was. See . . . you swung at the ball and didn't hit it. That's strike one. See, you in the batter's box now. You swung and you missed. That's strike one. Don't you strike out!

(*Lights fade to black.*)

ACT TWO
SCENE ONE

The following morning, CORY *is at the tree hitting the ball with the bat. He tries to mimic* TROY, *but his swing is awkward, less sure,* ROSE *enters from the house.*

ROSE. Cory, I want you to help me with this cupboard.

CORY. I ain't quitting the team. I don't care what Poppa say.

ROSE. I'll talk to him when he gets back. He had to go see about your Uncle Gabe. The police done arrested him. Say he was disturbing the peace. He'll be back directly. Come on in here and help me clean out the top of this cupboard.

(CORY *exits into the house.* ROSE *sees* TROY *and* BONO *coming down the alley.*)

Troy . . . what they say down there?

TROY. Ain't said nothing. I give them fifty dollars and they let him go. I'll talk to you about it. Where's Cory?

ROSE. He's in there helping me clean out these cupboards.

TROY. Tell him to get his butt out here.

(TROY *and* BONO *go over the pile of wood.* BONO *picks up the saw and begins sawing.*)

TROY. (*To* BONO.) All they want is the money. That makes six or seven times I done went down there and got him. See me coming they stick out their *hands.*

BONO. Yeah. I know what you mean. That's all they care about . . . that money. They don't care about what's right.

(*Pause.*)

Nigger, why you got to go and get some hard wood? You ain't done nothing but building a little old fence. Get you some soft pine wood. That's all you need.

TROY. I know what I'm doing. This is outside wood. You put pine wood inside the house. Pine wood is inside wood. This here is outside wood. Now you tell me where the fence is gonna be?

BONO. You don't need this wood. You can put it up with pine wood and it'll stand as long as you gonna be here looking at it.

TROY. How you know how long I'm gonna be here, nigger? Hell, I might just live forever. Live longer than old man Horsely.

BONO. That's what Magee used to say.

TROY. Magee's a damn fool. Now you tell me who you ever heard of gonna pull their own teeth with a pair of rusty pliers.

BONO. The old folks . . . my granddaddy used to pull his teeth with pliers. They ain't had no dentists for the colored folks back then.

TROY. Get clean pliers! You understand? Clean pliers! Sterlize them! Besides we ain't living back then. All Magee had to do was walk over to Doc Goldblums.

BONO. I see where you and that Tallahassee gal . . . that Alberta . . . I see where you all done got tight.

TROY. What you mean "got tight"?

BONO. I see where you be laughing and joking with her all the time.

TROY. I laughs and jokes with all of them, Bono. You know me.

BONO. That ain't the kind of laughing and joking I'm talking about.

(CORY *enters from the house.*)

CORY. How you doing, Mr. Bono?

TROY. Cory? Get that saw from Bono and cut some wood. He talking about the wood's too hard to cut. Stand back there, Jim, and let that young boy show you how it's done.

BONO. He's sure welcome to it.

(CORY *takes the saw and begins to cut the wood.*)

Whew-e-e! Look at that. Big old strong boy. Look like Joe Louis. Hell, must be getting old the way I'm watching that boy whip through that wood.

CORY. I don't see why Mama want a fence around the yard noways.

TROY. Damn if I know either. What the hell she keeping out with it? She ain't got nothing nobody want.

BONO. Some people build fences to keep people out . . . and other people build fences to keep people in. Rose wants to hold on to you all. She loves you.

TROY. Hell, nigger, I don't need nobody to tell me my wife loves me, Cory . . . go on in the house and see if you can find that other saw.

CORY. Where's it at?

TROY. I said find it! Look for it till you find it!

(CORY *exits into the house.*)

What's that supposed to mean? Wanna keep us in?

BONO. Troy . . . I done known you seem like damn near my whole life. You and Rose both, I done know both of you all for a long time. I remember when you met Rose. When you was hitting them baseball out the park. A lot of them old gals was after you then. You had the pick of the litter. When you picked Rose, I was happy for you. That was the first time I knew you had any sense. I said . . . My man Troy knows what he's doing . . . I'm gonna follow this nigger . . . he might take me somewhere. I been following you too. I done learned a whole heap of things about life watching you. I done learned how to tell where the shit lies. How to tell it from the alfalfa. You done learned me a lot of things. You showed me how to not make the same mistakes . . . to take life as it comes along and keep putting one foot in front of the other.

(*Pause.*)

Rose a good woman, Troy.

TROY. Hell, nigger, I know she a good woman. I been married to her for eighteen years. What you got on your mind, Bono?

BONO. I just say she a good woman. Just like I say anything. I ain't got to have nothing on my mind.

TROY. You just gonna say she a good woman and leave it hanging out there like that? Why you telling me she a good woman?

BONO. She loves you, Troy. Rose loves you.

TROY. You saying I don't measure up. That's what you trying to say. I don't measure up cause I'm seeing this other gal. I know what you trying to say.

BONO. I know what Rose means to you, Troy. I'm just trying to say I don't want to see you mess up.

TROY. Yeah, I appreciate that, Bono. If you was messing around on Lucille I'd be telling you the same thing.

BONO. Well, that's all I got to say. I just say that because I love you both.

TROY. Hell, you know me . . . I wasn't out there looking for nothing. You can't find a better woman than Rose. I know that. But seems like this woman just stuck onto me where I can't shake her loose. I done wrestled with it, tried to throw her off me . . . but she just stuck on tighter. Now she's stuck on for good.

BONO. You's in control . . . that's what you tell me all the time. You responsible for what you do.

TROY. I ain't ducking the responsibility of it. As long as it sets right in my heart . . . then I'm okay. Cause that's all I listen to. It'll tell me right from wrong every time. And I ain't talking about doing Rose no bad turn. I love Rose. She done carried me a long ways and I love and respect her for that.

BONO. I know you do. That's why I don't want to see you hurt her. But what you gonna do when she find out? What you got then? If you try and juggle both of them . . . sooner or later you gonna drop one of them. That's common sense.

TROY. Yeah, I hear what you saying, Bono. I been trying to figure a way to work it out.

BONO. Work it out right, Troy. I don't want to be getting all up between you and Rose's business . . . but work it so it come out right.

TROY. Aw hell, I get all up between you and Lucille's business. When you gonna get that woman that refrigerator she been wanting? Don't tell me you ain't got no money now. I know who your banker is. Mellon don't need that money bad as Lucille want that refrigerator. I'll tell you that.

BONO. Tell you what I'll do . . . when you finish building this fence for Rose . . . I'll buy Lucille that refrigerator.

TROY. You done stuck your foot in your mouth now!

(TROY *grabs up a board and begins to saw.* BONO *starts to walk out the yard.*)

Hey, nigger . . . where you going?

BONO. I'm going home. I know you don't expect me to help you now. I'm protecting my money. I wanna see you put that fence up by yourself. That's what I want to see. You'll be here another six months without me.

TROY. Nigger, you ain't right.

BONO. When it comes to my money . . . I'm right as fireworks on the Fourth of July.

TROY. Alright, we gonna see now. You better get out your bankbook.

(BONO *exits and* TROY *continues to work.* ROSE *enters from the house.*)

ROSE. What they say down there? What's happening with Gabe?

TROY. I went down there and got him out. Cost me fifty dollars. Say he was disturbing the peace. Judge set up a hearing for him in three weeks. Say to show cause why he shouldn't be re-committed.

ROSE. What was he doing that cause them to arrest him?

TROY. Some kids was teasing him and he run them off home. Say he was howling and carrying on. Some folks seen him and called the police. That's all it was.

ROSE. Well, what's you say? What'd you tell the judge?

TROY. Told him I'd look after him. It didn't make no sense to recommit the man. He stuck out his big greasy palm and told me to give him fifty dollars and take him on home.

ROSE. Where's he at now? Where'd he go off to?

TROY. He's gone on about his business. He don't need nobody to hold his hand.

ROSE. Well, I don't know. Seem like that would be the best place for him if they did put him into the hospital. I know what you're gonna say. But that's what I think would be best.

TROY. The man done had his life ruined fighting for what? And they wanna take and lock him up. Let him be free. He don't bother nobody.

ROSE. Well, everybody got their own way of looking at it I guess. Come on and get your lunch. I got a bowl of lima beans and some cornbread in the oven. Come on get something to eat. Ain't no sense you fretting over Gabe.

(ROSE *turns to go into the house.*)

TROY. Rose . . . got something to tell you.

ROSE. Well, come on . . . wait till I get this food on the table.

TROY. Rose!

(*She stops and turns around.*)

I don't know how to say this.

(*Pause.*)

I can't explain it none. It just sort of grows on you till it gets out of hand. It starts out like a little bush . . . and the next thing you know it's a whole forest.

ROSE. Troy . . . what is you talking about?

TROY. I'm talking, woman, let me talk. I'm trying to find a way to tell you . . . I'm gonna be a daddy. I'm gonna be somebody's daddy.

ROSE. Troy . . . you're not telling me this? You're gonna be . . . what?

TROY. Rose . . . now . . . see. . . .

ROSE. You telling me you gonna be somebody's daddy? You telling your *wife* this?

(GABRIEL *enters from the street. He carries a rose in his hand.*)

GABRIEL. Hey, Troy! Hey, Rose!

ROSE. I have to wait eighteen years to hear something like this.

GABRIEL. Hey, Rose . . . I got a flower for you.

(*He hands it to her.*)

That's a rose. Same rose like you is.

ROSE. Thanks, Gabe.

GABRIEL. Troy, you ain't mad at me is you? Them bad mens come and put me away. You ain't mad at me is you?

TROY. Naw, Gabe, I ain't mad at you.

ROSE. Eighteen years and you wanna come with this.

GABRIEL. (*Takes a quarter out of his pocket.*) See what I got? Got a brand new quarter.

TROY. Rose . . . it's just . . .

ROSE. Ain't nothing you can say, Troy. Ain't no way of explaining that.

GABRIEL. Fellow that give me this quarter had a whole mess of them. I'm gonna keep this quarter till it stop shining.

ROSE. Gabe, go on in the house there. I got some watermelon in the frigidaire. Go on and get you a piece.

GABRIEL. Say, Rose . . . you know I was chasing hellhounds and them bad mens come and get me and take me away. Troy helped me. He come down there and told them they better let me go before he beat them up. Yeah, he did!

ROSE. You go on and get you a piece of watermelon, Gabe. Them bad mens is gone now.

GABRIEL. Okay, Rose . . . gonna get me some watermelon. The kind with the stripes on it.

(GABRIEL *exits into the house.*)

ROSE. Why, Troy? Why? After all these years to come dragging this in to me now. It don't make no sense at your age. I could have expected this ten or fifteen years ago, but not now.

TROY. Age ain't got nothing to do with it, Rose.

ROSE. I done tried to be everything a wife should be. Everything a wife could be. Been married eighteen years and I got to live to see the day you tell me you been seeing another woman and done fathered a child by her. And you know I ain't never wanted no half nothing in my family. My whole family is half. Everybody got different fathers and mothers . . . my two sisters and my brother. Can't hardly tell who's who. Can't never sit down and talk about Papa and Mama. It's your papa and your mama and my papa and my mama. . .

TROY. Rose . . . stop it now.

ROSE. I ain't never wanted that for none of my children. And now you wanna drag your behind in here and tell me something like this.

TROY. You ought to know. It's time for you to know.

ROSE. Well, I don't want to know, goddamn it!

TROY. I can't just make it go away. It's done now. I can't wish the circumstance of the thing away.

ROSE. And you don't want to either. Maybe you want to wish me and my boy away. Maybe that's what you want? Well, you can't wish us away. I've got eighteen years of my life invested in you. You ought to have stayed upstairs in my bed where you belong.

TROY. Rose . . . now listen to me . . . we can get a handle on this thing. We can talk this out . . . come to an understanding.

ROSE. All of a sudden it's "we." Where was "we" at when you was down there rolling around with some god-forsaken woman? "We" should have come to an understanding before you started making a damn fool of yourself. You're a day late and a dollar short when it comes to an understanding with me.

TROY. It's just . . . She gives me a different idea . . . a different understanding about myself. I can step out of this house and get away from the pressures and problems . . . be a different man. I ain't got to wonder how I'm gonna pay the bills or get the roof fixed. I can just be a part of myself that I ain't never been.

ROSE. What I want to know . . . is do you plan to continue seeing her. That's all you can say to me.

TROY. I can sit up in her house and laugh. Do you understand what I'm saying. I can laugh out loud . . . and it feels good. It reaches all the way down to the bottom of my shoes.

(*Pause.*)

Rose, I can't give that up.

ROSE. Maybe you ought to go on and stay down there with her . . . if she a better woman than me.

TROY. It ain't about nobody being a better woman or nothing. Rose, you ain't the blame. A man couldn't ask for no woman to be a better wife than you've been. I'm responsible for it. I done locked myself into a pattern trying to take care of you all that I forgot about myself.

ROSE. What the hell was I there for? That was my job, not somebody else's.

TROY. Rose, I done tried all my life to live decent . . . to live a clean . . . hard . . . useful life. I tried to be a good husband to you. In every way I

knew how. Maybe I come into the world backwards. I don't know. But . . . you born with two strikes on you before you come to the plate. You got to guard it closely . . . always looking for the curve-ball on the inside corner. You can't afford to let none get past you. You can't afford a call strike. If you going down . . . you going down swinging. Everything lined up against you. What you gonna do. I fooled them, Rose. I bunted. When I found you and Cory and a halfway decent job . . . I was safe. Couldn't nothing touch me. I wasn't gonna strike out no more. I wasn't going back to the penitentiary. I wasn't gonna lay in the streets with a bottle of wine. I was safe. I had me a family. A job. I wasn't gonna get that last strike. I was on first looking for one of them boys to knock me in. To get me home.

ROSE. You should have stayed in my bed, Troy.

TROY. Then when I saw that gal . . . she firmed up my backbone. And I got to thinking that if I tried . . . I just might be able to steal second. Do you understand after eighteen years I wanted to steal second.

ROSE. You should have held me tight. You should have grabbed me and held on.

TROY. I stood on first base for eighteen years and I thought . . . well, goddamn it . . . go on for it!

ROSE. We're not talking about baseball! We're talking about you going off to lay in bed with another woman . . . and then bring it home to me. That's what we're talking about. We ain't talking about no baseball.

TROY. Rose, you're not listening to me. I'm trying the best I can to explain it to you. It's not easy for me to admit that I been standing in the same place for eighteen years.

ROSE. I been standing with you! I been right here with you, Troy. I got a life too. I gave eighteen years of my life to stand in the same spot with you. Don't you think I ever wanted other things? Don't you think I had dreams and hopes? What about my life? What about me. Don't you think it ever crossed my mind to want to know other men? That I wanted to lay up somewhere and forget about my responsibilities? That I wanted someone to make me laugh so I could feel good? You not the only one who's got wants and needs. But I held on to you, Troy. I took all my feelings, my wants and needs, my dreams . . . and I buried them inside you. I planted a seed and watched and prayed over it. I planted myself inside you and waited to bloom.

And it didn't take me no eighteen years to find out the soil was hard and rocky and it wasn't never gonna bloom.

But I held on to you, Troy. I held you tighter. You was my husband. I owed you everything I had. Every part of me I could find to give you. And upstairs in that room . . . with the darkness falling in on me . . . I gave everything I had to try and erase the doubt that you wasn't the finest man in the world. And wherever you was going . . . I wanted to be there with you. Cause you was my husband. Cause that's the only way I was gonna survive as your wife. You always talking about what you give . . . and what you don't have to give. But you take too. You take . . . and don't even know nobody's giving!

(ROSE *turns to exit into the house;* TROY *grabs her arm.*)

TROY. You say I take and don't give!

ROSE. Troy! You're hurting me!

TROY. You say I take and don't give.

ROSE. Troy . . . you're hurting my arm! Let go!

TROY. I done give you everything I got. Don't you tell that lie on me.

ROSE. Troy!

TROY. Don't you tell that lie on me!

(CORY *enters from the house.*)

CORY. Mama!

ROSE. Troy. You're hurting me.

TROY. Don't you tell me about no taking and giving.

(CORY *comes up behind* TROY *and grabs him.* TROY, *surprised, is thrown off balance just as* CORY *throws a glancing blow that catches him on the chest and knocks him down.* TROY *is stunned, as is* CORY.)

ROSE. Troy. Troy. No!

(TROY *gets to his feet and starts at* CORY.)

Troy . . . no. Please! Troy!

(ROSE *pulls on* TROY *to hold him back.* TROY *stops himself.*)

TROY. (*To* CORY.). Alright. That's strike two. You stay away from around me, boy. Don't you strike out. You living with a full count. Don't you strike out.

(TROY *exits out the yard as the lights go down.*)

ACT TWO
SCENE TWO

It is six months later, early afternoon. TROY *enters from the house and starts to exit the yard.* ROSE *enters from the house.*

ROSE. Troy, I want to talk to you.

TROY. All of a sudden, after all this time, you want to talk to me, huh? You ain't wanted to talk to me for months. You ain't wanted to talk to me last night. You ain't wanted no part of me then. What you wanna talk to me about now?

ROSE. Tomorrow's Friday.

TROY. I know what day tomorrow is. You think I don't know tomorrow's Friday? My whole life I ain't done nothing but look to see Friday coming and you got to tell me it's Friday.

ROSE. I want to know if you're coming home.

TROY. I always come home, Rose. You know that. There ain't never been a night I ain't come home.

ROSE. That ain't what I mean . . . and you know it. I want to know if you're coming straight home after work.

TROY. I figure I'd cash my check . . . hang out at Taylors' with the boys . . . maybe play a game of checkers . . .

ROSE. Troy I can't live like this. I won't live like this. You livin' on borrowed time with me. It's been going on six months now you ain't been coming home.

TROY. I be here every night. Every night of the year. That's 365 days.

ROSE. I want you to come home tomorrow after work.

TROY. Rose . . . I don't mess up my pay. You know that now. I take my pay and I give it to you. I don't have no money but what you give me back. I just want to have a little time to myself . . . a little time to enjoy life.

ROSE. What about me? When's my time to enjoy life?

TROY. I don't know what to tell you, Rose. I'm doing the best I can.

ROSE. You ain't been home from work but time enough to change your clothes and run out . . . and you wanna call that the best you can do?

TROY. I'm going over to the hospital to see Alberta. She went into the hospital this afternoon. Look like she might have the baby early. I won't be gone long.

ROSE. Well, you ought to know. They went over to Miss Pearl's and got Gabe today. She said you told them to go ahead and lock him up.

TROY. I ain't said no such thing. Whoever told you that is telling a lie. Pearl ain't doing nothing but telling a big fat lie.

ROSE. She ain't had to tell me. I read it on the papers.

TROY. I ain't told you nothing of the kind.

ROSE. I saw it right there on the papers.

TROY. What it say, huh?

ROSE. It said you told them to take him.

TROY. Then they screwed that up, just the way they screw up everything. I ain't worried about what they got on the paper.

ROSE. Say the government send part of his check to the hospital and the other part to you.

TROY. I ain't got nothing to do with that if that's the way it works. I ain't made up the rules about how it work.

ROSE. You did Gabe just like you did Cory. You wouldn't sign the paper for Cory . . . but you signed for Gabe. You signed that paper.

(*The telephone is heard ringing inside the house.*)

TROY. I told you I ain't signed nothing, woman! The only thing I signed was the release form. Hell, I can't read. I don't know what they had on that paper! I ain't signed nothing about sending Gabe away.

ROSE. I said send him to the hospital . . . you said let him be free . . . now you done went down there and signed him to the hospital for half his money. You went back on yourself, Troy. You gonna have to answer for that.

TROY. See now . . . you been over there talking to Miss Pearl. She done got mad cause she ain't getting Gabe's rent money. That's all it is. She's liable to say anything.

ROSE. Troy, I seen where you signed the paper.

TROY. You ain't seen nothing I signed. What she doing got papers on my brother anyway? Miss Pearl telling a big fat lie. And I'm gonna tell her about it too! You ain't seen nothing I signed. Say . . . you ain't seen nothing I signed.

(ROSE *exits into the house to answer the telephone. Presently she returns.*)

ROSE. Troy . . . that was the hospital. Alberta had the baby.

TROY. What she have? What is it?

ROSE. It's a girl.

TROY. I better get on down to the hospital to see her.

ROSE. Troy . . .

TROY. Rose . . . I got to go see her now. That's only right . . . what's the matter . . . the baby's alright, ain't it?

ROSE. Alberta died having the baby.

TROY. Died . . . you say she's dead? Alberta's dead?

ROSE. They said they done all they could. They couldn't do nothing for her.

TROY. The baby? How's the baby?

ROSE. They say it's healthy. I wonder who's gonna bury her.

TROY. She had family, Rose. She wasn't living in the world by herself.

ROSE. I know she wasn't living in the world by herself.

TROY. Next thing you gonna want to know if she had any insurance.

ROSE. Troy, you ain't got to talk like that.

TROY. That's the first thing that jumped out your mouth.
"Who's gonna bury her?" Like I'm fixing to take on that task for myself.

ROSE. I am your wife. Don't push me away.

TROY. I ain't pushing nobody away. Just give me some space. That's all. Just give me some room to breathe.

(ROSE *exits into the house,* TROY *walks about the yard.*)

TROY. (*With a quiet rage that threatens to consume him.*) Alright . . . Mr. Death. See now . . . I'm gonna tell you what I'm gonna do. I'm gonna take and build me a fence around this yard. See? I'm gonna build me a fence around what belongs to me. And then I want you to stay on the other side. See? You stay over there until you're ready for me. Then you come on. Bring your army. Bring

554

your sickle. Bring your wrestling clothes. I ain't gonna fall down on my vigilance this time. You ain't gonna sneak up on me no more. When you ready for me . . . when the top of your list say Troy Maxson . . . that's when you come around here. You come up and knock on the front door. Ain't nobody else got nothing to do with this. This is between you and me. Man to man. You stay on the other side of that fence until you ready for me. Then you come up and knock on the front door. Anytime you want. I'll be ready for you.

(*The lights go down to black.*)

ACT TWO
SCENE THREE

The lights come up on the porch. It is late evening three days later. ROSE sits listening to the ball-game waiting for TROY. The final out of the game is made and ROSE switches off the radio. TROY enters the yard carrying an infant wrapped in blankets. He stands back from the house and calls.

(ROSE *enters and stands on the porch. There is a long, awkward silence, the weight of which grows heavier with each passing second.*)

TROY. Rose . . . I'm standing here with my daughter in my arms. She ain't but a wee bittie little old thing. She don't know nothing about grownups' business. She innocent . . . and she ain't got no mama.

ROSE. What you telling me for, Troy?

(*She turns and exits into the house.*)

TROY. Well . . . I guess we'll just sit out here on the porch.

(*He sits down on the porch. There is an awkward indelicateness about the way he handles the baby. His largeness engulfs and seems to swallow it. He speaks loud enough for ROSE to hear.*)

A man's got to do what's right for him. I ain't sorry for nothing I done. It felt right in my heart.

(*To the baby.*)

What you smiling at? Your daddy's a big man. Got these great big old hands. But sometimes he's scared. And right now your daddy's scared cause we sitting out here and ain't got no home. Oh, I been homeless before. I ain't had no little baby with me. But I been homeless. You just be out on the road by your lonesome and you see one of them trains coming and you just kinda go like this.

(*He sings as a lullaby.*)

Please, Mr. Engineer let a man ride the line
Please, Mr. Engineer let a man ride the line
I ain't got no ticket please let me ride the blinds

(ROSE *enters from the house.* TROY *hearing her steps behind him, stands and faces her.*)

She's my daughter, Rose. My own flesh and blood. I can't deny her no more than I can deny them boys.

(*Pause.*)

You and them boys is my family. You and them and this child is all I got in the world. So I guess what I'm saying is . . . I'd appreciate it if you'd help me take care of her.

ROSE. Okay, Troy . . . you're right. I'll take care of your baby for you . . . cause . . . like you say . . . she's innocent . . . and you can't visit the sins of the father upon the child. A motherless child has got a hard time.

(*She takes the baby from him.*)

From right now . . . this child got a mother. But you a womanless man.

(ROSE *turns and exits into the house with the baby. Lights go down to black.*)

ACT TWO
SCENE FOUR

It is two months later. LYONS *enters from the street. He knocks on the door and calls.*

LYONS. Hey, Rose! (*Pause.*) Rose!

ROSE. (*From inside the house.*) Stop that yelling. You gonna wake up Raynell. I just got her to sleep.

LYONS. I just stopped by to pay Papa this twenty dollars I owe him. Where's Papa at?

ROSE. He should be here in a minute. I'm getting ready to go down to the church. Sit down and wait for him.

LYONS. I got to go pick up Bonnie over her mother's house.

ROSE. Well, sit it down there on the table. He'll get it.

LYONS. (*Enters the house and sets the money on the table.*) Tell Papa I said thanks. I'll see you again.

ROSE. Alright, Lyons. We'll see you.

(LYONS *starts to exit as* CORY *enters*)

CORY. Hey, Lyons.

LYONS. What's happening, Cory. Say man, I'm sorry I missed your graduation. You know I had a gig and couldn't get away. Otherwise, I would have been there, man. So what you doing?

CORY. I'm trying to find a job.

LYONS. Yeah I know how that go, man. It's rough out here. Jobs are scarce.

CORY. Yeah, I know.

LYONS. Look here, I got to run. Talk to Papa . . . he know some people. He'll be able to help get you a job. Talk to him . . . see what he say.

CORY. Yeah . . . alright, Lyons.

LYONS. You take care. I'll talk to you soon. We'll find some time to talk.

(LYONS *exits the yard.* CORY *wanders over to the tree, picks up the bat and assumes a batting stance. He studies an imaginary pitcher and swings. Dissatisfied with the result, he tries again.* TROY *enters. They eye each other for a beat.* CORY *puts the bat down and exits the yard.* TROY *starts into the house as* ROSE *exits with* RAYNELL. *She is carrying a cake.*)

TROY. I'm coming in and everybody's going out.

ROSE. I'm taking this cake down to the church for the bakesale. Lyons was by to see you. He stopped by to pay you your twenty dollars. It's laying in there on the table.

TROY. (*Going into his pocket.*) Well . . . here go this money.

ROSE. Put it in there on the table, Troy. I'll get it.

TROY. What time you coming back?

ROSE. Ain't no use in you studying me. It don't matter what time I come back.

TROY. I just asked you a question, woman. What's the matter . . . can't I ask you a question?

ROSE. Troy, I don't want to go into it. Your dinner's in there on the stove. All you got to do is heat it up. And don't you be eating the rest of them cakes in there. I'm coming back for them. We having a bakesale at the church tomorrow.

(ROSE *exits the yard.* TROY *sits down on the steps, takes a pint bottle from his pocket, opens it and drinks. He begins to sing.*)

TROY.
    Hear it ring! Hear it ring!
    Had an old dog his name was Blue
    You know Blue was mighty true
    You know Blue as a good old dog
    Blue trees a possum in a hollow log
    You know from that he was a good old dog

(BONO *enters the yard.*)

BONO. Hey, Troy.

TROY. Hey, what's happening, Bono?

BONO. I just thought I'd stop by to see you.

TROY. What you stop by and see me for? You ain't stopped by in a month of Sundays. Hell, I must owe you money or something.

BONO. Since you got your promotion I can't keep up with you. Used to see you everyday. Now I don't even know what route you working.

TROY. They keep switching me around. Got me out in Greentree now . . . hauling white folks' garbage.

BONO. Greentree, huh? You lucky, at least you ain't got to be lifting them barrels. Damn if they ain't getting heavier. I'm gonna put in my two years and call it quits.

TROY. I'm thinking about retiring myself.

BONO. You got it easy. You can *drive* for another five years.

TROY. It ain't the same, Bono. It ain't like working the back of the truck. Ain't got nobody to talk to . . . feel like you working by yourself. Naw, I'm thinking about retiring. How's Lucille?

BONO. She alright. Her arthritis get to acting up on her sometime. Saw Rose on my way in. She going down to the church, huh?

TROY. Yeah, she took up going down there. All them preachers looking for somebody to fatten their pockets.

(*Pause.*)

Got some gin here.

BONO. Naw, thanks. I just stopped by to say hello.

TROY. Hell, nigger . . . you can take a drink. I ain't never known you to say no to a drink. You ain't got to work tomorrow.

BONO. I just stopped by. I'm fixing to go over to Skinner's. We got us a domino game going over his house every Friday.

TROY. Nigger, you can't play no dominoes. I used to whup you four games out of five.

BONO. Well, that learned me. I'm getting better.

TROY. Yeah? Well, that's alright.

BONO. Look here . . . I got to be getting on. Stop by sometime, huh?

TROY. Yeah, I'll do that, Bono. Lucille told Rose you bought her a new refrigerator.

BONO. Yeah, Rose told Lucille you had finally built your fence . . . so I figured we'd call it even.

TROY. I knew you would.

BONO. Yeah . . . okay. I'll be talking to you.

TROY. Yeah, take care, Bono. Good to see you. I'm gonna stop over.

BONO. Yeah. Okay, Troy.

(BONO *exits.* TROY *drinks from the bottle.*)

TROY.
Old Blue died and I dig his grave
Let him down with a golden chain
Every night when I hear old Blue bark
I know Blue treed a possum in Noah's Ark.
Hear it ring! Hear it ring!

(CORY *enters the yard. They eye each other for a beat.* TROY *is sitting in the middle of the steps.* CORY *walks over.*)

CORY. I got to get by.

TROY. Say what? What's you say?

CORY. You in my way. I got to get by.

TROY. You got to get by where? This is my house. Bought and paid for. In full. Took me fifteen years. And if you wanna go in my house and I'm sitting on the steps . . . you say excuse me. Like your mamma taught you.

CORY. Come on, Pop . . . I got to get by.

(CORY *starts to maneuver his way past* TROY. TROY *grabs his leg and shoves him back.*)

TROY. You just gonna walk over top of me?

CORY. I live here too!

TROY. (*Advancing toward him.*) You just gonna walk over top of me in my own house?

CORY. I ain't scared of you.

TROY. I ain't asked if you was scared of me. I asked you if you was fixing to walk over top of me in my own house? That's the question. You ain't gonna say excuse me? You just gonna walk over top of me?

CORY. If you wanna put it like that.

TROY. How else am I gonna put it?

CORY. I was walking by you to go into the house cause you sitting on the steps drunk, singing to yourself. You can put it like that.

TROY. Without saying excuse me???

(CORY *doesn't respond.*)

I asked you a question. Without saying excuse me???

CORY. I ain't got to say excuse me to you. You don't count around here no more.

TROY. Oh, I see . . . I don't count around here no more. You ain't got to say excuse me to your daddy. All of a sudden you done got so grown that your daddy don't count around here no more . . . Around here in his own house and yard that he done paid for with the sweat of his brow. You done got so grown to where you gonna take over. You gonna take over my house. Is that right? You gonna wear my pants. You gonna go in there and stretch out on my bed. You ain't got to say excuse me cause I don't count around here no more. Is that right?

CORY. That's right. You always talking this dumb stuff. Now, why don't you just get out of my way.

TROY. I guess you got someplace to sleep and something to put in your belly. You got that, huh? You got that? That's what you need. You got that, huh?

CORY. You don't know what I got. You ain't got to worry about what I got.

TROY. You right! You one hundred percent right! I done spent the last seventeen years worrying about what you got. Now it's your turn, see? I'll tell you what to do. You grown . . . we done established that. You a man. Now, let's see you act like one. Turn your behind around and walk out this yard. And when you get out there in the alley . . . you can forget about this house. See? Cause this is my house. You go on and be a man and get your own house. You can forget about this. 'Cause this is mine. You go on and get yours cause I'm through with doing for you.

CORY. You talking about what you did for me . . . what'd you ever give me?

TROY. Them feet and bones! That pumping heart, nigger! I give you more than anybody else is ever gonna give you.

CORY. You ain't never gave me nothing! You ain't never done nothing but hold me back. Afraid I was gonna be better than you. All you ever did was try and make me scared of you. I used to tremble every time you called my name. Every time I heard your footsteps in the house. Wondering all the time . . . what's Papa gonna say if I do this? . . . What's he gonna say if I do that? . . . What's Papa gonna say if I turn on the radio? And Mama, too . . . she tries . . . but she's scared of you.

TROY. You leave your mama out of this. She ain't got nothing to do with this.

CORY. I don't know how she stand you . . . after what you did to her.

TROY. I told you to leave your mama out of this!

(*He advances toward* CORY.)

CORY. What you gonna do . . . give me a whupping? You can't whup me no more. You're too old. You just an old man.

TROY. (*Shoves him on his shoulder.*) Nigger! That's what you are. You just another nigger on the street to me!

CORY. You crazy! You know that?

TROY. Go on now! You got the devil in you. Get on away from me!

CORY. You just a crazy old man . . . talking about I got the devil in me.

TROY. Yeah, I'm crazy! If you don't get on the other side of that yard . . . I'm gonna show you how crazy I am! Go on . . . get the hell out of my yard.

CORY. It ain't your yard. You took Uncle Gabe's money he got from the army to buy this house and then you put him out.

TROY. (TROY *advances on* CORY.) Get your black ass out of my yard!

(TROY'*s advance backs* CORY *up against the tree.* CORY *grabs up the bat.*)

CORY. I ain't going nowhere! Come on . . . put me out! I ain't scared of you.

TROY. That's my bat!

CORY. Come on!

TROY. Put my bat down!

CORY. Come on, put me out.

(CORY *swings at* TROY, *who backs across the yard.*)

What's the matter? You so bad . . . put me out!

(TROY *advances toward* CORY.)

CORY. (*Backing up.*) Come on! Come on!

TROY: You're gonna have to use it! You wanna draw that bat back on me . . . you're gonna have to use it.

CORY. Come on! . . . Come on!

(CORY *swings the bat at* TROY a second time. He misses. TROY *continues to advance toward him.*)

TROY. You're gonna have to kill me! You wanna draw that bat back on me. You're gonna have to kill me.

(CORY, *backed up against the tree, can go no farther.* TROY *taunts him. He sticks out his head and offers him a target.*)

Come on! Come on!

(CORY *is unable to swing the bat.* TROY *grabs it.*)

TROY. Then I'll show you.

(CORY *and* TROY *struggle over the bat. The struggle is fierce and fully engaged.* TROY *ultimately is the stronger, and takes the bat from* CORY *and stands over him ready to swing. He stops himself.*)

Go on and get away from around my house.

(CORY, *stung by his defeat, picks himself up, walks slowly out of the yard and up the alley.*)

CORY. Tell Mama I'll be back for my things.

TROY. They'll be on the other side of that fence.

(CORY *exits.*)

TROY. I can't taste nothing. Helluljah! I can't taste nothing no more. (TROY *assumes a batting posture and begins to taunt Death, the fastball in the outside corner.*) Come on! It's between you and me now! Come on! Anytime you want! Come on! I be ready for you . . . but I ain't gonna be easy.

(*The lights go down on the scene.*)

ACT TWO
SCENE FIVE

The time is 1965. The lights come up in the yard. It is the morning of TROY's *funeral. A funeral plaque with a light hangs beside the door. There is a small garden plot off to the side. There is noise and activity in the house as* ROSE, GABRIEL *and* BONO *have gathered. The door opens and* RAYNELL, *seven years old, enters dressed in a flannel nightgown. She crosses to the garden and pokes around with a stick.* ROSE *calls from the house.*

ROSE. Raynell!

RAYNELL. Mam?

ROSE. What you doing out there?

RAYNELL. Nothing.

(ROSE *comes to the door.*)

ROSE. Girl, get in here and get dressed. What you doing?

RAYNELL. Seeing if my garden growed.

ROSE. I told you it ain't gonna grow overnight. You got to wait.

RAYNELL. It don't look like it never gonna grow. Dag!

ROSE. I told you a watched pot never boils. Get in here and get dressed.

RAYNELL. This ain't even no pot, Mama.

ROSE. You just have to give it a chance. It'll grow. Now you come on and do what I told you. We got to be getting ready. This ain't no morning to be playing around. You hear me?

RAYNELL. Yes, mam.

(ROSE *exits into the house.* RAYNELL *continues to poke at her garden with a stick.* CORY *enters. He is dressed in a Marine corporal's uniform, and carries a duffel bag. His posture is that of a military man, and his speech has a clipped sternness.*)

CORY. (*To* RAYNELL.) Hi.

(*Pause.*)

I bet your name is Raynell.

RAYNELL. Uh huh.

CORY. Is your mama home?

(RAYNELL *runs up on the porch and calls through the screendoor.*)

RAYNELL. Mama . . . there's some man out here. Mama?

(ROSE *comes to the door.*)

ROSE. Cory? Lord have mercy! Look here, you all!

(ROSE *and* CORY *embrace in a tearful reunion as* BONO *and* LYONS *enter from the house dressed in funeral clothes.*)

BONO. Aw, looka here . . .

ROSE. Done got all grown up!

CORY. Don't cry, Mama. What you crying about?

ROSE. I'm just so glad you made it.

CORY. Hey Lyons. How you doing, Mr. Bono.

(LYONS *goes to embrace* CORY.)

LYONS. Look at you, man. Look at you. Don't he look good, Rose. Got them Corporal stripes.

ROSE. What took you so long?

CORY. You know how the Marines are, Mama. They got to get all their paperwork straight before they let you do anything.

ROSE. Well, I'm sure glad you made it. They let Lyons come. Your Uncle Gabe's still in the hospital. They don't know if they gonna let him out or not. I just talked to them a little while ago.

LYONS. A Corporal in the United States Marines.

BONO. Your daddy knew you had it in you. He used to tell me all the time.

LYONS. Don't he look good, Mr. Bono?

BONO. Yeah, he reminded me of Troy when I first met him.

(*Pause.*)

Say, Rose, Lucille's down at the church with the choir. I'm gonna go down and get the pallbearers lined up. I'll be back to get you all.

ROSE. Thanks, Jim.

CORY. See you, Mr. Bono.

LYONS. (*With his arm around* RAYNELL.) Cory . . . look at Raynell. Ain't she precious? She gonna break a whole lot of hearts.

ROSE. Raynell, come and say hello to your brother. This is your brother, Cory. You remember Cory.

RAYNELL. No, Mam.

CORY. She don't remember me, Mama.

ROSE. Well, we talk about you. She heard us talk about you.
(*To* RAYNELL. This is your brother, Cory. Come on and say hello.

RAYNELL. Hi.

CORY. Hi. So you're Raynell. Mama told me a lot about you.

ROSE. You all come on into the house and let me fix you some breakfast. Keep up your strength.

CORY. I ain't hungry, Mama.

LYONS. You can fix me something, Rose. I'll be in there in a minute.

ROSE. Cory, you sure you don't want nothing. I know they ain't feeding you right.

CORY. No, Mama . . . thanks. I don't feel like eating. I'll get something later.

ROSE. Raynell . . . get on upstairs and get that dress on like I told you.

(ROSE *and* RAYNELL *exit into the house.*)

LYONS. So . . . I hear you thinking about getting married.

CORY. Yeah, I done found the right one, Lyons. It's about time.

LYONS. Me and Bonnie been split up about four years now. About the time Papa retired. I guess she just got tired of all them changes I was putting her through.

(*Pause.*)

I always knew you was gonna make something out yourself. Your head was always in the right direction. So . . . you gonna stay in . . . make it a career . . . put in your twenty years?

CORY. I don't know. I got six already, I think that's enough.

LYONS. Stick with Uncle Sam and retire early. Ain't nothing out here. I guess Rose told you what happened with me. They got me down the workhouse. I thought I was being slick cashing other people's checks.

CORY. How much time you doing?

LYONS. They give me three years. I got that beat now. I ain't got but nine more months. It ain't so bad. You learn to deal with it like anything else. You got to take the crookeds with the straights.

That's what Papa used to say. He used to say that when he struck out. I seen him strike out three times in a row . . . and the next time up he hit the ball over the grandstand. Right out there in Homestead Field. He wasn't satisfied hitting in the seats . . . he want to hit it over everything! After the game he had two hundred people standing around waiting to shake his hand. You got to take the crookeds with the straights. Yeah, Papa was something else.

CORY. You still playing?

LYONS. Cory . . . you know I'm gonna do that. There's some fellows down there we got us a band . . . we gonna try and stay together when we get out . . . but yeah, I'm still playing. It still helps me to get out of bed in the morning. As long as I do that I'm gonna be right there playing and trying to make some sense out of it.

ROSE. (*Calling.*) Lyons, I got these eggs in the pan.

LYONS. Let me go on and get these eggs, man. Get ready to go bury Papa.

(*Pause.*)

How you doing? You doing alright?

(CORY *nods.* LYONS *touches him on the shoulder and they share a moment of silent grief.* LYONS *exits into the house.* CORY *wanders about the yard.* RAYNELL *enters.*)

RAYNELL. Hi.

CORY. Hi.

RAYNELL. Did you used to sleep in my room?

CORY. Yeah . . . that used to be my room.

RAYNELL. That's what Papa call it. "Cory's room." It got your football in the closet.

(ROSE *comes to the door.*)

ROSE. Raynell, get in there and get them good shoes on.

RAYNELL. Mama, can't I wear these. Them other one hurt my feet.

ROSE. Well, they just gonna have to hurt your feet for a while. You ain't said they hurt your feet when you went down to the store and got them.

RAYNELL. They didn't hurt then. My feet done got bigger.

ROSE. Don't you give me no backtalk now. You get in there and get them shoes on.

(RAYNELL *exits into the house.*)

Ain't too much changed. He still got that piece of rag tied to that tree. He was out here swinging that bat. I was just ready to go back in the house. He swung that bat and and then he just fell over. Seem like he swung it and stood there with this grin on his face . . . and then he just fell over. They carried him on down to the hospital, but I knew there wasn't no need . . . why don't you come on in the house?

CORY. Mama . . . I got something to tell you. I don't know how to tell you this . . . but I've got to tell you . . . I'm not going to Papa's funeral.

ROSE. Boy, hush your mouth. That's your daddy you talking about. I don't want hear that kind of talk this morning. I done raised you to come to this? You standing there all healthy and grown talking about you ain't going to your daddy's funeral?

CORY. Mama . . . listen . . .

ROSE. I don't want to hear it, Cory. You just get that thought out of your head.

CORY. I can't drag Papa with me everywhere I go. I've got to say no to him. One time in my life I've got to say no.

ROSE. Don't nobody have to listen to nothing like that. I know you and your daddy ain't seen eye to eye, but I ain't got to listen to that kind of talk this morning. Whatever was between you and your daddy . . . the time has come to put it aside. Just take it and set it over there on the shelf and forget about it. Disrespecting your daddy ain't gonna make you a man, Cory. You got to find a way to come to that on your own. Not going to your daddy's funeral ain't gonna make you a man.

CORY. The whole time I was growing up . . . living in his house . . . Papa was like a shadow that followed you everywhere. It weighed on you and sunk into your flesh. It would wrap around you and lay there until you couldn't tell which one was you anymore. That shadow digging in your flesh. Trying to crawl in. Trying to live through you. Everywhere I looked, Troy Maxson was staring back at me . . . hiding under the bed . . . in the closet. I'm just saying I've got to find a way to get rid of that shadow, Mama.

ROSE. You just like him. You got him in you good.

CORY. Don't tell me that, Mama.

ROSE. You Troy Maxson all over again.

CORY. I don't want to be Troy Maxson. I want to be me.

ROSE. You can't be nobody but who you are, Cory. That shadow wasn't nothing but you growing into yourself. You either got to grow into it or cut it down to fit you. But that's all you got to make life with. That's all you got to measure yourself against that world out there. Your daddy wanted you to be everything he wasn't . . . and at the same time he tried to make you into everything he was. I don't know if he was right or wrong . . . but I do know he meant to do more good than he meant to do harm. He wasn't always right. Sometime when he touched he bruised. And sometimes when he took me in his arms he cut.

When I first met your daddy I thought . . . Here is a man I can lay down with and make a baby. That's the first thing I thought when I seen him. I was thirty years old and had done seen my share of men. But when he walked up to me and said, "I can dance a waltz that'll make you dizzy," I thought, Rose Lee, here is a man that you can open yourself up to and be filled to bursting. Here is a man that can fill all of them empty spaces you been tipping around the edges of. One of them empty spaces was being somebody's mother.

I married your daddy and settled down to cooking his supper and keeping clean sheets on the bed. When your daddy walked through the house he was so big he filled it up. That was my first mistake. Not to make him leave some room for me. For my part in the matter. But at that time I wanted that. I wanted a house that I could sing in. And that's what your daddy gave me. I didn't know to keep up his strength I had to give up little pieces of mine. I did that. I took on his life as mine and mixed up the pieces so that you couldn't hardly tell which was which anymore. It was my choice. It was my life and I didn't have to live it like that. But that's what life offered me in the way of being a woman and I took it. I grabbed hold of it with both hands.

By the time Raynell came into the house, me and your daddy had done lost touch with one another. I didn't want to make my blessing off of nobody's misfortune . . . but I took on to Raynell like she was all them babies I had wanted and never had.

(*The phone rings.*)

Like I'd been blessed to relive a part of my life. And if the Lord see fit to keep up my strength . . . I'm gonna do her just like your daddy did you . . . I'm gonna give her the best of what's in me.

RAYNELL. (*Entering, still with her old shoes.*) Mama . . . Reverend Tollivier on the phone.

(ROSE *exits into the house.*)

RAYNELL. Hi.

CORY. Hi.

RAYNELL. You in the Army or the Marines?

CORY. Marines.

RAYNELL. Papa said it was the Army. Did you know Blue?

CORY. Blue? Who's Blue?

RAYNELL. Papa's dog what he sing about all the time.

CORY. (*Singing.*) Hear it ring! Hear it ring!
    I had a dog his name was Blue
    You know Blue was mighty true
    You know Blue was a good old dog
    Blue treed a possum in a hollow log
    You know from that he was a good old dog.
    Hear it ring! Hear it ring!

(RAYNELL *joins in singing.*)

CORY and RAYNELL. Blue treed a possum out on a limb
    Blue looked at me and I looked at him
    Grabbed that possum and put him in a sack
    Blue stayed there till I came back
    Old Blue's feets was big and round
    Never allowed a possum to touch the ground.

    Old Blue died and I dug his grave
    I dug his grave with a silver spade
    Let him down with a golden chain
    And every night I call his name
    Go on Blue, you good dog you
    Go on Blue, you good dog you

RAYNELL. Blue laid down and died like a man
    Blue laid down and died . . .

BOTH. Blue laid down and died like a man
    Now he's treeing possums in the Promised Land
    I'm gonna tell you this to let you know
    Blue's gone where the good dogs go
    When I hear old Blue bark
    When I hear old Blue bark
    Blue treed a possum in Noah's Ark
    Blue treed a possum in Noah's Ark.

(ROSE *comes to the screen door.*)

ROSE. Cory, we gonna be ready to go in a minute.

CORY. (*To* RAYNELL.) You go on in the house and change them shoes like Mama told you so we can go to Papa's funeral.

RAYNELL. Okay, I'll be back.

(RAYNELL *exits into the house.* CORY *gets up and crosses over to the tree.* ROSE *stands in the screen door watching him.* GABRIEL *enters from the alley.*)

GABRIEL. (*Calling.*) Hey, Rose!

ROSE. Gabe?

GABRIEL. I'm here, Rose. Hey Rose, I'm here!

(ROSE *enters from the house.*)

ROSE. Lord . . . Look here, Lyons!

LYONS. See, I told you, Rose . . . I told you they'd let him come.

CORY. How you doing, Uncle Gabe?

LYONS. How you doing, Uncle Gabe?

GABRIEL. Hey, Rose. It's time. It's time to tell St. Peter to open the gates. Troy, you ready? You ready, Troy. I'm gonna tell St. Peter to open the gates. You get ready now.

(GABRIEL, *with great fanfare, braces himself to blow. The trumpet is without a mouthpiece. He puts the end of it into his mouth and blows with great force, like a man who has been waiting some twenty-odd years for this single moment. No sound comes out of the trumpet. He braces himself and blows again with the same result. A third time he blows. There is a weight of impossible description that falls away and leaves him bare and exposed to a frightful realization. It is a trauma that a sane and normal mind would be unable to withstand. He begins to dance. A slow, strange dance, eerie and lifegiving. A dance of atavistic signature and ritual.* LYONS *attempts to embrace him.* GABRIEL *pushes* LYONS *away. He begins to howl in what is an attempt at song, or perhaps a song turning back into itself in an attempt at speech. He finishes his dance and the gates of heaven stand open as wide as God's closet.*)

That's the way that go!

(*Blackout.*)

Richard Hamilton as Dodge in the 1978 New York production of *Buried Child*. (Photo courtesy of Shirley Herz.)

CHAPTER XVI

Contemporary American Theatre

The excitement and promise of the post-war theatre—embodied primarily in the works of Williams and Miller—had subsided by the end of the 1950s, and the American theatre was clearly in a state of decline. Not only was there a dearth of exciting plays, but the economics of the theatre suffered as well. While seventy-five legitimate theatres had operated on Broadway in 1929, only thirty-four were in existence in 1959. Similarly, fifty-six new productions in 1959 contrasted dramatically with two-hundred thirty-three which had opened in 1929. Production costs had risen dramatically, and a show had to run approximately one year to recoup its investments.

We have already seen, in Chapter XIV, how regional and off-Broadway theatres began to answer the changing needs of the cultural life of the country. By the 1960s the American theatre began to stir with a new energy, excitement, and political vision that had not been evidenced since the 1920s and 30s. It burst beyond Broadway and theatrical environments to streets, warehouses, churches, urban centers, and the rural communities. Its practitioners were often political activists rather than trained actors as the war in Vietnam and the civil rights movement inspired commitment on the part of American youth, Chicanos, native Americans, women and gays. It was no longer an establishment theatre. In our chapter on Artaud and Theatre of Cruelty, we saw how experimental groups like The Living Theatre, The Open Theatre, and the Performance Group devoted themselves to exploration of current issues, new spaces, new ways of working, communal effort, devaluation of text, and emphasis on freedom and ritual.

But this time of buoyant activity and passion was no less exciting for the literary playwright, and off-off Broadway was developed to offer the young dramatist a chance to be heard without commercial, political, or aesthetic restraints. Of the many off-off Broadway theatres that emerged after 1959—Cafe Cino, Cafe La Mama, Judson Poets' Theatre, Theatre Genesis, American Place Theatre and many others—one can be singled out as both representative and extraordinary: Cafe La Mama, now the La Mama Experimental Theatre Club, an organization under the distinguished and courageous leadership of Ellen Stewart, which has continued to flourish and prosper since its humble beginnings in 1959. Stewart, a dress designer, began to offer her East Village apartment as a place for young writers to try out their work because she said she was tired of their complaints about the state of theatre in New York. In those early days she said they did almost everything with a cot and a bottle of ketchup as their only props. Repeatedly in trouble with city officials because she was not licensed as a theatre and her basement room did not meet regulations, Stewart circumvented the law by offering light food and beverages. When an officer asked the name of her "restaurant" one of her proteges said, "Hey, Mama, what are you going to call it?" Hence, came the name: Cafe La Mama. As Stewart's skill at promoting young talent and obtaining grant money grew, so did the reputation of her theatre. In 1969 she produced more plays than appeared on Broadway, and in the same year acquired a building with two theatres, a facility that was extended and improved in 1974. La Mama, certainly the most important of all off-off Broadway enterprises, is first and foremost a playwrights' theatre where experimentation and individualism are fostered, and failure allowed. Of the many young playwrights who got both a start and encouragement from Ellen Stewart and similar off-off Broadway producers, many of them have continued to write and have become the established playwrights of the 1980s. Sam Shepard, first produced at Theatre Genesis and at La Mama, offers an important example.

Besides being off-off Broadway's most important playwright, Shepard has been extremely prolific, earning Obie Awards on eight occasions. From *Cowboys* (1964), through *Operation Sidewinder* (1970), *The Tooth of Crime* (1972), *Curse of the Starving Class* (1976), *Buried Child* (1978), *True West* (1980), *Fool for Love* (1982), and *A Lie of the Mind* (1985), Shepard continues to explore contemporary American myths—the cowboy, the West, the loner—in seemingly realistic frameworks which become charged with symbolism and meaning as we delve beneath surfaces. Shepard is fascinated by the destruction and destructive nature of the family in America, by the futile dreams and insubstantial reality of today's existence, by our obsession with material rather than spiritual values, and by our inability to escape our past. His plays are hard hitting, violent, eruptive, passionate; and his characters, are above all else, lonely and emotionally and spiritually starved. Shepard is fascinated by the world of popular art—radio, television, music, and comic books—and his characters are drawn not from the comfortable middle classes but from the rural, the poor, the lost and the weak. He creates a sharp sense of place, social class, the nuances of American rural speech, and the grotesqueness of contemporary life. His plays offer powerful metaphors for social and moral decay.

Another playwright who got his start with La Mama and Cafe Cino and then went on to pioneer off-off Broadway's Circle Repertory Company, with his colleague Marshall Mason as its artistic director, was Lanford Wilson. In *Balm in Gilead* (1965) and *The Hot L Baltimore* (1973), Wilson deals with the lost, forgotten, and disfranchised souls of America at a time when the country itself seems to have lost its direction. In *The Rimers of Eldridge* (1966) Wilson turns to the prejudice and provincialism in small town American life. One of Wilson's most interesting plays, although one that did not achieve success in production, was *The Mound Builders* (1976) which reveals a sophistication in Wilson's dramaturgy. He works in two time frames—one past and one present—as he explores the relationship between ancient mound builders and the archeologists who study them, between failed civilizations, failed archeological pursuits, and failed lives. The play, rich in symbolism and dramatic irony, becomes a complex statement about the disparity between the dreams and the achievements of humankind.

In recent years, Wilson has turned to his own family for inspiration and has written a series of plays about the Talleys of Southern Missouri: *The Fifth of July* (1978), *Talley's Folly* (1980), and *Talley and Son* (1985). These remarkable, almost Chekhovian plays, document contemporary American mid-western life, reflecting the changes in the spirit of America between World War II and Vietnam. In one play, *Talley's Folly,* two very different worlds unite when the quintessential WASP, Sally Talley, falls in love with Matt Friedman—a liberal Jew who is cognizant of the collision of old and new values. With his keen ability to chronicle contemporary American speech, character and behavior, and with his ability to capture both symbolically and literally the changing face of America, Lanford Wilson is a solid voice in our contemporary theatre.

The development of the off and off-off Broadway theatres that occured between 1960 and 1970 was phenomenal, injecting new life, spirit, freedom, and integrity into the theatre. At the peak of the movement, there were approximately 200 off-off Broadway theatres. Meanwhile the regional theatres continued to grow and prosper, and it is through this venue that many of our contemporary playwrights find an audience and a place to nurture their craft. A great training ground for young artists has emerged in Chicago where David Mamet's work has often originated. In fact, three of Mamet's most significant plays are about Chicago: *Sexual Perversity in Chicago* (1974), *American Buffalo* (1977), and the prize winning saga of ruthless Chicago real estate men selling property in Florida, *Glengarry Glen Ross* (1983). It is interesting that Mamet has maintained strong associations with college theatre, with regional theatre in Chicago, with off-off Broadway in New York, and even with the commercial Broadway theatre where many of his plays have ultimately been presented. Even liberal audience members are sometimes shocked at Mamet's language—a language that abounds in the rhythms, cliches, and obscenities of contemporary speech—yet his dramas exist as almost morality plays for our time. By presenting a world of corruption, insensitivity, power for money, dehumanization of people, destruction of moral and spiritual values, Mamet pleads for the preservation of our values and humanity. We may laugh at the stupidity, vulgarity, and blindness of Mamet's characters; at the same time we recognize them as lost souls, people who have been denied their fundamental needs and are left only their bluster, suppressed anger, and anguish. While they seem to function very well on a superficial and highly charged level, they have ceased to function as human beings of depth and real fibre.

Similar to Mamet in finding his way to the Broadway theatre through university, regional, and off Broadway houses is David Rabe, whose most recent play, *Hurly Burly* (1984) deals with the decadence, self destruction, and cruelty rampant in the Hollywood scene. Rabe is best known, however, for what is sometimes referred to as his Vietnam trilogy: *The Basic Training of Pavlo Hummel* (1971), *Sticks and Bones* (1971), and his finest play, *Streamers* (1976). *Streamers* takes place in a cadre room on an army base where young men of different backgrounds, race, and sexual orientation—a microcosm of our society—are thrown together in an environment as explosive as the war that awaits them in Vietnam. Like the symbolic title, they are men whose parachutes have failed to open, and they are plummeting to certain death. Rabe makes a strong statement that the precipitous violence surrounding war permeates every aspect of life until we are all consumed with violence and destructiveness. Like *Lysistrata* and *Mother Courage, Streamers* is a powerful and eloquent indictment of war.

Besides the regional theatres in cities like Chicago, three others should be mentioned as particularly significant in the development of new playwrights: the Yale Repertory Theatre, founded by Robert Brustein in 1966 and led by Lloyd Richards since 1978, where Athol Fugard has found an American audience, where August Wilson's works have been developed, and where a gifted young social satirist, Christopher Durang, received his first attention; the American Repertory Theatre, which Brustein has led at Harvard University since 1979 and which has fostered new playwrights, directors, and innovative production concepts; and finally the Actors Theatre of Louisville, under the direction of Jon Jory, which launched an annual new play festival in 1976, and produced early works of two of Americas most distinguished women playwrights, Beth Henley and Marsha Norman.

Henley's reputation rests almost entirely on one new play, *Crimes of the Heart* (1979), a bigger than life story of an idiosyncratic southern family and three sisters who are drawn together when the youngest, Babe, shoots her husband. The play was remounted for Broadway in 1981, won Henley a Pulitzer Prize, and was made into a successful motion picture in 1986 with Henley as the screen writer. Marsha Norman has written two successful plays—*Getting Out,* which Jory produced in 1977, and *'night, Mother,* which premiered at the American Repertory Theatre at

Harvard in 1981, moved to Broadway, and won the Pulitzer Prize in 1983. Both plays are about women's choices—Arlene of *Getting Out* to stay out of prison from which she has just been paroled and Jesse of *'night, Mother* to end her meaningless life. Norman is noted for her powerful language, the quality of her dialogue, her dry humor, and, above all, her honest and sensitive portraits of troubled women. Not since the work of Lillian Hellman in the 1930s and 40s have the voices of American women playwrights been as powerful and evident.

By the early 1970s the theatre seemed to be well again. The experimental movement offered a new freedom; new playwrights had emerged as a result of healthy off Broadway and off-off Broadway productions; and the flourishing resident or regional companies—producing an estimated 3,500 productions at some 200 independent, non-profit, professional theatres—were providing rich theatre fare throughout the country. The National Endowment for the Arts and a variety of private foundations seemed eager to subsidize the theatre. Even Broadway had created the Theatre Development Fund in 1967, to help students and special groups purchase tickets at reduced prices. In 1973 the Fund opened Tickets at Times Square where discount tickets could be purchased on the day of performance. But by the mid-1970s, the new energy of the theatre had begun to lose some of its momentum. A new conservatism, a preoccupation with economic wealth, a cynicism resulting from disillusion about Vietnam and Watergate—all seem to be reflected in a safe, conservative, careful approach to theatre. People of passionate commitment became computer programers while those devoted to experimental theatre found more money in packaging and selling the arts than producing new works. Those who continued to break new ground were known to only an elite few rather than to the general public, and most of our youth would rather attend a rock concert than a live theatrical event.

Broadway, "the ghetto of the theatre" as Harold Clurman calls it, continues to present safe theatre, predominantly musicals. The major exception to the commercial musical fare can be found in the extraordinary work of Stephen Sondheim and the development of the concept musical in which the songs, book, lyrics, setting, and production scheme all serve one unified purpose or objective. Beginning with *Company* in 1970 and developing through *Follies, A Little Night Music, Sweeney Todd,* and *Sunday in the Park with George* (1985) Sondheim has risked and endured failure to present social values, dark views of human behavior, and unattractive subject matter in order to make his complex musical statements. Critics begin to say that even Sondheim is repeating himself and that the center of musical theatre has moved away from Broadway to London where the popular works of Andrew Lloyd-Webber—*Jesus Christ Superstar, Evita, Cats, Starlight Express,* and *Phantom of the Opera*—are thrilling audiences with spectacular scenery and stage effects. Michael Bennett's *Chorus Line* has run for over ten years on Broadway, but little else of significance has been generated. Even the musical scene is turning to revivals of hits like Cole Porter's *Anything Goes* or Rodgers and Hart's *On Your Toes,* and reconstructions like the Gershwin musical, *My One and Only.* The price for a musical today is approximately fifty dollars per ticket as opposed to $4.50 in the 1930s.

Besides musicals, Broadway relies on revivals of popular plays, British imports, and a smattering of legitimate plays, primarily comedies. Of comedy writers who have found tremendous success on Broadway, we must acknowledge the work of Neil Simon whose first hit was *Come Blow Your Horn* (1961), followed by *Barefoot in the Park, Plaza Suite, The Odd Couple, The Last of the Red Hot Lovers, The Sunshine Boys,* and *Chapter Two.* Beginning in 1984 with *Brighton Beach Memoirs,* and continuing with *Biloxi Blues,* and *Broadway Bound,* Simon has explored his own youth, young adulthood, and early career with what critics perceive to be a growing depth and maturity. He seems to be willing to sacrifice his one line gags for a gentler humor and a more honest look at the pain and desperation that drives his comic characters.

Even the resident theatres have grown more conservative and careful. Instead of companies that can grow and work together, the professional resident theatres hire actors for single productions, and seem more willing to perform new plays by already established playwrights than take a risk on an unknown author. Budgets have shrunk under monetary stress, production costs have escalated, and economic failure always seems, and indeed sometimes is, imminent. American plays—and too few good ones are finding production—seem to dwell too exclusively on negative values and offer little in terms of heros and heroines for our time, and positive or uplifting statements. We are too delighted and satisfied with extravaganza and spectacular scenic effects in place of sound dramatic content. Indeed, the theatre scene looks bleak. But we must bear in mind that just as 1959 seemed to offer little vitality, a new vision, fervor, and commitment was just around the corner. In the midst of high ticket prices, astronomical production costs, and safe ventures, we have occasional intimations of new vigor such as the health that seems to be restored to the Vivian Beaumont Theatre in New York under the guidance of Gregory Mosher from Chicago's Goodman Theatre. Because the theatre has so traditionally mirrored the attitudes and perspectives of its times, we must not underestimate the capacity of this fabulous invalid for change, survival, and progress.

Sam Shepard

Sam Shepard was born, November 5, 1943 at Fort Sheridan in Illinois, after which the family moved from army base to army base wherever Shepard's father was stationed. In 1955 the family settled in California where Shepard went to school before joining Bishop's Company Repertory Players and touring the United States as an actor. In 1963, an angry young rebel, Shepard moved into East Greenwich Village in New York and began having his short plays produced at Theatre Genesis, La Mama Experimental Theatre Club, Cafe Cino, Judson Posts' Theatre, and any of the off-off Broadway playhouses who would have him. He won his first Obie Award for *Melodrama Play,* produced at La Mama in 1967, the same year he was to be awarded a Rockefeller Foundation grant. A Guggenheim Foundation grant followed, and in 1969, Shepard married O-Lan Johnson. A son, Jesse, was born in 1970, at about the same time Shepard was gaining a national reputation with works like *Operation Sidewinder* at the Vivian Beaumont in New York. In 1972 Shepard and his family moved to London for a time, and it was there that *Tooth of Crime* and *The Geography of a Horse Dreamer* premiered in the so-called fringe theatres. By this time Shepard was often directing his own works.

In 1974, Shepard returned to the United States and settled in California where his acting career gained great momentum. Contemporary followers of Shepard fear that he is selling out by his frequent appearances in and writing for film; but the truth of the matter is that Shepard, with almost volcanic energy, has written for and acted in films since the beginning of his career. With his role as Chuck Yeager in *The Right Stuff* in 1983 and his nomination for an Academy Award as best actor in a supporting role, Shepard has achieved the status of matinee idol with his rugged good looks and quiet strength. In films like *Francis* and *Country* Shepard has been coupled with his off-stage partner, Jessica Lange. Shepard has been playwright-in-residence at San Francisco's Magic Theatre where some of his finest work—*Buried Child,* for which he won the Pulitzer Prize in 1979, *True West* (1980), and *Fool for Love* (1983)—have originated. He has had plays performed at Yale Repertory Theatre, New York Public Theatre, and London's Royal Court Theatre, but he has never had a play performed on Broadway. Shepard continues to direct, act in film, write for film and for the stage with no indication of commercial sell-out or diminished creative energy.

Buried Child

While *Buried Child* by Sam Shepard has all the outward trappings of realistic drama—characters who are recognizable human portraits, a setting that represents a real enough farmhouse in the Mid West with its worn furniture and ancient television set, dialogue that approximates natural speech, stage business requiring real ears of corn to be shucked and real carrots to be scraped and pared—it is an obvious century away from the Realism of Ibsen. In its examination of the social scene, *Buried Child* is a direct descendant of the drama of Ibsen; but Shepard's play benefits immeasurably from the freedoms of form and content introduced into the drama by the Expressionists, the Absurdists, and the practitioners of the Theatre of Cruelty. It attempts to portray the subjective, inner reality of human experience; it certainly suggests that much of life is meaningless or at least difficult to fathom; it presents us with painful images and insidious violence which constantly remind us of the cruelty of the human condition. It is almost as though Ibsen, Strindberg, Beckett, Pinter and Artaud had harmoniously collaborated on one script. In a sense, we see most of the dominant trends of modern drama brought together in Sam Shepard's dramatic masterpiece.

Buried Child is a play that poses many questions but offers few, if any, real answers. It is a play of subtle innuendo, hint, suggestion and contradiction. Over and over again the viewer or reader arrives at points where he thinks he finally understands what is happening only to have his understanding shattered by a contradictory event or piece of information. Essentially, Shepard gives the theater-goer one set of expository "facts" only to contradict them almost entirely at a later point with a different set of "facts." But, while the plot may seem potentially confusing in its convoluted, non-linear development, the ultimate point made by the storyline—the ultimate action demonstrated—is remarkably clear. Shepard is writing, as he does in many of his plays, about the moral corruption of America. In some of his plays we see that corruption as it relates to the commercialization of our country; but in *Buried Child* the corruption is much more obviously psychological, social and domestic. In this instance, the family is the source *and* the victim of the moral decay in question. Sam Shepard is showing us some profound and devastating truths about the disintegration of the basic social unit—the family—in American society. He strongly hints that our salvation lies in reversing the trend of that moral decay within society, a decay which has now extended well beyond the family and given birth to political corruptions, assassinations, social injustices, denials of civil rights, Watergate, a war in Vietnam and on and on. In a very real sense, Shepard is saying that moral decay begins at home.

Buried Child shows us a family destroyed by the sins of the past and the crimes family members unwittingly or deliberately commit against one another. This is a lower middle-class family of that comic book-television-movie-pop music generation Shepard so often chooses to write about. Here is a family bound together by painful familial ties woven from threads of corruption and hidden evil so twisted and convoluted that it is impossible to sort them out. Dark and vile secrets infest the very air of the house. But of those secrets, which are truths and which are lies? Shepard chooses not to provide us with all the answers; at the end of the play we know as little of the truth as some of the characters. However, we do know that the secrets have all but destroyed the family; but somehow we sense in those final moments that the family must and can be saved by a confrontation with the truth.

Much of the fascination of the play lies in the highly theatrical and mysterious way Shepard offers us intriguing, provocative hints of the past crimes and sins—the dark secrets—within the family. The first half of the play in particular raises one compelling question after another. Has Halie, the mother, committed adultery at some time in the past in Florida? Or was it California? Did Tilden, the eldest son, get into trouble in New Mexico? If he did, what was the nature of the trouble? Has Tilden actually been in jail? Is he partially feeble-minded, or has he been severely damaged by the sins of the past? Why is Dodge, the father, afraid to be alone? Why is Dodge afraid of Bradley, another of his sons? And why does Bradley maliciously attack his father? (Bradley crops Dodge's hair while the old man sleeps. Is he, Delilah-fashion, depriving the old man of his physical vitality?) Was Bradley actually a football star? Why is Tilden afraid of going into town? Was Ansel, another son, really a basketball hero? Was Ansel really murdered by his wife's Mafia family? Or, for that matter, is Ansel real or only a figment of his mother's imagination? Could Ansel be the buried child?

And this is only the beginning. While the answers to these questions are uncertain, the possibilities are tremendous in their implications. While we are still in the dark about many issues, we become relatively sure of a few things as the story unfolds. Halie and Dodge live together in a state of estrangement. Halie may talk a great deal, but there is no substantial communication between man and wife. We know that Halie leaves for town for a purpose she chooses not to specify. We know that her grandson Vince, Tilden's son, arrives accompanied by his girl friend Shelly. He apparently has been away from the family for six years but has been drawn back to the scene of his youth. It does not take long for us to realize that he has returned searching for his roots or his place within the family structure.

But then, the questions continue. Why is Vince not recognized by his father and his grandfather? Why do they seem threatened by his unannounced appearance at one moment and then indifferent to him at the next? Why is Dodge resentful of Shelly's presence? Although Vince is not apparently recognized by either Tilden or Dodge, at a later point in the play he is recognized instantly by his grandmother Halie; at that point the rest of the family, including Tilden and Dodge, recognize him as well. Interestingly enough, the recognition closely follows Vince's violent entrance in Act Three. Is his violent nature his only real identity within the family? And the questions go on. Did Dodge really murder Halie's youngest son? Was he the father of the child? Or, was Tilden the incestuous father of the murdered child? Who is, or was, the child? Why does the family live in isolation from the rest of the world? Is there actually a cornfield and garden in back of the house? Is the child really buried there?

In Act Three Halie returns from her visit to town after an unexplained absence of an entire day. She is in the company of Father Dewis, the clergyman, who may or may not be her lover. This event naturally poses further questions. What is Father Dewis doing in the house and what is his real relationship with Halie? Is he part of the moral decay? Is that why he is such an ineffectual by-stander even when Halie appeals for his aid and assistance? Or, is Shepard telling us that when moral decay runs this deep even religion is of little help?

While the questions are numerous, there are certain guide posts in the play by which we can steer our course. Vince is, after all, obviously seeking his roots. And for a while we watch his efforts to establish his identity in the family. While there is some question as to whether or not the garden and cornfield actually exist behind the house, one thing is certain: Tilden believes in their reality. Furthermore, he brings corn and carrots into the house as concrete evidence of their existence. We sense somehow that the cornfield and the garden are manifestations or reminders of the past. When Tilden retreats to the garden and the cornfield, he is somehow seeking the past, perhaps searching through it for answers, possibly accepting it or even embracing it. At any rate, Tilden has a special affinity for the corn and the carrots—products of the very field and garden which possibly contain the body of the dead child. Perhaps this explains why he responds very positively to Shelly when she seems also to cherish the carrots or, at least, to find some special significance in them.

As the play draws to a close, other things become relatively certain as well. In the act of assuming Dodge's place on the old couch and taking over his role in the household, Vince seems to replace his grandfather and to inherit the sins of the family. There has been more than one reference in the play to the fact that the son is the image of the father and the father the image of the grandfather; they are, in effect, replications of one another. (Shepard says all of that so dramatically and brilliantly in a speech in which Vince tells of seeing his reflection in the windshield of his automobile—a reflection that quickly takes on the features of Tilden and then Dodge.) And so, the cycle of guilt and sin will go on.

Or, does the cycle go on? Does it have to go on? In the last moment of the play, just as we may be assuming that Vince is lost and destroyed, Tilden comes in carrying the body of the buried child wrapped in cerements. The crime has been unearthed, the sins of the past confronted. Was the child sacrificed for the family just as Christ was sacrificed for us? Is this a faint echo of the Resurrection? The Bible assures us that "a child shall lead them." Is this child leading the family toward some kind of salvation? At that moment, Halie, from her vantage point upstairs, sees the cornfield and the garden through the window. They do exist after all. Is this the Garden of Eden and, therefore, a new beginning? "A miracle," she declares. "I've never seen it like this. Maybe the rain did something. Maybe it was the rain." Perhaps the world has been cleansed once more by a deluge. It has, after all, happened before. In the course of Halie's speech Shepard draws parallels between the new life of a plant breaking through the hard earth ("tiny little shoot") and the buried child. The Christ image is reiterated. And again Halie asserts, "It's a miracle, Dodge. I've never seen a crop like this in my whole life. Maybe it's the sun. Maybe that's it. Maybe it's the sun."

The possibilities of meaning here are inviting. Halie, of course, could be referring to the Son of Man as the savior of the family. Or, perhaps it is her son—the buried child—who is the savior. Or, she could be speaking of the sun symbolically as the source of light and truth—the truth that sets Man free. (The same age-old symbolism is employed in *Oedipus Rex*.) Perhaps all of these possible meanings are valid and collectively convey Shepard's intentions at this point in the play. In any event, the message at the final moment is a hopeful one. Perhaps Vince does not have to assume the family mantle of sin. Perhaps there is hope for the future. There can be an end to sin, crime and corruption.

It cannot be denied that the family Shepard presents to us in *Buried Child* is a fascinating if frequently unpleasant one. It is also a familiar one. We have encountered it once before in Strindberg's *The Ghost Sonata*. The similarities between Strindberg's expressionistic masterpiece and Shepard's highly contemporary play are interesting to contemplate. The themes are almost identical. Youth is destroyed by the moral decay of the family. Human beings are bound together by a web of hideous relationships born of sin, crime and corruption. The sins of the past are visited upon the present just as the sins of the father are visited upon the son. Vince is much like the Hyacinth Girl in that he is the youth being destroyed by the sins of the family even though he may not be quite as innocent as his counterpart. Shelly is, like Strindberg's Student, the outsider who is suddenly immersed in a world of confusing evil and attempts to understand and to save; and she, like the Student, fails in her mission. Dodge, reminiscent of the Mummy, is worn out and half dead from exposure to sin but seeks in the final moments of the play to unveil the truth—or his version of the truth—in an effort to put an end to evil. Bradley with his wooden-leg and viciousness reminds one of Hummel, the psychological and physical cripple who seems to want to devour others. Halie, by virtue of the fact that she is the healthiest person in the household and manipulates the others, seems to be a latter-day version of the vampire cook.

While there is a danger in making too much of such comparisons, it is interesting, nonetheless, that *The Ghost Sonata* and *Buried Child* are highly reminiscent of one another especially in their actions which assert that Man must escape the sins, crimes and corruption of the past (hidden in both instances in twisted family relationships) or be destroyed by them. Shepard may not have been directly influenced by August Strindberg, but he undeniably shares a similar view of the world with the Swedish dramatist. They both embrace the same universal ideas in their work. They both write with tremendous insight and theatrical vigor. They both enrich world theatre with their drama. They both have something significant and cogent to tell us about the times in which they write. Shepard is a dramatist for our time just as Strindberg was the dramatist for his day.

Still, it is perhaps to be regretted that Shepard so doggedly insists on depicting the lives of lower middle-class people and drawing his images from the pop culture of that lower middle-class world. In a way, he limits the appeal of his drama. Many play-goers may reject the lower middle-class milieu as a valid and viable image of our culture as a whole. Besides, the very element of our society to which he speaks and about whom he speaks are ironically the very people who never see his plays because they would choose rather to stay at home and watch the latest sit-com or football game on television. That is, in the final analysis, highly regretable, for Shepard has so very much of importance to say to all Americans at this moment in time.

BURIED CHILD

by Sam Shepard

———— CHARACTERS ————

DODGE—In his seventies.
HALIE—His wife. Mid-sixties.
TILDEN—Their oldest son.
BRADLEY—Their next oldest son, an amputee.

VINCE—Tilden's son.
SHELLY—Vince's girl friend.
FATHER DEWIS—A Protestant minister.

ACT 1

SCENE. *Day. Old wooden staircase down left with pale, frayed carpet laid down on the steps. The stairs lead off stage left up into the wings with no landing. Up right is an old, dark green sofa with the stuffing coming out in spots. Stage right of the sofa is an upright lamp with a faded yellow shade and a small night table with several small bottles of pills on it. Down right of the sofa, with the screen facing the sofa, is a large, old-fashioned brown T.V. A flickering blue light comes from the screen, but no image, no sound. In the dark, the light of the lamp and the T.V. slowly brighten in the black space. The space behind the sofa, upstage, is a large, screened-in porch with a board floor; a solid interior door to stage right of the sofa, leading into the room on stage; and another screen door up left, leading from the porch to the outside. Beyond that are the shapes of dark elm trees.*

Gradually the form of DODGE *is made out, sitting on the couch, facing the T.V., the blue light flickering on his face. He wears a well-worn T-shirt, suspenders, khaki work pants and brown slippers. He's covered himself in an old brown blanket. He's very thin and sickly looking, in his late seventies. He just stares at the T.V. More light fills the stage softly. The sound of light rain.* DODGE *slowly tilts his head back and stares at the ceiling for a while, listening to the rain. He lowers his head again and stares at the T.V. He turns his head slowly to the left and stares at the cushion of the sofa next to the one he's sitting on. He pulls his left arm out from under the blanket, slides his hand under the cushion, and pulls out a bottle of whiskey. He looks down left toward the staircase, listens, then uncaps the bottle, takes a long swig and caps it again. He puts the bottle back under the cushion and stares at the T.V. He starts to cough slowly and softly. The coughing gradually builds. He holds one hand to his mouth and tries to stifle it. The coughing gets louder, then suddenly stops when he hears the sound of his wife's voice coming from the top of the staircase.*

HALIE'S VOICE. Dodge?

DODGE *just stares at the T.V. Long pause. He stifles two short coughs.*

HALIE'S VOICE. Dodge! You want a pill, Dodge?

He doesn't answer. Takes the bottle out again and takes another long swig. Puts the bottle back stares at T.V., pulls blanket up around his neck.

HALIE'S VOICE. You know what it is, don't you? It's the rain! Weather. That's it. Every time. Every time you get like this, it's the rain. No sooner does the rain start then you start. (*pause*) Dodge?

He makes no reply. Pulls a pack of cigarettes out from sweater and lights one. Stares at T.V. pause.

HALIE'S VOICE. You should see it coming down up here. Just coming down in sheets. Blue sheets. The bridge is pretty near flooded. What's it like down there? Dodge?

DODGE *turns his head back over his left shoulder and takes a look out through the porch. He turns back to the T.V.*

DODGE. (*to himself*) Catastrophic.

HALIE'S VOICE. What? What'd you say, Dodge?

DODGE. (*louder*) It looks like rain to me! Plain old rain!

374

HALIE'S VOICE. Rain? Of course it's rain! Are you having a seizure or something! Dodge? (*pause*) I'm coming down there in about five minutes if you don't answer me!

DODGE. Don't come down.

HALIE'S VOICE. What!

DODGE. (*louder*) Don't come down!

He has another coughing attack. Stops.

HALIE'S VOICE. You should take a pill for that! I don't see why you just don't take a pill. Be done with it once and for all. Put a stop to it.

He takes bottle out again. Another swig. Returns bottle.

HALIE'S VOICE. It's not Christian, but it works. It's not necessarily Christian, that is. We don't know. There's some things the ministers can't even answer. I, personally, can't see anything wrong with it. Pain is pain. Pure and simple. Suffering is a different matter. That's entirely different. A pill seems as good an answer as any. Dodge? (*pause*) Dodge, are you watching baseball?

DODGE. No.

HALIE'S VOICE. What?

DODGE. (*louder*) No!

HALIE'S VOICE. What're you watching? You shouldn't be watching anything that'll get you excited. No horse racing!

DODGE. They don't race on Sundays.

HALIE'S VOICE. What?

DODGE. (*louder*) They don't race on Sundays!

HALIE'S VOICE. Well they shouldn't race on Sundays.

DODGE. Well they don't!

HALIE'S VOICE. Good. I'm amazed they still have that kind of legislation. That's amazing.

DODGE. Yeah, it's amazing.

HALIE'S VOICE. What?

DODGE. (*louder*) It is amazing!

HALIE'S VOICE. It is. It truly is, I would've thought these days they'd be racing on Christmas even. A big flashing Christmas tree right down at the finish line.

DODGE. (*shakes his head*) No.

HALIE'S VOICE They used to race on New Year's! I remember that.

DODGE. They never raced on New Year's!

HALIE'S VOICE. Sometimes they did.

DODGE. They never did!

HALIE'S VOICE. Before we were married they did!

DODGE *waves his hand in disgust at the staircase. Leans back in sofa. Stares at T.V.*

HALIE'S VOICE. I went once. With a man.

DODGE. (*mimicking her*) Oh, a "man."

HALIE'S VOICE. What?

DODGE. Nothing!

HALIE'S VOICE. A wonderful man. A breeder.

DODGE. A what?

HALIE'S VOICE. A breeder! A horse breeder! Thoroughbreds.

DODGE. Oh, Thoroughbreds. Wonderful.

HALIE'S VOICE. That's right. He knew everything there was to know.

DODGE. I bet he taught you a thing or two huh? Gave you a good turn around the old stable!

HALIE'S VOICE. Knew everything there was to know about horses. We won bookoos of money that day.

DODGE. What?

HALIE'S VOICE. Money! We won every race I think.

DODGE. Bookoos?

HALIE'S VOICE. Every single race.

DODGE. Bookoos of money?

HALIE'S VOICE. It was one of those kind of days.

DODGE. New Year's!

HALIE'S VOICE. Yes! It might've been Florida. Or California! One of those two.

DODGE. Can I take my pick?

HALIE'S VOICE. It was Florida!

DODGE. Aha!

HALIE'S VOICE. Wonderful! Absolutely wonderful! The sun was just gleaming. Flamingos. Bougainvilleas. Palm trees.

DODGE. (*to himself, mimicking her*) Bougainvilleas. Palm trees.

HALIE'S VOICE. Everything was dancing with life! There were all kinds of people from everywhere. Everyone was dressed to the nines. Not like today. Not like they dress today.

DODGE. When was this anyway?

HALIE'S VOICE. This was long before I knew you.

DODGE. Must've been.

HALIE'S VOICE. Long before. I was escorted.

DODGE. To Florida?

HALIE'S VOICE. Yes. Or it might've been California. I'm not sure which.

DODGE. All that way you were escorted?

HALIE'S VOICE. Yes.

DODGE. And he never laid a finger on you I suppose? (*long silence*) Halie?

No answer. Long pause.

HALIE'S VOICE. Are you going out today?

DODGE. (*gesturing toward rain*) In this?

HALIE'S VOICE. I'm just asking a simple question.

DODGE. I rarely go out in the bright sunshine, why would I go out in this?

HALIE'S VOICE. I'm just asking because I'm not doing any shopping today. And if you need anything you should ask Tilden.

DODGE. Tilden's not here!

HALIE'S VOICE. He's in the kitchen.

DODGE *looks toward stage left, then back toward T.V.*

DODGE. All right.

HALIE'S VOICE. What?

DODGE. (*louder*) All right!

HALIE'S VOICE. Don't scream. It'll only get your coughing started.

DODGE. All right.

HALIE'S VOICE. Just tell Tilden what you want and he'll get it. (*pause*) Bradley should be over later.

DODGE. Bradley?

HALIE'S VOICE. Yes. To cut your hair.

DODGE. My hair? I don't need my hair cut!

HALIE'S VOICE. It won't hurt!

DODGE. I don't need it!

HALIE'S VOICE. It's been more than two weeks Dodge.

DODGE. I don't need it!

HALIE'S VOICE. I have to meet Father Dewis for lunch.

DODGE. You tell Bradley that if he shows up here with those clippers, I'll kill him!

HALIE'S VOICE. I won't be very late. No later than four at the very latest.

DODGE. You tell him! Last time he left me almost bald! And I wasn't even awake! I was sleeping! I woke up and he'd already left!

HALIE'S VOICE. That's not my fault!

DODGE. You put him up to it!

HALIE'S VOICE. I never did!

DODGE. You did too! You had some fancy, stupid meeting planned! Time to dress up the corpse for company! Lower the ears a little! Put up a little front! Surprised you didn't tape a pipe to my mouth while you were at it! That woulda' looked nice! Huh? A pipe? Maybe a bowler hat! Maybe a copy of the Wall Street Journal casually placed on my lap!

HALIE'S VOICE. You always imagine the worst things of people!

DODGE. That's not the worst! That's the least of the worst!

HALIE'S VOICE. I don't need to hear it! All day long I hear things like that and I don't need to hear more.

DODGE. You better tell him!

HALIE'S VOICE. You tell him yourself! He's your own son. You should be able to talk to your own son.

DODGE. Not while I'm sleeping! He cut my hair while I was sleeping!

HALIE'S VOICE. Well he won't do it again.

DODGE. There's no guarantee.

HALIE'S VOICE. I promise he won't do it without your consent.

DODGE. (*after pause*) There's no reason for him to even come over here.

HALIE'S VOICE. He feels responsible.

DODGE. For my hair?

HALIE'S VOICE. For your appearance.

DODGE. My appearance is out of his domain! It's even out of mine! In fact, it's disappeared! I'm an invisible man!

HALIE'S VOICE. Don't be ridiculous.

DODGE. He better not try it. That's all I've got to say.

HALIE'S VOICE. Tilden will watch out for you.

DODGE. Tilden won't protect me from Bradley!

HALIE'S VOICE. Tilden's the oldest. He'll protect you.

DODGE. Tilden can't even protect himself!

HALIE'S VOICE. Not so loud! He'll hear you. He's right in the kitchen.

DODGE. (*yelling off left*) Tilden!

HALIE'S VOICE. Dodge, what are you trying to do?

DODGE. (*yelling off left*) Tilden, get in here!

HALIE'S VOICE. Why do you enjoy stirring things up?

DODGE. I don't enjoy anything!

HALIE'S VOICE. That's a terrible thing to say.

DODGE. Tilden!

HALIE'S VOICE. That's the kind of statement that leads people right to the end of their rope.

DODGE. Tilden!

HALIE'S VOICE. It's no wonder people turn to Christ!

DODGE. TILDEN!!

HALIE'S VOICE. It's no wonder the messengers of God's word are shouted down in public places!

DODGE. TILDEN!!!!

DODGE *goes into a violent, spasmodic coughing attack as* TILDEN *enters from stage left, his arms loaded with fresh ears of corn.* TILDEN *is* DODGE'S *oldest son, late forties, wears heavy construction boots, covered with mud, dark green work pants, a plaid shirt and a faded brown windbreaker. He has a butch haircut, wet from the rain. Something about him is profoundly burned out and displaced. He stops center stage with the ears of corn in his arms and just stares at* DODGE *until he slowly finishes his coughing attack.* DODGE *looks up at him slowly. He stares at the corn. Long pause as they watch each other.*

HALIE'S VOICE. Dodge, if you don't take that pill nobody's going to force you.

The two men ignore the voice.

DODGE. (*to* TILDEN) Where'd you get that?

TILDEN. Picked it.

DODGE. You picked all that?

TILDEN *nods.*

DODGE. You expecting company?

TILDEN. No.

DODGE. Where'd you pick it from?

TILDEN. Right out back.

DODGE. Out back where!

TILDEN. Right out in back.

DODGE. There's nothing out there!

TILDEN. There's corn.

DODGE. There hasn't been corn out there since about nineteen thirty-five! That's the last time I planted corn out there!

TILDEN. It's out there now.

DODGE. (*yelling at stairs*) Halie!

HALIE'S VOICE. Yes dear!

DODGE. Tilden's brought a whole bunch of corn in here! There's no corn out in back is there?

TILDEN. (*to himself*) There's tons of corn.

HALIE'S VOICE. Not that I know of!

DODGE. That's what I thought.

HALIE'S VOICE. Not since about nineteen thirty-five!

DODGE. (to TILDEN) That's right. Nineteen thirty-five.

TILDEN. It's out there now.

DODGE. You go and take that corn back to wherever you got it from!

TILDEN. (*After pause, staring at* DODGE) It's picked. I picked it all in the rain. Once it's picked you can't put it back.

DODGE. I haven't had trouble with neighbors here for fifty-seven years. I don't even know who the neighbors are! And I don't wanna know! Now go put that corn back where it came from!

TILDEN *stares at* DODGE *then walks slowly over to him and dumps all the corn on* DODGE'S *lap and steps back.* DODGE *stares at the corn then back to* TILDEN. *Long pause.*

DODGE. Are you having trouble here, Tilden? Are you in some kind of trouble?

TILDEN. I'm not in any trouble.

DODGE. You can tell me if you are. I'm still your father.

TILDEN. I know you're still my father.

DODGE. I know you had a little trouble back in New Mexico. That's why you came out here.

TILDEN. I never had any trouble.

DODGE. Tilden, your mother told me all about it.

TILDEN. What'd she tell you?

TILDEN. *pulls some chewing tobacco out of his jacket and bites off a plug.*

DODGE. I don't have to repeat what she told me! She told me all about it!

TILDEN. Can I bring my chair in from the kitchen?

DODGE. What?

TILDEN. Can I bring in my chair from the kitchen?

DODGE. Sure. Bring your chair in.

> TILDEN *exits left.* DODGE *pushes all the corn off his lap onto the floor. He pulls the blanket off angrily and tosses it at one end of the sofa, pulls out the bottle and takes another swig.* TILDEN *enters again from left with a milking stool and a pail.* DODGE *hides the bottle quickly under the cushion before* TILDEN *sees it.* TILDEN *sets the stool down by the sofa, sits on it, puts the pail in front of him on the floor.* TILDEN *starts picking up the ears of corn one at a time and husking them. He throws the husks and silk in the center of the stage and drops the ears into the pail each time he cleans one. He repeats this process as they talk.*

DODGE. (*after a pause*) Sure is nice looking corn.

TILDEN. It's the best.

DODGE. Hybrid?

TILDEN. What?

DODGE. Some kinda fancy hybrid?

TILDEN. You planted it. I don't know what it is.

DODGE. (*pause*) Tilden, look, you can't stay here forever. You know that, don't you?

TILDEN. (*spits in spittoon*) I'm not.

DODGE. I know you're not. I'm not worried about that. That's not the reason I brought it up.

TILDEN. What's the reason?

DODGE. The reason is I'm wondering what you're gonna do.

TILDEN. You're not worried about me, are you?

DODGE. I'm not worried about you.

TILDEN. You weren't worried about me when I wasn't here. When I was in New Mexico.

DODGE. No, I wasn't worried about you then either.

TILDEN. You shoulda worried about me then.

DODGE. Why's that? You didn't do anything down there, did you?

TILDEN. I didn't do anything.

DODGE. Then why should I have worried about you?

TILDEN. Because I was lonely.

DODGE. Because you were lonely?

TILDEN. Yeah. I was more lonely than I've ever been before.

DODGE. Why was that?

TILDEN. (*pause*) Could I have some of that whiskey you've got?

DODGE. What whiskey? I haven't got any whiskey.

TILDEN. You've got some under the sofa.

DODGE. I haven't got anything under the sofa! Now mind your own damn business! Jesus God, you come into the house outa the middle of nowhere, haven't heard or seen you in twenty years and suddenly you're making accusations.

TILDEN. I'm not making accusations.

DODGE. You're accusing me of hoarding whiskey under the sofa!

TILDEN. I'm not accusing you.

DODGE. You just got through telling me I had whiskey under the sofa!

HALIE'S VOICE. Dodge?

DODGE. (*to* TILDEN) Now she knows about it!

TILDEN. She doesn't know about it.

HALIE'S VOICE. Dodge, are you talking to yourself down there?

DODGE. I'm talking to Tilden!

HALIE'S VOICE. Tilden's down there?

DODGE. He's right here!

HALIE'S VOICE. What?

578

DODGE. (louder) He's right here!

HALIE'S VOICE. What's he doing?

DODGE. (to TILDEN) Don't answer her.

TILDEN. (to DODGE) I'm not doing anything wrong.

DODGE. I know you're not.

HALIE'S VOICE. What's he doing down there?

DODGE. (to TILDEN) Don't answer.

TILDEN. I'm not.

HALIE'S VOICE. Dodge!

The men sit in silence. DODGE *lights a cigarette.* TILDEN *keeps husking corn, spits tobacco now and then in spittoon.*

HALIE'S VOICE. Dodge! He's not drinking anything, is he? You see to it that he doesn't drink anything! You've gotta watch out for him. It's our responsibility. He can't look after himself anymore, so we have to do it. Nobody else will do it. We can't just send him away somewhere. If we had lots of money we could send him away. But we won't. We never will. That's why we have to stay healthy. You and me. Nobody's going to look after us. Bradley can't look after us. Bradley can hardly look after himself. I was always hoping that Tilden would look out for Bradley when they got older. After Bradley lost his leg. Tilden's the oldest. I always though he'd be the one to take responsibility. I had no idea in the world that Tilden would be so much trouble. Who would've dreamed. Tilden was an All-American, don't forget. Don't forget that. Fullback. Or quarterback. I forget which.

TILDEN. (to himself) Fullback. (still husking)

HALIE'S VOICE. Then when Tilden turned out to be so much trouble, I put all my hopes on Ansel. Of course Ansel wasn't as handsome, but he was smart. He was the smartest probably. I think he probably was. Smarter than Bradley, that's for sure. Didn't go and chop his leg off with a chain saw. Smart enough not to go and do that. I think he was smarter than Tilden too. Especially after Tilden got in all that trouble. Doesn't take brains to go to jail. Anybody know that. Course then when Ansel died that left us all alone. Same as being alone. No different. Same as if they'd all died. He was the smartest. He could've earned lots of money. Lots and lots of money.

HALIE *enters slowly from the top of the staircase as she continues talking. Just her feet are seen at first as she makes her way down the stairs, a step at a time. She appears dressed completely in*

black, *as though in mourning. Black handbag, hat with a veil, and pulling on elbow length black gloves. She is about sixty-five with pure white hair. She remains absorbed in what she's saying as she descends the stairs and doesn't really notice the two men who continue sitting there as they were before she came down, smoking and husking.*

HALIE. He would've took care of us, too. He would've seen to it that we were repaid. He was like that. He was a hero. Don't forget that. A genuine hero. Brave. Strong. And very intelligent. Ansel could've been a great man. One of the greatest. I only regret that he didn't die in action. It's not fitting for man like that to die in a motel room. A soldier. He could've won a medal. He could've been decorated for valor. I've talked to Father Dewis about putting up a plaque for Ansel. He thinks it's a good idea. He agrees. He knew Ansel when he used to play basketball. Went to every game. Ansel was his favorite player. He even recommended to the City Council that they put up a statue of Ansel. A big, tall statue with a basketball in one hand and a rifle in the other. That's how much he thinks of Ansel.

HALIE *reaches the stage and begins to wander around, still absorbed in pulling on her gloves, brushing lint off her dress and continuously talking to herself as the men just sit.*

HALIE. Of course, he'd still be alive today if he hadn't married into the Catholics. The Mob. How in the world he never opened his eyes to that is beyond me. Just beyond me. Everyone around him could see the truth. Even Tilden. Tilden told him time and again. Catholic women are the Devil incarnate. He wouldn't listen. He was blind with love. Blind. I knew. Everyone knew. The wedding was more like a funeral. You remember? All those Italians. All that horrible black, greasy hair. The smell of cheap cologne. I think even the priest was wearing a pistol. When he gave her the ring I knew he was a dead man. I knew it. As soon as he gave her the ring. But then it was the honeymoon that killed him. The honeymoon. I knew he'd never come back from the honeymoon. I kissed him and he felt like a corpse. All white. Cold, Icey blue lips. He never used to kiss like that. Never before. I knew then that she'd cursed him. Taken his soul. I saw it in her eyes. She smiled at me with that Catholic sneer of hers. She told me with her eyes that she'd murder him in his bed. Murder my son. She told me. And there was nothing I could do. Absolutely nothing. He was going with her, thinking he was free. Thinking it was love. What could I do? I couldn't tell him she was a witch. I couldn't tell him that. He'd have turned on me. Hated me. I couldn't stand him hating me and then dying before he ever saw me again. Hating me in his death bed. Hating me and loving her! How could I do that? I had to let him go. I had to. I watched him leave. I watched him throw gardenias as he helped her into the limousine. I watched his face disappear behind the glass.

She stops abruptly and stares at the corn husks. She looks around the space as though just waking up. She turns and looks hard at TILDEN *and* DODGE *who continue sitting calmly. She looks at the corn husks.*

HALIE. (*pointing to the husks*) What's this in my house! (*kicks husks*) What's all this!

TILDEN *stops husking and stares at her.*

HALIE. (*to* DODGE) And you encourage him!

DODGE *pulls blanket over him again.*

DODGE. You're going out in the rain?

HALIE. It's not raining.

TILDEN *starts husking again.*

DODGE. Not in Florida it's not.

HALIE. We're not in Florida!

DODGE. It's not raining at the race track.

HALIE. Have you been taking those pills? Those pills always make you talk crazy. Tilden has he been taking those pills?

TILDEN. He hasn't took anything.

HALIE. (*to* DODGE) What've you been taking?

DODGE. It's not raining in California or Florida or the race track, only in Illinois. This is the only place it's raining. All over the rest of the world it's bright golden sunshine.

HALIE *goes to the night table next to the sofa and checks the bottle of pills.*

HALIE. Which ones did you take? Tilden, you must've seen him take something.

TILDEN. He never took a thing.

HALIE. Then why's he talking crazy?

TILDEN. I've been here the whole time.

HALIE. Then you've both been taking something!

TILDEN. I've just been husking the corn.

HALIE. Where'd you get that corn anyway? Why is the house suddenly full of corn?

DODGE. Bumper crop!

HALIE. (*moving center*) We haven't had corn here for over thirty years.

TILDEN. The whole back lot's full of corn. Far as the eye can see.

DODGE. (*to* HALIE) Things keep happening while you're upstairs, ya know. The world doesn't stop just because you're upstairs. Corn keeps growing. Rain keeps raining.

HALIE. I'm not unaware of the world around me! Thank you very much. It so happens that I have an over-all view from the upstairs. The back yard's in plain view of my window. And there's no corn to speak of. Absolutely none!

DODGE. Tilden wouldn't lie. If he says there's corn, there's corn.

HALIE. What's the meaning of this corn Tilden!

TILDEN. It's a mystery to me. I was out back there. And the rain was coming down. And I didn't feel like coming back inside. I didn't feel the cold so much. I didn't mind the wet. So I was just walking. I was muddy but I didn't mind the mud so much. And I looked up. And I saw this stand of corn. In fact I was standing in it. So, I was standing in it.

HALIE. There isn't any corn outside Tilden! There's no corn! Now, you must've either stolen this corn or you bought it.

DODGE. He doesn't have any money.

HALIE. (*to* TILDEN) So you stole it!

TILDEN. I didn't steal it. I don't want to get kicked out of Illinois. I was kicked out of New Mexico and I don't want to get kicked out of Illinois.

HALIE. You're going to get kicked out of this house, Tilden, if you don't tell me where you got that corn!

TILDEN *starts crying softly to himself but keeps husking corn. Pause.*

DODGE. (*to* HALIE) Why'd you have to tell him that? Who cares where he got the corn? Why'd you have to go and tell him that?

HALIE. (*to* DODGE) It's your fault you know! You're the one that's behind all this! I suppose you thought it'd be funny! Some joke! Cover the house with corn husks. You better get this cleaned up before Bradley sees it.

DODGE. Bradley's not getting in the front door!

HALIE. (*kicking husks, striding back and forth*) Bradley's going to be very upset when he sees this. He doesn't like to see the house in disarray. He can't stand it when one thing is out of place. The slightest thing. You know how he gets.

DODGE. Bradley doesn't even live here!

HALIE. It's his home as much as ours. He was born in this house!

DODGE. He was born in a hog wallow.

HALIE. Don't you say that! Don't you ever say that!

DODGE. He was born in a goddamn hog wallow! That's where he was born and that's where he belongs! He doesn't belong in this house!

HALIE. (*she stops*) I don't know what's come over you, Dodge. I don't know what in the world's come over you. You've become an evil man. You used to be a good man.

DODGE. Six of one, a half dozen of another.

HALIE. You sit here day and night, festering away! Decomposing! Smelling up the house with your putrid body! Hacking your head off til all hours of the morning! Thinking up mean, evil, stupid things to say about your own flesh and blood!

DODGE. He's not my flesh and blood! My flesh and blood's buried in the back yard!

They freeze. Long pause. The men stare at her.

HALIE. (*quietly*) That's enough, Dodge. That's quite enough. I'm going out now. I'm going to have lunch with Father Dewis. I'm going to ask him about a monument. A statue. At least a plaque.

She crosses to the door up right. She stops.

HALIE. If you need anything, ask Tilden. He's the oldest. I've left some money on the kitchen table.

DODGE. I don't need anything.

HALIE. No, I suppose not. (*she opens the door and looks out through porch*) Still raining. I love the smell just after it stops. The ground. I won't be too late.

She goes out door and closes it. She's still visible on the porch as she crosses toward stage left screen door. She stops in the middle of the porch, speaks to DODGE *but doesn't turn to him.*

HALIE. Dodge, tell Tilden not to go out in the back lot anymore. I don't want him back there in the rain.

DODGE. You tell him. He's sitting right here.

HALIE. He never listens to me Dodge. He's never listened to me in the past.

DODGE. I'll tell him.

HALIE. We have to watch him just like we used to now. Just like we always have. He's still a child.

DODGE. I'll watch him.

HALIE. Good.

She crosses to screen door, left, takes an umbrella off a hook and goes out the door. The door slams behind her. Long pause. TILDEN *husks corn, stares at pail.* DODGE *lights a cigarette, stares at T.V.*

TILDEN. (*still husking*) You shouldn't a told her that.

DODGE. (*staring at T.V.*) What?

TILDEN. What you told her. You know.

DODGE. What do you know about it?

TILDEN. I know. I know all about it. We all know.

DODGE. So what difference does it make? Everybody knows, everybody's forgot.

TILDEN. She hasn't forgot.

DODGE. She should've forgot.

TILDEN. It's different for a woman. She couldn't forget that. How could she forget that?

DODGE. I don't want to talk about it!

TILDEN. What do you want to talk about?

DODGE. I don't want to talk about anything! I don't want to talk about troubles or what happened fifty years ago or thirty years ago or the race track or Florida or the last time I seeded the corn! I don't want to talk!

TILDEN. You don't wanna die do you?

DODGE. No, I don't wanna die either.

TILDEN. Well, you gotta talk or you'll die.

DODGE. Who told you that?

TILDEN. That's what I know. I found that out in New Mexico. I thought I was dying but I just lost my voice.

DODGE. Were you with somebody?

TILDEN. I was alone. I thought I was dead.

DODGE. Might as well have been. What'd you come back here for.

TILDEN. I didn't know where to go.

DODGE. You're a grown man. You shouldn't be needing your parents at your age. It's un-natural. There's nothing we can do for you now anyway. Couldn't you make a living down there? Couldn't you find some way to make a living? Support yourself? What'd'ya come back here for? You expect us to feed you forever?

TILDEN. I didn't know where else to go.

DODGE. I never went back to my parents. Never. Never even had the urge. I was independent. Always independent. Always found a way.

TILDEN. I didn't know what to do. I couldn't figure anything out.

DODGE. There's nothing to figure out. You just forge ahead. What's there to figure out?

TILDEN *stands.*

TILDEN. I don't know.

DODGE. Where are you going?

TILDEN. Out back.

DODGE. You're not supposed to go out there. You heard what she said. Don't play deaf with me!

TILDEN. I like it out there.

DODGE. In the rain?

TILDEN. Especially in the rain. I like the feeling of it. Feels like it always did.

DODGE. You're supposed to watch out for me. Get me things when I need them.

TILDEN. What do you need?

DODGE. I don't need anything! But I might. I might need something any second. Any second now. I can't be left alone for a minute!

DODGE *starts to cough.*

TILDEN. I'll be right outside. You can just yell.

DODGE. (*between coughs*) No! It's too far! You can't go out there! It's too far! You might not ever hear me!

TILDEN. (*moving to pills*) Why don't you take a pill? You want a pill?
DODGE *coughs more violently, throws himself back against sofa, clutches his throat.* TILDEN *stands by helplessly.*

DODGE. Water! Get me some water!

TILDEN *rushes off left.* DODGE *reaches out for the pills, knocking some bottles to the floor, coughing in spasms. He grabs a small bottle, takes out pills and swallows them.* TILDEN *rushes back on with a glass of water.* DODGE *takes it and drinks, his coughing subsides.*

TILDEN. You all right now?

DODGE *nods. Drinks more water.* TILDEN *moves in closer to him.* DODGE *sets glass of water on the night table. His coughing is almost gone.*

TILDEN. Why don't you lay down for a while? Just rest a little.

TILDEN *helps* DODGE *lay down on the sofa. Covers him with blanket.*

DODGE. You're not going outside are you?

TILDEN. No.

DODGE. I don't want to wake up and find you not here.

TILDEN. I'll be here.

TILDEN *tucks blanket around* DODGE.

DODGE. You'll stay right here?

TILDEN. I'll stay in my chair.

DODGE. That's not a chair. That's my old milking stool.

TILDEN. I know.

DODGE. Don't call it a chair.

TILDEN. I won't.

TILDEN *tries to take* DODGE'S *baseball cap off.*

DODGE. What're you doing! Leave that on me! Don't take that offa me! That's my cap!

TILDEN *leaves the cap on* DODGE.

TILDEN. I know.

DODGE. Bradley'll shave my head if I don't have that on. That's my cap.

TILDEN. I know it is.

DODGE. Don't take my cap off.

TILDEN. I won't.

DODGE. You stay right here now.

TILDEN. (*sits on stool*) I will.

DODGE. Don't go outside. There's nothing out there.

TILDEN. I won't.

DODGE. Everything's in here. Everything you need. Money's on the table. T.V. Is the T.V. on?

TILDEN. Yeah.

DODGE. Turn it off! Turn the damn thing off! What's it doing on?

TILDEN. (*shuts off T.V., light goes out*) You left it on.

DODGE. Well turn it off.

TILDEN. (*sits on stool again*) It's off.

DODGE. Leave it off.

TILDEN. I will.

DODGE. When I fall asleep you can turn it on.

TILDEN. Okay.

DODGE. You can watch the ball game. Red Sox. You like the Red Sox don't you?

TILDEN. Yeah.

DODGE. You can watch the Red Sox. Pee Wee Reese. Pee Wee Reese. You remember Pee Wee Reese?

TILDEN. No.

DODGE. Was he with the Red Sox?

TILDEN. I don't know.

DODGE. Pee Wee Reese. (*falling asleep*) You can watch the Cardinals. You remember Stan Musial.

TILDEN. No.

DODGE. Stan Musial. (*falling into sleep*) Bases loaded. Top a' the sixth. Bases loaded. Runner on first and third. Big fat knuckle ball. Floater. Big as a blimp. Cracko! Ball just took off like a rocket. Just pulverized. I marked it. Marked it with my eyes. Straight between the clock and the Burma Shave ad. I was the first kid out there. First kid. I had to fight hard for that ball. I wouldn't give it up. They almost tore the ears right off me. But I wouldn't give it up.

DODGE *falls into deep sleep.* TILDEN *just sits staring at him for a while. Slowly he leans toward the sofa, checking to see if* DODGE *is well asleep. He reaches slowly under the cushion and pulls out the bottle of booze.* DODGE *sleeps soundly.* TILDEN *stands quietly, staring at* DODGE *as he uncaps the bottle and takes a long drink. He caps the bottle and sticks it in his hip pocket. He looks around at the husks on the floor and then back to* DODGE. *He moves center stage and gathers an armload of corn husks then crosses back to the sofa. He stands holding the husks over* DODGE *and*

looking down at him he gently spreads the corn husks over the whole length of DODGE'S *body. He stands back and looks at* DODGE. *Pulls out bottle, takes another drink, returns bottle to his hip pocket. He gathers more husks and repeats the procedure until the floor is clean of corn husks and* DODGE *is completely covered in them except for his head.* TILDEN *takes another long drink, stares at* DODGE *sleeping then quietly exits stage left. Long pause as the sound of rain continues.* DODGE *sleeps on. The figure of* BRADLEY *appears up left, outside the screen porch door. He holds a wet newspaper over his head as a protection from the rain. He seems to be struggling with the door then slips and almost falls to the ground.* DODGE *sleeps on, undisturbed.*

BRADLEY. Sonuvabitch! Sonuvagoddamnbitch!

BRADLEY *recovers his footing and makes it through the screen door onto the porch. He throws the newspaper down, shakes the water out of his hair, and brushes the rain off of his shoulders. He is a big man dressed in a grey sweat shirt, black suspenders, baggy dark blue pants and black janitor's shoes. His left leg is wooden, having been amputated above the knee. He moves with an exaggerated, almost mechanical limp. The squeaking sounds of leather and metal accompany his walk coming from the harness and hinges of the false leg. His arms and shoulders are extremely powerful and muscular due to a lifetime dependency on the upper torso doing all the work for the legs. He is about five years younger than* TILDEN. *He moves laboriously to the stage right door and enters, closing the door behind him. He doesn't notice* DODGE *at first. He moves toward the staircase.*

BRADLEY. (*calling to upstairs*) Mom!

He stops and listens. Turns upstage and sees DODGE *sleeping. Notices corn husks. He moves slowly toward sofa. Stops next to pail and looks into it. Looks at husks.* DODGE *stays asleep. Talks to himself.*

BRADLEY. What in the hell is this?

He looks at DODGE'S *sleeping face and shakes his head in disgust. He pulls out a pair of black electric hair clippers from his pocket. Unwinds the cord and crosses to the lamp. He jabs his wooden leg behind the knee, causing it to bend at the joint and awkwardly kneels to plug the cord into a floor outlet. He pulls himself to his feet again by using the sofa as leverage. He moves to* DODGE'S *head and again jabs his false leg. Goes down on one knee. He violently knocks away some of the corn husks then jerks off* DODGE'S *baseball cap and throws it down center stage.* DODGE *stays asleep.* BRADLEY *switches on the clippers. Lights start dimming.* BRADLEY *cuts* DODGE'S *hair while he sleeps. Lights dim slowly to black with the sound of clippers and rain.*

ACT 2

SCENE. *Same set as act 1. Night. Sound of rain.* DODGE *still asleep on sofa. His hair is cut extremely short and in places the scalp is cut and bleeding. His cap is still center stage. All the corn and husks, pail and milking stool have been cleared away. The lights come up to the sound of a young girl laughing off stage left.* DODGE *remains asleep.* SHELLY *and* VINCE *appear up left outside the screen porch door sharing the shelter of* VINCE'S *overcoat above their heads.* SHELLY *is about nineteen, black hair, very beautiful. She wears tight jeans, high heels, purple T-shirt and a short rabbit fur coat. Her makeup is exaggerated and her hair has been curled.* VINCE *is* TILDEN'S *son, about twenty-two, wears a plaid shirt, jeans, dark glasses, cowboy boots and carries a black saxophone case. They shake the rain off themselves as they enter the porch through the screen door.*

SHELLY. *(laughing, gesturing to house)* This is it? I don't believe this is it!

VINCE. This is it.

SHELLY. This is the house?

VINCE. This is the house.

SHELLY. I don't believe it!

VINCE. How come?

SHELLY. It's like a Norman Rockwell cover or something.

VINCE. What's a' matter with that? It's American.

SHELLY. Where's the milkman and the little dog? What's the little dog's name? Spot. Spot and Jane. Dick and Jane and Spot.

VINCE. Knock it off.

SHELLY. Dick and Jane and Spot and Mom and Dad and Junior and Sissy!

She laughs. Slaps her knee.

VINCE. Come on! It's my heritage. What dya' expect?

She laughs more hysterically, out of control.

SHELLY. "And Tuffy and Toto and Dooda and Bonzo all went down one day to the corner grocery store to buy a big bag of licorice for Mr. Marshall's pussy cat!"

She laughs so hard she falls to her knees holding her stomach. VINCE *stands there looking at her.*

VINCE. Shelly will you get up!

She keeps laughing. Staggers to her feet. Turning in circles holding her stomach.

SHELLY. *(continuing her story in kid's voice)* "Mr. Marshall was on vacation. He had no idea that the four little boys had taken such a liking to his little kitty cat."

VINCE. Have some respect would ya'!

SHELLY. *(trying to control herself)* I'm sorry.

VINCE. Pull yourself together.

SHELLY. *(salutes him)* Yes sir.

She giggles.

VINCE. Jesus Christ, Shelly.

SHELLY. *(pause, smiling)* And Mr. Marshall—

VINCE. Cut it out.

She stops. Stands there staring at him. Stifles a giggle.

VINCE. *(after pause)* Are you finished?

SHELLY. Oh brother!

VINCE. I don't wanna go in there with you acting like an idiot.

SHELLY. Thanks.

VINCE. Well, I don't.

SHELLY. I won't embarrass you. Don't worry.

VINCE. I'm not worried.

SHELLY. You are too.

VINCE. Shelly look, I just don't wanna go in there with you giggling your head off. They might think something's wrong with you.

SHELLY. There is.

VINCE. There is not!

SHELLY. Something's definitely wrong with me.

VINCE. There is not!

SHELLY. There's something wrong with you too.

VINCE. There's nothing wrong with me either!

SHELLY. You wanna know what's wrong with you?

VINCE. What?

SHELLY *laughs*.

VINCE. (*crosses back left toward screen door*) I'm leaving!

SHELLY. (*stops laughing*) Wait! Stop. Stop! (VINCE *stops*) What's wrong with you is that you take the situation too seriously.

VINCE. I just don't want to have them think that I've suddenly arrived out of the middle of nowhere completely deranged.

SHELLY. What do you want them to think then?

VINCE. (*pause*) Nothing. Let's go in.

He crosses porch toward stage right interior door. SHELLY *follows him.*

SHELLY. I mean I'll do anything you want. I'll pretend anything. I'm good at pretending. I can pretend I'm a Senator. How 'bout that?

They disappear from view behind the solid door. VINCE *knocks on the door.* DODGE *sleeps on.* VINCE *and* SHELLY'S *voices are heard without being seen.*

VINCE'S VOICE. Just do whatever you want! I don't care what you do.

SHELLY'S VOICE. I could tell them I'm a busboy. That's not so far fetched.

VINCE'S VOICE. Don't tell them anything, okay? Just let me do the talking.

The stage right door opens slowly. VINCE *sticks his head in, doesn't notice* DODGE *sleeping. Calls out toward staircase.*

VINCE. Grandma!

SHELLY *breaks into laughter, unseen behind* VINCE. VINCE *pulls his head back outside and pulls door shut. We hear their voices again without seeing them.*

SHELLY'S VOICE. (*stops laughing*) I'm sorry. I'm sorry Vince. I really am. I really am sorry. I won't do it again. I couldn't help it.

VINCE'S VOICE. It's not all that funny.

SHELLY'S VOICE. I know it's not. I'm sorry.

VINCE'S VOICE. I mean this is a tense situation for me! I haven't seen them for over six years. I don't know what to expect.

SHELLY'S VOICE. I know. I won't do it again.

VINCE'S VOICE. Can't you bite your tongue or something?

SHELLY'S VOICE. Just don't say "Grandma," okay? (*she giggles, stops*) I mean if you say "Grandma" I don't know if I can stop myself.

VINCE'S VOICE. Well try!

SHELLY'S VOICE. Okay. Sorry.

Door opens again. VINCE *sticks his head in then enters.* SHELLY *follows behind him.* VINCE *crosses to staircase, sets down saxophone case and overcoat, looks up staircase.* SHELLY *notices* DODGE'S *baseball cap. Crosses to it. Picks it up and puts it on her head.* VINCE *goes up the stairs and disappears at the top.* SHELLY *watches him then turns and sees* DODGE *on the sofa. She takes off the baseball cap.*

VINCE'S VOICE. (*from above stairs*) Grandma!

SHELLY *crosses over to* DODGE *slowly and stands next to him. She stands at his head, reaches out slowly and touches one of the cuts. The second she touches his head,* DODGE *jerks up to a sitting position on the sofa, eyes open.* SHELLY *gasps.* DODGE *looks at her, sees his cap in her hands, quickly puts his hand to his bare head. He glares at* SHELLY *then whips the cap out of her hands and puts it on.* SHELLY *backs away from him.* DODGE *stares at her.*

SHELLY. I'm uh—with Vince.

DODGE *just glares at her.*

SHELLY. He's upstairs.

DODGE *looks at the staircase then back to* SHELLY.

SHELLY. (*calling upstairs*) Vince!

VINCE'S VOICE. Just a second!

SHELLY. You better get down here!

VINCE'S VOICE. Just a minute! I'm looking at the pictures.

DODGE *keeps staring at her.*

585

SHELLY. (*to* DODGE) We just got here. Pouring rain on the freeway so we thought we'd stop by. I mean Vince was planning on stopping anyway. He wanted to see you. He said he hadn't seen you in a long time.

Pause. DODGE *just keeps staring at her.*

SHELLY. We were going all the way through to New Mexico. To see his father. I guess his father lives out there. We thought we'd stop by and see you on the way. Kill two birds with one stone, you know? (*she laughs,* DODGE *stares, she stops laughing*) I mean Vince has this thing about his family now. I guess it's a new thing with him. I kind of find it hard to relate to. But he feels it's important. You know. I mean he feels he wants to get to know you all again. After all this time.

Pause. DODGE *just stares at her. She moves nervously to staircase and yells up to* VINCE.

SHELLY. Vince will you come down here please!

VINCE *comes half way down the stairs.*

VINCE. I guess they went out for a while.

SHELLY *points to sofa and* DODGE. VINCE *turns and sees* DODGE. *He comes all the way down staircase and crosses to* DODGE. SHELLY *stays behind near staircase, keeping her distance.*

VINCE. Grandpa?

DODGE *looks up at him, not recognizing him.*

DODGE. Did you bring the whiskey?

VINCE *looks back at* SHELLY *then back to* DODGE.

VINCE. Grandpa, it's Vince. I'm Vince. Tilden's son. You remember?

DODGE *stares at him.*

DODGE. You didn't do what you told me. You didn't stay here with me.

VINCE. Grandpa, I haven't been here until just now. I just got here.

DODGE. You left. You went outside like we told you not to do. You went out there in back. In the rain.

VINCE *looks back at* SHELLY. *She moves slowly toward sofa.*

SHELLY. Is he okay?

VINCE. I don't know. (*takes off his shades*) Look, Grandpa, don't you remember me? Vince. Your Grandson.

DODGE *stares at him then takes off his baseball cap.*

DODGE. (*points to his head*) See what happens when you leave me alone? See that? That's what happens.

VINCE *looks at his head.* VINCE *reaches out to touch his head.* DODGE *slaps his hand away with the cap and puts it back on his head.*

VINCE. What's going on Grandpa? Where's Halie?

DODGE. Don't worry about her. She won't be back for days. She says she'll be back but she won't be. (*he starts laughing*) There's life in the old girl yet! (*stops laughing*)

VINCE. How did you do that to your head?

DODGE. I didn't do it! Don't be ridiculous!

VINCE. Well who did then?

Pause. DODGE *stares at* VINCE.

DODGE. Who do you think did it? Who do you think?

SHELLY *moves toward* VINCE.

SHELLY. Vince, maybe we oughta' go. I don't like this. I mean this isn't my idea of a good time.

VINCE. (*to* SHELLY) Just a second. (*to* DODGE) Grandpa, look, I just got here. I just now got here. I haven't been here for six years. I don't know anything that's happened.

Pause. DODGE *stares at him.*

DODGE. You don't know anything?

VINCE. No.

DODGE. Well that's good. That's good. It's much better not to know anything. Much, much better.

VINCE. Isn't there anybody here with you?

DODGE *turns slowly and looks off to stage left.*

DODGE. Tilden's here.

VINCE. No, Grandpa, Tilden's in New Mexico. That's where I was going. I'm going out there to see him.

DODGE *turns slowly back to* VINCE.

DODGE. Tilden's here.

VINCE *backs away and joins* SHELLY. DODGE *stares at them.*

SHELLY. Vince, why don't we spend the night in a motel and come back in the morning? We could have breakfast. Maybe everything would be different.

VINCE. Don't be scared. There's nothing to be scared of. He's just old.

SHELLY. I'm not scared!

DODGE. You two are not my idea of the perfect couple!

SHELLY. (*after pause*) Oh really? Why's that?

VINCE. Shh! Don't aggravate him.

DODGE. There's something wrong between the two of you. Something not compatible.

VINCE. Grandpa, where did Halie go? Maybe we should call her.

DODGE. What are you talking about? Do you know what you're talking about? Are you just talking for the sake of talking? Lubricating the gums?

VINCE. I'm trying to figure out what's going on here!

DODGE. Is that it?

VINCE. Yes. I mean I expected everything to be different.

DODGE. Who are you to expect anything? Who are you supposed to be?

VINCE. I'm Vince! Your Grandson!

DODGE. Vince. My Grandson.

VINCE. Tilden's son.

DODGE. Tilden's son, Vince.

VINCE. You haven't seen me for a long time.

DODGE. When was the last time?

VINCE. I don't remember.

DODGE. You don't remember?

VINCE. No.

DODGE. You don't remember. How am I supposed to remember if you don't remember?

SHELLY. Vince, come on. This isn't going to work out.

VINCE. (*to* SHELLY) Just take it easy.

SHELLY. I'm taking it easy! He doesn't even know who you are!

VINCE. (*crossing toward* DODGE) Grandpa, Look—

DODGE. Stay where you are! Keep your distance!

VINCE *stops. Looks back at* SHELLY *then to* DODGE.

SHELLY. Vince, this is really making me nervous. I mean he doesn't even want us here. He doesn't even like us.

DODGE. She's a beautiful girl.

VINCE. Thanks.

DODGE. Very Beautiful Girl.

SHELLY. Oh, my God.

DODGE. (*to* SHELLY) What's your name?

SHELLY. Shelly.

DODGE. Shelly. That's a man's name isn't it?

SHELLY. Not in this case.

DODGE. (*to* VINCE) She's a smart-ass too.

SHELLY. Vince! Can we go?

DODGE. She wants to go. She just got here and she wants to go.

VINCE. This is kind of strange for her.

DODGE. She'll get used to it. (*to* SHELLY) What part of the country do you come from?

SHELLY. Originally?

DODGE. That's right. Originally. At the very start.

SHELLY. L.A.

DODGE. L.A. Stupid country.

SHELLY. I can't stand this Vince! This is really unbelievable!

DODGE. It's stupid! L.A. is stupid! So is Florida! All those Sunshine States. They're all stupid! Do you know why they're stupid?

SHELLY. Illuminate me.

DODGE. I'll tell you why. Because they're full of smart-asses! That's why.

SHELLY *turns back to* DODGE, *crosses to staircase and sits on bottom step.*

DODGE. (*to* VINCE) Now she's insulted.

VINCE. Well you weren't very polite.

DODGE. She's insulted! Look at her! In my house she's insulted! She's over there sulking because I insulted her!

SHELLY. (*to* VINCE) This is really terrific. This is wonderful. And you were worried about me making the right first impression!

DODGE. (*to* VINCE) She's a fireball isn't she? Regular fireball. I had some a'them in my day. Temporary stuff. Never lasted more than a week.

VINCE. Grandpa—

DODGE. Stop calling me Grandpa will ya'! It's sickening. "Grandpa." I'm nobody's Grandpa!

DODGE *starts feeling around under the cushion for the bottle of whiskey.* SHELLY *gets up from the staircase.*

SHELLY. (*to* VINCE) Maybe you've got the wrong house. Did you ever think of that? Maybe this is the wrong address!

VINCE. It's not the wrong address! I recognize the yard.

SHELLY. Yeah but do you recognize the people? He says he's not your Grandfather.

DODGE. (*digging for bottle*) Where's that bottle!

VINCE. He's just sick or something. I don't know what's happened to him.

DODGE. Where's my goddamn bottle!

DODGE *gets up from sofa and starts tearing the cushions off it and throwing them downstage, looking for the whiskey.*

SHELLY. Can't we just drive on to New Mexico? This is terrible, Vince! I don't want to stay here. In this house. I thought it was going to be turkey dinners and apple pie and all that kinda stuff.

VINCE. Well I hate to disappoint you!

SHELLY. I'm not disappointed! I'm fuckin' terrified! I wanna' go!

DODGE *yells toward stage left.*

DODGE. Tilden! Tilden!

DODGE *keeps ripping away at the sofa looking for his bottle, he knocks over the night stand with the bottles.* VINCE *and* SHELLY *watch as he starts ripping the stuffing out of the sofa.*

VINCE. (*to* SHELLY) He's lost his mind or something. I've got to try to help him.

SHELLY. You help him! I'm leaving!

SHELLY *starts to leave.* VINCE *grabs her. They struggle as* DODGE *keeps ripping away at the sofa and yelling.*

DODGE. Tilden! Tilden get your ass in here! Tilden!

SHELLY. Let go of me!

VINCE. You're not going anywhere! You're going to stay right here!

SHELLY. Let go of me you sonuvabitch! I'm not your property!

Suddenly TILDEN *walks on from stage left just as he did before. This time his arms are full of carrots.* DODGE, VINCE *and* SHELLY *stop suddenly when they see him. They all stare at* TILDEN *as he crosses slowly center stage with the carrots and stops.* DODGE *sits on the sofa, exhausted.*

DODGE. (*panting, to* TILDEN) Where in the hell have you been?

TILDEN. Out back.

DODGE. Where's my bottle?

TILDEN. Gone.

TILDEN *and* VINCE *stare at each other.* SHELLY *backs away.*

DODGE. (*to* TILDEN) You stole my bottle!

VINCE. (*to* TILDEN) Dad?

TILDEN *just stares at* VINCE.

DODGE. You had no right to steal my bottle! No right at all!

VINCE. (*to* TILDEN) It's Vince. I'm Vince.

TILDEN *stares at* VINCE *then looks at* DODGE *then turns to* SHELLY.

TILDEN. (*after pause*) I picked these carrots. If anybody wants any carrots, I picked 'em.

SHELLY. (*to* VINCE) This is your father?

VINCE. (*to* TILDEN) Dad, what're you doing here?

TILDEN *just stares at* VINCE, *holding carrots,* DODGE *pulls the blanket back over himself.*

DODGE. (*to* TILDEN) You're going to have to get me another bottle! You gotta get me a bottle before Halie comes back! There's money on the table. (*points to stage left kitchen*)

TILDEN. (*shaking his head*) I'm not going down there. Into town.

SHELLY *crosses to* TILDEN. TILDEN *stares at her.*

SHELLY. (*to* TILDEN) Are you Vince's father?

TILDEN. (*to* SHELLY) Vince?

SHELLY. (*pointing to* VINCE) This is supposed to be your son! Is he your son? Do you recognize him? I'm just along for the ride here. I thought everybody knew each other!

TILDEN *stares at* VINCE. DODGE *wraps himself up in the blanket and sits on sofa staring at the floor.*

TILDEN. I had a son once but we buried him.

DODGE *quickly looks at* TILDEN. SHELLY *looks to* VINCE.

DODGE. You shut up about that! You don't know anything about that!

VINCE. Dad, I thought you were in New Mexico. We were going to drive down there and see you.

TILDEN. Long way to drive.

DODGE. (*to* TILDEN) You don't know anything about that! That happened before you were born! Long before!

VINCE. What's happened, Dad? What's going on here? I thought everything was all right. What's happened to Halie?

TILDEN. She left.

SHELLY. (*to* TILDEN) Do you want me to take those carrots for you?

TILDEN *stares at her. She moves in close to him. Holds out her arms.* TILDEN *stares at her arms then slowly dumps the carrots into her arms.* SHELLY *stands there holding the carrots.*

TILDEN. (*to* SHELLY) You like Carrots?

SHELLY. Sure. I like all kinds of vegetables.

DODGE. (*to* TILDEN) You gotta get me a bottle before Halie comes back!

DODGE *hits sofa with his fist.* VINCE *crosses up to* DODGE *and tries to console him.* SHELLY *and* TILDEN *stay facing each other.*

TILDEN. (*to* SHELLY) Back yard's full of carrots. Corn. Potatoes.

SHELLY. You're Vince's father, right?

TILDEN. All kinds of vegetables. You like vegetables?

SHELLY. (*laughs*) Yeah. I love vegetables.

TILDEN. We could cook these carrots ya' know. You could cut 'em up and we could cook 'em.

SHELLY. All right.

TILDEN. I'll get you a pail and a knife.

SHELLY. Okay.

TILDEN. I'll be right back. Don't go.

TILDEN *exits off stage left.* SHELLY *stands center, arms full of carrots.* VINCE *stands next to* DODGE. SHELLY *looks toward* VINCE *then down at the carrots.*

DODGE. (*to* VINCE) You could get me a bottle. (*pointing off left*) There's money on the table.

VINCE. Grandpa why don't you lay down for a while?

DODGE. I don't wanna lay down for a while! Every time I lay down something happens! (*whips off his cap, points at his head*) Look what happens! That's what happens! (*pulls his cap back on*) You go lie down and see what happens to you! See how you like it! They'll steal your bottle! They'll cut your hair! They'll murder your children! That's what'll happen.

VINCE. Just relax for a while.

DODGE. (*pause*) You could get me a bottle ya' know. There's nothing stopping you from getting me a bottle.

SHELLY. Why don't you get him a bottle Vince? Maybe it would help everybody identify each other.

DODGE. (*pointing to* SHELLY) There, see? She thinks you should get me a bottle.

VINCE *crosses to* SHELLY.

VINCE. What're you doing with those carrots.

SHELLY. I'm waiting for your father.

DODGE. She thinks you should get me a bottle!

VINCE. Shelly put the carrots down will ya'! We gotta deal with the situation here! I'm gonna need your help.

SHELLY. I'm helping.

VINCE. You're only adding to the problem! You're making things worse! Put the carrots down!

VINCE *tries to knock the carrots out of her arms. She turns away from him, protecting the carrots.*

SHELLY. Get away from me! Stop it!

VINCE *stands back from her. She turns to him still holding the carrots.*

VINCE. (*to* SHELLY) Why are you doing this! Are you trying to make fun of me? This is my family you know!

SHELLY. You coulda' fooled me! I'd just as soon not be here myself. I'd just as soon be a thousand miles from here. I'd rather be anywhere but here. You're the one who wants to stay. So I'll stay. I'll stay and I'll cut the carrots. And I'll cook the carrots. And I'll do whatever I have to do to survive. Just to make it through this.

VINCE. Put the carrots down Shelly.

TILDEN *enters from left with pail, milking stool and a knife. He sets the stool and pail center stage for* SHELLY. SHELLY *looks at* VINCE *then sits down on stool, sets the carrots on the floor and takes the knife from* TILDEN. *She looks at* VINCE *again then picks up a carrot, cuts the ends off, scrapes it and drops it in pail. She repeats this,* VINCE *glares at her. She smiles.*

DODGE. She could get me a bottle. She's the type a' girl that could get me a bottle. Easy. She'd go down there. Slink up to the counter. They'd probably give her two bottles for the price of one. She could do that.

SHELLY *laughs. Keeps cutting carrots.* VINCE *crosses up to* DODGE, *looks at him.* TILDEN *watches* SHELLY'S *hands. Long pause.*

VINCE. (*to* DODGE) I haven't changed that much. I mean physically. Physically I'm just about the same. Same size. Same weight. Everything's the same.

DODGE *keeps staring at* SHELLY *while* VINCE *talks to him.*

DODGE. She's a beautiful girl. Exceptional.

VINCE *moves in front of* DODGE *to block his view of* SHELLY. DODGE *keeps craning his head around to see her as* VINCE *demonstrates tricks from his past.*

VINCE. Look. Look at this. Do you remember this? I used to bend my thumb behind my knuckles. You remember? I used to do it at the dinner table.

VINCE *bends a thumb behind his knuckles for* DODGE *and holds it out to him.* DODGE *takes a short glance then looks back at* SHELLY. VINCE *shifts position and shows him something else.*

VINCE. What about this?

VINCE *curls his lips back and starts drumming on his teeth with his fingernails making little tapping sounds.* DODGE *watches a while.* TILDEN *turns toward the sound.* VINCE *keeps it up. He sees* TILDEN *taking notice and crosses to* TILDEN *as he drums on his teeth.* DODGE *turns T.V. on, watches it.*

VINCE. You remember this Dad?

VINCE *keeps on drumming for* TILDEN. TILDEN *watches a while, fascinated, then turns back to* SHELLY. VINCE *keeps up the drumming on his teeth, crosses back to* DODGE *doing it,* SHELLY *keeps working on carrots, talking to* TILDEN.

SHELLY. (*to* TILDEN) He drives me crazy with that sometimes.

VINCE. (*to* DODGE) I Know! Here's one you'll remember. You used to kick me out of the house for this one.

VINCE *pulls his shirt out of his belt and holds it tucked under his chin with his stomach exposed. He grabs the flesh on either side of his belly button and pushes it in and out to make it look like a mouth talking. He watches his belly button and makes a deep sounding cartoon voice to synchronize with the movement. He demonstrates it to* DODGE *then crosses down to* TILDEN *doing it. Both* DODGE *and* TILDEN *take short, uninterested glances then ignore him.*

VINCE. (*deep cartoon voice*) "Hello. How are you? I'm fine. Thank you very much. It's so good to see you looking well this fine Sunday morning. I was going down to the hardware to fetch a pail of water."

SHELLY. Vince, don't be pathetic will ya'!

VINCE *stops. Tucks his shirt back in.*

SHELLY. Jesus Christ. They're not gonna play. Can't you see that?

SHELLY *keeps cutting carrots.* VINCE *slowly moves toward* TILDEN. TILDEN *keeps watching* SHELLY. DODGE *watches T.V.*

VINCE. (*to* SHELLY) I don't get it. I really don't get it. Maybe it's me. Maybe I forgot something.

DODGE. (*from sofa*) You forgot to get me a bottle! That's what you forgot. Anybody in this house could get me a bottle. Anybody! But nobody will. Nobody understands the urgency! Peelin carrots is more important. Playin piano on your teeth! Well I hope you all remember this when you get up in years. When you find yourself immobilized. Dependent on the whims of others.

VINCE *moves up toward* DODGE. *Pause as he looks at him.*

VINCE. I'll get you a bottle.

DODGE. You will?

VINCE. Sure.

SHELLY *stands holding knife and carrot.*

SHELLY. You're not going to leave me here are you?

VINCE. (*moving to her*) You suggested it! You said, "why don't I go get him a bottle." So I'll go get him a bottle!

SHELLY. But I can't stay here.

VINCE. What is going on! A minute ago you were ready to cut carrots all night!

SHELLY. That was only if you stayed. Something to keep me busy, so I wouldn't be so nervous. I don't want to stay here alone.

DODGE. Don't let her talk you out of it! She's a bad influence. I could see it the minute she stepped in here.

SHELLY. (*to* DODGE) You were asleep!

TILDEN. (*to* SHELLY) Don't you want to cut carrots anymore?

SHELLY. Sure. Sure I do.

SHELLY *sits back down on stool and continues cutting carrots. Pause.* VINCE *moves around, stroking his hair, staring at* DODGE *and* TILDEN, VINCE *and* SHELLY *exchange glances.* DODGE *watches T.V.*

VINCE. Boy! This is amazing. This is truly amazing. (*keeps moving around*) What is this anyway? Am I in a time warp or something? Have I committed an unpardonable offence? It's true, I'm not married. (SHELLY *looks at him, then back to carrots*) But I'm also not divorced. I have been known to plunge into sinful infatuation with Alto Saxophone. Sucking on number 5 reeds deep into the wee wee hours. I did, luckily, avoid becoming a junkie by the skin of my teeth—

SHELLY. Vince, what are you doing that for? They don't care about any of that. They just don't recognize you, that's all.

VINCE. How could they not recognize me! How in the hell could they not recognize me! I'm their son!

DODGE. (*watching t.v.*) You're no son of mine. I've had sons in my time and you're not one of 'em.

Long pause. VINCE *stares at* DODGE *then looks at* TILDEN. *He turns to* SHELLY.

VINCE. Shelly, I gotta go out for a while. I just gotta go out. I'll get a bottle and I'll come right back. You'll be o.k. here. Really.

SHELLY. I don't know if I can handle this Vince.

VINCE. I just gotta think or something. I don't know. I gotta put this all together.

SHELLY. Can't we just go?

VINCE. No! I gotta find out what's going on.

SHELLY. Look, you think you're bad off, what about me? Not only don't they recognize me but I've never seen them before in my life. I don't know who these guys are. They could be anybody!

VINCE. They're not anybody!

SHELLY. That's what you say.

VINCE. They're my family for Christ's sake! I should know who my own family is! Now give me a break. It won't take that long. I'll just go out and I'll come right back. Nothing'll happen. I promise.

SHELLY *stares at him. Pause.*

SHELLY. All right.

VINCE. Thanks. (*he crosses up to* DODGE) I'm gonna go out now, Grandpa and I'll pick you up a bottle. Okay?

DODGE. Change of heart, huh? (*pointing off left*) Money's on the table. In the kitchen.

VINCE *moves toward* SHELLY.

VINCE. (*to* SHELLY) You be all right?

SHELLY. (*cutting carrots*) Sure. I'm fine. I'll just keep real busy while you're gone.

VINCE *looks at* TILDEN *who keeps staring down at* SHELLY'S *hands.*

DODGE. Persistence see? That's what it takes. Persistence. Persistence, fortitude and determination. Those are the three virtues. You stick with those three and you can't go wrong.

VINCE. (*to* TILDEN) You want anything, Dad?

TILDEN. (*looks up at* VINCE) Me?

VINCE. From the store? I'm gonna get grandpa a bottle.

TILDEN. He's not supposed to drink. Halie wouldn't like it.

VINCE. He wants a bottle.

TILDEN. He's not supposed to drink.

DODGE. (*to* VINCE) Don't negotiate with him! Don't make any transactions until you've spoken to me first! He'll steal you blind!

591

VINCE. (to DODGE) Tilden says you're not supposed to drink.

DODGE. Tilden's lost his marbles! Look at him! He's around the bend. Take a look at him.

VINCE *stares at* TILDEN. TILDEN *watches* SHELLY'S *hands as she keeps cutting carrots.*

DODGE. Now look at me. Look here at me!

VINCE *looks back to* DODGE.

DODGE. Now, between the two of us, who do you think is more trustworthy? Him or me? Can you trust a man who keeps bringing in vegetables from out of nowhere? Take a look at him.

VINCE *looks back at* TILDEN.

SHELLY. Go get the bottle Vince.

VINCE. (to SHELLY) You sure you'll be all right?

SHELLY. I'll be fine. I feel right at home now.

VINCE. You do?

SHELLY. I'm fine. Now that I've got the carrots everything is all right.

VINCE. I'll be right back.

VINCE *crosses stage left.*

DODGE. Where are you going?

VINCE. I'm going to get the money.

DODGE. Then where are you going?

VINCE. Liquor store.

DODGE. Don't go anyplace else. Don't go off some place and drink. Come right back here.

VINCE. I will.

VINCE *exits stage left.*

DODGE. (calling after VINCE) You've got responsibility now! And don't go out the back way either! Come out through this way! I wanna see you when you leave! Don't go out the back!

VINCE'S VOICE. (off left) I won't!

DODGE *turns and looks at* TILDEN *and* SHELLY.

DODGE. Untrustworthy. Probably drown himself if he went out the back. Fall right in a hole. I'd never get my bottle.

SHELLY. I wouldn't worry about Vince. He can take care of himself.

DODGE. Oh he can huh? Independent.

VINCE *comes on again from stage left with two dollars in his hand. He crosses stage right past* DODGE.

DODGE. (to VINCE) You get the money?

VINCE. Yeah. Two bucks.

DODGE. Two bucks. Two bucks is two bucks. Don't sneer.

VINCE. What kind do you want?

DODGE. Whiskey! Gold Star Sour Mash. Use your own discretion.

VINCE. Okay.

VINCE *crosses to stage right door. Opens it. Stops when he hears* TILDEN.

TILDEN. (to VINCE) You drove all the way from New Mexico?

VINCE *turns and looks at* TILDEN. *They stare at each other.* VINCE *shakes his head, goes out the door, crosses porch and exits out screen door.* TILDEN *watches him go. Pause.*

SHELLY. You really don't recognize him? Either one of you?

TILDEN *turns again and stares at* SHELLY'S *hands as she cuts carrots.*

DODGE. (watching t.v.) Recognize who?

SHELLY. Vince.

DODGE. What's to recognize?

DODGE *lights a cigarette, coughs slightly and stares at t.v.*

SHELLY. It'd be cruel if you recognized him and didn't tell him. Wouldn't be fair.

DODGE *just stares at t.v., smoking.*

TILDEN. I thought I recognized him. I thought I recognized something about him.

SHELLY. You did?

TILDEN. I thought I saw a face inside his face.

SHELLY. Well it was probably that you saw what he used to look like. You haven't seen him for six years.

TILDEN. I haven't?

SHELLY. That's what he says.

TILDEN *moves around in front of her as she continues with carrots.*

TILDEN. Where was it I saw him last?

SHELLY. I don't know. I've only known him for a few months. He doesn't tell me everything.

TILDEN. He doesn't?

SHELLY. Not stuff like that.

TILDEN. What does he tell you?

SHELLY. You mean in general?

TILDEN. Yeah.

TILDEN *moves around behind her.*

SHELLY. Well he tells me all kinds of things.

TILDEN. Like what?

SHELLY. I don't know! I mean I can't just come right out and tell you how he feels.

TILDEN. How come?

TILDEN *keeps moving around her slowly in a circle.*

SHELLY. Because it's stuff he told me privately!

TILDEN. And you can't tell me?

SHELLY. I don't even know you!

DODGE. Tilden, go out in the kitchen and make me some coffee! Leave the girl alone.

SHELLY. (*to* DODGE) He's all right.

TILDEN *ignores* DODGE, *keeps moving around* SHELLY. *He stares at her hair and coat.* DODGE *stares at t.v.*

TILDEN. You mean you can't tell me anything?

SHELLY. I can tell you some things. I mean we can have a conversation.

TILDEN. We can?

SHELLY. Sure. We are having a conversation right now.

TILDEN. We are?

SHELLY. Yes. That's what we're doing.

TILDEN. But there's certain things you can't tell me, right?

SHELLY. Right.

TILDEN. There's certain things I can't tell you either.

SHELLY. How come?

TILDEN. I don't know. Nobody's supposed to hear it.

SHELLY. Well, you can tell me anything you want to.

TILDEN. I can?

SHELLY. Sure.

TILDEN. It might not be very nice.

SHELLY. That's all right. I've been around.

TILDEN. It might be awful.

SHELLY. Well, can't you tell me anything nice?

TILDEN *stops in front of her and stares at her coat.* SHELLY *looks back at him. Long pause.*

TILDEN. (*after pause*) Can I touch your coat?

SHELLY. My coat? (*she looks at her coat then back to* TILDEN) Sure.

TILDEN. You don't mind?

SHELLY. No. Go ahead.

SHELLY *holds her arm out for* TILDEN *to touch.* DODGE *stays fixed on t.v.* TILDEN *moves in slowly toward* SHELLY, *staring at her arm. He reaches out very slowly and touches her arm, feels the fur gently then draws his hand back.* SHELLY *keeps her arm out.*

SHELLY. It's rabbit.

TILDEN. Rabbit.

He reaches out again very slowly and touches the fur on her arm then pulls back his hand again. SHELLY *drops her arm.*

SHELLY. My arm was getting tired.

TILDEN. Can I hold it?

SHELLY. (*pause*) The coat? Sure.

SHELLY *takes off her coat and hands it to* TILDEN. TILDEN *takes it slowly, feels the fur then puts it on.* SHELLY *watches as* TILDEN *strokes the fur slowly. He smiles at her. She goes back to cutting carrots.*

SHELLY. You can have it if you want.

TILDEN. I can?

SHELLY. Yeah. I've got a raincoat in the car. That's all I need.

TILDEN. You've got a car?

SHELLY. Vince does.

TILDEN *walks around stroking the fur and smiling at the coat.* SHELLY *watches him when he's not looking.* DODGE *sticks with t.v., stretches out on sofa wrapped in blanket.*

TILDEN. (*as he walks around*) I had a car once! I had a white car! I drove. I went everywhere. I went to the mountains. I drove in the snow.

SHELLY. That must've been fun.

TILDEN. (*still moving, feeling coat*) I drove all day long sometimes. Across the desert. Way out across the desert. I drove past towns. Anywhere. Past palm trees. Lightening. Anything. I would drive through it. I would drive through it and I would stop and I would look around and I would drive on. I would get back in and drive! I loved to drive. There was nothing I loved more. Nothing I dreamed of was better than driving.

DODGE. (*eyes on t.v.*) Pipe down would ya!

TILDEN *stops. Stares at* SHELLY.

SHELLY. Do you do much driving now?

TILDEN. Now? Now? I don't drive now.

SHELLY. How come?

TILDEN. I'm grown up now.

SHELLY. Grown up?

TILDEN. I'm not a kid.

SHELLY. You don't have to be a kid to drive.

TILDEN. It wasn't driving then.

SHELLY. What was it?

TILDEN. Adventure. I went everywhere.

SHELLY. Well you can still do that.

TILDEN. Not now.

SHELLY. Why not?

TILDEN. I just told you. You don't understand anything. If I told you something you wouldn't understand it.

SHELLY. Told me what?

TILDEN. Told you something that's true.

SHELLY. Like what?

TILDEN. Like a baby. Like a little tiny baby.

SHELLY. Like when you were little?

TILDEN. If I told you you'd make me give your coat back.

SHELLY. I won't. I promise. Tell me.

TILDEN. I can't. Dodge won't let me.

SHELLY. He won't hear you. It's okay.

Pause. TILDEN *stares at her. Moves slightly toward her.*

TILDEN. We had a baby. (*motioning to* DODGE) He did. Dodge did. Could pick it up with one hand. Put it in the other. Little baby. Dodge killed it.

SHELLY *stands.*

TILDEN. Don't stand up. Don't stand up!

SHELLY *sits again.* DODGE *sits up on sofa and looks at them.*

TILDEN. Dodge drowned it. Drowned it in the sink.

SHELLY. Don't tell me anymore! Okay?

TILDEN *moves closer to her.* DODGE *takes more interest.*

DODGE. Tilden? You leave that girl alone!

TILDEN. (*pays no attention*) Never told Halie. Never told anybody. Just drowned it.

DODGE. (*shuts off t.v.*) Tilden!

TILDEN. Nobody could find it. Just disappeared. Cops looked for it. Neighbors. Nobody could find it.

DODGE *struggles to get up from sofa.*

DODGE. Tilden, what're you telling her! Tilden!

DODGE *keeps struggling until he's standing.*

TILDEN. Finally everybody just gave up. Just stopped looking. Everybody had a different answer. Kidnap. Murder. Accident. Some kind of accident.

DODGE *struggles to walk toward* TILDEN *and falls.* TILDEN *ignores him.*

DODGE. Tilden you shut up! You shut up about it!

DODGE *starts coughing on the floor.* SHELLY *watches him from the stool.*

TILDEN. Little tiny baby just disappeared. It's not hard. It's so small. Almost invisible.

SHELLY *makes a move to help* DODGE. TILDEN *firmly pushes her back down on the stool.* DODGE *keeps coughing.*

TILDEN. He said he had his reasons. Said it went a long way back. But he wouldn't tell anybody.

594

DODGE. Tilden! Don't tell her anything! Don't tell her!

TILDEN. He's the only one who know where it's buried. The only one. Like a secret buried treasure. Won't tell any of us. Won't tell me or mother or even Bradley. Especially Bradley. Bradley tried to force it out of him but he wouldn't tell. Wouldn't even tell why he did it. One night he just did it.

DODGE'S *coughing subsides.* SHELLY *stays on stool staring at* DODGE. TILDEN *slowly takes* SHELLY'S *coat off and holds it out to her. Long pause.* SHELLY *sits there trembling.*

TILDEN. You probably want your coat back now.

SHELLY *stares at coat but doesn't move to take it. The sound of* BRADLEY'S *leg squeaking is heard off left. The others on stage remain still.* BRADLEY *appears up left outside the screen door wearing a yellow rain slicker. He enters through screen door, crosses porch to stage right door and enters stage. Closes door. Takes off rain slicker and shakes it out. He sees all the others and stops.* TILDEN *turns to him.* BRADLEY *stares at* SHELLY. DODGE *remains on floor.*

BRADLEY. What's going on here? (*motioning to* SHELLY) Who's that?

SHELLY *stands, moves back away from* BRADLEY *as he crosses toward her. He stops next to* TILDEN. *He sees coat in* TILDEN'S *hand and grabs it away from him.*

BRADLEY. Who's she supposed to be?

TILDEN. She's driving to New Mexico.

BRADLEY *stares at her.* SHELLY *is frozen.* BRADLEY *limps over to her with the coat in his fist. He stops in front of her.*

BRADLEY. (*to* SHELLY *after pause*) Vacation?

SHELLY *shakes her head "no", trembling.*

BRADLEY. (*to* SHELLY *motioning to* TILDEN) You taking him with you?

SHELLY *shakes her head "no".* BRADLEY *crosses back to* TILDEN.

BRADLEY. You oughta'. No use leaving him here. Doesn't do a lick a' work. Doesn't raise a finger. (*stopping, to* TILDEN) Do ya'. (*to* SHELLY) 'Course he used to be an All American. Quarterback or Fullback or somethin'. He tell you that?

SHELLY *shakes her head "no".*

BRADLEY. Yeah, he used to be a big deal. Wore lettermen's sweaters. Had medals hanging all around

his neck. Real purty. Big deal. (*he laughs to himself, notices* DODGE *on floor, crosses to him, stops*) This one too. (*to* SHELLY) You'd never think it to look at him would ya'? All boney and wasted away.

SHELLY *shakes her head again.* BRADLEY *stares at her, crosses back to her, clenching the coat in his fist. He stops in front of* SHELLY.

BRADLEY. Women like that kinda' thing don't they?

SHELLY. What?

BRADLEY. Importance. Importance in a man?

SHELLY. I don't know.

BRADLEY. Yeah. You know, you know. Don't give me that. (*moves closer to* SHELLY) You're with Tilden?

SHELLY. No.

BRADLEY. (*turning to* TILDEN) Tilden! She with you?

TILDEN *doesn't answer. Stares at floor.*

BRADLEY. Tilden!

TILDEN *suddenly bolts and runs off up stage left.* BRADLEY *laughs. Talks to* SHELLY. DODGE *starts moving his lips silently as though talking to someone invisible on the floor.*

BRADLEY. (*laughing*) Scared to death! He was always scared!

BRADLEY *stops laughing. Stares at* SHELLY.

BRADLEY. You're scared too, right? (*laughs again*) You're scared and you don't even know me. (*stops laughing*) You don't gotta be scared.

SHELLY *looks at* DODGE *on the floor.*

SHELLY. Can't we do something for him?

BRADLEY. (*looking at* DODGE) We could shoot him. (*laughs*) We could drown him! What about drowning him?

SHELLY. Shut up!

BRADLEY *stops laughing. Moves in closer to* SHELLY. *She freezes.* BRADLEY *speaks slowly and deliberately.*

BRADLEY. Hey! Missus. Don't talk to me like that. Don't talk to me in that tone a' voice. There was a time when I had to take that tone a' voice from pretty near everyone. (*motioning to* DODGE) Him, for one! Him and that half brain that just ran outa' here. They don't talk to me like that now. Not any more. Everything's turned around now. Full circle. Isn't that funny?

SHELLY. I'm sorry.

BRADLEY. Open your mouth.

SHELLY. What?

BRADLEY. (motioning for her to open her mouth) Open up.

She opens her mouth slightly.

BRADLEY. Wider.

She opens her mouth wider.

BRADLEY. Keep it like that.

She does. Stares at BRADLEY. With his free hand he puts his fingers into her mouth. She tries to pull away.

BRADLEY. Just stay put!

She freezes. He keeps his fingers in her mouth. Stares at her. Pause. He pulls his hand out. She closes her mouth, keeps her eyes on him. BRADLEY smiles. He looks at DODGE on the floor and crosses over to him. SHELLY watches him closely. BRADLEY stands over DODGE and smiles at SHELLY. He holds her coat up in both hands over DODGE, keeps smiling at SHELLY. He looks down at DODGE then drops the coat so that it lands on DODGE and covers his head. BRADLEY keeps his hands up in the position of holding the coat, looks over at SHELLY and smiles. The lights black out.

ACT 3

SCENE. *Same set. Morning. Bright sun. No sound of rain. Everything has been cleared up again. No sign of carrots. No pail. No stool. VINCE'S saxophone case and overcoat are still at the foot of the staircase. BRADLEY is asleep on the sofa under DODGE'S blanket. His head toward stage left. BRADLEY'S wooden leg is leaning against the sofa right by his head. The shoe is left on it. The harness hangs down. DODGE is sitting on the floor, propped up against the t.v. set facing stage left wearing his baseball cap. SHELLY'S rabbit fur coat covers his chest and shoulders. He stares off toward stage left. He seems weaker and more disoriented. The lights rise slowly to the sound of birds and remain for a while in silence on the two men. BRADLEY sleeps very soundly. DODGE hardly moves. SHELLY appears from stage left with a big smile, slowly crossing toward DODGE balancing a steaming cup of broth in a saucer. DODGE just stares at her as she gets close to him.*

SHELLY. (*as she crosses*) This is going to make all the difference in the world, Grandpa. You don't mind me calling you Grandpa do you? I mean I know you minded when Vince called you that but you don't even know him.

DODGE. He skipped town with my money ya' know. I'm gonna hold you as collateral.

SHELLY. He'll be back. Don't you worry.

She kneels down next to DODGE and puts the cup and saucer in his lap.

DODGE. It's morning already! Not only didn't I get my bottle but he's got my two bucks!

SHELLY. Try to drink this, okay? Don't spill it.

DODGE. What is it?

SHELLY. Beef bouillon. It'll warm you up.

DODGE. Bouillon! I don't want any goddamn bouillon! Get that stuff away from me!

SHELLY. I just got through making it.

DODGE. I don't care if you just spent all week making it! I ain't drinking it!

SHELLY. Well, what am I supposed to do with it then? I'm trying to help you out. Besides, it's good for you.

DODGE. Get it away from me!

SHELLY *stands up with cup and saucer.*

DODGE. What do you know what's good for me anyway?

She looks at DODGE then turns away from him, crossing to staircase, sits on bottom step and drinks the bouillon. DODGE stares at her.

DODGE. You know what'd be good for me?

SHELLY. What?

DODGE. A little massage. A little contact.

SHELLY. On no. I've had enough contact for a while. Thanks anyway.

She keeps sipping bouillon, stays sitting. Pause as DODGE stares at her.

DODGE. Why not? You got nothing better to do. That fella's not gonna be back here. You're not expecting him to show up again are you?

SHELLY. Sure. He'll shown up. He left his horn here.

DODGE. His horn? (*laughs*) You're his horn?

SHELLY. Very funny.

DODGE. He's run off with my money! He's not coming back here.

SHELLY. He'll be back.

DODGE. You're a funny chicken, you know that?

SHELLY. Thanks.

DODGE. Full of faith. Hope. Faith and hope. You're all alike you hopers. If it's not God then it's a man. If it's not a man then it's a woman. If it's not a woman then it's the land or the future of some kind. Some kind of future.

Pause.

SHELLY. (*looking toward porch*) I'm glad it stopped raining.

DODGE. (*looks toward porch then back to her*) That's what I mean. See, you're glad it stopped raining. Now you think everything's gonna be different. Just 'cause the sun comes out.

SHELLY. It's already different. Last night I was scared.

DODGE. Scared a' what?

SHELLY. Just scared.

DODGE. Bradley? (*looks at* BRADLEY) He's a push-over 'Specially now. All ya' gotta' do is take his leg and throw it out the back door. Helpless. Totally helpless.

SHELLY *turns and stares at* BRADLEY'S *wooden leg then looks at* DODGE. *She sips bouillon.*

SHELLY. You'd do that?

DODGE. Me? I've hardly got the strength to breath.

SHELLY. But you'd actually do it if you could?

DODGE. Don't be so easily shocked, girlie. There's nothing a man can't do. You dream it up and he can do it. Anything.

SHELLY. You've tried I guess.

DODGE. Don't sit there sippin' your bouillon and judging me! This is my house!

SHELLY. I forgot.

DODGE. You forgot? Whose house did you think it was?

SHELLY. Mine.

DODGE *just stares at her. Long pause. She sips from cup.*

SHELLY. I know it's not mine but I had that feeling.

DODGE. What feeling?

SHELLY. The feeling that nobody lives here but me. I mean everybody's gone. You're here, but it doesn't seem like you're supposed to be. (*pointing to* BRADLEY) Doesn't seem like he's supposed to be here either. I don't know what it is. It's the house or something. Something familiar. Like I know my way around here. Did you ever get that feeling?

DODGE *stares at her in silence. Pause.*

DODGE. No. No, I never did.

SHELLY *gets up. Moves around space holding cup.*

SHELLY. Last night I went to sleep up there in that room.

DODGE. What room?

SHELLY. That room up there with all the pictures. All the crosses on the wall.

DODGE. Halie's room?

SHELLY. Yeah. Whoever "Halie" is.

DODGE. She's my wife.

SHELLY. So you remember her?

DODGE. Whad'ya mean! 'Course I remember her! She's only been gone for a day—half a day. However long it's been.

SHELLY. Do you remember her when her hair was bright red? Standing in front of an apple tree?

DODGE. What is this, the third degree or something! Who're you to be askin' me personal questions about my wife!

SHELLY. You never look at those pictures up there?

DODGE. What pictures!

SHELLY. Your whole life's up there hanging on the wall. Somebody who looks just like you. Somebody who looks just like you used to look.

DODGE. That isn't me! That never was me! This is me. Right here. This is it. The whole shootin' match, sittin' right in front of you.

SHELLY. So the past never happened as far as you're concerned?

DODGE. The past? Jesus Christ. The past. What do you know about the past?

SHELLY. Not much. I know there was a farm.

Pause.

DODGE. A farm?

SHELLY. There's a picture of a farm. A big farm. A bull. Wheat. Corn.

DODGE. Corn?

SHELLY. All the kids are standing out in the corn. They're all waving these big straw hats. One of them doesn't have a hat.

DODGE. Which one was that?

SHELLY. There's a baby. A baby in a woman's arms. The same woman with red hair. She looks lost standing out there. Like she doesn't know how she got there.

DODGE. She knows! I told her a hundred times it wasn't gonna' be the city! I gave her plenty a' warning.

SHELLY. She's looking down at the baby like it was somebody else's. Like it didn't even belong to her.

DODGE. That's about enough outa' you! You got some funny ideas. Some damn funny ideas. You think just because people propogate they have to love their offspring? You never seen a bitch eat her puppies? Where are you from anyway?

SHELLY. L.A. We already went through that.

DODGE. That's right, L.A. I remember.

SHELLY. Stupid country.

DODGE. That's right! No wonder.

Pause.

SHELLY. What's happened to this family anyway?

DODGE. You're in no position to ask! What do you care? You some kinda' Social Worker?

SHELLY. I'm Vince's friend.

DODGE. Vince's friend! That's rich. That's really rich. "Vince"! "Mr. Vince"! "Mr. Thief" is more like it! His name doesn't mean a hoot in hell to me. Not a tinkle in the well. You know how many kids I've spawned? Not to mention Grand kids and Great Grand kids and Great Great Grand kids after them?

SHELLY. And you don't remember any of them?

DODGE. What's to remember? Halie's the one with the family album. She's the one you should talk to. She'll set you straight on the heritage if that's what you're interested in. She's traced it all the way back to the grave.

SHELLY. What do you mean?

DODGE. What do you think I mean? How far back can you go? A long line of corpses! There's not a living soul behind me. Not a one. Who's holding me in their memory? Who gives a damn about bones in the ground?

SHELLY. Was Tilden telling the truth?

DODGE *stops short. Stares at* SHELLY. *Shakes his head. He looks off stage left.*

SHELLY. Was he?

DODGE'S *tone changes drastically.*

DODGE. Tilden? (*turns to* SHELLY, *calmly*) Where is Tilden?

SHELLY. Last night. Was he telling the truth about the baby?

Pause.

DODGE. (*turns toward stage left*) What's happened to Tilden? Why isn't Tilden here?

SHELLY. Bradley chased him out.

DODGE. (*looking at* BRADLEY *asleep*) Bradley? Why is he on my sofa? (*turns back to* SHELLY) Have I been here all night? On the floor?

SHELLY. He wouldn't leave. I hid outside until he fell asleep.

DODGE. Outside? Is Tilden outside? He shouldn't be out there in the rain. He'll get himself into trouble. He doesn't know his way around here anymore. Not like he used to. He went out West and got himself into trouble. Got himself into bad trouble. We don't want any of that around here.

SHELLY. What did he do?

Pause.

DODGE. (*quietly stares at* SHELLY) Tilden? He got mixed up. That's what he did. We can't afford to leave him alone. Not now.

Sound of HALIE *laughing comes from off left.* SHELLY *stands, looking in direction of voice, holding cup and saucer, doesn't know whether to stay or run.*

DODGE. (*motioning to* SHELLY) Sit down! Sit back down!

SHELLY *sits. Sound of* HALIE'S *laughter again.*

DODGE. (*to* SHELLY *in a heavy whisper, pulling coat up around him*) Don't leave me alone now! Promise me? Don't go off and leave me alone. I need somebody here with me. Tilden's gone now and I need someone. Don't leave me! Promise!

SHELLY. (*sitting*) I won't.

HALIE *appears outside the screen porch door, up left with* FATHER DEWIS. *She is wearing a bright yellow dress, no hat, white gloves and her arms are full of yellow roses.* FATHER DEWIS *is dressed in traditional black suit, white clerical collar and shirt. He is a very distinguished grey haired man in his sixties. They are both slightly drunk and feeling giddy. As they enter the porch through the screen door,* DODGE *pulls the rabbit coat over his head and hides.* SHELLY *stands again.* DODGE *drops the coat and whispers intensely to* SHELLY. *Neither* HALIE *nor* FATHER DEWIS *are aware of the people inside the house.*

DODGE. (*to* SHELLY *in a strong whisper*) You promised!

SHELLY *sits on stairs again.* DODGE *pulls coat back over his head.* HALIE *and* FATHER DEWIS *talk on the porch as they cross toward stage right interior door.*

HALIE. Oh Father! That's terrible! That's absolutely terrible. Aren't you afraid of being punished?

She giggles.

DEWIS. Not by the Italians. They're too busy punishing each other.

They both break out in giggles.

HALIE. What about God?

DEWIS. Well, prayerfully, God only hears what he wants to. That's just between you and me of course. In our heart of hearts we know we're every bit as wicked as the Catholics.

They giggle again and reach the stage right door.

HALIE. Father, I never heard you talk like this in Sunday sermon.

DEWIS. Well, I save all my best jokes for private company. Pearls before swine you know.

They enter the room laughing and stop when they see SHELLY. SHELLY *stands.* HALIE *closes the door behind* FATHER DEWIS. DODGE'S *voice is heard under the coat, talking to* SHELLY.

DODGE. (*under coat, to* SHELLY) Sit down, sit down! Don't let 'em buffalo you!

SHELLY *sits on stair again.* HALIE *looks at* DODGE *on the floor then looks at* BRADLEY *asleep on sofa and sees his wooden leg. She lets out a shriek of embarrassment for* FATHER DEWIS.

HALIE. Oh my gracious! What in the name of Judas Priest is going on in this house!

She hands over the roses to FATHER DEWIS.

HALIE. Excuse me Father.

HALIE *crosses to* DODGE, *whips the coat off him and covers the wooden leg with it.* BRADLEY *stays asleep.*

HALIE. You can't leave this house for a second without the Devil blowing in through the front door!

DODGE. Gimme back that coat! Gimme back that goddamn coat before I freeze to death!

HALIE. You're not going to freeze! The sun's out in case you hadn't noticed!

DODGE. Gimme back that coat! That coat's for live flesh not dead wood!

HALIE *whips the blanket off* BRADLEY *and throws it on* DODGE. DODGE *covers his head again with blanket.* BRADLEY'S *amputated leg can be faked by having half of it under a cushion of the sofa. He's fully clothed.* BRADLEY *sits up with a jerk when the blanket comes off him.*

HALIE. (*as she tosses blanket*) Here! Use this! It's yours anyway! Can't you take care of yourself for once!

BRADLEY. (*yelling at* HALIE) Gimme that blanket! Gimme back that blanket! That's my blanket!

HALIE *crosses back toward* FATHER DEWIS *who just stands there with the roses.* BRADLEY *thrashes helplessly on the sofa trying to reach blanket.* DODGE *hides himself deeper in blanket.* SHELLY *looks on from staircase still holding cup and saucer.*

HALIE. Believe me, Father, this is not what I had in mind when I invited you in.

DEWIS. Oh, no apologies please. I wouldn't be in the ministry if I couldn't face real life.

He laughs self-consciously. HALIE *notices* SHELLY *again and crosses over to her.* SHELLY *stays sitting.* HALIE *stops and stares at her.*

BRADLEY. I want my blanket back! Gimme my blanket!

HALIE *turns toward* BRADLEY *and silences him.*

HALIE. Shut up Bradley! Right this minute! I've had enough!

BRADLEY *slowly recoils, lies back down on sofa, turns his back toward* HALIE *and whimpers softly.* HALIE *directs her attention to* SHELLY *again. Pause.*

HALIE. (*to* SHELLY) What're you doing with my cup and saucer?

SHELLY. (*looking at cup, back to* HALIE) I made some bouillon for Dodge.

HALIE. For Dodge?

SHELLY. Yeah.

HALIE. Well, did he drink it?

SHELLY. No.

HALIE. Did you drink it?

SHELLY. Yes.

HALIE *stares at her. Long pause. She turns abruptly away from* SHELLY *and crosses back to* FATHER DEWIS.

HALIE. Father, there's a stranger in my house. What would you advise? What would be the Christian thing?

DEWIS. (*squirming*) Oh, well . . . I . . . . I really—

HALIE. We still have some whiskey, don't we?

DODGE *slowly pulls the blanket down off his head and looks toward* FATHER DEWIS. SHELLY *stands.*

SHELLY. Listen, I don't drink or anything. I just—

HALIE *turns toward* SHELLY *viciously.*

HALIE. You sit back down!

SHELLY *sits again on stair.* HALIE *turns again to* DEWIS.

HALIE. I think we have plenty of whiskey left! Don't we Father?

DEWIS. Well, yes. I think so. You'll have to get it. My hands are full.

HALIE *giggles. Reaches into* DEWIS'S *pockets, searching for bottle. She smells the roses as she searches.* DEWIS *stands stiffly.* DODGE *watches* HALIE *closely as she looks for bottle.*

HALIE. The most incredible things, roses! Aren't they incredible, Father?

DEWIS. Yes. Yes they are.

HALIE. They almost cover the stench of sin in this house. Just magnificent! The smell. We'll have to put some at the foot of Ansel's statue. On the day of the unveiling.

HALIE *finds a silver flask of whiskey in* DEWIS'S *vest pocket. She pulls it out.* DODGE *looks on eagerly.* HALIE *crosses to* DODGE, *opens the flask and takes a sip.*

HALIE. (*to* DODGE) Ansel's getting a statue, Dodge. Did you know that? Not a plaque but a real live statue. A full bronze. Tip to toe. A basketball in one hand and a rifle in the other.

BRADLEY. (*his back to* HALIE) He never played basketball!

HALIE. You shut up, Bradley! You shut up about Ansel! Ansel played basketball better than anyone! And you know it! He was an All American! There's no reason to take the glory away from others.

HALIE *turns away from* BRADLEY, *crosses back toward* DEWIS *sipping on the flask and smiling.*

HALIE. (*to* DEWIS) Ansel was a great basketball player. One of the greatest.

DEWIS. I remember Ansel.

HALIE. Of course! You remember. You remember how he could play. (*she turns toward* SHELLY) Of course, nowadays they play a different brand of basketball. More vicious. Isn't that right, dear?

SHELLY. I don't know.

HALIE *crosses to* SHELLY, *sipping on flask. She stops in front of* SHELLY.

HALIE. Much, much more vicious. They smash into each other. They knock each other's teeth out. There's blood all over the court. Savages.

HALIE *takes the cup from* SHELLY *and pours whiskey into it.*

HALIE. They don't train like they used to. Not at all. They allow themselves to run amuck. Drugs and women. Women mostly.

HALIE *hands the cup of whiskey back to* SHELLY *slowly.* SHELLY *takes it.*

HALIE. Mostly women. Girls. Sad, pathetic little girls. (*she crosses back to* FATHER DEWIS) It's just a reflection of the time, don't you think Father? An indication of where we stand?

DEWIS. I suppose so, yes.

HALIE. Yes. A sort of bad omen. Our youth becoming monsters.

DEWIS. Well, I uh—

HALIE. Oh you can disagree with me if you want to, Father. I'm open to debate. I think argument only enriches both sides of the question don't you? (*she moves toward* DODGE) I suppose, in the long run, it doesn't matter. When you see the way things deteriorate before your very eyes. Everything running down hill. It's kind of silly to even think about youth.

DEWIS. No, I don't think so. I think it's important to believe in certain things.

HALIE. Yes. Yes, I know what you mean. I think that's right. I think that's true. (*she looks at* DODGE) Certain basic things. We can't shake certain basic things. We might end up crazy. Like my husband. You can see it in his eyes. You can see how mad he is.

DODGE *covers his head with the blanket again.* HALIE *takes a single rose from* DEWIS *and moves slowly over to* DODGE.

HALIE. We can't not believe in something. We can't stop believing. We just end up dying if we stop. Just end up dead.

HALIE *throws the rose gently onto* DODGE'S *blanket. It lands between his knees and stays there! Long pause as* HALIE *stares at the roses.* SHELLY *stands suddenly.* HALIE *doesn't turn to her but keeps staring at rose.*

SHELLY. (*to* HALIE) Don't you wanna' know who I am! Don't you wanna' know what I'm doing here! I'm not dead!

SHELLY *crosses toward* HALIE. HALIE *turns slowly toward her.*

HALIE. Did you drink your whiskey?

SHELLY. No! And I'm not going to either!

HALIE. Well that's a firm stand. It's good to have a firm stand.

SHELLY. I don't have any stand at all. I'm just trying to put all this together.

HALIE *laughs and crosses back to* DEWIS.

HALIE. (*to* DEWIS) Surprises, surprises! Did you have any idea we'd be returning to this?

SHELLY. I came here with your Grandson for a little visit! A little innocent friendly visit.

HALIE. My Grandson?

SHELLY. Yes! That's right. The one no one remembers.

HALIE. (*to* DEWIS) This is getting a little far fetched.

SHELLY. I told him it was stupid to come back here. To try to pick up from where he left off.

HALIE. Where was that?

SHELLY. Wherever he was when he left here! Six years ago! Ten years ago! Whenever it was. I told him nobody cares.

HALIE. Didn't he listen?

SHELLY. No! No he didn't. We had to stop off at every tiny little meatball town that he remembered from his boyhood! Every stupid little donut shop he ever kissed a girl in. Every Drive-In. Every Drag Strip. Every football field he ever broke a bone on.

HALIE. (*suddenly alarmed, to* DODGE) Where's Tilden?

SHELLY. Don't ignore me!

HALIE. Dodge! Where's Tilden gone?

SHELLY *moves violently toward* HALIE.

SHELLY. (*to* HALIE) I'm talking to you!

BRADLEY *sits up fast on the sofa,* SHELLY *backs away.*

BRADLEY. (*to* SHELLY) Don't you yell at my mother!

HALIE. Dodge! (*she kicks* DODGE) I told you not to let Tilden out of your sight! Where's he gone to!

DODGE. Gimme a drink and I'll tell ya'.

DEWIS. Halie, maybe this isn't the right time for a visit.

HALIE *crosses back to* DEWIS.

HALIE. (*to* DEWIS) I never should've left. I never, never should've left! Tilden could be anywhere by now! Anywhere! He's not in control of his faculties. Dodge knew that. I told him when I left here. I told him specifically to watch out for Tilden.

BRADLEY *reaches down, grabs* DODGE'S *blanket and yanks it off him. He lays down on sofa and pulls the blanket over his head.*

DODGE. He's got my blanket again! He's got my blanket!

HALIE. (*turning to* BRADLEY) Bradley! Bradley, put that blanket back!

HALIE *moves toward* BRADLEY. SHELLY *suddenly throw the cup and saucer against the stage right door.* DEWIS *ducks. The cup and saucer smash into pieces.* HALIE *stops, turns toward* SHELLY. *Everyone freezes.* BRADLEY *slowly pulls his head out from under blanket, looks toward stage right door, then to* SHELLY. SHELLY *stares at* HALIE. DEWIS *cowers with roses.* SHELLY *moves slowly toward* HALIE. *Long pause.* SHELLY *speaks softly.*

SHELLY. (*to* HALIE) I don't like being ignored. I don't like being treated like I'm not here. I didn't like it when I was a kid and I still don't like it.

BRADLEY. (*sitting up on sofa*) We don't have to tell you anything, girl. Not a thing. You're not the police are you? You're not the government. You're just some prostitute that Tilden brought in here.

HALIE. Language! I won't have that language in my house!

SHELLY. (*to* BRADLEY) You stuck your hand in my mouth and you call me a prostitute!

HALIE. Bradley! Did you put your hand in her mouth? I'm ashamed of you. I can't leave you alone for a minute.

BRADLEY. I never did. She's lying!

DEWIS. Halie, I think I'll be running along now. I'll just put the roses in the kitchen.

DEWIS *moves toward stage left.* HALIE *stops him.*

HALIE. Don't go now, Father! Not now.

BRADLEY. I never did anything, mom! I never touched her! She propositioned me! And I turned her down. I turned her down flat!

SHELLY *suddenly grabs her coat off the wooden leg and takes both the leg and coat down stage, away from* BRADLEY.

BRADLEY. Mom! Mom! She's got my leg! She's taken my leg! I never did anything to her! She's stolen my leg!

BRADLEY *reaches pathetically in the air for his leg.* SHELLY *sets it down for a second, puts on her coat fast and picks the leg up again.* DODGE *starts coughing softly.*

HALIE. (*to* SHELLY) I think we've had about enough of you young lady. Just about enough. I don't know where you came from or what you're doing here but you're no longer welcome in this house.

SHELLY. (*laughs, holds leg*) No longer welcome!

BRADLEY. Mom! That's my leg! Get my leg back! I can't do anything without my leg.

BRADLEY *keeps making whimpering sounds and reaching for his leg.*

HALIE. Give my son back his leg. Right this very minute!

DODGE *starts laughing softly to himself in between coughs.*

HALIE. (*to* DEWIS) Father, do something about this would you! I'm not about to be terrorized in my own house!

BRADLEY. Gimme back my leg!

HALIE. Oh, shut up Bradley! Just shut up! You don't need your leg now! Just lay down and shut up!

BRADLEY *whimpers. Lays down and pulls blanket around him. He keeps one arm outside blanket, reaching out toward his wooden leg.* DEWIS *cautiously approaches* SHELLY *with the roses in his arms.* SHELLY *clutches the wooden leg to her chest as though she's kidnapped it.*

DEWIS. (*to* SHELLY) Now, honestly dear, wouldn't it be better to try to talk things out? To try to use some reason?

SHELLY. There isn't any reason here! I can't find a reason for anything.

DEWIS. There's nothing to be afraid of. These are all good people. All righteous people.

SHELLY. I'm not afraid!

DEWIS. But this isn't your house. You have to have some respect.

SHELLY. You're the strangers here, not me.

HALIE. This has gone far enough!

DEWIS. Halie, please. Let me handle this.

SHELLY. Don't come near me. Don't anyone come near me. I don't need any words from you. I'm not threatening anybody. I don't even know what I'm doing here. You all say you don't remember Vince, okay, maybe you don't. Maybe it's Vince that's crazy. Maybe he's made this whole family thing up. I don't even care any more. I was just coming along for the ride. I thought it'd be a nice gesture. Besides, I was curious. He made all of you sound familiar to me. Every one of you. For every name, I had an image. Every time he'd tell me a name, I'd see the person. In fact, each of you was so clear in my mind that I actually believed it was you. I really believed when I walked through that door that the people who lived here would turn out to be the same people in my imagination. But I don't recognize any of you. Not one. Not even the slightest resemblance.

DEWIS. Well you can hardly blame others for not fulfilling your hallucination.

SHELLY. It was no hallucination! It was more like a prophecy. You believe in prophecy, don't you?

HALIE. Father, there's no point in talking to her any further. We're just going to have to call the police.

BRADLEY. No! Don't get the police in here. We don't want the police in here. This is our home.

SHELLY. That's right. Bradley's right. Don't you usually settle your affairs in private? Don't you usually take them out in the dark? Out in the back?

BRADLEY. You stay out of our lives! You have no business interfering!

SHELLY. I don't have any business period. I got nothing to lose.

She moves around, staring at each of them.

BRADLEY. You don't know what we've been through. You don't know anything!

SHELLY. I know you've got a secret. You've all got a secret. It's so secret in fact, you're all convinced it never happened.

HALIE *moves to* DEWIS.

HALIE. Oh, my God, Father!

DODGE. (*laughing to himself*) She thinks she's going to get it out of us. She thinks she's going to uncover the truth of the matter. Like a detective or something.

BRADLEY. I'm not telling her anything! Nothing's wrong here! Nothin's ever been wrong! Everything's the way it's supposed to be! Nothing ever happened that's bad! Everything is all right here! We're all good people!

DODGE. She thinks she's gonna suddenly bring everything out into the open after all these years.

DEWIS. (*to* SHELLY) Can't you see that these people want to be left in peace? Don't you have any mercy? They haven't done anything to you.

DODGE. She wants to get to the bottom of it. (*to* SHELLY) That's it, isn't it? You'd like to get right down to bedrock? You want me to tell ya'? You want me to tell ya' what happened? I'll tell ya'. I might as well.

BRADLEY. No! Don't listen to him. He doesn't remember anything!

DODGE. I remember the whole thing from start to finish. I remember the day he was born.

Pause.

HALIE. Dodge, if you tell this thing—if you tell this, you'll be dead to me. You'll be just as good as dead.

DODGE. That won't be such a big change, Halie. See this girl, this girl here, she wants to know. She wants to know something more. And I got this feeling that it doesn't make a bit a' difference. I'd sooner tell it to a stranger than anybody else.

BRADLEY. (*to* DODGE) We made a pact! We made a pact between us! You can't break that now!

DODGE. I don't remember any pact.

BRADLEY. (*to* SHELLY) See, he doesn't remember anything. I'm the only one in the family who remembers. The only one. And I'll never tell you!

SHELLY. I'm not so sure I want to find out now.

DODGE. (*laughing to himself*) Listen to her! Now she's runnin' scared!

SHELLY. I'm not scared!

DODGE *stops laughing, long pause.* DODGE *stares at her.*

DODGE. You're not huh? Well, that's good. Because I'm not either. See, we were a well established family once. Well established. All the boys were grown. The farm was producing enough milk to fill Lake Michigan twice over. Me and Halie here were pointed toward what looked like the middle part of our life. Everything was settled with us. All we had to do was ride it out. Then Halie got pregnant again. Outa' the middle a' nowhere, she got pregnant. We weren't planning on havin' any more boys. We had enough boys already. In fact, we hadn't been sleepin' in the same bed for about six years.

HALIE. (*moving toward stairs*) I'm not listening to this! I don't have to listen to this!

603

DODGE. (*stops* HALIE) Where are you going! Upstairs? You'll just be listenin' to it upstairs! You go outside, you'll be listenin' to it outside. Might as well stay here and listen to it.

HALIE *stays by stairs.*

BRADLEY. If I had my leg you wouldn't be saying this. You'd never get away with it if I had my leg.

DODGE. (*pointing to* SHELLY) She's got your leg. (*laughs*) She's gonna keep your leg too. (*to* SHELLY) She wants to hear this. Don't you?

SHELLY. I don't know.

DODGE. Well even if ya' don't I'm gonna' tell ya'. (*pause*) Halie had this kid. This baby boy. She had it. I let her have it on her own. All other boys I had had the best doctors, best nurses, everything. This one I let her have by herself. This one hurt real bad. Almost killed her, but she had it anyway. It lived, see. It lived. It wanted to grow up in this family. It wanted to be just like us. It wanted to be a part of us. It wanted to pretend that I was its father. She wanted me to believe in it. Even when everyone around us knew. Everyone. All our boys knew. Tilden knew.

HALIE. You shut up! Bradley, make him shut up!

BRADLEY. I can't

DODGE. Tilden was the one who knew. Better than any of us. He'd walk for miles with that kid in his arms. Halie let him take it. All night sometimes. He'd walk all night out there in the pasture with it. Talkin' to it. Singin' to it. Used to hear him singing to it. He'd make up stories. He'd tell that kid all kinds a' stories. Even when he knew it couldn't understand him. Couldn't understand a word he was sayin'. Never would understand him. We couldn't let a thing like that continue. We couldn't allow that to grow up right in the middle of our lives. It made everything we'd accomplished look like it was nothin'. Everything was cancelled out by this one mistake. This one weakness.

SHELLY. So you killed him?

DODGE. I killed it. I drowned it. Just like the runt of a litter. Just drowned it.

HALIE *moves toward* BRADLEY.

HALIE. (*to* BRADLEY) Ansel would've stopped him! Ansel would've stopped him from telling these lies! He was a hero! A man! A whole man! What's happened to the men in this family! Where are the men!

Suddenly VINCE *comes crashing through the screen porch door up left, tearing it off its hinges. Everyone but* DODGE *and* BRADLEY *back away from the porch and stare at* VINCE *who has landed on his stomach on the porch in a drunken stupor. He is singing loudly to himself and hauls himself slowly to his feet. He has a paper shopping bag full of empty booze bottles. He takes them out one at a time as he sings and smashes them at the opposite end of the porch, behind the solid interior door, stage right.* SHELLY *moves slowly toward stage right, holding wooden leg and watching* VINCE.

VINCE. (*singing loudly as he hurls bottles*) "From the Halls of Montezuma to the Shores of Tripoli. We will fight our country's battles on the land and on the sea."

He punctuates the words "Montezuma", "Tripoli", "battles" and "sea" with a smashed bottle each. He stops throwing for a seconds stares toward stage right of the porch, shades his eyes with his hand as though looking across to a battle field, then cups his hands around his mouth and yells across the space of the porch to an imaginary army. The others watch in terror and expectation.

VINCE. (*to imagined Army*) Have you had enough over there! 'Cause there's a lot more here where that came from! (*pointing to paper bag full of bottles*) A helluva lot more! We got enough over here to blow ya' from here to Kingdomcome!

He takes another bottle, makes high whistling sound of a bomb and throws it toward stage right porch. Sound of bottle smashing against wall. This should be the actual smashing of bottles and not tape sound. He keeps yelling and heaving bottles one after another. VINCE *stops for a while, breathing heavily from exhaustion. Long silence as the others watch him.* SHELLY *approaches tentatively in* VINCE'S *direction, still holding* BRADLEY'S *wooden leg.*

SHELLY. (*after silence*) Vince?

VINCE *turns toward her. Peers through screen.*

VINCE. Who? What? Vince who? Who's that in there?

VINCE *pushes his face against the screen from the porch and stares in at everyone.*

DODGE. Where's my goddamn bottle!

VINCE. (*looking in at* DODGE) What? Who is that?

604

DODGE. It's me! Your Grandfather! Don't play stupid with me! Where's my two bucks!

VINCE. Your two bucks?

HALIE *moves away from* DEWIS, *upstage, peers out at* VINCE, *trying to recognize him.*

HALIE. Vincent? Is that you, Vincent?

SHELLY *stares at* HALIE *then looks out at* VINCE.

VINCE. (*from porch*) Vincent who? What is this! Who are you people?

SHELLY. (*to* HALIE) Hey, wait a minute. Wait a minute! What's going on?

HALIE. (*moving closer to porch screen*) We thought you were a murderer or something. Barging in through the door like that.

VINCE. I am a murderer! Don't underestimate me for a minute! I'm the Midnight Strangler! I devour whole families in a single gulp!

VINCE *grabs another bottle and smashes it on the porch.* HALIE *backs away.*

SHELLY. (*approaching* HALIE) You mean you know who he is?

HALIE. Of course I know who he is! That's more than I can say for you.

BRADLEY. (*sitting up on sofa*) You get off our front porch you creep! What're you doing out there breaking bottles? Who are these foreigners anyway! Where did they come from?

VINCE. Maybe I should come in there and break them!

HALIE. (*moving toward porch*) Don't you dare! Vincent, what's got into you! Why are you acting like this?

VINCE. Maybe I should come in there and usurp your territory!

HALIE *turns back toward* DEWIS *and crosses to him.*

HALIE. (*to* DEWIS) Father, why are you just standing around here when everything's falling apart? Can't you rectify this situation?

DODGE *laughs, coughs.*

DEWIS. I'm just a guest here, Halie. I don't know what my position is exactly. This is outside my parish anyway.

VINCE *starts throwing more bottles as things continue.*

BRADLEY. If I had my leg I'd rectify it! I'd rectify him all over the goddamn highway! I'd pull his ears out if I could reach him!

BRADLEY *sticks his fist through the screening of the porch and reaches out for* VINCE, *grabbing at him and missing.* VINCE *jumps away from* BRADLEY'S *hand.*

VINCE. Aaah! Our lines have been penetrated! Tentacled animals! Beasts from the deep!

VINCE *strikes out at* BRADLEY'S *hand with a bottle.* BRADLEY *pulls his hand back inside.*

SHELLY. Vince! Knock it off will ya'! I want to get out of here!

VINCE *pushes his face against screen, looks in at* SHELLY.

VINCE. (*to* SHELLY) Have they got you prisoner in there, dear? Such a sweet young thing too. All her life in front of her. Nipped in the bud.

SHELLY. I'm coming out there, Vince! I'm coming out there and I want us to get in the car and drive away from here. Anywhere. Just away from here.

SHELLY *moves toward* VINCE'S *saxophone case and overcoat. She sets down the wooden leg, downstage left and picks up the saxophone case and overcoat.* VINCE *watches her through the screen.*

VINCE. (*to* SHELLY) We'll have to negotiate. Make some kind of a deal. Prisoner exchange or something. A few of theirs for one of ours. Small price to pay if you ask me.

SHELLY *crosses toward stage right door with overcoat and case.*

SHELLY. Just go and get the car! I'm coming out there now. We're going to leave.

VINCE. Don't come out here! Don't you dare come out here!

SHELLY *stops short of the door, stage right.*

SHELLY. How come?

VINCE. Off limits! Verboten! This is taboo territory. No man or woman has ever crossed the line and lived to tell the tale!

SHELLY. I'll take my chances.

SHELLY *moves to stage right door and opens it.* VINCE *pulls out a big folding hunting knife and pulls open the blade. He jabs the blade into the screen and starts cutting a hole big enough to climb through.* BRADLEY *cowers in a corner of the sofa as* VINCE *rips at the screen.*

VINCE. (*as he cuts screen*) Don't come out here! I'm warning you! You'll disintegrate!

DEWIS *takes* HALIE *by the arm and pulls her toward staircase.*

DEWIS. Halie, maybe we should go upstairs until this blows over.

HALIE. I don't understand it. I just don't understand it. He was the sweetest little boy!

DEWIS *drops the roses beside the wooden leg at the foot of the staircase then escorts* HALIE *quickly up the stairs.* HALIE *keeps looking back at* VINCE *as they climb the stairs.*

HALIE. There wasn't a mean bone in his body. Everyone loved Vincent. Everyone. He was the perfect baby.

DEWIS. He'll be all right after a while. He's just had a few too many that's all.

HALIE. He used to sing in his sleep. He'd sing. In the middle of the night. The sweetest voice. Like an angel. (*she stops for a moment*) I used to lie awake listening to it. I used to lie awake thinking it was all right if I died. Because Vincent was an angel. A guardian angel. He'd watch over us. He'd watch over all of us.

DEWIS *takes her all the way up the stairs. They disappear above.* VINCE *is now climbing through the porch screen onto the sofa.* BRADLEY *crashes off the sofa, holding tight to his blanket, keeping it wrapped around him.* SHELLY *is outside on the porch.* VINCE *holds the knife in his teeth once he gets the hole wide enough to climb through.* BRADLEY *starts crawling slowly toward his wooden leg, reaching out for it.*

DODGE. (*to* VINCE) Go ahead! Take over the house! Take over the whole goddamn house! You can have it! It's yours. It's been a pain in the neck ever since the very first mortgage. I'm gonna die any second now. Any second. You won't even notice. So I'll settle my affairs once and for all.

As DODGE *proclaims his last will and testament,* VINCE *climbs into the room, knife in mouth and strides slowly around the space, inspecting his inheritance. He casually notices* BRADLEY *as he crawls toward his leg.* VINCE *moves to the leg and keeps pushing with his foot so that it's out of* BRADLEY'S *reach then goes on with his inspection. He picks up the roses and carries them around smelling them.* SHELLY *can be seen outside on the porch, moving slowly center and staring in at* VINCE. VINCE *ignores her.*

DODGE. The house goes to my Grandson, Vincent. All the furnishings, accoutrements and paraphanalia therein. Everything tacked to the walls or otherwise resting under this roof. My tools— namely my band saw, my skill saw, my drill press, my chain saw, my lathe, my electric sander, all go to my eldest son, Tilden. That is, if he ever shows up again. My shed and gasoline powered equipment, namely my tractor, my dozer, my hand tiller plus all the attachments and riggings for the above mentioned machinery, namely my spring tooth harrow, my deep plows, my disk plows, my automatic fertilizing equipment, my reaper, my swathe, my seeder, my John Deere Harvester, my post hole digger, my jackhammer, my lathe—(*to himself*) Did I mention my lathe? I already mentioned my lathe—my Bennie Goodman records, my harnesses, my bits, my halters my brace, my rough rasp, my forge, my welding equipment, my shoeing nails, my levels and bevels, my milking stool—no, not my milking stool—my hammers and chisels, my hinges, my cattle gates, my barbed wire, self-tapping augers, my horse hair ropes and all related materials are to be pushed into a gigantic heap and set ablaze in the very center of my fields. When the blaze is at its highest, preferably on a cold, windless night, my body is to be pitched into the middle of it and burned til nothing remains but ash.

Pause. VINCE *takes the knife out of his mouth and smells the roses. He's facing toward audience and doesn't turn around to* SHELLY. *He folds up knife and pockets it.*

SHELLY. (*from porch*) I'm leaving, Vince. Whether you come or not, I'm leaving.

VINCE. (*smelling roses*) Just put my horn on the couch there before you take off.

SHELLY. (*moving toward hole in screen*) You're not coming?

VINCE *stays downstage, turns and looks at her.*

VINCE. I just inherited a house.

SHELLY. (*through hole, from porch*) You want to stay here?

606

VINCE. (as he pushes BRADLEY'S *leg out of reach*) I've gotta carry on the line. I've gotta see to it that things keep rolling.

BRADLEY *looks up at him from floor, keeps pulling himself toward his leg.* VINCE *keeps moving it.*

SHELLY. What happened to you Vince? You just disappeared.

VINCE. (*pause, delivers speech front*) I was gonna run last night. I was gonna run and keep right on running. I drove all night. Clear to the Iowa border. The old man's two bucks sitting right on the seat beside me. It never stopped raining the whole time. Never stopped once. I could see myself in the windshield. My face. My eyes. I studied my face. Studied everything about it. As though I was looking at another man. As though I could see his whole race behind him. Like a mummy's face. I saw him dead and alive at the same time. In the same breath. In the windshield, I watched him breathe as though he was frozen in time. And every breath marked him. Marked him forever without him knowing. And then his face changed. His face became his father's face. Same bones. Same eyes. Same nose. Same breath. And his father's face changed to his Grandfather's face. And it went on like that. Changing. Clear on back to faces I'd never seen before but still recognized. Still recognized the bones underneath. The eyes. The breath. The mouth. I followed my family clear into Iowa. Every last one. Straight into the Corn Belt and further. Straight back as far as they'd take me. Then it all dissolved. Everything dissolved.

SHELLY *stares at him for a while then reaches through the hole in the screen and sets the saxophone case and* VINCE'S *overcoat on the sofa. She looks at* VINCE *again.*

SHELLY. Bye Vince.

She exits left off the porch. VINCE *watches her go.* BRADLEY *tries to make a lunge for his wooden leg.* VINCE *quickly picks it up and dangles it over* BRADLEY'S *head like a carrot.* BRADLEY *keeps making desperate grabs at the leg.* DEWIS *comes down the staircase and stops halfway, staring at* VINCE *and* BRADLEY. VINCE *looks up at* DEWIS *and smiles. He keeps moving backwards with the leg toward upstage left as* BRADLEY *crawls after him.*

VINCE. (*to* DEWIS *as he continues torturing Bradley*) Oh, excuse me Father. Just getting rid of some of the vermin in the house. This is my house now, ya' know? All mine. Everything. Except for the power tools and stuff. I'm gonna get all new equipment anyway. New plows, new tractor, everything. All brand new. (VINCE *teases* BRADLEY *closer to the up left corner of the stage.*) Start right off on the ground floor.

VINCE *throws* BRADLEY'S *wooden leg far off stage left.* BRADLEY *follows his leg off stage, pulling himself along on the ground, whimpering. As* BRADLEY *exits* VINCE *pulls the blanket off him and throws it over his own shoulder. He crosses toward* DEWIS *with the blanket and smelling the roses.* DEWIS *comes to the bottom of the stairs.*

DEWIS. You better go up and see your Grandmother.

VINCE. (*looking up stairs, back to* DEWIS) My Grandmother? There's nobody else in this house. Except for you. And you're leaving aren't you?

DEWIS *crosses toward stage right door. He turns back to* VINCE.

DEWIS. She's going to need someone. I can't help her. I don't know what to do. I don't know what my position is. I just came in for some tea. I had no idea there was any trouble. No idea at all.

VINCE *just stares at him.* DEWIS *goes out the door, crosses porch and exits left.* VINCE *listens to him leaving. He smells roses, looks up the staircase then smells roses again. He turns and looks upstage at* DODGE. *He crosses up to him and bends over looking at* DODGE'S *open eyes.* DODGE *is dead. His death should have come completely unnoticed by the audience.* VINCE *covers* DODGE'S *body with the blanket, then covers his head. He sits on the sofa. Smelling roses and staring at* DODGE'S *body. Long pause.* VINCE *places the roses on* DODGE'S *chest then lays down on the sofa, arms folded behind his head, staring at the ceiling. His body is in the same relationship to* DODGE'S. *After a while* HALIE'S *voice is heard coming from above the staircase. The lights start to dim almost imperceptively as* HALIE *speaks.* VINCE *keeps staring at the ceiling.*

HALIE'S VOICE. Dodge? Is that you Dodge? Tilden was right about the corn you know. I've never seen such corn. Have you taken a look at it lately? Tall as a man already. This early in the year. Carrots too. Potatoes. Peas. It's like a paradise out there, Dodge. You oughta' take a look. A miracle. I've never seen it like this. Maybe the rain did something. Maybe it was the rain.

As HALIE *keeps talking off stage,* TILDEN *appears from stage left, dripping with mud from the knees down. His arms and hands are covered with mud. In his hands he carries the corpse of a small child at chest level, staring down at it. The corpse mainly consists of bones wrapped in muddy, rotten cloth. He moves slowly downstage toward the staircase, ignoring* VINCE *on the sofa.* VINCE *keeps staring at the ceiling as though* TILDEN *wasn't there. As* HALIE'S *voice continues,* TILDEN *slowly makes his way up the stairs. His eyes never leave the corpse of the child. The lights keep fading.*

HALIE'S VOICE. (*contd.*) Good hard rain. Takes everything straight down deep to the roots. The rest takes care of itself. You can't force a thing to grow. You can't interfere with it. It's all hidden. It's all unseen. You just gotta wait til it pops up out of the ground. Tiny little shoot. Tiny little white shoot. All hairy and fragile. Strong though. Strong enough to break the earth even. It's a miracle, Dodge. I've never seen a crop like this in my whole life. Maybe it's the sun. Maybe that's it. Maybe it's the sun.

TILDEN *disappears above. Silence. Lights go to black.*

Act One of *Cloud Nine,* a University Resident Theatre production at Penn State University. William Kelly, director.

CHAPTER XVII

Post-Modernism

Perhaps the most difficult questions to answer in the theatre are these: Where are we now and where are we going? Not only is it often impossible to "see the forest for the trees" but taste, customs, and conventions change, and we are often lured into declaring that what is contemporary and avante-garde is, on the one hand, the only theatre worth seeing and, on the other, fakery, sham, and utter nonsense. There is a delightful story in theatre lore that when a now all-but-forgotten play titled *Douglas* by John Home, a Scots Presbyterian minister, opened in Edinburgh in 1756, an ardent supporter in the audience stood up at the final curtain and called out in a thick brogue, "Where's yer Willy Shakespeare now?" Somehow in the excitement of the moment, the spectator was blind to the glory of the past and the limitations of the present. While we, like the enthusiastic Scot, may not have the perspective of time to evaluate today's theatre and while practitioners overlooked here may be the champions of the future or, conversely, those included may rapidly fade into obscurity, nevertheless, several observations can be made with some degree of certainty.

First, just as our establishment theatre today has evolved as a result of the resident theatre and off-off Broadway movements of the 1960s and 1970s, so much of our avante-garde theatre has grown out of the activity of experimental groups of the same period. Let us take as an example The Wooster Group, in Massachusetts, which was formed in 1975 by members of Richard Schechner's Performance Group. Elizabeth LeCompte is artistic director, and Spalding Gray, writer and actor, one of its principle members. The group's work is highly controversial and provocative, evidencing a documentary style mixed with bold theatricality. In 1981, Spalding Gray developed *Route 1 & 9* which juxtaposes portions of *Our Town* with black-face minstrel routines and pornography. The group seems to be commenting on what they consider the provincialism and narrow perspective of Wilder's play, yet they resist manipulating audience response or forcing the spectator to arrive at a preconceived point of view. It is interesting that the use of blackface was interpreted as racism and brought the group severe criticism. Director LeCompte felt that if a character had responded to the blackface with a comment like, "I deplore this," no problem would have existed. Similarly, *L.S.D.* (1986) chronicles the period of the Communist witch hunts in the 1950s. Originally the text drew largely from Arthur Miller's *The Crucible,* but had to be reshaped when Miller threatened to sue for distortion of his text. Drawing from a variety of sources, the work explores both victims and accusors, the voices of the right and the left, the culture and the counter-culture, the written history and the suppressed history; yet no conclusions are drawn. *L.S.D.* is a panoramic, multi-faceted exploration of a political and cultural event not a judgment on that event. In spite of controversy, The Wooster Group was selected for a Continuing Ensembles Grant from the National Endowment of the Arts and remains in the forefront of the current avante-garde.

Besides evolving from the experimental theatre of the 1960s, we can accurately observe that the new theatre is profoundly influenced by technology. We live in an age when the computer, the laser, state of the art audio and video equipment are commonplaces. The new theatre makes exhaustive use of such technology, and a number of designers have led the way in the integration of advanced technology in the theatre. Three examples will serve. In America, designer Ming Cho Lee has been in the forefront of scenic advancements. When Patrick Meyer's *K2,* a play about two men lost on the world's second largest mountain, premiered in New York, Lee's setting of styrofoam extended both above and below the proscenium opening. Not only was there a graphic depiction of the ice cliff on which the two explorers were stranded but an avalanche achieved with lighting and projections, a subtle sound re-creation of falling and crackling ice, and a gleaming icy surface achieved by light. The real star of the production was the setting. Similarly, among the most lavish and spectacular design work in the world is that of John Napier of the Royal Shakespeare Company in England, who combines skills in all three areas: scenic design, lighting, and costuming. Napier's designs for *Nicholas Nickleby, Cats, Starlight Express,* and *Les Miserables* have attracted international attention and universal praise.

Perhaps the most important designer in the world today, however, is Czechoslovakian Josef Svoboda, who has established an international reputation for his integration of film, slides, and projections—in fact, all that contemporary media can offer—to the stage. Through these devices, Svoboda creates a completely flexible stage, capable of instant change and alteration. Besides filmic techniques, Svoboda has developed electronic platforms that are capable of movement horizontally, vertically, and laterally; he has explored mirrors, netting, screening apparatus to reflect action from above, below, the sides, and at unique angles. Svoboda's pioneering work, which has dominated both the opera and theatre worlds on two continents, has opened unlimited possibilities of media and technology to the designers he has influenced.

Our third observation about the avante-garde theatre today is that it is dominated, not by actors and playwrights, but by directors. Although this trend was certainly evident by the 1950s with the work of such distinctive directors as Tyrone Guthrie and Elia Kazan, it was probably the extraordinary vision and freshness of approach of Peter Brook at the Royal Shakespeare Company in England that established the model for younger directors. Brook's theatre of cruelty interpretations of *Marat/Sade* and *King Lear,* his acrobatic and minimalistic approach to *A Midsummer Night's Dream,* and his stark and sensual *la tragédie de Carmen* are landmarks of directorial vision and inventiveness. While there is probably no direct influence from Brook, Russian director Yuri Lyubimov staged a nightmare version of Dostoyevsky's novel *Crime and Punishment* at the Arena Stage in Washington, D.C. in 1986. With a powerful central metaphor of a white door smeared with blood, Lyubimov created a theatrical score of text, lighting, music, choreography, and presentationalism. At the American Repertory Theatre in Boston, director Jo Anne Akalaitis made an individual statement by placing Beckett's *Endgame* in a subway station littered with debris. Andre Serban, a Rumanian director, recreated his *Fragments of a Greek Trilogy* as a part of La Mama's twenty-fifth anniversary (1987). Drawing from *Medea, Trojan Women,* and *Electra* and combining the original Greek and Latin of Euripides and Seneca's texts, Serban explored the purely emotional quality of sound rather than the literal meaning of words. With a score of western and non-western music and sound by Elizabeth Swados, the actors sing, speak in foreign tongues, chant, shriek, and whisper in this highly charged avante-garde classic.

One young director in the American theatre has been extoled as boy genius and condemned as utter fraud: Peter Sellars, a graduate of Harvard and student at the American Repertory Theatre, hired in 1984 to create an American National Theatre at the Kennedy Center in Washington. As at home with opera as with theatre, Sellars has created a *Mikado* in the board room of a contemporary Japanese corporation, Handel's *Julius Caesar* in the troubled Middle East, and Handel's *Orlando* peopled with astronauts. Whether right or wrong, directors like Sellars attempt to make works alive, contemporary, and immediate to audience members who might otherwise reject classics as antiquated and stodgy.

Our fourth and final observation about the avante-garde theatre in America is that it draws from a variety of sources, primarily Artaud's Theatre of Cruelty, Brecht's Epic Theatre, Absurdism, and the popular arts—television, radio, film, computer graphics, stereo technology, and contemporary music. Its practitioners form a kind of family whose work dissects, intersects, builds upon, refutes, and compliments one another's. Just as we seem to be moving away from a verbal culture of printed and oral words, so our theatre is moving away from language to a more visually-oriented experience. Some critics refer to the avante-garde theatre today as the new theatre, post-modernism, theatre of images, or performance art. Whatever label one may choose, certain characteristics are shared by this avante-garde front. There is an absence or minimalizing of dialogue; there is a clear relationship—as was true of the happenings of the 1960s—with other art forms: dance, music, painting, sculpture, and media; and there is an emphasis on the process itself and not just on the result of that process.

Drawing as it does from the art world, the theatre of images focuses on composition and even more specifically on tableaux, frozen moments suggesting painting or sculpture, or moments accelerated or retarded in time. As in expressionism, time and space are manipulated and distorted. Language is similarly distorted or fragmented: an image in space becomes an interior monologue or an actor's thoughts; lines overlap, are cacophonic and amplified through the use of tape recorders; choral passages and narration are also used; but language is part of the image rather than a tool to convey literal meanings. Similarly, stereo speakers surround audiences and bombard them with audio impressions. "The significance of the Theatre of Images," Bonnie Marranca tells us, "is its expansion of the audience's capacity to perceive. It is a theatre devoted to the creation of a new stage language, a visual grammar 'written' in sophisticated perceptual codes. To break these codes is to enter the refined, sensual worlds this theatre offers." These experiences do away with clear-cut differentiations—among people, the sexes, art forms, performance styles, and dramatic genres. More and more performance art gains critical and popular attention; for example, Stuart Sherman's brief work, "The Yellow Chair" (1987), a study about dualities, and Martha Clark's *The Garden of Earthly Delights,* a visual interpretation of the famous Hieronymus Bosch painting. Clark's previous work included *Vienna: Lusthaus,* a presentation in movement, dance, song, and theatre of the deterioration of the quality of life and the growing decadence that pervaded turn-of-the-century Vienna. But the reputation of post-modernism rests primarily with three artists: Richard Foreman, Lee Breuer, and Robert Wilson, each of whom functions on all levels of theatre—as originators, writers, directors, and designers.

Foreman established the Ontological-Hysteric Theatre in 1968. Two of his most provocative productions have been *Pandering to the Masses* (1975) and *Africanis Instructus* (1985). Perhaps the most influenced by Brecht of the performance artists, Foreman is didactic, radical, and doggedly opposed to establishment theatre. Like Brecht he employs recorded dialogue and projected slides, and he chooses to make his audiences aware of their moment-to-moment existence in the theatre, the fact that they are seeing art made and not merely observing art. Like the absurdists, Foreman is fascinated by the condition of existence and will not let his plays be destroyed by the need to mean something. Finally, like the expressionists and surrealists, Foreman is fascinated by the subconscious and claims a real debt to Gertrude Stein. In his arranged, focused, and meticulously organized pictures, Foreman presents visions of his own sub-conscious.

Very different in approach and objective is Lee Breuer, whose comic *The Red Horse Imitation* (1970) is perhaps his most popular production. Employing the techniques of both film and the comic book, Breuer's work, which he calls "performance poetry," is technically advanced but somehow closer to theatre as we know it than Foreman's. One of his hallmarks is the use of holography, a special photographic technique employing lasers. A founder of a theatre collaborative, Mabou Mines Ensemble, Breuer was trained at the Actors' Workshop of San Francisco and the Berliner Ensemble. His *Prelude to Death in Venice* (1979) is a collage on youth, growing old, and death drawing from Thomas Mann's novel, images of Dracula, esoteric references and electronic tricks. At the American Repertory Theatre in 1980 he adapted Frank Wedekind's German expressionistic play, *Lulu,* translating it to a punk rock idiom. His most striking and accessible work is probably his epic collage, *Gospel at Colonus* (1984), which combines the essence of Greek tragedy—with much of the dialogue from Sophocles tragedies on the Oedipus myth intact—with the spirit and fervor of a gospel revival. The black cast, use of two large gospel choirs, glittering contemporary dress, church-like setting—all contribute to an emotional involvement, spectacle, and cathartic impact that must be very like that achieved in the ancient theatre of the 4th century B.C.

The most visible and prolific of the performance artists is Robert Wilson who concerns himself primarily with American cultural myths. Although he is best known for *Einstein on the Beach* (1976), written with composer Philip Glass, Wilson's most ambitious work to date is his opera, the *CIVIL warS* (1983–84), originally intended for the 1984 Olympic Games in Los Angeles. Designed as a twelve hour multi-lingual event, the work is a collaboration of many artists including German playwright Heiner Muller, in which images of the American Civil War are expanded to embrace all potential struggles. Perhaps Wilson's most accessible work is *Alcestis* staged at the American Repertory Theatre in 1986. When Alcestis decides to sacrifice herself to death so that her husband might live, Wilson slows the scene down so that the audience may share Alcestis's torturous experience. Peasants, both masked and with horror painted on real faces, pass by. Amplified voices, barking dogs, a howling wind, a ticking clock, the sound of a helicopter invade the auditorium. Three Alcestis characters—one exemplifying marital love, one maternal love, and a third anguish—move in space. A white drapery stirs in the breeze, and Alcestis is enveloped by death, a gigantic bat behind her. Three figures like the prop men of the Japanese Noh or Kabuki theatre carry Alcestis off stage, a magnificent painted backdrop appears, and a boulder is dislodged and tumbles down a mountain in ghostly stillness—a painful and eerie series of separate and yet related images, an evocative visual and sensual poem about death.

It is interesting that many of the elements of the performance art in America manifest themselves in the post-modern scene of Great Britain, perhaps the healthiest theatre in the world today. With low ticket prices, generous subsidy by the Arts Council of Great Britain, tremendous popularity among the young, two splendid national theatres—the National and the Royal Shakespeare Company—theatre seems much more a way of life in Great Britain than in the United States.

Great Britain has always nurtured great playwrights from Shakespeare to George Bernard Shaw, and the present is no exception. As with the American avante-garde, the British show a profound influence from Brecht, Artaud, and the Absurdists, but their drama has remained a literary one. The list of brilliant dramatists working in the theatre today is astounding, and any one of them could provide the basis for lengthy discussion: Alan Aychbourn, Howard Barker, Howard Brenton, Michael Frayn, Pam Gems, Simon Gray, Trevor Griffiths, Christopher Hampton, David Hare, Peter Nichols, Louise Page, Harold Pinter, David Pownall, Peter Shaffer, Tom Stoppard, and David Storey. The list is included only to provide some sense of the dynamic activity, productivity, and creativity flourishing in England today.

Four playwrights may be selected as excellent examples of the post-modern drama in Great Britain: David Edgar, Edward Bond, Peter Barnes, and Caryl Churchill. All of them share a number of characteristics which clarify and distill current trends in post-modern work. First, they show the influence or at least an awareness of the writings of Artaud, Brecht, and the Absurdists. They employ sexually explicit dialogue (Great Britain has only been free of censorship in very recent years), and they employ scenes of explicit physical violence, reflecting the violence of our contemporary society. The plays are anti-realistic without being anti-truthful; a variety of styles, multiple settings, and loose structure stand in sharp contrast to the single set shows and three act structure of the past. The works move freely in time and space; they are filmic. (It may not be altogether coincidental that most of Britain's playwrights have apprenticed or still work in film, radio, and television.) They display a marked interest in social and political issues, and most of the dramatists are liberal, if not clearly socialistic, in their political pursuasions. Finally, the dramas are marked by bold and inventive theatricality. Because of these characteristics, some critics have called the contemporary British drama theatrical eclecticism, yet another title that shows us searching for a label by which to organize or categorize the work of today's playwrights.

David Edgar's eight hour dramatization of Charles Dicken's rambling novel, *Nicholas Nickleby,* is believed by many to be the outstanding theatrical event of the eighties. Created in a workshop situation and employing approximately fifty actors from the Royal Shakespeare Company, the work was directed by John Caird and Trevor Nunn with costumes and scenery by John Napier. Meeting first for discussions and research on the England of Dickens's day, improvising extensively, doubling and tripling in roles, both narrating and acting, creating sounds and stunning visual effects like a stagecoach created of boxes, chairs, and tables, the actors and directors worked together as a real ensemble to create a theatrical and yet very intimate and moving experience. The production proved so popular that it was recreated with a different cast in 1986, where it again played both in London and on Broadway. Although the play is political in its attack on capitalism, audiences were willing to pay one-hundred dollars per ticket, the highest price in the history of the American theatre.

Far more political than *Nicholas Nickleby,* however, is the work of Edward Bond, a prolific playwright and outspoken Marxist. Coming from the North London suburb of Holloway, Bond left school when he was fourteen. He first attracted attention with *The Pope's Wedding* in 1962, but it was *Saved* in 1965, with its naturalistic and cruel stoning of an infant in a baby carriage, that shocked and astounded audiences. Since then Bond, who considers himself a social satirist, has continued to flood the British stage with his socialistic vision, his outspoken attacks on capitalism, his hatred of war, his depictions of power struggles and oppression, and his compassionate championing of the poor. His more recent works include: *Early Morning* (1968), *Narrow Road to the Deep North* (1968), *Lear* (1971), *The Fool* (1975), *The Bundle* (1978), *The Women* (1978),

Restoration (1981), and *The War Plays* (1985). Bond's plays are violent, didactic, boldly theatrical, and profoundly moral. In *Restoration,* for example, an innocent man goes to the gallows for his guilty master simply because he is ignorant, has never learned to read, and lacks the ability to defend himself against injustice. Only his wife, Rose, is capable of understanding that man is what he knows. She cannot save her husband from the gallows but she may ultimately save herself.

Almost as controversial as Bond is playwright Peter Barnes, who made his reputation with *The Ruling Class* (1968), the story of a mad man who is shocked out of his role of Christ into that of Jack the Ripper. Considered insane when teaching Christian love, the leading character is thought quite normal when he assumes the role of an autocratic sadist. Barnes's plays crackle with irony. His most recent, *Red Noses* (1985), explores the humanity of mirth in a time of fear and crisis. Set in France during the Black Plague, *Red Noses* is a wild and deliberate conglomeration of socialist theory, vaudeville and music hall routines, puns, songs, elegant literary conceits, Christian symbolism, zanni characters, anachronisms, history, cheap jokes, lyric poetry, violence and cruelty, and bold theatricality.

Representative of these daring political and theatrical dramatists in England today is the single woman playwright included in this volume, Caryl Churchill. It is noteworthy that as we select what we consider to be the best of any period or genre, we are able in our own time to offer the work of this outstanding woman playwright. At one time in 1983, three of Churchill's plays were running in New York: *Cloud Nine, Top Girls,* and *Fen.* Churchill continues to be a prolific playwright: *Serious Money, Ice Cream,* and *Mad Forest* are examples of recent work. An ardent feminist, Churchill recognizes that justice for women is justice for men as well. Her plays are a curious mixture of styles, time frames, cross-sexual casting, outrageous comedy, and biting social criticism. All of these British playwrights—of whom we have mentioned all too few—bespeak the health and vitality of the British theatre. Perhaps a major lesson can be learned by Americans: no theatre in the world has ever been able to thrive without patronage or support of some kind. Moreover when one goes to England, one is keenly aware of theatre as a reflection of our own times and perceptions, as a vigorous institution in which the young, the old, the members of all social classes join in a common bond of experience, and where playwrights are free to fail and to speak their beliefs boldly without financial or commercial restraints.

Caryl Churchill

Caryl Churchill's father was a cartoonist and her mother a model and minor film actress; so the playwright, born in London on September 3, 1938, comes quite naturally to her creative talents. She sees her characters and situations with the bold satiric vision of the cartoonist, and she certainly inherited an actor's ability to feel into other people's lives and situations. After spending the war years in London with her family, Churchill went to school in Montreal, Canada and then returned for a B.A. degree in English at Oxford, from which she graduated in 1960. In spite of a love of making up and putting on pantomimes as a child and working backstage in a summer theatre, Churchill had no thought of a career in the theatre when she married David Harter in 1961. During the 1960s Churchill stayed at home, raised three sons, and played her role as a young barrister's wife. She says that her own consciousness was raised and her political awareness began when her husband left private practice for work with legal aid in 1972.

With some experience as a radio writer, Churchill turned to playwriting in 1972 and found her first play, *Owners,* produced by the Royal Court Theatre, Upstairs. *Objections to Sex and Violence* (1975) marks the beginning of her emerging feminism. In 1976 Churchill began working with a theatre collective, the Joint Stock Theatre Group, and started to approach her scripts in a different way. After a period of personal exploration and improvisation on the part of the actors, Churchill goes off alone to write, drawing from the input of the actors, the improvisations, and sharing. In 1976, Churchill wrote *Vinegar Tom* about witchcraft and moved to more theatrical devises such as the interpolation of songs between scenes. *Traps* in 1977 seems to derive inspiration from the works of Pirandello and Pinter and involves six people trapped in a room and the fact that their experience was "real while it happened." *Cloud Nine* (1979) was again written as a result of a Joint Stock Workshop and like many of Churchill's plays performed at the Royal Court Theatre, this time on the main stage. It was revived for a second run and played successfully in New York at the Theatre deLys in 1981. *More Sleepless Nights* (1980), *Top Girls* (1982), *Fen* (1983), *Softcops* (1984) for the Royal Shakespeare, *Serious Money* (1987) and *Mad Forest* (1991) exemplify Churchill's repertoire. Her audacity, bold theatricality, vibrant humor, and social awareness place her among the leading dramatists in Britain today. Judith Thurman wrote an article for *Ms.* Magazine, the title of which delightfully summarizes the work of the dramatist, "Caryl Churchill: The Playwright Who Makes You Laugh About Orgasm, Racism, Class Struggle, Homophobia, Women-Hating, the British Empire, and the Irrepressible Strangeness of the Human Heart."

Cloud Nine

Cloud Nine is not only an ideal representation of the work of Caryl Churchill; it is also an ideal example of the contemporary drama for the manner in which it demonstrates the many characteristics of plays written in the last decades of the twentieth century. Here is a play, like *Buried Child,* which profits from the achievements of Ibsen, Strindberg, Brecht, Beckett and Artaud. Their influences can be found on practically every page and in every stage moment of *Cloud Nine.* But that is not to say that Churchill is in anyway slavish and imitative where her models are concerned. On the contrary, she is very much her own playwright.

Like Ibsen, Caryl Churchill centers her play around the social and political issues of the day. *Cloud Nine* is unmistakably a contemporary play in its consideration of civil rights issues, the women's movement, colonialism, sexual mores and sexual freedoms. To a large extent, the play may be regarded as an examination of the changing role of women in society through its juxtaposition and contrast of a Victorian family in Act One and its present-day descendents in Act II. In this regard the play is very timely.

The play is remarkably contemporary, too, in its use of sexually explicit dialogue. Four-letter words are a natural part of the vocabulary of Churchill's characters; the most potent of all four-letter words is frequently used as an expletive and just as frequently employed in a literal sense. There is frank discussion of masturbation and both hetrosexual and homosexual acts of physical gratification. Such frank speech is a highly vivid reflection of our times in more ways than one. It is liberated speech, to be sure; but it is also meaningless verbage. The Absurdists had much to say about the devaluation of our language as specific words lose their meaning through our verbal abuse and over-use of them. Churchill provides us with a highly amusing, touching and frightening scene when a dead soldier appears on stage to rage about his truncated, unfulfilled and painful life; the meaninglessness of his life is theatrically and movingly reflected in the meaninglessness of his language in which the four-letter word is so over-used that its meaning and impact are nullified.

The violence of the imagery and the emotion in the soldier's scene is evidence of the influence of Artaud's vision. Physical violence is very much a part of *Cloud Nine* just as it is a part of contemporary life. However, unlike many of her fellow playwrights, Churchill keeps a tight rein on the actual performance of violence. A mother actually strikes a child on stage; and there is a sexual encounter between Clive and Mrs. Saunders in Act One that leaves little to the imagination. But, for the most part, the violence is tastefully off-stage (as in the case of the physical punishment of the African natives in Act One) or is reported second-hand (as evidenced in Gerry's vivid chronicle of a homosexual encounter). Nonetheless, it is dramatically there as a part of the play and as a part of our everyday lives.

Our contemporary theatre is notable also for its anti-realistic approach and for its inventive theatricality. Each of these characteristics are amply present in Caryl Churchill's play. The setting itself is a radical departure from slavish Realism. Act One transpires on an entire colonial estate in Africa during the Victorian era. As the action progresses, we are somewhere on the grounds near the house at one moment, near the barns at another and in some more remote spot at yet another time. Exact areas are not specified. Sometimes what happens can be seen from the house; at other times we must assume that what happens most certainly cannot be seen from the house. This, of course, allows the play to move quickly and crisply from moment to moment without the necessity of curtains, blackouts, set changes, and dead intervals between scenes. Just as Churchill's play moves freely in space, so does it move freely in time. It would be impossible to say how much time elapses during either Act One or Act Two. Furthermore, the lapse of time between the acts is vague to say the least. We move from the Victorian era in the middle of the nineteenth century to the present day; and yet we must assume that some of the characters—like Betty, Edward and Victoria—who are common to both acts have aged only thirty years or so. Obviously, the dramatist's focus is not on telling a realistic tale; she is far more interested in the audience understanding her message. The odd juxtaposition of time helps her to get her point across by graphically telling us that people do not change much from one period of time to the next.

Because the play makes no attempt to be realistic, the spectator is not disturbed by the fact that the first act is strongly farcical while the second act is noticeably more serious in tone. Such freedom allows Churchill to perform some startling and highly effective theatrical stunts as a means of vivifying her themes and messages. For instance, Victoria in Act One is played by a puppet or rag doll rather than by an actress. There could scarcely be a more direct and viably dramatic way of saying that this female child in the Victorian family is of little consequence; women are, in this society, attractive but insignificant appendages—dolls to be possessed, fondled, adored and humored but not taken seriously. (One hears echoes of Ibsen's *A Doll House* without a word being said.) This, of course, pays off with large, unstated dividends in Act Two when Cathy, Victoria's counterpart, is an obstreperous brat at times and allowed to be one by her modern mother. The employment of a puppet to play a character is not, however, the only theatrical effect in the casting of the play. A black servant in the first act is played by a white actor. The dramatist insists upon that for it is a subtle and subliminal way to comment on Uncle Tomism and to underscore the plight of the black man in a dominantly white society. One of the boldest theatrical strokes in the play is the casting of a man in the role of Betty as well as the shuffling of roles between the two acts. With this device, the playwright—and the actors, to be sure—makes certain that one character's experiences and attitudes will comment on those of another. If, for example, one actress plays the mother in both acts (Maud in Act One and Betty in Act Two), the audience becomes much more poignantly aware of the changing attitudes of women—and toward women—in our present-day society. Notice, incidentally, how this casting arrangement makes a profound point and marks *Cloud Nine* as distinctively dramatic in the purest sense of the word. The audience is not *told* the idea; it is *shown* it. This is not narration or exposition; this is drama. The point or message is not stated directly in the dialogue and, therefore, does not appear on the printed page of the manuscript. The play only makes its meaning clear and fulfills its dramatic intention in the moment of actual production as one actress embodies both characters. Once again, it demands an enormously perceptive and imaginative reader to get the full impact of *Cloud Nine* in the reading of it.

It cannot be denied that Caryl Churchill manipulates the contemporary form of her play with incredible skill. But what is even more surprising and rewarding is that she provides us with such rich content while doing so. Few other plays—very few, indeed—say as much as *Cloud Nine* says about our life of the moment. And much of what is said is so simply accomplished through the device of contrasting the Victorian society of Act One with the present-day society of Act Two. The differences do not have to be discussed; they are there for us to see, to feel, and to experience.

Early in the first act Clive sets the Victorian attitude by asserting: "We are not in this country [*read: this life*] to enjoy ourselves." Man's highest duty on earth is apparently to control and obliterate his baser urges; his actual duty, as it becomes evident, is to keep them well concealed while still seeking to satisfy them. Woman, of course, must do the same. But Woman has the additional burden of denying herself *totally* in order to be what Man says she must be: Subservient. Insignificant. Weak. Unintelligent. Dependent. Attractive. Second-class. Without passion (except that which she should fake to satisfy the male sex drive and male vanity). Procreate for Merry Old England, not for pleasure. Little wonder, then, that no one, male or female, in this society is fulfilled or truly understands oneself. Everything and everyone is exceedingly proper on the surface. Betty, for example, behaves like a proper lady; she reads a little, plays the piano a little and conceals her true self. However, Betty has an affair with Harry. Betty also has a rather unique friendship with Ellen. (She hints at the true nature of that relationship in Act Two.) In the meantime, Harry has homosexual relationships with Joshua and Edward. Edward wants Harry. Ellen wants Betty. Betty wants Harry *and* Clive *and* respectability. Clive has Betty but lusts after Mrs. Saunders—and gets her. Mrs. Saunders seems to want anyone who will suit her immediate purpose. No one, with the possible exception of Maud, is what he or she pretends to be. No one is fulfilled. No one has achieved even a hint of self-awareness or self-identity. Everyone is striving to live up to someone else's or society's image of what he or she should be. Yes, the Victorians, especially Victorian women, were terribly repressed.

But . . . is the situation really any better today? According to Caryl Churchill in her second act, things have not improved much in spite of all our sexual freedoms. Edward is out of the closet but that does not mean he has found happiness. Victoria may experiment with bi-sexual relationships and struggle for identity in a career; but none of that has made her life any richer or more rewarding. Betty is striving very hard to liberate herself, but she cannot escape feeling guilty about doing things for herself rather than doing them for a man. Betty finds the company of other women rather unrewarding because she is still convinced that men's lives are of more interest and value than women's. Gerry (an extension of the character of Harry from Act One) is frankly and openly homosexual, and yet all of his promiscuity does not make him a complete human being or lead him to a truly meaningful relationship with another male. Martin, Victoria's husband, is struggling to be an understanding and supportive mate; but an inherent male chauvinism still causes him problems. Tommy and Cathy, the children, are certainly no better off than their Victorian counterparts. Perhaps Lin, a mother and divorcee and Victoria's lesbian lover, says it best when she confesses, "I've changed who I sleep with. I can't change everything."

And yet, this is not a hopeless world. In the final moments of the play, Betty reaches out feebly to make real contact with other human beings—her daughter, her son, her son-in-law and even a stranger (who turns out to be her son's homosexual lover). In the isolation and loneliness of her new-found freedom—primarily her divorce from Clive and her own gainful employment which gives her financial independence—she learns a vital lesson. Real rewarding human relationships have to begin with an acceptance of others. But an acceptance of others can only begin with an acceptance of yourself. Social freedoms will not guarantee individual fulfillment. That has to begin with the individual. As Betty learns to know and accept herself for the first time there is hope that she will find fulfillment and happiness.

In the final analysis, Churchill, like Ibsen, has scrutinized the social and domestic scene, analyzed it with care, dramatized it for us with incredible clarity and theatrical interest, and sent us out of the theatre with something to think about. And unlike so many of her contemporaries, Caryl Churchill has not only given us a great deal to contemplate, she has given us some answers as well. It is wonderfully refreshing to find that some answers are still possible in today's world in spite of what the Absurdists have told us. In that regard, Caryl Churchill and *Cloud Nine* are good for the soul.

CLOUD NINE

by Caryl Churchill

———— CHARACTERS ————

ACT I

Clive
Betty, *his wife, played by a man*
Joshua, *his black servant, played by a white*
Edward, *his son, played by a woman*
Victoria, *his daughter, a dummy*
Maud, *his mother-in-law*
Ellen, *Edward's governess*
Harry Bagley, *an explorer*
Mrs. Saunders, *a widow*

ACT II

Betty
Edward, *her son*
Victoria, *her daughter*
Martin, *Victoria's husband*
Lin
Cathy, *Lin's daughter age 5, played by a man*
Gerry, *Edward's lover*

Except for Cathy, characters in Act II are played by actors of their own sex.

Act I takes place in a British colony in Africa in Victorian times.

Act II takes place in London in the present, but for the characters it is twenty-five years later.

ACT I
SCENE 1

Low bright sun. Verandah. Flagpole with Union Jack.
The Family—CLIVE, BETTY, EDWARD, VICTORIA, MAUD, ELLEN, JOSHUA.

ALL (*sung*).
Come gather, sons of England, come gather in your
  pride,
Now meet the world united, now face it side by side;
Ye who the earth's wide corners, from veldt to prairie
  roam.
From bush and jungle muster all who call England
  'home'.

Then gather round for England,
Rally to the flag,
From North and South and East and West
Come one and all for England!

CLIVE. This is my family. Though far from home
We serve the Queen wherever we may roam
I am a father to the natives here,
And father to my family so dear.

He presents Betty. She is played by a man.

My wife is all I dreamt a wife should be,
And everything she is she owes to me.

BETTY. I live for Clive. The whole aim of my life
Is to be what he looks for in a wife.
I am a man's creation as you see,
And what men want is what I want to be.

Clive presents Joshua. He is played by a white.

CLIVE. My boy's a jewel. Really has the knack.
You'd hardly notice that the fellow's black.

JOSHUA. My skin is black but oh my soul is white.
I hate my tribe. My master is my light.
I only live for him. As you can see,
What white men want is what I want to be.

Clive presents Edward. He is played by a woman.

CLIVE. My son is young. I'm doing all I can
To teach him to grow up to be a man.

EDWARD. What father wants I'd dearly like to be.
I find it rather hard as you can see.

Clive presents Victoria, who is a dummy, Maud, and Ellen.

CLIVE. No need for any speeches by the rest.
My daughter, mother-in-law, and governess.

ALL (*sung*).
O'er countless numbers she, our Queen,
Victoria reigns supreme;
O'er Afric's sunny plains, and o'er
Canadian frozen stream;
The forge of war shall weld the chains of brother-
  hood secure;
So to all time in ev'ry clime our Empire shall endure.

Then gather round for England,
Rally to the flag,
From North and South and East and West
Come one and all for England!

All go except Betty.

Clive comes.

BETTY. Clive?

CLIVE. Betty. Joshua!

Joshua comes with a drink for Clive.

BETTY. I thought you would never come. The day's
so long without you.

CLIVE. Long ride in the bush.

BETTY. Is anything wrong? I heard drums.

CLIVE. Nothing serious. Beauty is a damned good
mare. I must get some new boots sent from home.
These ones have never been right. I have a blister.

BETTY. My poor dear foot.

CLIVE. It's nothing.

BETTY. Oh but it's sore.

CLIVE. We are not in this country to enjoy ourselves. Must have ridden fifty miles. Spoke to three
different headmen who would all gladly chop off
each other's heads and wear them round their
waists.

BETTY. Clive!

CLIVE. Don't be squeamish, Betty, let me have my
joke. And what has my little dove done today?

BETTY. I've read a little.

CLIVE. Good. Is it good?

BETTY. It's poetry.

CLIVE. You're so delicate and sensitive.

BETTY. And I played the piano. Shall I send for the
children?

CLIVE. Yes, in a minute. I've a piece of news for you.

BETTY. Good news?

CLIVE. You'll certainly think it's good. A visitor.

BETTY. From home?

CLIVE. No. Well of course originally from home.

BETTY. Man or woman?

CLIVE. Man.

BETTY. I can't imagine.

CLIVE. Something of an explorer. Bit of a poet. Old chap but brave as a lion. And a great admirer of yours.

BETTY. What do you mean? Whoever can it be?

CLIVE. With an H and a B. And does conjuring tricks for little Edward.

BETTY. That sounds like Mr. Bagley.

CLIVE. Harry Bagley.

BETTY. He certainly doesn't admire me, Clive, what a thing to say. How could I possibly guess from that. He's hardly explored anything at all, he's just been up a river, he's done nothing at all compared to what you do. You should have said a heavy drinker and a bit of a bore.

CLIVE. But you like him well enough. You don't mind him coming?

BETTY. Anyone at all to break the monotony.

CLIVE. But you have your mother. You have Ellen.

BETTY. Ellen is a governess. My mother is my mother.

CLIVE. I hoped when she came to visit she would be company for you.

BETTY. I don't think mother is on a visit. I think she lives with us.

CLIVE. I think she does.

BETTY. Clive you are so good.

CLIVE. But are you bored my love?

BETTY. It's just that I miss you when you're away. We're not in this country to enjoy ourselves. If I lack society that is my form of service.

CLIVE. That's a brave girl. So today has been all right? No fainting? No hysteria?

BETTY. I have been very tranquil.

CLIVE. Ah what a haven of peace to come home to. The coolth, the calm, the beauty.

BETTY. There is one thing, Clive, if you don't mind.

CLIVE. What can I do for you, my dear?

BETTY. It's about Joshua.

CLIVE. I wouldn't leave you alone here with a quiet mind if it weren't for Joshua.

BETTY. Joshua doesn't like me.

CLIVE. Joshua has been my boy for eight years. He has saved my life. I have saved his life. He is devoted to me and to mine. I have said this before.

BETTY. He is rude to me. He doesn't do what I say. Speak to him.

CLIVE. Tell me what happened.

BETTY. He said something improper.

CLIVE. Well, what?

BETTY. I don't like to repeat it.

CLIVE. I must insist.

BETTY. I had left my book inside on the piano. I was in the hammock. I asked him to fetch it.

CLIVE. And did he not fetch it?

BETTY. Yes, he did eventually.

CLIVE. And what did he say?

BETTY. Clive—

CLIVE. Betty.

BETTY. He said Fetch it yourself. You've got legs under that dress.

CLIVE. Joshua!

Joshua comes.

Joshua, madam says you spoke impolitely to her this afternoon.

JOSHUA. Sir?

CLIVE. When she asked you to pass her book from the piano.

JOSHUA. She has the book, sir.

BETTY. I have the book now, but when I told you—

CLIVE. Betty, please let me handle this. You didn't pass it at once?

JOSHUA. No sir, I made a joke first.

CLIVE. What was that?

JOSHUA. I said my legs were tired, sir. That was funny because the book was very near, it would not make my legs tired to get it.

623

BETTY. That's not true.

JOSHUA. Did madam hear me wrong?

CLIVE. She heard something else.

JOSHUA. What was that, madam?

BETTY. Never mind.

CLIVE. Now Joshua, it won't do you know. Madam doesn't like that kind of joke. You must do what madam says, just do what she says and don't answer back. You know your place, Joshua. I don't have to say any more.

JOSHUA. No sir.

BETTY. I expect an apology.

JOSHUA. I apologise, madam.

CLIVE. There now. It won't happen again, my dear. I'm very shocked Joshua, very shocked.

Clive winks at Joshua, unseen by Betty.
Joshua goes.

CLIVE. I think another drink, and send for the children, and isn't that Harry riding down the hill? Wave, wave. Just in time before dark. Cuts it fine, the blighter. Always a hothead, Harry.

BETTY. Can he see us?

CLIVE. Stand further forward. He'll see your white dress. There, he waved back.

BETTY. Do you think so? I wonder what he saw. Sometimes sunset is so terrifying I can't bear to look.

CLIVE. It makes me proud. Elsewhere in the empire the sun is rising.

BETTY. Harry looks so small on the hillside.

Ellen comes.

ELLEN. Shall I bring the children?

BETTY. Shall Ellen bring the children?

CLIVE. Delightful.

BETTY. Yes, Ellen, make sure they're warm. The night air is deceptive. Victoria was looking pale yesterday.

CLIVE. My love.

Maud comes from inside the house.

MAUD. Are you warm enough Betty?

BETTY. Perfectly.

MAUD. The night air is deceptive.

BETTY. I'm quite warm. I'm too warm.

MAUD. You're not getting a fever, I hope? She's not strong, you know, Clive. I don't know how long you'll keep her in this climate.

CLIVE. I look after Her Majesty's domains, I think you can trust me to look after my wife.

Ellen comes carrying Victoria, age 2, Edward, aged 9, lags behind.

BETTY. Victoria, my pet, say good evening to papa.

Clive takes Victoria on his knee.

CLIVE. There's my sweet little Vicky. What have we done today?

BETTY. She wore Ellen's hat.

CLIVE. Did she wear Ellen's big hat like a lady? What a pretty.

BETTY. And Joshua gave her a piggy back. Tell papa. Horsy with Joshy?

ELLEN. She's tired.

CLIVE. Nice Joshy played horsy. What a big strong Joshy. Did you have a gallop? Did you make him stop and go? Not very chatty tonight are we?

BETTY. Edward, say good evening to papa.

CLIVE. Edward my boy. Have you done your lessons well?

EDWARD. Yes papa.

CLIVE. Did you go riding?

EDWARD. Yes papa.

CLIVE. What's that you're holding?

EDWARD. It's Victoria's doll.

CLIVE. What are you doing with it, Edward?

EDWARD. Minding her.

BETTY. Well I should give it to Ellen quickly. You don't want papa to see you with a doll.

CLIVE. No, we had you with Victoria's doll once before, Edward.

ELLEN. He's minding it for Vicky. He's not playing with it.

BETTY. He's not playing with it, Clive. He's minding it for Vicky.

CLIVE. Ellen minds Victoria, let Ellen mind the doll.

ELLEN. Come, give it to me.

Ellen takes the doll.

EDWARD. Don't pull her apart. Vicky's very fond of her. She likes me to have her.

BETTY. He's a very good brother.

CLIVE. Yes, it's manly of you Edward, to take care of your little sister. We'll say no more about it. Tomorrow I'll take you riding with me and Harry Bagley. Would you like that?

EDWARD. Is he here?

CLIVE. He's just arrived. There Betty, take Victoria now. I must go and welcome Harry.

Clive tosses Victoria to Betty, who gives her to Ellen.

EDWARD. Can I come, papa?

BETTY. Is he warm enough?

EDWARD. Am I warm enough?

CLIVE. Never mind the women, Ned. Come and meet Harry.

They go. The women are left.
There is a silence.

MAUD. I daresay Mr. Bagley will be out all day and we'll see nothing of him.

BETTY. He plays the piano. Surely he will sometimes stay at home with us.

MAUD. We can't expect it. The men have their duties and we have ours.

BETTY. He won't have seen a piano for a year. He lives a very rough life.

ELLEN. Will it be exciting for you, Betty?

MAUD. Whatever do you mean, Ellen?

ELLEN. We don't have very much society.

BETTY. Clive is my society.

MAUD. It's time Victoria went to bed.

ELLEN. She'd like to stay up and see Mr. Bagley.

MAUD. Mr. Bagley can see her tomorrow.

Ellen goes.

MAUD. You let that girl forget her place, Betty.

BETTY. Mother, she is governess to my son. I know what her place is. I think my friendship does her good. She is not very happy.

MAUD. Young women are never happy.

BETTY. Mother, what a thing to say.

MAUD. Then when they're older they look back and see that comparatively speaking they were ecstatic.

BETTY. I'm perfectly happy.

MAUD. You are looking very pretty tonight. You were such a success as a young girl. You have made a most fortunate marriage. I'm sure you will be an excellent hostess to Mr. Bagley.

BETTY. I feel quite nervous at the thought of entertaining.

MAUD. I can always advise you if I'm asked.

BETTY. What a long time they're taking. I always seem to be waiting for the men.

MAUD. Betty you have to learn to be patient. I am patient. My mama was very patient.

Clive approaches, supporting Caroline Saunders.

CLIVE. It is a pleasure. It is an honour. It is positively your duty to seek my help. I would be hurt, I would be insulted by any show of independence. Your husband would have been one of my dearest friends if he had lived. Betty, look who has come, Mrs. Saunders. She has ridden here all alone, amazing spirit. What will you have? Tea or something stronger? Let her lie down, she is overcome. Betty, you will know what to do.

Mrs. Saunders lies down.

MAUD. I knew it. I heard drums. We'll be killed in our beds.

CLIVE. Now, please, calm yourself.

MAUD. I am perfectly calm. I am just outspoken. If it comes to being killed I shall take it as calmly as anyone.

CLIVE. There is no cause for alarm. Mrs. Saunders has been alone since her husband died last year, amazing spirit. Not surprisingly, the strain has told. She has come to us as her nearest neighbours.

MAUD. What happened to make her come?

CLIVE. This is not an easy country for a woman.

MAUD. Clive, I heard drums. We are not children.

CLIVE. Of course you heard drums. The tribes are constantly at war, if the term is not too grand to grace their squabbles. Not unnaturally Mrs. Saunders would like the company of white women. The piano. Poetry.

BETTY. We are not her nearest neighbours.

CLIVE. We are among her nearest neighbours and I was a dear friend of her late husband. She knows that she will find a welcome here. She will not be disappointed. She will be cared for.

MAUD. Of course we will care for her.

BETTY. Victoria is in bed. I must go and say goodnight. Mother, please, you look after Mrs. Saunders.

CLIVE. Harry will be here at once.

Betty goes.

MAUD. How rash to go out after dark without a shawl.

CLIVE. Amazing spirit. Drink this.

MRS. SAUNDERS. Where am I?

MAUD. You are quite safe.

MRS. SAUNDERS. Clive? Clive? Thank God. This is very kind. How do you do? I am sorry to be a nuisance. Charmed. Have you a gun? I have a gun.

CLIVE. There is no need for guns I hope. We are all friends here.

MRS. SAUNDERS. I think I will lie down again.

Harry Bagley and Edward have approached.

MAUD. Ah, here is Mr. Bagley.

EDWARD. I gave his horse some water.

CLIVE. You don't know Mrs. Saunders, do you Harry? She has at present collapsed, but she is recovering thanks to the good offices of my wife's mother who I think you've met before. Betty will be along in a minute. Edward will go home to school shortly. He is quite a young man since you saw him.

HARRY. I hardly knew him.

MAUD. What news have you for us, Mr. Bagley?

CLIVE. Do you know Mrs. Saunders, Harry? Amazing spirit.

EDWARD. Did you hardly know me?

HARRY. Of course I knew you. I mean you have grown.

EDWARD. What do you expect?

HARRY. That's quite right, people don't get smaller.

MAUD. Edward. You should be in bed.

EDWARD. No, I'm not tired, I'm not tired am I Uncle Harry?

HARRY. I don't think he's tired.

CLIVE. He is overtired. It is past his bedtime. Say goodnight.

EDWARD. Goodnight, sir.

CLIVE. And to your grandmother.

EDWARD. Goodnight, grandmother.

Edward goes.

MAUD. Shall I help Mrs. Saunders indoors? I'm afraid she may get a chill.

CLIVE. Shall I give her an arm?

MAUD. How kind of you Clive. I think I am strong enough.

Maud helps Mrs. Saunders into the house.

CLIVE. Not a word to alarm the women.

HARRY. Absolutely.

CLIVE. I did some good today I think. Kept up some alliances. There's a lot of affection there.

HARRY. They're affectionate people. They can be very cruel of course.

CLIVE. Well they are savages.

HARRY. Very beautiful people many of them.

CLIVE. Joshua! (*to* HARRY) I think we should sleep with guns.

HARRY. I haven't slept in a house for six months. It seems extremely safe.

Joshua comes.

CLIVE. Joshua, you will have gathered there's a spot of bother. Rumours of this and that. You should be alarmed I think.

JOSHUA. There are many bad men, sir. I pray about it. Jesus will protect us.

CLIVE. He will indeed and I'll also get you a weapon. Betty, come and keep Harry company. Look in the barn, Joshua, every night.

Clive and Joshua go. Betty comes.

HARRY. I wondered where you were.

BETTY. I was singing lullabies.

HARRY. When I think of you I always think of you with Edward in your lap.

BETTY. Do you think of me sometimes then?

HARRY. You have been thought of where no white woman has ever been thought of before.

BETTY. It's one way of having adventures. I suppose I will never go in person.

HARRY. That's up to you.

BETTY. Of course it's not. I have duties.

HARRY. Are you happy, Betty?

BETTY. Where have you been?

HARRY. Built a raft and went up the river. Stayed with some people. The king is always very good to me. They have a lot of skulls around the place but not white men's I think. I made up a poem one night. If I should die in this forsaken spot, There is a loving heart without a blot, Where I will live— and so on.

BETTY. When I'm near you it's like going out into the jungle. It's like going up the river on a raft. It's like going out in the dark.

HARRY. And you are safety and light and peace and home.

BETTY. But I want to be dangerous.

HARRY. Clive is my friend.

BETTY. I am your friend.

HARRY. I don't like dangerous women.

BETTY. Is Mrs. Saunders dangerous?

HARRY. Not to me. She's a bit of an old boot.

Joshua comes, unobserved.

BETTY. Am I dangerous?

HARRY. You are rather.

BETTY. Please like me.

HARRY. I worship you.

BETTY. Please want me.

HARRY. I don't want to want you. Of course I want you.

BETTY. What are we going to do?

HARRY. I should have stayed on the river. The hell with it.

He goes to take her in his arms, she runs away into the house. Harry stays where he is. He becomes aware of Joshua.

HARRY. Who's there?

JOSHUA. Only me sir.

HARRY. Got a gun now have you?

JOSHUA. Yes sir.

HARRY. Where's Clive?

JOSHUA. Going round the boundaries sir.

HARRY. Have you checked there's nobody in the barns?

JOSHUA. Yes sir.

HARRY. Shall we go in a barn and fuck? It's not an order.

JOSHUA. That's all right, yes.

They go off.

SCENE 2

An open space some distance from the house. MRS. SAUNDERS *alone, breathless.* CLIVE *arrives.*

CLIVE. Why? Why?

MRS. SAUNDERS. Don't fuss, Clive, it makes you sweat.

CLIVE. Why ride off now? Sweat, you would sweat if you were in love with somebody as disgustingly capricious as you are. You will be shot with poisoned arrows. You will miss the picnic. Somebody will notice I came after you.

MRS. SAUNDERS. I didn't want you to come after me. I wanted to be alone.

CLIVE. You will be raped by cannibals.

MRS. SAUNDERS. I just wanted to get out of your house.

CLIVE. My God, what women put us through. Cruel, cruel. I think you are the sort of woman who would enjoy whipping somebody. I've never met one before.

MRS. SAUNDERS. Can I tell you something, Clive?

CLIVE. Let me tell you something first. Since you came to the house I have had an erection twenty-four hours a day except for ten minutes after the time we had intercourse.

MRS. SAUNDERS. I don't think that's physically possible.

CLIVE. You are causing me appalling physical suffering. Is this the way to treat a benefactor?

MRS. SAUNDERS. Clive, when I came to your house the other night I came because I was afraid. The cook was going to let his whole tribe in through the window.

CLIVE. I know that, my poor sweet. Amazing—

MRS. SAUNDERS. I came to you although you are not my nearest neighbour—

CLIVE. Rather than to the old major of seventy-two.

MRS. SAUNDERS. Because the last time he came to visit me I had to defend myself with a shotgun and I thought you would take no for an answer.

CLIVE. But you've already answered yes.

MRS. SAUNDERS. I answered yes once. Sometimes I want to say no.

CLIVE. Women, my God. Look the picnic will start, I have to go to the picnic. Please Caroline—

MRS. SAUNDERS. I think I will have to go back to my own house.

CLIVE. Caroline, if you were shot with poisoned arrows do you know what I'd do? I'd fuck your dead body and poison myself. Caroline, you smell amazing. You terrify me. You are dark like this continent. Mysterious. Treacherous. When you rode to me through the night. When you fainted in my arms. When I came to you in your bed, when I lifted the mosquito netting, when I said let me in, let me in. Oh don't shut me out, Caroline, let me in.

He has been caressing her feet and legs. He disappears completely under her skirt.

MRS. SAUNDERS. Please stop. I can't concentrate. I want to go home. I wish I didn't enjoy the sensation because I don't like you, Clive. I do like living in your house where there's plenty of guns. But I don't like you at all. But I do like the sensation. Well I'll have it then. I'll have it, I'll have it—

Voices are heard singing The First Noel.

Don't stop. Don't stop.

Clives comes out from under her skirt.

CLIVE. The Christmas picnic. I came.

MRS. SAUNDERS. I didn't.

CLIVE. I'm all sticky.

MRS. SAUNDERS. What about me? Wait.

CLIVE. All right, are you? Come on. We mustn't be found.

MRS. SAUNDERS. Don't go now.

CLIVE. Caroline, you are so voracious. Do let go. Tidy yourself up. There's a hair in my mouth.

Clive and Mrs. Saunders go off. Betty and Maud come, with Joshua carrying hamper.

MAUD. I never would have thought a guinea fowl could taste so like a turkey.

BETTY. I had to explain to the cook three times.

MAUD. You did very well dear.

Joshua sits apart with gun. Edward and Harry with Victoria on his shoulder, singing The First Noel. Maud and Betty are unpacking the hamper. Clive arrives separately.

MAUD. This tablecloth was one of my mama's.

BETTY. Uncle Harry playing horsy.

EDWARD. Crackers crackers.

BETTY. Not yet, Edward.

CLIVE. And now the moment we have all been waiting for.

Clive opens champagne. General acclaim.

CLIVE. Oh dear, stained my trousers, never mind.

EDWARD. Can I have some?

MAUD. Oh no Edward, not for you.

CLIVE. Give him half a glass.

MAUD. If your father says so.

CLIVE. All rise please. To Her Majesty Queen Victoria, God bless her, and her husband and all her dear children.

ALL. The Queen.

EDWARD. Crackers crackers.

General cracker pulling, hats. Clive and Harry discuss champagne.

HARRY. Excellent, Clive, wherever did you get it?

CLIVE. I know a chap in French Equatorial Africa.

EDWARD. I won, I won mama.

Ellen arrives.

BETTY. Give a hat to Joshua, he'd like it.

Edward takes hat to Joshua. Betty takes a ball from the hamper and plays catch with Ellen. Murmurs of surprise and congratulations from the men whenever they catch the ball.

EDWARD. Mama, don't play. You know you can't catch a ball.

BETTY. He's perfectly right. I can't throw either.

Betty sits down. Ellen has the ball.

EDWARD. Ellen, don't you play either. You're no good. You spoil it.

Edward takes Victoria from Harry and gives her to Ellen. He takes the ball and throws it to Harry. Harry, Clive and Edward play ball.

BETTY. Ellen come and sit with me. We'll be spectators and clap.

Edward misses the ball.

CLIVE. Butterfingers.

EDWARD. I'm not.

HARRY. Throw straight now.

EDWARD. I did, I did.

CLIVE. Keep your eye on the ball.

EDWARD. You can't throw.

CLIVE. Don't be a baby.

EDWARD. I'm not, throw a hard one, throw a hard one—

CLIVE. Butterfingers. What will Uncle Harry think of you?

EDWARD. It's your fault. You can't throw. I hate you.

He throws the ball wildly in the direction of Joshua.

CLIVE. Now you've lost the ball. He's lost the ball.

EDWARD. It's Joshua's fault. Joshua's butterfingers.

CLIVE. I don't think I want to play any more. Joshua, find the ball will you?

EDWARD. Yes, please play. I'll find the ball. Please play.

CLIVE. You're so silly and you can't catch. You'll be no good at cricket.

MAUD. Why don't we play hide and seek?

EDWARD. Because it's a baby game.

BETTY. You've hurt Edward's feelings.

CLIVE. A boy has no business having feelings.

HARRY. Hide and seek. I'll be it. Everybody must hide. This is the base, you have to get home to base.

EDWARD. Hide and seek, hide and seek.

HARRY. Can we persuade the ladies to join us?

MAUD. I'm playing. I love games.

BETTY. I always get found straight away.

ELLEN. Come on, Betty, do. Vicky wants to play.

EDWARD. You won't find me ever.

They all go except Clive, Harry, Joshua.

HARRY. It is safe, I suppose?

CLIVE. They won't go far. This is very much my territory and it's broad daylight. Joshua will keep an open eye.

HARRY. Well I must give them a hundred. You don't know what this means to me Clive. A chap can only go on so long alone. I can climb mountains and go down rivers, but what's it for? For Christmas and England and games and women singing. This is the empire, Clive. It's not me putting a flag in new lands. It's you. The empire is one big family. I'm one of its black sheep, Clive. And I know you think my life is rather dashing. But I want you to know I admire you. This is the empire, Clive and I serve it. With all my heart.

CLIVE. I think that's about a hundred.

HARRY. Ready or not, here I come!

He goes.

CLIVE. Harry Bagley is a fine man, Joshua. You should be proud to know him. He will be in history books.

JOSHUA. Sir, while we are alone.

CLIVE. Joshua of course, what is it? You always have my ear. Any time.

JOSHUA. Sir, I have some information. The stable boys are not to be trusted. They whisper. They go out at night. They visit their people. Their people are not my people. I do not visit my people.

CLIVE. Thank you, Joshua. They certainly look after Beauty. I'll be sorry to have to replace them.

JOSHUA. They carry knives.

CLIVE. Thank you, Joshua.

JOSHUA. And, sir.

CLIVE. I appreciate this, Joshua, very much.

JOSHUA. Your wife.

CLIVE. Ah, yes?

JOSHUA. She also thinks Harry Bagley is a fine man.

CLIVE. Thank you, Joshua.

JOSHUA. Are you going to hide?

CLIVE. Yes, yes I am. Thank you. Keep your eyes open, Joshua.

JOSHUA. I do, sir.

Clive goes. Joshua goes. Harry and Betty race back to base.

BETTY. I can't run, I can't run at all.

HARRY. There, I've caught you.

BETTY. Harry, what are we going to do?

HARRY. It's impossible, Betty.

BETTY. Shall we run away together?

Maud comes.

MAUD. I give up. Don't catch me. I have been stung.

HARRY. Nothing serious I hope.

MAUD. I have ointment in my bag. I always carry ointment. I shall just sit down and rest. I am too old for all this fun. Hadn't you better be seeking, Harry?

Harry goes. Maud and Betty are alone for some time. They don't speak. Harry and Edward race back.

EDWARD. I won, I won, you didn't catch me.

HARRY. Yes I did.

EDWARD. Mama, who was first?

BETTY. I wasn't watching. I think it was Harry.

EDWARD. It wasn't Harry. You're no good at judging. I won, didn't I grandma?

MAUD. I expect so, since it's Christmas.

EDWARD. I won, Uncle Harry. I'm better than you.

BETTY. Why don't you help Uncle Harry look for the others?

EDWARD. Shall I?

HARRY. Yes, of course.

BETTY. Run along then. He's just coming.

Edward goes.

Harry, I shall scream.

HARRY. Ready or not, here I come.

Harry runs off.

BETTY. Why don't you go back to the house, mother, and rest your insect-bite?

MAUD. Betty, my duty is here. I don't like what I see. Clive wouldn't like it, Betty. I am your mother.

BETTY. Clive gives you a home because you are my mother.

Harry comes back.

HARRY. I can't find anyone else. I'm getting quite hot.

BETTY. Sit down a minute.

HARRY. I can't do that. I'm it. How's your sting?

MAUD. It seems to be swelling up.

BETTY. Why don't you go home and rest? Joshua will go with you. Joshua!

HARRY. I could take you back.

MAUD. That would be charming.

BETTY. You can't go. You're it.

Johsua comes.

BETTY. Joshua, my mother wants to go back to the house. Will you go with her please.

JOSHUA. Sir told me I have to keep an eye.

BETTY. I am telling you to go back to the house. Then you can come back here and keep an eye.

MAUD. Thank you Betty. I know we have our little differences, but I always want what is best for you.

Joshua and Maud go.

HARRY. Don't give way. Keep calm.

BETTY. I shall kill myself.

HARRY. Betty, you are a star in my sky. Without you I would have no sense of direction. I need you, and I need you where you are, I need you to be Clive's wife. I need to go up rivers and know you are sitting here thinking of me.

BETTY. I want more than that. Is that wicked of me?

HARRY. Not wicked, Betty. Silly.

Edward calls in the distance.

EDWARD. Uncle Harry, where are you?

BETTY. Can't we ever be alone?

HARRY. You are a mother. And a daughter. And a wife.

BETTY. I think I shall go and hide again.

Betty goes. Harry goes. Clive chases Mrs. Saunders across the stage. Edward and Harry call in the distance.

EDWARD. Uncle Harry!

HARRY. Edward!

Edward comes.

EDWARD. Uncle Harry!

Harry comes.

There you are. I haven't found anyone have you?

HARRY. I wonder where they all are.

EDWARD. Perhaps they're lost forever. Perhaps they're dead. There's trouble going on isn't there, and nobody says because of not frightening the women and children.

HARRY. Yes, that's right.

EDWARD. Do you think we'll be killed in our beds?

HARRY. Not very likely.

EDWARD. I can't sleep at night. Can you?

HARRY. I'm not used to sleeping in a house.

EDWARD. If I'm awake at night can I come and see you? I won't wake you up. I'll only come in if you're awake.

HARRY. You should try to sleep.

EDWARD. I don't mind being awake because I make up adventures. Once we were on a raft going down to the rapids. We've lost the paddles because we used them to fight off the crocodiles. A crocodile comes at me and I stab it again and again and the blood is everywhere and it tips up the raft and it has you by the leg and it's biting your leg right off and I take my knife and stab it in the throat and rip open its stomach and it lets go of you but it bites my hand but it's dead. And I drag you onto the river bank and I'm almost fainting with pain and we lie there in each other's arms.

HARRY. Have I lost my leg?

EDWARD. I forgot about the leg by then.

HARRY. Hadn't we better look for the others?

EDWARD. Wait. I've got something for you. It was in mama's box but she never wears it.

Edward gives Harry a necklace.

You don't have to wear it either but you might like it to look at.

HARRY. It's beautiful. But you'll have to put it back.

EDWARD. I wanted to give it to you.

HARRY. You did. It can go back in the box. You still gave it to me. Come on now, we have to find the others.

EDWARD. Harry, I love you.

HARRY. Yes I know. I love you too.

EDWARD. You know what we did when you were here before. I want to do it again. I think about it all the time. I try to do it myself but it's not as good. Don't you want to any more?

HARRY. I do, but it's a sin and a crime and it's also wrong.

EDWARD. But we'll do it anyway won't we?

HARRY. Yes of course.

EDWARD. I wish the others would all be killed. Take it out now and let me see it.

HARRY. No.

EDWARD. Is it big now?

HARRY. Yes.

EDWARD. Let me touch it.

HARRY. No.

EDWARD. Just hold me.

HARRY. When you can't sleep.

EDWARD. We'd better find the others then. Come on.

HARRY. Ready or not, here we come.

They go out with whoops and shouts. Betty and Ellen come.

BETTY. Ellen, I don't want to play any more.

ELLEN. Nor do I, Betty.

BETTY. Come and sit here with me. Oh Ellen, what will become of me?

ELLEN. Betty, are you crying? Are you laughing?

BETTY. Tell me what you think of Harry Bagley.

ELLEN. He's a very fine man.

BETTY. No, Ellen, what you really think.

ELLEN. I think you think he's very handsome.

BETTY. And don't you think he is? Oh Ellen, you're so good and I'm so wicked.

ELLEN. I'm not so good as you think.

Edward comes.

EDWARD. I've found you.

ELLEN. We're not hiding Edward.

EDWARD. But I found you.

ELLEN. We're not playing, Edward, now run along.

EDWARD. Come on, Ellen, do play. Come on, mama.

ELLEN. Edward, don't pull your mama like that.

BETTY. Edward, you must do what your governess says. Go and play with Uncle Harry.

EDWARD. Uncle Harry!

Edward goes.

BETTY. Ellen, can you keep a secret?

ELLEN. Oh yes, yes please.

BETTY. I love Harry Bagley. I want to go away with him. There, I've said it, it's true.

ELLEN. How do you know you love him?

BETTY. I kissed him.

ELLEN. Betty.

BETTY. He held my hand like this. Oh I want him to do it again. I want him to stroke my hair.

ELLEN. Your lovely hair. Like this, Betty?

BETTY. I want him to put his arm around my waist.

ELLEN. Like this, Betty?

BETTY. Yes, oh I want him to kiss me again.

ELLEN. Like this Betty?

Ellen kisses Betty.

BETTY. Ellen, whatever are you doing? It's not a joke.

ELLEN. I'm sorry, Betty. You're so pretty. Harry Bagley doesn't deserve you. You wouldn't really go away with him?

BETTY. Oh Ellen, you don't know what I suffer. You don't know what love is. Everyone will hate me, but it's worth it for Harry's love.

ELLEN. I don't hate you, Betty, I love you.

BETTY. Harry says we shouldn't go away. But he says he worships me.

ELLEN. I worship you Betty.

BETTY. Oh Ellen, you are my only friend.

They embrace. The others have all gathered together. Maud has rejoined the party, and Joshua.

CLIVE. Come along everyone, you mustn't miss Harry's conjuring trick.

Betty and Ellen go to join the others.

MAUD. I didn't want to spoil the fun by not being here.

HARRY. What is it that flies all over the world and is up my sleeve?

Harry produces a union jack from up his sleeve. General acclaim.

CLIVE. I think we should have some singing now. Ladies, I rely on you to lead the way.

ELLEN. We have a surprise for you. I have taught Joshua a Christmas carol. He has been singing it at the piano but I'm sure he can sing it unaccompanied, can't you, Joshua?

JOSHUA. In the deep midwinter
Frosty wind made moan,
Earth stood hard as iron,
Water like a stone.
Snow had fallen snow on snow
Snow on snow,
In the deep midwinter
Long long ago.

What can I give him
Poor as I am
If I were a shepherd
I would bring a lamb.
If I were a wise man
I would do my part
What I can I give him,
Give my heart.

SCENE 3

Inside the house. BETTY, MRS. SAUNDERS, MAUD *with* VICTORIA. *The blinds are down so the light isn't bright though it is day outside.* CLIVE *looks in.*

CLIVE. Everything all right? Nothing to be frightened of.

Clive goes. Silence.

MAUD. Clap hands, daddy comes, with his pockets full of plums. All for Vicky.

Silence.

MRS. SAUNDERS. Who actually does the flogging?

MAUD. I don't think we want to imagine.

MRS. SAUNDERS. I imagine Joshua.

BETTY. Yes I think it would be Joshua. Or would Clive do it himself?

MRS. SAUNDERS. Well we can ask them afterwards.

MAUD. I don't like the way you speak of it, Mrs. Saunders.

MRS. SAUNDERS. How should I speak of it?

MAUD. The men will do it in the proper way, whatever it is. We have our own part to play.

MRS. SAUNDERS. Harry Bagley says they should just be sent away. I don't think he likes to see them beaten.

BETTY. Harry is so tender-hearted. Perhaps he is right.

MAUD. Harry Bagley is not altogether—He has lived in this country a long time without any responsibilities. It is part of his charm but it hasn't improved his judgment. If the boys were just sent away they would go back to the village and make more trouble.

MRS. SAUNDERS. And what will they say about us in the village if they've been flogged?

BETTY. Perhaps Clive should keep them here.

MRS. SAUNDERS. That is never wise.

BETTY. Whatever shall we do?

MAUD. I don't think it is up to us to wonder. The men don't tell us what is going on among the tribes, so how can we possibly make a judgment?

MRS. SAUNDERS. I know a little of what is going on.

BETTY. Tell me what you know. Clive tells me nothing.

MAUD. You would not want to be told about it, Betty. It is enough for you that Clive knows what is happening. Clive will know what to do. Your father always knew what to do.

BETTY. Are you saying you would do something different, Caroline?

MRS. SAUNDERS. I would do what I did at my own home. I left. I can't see any way out except to leave. I will leave here. I will keep leaving everywhere I suppose.

MAUD. Luckily this household has a head. I am squeamish myself. But Clive is not.

BETTY. You are leaving here then Caroline?

MRS. SAUNDERS. Not immediately. I'm sorry.

Silence.

MRS. SAUNDERS. I wonder if it's over.

Edward comes in.

BETTY. Shouldn't you be with the men, Edward?

EDWARD. I didn't want to see any more. They got what they deserved. Uncle Harry said I could come in.

MRS. SAUNDERS. I never allowed the servants to be beaten in my own house. I'm going to find out what's happening.

Mrs. Saunders goes out.

BETTY. Will she go and look?

MAUD. Let Mrs. Saunders be a warning to you, Betty. She is alone in the world. You are not, thank God. Since your father died, I know what it is to be unprotected. Vicky is such a pretty little girl. Clap hands, daddy comes, with his pockets full of plums. All for Vicky.

Edward, meanwhile, has found the doll and is playing clap hands with her.

BETTY. Edward, what have you got there?

EDWARD. I'm minding her.

BETTY. Edward, I've told you before, dolls are for girls.

MAUD. Where is Ellen? She should be looking after Edward. (*She goes to the door.*) Ellen! Betty, why do you let that girl mope about in her own room? That's not what she's come to Africa for.

BETTY. You must never let the boys at school know you like dolls. Never, never. No one will talk to you, you won't be on the cricket team, you won't grow up to be a man like your papa.

EDWARD. I don't want to be like papa. I hate papa.

MAUD. Edward! Edward!

BETTY. You're a horrid wicked boy and papa will beat you. Of course you don't hate him, you love him. Now give Victoria her doll at once.

EDWARD. She's not Victoria's doll, she's my doll. She doesn't love Victoria and Victoria doesn't love her. Victoria never even plays with her.

MAUD. Victoria will learn to play with her.

EDWARD. She's mine and she loves me and she won't be happy if you take her away, she'll cry, she'll cry, she'll cry.

Betty takes the doll away, slaps him, bursts into tears. Ellen comes in.

BETTY. Ellen, look what you've done. Edward's got the doll again. Now, Ellen, will you please do your job.

ELLEN. Edward, you are a wicked boy. I am going to lock you in the nursery until supper time. Now go upstairs this minute.

She slaps Edward, who bursts into tears and goes out.

I do try to do what you want. I'm so sorry.

Ellen bursts into tears and goes out.

MAUD. There now, Vicky's got her baby back. Where did Vicky's naughty baby go? Shall we smack her? Just a little smack? (MAUD *smacks the doll hard.*) There, now she's a good baby. Clap hands, daddy comes, with his pockets full of plums. All for Vicky's baby. When I was a child we honoured our parents. My mama was an angel.

Joshua comes in. He stands without speaking.

BETTY. Joshua?

JOSHUA. Madam?

BETTY. Did you want something?

JOSHUA. Sent to see the ladies are all right, madam.

Mrs. Saunders comes in.

MRS. SAUNDERS. We're very well thank you Joshua, and how are you?

JOSHUA. Very well thank you Mrs. Saunders.

MRS. SAUNDERS. And the stable boys?

JOSHUA. They have had justice, madam.

MRS. SAUNDERS. So I saw. And does your arm ache?

MAUD. This is not a proper conversation, Mrs. Saunders.

MRS. SAUNDERS. You don't mind beating your own people?

JOSHUA. Not my people, madam.

MRS. SAUNDERS. A different tribe?

JOSHUA. Bad people.

Harry and Clive come in.

CLIVE. Well this is all very gloomy and solemn. Can we have the shutters open? The heat of the day has gone, we could have some light, I think. And cool drinks on the verandah, Joshua. Have some lemonade yourself. It is most refreshing.

Sunlight floods in as the shutters are opened. Edward comes.

EDWARD. Papa, papa, Ellen tried to lock me in the nursery. Mama is going to tell you of me. I'd rather tell you myself. I was playing with Vicky's doll again and I know it's very bad of me. And I said I didn't want to be like you and I said I hated you. And it's not true and I'm sorry, I'm sorry and please beat me and forgive me.

CLIVE. Well there's a brave boy to own up. You should always respect and love me, Edward, not for myself, I may not deserve it, but as I respected and loved my own father, because he was my father. Through our father we love our Queen and our God, Edward. Do you understand? It is something men understand.

EDWARD. Yes papa.

CLIVE. Then I forgive you and shake you by the hand. You spend too much time with the women. You may spend more time with me and Uncle Harry, little man.

EDWARD. I don't like women. I don't like dolls. I love you, papa, and I love you, Uncle Harry.

CLIVE. There's a fine fellow. Let us go out onto the verandah.

They all start to go. Edward takes Harry's hand and goes with him. Clives draws Betty back. They embrace.

BETTY. Poor Clive.

CLIVE. It was my duty to have them flogged. For you and Edward and Victoria, to keep you safe.

BETTY. It is terrible to feel betrayed.

CLIVE. You can tame a wild animal only so far. They revert to their true nature and savage your hand. Sometimes I feel the natives are the enemy. I know that is wrong. I know I have a responsibility towards them, to care for them and bring them all to be like Joshua. But there is something dangerous. Implacable. This whole continent is my enemy. I am pitching my whole mind and will and

reason and spirit against it to tame it, and I sometimes feel it will break over me and swallow me
up.

BETTY. Clive, Clive, I am here. I have faith in you.

CLIVE. Yes, I can show you my moments of weakness, Betty, because you are my wife and because
I trust you. I trust you, Betty, and it would break
my heart if you did not deserve that trust. Harry
Bagley is my friend. It would break my heart if
he did not deserve my trust.

BETTY. I'm sorry, I'm sorry. Forgive me. It is not
Harry's fault, it is all mine. Harry is noble. He has
rejected me. It is my wickedness, I get bored, I get
restless, I imagine things. There is something so
wicked in me Clive.

CLIVE. I have never thought of you having the
weakness of your sex, only the good qualities.

BETTY. I am bad, bad, bad—

CLIVE. You are thoughtless, Betty, that's all. Women
can be treacherous and evil. They are darker and
more dangerous than men. The family protects us
from that, you protect me from that. You are not
that sort of woman. You are not unfaithful to me,
Betty. I can't believe you are. It would hurt me so
much to cast you off. That would be my duty.

BETTY. No, no, no.

CLIVE. Joshua has seen you kissing.

BETTY. Forgive me.

CLIVE. But I don't want to know about it. I don't
want to know. I wonder of course, I wonder constantly. If Harry Bagley was not my friend I would
shoot him. If I shot you every British man and
woman would applaud me. But no. It was a
moment of passion such as women are too weak
to resist. But you must resist it, Betty, or it will
destroy us. We must fight against it. We must resist
this dark female lust, Betty, or it will swallow us
up.

BETTY. I do, I do resist. Help me. Forgive me.

CLIVE. Yes I do forgive you. But I can't feel the same
about you as I did. You are still my wife and we
still have duties to the household.

*They go out arm in arm. As soon as they have gone
Edward sneaks back to get the doll, which has been
dropped on the floor. He picks it up and comforts
it. Joshua comes through with a tray of drinks.*

JOSHUA. Baby. Sissy. Girly.

Joshua goes. Betty calls from off.

BETTY. Edward?

Betty comes in.

BETTY. There you are, my darling. Come, papa
wants us all to be together. Uncle Harry is going
to tell how he caught a crocodile. Mama's sorry
she smacked you.

*They embrace. Joshua comes in again, passing
through.*

BETTY. Joshua, fetch me some blue thread from my
sewing box. It is on the piano.

JOSHUA. You've got legs under that skirt.

BETTY. Joshua.

JOSHUA. And more than legs.

BETTY. Edward, are you going to stand there and
let a servant insult your mother?

EDWARD. Joshua, get my mother's thread.

JOSHUA. Oh little Eddy, playing at master. It's only
a joke.

EDWARD. Don't speak to my mother like that again.

JOSHUA. Ladies have no sense of humour. You like
a joke with Joshua.

EDWARD. You fetch her sewing at once, do you hear
me?
You move when I speak to you, boy.

JOSHUA. Yes sir, master Edward sir.

Joshua goes.

BETTY. Edward, you were wonderful.

She goes to embrace him but he moves away.

EDWARD. Don't touch me.

SONG—*A Boy's Best Friend*—ALL.

While plodding on our way, the toilsome road of life,
How few the friends that daily there we meet!
Not many will stand by in trouble and in strife,
With counsel and affection ever sweet!
But there is one whose smile will ever on us beam,
Whose love is dearer far than any other;
And wherever we may turn
This lesson we will learn
A boy's best friend is his mother.

Then cherish her with care
And smooth her silv'ry hair,
When gone you will never get another.
And wherever we may turn
This lesson we shall learn,
A boy's best friend is his Mother.

SCENE 4

The verandah as in Scene 1. Early morning. Nobody there. JOSHUA *comes out of the house slowly and stands for some time doing nothing.* EDWARD *comes out.*

EDWARD. Tell me another bad story, Joshua. Nobody else is even awake yet.

JOSHUA. First there was nothing and then there was the great goddess. She was very large and she had golden eyes and she made the stars and the sun and the earth. But soon she was miserable and lonely and she cried like a great waterfall and her tears made all the rivers in the world. So the great spirit sent a terrible monster, a tree with hundreds of eyes and a long green tongue, and it came chasing after her and she jumped into a lake and the tree jumped in after her, and she jumped right up into the sky. And the tree couldn't follow, he was stuck in the mud. So he picked up a big handful of mud and he threw it at her, up among the stars, and it hit her on the head. And she fell down onto the earth into his arms and the ball of mud is the moon in the sky. And then they had children which is all of us.

EDWARD. It's not true, though.

JOSHUA. Of course it's not true. It's a bad story. Adam and Eve is true. God made man white like him and gave him the bad woman who liked the snake and gave us all this trouble.

Clive and Harry come out.

CLIVE. Run along now, Edward. No, you may stay. You mustn't repeat anything you hear to your mother or your grandmother or Ellen.

EDWARD. Or Mrs. Saunders.

CLIVE. Mrs. Saunders is an unusual woman and does not require protection in the same way. Harry, there was trouble last night where we expected it. But it's all over now. Everything is under control but nobody should leave the house today I think.

HARRY. Casualties?

CLIVE. No, none of the soldiers hurt thank God. We did a certain amount, set a village on fire and so forth.

HARRY. Was that necessary?

CLIVE. Obviously, it was necessary, Harry, or it wouldn't have happened. The army will come and visit, no doubt. You'll like that, eh, Joshua, to see the British army? And a treat for you, Edward, to see the soldiers. Would you like to be a soldier?

EDWARD. I'd rather be an explorer.

CLIVE. Ah, Harry, like you, you see. I didn't know an explorer at his age. Breakfast, I think, Joshua.

Clive and Joshua go in. Harry is following.

EDWARD. Uncle.

Harry stops.

EDWARD. Harry, why won't you talk to me?

HARRY. Of course I'll talk to you.

EDWARD. If you won't be nice to me I'll tell father.

HARRY. Edward, no, not a word, never, not to your mother, nobody, please. Edward, do you understand? Please.

EDWARD. I won't tell. I promise I'll never tell. I've cut my finger and sworn.

HARRY. There's no need to get so excited Edward. We can't be together all the time. I will have to leave soon anyway, and go back to the river.

EDWARD. You can't, you can't go. Take me with you.

ELLEN. Edward!

HARRY. I have my duty to the Empire.

Harry goes in. Ellen comes out.

ELLEN. Edward, breakfast time. Edward.

EDWARD. I'm not hungry.

ELLEN. Betty, please come and speak to Edward.

Betty comes.

BETTY. Why what's the matter?

ELLEN. He won't come in for breakfast.

BETTY. Edward, I shall call your father.

EDWARD. You can't make me eat.

He goes in. Betty is about to follow.

ELLEN. Betty.

Betty stops.

ELLEN. Betty, when Edward goes to school will I have to leave?

BETTY. Never mind, Ellen dear, you'll get another place. I'll give you an excellent reference.

ELLEN. I don't want another place, Betty. I want to stay with you forever.

BETTY. If you go back to England you might get married, Ellen. You're quite pretty, you shouldn't despair of getting a husband.

ELLEN. I don't want a husband. I want you.

BETTY. Children of your own, Ellen, think.

ELLEN. I don't want children, I don't like children. I just want to be alone with you, Betty, and sing for you and kiss you because I love you, Betty.

BETTY. I love you too, Ellen dear. But women have their duty as soldiers have. You must be a mother if you can.

ELLEN. Betty, Betty, I love you so much. I want to stay with you forever, my love for you is eternal, stronger than death. I'd rather die than leave you, Betty.

BETTY. No you wouldn't. Ellen, don't be silly. Come, don't cry. You don't feel what you think you do. It's the loneliness here and the climate is very confusing. Come and have breakfast, Ellen dear, and I'll forget all about it.

Ellen goes, Clive comes.

BETTY. Clive, please forgive me.

CLIVE. Will you leave me alone?

Betty goes back into the house. Harry comes.

CLIVE. Women, Harry. I envy you going into the jungle, a man's life.

HARRY. I envy you.

CLIVE. Harry, I know you do. I have spoken to Betty.

HARRY. I assure you, Clive—

CLIVE. Please say nothing about it.

HARRY. My friendship is for you—

CLIVE. Absolutely. I know the friendship between us, Harry, is not something that could be spoiled by the weaker sex. Friendship between men is a fine thing. It is the noblest form of relationship.

HARRY. I agree with you.

CLIVE. There is the necessity of reproduction. The family is all important. And there is the pleasure. But what we put ourselves through to get that pleasure, Harry. When I heard about our fine fellows last night fighting those savages to protect us I thought yes, that is what I aspire to. I tell you Harry, in confidence, I suddenly got out of Mrs. Saunders' bed and came out here on the verandah and looked at the stars.

HARRY. I couldn't sleep last night either.

CLIVE. There is something dark about women, that threatens what is best in us. Between men that light burns brightly.

HARRY. I didn't know you felt like that.

CLIVE. Women are irrational, demanding, inconsistent, treacherous, lustful, and they smell different from us.

HARRY. Clive—

CLIVE. Think of the comradeship of men, Harry, sharing adventures, sharing danger, risking their lives together.

Harry takes hold of Clive.

CLIVE. What are you doing?

HARRY. Well, you said—

CLIVE. I said what?

HARRY. Between men.

Clive is speechless.

I'm sorry, I misunderstood, I would never have dreamt, I thought—

CLIVE. My God, Harry, how disgusting.

HARRY. You will not betray my confidence.

CLIVE. I feel contaminated.

HARRY. I struggle against it. You cannot imagine the shame. I have tried everything to save myself.

CLIVE. The most revolting perversion. Rome fell, Harry, and this sin can destroy an empire.

HARRY. It is not a sin, it is a disease.

CLIVE. A disease more dangerous than diphtheria. Effeminacy is contagious. How I have been deceived. Your face does not look degenerate. Oh Harry, how did you sink to this?

HARRY. Clive, help me, what am I to do?

CLIVE. You have been away from England too long.

HARRY. Where can I go except into the jungle to hide?

CLIVE. You don't do it with the natives, Harry? My God, what a betrayal of the Queen.

HARRY. Clive, I am like a man born crippled. Please help me.

CLIVE. You must repent.

HARRY. I have thought of killing myself.

CLIVE. That is a sin too.

HARRY. There is no way out. Clive I beg of you do not betray my confidence.

CLIVE. I cannot keep a secret like this. Rivers will be named after you, it's unthinkable. You must save yourself from depravity. You must get married. You are not unattractive to women. What a relief that you and Betty were not after all—good God, how disgusting. Now Mrs. Saunders. She's a woman of spirit, she could go with you on your expeditions.

HARRY. I suppose getting married wouldn't be any worse than killing myself.

CLIVE. Mrs. Saunders! Mrs. Saunders! Ask her now, Harry. Think of England.

Mrs. Saunders comes.

Clive withdraws. Harry goes up to Mrs. Saunders.

HARRY. Mrs. Saunders, will you marry me?

MRS. SAUNDERS. Why?

HARRY. We are both alone.

MRS. SAUNDERS. I choose to be alone, Mr. Bagley. If I can look after myself, I'm sure you can. Clive, I have something important to tell you. I've just found Joshua putting earth on his head. He tells me his parents were killed last night by the British soldiers. I think you owe him an apology on behalf of the Queen.

CLIVE. Joshua! Joshua!

MRS. SAUNDERS. Mr. Bagley, I could never be a wife again. There is only one thing about marriage that I like.

Joshua comes.

CLIVE. Joshua, I am horrified to hear what has happened. Good God!

MRS. SAUNDERS. His father was shot. His mother died in the blaze.

Mrs. Saunders goes.

CLIVE. Joshua, do you want a day off? Do you want to go to your people?

JOSHUA. Not my people, sir.

CLIVE. But you want to go to your parents' funeral?

JOSHUA. No sir.

CLIVE. Yes, Joshua, yes, your father and mother. I'm sure they were loyal to the crown. I'm sure it was all a terrible mistake.

JOSHUA. My mother and father were bad people.

CLIVE. Joshua, no.

JOSHUA. You are my father and mother.

CLIVE. Well really. I don't know what to say. That's very decent of you. Are you sure there's nothing I can do? You can have the day off you know.

Betty comes out followed by Edward.

BETTY. What's the matter? What's happening?

CLIVE. Something terrible has happened. No, I mean some relatives of Joshua's met with an accident.

JOSHUA. May I go sir?

CLIVE. Yes, yes of course. Good God, what a terrible thing. Bring us a drink will you Joshua?

Joshua goes.

EDWARD. What? What?

BETTY. Edward, go and do your lessons.

EDWARD. What is it, Uncle Harry?

HARRY. Go and do your lessons.

ELLEN. Edward, come in here at once.

EDWARD. What's happened, Uncle Harry?

Harry has moved aside, Edward follows him. Ellen comes out.

HARRY. Go away. Go inside. Ellen!

ELLEN. Go inside, Edward. I shall tell your mother.

BETTY. Go inside, Edward at once. I shall tell your father.

CLIVE. Go inside, Edward. And Betty you go inside too.

Betty, Edward and Ellen go. Maud comes out.

CLIVE. Go inside. And Ellen, you come outside.

Ellen comes out.

Mr. Bagley has something to say to you.

HARRY. Ellen. I don't suppose you would marry me?

ELLEN. What if I said yes?

CLIVE. Run along now, you two want to be alone.

Harry and Ellen go out. Joshua brings Clive a drink.

JOSHUA. The governess and your wife, sir.

CLIVE. What's that, Joshua?

JOSHUA. She talks of love to your wife, sir. I have seen them. Bad women.

CLIVE. Joshua, you go too far. Get out of my sight.

SCENE 5

The verandah. A table with a white cloth. A wedding cake and a large knife. Bottles and glasses. JOSHUA *is putting things on the table.* EDWARD *has the doll.* JOSHUA *sees him with it. He holds out his hand.* EDWARD *gives him the doll.* JOSHUA *takes the knife and cuts the doll open and shakes the sawdust out of it.* JOSHUA *throws the doll under the table.*

MAUD. Come along Edward, this is such fun.

Everyone enters, triumphal arch for Harry and Ellen.

MAUD. Your mama's wedding was a splendid occasion, Edward. I cried and cried.

Ellen and Betty go aside.

ELLEN. Betty, what happens with a man? I don't know what to do.

BETTY. You just keep still.

ELLEN. And what does he do?

BETTY. Harry will know what to do.

ELLEN. And is it enjoyable?

BETTY. Ellen, you're not getting married to enjoy yourself.

ELLEN. Don't forget me, Betty.

Ellen goes.

BETTY. I think my necklace has been stolen Clive. I did so want to wear it at the wedding.

EDWARD. It was Joshua. Joshua took it.

CLIVE. Joshua?

EDWARD. He did, he did, I saw him with it.

HARRY. Edward, that's not true.

EDWARD. It is, it is.

HARRY. Edward, I'm afraid you took it yourself.

EDWARD. I did not.

HARRY. I have seen him with it.

CLIVE. Edward, is that true? Where is it? Did you take your mother's necklace? And to try and blame Joshua, good God.

Edward runs off.

BETTY. Edward, come back. Have you got my necklace?

HARRY. I should leave him alone. He'll bring it back.

BETTY. I wanted to wear it. I wanted to look my best at your wedding.

HARRY. You always look your best to me.

BETTY. I shall get drunk.

Mrs. Saunders comes.

MRS. SAUNDERS. The sale of my property is completed. I shall leave tomorrow.

CLIVE. That's just as well. Whose protection will you seek this time?

MRS. SAUNDERS. I shall go to England and buy a farm there. I shall introduce threshing machines.

CLIVE. Amazing spirit.

He kisses her. Betty launches herself on Mrs. Saunders. They fall to the ground.

CLIVE. Betty—Caroline—I don't deserve this—Harry, Harry.

Harry and Clive separate them. Harry holding Mrs. Saunders, Clive Betty.

CLIVE. Mrs. Saunders, how can you abuse my hospitality? How dare you touch my wife? You must leave here at once.

BETTY. Go away, go away. You are a wicked woman.

MAUD. Mrs. Saunders, I am shocked. This is your hostess.

CLIVE. Pack your bags and leave the house this instant.

MRS. SAUNDERS. I was leaving anyway. There's no place for me here. I have made arrangements to leave tomorrow, and tomorrow is when I will leave. I wish you joy, Mr. Bagley.

Mrs. Saunders goes.

CLIVE. No place for her anywhere I should think. Shocking behaviour.

BETTY. Oh Clive, forgive me, and love me like you used to.

CLIVE. Were you jealous my dove? My own dear wife!

MAUD. Ah, Mr. Bagley, one flesh, you see.

Edward comes back with the necklace.

CLIVE. Good God, Edward, it's true.

EDWARD. I was minding it for mama because of the troubles.

CLIVE. Well done, Edward, that was very manly of you. See Betty? Edward was protecting his mama's jewels from the rebels. What a hysterical fuss over nothing. Well done, little man. It is quite safe now. The bad men are dead. Edward, you may do up the necklace for mama.

Edward does up Betty's necklace, supervised by Clive, Joshua is drinking steadily. Ellen comes back.

MAUD. Ah, here's the bride. Come along, Ellen, you don't cry at your own wedding, only at other people's.

CLIVE. Now, speeches, speeches. Who is going to make a speech? Harry, make a speech.

HARRY. I'm no speaker. You're the one for that.

ALL. Speech, speech.

HARRY. My dear friends—what can I say—the empire—the family—the married state to which I have always aspired—your shining example of domestic bliss—my great good fortune in winning Ellen's love—happiest day of my life.

Applause.

CLIVE. Cut the cake, cut the cake.

Harry and Ellen take the knife to cut the cake. Harry steps on the doll under the table.

HARRY. What's this?

ELLEN. Oh look.

BETTY. Edward.

EDWARD. It was Joshua. It was Joshua. I saw him.

CLIVE. Don't tell lies again.

He hits Edward across the side of the head.

CLIVE. Unaccustomed as I am to public speaking—

Cheers.

Harry, my friend. So brave and strong and supple.
Ellen, from neath her veil so shyly peeking.
I wish you joy. A toast—the happy couple.

Dangers are past. Our enemies are killed.
—Put your arm round her, Harry, have a kiss—
All murmuring of discontent is stilled.
Long may you live in peace and joy and bliss.

While he is speaking Joshua raises his gun to shoot Clive. Only Edward sees. He does nothing to warn the others. He puts his hands over his ears.
BLACK.

ACT II
SCENE 1

Winter afternoon. Inside the hut of a one o'clock club, a children's playcentre in a park, VICTORIA *and* LIN, *mothers.* CATHY, LIN's *daughter, age 4, played by a man, clinging to* LIN. VICTORIA *reading a book.*

CATHY. Yum yum bubblegum.
Stick it up your mother's bum
When it's brown
Pull it down
Yum yum bubblegum.

LIN. Like your shoes, Victoria.

CATHY. Jack be nimble, Jack be quick
Jack jump over the candlestick.
Silly Jack, he should jump higher
Goodness gracious, great balls of fire.

LIN. Cathy, do stop. Do a painting.

CATHY. You do a painting.

LIN. You do a painting.

CATHY. What shall I paint?

LIN. Paint a house.

CATHY. No.

LIN. Princess.

CATHY. No.

LIN. Pirates.

CATHY. Already done that.

LIN. Spacemen.

CATHY. I never paint spacemen. You know I never.

LIN. Paint a car crash and blood everywhere.

CATHY. No, don't tell me. I know what to paint.

LIN. Go on then. You need an apron, where's an apron. Here.

CATHY. Don't want an apron.

LIN. Lift up your arms. There's a good girl.

CATHY. I don't want to paint.

LIN. Don't paint. Don't paint.

CATHY. What shall I do? You paint. What shall I do mum?

VICTORIA. There's nobody on the big bike, Cathy, quick.

Cathy goes out. Victoria is watching the children playing outside.

VICTORIA. Tommy, it's Jimmy's gun. Let him have it. What the hell.

She goes on reading. She reads while she talks.

LIN. I don't know how you can concentrate.

VICTORIA. You have to or you never do anything.

LIN. Yeh, well. It's really warm in here, that's one thing. It's better than standing out there. I got chilblains last winter.

VICTORIA. It is warm.

LIN. I suppose Tommy doesn't let you read much. I expect he talks to you while you're reading.

VICTORIA. Yes, he does.

LIN. I didn't get very far with that book you lent me.

VICTORIA. That's all right.

LIN. I was glad to have it, though. I sit with it on my lap while I'm watching the telly. Well, Cathy's off. She's frightened I'm going to leave her. It's the babyminder didn't work out when she was two, she still remembers. You can't get them used to other people if you're by yourself. It's no good blaming me. She clings round my knees every morning up the nursery and they don't say anything but they make you feel you're making her do it. But I'm desperate for her to go to school. I did cry when I left her the first day. You wouldn't, you're too fucking sensible. You'll call the teacher by her first name. I really fancy you.

VICTORIA. What?

LIN. Put your book down will you for five minutes. You didn't hear a word I said.

VICTORIA. I don't get much time to myself.

LIN. Do you ever go to the movies?

VICTORIA. Tommy's very funny who he's left with. My mother babysits sometimes.

LIN. Your husband could babysit.

VICTORIA. But then we couldn't go to the movies.

LIN. You could go to the movies with me.

VICTORIA. Oh I see.

LIN. Couldn't you?

VICTORIA. Well yes, I could.

LIN. Friday night?

VICTORIA. What film are we talking about?

LIN. Does it matter what film?

VICTORIA. Of course it does.

LIN. You choose then. Friday night.

Cathy comes in with gun, shoots them saying Kiou kiou kiou, and runs off again.

LIN. Not in a foreign language, ok. You don't go to the movies to read.

Lin watches the children playing outside.

Don't hit him. Cathy, kill him. Point the gun, kiou, kiou, kiou. That's the way.

VICTORIA. They've just banned war toys in Sweden.

LIN. The kids'll just hit each other more.

VICTORIA. Well psychologists do differ in their opinions as to whether or not aggression is innate.

LIN. Yeh?

VICTORIA. I'm afraid I do let Tommy play with guns and just hope he'll get it out of his system and not end up in the army.

LIN. I've got a brother in the army.

VICTORIA. Oh I'm sorry. Whereabouts is he stationed?

LIN. Belfast.

VICTORIA. Oh dear.

LIN. I've got a friend who's Irish and we went on a Troops Out march. Now my dad won't speak to me.

VICTORIA. I don't get on too well with my father either.

LIN. And your husband? How do you get on with him?

VICTORIA. Oh, fine. Up and down. You know. Very well. He helps with the washing up and everything.

LIN. I left mine two years ago. He let me keep Cathy and I'm grateful for that.

VICTORIA. You shouldn't be grateful.

LIN. I'm a lesbian.

VICTORIA. You still shouldn't be grateful.

LIN. I'm grateful he didn't hit me harder than he did.

VICTORIA. I suppose I'm very lucky with Martin.

LIN. Don't get at me about how I bring up Cathy, ok?

VICTORIA. I didn't.

LIN. Yes you did. War toys. I'll give her a rifle for Christmas and blast Tommy's pretty head off for a start.

Victoria goes back to her book.

LIN. I hate men.

VICTORIA. You have to look at it in a historical perspective in terms of learnt behaviour since the industrial revolution.

LIN. I just hate the bastards.

VICTORIA. Well it's a point of view.

By now Cathy has come back in and started painting in many colours, without an apron. Edward comes in.

EDWARD. Victoria, mother's in the park. She's walking round all the paths very fast.

VICTORIA. By herself?

EDWARD. I told her you were here.

VICTORIA. Thanks.

EDWARD. Come on.

VICTORIA. Ten minutes talking to my mother and I have to spend two hours in a hot bath.

Victoria goes out.

LIN. Shit, Cathy, what about an apron. I don't mind you having paint on your frock but if it doesn't wash off just don't tell me you can't wear your frock with paint on, ok?

CATHY. Ok.

LIN. You're gay, aren't you?

EDWARD. I beg your pardon?

LIN. I really fancy your sister. I thought you'd understand. You do but you can go on pretending you don't, I don't mind. That's lovely Cathy, I like the green bit.

EDWARD. Don't go around saying that. I might lose my job.

LIN. The last gardener was ever so straight. He used to flash at all the little girls.

EDWARD. I wish you hadn't said that about me. It's not true.

LIN. It's not true and I never said it and I never thought it and I never will think it again.

EDWARD. Someone might have heard you.

LIN. Shut up about it then.

Betty and Victoria come up.

BETTY. It's quite a nasty bump.

VICTORIA. He's not even crying.

BETTY. I think that's very worrying. You and Edward always cried. Perhaps he's got concussion.

VICTORIA. Of course he hasn't mummy.

BETTY. That other little boy was very rough. Should you speak to somebody about him?

VICTORIA. Tommy was hitting him with a spade.

BETTY. Well he's a real little boy. And so brave not to cry. You must watch him for signs of drowsiness. And nausea. If he's sick in the night, phone an ambulance. Well, you're looking very well darling, a bit tired, a bit peaky. I think the fresh air agrees with Edward. He likes the open air life because of growing up in Africa. He misses the sunshine, don't you, darling? We'll soon have Edward back on his feet. What fun it is here.

VICTORIA. This is Lin. And Cathy.

BETTY. Oh Cathy what a lovely painting. What is it? Well I think it's a house on fire. I think all that red is a fire. Is that right? Or do I see legs, is it a horse? Can I have the lovely painting or is it for mummy? Children have such imagination, it makes them so exhausting. (*to* LIN) I'm sure you're wonderful, just like Victoria. I had help with my children. One does need help. That was in Africa of course so there wasn't the servant problem. This is my son Edward. This is—

EDWARD. Lin.

BETTY. Lin, this is Lin. Edward is doing something such fun, he's working in the park as a gardener. He does look exactly like a gardener.

EDWARD. I am a gardener.

BETTY. He's certainly making a stab at it. Well it will be a story to tell. I expect he will write a novel about it, or perhaps a television series. Well what a pretty child Cathy is. Victoria was a pretty child just like a little doll—you can't be certain how they'll grow up. I think Victoria's very pretty but she doesn't make the most of herself, do you darling, it's not the fashion I'm told but there are still women who dress out of *Vogue,* well we hope that's not what Martin looks for, though in many ways I wish it was, I don't know what it is Martin looks for and nor does he I'm afraid poor Martin. Well I am rattling on. I like your skirt dear but your shoes won't do at all. Well do they have lady gardeners, Edward, because I'm going to leave your father and I think I might need to get a job, not a gardener really of course. I haven't got green fingers I'm afraid, everything I touch shrivels straight up. Vicky gave me a poinsettia last Christmas and the leaves all fell off on Boxing Day. Well good heavens, look what's happened to that lovely painting.

Cathy has slowly and carefully been going over the whole sheet with black paint. She has almost finished.

LIN. What you do that for silly? It was nice.

CATHY. I like your earrings.

VICTORIA. Did you say you're leaving Daddy?

BETTY. Do you darling? Shall I put them on you? My ears aren't pierced, I never wanted that, they just clip on the lobe.

LIN. She'll get paint on you, mind.

BETTY. There's a pretty girl. It doesn't hurt does it? Well you'll grow up to know you have to suffer a little bit for beauty.

CATHY. Look mum I'm pretty, I'm pretty, I'm pretty.

LIN. Stop showing off Cathy.

VICTORIA. It's time we went home. Tommy, time to go home. Last go then, all right.

EDWARD. Mum did I hear you right just now?

CATHY. I want my ears pierced.

BETTY. Ooh, not till you're big.

CATHY. I know a girl got her ears pierced and she's three. She's got real gold.

BETTY. I don't expect she's English, darling. Can I give her a sweety? I know they're not very good for the teeth, Vicky gets terribly cross with me. What does mummy say?

LIN. Just one, thank you very much.

CATHY. I like your beads.

BETTY. Yes they are pretty. Here you are.

LIN. Don't get paint on it.

It is the necklace from ACT I.

CATHY. Look at me, look at me. Vicky, Vicky, Vicky look at me.

LIN. You look lovely, come on now.

CATHY. And your hat, and your hat.

LIN. No, that's enough.

BETTY. Of course she can have my hat.

CATHY. Yes, yes, hat, hat.

CATHY. Look look look.

LIN. That's enough, please, stop it now. Hat off, bye bye hat.

CATHY. Give me my hat.

LIN. Bye bye beads.

BETTY. It's just fun.

LIN. It's very nice of you.

CATHY. I want my beads.

LIN. Where's the other earring?

CATHY. I want my beads.

Cathy has the other earring in her hand. Meanwhile Victoria and Edward look for it.

EDWARD. Is it on the floor?

VICTORIA. Don't step on it.

EDWARD. Where?

CATHY. I want my beads. I want my beads.

LIN. You'll have a smack.

Lin gets the earring from Cathy.

CATHY. I want my beads

BETTY. Oh dear oh dear. Have you got the earring? Thank you darling.

CATHY. I want my beads, you're horrid, I hate you, mum, you smell.

BETTY. This is the point you see where one had help. Well it's been lovely seeing you dears and I'll be off again on my little walk.

VICTORIA. You're leaving him? Really?

BETTY. Yes you heard aright, Vicky, yes, I'm finding a little flat, that will be fun.

Betty goes.

Bye bye Tommy, granny's going now. Tommy don't hit that little girl, say goodbye to granny.

VICTORIA. Fucking hell.

EDWARD. Puking Jesus.

LIN. That was news was it, leaving your father?

EDWARD. They're going to want so much attention.

VICTORIA. Does everybody hate their mothers?

EDWARD. Mind you, I wouldn't live with him.

LIN. Stop snivelling, pigface. Where's your coat? Be quiet now and we'll have doughnuts for tea and if you keep on we'll have dogshit on toast.

Cathy laughs so much she lies on the floor.

VICTORIA. Tommy, you've had two last goes. Last last last last go.

LIN. Not that funny, come on, coat on.

EDWARD. Can I have your painting?

CATHY. What for?

EDWARD. For a friend of mine.

CATHY. What's his name?

EDWARD. Gerry.

CATHY. How old is he?

EDWARD. Thirty-two.

CATHY. You can if you like. I don't care. Kiou kiou kiou kiou.

Cathy goes out. Edward takes the painting and goes out.

LIN Will you have sex with me?

VICTORIA. I don't know what Martin would say. Does it count as adultery with a woman?

LIN. You'd enjoy it.

SCENE 2

Spring, Swing, bench, pond nearby. EDWARD *is gardening.* GERRY *sitting on a bench.*

EDWARD. I sometimes pretend we don't know each other. And you've come to the park to eat your sandwiches and look at me.

GERRY. That would be more interesting, yes. Come and sit down.

EDWARD. If the superintendent comes I'll be in trouble. It's not my dinner time yet. Where were you last night? I think you owe me an explanation. We always do tell each other everything.

GERRY. Is that a rule?

EDWARD. It's what we agreed.

GERRY. It's a habit we've got into. Look, I was drunk. I woke up at 4 o'clock on somebody's floor. I was sick. I hadn't any money for a cab. I went back to sleep.

EDWARD. You could have phoned.

GERRY. There wasn't a phone.

EDWARD. Sorry.

GERRY. There was a phone and I didn't phone you. Leave it alone, Eddy, I'm warning you.

EDWARD. What are you going to do to me, then?

GERRY. I'm going to the pub.

EDWARD. I'll join you in ten minutes.

GERRY. I didn't ask you to come. Two years I've been with Edward. You have to get away sometimes or you lose sight of yourself. The train from Victoria to Clapham still has those compartments without a corridor. As soon as I got on the platform I saw who I wanted. Slim hips, tense shoulders, trying not to look at anyone. I put my hand on my packet just long enough so that he couldn't miss it. The train came in. You don't want to get in too fast or some straight dumbo might get in with you. I sat by the window. I couldn't see where the fuck he'd got to. Then just as the whistle went he got in. Great. It's a six-minute journey so you can't start anything you can't finish. I stared at him and he unzipped his flies. Then he stopped. So I stood up and took my cock out. He took me in his mouth and shut his eyes tight. He was sort of mumbling it about as if he wasn't sure what to do, so I said, 'A bit tighter son' and he said 'Sorry' and then got on with it. He was jerking off with his left hand, and I could see he'd got a fairsized one. I wished he's keep still so I could see his watch. I was getting really turned on. What if we pulled into Clapham Junction now. Of course by the time we sat down again the train was just slowing up. I felt wonderful. Then he started talking. It's better if nothing is said. Once you find he's a librarian in Walthamstow with a special interest in science fiction and lives with his aunt, then forget it. He said I hope you don't think I do this all the time. I said I hope you will from now on. He said he would if I was on the train, but why don't we go out for a meal? I opened the door before the train stopped. I told him I live with somebody, I don't want to know. He was jogging sideways to keep up. He said what's your phone number, you're my ideal physical type, what sign of the zodiac are you? Where do you live? Where are you going now? It's not fair. I saw him at Victoria a couple of months later and I went straight down to the end of the platform and I picked up somebody really great who never said a word, just smiled.

Cathy is on the swing.

CATHY. Batman and Robin
Had a batmobile
Robin done a fart
And paralysed the wheel
The wheel couldn't take it
The engine fell apart
All because of Robin
And his supersonic fart

Cathy goes. Martin, Victoria and Betty walking slowly.

MARTIN. Tom!

BETTY. He'll fall in.

VICTORIA. No he won't.

MARTIN. Don't go too near the edge Tom. Throw the bread from there. The ducks can get it.

BETTY. I'll never be able to manage. If I can't even walk down the street by myself. Everything looks so fierce.

VICTORIA. Just watch Tommy feeding the ducks.

BETTY. He's going to fall in. Make Martin make him move back.

VICTORIA. He's not going to fall in.

BETTY. It's since I left your father.

VICTORIA. Mummy, it really was the right decision.

BETTY. Everything comes at me from all directions. Martin despises me.

VICTORIA. Of course he doesn't, mummy.

BETTY. Of course he does.

MARTIN. Throw the bread. That's the way. The duck can get it. Quack quack quack quack quack.

BETTY. I don't want to take pills. Lin says you can't trust doctors.

VICTORIA. You're not taking pills. You're doing very well.

BETTY. But I'm so frightened.

VICTORIA. What are you frightened of?

BETTY. Victoria, you always ask that as if there was suddenly going to be an answer.

VICTORIA. Are you all right sitting there?

BETTY. Yes, yes. Go and be with Martin.

Victoria joins Martin, Betty stays sitting on the bench.

MARTIN. You take the job, you go to Manchester. You turn it down, you stay in London. People are making decisions like this every day of the week. It needn't be for more than a year. You get long vacations. Our relationship might well stand the strain of that, and if it doesn't we're better out of it. I don't want to put any pressure on you. I'd just like to know so we can sell the house. I think we're moving into an entirely different way of life if you go to Manchester because it won't end there. We could keep the house as security for Tommy but he might as well get used to the fact that life nowadays is insecure. You should ask your mother what she thinks and then do the opposite. I could just take that room in Barbara's house, and then we could babysit for each other. You think that means I want to fuck Barbara. I don't. Well, I do, but I won't. And even if I did, what's a fuck between friends? What are we meant to do it with, strangers? Whatever you want to do, I'll be delighted. If you could just let me know what it is I'm to be delighted about. Don't cry again, Vicky, I'm not the sort of man who makes women cry.

Lin has come in and sat down with Betty, Cathy joins them. She is wearing a pink dress and carrying a rifle.

LIN. I've bought her three new frocks. She won't wear jeans to school any more because Tracy and Mandy called her a boy.

CATHY. Tracy's got a perm.

LIN. You should have shot them.

CATHY. They're coming to tea and we've got to have trifle. Not trifle you make, trifle out of a packet. And you've got to wear a skirt. And tights.

LIN. Tracy's mum wears jeans.

CATHY. She does not. She wears velvet.

BETTY. Well I think you look very pretty. And if that gun has caps in it please take it a long way away.

CATHY. It's got red caps. They're louder.

MARTIN. Do you think you're well enough to do this job? You don't have to do it. No one's going to think any the less of you if you stay here with me. There's no point being so liberated you make yourself cry all the time. You stay and we'll get everything sorted out. What it is about sex, when we talk while it's happening I get to feel it's like a driving lesson. Left, right, a little faster, carry on. slow down—

Cathy shoots Victoria.

CATHY. You're dead Vicky.

VICTORIA. Aaaargh.

CATHY. Fall over.

VICTORIA. I'm not falling over, the ground's wet.

CATHY. You're dead.

VICTORIA. Yes, I'm dead.

CATHY. The Dead Hand Gang fall over. They said I had to fall over in the mud or I can't play. That duck's a mandarin.

MARTIN. Which one? Look, Tommy.

CATHY. That's a diver. It's got a yellow eye and it dives. That's a goose. Tommy doesn't know it's a goose, he thinks it's a duck. The babies get eaten by weasels. Kiou kiou.

Cathy goes.

MARTIN. So I lost my erection last night not because I'm not prepared to talk, it's just that taking in technical information in a different part of the brain and also I don't like to feel that you do it better to yourself. I have read the Hite report. I do know that women have to learn to get their pleasure despite our clumsy attempts at expressing undying devotion and ecstasy, and that what we spent our adolescence thinking was an animal urge we had to suppress is in fact a fine art we have to acquire. I'm not like whatever percentage of American men have become impotent as a direct result of women's liberation, which I am totally in favour of, more I sometimes think

than you are yourself. Nor am I one of your villains who sticks it in, bangs away, and falls asleep. My one aim is to give you pleasure. My one aim is to give you rolling orgasms like I do other women. So why the hell don't you have them? My analysis for what it's worth is that despite all my efforts you still feel dominated by me. I in fact think it's very sad that you don't feel able to take that job. It makes me feel very guilty. I don't want you to do it just beause I'd encourage you to do it. But don't you think you'd feel better if you did take the job? You're the one who's talked about freedom. You're the one who's experimenting with bisexuality, and I don't stop you, I think women have something to give each other. You seem to need the mutual support. You find me too overwhelming. So follow it through, go away, leave me and Tommy alone for a bit, we can manage perfectly well without you. I'm not putting any pressure on you but I don't think you're being a whole person. God knows I do everything I can to make you stand on your own two feet. Just be yourself. You don't seem to realise how insulting it is to me that you can't get yourself together.

Martin and Vic go.

BETTY. You must be very lonely yourself with no husband. You don't miss him?

LIN. Not really, no.

BETTY. Maybe you like being on your own.

LIN. I'm seeing quite a lot of Vicky. I don't live alone. I live with Cathy.

BETTY. I would have been frightened when I was your age. I thought, the poor children, their mother all alone.

LIN. I've a lot of friends.

BETTY. I find when I'm making tea I put out two cups. It's strange not having a man in the house. You don't know who to do things for.

LIN. Yourself.

BETTY. Oh, that's very selfish.

LIN. Have you any women friends?

BETTY. I've never been so short of men's company that I've had to bother with women.

LIN. Don't you like women?

BETTY. They don't have such interesting conversations as men. There has never been a woman composer of genius. They don't have a sense of humour. They spoil things for themselves with their emotions. I can't say I do like women very much, no.

LIN. But you're a woman.

BETTY. There's nothing says you have to like your-self.

LIN. Do you like me?

BETTY. There's no need to take it personally, Lin.

Martin and Vic come back.

MARTIN. Did you know if you put cocaine on your prick you can keep it up all night? The only thing is of course it goes numb so you don't feel any-thing. But you would, that's the main thing. I just want to make you happy.

BETTY. Vicky I'd like to go home.

VICTORIA. Yes, mummy, of course.

BETTY. I'm sorry dear.

VICTORIA. I think Tommy would like to stay out a bit longer.

LIN. Hello, Martin. We do keep out of each other's way.

MARTIN. I think that's the best thing to do.

BETTY. Perhaps you'd walk home with me, Martin. I do feel safer with a man. The park is so large the grass seems to tilt.

MARTIN. Yes, I'd like to go home and do some work. I'm writing a novel about women from the wom-en's point of view.

Martin and Betty go. Lin and Victoria are alone, They embrace.

VICTORIA. Why the hell can't he just be a wife and come with me? Why does Martin make me tie myself in knots? No wonder we can't just have a simple fuck. No, not Martin, why do I make myself tie myself in knots. It's got to stop, Lin. I'm not like that with you. Would you love me if I went to Manchester?

LIN. Yes.

VICTORIA. Would you love me if I went on a climbing expedition in the Andes mountains?

LIN. Yes.

VICTORIA. Would you love me if my teeth fell out?

LIN. Yes.

VICTORIA. Would you love me if I loved ten other people?

LIN. And me?

VICTORIA. Yes.

LIN. Yes.

VICTORIA. And I feel apologetic for not being quite so subordinate as I was. I am more intelligent than him. I am brilliant.

LIN. Leave him Vic. Come and live with me.

VICTORIA. Don't be silly.

LIN. Silly, Christ, don't then. I'm not asking be-cause I need to live with someone. I'd enjoy it, that's all, we'd both enjoy it. Fuck you. Cathy, for fuck's sake stop throwing stones at the ducks. The man's going to get you.

VICTORIA. What man? Do you need a man to frighten your child with?

LIN. My mother said it.

VICTORIA. You're so inconsistent, Lin.

LIN. I've changed who I sleep with, I can't change everything.

VICTORIA. Like when I had to stop you getting a job in a boutique and collaborating with sexist consumerism.

LIN. I should have got that job, Cathy would have liked it. Why shouldn't I have some decent clothes? I'm sick of dressing like a boy, why can't I look sexy, wouldn't you love me?

VICTORIA. Lin, you've no analysis.

LIN. No but I'm good at kissing aren't I? I give Cathy guns, my mum didn't give me guns. I dress her in jeans, she wants to wear dresses. I don't know. I can't work it out, I don't want to. You read too many books, you get at me all the time, you're worse to me than Martin is to you, you piss me off, my brother's been killed, I'm sorry to win the argument that way but there it is.

VICTORIA. What do you mean win the argument?

LIN. I mean be nice to me.

VICTORIA. In Belfast?

LIN. I heard this morning. Don't don't start. I've hardly seen him for two years. I rung my father. You'd think I'd shot him myself. He doesn't want me to go to the funeral.

Cathy approaches.

VICTORIA. What will you do?

LIN. Go of course.

CATHY. What is it? Who's killed? What?

LIN. It's Bill. Your uncle. In the army. Bill that gave you the blue teddy.

CATHY. Can I have his gun?

LIN. It's time we went home. Time you went to bed.

CATHY. No it's not.

LIN. We go home and you have tea and you have a bath and you go to bed.

CATHY. Fuck off.

LIN. Cathy shut up.

VICTORIA. It's only half past five, why don't we—

LIN. I'll tell you why she has to go to bed—

VICTORIA. She can come home with me.

LIN. Because I want her out of the fucking way.

VICTORIA. She can come home with me.

CATHY. I'm not going to bed.

LIN. I want her home with me not home with you, I want her in bed, I want today over.

CATHY. I'm not going to bed.

Lin hits Cathy, Cathy cries.

LIN. And shut up or I'll give you something to cry for.

CATHY. I'm not going to bed.

VICTORIA. Cathy—

LIN. You keep out of it.

VICTORIA. Lin for God's sake.

They are all shouting. Cathy runs off. Lin and Victoria are silent. Then they laugh and embrace.

LIN. Where's Tommy?

VICTORIA. What? Didn't he go with Martin?

LIN. Did he?

VICTORIA. God oh God.

LIN. Cathy! Cathy!

VICTORIA. I haven't thought about him. How could I not think about him? Tommy!

LIN. Cathy! Come on, quick, I want some help.

VICTORIA. Tommy! Tommy!

Cathy comes back.

LIN. Where's Tommy? Have you seen him? Did he go with Martin? Do you know where he is?

CATHY. I showed him the goose. We went in the bushes.

LIN. Then what?

CATHY. I came back on the swing.

VICTORIA. And Tommy? Where was Tommy?

CATHY. He fed the ducks.

LIN. No that was before.

CATHY. He did a pee in the bushes. I helped him with his trousers.

VICTORIA. And after that?

CATHY. He fed the ducks.

VICTORIA. No no.

CATHY. He liked the ducks. I expect he fell in.

LIN Did you see him fall in?

VICTORIA. Tommy! Tommy!

LIN. What's the last time you saw him?

CATHY. He did a pee.

VICTORIA. Mummy said he would fall in. Oh God, Tommy!

LIN. We'll go round the pond. We'll go opposite ways round the pond.

ALL. (*Shout*) Tommy!

Victoria and Lin go off opposite sides. Cathy goes on the swing, standing up.

CATHY. Georgy Best superstar
Walks like a woman and wears a bra.
There he is! I see him! Mum! Vicky! There he is? He's in the bushes.

Lin comes back.

LIN. Come on Cathy love, let's go home.

CATHY. Vicky's got him.

LIN. Come on.

CATHY. Is she cross?

LIN. No. Come on.

CATHY. I found him.

LIN. Yes. Come on.

Cathy gets off the bench. Cathy and Lin hug.

CATHY. I'm watching telly.

LIN. Ok.

CATHY. After the news.

LIN. Ok.

CATHY. I'm not going to bed.

LIN. Yes you are.

CATHY. I'm not going to bed now.

LIN. Not now but early.

CATHY. How early?

LIN. Not late.

CATHY. How not late?

LIN. Early.

CATHY. How early?

LIN. Not late.

They go off together. Gerry comes on. He waits. Edward comes. He has changed out of his work clothes.

EDWARD. I've got some fish for dinner. I thought I'd make a cheese sauce.

GERRY. I won't be in.

EDWARD. Where are you going?

GERRY. For a start I'm going to a sauna. Then I'll see.

EDWARD. All right. What time will you be back? We'll eat then.

GERRY. You're getting like a wife.

EDWARD. I don't mind that.

GERRY. Why don't I do the cooking sometime?

EDWARD. You can if you like. You're just not so good at it that's all. Do it tonight.

GERRY. I won't be in tonight.

EDWARD. Do it tomorrow. If we can't eat it we can always go to a restaurant.

GERRY. Stop it.

EDWARD. Stop what?

GERRY. Just be yourself.

EDWARD. I don't know what you mean. Everyone's always tried to stop me being feminine and now you are too.

GERRY. You're putting it on.

EDWARD. I like doing the cooking. I like being fucked. You do like me like this really.

GERRY. I'm bored Eddy.

EDWARD. Go to the sauna.

GERRY. And you'll stay home and wait up for me.

EDWARD. No, I'll go to bed and read a book.

GERRY. Or knit. You could knit me a pair of socks.

EDWARD. I might knit. I like knitting.

GERRY. I don't mind if you knit. I don't want to be married.

EDWARD. I do.

GERRY. Well I'm divorcing you.

EDWARD. I wouldn't want to keep a man who wants his freedom.

GERRY. Eddy, do stop playing the injured wife, it's not funny.

EDWARD. I'm not playing. It's true.

GERRY. I'm not the husband so you can't be the wife.

EDWARD. I'll always be here, Gerry, if you want to come back. I know you men like to go off by yourselves. I don't think I could love deeply more than once. But I don't think I can face life on my own so don't leave it too long or it may be too late.

GERRY. What are you trying to turn me into?

EDWARD. A monster, darling, which is what you are.

GERRY. I'll collect my stuff from the flat in the morning.

Gerry goes. Edward sits on the bench. It gets darker. Victoria comes.

VICTORIA. Tommy dropped a toy car somewhere, you haven't seen it? It's red. He says its his best one. Oh the hell with it. Martin's reading him a story. There, isn't it quiet?

They sit on the bench, holding hands.

EDWARD. I like women.

VICTORIA. That should please mother.

EDWARD. No listen Vicky. I'd rather be a woman. I wish I had breasts like that, I think they're beautiful. Can I touch them?

VICTORIA. What, pretending they're yours?

EDWARD. No, I know it's you.

649

VICTORIA. I think I should warn you I'm enjoying this.

EDWARD. I'm sick of men.

VICTORIA. I'm sick of men.

EDWARD. I think I'm a lesbian.

SCENE 3

The park. Summer night. VICTORIA, LIN *and* EDWARD *drunk.*

LIN. Where are you?

VICTORIA. Come on.

EDWARD. Do we sit in a circle?

VICTORIA. Sit in a triangle.

EDWARD. You're good at mathematics. She's good at mathematics.

VICTORIA. Give me your hand. We all hold hands.

EDWARD. Do you know what to do?

LIN. She's making it up.

VICTORIA. We start off by being quiet.

EDWARD. What?

LIN. Hush.

EDWARD. Will something appear?

VICTORIA. It was your idea.

EDWARD. It wasn't my idea. It was your book.

LIN. You said call up the goddess.

EDWARD. I don't remember saying that.

LIN. We could have called her on the telephone.

EDWARD. Don't be so silly, this is meant to be frightening.

LIN. Kiss me.

VICTORIA. Are we going to do it?

LIN. We're doing it.

VICTORIA. A ceremony.

LIN. It's very sexy, you said it is. You said the women were priests in the temples and fucked all the time. I'm just helping.

VICTORIA. As long as it's sacred.

LIN. It's very sacred.

VICTORIA. Innin, Innana, Nana, Nut, Anat, Anahita, Istar, Isis.

LIN. I can't remember all that.

VISTORIA. Lin! Innin, Innana, Nana, Nut, Anat, Anahita, Istar, Isis.

Lin and Edward join in and continue the chant under Victoria's speech.

Goddess of many names, oldest of the old, who walked in chaos and created life, hear us calling you back through time, before Jehovah, before Christ, before men drove you out and burnt your temples, hear us, Lady, give us back what we were, give us the history we haven't had, make us the women we can't be.

ALL. Innin, Innana, Nana, Nut, Anat, Anahita, Istar, Isis.

Chant continues under other speeches.

LIN. Come back, goddess.

VICTORIA. Goddess of the sun and the moon her brother, little goddess of Crete with snakes in your hands.

LIN. Goddess of breasts.

VICTORIA. Goddess of cunts.

LIN. Goddess of fat bellies and babies, And blood blood blood.

Chant continues.

LIN. I see her.

EDWARD. What?

They stop chanting.

LIN. I see her. Very tall. Snakes in her hands. Light light light—look out! Did I give you a fright?

EDWARD. I was terrified.

VICTORIA. Don't spoil it Lin.

LIN. It's all out of a book.

VICTORIA. Innin Innana—I can't do it now. I was really enjoying myself.

LIN. She won't appear with a man here.

VICTORIA. They had men, they had sons and lovers.

EDWARD. They had eunuchs.

LIN. Don't give us ideas.

VICTORIA. There's Attis and Tammuz, they're torn to pieces.

EDWARD. Tear me to pieces, Lin.

VICTORIA. The priestess chose a lover for a year and he was king because she chose him and then he was killed at the end of the year.

EDWARD. Hurray.

VICTORIA. And the women had the children and nobody knew it was done by fucking so they didn't know about fathers and nobody cared who the father was and the property was passed down through the maternal line—

LIN. Don't turn it into a lecture, Vicky, it's meant to be an orgy.

VICTORIA. It never hurts to understand the theoretical background. You can't separate fucking and economics.

LIN. Give us a kiss.

EDWARD. Shut up, listen.

LIN. What?

EDWARD. There's somebody there.

LIN. Where?

EDWARD. There.

VICTORIA. The priestesses used to make love to total strangers.

LIN. Go on then, I dare you.

EDWARD. Go on, Vicky.

VICTORIA. He won't know it's a sacred rite in honour of the goddess.

EDWARD. We'll know.

LIN. We can tell him.

EDWARD. It's not what he thinks, it's what we think.

LIN. Don't tell him till after, he'll run a mile.

VICTORIA. Hello, We're having an orgy. Do you want me to suck your cock?

The stranger approaches. It is Martin.

MARTIN. There you are. I've been looking everywhere. What the hell are you doing? Do you know what the time is? You're all pissed out of your minds.

They leap on Martin, pull him down and start to make love to him.

MARTIN. Well that's all right. If all we're talking about is having a lot of sex there's no problem. I was all for the sixties when liberation just meant fucking.

Another stranger approaches.

LIN. Hey you, come here. Come and have sex with us.

VICTORIA. Who is it?

The stranger is a soldier.

LIN. It's my brother.

EDWARD. Lin, don't.

LIN. It's my brother.

VICTORIA. It's her sense of humour, you get used to it.

LIN. Shut up Vicky, it's my brother. Isn't it? Bill?

SOLDIER. Yes it's me.

LIN. And you are dead.

SOLIDER. Fucking dead all right yeh.

LIN. Have you come back to tell us something?

SOLDIER. No I've come for a fuck. That was the worst thing in the fucking army. Never fucking let out. Can't fucking talk to Irish girls. Fucking bored out of my fucking head. That or shit scared. For five minutes I'd be glad I wasn't bored, then I was fucking scared. Then we'd come in and I'd be glad I wasn't scared and then I was fucking bored. Spent the day reading fucking porn and the fucking night wanking. Man's fucking life in the fucking army? No fun when the fucking kids hate you. I got so I fucking wanted to kill someone and I got fucking killed myself and I want a fuck.

LIN. I miss you. Bill. Bill.

Lin collapses. Soldier goes. Victoria comforts Lin.

EDWARD. Let's go home.

LIN. Victoria, come home with us. Victoria's coming to live with me and Edward.

MARTIN. Tell me about it in the morning.

LIN. It's true.

VICTORIA. It is true.

MARTIN. Tell me when you're sober.

Edward, Lin, Victoria go off together. Martin goes off alone. Gerry comes on.

GERRY. I come here sometimes at night and pick somebody up. Sometimes I come here at night and don't pick anybody up. I do also enjoy walking about at night. There's never any trouble finding someone. I can have sex any time. You might not find the type you most fancy every day of the week, but there's plenty of people about who just enjoy having a good time. I quite like living alone. If I live with someone I get annoyed with them. Edward always put on Capital radio when he got up. The silence gets wasted. I wake up at four o'clock sometimes. Birds. Silence. If I bring somebody home I never let them stay the night. Edward! Edward!

Edward from Act I comes on.

EDWARD. Gerry I love you.

GERRY. Yes, I know. I love you, too.

EDWARD. You know what we did? I want to do it again. I think about it all the time. Don't you want to any more?

GERRY. Yes, of course.

SONG Cloud Nine

It'll be fine when you reach Cloud 9.

Mist was rising and the night was dark
Me and my baby took a walk in the park
He said Be mine and you're on Cloud 9.

Better watch out when you're on Cloud 9.

Smoked some dope on the playground swings
Higher and higher on true love's wings
He said Be mine and you're on Cloud 9.

Twenty five years on the same Cloud 9.
Who did she meet on her first blind date?
The guys were no surprise but the lady was great
They were women in love, they were on Cloud 9.

Two the same, they were on Cloud 9.

The bride was sixtyfive, the groom was seventeen,
They fucked in the back of the black limousine.
It was divine in their silver Cloud 9.

Simply divine in their silver Cloud 9.

The wife's lover's children and my lover's wife,
Cooking in my kitchen, confusing my life.
And it's upside down when you reach Cloud 9.

Upside down when you reach Cloud 9.

SCENE 4

The park. Afternoon in late summer. MARTIN, CATHY, EDWARD.

CATHY. Under the bramble bushes
Under the sea boom boom boom
True love for you my darling

True love for me my darling
When we are married
We'll raise a family
Boy for you, girl for me,
Boom tiddley oom boom.
SEXY

EDWARD. You'll have Tommy and Cathy tonight then ok? Tommy's still on antibiotics, do make him finish the bottle, he takes it in Ribena. It's no good in orange, he spits it out. Remind me to give you Cathy's swimming things.

CATHY. I did six strokes, didn't I Martin? Did I do a width? How many strokes is a length? How many miles is a swimming pool? I'm going to take my bronze and silver and gold and diamond.

MARTIN. Is Tommy still wetting the bed?

EDWARD. Don't get angry with him about it.

MARTIN. I just need to go to the launderette so I've got a spare sheet. Of course I don't get fucking angry, Eddy, for God's sake. I don't like to say he is my son but he is my son. I'm surprised I'm not wetting the bed myself.

CATHY. I don't wet the bed ever. Do you wet the bed Martin?

MARTIN. No.

CATHY. You said you did.

Betty comes.

BETTY. I do miss the sun living in England but today couldn't be more beautiful. You appreciate the weekend when you're working. Betty's been at work this week, Cathy. It's terribly tiring, Martin, I don't know how you've done it all these years. And the money, I feel like a child with the money, Clive always paid everything but I do understand it perfectly well. Look Cathy let me show you my money.

CATHY. I'll count it. Let me count it. What's that?

BETTY. Five pounds. Five and five is—?

CATHY. One two three—

BETTY. Five and five is ten, and five—

CATHY. If I get it right can I have one?

EDWARD. No you can't.

Cathy goes on counting the money.

BETTY. I never like to say anything, Martin, or you'll think I'm being a mother-in-law.

EDWARD. Which you are.

BETTY. Thank you, Edward, I'm not talking to you. Martin, I think you're being wonderful. Vicky will come back. Just let her stay with Lin till she sorts herself out. It's very nice for a girl to have a friend; I had friends at school, that was very nice. But I'm sure Lin and Edward don't want her with them all the time. I'm not at all shocked that Lin and Edward aren't married and she already has a child, we all know first marriages don't always work out. But really Vicky must be in the way. And poor little Tommy. I hear he doesn't sleep properly and he's had a cough.

MARTIN. No, he's fine, Betty, thank you.

CATHY. My bed's horrible. I want to sleep in the big bed with Lin and Vicky and Eddy and I do get in if I've got a bad dream, and my bed's got a bump right in my back. I want to sleep in a tent.

BETTY. Well Tommy has got a nasty cough, Martin, whatever you say.

EDWARD. He's over that. He's got some medicine.

MARTIN. He takes it in Ribena.

BETTY. Well I'm glad to hear it. Look what a lot of money, Cathy, and I sit behind a desk of my own and I answer the telephone and keep the doctor's appointment book and it really is great fun.

CATHY. Can we go camping, Martin, in a tent? We could take the Dead Hand Gang.

BETTY. Not those big boys, Cathy? They're far too big and rough for you. They climb back into the park after dark. I'm sure mummy doesn't let you play with them, does she Edward? Well I don't know.

Ice cream bells.

CATHY. Ice cream. Martin you promised. I'll have a double ninety nine. No I'll have a shandy lolly. Betty, you have a shandy lolly and I'll have a lick. No, you have a double ninety nine and I'll have the chocolate.

Martin, Cathy and Betty go, leaving Edward. Gerry comes.

GERRY. Hello, Eddy. Thought I might find you here.

EDWARD. Gerry.

GERRY. Not working today then?

EDWARD. I don't work here any more.

GERRY. Your mum got you into a dark suit?

EDWARD. No of course not. I'm on the dole. I am working, though, I do housework.

GERRY. Whose wife are you now then?

EDWARD. Nobody's. I don't think like that any more. I'm living with some women.

GERRY. What women?

EDWARD. It's my sister, Vic, and her lover. They go out to work and I look after the kids.

GERRY. I thought for a moment you said you were living with women.

EDWARD. We do sleep together, yes.

GERRY. I was passing the park anyway so I thought I'd look in. I was in the sauna the other night and I saw someone who looked like you but it wasn't. I had sex with him anyway.

EDWARD. I do go to the sauna sometimes.

Cathy comes, gives Edward an ice cream, goes.

GERRY. I don't think I'd like living with children. They make a lot of noise don't they?

EDWARD. I tell them to shut up and they shut up. I wouldn't want to leave them at the moment.

GERRY. Look why don't we go for a meal sometime?

EDWARD. Yes I'd like that.

Edward goes. Harry comes. Harry and Gerry pick each other up. They go off. Betty comes back.

BETTY. No, the ice cream was my treat, Martin. Off you go. I'm going to have a quiet sit in the sun.

Maud comes.

MAUD. Let Mrs. Saunders be a warning to you, Betty. I know what it is to be unprotected.

BETTY. But mother, I have a job. I earn money.

MAUD. I know we have our little differences but I always want what is best for you.

Ellen comes.

ELLEN. Betty, what happens with a man?

BETTY. You just keep still.

ELLEN. And is it enjoyable? Don't forget me, Betty.

Maud and Ellen go.

BETTY. I used to think Clive was the one who liked sex. But then I found I missed it. I used to touch myself when I was very little, I thought I'd invented something wonderful. I used to do it to go to sleep with or to cheer myself up, and one day it was raining and I was under the kitchen table, and my mother saw me with my hand under my dress rubbing away, and she dragged me out so quickly I hit my head and it bled and I was sick, and nothing was said, and I never did it again till this year. I thought if Clive wasn't looking at me there wasn't a person there. And one night in bed in my flat I was so frightened I started touching myself. I thought my hand might go through into space. I touched my face, it was there, my arm, my breast, and my hand went down where I thought it shouldn't, and I thought well there is somebody there. It felt very sweet, it was a feeling from a very long ago, it was very soft, just barely touching, and I felt myself gathering together more and more and I felt angry with Clive and angry with my mother and I went on and on defying them, and there was this vast feeling growing in me and all round me and they couldn't stop me and no one could stop me and I was there and coming and coming. Afterwards I thought I'd betrayed Clive. My mother would kill me. But I felt triumphant because I was a separate person from them. And I cried because I didn't want to be. But I don't cry about it any more. Sometimes I do it three times in one night and it really is great fun.

Victoria and Lin comes in.

VICTORIA. So I said to the professor, I don't think this is an occasion for invoking the concept of structural causality—oh hello mummy.

BETTY. I'm going to ask you a question, both of you. I have a little money from your grandmother. And the three of you are living in that tiny flat with two children. I wonder if we could get a house and all live in it together? It would give you more room.

VICTORIA. But I'm going to Manchester anyway.

LIN. We'd have a garden, Vicky.

BETTY. You do seem to have such fun all of you.

VICTORIA. I don't want to.

BETTY. I didn't think you would.

LIN. Come on, Vicky, she knows we sleep together, and Eddy.

BETTY. I think I've known for quite a while but I'm not sure. I don't usually think about it, so I don't know if I know about it or not.

VICTORIA. I don't want to live with my mother.

LIN. Don't think of her as your mother, think of her as Betty.

VICTORIA. But she thinks of herself as my mother.

BETTY. I am your mother.

VICTORIA. But mummy we don't even like each other.

BETTY. We might begin to.

Cathy comes on howling with a nosebleed.

LIN. Oh Cathy what happened?

BETTY. She's been assaulted.

VICTORIA. It's a nosebleed.

CATHY. Took my ice cream.

LIN. Who did?

CATHY. Took my money.

Martin comes.

MARTIN. Is everything all right?

LIN. I thought you were looking after her.

CATHY. They hit me. I can't play. They said I'm a girl.

BETTY. Those dreadful boys, the gang, the Dead Hand.

MARTIN. What do you mean you thought I was looking after her?

LIN. Last I saw her she was with you getting an ice cream. It's your afternoon.

MARTIN. Then she went off to play. She goes off to play. You don't keep an eye on her every minute.

LIN. She doesn't get beaten up when I'm looking after her.

CATHY. Took my money.

MARTIN. Why the hell should I look after your child anyway? I just want Tommy. Why should he live with you and Vicky all week?

LIN. I don't mind if you don't want to look after her but don't say you will and then this happens.

VICTORIA. When I go to Manchester everything's going to be different anyway, Lin's staying here, and you're staying here, we're all going to have to sit down and talk it through.

MARTIN. I'd really enjoy that.

CATHY. Hit me on the face.

LIN. You were the one looking after her and look at her now, that's all.

MARTIN. I've had enough of you telling me.

LIN. Yes you know it all.

MARTIN. Now stop it. I work very hard at not being like this, I could do with some credit.

LIN. Ok you're quite nice, try and enjoy it. Don't make me sorry for you, Martin, It's hard for me too. We've better things to do than quarrel. I've got to go and sort those little bastards out for a start. Where are they, Cathy?

CATHY. Don't kill them, mum, hit them. Give them a nosebleed, mum.

Lin goes.

VICTORIA. Tommy's asleep in the pushchair. We'd better wake him up or he won't sleep tonight.

MARTIN. Sometimes I keep him up watching television till he falls asleep on the sofa so I can hold him. Come on, Cathy, we'll get another ice cream.

CATHY. Chocolate sauce and nuts.

VICTORIA. Betty, would you like an ice cream?

BETTY. No thank you, the cold hurts my teeth, but what a nice thought, Vicky, thank you.

Vicky goes. Betty alone. Gerry comes.

BETTY. I think you used to be Edward's flatmate.

GERRY. You're his mother. He's talked about you.

BETTY. Well never mind. Children are always wrong about their parents. It's great problem knowing where to live and who to share with. I live by myself just now.

GERRY. Good. So do I. You can do what you like.

BETTY. I don't really know what I like.

GERRY. You'll soon find out.

BETTY. What do you like?

GERRY. Waking up at four in the morning.

BETTY. I like listening to music in bed and sometimes for supper I just have a big piece of bread and dip it in very hot lime pickle. So you don't get lonely by yourself? Perhaps you have a lot of visitors. I've been thinking I should have some visitors, I could give a little dinner party. Would you come? There wouldn't just be bread and lime pickle.

GERRY: Thank you very much.

BETTY. Or don't wait to be asked to dinner. Just drop in informally. I'll give you the address shall I? I don't usually give strange men my address but then you're not a strange man, you're a friend of Edward's. I suppose I seem a different generation to you but you are older than Edward. I was married for so many years it's quite hard to know how to get acquainted. But if there isn't a right way to do things you have to invent one. I always thought my mother was far too old to be attractive but when you get to an age yourself it feels quite different.

GERRY. I think you could be quite attractive.

BETTY. If what?

GERRY. If you stop worrying.

BETTY. I think when I do more about things I worry about them less. So perhaps you could help me do more.

GERRY. I might be going to live with Edward again.

BETTY. That's nice, but I'm rather surprised if he wants to share a flat. He's rather involved with a young woman he lives with, or two young women, I don't understand Edward but never mind.

GERRY. I'm very involved with him.

BETTY. I think Edward did try to tell me once but I didn't listen. So what I'm being told now is that Edward is 'gay' is that right? And you are too. And I've being making rather a fool of myself. But Edward does also sleep with women.

GERRY. He does, yes, I don't.

BETTY. Well people always say it's the mother's fault but I don't intend to start blaming myself. He seems perfectly happy.

GERRY. I could still come and see you.

BETTY. So you could, yes. I'd like that. I've never tried to pick up a man before.

GERRY. Not everyone's gay.

BETTY. No, that's lucky isn't it.

Gerry goes. Clive comes.

CLIVE. You are not that sort of woman, Betty. I can't believe you are. I can't feel the same about you as I did. And Africa is to be communist I suppose. I used to be proud to be British. There was a high ideal. I came out onto the verandah and looked at the stars.

Clive goes. Betty from Act I comes. Betty and Betty embrace.

CHAPTER XVIII

As the Curtain Descends

It is very possible that Caryl Churchill and playwrights like her are showing us the way our drama must go. Think back for a moment to where we began with *Antigone*. Here was drama about people and issues that mattered. While centuries passed and the political world became more and more democratic as Common People asserted their rights, so the drama, reflecting its world, became increasingly more democratic. At first, only kings and queens and aristocrats seemed to warrant attention. But, then, by the middle of the eighteenth century—as we saw in *The Beaux' Stratagem*—the middle-class began to assert itself in drama. By Ibsen's time the middle-class citizen was the protagonist of the play. The trend continued at a rather alarming pace until by the beginning of the twentieth century dramatists were writing about the inhabitants of the lowest rung of the socio-economic ladder as was the case in Gorky's *The Lower Depths* and in much of the socially aware drama of the American and German theatres of the 1920's and 1930's. By the time we reach our contemporary theatre and the plays of Sam Shepard (or plays such as *'night, Mother*), dramatists are focusing attention on the emotionally and psychologically crippled in our culture.

An unfortunate by-product of this ever-increasing democratization of drama is the fact that we now are innundated with plays about an almost sub-human sub-culture—as in most Theatre of the Absurd drama. These are plays peopled with characters for whom it is extremely difficult to develop any genuine empathic response. It is, after all, difficult to care about what happens to someone who doesn't care himself. We can conclude that such people are pathetic. But is there really much we can do for them when they seem so incapable of growth or improvement? Caryl Churchill finds a way to stress the humanity of her characters and to make us feel that what happens to them is important because they so vividly represent or reflect facets of ourselves. The dramatic character does not have to be a king to matter; but he absolutely has to have a soul and a yearning to be something more than dirt or animal waste. Perhaps it is time in our drama to stop being content with wallowing in our pity for the down-trodden and unfortunate. After all, this comes dangerously close to melodramatic self-pity, and that could be counter-productive. Perhaps we need more playwrights like Caryl Churchill who can tell us not only that "This is how it is" but also "This is how it could be."

And perhaps we also need more playwrights like Caryl Churchill who are not afraid to make sense. Too many practitioners in the theatre today deliberately aschew sense sometimes with the assertion that meaning has no place in our theatre since our life is meaningless. One suspects that those directors, playwrights and actors are subtly protecting themselves from failure. After all, when their product fails to make its point with an audience in the theatre, it becomes conveniently face-saving to insist that there was no point to be made. Drama from the days of Aeschylus, Sophocles and Euripides—nay, even the drama of pagan religious ritual which preceded them—had its purpose and made its point. Shakespeare and Molière and Ibsen and Strindberg and Chekhov—they all made their point. They were never ashamed of making sense.

In fact, from the middle of the nineteenth century forward drama quite emphatically pursued a course of the revelation of Truth. Realism and Naturalism were born of this need to reveal Truth in its many faces, contradictory as those faces may be. Expressionism, even though it superficially seems so removed from real experience, was striving to reveal the ultimate truth or reality which lay beneath the surface of life—the reality of the subjective world. Absurdism and the Theatre of Cruelty pursue exactly the same objective in their quest for an ultimate Truth about the human condition, the human experience.

Drama is, after all, about Man and Woman! All men and all women. When the drama moves us, it is because we perceive it as an image of life. We understand it as an imitation of life. Despite the unique form and convention of Greek drama, we still understand the play as human experience; Antigone is a woman, and we perceive her as such. Othello is a man, and he speaks to us through his play as a man. Strindberg's expressionistic characters, for all of their oddity and quaintness, never stray so far from human form that we cannot recognize them as metaphors for Humankind.

Perhaps all of this tells us that drama, in order to be meaningful and great—in order to deserve its name—must keep one foot in the world of reality. That is not to say it has to be realistic. But it must remain an intrinsically recognizable image of life. Much of experimental theatre of today, with its emphasis on technological display, runs the risk of losing sight of the human figure in drama. When that happens, the product ceases to be drama at all even though it may remain an interesting theatrical event or spectacle. Perhaps playwrights like Wilder, Shepard, and Churchill are telling us that we must take full advantage of all the freedoms of form and content and all the technical know-how that are part of our present-day theatre, but that we must not for a moment lose sight of the fact that drama is an imitation of the deeds, thoughts, dreams, feelings and aspirations of human beings. So, the human being—and the actors who represent him on stage—had better remain the center of our theatre.

Bibliography

General References

The following books have been used throughout the study and therefore will not be listed in individual chapters.

Brockett, Oscar and Findlay, Robert R. *Century of Innovation.* Englewood Cliffs, New Jersey: Prentice-Hall, Inc., 1973.

Brockett, Oscar G. *History of the Theatre.* 5th ed. Boston: Allyn and Bacon, Inc., 1987.

Downer, Alan S. *The British Drama.* New York: Appleton-Century, Crofts, Inc., 1950.

Gassner, John (ed.). *Masters of the Drama.* 3rd rev. ed. New York: Dover Publications, 1954.

Hartnoll, Phyllis (ed.). *The Oxford Companion to the Theatre.* Oxford: Oxford University Press, 1972.

Harwood, Ronald. *All the World's a Stage.* London: Methuen, 1984.

Langer, William L. *Encyclopedia of World History.* Rev. ed. Boston: Houghton Mifflin Company, 1962.

MacGowan, Kenneth, and Melnitz, William, with Armstrong, Gordon. *Golden Ages of the Theatre.* Rev. ed. Englewood Cliffs, New Jersey: Prentice-Hall, Inc., 1979.

Nicoll, Allardyce. *World Drama from Aeschylus to Anouilh.* New York: Harcourt, Brace, 1950.

Nicoll, Allardyce. *The Development of the Theatre.* 5th ed., rev. New York: Harcourt, Brace and World, 1967.

Chapter 1

Butcher, S. H. *Aristotle's Theory of Poetry and Fine Art.* 4th ed. New York: Dover Publications, 1951.

Butcher, S. H. (ed. and trans.). *The Poetics of Aristotle.* 4th ed. London: Macmillan and Co., 1911.

Clark, Barrett H. (ed.). *European Theories of the Drama.* New York: Crown Publishers, 1965.

Dukore, Bernard Frank. *Dramatic Theory and Criticism: Greeks to Grotowski.* New York: Holt, Rinehart and Winston, 1974.

Fergusson, Francis. *The Idea of a Theatre.* Garden City, New York: Doubleday, 1949.

Chapter II

Arnott, Peter D. *An Introduction to the Greek Theatre.* London: Macmillan and Company Limited. 1961.

Bieber, Margarete. *The History of the Greek and Roman Theatre.* 2nd ed. Princeton, N.J.: Princeton University Press, 1961.

Butler, James H. *The Theatre and Drama of Greece and Rome.* San Francisco: Chandler Publishing Co., 1972.

Fleckinger, R. C. *The Greek Theatre and Its Drama.* 6th ed. Chicago: University of Chicago Press, 1960.

Hamilton, Edith. *The Greek Way.* New York: W. W. Norton and Co., Inc. (A Mentor Book), 1954.

Jones, Robert Edmond. *The Dramatic Imagination.* New York: Duell, Sloan and Pearce, 1941.

Kitto, H. D. F. *The Greeks.* Edinburgh: Penguin Books, 1956.

Kitto, H. D. F. *Greek Tragedy.* 2nd ed. London: Methuen and Co., Ltd., 1950.

National Geographic Society. *Greece and Rome: Builders of Our World.* Washington, D.C.: National Geographic Society, 1968.

Pickard-Cambridge, A. W. *The Dramatic Festivals of Athens.* 2nd ed. rev. by J. Gould and D. M. Lewis. Oxford: Clarendon Press, 1968.

Pickard-Cambridge, A. W. *The Theatre of Dionysus in Athens.* Oxford: The Clarendon Press, 1946.

Renault, Mary. *The Mask of Apollo.* New York: Pantheon Books, 1966.

Trendall, A. D. and Webster, T. B. L. *Illustrations of Greek Drama..* London: Phaidon, 1971.

Chapter III

Burton, E. J. *The British Theatre: Its Repertory and Practice, 1100–1900.* London: Herbert Jenkins, 1960.

Cawley, A. C. (ed.). *Everyman and Medieval Miracle Plays.* New York: E. P. Dutton and Co., 1959.

Gassner, John (ed.). *Medieval and Tudor Drama.* New York: Bantam Books, 1963.

Hardison, O. E., Jr. *Christian Rite and Christian Drama in the Middle Ages.* Baltimore: The Johns Hopkins Press, 1965.

Hunninger, Benjamin. *The Origin of the Theatre.* New York: Hill and Wang, 1961.

Kolve, V. A. *The Play Called Corpus Christi.* Stanford: Stanford University Press, 1966.

Nagler, A. M. *A Source Book in Theatre History.* New York: Dover Publications, Inc., 1952.

Prosser, Eleanor. *Drama and Religion in the English Mystery Plays: A Re-evaluation.* Stanford: Stanford University Press, 1961.

Rose, Martial (ed.). *The Wakefield Mystery Plays.* Garden City: Doubleday and Co., Inc., 1962.

Salter, F. M. *Medieval Drama in Chester.* Toronto: University of Toronto Press, 1965.

Southern, Richard. *The Seven Ages of the Theatre.* New York: Hill and Wang, 1963.

Chapter IV

Barnet, Sylvan (ed.). *The Complete Signet Classic Shakespeare.* New York: Harcourt Brace Jovanovich, Inc., 1972.

Beckerman. Bernard. *Shakespeare at the Globe: 1599–1609.* New York: The Macmillan Company, 1962.

Chambers, E. K. *The Elizabethan Stage.* 4 vols. Oxford: Oxford University Press, 1923.

Chute, Marchette. *Shakespeare of London.* New York: E. P. Dutton and Company, Inc., 1949.

Cunningham, J. V. *The Renaissance in England.* New York: Harcourt, Brace and World, Inc., 1966.

Evans, G. Blakemore (ed.). *The Riverside Shakespeare.* Boston: Houghton Mifflin Company, 1974.

Harrison, G. B. *Elizabethan Plays and Players.* Ann Arbor: University of Michigan Press, 1956.

Hurstfield, Joel. *The Elizabethan Nation.* New York: Harper and Row, 1964.

Nagler, A. M. *Shakespeare's Stage.* New Haven: Yale University Press, 1969.

Sprague, A. C. *Shakespearean Players and Performances.* Cambridge: Harvard University Press, 1953.

Tillyard, E. M. W. *The Elizabethan World Picture.* New York: The Macmillan Company, 1943.

Wickham, Glynne. *Early English Stages, 1300 to 1660.* 3 Vols. New York: Columbia University Press, 1959–1979.

Wilson, John Dover. *Life in Shakespeare's England.* Baltimore, Maryland: Penguin Books, 1968.

Chapter V

Ducharte, Pierre L. *The Italian Comedy.* New York: Dover Publications, Inc. 1966.

Fergusson, Francis (ed.). *Plays by Molière.* New York: Random House (The Modern Library), 1950.

Hewitt, Barnard (ed.). *The Renaissance Stage: Documents of Serlio, Sabbattini, and Furttenbach.* Coral Gables, Florida: University of Miami Press, 1958.

Kernodle, George. *From Art to Theatre: Form and Convention in the Renaissance.* Chicago: University of Chicago Press, 1943.

Moore, W. G. *Molière, A New Criticism.* New York: Doubleday and Company, Inc., 1962.

Molière. *The Miser.* Adapted by Miles Mallison. London: Samuel French, 1950.

Sypher, Wylie. *Four Stages of Renaissance Style.* New York: Doubleday and Company, Inc., 1955.

Chapter VI

Burnim, Kalman. *David Garrick, Director.* Pittsburgh: Pittsburgh University Press, 1961.

Cibber, Colley. *An Apology for the Life of Colley Cibber.* Edited by B. R. S. Fone. Ann Arbor: University of Michigan Press, 1968.

Davis, Thomas. *Memories of Mr. David Garrick.* Vol. I and II. London: Longman, Hurst, Reese and Orme, 1809.

Dobbs, Brian. *Drury Lane.* London: Cassell, 1971.

Fitzgerald, Percy H. *The Sheridans.* Vols I and II. London: R. Bentley, 1886.

Gibbs, Lewis. *Sheridan.* London: J. M. Dent and Sons, Ltd., 1947.

Glawgow, Alice. *Sheridan of Drury Lane.* New York: Frederich A. Stokes Co., 1940.

Hughes, Leo. *The Drama's Patrons.* Austin: University of Texas Press, 1971.

Knapp, Mary E. *Prologues and Epilogues of the Eighteenth Century.* New Haven: Yale University Press, 1961.

Krutch, Joseph Wood. *Comedy and Conscience after the Restoration.* New York: Columbia University Press, 1924.

Lynch, James J. *Box, Pit, and Gallery.* Berkeley and Los Angeles: University of Califonia Press, 1953.

Nettleton, George H. and Case, Arthur E. (eds.). *British Dramatists from Dryden to Sheridan.* Boston: Houghton Mifflin Company, 1939.

Nettleton, George Henry. *English Drama of the Restoration and Eighteenth Century.* New York: The Macmillan Company, 1914.

Oman, Carola. *David Garrick.* London: Hodder and Stoughton, 1958.

Parsons, Mrs. Clement. *Garrick and his Circle.* 2nd ed. London: Methuen and Co., 1906.

Sanders, Lloyd C. *Life of Richard Brindley Sheridan.* London: Walter Scott, n.d.

Chapter VII

Bentley, Eric. *The Playwright as Thinker*. New York: Reynal and Company, Inc., 1946.

Bjorkman, Edwin A. *Voices of Tomorrow*. New York: Mitchell Kennerley, 1913.

Darwin, Charles. *The Origin of the Species*. New York: W. W. Norton and Company, Inc., 1975.

Downs, Brian W. *A Study of Six Plays by Ibsen*. Cambridge: Harvard University Press, 1946.

Downs, Brian W. *Ibsen: The Intellectual Background*. Cambridge: Harvard University Press, 1946.

Gassner, John. *The Theatre in Our Times: A Survey of the Men, Materials and Movements in the Modern Theatre*. New York: Crown Publishers, Inc., 1854.

Gustafson, Alrik. "The Scandinavian Countries," *A History of Modern Drama*. ed. by Barrett H. Clark and George Freedley. New York: D. Appleton-Century Company, Inc., 1947.

Heller, Otto. *Henrik Ibsen: Plays and Problems*. Boston: Houghton Mifflin Co., 1912.

Ibsen, Berliot. *The Three Ibsen's*. London: Hutchinson and Co., Ltd., 1951.

Ibsen, Henrik. *The Complete Major Prose Plays*. Trans. and Intro. by Rolf Fjelde. New York: New American Library, 1978.

Meyer, Michael. *Ibsen: A Biography*. Garden City, New York: Doubleday and Company, Inc., 1971.

Weigand, M. J. *The Modern Ibsen: A Reconsideration*. New York: Henry Holt, 1925.

Zucker, A. E. *Ibsen the Master Builder*. New York: Henry Holt, 1929.

Chapter VIII

Chekhov, Anton. *Anton Chekhov: Four Plays*. Trans. by David Magarshack. New York: Hill and Wang (A Mermaid Drama Book), 1969.

Chekhov, Anton. *The Three Sisters*. Trans. by Michael Frayn. London: Methuen's Theatre Classics, 1983.

Gassner, John. *Form and Idea in the Modern Theatre*. New York: Holt, Rinehart and Winston, Inc., 1956.

Gorchakov, Nikolai A. *The Theatre in Soviet Russia*. Trans. by Edgar Lehman. New York: Columbia University Press, 1957.

Lumley, Frederick. *Trends in Twentieth Century Drama: A Survey Since Ibsen and Shaw*. 2nd ed. London: Barrie and Rockliff, 1960.

Magarshack, David. *Chekhov, a Life*. New York: Grove Press, 1952.

Magarshack, David. *Chekhov the Dramatist*. New York: Hill and Wang, 1960.

Matlow, Myron. *Modern World Drama: An Encyclopedia*. New York: E. P. Dutton and Co., Inc., 1972.

Meyerhold, Vsevolad. *Meyerhold on Theatre*. Ed. by Edward Braun. New York: Hill and Wang, Inc., 1969.

Slonin, Marc. *Russian Theatre from the Empire to the Soviets*. Cleveland: World Publishing Company, 1961

Stanislavsky, Constantin. *An Actor Prepares*. Trans. by Elizabeth R. Hapgood. New York: Theatre Arts Books, c. 1948.

Stanislavsky, Constantin. *My Life in Art*. Trans. by J. J. Robbins. New York: Theatre Arts Books, c. 1952.

Chapter IX

"August Strindberg, 1912–1962." Special issue of *World Theatre*. Brussels: International Theatre Institute and UNESCO, 1963.

Bjorkman, Edwin. "August Strindberg," *Voices of Tomorrow*. New York: Mitchell Kennerley, 1913.

Gustafson, Alrik. *August Strindberg: 1849–1912*. Stockholm: The Swedish Institute, 1962.

Lagercrantz, Olof. *August Strindberg*. Trans. by Anselm Hollo. New York: Farrar, Straus, Giroux, 1984.

McGill, V. J. *August Strindberg, the Bedeviled Viking*. New York: Brentano, 1930.

Sprigge, Elizabeth. *The Strange Life of August Strindberg*. New York: The Macmillan Company, 1949.

Strindberg, August. *Letters to Harriet Bosse*. Ed. and trans. by Arvid Paulson. New York: Grosset and Dunlap, 1959.

Strindberg, August. *Selected Plays*. Trans. by Evert Sprinchorn. Vols. I and II. Minneapolis: University of Minnesota Press, 1986.

Chapter X

Brecht, Bertolt. *Seven Plays*. Ed. and with an intro. by Eric Bentley. New York: Grove Press, 1961.

Brecht, Bertolt. *Parables for the Theatre*. Trans. by Eric and Maja Bentley. New York: Grove Press, n.d.

Brecht, Bertolt. *Mother Courage*. Trans. by Eric Bentley, New York: Grove Press, 1963.

Brecht, Bertolt. *Brecht on Theatre*. Trans. by John Willett. London: Methuen, 1964.

Brecht, Bertolt. *Fear and Misery of the Third Reich*. Trans. by John Willett and Wolfgang Sauerlander, ed. by John Willett and Ralph Manheim. Vol. 4 of *Brecht's Collected Works*. London: Methuen, 1983.

Brecht, Bertolt. *Private Life of the Master Race*. Trans. by Eric Bentley. New York: New Directions, 19—.

Esslin, Martin. *Bertolt Brecht*. New York: Columbia University Press, 1969.

Esslin, Martin. *Brecht: The Man and his Work*. Garden City, New York: Doubleday, 1960.

Ewen, Frederic. *Bertolt Brecht: His Life, His Art and His Times*. New York: Citadel Press, 1967.

Manfull, Helen (ed.). *Additional Dialogue: The Letters of Dalton Trumbo, 1942–1962*. New York: M. Evans and Company, Inc., 1970.

Spalter, Max. *Brecht's Tradition*. Baltimore: Johns Hopkins Press, 1967.

Willett, John. *The Theatre of Bertolt Brecht*. Norfolk, Conn.: New Directions, 1959.

Chapter XI

Artaud, Antonin. *Collected Works*. 3 Vols. Trans. by Victor Corti. London: Calder and Boyers Ltd., 1968.

Artaud, Antonin. *The Theatre and Its Double*. Trans. by Mary C. Richards. New York: Grove Press, 1958.

Biner, Pierre. *The Living Theatre*. New York: Horizon Press, 1972.

Brook, Peter. *The Empty Space*. New York: Atheneum, 1968.

Croyden, Margaret. *Lunatics, Lovers, and Poets*. New York: McGraw Hill, 1974.

Grotowski, Jerzy. *Towards a Poor Theatre*. New York: Simon and Schuster, 1968.

Kirby, Michael. *Happenings*. New York: E. P. Dutton and Co., Inc., 1965.

Pascoli, Robert. *A Book on the Open Theatre*. New York: Avon, 1970.

Schechner, Richard. *Environmental Theatre*. New York: Hawthorn Books, Inc, 1973.

Schechner, Richard (ed.). *The Performance Group: Dionysus in 69*. New York: Farrar, Straus and Giroux, 1970.

Chapter XII

Beckett, Samuel. *Waiting for Godot*. New York: Grove Press, 1954.

Benedikt, Michael and George Wellwarth (eds.). *Modern French Theatre: The Avante-Garde, Dada, and Surrealism*. New York: E. P. Dutton and Co., Inc., 1964.

Bentley, Eric. *The Theory of the Modern Stage*. New York: Penguin Books, Inc., 1976.

Brustein, Robert. *The Theatre of Revolt: An Approach to Modern Drama*. Boston: Little, Brown and Co., 1964.

Esslin, Martin. *The Theatre of the Absurd*. Rev. ed. Garden City, New York: Doubleday and Company, Inc., 1969.

Kalb, Jonathan. "Acting Beckett," *American Theatre*, IV. December, 1987.

Chapters XIII and XIV

Bordman, Gerald. *American Musical Theatre*. New York: Oxford University Press, 1978.

Broun, Heywood. "Preface," *The Show-Off* by George Kelly. New York: Samuel French, 1924.

Clark, Barrett H. "The United States," *A History of Modern Drama*. Ed. by Barrett H. Clark and George Freedley. New York: D. Appleton-Century Company, Inc., 1947.

Clurman, Harold. *The Fervent Years: The Story of the Group Theater in the 1930's*. New York: Harcourt Brace Jovanovich, Inc., 1957.

Downer, Alan S. *Fifty Years of American Drama, 1900–1950*. Chicago: Henry Regnery Company, 1951.

Gallup, Donald (ed.). *The Journals of Thornton Wilder: 1939–1961*. New Haven: Yale University Press, 1985.

Green, Stanley. *Encyclopedia of the Musical Theatre*. New York: DaCapo Press, Inc., 1976.

Guthrie, Tyrone. *A Life in the Theatre*. New York: McGraw-Hill Book Company, Inc., 1959.

Hart, Moss. *Act One*. New York: Random House, 1959.

Hewitt, Barnard. *Theatre U.S.A., 1668 to 1957*. New York: McGraw Hill Book Company, Inc., 1959.

Hirsch, Foster. George Kelly. Boston: Twayne Publishers, 1975

Hughes, Glenn. *A History of the American Theatre, 1700–1950*. New York: Samuel French, Inc., 1951.

Kronenberger, Louis (ed.) *Cavalcade of Comedy*. New York: Simon and Schuster, 1953.

Krutch, Joseph Wood. *The American Drama since 1918*. New York: Random House, 1939.

Mantle, Burns. *American Playwrights of Today*. New York: Dodd, Mead and Company, 1929.

Mantle, Burns. *The Best Plays of 1926–27*. New York: Dodd, Mead and Company, 1927.

Mates, Julian. *America's Musical Stage*. New York: Praeger, 1985.

Meredith, Scott. *George S. Kaufman and his Friends*. Garden City, N.Y.: Doubleday & Company, Inc., 1974.

Moses, Montrose J., and Brown, John Mason (eds.). *The American Theatre as Seen By Its Critics, 1752–1934*. New York: W. W. Norton and Company, Inc., 1934.

Pollack, Rhoda-Gale. *George S. Kaufman*. Boston: Twayne Publishers, 1988.

Quinn, Arthur Hobson. *A History of the American Drama from the Civil War to the Present Day*. 2 Vols. Rev. ed. New York: Appleton-Century-Crofts, Inc., 1957.

Rice, Elmer. *The Living Theatre*. New York: Harper and Brothers, 1959.

Sheaffer, Louis. *O'Neill*. 2 Vols. Boston: Little, Brown and Company, 1968 and 1973.

Sullivan, Mark. *Our Times*. 6 Vols. New York: Charles Scribner's Sons, 1926–1937.

Williams, Tennessee. *Eight Plays*. Intro. by Harold Clurman Garden City, New York: Nelson Doubleday, Inc., 1979.

Chapter XV

Abramson, Doris E. *Negro Playwrights in the American Theatre*. New York: Columbia University Press, 1969.

Brown, Sterling A. *The Negro in American Fiction*. New York: Argosy-Antiquarian, 1969.

DeVries, Hilary. "A Song in Search of Itself," *American Theatre*. III. January 1987.

Gussow, Mel. "Blacks on Stage: The Progress is Deceptive," *The New York Times*, Sect. 2, August 3, 1986.

Isaacs, Edith Juliet Rich. *The Negro in the American Theatre*. Rev. ed. College Park, Md.: McGrath Publishing Co., 1968.

Lindsay, Patterson (ed.). *Black Theatre, A Twentieth Century Collection of the Works of It's Best Playwrights*. New York: Dodd, Mead., 1971.

Molette, Carlton W. and Barbara J. *Black Theatre, Premise and Presentation*. Bristol, Ind.: Wyndham Hall Press, 1986.

Ward, Douglas Turner. "For Whites Only." *American Theatre*. III. November, 1986.

Wilson, August. *Fences*. New York and Scarborough, Ontario: New American Library (A Plume Book), 1986.

Wilson, August. *Ma Rainey's Black Bottom*. New York and Scarborough, Ontario: New American Library, 1985.

Chapter XVI

Bigsley, C. W. E. *A Critical Introduction to Twentieth Century American Drama*. Vol. III. *Beyond Broadway*. Cambridge: Cambridge University Press, 1985.

Bock, Hedwig and Wertheim, Albert (eds.). *Essays on Contemporary American Drama*. Munchen: Max Hueber Verlag, 1984.

Little, Stuart. *Enter Joseph Papp: In Search of a New American Theatre*. New York: Coward, McCann and Geoghegan, Inc., 1974.

Mottram, Ron. *Inner Landscapes: The Theatre of Sam Shepard*. Columbia, Missouri: University of Missouri Press, 1984.

Novick, Julius. *Beyond Broadway*. New York: Hill and Wang, 1968.

Shephard, Sam. *Buried Child*. New York: Urizon Brooks, 1976.

Ziegler, Joseph. *Regional Theatre: The Revolutionary Stage*. Minneapolis: University of Minnesota Press, 1973.

Chapter XVII

Addenbrooke, David. *The Royal Shakespeare Company: The Peter Hall Years*. London: William Kimber, 1974.

Blumentha, Eileen. "Serban Recreates His Landmark 'Trilogy'," *American Theatre*. IV. February, 1987.

Breuer, Lee. "The Theatre and Its Trouble," *American Theatre*. IV. November, 1986.

Browne, Terry. *Playwrights' Theatre: The English Stage Company at the Royal Court*. London: Pitman, 1975.

Burian, Jarka. *The Scenography of Josef Svoboda*. Middletown, Conn.: Wesleyan University Press, 1971.

Churchill, Caryl. *Plays: One*. London: Methuen, 1985.

Cook, Judith. *The National Theatre*. London: Harrop, 1976.

Cornish, Roger and Ketels, Violet (eds.). *Landmarks of Modern British Drama*. Vols. 1 and II. London: Methuen, 1985 and 1986.

Dukore, Bernard F. *The Theatre of Peter Barnes*. London: Heinemann, 1981.

Hay, Malcolm and Roberts, Philip. *Bond: A Study of His Plays:* London and New York: Eyre Methuen, 1980.

Honan, William H. "Theatre of Images Discovers the Word," *The New York Times,* Sect. H, August 10, 1986.

Kaufman, David. "Stuart Sherman Performs with Paradox," *The New York Times,* Sect. H, July 1987.

Marranca, Bonnie (ed.). *The Theatre of Images*. New York: Drama Book Specialists, 1977.

Novick, Julius. "Interlopers in the Opera House," *American Theatre*. III. May, 1986.

Rubin, Leon. *The Nicholas Nickleby Story*. London: Penguin Books, 1981.

Savran, David. "Terrorists of the Text," *American Theatre*. III. December, 1986.

Thurman, Judith. "Caryl Churchill: The Playwright Who Makes You Laugh about Orgasm, Racism, Class Struggle, Homophobia, Woman-Hating, the British Empire, and the Irrepressible Strangeness of the Human Heart," *Ms. Magazine,* May, 1972.

Volkov, Soloman. "At the Scene of Lyubimov's 'Crime'," *American Theatre*. IV. April, 1987.

Weintraub, Erica Beth. "Caryl Churchill," *Dictionary of Literary Biography,* XIII, Pt. I. *British Dramatists Since World War II,* ed. by Stanley Weintraub. Detroit: Gale Research Co., 1982.